BLACKSTONE'S

CRIMINAL PRACTICE

BLACKSTONE'S

CRIMINAL PRACTICE

2014

SUPPLEMENT 3

GENERAL EDITORS

THE RIGHT HONOURABLE SIR ANTHONY HOOPER
FORMERLY A LORD JUSTICE OF APPEAL

DAVID ORMEROD QC
LAW COMMISSIONER, BARRISTER, BENCHER OF MIDDLE
TEMPLE, PROFESSOR OF CRIMINAL JUSTICE, QUEEN MARY,
UNIVERSITY OF LONDON

FOUNDING EDITOR

HHJ PETER MURPHY

CONSULTANT EDITOR

HHJ JOHN PHILLIPS CBE

ADVISORY EDITORIAL BOARD
SIR BRIAN LEVESON, PRESIDENT OF THE QUEEN'S BENCH DIVISION,
THE HONOURABLE MR JUSTICE GLOBE,
HHJ ROBERT ATHERTON, HH PETER BEAUMONT QC, CBE,
HHJ SALLY CAHILL QC, HHJ RICHARD MARKS QC,
HHJ JEFFREY PEGDEN QC, HOWARD RIDDLE, MICHAEL BOWES QC,
ALISON LEVITT QC, TIM OWEN QC, DAVID PERRY QC,
ROBERT SMITH QC, ADRIAN WATERMAN QC, HH ERIC STOCKDALE

CONTRIBUTORS
DUNCAN ATKINSON, ALEX BAILIN QC, DIANE BIRCH, ED CAPE,
ANAND DOOBAY, ANTHONY EDWARDS, RUDI FORTSON QC,
MICHAEL HIRST, LAURA C. H. HOYANO, PETER HUNGERFORD-WELCH,
ADRIAN KEANE, MICHAEL LEREGO QC, RICHARD MCMAHON QC,
VALSAMIS MITSILEGAS, TIM MOLONEY QC, STEPHEN PARKINSON,
DUNCAN PENNY, AMANDA PINTO QC, EDWARD REES QC,
HHJ PETER ROOK QC, MAYA SIKAND, RICHARD D. TAYLOR,
MARK TOPPING, MARTIN WASIK CBE

OXFORD
UNIVERSITY PRESS

OXFORD
UNIVERSITY PRESS

Great Clarendon Street, Oxford, OX2 6DP,
United Kingdom

Oxford University Press is a department of the University of Oxford.
It furthers the University's objective of excellence in research, scholarship,
and education by publishing worldwide. Oxford is a registered trade mark of
Oxford University Press in the UK and in certain other countries

© Oxford University Press, 2014

The moral rights of the authors have been asserted

First Edition published in 2014

Impression: 1

Published in the United States of America by Oxford University Press
198 Madison Avenue, New York, NY 10016, United States of America

British Library Cataloguing in Publication Data

Data available

ISBN 978–0–19–968144–0

Printed and bound in Great Britain by
Ashford Colour Press Ltd, Gosport, Hampshire

Introduction

This supplement is the third of three cumulative updating supplements to *Blackstone's Criminal Practice 2014*.

This supplement updates *Blackstone's Criminal Practice 2014*, taking account of legislative developments and leading cases since the publication of the 2014 edition. It follows the headings and the paragraph numbering used in the 2014 edition and is up to date to 7 March 2014.

This supplement also contains the complete text of the Criminal Procedure Rules 2013, as amended, and the Sentencing Guidelines as at 21 March 2014. This supplement also contains the new Criminal Practice Directions. The Criminal Procedure Rules and the relevant Practice Directions are presented as a single integrated document.

David Ormerod is the Criminal Law Commissioner for England and Wales, but nothing in this work should be taken as representing the views of the Law Commission unless expressly stated to do so.

Please visit the *Blackstone's Criminal Practice 2014* companion website at www.oup.com/black-stones/criminal for free online monthly updates, and an updated version of the Criminal Practice Rules and Criminal Practice Directions, taking in any amendments made in the course of the practice year. You may also register to receive the *Blackstone's Criminal Practice Update*, a free quarterly newsletter. If you have any queries, please contact blackstonescriminal@oup.com.

Contents

Contents

Table of Cases

Table of Statutes

Table of Statutory Instruments

Table of Practice Directions

Table of Codes of Conduct

Table of Guidelines

Table of Protocols and Circulars

Table of International Treaties and Conventions and other Legal Instruments

Table of European Legislation

Directives

SUPPLEMENT TO PART A
CRIMINAL LAW

Section A2   *Mens Rea*

STRICT LIABILITY

The Imposition of Strict Liability

Human Rights Compatibility   The policy illustrated in the House of Lords' decision in A2.28
G [2009] 1 AC 92 (which was approved in *G v UK* [2011] ECHR 1308), that those who have
sexual intercourse with young children under 13 are strictly liable and that there is no defence
of reasonable belief that the child is over that age, has been further illustrated in *Brown* [2013]
UKSC 43. The offence of unlawful carnal knowledge of a girl under the age of 14 years, contrary
to the Criminal Law Amendment Acts (Northern Ireland) 1885–1923, s. 4, is also an offence
of strict liability in relation to which the presumption of *mens rea* is displaced.

See also *Robinson-Pierre* [2013] EWCA Crim 2396 (strict liability in relation to dangerous
dogs) at **B20.6** in this supplement.

TRANSFERRED *MENS REA*

Accessories   In *Grant* [2014] EWCA Crim 143 the Court of Appeal applied the transferred A2.33
mens rea principle to the conviction of a principal and two accessories in an attempted murder
by shooting which also resulted in grievous bodily harm to two innocent bystanders. A finding
of an intent to kill a specific individual forming the basis of the conviction on the attempted
murder count would inevitably encompass within it an intent to cause grievous bodily harm
which could be the basis also of a conviction or convictions for causing grievous bodily harm to
the bystanders under the OAPA 1861, s. 18, using the transferred *mens rea* rule. The argument
that the intent to kill for attempted murder and the intent to cause grievous bodily harm for the
purpose of s. 18 were mutually exclusive or inconsistent with one another was roundly rejected —
the former included the latter and conviction for the attempted killing of A plus conviction for
the grievous bodily harm caused to B and C when the plan miscarried was perfectly proper for
all three defendants.

Section A3   General Defences

DEFENCES DENYING BASIC ELEMENTS OF LIABILITY

Insanity: General Principles: The M'Naghten Rules

In *Oye* [2013] EWCA Crim 1725 the Court of Appeal has decided that the special verdict of not A3.23
guilty by reason of insanity is available and appropriate where there is agreed psychiatric evidence
that the accused was suffering at the time of the offence from insane delusions that he was being
confronted by 'evil spirits' intent on harming him. If, as was agreed, he did not know the nature
and quality of his actions due to a defect of reason from disease of the mind, the special verdict is
still available notwithstanding that the subjective belief part of the complete defence of self-defence
may be made out. Davis LJ in the Court of Appeal did not find it necessary to decide on the facts
whether the appellant could ask to have the complete defence of self-defence put to the jury first.
That would involve the objective question of whether the force was reasonable in the circumstances as D believed them to be (which would, in any event, set D serious problems in such a case
and the actual evidence did not clearly address this) and the jury by their verdict had in fact rejected
its reasonableness so the question of which defence ought to be put first, or which took precedence,
did not arise. The judge could not instruct a jury to return a special verdict even though the prosecution accepted that the accused was insane at the relevant time and, for some reason, the jury
had instead returned verdicts of guilty on the two counts of affray and on a third count of inflicting
grievous bodily harm contrary to the OAPA 1861, s. 20. However, the Court of Appeal had power
to substitute special verdicts under the Criminal Appeal Act 1968, s. 6, and the Court was of the
clear opinion that it should intervene to do so on the facts.

Part A   Criminal Law

A

DEFENCES INVOLVING OTHER EXCUSES AND JUSTIFICATIONS

Self-defence, Prevention of Crime and Related Defences Generally

A3.56 **'Reasonable Force'** The cases of *Oye* [2013] EWCA Crim 1725 and *Press and Thompson* [2013] EWCA Crim 1849 (see **A3.63** in this supplement) turn on the interpretation of the CJIA 2008, s. 76, but the version of s. 76 displayed in the main work is incomplete. The version set out below includes all changes now implemented.

Criminal Justice and Immigration Act 2008, s. 76

(1) This section applies where in proceedings for an offence—
    (a) an issue arises as to whether a person charged with the offence ('D') is entitled to rely on a defence within subsection (2), and
    (b) the question arises whether the degree of force used by D against a person ('V') was reasonable in the circumstances.

(2) The defences are—
    (a) the common law defence of self-defence;.
    (aa) the common law defence of defence of property; and
    (b) the defences provided by section 3(1) of the Criminal Law Act 1967 or section 3(1) of the Criminal Law Act (Northern Ireland) 1967 (use of force in prevention of crime or making arrest).

(3) The question whether the degree of force used by D was reasonable in the circumstances is to be decided by reference to the circumstances as D believed them to be, and subsections (4) to (8) also apply in connection with deciding that question.

(4) If D claims to have held a particular belief as regards the existence of any circumstances—
    (a) the reasonableness or otherwise of that belief is relevant to the question whether D genuinely held it; but
    (b) if it is determined that D did genuinely hold it, D is entitled to rely on it for the purposes of subsection (3), whether or not—
        (i) it was mistaken, or
        (ii) (if it was mistaken) the mistake was a reasonable one to have made.

(5) But subsection (4)(b) does not enable D to rely on any mistaken belief attributable to intoxication that was voluntarily induced.

(5A) In a householder case, the degree of force used by D is not to be regarded as having been reasonable in the circumstances as D believed them to be if it was grossly disproportionate in those circumstances.

(6) In a case other than a householder case, the degree of force used by D is not to be regarded as having been reasonable in the circumstances as D believed them to be if it was disproportionate in those circumstances.

(6A) In deciding the question mentioned in subsection (3), a possibility that D could have retreated is to be considered (so far as relevant) as a factor to be taken into account, rather than as giving rise to a duty to retreat.

(7) In deciding the question mentioned in subsection (3) the following considerations are to be taken into account (so far as relevant in the circumstances of the case)—
    (a) that a person acting for a legitimate purpose may not be able to weigh to a nicety the exact measure of any necessary action; and
    (b) that evidence of a person's having only done what the person honestly and instinctively thought was necessary for a legitimate purpose constitutes strong evidence that only reasonable action was taken by that person for that purpose.

(8) Subsections (6A) and (7) are not to be read as preventing other matters from being taken into account where they are relevant to deciding the question mentioned in subsection (3).

(8A) For the purposes of this section 'a householder case' is a case where—
    (a) the defence concerned is the common law defence of self-defence,
    (b) the force concerned is force used by D while in or partly in a building, or part of a building, that is a dwelling or is forces accommodation (or is both),
    (c) D is not a trespasser at the time the force is used, and
    (d) at that time D believed V to be in, or entering, the building or part as a trespasser.

(8B) Where—
    (a) a part of a building is a dwelling where D dwells,

(b)   another part of the building is a place of work for D or another person who dwells in the first part, and

(c)   that other part is internally accessible from the first part, that other part, and any internal means of access between the two parts, are each treated for the purposes of subsection (8A) as a part of a building that is a dwelling.

(8C) Where—

(a)   a part of a building is forces accommodation that is living or sleeping accommodation for D,

(b)   another part of the building is a place of work for D or another person for whom the first part is living or sleeping accommodation, and

(c)   that other part is internally accessible from the first part,

that other part, and any internal means of access between the two parts, are each treated for the purposes of subsection (8A) as a part of a building that is forces accommodation.

(8D) Subsections (4) and (5) apply for the purposes of subsection (8A)(d) as they apply for the purposes of subsection (3).

(8E) The fact that a person derives title from a trespasser, or has the permission of a trespasser, does not prevent the person from being a trespasser for the purposes of subsection (8A).

(8F) In subsections (8A) to (8C)—

'building' includes a vehicle or vessel, and

'forces accommodation' means service living accommodation for the purposes of Part 3 of the Armed Forces Act 2006 by virtue of section 96(1)(a) or (b) of that Act.

(9)   This section, except so far as making different provision for householder cases, is intended to clarify the operation of the existing defences mentioned in subsection (2).

(10)   In this section—

(a)   'legitimate purpose' means—

(i)   the purpose of self-defence under the common law, . . .

[(ia) the purpose of defence of property under the common law, or]

(ii)   the prevention of crime or effecting or assisting in the lawful arrest of persons mentioned in the provisions referred to in subsection (2)(b);

(b)   references to self-defence include acting in defence of another person; and

(c)   references to the degree of force used are to the type and amount of force used.

The Degree of Force Permitted   In *Oye* [2013] EWCA Crim 1725 (see also **A3.23** in this supplement) the Court of Appeal commented on the ruling in *Martin* [2002] 2 WLR 1 that it would not be appropriate, 'except in exceptional circumstances which would make the evidence especially probative', to take into account, when deciding whether excessive force was used in self-defence, that the defendant was suffering from a psychiatric condition. The Court referred to *Canns* [2005] EWCA Crim 2264, where three highly experienced members of the Court of Appeal found it 'impossible to identify the sort of exceptional circumstances in which it would be appropriate to take a psychiatric condition from which a defendant is suffering into account, when addressing the question of whether excessive force is used'. The Court pointed out that the enactment of the CJIA 2008, s. 76, was only to clarify the law and therefore did not change the position that considered that it was difficult to see in what circumstances, even exceptionally, a psychiatric condition can (or on policy grounds, ought to) be relevant to the question of excessive force. Note, however, *Press and Thompson* [2013] EWCA Crim 1849, which provides some indication.

A3.63

In *Press and Thompson* the Court of Appeal also considered the relationship between psychiatric conditions and the objective question of whether the degree of force used by D was reasonable in the circumstances. This was a different set of circumstances to *Oye* and was characterised as one where 'the defendant was acting under an insane delusion as to the nature of the threat'. In the instant case, there was evidence that D's post-traumatic stress disorder (a consequence of military service in Afghanistan) may have caused him to react over-sensitively to perceived threats. The trial judge had been correct to invite the jury to consider the psychiatric evidence when resolving the question whether D did only what he honestly believed was necessary in the circumstances, which under *Palmer v The Queen* [1971] AC 814, at common law, and now by statute under the CJIA 2008, s. 76(7)(b), 'constitutes strong evidence that only reasonable action was taken'. However, strong evidence is not conclusive evidence and it was for the jury, not the defendant, to resolve the ultimate and objective question of whether the degree of force used was reasonable. The appeal was dismissed as the jury had been able to 'assess for themselves from the contents of the CCTV film whether Thompson, even upon his understanding, had gone grossly beyond what was reasonable in the circumstances' (at [39]).

The reference to going 'grossly beyond' what is reasonable is intriguing as this is the expression used to denote where force is not to be regarded as reasonable in 'householder cases' following the insertion of subsection (5A) into s. 76 as from 25 April 2013, but the case was not a householder case. The parallel may be that a householder is in effect ordinarily presumed to be honestly and instinctively using reasonable force in self-defence but the force used will nonetheless be unreasonable if it is grossly disproportionate.

Mistakes of Fact and Self-defence

A3.68   In *Ibrahim* [2014] EWCA Crim 121 the Court of Appeal had to decide whether the trial judge had been correct to exclude a late medical report relating to the general effects of Attention Deficit Hyperactivity Disorder (ADHD) in a case which turned on self-defence. In agreeing that the evidence was not relevant on the facts of the case, the Court noted that the case before it was *not* a case like *Oye* [2013] EWCA Crim 1725 (see **A3.63** in this supplement), 'in which the defendant suffered from a psychiatric condition that caused him to believe in a state of affairs which did not exist. In such case, as the authorities show, expert medical evidence is admissible in relation to the first limb of the defence of self-defence in order to establish what state of affairs the defendant genuinely believed to exist.'

It should be noted that the actual decision in *Oye* was that the medical evidence, while relevant to the question of the circumstances believed by D to exist, was not legally relevant to the separate question of the degree of force which it was reasonable to use in those perceived circumstances. However, in the instant case the main point at issue was whether the accused had initiated the violence and the medical evidence was rightly excluded for the separate reason that it 'would not have assisted the jury one way or the other on the main issue in the case. If the appellant was the sole aggressor, then his ADHD and its possible manifestations were irrelevant. In those circumstances no question of self-defence arose.'

One can perhaps add that of the three effects referred to in the medical report (poor impulse control, exaggerated response to threats, reduced capacity to evaluate current circumstances) only the last could really have been relevant to the subjective question of the facts as believed to exist by D, even in a case where that was a live issue.

Section A4   Parties to Offences

LIABILITY OF PRINCIPALS AND ACCESSORIES GENERALLY

A4.1   *Banfield* [2013] EWCA Crim 1394 provides yet another illustration of the complications that can arise where there are two accused who may potentially have been responsible (in this case for murder); either might be guilty as principal or accessory, but it is not clear which. As *Giannetto* [1997] 1 Cr App R 1 and *Morton* [2003] EWCA Crim 1501 show, a person can be convicted if it is clear that he was either the principal or, if not, that he was an accessory (provided that the possibility that he was not responsible on either basis can be ruled out). However, if (as in *Banfield*) the jury cannot rule out that the killing may have been the work of B without the assistance or encouragement of A or, alternatively, that it may have been the work of A without the assistance or encouragement of B then, even though there are also inculpatory possibilities that they killed jointly or that one of them encouraged the other to kill, neither of them can safely be convicted. The slightly curious thing about the case is that the question of whether either of the parties could have been liable on the basis of encouragement seems to have been equated with the question of whether it could be proved they were present. It was said by Rafferty LJ, giving the judgment of the Court of Appeal, that it would be different if a conspiracy had been alleged but it is difficult to see why there could not be prior encouragement by either party without there being a conspiracy to commit murder. However, the fact remains that the evidence against any one individual was very largely circumstantial and no body had been found. Notwithstanding the concession on appeal that there had been a murder perpetrated by one of the accused, since it could not be shown which one it was and it could not be proved that the other assisted or encouraged the principal or acted in concert with him, the convictions of each inevitably had to be quashed.

That the question of whether the accused is liable on the basis of being a principal or as an accessory is often of little importance (provided it is clear he was liable as one or the other) was also reiterated in *Montague* [2013] EWCA Crim 1781, a case concerning possession of false documents (driving licences bearing D's photograph) for use in connection with frauds. The Court of Appeal agreed with what was said in *DPP for Northern Ireland v Maxwell* [1978] 3 All ER 1140, about it being important that the accused knew the real nature of the case that he has to answer and noted that in this case the prosecution had indicated that their case was based on D being in joint possession and control with other defendants as opposed to being a secondary party to the possession by others. However, the judge summed up the case to the jury on the basis that he could be liable either as a principal (in joint possession) or as a secondary party to the possession by others. *Taylor* [1998] Crim LR 582 shows that this may be a material misdirection but, on the facts of the instant case, 'the reality of the allegation he had to face was unaffected by the precise legal label attached to his participation'. The judge had told the jury, as the defence requested, that he could not be liable simply on the basis that he had supplied the photographs to be used in the driving licences and the essence of his defence was that 'he had not been involved, either alone or on a joint enterprise basis, in the possession or control of the relevant items after he supplied the photographs to his co-accused'. Therefore 'it was not of significance whether he was in joint possession of the items... or, instead, assisted others who were in possession of them'.

THE MENTAL ELEMENT FOR ACCESSORIES

The mental element for accessories has recently arisen in a civil case (*O'Neil v Gale* [2013]   **A4.5**
EWCA Civ 1554) in relation to the question of whether a person is acting unlawfully for the purposes of a defence to restitution claim. The Court of Appeal (civil division) applied the test for intention as propounded in *Bryce* [2004] 2 Cr App R 592 and confirmed that, for a person to be convicted of assisting, he must at least know the essential matters which constitute the offence. If a person does know all the facts and is intentionally assisting another person to do certain things, and it turns out that the doing of those things constitutes an offence, the person who is assisting is guilty of aiding and abetting that offence irrespective of any lack of knowledge of the law (in this case the Financial Services and Markets Act 2000) rendering the acts criminal.

THE SCOPE OF THE JOINT VENTURE

The Contemplation Test

Bristow [2013] EWCA Crim 1540 throws up the difficult question of what are 'the essential   **A4.10**
matters constituting the offence', which the accessory has to contemplate, in relation to unlawful act manslaughter arising from a burglary. In this case the relevant facts were that the burglary was to be carried out using vehicles at a farm with residential buildings from which there was only one way out via vehicular track and that there was a risk of being interrupted by a resident of the farm. A resident who did intervene was knocked down and run over and killed by escaping vehicles driven by the defendants although it was not clear which defendant or defendants did the driving. The trial judge found that it was open for the jury 'to conclude that each burglar intended the vehicular escape, should it arise in those circumstances, that that escape should be achieved at speed and with determination and, if necessary, with no respect for property or person that might get in the way'. One of the points raised by the appellant was that the actual

driver, whoever he was, might in seeking to escape have deliberately driven over the victim intending to kill or cause grievous bodily harm rather than simply intending to escape and that would have taken what the principal did outside the scope of the joint venture. The Court of Appeal rejected this argument referring (at [41]) to *Rahman* [2009] 1 AC 129 and *Carpenter* [2012] QB 722, which 'demonstrate that the test of an accessory's liability is one of foresight, namely foresight of what the principal might do, rather than foresight of the intention with which the principal might perform such acts'. Although it seems that the accessory was required to contemplate that the driver might, if necessary, make a rapid vehicular escape from an intervener, there was no need for the accessory to contemplate the danger arising from that contemplated action, it being sufficient that the reasonable man would contemplate the danger. As Treacy LJ put it (at [36]):

> The factual questions for the jury, given that the appellants were involved in the unlawful act of burglary, were whether each appellant foresaw the risk of intervention by a third party, and whether the reasonable bystander would consider the venture dangerous in the *Church* sense.

A4.12 **Contemplation of the *Mens Rea* of Murder**   In *Jogee* [2013] EWCA Crim 1725 the Court of Appeal rejected an argument that the principle, that an accessory is liable for murder where he realises that the principal may use a knife with intent to kill or cause grievous bodily harm, applies only to cases of active participation as opposed to encouragement. Laws LJ referred to the well-known passage from Lord Brown's judgment in *Rahman* [2009] 1 AC 129 (quoted at A4.16 in the main work) and then cogently commented (at [23]) that there is:

> ...no principled basis on which this reasoning should be applied only to cases of participation and not to cases of encouragement. Indeed, the distinction between the two is, to say the least, permeable. Encouragement is a form of participation; that is why it is enough to convict a secondary party. The *actus reus* of the secondary party's crime is lending support to the primary actor, whether by active participation or encouragement or both. The mental element, the *mens rea*, of the secondary party's crime is an appreciation that the primary actor might inflict grievous bodily harm and a willingness to lend his support notwithstanding.

A4.16 **Departures from the Contemplated Method**   That to be guilty of murder, the accessory must contemplate not only the act of the principal (e.g., the use of a knife) but also that the act will be done with the *mens rea* for murder (i.e. that the knife will be used with an intention to kill or cause grievous bodily harm) has been re-emphasised in *Ellis* [2013] EWCA Crim 2554. Although in *A (Joint Enterprise)* [2010] 2 Cr App R 369 it was commented that once the use of a knife is foreseen, 'in a great many cases' this will almost inevitably carry with it foresight of an intention to kill or at least to cause really serious injury, that did not mean that the inference was inevitable in all cases or that directions to juries should not make clear that the accessory must have contemplated the murderous intent with which the knife might be used. In the judgment of the Court of Appeal in *Ellis*, 'the failure to include the requisite knowledge of the stabber's intention, that is to say knowledge or realisation that the stabber intended to kill or cause really serious harm', constituted a defect in the direction to the jury which, on the facts of the case, rendered the convictions for murder unsafe.

MISCELLANEOUS ISSUES

Presence at the Scene of the Crime: Omissions

A4.28 *L v CPS* [2013] EWHC 4127 (Admin) provides a further illustration of the principle that presence at the scene of a crime, even as a member of an intimidatory group, does not provide conclusive evidence of aiding and abetting any particular crime, in this case the attempted robbery of a mobile phone produced by the victim, which happens to be committed by a member of the group.

Section A5   Inchoate Offences
CONSPIRACY GENERALLY
Common Law and Statutory Conspiracies

The Court of Appeal in *Dosanjh* [2013] EWCA Crim 2366 refers in several places to a supposed offence of: **A5.39**

> Common law conspiracy to cheat, which was abolished by section 32(1)(a) of the Theft Act 1968 except as regards offences relating to the public revenue.

The transcript gives the impression that the appellant was indeed convicted of such a 'common law' conspiracy to cheat the revenue. This cannot be correct. No such species of common-law conspiracy survived the enactment of the CLA 1977. The common-law offence preserved by the Theft Act 1968, s. 32(1)(a), was the substantive offence of cheating the public revenue (as to which see the main work at **B16.3**). Any conspiracy to commit an offence (common law or statutory) must now be charged either as a statutory conspiracy under the CLA 1977, s. 1, or (in appropriate cases) as a conspiracy to defraud.

The Court in *Dosanjh* was, however, right to conclude that a charge of conspiracy to cheat the public revenue potentially exposes convicted defendants to higher sentences than either a charge of conspiracy to defraud or a charge of conspiracy to commit an offence under the Fraud Act 2006. This is because the penalty for the substantive offence is at large, and under the CLA 1977, s. 3, a person guilty of conspiracy to commit an indictable offence punishable with imprisonment where no maximum term is specified is subject to a maximum penalty of life imprisonment.

Moreover, there may sometimes be good reasons, as in this case, for charging the alleged perpetrators of major revenue frauds either with the substantive common-law offence of cheating or with a conspiracy to commit that offence, thereby extending the sentencing powers of the court in the event of a conviction.

STATUTORY CONSPIRACY
Indictment

The guidance formerly contained in the *Consolidated Criminal Practice Direction*, para. 34.3, as to the use of conspiracy charges is reproduced with only minor changes in the *Criminal Practice Directions* [2013] EWCA Crim 1631 at 14A.3 (see **PD-17** in this supplement).   **A5.44**

CONSPIRACY TO DEFRAUD
Indictment, Sentence and Procedure

The Sentencing Council has published a new sentencing guideline for the sentencing of organisations convicted, *inter alia*, of conspiracy to defraud. The new guideline, entitled 'Fraud, bribery and money laundering: corporate offenders', has effect from 1 October 2014.   **A5.63**

ATTEMPT
Mens Rea as to Circumstances

In *Pace* [2014] EWCA Crim 186, the Court of Appeal held that on a charge of attempting to commit an offence of converting criminal property, contrary to the POCA 2002, s. 327(1)(c), it is not sufficient for the prosecution to prove that D merely suspected the property in question   **A5.76** to be criminal property. Suspicion as to this suffices for the substantive offence (as it does for all such offences under ss. 327 to 329) but it cannot suffice for an attempt.

The Court was prepared to distinguish *Khan* [1990] 2 All ER 783, on the basis, *inter alia*, that 'in *Khan*, the substantive offence admitted of recklessness as the *mens rea*: which is not the case here', but this (with respect) is not an obvious or coherent reason for distinguishing the two cases. The Court's preferred approach in *Pace* would seem to be one of equating the *mens rea* of attempt in this respect with that of conspiracy where, by the CLA 1977, s. 1(2) (see **A5.55** in the main work), an alleged conspirator must be proved to have known or intended any circumstances necessary for the commission of the substantive offence. If that were so then neither *Khan* nor *A-G's Ref (No. 3 of 1992)* [1994] 2 All ER 121 would remain good law.

Pace may perhaps best be understood as a case on 'attempting the impossible' and this may be a better way to distinguish it from *Khan,* which the Court in *Pace* had no power to overrule. See also **A5.80** in this supplement.

Impossibility

A5.80   In *Pace* [2014] EWCA Crim 186, the Court of Appeal held that, on a charge of attempting to commit an offence of converting criminal property, contrary to the POCA 2002, s. 327(1)(c), it was not sufficient for the prosecution to prove that D merely suspected the property in question to be criminal property, when it was in fact police property that was being used as 'bait' in the course of an undercover 'sting' operation designed to expose dishonest scrap metal dealers.

Undercover officers in this case had purported to be dishonest characters and had repeatedly approached the defendants at their scrapyard with consignments of what they pretended or suggested to be stolen goods, such as cable that one of them had supposedly stolen from a van while the other distracted the driver. In almost every case the defendants had purchased the material offered, complaining in one case that they would 'pretend not to hear where it came from because they would get into trouble for buying stolen metal'.

One might in the circumstances have expected the prosecution to have presented the case as one in which the defendants mistakenly *believed* the property to be criminal property, in which case by virtue of the CAA 1981, s. 1(3), they could have been regarded as having had an intent to commit a s. 327 offence on the basis of the facts as they believed them to be. But for one reason or another the case was presented and summed-up as one in which they would be guilty if they merely suspected it to be criminal property, and the Court of Appeal was clearly right in holding that mere suspicion is not enough for an attempt, either under s. 1(1) or under s. 1(3), even though it would have sufficed (if well-founded) for the commission of a substantive offence under s. 327.

Section A7   Human Rights

SENTENCE

Preventative Sentences

A7.108   A five-member Court of Appeal in *A-G's Ref (No. 69 of 2013)* [2014] EWCA Crim 188, was specially constituted to consider a number of appeals in the light of *Vinter v UK* [2013] ECHR 645, in which the ECtHR had held that whole life minimum terms violated the ECHR, Article 3, on the basis that they were not reducible. For discussion, see **E3.3** in this supplement.

Section A8   Territorial and Extra-territorial Jurisdiction

EXTRA-TERRITORIAL JURISDICTION

Offences Committed in 'Convention Countries' or by Nationals of Convention Countries

Venclovas [2013] EWCA Crim 2182 appears to be the first case to be brought under the   **A8.23**
Suppression of Terrorism Act 1978, s. 4. It demonstrates the potential breadth of that provision,
and confirms that prosecutions brought by virtue of this provision need not have any connection with terrorism, but need only involve one of the offences specified in the relevant part of
s. 4 and sch. 1. The need for the A-G to authorise any prosecution may provide a check on the
inappropriate use of s. 4, but *Venclovas* demonstrates that consent may sometimes be given even
in a non-terrorist case.

Venclovas also confirms that s. 4 creates no new offence, but only extends the jurisdictional
ambit of specified statutory and common law offences. So, where D (a Lithuanian national) was
charged with the murder of his estranged wife, either in England (where he had abducted her)
or in Poland (where her body was found), or in one of the countries he had driven through
between England and Poland (all being Convention countries for the purposes of the 1978
Act), he could properly be convicted of murder at common law, even though the place of the
murder could not satisfactorily be established. If the murder had indeed been committed in
England then s. 4 would not be needed, but it would be the same common-law offence of murder in any event.

The Court of Appeal noted that the OAPA 1861, s. 9, operates in the same way, so the outcome
would have been the same had D been a British citizen or UK national charged under that provision.

Contrast the position under the Armed Forces Act 2006, s. 42, as used in the case of Sergeant
Blackwell (*Marine A* [2013] EWCA Crim 2367). The s. 42 offence with which Blackwell was
charged and convicted in that case following the murder of a wounded prisoner in Afghanistan
is legally distinct from the common-law offence of murder on which it is based. See the main
work at **A8.21**.

Part A   Criminal Law

SUPPLEMENT TO PART B
OFFENCES

Section B1   Homicide and Related Offences

MURDER

Elements

Direction on Foresight Rarely Needed   *Royle* [2013] EWCA Crim 1461 provides another **B1.14**
example of where the use of the tried and tested formula of foresight of virtual certainty may not
be necessary if the direction actually given is appropriate to the facts of the case, especially
where, if anything, it involves a higher hurdle than foresight of virtual certainty. The trial judge
had told the jury 'You must be sure that he did not just realise that it [really serious harm] *could
happen* but acted on the basis that it *would* or that he intended that it would' (emphasis added).
Rafferty LJ said of this direction (at [27]) that it:

> . . . arguably set a hurdle higher than that in *Woollin* and *Nedrick*. It contemplates not virtual cer-
> tainty but certainty. We find it difficult to see how it can be a misdirection since it is to the benefit
> of the appellant. In any event, the appellant's case was not that this was a robbery that went wrong.
> That was a phrase used by the judge in sentencing once the jury had convicted. The appellant's
> case was complete denial. Consequently the direction upon intent avoided unnecessary elabora-
> tion and there was no need for further assistance or amplification in the *Nedrick/Woollin* tradition.

DIMINISHED RESPONSIBILITY

Basis of Defence

Abnormality of Mental Functioning   As under the previous version of the defence, it **B1.19**
remains a 'practical necessity' that there should be medical evidence adduced by the accused
and this evidence must be capable of discharging the burden on the accused to show on the
balance of probabilities that each ingredient of the defence is made out. In *Bunch* [2013]
EWCA Crim 2498 leave to appeal was refused since the trial judge had been wholly correct
to rule that the very limited indirect evidence given of alcohol dependency, even if it could
establish that condition, provided 'no evidence on which the jury could find that the applicant was suffering from an abnormality of mental functioning which arose from that medical condition and which substantially impaired one of the three capacities mentioned in the
Act'.

CONSTRUCTIVE MANSLAUGHTER (KILLING BY AN UNLAWFUL ACT LIKELY TO CAUSE BODILY HARM)

Likely to Cause Bodily Harm

The Objective Nature of the Test   *Bristow* [2013] EWCA Crim 1540 shows again that bur- **B1.56**
glary in certain circumstances may be an unlawful act likely to cause bodily harm (see also
A4.10 in this supplement). The relevant circumstances were that the burglary was to be carried
out using powerful vehicles at a farm with residential buildings from which there was only one
way out via vehicular track and that there was a risk of being interrupted by a resident of the
farm. A resident who did intervene was knocked down and run over and killed by escaping
vehicles driven by one or more of the defendants. In upholding convictions for unlawful act
manslaughter on the basis that D was at the least an accessory, Treacy LJ said (at [34]):

> Whilst burglary of itself is not a dangerous crime, a particular burglary may be dangerous because
> of the circumstances surrounding its commission. We consider that the features identified by the
> Crown . . . were capable of making this burglary dangerous when coupled with foresight of the risk
> of intervention to prevent escape.

Although the reference to foresight may seem at first glance to depart somewhat from an objective test and thus be more favourable to the accused, this may be partly explicable on the basis
that the case concerned liability as an accessory where 'knowledge of the essential matters' is
required even in relation to strict liability offences (see **A4.6** in the main work). Furthermore,

a more detailed reading of the judgment shows that the Court of Appeal was well aware of the objective nature of the test for dangerousness and commented on the fact that the trial judge had in effect been too generous to the accused in conflating 'the role of the reasonable bystander and that of a burglar'. Treacy LJ went on to distinguish two questions for the jury (at [36]):

> The factual questions for the jury, given that the appellants were involved in the unlawful act of burglary, were whether each appellant foresaw the risk of intervention by a third party, and whether the reasonable bystander would consider the venture dangerous in the *Church* sense.

The decision in effect requires D to be aware of the facts and circumstances which turn the burglary into a dangerous unlawful act (the possibility of third-party intervention in a situation of closely confined powerful escape vehicles) which the objective bystander would recognise as dangerous, but D does not subjectively have to recognise the danger, he just has to be aware of the facts which objectively give rise to the danger.

CAUSING OR ALLOWING THE DEATH OF A CHILD OR VULNERABLE ADULT

Procedure

B1.74   In *Hopkinson* [2014] 1 Cr App R 22 (3) the Court of Appeal commented that, while special verdicts may on rare occasions be appropriately sought in murder trials where there are a number of alternative defences, 'it is inappropriate for a special verdict [as to whether a particular defendant actually caused as opposed to allowed the death] to be sought in the context of the legislation in section 5 of the 2004 Act which was deliberately created just because of the inevitable difficulties of proving which of two defendants was responsible for the infliction of fatal injuries on a child when there are no other candidates, and neither defendant appears to be willing to tell the truth about the incident'.

ENCOURAGING OR ASSISTING SUICIDE

Sentencing Guidelines

B1.140   In *Howe* [2014] EWCA 114 the Court of Appeal gave guidance (at [23]–[29]) on the appropriate level of sentencing for the offence of encouraging or assisting suicide. This was the first prosecution since the DPP's guidance was issued following the judgment of the House of Lords in *R (Purdy) v DPP* [2010] 1 AC 345. Treacy LJ stated that the guidance related to face-to-face encouragement or assistance, as opposed to internet-based encouragement. The Court indicates that, where the custodial threshold is crossed, the range of sentence would run 'from 3 years to 12 years or more where an attempt at suicide or actual suicide has taken place'. In the instant case, where the offender had bought petrol from a garage at the request of W, who was seeking to commit suicide by setting himself alight, a sentence of ten years' detention was thought appropriate. Although death had not resulted, W suffered horrific burns. The offender lacked remorse but, in determining his sentence, the Court took account of his age (19) and immaturity.

Section B2   Non-fatal Offences Against the Person

WOUNDING OR CAUSING GRIEVOUS BODILY HARM WITH INTENT

Sentence

B2.67   An example of offending falling into the highest category of seriousness, without being the very worst type of offence within that category, is provided by *Finn* [2013] EWCA Crim 1643, where the offender had attacked a woman with a fencepost, hitting her in the face and blinding her in one eye. There were many aggravating features in this case, including the offender's previous offending, his commission of the offence whilst on bail and the gravity of the attack, which caused extensive and permanent injuries. But the weapon had not been a lethal one and had not been used with lethal intent. Only one blow had been struck with it.

An extended sentence of 17 years and two months' imprisonment comprising a custodial term of 14 years and two months' imprisonment and an extension period (an extended period of licence) of three years was quashed on appeal and substituted with a slightly reduced sentence of 17 years comprising a custodial term of 13 years and an extension period of four years.

CHILD ABDUCTION

Abduction of Child by Other Persons

Sentence   In *Sivillica* [2013] EWCA Crim 1591, the offender (aged 20) formed a liaison with   **B2.112**
a boy of 14, M. This appeared improper and unhealthy and D was served with a 'Harbouring' notice requiring him not to associate with M. The notice stated that if he allowed M 'to be at an address at which you reside or are at and/or associate with this child, you will be arrested for child abduction'. He repeatedly defied this notice, even when on bail for other breaches, and eventually pleaded guilty to three counts of child abduction, for which he was sentenced to a total of 22 months' imprisonment. This was reduced on appeal to 16 months in light of substantial personal mitigation, notably the offender's genuine friendship with M and unhappy childhood and adolescence, which probably contributed to his feelings of isolation and loneliness at the time of the offences.

CHILD CRUELTY

Sentence

Mason [2013] EWCA Crim 1666 was a case in which the judge had faced a difficult sentencing   **B2.133**
exercise. The offender's son (aged 22 months) had fallen from a worktop and suffered a head injury. When the child showed signs of fitting, the offender called an ambulance but did not tell the paramedics or doctors what had happened. The child died, but might possibly have been saved had the truth been told at once. The offender pleaded guilty to wilful neglect. He had no relevant previous convictions and expressed deep and genuine remorse for what had happened. A sentence of 15 months' imprisonment was reduced on appeal to ten months, but the Court of Appeal declined to suspend that sentence. D's neglect to tell the truth may not have caused his son's death but had, to some unquantifiable extent, exposed the child to a higher risk of serious injury and death.

ILL-TREATMENT OF MENTAL PATIENTS OR
PERSONS WHO LACK CAPACITY

Ill-treatment or Neglect of Persons who Lack Capacity

Sentence   In *Kenyon* [2013] EWCA Crim 2123, a care assistant at a residential home was   **B2.148**
upset that she had been denied promotion and took out her anger on the elderly residents in her care, leaving them unfed, unchanged and uncared for throughout her six-hour shift. Many were incontinent and were left in a pitiful state. A sentence of eight months' immediate imprisonment was upheld on appeal. Her offending was considered even more serious than that in *Heaney* [2011] EWCA Crim 2682 (another case of wilful neglect and cruelty by a care assistant), where the total sentence had been six months' imprisonment.

Elements   *Sheppard* [1981] AC 394 and *Patel* [2013] All ER (D) 216 (May) were considered   **B2.149**
in *Turbill* [2013] EWCA Crim 1422. The Court of Appeal quashed a conviction for wilful neglect on the basis of errors in the trial judge's summing-up. Hallett LJ said:

> In some of the passages to which we have referred, [the judge] appears to equate carelessness or negligence with wilful neglect. They are not the same. Parliament has decreed that neglect is not enough to constitute a criminal offence, even of a vulnerable patient...The neglect must be 'wilful' and that

means something more is required than a duty and what a reasonable person would regard as a reckless breach of that duty.

OFFENCES OF HARASSMENT

Definition of Harassment

B2.165   *Majrowski v Guy's & St Thomas's NHS Trust* [2007] 1 AC 224 was considered in *Plavelil v DPP* [2014] EWHC 736 (Admin), in which it was held that the repeated making of false and malicious assertions against a doctor in connection with an investigation by the GMC could amount to a course of harassment. The Divisional Court unsurprisingly rejected the argument that malicious allegations could not be oppressive if they could easily be rebutted.

Section B3   Sexual Offences

INTRODUCTION

B3.1   The DPP has issued comprehensive new guidelines and protocols on prosecuting cases of child sexual abuse. See www.cps.gov.uk/legal/a_to_c/child_sexual_abuse/. Guidance is provided for each stage of a prosecution, from early consultation between the CPS and the police through to trial. A link is also provided for guidance as to inter-agency working to safeguard and promote the welfare of children.

In October 2013, the '2013 Protocol and Good Practice Model: Disclosure of information in cases of alleged child abuse and linked criminal and care directions' was issued, having effect from 1 January 2014. It is of special importance where concurrent criminal and care proceedings are taking place. It can be accessed at www.judiciary.gov.uk/publications-and-reports/guidance/2013/protocol-good-practice-model-2013 (see also **D9.5** in this supplement).

Sentencing under the Sexual Offences Act 2003 and Historic Cases: General

B3.3   The Sentencing Council has published new guidelines which have effect from 1 April 2014 (see part 26 of the Sentencing Guidelines at **SG-528** in this supplement) whenever the offence was committed. The new guidelines apply to all adult offenders but not to those aged under 18. The new guideline was produced following a thorough consultation with victims, criminal justice professionals and the public. (See Sexual Offences: The New Definitive Guideline by HHJ Peter Rook QC and others in *Blackstone's Criminal Practice Quarterly Update*, March 2014 for analysis of the key changes implemented by the new guideline.)

In *A-G's Ref (No. 38 of 2013) (Hall)* [2013] EWCA Crim 1450, the Court of Appeal increased the sentence on a well-known television personality for a large number of historic offences of sexual assault committed against young girls (aged between 10 and 17), which were committed over a number of years whilst the offender was middle-aged. The offender had been sentenced to a total of 15 months' imprisonment following guilty pleas that were acceptable to the prosecution. Giving the judgment of the Court, Lord Judge CJ observed (at [75]):

> The offender's successful career provides no mitigation. On the contrary, it was the career that put him in a position of trust which he was then able to exploit and which contributed to his image as a cheerful, fun-loving, fundamentally decent man. This contributed to the view that he could be trusted; and second, if he could not be trusted, effectively he was untouchable. It is true that he has no previous convictions of any kind. It is true that he has behaved decently on occasions and deserves credit for that. But we now know, as the world at large knows, that since the mid-1960s he molested children and growing girls and therefore that he lived a lie — a lie for more than half his life; a lie repeated on the steps of the magistrates' court for the benefit of the accompanying media.

His attacks on the victims to the media constituted an aggravating feature of his offences. A damaging effect of his crimes was that it had caused difficulties between the victims and their parents because the matters were not reported to the police. Moreover, the Court of Appeal explained that the principle of double jeopardy did not apply in the offender's case as he was already serving a custodial sentence and was aware that the A-G intended to refer the sentence to the Court of Appeal. The sentence of 15 months' imprisonment was increased to one of 30 months.

RAPE

Sentencing Guidelines

Life Imprisonment: Automatic and Discretionary Life Sentences   *Saunders* [2013]   **B3.16**
EWCA Crim 1027 is an instructive recent example of the Court of Appeal upholding a discretionary life sentence in a very serious rape case. The Court took the view that a life sentence was correctly imposed even though the option of an IPP or an extended sentence had been available to the judge. Lord Judge CJ noted the appalling nature of the offences. He observed that the evidence underlined that, for an indefinite period, the offender would represent a very high risk to children. There was no getting away from the stark, profoundly disturbing facts.

The offender had been sentenced to life imprisonment with a minimum term of eight years for the rape of a child under 13, contrary to the SOA 2003, s. 5. He was given concurrent sentences for various other sexual offences. There were two child victims. The appellant, a photography student, was aged 23. In 2005, when he was only 16, he was convicted of a sexual assault upon a five-year-old girl. He had admitted downloading sexual images of children since he was 12. The probation officer described him as having an entrenched pattern of sexual offending against children.

The offender had answered an advertisement on the internet for a babysitter for G, a girl then aged six. He provided the parents with a bogus employment history and bogus references. He claimed that he would provide the relevant criminal records check when it was available. To the parents and prospective employers, he appeared plausible, even charming; he seemed to interact with the child in a natural way. This was all a front, for he had always intended to abuse G whilst the parents were out, indeed, he wrote a script in advance describing what he planned to do. The offender also obtained similar employment with another family who had a daughter, aged seven. Again he wrote himself a script and filmed and edited the acts amounting to offences, including oral rape of a child aged under 13.

When police searched his house, they found the films and 4,000 indecent images of children, some at level 4 or 5 on the Copine scale. He told the writer of the pre-sentence report that, after a time, viewing was not enough and he wanted to be part of it. Police also found a diary in which the appellant set out in disturbing detail how to abduct, sexually abuse, kill and dispose of a child. The author of the pre-sentence report did not accept that his expressions of remorse were genuine. He was plainly dangerous.

In his sentencing remarks the judge observed that these were truly grave sexual offences and concluded that the public would consider this offence warranted a sentence of denunciatory value and accordingly imposed a sentence of life imprisonment on the s. 5 count. If sentence had been passed one month later, after the coming into force of the relevant provisions of the LASPO 2012 and the abolition of IPP, it would no longer have been apposite to identify a 'denunciatory' ingredient to distinguish between the circumstances in which discretionary life should be imposed rather than IPP. However, the Court of Appeal agreed with the judge's decision — even if the judge had not found the 'denunciatory' element, its absence would not have precluded the imposition of a life sentence. (See **E4.6**, **E4.9** and **E4.14** in the main work for important discussion in *Saunders* of the principles applying to the imposition of discretionary life sentences after the abolition of the sentence of imprisonment for public protection by the LASPO 2012.)

Absence of Consent

B3.23   In *Kamki* [2013] EWCA Crim 2335, the Court of Appeal observed that, when the elements of capacity to consent have been fully explained in a summing-up, there is no necessity to say the simple words that 'a drunken consent remains a consent' in every case.

SEX OFFENCES AGAINST CHILDREN AGED 13 TO 16

Causing or Inciting a Child to Engage in Sexual Activity

B3.105   **Sentencing**   The Court of Appeal considered a reference by the A-G of sentences for 'cyber sex' offences in *Knight* [2013] EWCA Crim 1757. The offender had pleaded guilty at a plea and case management hearing to an indictment containing 17 counts. Counts 1 to 14 involved inciting or attempting to incite children to engage in sexual activities, contrary to the SOA 2003, ss. 8(1) and 10(1), count 15 charged attempting to incite a child to engage in sexual activity, and counts 16 and 17 concerned the making of indecent photographs of children. Eight offences similar in nature to those pleaded in counts 1 to 15 were asked to be taken into consideration. He was sentenced to a total of 16 months' imprisonment.

The offender described himself on 'Facebook' as a teenage girl or boy and thereby befriended younger boys, and incited and/or caused eight of them to perform sexual activities such as masturbating in front of a web camera so that he could see them. Count 15 arose from the fact that he also unsuccessfully incited more than 200 others to indulge in similar behaviour. A number of the offences were committed whilst on bail for others.

The Solicitor General submitted that the aggravating features of the case were that the offender committed a number of the offences whilst on bail, the high number of victims and the high degree of sophisticated planning. The acknowledged mitigating features were the full admissions in interview and the early guilty pleas.

As there was no specific sentencing guideline related to these offences, the Solicitor General submitted that guidance should be derived from that directed to the closest analogy on the facts, namely the guideline relating to the offences under the SOA 2003, s. 8. The starting point there where there is one victim and the offender is a person of good character is five years' imprisonment with a range of four to eight years. Before discounting for plea, the sentencing judge had taken a starting point of two years. The Court of Appeal noted that in *A-G's Ref (No. 24 of 2011)* [2011] EWCA Crim 1960 Hughes LJ had observed that the Sentencing Guidelines Council's work was concerned with contact sexual offences rather than 'cyber sex' offences and had approved the approach in *Butcher* [2009] EWCA Crim 1458. That involved looking at the nearest applicable guideline and deriving general assistance from it, but no more. Moreover, a sentencing court should remember that offences of cyber sex, serious as they were, were ordinarily likely to be less serious than physical contact offences. However, Rafferty LJ said (at [21]–[24]):

> We do not construe the words of the Vice-President as intending in any way to dilute the seriousness on their own facts of offences such as these.
>
> The Solicitor General suggests that these offences, although in one sense less serious than physical contact, are arguably more difficult to prevent. Additionally, one could readily envisage some contact offences which were themselves less serious than some cyber sex offences, particularly if, as here, the latter are in number. The long-term effect on a child confronting personal exposure to a stranger is likely to be severe, the Solicitor General suggests, conceding that inevitably only time will tell.
>
> ...
>
> In our judgment the submissions of Her Majesty's Solicitor General are unanswerable.

The total sentence was increased to one of four years' imprisonment.

EXTREME PORNOGRAPHIC IMAGES

Sentencing

In *Livesey* [2013] All ER (D) 179 (Aug) the Court of Appeal reduced the sentence for an offender **B3.339**
who had pleaded guilty to three offences of possessing extreme pornographic images contrary
to the CJIA 2008, s. 63, from a total of 14 months' imprisonment to four months. The offender
had a large number of still and moving images on his laptop of horses and dogs penetrating
women. He admitted the offences immediately upon police officers arriving at his home. The
Court decided that, even though the number of extreme images involved was large and the
offender had deliberately sought them out, since he had no previous convictions, was of good
character and had demonstrated remorse for his actions and there were no other aggravating
features in his case and the personal mitigation was extremely strong, an element of leniency was
justified.

Section B4   Theft, Handling Stolen Goods and Related Offences

THEFT

Sentence

Offences of Theft Generally   Thefts that create danger to the public (e.g., theft of manhole **B4.6**
covers from public roads at night, as in *Leith* [2013] EWCA Crim 1971) will ordinarily merit
severe sentences in order to deter others. In *Leith,* the Court of Appeal approved a starting point
of four years' imprisonment for the theft of 185 such manhole covers.

Theft in Breach of Trust   In *Griffiths* [2013] EWCA Crim 2507 the Court of Appeal quashed **B4.9**
a sentence of 16 months' imprisonment imposed for two offences of theft, committed at the
houses of elderly and disabled people to whom the offender was providing her services as a carer.
The Court held that the judge ought to have reduced the starting point indicated in the relevant
sentencing guidelines in order to reflect the personal circumstances of the offender and the
motives which had driven her. Accordingly, the sentence would be reduced on each count to ten
months' imprisonment, to be served concurrently.

BURGLARY

Sentence

Burglary from Dwellings   In *A-G's Ref (Nos. 44 and 45 of 2013) (Connors)* [2013] EWCA **B4.81**
Crim 1460, sentences of five and seven years (on guilty pleas) were held to be unduly lenient in a
case of conspiracy to commit domestic burglaries in which at least 34 dwellings had been bur-
gled. The offences exhibited a number of similarities, namely: (i) in the vast majority, the offenders targeted the homes of elderly people; (ii) burglaries would be committed either by using force
to break in through windows or doors or by a method of distraction on the part of the offenders;
and (iii) money and jewellery were targeted which were of a high monetary and/or sentimental value.

During the commission of some of the offences, the victims were at home and were either too
scared or too vulnerable to stop the offenders. Many were cowed and frightened. Some of the
victims were particularly vulnerable and suffered from dementia. This could properly be said to
put the offences into the top category of offending of that type. Sentences of six and nine years
were substituted.

Section B5   Fraud and Blackmail

THE OFFENCE OF FRAUD

Sentencing for Fraud Offences Generally

B5.7   False whiplash injury claims in motor insurance cases were featured in *McKenzie* [2013] EWCA Crim 1544, where the offender pleaded guilty to fraudulently claiming in respect of an accident that had never occurred. He received a sentence of 15 months' imprisonment, which reflected the fact that it was part of a wider conspiracy involving many such cases and in which the ringleader received a seven-year sentence. He argued that he should have been sentenced in respect of a single fraudulent transaction with a starting point of 26 weeks' imprisonment but the Court of Appeal disagreed. Moreover, a deterrent sentence was justified on the facts. Such frauds cost the insurance industry millions and add £50 a year to each driver's premium. See also *M* [2013] EWCA Crim 206, which involved other parties to this wider conspiracy.

The Sentencing Council has published a new sentencing guideline for the sentencing of organisations convicted, *inter alia*, of fraud. The new guideline, entitled 'Fraud, bribery and money laundering: corporate offenders', has effect from 1 October 2014.

POSSESSION OR CONTROL OF ARTICLES FOR USE IN FRAUD

B5.21   The observations made by the Court of Appeal in *Ellames* [1974] 3 All ER 130 as to the application of the Theft Act 1968, s. 25, apply with equal force to offences under the Fraud Act 2006, s. 6. It follows that possession or control of items previously used in frauds does not of itself suffice to create liability under s. 6. See *Sakalauskas* [2014] 1 All ER 1231.

Procedure, Sentence and Jurisdiction

B5.22   The Sentencing Council has published a new sentencing guideline for the sentencing of organisations convicted, *inter alia*, of possession of articles for use in fraud. The new guideline, entitled 'Fraud, bribery and money laundering: corporate offenders', has effect from 1 October 2014.

MAKING OR SUPPLYING ARTICLES FOR USE IN FRAUD

Procedure, Sentence and Jurisdiction

B5.24   The Sentencing Council has published a new sentencing guideline for the sentencing of organisations convicted, *inter alia*, of making or supplying articles for use in fraud. The new guideline, entitled 'Fraud, bribery and money laundering: corporate offenders', has effect from 1 October 2014.

Section B6   Falsification, Forgery and Counterfeiting

FALSE ACCOUNTING

Sentence

B6.6   The Sentencing Council has published a new sentencing guideline for the sentencing of organisations convicted, *inter alia*, of false accounting. The new guideline, entitled 'Fraud, bribery and money laundering: corporate offenders', has effect from 1 October 2014.

Section B7   Company, Commercial and Insolvency Offences

FRAUDULENT TRADING

Liability of Parties

In *Bilta (UK) Ltd v Nazir (No. 2)* [2013] 3 WLR 1167 (at [84]–[93]) the Court of Appeal decided that the Insolvency Act 1986, s. 213, has extra-territorial effect and extends to persons outside the jurisdiction.   **B7.9**

THE CARTEL OFFENCE

Section 188 of the Enterprise Act 2002 is amended by the Enterprise and Regulatory Reform Act 2013, s. 47(1) to (4), and new ss. 188A and 188B are inserted by s. 47(5) and (6) of the 2013 Act. Section 47 of the 2013 Act is not yet in force but, when it comes into force, the Enterprise Act 2002, ss. 188 to 188B, will provide as follows: **B7.40**

188.—(1) An individual is guilty of an offence if he agrees with one or more other persons to make or implement, or to cause to be made or implemented, arrangements of the following kind relating to at least two undertakings (A and B).

(2) The arrangements must be ones which, if operating as the parties to the agreement intend, would—

    (a)   directly or indirectly fix a price for the supply by A in the United Kingdom (otherwise than to B) of a product or service,

    (b)   limit or prevent supply by A in the United Kingdom of a product or service,

    (c)   limit or prevent production by A in the United Kingdom of a product,

    (d)   divide between A and B the supply in the United Kingdom of a product or service to a customer or customers,

    (e)   divide between A and B customers for the supply in the United Kingdom of a product or service, or

    (f)   be bid-rigging arrangements.

(3) Unless subsection (2)(d), (e) or (f) applies, the arrangements must also be ones which, if operating as the parties to the agreement intend, would—

    (a)   directly or indirectly fix a price for the supply by B in the United Kingdom (otherwise than to A) of a product or service,

    (b)   limit or prevent supply by B in the United Kingdom of a product or service, or

    (c)   limit or prevent production by B in the United Kingdom of a product.

(4) In subsections (2)(a) to (d) and (3), references to supply or production are to supply or production in the appropriate circumstances (for which see section 189).

(5) 'Bid-rigging arrangements' are arrangements under which, in response to a request for bids for the supply of a product or service in the United Kingdom, or for the production of a product in the United Kingdom—

    (a)   A but not B may make a bid, or

    (b)   A and B may each make a bid but, in one case or both, only a bid arrived at in accordance with the arrangements.

(6) [Repealed.]

(7) 'Undertaking' has the same meaning as in Part 1 of the 1998 Act.

(8) This section is subject to section 188A.

188A.—(1) An individual does not commit an offence under section 188(1) if, under the arrangements—

    (a)   in a case where the arrangements would (operating as the parties intend) affect the supply in the United Kingdom of a product or service, customers would be given relevant information about the arrangements before they enter into agreements for the supply to them of the product or service so affected,

    (b)   in the case of bid-rigging arrangements, the person requesting bids would be given relevant information about them at or before the time when a bid is made, or

    (c)   in any case, relevant information about the arrangements would be published, before the arrangements are implemented, in the manner specified at the time of the making of the agreement in an order made by the Secretary of State.

(2) In subsection (1), 'relevant information' means—

    (a)   the names of the undertakings to which the arrangements relate,

    (b) a description of the nature of the arrangements which is sufficient to show why they are or might be arrangements of the kind to which section 188(1) applies,

    (c) the products or services to which they relate, and

    (d) such other information as may be specified in an order made by the Secretary of State.

(3) An individual does not commit an offence under section 188(1) if the agreement is made in order to comply with a legal requirement.

(4) In subsection (3), 'legal requirement' has the same meaning as in paragraph 5 of Schedule 3 to the Competition Act 1998.

(5) A power to make an order under this section—

    (a) is exercisable by statutory instrument,

    (b) may be exercised so as to make different provision for different cases or different purposes, and

    (c) includes power to make such incidental, supplementary, consequential, transitory, transitional or saving provision as the Secretary of State considers appropriate.

(6) A statutory instrument containing an order under this section is subject to annulment in pursuance of a resolution of either House of Parliament.

188B.—(1) In a case where the arrangements would (operating as the parties intend) affect the supply in the United Kingdom of a product or service, it is a defence for an individual charged with an offence under section 188(1) to show that, at the time of the making of the agreement, he or she did not intend that the nature of the arrangements would be concealed from customers at all times before they enter into agreements for the supply to them of the product or service.

(2) It is a defence for an individual charged with an offence under section 188(1) to show that, at the time of the making of the agreement, he or she did not intend that the nature of the arrangements would be concealed from the [Competition and Markets Authority].

(3) It is a defence for an individual charged with an offence under section 188(1) to show that, before the making of the agreement, he or she took reasonable steps to ensure that the nature of the arrangements would be disclosed to professional legal advisers for the purposes of obtaining advice about them before their making or (as the case may be) their implementation.

BANKRUPTCY OFFENCES

Fraudulent Disposal or Concealment of Property

B7.66   On sentencing for an offence contrary to the Insolvency Act 1986, s. 357, see also *Ferguson* [2013] EWCA Crim 1089.

Obtaining Credit: Engaging in Business

B7.71   **Obtaining**   For an offence to be committed by a bankrupt contrary to the Insolvency Act 1986, s. 360, the agreement to provide credit does not have to be enforceable (*Roder Ltd v West* [2012] QB 752 at [17]).

SENTENCING: INSOLVENCY AND BANKRUPTCY OFFENCES

B7.77   See also *Hussain* [2013] EWCA Crim 2243 (six months' imprisonment, not suspended, imposed on a bankrupt for making a false statement and fraudulent concealment of property).

Section B10   Terrorism, Piracy and Hijacking

TERRORISM: OVERVIEW

Definition of Terrorism

B10.2   In *Gul* [2013] 3 WLR 1207 the Supreme Court reviewed the definition of terrorism in the TA 2000, s. 1. The Court noted, but did not restrict, the very wide ambit of the definition.

G appealed against a decision ([2012] EWCA Crim 280) dismissing his appeal against his conviction for dissemination of terrorist publications contrary to the TA 2006, s. 2. The certified question was whether the definition of 'terrorism' in the TA 2000, s. 1, operated so as to include any or all military attacks by a non-state armed group against any or all state or inter-governmental organisation armed forces in the context of a non-international armed conflict.

The Court concluded that, although it had concerns about the breadth of the definition (referring to the reports of the Independent Reviewer and the comments on this issue from David Anderson QC in particular), there was no basis in domestic law to restrict the statutory definition in the way advanced by the appellant.

The appellant advanced arguments based in international law that:

(a) some provisions of the 2000 and 2006 Acts were enacted to give effect to the UK's treaty obligations concerned with the suppression of terrorism, and that 'terrorism' should accordingly be given a meaning in those statutes which accords with the international law norm, consistent with the definition in the treaty to which effect is being given, and

(b) that, as the 2000 and 2006 Acts criminalise certain 'terrorist' actions committed outside the UK, the meaning of 'terrorism' in those statutes should not be wider than what is accepted as an international norm.

The Court noted the absence of any accepted norm in international law as to what constitutes terrorism, citing its recent decision in *Al-Sirri v Secretary of State for the Home Department* [2013] 1 AC 745. It observed that, whilst some UN and other texts provided significant support for the argument that terrorism did not extend to the acts of insurgents or 'freedom fighters' in non-international armed conflicts, it was insufficient to demonstrate a rule of international law requiring the definition to be read down as being in conflict with the UK's ECHR or other international law obligations. It reiterated the point made in *Al-Sirri*, that 'an attack on ISAF in Afghanistan is in principle capable of being an act contrary to the purposes and principles of the United Nations', and such an attack therefore can constitute 'terrorism'. The Court pointed to UN resolutions which referred to the activities of Al-Qa'ida and the Taliban as 'terrorism', even though their actions involved insurgents attacking forces of states and inter-governmental organisations in non-international armed conflict and noted that insurgents do not benefit from combatant immunity in non-international armed conflicts.

Next, the Court considered the argument that the TA 2000, ss. 62 to 64, and some provisions of the TA 2006, gave effect to the UK's obligations under international conventions, two of which exclude insurgent attacks on military forces in non-international armed conflicts from their definitions. However, the Court declined to read down the definition of terrorism because some of the activities which became offences under the TA 2000 were included in order to fulfil international law obligations. This was because the UK can go beyond its international law obligations in criminalising conduct. And, even if the wide definition of terrorism in s. 1 had to be read down for the purposes of ss. 62 to 64, it did not have to be read down when interpreting the rest of the Act. This was the approach in *Al-Sirri*, where the Court held that, if the application of the wide definition of terrorism in s. 1 led to another provision of the Act being found to be in conflict with the UK's obligations under the Geneva Convention, then the definition should be read down when applied to the provision in question only.

Finally, the Court made two general points about the two Acts. First, the Court observed that the definition of terrorism was concerningly wide and that serious consideration should be given to legislative narrowing of that definition, provided that it was done in a way which was consistent with public protection. Secondly, the Court expressed concern about the substantial and unrestricted intrusive powers granted to the police and to immigration officers, including stop and search and the powers under the TA 2000, sch. 7 ('port stop' procedures), which depend upon very broad discretion on their part.

COUNTER-TERRORISM POWERS UNDER THE TERRORISM ACT 2000

Port and Border Controls

B10.27 In *Beghal v DPP* [2013] EWHC 2573 (Admin) the Divisional Court ruled that the operation of the TA 2000, sch. 7, did not breach either Article 6 or 8 of the ECHR. The Court observed (at [151]):

> ...although the Independent Reviewer has drawn attention to the increase in litigation concerning the schedule 7 powers, he has reiterated the utility of these powers as an 'essential tool' in the fight against terrorism: see, for instance, paras. 10.35 and 10.63. At para. 10.91, the 2013 [Independent Reviewer's] Report says this:
>
> > 'The power remains of unquestioned utility; and as I have recorded in previous years, examinations are for the most part exercised with good humour, good judgment and restraint. The decreasing use of schedule 7 in recent years contrasts markedly with the explosion in the use of section 44 during the second half of the last decade. Senior ports officers are well aware not only of the value of the power, but of the fact that like all valuable things, it needs careful handling.'

SUBSTANTIVE TERRORISM OFFENCES UNDER THE TERRORISM ACT 2000

Membership of a Proscribed Organisation

B10.34 **Elements** By virtue of the Proscribed Organisations (Name Changes) (No. 2) Order 2013 (SI 2013 No. 2742), from 29 October 2013, the organisation 'Ahle Sunnat wal Jamaat' is to be treated as another name for the proscribed organisations Lashkar-e Jhangvi and Sipah-e Sahaba Pakistan. By virtue of the Terrorism Act 2000 (Proscribed Organisations) (Amendment) (No. 2) Order 2013 (SI 2013 No. 3172), with effect from 13 December 2013, the organisation 'Imarat Kavkaz (Caucasus Emirate)' is designated a proscribed organisation under the TA 2000, sch. 2.

Section B11   Offences Affecting Public Order

HARASSMENT, ALARM OR DISTRESS

B11.69 The Crime and Courts Act 2013 (Commencement No. 6) Order 2013 (SI 2013 No. 2981) brought the CCA 2013, s. 57, into force on 1 February 2014.

B11.70 **ECHR, Article 10** The Divisional Court in *Gough v DPP* [2013] EWHC 3267 (Admin) upheld the finding of the District Judge in the court below that being naked was a form of expression such that the ECHR, Article 10, was engaged but that there was a pressing social need for the restriction of his right to be naked in the context of this case (the appellant had walked naked in the centre of Halifax in the daytime for around 15 minutes before being arrested). The restriction imposed as a consequence of the POA 1986, s. 5, corresponded to this social need; as a summary-only offence, it was a proportionate response to it.

Threatening, Abusive or Insulting Words or Behaviour; Disorderly Behaviour; Writing

B11.74 The Crime and Courts Act 2013 (Commencement No. 6) Order 2013 (SI 2013 No. 2981) brought the CCA 2013, s. 57, into force on 1 February 2014.

Mens Rea

B11.79 The Crime and Courts Act 2013 (Commencement No. 6) Order 2013 (SI 2013 No. 2981) brought the CCA 2013, s. 57, into force on 1 February 2014.

CONTROL OF PROCESSIONS, ASSEMBLIES AND MEETINGS

Failure to Comply with Conditions Imposed on Public Procession

The power to direct conditions as to the route of a procession is not confined to processions **B11.112** whose routes have been designated under the POA 1986, s. 11. In *Powlesland v DPP* [2013] EWHC 3846 (Admin), the Divisional Court held that s. 12 plainly covered processions and proposed routes which had not been notified. This case arose from another critical mass ride (as to which see *R (Kay) v Commissioner of Police of the Metropolis* [2008] 2 All ER 935 at **B11.111** in the main work, in which it was established that no notification was necessary where the mass ride took place at the same time and same place every month but with no predetermined route). The senior police officer had made a direction specifying that the ride must go north of the Thames. The Court found the order was lawful and the appellant had been properly convicted of the offence under s. 12(5). Where the police reasonably believed the procession might take a seriously disruptive route, it was open to them to use the power in s. 12: it was not necessary for them to know the actual route at the time the direction was given.

USING WORDS OR BEHAVIOUR OR DISPLAYING WRITTEN MATERIAL STIRRING UP HATRED ON RELIGIOUS GROUNDS OR ON GROUNDS OF SEXUAL ORIENTATION

Elements

The Marriage (Same Sex Couples) Act 2013 (Commencement No. 2 and Transitional **B11.183** Provisions) Order 2014 (SI 2014 No. 93) brought the Marriage (Same Sex Couples) Act 2013, sch. 7, para. 28 into force on 13 March 2014.

Section B12   Offences Relating to Weapons

FIREARM OFFENCES GENERALLY

As to the power of the Court of Appeal to substitute a firearms offence, pursuant to the Criminal **B12.1** Appeal Act 1968, s. 3A, see *Lawrence* [2014] 1 WLR 106.

GENERAL DEFINITIONS

Meaning of 'Firearm'

Any Component Part   See also the Home Office 'Guide on Firearms Licensing Law' **B12.13** (November 2013), para. 13.74.

Meaning of 'Ammunition'

See also the Home Office 'Guide on Firearms Licensing Law' (November 2013), para. 2.12.   **B12.20**

OFFENCES RELATING TO IMITATION FIREARMS

Offences Applying to Imitation Firearms by virtue of the Firearms Act 1982

For a commentary to *Williams* [2013] 2 All ER 787, see [2013] Crim LR 981, at p. 984.   **B12.26**

POSSESSING ETC. FIREARM OR AMMUNITION
WITHOUT FIREARM CERTIFICATE

Possession Generally

B12.40   The distinction in the FA 1968 between being in 'possession' of a firearm and 'having a firearm with him' is reinforced (it is submitted) by the observations of the Court in *Veira* [2013] EWCA Crim 1823 at [15].

EXEMPTIONS AND DEFENCES FOR THE PURPOSES
OF THE FIREARMS ACT 1968, s. 1

B12.43   Note the amendments made to the Firearms Rules 1998 (SI 1998 No. 1941) by the Firearms (Amendment) Rules 2013 (SI 2013 No. 1945) and the Firearms (Amendment) (No. 2) Rules 2013 (SI 2013 No. 2970), both in force from 1 December 2013.

OFFENCES RELATING TO SHOT GUNS

Possessing etc. Shot Gun without Shot Gun Certificate

B12.46   Note the amendments made to the Firearms Rules 1998 (SI 1998 No. 1941) by the Firearms (Amendment) Rules 2013 (SI 2013 No. 1945) and the Firearms (Amendment) (No. 2) Rules 2013 (SI 2013 No. 2970), both in force from 1 December 2013.

POSSESSING OR DISTRIBUTING PROHIBITED
WEAPONS OR AMMUNITION

Specific Issues Associated with Particular Prohibited Weapons

B12.65   See also the Home Office 'Guide on Firearms Licensing Law' (November 2013), para. 2.55, and chapter 3.

POSSESSION OF FIREARM WITH INTENT TO ENDANGER LIFE

Virtual Certainty and Intention

B12.88   In *Royle* [2013] EWCA Crim 1461, the Court of Appeal, having regard to *Nedrick* [1986] 3 All ER 1 and *Woollin* [1999] AC 82, held that the direction '[y]ou must be sure that he did not just realise that it could happen but acted on the basis that it would or that he intended that it would' was far from being a misdirection but, arguably, set a hurdle higher than that in *Woollin* and *Nedrick*. It contemplated not virtual certainty but certainty.

Section B13   Offences Affecting Enjoyment of Premises

AGGRAVATED TRESPASS

Elements

B13.47   Upholding the decision of the Divisional Court (see **B13.47** in the main work), the Supreme Court in *Richardson v DPP* [2014] UKSC 8 held that the intention of the CJPO 1994, s. 68, is plainly to add the sanction of the criminal law to a trespass where, in addition to the defendant invading the property of someone else where he is not entitled to be, he there disrupts an activity which the occupant is entitled to pursue. Section 68(2) therefore must mean that the additional criminal sanction is removed when the activity which is disrupted is, in itself, unlawful, which may be either because the occupant is himself trespassing, or because his activity is criminal. Not every incidental or collateral criminal offence can properly be said to affect the lawfulness of the activity, nor to render it criminal. It will do so only when the criminal offence is integral to the core activity carried on. It will not do so when there is some incidental or collateral offence which is remote from the activity. If, however, a criminal offence integral to the core activity is raised, it may involve the court investigating extraneous facts, or the conduct of third parties.

TRESPASS ON A PROTECTED SITE

Elements

The Serious Organised Crime and Police Act 2005 (Designated Sites under Section 128) (Amendment) Order 2014 (SI 2014 No. 411), which has effect from 26 March 2014, amends the principal Order of 2007 (SI 2007 No. 930) with the effect of removing the GCHQ site at Cheltenham from the list of designated sites. **B13.81**

Section B14   Offences Against the Administration of Justice

General: Criminal Practice Directions

The *Criminal Practice Directions* [2013] EWCA Crim 1631, as amended (see [2013] EWCA Crim 2328), revoked and replaced the greater part of the *Consolidated Criminal Practice Direction* [2002] 1 WLR 2870. References in the main work to directions which have been revoked should now refer to the new *Criminal Practice Directions* as follows:

B14.34   *Consolidated Criminal Practice Direction*, para. III.21 — New *Criminal Practice Directions*, II Preliminary Matters, Part 14 Settling the Indictment, para. 14A.3 (see **PD-17** in this supplement).

B14.110 *Consolidated Criminal Practice Direction*, para. I.2 — New *Criminal Practice Directions*, II Preliminary Matters, Part 16 Reporting etc. Restrictions, para. 16A.2 (see **PD-19** in this supplement).

B14.114 *Consolidated Criminal Practice Direction*, para. I.3 — New *Criminal Practice Directions*, II Preliminary Matters, Part 16 Reporting etc. Restrictions (see **PD-19** in this supplement).

PERVERTING THE COURSE OF JUSTICE

Sentence

In *Evans-Keady* [2013] EWCA Crim 1546 the Court of Appeal held that in sentencing for **B14.33** perverting or conspiracy to pervert the course of justice a court must always consider: (i) the seriousness of the underlying offence; (ii) the degree to which the conspiracy or offence persisted; and (iii) the effect it had upon the course of justice. Where (as in *Evans-Keady*) the offender was a police officer, that must be an aggravating feature. But this case was unusual in that D first arrested a woman on suspicion of drug dealing and then (together with his co-accused, a civilian police employee) falsified the positive basic drug-test result as negative merely because he felt sorry for her. He never sought to gain from this and acted spontaneously out of misplaced sympathy. A sentence of two years' imprisonment on a late guilty plea was reduced to one of 12 months. The civilian employee had received a suspended sentence.

In *Shipman* [2013] EWCA Crim 1698 the partner of a recently convicted rapist manufactured false evidence in an attempt to destroy the credibility of the two complainants who had testified against her partner. This involved creating false Facebook accounts in the names of the two complainants, from which she then 'received' admissions that their evidence had been false. Her deception initially led to the arrest of the two complainants, but was soon exposed, and she pleaded guilty at the first opportunity. It was accepted that a custodial sentence was inevitable, but the Court of Appeal reduced this from 30 months to 20 months. Various mitigating features were noted, including the offender's youth (22) and previous good character, the fact that she had been abused and manipulated by her partner and the inexplicably long delay (30 months) in bringing her case to court. The sentencing judge had been aware of all this, but 'had not correctly assessed' the effect of the attempt to pervert the course of justice (see the note on *Evans-Keady*, above). This particular attempt never had any real prospect of success, although it caused distress and anxiety to the complainants.

CONTEMPT OF COURT

Forms of Contempt: Misuse of Tape Recorders in Court

B14.110 The Court of Appeal (Recording and Broadcasting) Order 2013 (SI 2013 No. 2786), which has effect from 21 November 2013, sets out the regime for the recording and broadcasting of certain proceedings in the Court of Appeal and, subject to compliance with that regime, provides that the Contempt of Court Act 1981, s. 9, will not apply in that context.

Forms of Contempt: Photography, Sketching, Tweeting and Mobile Telephones

B14.111 The Court of Appeal (Recording and Broadcasting) Order 2013 (SI 2013 No. 2786), which has effect from 21 November 2013, sets out the regime for the recording and broadcasting of certain proceedings in the Court of Appeal and, subject to compliance with that regime, provides that the CJA 1925, s. 41, will not apply in that context.

Section B15   Corruption

OFFENCES UNDER THE BRIBERY ACT 2010

The Structure of the Act

B15.2 The Sentencing Council has published a new sentencing guideline for the sentencing of organisations convicted, *inter alia*, of offences under the Bribery Act 2010, ss. 1, 2 and 6. The new guideline, entitled 'Fraud, bribery and money laundering: corporate offenders', has effect from 1 October 2014.

MISCONDUCT IN PUBLIC OFFICE

B15.27 In *King* [2013] EWCA Crim 1599, D, a prison officer, became involved with an ex-prisoner (E) without notifying her employers, as was required in such cases. E was later arrested again on serious drugs charges. D was also arrested and large sums of cash were found in her possession. After E was remanded in custody, D continued to make contact with him by means of a mobile phone that he had managed to obtain and conceal in his cell. D pleaded guilty (but not at the first opportunity) to charges of misconduct in public office and concealing criminal property. In respect of the former, sentences totalling three years' imprisonment (based on a starting point of four years) were reduced on appeal to 27 months. The Court of Appeal took account of the fact that D's relationship with E had not overlapped at any stage with an occasion when she was a prison officer at the prison where he was detained. Where there is such an overlap, there is an obvious danger of the officer being subjected to pressure or blackmail, but that was not the case here.

In *Bunyan* [2013] EWCA Crim 1885, a police community support officer was convicted after trial on eight counts of misconduct in public office in that, while on duty, he engaged in consensual sexual relationships with vulnerable women with whom he came into contact as a result of his position, improperly accessed police records, sent text messages of a sexual nature, and neglected his legitimate police work. A sentence of seven years' imprisonment in total was reduced on appeal to three years. The Court of Appeal observed that the offending was:

> ...to be clearly distinguished from those cases where police officers have taken blatant advantage of vulnerable women in the course of their duties: see *Fletcher* [2012] 1 Cr App R (S) 356. Further, the accessing of police records was to obtain personal information about the women and information about [another person] — none of it criminal intelligence. So that offending, while serious, is to be clearly distinguished from those cases where police officers have provided information to criminals: see *A-G's Ref (No 30 of 2010); Bohannan* [2011] 1 Cr App R 624; or accessed police computers to trace women for the purposes of having sexual relationships with them: see *Lewis* [2010] 2 Cr App R (S) 666.

An ambulance driver is not the holder of a public office for the purpose of this offence (*Mitchell* [2014] EWCA Crim 318).

OLD OFFENCE OF CORRUPTION IN PUBLIC OFFICE

Meaning of 'Corruptly'

Wellburn (1979) 69 Cr App R 254 was applied in *J* [2013] EWCA Crim 2287. In a prosecution brought under the Prevention of Corruption Act 1906, s. 1, alleging a conspiracy by agents of a company to bribe the tax officials of a Commonwealth country on behalf of that company, the prosecution did not have to prove that the company was unaware of the bribery. The prosecution needed only to prove that the payment had been made corruptly. As Lord Thomas CJ explained: **B15.36**

> In determining whether the payment was made corruptly in the case of transactions between commercial agents and principals any evidence relating to what was disclosed to the principal and what the principal knew and any informed consent may...be highly material to the issue of whether they acted corruptly. In such cases, the evidential inquiry may give rise to the factual issue of identifying the actual principal who is entitled to give informed consent after full disclosure. In the case of an overseas body corporate this may raise difficult factual inquiries in the light of the applicable law as determined by the judge. These are, however, all matters of evidence that may go to the issue of whether the payment for the prohibited purpose in transactions between commercial agents and commercial principals was made or received corruptly. However, by way of a contrary example, where there was a payment to a public official in the UK for the prohibited purpose, evidence as to knowledge and consent will...not arise. What the Crown has to prove remains the same in each case — that the payment for the prohibited purpose was made corruptly; evidence as to the informed consent of the actual principal may or may not be material or highly material depending on the facts of the case.

Section B16   Revenue, Customs and Social Security Offences

CHEATING THE PUBLIC REVENUE

For further cases on sentencing for carousel frauds, see *Bajwa* [2013] EWCA Crim 811 and *Hackney* [2013] EWCA Crim 1156.   **B16.3**

In *Dosanjh* [2013] EWCA Crim 2366 the Court of Appeal decided that Parliament had deliberately left the common-law offence of cheating the public revenue untouched by statutory changes. It therefore remains appropriate to charge this offence for the most serious revenue frauds for which statutory offences do not adequately reflect the criminality involved. The Court discussed current sentencing levels for the offence and imposed sentences on three offenders of imprisonment for 13 years, ten years and eight years respectively for conspiring to cheat the public revenue by a missing trader VAT fraud involving a loss to the public purse of £39 million. The Court pointed out that the offences in *Randhawa* [2012] 2 Cr App R (S) 298 were aggravated by the fact that at the time of the offence the offenders were on bail for offences of money laundering and deception.

The Sentencing Council has published a new sentencing guideline for the sentencing of organisations convicted, *inter alia*, of cheating the public revenue. The new guideline, entitled 'Fraud, bribery and money laundering: corporate offenders', has effect from 1 October 2014.

CUSTOMS AND EXCISE: PROCEDURAL PROVISIONS

B16.15 The decisions of the Court of Appeal in *Chambers, Khan, White, Bell* and *Bajwa* (all referred to at **B16.15** in the main work) were discussed and applied by the Supreme Court in *Mackle* [2014] 2 WLR 267. Not all persons knowingly involved in the fraudulent evasion of duty contrary to the Customs and Excise Management Act 1979, s. 170(2) are chargeable with duty. Under the Tobacco Products Regulations 2001 (SI 2001 No. 1712), duty on tobacco products brought by sea becomes chargeable when the ship carrying them comes within the limits of a port. Regulation 13 identifies the persons liable to pay the duty. Confiscation orders cannot be made against other offenders solely on the basis that they have obtained a benefit in evading duty to the value of the amount of duty unpaid.

OFFENCES IN CONNECTION WITH COMMISSIONERS AND OFFICERS

Obstruction of and Assaults upon Officers etc.

B16.25 The power to seize and detain goods was further discussed in *Customs and Excise Commissioners v First Stop Wholesale Ltd* [2013] EWCA Civ 183 and *R (Blackside Ltd) v Secretary of State for the Home Department* [2013] EWHC 2087 (Admin).

SENTENCING GUIDELINES FOR REVENUE FRAUD

B16.50 On sentencing for smuggling, see also *Lamb* [2013] EWCA Crim 1365 (sentences of six and five years' imprisonment on former police officers for conspiracy to evade duty on cigarettes), *Lachman* [2013] EWCA Crim 1528 (sentence of five and a half years' imprisonment on a drugs courier importing 1.18 kg of cocaine) and *Sedani* [2013] EWCA Crim 1763 (sentence of 20 months' imprisonment for evading duty on tobacco suspended for reasons of serious ill-health).

The Sentencing Council has published a new sentencing guideline for the sentencing of organisations convicted, *inter alia*, of fraudulent evasion of VAT and fraudulent evasion of duty. The new guideline, entitled 'Fraud, bribery and money laundering: corporate offenders', has effect from 1 October 2014.

SOCIAL SECURITY FRAUDS

Elements

B16.52 In cases under the Social Security Administration Act 1992, s. 111A, involving a change of circumstances, the prosecution must prove that the accused knew that the change affected entitlement to benefit (*Webster* [2013] EWCA Crim 1714 at [41]).

Procedure

B16.53 The Secretary of State may delegate the power to issue a certificate under the Social Security Administration Act 1992, s. 116, to a lawyer or prosecutor (*Mohammed v Department for Work and Pensions* [2012] EWHC 4220 (Admin)).

Sentencing Guidelines for Social Security Fraud

See also *Jairam* [2013] EWCA Crim 1140 (elderly offender), *Bonner* [2013] EWCA Crim 1534 **B16.54**
(mother of a young child) and *Taylor* [2013] EWCA Crim 1668 (on whether to suspend a sentence of imprisonment).

Section B17   Offences Involving Misuse of Computers

SENTENCING FOR OFFENCES UNDER
THE COMPUTER MISUSE ACT 1990

The 21-year-old offender in *Martin* [2013] EWCA Crim 1420 committed a range of offences **B17.14**
under the Computer Misuse Act 1990 (one under s. 1, one under s. 2, five under s. 3 and two
under s. 3A). These included serious and damaging denial of service attacks on university websites and a further attack on a website belonging to Kent Police. He also obtained the bank
account and personal details of a named individual requiring that individual to change his bank
cards and passwords. On appeal against sentence, the Court of Appeal said that a total sentence
of two years' imprisonment was amply justified. Leveson LJ noted that offences under the Act
are comparatively easy to commit by those with the relevant expertise and they are increasingly
prevalent. Sentencing should contain a real element of deterrence. In this case there were a
number of aggravating factors — planning, persistence, offences committed on bail, damage
caused (in terms of the time taken to deal with the attack), the serious potential consequences
for the organisations and the invasion of privacy of individual victims. His lordship said that
Mangham [2013] 1 Cr App R (S) 62 (11) (see **B17.14** in the main work) should not be considered a benchmark for sentencing in cases under the Act; there were a number of factors of personal mitigation in that case. For offending on the scale exhibited in *Martin*, sentences should
be measured in years and not months.

Section B19   Offences Related to Drugs

CONTROLLED DRUGS

'Substances and Products' Specified as Controlled Drugs in Class A, B, or C

'Preparations' and 'Products' which Contain a Controlled Drug are Controlled   Although **B19.10**
obiter, it was remarked by the Divisional Court in *Jama v Senior Public Prosecutor, Germany*
[2013] EWHC 3276 (Admin), that *Hodder v DPP* [1990] Crim LR 261 'does not sit comfortably' with the observations of Lord Diplock in *DPP v Goodchild* [1978] 2 All ER 161 (at [37]).
It did not seem to the Court (*obiter*) that bundles of khat plants (as described in a European
Arrest Warrant) could properly be regarded as a 'preparation or other product' containing cathinone, within the meaning of the MDA 1971, sch. 2, part III, para. 4, so as to bring the importation, exportation and supply of the plants themselves within the scope of the offences in ss. 3(1)
and 4(1). The warrant did not suggest that anything had been done to the khat beyond picking
it and bundling it up in parcels. In the opinion of the Court, it remained the natural plant, not
a 'product' within the meaning of the statute (per Richards LJ at [38]).

Note that the government has announced its intention to classify khat (namely, the leaves, stems
or shoots of the plant of the species *Catha edulis*) as a Class C drug.

SUPPLYING OR OFFERING TO SUPPLY ETC. CONTROLLED DRUG

Meaning of 'Supply'

Maginnis [1987] AC 303 was considered in *Watson* [2014] EWCA Crim 196. The Court of **B19.40**
Appeal agreed with the single judge that questions of joint possession were irrelevant, and that,

on the facts of that case, the key elements of unlawful possession and intent to supply were established.

POSSESSION OF CONTROLLED DRUG WITH INTENT TO SUPPLY

Alternative Verdicts

B19.51   In *Johnson* [2013] EWCA Crim 2001, the Court of Appeal, when quashing a conviction for an offence under the MDA 1971, s. 5(3), held that it did not suggest, any more than did the Court in *Hodson* [2009] EWCA Crim 1590, that every time that a jury is considering a count under s. 5(3) it will be necessary to leave simple possession in the alternative. It depends on the circumstances and the assessment of the trial judge as to what is fair. In the instant case, the jury should, at the least, have received assistance as to the evidence that was capable of establishing an intention to supply.

Section B20   Offences Relating to Dangerous Dogs and Animal Welfare

OFFENCES UNDER THE DANGEROUS DOGS ACT 1991

Failing to Keep Dogs under Proper Control

B20.6   **Elements**   *Bezzina* [1994] 3 All ER 964 and *Hughes* [2013] UKSC 56 (as to which see **A1.28** in the main work) were considered in *Robinson-Pierre* [2013] EWCA Crim 2396, in which D's pit bull terrier attacked police officers who had forcefully entered D's house in order to execute a warrant. Prior to the entry by the police, the dog had been securely enclosed in a locked house, but the police officers left the house and the dog followed them onto the road. D was convicted of being the owner of a dog which caused injury while dangerously out of control in a public place, contrary to the Dangerous Dogs Act 1991, s. 3(1). He appealed on the basis that the direction to the jury, that it did not matter if the dog had become out of control in a public place through no fault of D but through the action of a third party, was incorrect. The issue was not merely one of strict liability, but one of causation.

The appeal was allowed. Pitchford LJ said:

> While there is no doubt that s. 3(1) creates a strict liability offence, the question remains whether Parliament intended liability to be absolute in the sense that criminal liability may follow notwithstanding the absence of any act or omission of the defendant contributing to the prohibited state of affairs.

In the Court of Appeal's view, the offence required proof of an act or omission by D (with or without fault) that to some more than minimal degree caused or permitted the prohibited state of affairs to come about. The jury had not been invited to consider that question so the conviction was unsafe.

Section B21   Offences Relating to Money Laundering and the Proceeds of Criminal Conduct

OFFENCES UNDER THE PROCEEDS OF CRIME ACT 2002

Offences of Concealment, etc.

B21.12   **Procedure and Sentence**   The Sentencing Council has published a new sentencing guideline for the sentencing of organisations convicted, *inter alia*, of offences under the Proceeds of

Crime Act 2002, ss. 327 to 329. The new guideline, entitled 'Fraud, bribery and money laundering: corporate offenders', has effect from 1 October 2014.

Section B22   Immigration Offences

ILLEGAL ENTRY AND DECEPTION

Defences

Article 31 of the Convention Relating to the Status of Refugees   *Mateta* [2014] 1 All ER 152   **B22.7**
is another recent case to apply the principles already established in *Mohamed* [2011] 1 Cr App
R 432 (see **B22.8** in the main work). The issue in each of the appeals heard together was the
approach to be taken by the Court of Appeal when an accused, following incorrect legal advice,
has pleaded guilty to an offence under the Identity Cards Act 2006, s. 25(1), or the Identity
Documents Act 2010, s. 4, when a defence under the Immigration and Asylum Act 1999, s. 31,
was or may have been available to him. The Court revisited the case law to date and made a
number of observations on the operation of the s. 31 defence and then summarised the main
elements of the operation of the defence (at [21]). The Court then went on to consider the
parameters of the advice that it expected lawyers representing such defendants to give (at [22]
et seq.). Where no such advice was given, the Court will assess whether the defence would 'quite
probably' have succeeded (as per *Mohamed*). The Court confirmed that it is appropriate for it to
assess the prospects of an asylum defence succeeding by reference to the findings of the First Tier
Tribunal (Immigration and Asylum Chamber), if available (as per *Sadighpour* [2013] 1 Cr App
R 269 (20)).

B

Part B Offences

SUPPLEMENT TO PART C
ROAD TRAFFIC OFFENCES

Section C2　Procedure and Evidence in Road Traffic Cases

EVIDENCE

Admissibility of Evidence from Prescribed Devices

The Road Traffic Offenders (Additional Offences) Order 2014 (SI 2014 No. 260), which has **C2.22** effect from 1 April 2014, amends the RTOA 1988, s. 20, so as to add the offence contrary to the HGV Road User Levy Act 2013, s. 11 (using or keeping heavy goods vehicle if levy not paid), to the list of offences to which s. 20 applies.

Section C3　Offences Relating to Driving Triable on Indictment

CAUSING DEATH BY DANGEROUS DRIVING

Sentencing

Being distracted through mobile telephone use during the time shortly before committing an **C3.19** offence is something avoidable and so is an aggravating feature that can be taken into account when considering the appropriate starting point in sentencing for the offence (*Arora* [2014] EWCA Crim 104).

In *Paul* [2013] EWCA 2034, the Court of Appeal explained (at [27]) that sentencing guidelines like those relating to causing death by driving are to be interpreted in a flexible way and with a degree of nuance which is sensitive to the facts of the case, adding, in *Torkington* [2013] EWCA Crim 2183 (at [15]), that 'it is not possible to fit each individual offence precisely into the types of driving described in the Guideline. The list of circumstances which appear in paragraph 3 in respect of each of the Levels of offence is not exhaustive. It is necessary to look at the circumstances of each case in their entirety to determine where an offence is best placed.'

CAUSING DEATH BY CARELESS DRIVING WHEN UNDER THE INFLUENCE OF DRINK OR DRUGS

Elements

In *Beach* [2013] EWCA Crim 1783, the Court of Appeal emphasised the need to consider the **C3.22** evidence as a totality and not to compartmentalise it. In relation to a drug such as phenazepam that was not used in the UK, so that there were no guidelines concerning it, it did not automatically mean it was illegal to drive having taken it but rather that the jury needed to consider whether its presence in the defendant's body made him unfit to do so.

Sentencing

The action of the defendant being shepherded away from the scene as an act of compassion **C3.26** should not be equated to attempting to escape the wrongdoing and so does not represent an aggravating feature (*Williams* [2014] EWCA Crim 147).

CAUSING DEATH BY CARELESS, OR INCONSIDERATE, DRIVING

Sentencing

It is potentially less culpable for a foreign driver to execute a U-turn in the dark and then drive **C3.32** on the right-hand side of the road in a moment of forgetfulness than such a manoeuvre would be for a British driver (*Fleury* [2013] EWCA Crim 2273).

DANGEROUS DRIVING

C3.39 The *Criminal Practice Directions* [2013] EWCA Crim 1631, paras. 9A.1 to 9A.3 (see **PD-15** in this supplement) contain further guidance on the approach to be taken when considering whether or not to send defendants for trial in the Crown Court, with the consequence that the specific factors applicable to dangerous driving mentioned in the *Consolidated Criminal Practice Direction* have been superseded.

Sentencing

C3.45 *Wilson* [2013] EWCA Crim 1745 provides further guidance about the importance of being realistic about just how bad the driving was when selecting the corresponding starting point.

CAUSING DEATH BY DRIVING: UNLICENSED, DISQUALIFIED OR UNINSURED DRIVERS

Elements

C3.48 In *Uthayakmar* [2014] EWCA Crim 123, an appeal following a guilty plea which was entered relying on legal advice given based on the position preceding *Hughes* [2013] UKSC 123 was allowed.

Section C7   Sentencing

GENERAL PRINCIPLES

Fixed Penalties

C7.3 With effect from 1 April 2014, the Fixed Penalty (Amendment) Order 2014 (SI 2014 No. 259) adds the offence under the HGV Road User Levy Act 2013, s. 11, to the list of offences for which a fixed penalty may be imposed.

Financial Penalty Deposits

C7.5 The appropriate amounts to be deposited were increased with effect from 16 August 2013 by the Road Safety (Financial Penalty Deposit) (Amendment) Order 2013 (SI 2013 No. 2025), under which £500 has been substituted for £300 and £1,500 for £900.

With effect from 1 April 2014, the Road Safety (Financial Penalty Deposit) (Amendment) Order 2014 (SI 2014 No. 267) adds the offence under the HGV Road User Levy Act 2013, s. 11, to the list of offences for which a financial penalty deposit may be required.

DISQUALIFICATION GENERALLY

Disqualification Pending Passing of Driving Test

C7.33 The principle from *Abdullahi* [2010] EWCA Crim 1886, etc. was repeated in *Green* [2013] EWCA Crim 2517.

Under the RTOA 1988, s. 36(5), when imposing a discretionary disqualification for driving while disqualified, the sentencing court cannot disqualify until an extended driving test is passed; all that can be imposed is the requirement to pass an ordinary driving test (*Watson* [2013] EWCA Crim 2316).

Length of Disqualification

C7.36 *Dadson* [2013] EWCA Crim 1887 confirms that care needs to be taken not to over-sentence when disqualifying for what appears to be a one-off incident where there is no basis for concluding that there is an appreciable risk to the public. In that case, a three-year disqualification was halved.

Where the public is not in need of protection from bad driving, it is desirable not to prevent people of working age from driving for very long periods (*Zar* [2013] EWCA Crim 1897). A similar approach was taken in *Bell* [2013] EWCA Crim 2549, emphasising that 'the purpose of disqualification is not to punish but to seek to protect from harm in the future'.

SUPPLEMENT TO PART D
PROCEDURE

Section D1   Powers of Investigation

POLICE POWERS IN THE INVESTIGATION OF CRIME

Revised PACE Codes of Practice A, B, C, E, F and H were introduced on 27 October 2013 by **D1.1** the Police and Criminal Evidence Act 1984 (Codes of Practice) (Revisions to Codes A, B, C, E, F and H) Order 2013 (SI 2013 No. 2685). Most of the changes to Codes A and B reflect changes to legislation concerning terrorism powers. Whilst powers of stop and search under the TA 2000 are now governed by a code of practice issued under that Act in July 2012, the revised Code A governs powers to search persons without them being arrested which were introduced by the Terrorism Prevention and Investigation Measures Act 2011. Code B now includes powers to enter and search premises for the purposes of serving, monitoring and enforcing TPIM notices. The main changes to Codes C and H are designed to give effect to *R (HC) v Secretary of State for the Home Department* [2013] EWHC 983 (Admin) (treating 17-year-olds as juveniles) and to the EU Directive 2010/64/EU on the right to interpretation and translation in criminal proceedings. Note, in respect of the former, that the PACE 1984 has not been amended, so that s. 38(6) (transfer of persons aged 16 years or younger to local authority accommodation pending appearance at court), and s. 65 (consent to fingerprints, etc., by those aged 16 years and under) remain unaffected. The main changes to Codes E and F complement the 2012 revisions to Codes C and G and concern the conduct and recording of voluntary interviews of suspects who are not under arrest. A summary of the changes can be found in the Explanatory Memorandum to the Order, available at www.legislation.gov.uk/uksi/2013/2685/memorandum/contents.

Further revisions are expected to be made to Code C, in order to give effect to Directive 2012/13/EU on the right to information in criminal proceedings, which must be in force by 2 June 2014. The major changes are likely to be in respect of the information to be provided to suspects in police detention regarding the suspected offence, and a revised Notice of Rights.

POWERS TO STOP AND SEARCH

Stop and Search Powers Not Requiring Reasonable Suspicion

The Divisional Court decision in *R (Roberts) v Commissioner of Police of the Metropolis* [2012] **D1.12** EWHC 1977 (Admin) was upheld by the Court of Appeal in *R (Roberts) v Commissioner of Police of the Metropolis* [2014] EWCA Civ 69. Notwithstanding the exceptional nature of the power of stop and search under the CJPOA 1994, s. 60, it is circumscribed by specific requirements so that it is justified pursuant to the ECHR, Article 8(2).

ARREST WITHOUT WARRANT

Arrest for Breach of the Peace

In *R (Hicks) v Commissioner of Police of the Metropolis* [2014] EWCA Civ 3, the Court of **D1.34** Appeal, overruling the Divisional Court on this point, held that arrest and detention for an anticipated breach of the peace is governed by the ECHR, Article 5(1)(c), which provides, *inter alia*, that a person may be deprived of his liberty by lawful arrest or detention effected for the purpose of preventing him from committing an offence. Article 5(1)(c) is to be interpreted as meaning that the arrest or detention must be carried out for the purpose of bringing the person before the competent legal authority. However, applying *Brogan v UK* (1989) 11 EHRR 117, the mere fact that a court appearance does not ensue before detention comes to an end does not necessarily negate the existence of such a purpose at the time of arrest or detention. On the facts, the Court concluded that the appellants were arrested and detained for the purpose of bringing them before the competent legal authority 'if that were to become necessary'.

DETENTION AND TREATMENT OF SUSPECTS

The Decision to Detain

D1.50 **The Procedural Requirements** As to the revised PACE Code of Practice C (see **D1.1** in this supplement) and the treatment of persons aged 17, see **D1.63** in this supplement.

Juveniles and Mentally Disordered or Vulnerable Persons

D1.63 Revised PACE Code of Practice C (see **D1.1** in this supplement), para. 1.5A (giving effect to *R (HC) v Secretary of State for the Home Department* [2013] EWHC 983 (Admin)), provides that if a person appears to have attained the age of 17 and to be under the age of 18, he shall, in the absence of clear evidence that he is older, be treated as a 17-year-old for the purposes of this and any other Code. The provisions and notes for guidance of any of the PACE Codes of Practice that apply to persons under age 17 also apply to those aged 17 years. This is subject to the exceptions noted in **D1.1** in this supplement.

INTERROGATION OF SUSPECTS

Interviews Generally

D1.89 **When Interviews Should Cease** For application of the provision regarding rest periods, see *Beeres v CPS* [2014] EWHC 283 (Admin).

Special Categories of Persons

D1.91 The special rules applying where a child who is to be interviewed is a ward of court are now contained in the *Criminal Practice Directions*, part 28A (see **PD-33** in this supplement).

PACE Code of Practice C has been amended to give effect to the EU Directive 2010/64/EU on the right to interpretation and translation (see **D1.1** in this supplement). The custody officer, or other custody staff as directed by the custody officer, must determine whether a detainee requires an interpreter (Code C, para. 3.5(c)(ii)), and if he appears not to speak or understand English the custody officer must call an interpreter for assistance without delay (para. 3.12). This also applies where a person attends a police station voluntarily (para. 3.21). A person who requires an interpreter must not be interviewed without the interpreter being present, although this is subject to an exception in urgent circumstances (paras. 11.18(c) and 13.2). 'Essential documents' must be translated, in writing or orally (para. 13.10B). The documents that are 'essential' are set out in Annex M, and include the grounds for detention before and after charge, the written notice showing the offence charged and written interview records. A person may waive the right to translation of documents, but only if he does so voluntarily after receiving legal advice or having full knowledge of the consequences, and gives his unconditional and fully informed consent in writing (Annex M, para. 4). Chief officers are responsible for making arrangements to provide appropriately qualified independent persons to act as interpreters and to provide translations of essential documents (paras. 13.1 and 13.1A).

BIOMETRIC IMPRESSIONS AND SAMPLES

Body Samples and Dental or Skin Impressions

D1.112 **Non-intimate Samples** Various offences were added to the list of 'qualifying offences' in the PACE 1984, s. 65A, by the Police and Criminal Evidence Act 1984 (Amendment: Qualifying Offences) Order 2013 (2013 No. 2774), which came into effect on 11 November 2013.

Powers to Require Attendance at Police Station

D1.114 It was held in *R (R) v A Chief Constable* [2013] EWHC 2864 (Admin) that a demand to attend a police station to provide a non-intimate sample under the PACE 1984, sch. 2A, para. 11, which was made before an authorisation by an inspector or an officer of a higher rank was given, as required by s. 63(3B)(b), was unlawful. The guidance note published by ACPO in July 2012 was, in this respect, misleading in that it implied that the requirement to attend could be issued before the authorisation was given. However, whilst a properly issued demand engaged the ECHR, Article 8, it did not breach the applicant's Article 8 rights because, in the circumstances, it was a proportionate response to the objective of solving crime.

Retention or Destruction of Biometric Data

The Protection of Freedoms Act 2012 (Destruction, Retention and Use of Biometric Data) (Transitional, Transitory and Saving Provisions) (Amendment) (No. 2) Order 2013 (SI 2013 No. 2770) amends, as from 31 October 2013, the original Order (SI 2013 No. 2580). In particular, it inserts a new article into the original Order, making provision in relation to a person whose DNA profile or fingerprints are taken before 30 September 2014. If the person is arrested for or charged with a subsequent offence, or is convicted or given a penalty notice for a subsequent offence, that person's profile or fingerprints can be retained by reference to the rules applicable to that subsequent offence.

D1.117

The Police and Criminal Evidence Act 1984 (Armed Forces) (Amendment) Order 2013 (SI 2013 No. 2554), in force from 31 October 2013, makes equivalent provision (subject to modifications) in respect of the investigation of service offences under the Armed Forces Act 2006 to those contained in the PACE 1984, part V, as amended by the Protection of Freedoms Act 2012, part 1, chapter 1 (provisions regarding the retention and destruction of fingerprints, footwear impressions and DNA samples and profiles).

The Protection of Freedoms Act 2012 (Consequential Amendments) (No. 3) Order 2013 (SI 2013 No. 2343), in force from 31 October 2013, makes consequential amendments to the Police and Criminal Evidence Act 1984 (Application to Immigration Officers and Designated Customs Officials in England and Wales) Order 2013 (SI 2013 No. 1542) (the principal Order). The principal Order applies specified provisions of the PACE 1984 to criminal investigations conducted by immigration officers and designated customs officials and to persons detained by designated customs officials (see **D1.3** in the main work). The principal Order is amended to give effect to the amendment of the retention and destruction of fingerprints, footwear impressions and DNA samples and profiles provisions in the PACE 1984, part V, by the Protection of Freedoms Act 2012, part 1, chapter 1. Only the provisions which apply to the destruction, retention and use of samples (not fingerprints) are to be applied under the principal Order and they are only to apply to criminal investigations conducted by designated customs officials (not immigration officers) and to persons detained by designated customs officials.

ENTRY AND SEARCH UNDER WARRANT

Access to Excluded or Special Procedure Material

Procedure   In *R (S) v Chief Constable of the British Transport Police* [2014] 1 All ER 268, search warrants for excluded material and special procedure material at solicitors' premises were quashed. The information laid in support of the warrant relating to S's premises set out verbatim the terms of the PACE 1984, sch. 1, para. 2(b) and (c) and, in the alternative, para. 3, without any statement of the facts or matters on which the assertions were said to be made. Furthermore, the warrant was drawn too widely, and the powers under the CJPA 2001, s. 50, should have been used instead. In respect of the application for a warrant relating to the offices of the third applicant, L, the police had relied on sch. 1, para. 14(d), without providing any evidence which could have given the court a rational basis on which it could be satisfied that service of a notice on L under para. 4 could seriously prejudice the investigation. Furthermore, the police had told the court that they would only search L's premises if the material they were seeking was not found on searching the premises of F, the second applicant. However, when the warrant for the search of L's premises was executed, the police did not know whether the file that they had seized from F's premises contained the material.

D1.157

Procedural Requirements and Safeguards

D1.163　**The Application**　The importance of compliance with the requirements of the PACE 1984, s. 15, was confirmed in *R (Lees) v Solihull Magistrates' Court* [2013] EWHC 3779 (Admin), where warrants granted to the Revenue and Customs Commissioners were declared unlawful because they were too vague and general and failed properly to identify the items to which they related. There had been reasonable grounds for believing that an indictable offence had been committed and that the material on the relevant premises had been likely to be relevant evidence, so the warrants were not quashed, but the Divisional Court ordered the Revenue to return all property and any copies which had been taken of such material seized pursuant to the warrants and retained in its possession within 14 days, unless within that period they made an application to the Crown Court pursuant to the CJPA 2001, s. 59, for the retention of the material on the grounds that the conditions in s. 59(7) were satisfied. See also *Cheema v Nottingham and Newark Magistrates' Court* [2013] EWHC 3790 (Amin), and see **D1.180** in this supplement.

D1.167　**Execution of the Warrant**　It was held in *R (Pearce) v Commissioner of Police of the Metropolis* [2013] EWCA Civ 866 that a distinction can be made between the timing of the execution of search warrants and the operational decision as to timing of execution of the warrants. Whilst undoubtedly the timing of the execution of the warrants was related to the Royal wedding in April 2011, they were executed for the purpose for which they had been obtained. If police officers were not permitted to decide upon the timing for the execution of a lawfully obtained warrant with an eye on a collateral advantage, their operational freedom of manoeuvre would be unjustifiably inhibited.

SEIZURE OF, ACCESS TO AND RETENTION OF MATERIALS

Access to and Retention of Seized Material

D1.180　In *R (Chief Constable of South Yorkshire) v Sheffield Crown Court* [2014] EWHC 81 (Admin), it was held that the judge had erred in ordering the return of a portion of the property seized on the grounds that it was likely that the defendant had legitimately owned that portion. Section 53(2) of the CJPA 2001 imposes a duty on the police to ensure that an initial examination of property is carried out as soon as reasonably practicable after seizure, and to return anything that does not fall within s. 53(3). However, under s. 53(3)(b), such property may be retained if its retention is authorised by s. 56(2)(b) (there are reasonable grounds for believing that the property was obtained as the result of an offence and its retention is necessary to prevent it being concealed, lost, damaged, altered or destroyed). The judge had erred in thinking that, if he found on the balance of probabilities that not all the property was stolen, he was under a duty to order the return of such amount of the property as he believed might be legitimate. The actual question for him to determine under s. 59(3)(d) was whether the seized property was or contained something which did not fall within s. 53(3). On the facts, there were reasonable grounds for believing that the property was stolen, despite the police accepting that some of it might be legitimate property, and for believing that it would be lost, given that the defendant sought its return in order to sell it.

Section D2　The Decision to Prosecute and Diversion

THE DECISION TO PROSECUTE

The Tests for Deciding Whether to Charge

D2.10　**The Evidential Stage**　In *R (O'Brien) v DPP* [2013] EWHC 3741 (Admin) a decision not to prosecute a police officer for perverting the course of justice, perjury and misconduct in public office was challenged by way of judicial review. The test to be applied was whether it had been unreasonable of the prosecutor to conclude that there was no realistic prospect that a reasonable jury, properly directed, would be able to be sure of guilt. On the facts, the decision of the prosecutor was not only reasonable, but also correct.

ALTERNATIVES TO PROSECUTION

Simple Cautions (Adults)

A revised version of the Ministry of Justice guidance, *Simple Cautions for Adult Offenders*, was issued in November 2013 (available at www.justice.gov.uk/downloads/oocd/adult-simple-caution-guidance-oocd.pdf). See **D2.27** in this supplement.

D2.24

Repeat Cautions   Under the revised Ministry of Justice guidance (see **D2.24** in this supplement), a simple caution should not be given where the person has been cautioned for or convicted of the same or similar offences within two years of the commission of the current offence unless there are exceptional circumstances. In such circumstances the decision should normally be made only by an officer of at least the rank of inspector (paras. 46 and 47).

D2.27

Conditional Cautions

Conditions that May be Imposed   The Home Office issued guidance in November 2013 on attaching sobriety conditions to a conditional caution. See *Using Conditional Cautions with Sobriety requirements: Guidance* (available at www.gov.uk/government/publications/using-conditional-cautions-with-sobriety-requirements).

D2.38

DETENTION FOLLOWING CHARGE

Detention of Juveniles after Charge

Note that the definition of juvenile for the purposes of the PACE 1984, s. 38, is not affected by the revisions to Code of Practice C (see **D1.1** in this supplement). See further Code of Practice C, paras. 1.5 and 1.5A.

D2.52

Section D3   Courts, Parties and Abuse of Process

General: Criminal Practice Directions

The *Criminal Practice Directions* [2013] EWCA Crim 1631, as amended (see [2013] EWCA Crim 2328), revoked and replaced the greater part of the *Consolidated Criminal Practice Direction* [2002] 1 WLR 2870. As a consequence, most references in the main work to directions which have been revoked should now refer to the new *Criminal Practice Directions*, but note that there are some saved provisions. The position as regards **D3** is as follows:

D3.2   *Consolidated Criminal Practice Direction*, para. III.21 — Saved (see **PD-87** in this supplement).

D3.5   *Consolidated Criminal Practice Direction*, para. IV.33 — Saved (see **PD-90** in this supplement).

D3.11   *Consolidated Criminal Practice Direction*, para. IV.30 — New *Criminal Practice Directions*, XII General application, B (see **PD-81** in this supplement).

D3.111   *Consolidated Criminal Practice Direction*, para. IV.36 — New *Criminal Practice Directions*, I General matters, part 3C (see **PD-4** in this supplement)

D3.128   *Consolidated Criminal Practice Direction*, para. I.3.3 — New *Criminal Practice Directions*, II Preliminary proceedings, paras. 16B.1 to 16B.7 (see **PD-20** and **D3.128** in this supplement).

D3.136   *Consolidated Criminal Practice Direction*, para. I.3 — New *Criminal Practice Directions*, II Preliminary proceedings, part 16B (see **PD-20** and **D3.128** in this supplement).

PARTIES TO CRIMINAL PROCEEDINGS

Prosecution by Other Persons

D3.55   In *R (Virgin Media Ltd) v Zinga* [2014] EWCA Crim 52, it was held that a private prosecutor is entitled to initiate confiscation proceedings under the POCA 2002, s. 6.

ABUSE OF PROCESS: THE POWER TO STAY PROCEEDINGS

D3.70   In *Fawcett* [2013] EWCA Crim 1399, F had been charged with two offences of handling stolen property. He was later also charged with two counts of burglary in relation to the same goods. He entered guilty pleas to all the counts. Subsequently, it was argued that the two burglary counts amounted to an abuse of process. Laws LJ (at [12]) said that to allow the appeal 'would sanction the triumph of technicality over justice'. Whilst it was true that F could not remain convicted both of handling and of burglary, the Court had the power to vacate the plea to the handling counts, even if the defence had not applied to vacate the pleas (at [14]). It followed that F faced no risk of being proceeded against twice for the same offending. Laws LJ concluded (at [15]):

> The basis of the abuse jurisdiction is the protection of criminal defendants from unfairness and oppression. This appellant will not remotely be at risk of either if the handling pleas are vacated and the court proceeds to sentence him for the burglaries. That is what should happen. For these reasons this appeal is dismissed.

Failing to Obtain, Losing or Destroying Evidence

D3.90   In *Clay* [2014] EWHC 321 (Admin), the accused had been driving a lorry which collided with the rear of a car. The police had released the car and allowed the insurer to dispose of it. The accused argued that, because he had been deprived of the ability to examine the state of the car (in particular whether the brake lights were working), the failure by the police to retain the vehicle resulted in the proceedings amounting to an abuse of process. Pitchford LJ (at [48]–[50]) considered the decision in *R (Ebrahim) Feltham Magistrates' Court* [2001] 1 All ER 831:

> With great respect to the court in *Ebrahim*, it seems to me that the question of whether the defendant can have a fair trial does not logically depend upon whether anyone was 'at fault' in causing the exigency that created the unfairness. If vital evidence has as a matter of fact been lost to the defendant whether occasioned by the fault of the police or not, the issue is whether that disadvantage can be accommodated at his trial so as to ensure that his trial is fair. There is in this respect no difference between an unfair trial occasioned by delay and an unfair trial occasioned by the loss of vital evidence.

Burton J added (at [77]) that the justices in the present case were entitled to conclude that 'injustice to the defendant could be avoided by judicious regulation of the trial'.

Going Back on a Promise, Legitimate Expectation and Double Jeopardy

D3.96   **Prosecution Changes of Mind**   In *R (Gavigan) v Enfield Magistrates' Court* (2013) 177 JP 609, Mitting J said (at [15]) that there is no principle or policy reason that requires that a person who has rejected the opportunity to pay a fixed penalty should not thereafter be prosecuted for any offence arising out of the same set of facts for those in respect of which the fixed penalty notice was issued.

OPEN JUSTICE

Freedom of the Media to Report Court Proceedings

D3.128   **Scope of Order**   The *Criminal Practice Directions* [2013] EWCA Crim 1631, as amended (see [2013] EWCA Crim 2328), include new guidance on the making of orders restricting the reporting of proceedings (see paras. 16B.1 to 16B.7 at **PD-20**). Paragraph 16B.3 emphasises the importance of the court following precisely the statutory provisions under which the order is to be made, paying particular regard to what has to be established, by whom and to what standard. Paragraph 16B.4 makes the point that the court must be satisfied that the purpose of the proposed order cannot be achieved by some lesser measure and that the terms of the order must be proportionate (in order to comply with the ECHR, Article 10).

In *R (Guardian News and Media Ltd) v City of Westminster Magistrates' Court* [2013] QB 618, Toulson LJ said (at [85]):

> In a case where documents have been placed before a judge and referred to in the course of proceedings, in my judgment the default position should be that access should be permitted on the open justice principle; and where access is sought for a proper journalistic purpose, the case for allowing it will be particularly strong. However, there may be countervailing reasons…The court has to carry out a proportionality exercise which will be fact-specific. Central to the court's evaluation will be the purpose of the open justice principle, the potential value of the material in advancing that purpose and, conversely, any risk of harm which access to the documents may cause to the legitimate interests of others.

This case was cited in *Marine A* [2013] EWCA Crim 2367, where Lord Thomas CJ (at [52]), applying the *Criminal Practice Directions*, para. 5B.9, said that the court is bound to 'have regard to the rights of victims, parties, witnesses and any third parties whose rights may be engaged by the release to the public of material presented in court'. His lordship went on to consider the position of journalists, saying (at [56]) that:

> …it is clear that those who inform public debate on matters of public interest as journalists (whether in the print, broadcasting or internet media) are accorded a special position, given the role of journalism in enabling proper and effective participation in a democratic society.

Lord Thomas considered the test to be applied where restrictions on publication of the identity of the accused are sought. His lordship said (at [84]) that 'a defendant in a criminal trial must be named save in rare circumstances'. However, 'the Court has a power to withhold the name and address of a defendant in cases where circumstances justify that', although 'such cases would be rare. Any derogation from open justice, and any interference with the right to report a criminal trial, must be both necessary and proportionate' (at [85]).

His lordship added (at [88]) that an order that an accused should not be identified 'will not be necessary, if some other measure is available to protect those rights of the individuals, and that other measure would be proportionate'.

Imposition of a Permanent Ban on Reporting Certain Matters

Juveniles   In *Jolleys* [2013] EWCA Crim 1135, Leveson LJ said (at [19]) that orders made **D3.138** under the CYPA 1933, s. 39, 'should be restricted to the language of the legislation'. It is submitted that this dictum applies to orders made under any legislation which restricts the freedom of the press to report court proceedings.

Section D4   Criminal Procedure Rules and Case Management

THE EVOLUTION OF THE RULES

The *Criminal Practice Directions* [2013] EWCA Crim 1631 revoked and replaced the greater part **D4.1** of the *Consolidated Criminal Practice Direction* [2002] 1 WLR 2870. The aim of the new *Criminal Practice Directions* is that they will work hand in hand with the CrimPR. They address, under the heading of general matters, both the overriding objective (para. 1A.1) and case management (part 3A). The *Criminal Practice Directions* were amended by *Practice Direction (Criminal Proceedings: Various Changes)* [2013] EWCA Crim 2328 with effect from 10 December 2013.

CASE MANAGEMENT

Practical Case Management

The *Criminal Practice Directions* [2013] EWCA Crim 1631, as amended (see [2013] EWCA **D4.12** Crim 2328), revoked and replaced the greater part of the *Consolidated Criminal Practice*

Direction [2002] 1 WLR 2870. The directions relating to case management are to be found in part 3A of the new *Criminal Practice Directions* (see **PD-2** in this supplement).

Section D5 Preliminary Proceedings in Magistrates' Courts

ADJOURNMENTS AND REMANDS

Power to Adjourn

D5.25 **Approach Where Accused Claims to be Unfit to Attend** The *Criminal Practice Directions* [2013] EWCA Crim 1631, para. 19B.2 (see **PD-22** in this supplement), provides that, where an accused is on bail and is unable, for medical reasons, to attend court, he must (in advance of the hearing) obtain a certificate from his general practitioner (or another appropriate medical practitioner, such as the doctor with care of the accused at a hospital). Without a medical certificate (or if an unsatisfactory certificate is provided), the court is likely to consider that the accused has failed to surrender to bail (para. 19B.3).

Section D6 Classification of Offences and Determining Mode of Trial

FAILURE TO COMPLY WITH THE MODE OF TRIAL PROCEDURE

D6.29 Failure to follow the statutory procedure for allocation was considered in *R (Rahmdezfouli) v Wood Green Crown Court* [2013] EWHC 2998 (Admin). Mackay J said (at [16]):

> [T]he legislature in enacting s. 17A must have intended . . . that where a magistrates' court declined or failed to follow the requirements of the section it was acting without jurisdiction every bit as much as if, for instance, it had purported to try a defendant on a charge of homicide.

Section D7 Bail

General: Criminal Practice Directions

The *Criminal Practice Directions* [2013] EWCA Crim 1631, as amended (see [2013] EWCA Crim 2328), revoked and replaced the greater part of the *Consolidated Criminal Practice Direction* [2002] 1 WLR 2870. As a consequence, references in the main work to directions which have been revoked should now refer to the new Practice Directions but take note of changes in wording. The position as regards **D7** is as follows:

D7.87 *Consolidated Criminal Practice Direction*, paras. III.25.2 to 5 — New *Criminal Practice Directions*, III Custody and bail, paras. 19G.2 to 19G.4 (see **PD-27** in this supplement), but note that there is no longer any reminder equivalent to *Consolidated Criminal Practice Direction*, para. III.25.4

D7.114 *Consolidated Criminal Practice Direction*, para. I.13 — New *Criminal Practice Directions*, III Custody and bail, paras. 19B.2 to 19E.4 (see **PD-22** *et seq.* in this supplement).

D7.115 *Consolidated Criminal Practice Direction*, para. I.13.9 — New *Criminal Practice Directions*, III Custody and bail, para. 19C.4 (see **PD-23** in this supplement).
Consolidated Criminal Practice Direction, para. I.13.8 — New *Criminal Practice Directions*, III Custody and bail, para. 19C.3 (see **PD-23** in this supplement).
Consolidated Criminal Practice Direction, para. I.13.5 — New *Criminal Practice Directions*, III Custody and bail, para. 19C.5 (see **PD-23** in this supplement).

D7.119 *Consolidated Criminal Practice Direction*, para. I.13.13 — New *Criminal Practice Directions*, III Custody and bail, part 19C (see **PD-23** in this supplement), but note the changes in approach arising from the definitive sentencing guidelines for the offence.

PROCEDURE FOR BAIL APPLICATIONS IN THE CROWN COURT

Notice of Appeal

The *Criminal Practice Directions* [2013] EWCA Crim 1631, para. 19A.2 (see **PD-21**), stipu-   **D7.83**
lates that applications should be made to the court to which the defendant will be, or would
have been, sent for trial. In the event of an application in a purely summary case, it should be
made to the Crown Court centre which normally receives Class 3 work. The hearing will be
listed as a chambers matter, unless a judge has directed otherwise.

BAIL BY THE HIGH COURT

Challenging Refusal of Bail by Way of Judicial Review

The SCA 1981, s. 29(3), prevents a judicial review challenge to a decision by a trial judge during   **D7.89**
a trial to revoke bail of a defendant (*R (Uddin) v Leeds Crown Court* [2013] EWHC 2752
(Admin)).

R (Lahooty) v Kingston Crown Court [2013] EWHC 2895 (Admin) provides an example of a
successful claim for judicial review on the ground, *inter alia*, that the judge, when refusing bail,
took into account a factor that was not open to her on the evidence, namely the effectiveness or
otherwise of a curfew, reporting and tagging, because this was based upon the judge's personal
experience, had not been relied upon by the prosecution and there was no evidence about it.

Section D8   Assets Recovery

MAGISTRATES' COURTS: CASH SEIZURE AND FORFEITURE

Forfeiture

In *Fletcher v Chief Constable of Leicestershire Constabulary* [2013] EWHC 3357 (Admin), a   **D8.13**
single judge of the Administrative Court (Lewis J) considered the relationship between the
POCA 2002, s. 298(2)(a) and (b), in circumstances where the appellant, acting innocently and
in good faith, found cash which he delivered to a police officer. The Court was clearly right to
say (at [31]) that it is not possible to regard s. 298(2)(b) as inapplicable in situations when an
innocent finder intends to use the money because the subsection applies when 'any' person
intends to use the money for criminal conduct. The Court considered two tests for proving that
property is derived from crime: the first relates to civil recovery (*Angus v UK Border Agency*
[2011] EWHC 461 (Admin)), whereas the second test relates to criminal proceedings for a
money laundering offence (*Anwoir* [2008] EWCA Crim 1354). The Court concluded, notwithstanding *Angus*, that on a proper construction of s. 298(b) it was permissible to find (from
the circumstances in which the money was found and kept) that the money had been obtained
by unlawful conduct of some unspecified kind.

RESTRAINT ORDERS

External Requests and Orders

The Proceeds of Crime Act 2002 (External Requests and Orders) (Amendment) Order 2013   **D8.44**
(SI 2013 No. 2604), in force from 11 November 2013, amends the Proceeds of Crime Act 2002
(External Requests and Orders) Order 2005 by adding part 4A which makes provision for a
prohibition on dealing with relevant property which is the subject of an external request, within
the meaning of the POCA 2002, s. 447(1). Proceedings in England and Wales or Northern
Ireland are initiated in the High Court. The provisions correspond (with some modification) to
the civil recovery provisions in part V. Part 1 of the Proceeds of Crime Act 2002 (External
Investigations) Order 2013 (SI 2013 No. 2605), also in force from 11 November 2013, which
applies to England, Wales and Northern Ireland only, enables the Director General of the
National Crime Agency or a relevant Director to assist an external investigation by obtaining
orders and warrants from the High Court.

D

Part D   Procedure

Procedure

D8.47   In relation to an exclusion under the terms of a freezing order for the payment of legal expenses in respect of proceedings for civil recovery under the POCA 2002, part 5, see *SOCA v Azam* [2013] EWCA Civ 970. *SOCA v Azam* was applied in *NCA v Surin* [2013] EWHC 3784 (QB).

Section D9   Disclosure

INTRODUCTION

The Scheme of the Legislation

D9.5   **Secondary Sources**   The Judicial Protocol on the Disclosure of Unused Material in Criminal Cases (the Judicial Disclosure Protocol) was published in December 2013 and is set out in full in this supplement (see **appendix** 4). It has been prepared following the recommendations of Gross LJ in his 2011 and 2012 reviews of disclosure in criminal proceedings, the latter one carried out with Treacy LJ. The Judicial Disclosure Protocol replaces the Crown Court Protocol and section 4 of the Lord Chief Justice's Protocol for the Control and Management of Heavy Fraud and other Complex Cases. It sets out the principles to be applied to, and the importance of, disclosure; the expectations of the court and its role in disclosure, in particular in relation to case management; and the consequences if there is a failure of the prosecution or defence to comply with their obligations. Its emphasis is on prosecution-led disclosure, a constructive approach on both sides, supported by robust judicial case management. All requests by the defence for disclosure should now be made on the section 8 application form, even if no hearing is sought in the first instance. There is extensive new guidance in the protocol on material held by third parties, and the 2013 Protocol and Good Practice Model on Disclosure of Information in Cases of Alleged Child Abuse and Linked Criminal and Care Directions Hearings (www.judiciary.gov.uk/publications-and-reports/guidance/2013/protocol-good-practice-model-2013) is commended as representing best practice and should therefore be consulted in all cases.

Alongside the Judicial Disclosure Protocol, revised A-G's Guidelines on Disclosure for investigators, prosecutors and defence practitioners have been published and are also set out in full in **appendix** 4 of this supplement. For ease of reference they are structured in the same way as the Judicial Disclosure Protocol and complement the messages in it. In particular, the guidelines emphasise the importance of prosecution-led disclosure and of applying the CPIA regime thoughtfully, tailored where appropriate to the type of investigation or prosecution in question. The A-G's Supplementary Guidelines on Digitally Stored Material (2011) are annexed to the new guidelines.

Part 22 of the *Criminal Practice Directions* [2013] EWCA Crim 1631 (see **PD-29** in this supplement) deals with disclosure. It states that all parties must be familiar with their obligations, in particular under the CPIA and the Code issued under that Act, and must comply with the relevant judicial protocol and guidelines from the A-G (para. 22A.1).

PROSECUTION DISCLOSURE

Consequences of Non-disclosure

D9.28   In *DPP v Gowing* [2013] EWHC 4614 (Admin), the Divisional Court allowed an appeal by the DPP against a decision by magistrates to stay a case on the ground that disclosure had not been served. The material had been sent in error to the wrong address. There was no suggestion of bad faith or failure to comply with s.3 of the CPIA. The Court found that the magistrates had fallen into error by overlooking the overriding objective of the CrimPR to deal with criminal cases justly and to treat the prosecution and defence fairly. It stated that while proceedings should be efficient and expeditious, the power to stop them should not be used to punish the prosecution.

Section D10   Sending Cases from the Magistrates' Court to the Crown Court

SENDING CASES TO THE CROWN COURT UNDER THE CRIME AND DISORDER ACT 1998, s. 51

Appearance in the Crown Court

The *Criminal Practice Directions* [2013] EWCA Crim 1631, para. 3A.6 (see **PD-2** in this sup-   **D10.21**
plement), makes provision for early guilty plea hearings, to allow the Crown Court to deal
promptly with a case where the accused wishes to plead guilty. This will be of relevance principally to indictable-only offences (since the accused can enter a guilty plea in the magistrates'
court, at the plea before venue hearing, if the offence is triable either way). Sentence should
normally be passed at an early guilty plea hearing (para. 3A.7), and any issues related to the basis
of plea need to be sorted out beforehand, and a pre-sentence report (if required) obtained prior
to the hearing.

By virtue of para. 3A.9, if no early guilty plea hearing is ordered, the magistrates' court or the
Crown Court should order a preliminary hearing (to take place between 14 and 21 days after
the case is sent for trial) if there are case management issues which call for such a hearing, or the
trial is likely to last for more than four weeks, or the accused is a juvenile.

If the magistrates' court does not order an early guilty plea hearing or a preliminary hearing,
it should order a plea and case management hearing to be held, usually within 13 weeks of
the case being sent for trial if the accused is in custody or within 16 weeks if he is on bail
(para. 3A.10).

VOLUNTARY BILLS OF INDICTMENT

Procedure for Obtaining a Voluntary Bill

The procedure for obtaining a voluntary bill of indictment is now set out in the *Criminal*   **D10.44**
Practice Directions [2013] EWCA Crim 1631, paras. 14B.2, 14B.3 and 14B.5 to 14B.8 (see
PD-18 in this supplement). There are no changes of substance from the provisions formerly
contained in the *Consolidated Criminal Practice Direction*.

Circumstances in which it is Appropriate to Apply for a Voluntary Bill

The exceptional nature of the voluntary bill procedure is emphasised in the *Criminal Practice*   **D10.47**
Directions [2013] EWCA Crim 1631, para. 14B.4 (see **PD-18** in this supplement).

Section D11   The Indictment

General: Criminal Practice Directions

The *Criminal Practice Directions* [2013] EWCA Crim 1631, as amended (see [2013] EWCA
Crim 2328), revoked and replaced the greater part of the *Consolidated Criminal Practice
Direction* [2002] 1 WLR 2870. As a consequence, references in the main work to directions
which have been revoked should now refer to the new Practice Directions but take note of
changes in wording. The position as regards **D11** is as follows:

D11.1   *Consolidated Criminal Practice Direction*, para. IV.34 — New *Criminal Practice
         Directions*, II Preliminary Proceedings, part 14A (see **PD-17** in this supplement).
D11.8   *Consolidated Criminal Practice Direction*, para. IV.34.1 — New *Criminal Practice
         Directions*, II Preliminary Proceedings, para. 14A.1 (see **PD-17** in this supplement).
D11.14   *Consolidated Criminal Practice Direction*, para. IV.34.1 — New *Criminal Practice
         Directions*, II Preliminary Proceedings, para. 14A.1 (see **PD-17** in this supplement).

D11.16   *Consolidated Criminal Practice Direction*, para. IV.34.2 — New *Criminal Practice Directions*, II Preliminary Proceedings, para. 14A.2 (see **PD-17** in this supplement).

D11.22   *Consolidated Criminal Practice Direction*, para. IV.34.2 — New *Criminal Practice Directions*, II Preliminary Proceedings, para. 14A.2 (see **PD-17 and D11.22** in this supplement).

D11.35   *Consolidated Criminal Practice Direction*, para. IV.34.10 — New *Criminal Practice Directions*, II Preliminary Proceedings, para. 14A.10 (see **PD-17** in this supplement).

D11.39   *Consolidated Criminal Practice Direction*, paras. IV.34.4 to 34.9 — New *Criminal Practice Directions*, II Preliminary Proceedings, paras. 14A.4 to 14A.9 (see **PD-17** in this supplement).

D11.95   *Consolidated Criminal Practice Direction*, para. IV.34.3 — New *Criminal Practice Directions*, II Preliminary Proceedings, para. 14A.4 (see **PD-17** in this supplement).

DUPLICATION OF INDICTMENTS

D11.22   The *Criminal Practice Directions* [2013] EWCA Crim 1631, para. 14A.2, makes clear that there can be more than one indictment before the court, but that the court should only allow the prosecution to proceed with one of them.

SEVERANCE

Overloading Indictments

D11.91   The *Criminal Practice Directions* [2013] EWCA Crim 1631, para. 14A.3, enunciates the undesirability of there being too many counts on an indictment and suggests a number of remedies, including requiring the prosecution to elect between conspiracy and substantive charges.

DEFECTS IN THE INDICTMENT AS A GROUND OF APPEAL

D11.114   In *Wilson* [2014] 1 Cr App R 127 (10), the Court of Appeal repeated that, even where there was a material irregularity in the drafting of the indictment on which an accused had been convicted, where the error constituted a mis-labelling of the offence, whether it be a misdescription in the statement or particulars of the offence as to the source of criminality, that would not result in the indictment being regarded as a nullity and a conviction based on that indictment would be safe unless there was unfairness occasioned to the accused by the error. Similarly, in *Stocker* [2013] EWCA Crim 1993, the Court of Appeal declined to quash a conviction where, through error, the statement of offence was identified under the wrong statute. The Court considered this was an error that could easily have been cured at the time, and caused no prejudice to the accused.

Section D12   Arraignment and Pleas

General: Criminal Practice Directions

The *Criminal Practice Directions* [2013] EWCA Crim 1631, as amended (see [2013] EWCA Crim 2328), revoked and replaced the greater part of the *Consolidated Criminal Practice Direction* [2002] 1 WLR 2870. As a consequence, references in the main work to directions which have been revoked should now refer to the new Practice Directions but take note of changes in wording. The position as regards **D12** is as follows:

D12.54   *Consolidated Criminal Practice Direction*, para. IV.34.6 — New *Criminal Practice Directions*, II Preliminary Proceedings, para. 14A.6 (see **PD-17** in this supplement).

D12.60   *Consolidated Criminal Practice Direction*, para. IV.45 — New *Criminal Practice Directions*, VII Sentencing, part B (see **PD-56** in this supplement).

D12.61   *Consolidated Criminal Practice Direction*, para. IV.45.29 — New *Criminal Practice Directions*, VII Sentencing, part C (see **PD-57** in this supplement).

D12.75   *Consolidated Criminal Practice Direction*, para. IV.45 — New *Criminal Practice Directions*, VII Sentencing, parts A to D (see **PD-55** *et seq.* in this supplement).

UNFITNESS TO PLEAD AND OTHER REASONS
FOR FAILING TO PLEAD

Unfitness to Plead

Relevance of the Mental Element of an Offence at the Trial of the Facts   In *Antoine* [2001] 1   **D12.11**
AC 340, while addressing the availability of the defence of diminished responsibility for an
accused found to be under a disability, the House of Lords (Lord Hutton) also observed that
careful consideration would always have to be given as to whether an accused found to be under
a disability should be called to give evidence at the hearing under the Criminal Procedure
(Insanity) Act 1964, s. 4A(2). Applying that approach, the Court of Appeal in *Swinbourne*
[2013] EWCA Crim 2329 concluded that the interview under caution of such an accused
should not be adduced at the s. 4A hearing, there being grounds to doubt that he would have
understood the caution or the interview process.

AUTREFOIS ACQUIT AND AUTREFOIS CONVICT

Meaning of 'Acquittal' and 'Conviction' in Context of Autrefois Pleas

In *DPP v Jarman* [2013] EWHC 4391 (Admin) the Administrative Court found that the dis-   **D12.21**
missal of proceedings for want of prosecution did not constitute an acquittal for the purposes of
a plea of autrefois. Moreover, the Court found on the facts of the case that the plea would have
been unlikely to succeed even if it had been available because the court did not consider the
merits of the evidence at the hearing at which the case was dismissed.

Scope of the Pleas

Findings that Cannot Form Basis for Plea of Autrefois Acquit   In *Fawcett* [2013] EWCA   **D12.26**
Crim 1399 the Court of Appeal rejected the contention that it had been an abuse of process to
prosecute the accused for burglary when he had earlier pleaded guilty to offences of handling
stolen goods relating to the same conduct on an indictment that had been preferred in error.
The Court found that the guilty pleas to that indictment could be vacated and the accused
arraigned on the proper burglary indictment without any injustice.

DEFERRED PROSECUTION AGREEMENTS

By virtue of the Crime and Courts Act (Commencement No. 8) Order 2014 (SI 2014 No. 258),   **D12.106**
the deferred prosecution agreement provisions are in force, with effect from 24 February 2014.
Rules relating to their application (see **R-101A** in this supplement) are to be found in part 12 of
the CrimPR, added by the Criminal Procedure (Amendment No. 2) Rules 2013 (SI 2013
No. 3183).

The Sentencing Council has also published a new sentencing guideline for the sentencing of
organisations convicted of fraud, money laundering, and bribery offences (see **E1.3** in this
supplement and Part 27 of the Sentencing Guidelines at **SG-662**). The new guideline, entitled
'Fraud, Bribery and Money Laundering Offences: Corporate Offenders', has effect from 1
October 2014. The guideline is said to be intended to assist in any decision related to a deferred
prosecution agreement.

Section D13   Juries

General: Criminal Practice Directions

The *Criminal Practice Directions* [2013] EWCA Crim 1631, as amended (see [2013] EWCA
Crim 2328), revoked and replaced the greater part of the *Consolidated Criminal Practice
Direction* [2002] 1 WLR 2870. As a consequence, references in the main work to directions

D

Part D Procedure

which have been revoked should now refer to the new Practice Directions but take note of changes in wording. The position as regards **D13** is as follows:

D13.2   *Consolidated Criminal Practice Direction*, paras. IV.42.1 to 42.3 — New *Criminal Practice Directions*, VI Trial, parts 39B to 39D and 39H (see **PD-41** *et seq.* in this supplement), but note that there is no longer any reminder equivalent to *Consolidated Criminal Practice Direction*, para. III.25.4.

D13.7   *Consolidated Criminal Practice Direction*, paras. IV.42.1 to 42.3 — New *Criminal Practice Directions*, VI Trial, parts 39B and 39C (see **PD-41** *et seq.* in this supplement).

D13.19   *Consolidated Criminal Practice Direction*, paras. I.13.9 to IV.42.4 — New *Criminal Practice Directions*, VI Trial, para. 39E.3 (see **PD-44** in this supplement), but note that the form of oath is no longer set out and may vary according to the faith indicated to the court.

D13.21   *Consolidated Criminal Practice Direction*, paras. IV.42.6 to 42.9 — New *Criminal Practice Directions*, VI Trial, part 39G (see **PD-46 and D13.21** in this supplement).

D13.51   *Consolidated Criminal Practice Direction*, para. IV.42 — New *Criminal Practice Directions*, VI Trial, part 39G (see **PD-46** in this supplement), and note para. 39G.3(iv) in particular.

SELECTION OF JURY FOR A PARTICULAR CASE

Ballot in Open Court

D13.20   **Anonymity of Jurors**   *Comerford* [1998] 1 All ER 823 was considered in *Baybasin* [2014] 1 Cr App R 264 (19), in which complaint was made that the jury had been selected following a ballot by number, and other measures had been adopted to protect the jury. The Court of Appeal considered the measures, such as collecting the jury from a city-centre pickup point and remaining in their room when not in court, did not affect the fairness of the trial and that ballot by numbers had not inhibited the accused's right of challenge. The Court did, however, observe that the permissible measures for jury management were now those promulgated by the Criminal Procedure Rules Committee, and that local initiatives ought to be referred to that committee for its approval.

D13.21   **Warnings to the Jury on Empanelment**   The *Criminal Practice Directions* [2013] EWCA Crim 1631 address preliminary instructions to a jury on empanelment at part 39G (see **PD-46** in this supplement). This covers a list of matters as to which a jury should receive 'clear guidance', such as the prohibition on conducting their own researches via the internet and their collective responsibility for their verdict.

DISCHARGE OF JURORS OR ENTIRE JURY

Discharge of Individual Jurors

D13.53   **Judicial Discretion to Discharge a Juror**   The approach to the discharge of a juror for personal reasons is addressed in the *Criminal Practice Directions* [2013] EWCA Crim 1631, part 39H (see **PD-47** in this supplement).

Investigation of Misconduct

D13.69   The investigation of jury irregularities is addressed in the *Criminal Practice Directions* [2013] EWCA Crim 1631, part 39M (see **PD-51** in this supplement).

Section D14   Special Measures and Anonymity Orders

General: Criminal Practice Directions

The *Criminal Practice Directions* [2013] EWCA Crim 1631, as amended (see [2013] EWCA Crim 2328), revoked and replaced the greater part of the *Consolidated Criminal Practice Direction* [2002] 1 WLR 2870. As a consequence, references in the main work to directions which have been revoked should now refer to the new Practice Directions but take note of changes in wording which, as regards special measures and vulnerable defendants especially, may be substantial. The position as regards **D14** is as follows:

D14.21   *Consolidated Criminal Practice Direction*, para. III.30 — New *Criminal Practice Directions*, I General Matters, parts 3D to 3F (see **PD-5** *et seq.* in this supplement).

D14.23   *Consolidated Criminal Practice Direction*, para. III.30.13 — New *Criminal Practice Directions*, I General Matters, para. 3G.11 (see **PD-8** in this supplement), but see also para. 3G.4.

D14.33   *Consolidated Criminal Practice Direction*, para. IV.40 — New *Criminal Practice Directions*, V Evidence, part 27B (see **PD-31** in this supplement).

D14.35   *Consolidated Criminal Practice Direction*, para. IV.40.3 — New *Criminal Practice Directions*, V Evidence, para. 27B.3 (see **PD-31** in this supplement).

D14.40   *Consolidated Criminal Practice Direction*, para. III.29.2 — New *Criminal Practice Directions*, V Evidence, part 29B (see **PD-35** in this supplement).

D14.42   *Consolidated Criminal Practice Direction*, para. III.30.14 — New *Criminal Practice Directions*, I General Matters, para. 3G.12 (see **PD-8** in this supplement), but note the significant change in emphasis.

D14.47   *Consolidated Criminal Practice Direction*, para. III.30.15 — New *Criminal Practice Directions*, I General Matters, para. 3G.13 (see **PD-8** in this supplement), but note the additional guidance on reporting of the proceedings.

D14.51   *Consolidated Criminal Practice Direction*, para. I.15 — New *Criminal Practice Directions*, V Evidence, part 29D (see **PD-37** in this supplement).

SPECIAL MEASURES FOR WITNESSES: GENERAL

Introduction

The *Equal Treatment Bench Book 2013* was published by the Judicial College in November **D14.1** 2013, to bring court practice into line with the Equality Act 2010. The protected characteristics of age, disability, race and religion are particularly relevant to special measures for vulnerable witnesses and defendants. The new guidance is extremely detailed compared to its predecessors. It requires the judiciary to be alert to vulnerability even if not previously flagged up, indicators including demeanour, language, circumstances of the alleged offence, a child being looked after by the local authority, or a witness coming from a group with moral or religious proscriptions on speaking about sexual activities. Creative flexibility on the part of all those involved in adjusting the adversarial process to the circumstances, instead of giving up on the witness, is the dominant theme. Pragmatic solutions are suggested to commonly encountered difficulties with special measures, so counsel should consult the *Equal Treatment Bench Book* in advance of any trial involving witnesses with special needs.

ESTABLISHING ELIGIBILITY FOR SPECIAL MEASURES

Child Witnesses

Deemed Eligibility   The Special Measures for Child Witnesses (Sexual Offences) **D14.13** Regulations 2013 (SI 2013 No. 2971) amend the YJCEA 1999, s. 33, with effect from 18 December 2013. By virtue of the amendments, a complainant of a 'relevant offence' whose age is uncertain will be presumed to be under the age of 18 if there are reasons to believe that person is under the age of 18. An offence is a 'relevant offence' if it is a sexual offence, an offence under the Protection of Children Act 1978, s. 1, an offence under the CJA 1988, s. 160, or an offence under the Asylum and Immigration (Treatment of Claimants, etc.) Act 2004, s. 4. The effect is that a complainant to whom the presumption applies will be eligible for special measures under s. 16.

Adult Witnesses with Physical or Mental Impairment

The *Equal Treatment Bench Book 2013* contains background discussion and recommendations **D14.16** for the handling of witnesses and defendants with physical or mental disabilities. Lawyers dealing with witnesses and clients with physical or mental disabilities should have reference to that and in some cases may need to seek expert advice tailored to the needs of those particular individuals.

Child and Other Vulnerable Defendants

D14.21   Vulnerable defendants are entitled to special consideration throughout the trial to enable their effective participation (*Dixon* [2013] EWCA Crim 465). The *Equal Treatment Bench Book 2013* provides specific examples of what unorthodox practices that consideration may entail. Paragraph 52 helpfully clarifies the fraught issue of funding for *ad hoc* appointments of intermediaries for vulnerable defendants pursuant to an agreement between the relevant agencies: the Legal Aid Agency pays for the assessment and pre-trial involvement, subject to prior authority, whilst the intermediary's attendance at trial is paid for by HM Courts and Tribunal Service. Regrettably, the matching service run by the Ministry of Justice and National Crime Agency remains unavailable to defence lawyers.

THE SPECIAL MEASURES

Video-recorded Evidence-in-chief

D14.27   **ECHR Compliance**   The *Equal Treatment Bench Book 2013*, echoing the new *Criminal Practice Directions* [2013] EWCA Crim 1631, para. 29A.2, states that, if a witness testifying by live link so wishes, the defendant can be prevented from seeing the live-link screen, as would occur with a screen in the courtroom (although a camera has been used to enable the defendant to see a witness using the screen in court: *Taylor* [1995] Crim LR 253). This raises an issue of compliance with the ECHR, Article 6(1) and (3)(d): arguably, if seeing the witness testify is important for the jury, the defendant is equally entitled to see the same thing, in order to instruct counsel and participate effectively in the trial (YJCEA 1999, ss. 18(3)(b) and 25(2)(a)). The Court of Appeal has held that the default rule that the accused should be able to see his accusers should be denied only in rare or exceptional circumstances (*Taylor* [1995] Crim LR 253); the point remains open under the HRA 1998.

Intermediaries

D14.43   The *Equal Treatment Bench Book 2013* directs that assessment by an intermediary is to be considered if the person seems unlikely to be able to recognise a problematic question or to say so to a questioner in authority.

A discussion of the role and duties of an intermediary can be found in the Court of Appeal's judgment in *IA* [2013] EWCA Crim 1308 at [27] *et seq*. F, the intermediary in that case, acted for a child complainant (RB) who was profoundly deaf and without speech, and in the course of the trial and appeal attacks were made on his role, performance and professional integrity. Treacy LJ said (at [35]–[36]):

> As s 29(2) of the [YJCEA 1999] makes clear, the function of the intermediary is to communicate (a) to the witness, questions put to the witness, and (b) to any person asking such questions, the answers given by the witness in reply to them. The intermediary must explain such questions or answers so far as is necessary to enable them to be understood by the witness or person in question... [F] was entitled to interject in order to ensure that RB could understand what she was being asked. We do not consider that his interjections have been shown to be intended to be disruptive, nor were they widespread... we are unpersuaded that they had disruptive effect which resulted in an unfair handicap to the defence. If anything, the extremely lengthy cross-examinations of RB were permitted to go on far too long.

Video-recorded Cross-examination and Re-examination

D14.46   A pilot scheme implementing the YJCEA 1999, s. 28, in respect of relevant proceedings in the Crown Court at Kingston-upon-Thames, Leeds and Liverpool came into force on 30 December 2013. See the Youth Justice and Criminal Evidence Act 1999 (Commencement No. 13) Order 2013 (SI 2013 No. 3236).

BEST PRACTICE IN QUESTIONING CHILD AND VULNERABLE WITNESSES

The *Equal Treatment Bench Book 2013* implies that counsel can now expect even more **D14.48** emphasis on the paramount importance of a ground rules hearing in any case involving a young or vulnerable witness (it is now mandatory in all intermediary trials), using the agenda set by the *Bench Book*, and to have their cross-examination firmly controlled in language, length, and even content, to ensure effective and fair testimony. Paragraph 64 describes types of questions which can be prohibited as being likely to produce unreliable answers, requiring an advocate to prepare cross-examination very carefully to avert judicial intervention, or even directions to the jury about any persistent failure to comply with the ground rules.

Section D15   Trial on Indictment: General Matters and Pre-trial Procedure

General: Criminal Practice Directions

The *Criminal Practice Directions* [2013] EWCA Crim 1631, as amended (see [2013] EWCA Crim 2328), revoked and replaced the greater part of the *Consolidated Criminal Practice Direction* [2002] 1 WLR 2870, although certain provisions have been saved. As a consequence, references in the main work to directions which have been revoked should now refer to the new Practice Directions but take note of changes in wording. The position as regards **D15** is as follows:

D15.3   *Consolidated Criminal Practice Direction*, paras. III.21 and IV.33 — Saved (see **PD-87** and **PD-90** in this supplement).

D15.41   *Consolidated Criminal Practice Direction*, para. IV.41 — New *Criminal Practice Directions*, I General Matters, parts 3A and 3B (see **PD-2** and **PD-3** in this supplement), but note that para. IV.41.9 has been saved (see **PD-92** in this supplement).

D15.42   *Consolidated Criminal Practice Direction*, para. V.56.3 — New *Criminal Practice Directions*, I General Matters, para. 3A.2 (see **PD-2** in this supplement).

D15.44   *Consolidated Criminal Practice Direction*, para. IV.41.3 — New *Criminal Practice Directions*, I General Matters, para. 3A.9 (see **PD-2** in this supplement).

D15.45   *Consolidated Criminal Practice Direction*, para. IV.41 — New *Criminal Practice Directions*, I General Matters, parts 3A and 3B (see **PD-2** and **PD-3** in this supplement), but note that para. IV.41.9 has been saved (see **PD-92** in this supplement).

D15.47   *Consolidated Criminal Practice Direction*, para. IV.41.8 — New *Criminal Practice Directions*, I General Matters, para. 3A.13 (see **PD-2** in this supplement).

D15.48   *Consolidated Criminal Practice Direction*, para. IV.41.11 — New *Criminal Practice Directions*, I General Matters, para. 3A.15 (see **PD-2** in this supplement).

PRE-TRIAL AND PLEA AND CASE MANAGEMENT HEARINGS

The *Criminal Practice Directions* [2013] EWCA Crim 1631 address pre-trial hearings **D15.39** under the heading of case management in part 3A. This includes the procedure for early guilty plea hearings (para. 3A.6) in cases where a guilty plea is anticipated, for preliminary hearings in cases that have been sent for trial pursuant to the CDA 1998, s. 51, and for plea and case management hearings (para. 3A.10). In relation to the latter, the *Criminal Practice Directions* make explicit (at para. 3A.11) a list of matters that ought to have been addressed by the parties, by reference to the relevant parts of the CrimPR, before a plea and case management hearing takes place. These include the service of the prosecution case, the preferring of the indictment, the service of a defence statement and the making of any application to dismiss.

D

Part D   Procedure

PRESENCE OF THE ACCUSED AT TRIAL

Exceptions to the Principle

D15.88 **The Principles to be Considered** *Jones* [2003] 1 AC 1 was applied in *Lopez* [2013] EWCA Crim 1744. The Court of Appeal observed that the decision to proceed with a trial in the absence of an accused was one that had to be approached with the utmost care and that such a course should be adopted only in rare cases and only after consideration had been given to all relevant matters and in particular the fairness of the trial. Where the accused's defence involved the retraction of admissions made to the police in interview, his presence at his trial was of importance. The *Criminal Practice Directions* [2013] EWCA Crim 1631 also address trials in the absence of the accused at para. 19E.1 *et seq.* (see **PD-25** in this supplement).

ATTENDANCE OF WITNESSES

Live Link

D15.99 **Further Use of Live Links in the Interests of Justice** Although the CJA 2003, s. 51, sought to increase the availability of live links, their availability remained under statutory control. Accordingly, it was not permissible for a court to permit a witness to give evidence by telephone where such a link was not available (*Hampson* [2014] 1 Cr App R 28 (4)).

Section D16   Trial on Indictment: The Prosecution Case

OBJECTIONS TO PROSECUTION EVIDENCE

Editing of Prosecution Evidence

D16.52 Reference to the *Consolidated Criminal Practice Direction*, para. III.24, should now be read as reference to the *Criminal Practice Directions* [2013] EWCA Crim 1631, part 27A. See also part 3B, where guidance is given as to the pagination and indexing of served evidence, and para. 27A.3, which addresses the editing of witness statements.

SUBMISSION OF NO CASE TO ANSWER

Prima Facie Case against Two Accused

D16.63 The approach enunciated by Lord Goddard CJ in *Abbott* [1955] 2 QB 497 was restated by the Court of Appeal in *Banfield* [2013] EWCA Crim 1394. Where two accused were charged with murder, as opposed to conspiracy to murder, and the evidence was inconclusive as to whether the killing had been the responsibility of one, the other or both, the trial judge ought to have stopped the case against both.

Section D17   Trial on Indictment: The Defence Case

THE DEFENCE CASE

The Accused as a Witness

D17.13 **Failure to Give Evidence** Reference to the *Consolidated Criminal Practice Direction*, para. IV.44.3 should now be read as reference to the *Criminal Practice Directions* [2013] EWCA Crim 1631, paras. 39P.2 and 39P.3.

TREATMENT BY COURT OF UNREPRESENTED ACCUSED

The Accused's Right to Give or Call Evidence

D17.18 Reference to the *Consolidated Criminal Practice Direction*, para. IV.44 should now be read as reference to the *Criminal Practice Directions* [2013] EWCA Crim 1631, paras. 39P.4 and 39P.5.

Section D18   Trial on Indictment: Procedure between Close of Defence Evidence and Retirement of Jury

CLOSING SPEECHES

Restrictions on Prosecution Closing Speeches

In *Paul* [2013] 2 Cr App R 282 (26) the Court of Appeal emphasised that the convention that   **D18.17**
the prosecution should not make a closing speech where the defendant was unrepresented
was 'more than a convention, and that both prosecution and court should be careful to
observe it'.

SUMMING-UP

Unanimity

Reference to the *Consolidated Criminal Practice Direction*, para. IV.46.1 should now be read as   **D18.43**
reference to the *Criminal Practice Directions* [2013] EWCA Crim 1631, para. 39Q.1 (see
PD-54 in this supplement).

Section D19   Trial on Indictment: Procedure Relating to Retirement of the Jury and Verdict

General: Criminal Practice Directions

The *Criminal Practice Directions* [2013] EWCA Crim 1631, as amended (see [2013] EWCA
Crim 2328), revoked and replaced the greater part of the *Consolidated Criminal Practice
Direction* [2002] 1 WLR 2870. As a consequence, references in the main work to directions
which have been revoked should now refer to the new Practice Directions but take note of
changes in wording. The position as regards **D19** is as follows:

D19.31 *Consolidated Criminal Practice Direction*, paras. IV.42.5 to IV.42.9 — New *Criminal
Practice Directions*, VI Trial, para. 39G.3 (see **PD-46** in this supplement).
D19.34 *Consolidated Criminal Practice Direction*, para. IV.46.1 — New *Criminal Practice
Directions*, VI Trial, para. 39K.1 (see **PD-49** in this supplement).
D19.35 *Consolidated Criminal Practice Direction*, para. IV.46 — New *Criminal Practice
Directions*, VI Trial, part 39Q (see **PD-54** in this supplement).
D19.36 *Consolidated Criminal Practice Direction*, para. IV.46.3 — New *Criminal Practice
Directions*, VI Trial, para. 39Q.3 (see **PD-54** in this supplement).
D19.40 *Consolidated Criminal Practice Direction*, para. IV.46 — New *Criminal Practice
Directions*, VI Trial, part. 39Q (see **PD-54** in this supplement).
D19.70 *Consolidated Criminal Practice Direction*, para. IV.46.2 — New *Criminal Practice
Directions*, VI Trial, para. 39Q.2 (see **PD-54** in this supplement).
D19.73 *Consolidated Criminal Practice Direction*, para. IV.46 — New *Criminal Practice
Directions*, VI Trial, part. 39Q (see **PD-54** in this supplement).

RETIREMENT OF THE JURY

Custody of the Jury Bailiff

Communication with the Jury   As to an extraordinary breach of the limitation on communi-   **D19.6**
cation between the jury bailiff and the jury in retirement, and the obstruction of communication between such a jury and the trial judge, see *Mole* [2013] EWCA Crim 2420.

Questions from the Jury

See *Mole* [2013] EWCA Crim 2420 at **D19.6** in this supplement as to obstruction of communi-   **D19.18**
cation between the jury and the trial judge.

D

Part D Procedure

TYPES OF VERDICT

D19.34 In *Hopkinson* [2014] 1 Cr App R 22 (3), the Court of Appeal repeated that the taking of special verdicts, by which the jury were required to indicate the basis for their finding of guilt, should be used only in the context of a trial for murder where there were a number of alternative defences available, such as loss of control or diminished responsibility, and even then only rarely.

MAJORITY VERDICTS

D19.35 The Court of Appeal in *Arthur* [2013] EWCA Crim 1852 underlined the importance of following the approved wording for a majority direction, so that no pressure was placed on, or perceived to be placed on, the jury when that direction was given. The trial judge had erroneously included words in his direction that had the effect of giving a partial *Watson* direction as part of the majority direction. Such a merging of the two directions was undesirable. The majority direction is now dealt with in the *Criminal Practice Directions* [2013] EWCA Crim 1631, part 39Q.

Section D20   Trial on Indictment: Sentencing Procedure

General: Criminal Practice Directions

The *Criminal Practice Directions* [2013] EWCA Crim 1631, as amended (see [2013] EWCA Crim 2328), revoked and replaced the greater part of the *Consolidated Criminal Practice Direction* [2002] 1 WLR 2870. As a consequence, references in the main work to directions which have been revoked should now refer to the new Practice Directions but take note of changes in wording. The position as regards **D20** is as follows:

D20.45   *Consolidated Criminal Practice Direction*, para. III.27 — New *Criminal Practice Directions*, II Preliminary Proceedings, part 10A (see **PD-16** in this supplement).

D20.47   *Consolidated Criminal Practice Direction*, para. III.27 — New *Criminal Practice Directions*, II Preliminary Proceedings, part 10A (see **PD-16** in this supplement).

D20.49   *Consolidated Criminal Practice Direction*, para. I.6 — New *Criminal Practice Directions*, V Evidence, part 35A (see **PD-38** in this supplement).

D20.50   *Consolidated Criminal Practice Direction*, para. I.6 — New *Criminal Practice Directions*, V Evidence, part 35A (see **PD-38** in this supplement).

D20.65   *Consolidated Criminal Practice Direction*, para. IV.45.29 — New *Criminal Practice Directions*, VII Sentencing, para. C.1 (see **PD-57** in this supplement).

D20.93   *Consolidated Criminal Practice Direction*, para. I.7 — This provision is revoked but there is no equivalent provision is made.

DISPUTES ABOUT THE FACTS FOLLOWING A PLEA OF GUILTY

Newton Hearings

D20.8 In *Sheard* [2013] EWCA Crim 1161, in the context of a reference by the A-G under the CJA 1988, s. 36, of the accused's sentence as unduly lenient, the Court of Appeal expressed concern that the sentencing judge had been invited to resolve a factual dispute as to whether or not certain aggravating features of the seriousness of the offence were present without hearing any live evidence. This was especially of concern where those factors might be determinative of whether a sentence of imprisonment was required. See also *Nicholls v DPP* [2013] EWHC 4365 (Admin), in which the purposes of, and limitations to, a *Newton* hearing were restated by the Administrative Court.

SENTENCING THE OFFENDER FOR MATTERS
OF WHICH HE HAS NOT BEEN CONVICTED

Sample Offences

D20.56 The approach to sentence where an accused is to be sentenced on less than the full indictment, following the prosecution's acceptance of pleas, is now addressed in the *Criminal Practice Directions* [2013] EWCA Crim 1631, Sentencing, paras. B.1 and B.18 (see **PD-56** in this supplement).

Section D21   Summary Trial: General and Preliminary Matters

THE INFORMATION OR WRITTEN CHARGE

Rule against Duplicity

The rule against duplicity was considered in *Euro Foods Group v Cumbria County Council* (2013)   **D21.8**
177 JP 614. However, it is submitted that the case should not be regarded as authoritative as the
court applied r. 12 of the Magistrates' Courts Rules 1981, rather than the CrimPR, r. 7(3).

AMENDMENT OF INFORMATION OR WRITTEN CHARGE

Defects which Require Amendment but which Are Not Incurable

In *Foster v DPP* [2013] EWHC 2039 (Admin), the accused was charged with an offence alleg-   **D21.14**
edly committed on 18 April. In fact, the nature of the offence charged could not have been
committed before the period of 28 days from 28 March had expired. It followed that the accused
could not be guilty of the offence charged. Wilkie J said (at [23]) that:

> …a discrepancy of the nature which we see in this case, where the information on the basis of which the
> defendant before the magistrates had been brought to court does not disclose any offence at all, must
> be of sufficient substance that it requires amendment in order for the magistrates properly then to try
> the information. It would be an extremely odd set of circumstances if the magistrates could lawfully try
> a case and convict someone of an offence where the statement of the offence does not in fact, on the
> evidence, on any view, disclose the commission of the offence of which they convict the defendant.

CASE MANAGEMENT

The *Criminal Practice Directions* [2013] EWCA Crim 1631, para. 3A.3 (see **PD-2** in this sup-   **D21.39**
plement), states that, where a case is to be tried in a magistrates' court or a youth court, the
prescribed trial preparation form must be used.

SPECIAL PLEAS IN THE CONTEXT OF SUMMARY TRIALS

Double Jeopardy

In *DPP v Jarman* [2013] EWHC 4391 (Admin), the prosecutor failed to attend and the magistrates   **D21.50**
dismissed the case for want of prosecution under the MCA 1980, s. 15. Fresh proceedings were then
instituted. Griffith Williams J (at [30]) reiterated that 'the scope of the key of autrefois acquit is nar-
rowly confined to those cases where the accused is put in peril of conviction for the same offence as
that with which he is then charged'. It follows that 'the court must be in a position to conduct a
hearing and so it follows that there must be a prosecutor to prosecute and a defendant to defend
unless, of course, the defendant has wilfully absented himself or herself and so the trial proceeds in
his or her absence' (at [31]). In *Jarman*, the accused 'was in no way in peril because while the court
was competent to try him and there was a valid charge upon which he was to be tried, the dismissal
was not on the merits; there was no prosecutor and the magistrates had heard no evidence' (at [32]).

Section D22   Summary Trial: The Course of the Trial

FAILURE OF PARTIES TO APPEAR

Failure of Prosecutor to Appear

In *DPP v Jarman* [2013] EWHC 4391 (Admin), the prosecutor failed to attend and the magis-   **D22.29**
trates dismissed the case for want of prosecution under the MCA 1980, s. 15. Griffith Williams J
(at [36]) said that:

> While the overriding objective includes also the requirement to deal with cases efficiently and expedi-
> tiously, the use of the power to dismiss proceedings pursuant to s. 15 of the Act must not, in my judg-
> ment, be used, save in the most exceptional cases, to, in effect, punish the prosecution for its
> inefficiency.

D

Part D Procedure

WRITTEN EVIDENCE AT SUMMARY TRIAL: CRIMINAL JUSTICE ACT 1967, s. 9

D22.38   The principles applicable to evidence by written statement are now to be found in the *Criminal Practice Directions* [2013] EWCA Crim 1631, part 27A (see **PD-30** in this supplement). There are no changes in substance from the provisions formerly contained in the *Consolidated Criminal Practice Direction*.

THE ROLE OF THE JUSTICES' CLERK/LEGAL ADVISER

Introduction

D22.78 to
D22.84   Guidance on the role of the justices' clerk/court legal adviser is now to be found in the *Criminal Practice Directions* [2013] EWCA Crim 1631, part 37A (see **PD-39** in this supplement). There are no major changes in substance from the provisions formerly contained in the *Consolidated Criminal Practice Direction*.

Section D23   Sentencing in the Magistrates' Court

COMMITTAL FOR SENTENCE

Committal under the Powers of Criminal Courts (Sentencing) Act 2000, s. 6

D23.60   *Ayhan* [2012] 1 WLR 1775 was followed in *Luff* [2013] EWCA Crim 1958, where the committal purported to be under the PCC(S)A 2000, s. 6, but the Court of Appeal held that the reference to s. 6 was a mistake, and that the committal should be treated as having been under s. 4.

Section D24   Trial of Juveniles

DETERMINING MODE OF TRIAL OF JUVENILES

Where Juvenile is Charged with an Adult

D24.56   **Severance**   The *Criminal Practice Directions* [2013] EWCA Crim 1631, para. 3G.1 (see **PD-8** in this supplement), replacing the *Consolidated Criminal Practice Direction*, para. III.30.4, provides that, if a vulnerable defendant (especially one who is young) is to be tried jointly with one who is not, the court should consider whether the vulnerable defendant should be tried on his own. Such an order should be made only if the court is satisfied that a fair trial cannot be achieved by use of appropriate special measures or other support for the vulnerable defendant.

TRIAL OF JUVENILES ON INDICTMENT

Reporting Restrictions

D24.78   In *Jolleys* [2013] EWCA Crim 1135, Leveson LJ (at [12]–[13]), confirmed that a person is 'concerned in the proceedings' for the purposes of the CYPA 1933, s. 39, if, and only if, he is 'the person by or against or in respect of whom the proceedings are taken or as being a witness herein'. In relation to criminal proceedings, this can only include a child or young person who is the victim of an alleged offence, or the defendant or a witness. It does not extend to children or young persons simply on the basis that they may be concerned in the more general sense of being affected thereby.

VULNERABLE DEFENDANTS: ADAPTATIONS TO NORMAL TRIAL PROCESS

Ensuring Fairness of the Trial Process

D24.93
and D24.94   The *Criminal Practice Directions* [2013] EWCA Crim 1631, paras. 3G.7 to 3G.14 (see **PD-8** in this supplement), set out the special arrangements which should made where a vulnerable

defendant is being tried: this includes a juvenile being tried in the Crown Court or in an adult magistrates' court. There are no major changes in substance from the provisions formerly contained in the *Consolidated Criminal Practice Direction*, para. III.30.

Section D26   Appeal to the Court of Appeal (Criminal Division) Following Trial on Indictment

APPEAL AGAINST CONVICTION

Statutory Basis of Appeal against Conviction

The circumstances in which a certificate of fitness for appeal may be granted by a Crown Court are now governed by the *Criminal Practice Directions* [2013] EWCA Crim 1631, part 19H (see **PD-28** in this supplement).   **D26.7**

Directions Concerning Loss of Time and Frivolous and Vexatious Appeals

The *Criminal Practice Directions* [2013] EWCA Crim 1631, part 68E (see **PD-76** in this supplement), now governs the procedure for directions in relation to loss of time served after service of the notice of appeal, replacing the *Consolidated Criminal Practice Direction*, para. II.16.1 but also including a reminder of the warning given by the Court of Appeal in *Hart* [2007] 1 Cr App R 412 (31) that it may order that time be lost even where counsel has advised that there are good grounds for appeal.   **D26.12**

Appellant who Absconds

See *Okedare* [2014] EWCA Crim 228 for a recent review of whether the Court of Appeal should consider an appeal where the appellant has absconded, including the extent of the authority of solicitors acting for the appellant.   **D26.13**

APPROACH OF COURT OF APPEAL TO COMMONLY OCCURRING ERRORS IN THE COURSE OF A TRIAL

Inconsistent Verdicts

The Court of Appeal held in *Gilmartin* [2013] EWCA Crim 2631 that a jury had not given inconsistent verdicts by acquitting two offenders of possession of an offensive weapon but convicting them of an affray during which they were said to have threatened the victims with weapons. The jury must have been sure that they had used weapons, but could have been unsure about the nature of the weapons and which offender had used which weapon.   **D26.27**

In *Formhals* [2013] EWCA Crim 2624, the Court of Appeal considered whether there could be inconsistent verdicts when verdicts were reached on some counts while a jury failed to agree on others. The appeal was dismissed; Davis LJ said (at [27]–[28]):

> Overall in this context what the Court of Appeal ultimately has to consider is whether or not a conviction is safe. The failure of a jury to agree on a verdict is…self-evidently not a verdict. But…linguistics should not be allowed to triumph over justice…[I]n our view, the principles applicable to inconsistent verdicts are capable of applying by analogy where it simply is logically inexplicable as to how a jury could not reach a verdict on one count when set against a verdict of guilt they had reached on another count. We thus think it would be going too far to preclude a defendant in such a situation from even being permitted to argue that the resulting situation gives rise to an unsafe conviction…

> It will be a rare case indeed where a failure to reach a verdict can be said to be logically inexplicable when contrasted with or set against a verdict or verdicts which have been reached. If such an argument is to be run, it will have to be run in cases which will call for the closest scrutiny by the court.

D

Part D Procedure

RIGHT OF APPEAL AGAINST SENTENCE

Statutory Basis of Appeal against Sentence

D26.41   The *Criminal Practice Directions* [2013] EWCA Crim 1631, part 68E (see **PD-76** in this supplement), and paras. 19H.5 and 19H.6, replacing the *Consolidated Criminal Practice Direction*, para. IV.50, now cover the grant of bail pending appeal.

Section D27   Procedure on Appeal to the Court of Appeal (Criminal Division)

General: Criminal Practice Directions

The *Criminal Practice Directions* [2013] EWCA Crim 1631, as amended (see [2013] EWCA Crim 2328), revoked and replaced the greater part of the *Consolidated Criminal Practice Direction* [2002] 1 WLR 2870. As a consequence, references in the main work to directions which have been revoked should now refer to the new Practice Directions but take note of changes in wording. The position as regards **D27** is as follows:

D27.4   *Consolidated Criminal Practice Direction*, paras. II.2.2 and 2.5 — New *Criminal Practice Directions*, X Appeal, paras. 68B.2 and 68B.6 (see **PD-73** in this supplement).

D27.18   *Consolidated Criminal Practice Direction*, para. IV.50 — New *Criminal Practice Directions*, III Custody and bail, part 19H (see **PD-28** in this supplement).

D27.22   *Consolidated Criminal Practice Direction*, paras. II.17 and II.18 — New *Criminal Practice Directions*, X Appeal, part 68F (see **PD-77** in this supplement).

BAIL PENDING APPEAL

Bail by the Court of Appeal

D27.15   The *Criminal Practice Directions* [2013] EWCA Crim 1631, paras. 19H.5 and 19H.6, now cover the grant of bail pending appeal, replacing the *Consolidated Criminal Practice Direction*, para. IV.50, but there is no equivalent provision to para. IV.50.6.

Bail Granted by the Crown Court

D27.18   The *Criminal Practice Directions* [2013] EWCA Crim 1631, part 19H, governs the granting of a certificate of fitness for appeal and associated bail by a Crown Court judge. It is in significantly different terms to the *Consolidated Criminal Practice Direction*, para. IV.50, which it replaces.

HEARING OF AN APPEAL

Practice in Usual Case

D27.23   The guidance as to citation of authority set out in *Erskine* [2010] 1 All ER 1196 is now embodied in the *Criminal Practice Directions* [2013] EWCA Crim 1631, XII General Application, paras. D.2 to D.13.

ABANDONING AN APPEAL

D27.33   In *Smith* [2013] EWCA Crim 2388, the Court of Appeal revisited the question of when an abandonment of appeal was a nullity because it came about as a result of wrong legal advice. The Court observed (at [58]) that there were four propositions which applied to the case:

  i) A notice of abandonment of appeal is irrevocable, unless the Court of Appeal treats that notice as a nullity.

  ii) A notice of abandonment is a nullity if the applicant's mind does not go with the notice which he signs.

iii) If the applicant abandons his appeal after and because of receiving incorrect legal advice, then his mind may not go with the notice which he signs. Whether this is the case will depend upon the circumstances.

iv) Incorrect legal advice...means advice which is positively wrong. It does not mean the expression of opinion on a difficult point, with which some may agree and others may disagree.

The conviction was challenged on the basis that defence counsel had failed properly to conduct the accused's defence at trial. Queen's Counsel had advised that the appeal was not arguable and the accused consequently abandoned his appeal. He then sought to argue that the abandonment was a nullity because that advice was wrong. The Court dismissed the appeal. The Court (at [90]–[92]) criticised 'a growing and unwelcome tendency of convicted defendants to dismiss their original counsel and then to bring in new counsel to criticise their predecessors'. Such a strategy was described as 'an attempt to circumvent the restriction on calling fresh evidence' enabling the accused 'to get the best of both worlds' because:

> He tries one defence before the jury. If that fails, he tries the alternative defence before the Court of Appeal and possibly before a new jury at his re-trial. We deplore this strategy. Members of the Bar should not lend their support to this strategy unless there really is a proper basis for impugning the conduct of previous counsel...

> Criminal litigation is a process in which the defendant is required to make a series of irrevocable (or usually irrevocable) decisions: for example, whether to plead guilty, whether to give evidence and so forth. If things go badly for the defendant, he cannot simply go back to square one and try a different tack. Criminal litigation is not a tactical exercise.

Section D31   Extradition

THE EXTRADITION HEARING

Validity of Part 1 Warrant

The Supreme Court has considered in conjoined appeals whether a Ministry of Justice which issues a part 1 warrant for a convicted person is a judicial authority (*Ministry of Justice, Lithuania v Bucnys* [2013] UKSC 71). The Court started from the premise that the concept of 'judicial authority' embraces courts, judges, magistrates and (in light of *Assange v Swedish Prosecution Authority* [2012] 2 AC 471) public prosecutors (at [34]). Lord Mance, giving the judgment of the Court, considered (at [48]) that:

D31.12

> ...accusation and conviction warrants do not necessarily raise the same considerations...If the court responsible for the conviction or execution of the sentence considers that the European arrest warrant should be sought, and the issue of the warrant follows from its decision, then the issue of the warrant can be regarded as the result of a judicial decision even though the issue takes place by and in the name of a different authority.

Therefore, if a Ministry of Justice issues a EAW at the request of a court responsible for the sentence then it is a judicial authority. Furthermore, a Ministry of Justice will be acting as a judicial authority if it issues the warrant at the request of, and by way of an endorsement of, some other person properly regarded as a judicial authority — in some circumstances this could be a public prosecutor (see [57] and [66]). In these situations, the discretion of the Ministry of Justice not to issue a EAW is not relevant. The Court concluded by stating (at [66]) that 'a Ministry which has power to issue and issues a European arrest warrant of its own motion or at the request of a non-judicial authority, including an executive agency such as a prison department, cannot be regarded as a judicial authority'. (However, the Court did not reach a conclusion as to whether an individual decision-maker in a Ministry of Justice could be functionally independent and, therefore, a judicial authority, as this did not arise on the facts of the appeals (at [47] and [66]).

D

Part D Procedure

Following this decision, there were a number of challenges which sought to argue that the Supreme Court's reasoning in *Assange* had been held to be flawed in *Bucnys* and so a public prosecutor could not be considered to be a judicial authority. However, in *Binder v Public Prosecutor's Office, Memminghem, Germany* [2014] EWHC 133 (Admin) the Divisional Court confirmed (at [25]) that the conclusion in *Assange* that a public prosecutor is a judicial authority remains valid.

EXTRADITION OFFENCE

D31.17   The framework list on the EAW has 32 categories of offences, described in general terms, for which dual criminality is not required. In *Jama v Senior Public Prosecutor Gera, Germany* [2013] EWHC 3276 (Admin), the Divisional Court said (at [26]) that 'one should be very cautious about cutting down the scope of such general terms by reading implied limitations into them, whether by reference to international instruments or otherwise'.

D31.18   The court must determine the issue of dual criminality only on the basis of what is set out in the extradition request. It cannot take into account evidence put forward by the requested person contradicting the extradition request (*Government of the USA v Shlesinger* [2013] EWHC 2671 (Admin) at [12]). It is possible for the court to consider evidence put forward by the requested person if considering whether the fairness or accuracy of the description of the extradition offence gives rise to an abuse of process (*Shlesinger* at [12] and [14]–[15]). See also **D31.14** and **D31.34** in the main work.

BARS TO EXTRADITION

Speciality

D31.25   The Divisional Court considered the issue of speciality in four linked appeals concerning requests from Poland for conviction cases which involved aggregate sentences. The sentences had been imposed for multiple offences which, at least arguably, included one or more offences which did not qualify as an extradition offence (*Brodziak v Circuit Court in Warsaw, Poland* [2013] EWHC 3394 (Admin)). The Court considered that the Polish Criminal Procedure Code provided for the protection of speciality and did not find that the application of the Polish legislation would lead in practice to a breach of the speciality rule.

Additional Potential Bars

D31.26   The forum bar for accusation cases enacted by the CCA 2013, sch. 20, paras. 1 to 7, was brought into force on 14 October 2013 (Crime and Courts Act 2013 (Commencement No. 5) Order 2013 (SI 2013 No. 2349)).

The Secretary of State has the power to designate prosecutors who, in addition to members of the CPS, can issue a certificate which stops a judge finding that extradition is barred by reason of forum (ss. 19F(2) and 83E(2)). The Secretary of State has exercised this power to designate the Competition and Markets Authority Board, the DPP for Northern Ireland, the Director of Revenue and Customs Prosecutions, the Director of the SFO, the Director of Service Prosecutions, the Financial Conduct Authority or a chief or deputy chief prosecutor (or the equivalent) appointed by them (Extradition Act 2003 (Designation of Prosecutors) (England and Wales and Northern Ireland) Order 2013 (SI 2013 No. 2388)). The Secretary of State has also designated the Secretary of State for Business, Innovation and Skills, but only acting personally.

HUMAN RIGHTS

D31.30   In *Aleksynas v Minister of Justice, Republic of Lithuania* [2014] EWHC 437 (Admin) the Divisional Court conducted a detailed exercise to consider the assurances given in a number of linked appeals concerning whether detention conditions in Lithuania would give rise to a breach of Article 3 (see **D31.31** in this supplement).

The ECHR, Article 3, may be violated if a person who is ill could be detained after his extradition and would not receive appropriate medical care (*Aswat v UK* (2014) 58 EHRR 1 at [50]). The ECtHR has said that particular care must be taken in the case of mentally ill persons to consider their vulnerability and their inability, in some cases, to complain coherently or at all about how they are affected by their treatment. 'The feeling of inferiority and powerlessness which is typical of persons who suffer from a mental disorder calls for increased vigilance in reviewing whether the Convention has (or will be) complied with.' The Court has specified three particular elements to be considered when examining whether a person's health is compatible with his detention: his medical condition, the adequacy of the medical assistance and care provided in detention and the advisability of maintaining the detention given the person's health.

D31.31

In 2013, both the Queen's Bench Division in Northern Ireland (*Lithuania v Liam Campbell* [2013] NIQB 19) and the High Court in the Republic of Ireland (*Minister of Justice v McGuigan* [2013] EIEHC 216) held that the detention conditions in a Lithuanian remand prison would amount to a violation of the ECHR, Article 3. A number of linked appeals have now been heard which considered this issue in the context of evidence and assurances provided by Lithuania, and the Divisional Court has found that extradition in these cases would not lead to a violation of Article 3 (*Aleksynas v Minister of Justice, Republic of Lithuania* [2014] EWHC 437 (Admin)).

PHYSICAL OR MENTAL CONDITION

Amongst the factors to be considered on an application for extradition is what might happen to a requested person after extradition (*Government of South Africa v Dewani* [2014] EWHC 153 (Admin) at [50]). It might be unjust and oppressive to order the extradition of a person who it was agreed was unfit to stand trial at the time of the extradition proceedings if there was a prospect that he might remain permanently unfit. A court would need to consider whether an undertaking to allow his return, if after a reasonable time for further treatment he was still likely to remain unfit, should be required from the requesting territory (at [60]).

D31.33

If there is a genuine and legitimate dispute between medical experts as to a requested person's fitness to plead or stand trial then this is normally an issue which the court in the requesting State should determine as part of the trial process, although the English court can consider whether in a particular case this would result in injustice or oppression (*Edwards v Government of the USA* [2013] EWHC 1906 (Admin) at [54]–[58]).

APPEALS

Further Appeal or Remedy

The Divisional Court has stressed the professional obligations which apply to legal representatives who apply to the out-of-hours judge for urgent injunctions or similar orders, emphasising the strict obligation of candour and the need to draw to the judge's attention points which are potentially adverse to their application (*R (Kozlowski) v Serious Organised Crime Agency and CPS Extradition Unit* [2013] EWHC 1741 (Admin) at [23]–[26]).

D31.42

The Divisional Court used its residual discretion to reopen a final determination of an appeal under the Civil Procedure Rules, r. 52.17, in a part 2 case where it had directed a judge to reconsider a question he had decided (*Government of South Africa v Dewani* [2014] EWHC 153 (Admin) at [50]). The judge came to the same conclusion and the appeal was taken to have been dismissed by a decision of the High Court. However, the High Court reopened the appeal as it considered it would be in the interests of justice for it to consider an issue which it had previously declined to decide (at [17]).

The Extradition Appeals (England, Wales and Northern Ireland) Order 2013 (SI 2013 No. 2384), which has effect from 14 October 2013, modifies s. 109(2) to (4) of the Extradition Act 2003. Those subsections provide that, on an appeal under s. 108 against a decision of the Secretary of State to order a person's extradition, the High Court is to consider the questions which were before the Secretary of State. However, as s. 70(11) provides that the Secretary of State is not to consider whether the extradition would be compatible with the human rights of the person extradited, this Order modifies s. 109 to make it clear that the High Court is able to allow or dismiss an appeal brought on human rights grounds where human rights questions were not considered by the Secretary of State because of the effect of s. 70.

Section D32   Public Funding

REPRESENTATION ORDERS

Applying for a Representation Order in a Magistrates' Court

D32.6   The rules as to eligibility to receive criminal legal aid in the magistrates' court will, in relation to applications for a representation order made on or after 27 January 2014, also apply to proceedings in the Crown Court. A means test will then apply to the obtaining of criminal legal aid in the Crown Court (Criminal Legal Aid (Financial Resources) (Amendment) Regulations 2103 (SI 2013 No. 2791)). The rules on contribution orders are amended from the same date by the Criminal Legal Aid (Contribution Orders) (Amendment) Regulations 2013 (SI 2013 No. 2792).

In order to recover costs from central funds on acquittal in the Crown Court, an application for legal aid must have been made and refused, however inevitable an outcome such a refusal may be (Costs in Criminal Cases (Legal Costs) (Exceptions) Regulations 2014 (SI 2014 No. 130)).

No changes are made in relation to the Court of Appeal so that legal aid, albeit (when appropriate) with a contribution, will always be available, However, as a consequence, successful appellants paying privately cannot recover their costs at all from central funds.

Nature of Representation

D32.10   The Criminal Legal Aid (Determinations by a Court and Choice of Representative) Regulations 2013 are amended by SI 2013 No. 2814 in relation to representation orders granted on or after 2 December 2013.

Regulation 18(7) is amended so that after the present definition of 'the prosecution condition' there is added:

> and the relevant court is satisfied that the individual will be, or will be likely to be, prejudiced if they too are not represented by two or more advocates.

Regulation 19 is also substituted by SI 2013 No 2814:

> 19.—(1) A determination that an individual is entitled to select a Queen's Counsel or more than one advocate under regulation 18 may only be made by the following judges—
> (a) subject to paragraph (2), in the course of a trial or a preliminary hearing, pre-trial review or plea and directions hearing, the judge who has been assigned as the trial judge;
> (b) where a trial judge has not been assigned, by—
>   (i) a High Court judge; or
>   (ii) subject to paragraph (2), a resident judge of the Crown Court or, in the absence of a resident judge, a judge nominated by a resident judge of the Crown Court for the purpose of making such a determination; or
> (c) where the proceedings are in the Court of Appeal, by the Registrar of Criminal Appeals, a High Court judge or a judge of the Court of Appeal.
> (2) A determination made by a judge referred to in paragraph (1)(a) or (b)(ii) does not take effect unless it is approved by a presiding judge of the circuit or by a judge nominated by a presiding judge of the circuit for the purpose of giving such approval.

Section D33   Costs

General: New Costs Practice Direction

Throughout this section the *Practice Direction (Criminal Proceedings: Costs)* [2010] 1 WLR 2351 has been replaced by the *Practice Direction (Costs in Criminal Proceedings)* [2013] EWCA Crim 1632. There is however no change of substance and the paragraph numbering remains unchanged.

POWER TO AWARD COSTS

D33.1 Under the Criminal Procedure (Attendance of Witnesses) Act 1965, s. 2, there is a power to award costs to a person who successfully applies to set aside an order for a witness summons under the provisions of s. 2. This power was considered in *DLA Piper UK LLP v BDO LLP* [2013] EWHC 3970 (Admin). The Divisional Court held that the statute had a lacuna. No costs can be awarded to a party who successfully resists the original application for a summons. While costs may be awarded to a successful applicant to set aside such an order, this could be done only if that person was not notified of the original application. There is no inherent jurisdiction to make a costs order. In any event an order could not be made against the solicitors acting; they were not a party to the proceedings, and only a party can issue an application for a witness summons (1965 Act, s. 2(8) and CrimPR, r. 28.1). On the facts, the solicitors had not been guilty of any act or omission that would have justified a wasted costs order.

DEFENDANT'S COSTS ORDERS

Jurisdiction to Make a Defendant's Costs Order

D33.2 The Costs in Criminal Cases (Legal Costs) (Exceptions) Regulations 2014 (SI 2014 No. 130) amend the Prosecution of Offences Act 1985, s. 16A, which provides that a defendant's costs order made under s. 16 of that Act may not require the payment out of central funds of an amount that includes an amount in respect of the accused's legal costs, unless an exception applies. Regulation 2 inserts a new exception (condition D) into s. 16A which would enable an individual who is financially ineligible for legal aid in certain Crown Court proceedings to receive a payment out of central funds in respect of his legal costs if he is acquitted. See **D33.38** in this supplement. The Regulations came into force on 27 January 2014.

By virtue of the Costs in Criminal Cases (General) (Amendment) (No. 2) Regulations 2013 (SI 2013 No. 2830), in relation to cases in which an application for a representation order is made on or after 27 January 2013, the power for a Crown Court to make a defendant's costs order is restored in favour of those who are not tried for an offence for which they were sent or transferred for trial, or who are acquitted of any offence at trial. However, the value of such orders is limited to the value of the claim at legal aid rates. The same regime will therefore apply in both magistrates' court and Crown Court proceedings for those who are ineligible for public funding.

Proper Approach to Making of a Defendant's Costs Order

D33.5 When the Crown would not accept a proposal from the defence to be bound over to keep the peace until it became apparent, on the day of trial, that the complainant would not give evidence, it was wrong for the judge to limit the amount of the defendant's costs order to the cost of that day alone (*Newcombe v CPS* [2013] EWHC 2180 (Admin)).

Effect of Defendant's Costs Order: the General Rule

D33.11 There are conflicting decisions in relation to the payment of agency fees. If these are claimed as a disbursement a reasonable payment can be recovered, subject to the statutory limits now in place. However, if the time spent is charged to profit costs, *Murray* [2013] Costs LR 867 suggests that where an agent is instructed it is not possible to recover an amount greater than that charged to the principals by the agent. However, that decision is inconsistent with a series of earlier decisions (*Duxbury* [1997] Costs LR (Core Vol) 423; *Pullum* [1997] Costs LR (Core Vol) 413; *Smith and Graham v Lord Chancellor* [1999] All ER (D) 957). The decision in *Murray* fails to acknowledge that the issue is the contractual liability accepted by the client to the principal firm and not the liability incurred by that firm.

Murray confirms that a former senior solicitor, requalified as a barrister, may recover hourly remuneration at the rate appropriate to a senior solicitor.

Order in Favour of a Publicly Funded Accused

D33.15 Where the same firm continues to act privately for a client who has the benefit of a representation order, the effect of the Criminal Legal Aid (Remuneration) Regulations 2013, reg. 9, is that payment cannot be recovered from central funds for legal expenses incurred until the representation order is withdrawn notwithstanding the agreement of the client (*McCatty* [2013] Costs LR 863).

COSTS AGAINST LEGAL REPRESENTATIVES

Procedure and Practice in Making Order

D33.34 The reference to the Civil Procedure Rules, r. 48.7, should now be to r. 46.8. As to an order sought against solicitors in relation to the issuing of a witness summons, see *DLA Piper UK LLP v BDO LLP* [2013] EWHC 3970 (Admin), discussed at **D33.1** in this supplement.

STATUTES AND REGULATIONS RELATING TO COSTS

D33.38   The Costs in Criminal Cases (Legal Costs) (Exceptions) Regulations 2014 (SI 2014 No. 130) amend the Prosecution of Offences Act 1985, s. 16A. The Regulations came into force on 27 January 2014. Regulation 2 inserts a new exception (condition D) into s. 16A which would enable an individual who is financially ineligible for legal aid in certain Crown Court proceedings to receive a payment out of central funds in respect of his legal costs if he is acquitted. New subsections (5A) and (11) are inserted, which provide as follows:

> (5A) Condition D is that—
> (a) the accused is an individual,
> (b) the order is made under section 16(2),
> (c) the legal costs were incurred in relevant Crown Court proceedings, and
> (d) the Director of Legal Aid Casework has made a determination of financial ineligibility in relation to the accused and those proceedings
> (and condition D continues to be met if the determination is withdrawn).
>
> (11) In subsection (5A)—
> 'determination of financial ineligibility', in relation to an individual and proceedings, means a determination under section 21 of the Legal Aid, Sentencing and Punishment of Offenders Act 2012 that the individual's financial resources are such that the individual is not eligible for representation under section 16 of that Act for the purposes of the proceedings;
> 'Director of Legal Aid Casework' means the civil servant designated under section 4(1) of the Legal Aid, Sentencing and Punishment of Offenders Act 2012;
> 'relevant Crown Court proceedings' means any of the following—
> (a) proceedings in the Crown Court in respect of an offence for which the accused has been sent by a magistrates' court to the Crown Court for trial;
> (b) proceedings in the Crown Court relating to an offence in respect of which a bill of indictment has been preferred by virtue of section 2(2)(b) of the Administration of Justice (Miscellaneous Provisions) Act 1933(2);
> (c) proceedings in the Crown Court following an order by the Court of Appeal or the Supreme Court for a retrial.

The Costs in Criminal Cases (General) (Amendment) Regulations 2013 (SI 2013 No. 2526), which have effect from 27 October 2013, make minor amendments to the principal Regulations (SI 1986 No. 1335); *inter alia*, regs. 15 and 16 are amended. In reg. 15 (definitions) 'sent' is substituted for 'committed' at para. (b) and reg. 16(1) has inserted after (b) '(bb) an intermediary is required to assist the defendant; or'.

SUPPLEMENT TO PART E
SENTENCING

Section E1   Sentencing: General Provisions

PURPOSES OF SENTENCING

In *Sellafield Ltd, Network Rail Infrastructure Ltd* [2014] EWCA Crim 49, the Court of Appeal **E1.1**
pointed out that the purposes of sentencing listed in the CJA 2003, s.142 (see **E1.1** in the main
work), applied to corporate defendants just as much as they applied to individuals.

SENTENCING GUIDELINES

The Sentencing Council published its definitive guideline on Sexual Offences in December **E1.3**
2013. It replaced the existing SGC guideline on 1 April 2014. The guidelines will apply to all
adult offenders, regardless of when the offences took place, so while offenders will be subject to
the law at the time of the offence, the guideline will bring what is described as a 'modern and
victim-focused approach' to how historic offenders are dealt with by the courts. The guidelines
are very similar in structure to earlier Sentencing Council guidelines, and contain the series of
Steps with which judges have become familiar. At Step One, however, the language changes
from earlier guidelines which express harm and culpability as 'greater' and 'lesser' harm, and
'higher' and 'lower' culpability. Culpability in the rape guideline, for example, is assessed as 'A'
or 'B' rather than 'higher' or 'lower', and harm at Categories 1, 2 or 3. The Council says that this
reflects 'the baseline of harm and culpability inherent in the act of rape', and has been 'specifically tailored to sexual offences'. The Council has included 'previous good character and/or
exemplary conduct' as a mitigating factor in all its previous guidelines. In the context of sexual
offences the approach has changed, and the Council says that judges must assess carefully how
relevant previous good character is. The new guidelines are set out in part 26 of the Sentencing
Guidelines at **SG-528** in this supplement.

The Sentencing Council has also published new sentencing guidelines for environmental
crimes (see part 28 of the Sentencing Guidelines at **SG-674** in this supplement), which have
effect from 1 July 2014. The guideline covers a variety of offences related to the disposal of waste
and rubbish (e.g., fly-tipping), mostly covered by the Environmental Protection Act 1990 and
the Environmental Permitting (England and Wales) Regulations 2010. It also covers waste
handling or disposal offences and nuisance offenders.

The Sentencing Council has also published a new sentencing guideline for the sentencing of
organisations convicted of fraud, money laundering and bribery offences (see part 27 of the
Sentencing Guidelines at **SG-662** in this supplement). The new guideline, entitled 'Fraud,
bribery and money laundering: corporate offenders', has effect from 1 October 2014. The
guideline is said to be part of the wider development of guidelines for all fraud offences, including those committed by individuals, which will be published later in 2014.

In *Dyer* [2013] EWCA Crim 2114 Leveson LJ in the Court of Appeal said (in the context **E1.4**
of the Sentencing Council definitive guideline on *Drugs Offences*) that pre-guideline case
authority was overtaken by the guideline, so reliance on *Afonso* [2005] 1 Cr App R
(S) 560 and other pre-guideline cases is no longer appropriate. His lordship said that while
the guideline set out the approach for the courts to follow, subsequent appellate decisions
might help to interpret the guideline, provide practical illustrations of its application, and
indicate when the interests of justice might justify a departure from it. If the Court identified areas not covered by the guideline it was for the Sentencing Council to reconsider it.
Most of the arguments in the instant case advanced alleged disparity of sentences with
those passed on different offenders, by different judges, at different times. The purpose of
the guideline was to introduce what is hoped to be an increasingly consistent approach to
sentence. That is not the same as saying that the outcome in each case must be the same.
Following the approach in the guideline in each case effectively removed any arguments
about disparity of sentence.

REQUIRED REDUCTIONS IN SENTENCE

Reduction in Sentence for Guilty Plea

E1.9 The *Criminal Practice Directions* [2013] EWCA Crim 1631 include new guidance on early guilty plea hearings at paras. 3A.6 to 3A.8 (see **PD-2** in this supplement).

The *Criminal Practice Directions* also include new guidance on pleas of guilty in the Crown Court, at Sentencing, para. A.1 and paras. B.1 to B.27. Matters covered include: where a guilty plea is offered to less than the whole indictment and the prosecution is minded to accept pleas tendered to some counts or to lesser alternative counts; a range of situations where a guilty plea is offered on a limited basis; the procedure to be followed on agreed bases of plea; the status of plea agreement and joint sentencing submissions.

E1.10 The Court of Appeal in *Nelson* [2013] EWCA Crim 2410 considered the case of an offender who came within the terms of the PCC(S)A 2000, s. 111, and qualified for the minimum sentence of three years' imprisonment (three-strikes burglary) but who had also taken advantage of the early guilty plea scheme. The Court took a sentencing starting point of four years and three months and was able to give the full one-third reduction for the guilty plea without infringing the rule in the CJA 2003, s. 144(2) (see **E1.8** in the main work) that the final sentence must not be less than 80 per cent of three years. It seems that if a starting point closer to three years had been appropriate on the facts then the level of discount would have been limited by the rule in s. 144(2) and the normal full credit could not have been given under the early guilty plea scheme.

AGGRAVATING FACTORS

Previous Convictions

E1.14 The decision of the Court of Appeal in *Bailey* [2013] EWCA Crim 1779 provides further authority for the proposition that, however bad the record of the offender, the sentencing court must keep the sentence imposed for the latest offence in some reasonable proportion to the seriousness of that offence.

The *Criminal Practice Directions* [2013] EWCA Crim 1631 include new guidance on the provision of information relating to the defendant's record at paras. 10A.1 to 10A.8. The *Consolidated Criminal Practice Direction*, para. III.27, is revoked and replaced. As to spent convictions, see **E24.1** in this supplement.

PREVALENCE

E1.22 The *Criminal Practice Directions* [2013] EWCA Crim 1631, paras. H.1 to H.6 (see **PD-62** in this supplement), include new guidance on community impact statements, which may be prepared by the police to make the court aware of particular crime trends in the local area and the impact of these on the local community.

REPORTS

Victim Personal Statements

E1.31 In relation to sub-paragraph (e) of the listed guidance in the main work (opinions of the victim and victim's close relatives on the appropriate level of sentence), see *A-G's Ref (No. 36 of 2013) (Hall)* [2013] EWCA Crim 1450, where some victims of the sexual offences committed by the offender wrote to the Court of Appeal to say that they were content with the original sentence(s). Lord Judge CJ said that these views could not determine what was appropriate, and the total sentence was increased from 15 months to 30 months.

The *Criminal Practice Directions* [2013] EWCA Crim 1631 include new guidance on victim personal statements at paras. F.1 to F.3 (see **PD-60** in this supplement), and on families bereaved by homicide and other criminal conduct at paras. G.1 to G.3 (see **PD-61** in this supplement). The *Consolidated Criminal Practice Direction*, para. III.28, is revoked and replaced.

The *Criminal Practice Directions* [2013] EWCA Crim 1631 were amended by the Amendment to the Criminal Practice Directions [2013] EWCA Crim 2328 (in force from 7 October 2013). The Amendment, *inter alia*, creates a presumption that victim personal statements will be read to the court if the victim so requests, subject to judicial discretion, in line with the revised *Code of Practice for Victims of Crime*, which was issued on 29 October 2013 (see **PD-60** in this supplement).

The Amendment also creates a new Practice Direction on impact statements where the victim, or one of the victims, is a business or enterprise (Impact Statement for Business, or ISB) (see **PD-63** in this supplement).

Section E2   Custodial Sentences: General Provisions

LENGTH OF SENTENCE

Crediting Periods of Remand on Bail

In *Leacock* [2013] EWCA Crim 1994, endorsing *Hoggard* [2013] EWCA Crim 1024, the **E2.17** Court of Appeal said that it was the duty of advocates to make proper inquiries and to ensure that full and accurate information was before the court about the period of time spent by the offender under a qualifying curfew. Solicitors and counsel had specifically to ask the offender whether he had been the subject of 'tagging'. If an error had been made, it was the advocate's duty to apply to the court within the time-limit applicable. In future, the Court of Appeal would apply the time-limits strictly.

Concurrent and Consecutive Custodial Sentences

The *Criminal Practice Directions* [2013] EWCA Crim 1631, paras. E.1 to E.3 (see **PD-59** in **E2.19** this supplement) include new guidance on the appropriate form of words to be used when imposing a consecutive sentence on an offender already serving one or more custodial sentences.

Section E3   Mandatory Life Sentences

MURDER: LIFE IMPRISONMENT

The *Criminal Practice Directions* [2013] EWCA Crim 1631, paras. P.1 to P.3 (see **PD-69** in this **E3.2** supplement) provide guidance on the procedure for announcing the minimum term in open court.

Schedule 21 Principles

A five-member Court of Appeal in *A-G's Ref (No. 69 of 2013)* [2014] EWCA Crim 188, was **E3.3** specially constituted to consider a number of appeals in the light of *Vinter v UK* [2013] ECHR 645, in which the Grand Chamber of the ECtHR had held that whole life minimum terms violated the ECHR, Article 3, on the basis that they were not reducible. The ECtHR had said that for a life sentence to be compatible with Article 3, there had to be a prospect of release and a possibility of review, and that, while a judge could impose a whole life order, a legal regime for review had to be in place at the time the sentence was passed. The Court of Appeal found that whole life minimum terms imposed pursuant to the CJA 2003, s. 269 and sch. 21, were

E

Part E Sentencing

not incompatible with Article 3. This was because the review regime provided for by the Crime (Sentences) Act 1997, s. 30, which gave power to the Secretary of State to release a life sentence prisoner early on compassionate grounds, did provide offenders with the possibility of release in exceptional circumstances. Lord Thomas CJ said that it was consistent with the rule of law that applications under s. 30 were considered by the Secretary of State on an individual basis against the criteria that circumstances had changed to such an extent that the punishment was no longer justifiable. It followed that judges should continue to apply the CJA 2003 regime and to impose, in exceptional cases, whole-life orders in accordance with sch. 21 of that Act.

This is an important decision, in which the Court adopts the same line, and essentially the same reasoning, as it did in its earlier decision in *Oakes* [2013] 2 All ER 30 (again a five-strong Court). The basic question here is whether s. 30 (regarded by many as a discretionary 'long-stop' power allowing some terminally ill prisoners to spend their last few weeks outside the prison environment) really amounts to the 'legal regime for review' of the whole life order which the ECtHR seems to have had in mind in *Vinter*. If the Court of Appeal had agreed with the ECtHR, and found that the CJA 2003 regime was incompatible with Article 3, it would have had to issue a declaration of incompatibility under the HRA 1998, s. 4, which in turn would have required Parliament to amend the statute to remedy the situation. This issue may yet require the consideration of the Supreme Court.

E3.5   The *Criminal Practice Directions* [2013] EWCA Crim 1631, paras. M.1 to M.14 (see **PD-67** in this supplement) provide guidance on the imposition of the mandatory life sentence for murder. The *Consolidated Criminal Practice Direction*, para. IV.49, is revoked and replaced.

Section E4   Dangerous Offenders

PERIOD SPECIFIED UNDER THE POWERS OF CRIMINAL COURTS (SENTENCING) ACT 2000, s. 82A

Procedure

E4.17   The *Criminal Practice Directions* [2013] EWCA Crim 1631, paras. L.1 to L.5 (see **PD-66** in this supplement) provide guidance on the imposition of life sentences and the PCC(S)A 2000, s. 82A. The *Consolidated Criminal Practice Direction*, para. IV.47, is revoked and replaced.

Section E5   Prescribed Custodial Sentences

MINIMUM CUSTODIAL SENTENCES FOR DOMESTIC BURGLARY

E5.4   The Court of Appeal in *Andrews* [2013] 2 Cr App R (S) 274 (5) said that a court proceeding to sentence an offender for an offence of domestic burglary where the PCC(S)A 2000, s. 111, was engaged should first work through the Sentencing Council guideline in the normal way and then cross-check to ensure that the provisional sentence arrived at was not less than the minimum sentence required by s. 111. The three-year prescribed sentence was not the starting point for sentence. *Andrews* was followed and applied in *Silvera* [2013] EWCA Crim 1764.

Guilty Plea

E5.7   In *Nelson* [2013] EWCA Crim 2401 the Court of Appeal considered the case of an offender who qualified for the minimum custodial sentence under the PCC(S)A 2000, s. 111, but had also taken advantage of the early guilty plea scheme. See **E1.10** in this supplement for discussion.

Section E8   Community Orders

POWER TO MAKE A COMMUNITY ORDER

Criteria for the Imposition of Community Order

The Crime and Courts Act 2013 (Commencement No. 6) Order 2013 (SI 2013 No. 2981) **E8.2**
brought the CCA 2013, sch. 16 (except part 4), into force on 11 December 2013. **and E8.4**

Community Order Requirements

The Crime and Courts Act 2013 (Commencement No. 6) Order 2013 (SI 2013 No. 2981) **E8.10**
brought the CCA 2013, sch. 16 (except part 4), into force on 11 December 2013.

Section E12   Absolute and Conditional Discharges

POWER TO GRANT ABSOLUTE AND CONDITIONAL DISCHARGES

The *Criminal Practice Directions* [2013] EWCA Crim 1631, para. J.20 (see **PD-64** in this **E12.1**
supplement), includes guidance on the power under the PCC(S)A 2000, s. 12(6), to allow a
person who consents to do so to give security for the good behaviour of the offender.

Combining Discharge with Other Sentences or Orders

The Prevention of Social Housing Fraud Act 2013 was brought into force in England on 15 **E12.4**
October 2013 (Prevention of Social Housing Fraud Act 2013 (Commencement) (England)
Order 2013 (SI 2013 No. 2622)) and was brought into force in Wales on 5 November 2013
(Prevention of Social Housing Fraud Act 2013 (Commencement) (Wales) Order 2013 (SI 2013
No. 2861)).

Section E13   Binding Over

BINDING OVER TO KEEP THE PEACE

Power to Bind Over to Keep the Peace

The *Criminal Practice Directions* [2013] EWCA Crim 1631, paras. J.1 to J.15 (see **PD-64** **E13.2**
et seq. in this supplement), include guidance on the imposition of an order to bind over to keep
the peace.

BINDING OVER TO COME UP FOR JUDGMENT

Powers to Bind Over to Come Up for Judgment

The *Criminal Practice Directions* [2013] EWCA Crim 1631, paras. J.17 to J.18 (see **PD-64** **E13.8**
in this supplement), include guidance on the use of the power to bind over to come up for
judgment.

Section E14   Orders Against Parents

BINDING OVER OF PARENT OR GUARDIAN
OF OFFENDER AGED UNDER 18

The *Criminal Practice Directions* [2013] EWCA Crim 1631, para. J.19 (see **PD-64** in this **E14.6**
supplement), includes guidance on the imposition of an order to bind over a parent or
guardian.

E

Part E Sentencing

Section E15   Fines

FINES: SENTENCING PRINCIPLES

E15.15   For detailed discussion of the principles applicable to the imposition of a fine on a large corporation, see *Sellafield Ltd, Network Rail Infrastructure Ltd* [2014] EWCA Crim 49 and *Southern Water Services Ltd* [2014] EWCA Crim 120.

Taking into Account Means of Offender

E15.20   For consideration of the level of fine appropriate for public corporations of various kinds and the requirements imposed on such companies to provide full details of their financial position, see *Sellafield Ltd, Network Rail Infrastructure Ltd* [2014] EWCA Crim 49 and *Southern Water Services Ltd* [2014] EWCA Crim 120.

Surcharge

E15.24   The Prevention of Social Housing Fraud Act 2013 was brought into force in England on 15 October 2013 (Prevention of Social Housing Fraud Act 2013 (Commencement) (England) Order 2013 (SI 2013 No. 2622)) and was brought into force in Wales on 5 November 2013 (Prevention of Social Housing Fraud Act 2013 (Commencement) (Wales) Order 2013 (SI 2013 No. 2861)).

In *Holden* [2013] EWCA Crim 2017 the Court of Appeal observed that it is *not* permissible to fix a term in default when making the order for a surcharge. Section 139 of the PCC(S)A 2000 empowers the fixing of a default term for a fine, but has not been amended to include surcharges. On the other hand, there *is* power to give time to pay a surcharge. That is provided by the PCC(S)A 2000, s. 141, and the Administration of Justice Act 1970, sch. 9, para. 13.

Section E16   Compensation Orders

POWER TO MAKE COMPENSATION ORDERS

E16.2   The Crime and Courts Act 2013 (Commencement No. 6) Order 2013 (SI 2013 No. 2981) brought the CCA 2013, sch. 16 (except part 4), into force on 11 December 2013.

Payment, Discharge and Review

E16.9   The PCC(S)A 2000, s. 133, is amended by the Prevention of Social Housing Fraud Act 2013 by the insertion, after the reference to a confiscation order under the POCA 2002, of the words 'or an unlawful profit order under section 4 of the Prevention of Social Housing Fraud Act 2013 (or both)'. The 2013 Act was brought into force in England on 15 October 2013 (Prevention of Social Housing Fraud Act 2013 (Commencement) (England) Order 2013 (SI 2013 No. 2622)) and was brought into force in Wales on 5 November 2013 (Prevention of Social Housing Fraud Act 2013 (Commencement) (Wales) Order 2013 (SI 2013 No. 2861)).

Section E19   Confiscation Orders

GENERAL

E19.1   *Evwierhowa* [2011] 2 Cr App R (S) 442 was considered in *Onuigbo* [2014] EWCA Crim 65 (a decision that turned on its facts); see also *Boughton-Fox* [2014] EWCA Crim 227.

The Process: A Summary

E19.7   The Prevention of Social Housing Fraud Act 2013 was brought into force in England on 15 October 2013 (Prevention of Social Housing Fraud Act 2013 (Commencement) (England)

Order 2013 (SI 2013 No. 2622)) and was brought into force in Wales on 5 November 2013 (Prevention of Social Housing Fraud Act 2013 (Commencement) (Wales) Order 2013 (SI 2013 No. 2861)).

MAKING OF CONFISCATION ORDER

Stage Two—Determination of Benefit from Criminal Conduct

Obtaining   The leading cases of *Mitchell* [2009] EWCA Crim 214, *White* [2010] EWCA   **E19.24** Crim 978, *Bajwa* [2012] 1 WLR 601 and *Taylor* [2013] EWCA Crim 1151 were considered in *Tatham* [2014] EWCA Crim 226. See also *Mackle* [2014] UKSC 5.

Joint Enterprise and Individual Benefit   In *Fields* [2013] EWCA Crim 2042, the Court of   **E19.26** Appeal reviewed a large number of decisions including *Porter* [1990] 1 WLR 1260, *May* [2008] 1 AC 1028, *Lambert* [2012] 2 Cr App R (S) 535, and *Waya* [2013] 1 AC 294 (but not *Rooney* [2010] EWCA Crim 2). In relation to the determination of the 'recoverable amount', the Court rejected the argument that it would be disproportionate to order each defendant to pay the total amount of the benefit, on the footing that each had failed to disprove that he had available assets sufficient to discharge payment in that amount (Davis LJ at [72]–[90]). Less clear (it is submitted) is what the court's approach should be when determining a defendant's 'available amount' under the POCA 2002, s. 9, in circumstances where the extent of the defendant's wealth is ostensibly no more than the value of his share of the proceeds of the criminal conduct in question. In *Fields*, the Court said that to embrace concepts of apportionment 'at any stage' would 'potentially involve impracticable inquiries into financial dealings between criminals and could lead to evasion, manoeuvring and chicanery on the part of defendants' (per Davis LJ at [82](iv)).

Connection with Criminal Conduct   There is nothing in the principle established in *Waya*   **E19.29** [2012] UKSC 51 that undermines what would seem, with respect, to be the common sense of the conclusion in *Pattison* [2007] EWCA Crim 1536, namely, that rental income from a property does constitute a 'benefit' in the hands of the recipient (*Oyebola* [2013] EWCA Crim 1052).

Proportionality and Abuse of Process   It was held in *Morgan* [2013] EWCA Crim 1307   **E19.31** (among other things) that the concept of 'abuse of process' was not appropriate to the argument advanced by the appellant, namely, that the judge's finding of the benefit that he had obtained resulted in a confiscation order that was 'oppressive'. Rather, the key question is whether the confiscation order made was 'disproportionate' so as to amount to a breach of M's rights under the ECHR, Protocol 1, Article 1.

Where HM Revenue and Customs had seized cigarettes 'smuggled' by the accused, the cigarettes had not been restored to them as true owners. The seizure was administrative or possibly penal, but it was not compensatory (*Louca* [2013] EWCA Crim 2090).

In considering whether to grant an extension of time within which to appeal the making and enforcement of a confiscation order when the effect would be to permit the applicant to take advantage of the change in the application of the law arising from the Supreme Court's decision in *Waya* [2013] 1 AC 294, the Court of Appeal in *Bestel* [2013] 2 Cr App R 317 (36) held (at [42]) that the Court does not 'apply the finality principle in isolation from the justice of the case ... [T]he practice of this Court, almost without exception, has been to examine the underlying justice of a conviction for a criminal offence.'

Stage Three—Determination of the Recoverable Amount

The Prevention of Social Housing Fraud Act 2013 was brought into force in England on 15   **E19.43** October 2013 (Prevention of Social Housing Fraud Act 2013 (Commencement) (England) Order 2013 (SI 2013 No. 2622)) and was brought into force in Wales on 5 November 2013 (Prevention of Social Housing Fraud Act 2013 (Commencement) (Wales) Order 2013 (SI 2013 No. 2861)).

Where the value of property (at the time the person obtained it) is adjusted pursuant to the POCA 2002, s. 80(2)(a), to take account of later changes in the value of money, the use of the Retail Price Index continues to be appropriate in confiscation proceedings rather than the Consumer Price Index (*Shepherd* [2014] EWCA Crim 179).

E19.44　**The Amount of Benefit**　In *Harvey* [2014] 1 WLR 124, the Court of Appeal expressed the following conclusions as to the status of cases decided prior to *Waya* [2013] 1 AC 294 (per Jackson LJ at [65]):

　　i)　*Smith* [[2001] UKHL 68] and *May* [[2008] 1 AC 1028] are still good law as the Supreme Court has expressly approved them.
　　ii)　*Singh* [[2008] EWCA Crim 243] was correctly decided in the light of *Waya* paragraphs 25 and 26.
　　iii)　*Morgan* [[2008] EWCA Crim 1323] is still good law because the Supreme Court has approved it. The only reason why *Morgan* survives is that M had failed to make *full* restoration by the date of the hearing and had not indicated any willingness to make *full* restoration: see paragraph 39 of Hughes LJ's judgment in *Morgan*. Even so we are bound to say that *Morgan* seems to be a decision which is close to the line, since M had restored to V 81% of the money which M had taken from her.
　　iv)　*Xu and Xu* [[2008] EWCA Crim 2372] is still good law as the reasoning of the Court of Appeal seems to be entirely consistent with *Waya*.
　　v)　*Baden Lowe* [[2009] EWCA Crim 194] is probably no longer good law, as this was a case in which there was full restoration of the relevant property to V.
　　vi)　*Del Basso* [[2010] EWCA Crim 1119] is another case which is close to the line. This was a 'criminal lifestyle' case where the statutory assumptions applied. The Court of Appeal proceeded on the basis that the expenses which D incurred in administering the car park and the football club should not be deducted. Thus paragraphs 25 and 26 of *Waya* would seem to suggest that *Del Basso* was correctly decided. On the other hand the final decision does seem excessively harsh and may arguably be characterised as disproportionate.
　　vii)　*James and Blackburn* [[2011] EWCA Crim 2991] must still stand as it is consistent with *Waya*.
　　viii)　*Ahmad* [[2012] 1 WLR 2335] would also appear to be consistent with the decision in *Waya*.

For the purposes of determining the amount of a defendant's benefit (as well as the 'available amount' under the POCA 2002, s. 9: see **E19.49** in the main work), there may be circumstances in which it would be appropriate to pierce the corporate veil in respect of a company controlled by the defendant (consider *Jennings v CPS* [2008] 2 Cr App R 414 and *Seager* [2010] 1 WLR 815). In *Sale* [2013] EWCA Crim 1306, the Court of Appeal discussed the Supreme Court decision in *Prest v Petrodel Resources Ltd* [2013] UKSC 34. The Court could see no reason why the analysis relevant to criminal confiscation proceedings at [76] of *Seager* should not continue to apply in criminal confiscation proceedings, subject to an understanding of *Prest*. The Court opined that 'it may be that the three situations identified by the court in *Seager* … might be prefaced as if the preceding sentence read … In the context of criminal cases the courts have identified at least three situations when *a benefit obtained by a company is also treated in law by POCA as a benefit obtained by the individual criminal*' (per Treacy LJ at [41]).

E19.47　**Valuation of Benefit**　For the purposes of the POCA 220, s. 79(2), it is perfectly consistent with the notion of 'market value' that the value of particular property may vary, depending for example on the time at which it is obtained or the capacity or role of the person obtaining it (*Elsayed* [2014] EWCA Crim 333).

Stage Four – Determination of the Available Amount

E19.51　As to piercing the corporate veil for the purpose of determining the available amount, see *Sale* [2013] EWCA Crim 1306 at **E19.44** in this supplement.

See also *Fields* [2013] EWCA Crim 2042 at **E19.26** in this supplement.

E19.54　**Tainted Gifts**　On an application made to enforce a confiscation order, it was open to the court to proceed on the basis that a confiscation order treated an item of property in the hands of the recipient as a tainted gift, even if the judge, when making the confiscation order, had not expressly found as a fact that it was a 'tainted gift' (*Heron v SOCA* [2013] EWCA Civ 1106).

Confiscation Orders and Sentence

The Prevention of Social Housing Fraud Act 2013 was brought into force in England on 15 **E19.59** October 2013 (Prevention of Social Housing Fraud Act 2013 (Commencement) (England) Order 2013 (SI 2013 No. 2622)) and was brought into force in Wales on 5 November 2013 (Prevention of Social Housing Fraud Act 2013 (Commencement) (Wales) Order 2013 (SI 2013 No. 2861)).

ENFORCEMENT, RECONSIDERATION AND APPEALS

Enforcement

In *Gibson v Secretary of State for Justice* [2013] EWHC 2481 (Admin), it was held that (in the **E19.67** context of the Drug Trafficking Act 1994) the words 'at the time the period of detention was imposed' in the MCA 1980, s. 79(2), mean the time when the default term was activated by the magistrates' court and not the time when the period to be served in default was fixed by the Crown Court. The answer is relevant to the number of days that the defaulting defendant is entitled to have remitted against the default term. In relation to the POCA 2002, the Court observed that in one respect the POCA 2002 is even more draconian than its predecessor because if s. 37 applies:

> ...then it would appear that interest continues to run throughout the term of both the original and default term of imprisonment and there is no cut-off so far as interest is concerned at the point of imposition of the default term. This...is as a consequence of the exclusion of section 79(2) MCA 1980 from the process (per His Honour Judge Gosnell at [17]).

Care needs to be taken regarding this point because s. 37 was repealed by the Serious Crime Act 2007 on 1 April 2008.

Reconsideration

It was held in *Padda* [2013] EWCA Crim 2330, that the POCA 2002, s. 22, was of similar effect **E19.70** to the provisions of the Drug Trafficking Act 1994, s. 16. The obligation of a court under s. 22(4)(a) of the POCA 2002 is to exercise its discretion to make a 'just' order. Accordingly, it is unlikely that any order which is 'just' will be found to be disproportionate, so as to infringe the ECHR, Protocol 1, Article 1. See also *Ludlam v Department of Business Innovation and Skills* [2013] EWCA Civ 1282.

Appeals

It was held in *Mackle* [2014] UKSC 5 (citing *Emmett* [1998] AC 773 and *Bell* [2011] EWCA **E19.73** Crim 6) that a defendant is not precluded from appealing against a confiscation order made by consent on the ground that the consent was based on a mistake of law, as a result of wrong legal advice.

MISCELLANEOUS

Absent Defendants

Inability to Attend   *Bhanji* [2011] EWCA Crim 1198 and *Gavin and Tasie* [2011] 1 Cr App **E19.74** R (S) 731 were considered and discussed in *Robb v NCA* [2014] EWCA Civ 171, albeit in the context of the POCA 2002, part 2.

E

Part E Sentencing

Section E20   Recommendation for Deportation

POWER TO RECOMMEND FOR DEPORTATION

E20.1   In *Gheorghiu* [2013] 2 Cr App R (S) 497 (74) the Court of Appeal confirmed that it was no longer appropriate for a court to make a recommendation for deportation in the case of an offender falling within the definition of 'foreign criminal' for the purposes of the UK Borders Act 2007. The Court also confirmed that, in the exceptional cases where a court might consider making such a recommendation, the appropriate test to apply was whether the offender's continued presence in the UK is to its detriment. In the instant case, the judge had considered whether the offender's continued presence in the UK was not conducive to the public good. That was the wrong test to apply.

Section E21   Exclusions and Disqualifications

SEXUAL OFFENCES PREVENTION ORDERS

Restraining Orders under the Protection from Harassment Act 1997

E21.28   In *James* [2013] 2 Cr App R (S) 542 (85) the Court of Appeal considered an appeal against a restraining order imposed in addition to a community order following the offender's conviction for assault occasioning actual bodily harm on his adult stepdaughter. The complainant had asserted that the offender had assaulted her sexually, but the offender had denied that, claiming that he had struck her when she had provoked him by stabbing him with a screwdriver. The jury acquitted of sexual assault and the Court said that on the main contested issues at trial the jury had believed the offender. The stepdaughter had a history of making false allegations. In the circumstances, a restraining order was inappropriate. Far from mending the relationship between the offender and the complainant it might well provide an opportunity for further problems to arise.

Section E22   Mentally Disordered Offenders

HOSPITAL AND LIMITATION DIRECTIONS

E22.13   In *Fort* [2013] EWCA Crim 2332 the Court of Appeal noted, when dealing with an appeal against sentence by an 18-year-old offender who had pleaded guilty to diminished responsibility manslaughter, that the power to make hospital and limitation directions under the Mental Health Act 1983, ss. 45A and 45B, is available only in the case of an offender aged 21 and over. Those sections apply where a court is considering the imposition of a 'sentence of imprisonment' on an offender. In the context of the Mental Health Act 1983, the term 'sentence of imprisonment' does *not* include the equivalent custodial sentences for offenders aged 18, 19 or 20. The Court could find no good reason why the power under ss. 45A and 45B was not available for that age group, and recommended that it should be so extended.

Section E23   Notification Requirements under the Sexual Offences Act 2003

INTRODUCTION

E23.1   In *R (Prothero) v Secretary of State* [2013] EWHC 2830 (Admin) the Divisional Court considered the Sexual Offences Act 2003 (Notification Requirements) (England and Wales) Regulations 2012 (SI 2012 No. 1876) which, *inter alia*, by reg. 12 require the offender to provide details of his bank, debit or credit card accounts. The claimant sought a declaration that reg. 12 was incompatible with the ECHR, Article 8. The Court refused the application, holding that reg. 12 was a practical and proportionate way of preventing other people becoming victims and that the means employed to do so were not inappropriate or disproportionate.

Section E24   Rehabilitation of Offenders

GENERAL PRINCIPLE

The *Criminal Practice Directions* [2013] EWCA Crim 1631, paras. 35A.1 to 35A.3 (see **PD-38**   **E24.1** in this supplement), include guidance on the proper treatment in court of spent convictions, The *Consolidated Criminal Practice Direction*, para. I.6, is revoked and replaced.

REHABILITATION PERIODS

Pending Change to Rehabilitation Periods

By virtue of the Legal Aid, Sentencing and Punishment of Offenders Act 2012 (Commencement   **E24.5** No. 9, Saving Provision and Specification of Commencement Date) Order 2014 (SI 2014 No. 423), the LASPO 2012, s. 139, was brought into force with effect from 10 March 2014. It should be noted that, from that date, all rehabilitation periods will change to those set out in the table in **E24.5** in the main work. This change to rehabilitation periods is retrospective, and applies to all convictions, whether they were incurred before or after the Rehabilitation of Offenders Act 1974 came into force on 1 July 1975.

SUPPLEMENT TO PART F
EVIDENCE

Section F1　General Principles of Evidence in Criminal Cases

QUESTIONS OF LAW AND FACT

In Summary Trials

As to the proper role of the justices' clerk in a summary trial, see now the *Criminal Practice* **F1.38**
Directions [2013] EWCA Crim 1631, part 37A (see **PD-39** in this supplement).

Section F2　The Discretion to Exclude Evidence; Evidence Unlawfully, Improperly or Unfairly Obtained

ADMISSIBILITY OF EVIDENCE OBTAINED UNLAWFULLY, IMPROPERLY OR UNFAIRLY

Procedures for Obtaining Evidence Prescribed by Statute

Scott v Baker [1969] 1 QB 659 was distinguished in *Public Prosecution Service of Northern* **F2.13**
Ireland v Elliott [2013] 2 Cr App R 180 (17): see **F3.71** in this supplement.

DISCRETIONARY EXCLUSION OF EVIDENCE OBTAINED UNLAWFULLY, IMPROPERLY OR UNFAIRLY

Police and Criminal Evidence Act 1984, s. 78

Undercover Operations after Commission of the Offence　In *Plunkett* [2013] EWCA Crim **F2.42**
261, a case of aggravated burglary, false imprisonment and possession of a firearm, evidence was
admitted of damaging admissions made by the accused, after their arrest, in a police van en
route to a police station. The admissions were covertly recorded following authorisation under
the RIPA 2000. Some of the admissions were made when the accused were left in the van on
their own during a deliberately built-in delay. Under the PACE 1984, s. 30(1A), a person
arrested must be taken by a constable to a police station as soon as practicable after the arrest. It
was held that, even if there had been a breach of the RIPA 2000 or s. 30(1A), the breaches would
have been minor, given the immense seriousness of the crime and the need to protect the victims
of the crime. The evidence had been properly admitted and there was no ground to exclude it
under s. 78.

In *Khan* [2013] EWCA Crim 2230, a covert recording, carried out in good faith, exceeded **F2.43**
the authority granted under the RIPA 2000 because the authority had been sought to
obtain evidence to prove or disprove the involvement of the accused in the offence but the
recording was carried out after the accused had been charged. It was held that, although
there had been a breach of the ECHR, Article 8, fairness of the criminal trial process is the
touchstone of the law and the trial judge had not erred in refusing to exclude the evidence
under s. 78.

Telephone Interceptions

In *Mahmood* [2013] EWCA Crim 2356, it was held that a blanket interception and record- **F2.52**
ing of the telephone calls of prisoners at two prisons did not constitute a breach of the RIPA
2000. Under s. 4(4) of the Act, interception of a communication is authorised if it is in
exercise of a power conferred by or under rules made under the Prison Act 1952, s. 47. The
Court of Appeal held that, under the Prison Rules 1999, rr. 34 and 35A, the Secretary of
State is empowered to impose restrictions and conditions on the telephone calls made by
prisoners either across the entire prison estate or in relation to particular prisoners or classes
of prisoners.

Section F3   Burden and Standard of Proof and Presumptions

REBUTTABLE PRESUMPTIONS OF LAW

Presumption of Regularity

F3.71   *Scott v Baker* [1969] 1 QB 659 was distinguished in *Public Prosecution Service of Northern Ireland v Elliott* [2013] 2 Cr App R 180 (17) in relation to fingerprints taken using an electronic reader that had not been approved for use, as it should have been, by the Secretary of State. The Supreme Court held that the well-established English rule of law that evidence which is relevant is admissible, even if it has been obtained illegally, extends to evidence created by an unlawful process. The Court also held that the statutory requirement for approval of an electronic fingerprint reader is not analogous to the approval requirements in the case of breath test or speed gun devices, because whereas breath tests, like speed guns, are means of measuring something that cannot subsequently be re-measured, fingerprints can be reproduced subsequently and the accuracy of the initial readings, if disputed, can be checked by the provision of more samples.

Section F4   Competence and Compellability of Witnesses and Oaths and Affirmations

GENERAL

Wards of Court as Witnesses

F4.4   Concerning interviews with wards of court, see now the *Criminal Practice Directions* [2013] EWCA Crim 1631, part 28A (see **PD-33** in this supplement).

OTHER WITNESSES

Children and Persons with a Disorder or Disability of the Mind

F4.22   The dictum in *Barker* [2010] EWCA Crim 4 that a witness, in order to be competent, does not need to understand every single question or give a readily understood answer to every question, was applied in *IA* [2013] EWCA Crim 1308 (see also **D14.43** in this supplement).

Section F7   Cross-examination and Re-examination

PROTECTION OF COMPLAINANTS IN PROCEEDINGS FOR SEXUAL OFFENCES

The Restriction

F7.22   In *P (RP)* [2013] EWCA Crim 2331, it was held that, although in some cases a question about an abortion might be a way of asking about a complainant's sexual history and therefore about her 'sexual behaviour', questions about the accused's emotional succour and financial support for the complainant in relation to an abortion that was performed some years after the offences, and which were relevant as tending to detract from her account that she viewed him with distaste because of the offences, were not questions about 'sexual behaviour'.

Section 41(5): Evidence or a Question Relating to Evidence Adduced by the Prosecution

F7.39   Where evidence is adduced by the prosecution about sexual behaviour of the complainant and the prosecution also has material that would enable the evidence to be rebutted, the material should be disclosed to the defence (*Abdul-Majoud* [2013] EWCA Crim 2622).

Procedure on Applications under s. 41

In *Crossland* [2013] EWCA Crim 2313 it was held that failure to comply with the rules relat-   **F7.41**
ing to applications under the YJCEA 1999, s. 41, makes it more likely that things will go
wrong at the trial, either because the statutory protection given to the complainant will be
undermined or because the defence will be prohibited from pursuing a legitimate line of questioning.

RULE OF FINALITY OF ANSWERS TO QUESTIONS ON COLLATERAL MATTERS

Previous Convictions

Consolidated Criminal Practice Direction, para. I.6, has been replaced by the *Criminal Practice*   **F7.55**
Directions [2013] EWCA Crim 1631, part 35A (see **PD-38** in this supplement). Under para.
35A.2, when considering bad character applications under the CJA 2003, regard should always
be had to the general principles of the Rehabilitation of Offenders Act 1974. In civil proceedings, cross-examination of any witness about a spent conviction is prohibited by s. 4(1) of the
1974 Act unless the judge is satisfied that it is not possible for justice to be done except by admitting the conviction (s. 7(3) of the 1974 Act).

Section F8   Documentary Evidence and Real Evidence

PROOF OF PUBLIC AND JUDICIAL DOCUMENTS

Births, Deaths and Marriages

Foreign Records   The repeal of the Foreign Marriage Act 1892, s. 16, by the Marriage (Same   **F8.25**
Sex Couples) Act 2013, s. 13(2), is brought into force on 3 June 2014 (Marriage (Same Sex
Couples) Act 2013 (Commencement No. 2 and Transitional Provision) Order 2014
(SI 2014 No. 93), art. 5(b)).

REAL EVIDENCE

Tape Recordings and Transcripts

Consolidated Criminal Practice Direction, para. IV.43, has been replaced by the *Criminal Practice*   **F8.53**
Directions [2013] EWCA Crim 1631, part 27C (see **PD-32** in this supplement).

Section F9   Public Policy and Privilege

LEGAL PROFESSIONAL PRIVILEGE

Communications in Furtherance of Crime or Fraud

In *Minchin* [2013] EWCA Crim 2412, a case of conspiracy to pervert the course of justice relat-   **F9.65**
ing to an allegedly false alibi, it was held that material in support of the purported alibi and held
by solicitors was not protected by the privilege because there was 'free-standing and independent' evidence of the conspiracy.

Section F12   Character Evidence: Evidence of Bad Character of Accused

CODIFICATION OF EVIDENCE OF BAD CHARACTER BY THE CRIMINAL JUSTICE ACT 2003

Bad Character

F12.10   **'Has to do with' Alleged Facts**   Comments in *Fox* [2009] EWCA Crim 653, to the effect that the exception in the CJA 2003, s. 98(a), relates only to the *actus reus* of the offence were disapproved in *IA* [2013] EWCA Crim 1308. The correct approach was said to be that the 'evidence must relate directly to the offence charged, be reasonably contemporaneous with it, and be associated closely with it. It is not a requirement that the misconduct is essential to proof of guilt: direct relevance will be sufficient.'

WEIGHT OF CHARACTER EVIDENCE AND JUDICIAL DIRECTION

Evidence Once Admitted can be Used for All Relevant Purposes

F12.23   *Tollady* [2010] EWCA Crim 2614, *Campbell* [2007] 1 WLR 2798 and *Singh* [2007] EWCA Crim 2140 were considered in *Speed* [2013] EWCA Crim 1650. The accused was charged with three counts of indecent exposure to a child. He had adduced evidence of a variety of convictions relating to robbery, burglary and drugs offences, part of the relevance of which was to show that, at the age of 60, he had no previous convictions for any sexual offences. It was held not to be unfair for the trial judge to suggest to the jury that the conduct of the accused in pleading not guilty in the past when facing charges of which he knew he was guilty was something which the jury could take into account in relation to the accused's credibility as a witness, although he had not given evidence in those proceedings. The accused, in cross-examination, had acceded to counsel's suggestion that he had 'tried it on' in relation to the instructions he had given in those cases, but it is far from clear that he had done anything more than put the prosecution to proof of its case. Although the Court of Appeal claims not to have been concerned with this constitutional principle, but only with the overall fairness of the judge's direction in relation to the evidence that was properly before the jury, it seems that the court is out of sympathy with the defence objection, referring to the cross-examination as showing the accused's 'dishonest lack of responsibility in connection with earlier trials'. This seems to overstate the basis for an inference about credibility. It may be that the accused's later and more general admission 'I have lied all my life' provides a better basis for declaring the overall thrust of the judge's comments not to have been unfair.

EVIDENCE OF BAD CHARACTER ADDUCED BY PROSECUTION TO PROVE GUILT OR UNTRUTHFULNESS

Criminal Justice Act 2003: Admissibility under s. 101(1)(d)

F12.39   **Propensity as an Issue**   In *Laws-Chapman* [2013] EWCA Crim 1851, the accused was charged with historic offences of indecency with a child and buggery, the latter offence involving 'violent paedophile behaviour' against a non-consenting child in the company of a group of other men. He had one previous conviction for buggery in 1985, the details of which were unknown, but the offence appeared (from the sentence given) to have been consensual, and it was 'highly likely' that it would have been no offence at all under the current law. The admission of the conviction to show that the accused had a sexual interest in boys on which he was inclined to act 'even to the extent of buggery' was wrong and based on flawed reasoning: mutually agreed sexual relations between individuals over the age of consent do not, without more, tend to prove that the older participant is a violent paedophile.

In *Kane* [2013] EWCA Crim 1487 the Court of Appeal was concerned with an 'undifferentiated mass' of bad character evidence, which appeared to have been accumulated in anticipation that the accused would face a number of charges more serious than the offence of blackmail for which he ultimately stood trial, he having pleaded guilty to the other offences. On appeal an attempt was made to justify the admission of the bad character evidence because, taken cumulatively, it showed 'the nature of the man with whom [the jury] were dealing'. However, this cannot in itself be a ground for admitting evidence under the CJA 2003 without specific consideration of the relevance of the individual items of evidence. Nor is 'propensity' in s. 103 to be equated with 'some kind of propensity to commit offences generally'. The Court was very clear that '[p]oints which are devoid of content as legitimate bad character evidence cannot acquire such a status simply by heaping them together with other points which themselves also have no proper claim to admissibility as bad character evidence under the requirements of the 2003 Act'.

Identifying the Accused by Evidence of Bad Character under the Criminal Justice Act 2003, s. 101(1)(d)

Smith [2009] 1 Cr App R 521 and *Elliott* (2011) 175 JP 39 were applied in *Lewis* [2014] EWCA **F12.49**
Crim 48 where it was said to be 'well-established' that evidence of membership of a criminal gang may be admissible under the CJA 2003, s. 101(1)(d). In *Lewis* the evidence served not only to identify those taking part in a riot, but also to provide evidence of common purpose and to rebut innocent presence. As in *Elliott*, the Court of Appeal paid careful attention to the risk of prejudice arising from evidence of membership. Of particular importance was the risk that the showing of gang-related videos posted on the internet might have an overly-emotive effect on the jury, out of proportion to its probative value. On the facts, however, and given the other evidence of participation, the evidence was rightly admitted.

Multiple Charges and Accusations under the Criminal Justice Act 2003, s. 101(1)(d)

Freeman [2009] 2 All ER 18 was applied in *O'Leary* [2013] EWCA Crim 1371, in which the **F12.60**
accused faced two sets of charges relating to the deception of elderly and vulnerable victims, both of whom were suffering from dementia. It was held that the circumstances of the two transactions were admissible in relation to one another on the issue whether the accused acted dishonestly and had targeted the victims because they were vulnerable. The evidence was not used to establish propensity, and is a case of holistic rather than sequential reasoning (see the other authorities considered at **F12.60** in the main work for examples of sequential reasoning).

Acquittals: Special Considerations

Z [2000] 2 AC 483 was considered in *T (P)* [2013] EWCA Crim 2398, where some 30 years **F12.66**
had passed since the original acquittals for sexual offences. A challenge based on the fact that there no longer existed relevant material that would have assisted the jury in assessing the reliability of the evidence was dismissed. On the facts, it appears that the portions of the evidence that were significant in the later prosecution (for a series of serious sexual offences together with the murder of one victim) were supported by statements of the accused, including what amounted to an admission of one of the rapes. The lapse of time, which might in other circumstances have proved critical, did not appear to provide a genuine impediment to challenging the relevant parts of the evidence of the two complainants.

Section F13   Character Evidence: Admissibility of Evidence of Accused's Good Character

MEANING OF GOOD CHARACTER

Absence of Previous Convictions, Cautions etc. and 'Effective' Good Character

Other Discreditable Matters   Where a trial judge is minded to qualify either or both limbs **F13.20**
of a good character direction it is better to give the conventional direction, followed by the

qualification, rather than to modify the direction (*Press* [2013] EWCA Crim 1849, where the credibility direction was qualified in relation to lies told by the accused at interview, and the propensity direction by reference to evidence that the accused had been drinking heavily at the time he claimed to be acting in self-defence).

Section F14   Character Evidence: Evidence of Bad Character of Persons Other than the Accused

CRIMINAL JUSTICE ACT 2003, s. 100

Gateways to Admissibility

F14.11   Matters Relevant to Assessment of Probative Value   In *Matthews* [2013] EWCA Crim 2238, it was held that one matter of relevance to the question whether evidence is of substantial probative value is whether it is hearsay. In that case, the defence of M, who was charged with assault by penetration of a child, was that the offence had been committed by R, the child's mother. An application under the CJA 2003, s. 100, was granted to enable M to put to R that she had previously slapped the penis of another child, which he did, but a later hearsay application to admit the supporting evidence of the complaint made by that child to his mother and grandmother did not meet the standard of 'substantial probative value'. As the Court of Appeal pointed out, had the applications been heard together, as perhaps they should have been, the result would have been to deprive the allegation of any probative value.

Section F15   The Rule Against Hearsay: General Principles

COMMON DEFINITIONAL CHALLENGES

Illustrations of Non-hearsay Evidence

F15.13   In *Minchin* [2013] EWCA Crim 2412 the Court of Appeal accepted that a statement containing the details of an alibi alleged to be false could be tendered by the prosecution without breaching the hearsay rule: 'What mattered was the fact that it was said.'

HEARSAY AND 'MATTERS STATED'

Matters Not Intended to be Believed or Acted Upon

F15.19   *Twist* [2011] 3 All ER 1055 was applied in *Khan* [2013] EWCA Crim 2230, where the question was whether one of two parties to a conversation was acquainted with K. The fact that both parties referred to K by his nickname, Bana, suggested that he was well-known to both. No question of hearsay was involved, as the intention of the speaker was not for the purpose of causing the listener to believe that the speaker knew 'Bana'. The Court of Appeal also noted that the fact that the conversation took place in the absence of K was not of itself a reason for excluding it, unless it was inadmissible hearsay or for some other reason prejudicial.

Section F16   Exceptions to the Rule Against Hearsay (Excluding Confessions)

CRIMINAL JUSTICE ACT 2003: UNAVAILABLE WITNESSES; BUSINESS AND OTHER DOCUMENTS AND DISCRETIONARY EXCLUSION

Business and Other Documents

Unavailability of Maker of Statement Prepared for Purposes of Criminal Proceedings or Investigation   In *Minchin* [2013] EWCA Crim 2412, M was charged with conspiracy to pervert the course of justice for providing a false alibi for his son. The Court of Appeal accepted that a solicitor's file note recording a meeting that had taken place with M and his son was inadmissible under the CJA 2003, s. 117, as it had been prepared for the purposes of criminal proceedings (s. 117(4)) and none of the statutory reasons for not calling the maker applied (s. 117(5)). However, the probative value of the note ultimately led to its admission under s. 114(1)(d) in the interests of justice (see **F16.38** in the main work). The Court recognised the importance of the general rule that s. 114(1)(d) should not be used to circumvent restrictions imposed by other exceptions to the hearsay rule such as those contained in s. 117, but also commented that there was an 'element of unreality' in the defence case, in that the only reason for the unavailability of the maker of the note was the refusal of the defence to waive legal privilege.   **F16.29**

Discretionary Exclusion of Statements Admissible under the Criminal Justice Act 2003, ss. 116 and 117

Hearsay, Loss of Right to Cross-examine and Fair Trial Provisions   *Horncastle* [2010] 2 AC 373 and *Riat* [2013] 1 All ER 349 were applied in *T (P)* [2013] EWCA Crim 2398, where it was reaffirmed that *Horncastle* does not require that admissible hearsay evidence must be demonstrably reliable. Article 6 of the ECHR requires a fair trial, but this is possible either where the evidence is demonstrably reliable or where there are sufficient tools available to the jury to assess the extent of its reliability. Features which tend to demonstrate reliability include the disinterest (lack of bias) of the maker of the statement and evidence independent of the hearsay which dovetails with it. In *T (P)* the Court of Appeal stated that acceptance of this principle 'embraces with particular force the evidence of witnesses who had died or who could not be expected to have any present recollection of events described in witness statements made over 30 years previously'. However, none of the hearsay evidence in that case was of 'sole or decisive' importance to the success of the prosecution.   **F16.33**

Riat and *Shabir* (2013) 177 JP 271 were applied in *Harvey* [2014] EWCA Crim 54. Although the evidence of the two witnesses who were absent through fear was central to the prosecution in that case, there was strong evidence that supported the reliability of their accounts. This included the *res gestae* statement of the two witnesses themselves, made while they were still under the influence of the effect of an armed robbery (for *res gestae*, see **F16.55** in the main work) and the extent to which the accounts subsequently given by the two tallied with one another, despite their lack of opportunity to confer immediately after the event. The Court also drew attention to the availability for the defence of a significant amount of evidence regarding the bad character of the two witnesses, who had links to the gangland fraternity, that could be deployed in support of a possible alternative explanation for the presence of firearms in the home of one of them, which was also the location for the alleged armed robbery. However, the wide powers provided by the CJA 2003, s. 124 (see **F16.92** in the main work), to admit evidence to discredit the two were rightly limited at trial so as to exclude bad character evidence that was of no substantial probative value: the evidence that may be admitted under s. 124 is subject to the same controls as where the witness attends to give evidence, i.e. the provisions of s. 100 apply (see **F14.9** in the main work).

CRIMINAL JUSTICE ACT 2003: HEARSAY ADMISSIBLE IN THE INTERESTS OF JUSTICE

Relationship with Other Hearsay Exceptions

F16.41 **Exclusionary Rules and Cautious Application of Interests of Justice Exception**   The proposition that the CJA 2003, s. 114(1)(d), was not to be applied so as to circumvent the provisions of s. 116 was reaffirmed in *Warnick* [2013] EWCA Crim 2320. Having concluded that one of the conditions for admitting the evidence of an allegedly fearful witness under s. 116 was missing, the judge was wrong to admit the same evidence under s. 114(1)(d) where to do so 'would nullify the purpose of the conditions specified by Parliament in s. 116'. See however *Minchin* [2013] EWCA Crim 2412 (at **F16.29** in this supplement), where a different view was taken (rightly, it is submitted) of a decision to admit under s. 114(1)(d) a solicitor's file note that was inadmissible under s. 117 because the defence refused to waive legal privilege in order to allow the solicitor to give evidence of a matter that would have shown that there was a conspiracy between the defendants to fabricate an alibi.

CRIMINAL JUSTICE ACT 2003: EVIDENCE AFFECTING THE CREDIBILITY OF ADMISSIBLE HEARSAY

F16.92   In *Harvey* [2014] EWCA Crim 54 it was held that the CJA 2003, s. 124, could not be deployed so as to admit bad character evidence to discredit hearsay witnesses where the evidence was of no substantial probative value: the evidence that may be admitted under s. 124 is subject to the same controls as where the witness attends to give evidence, i.e. the provisions of s. 100 apply (see **F14.9** in the main work).

Section F17   The Rule Against Hearsay: Confessions

EDITING OF CONFESSIONS

Pre-trial Editing of Witness Statement Made by Suspect

F17.92   The *Consolidated Criminal Practice Direction*, paras. III.24.4 and III.24.5, have been replaced by the *Criminal Practice Directions* [2013] EWCA Crim 1631, paras. 27A.4 and 27A.5C (see **PD-30** in this supplement).

MIXED STATEMENTS

Prosecution Placing No Reliance on Admission Contained in Mixed Statement

F17.98   *Papworth* [2008] 1 Cr App R 439 and *Garrod* [1997] Crim LR 445 were applied in *Shirley* [2013] EWCA Crim 1990. The prosecution in that case relied on only very limited admissions (that the accused was known by his middle name of Mark, and that he told people he had served in the army when he had not). As it was open to the judge to conclude that these were not 'significant' statements in the prosecution's case (and both could, it appears, have been proved by other evidence had they been contested), the interview in which S made the concessions could not be viewed, taken as a whole, as a mixed statement. S, who did not testify, was therefore rightly precluded from relying on any self-serving statements made in the same interviews.

Section F18   Evidence of Identification

VISUAL IDENTIFICATION

Turnbull [1977] QB 224, *Forbes* [2001] AC 473 and *Gojra* [2010] EWCA Crim 1939 were considered in *Laing* [2013] EWCA Crim 1836.

F18.1 to F18.18

DNA EVIDENCE

Evaluating DNA Matches   The difficulty of using DNA evidence to prove guilt in the absence of other incriminating evidence was noted in *Ogden* [2013] EWCA Crim 1294, although in that case the position was complicated by the fact that the scarf found at the scene of a burglary had mistakenly been destroyed following the obtaining of D's DNA from one of two small blood stains found on it. This DNA was the only evidence linking D with the crime, but, as Elias LJ noted (at [3]):

F18.30

> There were a number of admissions before the jury in relation to this forensic evidence. They included the fact that it was not possible to date the DNA. It was therefore possible that another person had carried the scarf to the scene of the burglary, the defendant's DNA already being on it. It was not possible either to say how the DNA came to be on the scarf, whether it was by direct contact with somebody or by airborne droplets. There was no independent evidence that the burglar had cut himself on the window. It was agreed that the remainder of the scarf had not been tested and nor . . . was the other patch of blood.

In those circumstances a submission of no case to answer ought to have been accepted. See also *Grant* [2008] EWCA Crim 1890.

Section F19   Inferences from Silence and the Non-production of Evidence

OUT-OF-COURT SILENCE UNDER THE 1994 ACT

Facts which Should Have Been Mentioned

In *Walton* [2013] EWCA Crim 2536 the accused was not asked at any point about his failure to answer questions at interview (where he had tendered a prepared statement). Nor does it appear that he was invited to deal with the question why he had made no previous mention of particular facts later relied on in his defence. Although counsel for the prosecution did not seek a direction on adverse inference, the trial judge elected to give one. The Court of Appeal considered the direction to be both wrong and unfair in the circumstances: '[T]he jury were invited to consider an adverse inference without knowing what if anything the appellant might have had to say about his silence'. See further *T v DPP* (2007) 171 JP 605, *Webber* [2004] 1 All ER 770 and the other authorities referred to in the main work. An adverse inference is appropriate only where the accused's non-disclosure is indicative of guilt. It must follow that he should be given the opportunity to put forward an innocent explanation.

F19.23

FAILURE OF ACCUSED TO TESTIFY

Failure to Testify following the 1994 Act

Procedure   The procedure for determining whether an accused person has voluntarily decided not to testify was considered in *Farooqi* [2013] EWCA Crim 1649. The Court of Appeal noted that 'where an appellant wishes to assert that he has not been given appropriate advice in a particular respect, or has not been able to make an informed decision about a matter of materiality in the trial, he must provide the court with a statement setting out the relevant history'. That had not been done in this case. Despite the failings, in other respects, of leading counsel at trial, the available evidence suggested F's decision not to give evidence was made with his full understanding and after significant discussion of the advantages and disadvantages of doing so.

F19.43

The *Criminal Practice Directions* [2013] EWCA Crim 1631 revoked and replaced the greater part of the *Consolidated Criminal Practice Direction* [2002] 1 WLR 2870, including para. IV.44 on the right to give or not give evidence. The procedure to be followed by the court at the close of the prosecution case is now to be found in *Criminal Practice Directions* [2013] EWCA Crim 1631, paras. 39P.1 to 39P.5 (see **PD-53** in this supplement). The new procedure is very similar, but specifically recognises the desirability of an adjournment, if requested by the defence at that point in the trial, to advise their client. Likewise, if the accused is unrepresented, he should now be advised in the absence of the jury of the direction that will be given if he chooses not to testify, and be given a brief adjournment, if he wishes, to consider his position.

'Proper' Inferences of Guilt

F19.45 The *Criminal Practice Directions* [2013] EWCA Crim 1631 revoked and replaced the greater part of the *Consolidated Criminal Practice Direction* [2002] 1 WLR 2870, including para. IV.44 on the right to give or not give evidence. The procedure to be followed by the court at the close of the prosecution case is now to be found in *Criminal Practice Directions* [2013] EWCA Crim 1631, paras. 39P.1 to 39P.5 (see **PD-53** in this supplement). The new procedure is very similar, but specifically recognises the desirability of an adjournment, if requested by the defence at that point in the trial, to advise their client. Likewise, if the accused is unrepresented, he should now be advised in the absence of the jury of the direction that will be given if he chooses not to testify, and be given a brief adjournment, if he wishes, to consider his position.

SUPPLEMENT TO APPENDICES

Appendix 1   Codes of Evidence Under the Police and Criminal Evidence Act 1984

PACE CODE A
CODE OF PRACTICE FOR THE EXERCISE BY: POLICE OFFICERS OF STATUTORY POWERS OF STOP AND SEARCH
POLICE OFFICERS AND POLICE STAFF OF REQUIREMENTS TO RECORD PUBLIC ENCOUNTERS

By virtue of the Police and Criminal Evidence Act 1984 (Codes of Practice) (Revisions to Codes A, B, C, E, F and H) Order 2013 (SI 2013 No. 2685), a revised Code A has effect. It applies to any search by a police officer and the recording of public encounters taking place after 00.00 on 27 October 2013. The revised Code is available via https://www.gov.uk/government/publications/pace-code-a-2013. The following changes are made to the Code.

1. The paragraphs under the heading '**General**' are numbered (1.01 to 1.03) and in 1.03 a new sub-paragraph (c) adds to the list of search powers to which Code A does not apply, namely 'the powers to search persons and vehicles and to stop and search in specified locations to which the Code of Practice issued under section 47AB of the Terrorism Act 2000 applies'.
2. Paragraph 1.1 is amended to clarify the reminder about unlawful discrimination and the protected characteristics relevant to the Code to which the Equality Act 2010 applies. It now reads as follows:
    1.1 Powers to stop and search must be used fairly, responsibly, with respect for people being searched and without unlawful discrimination. Under the Equality Act 2010, section 149, when police officers are carrying out their functions, they also have a duty to have due regard to the need to eliminate unlawful discrimination, harassment and victimisation, to advance equality of opportunity between people who share a relevant protected characteristic and people who do not share it, and to take steps to foster good relations between those persons. (*See Notes 1 and 1A.*)
3. Paragraph 2.1 is amended to read as follows:
    2.1 This code applies, subject to paragraph 1.03, to powers of stop and search as follows:
    (a) powers which require reasonable grounds for suspicion, before they may be exercised; that articles unlawfully obtained or possessed are being carried;
    (b) authorised under section 60 of the Criminal Justice and Public Order Act 1994, based upon a reasonable belief that incidents involving serious violence may take place or that people are carrying dangerous instruments or offensive weapons within any locality in the police area, or that it is expedient to use the powers to find such instruments or weapons that have been used in incidents of serious violence;
    (c) Not used.
    (d) powers to search a person who has not been arrested in the exercise of a power to search premises (see Code B paragraph 2.4); and
    (e) the powers in Schedule 5 to the Terrorism Prevention and Investigation Measures (TPIM) Act 2011 to search an individual who has not been arrested, conferred by:
      (i) paragraph 6(2)(a) at the time of serving a TPIM notice;
      (ii) paragraph 8(2)(a) under a search warrant for compliance purposes; and
      (iii) paragraph 10 for public safety purposes.
    See paragraph 2.18A.
4. Paragraph 2.2 is amended so as to remove the reference to searches under the Terrorism Act 2000, s. 43, and so as to include a reference to Note 1A.
5. Paragraph 2.3 is amended so as to remove the references to searches under the Terrorism Act 2000, s. 43.
6. Paragraph 2.8, which referred to powers under the Terrorism Act 2000, is now simply 'Not used'.
7. Instead of the provisions in paras. 2.18A to 2.26 (which dealt with searches authorised under the Terrorism Act 2000, s. 44), new provisions outline the powers to search persons without them having to be arrested, introduced by the TPIM Act 2011. These are outside the scope of the new terrorism Code but within the statutory scope of the PACE 1984, ss. 2 and 3 and Code A. The additions are as follows:

Searches under Schedule 5 to the Terrorism Prevention and Investigation Measures Act 2011

2.18A Paragraph 3 of Schedule 5 to the TPIM Act 2011 allows a constable to detain an individual to be searched under the following powers:

(i) paragraph 6(2)(a) when a TPIM notice is being, or has just been, served on the individual for the purpose of ascertaining whether there is anything on the individual that contravenes measures specified in the notice;

(ii) paragraph 8(2)(a) in accordance with a warrant to search the individual issued by a justice of the peace in England and Wales, a sheriff in Scotland or a lay magistrate in Northern Ireland who is satisfied that a search is necessary for the purpose of determining whether an individual in respect of whom a TPIM notice is in force is complying with measures specified in the notice (see *paragraph 2.20*); and

(iii) paragraph 10 to ascertain whether an individual in respect of whom a TPIM notice is in force is in possession of anything that could be used to threaten or harm any person.

See *paragraph 2.1(e)*.

2.19 The exercise of the powers mentioned in paragraph 2.18A does not require the constable to have reasonable grounds to suspect that the individual:

(a) has been, or is, contravening any of the measures specified in the TPIM notice; or

(b) has on them anything which:

- in the case of the power in sub-paragraph (i), contravenes measures specified in the TPIM notice;
- in the case of the power in sub-paragraph (ii) is not complying with measures specified in the TPIM notice; or
- in the case of the power in sub-paragraph (iii), could be used to threaten or harm any person.

2.20 A search of an individual on warrant under the power mentioned in paragraph 2.18A(ii) must carried out within 28 days of the issue of the warrant and:

- the individual may be searched on one occasion only within that period;
- the search must take place at a reasonable hour unless it appears that this would frustrate the purposes of the search.

[2.21 to 2.25 *Not used.*]

2.26 The powers under Schedule 5 only allow a constable to conduct a search of an individual only for specified purposes relating to a TPIM notice as set out above. However, anything found may be seized and retained if there are reasonable grounds for believing that it is or it contains evidence of any offence for use at a trial for that offence or to prevent it being concealed, lost, damaged, altered, or destroyed. However, this would not prevent a search being carried out under other search powers if, in the course of exercising these powers, the officer formed reasonable grounds for suspicion.

8. Paragraph 2.28 is amended in light of the fact that the statutory threshold for exercising the power to search for weapons under the CJA 1988, s. 139B, has switched from 'reasonable belief' to 'reasonable suspicion' (see the VCRA 2006, s. 48) and to take account of the new offence under s. 139AA (see **B12.175** in the main work). Paragraph 2.28 now reads as follows:

Before the power under section 139B of the Criminal Justice Act 1988 may be exercised, the constable must have reasonable grounds to suspect that an offence under section 139A or 139AA of the Criminal Justice Act 1988 (having a bladed or pointed article or offensive weapon on school premises) has been or is being committed. A warrant to search premises and persons found therein may be issued under section 23(3) of the Misuse of Drugs Act 1971 if there are reasonable grounds to suspect that controlled drugs or certain documents are in the possession of a person on the premises.

9. Paragraph 3.6 is amended so that the reference to Annex F is replaced by a reference to Annex L.

10. Paragraph 3.8 is amended so that paragraph (d) specifies the information to be given before a search under the TPIM powers. The material in para. 3.8(d) relating to the Terrorism Act 2000, s. 44 is deleted.

11. Paragraph 4.3 is amended so that paragraph (d) specifies what is to be contained in the record of a search under the TPIM powers and the information to be included in the search record. The material in para. 4.3(d) relating to the Terrorism Act 2000, s. 44 is deleted.

12. In para. 5.4 the reference to 'police authorities' is amended to 'police and crime commissioners'.

13. A new note for guidance 1A reads

In paragraphs 1.1 and *2.2*, *'relevant protected characteristic' includes: age, disability, gender reassignment, pregnancy and maternity, race, religion/belief, sex and sexual orientation.*

14. In the summary of the main stop and search powers in Annex A, references to TPIM search powers replace references to repealed search powers under the Terrorism Act 2000.

15. In Annex C, the previous first entry, which related to the search powers of CSOs under the Terrorism Act 2000, is deleted.

PACE CODE B
CODE OF PRACTICE FOR SEARCHES OF PREMISES BY POLICE OFFICERS AND THE SEIZURE OF PROPERTY FOUND BY POLICE OFFICERS ON PERSONS OR PREMISES

By virtue of the Police and Criminal Evidence Act 1984 (Codes of Practice) (Revisions to Codes A, B, C, E, F and H) Order 2013 (SI 2013 No. 2685), a revised Code B has effect. It applies to applications for warrants made after 00.00 on 27 October 2013 and to searches and seizures taking place after 00.00 on 27 October 2013. The revised Code is available via https://www.gov.uk/government/publications/pace-code-b-2013. The following changes are made to the Code.

1. Paragraph 1.3A is amended to clarify the reminder about unlawful discrimination and the protected characteristics relevant to the Code to which the Equality Act 2010 applies. It now reads as follows:

    Powers to search and seize must be used fairly, responsibly, with respect for people who occupy premises being searched or are in charge of property being seized and without unlawful discrimination. Under the Equality Act 2010, section 149, when police officers are carrying out their functions, they also have a duty to have due regard to the need to eliminate unlawful discrimination, harassment and victimisation, to advance equality of opportunity between people who share a relevant protected characteristic and people who do not share it, and to take steps to foster good relations between those persons. *See Note 1A.*

2. A new Note for Guidance 1A is added. This states:

    In paragraph 1.3A, 'relevant protected characteristic' includes: age, disability, gender *reassignment, pregnancy and maternity, race, religion/belief, sex and sexual orientation.*

3. In Notes for Guidance 2A and 2B, a reference to the power to enter and search premises under the TPIM Act 2011, sch. 5 for the purposes of serving, monitoring and enforcing TPIM notices replaces the reference to the repealed 'control order' provisions under the Prevention of Terrorism Act 2005.

4. Note for Guidance 2C is amended in light of the fact that the statutory threshold for exercising the power to search for weapons under the CJA 1988, s. 139B, has switched from 'reasonable belief' to 'reasonable suspicion' (see the VCRA 2006, s. 48) and to take account of the new offence under s. 139AA (see **B12.175** in the main work).

5. Paragraph 6.1 is amended so as to take account of warrants where the issuing enactment specifies a period less than three calendar months within which it must be executed (e.g., warrants under the MDA 1971, s. 23) and now reads:

    Searches made under warrant must be made within three calendar months of the date the warrant is issued or within the period specified in the enactment under which the warrant is issued if this is shorter.

6. Section 10 is replaced to take account of the power to enter and search premises under the TPIM Act 2011, sch. 5, for the purposes of serving, monitoring and enforcing TPIM notices. It now reads as follows:

    10   Searches under Schedule 5 to the Terrorism Prevention and Investigation Measures Act 2011

    10.1 This Code applies to the powers of constables under Schedule 5 to the Terrorism Prevention and Investigation Measures Act 2011 relating to TPIM notices to enter and search premises subject to the modifications in the following paragraphs.

    10.2 In paragraph 2.3(d), the reference to the investigation into an alleged or suspected offence include the enforcement of terrorism prevention and investigation measures which may be imposed on an individual by a TPIM notice in accordance with the Terrorism Prevention and Investigation Measures Act 2011.

    10.3 References to the purpose and object of the entry and search of premises, the nature of articles sought and what may be seized and retained include (as appropriate):

    (a) in relation to the power to search *without a search warrant in paragraph 5* (for purposes of serving TPIM notice), finding the individual on whom the notice is to be served.

    (b) in relation to the power to search *without a search warrant in paragraph 6* (at time of serving TPIM notice), ascertaining whether there is anything in the premises, that contravenes measures specified in the notice. (See *Note 10A.*)

    (c) in relation to the power to search *without a search warrant* under *paragraph 7* (suspected absconding), ascertaining whether a person has absconded or if there is anything on the premises which will assist in the pursuit or arrest of an individual in respect of whom a TPIM notice is in force who is reasonably suspected of having absconded.

    (d) in relation to the power to search *under a search warrant* issued under *paragraph 8* (for compliance purposes), determining whether an individual in respect of whom a TPIM notice is in force is complying with measures specified in the notice. (See *Note 10A.*)

Note for guidance

10A   *Searches of individuals under Schedule 5, paragraphs 6(2)(a) (at time of serving TPIM notice) and 8(2)(a) (for compliance purposes) must be conducted and recorded in accordance with Code A. See Code A paragraph 2.18A for details.*

PACE CODE C
CODE OF PRACTICE FOR THE DETENTION, TREATMENT AND QUESTIONING OF PERSONS BY POLICE OFFICERS

By virtue of the Police and Criminal Evidence Act 1984 (Codes of Practice) (Revisions to Codes A, B, C, E, F and H) Order 2013 (SI 2013 No. 2685), a revised Code C has effect. It applies to people in police detention after 00.00 on 27 October 2013, notwithstanding that their period of detention may have commenced before that time. The main changes in Code C have been made in order to:

(a) comply with the Divisional Court judgment concerning safeguards for 17-year-olds, in *R (HC) v Secretary of State for the Home Department* [2013] EWHC 982 (Admin), and

(b) implement the EU Directive on the right to interpretation and translation in criminal proceedings (see EU Directive 2010/64).

The revised Code is available via https://www.gov.uk/government/publications/pace-code-c-2013. The following changes are made to the Code.

1. Paragraph 1.0 is amended to clarify the reminder about unlawful discrimination and the protected characteristics relevant to the Code to which the Equality Act 2010 applies. It now reads as follows:

   The powers and procedures in this Code must be used fairly, responsibly, with respect for the people to whom they apply and without unlawful discrimination. Under the Equality Act 2010, section 149, when police officers are carrying out their functions, they also have a duty to have due regard to the need to eliminate unlawful discrimination, harassment and victimisation, to advance equality of opportunity between people who share a relevant protected characteristic and people who do not share it, and to take steps to foster good relations between those persons. See *Notes 1A* and *1AA*.

2. Paragraph 1.5 is amended and a new C1.5A is added to extend the safeguards for juveniles to 17-year-olds unless precluded by statutory provisions. These paragraphs now read as follows:

   1.5   If anyone appears to be under 17, they shall in the absence of clear evidence that they are older, be treated as a juvenile for the purposes of this Code and any other Code.

   1.5A   If anyone appears to have attained the age of 17 and to be under the age of 18, they shall in the absence of clear evidence that they are older, be treated as a 17-year-old for the purposes of this and any other Code. The provisions and *Notes for Guidance* which in accordance with *paragraph 1.5* apply to a juvenile and the way they are to be treated shall also apply to them, *except* as described in sub-paragraphs (a) and (b) below:

       (a) The *statutory* provisions in section 38 of PACE (Detention after charge) which apply only to an *arrested juvenile* as defined in section 37(15) of PACE and to which paragraphs *16.7* and *16.10* and *Note 16D* of this Code relate, shall *not apply* to a person who appears to have attained the age of 17 for the purposes of:

          (i) the grounds to keep them in police detention after charge; and

          (ii) the requirement to transfer a person who has been kept in police detention after charge to local authority accommodation and the power of the local authority to detain them pending appearance at court.

3. Paragraph 1.7(a) has been amended to add 'Note: *Paragraph 1.5A* extends sub-paragraph (a) to the person called to fulfil the role of the appropriate adult for a 17-year-old detainee.' And references to Notes 1B and 1C have been added for clarity.

4. Note 1F has been amended (so as to remove the reference to lay visitors) and the following new notes have been added:

   1AA   *In paragraph 1.0, 'relevant protected characteristic' includes: age, disability, gender reassignment, pregnancy and maternity, race, religion/belief, sex and sexual orientation.*

   1L   *Paragraph 1.5A does not amend section 37(15) of PACE which defines the term 'arrested juvenile' for the purposes of sections 34 to 51 of PACE, or provisions in any other enactment which expressly refer and apply to persons under the age of 17. Until amended by Parliament, these statutory provisions alone do not extend to persons who have attained the age of 17.*

   1M   *The purpose of paragraph 1.5A is to extend the safeguards for juveniles to 17-year-olds unless this is precluded by any statutory provisions. Sub-paragraphs 1.5A(a) and (b) identify the provisions of sections 38 and 65 of PACE concerning detention after charge and appropriate consent which for this reason do not extend to 17-year-olds. All other safeguards in this and other Codes are extended and the requirements which are indicated in the relevant provisions and Notes for Guidance are as follows:*

(a) under paragraph 3.13 of this Code, to identify and inform someone responsible for the welfare of a 17-year-old which is in addition to their right in section 5 of this Code not to be held incommunicado;

(b) under paragraph 3.14 of this Code to notify a person who has statutory responsibility under a court order to supervise or monitor a 17-year-old;

(c) under paragraph 8.8 with regard to cell accommodation and keeping 17-year-old detainees separate from adults;

(d) to call a person described by paragraph 1.7(a) or Note 17G in relation to testing for the presence of Class A drugs, to fulfil the role of the appropriate adult for the purposes of this or any other Code to support and assist a 17-year-old:

(i) by being present when:
- *they are informed of their rights and entitlements and the grounds for their detention (see paragraphs 3.17 and 3.18);*
- *they are cautioned or given a special warning (see paragraphs 10.12 and 10.11A);*
- *they are being interviewed in accordance with this Code (see sections 11 and 12) or Codes E or F unless paragraph 11.15 of this Code allows the interview to go ahead without the adult being present;*
- *their detention is being reviewed or an extension is being considered (see paragraphs 15.3(c) and 15.3C(a)):*
- *they are charged and related action is taken (see paragraphs 16.1, 16.3, 16.4A and 16.6);*
- *samples to test for Class A drugs are requested from a person who has not attained the age of 18 (see paragraph 17.7);*
- *an intimate search is carried out (see Annex A paragraphs 2A, 2B and 5);*
- *a strip search is carried out (see Annex A paragraph 11(c));*
- *an x-ray or ultrasound scan is carried out (see Annex K paragraphs 2 and 3);*
- *procedures in Code D involving witness identification, taking fingerprints, samples, footwear impressions and photographs and when evidential searches and examinations are carried out (see paragraphs 2.14 and 2.15).*

(ii) by allowing:
- *the adult to inspect their custody record and to have a copy of their record (see paragraphs 2.4, 2.4A and 2.5);*
- *a 17-year-old to consult the adult in private (see paragraph 3.18);*
- *the adult to request legal advice on their behalf to advise and assist them (see paragraphs 3.19, 6.5A and 11.17).*

5. Paragraphs 2.4, 2.4A and 2.5 all have notes added to point out that C1.5A extends requirements concerning access to custody records to the person called to fulfil the role of the appropriate adult for 17-year-old detainees.

6. Paragraph 3.5(c)(ii) is revised so as to add various references, by way of notes, to the substantial amendments made on this revision.

7. Paragraph 3.12 is amended to accord with the terms of EU Directive 2010/64 in respect of persons who require an interpreter. It now reads as follows:

   If the detainee appears to be someone who does not speak or understand English or who has a hearing or speech impediment, the custody officer must, without delay, call an interpreter for assistance in the action under *paragraphs 3.1 to 3.5*. If the person appears to have a hearing or speech impediment, the reference to 'interpreter' includes appropriate assistance necessary to comply with *paragraphs 3.1 to 3.5*. See *paragraph 13.1C* if the detainee is in Wales. See *section 13* and *Note 13B*.

8. Paragraphs 3.13, 3.14, 3.15, 3.17 and 3.18 all have notes added to point out that para. 1.5A extends their requirements and obligations to 17-year-old detainees.

9. Paragraph 3.19 has a note added as follows: 'Note: *Paragraph 1.5A* extends the obligations in this paragraph to 17-year-old detainees.'

10. Paragraph 3.21 is amended and references to para. 3.12 and section 13 (interpreters) are added to make it clear that the need for an interpreter also applies to suspects who have not been arrested.

11. The reference in Note 3E to Home Office Circular 32/2000 is replaced with a reference to the Detention and Custody Authorised Professional Practice (APP) produced by the College of Policing (see http://www.college.police.uk/en/19723.htm).

12. Note 5F is replaced with the following:

> Prison Service Instruction 26/2012 (Production of Prisoners at the Request of Warranted Law Enforcement Agencies) provides detailed guidance and instructions for police officers and Governors and Directors of Prisons regarding applications for prisoners to be transferred to police custody and their safe custody and treatment while in police custody.

13. Paragraph 6.5 is amended to include in the list or required reminders a reference to the new Annex M5 which requires suspects to be reminded of their right to legal advice before waiving the right to a written translation of an essential document.

14. Paragraph 6.5A has a note added as follows: 'Note: *Paragraph 1.5A* applies this paragraph to 17-year-old detainees.'

15. Paragraph 7.2 updates the reference to a URL for contact information for embassies etc. relevant to detainees who are foreign nationals.

16. Paragraphs 7. 4 and 7.5 are amended to reflect the transfer of the functions of the United Kingdom Borders Agency to the Home Office.

17. Paragraphs 8.8 and 8.10 have a note added to point out that para. 1.5A extends requirement concerning cell accommodation and keeping juveniles and adults separate to 17-year-old detainees.

18. Note 8C is revised so as to refer to new guidance, namely the Detention and Custody Authorised Professional Practice (APP) produced by the College of Policing *(see* http://www.college.police.uk/en/19723.htm).

19. Note 9B is amended to point out that para. 1.5A extends its effect to 17-year-old detainees.

20. A new para. 10.12A points out that para. 1.5A extends the effect of paras. 10.11A and 10.12 to 17-year-old detainees.

21. Notes are added to paras. 11.12, 11.15, 11.16 and 11.18(a) to point out that para. 1.5A extends their requirements and obligations to 17-year-old detainees.

22. Paragraph 11.18(c) is amended to read:

> an interview, without an interpreter being present, of a person whom the custody officer has determined requires an interpreter (see *paragraphs 3.5(c)(ii)* and *3.12*) which is carried out by an interviewer speaking the suspect's own language or (as the case may be) otherwise establishing effective communication which is sufficient to enable the necessary questions to be asked and answered in order to avert the consequences. See *paragraphs 13.2* and *13.5*.

23. Section 13 (Interpreters) is very substantially amended and is set out in full below:

(a) General

13.1 Chief officers are responsible for making arrangements to provide appropriately qualified independent persons to act as interpreters and to provide translations of essential documents for:
(a) detained suspects who, in accordance with *paragraph 3.5(c)(ii)*, the custody officer has determined require an interpreter, and
(b) suspects who are not under arrest but are cautioned as in *section 10* who, in accordance with *paragraph 3.21*, the interviewer has determined require an interpreter. In these cases, the responsibilities of the custody officer are, if appropriate, assigned to the interviewer. An interviewer who has any doubts about whether an interpreter is required or about how the provisions of this section should be applied to a suspect who is not under arrest should seek advice from an officer of the rank of sergeant or above.
If the suspect has a hearing or speech impediment, references to 'interpreter' and 'interpretation' in this Code include appropriate assistance necessary to establish effective communication with that person. See *paragraph 13.1C* below if the person is in Wales.

13.1A The arrangements must comply with the minimum requirements set out in Directive 2010/64/EU of the European Parliament and of the Council of 20 October 2010 on the right to interpretation and translation in criminal proceedings (see *Note 13A*). The provisions of this Code implement the requirements for those to whom this Code applies. These requirements include the following:
• That the arrangements made and the quality of interpretation and translation provided shall be sufficient to '*safeguard the fairness of the proceedings, in particular by ensuring that suspected or accused persons have knowledge of the cases against them and are able to exercise their right of defence*'. This term which is used by the Directive means that the suspect must be able to understand their position and be able to communicate effectively with police officers, interviewers, solicitors and appropriate adults as provided for by this and any other Code in the same way as a suspect who can speak and understand English and who does not have a hearing or speech impediment and who would therefore not require an interpreter.
• The provision of a written translation of all documents considered essential for the person to exercise their right of defence and to '*safeguard the fairness of the proceedings*' as

described above. For the purposes of this Code, this includes any decision to authorise a person to be detained and details of any offence(s) with which the person has been charged or for which they have been told they may be prosecuted, see *Annex M*.
- Procedures to help determine:
  - whether a suspect can speak and understand English and needs the assistance of an interpreter, *see paragraph 13.1* and *Notes 13B and 13C*; and
  - whether another interpreter should be called or another translation should be provided when a suspect complains about the quality of either or both, see *paragraphs 13.10A* and *13.10C*.

13.1B All reasonable attempts should be made to make the suspect understand that interpretation and translation will be provided at public expense.

13.1C With regard to persons in Wales, nothing in this or any other Code affects the application of the Welsh Language Schemes produced by police and crime commissioners in Wales in accordance with the Welsh Language Act 1993. See paragraphs *3.12 and 13.1*.

(b) Interviewing suspects – foreign languages

13.2 Unless *paragraphs 11.1 or 11.18(c)* apply, a suspect who for the purposes of this Code requires an interpreter because they do not appear to speak or understand English (see *paragraphs 3.5(c)(ii)* and *3.12*) must not be interviewed in the absence of a person capable of interpreting.

13.2A An interpreter should also be called if a juvenile is interviewed and their parent or guardian, present as the appropriate adult, does not appear to speak or understand English, unless the interview is urgent and *paragraphs 11.1 or 11.18(c)* apply.

  Note: *Paragraph 1.5A* extends the requirement in this paragraph to interviews of 17-year-old suspects.

13.3 When a written record of the interview is made (see *paragraph 11.7*), the interviewer shall make sure the interpreter makes a note of the interview at the time in the person's language for use in the event of the interpreter being called to give evidence, and certifies its accuracy. The interviewer should allow sufficient time for the interpreter to note each question and answer after each is put, given and interpreted. The person should be allowed to read the record or have it read to them and sign it as correct or indicate the respects in which they consider it inaccurate. If an audio or visual record of the interview is made, the arrangements in Code E or F shall apply.

13.4 In the case of a person making a statement under caution to a police officer or other police staff other than in English:
  (a) the interpreter shall record the statement in the language it is made;
  (b) the person shall be invited to sign it;
  (c) an official English translation shall be made in due course.

(c) Interviewing suspects who have a hearing or speech impediment

13.5 Unless *paragraphs 11.1 or 11.18(c)* (urgent interviews) apply, a suspect who for the purposes of this Code requires an interpreter or other appropriate assistance to enable effective communication with them because they appear to have a hearing or speech impediment (see *paragraphs 3.5(c)(ii)* and *3.12*) must not be interviewed in the absence of an independent person capable of interpreting or without that assistance.

13.6 An interpreter should also be called if a juvenile is interviewed and their parent or guardian, present as the appropriate adult, appears to have a hearing or speech impediment, unless the interview is urgent and *paragraphs 11.1 or 11.18(c)* apply.

  Note: *Paragraph 1.5A* extends the requirement in this paragraph to interviews of 17-year-old suspects.

13.7 The interviewer shall make sure the interpreter is allowed to read the interview record and certify its accuracy in the event of the interpreter being called to give evidence. If the interview is audibly recorded or visually recorded, the arrangements in Code E or F apply.

(d) Additional rules for detained persons

13.8 *Not used.*

13.9 If *paragraph 6.1* applies and the detainee cannot communicate with the solicitor because of language, hearing or speech difficulties, an interpreter must be called. A police officer or any other police staff may not be used for this purpose.

13.10 After the custody officer has determined that a detainee requires an interpreter (see *paragraph 3.5(c)(ii)*) and following the initial action in *paragraphs 3.1 to 3.5*, arrangements must also be made for an interpreter to:

- explain the grounds and reasons for any authorisation for their *continued* detention, before or after charge and any information about the authorisation given to them by the authorising officer and which is recorded in the custody record. See *paragraphs 15.3, 15.4* and *15.16(a)* and *(b)*;
- be present at the magistrates' court for the hearing of an application for a warrant of further detention or any extension or further extension of such warrant to explain any grounds and reasons for the application and any information about the authorisation of their further detention given to them by the court (see PACE, sections 43 and 44 and *paragraphs 15.2* and *15.16(c)*), and
- explain any offence with which the detainee is charged or for which they are informed they may be prosecuted and any other information about the offence given to them by or on behalf of the custody officer, see *paragraphs 16.1* and *16.3*.

13.10A If a detainee complains that they are not satisfied with the quality of interpretation, the custody officer or (as the case may be) the interviewer, is responsible for deciding whether a different interpreter should be called in accordance with the procedures set out in the arrangements made by the chief officer, *see paragraph 13.1A*.

(e) Translations of essential documents

13.10B Written translations, oral translations and oral summaries of essential documents in a language the detainee understands shall be provided in accordance with Annex M (Translations of documents and records).

13.10C If a detainee complains that they are not satisfied with the quality of the translation, the custody officer or (as the case may be) the interviewer, is responsible for deciding whether a further translation should be provided in accordance with the procedures set out in the arrangements made by the chief officer, *see paragraph 13.1A*.

(f) Decisions not to provide interpretation and translation.

13.10D If a suspect challenges a decision:
- made by the custody officer or (as the case may be) by the interviewer, in accordance with this Code (see *paragraphs 3.5(c)(ii)* and *3.21)* that they do not require an interpreter; or
- made in accordance with *paragraphs 13.10A, 13.10B* or *13.10C* not to provide a different interpreter or another translation or not to translate a requested document, the matter shall be reported to an inspector to deal with as a complaint for the purposes of *paragraph 9.2* or *12.9* if the challenge is made during an interview.

(g) Documentation

13.11 The following must be recorded in the custody record or, as applicable, the interview record:
  (a) Action taken to call an interpreter;
  (b) Action taken when a detainee is not satisfied about the standard of interpretation or translation provided, see *paragraphs 13.10A* and *13.10C*;
  (c) When an urgent interview is carried out in accordance with *paragraph 13.2* or *13.5* in the absence of an interpreter;
  (d) When a detainee has been assisted by an interpreter for the purpose of providing or being given information or being interviewed;
  (e) Action taken in accordance with Annex M when:
    - a written translation of an essential document is provided;
    - an oral translation or oral summary of an essential document is provided instead of a written translation and the authorising officer's reason(s) why this would not prejudice the fairness of the proceedings (see *Annex M, paragraph 3*);
    - a suspect waives their right to a translation of an essential document (see *Annex M, paragraph 4*);
    - when representations that a document which is not included in the table is essential and that a translation should be provided are refused and the reason for the refusal (see *Annex M, paragraph 8*).

Notes for Guidance

13A Chief officers have discretion when determining the individuals or organisations they use to provide interpretation and translation services for their forces provided that these services are compatible with the requirements of the Directive. One example which chief officers may wish to consider is the Ministry of Justice Framework Agreement for interpretation and translation services.

13B   A procedure for determining whether a person needs an interpreter might involve a telephone interpreter service or using cue cards or similar visual aids which enable the detainee to indicate their ability to speak and understand English and their preferred language. This could be confirmed through an interpreter who could also assess the extent to which the person can speak and understand English.

13C   There should also be a procedure for determining whether a suspect who requires an interpreter requires assistance in accordance with paragraph 3.20 to help them check and if applicable, sign any documentation.

24. Notes are added to paras. 15.2A, 15.3(c) and 15.3C(a) to point out that para. 1.5A extends the requirements concerning appropriate adults to 17-year-old detainees.
25. Note 15B(f) is amended to reflect the transfer of responsibilities for immigration to the Home Office.
26. Notes are added to paras. 16.1, 16.3, 16.4A and 16.6 to point out that para. 1.5A extends the requirements concerning appropriate adults to 17-year-old detainees.
27. A note is added to para. 16.7 to point out that the requirement to transfer a juvenile detained after charge to local authority accommodation does not apply to 17-year-olds.
28. Note 16A is amended so as to remove the reference to reprimands and warnings.
29. Notes are added to para. 17.7 and Note 17G to point out that para. 1.5A extends the requirements concerning appropriate adults to 17-year-old detainees.
30. In Annex A, paras. 2B, 5 and 11(c) are amended to point out that para. 1.5A extends the requirements concerning appropriate adults to 17-year-old detainees.
31. A new Annex M deals with documents and records to be translated.

PACE CODE E
CODE OF PRACTICE ON AUDIO RECORDING INTERVIEWS WITH SUSPECTS AND PACE CODE F CODE OF PRACTICE ON VISUAL RECORDING WITH SOUNDS OF INTERVIEWS WITH SUSPECTS

By virtue of the Police and Criminal Evidence Act 1984 (Codes of Practice) (Revisions to Codes A, B, C, E, F and H) Order 2013 (SI 2013 No. 2685), revised Codes E and F have effect. They apply to any interview carried out after 00.00 on 27 October 2013 (even where the interview commenced before that time). The revised Codes are available via https://www.gov.uk/government/publications/pace-code-e-2013 and https://www.gov.uk/government/publications/pace-code-f-2013. The Codes relating to audio recording and visual recording of interviews with suspects are revised principally to reflect:

• the requirement in Code C, para. 1.5A, to call someone to fulfil the role of the appropriate adult for 17-year-old suspects;
• the requirement that the conduct and recording of interviews in terrorism cases must accord with a separate terrorism Code;
• recent revisions to Code G (Arrest) and changes to Code C, paras. 3.21 and C3.22, which support the use of voluntary interviews to ensure that voluntary interviews are subject to Code E and distinguish them from custody cases;
• new requirements concerning security of master recordings to ensure consistency across the interview recording provisions in Codes E and F and the corresponding terrorism provisions.

PACE CODE H
CODE OF PRACTICE IN CONNECTION WITH THE DETENTION, TREATMENT AND QUESTIONING BY POLICE OFFICERS OF PERSONS UNDER SECTION 41 OF, AND SCHEDULE 8 TO, THE TERRORISM ACT 2000

By virtue of the Police and Criminal Evidence Act 1984 (Codes of Practice) (Revisions to Codes A, B, C, E, F and H) Order 2013 (SI 2013 No. 2685), a revised Code H has effect. It applies to people in police detention after 00.00 on 27 October 2013, notwithstanding that their period of detention may have commenced before that time. The main changes in Code H have been made in order to:

(a) comply with the Divisional Court judgment concerning safeguards for 17-year-olds; and
(b) implement the EU Directive on the right to interpretation and translation in criminal proceedings (see EU Directive 2010/64).

These changes mirror the changes to Code C.

The revised Code is available via https://www.gov.uk/government/publications/pace-code-h-2013.

Appendix 4   Disclosure

ATTORNEY-GENERAL'S GUIDELINES ON DISCLOSURE FOR INVESTIGATORS, PROSECUTORS AND DEFENCE PRACTITIONERS

December 2013

Foreword

We are pleased to publish a revised judicial protocol and revised guidance on the disclosure of unused material in criminal cases. Proper disclosure of unused material, made through a rigorous and carefully considered application of the law, remains a crucial part of a fair trial, and essential to avoiding miscarriages of justice. These new documents are intended to clarify the procedures to be followed and to encourage the active participation of all parties.

They have been prepared following the recommendations of Lord Justice Gross in his September 2011 'Review of Disclosure in Criminal Proceedings' and take account of Lord Justice Gross and Lord Justice Treacy's 'Further review of disclosure in criminal proceedings: sanctions for disclosure failure', published in November 2012.

There are important roles for the prosecution, the defence and the court in ensuring that disclosure is conducted properly, including on the part of the investigating, case progression and disclosure officers, as well as the lawyers and advocates. Lord Justice Gross particularly recommended that the guidance on disclosure of unused material in criminal cases should be consolidated and abbreviated. Given all of those involved in this process have separate constitutional roles, the judiciary and the Attorney-General have worked together to produce complementary guidance that is shorter than the previous iterations, but remains comprehensive. The two documents are similarly structured for ease of reference and should be read together.

The Rt. Hon. Dominic Grieve QC MP

Attorney General

The Rt. Hon. The Lord Thomas

Lord Chief Justice of England and Wales

Introduction

These Guidelines are issued by the Attorney General for investigators, prosecutors and defence practitioners on the application of the disclosure regime contained in the Criminal Procedure and Investigations Act 1996 ('CPIA'). The Guidelines emphasise the importance of prosecution-led disclosure and the importance of applying the CPIA regime in a 'thinking manner', tailored, where appropriate, to the type of investigation or prosecution in question.

The Guidelines do not contain the detail of the disclosure regime; they outline the high level principles which should be followed when the disclosure regime is applied.

These Guidelines replace the existing Attorney General's Guidelines on Disclosure issued in 2005 and the Supplementary Guidelines on Digital Material issued in 2011, which is an annex to the general guidelines.

The Guidelines are intended to operate alongside the Judicial Protocol on the Disclosure of Unused Material in Criminal Cases. They are not designed to be an unequivocal statement of the law at any one time, nor are they a substitute for a thorough understanding of the relevant legislation, codes of practice, case law and procedure.

Readers should note that a review of disclosure in the magistrates' courts is currently being undertaken by HHJ Kinch QC and the Chief Magistrate, on behalf of Lord Justice Gross, the Senior Presiding Judge. Amendments may therefore be made to these documents following the recommendations of that review, and in accordance with other forthcoming changes to the criminal justice system.

The Importance of Disclosure

1. The statutory framework for criminal investigations and disclosure is contained in the Criminal Procedure and Investigations Act 1996 (the CPIA) and the CPIA Code of Practice. The CPIA aims to ensure that criminal investigations are conducted in a fair, objective and thorough manner, and

requires prosecutors to disclose to the defence material which has not previously been disclosed to the accused and which might reasonably be considered capable of undermining the case for the prosecution against the accused or of assisting the case for the accused. The CPIA requires a timely dialogue between the prosecution, defence and the court to enable the prosecution properly to identify such material.

2. Every accused person has a right to a fair trial, a right long embodied in our law and guaranteed by Article 6 of the European Convention on Human Rights (ECHR). A fair trial is the proper object and expectation of all participants in the trial process. Fair disclosure to the accused is an inseparable part of a fair trial. A fair trial should not require consideration of irrelevant material and should not involve spurious applications or arguments which serve to divert the trial process from examining the real issues before the court.

3. Properly applied, the CPIA should ensure that material is not disclosed which overburdens the participants in the trial process, diverts attention from the relevant issues, leads to unjustifiable delay, and is wasteful of resources. Consideration of disclosure issues should be an integral part of a good investigation and not something that exists separately.

Disclosure: general principles

4. Disclosure refers to providing the defence with copies of, or access to, any prosecution material which might reasonably be considered capable of undermining the case for the prosecution against the accused, or of assisting the case for the accused, and which has not previously been disclosed (section 3 CPIA).

5. Prosecutors will only be expected to anticipate what material might undermine their case or strengthen the defence in the light of information available at the time of the disclosure decision, and they may take into account information revealed during questioning.

6. In deciding whether material satisfies the disclosure test, consideration should be given amongst other things to:
   (a) the use that might be made of it in cross-examination;
   (b) its capacity to support submissions that could lead to:
       (i) the exclusion of evidence;
       (ii) a stay of proceedings, where the material is required to allow a proper application to be made;
       (iii) a court or tribunal finding that any public authority had acted incompatibly with the accused's rights under the ECHR;
   (c) its capacity to suggest an explanation or partial explanation of the accused's actions;
   (d) the capacity of the material to have a bearing on scientific or medical evidence in the case.

7. It should also be borne in mind that while items of material viewed in isolation may not be reasonably considered to be capable of undermining the prosecution case or assisting the accused, several items together can have that effect.

8. Material relating to the accused's mental or physical health, intellectual capacity, or to any ill treatment which the accused may have suffered when in the investigator's custody is likely to fall within the test for disclosure set out in paragraph 4 above.

9. Disclosure must not be an open-ended trawl of unused material. A critical element to fair and proper disclosure is that the defence play their role to ensure that the prosecution are directed to material which might reasonably be considered capable of undermining the prosecution case or assisting the case for the accused. This process is key to ensuring prosecutors make informed determinations about disclosure of unused material. The defence statement is important in identifying the issues in the case and why it is suggested that the material meets the test for disclosure.

10. Disclosure should be conducted in a thinking manner and never be reduced to a box-ticking exercise[1]; at all stages of the process, there should be consideration of **why** the CPIA disclosure regime requires a particular course of action and what should be done to achieve that aim.

11. There will always be a number of participants in prosecutions and investigations: senior investigation officers, disclosure officers, investigation officers, reviewing prosecutors, leading counsel, junior counsel, and sometimes disclosure counsel. Communication within the 'prosecution team' is vital to ensure that all matters which could have a bearing on disclosure issues are given sufficient attention by the right person. This is especially so given many reviewing lawyers will be unable to sit behind the trial advocate throughout the trial. In practice, this is likely to mean that a full log of disclosure decisions (with reasons) must be kept on the file and made available as appropriate to the prosecution team.

---

[1] *R v Olu, Wilson and Brooks* [2010] EWCA Crim 2975 at paragraph 42

12. The role of the reviewing lawyer will be central to ensuring all members of the prosecution team are aware of, and carry out, their duties and role(s). Where this involves counsel or more than one reviewing lawyer, this should be done by giving clear written instructions and record keeping.

13. The centrality of the reviewing lawyer does not mean that he or she has to do all the work personally; on the contrary, it will often mean effective delegation. Where the conduct of a prosecution is assigned to more than one prosecutor, steps must be taken to ensure that all involved in the case properly record their decisions. Subsequent prosecutors must be able to see and understand previous disclosure decisions before carrying out their continuous review function.

14. Investigators must always be alive to the potential need to reveal and prosecutors to the potential need to disclose material, in the interests of justice and fairness in the particular circumstances of any case, after the commencement of proceedings but before their duty arises under the Act. For instance, disclosure ought to be made of significant information that might affect a bail decision. This is likely to depend on what the defence chooses to reveal at that stage.

Investigators and Disclosure Officers

15. Investigators and disclosure officers must be fair and objective and must work together with prosecutors to ensure that disclosure obligations are met. Investigators and disclosure officers should be familiar with the CPIA Code of Practice, in particular their obligations to **retain** and **record** relevant material, to **review** it and to **reveal** it to the prosecutor.

16. Whether a case is a summary only matter or a long and complex trial on indictment, it is important that investigators and disclosure officers should approach their duties in a 'thinking manner' and not as a box ticking exercise. Where necessary, the reviewing lawyer should be consulted. It is important that investigators and disclosure officers are deployed on cases which are commensurate with their training, skills and experience. The conduct of an investigation provides the foundation for the entire case, and may even impact the conduct of linked cases. It is vital that there is always consideration of disclosure matters at the outset of an investigation, regardless of its size.

17. A fair investigation involves the pursuit of material following all reasonable lines of enquiry, whether they point towards or away from the suspect. What is 'reasonable' will depend on the context of the case. A fair investigation does not mean an endless investigation: investigators and disclosure officers must give thought to defining, and thereby limiting, the scope of their investigations, seeking the guidance of the prosecutor where appropriate

18. Where there are a number of disclosure officers assigned to a case, there should be a lead disclosure officer who is the focus for enquiries and whose responsibility it is to ensure that the investigator's disclosure obligations are complied with. Where appropriate, regular case conferences and other meetings should be held to ensure prosecutors are apprised of all relevant developments in investigations. Full records should be kept of such meetings.

19. The CPIA Code of Practice encourages investigators and disclosure officers to seek advice from prosecutors about whether any particular item of material may be relevant to the investigation, and if so, how. Investigators and disclosure officers should record key decisions taken on these matters and be prepared to account for their actions later. An identical approach is not called for in each and every case.

20. Investigators are to approach their task seeking to establish what actually happened. They are to be fair and objective.

21. Disclosure officers (or their deputies) must inspect, view, listen to or search all relevant material that has been retained by the investigator and the disclosure officer must provide a personal declaration to the effect that this task has been undertaken. In some cases, a detailed examination of all material seized may be required. In others, however, a detailed examination of every item of material seized would be virtually impossible: see the **Annex**.

22. Prosecutors only have knowledge of matters which are revealed to them by investigators and disclosure officers, and the schedules are the written means by which that revelation takes place. Whatever the approach taken by investigators or disclosure officers to examining the material gathered or generated in the course of an investigation, it is crucial that disclosure officers record their reasons for a particular approach in writing.

23. In meeting the obligations in paragraph 6.9 and 8.1 of the Code, schedules must be completed in a form which not only reveals sufficient information to the prosecutor, but which demonstrates a transparent and thinking approach to the disclosure exercise, to command the confidence of the defence and the court. Descriptions on non-sensitive schedules must be clear and accurate, and must contain sufficient detail to enable the prosecutor to make an informed decision on disclosure. The use of abbreviations and acronyms can be problematic and lead to difficulties in appreciating the significance of the material.

24. Sensitive schedules must contain sufficiently clear descriptions to enable the prosecutor to make an informed decision as to whether or not the material itself should be viewed, to the extent possible without compromising the confidentiality of the information.

25. It may become apparent to an investigator that some material obtained in the course of an investigation, either because it was considered to be potentially relevant, or because it was inextricably linked to material that was relevant, is, in fact, incapable of impact. It is not necessary to retain such material, although the investigator should err on the side of caution in reaching that conclusion and should be particularly mindful of the fact that some investigations continue over some time and that what is incapable of impact may change over time. The advice of the prosecutor should be sought where appropriate.

26. Disclosure officers must specifically draw material to the attention of the prosecutor for consideration where they have any doubt as to whether it might reasonably be considered capable of undermining the prosecution case or of assisting the case for the accused.

27. Disclosure officers must seek the advice and assistance of prosecutors when in doubt as to their responsibility as early as possible. They must deal expeditiously with requests by the prosecutor for further information on material, which may lead to disclosure.

Prosecutors

28. Prosecutors are responsible for making proper disclosure in consultation with the disclosure officer. The duty of disclosure is a continuing one and disclosure should be kept under review. In addition, prosecutors should ensure that advocates in court are properly instructed as to disclosure issues. Prosecutors must also be alert to the need to provide advice to, and where necessary probe actions taken by, disclosure officers to ensure that disclosure obligations are met. There should be no aspects of an investigation about which prosecutors are unable to ask probing questions.

29. Prosecutors must review schedules prepared by disclosure officers thoroughly and must be alert to the possibility that relevant material may exist which has not been revealed to them or material included which should not have been. If no schedules have been provided, or there are apparent omissions from the schedules, or documents or other items are inadequately described or are unclear, the prosecutor must at once take action to obtain properly completed schedules. Likewise schedules should be returned for amendment if irrelevant items are included. If prosecutors remain dissatisfied with the quality or content of the schedules they must raise the matter with a senior investigator to resolve the matter satisfactorily.

30. Where prosecutors have reason to believe that the disclosure officer has not discharged the obligation in paragraph 21 to inspect, view, listen to or search relevant material, they must at once raise the matter with the disclosure officer and request that it be done. Where appropriate the matter should be raised with the officer in the case or a senior officer.

31. Prosecutors should copy the defence statement to the disclosure officer and investigator as soon as reasonably practicable and prosecutors should advise the investigator if, in their view, reasonable and relevant lines of further enquiry should be pursued. If the defence statement does point to other reasonable lines of enquiry, further investigation is required and evidence obtained as a result of these enquiries may be used as part of the prosecution case or to rebut the defence.

32. It is vital that prosecutors consider defence statements thoroughly. Prosecutors cannot comment upon, or invite inferences to be drawn from, failures in defence disclosure otherwise than in accordance with section 11 of the CPIA. Prosecutors may cross-examine the accused on differences between the defence case put at trial and that set out in his or her defence statement. In doing so, it may be appropriate to apply to the judge under section 6E of the CPIA for copies of the statement to be given to a jury, edited if necessary to remove inadmissible material. Prosecutors should examine the defence statement to see whether it points to other lines of enquiry.

33. Prosecutors should challenge the lack of, or inadequate, defence statements in writing, copying the document to the court and the defence and seeking directions from the court to require the provision of an adequate statement from the defence.

34. If the material does not fulfil the disclosure test there is no requirement to disclose it. For this purpose, the parties' respective cases should not be restrictively analysed but must be carefully analysed to ascertain the specific facts the prosecution seek to establish and the specific grounds on which the charges are resisted.

Prosecution advocates

35. Prosecution advocates should ensure that all material which ought to be disclosed under the Act is disclosed to the defence. However, prosecution advocates cannot be expected to disclose material if

they are not aware of its existence. As far as is possible, prosecution advocates must place themselves in a fully informed position to enable them to make decisions on disclosure.

36. Upon receipt of instructions, prosecution advocates should consider as a priority all the information provided regarding disclosure of material. Prosecution advocates should consider, in every case, whether they can be satisfied that they are in possession of all relevant documentation and that they have been fully instructed regarding disclosure matters. If as a result the advocate considers that further information or action is required, written advice should promptly be provided setting out the aspects that need clarification or action.

37. The prosecution advocate must keep decisions regarding disclosure under review until the conclusion of the trial, whenever possible in consultation with the reviewing prosecutor. The prosecution advocate must in every case specifically consider whether he or she can satisfactorily discharge the duty of continuing review on the basis of the material supplied already, or whether it is necessary to inspect further material or to reconsider material already inspected. Prosecution advocates must not abrogate their responsibility under the CPIA by disclosing material which does not pass the test for disclosure, set out in paragraph 4, above.

38. There remains no basis in practice or law for counsel to counsel disclosure.

Defence

39. Defence engagement must be early and meaningful for the CPIA regime to function as intended. Defence statements are an integral part of this and are intended to help focus the attention of the prosecutor, court and co-defendants on the relevant issues in order to identify exculpatory unused material. Defence statements should be drafted in accordance with the relevant provisions of the CPIA.

40. Defence requests for further disclosure should ordinarily only be answered by the prosecution if the request is relevant to and directed to an issue identified in the defence statement. If it is not, then a further or amended defence statement should be sought by the prosecutor and obtained before considering the request for further disclosure.

41. In some cases that involve extensive unused material that is within the knowledge of a defendant, the defence will be expected to provide the prosecution and the court with assistance in identifying material which is suggested to pass the test for disclosure.

42. The prosecution's continuing duty to keep disclosure under review is crucial, and particular attention must be paid to understanding the significance of developments in the case on the unused material and earlier disclosure decisions. Meaningful defence engagement will help the prosecution to keep disclosure under review. The continuing duty of review for prosecutors is less likely to require the disclosure of further material to the defence if the defence have clarified and articulated their case, as required by the CPIA.

43. In the magistrates' courts, where the provision of a defence statement is not mandatory, early identification of the material issues by the defence, whether through a defence statement, case management form or otherwise, will help the prosecution to focus its preparation of the case and allow any defence disclosure queries to be dealt with promptly and accurately.

Magistrates' Courts (including the Youth Court)

44. The majority of criminal cases are heard in the magistrates' court. The requirement for the prosecution to provide initial disclosure only arises after a not guilty plea has been entered but prosecutors should be alert to the possibility that material may exist which should be disclosed to the defendant prior to the CPIA requirements applying to the case[2].

45. Where a not guilty plea is entered in the magistrates' court, prosecutors should ensure that any issues of dispute which are raised are noted on the file. They should also seek to obtain a copy of any Magistrates' Court Trial Preparation Form. Consideration of the issues raised in court and on the Trial Preparation Form will assist in deciding what material undermines the prosecution case or assists the defendant.

46. Where a matter is set down for trial in the magistrates' court, prosecutors should ensure that the investigator is requested to supply any outstanding disclosure schedules as a matter of urgency. Prosecutors should serve initial disclosure in sufficient time to ensure that the trial date is effective.

47. There is no requirement for a defence statement to be served in the magistrates' court but it should be noted that if none is given the court has no power to hear an application for further prosecution disclosure under section 8 of the CPIA and the Criminal Procedure Rules.

---

[2] See for example *R v DPP ex parte Lee [1999] 2 All ER 737*

Cases in the Crown Court

48. The exponential increase in the use of technology in society means that many routine Crown Court cases are increasingly likely to have to engage with digital material of some form. It is not only in large and complex cases that there may be large quantities of such material. Where such investigations involve digital material, it will be virtually impossible for investigators (or prosecutors) to examine every item of such material individually and there should be no expectation that such material will be so examined. Having consulted with the prosecution as appropriate, disclosure officers should determine what their approach should be to the examination of the material. Investigators or disclosure officers should decide how best to pursue a reasonable line of enquiry in relation to the relevant digital material, and ensure that the extent and manner of the examination are commensurate with the issues in the case.

49. Consideration should be given to any local or national agreements in relation to disclosure in 'Early Guilty Plea Scheme' cases.

Large and complex cases in the Crown Court

50. The particular challenges presented by large and complex criminal prosecutions require an approach to disclosure which is specifically tailored to the needs of such cases. In these cases more than any other is the need for careful thought to be given to prosecution-led disclosure matters from the very earliest stage. It is essential that the prosecution takes a grip on the case and its disclosure requirements from the very outset of the investigation, which must continue throughout all aspects of the case preparation.

Disclosure Management Documents

51. Accordingly, investigations and prosecutions of large and complex cases should be carefully defined and accompanied by a clear investigation and prosecution strategy. The approach to disclosure in such cases should be outlined in a document which should be served on the defence and the court at an early stage. Such documents, sometimes known as Disclosure Management Documents, will require careful preparation and presentation, tailored to the individual case. They may include:

   (a)   Where prosecutors and investigators operate in an integrated office, an explanation as to how the disclosure responsibilities have been managed;

   (b)   A brief summary of the prosecution case and a statement outlining how the prosecutor's general approach will comply with the CPIA regime, these Guidelines and the Judicial Protocol on the Disclosure of Unused Material in Criminal Cases;

   (c)   The prosecutor's understanding of the defence case, including information revealed during interview;

   (d)   An outline of the prosecution's general approach to disclosure, which may include detail relating to:

   (i)   Digital material: explaining the method and extent of examination, in accordance with the **Annex** to these Guidelines;

   (ii)   Video footage;

   (iii) Linked investigations: explaining the nexus between investigations, any memoranda of understanding or disclosure agreements between investigators;

   (iv)   Third party and foreign material, including steps taken to obtain the material;

   (v)   Reasonable lines of enquiry: a summary of the lines pursued, particularly those that point away from the suspect, or which may assist the defence;

   (vi)   Credibility of a witness: confirmation that witness checks, including those of professional witnesses have, or will be, carried out.

52. Thereafter the prosecution should follow the Disclosure Management Document. They are living documents and should be amended in light of developments in the case; they should be kept up to date as the case progresses. Their use will assist the court in its own case management and will enable the defence to engage from an early stage with the prosecution's proposed approach to disclosure.

Material not held by the prosecution

Involvement of other agencies: material held by other Government departments and third parties

53. Where it appears to an investigator, disclosure officer or prosecutor that a Government department or other Crown body has material that may be relevant to an issue in the case, reasonable steps should be taken to identify and consider such material. Although what is reasonable will vary from case to

case, the prosecution should inform the department or other body of the nature of its case and of relevant issues in the case in respect of which the department or body might possess material, and ask whether it has any such material.

54. It should be remembered that investigators, disclosure officers and prosecutors cannot be regarded to be in constructive possession of material held by Government departments or Crown bodies simply by virtue of their status as Government departments or Crown bodies.

55. Where, after reasonable steps have been taken to secure access to such material, access is denied, the investigator, disclosure officer or prosecutor should consider what if any further steps might be taken to obtain the material or inform the defence. The final decision on any further steps will be for the prosecutor.

Third party material: other domestic bodies

56. There may be cases where the investigator, disclosure officer or prosecutor believes that a third party (for example, a local authority, a social services department, a hospital, a doctor, a school, a provider of forensic services) has material or information which might be relevant to the prosecution case. In such cases, investigators, disclosure officers and prosecutors should take reasonable steps to identify, secure and consider material held by any third party where it appears to the investigator, disclosure officer or prosecutor that (a) such material exists and (b) that it may be relevant to an issue in the case.

57. If the investigator, disclosure officer or prosecutor seeks access to the material or information but the third party declines or refuses to allow access to it, the matter should not be left. If despite any reasons offered by the third party it is still believed that it is reasonable to seek production of the material or information, and the requirements of section 2 of the Criminal Procedure (Attendance of Witnesses) Act 1965 or as appropriate section 97 of the Magistrates Courts Act 1980 are satisfied (or any other relevant power), then the prosecutor or investigator should apply for a witness summons causing a representative of the third party to produce the material to the court.

58. Sometimes, for example through multi-agency working arrangements, investigators, disclosure officers or prosecutors may become aware of the content or nature of material held by a third party. Consultation with the relevant third party must always take place before disclosure is made; there may be public interest reasons to apply to the Court for an order for non-disclosure in the public interest, in accordance with the procedure outlined in paragraph 65 and following.

International matters

59. The obligations under the CPIA Code to pursue all reasonable lines of enquiry apply to material held overseas.

60. Where it appears that there is relevant material, the prosecutor must take reasonable steps to obtain it, either informally or making use of the powers contained in the Crime (International Co-operation) Act 2003 and any EU and international conventions. See CPS Guidance 'Obtaining Evidence and Information from Abroad'.

61. There may be cases where a foreign state or a foreign court refuses to make the material available to the investigator or prosecutor. There may be other cases where the foreign state, though willing to show the material to investigators, will not allow the material to be copied or otherwise made available and the courts of the foreign state will not order its provision.

62. It is for these reasons that there is no absolute duty on the prosecutor to disclose relevant material held overseas by entities not subject to the jurisdiction of the courts in England and Wales. However consideration should be given to whether the type of material believed to be held can be provided to the defence.

63. The obligation on the investigator and prosecutor under the CPIA is to take reasonable steps. Where investigators are allowed to examine files of a foreign state but are not allowed to take copies or notes or list the documents held, there is no breach by the prosecution in its duty of disclosure by reason of its failure to obtain such material, provided reasonable steps have been taken to try and obtain the material. Prosecutors have a margin of consideration as to what steps are appropriate in the particular case but prosecutors must be alive to their duties and there may be some circumstances where these duties cannot be met. Whether the prosecutor has taken reasonable steps is for the court to determine in each case if the matter is raised.

64. In these circumstances it is important that the position is clearly set out in writing so that the court and the defence know what the position is. Investigators and prosecutors must record and explain the situation and set out, insofar as they are permitted by the foreign state, such information as they can and the steps they have taken.

Applications for non-disclosure in the public interest

65. The CPIA allows prosecutors to apply to the court for an order to withhold material which would otherwise fall to be disclosed if disclosure would give rise to a real risk of serious prejudice to an important public interest. Before making such an application, prosecutors should aim to disclose as much of the material as they properly can (for example, by giving the defence redacted or edited copies or summaries). Neutral material or material damaging to the defendant need not be disclosed and there is no need to bring it to the attention of the court. Only in truly borderline cases should the prosecution seek a judicial ruling on whether material in its possession should be disclosed.

66. Prior to the hearing, the prosecutor and the prosecution advocate must examine all material which is the subject matter of the application and make any necessary enquiries of the investigator. The investigator must be frank with the prosecutor about the full extent of the sensitive material. Prior to or at the hearing, the court must be provided with full and accurate information about the material

67. The prosecutor (or representative) and/or investigator should attend such applications. Section 16 of the CPIA allows a person claiming to have an interest in the sensitive material to apply to the court for the opportunity to be heard at the application.

68. The principles set out at paragraph 36 of *R v H & C* [2004] 2 Cr. App. R. 10 [2004] UKHL 3 should be applied rigorously, firstly by the prosecutor and then by the court considering the material. It is essential that these principles are scrupulously adhered to, to ensure that the procedure for examination of material in the absence of the accused is compliant with Article 6.

69. If prosecutors conclude that a fair trial cannot take place because material which satisfies the test for disclosure cannot be disclosed, and that this cannot be remedied by the above procedure; how the case is presented; or by any other means, they should not continue with the case.

Other disclosure

70. Disclosure of any material that is made outside the ambit of CPIA will attract confidentiality by virtue of *Taylor v SFO* [1999] 2 AC 177.

Material relevant to sentence

71. In all cases the prosecutor must consider disclosing in the interests of justice any material which is relevant to sentence (e.g. information which might mitigate the seriousness of the offence or assist the accused to lay blame in part upon a co-accused or another person).

Post-conviction

72. Where, after the conclusion of the proceedings, material comes to light, that might cast doubt upon the safety of the conviction, the prosecutor must consider disclosure of such material.

Applicability of these Guidelines

73. These Guidelines shall have immediate effect.

Annex: Attorney General's Guidelines on Disclosure: Supplementary Guidelines on Digitally Stored Material (2011)

[The Annex repeats the supplementary guidelines published in 2011 and reproduced in the main work in appendix 4 under the heading 'Supplementary Attorney-General's Guidelines on Disclosure']

Annexed to the revised Attorney General's Guidelines on Disclosure December 2013

JUDICIAL PROTOCOL ON THE DISCLOSURE OF UNUSED MATERIAL IN CRIMINAL CASES

Introduction

This protocol is prescribed for use by CPD IV Disclosure 22A: Disclosure of Unused Material. It is applicable in all the criminal courts of England and Wales, including the Crown Court, the Court Martial[3] and the magistrates' courts. It replaces the previous judicial document 'Disclosure: a Protocol for the Control

---

[3] The timetables given here may vary in the Court Martial and reference should be made to the Criminal Procedure and Investigations Act 1996 (Application to the Armed Forces) Order 2009 and to any practice note issued by the Judge Advocate General.

and Management of Unused Material in the Crown Court'[4] and it also replaces section 4 'Disclosure' of the Lord Chief Justice's Protocol on the Control and Management of Heavy Fraud and Other Complex Criminal Cases, dated 22 March 2005.[5]

This protocol is intended to provide a central source of guidance for the judiciary, although that produced by the Attorney General also requires attention.

In summary, this judicial protocol sets out the principles to be applied to, and the importance of, disclosure; the expectations of the court and its role in disclosure, in particular in relation to case management; and the consequences if there is a failure by the prosecution or defence to comply with their obligations.

Readers should note that a review of disclosure in the magistrates' courts is currently being undertaken by HHJ Kinch QC and the Chief Magistrate, on behalf of Lord Justice Gross, the Senior Presiding Judge. Amendments may therefore be made following the recommendations of that review, and in accordance with other forthcoming changes to the criminal justice system.

The importance of disclosure for fair trials

1. Disclosure remains one of the most important – as well as one of the most misunderstood and abused – of the procedures relating to criminal trials. Lord Justice Gross' review has re-emphasised the need for all those involved to understand the statutory requirements and to undertake their roles with rigour, in a timely manner.

2. The House of Lords stated in *R v H and C* [2004] UKHL 3; [2004] 2 AC 134; [2004] 2 Cr App R 10:

    > Fairness ordinarily requires that any material held by the prosecution which weakens its case or strengthens that of the defendant, if not relied on as part of its formal case against the defendant, should be disclosed to the defence. Bitter experience has shown that miscarriages of justice may occur where such material is withheld from disclosure. The golden rule is that full disclosure of such material should be made. ([2004] 2 AC 134, at 147)

    The Criminal Cases Review Commission has recently noted that failure to disclose material to the defence to which they were entitled remains the biggest single cause of miscarriages of justice.

3. However, it is also essential that the trial process is not overburdened or diverted by erroneous and inappropriate disclosure of unused prosecution material or by misconceived applications. Although the drafters of the Criminal Procedure and Investigations Act 1996 ('CPIA 1996') cannot have anticipated the vast increase in the amount of electronic material that has been generated in recent years, nevertheless the principles of that Act still hold true. Applications by the parties or decisions by judges based on misconceptions of the law or a general laxity of approach (however well-intentioned) which result in an improper application of the disclosure regime have, time and again, proved unnecessarily costly and have obstructed justice. As Lord Justice Gross noted, the burden of disclosure must not be allowed to render the prosecution of cases impracticable.

4. The overarching principle is that unused prosecution material will fall to be disclosed if, and only if, it satisfies the test for disclosure applicable to the proceedings in question, subject to any overriding public interest considerations. The test for disclosure will depend on the date the criminal investigation in question commenced, as this will determine whether the common law disclosure regime applies, or either of the two disclosure regimes under the CPIA 1996.

5. The test for disclosure under section 3 of the CPIA 1996 as amended will be applicable in nearly every case and all those involved in the process will need to be familiar with it. Material fulfils the test if – but only if – it 'might reasonably be considered capable of undermining the case for the prosecution ... or of assisting the case for the accused.'

6. The disclosure process must be led by the prosecution so as to trigger comprehensive defence engagement, supported by robust judicial case management. Active participation by the court in the disclosure process is a critical means of ensuring that delays and adjournments are avoided, given failures by the parties to comply with their obligations may disrupt and (in some cases) frustrate the course of justice.

---

[4] The previous judicial protocol was endorsed by the Court of Appeal in *R v K* [2006] EWCA Crim 724; [2006] 2 All ER 552 (Note); [2006] Crim LR 1012.
[5] This protocol also replaces the Protocol for the Provision of Advance Information, Prosecution Evidence and Disclosure of Unused Material in the Magistrates' Courts, dated 12 May 2006, which was adopted as part of the Stop Delaying Justice initiative.

Disclosure of unused material in criminal cases

7. The court should keep the timetable for prosecution and defence disclosure under review from the first hearing. Judges should as a matter of course ask the parties to identify the issues in the case, and invite the parties to indicate whether further disclosure is sought, and on what topics. For example, it is not enough for the judge to rely on the content of the PCMH form. Proper completion of the disclosure process is a vital part of case preparation, and it may well affect the progress of the case. The court will expect disclosure to have been considered from the outset; the prosecution and defence advocates need to be aware of any potential problems and substantive difficulties should be explained to the judge; and the parties should propose a sensible timetable. Realism is preferable to optimistic but unachievable deadlines which may dislocate the court schedule and imperil the date of trial. It follows that judges should not impose deadlines for service of the case papers or disclosure until they are confident that the prosecution advocate has taken instructions from the individuals who are best placed to evaluate the work to be undertaken.

8. The advocates – both prosecution and defence – must be kept fully informed throughout the course of the proceedings as to any difficulties which may prevent them from complying with their disclosure obligations. When problems arise or come to light after directions have been given, the advocates should notify the court and the other party (or parties) immediately rather than waiting until the date set by the court for the service of the material is imminent or has passed, and they must provide the court with a suggested timetable in order to resolve the problem. The progress of the disclosure process should be reviewed at every hearing. There remains no basis in practice or law for Counsel to Counsel disclosure.

9. If there is a preliminary hearing the judge should seize the opportunity to impose an early timetable for disclosure and to identify any likely problems including as regards third party material and material that will require an application to the Family Court. In an appropriate case the court should consider holding a Joint Criminal/Care Directions Hearing. See Material held by Third Parties, from paragraph 44 below.

10. For the PCMH to be effective, the defence must have a proper opportunity to review the case papers and consider initial disclosure, with a view to preparing a properly completed defence statement which will inform the judge's conduct of the PCMH, and inform the prosecution of the matters required by sections 5, 6A and 6C of the CPIA. As the Court of Appeal noted in *R v Newell* [2012] EWCA Crim 650; [2012] 2 Cr App R 10, 'a typed defence statement must be provided before the PCMH. If there is no defence statement by the time of the PCMH, then a judge will usually require the trial advocate to see that such a statement is provided and not proceed with the PCMH until that is done. In the ordinary case the trial advocate will be required to do that at the court and the PCMH resumed later in the day to avoid delay'. There may be some instances when there will be a well-founded defence application to extend the 28-day time limit for serving a proper defence statement. In a proper case (but never routinely), it may be appropriate to put the PCMH back by a week or more, to enable an appropriate defence statement to be filed.

11. The defence statement can be admitted into evidence under section 6E(4) of the CPIA 1996. However, information included on the PCMH form (which is primarily an administrative form) will not usually be admitted in evidence when the defence advocate has complied with the letter and the spirit of the Criminal Procedure Rules.[6] Introducing the PCMH form (or part of it) during the trial is likely to be an exceptional event. The status of the trial preparation form in the magistrates' court is somewhat different, as discussed below.

12. The court should not extend time lightly or as a matter of course. If an extension is sought, it ought to be accompanied by an appropriate explanation. For instance, it is not sufficient for the prosecutor merely to say that the investigator has delivered the papers late: the underlying reasons are to be provided to the court. The same applies if the defence statement is delayed. Whichever party is at fault, realistic proposals for service are to be set out.

13. Judges should not allow the prosecution to avoid their statutory responsibility for reviewing the unused material by the expedient of permitting the defence to have access to (or providing the defence with copies of) the material listed in the schedules of non-sensitive unused prosecution material irrespective of whether it satisfies, wholly or in part, the relevant test for disclosure. Additionally, it is for the prosecutor to decide on the manner of disclosure, and it does not have to mirror the form in which the information was originally recorded. Rose LJ gave guidance on case

---

[6] *R v Newell* [2012] EWCA Crim 650; [2012] 2 Cr App R 10.

management issues in this context in *R v CPS* (Interlocutory Application under sections 35/36 CPIA) [2005] EWCA Crim 2342. Allowing the defence to inspect items that fulfil the disclosure test is also a valid means of providing disclosure.

14. The larger and more complex the case, the more important it is for the prosecution to adhere to the overarching principle and ensure that sufficient prosecution attention and resources are allocated to the task. Handing the defendant the 'keys to the warehouse' has been the cause of many gross abuses in the past, resulting in considerable expenditure by the defence without any material benefit to the course of justice. The circumstances relating to large and complex cases are outlined below.

15. The court will require the defence to engage and assist in the early identification of the real issues in the case and, particularly in the larger and more complex cases, to contribute to the search terms to be used for, and the parameters of, the review of any electronically held material (which can be very considerable). Any defence criticisms of the prosecution approach to disclosure should be timely and reasoned; there is no place for disclosure 'ambushes' or for late or uninformative defence statements. Admissions should be used so far as possible to narrow the real issues in dispute.

16. A constructive approach to disclosure is a necessary part of professional best practice, for the defence and prosecution. This does not undermine the defendant's legitimate interests, it accords with his or her obligations under the Rules and it ensures that all the relevant material is provided. Delays and failures by the prosecution and the defence are equally damaging to a timely, fair and efficient trial, and judges should be vigilant in preventing and addressing abuses. Accordingly, whenever there are potential failings by either the defence or the prosecution, judges, in exercising appropriate oversight of disclosure, should carefully investigate the suggested default and give timely directions.

17. In the Crown Court, the defence statement is to be served within 28 days of the date when the prosecution complies with its duty of initial disclosure (or purports to do so) and whenever section 5(5) of the CPIA applies to the proceedings, and the defence statement must comply with section 6A of the CPIA. Service of the defence statement is a most important stage in the disclosure process, and timely service is necessary to facilitate proper consideration of the disclosure issues well in advance of the trial date. Judges expect a defence statement to contain a clear and detailed exposition of the issues of fact and law. Defence statements that merely rehearse the suggestion that the defendant is innocent do not comply with the requirements of the CPIA.

18. The prosecutor should consider the defence statement carefully and promptly provide a copy to the disclosure officer, to assist the prosecution in its continuing disclosure obligations. The court expects the Crown to identify any suggested deficiencies in the defence statement, and to draw these to the attention of the defence and the court; in particular in large and complex cases, it will assist the court if this is in writing. Although the prosecution's ability to request, and the court's jurisdiction to give, an adverse inference direction under section 11 of CPIA is not contingent on the prosecution having earlier identified any suggested deficiencies, nevertheless the prosecutor must provide a timely written explanation of its position.

19. Judges should examine the defence statement with care to ensure that it complies with the formalities required by the CPIA. As stated in *R v H and C* (supra) (paragraph 35):

> If material does not weaken the prosecution case or strengthen that of the defendant, there is no requirement to disclose it. For this purpose the parties' respective cases should not be restrictively analysed. But they must be carefully analysed, to ascertain the specific facts the prosecution seek to establish and the specific grounds on which the charges are resisted. The trial process is not well served if the defence are permitted to make general and unspecified allegations and then seek far-reaching disclosure in the hope that material may turn up to make them good. Neutral material or material damaging to the defendant need not be disclosed and should not be brought to the attention of the court.

20. If no defence statement – or an inadequate defence statement – is served within the relevant time limits, the judge should investigate the position. At every PCMH where there is no defence statement, including those where an extension has been given, or the time for filing has not yet expired, the defence should be warned in appropriate terms that pursuant to section 6E(2) of the CPIA an adverse inference may be drawn during the trial, and this result is likely if there is no justification for the deficiency. The fact that a warning has been given should be noted.

21. An adverse inference may be drawn under section 11 of the CPIA if the accused fails to discharge his or her disclosure obligations. Whenever the amended CPIA regime applies, the prosecution may comment on any failure in defence disclosure (except where the failure relates to a point of law) without leave of the court, but counsel should use a measure of judgment as to whether it is wise to embark on cross-examination about such a failure.[7] If the accused is cross-examined about discrepan-

---

[7] *R v Essa* [2009] EWCA Crim 43, paragraph 22.

cies between his evidence and his defence statement, or if adverse comment is made, the judge must give appropriate guidance to the jury.[8]

22. In order to secure a fair trial, it is vital that the prosecution is mindful of its continuing duty of disclosure. Once the defence statement has been received, the Crown must review disclosure in the light of the issues identified in the defence statement. In cases of complexity, the following steps are then likely to be necessary:

    (i) Service by the prosecution of any further material due to the defence following receipt of the defence statement.

    (ii) Any defence request to the prosecution for service of additional specific items. As discussed below, these requests must be justified by reference to the defence statement and they should be submitted on the section 8 form.

    (iii) Prosecution response to the defence request.

    (iv) If the defence considers that disclosable items are still outstanding, a section 8 application should be made using the appropriate form.

23. It follows that all requests by the defence to the prosecution for disclosure should be made on the section 8 application form, even if no hearing is sought in the first instance. Discussion and co-operation between the parties outside of court is encouraged in order to ensure that the court is only asked to issue a ruling when strictly necessary. However, use of the section 8 form will ensure that focussed requests are clearly set out in one place.

24. The judge should set a date as part of the timetabling exercise by which any application under section 8 is to be made, if this appears to be a likely eventuality.

25. The Court will require the section 8 application to be served on the prosecution well in advance of the hearing – indeed, prior to requesting the hearing – to enable the Crown to identify and serve any items that meet the test for disclosure.

26. Service of a defence statement is an essential precondition for an application under section 8, and applications should not be heard or directions for disclosure issued in the absence of a properly completed statement (see Part 22 of the Criminal Procedure Rules). In particular, blanket orders in this context are inconsistent with the statutory framework for disclosure laid down by the CPIA and the decision of the House of Lords in *R v H and C* (supra). It follows that defence requests for disclosure of particular pieces of unused prosecution material which are not referable to any issue in the case identified in the defence statement should be rejected.

27. Judges must ensure that defendants are not prejudiced on account of the failures of their lawyers, and, when necessary, the professions should be reminded that if justice is to be done, and if disclosure is to be dealt with fairly in accordance with the law, a full and careful defence statement and a reasoned approach to section 8 applications are essential. In exploring the adequacy of the defence statement, a judge should always ask what the issues are and upon what matters of fact the defendant intends to rely[9] and on what matters of fact the defendant takes issue.

Listing

28. Sufficient time is necessary for the judge properly to undertake the PCMH, and this is a paramount consideration when listing cases. Unless the court is able to sit early, judges who are part heard on trials are probably not best placed to conduct PCMHs.

29. Cases that raise particularly difficult issues of disclosure should be referred to the Resident Judge for directions (unless a trial judge has been allocated) and, for trials of real complexity, the trial judge should be identified at an early stage, prior to the PCMH if possible. Listing officers, working in consultation with the Resident Judge and, if allocated, the trial judge, should ensure that sufficient time is allowed for judges to prepare and deal with prosecution and defence applications relating to disclosure, particularly in the more complex cases.

Magistrates' Courts (including the Youth Court)

30. The principles relating to disclosure apply equally in the magistrates' courts. It follows that whilst disclosure of unused material in compliance with the statutory test is undoubtedly essential in order to achieve justice, it is critical that summary trials are not delayed or made over-complicated by misconceived applications for, or inappropriate disclosure of, prosecution material.

31. Magistrates will rely on their legal advisers for guidance, and the latter should draw the attention of the parties and the court to the statutory provisions and the applicable case law. Cases raising disclo-

[8] *R v Hanyes* [2011] EWCA Crim 3281.
[9] *R v Rochford* [2010] EWCA Crim 1928; [2011] 1 Cr App R 11

sure issues of particular complexity should be referred to a District Judge (Magistrates' Courts), if available.

32. Although service of a defence statement is voluntary for summary trials (section 6 CPIA), the defendant cannot make an application for specific disclosure under section 8 CPIA, and the court cannot make any orders in this regard, unless a proper defence statement has been provided. It follows that although providing a defence statement is not mandatory, it remains a critical stage in the disclosure process. If disclosure issues are to be raised by the defence, a defence statement must be served well in advance of the trial date. Any section 8 application must be made in strict compliance with the Rules.

33. The case-management forms used in the magistrates' courts fulfil some of the functions of a defence statement, and the prosecution must take into account the information provided as to the defence case when conducting its on-going review of unused material. As the Court of Appeal noted in *R v Newell* (supra), admissions can be made in the Trial Preparation Form and the defence is able to identify the matters that are not in issue. Admissions made in these circumstances may be admissible during the trial. However, other information on the form that does not come within the section relating to admissions should be treated in the same way as the contents of a PCMH form in the Crown Court and it should not generally be introduced as part of the evidence at trial. However, the contents of the Trial Preparation Form do not replace the need to serve a defence statement if the defendant seeks to apply for disclosure under section 8 CPIA.

34. The standard directions require that any defence statement is to be served within 14 days of the date upon which the prosecution has complied with, or purported to comply with, the duty to provide initial disclosure. There may be some instances when there will be a well-founded defence application to extend the 14-day time limit for serving the defence statement. These applications must be made in accordance with the Criminal Procedure Rules, in writing and before the time limit expires.

35. Although CCTV footage frequently causes difficulties, it is to be treated as any other category of unused material and it should only be disclosed if the material meets the appropriate test for disclosure under the CPIA. The defence should either be provided with copies of the sections of the CCTV or afforded an opportunity to view them. If the prosecution refuses to disclose CCTV material that the defence considers to be discloseable, the courts should not make standard or general directions requiring the prosecutor to disclose material of this kind in the absence of an application under section 8. When potentially relevant CCTV footage is not in the possession of the police, the guidance in relation to third party material will apply, although the police remain under a duty to pursue all reasonable lines of inquiry, including those leading away from a suspect, whether or not defence requests are made.

36. The previous convictions of witnesses and any disciplinary findings against officers in the case are frequently discloseable and care should be taken to disclose them as appropriate. Documents such as crime reports or records of emergency calls should not be provided on a routine basis, for instance as part of a bundle of disclosed documents, irrespective of whether the material satisfies the appropriate test for disclosure. Defence advocates should not request this material in standard or routine correspondence, and instead focussed consideration should be given to the circumstances of the particular case. Unjustified requests for disclosure of material of this kind are routinely made, frequently leading to unnecessary delays and adjournments. The prosecution should always consider whether the request is properly made out.

37. The supervisory role of the courts is critical in this context, and magistrates must guard against granting unnecessary adjournments and issuing unjustified directions.

Large and complex cases in the Crown Court

38. Disclosure is a particular problem with the larger and more complex cases, which require a scrupulous approach by the parties and robust case management by the judiciary. If possible, the trial judge should be identified at the outset.

39. The legal representatives need to fulfil their duties in this context with care and efficiency; they should co-operate with the other party (or parties) and the court; and the judge and the other party (or parties) are to be informed of any difficulties, as soon as they arise. The court should be provided with an up-to date timetable for disclosure whenever there are material changes in this regard. A disclosure-management document, or similar, prepared by the prosecution will be of particular assistance to the court in large and complex cases.

40. Judges should be prepared to give early guidance as to the prosecution's approach to disclosure, thereby ensuring early engagement by the defence.

41. Cases of this nature frequently include large volumes of digitally stored material. The Attorney General's 2011 guidance is of particular relevance and assistance in this context: https://www.gov.uk/government/uploads/system/uploads/attachment_data/file/16239/Attorney_General_s_guidelines_on_disclosure_2011.pdf

42. Applications for witness anonymity orders require particular attention; as the Court of Appeal noted in *R v Mayers and Others* [2008] EWCA Crim 2989; [2009] 1 Cr App R 30, in making such an application, the prosecution's obligations of disclosure 'go much further than the ordinary duties of disclosure'.

43. If the judge considers that there are reasonable grounds to doubt the good faith of the investigation, he or she will be concerned to see that there has been independent and effective appraisal of the documents contained in the disclosure schedule and that its contents are adequate. In appropriate cases where this issue has arisen and there are grounds which show there is a real issue, consideration should be given to receiving evidence on oath from the senior investigating officer at an early case management hearing.

Material held by Third Parties

44. Where material is held by a third party such as a local authority, a social services department, hospital or business, the investigators and the prosecution may need to make enquiries of the third party, with a view to inspecting the material and assessing whether the relevant test for disclosure is met and determining whether any or all of the material should be retained, recorded and, in due course, disclosed to the accused. If access by the prosecution is granted, the investigators and the prosecution will need to establish whether the custodian of the material intends to raise PII issues, as a result of which the material may have to be placed before the court for a decision. This does not obviate the need for the defence to conduct its own enquiries as appropriate. Speculative enquiries without any proper basis in relation to third party material – whether by the prosecution or the defence – are to be discouraged, and, in appropriate cases, the court will consider making an order for costs where an application is clearly unmeritorious and misconceived.

45. The 2013 Protocol and Good Practice Model on Disclosure of Information in Cases of Alleged Child Abuse and Linked Criminal and Care Directions Hearings has recently been published. It provides a framework and timetable for the police and CPS to obtain discloseable material from local authorities, and for applications to be made to the Family Court. It is applicable to all cases of alleged child abuse where the child is aged 17 years or under. It is not binding on local authorities, but it does represent best practice and therefore should be consulted in all such cases. Delays in obtaining this type of material have led to unacceptable delays to trials involving particularly vulnerable witnesses and every effort must be made to ensure that all discloseable material is identified at an early stage so that any necessary applications can be made and the defence receive material to which they are entitled in good time.

46. There is no specific procedure for disclosure of material held by third parties in criminal proceedings, although the procedure established under section 2 of the Criminal Procedure (Attendance of Witnesses) Act 1965 or section 97 of the Magistrates' Courts Act 1980 is often used for this purpose. Where the third party in question declines to allow inspection of the material, or requires the prosecution to obtain an order before providing copies, the prosecutor will need to consider whether it is appropriate to obtain a witness summons under either section 2 of the Criminal Procedure (Attendance of Witnesses) Act 1965 or section 97 of the Magistrates' Court Act 1980. Part 28 of the Criminal Procedure Rules and paragraphs 3.5 and 3.6 of the Code of Practice under the CPIA 1996 should be followed.

47. Applications for third party disclosure must identify the documents that are sought and provide full details of why they are discloseable. This is particularly relevant when access is sought to the medical records of those who allege they are victims of crime. It should be appreciated that a duty to assert confidentiality may arise when a third party receives a request for disclosure, or the right to privacy may be claimed under article 8 of the ECHR (see in particular Crim PR Part 28.6). Victims do not waive the confidentiality of their medical records, or their right to privacy under article 8 of the ECHR, by making a complaint against the accused. The court, as a public authority, must ensure that any interference with the right to privacy under article 8 is in accordance with the law, and is necessary in pursuit of a legitimate public interest. General and unspecified requests to trawl through such records should be refused. Confidentiality rests with the subject of the material, not with the authority holding it. The subject is entitled to service of the application and has the right to make representations: Criminal Procedure Rule 22.3 and *R (on the application of B) v Stafford Combined Court* [2006] EWHC 1645 (Admin); [2006] 2 Cr App R 34. The 2013 Protocol and Good Practice Model at paragraph 13 should be followed. It is likely that the judge will need to issue directions when issues of this kind are raised (e.g. whether enquiries with the third party are likely to be appropriate; who is to make the request; what material is to be sought, and from whom; and a timetable should be set).

48. The judge should consider whether to take any steps if a third party fails, or refuses, to comply with a request for disclosure, including suggesting that either of the parties pursue the request and, if necessary, make an application for a witness summons. In these circumstances, the court will need to set an appropriate timetable for compliance with Part 28 of the Rules. Any failure to comply with the timetable must immediately be referred back to the court for further directions, although a hearing will not always be necessary. Generally, it may be appropriate for the defence to pursue requests of this kind when the prosecution, for good reason, decline to do so and the court will need to ensure that this procedure does not delay the trial.

49. There are very limited circumstances in which information relating to Family Court proceedings (e.g. where there have been care proceedings in relation to a child who has complained to the police of mistreatment) may be communicated without a court order: see the Family Procedure Rules 12.73. Reference should be made to the 2013 Protocol and Good Practice Model. In most circumstances, a court order will be required and paragraph 11 of the Protocol which sets out how an application should be made should be followed.

Other Government Departments

50. Material held by other government departments or other Crown agencies will not be prosecution material for the purposes of section 3(2) or section 8(4) of the CPIA if it has not been inspected, recorded and retained during the course of the relevant criminal investigation. The CPIA Code of Practice and the Attorney General's Guidelines on Disclosure, however, impose a duty upon the investigators and the prosecution to pursue all reasonable lines of inquiry and that may involve seeking disclosure from the relevant body.

International matters

51. The obligations of the Crown in relation to relevant third-party material held overseas are as set out in *R v Flook* [2009] EWCA Crim 682; [2010] 1 Cr App R 30: the Crown must pursue reasonable lines of enquiry and if it appears there is relevant material, all reasonable steps must be taken to obtain it, whether formally or otherwise. To a great extent, the success of these enquiries will depend on the laws of the country where the material is held and the facts of the individual case. It needs to be recognised that when the material is held in a country outside of the European Union, the power of the Crown and the courts of England and Wales to obtain third-party material may well be limited. If informal requests are unsuccessful, the avenues are limited to the Crime (International Co-operation) Act 2003 and any applicable international conventions. It cannot, in any sense, be guaranteed that a request to a foreign government, court or body will produce the material sought. Additionally, some foreign authorities may be prepared to show the material in question to the investigating officers, whilst refusing to allow the material to be copied or otherwise made available.

52. As the Court of Appeal observed in *R v Khyam* [2008] EWCA Crim 1612; [2009] 1 Cr App R (S) 77:

> The prosecuting authorities in this jurisdiction simply cannot compel authorities in a foreign country to acknowledge, let alone comply with, our disclosure principles. ([2008] EWCA Crim 1612, at paragraph 37)

The obligation is therefore to take reasonable steps. Whether the Crown has complied with that obligation is for the courts to judge in each case.

53. It is, therefore, important that the prosecution sets out the position clearly in writing, including any inability to inspect or retrieve any material that potentially ought to be disclosed, along with the steps that have been taken.

Applications for Non-Disclosure in the Public Interest

54. Applications in this context, whenever possible, should be considered by the trial judge. The House of Lords in *R v H and C* (supra) has provided useful guidance as to the proper approach to be applied (paragraph 36):

> When any issue of derogation from the golden rule of full disclosure comes before it, the court must address a series of questions:
>
> (1) What is the material which the prosecution seek to withhold? This must be considered by the court in detail.
>
> (2) Is the material such as may weaken the prosecution case or strengthen that of the defence? If No, disclosure should not be ordered. If Yes, full disclosure should (subject to (3), (4) and (5) below) be ordered.
>
> (3) Is there a real risk of serious prejudice to an important public interest (and, if so, what) if full disclosure of the material is ordered? If No, full disclosure should be ordered.

(4)   If the answer to (2) and (3) is Yes, can the defendant's interest be protected without disclosure or disclosure be ordered to an extent or in a way which will give adequate protection to the public interest in question and also afford adequate protection to the interests of the defence?

This question requires the court to consider, with specific reference to the material which the prosecution seek to withhold and the facts of the case and the defence as disclosed, whether the prosecution should formally admit what the defence seek to establish or whether disclosure short of full disclosure may be ordered. This may be done in appropriate cases by the preparation of summaries or extracts of evidence, or the provision of documents in an edited or anonymised form, provided the documents supplied are in each instance approved by the judge. In appropriate cases the appointment of special counsel may be a necessary step to ensure that the contentions of the prosecution are tested and the interests of the defendant protected (see para 22 above). In cases of exceptional difficulty the court may require the appointment of special counsel to ensure a correct answer to questions (2) and (3) as well as (4).

(5)   Do the measures proposed in answer to (4) represent the minimum derogation necessary to protect the public interest in question? If No, the court should order such greater disclosure as will represent the minimum derogation from the golden rule of full disclosure.

(6)   If limited disclosure is ordered pursuant to (4) or (5), may the effect be to render the trial process, viewed as a whole, unfair to the defendant? If Yes, then fuller disclosure should be ordered even if this leads or may lead the prosecution to discontinue the proceedings so as to avoid having to make disclosure.

(7)   If the answer to (6) when first given is No, does that remain the correct answer as the trial unfolds, evidence is adduced and the defence advanced?

It is important that the answer to (6) should not be treated as a final, once-and-for-all, answer but as a provisional answer which the court must keep under review. ([2004] 2 AC 134, at 155-156)

55.   In this context, the following matters are to be emphasised:

(a)   The procedure for making applications to the court is set out in the Criminal Procedure Rules, Part 22;

(b)   When the PII application is a Type 1 or Type 2 application, proper notice to the defence is necessary to enable the accused to make focused submissions to the court and the notice should be as specific as the nature of the material allows. It is appreciated that in some cases only the generic nature of the material can be identified. In some wholly exceptional cases (Type 3 cases) it may be justified to give no notice at all. The judge should always ask the prosecution to justify the form of notice (or the decision to give no notice at all).

(c)   The prosecution should be alert to the possibility of disclosing a statement in a redacted form by, for example, simply removing personal details. This may obviate the need for a PII application, unless the redacted material satisfies the test for disclosure.

(d)   Except when the material is very short (for instance only a few sheets), or for reasons of sensitivity, the prosecution should supply securely sealed copies to the judge in advance, together with a short statement explaining the relevance of each document, how it satisfies the disclosure test and why it is suggested that disclosure would result in a real risk of serious prejudice to an important public interest; in undertaking this task, the use of merely formulaic expressions is to be discouraged. In any case of complexity a schedule of the material should be provided, identifying the particular objection to disclosure in relation to each item, and leaving a space for the judge's decision.

(e)   The application, even if held in private or in secret, should be recorded. The judge should give some short statement of reasons; this is often best done document by document as the hearing proceeds.

(f)   The recording, copies of the judge's orders (and any copies of the material retained by the court) should be clearly identified, securely sealed and kept in the court building in a safe or locked cabinet consistent with its security classification, and there should be a proper register of the contents. Arrangements should be made for the return of the material to the prosecution once the case is concluded and the time for an appeal has elapsed.

Conclusion

56. Historically, disclosure was viewed essentially as being a matter to be resolved between the parties, and the court only became engaged if a particular issue or complaint was raised. That perception is now wholly out of date. The regime established under the Criminal Justice Act 2003 and the Criminal Procedure Rules gives judges the power – indeed, it imposes a duty on the judiciary – actively to manage disclosure in every case. The efficient, effective and timely resolution of these issues is a critical element in meeting the overriding objective of the Criminal Procedure Rules of dealing with cases justly.

New Protocol in Child Abuse Cases

In October 2013, the '2013 Protocol and Good Practice Model: Disclosure of information in cases of alleged child abuse and linked criminal and care directions' was issued, having effect from 1 January 2014. It is of special importance where concurrent criminal care proceedings are taking place. It can be accessed at http://www.cps.gov.uk/legal/a_to_c#lgC.

CRIMINAL PROCEDURE RULES 2013 AND CRIMINAL PRACTICE DIRECTIONS

Criminal Procedure Rules 2013 (SI 2013 No. 1554) and Criminal Practice Directions [2013] EWCA Crim 1631

The following text reproduces the Criminal Procedure Rules 2013 and the Criminal Practice Directions which came into force on 7 October 2013. The Rules are shown as amended by the Criminal Procedure (Amendment) Rules 2013 (SI 2013 No. 2525), which have effect from 27 October 2013, and the Criminal Procedure (Amendment No. 2) Rules 2013 (SI 2013 No. 3183), which have effect from 24 February 2014 (the new Part 12) and 7 April 2014. The objective of the restructuring and revision of the new Practice Direction is to make it more accessible and useful to practitioners and a key part of that is arranging the Practice Direction so as to correspond so far as practicable with the related parts of the Criminal Procedure Rules. We have integrated the texts of the Rules and the Practice Direction so far as possible. The text of the Rules is displayed in black text and is accompanied by a number (e.g., **R-36**) in addition to the numbering in the rules themselves. The text of the Practice Direction is displayed in grey boxes and follows the relevant text of the Rules (save where this is impracticable) and is accompanied by a number (e.g., **PD-18**) in addition to the number used in the Practice Direction itself.

CRIMINAL PRACTICE DIRECTIONS   GENERAL MATTERS

CPD I General matters A
PD-0

A.1   The Lord Chief Justice has power, including power under section 74 of the Courts Act 2003 and Part 1 of Schedule 2 of the Constitutional Reform Act 2005, to make directions as to the practice and procedure of the criminal courts. The following directions are made accordingly.

A.2   These Practice Directions replace the Consolidated Criminal Practice Direction of 8 July 2002 ([2002] 1 W L.R 2870; [2002] 2 Cr App R 35), as amended, which is hereby revoked, with the exception of sections III.21, IV.31, IV.32, IV. 33, IV.38 and IV.41.9. The Practice Directions, Practice Notes and Practice Statements listed in Annex A and Annex B of the 2002 consolidation, with the exception of Practice Direction: (Supreme Court) (Devolution Issues) [1999] 1 WLR 1592; [1999] 3 All ER 466; [1999] 2 Cr App R 486, are also revoked. Annexes D, E and F remain in force.

A.3   These Practice Directions, which shall be known as the Criminal Practice Directions, take effect from the 7th October 2013. They apply to all cases in all the criminal courts of England and Wales from that date.

CRIMINAL PROCEDURE RULES   PART 1   THE OVERRIDING OBJECTIVE

The overriding objective
R-1

1.1   (1)   The overriding objective of this new code is that criminal cases be dealt with justly.

(2)   Dealing with a criminal case justly includes—

  (a)   acquitting the innocent and convicting the guilty;

  (b)   dealing with the prosecution and the defence fairly;

  (c)   recognising the rights of a defendant, particularly those under Article 6 of the European Convention on Human Rights;

  (d)   respecting the interests of witnesses, victims and jurors and keeping them informed of the progress of the case;

  (e)   dealing with the case efficiently and expeditiously;

  (f)   ensuring that appropriate information is available to the court when bail and sentence are considered; and

  (g)   dealing with the case in ways that take into account—

    (i)   the gravity of the offence alleged,

    (ii)   the complexity of what is in issue,

    (iii)   the severity of the consequences for the defendant and others affected, and

    (iv)   the needs of other cases.

The duty of the participants in a criminal case
R-2

1.2   (1)   Each participant, in the conduct of each case, must—

  (a)   prepare and conduct the case in accordance with the overriding objective;

  (b)   comply with these Rules, practice directions and directions made by the court; and

  (c)   at once inform the court and all parties of any significant failure (whether or not that participant is responsible for that failure) to take any procedural step required by these Rules, any practice direction or any direction of the court. A failure is significant if it might hinder the court in furthering the overriding objective.

(2) Anyone involved in any way with a criminal case is a participant in its conduct for the purposes of this rule.

R-3   The application by the court of the overriding objective

1.3   The court must further the overriding objective in particular when—

(a) exercising any power given to it by legislation (including these Rules);

(b) applying any practice direction; or

(c) interpreting any rule or practice direction.

Criminal Practice Directions   Part 1   The Overriding Objective

PD-1   CPD I General matters 1A

1A.1   The presumption of innocence and an adversarial process are essential features of English and Welsh legal tradition and of the defendant's right to a fair trial. But it is no part of a fair trial that questions of guilt and innocence should be determined by procedural manoeuvres. On the contrary, fairness is best served when the issues between the parties are identified as early and as clearly as possible. As Lord Justice Auld noted, a criminal trial is not a game under which a guilty defendant should be provided with a sporting chance. It is a search for truth in accordance with the twin principles that the prosecution must prove its case and that a defendant is not obliged to inculpate himself, the object being to convict the guilty and acquit the innocent.

1A.2   Further, it is not just for a party to obstruct or delay the preparation of a case for trial in order to secure some perceived procedural advantage, or to take unfair advantage of a mistake by someone else. If courts allow that to happen it damages public confidence in criminal justice. The Rules and the Practice Direction, taken together, make it clear that courts must not allow it to happen.

CRIMINAL PROCEDURE RULES   PART 2   UNDERSTANDING AND APPLYING THE RULES

R-4   When the Rules apply

2.1   (1) In general, the Criminal Procedure Rules apply—

(a) in all criminal cases in magistrates' courts and in the Crown Court; and

(b) in all cases in the criminal division of the Court of Appeal.

(2) If a rule applies only in one or two of those courts, the rule makes that clear.

(3) The Rules apply on and after 7th October 2013, but unless the court otherwise directs they do not affect a right or duty existing under The Criminal Procedure Rules 2012.

(4) In a case in which a request for extradition was received by a relevant authority in the United Kingdom on or before 31st December, 2003—

(a) the rules in Part 17 (Extradition) do not apply; and

(b) the rules in Part 17 of The Criminal Procedure Rules 2012 continue to apply as if those rules had not been revoked.

R-5   Definitions

2.2   (1) In these Rules, unless the context makes it clear that something different is meant:

'business day' means any day except Saturday, Sunday, Christmas Day, Boxing Day, Good Friday, Easter Monday or a bank holiday;

'court' means a tribunal with jurisdiction over criminal cases. It includes a judge, recorder, District Judge (Magistrates' Courts), lay justice and, when exercising their judicial powers, the Registrar of Criminal Appeals, a justices' clerk or assistant clerk;

'court officer' means the appropriate member of the staff of a court;

'justices' legal adviser' means a justices' clerk or an assistant to a justices' clerk;

'live link' means an arrangement by which a person can see and hear, and be seen and heard by, the court when that person is not in court;

'Practice Direction' means the Lord Chief Justice's Criminal Practice Directions, as amended, and 'Criminal Costs Practice Direction' means the Lord Chief Justice's Practice Direction (Costs in Criminal Proceedings), as amended;

'public interest ruling' means a ruling about whether it is in the public interest to disclose prosecution material under sections 3(6), 7A(8) or 8(5) of the Criminal Procedure and Investigations Act 1996; and

'Registrar' means the Registrar of Criminal Appeals or a court officer acting with the Registrar's authority.

(2) Definitions of some other expressions are in the rules in which they apply.

References to Acts of Parliament and to Statutory Instruments   R-6

2.3   In these Rules, where a rule refers to an Act of Parliament or to subordinate legislation by title and year, subsequent references to that Act or to that legislation in the rule are shortened: so, for example, after a reference to the Criminal Procedure and Investigations Act 1996 that Act is called 'the 1996 Act'; and after a reference to the Criminal Procedure and Investigations Act 1996 (Defence Disclosure Time Limits) Regulations 2011 those Regulations are called 'the 2011 Regulations'.

Representatives   R-7

2.4   (1) Under these Rules, unless the context makes it clear that something different is meant, any-thing that a party may or must do may be done—
         (a) by a legal representative on that party's behalf;
         (b) by a person with the corporation's written authority, where that corporation is a defendant;
         (c) with the help of a parent, guardian or other suitable supporting adult where that party is a defendant—
              (i)   who is under 18, or
              (ii) whose understanding of what the case involves is limited.
       (2) A member, officer or employee of a prosecutor may, on the prosecutor's behalf—
         (a) serve on the magistrates' court officer, or present to a magistrates' court, an information under section 1 of the Magistrates' Courts Act 1980; or
         (b) issue a written charge and requisition under section 29 of the Criminal Justice Act 2003.

CRIMINAL PROCEDURE RULES   PART 3   CASE MANAGEMENT

The scope of this Part   R-8

3.1   This Part applies to the management of each case in a magistrates' court and in the Crown Court (including an appeal to the Crown Court) until the conclusion of that case.

The duty of the court   R-9

3.2   (1) The court must further the overriding objective by actively managing the case.
       (2) Active case management includes—
         (a) the early identification of the real issues;
         (b) the early identification of the needs of witnesses;
         (c) achieving certainty as to what must be done, by whom, and when, in particular by the early setting of a timetable for the progress of the case;
         (d) monitoring the progress of the case and compliance with directions;
         (e) ensuring that evidence, whether disputed or not, is presented in the shortest and clearest way;
         (f) discouraging delay, dealing with as many aspects of the case as possible on the same occasion, and avoiding unnecessary hearings;
         (g) encouraging the participants to co-operate in the progression of the case; and
         (h) making use of technology.
       (3) The court must actively manage the case by giving any direction appropriate to the needs of that case as early as possible.

The duty of the parties   R-10

3.3   Each party must—
         (a) actively assist the court in fulfilling its duty under rule 3.2, without or if necessary with a direction; and
         (b) apply for a direction if needed to further the overriding objective.

Case progression officers and their duties   R-11

3.4   (1) At the beginning of the case each party must, unless the court otherwise directs—
         (a) nominate an individual responsible for progressing that case; and
         (b) tell other parties and the court who he is and how to contact him.
       (2) In fulfilling its duty under rule 3.2, the court must where appropriate—
         (a) nominate a court officer responsible for progressing the case; and
         (b) make sure the parties know who he is and how to contact him.
       (3) In this Part a person nominated under this rule is called a case progression officer.
       (4) A case progression officer must—
         (a) monitor compliance with directions;
         (b) make sure that the court is kept informed of events that may affect the progress of that case;
         (c) make sure that he can be contacted promptly about the case during ordinary business hours;

(d) act promptly and reasonably in response to communications about the case; and

(e) if he will be unavailable, appoint a substitute to fulfil his duties and inform the other case progression officers.

R-12   **The court's case management powers**

3.5   (1) In fulfilling its duty under rule 3.2 the court may give any direction and take any step actively to manage a case unless that direction or step would be inconsistent with legislation, including these Rules.

(2) In particular, the court may—

(a) nominate a judge, magistrate or justices' legal adviser to manage the case;

(b) give a direction on its own initiative or on application by a party;

(c) ask or allow a party to propose a direction;

(d) for the purpose of giving directions, receive applications and representations by letter, by telephone or by any other means of electronic communication, and conduct a hearing by such means;

(e) give a direction—

(i) at a hearing, in public or in private, or

(ii) without a hearing;

(f) fix, postpone, bring forward, extend or cancel a hearing;

(g) shorten or extend (even after it has expired) a time limit fixed by a direction;

(h) require that issues in the case should be—

(i) identified in writing,

(ii) determined separately, and decide in what order they will be determined; and

(i) specify the consequences of failing to comply with a direction.

(3) A magistrates' court may give a direction that will apply in the Crown Court if the case is to continue there.

(4) The Crown Court may give a direction that will apply in a magistrates' court if the case is to continue there.

(5) Any power to give a direction under this Part includes a power to vary or revoke that direction.

(6) If a party fails to comply with a rule or a direction, the court may—

(a) fix, postpone, bring forward, extend, cancel or adjourn a hearing;

(b) exercise its powers to make a costs order; and

(c) impose such other sanction as may be appropriate.

R-13   **Application to vary a direction**

3.6   (1) A party may apply to vary a direction if—

(a) the court gave it without a hearing;

(b) the court gave it at a hearing in his absence; or

(c) circumstances have changed.

(2) A party who applies to vary a direction must—

(a) apply as soon as practicable after he becomes aware of the grounds for doing so; and

(b) give as much notice to the other parties as the nature and urgency of his application permits.

R-14   **Agreement to vary a time limit fixed by a direction**

3.7   (1) The parties may agree to vary a time limit fixed by a direction, but only if—

(a) the variation will not—

(i) affect the date of any hearing that has been fixed, or

(ii) significantly affect the progress of the case in any other way;

(b) the court has not prohibited variation by agreement; and

(c) the court's case progression officer is promptly informed.

(2) The court's case progression officer must refer the agreement to the court if he doubts the condition in paragraph (1)(a) is satisfied.

R-15   **Case preparation and progression**

3.8   (1) At every hearing, if a case cannot be concluded there and then the court must give directions so that it can be concluded at the next hearing or as soon as possible after that.

(2) At every hearing the court must, where relevant—

(a) if the defendant is absent, decide whether to proceed nonetheless;

(b) take the defendant's plea (unless already done) or if no plea can be taken then find out whether the defendant is likely to plead guilty or not guilty;

(c) set, follow or revise a timetable for the progress of the case, which may include a timetable for any hearing including the trial or (in the Crown Court) the appeal;

(d) in giving directions, ensure continuity in relation to the court and to the parties' representatives where that is appropriate and practicable; and

(e) where a direction has not been complied with, find out why, identify who was responsible, and take appropriate action.

(3) In order to prepare for a trial in the Crown Court—

    (a) the court must conduct a plea and case management hearing unless the circumstances make that unnecessary;

    (b) the defendant must notify the court officer of the identity of the intended defence trial advocate—

        (i) as soon as practicable, and in any event no later than the day of the plea and case management hearing (if there is one),

        (ii) in writing, or orally at the plea and case management hearing (if there is one);

    (c) the defendant must notify the court officer in writing of any change in the identity of the intended defence trial advocate as soon as practicable, and in any event not more than 5 business days after that change.

(4) In order to prepare for the trial, the court must take every reasonable step—

    (a) to encourage and to facilitate the attendance of witnesses when they are needed; and

    (b) to facilitate the participation of any person, including the defendant.

(5) Facilitating the participation of the defendant includes finding out whether the defendant needs interpretation because—

    (a) the defendant does not speak or understand English; or

    (b) the defendant has a hearing or speech impediment.

(6) Where the defendant needs interpretation—

    (a) the court officer must arrange for interpretation to be provided at every hearing which the defendant is due to attend;

    (b) interpretation may be by an intermediary where the defendant has a speech impediment, without the need for a defendant's evidence direction;

    (c) on application or on its own initiative, the court may require a written translation to be provided for the defendant of any document or part of a document, unless—

        (i) translation of that document, or part, is not needed to explain the case against the defendant, or

        (ii) the defendant agrees to do without and the court is satisfied that the agreement is clear and voluntary and that the defendant has had legal advice or otherwise understands the consequences;

    (d) on application by the defendant, the court must give any direction which the court thinks appropriate, including a direction for interpretation by a different interpreter, where —

        (i) no interpretation is provided,

        (ii) no translation is ordered or provided in response to a previous application by the defendant, or

        (iii) the defendant complains about the quality of interpretation or of any translation.

Readiness for trial or appeal   R-16

3.9 (1) This rule applies to a party's preparation for trial or appeal, and in this rule and rule 3.10 trial includes any hearing at which evidence will be introduced.

    (2) In fulfilling his duty under rule 3.3, each party must—

        (a) comply with directions given by the court;

        (b) take every reasonable step to make sure his witnesses will attend when they are needed;

        (c) make appropriate arrangements to present any written or other material; and

        (d) promptly inform the court and the other parties of anything that may—

            (i) affect the date or duration of the trial or appeal, or

            (ii) significantly affect the progress of the case in any other way.

    (3) The court may require a party to give a certificate of readiness.

Conduct of a trial or an appeal   R-17

3.10 In order to manage the trial or an appeal, the court—

    (a) must establish, with the active assistance of the parties, what are the disputed issues;

    (b) must consider setting a timetable that—

        (i) takes account of those issues and any timetable proposed by a party, and

        (ii) may limit the duration of any stage of the hearing;

    (c) may require a party to identify—

        (i) which witnesses that party wants to give evidence in person,

        (ii) the order in which that party wants those witnesses to give their evidence, (iii)　whether that party requires an order compelling the attendance of a witness,

(iv)　what arrangements are desirable to facilitate the giving of evidence by a witness,

(v)　what arrangements are desirable to facilitate the participation of any other person, including the defendant,

(vi)　what written evidence that party intends to introduce,

(vii)　what other material, if any, that person intends to make available to the court in the presentation of the case,

(viii)　whether that party intends to raise any point of law that could affect the conduct of the trial or appeal, and

(d)　may limit—

(i)　the examination, cross-examination or re-examination of a witness, and

(ii)　the duration of any stage of the hearing.

R-18　Case management forms and records

3.11　(1)　The case management forms set out in the Practice Direction must be used, and where there is no form then no specific formality is required.

(2)　The court must make available to the parties a record of directions given.

(3)　Where a person is entitled or required to attend a hearing, the court officer must give as much notice as reasonably practicable to—

(a)　that person; and

(b)　that person's custodian (if any).

Criminal Practice Directions　　Part 3　　Case Management

PD-2　CPD I General matters 3A: CASE MANAGEMENT

3A.1　To avoid unnecessary and wasted hearings, the parties should be allowed adequate time to prepare, having regard to the time limits for applications and notices set by the Criminal Procedure Rules and by other legislation. When those time limits have expired, the parties will be expected to be fully prepared.

3A.2　The required forms and guidance notes can all be found in Annex D. PDF and Word versions are available on the Criminal Procedure Rules pages of the Ministry of Justice website. The forms to be used in magistrates' courts contain directions some of which are determined by Criminal Procedure Rules or other legislation and some of which are discretionary, as explained in the guidance notes. All those directions apply in every case unless the court otherwise orders.

Cases to be tried in a magistrates' court or a youth court

3A.3　The trial preparation form authorised for use must be used. The form, read with the notes, constitutes a timetable for the effective preparation of a case and provides a list of all the matters that the court should consider in giving directions for trial.

Cases sent for trial in the Crown Court

3A.4　The magistrates' court that sends a case for trial should remind the parties of the time limits set by the Criminal Procedure Rules and other legislation applicable, in the standard form produced for the court by Her Majesty's Courts and Tribunals Service.

3A.5　In the magistrates' court's discretion, having consulted the Crown Court, it may give other directions for the preparation of the case: see rule 3.5(3) of the Criminal Procedure Rules. In particular, the magistrates' court may give directions for the case to be listed in the Crown Court for an early guilty plea hearing, a preliminary hearing or a plea and case management hearing, as appropriate.

Early guilty plea hearing

3A.6　The magistrates' court or the Crown Court may order an early guilty plea hearing, in accordance with directions given by the presiding judges, where a guilty plea is anticipated, to allow the Crown Court promptly to deal with such a case.

3A.7　Sentence should normally be passed at an early guilty plea hearing. The parties must prepare accordingly in advance of the hearing. This may include:

i)　addressing any issue arising from a basis of plea,

ii)　making timely application for a pre-sentence report and, if granted, ensuring that the Probation Service is provided with details of the offence(s) in respect of which the defendant intends to plead guilty, the details of any basis of plea(s) and of the defendant's current address and telephone number(s),

iii)　obtaining medical or other material necessary for sentencing, and

iv)　quantifying costs.

3A.8　The court must be notified promptly of any difficulty which may mean that sentence cannot be passed at the hearing so that an alternative date can be considered.

Preliminary hearings for cases sent for trial

3A.9 If no early guilty plea hearing is ordered, the magistrates' court or the Crown Court should order a preliminary hearing where:
  (a) there are case management issues which call for such a hearing;
  (b) the trial is likely to last for more than 4 weeks;
  (c) it would be desirable to set an early trial date; or
  (d) the defendant is a child or young person.
  If there is to be a preliminary hearing, it is preferable for this to be held between 14 and 21 days after the case is sent for trial.

Plea and case management hearings ('PCMH')

3A.10 Where the magistrates' court does not order an early guilty plea hearing or a preliminary hearing, it should order a plea and case management hearing to be held within about:
  (a) 13 weeks after sending for trial, where a defendant is in custody; or
  (b) 16 weeks after sending for trial, where a defendant is on bail.

3A.11 Those periods accommodate the periods fixed by the relevant rules and other legislation for the service of:
  (a) the prosecution case papers (see rule 9.15 of the Criminal Procedure Rules, and the regulations to which that rule refers);
  (b) prosecution initial disclosure (see rule 22.2 of the Criminal Procedure Rules, and the legislation to which that rule refers);
  (c) the indictment (see rule 14.1 of the Criminal Procedure Rules);
  (d) the defence statement and witness notice (see rule 22.4 of the Criminal Procedure Rules, and the legislation to which that rule refers);
  (e) any defence application to dismiss the charges (see rule 9.16 of the Criminal Procedure Rules, and the legislation to which that rule refers);
  (f) any defence application for prosecution disclosure (see rule 22.5 of the Criminal Procedure Rules, and the legislation to which that rule refers);
  (g) any defence application under Part 36 of the Criminal Procedure Rules (evidence of a complainant's previous sexual behaviour); and
  (h) the prosecution response to any such application.

3A.12 Where the parties realistically expect to have completed these preparatory steps in less time than that, then the magistrates' court should order the PCMH to be held earlier. But it will not normally be appropriate to order that the PCMH be held on a date before the expiry of at least 4 weeks from the date on which the prosecutor expects to serve the prosecution case papers, to allow the defence a proper opportunity to consider them and give a defence statement. To order that a PCMH be held before the parties have had a reasonable opportunity to complete their preparation in accordance with the Criminal Procedure Rules risks compromising the effectiveness of this most important pre-trial hearing and risks wasting their time and that of the court.

3A.13 Active case management at the PCMH is essential, to reduce the number of ineffective, cracked and vacated trials and delays during the trial to resolve legal issues. The effectiveness of a PCMH hearing in a contested case depends in large measure upon preparation by all concerned and upon the presence of the trial advocate, or an advocate who is able to make decisions and give the court the assistance which the trial advocate could be expected to give. Resident Judges, in setting the listing policy, should ensure that list officers fix cases as far as possible to enable the trial advocate to conduct the PCMH and the trial.

3A.14 The PCMH form authorised for use provides a list of all the matters that the court should consider in giving directions for trial.

3A.15 Additional pre-trial hearings should be held only if needed for some compelling reason. Such hearings – often described informally as 'mentions' – are expensive and should actively be discouraged. Where necessary the power to give, vary or revoke a direction without a hearing should be used. Rule 3.9(3) of the Criminal Procedure Rules enables the court to require the parties' case progression officers to inform the Crown Court case progression officer that the case is ready for trial, that it will proceed as a trial on the date fixed and will take no more or less time than that previously ordered.

CPD I General matters 3B: Pagination and Indexing of Served Evidence

3B.1 The following directions apply to matters before the Crown Court, where:
  (a) there is an application to prefer a bill of indictment in relation to the case;
  (b) a person is sent for trial under section 51 of the Crime and Disorder Act 1998 (sending cases to the Crown Court), to the service of copies of the documents containing the evidence on which the charge or charges are based under Paragraph 1 of Schedule 3 to that Act; or
  (c) a defendant wishes to serve evidence.

PD-3

3B.2 A party who serves documentary evidence in the Crown Court should:

    (a) paginate each page in any bundle of statements and exhibits sequentially;

    (b) provide an index to each bundle of statements produced including the following information:

        i. the name of the case;

        ii. the author of each statement;

        iii. the start page number of the witness statement;

        iv. the end page number of the witness statement.

    (c) provide an index to each bundle of documentary and pictorial exhibits produced, including the following information:

        i. the name of the case;

        ii. the exhibit reference;

        iii. a short description of the exhibit;

        iv. the start page number of the exhibit;

        v. the end page number of the exhibit;

        vi. where possible, the name of the person producing the exhibit should be added.

3B.3 Where additional documentary evidence is served, a party should paginate following on from the last page of the previous bundle or in a logical and sequential manner. A party should also provide notification of service of any amended index.

3B.4 The prosecution must ensure that the running total of the pages of prosecution evidence is easily identifiable on the most recent served bundle of prosecution evidence.

3B.5 For the purposes of these directions, the number of pages of prosecution evidence served on the court includes all:

    (a) witness statements;

    (b) documentary and pictorial exhibits;

    (c) records of interviews with the defendant; and

    (d) records of interviews with other defendants which form part of the served prosecution documents or which are included in any notice of additional evidence,

but does not include any document provided on CD-ROM or by other means of electronic communication.

PD-4   **CPD I General matters 3C: Abuse of Process Stay Applications**

3C.1 In all cases where a defendant in the Crown Court proposes to make an application to stay an indictment on the grounds of abuse of process, written notice of such application must be given to the prosecuting authority and to any co-defendant as soon as practicable after the defendant becomes aware of the grounds for doing so and not later than 14 days before the date fixed or warned for trial ("the relevant date"). Such notice must:

    (a) give the name of the case and the indictment number;

    (b) state the fixed date or the warned date as appropriate;

    (c) specify the nature of the application;

    (d) set out in numbered sub-paragraphs the grounds upon which the application is to be made;

    (e) be copied to the chief listing officer at the court centre where the case is due to be heard.

3C.2 Any co-defendant who wishes to make a like application must give a like notice not later than seven days before the relevant date, setting out any additional grounds relied upon.

3C.3 In relation to such applications, the following automatic directions shall apply:

    (a) the advocate for the applicant(s) must lodge with the court and serve on all other parties a skeleton argument in support of the application, at least five clear working days before the relevant date. If reference is to be made to any document not in the existing trial documents, a paginated and indexed bundle of such documents is to be provided with the skeleton argument;

    (b) the advocate for the prosecution must lodge with the court and serve on all other parties a responsive skeleton argument at least two clear working days before the relevant date, together with a supplementary bundle if appropriate.

3C.4 All skeleton arguments must specify any propositions of law to be advanced (together with the authorities relied upon in support, with paragraph references to passages relied upon) and, where appropriate, include a chronology of events and a list of dramatis personae. In all instances where reference is made to a document, the reference in the trial documents or supplementary bundle is to be given.

3C.5 The above time limits are minimum time limits. In appropriate cases, the court will order longer lead times. To this end, in all cases where defence advocates are, at the time of the preliminary hearing or as soon as practicable after the case has been sent, considering the possibility of an abuse of process application, this must be raised with the judge dealing with the matter, who will order a different timetable if appropriate, and may wish, in any event, to give additional directions about the conduct of the application. If the trial judge has not been identified, the matter should be raised with the Resident Judge.

CPD I General matters 3D: Vulnerable People in the Courts

PD-5

3D.1 In respect of eligibility for special measures, 'vulnerable' and 'intimidated' witnesses are defined in sections 16 and 17 of the Youth Justice and Criminal Evidence Act 1999 (as amended by the Coroners and Justice Act 2009); 'vulnerable' includes those under 18 years of age and people with a mental disorder or learning disability; a physical disorder or disability; or [who] are likely to suffer fear or distress in giving evidence because of their own circumstances or those relating to the case.

3D.2 However, many other people giving evidence in a criminal case, whether as a witness or defendant, may require assistance: the court is required to take 'every reasonable step' to encourage and facilitate the attendance of witnesses and to facilitate the participation of any person, including the defendant (Rule 3.8(4) (a) and (b)). This includes enabling a witness or defendant to give their best evidence, and enabling a defendant to comprehend the proceedings and engage fully with his or her defence. The pre-trial and trial process should, so far as necessary, be adapted to meet those ends. Regard should be had to the welfare of a young defendant as required by section 44 of the Children and Young Persons Act 1933, and generally to Parts 1 and 3 of the Criminal Procedure Rules (the overriding objective and the court's powers of case management).

3D.3 Under Part 3 of the Rules, the court must identify the needs of witnesses at an early stage (Rule 3.2(2) (b)) and may require the parties to identify arrangements to facilitate the giving of evidence and participation in the trial (Rule 3.10(c) (iv) and (v)). There are various statutory special measures that the court may utilise to assist a witness in giving evidence. Part 29 of the Rules gives the procedures to be followed. Courts should note the 'primary rule' which requires the court to give a direction for a special measure to assist a child witness or qualifying witness and that in such cases an application to the court is not required (rule 29.9).

3D.4 Court of Appeal decisions on this subject include a judgment from the Lord Chief Justice, Lord Judge in *R v Cox* [2012] EWCA Crim 549, [2012] 2 Cr App R 6; *R v Wills* [2011] EWCA Crim 1938, [2012] 1 Cr App R 2; and *R v E* [2011] EWCA Crim 3028, [2012] Crim LR 563.

3D.5 In *R v Wills*, the Court endorsed the approach taken by the report of the Advocacy Training Council (ATC) 'Raising the Bar: the Handling of Vulnerable Witnesses, Victims and Defendants in Court' (2011). The report includes and recommends the use of 'toolkits' to assist advocates as they prepare to question vulnerable people at court: http://www.advocacytrainingcouncil.org/vulnerable-witnesses/raising-the-bar

3D.6 Further toolkits are available through the Advocate's Gateway which is managed by the ATC's Management Committee: http://www.theadvocatesgateway.org/

3D.7 These toolkits represent best practice. Advocates should consult and follow the relevant guidance whenever they prepare to question a young or otherwise vulnerable witness or defendant. Judges may find it helpful to refer advocates to this material and to use the toolkits in case management.

3D.8 'Achieving Best Evidence in Criminal Proceedings' (Ministry of Justice 2011) describes best practice in preparation for the investigative interview and trial: http://www.cps.gov.uk/publications/docs/best_ evidence_in_criminal_proceedings.pdf.

CPD I General matters 3E: Ground Rules Hearings to Plan the Questioning of a Vulnerable Witness or Defendant

PD-6

3E.1 The judiciary is responsible for controlling questioning. Over-rigorous or repetitive cross-examination of a child or vulnerable witness should be stopped. Intervention by the judge, magistrates or intermediary (if any) is minimised if questioning, taking account of the individual's communication needs, is discussed in advance and ground rules are agreed and adhered to.

3E.2 Discussion of ground rules is required in all intermediary trials where they must be discussed between the judge or magistrates, advocates and intermediary before the witness gives evidence. The intermediary must be present but is not required to take the oath (the intermediary's declaration is made just before the witness gives evidence).

3E.3 Discussion of ground rules is good practice, even if no intermediary is used, in all young witness cases and in other cases where a witness or defendant has communication needs. Discussion before the day of trial is preferable to give advocates time to adapt their questions to the witness' needs. It may be helpful for a trial practice note of boundaries to be created at the end of the discussion. The judge may use such a document in ensuring that the agreed ground rules are complied with.

3E.4　All witnesses, including the defendant and defence witnesses, should be enabled to give the best evidence they can. In relation to young and/or vulnerable people, this may mean departing radically from traditional cross-examination. The form and extent of appropriate cross-examination will vary from case to case. For adult non vulnerable witnesses an advocate will usually put his case so that the witness will have the opportunity of commenting upon it and/or answering it. When the witness is young or otherwise vulnerable, the court may dispense with the normal practice and impose restrictions on the advocate 'putting his case' where there is a risk of a young or otherwise vulnerable witness failing to understand, becoming distressed or acquiescing to leading questions. Where limitations on questioning are necessary and appropriate, they must be clearly defined. The judge has a duty to ensure that they are complied with and should explain them to the jury and the reasons for them. If the advocate fails to comply with the limitations, the judge should give relevant directions to the jury when that occurs and prevent further questioning that does not comply with the ground rules settled upon in advance. Instead of commenting on inconsistencies during cross-examination, following discussion between the judge and the advocates, the advocate or judge may point out important inconsistencies after (instead of during) the witness's evidence. The judge should also remind the jury of these during summing up. The judge should be alert to alleged inconsistencies that are not in fact inconsistent, or are trivial.

3E.5　If there is more than one defendant, the judge should not permit each advocate to repeat the questioning of a vulnerable witness. In advance of the trial, the advocates should divide the topics between them, with the advocate for the first defendant leading the questioning, and the advocate(s) for the other defendant(s) asking only ancillary questions relevant to their client's case, without repeating the questioning that has already taken place on behalf of the other defendant(s).

3E.6　In particular in a trial of a sexual offence, 'body maps' should be provided for the witness' use. If the witness needs to indicate a part of the body, the advocate should ask the witness to point to the relevant part on the body map. In sex cases, judges should not permit advocates to ask the witness to point to a part of the witness' own body. Similarly, photographs of the witness' body should not be shown around the court while the witness is giving evidence.

PD-7　CPD I General matters 3F: Intermediaries

3F.1　Intermediaries are communication specialists (not supporters or expert witnesses) whose role is to facilitate communication between the witness and the court, including the advocates. Intermediaries are independent of the parties and owe their duty to the court (see Registered Intermediaries Procedural Guidance Manual, Ministry of Justice, 2012): http://www.cps.gov.uk/publications/docs/RI_ProceduralGuidanceManual_2012.pdf

3F.2　Intermediaries for witnesses, with the exception of defendants, are one of the special measures available under the Youth Justice and Criminal Evidence Act 1999 and Part 29 of the Criminal Procedure Rules.

3F.3　There is currently no statutory provision in force for intermediaries for defendants. Section 104 of the Coroners and Justice Act 2009 (not yet implemented) creates a new section 33BA of the Youth Justice and Criminal Evidence Act 1999. This will provide an intermediary to an eligible defendant only while giving evidence. A court may use its inherent powers to appoint an intermediary to assist the defendant's communication at trial (either solely when giving evidence or throughout the trial) and, where necessary, in preparation for trial: *R (AS) v Great Yarmouth Youth Court* [2011] EWHC 2059 (Admin), [2012] Crim LR 478; *R v H* [2003] EWCA Crim 1208, Times, April 15, 2003; *R (C) v Sevenoaks Youth Court* [2009] EWHC 3088 (Admin), [2010] 1 All ER 735; *R (D) v Camberwell Green Youth Court*, [2005] UKHL 4, [2005] 1 WLR 393, [2005] 2 Cr App R 1; *R (TP) v West London Youth Court* [2005] EWHC 2583 (Admin), [2006] 1 WLR 1219, [2006] 1 Cr App R 25.

3F.4　Ministry of Justice regulation only applies to Registered Intermediaries appointed for prosecution and defence witnesses through its Witness Intermediary Scheme. All defendant intermediaries – professionally qualified or otherwise – are 'non-registered' in this context, even though they may be a Registered Intermediary in respect of witnesses. Even where a judge concludes he has a common law power to direct the provision of an intermediary, the direction will be ineffective if no intermediary can be identified for whom funding would be available.

3F.5　Assessment should be considered if a child or young person under 18 seems unlikely to be able to recognise a problematic question or, even if able to do so, may be reluctant to say so to a questioner in a position of authority. Studies suggest that the majority of young witnesses, across all age groups, fall into one or other of these categories. For children aged 11 years and under in particular, there should be a presumption that an intermediary assessment is appropriate. Once the child's individual requirements are known and discussed at the ground rules hearing, the intermediary may agree that his or her presence is not needed for the trial.

3F.6 In the absence of an intermediary for the defendant, trials should not be stayed where an asserted unfairness can be met by the trial judge adapting the trial process with appropriate and necessary caution (*R v Cox* [2012] EWCA Crim 549, [2012] 2 Cr App R 6). This includes setting ground rules for all witness testimony to help the defendant follow proceedings; for example, directing that all witness evidence be adduced by simple questions, with witnesses asked to answer in short sentences; and short periods of evidence, followed by breaks to enable the defendant to relax and for counsel to summarise the evidence for him and to take further instructions.

Photographs of court facilities

3F.7 Resident Judges in the Crown Court or the Chief Clerk or other responsible person in the magistrates' courts should, in consultation with HMCTS managers responsible for court security matters, develop a policy to govern under what circumstances photographs or other visual recordings may be made of court facilities, such as a live link room, to assist vulnerable or child witnesses to familiarise themselves with the setting, so as to be enabled to give their best evidence. For example, a photograph may provide a helpful reminder to a witness whose court visit has taken place sometime earlier. Resident Judges should tend to permit photographs to be taken for this purpose by intermediaries or supporters, subject to whatever restrictions the Resident Judge or responsible person considers to be appropriate, having regard to the security requirements of the court.

CPD I General matters 3G: Vulnerable Defendants

PD-8

Before the trial, sentencing or appeal

3G.1 If a vulnerable defendant, especially one who is young, is to be tried jointly with one who is not, the court should consider at the plea and case management hearing, or at a case management hearing in a magistrates' court, whether the vulnerable defendant should be tried on his own, but should only so order if satisfied that a fair trial cannot be achieved by use of appropriate special measures or other support for the defendant. If a vulnerable defendant is tried jointly with one who is not, the court should consider whether any of the modifications set out in this direction should apply in the circumstances of the joint trial and, so far as practicable, make orders to give effect to any such modifications.

3G.2 It may be appropriate to arrange that a vulnerable defendant should visit, out of court hours and before the trial, sentencing or appeal hearing, the courtroom in which that hearing is to take place so that he or she can familiarise him or herself with it.

3G.3 Where an intermediary is being used to help the defendant to communicate at court, the intermediary should accompany the defendant on his or her pre-trial visit. The visit will enable the defendant to familiarise him or herself with the layout of the court, and may include matters such as: where the defendant will sit, either in the dock or otherwise; court officials (what their roles are and where they sit); who else might be in the court, for example those in the public gallery and press box; the location of the witness box; basic court procedure; and the facilities available in the court.

3G.4 If the defendant's use of the live link is being considered, he or she should have an opportunity to have a practice session.

3G.5 If any case against a vulnerable defendant has attracted or may attract widespread public or media interest, the assistance of the police should be enlisted to try and ensure that the defendant is not, when attending the court, exposed to intimidation, vilification or abuse. Section 41 of the Criminal Justice Act 1925 prohibits the taking of photographs of defendants and witnesses (among others) in the court building or in its precincts, or when entering or leaving those precincts. A direction reminding media representatives of the prohibition may be appropriate. The court should also be ready at this stage, if it has not already done so, where relevant to make a reporting restriction under section 39 of the Children and Young Persons Act 1933 or, on an appeal to the Crown Court from a youth court, to remind media representatives of the application of section 49 of that Act.

3G.6 The provisions of the Practice Direction accompanying Part 16 should be followed.

The trial, sentencing or appeal hearing

3G.7 Subject to the need for appropriate security arrangements, the proceedings should, if practicable, be held in a courtroom in which all the participants are on the same or almost the same level.

3G.8   Subject again to the need for appropriate security arrangements, a vulnerable defendant, especially if he is young, should normally, if he wishes, be free to sit with members of his family or others in a like relationship, and with some other suitable supporting adult such as a social worker, and in a place which permits easy, informal communication with his legal representatives. The court should ensure that a suitable supporting adult is available throughout the course of the proceedings.

3G.9   It is essential that at the beginning of the proceedings, the court should ensure that what is to take place has been explained to a vulnerable defendant in terms he or she can understand and, at trial in the Crown Court, it should ensure in particular that the role of the jury has been explained. It should remind those representing the vulnerable defendant and the supporting adult of their responsibility to explain each step as it takes place and, at trial, explain the possible consequences of a guilty verdict and credit for a guilty plea. The court should also remind any intermediary of their responsibility to ensure that the vulnerable defendant has understood the explanations given to him/her. Throughout the trial the court should continue to ensure, by any appropriate means, that the defendant understands what is happening and what has been said by those on the bench, the advocates and witnesses.

3G.10   A trial should be conducted according to a timetable which takes full account of a vulnerable defendant's ability to concentrate. Frequent and regular breaks will often be appropriate. The court should ensure, so far as practicable, that the whole trial is conducted in clear language that the defendant can understand and that evidence in chief and cross-examination are conducted using questions that are short and clear. The conclusions of the 'ground rules' hearing should be followed, and advocates should use and follow the 'toolkits' as discussed above.

3G.11   A vulnerable defendant who wishes to give evidence by live link, in accordance with section 33A of the Youth Justice and Criminal Evidence Act 1999, may apply for a direction to that effect; the procedure in Section 4 of Part 29 of the Rules should be followed. Before making such a direction, the court must be satisfied that it is in the interests of justice to do so and that the use of a live link would enable the defendant to participate more effectively as a witness in the proceedings. The direction will need to deal with the practical arrangements to be made, including the identity of the person or persons who will accompany him or her.

3G.12   In the Crown Court, the judge should consider whether robes and wigs should be worn, and should take account of the wishes of both a vulnerable defendant and any vulnerable witness. It is generally desirable that those responsible for the security of a vulnerable defendant who is in custody, especially if he or she is young, should not be in uniform, and that there should be no recognisable police presence in the courtroom save for good reason.

3G.13   The court should be prepared to restrict attendance by members of the public in the courtroom to a small number, perhaps limited to those with an immediate and direct interest in the outcome. The court should rule on any challenged claim to attend. However, facilities for reporting the proceedings (subject to any restrictions under section 39 or 49 of the Children and Young Persons Act 1933) must be provided. The court may restrict the number of reporters attending in the courtroom to such number as is judged practicable and desirable. In ruling on any challenged claim to attend in the court room for the purpose of reporting, the court should be mindful of the public's general right to be informed about the administration of justice.

3G.14   Where it has been decided to limit access to the courtroom, whether by reporters or generally, arrangements should be made for the proceedings to be relayed, audibly and if possible visually, to another room in the same court complex to which the media and the public have access if it appears that there will be a need for such additional facilities. Those making use of such a facility should be reminded that it is to be treated as an extension of the courtroom and that they are required to conduct themselves accordingly.

PD-9   **CPD I General matters 3H: Wales and the Welsh Language: Devolution Issues**

3H.1   These are the subject of Practice Direction: (Supreme Court) (Devolution Issues) [1999] 1 WLR 1592; [1999] 3 All ER 466; [1999] 2 Cr App R 486, to which reference should be made.

PD-10   **CPD I General matters 3J: Wales and the Welsh Language: Applications for Evidence to be given in Welsh**

3J.1   If a defendant in a court in England asks to give or call evidence in the Welsh language, the case should not be transferred to Wales. In ordinary circumstances, interpreters can be provided on request.

**CPD I General matters 3K: Wales and the Welsh Language: Use of the Welsh Language in Courts   PD-11
in Wales**

3K.1   The purpose of this direction is to reflect the principle of the Welsh Language Act 1993 that, in the
administration of justice in Wales, the English and Welsh languages should be treated on a basis of
equality.

General

3K.2   It is the responsibility of the legal representatives in every case in which the Welsh language may be
used by any witness or party, or in any document which may be placed before the court, to inform
the court of that fact, so that appropriate arrangements can be made for the listing of the case.

3K.3   Any party or witness is entitled to use Welsh in a magistrates' court in Wales without giving prior
notice. Arrangements will be made for hearing such cases in accordance with the 'Magistrates'
Courts' Protocol for Listing Cases where the Welsh Language is used' (January 2008) which is available on the Judiciary's website: http://www.judiciary.gov.uk/NR/exeres/57AD4763-F265-47B9-8
A35-0442E08160E6. See also rule 37.13.

3K.4   If the possible use of the Welsh language is known at the time of sending or appeal to the Crown
Court, the court should be informed immediately after sending or when the notice of appeal is
lodged. Otherwise, the court should be informed as soon as the possible use of the Welsh language
becomes known.

3K.5   If costs are incurred as a result of failure to comply with these directions, a wasted costs order may
be made against the defaulting party and/or his legal representatives.

3K.6   The law does not permit the selection of jurors in a manner which enables the court to discover
whether a juror does or does not speak Welsh, or to secure a jury whose members are bilingual, to
try a case in which the Welsh language may be used.

Preliminary and plea and case management hearings

3K.7   An advocate in a case in which the Welsh language may be used must raise that matter at the preliminary and/or the plea and case management hearing and endorse details of it on the advocates'
questionnaire, so that appropriate directions may be given for the progress of the case.

Listing

3K.8   The listing officer, in consultation with the resident judge, should ensure that a case in which the
Welsh language may be used is listed:
(a)   wherever practicable before a Welsh speaking judge; and
(b)   in a court in Wales with simultaneous translation facilities.

Interpreters

3K.9   Whenever an interpreter is needed to translate evidence from English into Welsh or from Welsh into
English, the court listing officer in whose court the case is to be heard shall contact the Welsh
Language Unit who will ensure the attendance of an accredited interpreter.

Jurors

3K.10   The jury bailiff, when addressing the jurors at the start of their period of jury service, shall inform
them that each juror may take an oath or affirm in Welsh or English as he wishes.

3K.11   After the jury has been selected to try a case, and before it is sworn, the court officer swearing in the
jury shall inform the jurors in open court that each juror may take an oath or affirm in Welsh or
English as he wishes. A juror who takes the oath or affirms in Welsh should not be asked to repeat
it in English.

3K.12   Where Welsh is used by any party or witness in a trial, an accredited interpreter will provide simultaneous translation from Welsh to English for the jurors who do not speak Welsh. There is no provision for the translation of evidence from English to Welsh for a Welsh speaking juror.

3K.13   The jury's deliberations must be conducted in private with no other person present and therefore
no interpreter may be provided to translate the discussion for the benefit of one or more of the
jurors.

Witnesses

3K.14   When each witness is called, the court officer administering the oath or affirmation shall inform
the witness that he may be sworn or affirm in Welsh or English, as he wishes. A witness who takes
the oath or affirms in Welsh should not be asked to repeat it in English.

Opening/closing of Crown Courts

3K.15 Unless it is not reasonably practicable to do so, the opening and closing of the court should be performed in Welsh and English.

Role of Liaison Judge

3K.16 If any question or problem arises concerning the implementation of these directions, contact should in the first place be made with the Liaison Judge for the Welsh language through the Wales Circuit Office:

> HMCTS WALES / GLITEM CYMRU
> 3rd Floor, Churchill House / 3ydd Llawr Tŷ Churchill
> Churchill Way / Ffordd Churchill
> Cardiff / Caerdydd
> CF10 2HH
> 029 2067 8300

CRIMINAL PROCEDURE RULES   PART 4   SERVICE OF DOCUMENTS

R-19 **When this Part applies**

4.1   The rules in this Part apply to the service of every document in a case to which these Rules apply, subject to any special rules in other legislation (including other Parts of these Rules) or in the Practice Direction.

R-20 **Methods of service**

4.2   (1) A document may be served by any of the methods described in rules 4.3 to 4.6 (subject to rule 4.7), or in rule 4.8.

       (2) Where a document may be served by electronic means, the general rule is that the person serving it must use that method.

R-21 **Service by handing over a document**

4.3   (1) A document may be served on—

       (a) an individual by handing it to him or her;

       (b) a corporation by handing it to a person holding a senior position in that corporation;

       (c) an individual or corporation who is legally represented in the case by handing it to that representative;

       (d) the prosecution by handing it to the prosecutor or to the prosecution representative;

       (e) the court officer by handing it to a court officer with authority to accept it at the relevant court office; and

       (f) the Registrar of Criminal Appeals by handing it to a court officer with authority to accept it at the Criminal Appeal Office.

       (2) If an individual is under 18, a copy of a document served under paragraph (1)(a) must be handed to his or her parent, or another appropriate adult, unless no such person is readily available.

R-22 **Service by leaving or posting a document**

4.4   (1) A document may be served by addressing it to the person to be served and leaving it at the appropriate address for service under this rule or by sending it to that address by first class post or by the equivalent of first class post.

       (2) The address for service under this rule on—

       (a) an individual is an address where it is reasonably believed that he or she will receive it;

       (b) a corporation is its principal office, and if there is no readily identifiable principal office then any place where it carries on its activities or business;

       (c) an individual or corporation who is legally represented in the case is that representative's office;

       (d) the prosecution is the prosecutor's office;

       (e) the court officer is the relevant court office; and

       (f) the Registrar of Criminal Appeals is the Criminal Appeal Office, Royal Courts of Justice, Strand, London WC2A 2LL.

R-23 **Service by document exchange**

4.5   (1) This rule applies where—

       (a) the person to be served—

          (i) has given a DX box number, and

          (ii) has not refused to accept service by DX; or

     (b) the person to be served is legally represented in the case and the representative has given a DX box number.

(2) A document may be served by—

     (a) addressing it to that person or representative, as appropriate, at that DX box number; and

     (b) leaving it at—

         (i) the document exchange at which the addressee has that DX box number, or

         (ii) a document exchange at which the person serving it has a DX box number.

Service by electronic means   R-24

4.6 (1) This rule applies where—

     (a) the person to be served—

         (i) has given an electronic address, and

         (ii) has not refused to accept service by electronic means; or

     (b) the person to be served is legally represented in the case and the representative has given an electronic address.

(2) A document may be served by transmitting it by electronic means to that person or representative, as appropriate, at that address.

(3) Where a document is served under this rule the person serving it need not provide a paper copy as well.

Documents that must be served by specified methods   R-25

4.7 (1) The documents listed in paragraph (2) may be served—

     (a) on an individual, only under rule 4.3(1)(a) (handing over) or rule 4.4(1) and (2)(a) (leaving or posting); and

     (b) on a corporation only under rule 4.3(1)(b) (handing over) or rule 4.4(1) and (2)(b) (leaving or posting).

(2) Those documents are—

     (a) a summons, requisition or witness summons;

     (b) notice of an order under section 25 of the Road Traffic Offenders Act 1988;

     (c) a notice of registration under section 71(6) of that Act;

     (d) notice of a hearing to review the postponement of the issue of a warrant of detention or imprisonment under section 77(6) of the Magistrates' Courts Act 1980;

     (e) notice under section 86 of that Act of a revised date to attend a means inquiry;

     (f) any notice or document served under Part 19 (Bail and custody time limits);

     (g) notice under rule 37.15 of when and where an adjourned hearing will resume;

     (h) notice under rule 42.5(3) of an application to vary or discharge a compensation order;

     (i) notice under rule 42.10(2) of the location of the sentencing or enforcing court;

     (j) a collection notice, or notice requiring payment, served under rule 52.2(a).

(3) An application or written statement, and notice, under rule 62.9 alleging contempt of court may be served—

     (a) on an individual, only under rule 4.3(1)(a) (by handing it to him or her);

     (b) on a corporation, only under rule 4.3(1)(b) (by handing it to a person holding a senior position in that corporation).

Service by person in custody   R-26

4.8 (1) A person in custody may serve a document by handing it to the custodian addressed to the person to be served.

(2) The custodian must—

     (a) endorse it with the time and date of receipt;

     (b) record its receipt; and

     (c) forward it promptly to the addressee.

Service by another method   R-27

4.9 (1) The court may allow service of a document by a method—

     (a) other than those described in rules 4.3 to 4.6 and in rule 4.8;

     (b) other than one specified by rule 4.7, where that rule applies.

(2) An order allowing service by another method must specify—

     (a) the method to be used; and

     (b) the date on which the document will be served.

R-28   **Date of service**

4.10   (1)   A document served under rule 4.3 or rule 4.8 is served on the day it is handed over.

       (2)   Unless something different is shown, a document served on a person by any other method is served—

          (a)   in the case of a document left at an address, on the next business day after the day on which it was left;

          (b)   in the case of a document sent by first class post or by the equivalent of first class post, on the second business day after the day on which it was posted or despatched;

          (c)   in the case of a document served by document exchange, on the second business day after the day on which it was left at a document exchange allowed by rule 4.5;

          (d)   in the case of a document transmitted by electronic means, on the next business day after it was transmitted; and

          (e)   in any case, on the day on which the addressee responds to it if that is earlier.

       (3)   Unless something different is shown, a document produced by a court computer system is to be taken as having been sent by first class post or by the equivalent of first class post to the addressee on the business day after the day on which it was produced.

       (4)   Where a document is served on or by the court officer, 'business day' does not include a day on which the court office is closed.

R-29   **Proof of service**

4.11   The person who serves a document may prove that by signing a certificate explaining how and when it was served.

R-30   **Court's power to give directions about service**

4.12   (1)   The court may specify the time as well as the date by which a document must be—

          (a)   served under rule 4.3 or rule 4.8; or

          (b)   transmitted by electronic means, if it is served under rule 4.6.

       (2)   The court may treat a document as served if the addressee responds to it even if it was not served in accordance with the rules in this Part.

CRIMINAL PROCEDURE RULES   PART 5   FORMS AND COURT RECORDS

Section 1: forms

R-31   **Forms**

5.1   The forms set out in the Practice Direction and in the Criminal Costs Practice Direction must be used as appropriate in connection with the rules to which they apply.

R-32   **Forms in Welsh**

5.2   (1)   Any Welsh language form set out in the Practice Direction, or in the Criminal Costs Practice Direction, is for use in connection with proceedings in courts in Wales.

       (2)   Both a Welsh form and an English form may be contained in the same document.

       (3)   Where only a Welsh form, or only the corresponding English form, is served—

          (a)   the following words in Welsh and English must be added:

             'Darperir y ddogfen hon yn Gymraeg / Saesneg os bydd arnoch ei heisiau. Dylech wneud cais yn ddi-oed i (swyddog y llys) (rhodder yma'r cyfeiriad)

             This document will be provided in Welsh / English if you require it. You should apply immediately to (the court officer) (address)'; and

          (b)   the court officer, or the person who served the form, must, on request, supply the corresponding form in the other language to the person served.

R-33   **Signature of forms**

5.3   (1)   This rule applies where a form provides for its signature.

       (2)   Unless other legislation otherwise requires, or the court otherwise directs, signature may be by any written or electronic authentication of the form by, or with the authority of, the signatory.

Section 2: court records

R-34   **Duty to make records**

5.4   (1)   For each case, as appropriate, the court officer must record, by such means as the Lord Chancellor directs—

          (a)   each charge or indictment against the defendant;

          (b)   the defendant's plea to each charge or count;

(c) each acquittal, conviction, sentence, determination, direction or order;

(d) each decision about bail;

(e) the power exercised where the court commits or adjourns the case to another court—

    (i) for sentence, or

    (ii) for the defendant to be dealt with for breach of a community order, a deferred sentence, a conditional discharge, or a suspended sentence of imprisonment, imposed by that other court;

(f) the court's reasons for a decision, where legislation requires those reasons to be recorded;

(g) any appeal;

(h) each party's presence or absence at each hearing;

(i) any consent that legislation requires before the court can proceed with the case, or proceed to a decision;

(j) in a magistrates' court—

    (i) any indication of sentence given in connection with the allocation of a case for trial, and

    (ii) the registration of a fixed penalty notice for enforcement as a fine, and any related endorsement on a driving licence;

(k) in the Crown Court, any request for assistance or other communication about the case received from a juror;

(l) the identity of—

    (i) the prosecutor,

    (ii) the defendant,

    (iii) any other applicant to whom these Rules apply,

    (iv) any interpreter or intermediary;

    (v) the parties' legal representatives, if any, and

    (vi) the judge, magistrate or magistrates, justices' legal adviser or other person who made each recorded decision.

(m) where a defendant is entitled to attend a hearing, any agreement by the defendant to waive that right; and

(n) where interpretation is required for a defendant, any agreement by that defendant to do without the written translation of a document.

(2) Such records must include—

(a) each party's and representative's address, including any electronic address and telephone number available;

(b) the defendant's date of birth, if available; and

(c) the date of each event and decision recorded.

Recording and transcription of proceedings in the Crown Court   R-35

5.5 (1) Where someone may appeal to the Court of Appeal, the court officer must—

(a) arrange for the recording of the proceedings in the Crown Court, unless the court otherwise directs; and

(b) arrange for the transcription of such a recording if—

    (i) the Registrar wants such a transcript, or

    (ii) anyone else wants such a transcript (but that is subject to the restrictions in paragraph (2)).

(2) Unless the court otherwise directs, a person who transcribes a recording of proceedings under such arrangements—

(a) must not supply anyone other than the Registrar with a transcript of a recording of—

    (i) a hearing in private, or

    (ii) information to which reporting restrictions apply;

(b) subject to that, must supply any person with any transcript for which that person asks—

    (i) in accordance with the transcription arrangements made by the court officer, and

    (ii) on payment by that person of any fee prescribed.

(3) A party who wants to hear a recording of proceedings must—

(a) apply—

    (i) in writing to the Registrar, if an appeal notice has been served where Part 65 applies (Appeal to the Court of Appeal: general rules), or

    (ii) orally or in writing to the Crown Court officer;

(b) explain the reasons for the request; and

(c) pay any fee prescribed.

    (4) If the Crown Court or the Registrar so directs, the Crown Court officer must allow that party to hear a recording of—
        (a) a hearing in public;
        (b) a hearing in private, if the applicant was present at that hearing.

R-36   **Custody of case materials**

    5.6   Unless the court otherwise directs, in respect of each case the court officer may—
        (a) keep any evidence, application, representation or other material served by the parties; or
        (b) arrange for the whole or any part to be kept by some other appropriate person, subject to—
            (i) any condition imposed by the court, and
            (ii) the rules in Part 63 (Appeal to the Crown Court) and Part 65 (Appeal to the Court of Appeal: general rules) about keeping exhibits pending any appeal.

R-37   **Supply to a party of information or documents from records or case materials**

    5.7   (1) This rule applies where—
        (a) a party wants information, or a copy of a document, from records or case materials kept by the court officer (for example, in case of loss, or to establish what is retained); or
        (b) a person affected by an order made, or warrant issued, by the court wants such information or such a copy.
      (2) Such a party or person must—
        (a) apply to the court officer;
        (b) specify the information or document required; and
        (c) pay any fee prescribed.
      (3) The application—
        (a) may be made orally, giving no reasons, if paragraph (4) requires the court officer to supply the information or document requested;
        (b) must be in writing, unless the court otherwise permits, and must explain for what purpose the information is required, in any other case.
      (4) The court officer must supply to the applicant party or person —
        (a) a copy of any document served by, or on, that party or person (but not of any document not so served);
        (b) by word of mouth, or in writing, as requested—
            (i) information that was received from that party or person in the first place,
            (ii) information about the terms of any direction or order directed to that party or person, or made on an application by that party or person, or at a hearing in public,
            (iii) information about the outcome of the case.
      (5) If the court so directs, the court officer must supply to the applicant party or person, by word of mouth or in writing, as requested, information that paragraph (4) does not require the court officer to supply.
      (6) Where the information requested is about the grounds on which an order was made, or a warrant was issued, in the absence of the party or person applying for that information—
        (a) that party or person must also serve the request on the person who applied for the order or warrant;
        (b) if the person who applied for the order or warrant objects to the supply of the information requested, that objector must—
            (i) give notice of the objection not more than 14 days after service of the request (or within any longer period allowed by the court),
            (ii) serve that notice on the court officer and on the party or person requesting the information, and
            (iii) if the objector wants a hearing, explain why one is needed;
        (c) the court may determine the application for information at a hearing (which must be in private unless the court otherwise directs), or without a hearing;
        (d) the court must not permit the information requested to be supplied unless the person who applied for the order or warrant has had at least 14 days (or any longer period allowed by the court) in which to make representations.
      (7) A notice of objection under paragraph (6) must explain—
        (a) whether the objection is to the supply of any part of the information requested, or only to the supply of a specified part, or parts, of it;
        (b) whether the objection is to the supply of the information at any time, or only to its supply before a date or event specified by the objector; and
        (c) the grounds of the objection.

(8) Where a notice of objection under paragraph (6) includes material that the objector thinks ought not be revealed to the party or person applying for information, the objector must—
    (a) omit that material from the notice served on that party or person;
    (b) mark the material to show that it is only for the court; and
    (c) with that material include an explanation of why it has been withheld.

Supply to the public, including reporters, of information about a case   R-38

5.8 (1) This rule—
    (a) applies where a member of the public, including a reporter, wants information about a case from the court officer;
    (b) requires the court officer to publish information about cases due to be heard.
(2) A person who wants information about a case from the court officer must—
    (a) apply to the court officer;
    (b) specify the information requested; and
    (c) pay any fee prescribed.
(3) The application—
    (a) may be made orally, giving no reasons, if paragraph (4) requires the court officer to supply the information requested;
    (b) must be in writing, unless the court otherwise permits, and must explain for what purpose the information is required, in any other case.
(4) The court officer must supply to the applicant—
    (a) any information listed in paragraph (6), if—
        (i) the information is available to the court officer,
        (ii) the supply of the information is not prohibited by a reporting restriction, and
        (iii) the trial has not yet concluded, or the verdict was not more than 6 months ago; and
    (b) details of any reporting or access restriction ordered by the court.
(5) The court officer must supply that information—
    (a) by word of mouth; or
    (b) by such other arrangements as the Lord Chancellor directs.
(6) The information that paragraph (4) requires the court officer to supply is—
    (a) the date of any hearing in public, unless any party has yet to be notified of that date;
    (b) each alleged offence and any plea entered;
    (c) the court's decision at any hearing in public, including any decision about—
        (i) bail, or
        (ii) the committal, sending or transfer of the case to another court;
    (d) whether the case is under appeal;
    (e) the outcome of any trial and any appeal; and
    (f) the identity of—
        (i) the prosecutor,
        (ii) the defendant,
        (iii) the parties' representatives, including their addresses, and
        (iv) the judge, magistrate or magistrates, or justices' legal adviser by whom a decision at a hearing in public was made.
(7) If the court so directs, the court officer must—
    (a) supply to the applicant, by word of mouth, other information about the case; or
    (b) allow the applicant to inspect or copy a document, or part of a document, containing information about the case.
(8) The court may determine an application to which paragraph (7) applies—
    (a) at a hearing, in public or in private; or
    (b) without a hearing.
(9) The court officer must publish the information listed in paragraph (11) if—
    (a) the information is available to the court officer;
    (b) the hearing to which the information relates is due to take place in public; and
    (c) the publication of the information is not prohibited by a reporting restriction.
(10) The court officer must publish that information—
    (a) by notice displayed somewhere prominent in the vicinity of the court room in which the hearing is due to take place;
    (b) by such other arrangements as the Lord Chancellor directs, including arrangements for publication by electronic means; and
    (c) for no longer than 2 business days.

(11) The information that paragraph (9) requires the court officer to publish is—

    (a) the date, time and place of the hearing;

    (b) the identity of the defendant; and

    (c) such other information as it may be practicable to publish concerning—

        (i) the type of hearing,

        (ii) the identity of the court,

        (iii) the offence or offences alleged, and

        (iv) whether any reporting restriction applies.

R-39 **Supply of written certificate or extract from records**

5.9 (1) This rule applies where legislation—

    (a) allows a certificate of conviction or acquittal, or an extract from records kept by the court officer, to be introduced in evidence in criminal proceedings; or

    (b) requires such a certificate or extract to be supplied by the court officer to a specified person for a specified purpose.

  (2) A person who wants such a certificate or extract must—

    (a) apply in writing to the court officer;

    (b) specify the certificate or extract required;

    (c) explain under what legislation and for what purpose it is required; and

    (d) pay any fee prescribed.

  (3) If the application satisfies the requirements of that legislation, the court officer must supply the certificate or extract requested—

    (a) to a party;

    (b) unless the court otherwise directs, to any other applicant.

Criminal Practice Directions   Part 5   Forms and Court Records

PD-12 **CPD I General matters 5A: Forms**

5A.1 The forms at Annex E, or forms to that effect, are to be used in the criminal courts, in accordance with Rule 5.1.

5A.2 The forms at Annex D, the case management forms, must be used in the criminal courts, in accordance with Rule 3.11(1).

5A.3 The table at the beginning of each section lists the forms and:

    (a) shows the Rule in connection with which each applies;

    (b) describes each form.

5A.4 The forms may be amended or withdrawn from time to time, or new forms added, under the authority of the Lord Chief Justice.

PD-13 **CPD I General matters 5B: Access to Information Held by the Court**

5B.1 Open justice, as Lord Justice Toulson recently re-iterated in the case of *R (Guardian News and Media Ltd) v City of Westminster Magistrates' Court* [2012] EWCA Civ 420, [2013] QB 618, is a 'principle at the heart of our system of justice and vital to the rule of law.' There are exceptions but these 'have to be justified by some even more important principle.' However, the practical application of that undisputed principle, and the proper balancing of conflicting rights and principles, call for careful judgments to be made. The following is intended to provide some assistance to courts making decisions when asked to provide the public, including journalists, with access to or copies of information and documents held by the court. It is not a prescriptive list, as the court will have to consider all the circumstances of each individual case.

5B.2 It remains the responsibility of the recipient of information or documents to ensure that they comply with any and all restrictions such as reporting restrictions (see Part 16 and the accompanying Practice Direction).

5B.3 For the purposes of this direction, the word document includes images in photographic, digital including DVD format, video, CCTV or any other form.

5B.4 Certain information can and should be provided to the public on request, unless there are restrictions, such as reporting restrictions, imposed in that particular case. Rule 5.8(4) and 5.8(6) read together specify the information that the court officer will supply to the public; an oral application is acceptable and no reason need be given for the request. There is no requirement for the court officer to consider the non-disclosure provisions of the Data Protection Act 1998 as the exemption under section 35 applies to all disclosure made under 'any enactment. . .or by the order of a court', which includes under the Criminal Procedure Rules.

5B.5 If the information sought is not listed at Rule 5.8(6), Rule 5.8(7) will apply, and the provision of information is at the discretion of the court. The following guidance is intended to assist the court in exercising that discretion.

5B.6 A request for access to documents used in a criminal case should first be addressed to the party who presented them to the court. Prosecuting authorities are subject to the Freedom of Information Act 2000 and the Data Protection Act 1998 and their decisions are susceptible to review.

5B.7 If the request is from a journalist or media organisation, note that there is a protocol between ACPO, the CPS and the media entitled 'Publicity and the Criminal Justice System': http://www.cps.gov.uk/publications/agencies/mediaprotocol.html

There is additionally a protocol made under Rule 5.8(5)(b) between the media and HMCTS: http://www.newspapersoc.org.uk/sites/default/files/Docs/Protocol-for-Sharing-Court- Registers-and-C ourt-Lists-with-Local-Newspapers_September-2011.doc

This Practice Direction does not affect the operation of those protocols. Material should generally be sought under the relevant protocol before an application is made to the court.

5B.8 An application to which Rule 5.8(7) applies must be made in accordance with Rule 5.8; it must be in writing, unless the court permits otherwise, and 'must explain for what purpose the information is required.' A clear, detailed application, specifying the name and contact details of the applicant, whether or not he or she represents a media organisation, and setting out the reasons for the application and to what use the information will be put, will be of most assistance to the court. Applicants should state if they have requested the information under a protocol and include any reasons given for the refusal. Before considering such an application, the court will expect the applicant to have given notice of the request to the parties.

5B.9 The court will consider each application on its own merits. The burden of justifying a request for access rests on the applicant. Considerations to be taken into account will include:

  i. whether or not the request is for the purpose of contemporaneous reporting; a request after the conclusion of the proceedings will require careful scrutiny by the court;
  ii. the nature of the information or documents being sought;
  iii. the purpose for which they are required;
  iv. the stage of the proceedings at the time when the application is made;
  v. the value of the documents in advancing the open justice principle, including enabling the media to discharge its role, which has been described as a 'public watchdog', by reporting the proceedings effectively;
  vi. any risk of harm which access to them may cause to the legitimate interests of others; and
  vii. any reasons given by the parties for refusing to provide the material requested and any other representations received from the parties.

Further, all of the principles below are subject to any specific restrictions in the case. Courts should be aware that the risk of providing a document may reduce after a particular point in the proceedings, and when the material requested may be made available.

Documents read aloud in their entirety

5B.10 If a document has been read aloud to the court in its entirety, it should usually be provided on request, unless to do so would be disruptive to the court proceedings or place an undue burden on the court, the advocates or others. It may be appropriate and convenient for material to be provided electronically, if this can be done securely.

5B.11 Documents likely to fall into this category are:

  i. Opening notes;
  ii. Statements agreed under section 9 of the Criminal Justice Act 1967, including experts' reports, if read in their entirety;
  iii. Admissions made under section 10 of the Criminal Justice Act 1967.

Documents treated as read aloud in their entirety

5B.12 A document treated by the court as if it had been read aloud in public, though in fact it has been neither read nor summarised aloud, should generally be made available on request. The burden on the court, the advocates or others in providing the material should be considered, but the presumption in favour of providing the material is greater when the material has only been treated as having been read aloud. Again, subject to security considerations, it may be convenient for the material to be provided electronically.

5B.13 Documents likely to fall into this category include:

    i. Skeleton arguments;

    ii. Written submissions.

Documents read aloud in part or summarised aloud

5B.14 Open justice requires only access to the part of the document that has been read aloud. If a member of the public requests a copy of such a document, the court should consider whether it is proportionate to order one of the parties to produce a suitably redacted version. If not, access to the document is unlikely to be granted; however open justice will generally have been satisfied by the document having been read out in court.

5B.15 If the request comes from an accredited member of the press (see *Access by reporters* below), there may be circumstances in which the court orders that a copy of the whole document be shown to the reporter, or provided, subject to the condition that those matters that had not been read out to the court may not be used or reported. A breach of such an order would be treated as a contempt of court.

5B.16 Documents in this category are likely to include:

    i. Section 9 statements that are edited.

Jury bundles and exhibits (including video footage shown to the jury)

5B.17 The court should consider:

    i. whether access to the specific document is necessary to understand or effectively to report the case;

    ii. the privacy of third parties, such as the victim (in some cases, the reporting restriction imposed by section 1 of the Judicial Proceedings (Regulation of Reports) Act 1926 will apply (indecent or medical matter));

    iii. whether the reporting of anything in the document may be prejudicial to a fair trial in this or another case, in which case whether it may be necessary to make an order under section 4(2) of the Contempt of Court Act 1981.

The court may order one of the parties to provide a copy of certain pages (or parts of the footage), but these should not be provided electronically.

Statements of witnesses who give oral evidence

5B.18 A witness statement does not become evidence unless it is agreed under section 9 of the Criminal Justice Act 1967 and presented to the court. Therefore the statements of witnesses who give oral evidence, including ABE interview and transcripts and experts' reports, should not usually be provided. Open justice is generally satisfied by public access to the court.

Confidential documents

5B.19 A document the content of which, though relied upon by the court, has not been communicated to the public or reporters, nor treated as if it had been, is likely to have been supplied in confidence and should be treated accordingly. This will apply even if the court has made reference to the document or quoted from the document. There is most unlikely to be a sufficient reason to displace the expectation of confidentiality ordinarily attaching to a document in this category, and it would be exceptional to permit the inspection or copying by a member of the public or of the media of such a document. The rights and legitimate interests of others are likely to outweigh the interests of open justice with respect these documents.

5B.20 Documents in this category are likely to include:

    i. Pre-sentence reports;

    ii. Medical reports;

    iii. Victim Personal Statements;

    iv. Reports and summaries for confiscation.

Prohibitions against the provision of information

5B.21 Statutory provisions may impose specific prohibitions against the provision of information. Those most likely to be encountered are listed in the note to rule 5.8 and include the Rehabilitation of Offenders Act 1974, section 18 of the Criminal Procedure and Investigations Act 1996 ("unused material" disclosed by the prosecution), sections 33, 34 and 35 of the Legal Aid, Sentencing and Punishment of Offenders Act 2012 ('LASPO Act 2012') (privileged information furnished to the Legal Aid Agency) and reporting restrictions generally.

5B.22 Reports of allocation or sending proceedings are restricted by section 52A of the Crime and Disorder Act 1998, so that only limited information, as specified in the statute, may be reported, whether it is referred to in the court room or not. The magistrates' court has power to order that the restriction shall not apply; if any defendant objects the court must apply the interests of justice test as specified in section 52A. The restriction ceases to apply either after all defendants indicate a plea of guilty, or after the conclusion of the trial of the last defendant to be tried. If the case does not result in a guilty plea, a finding of guilt or an acquittal, the restriction does not lift automatically and an application must be made to the court.

5B.23 Extradition proceedings have some features in common with committal proceedings, but no automatic reporting restrictions apply.

5B.24 Public Interest Immunity and the rights of a defendant, witnesses and victims under Article 6 and 8 of the European Convention on Human Rights may also restrict the power to release material to third parties.

Other documents

5B.25 The following table indicates the considerations likely to arise on an application to inspect or copy other documents.

Document	Considerations
Charge sheet Indictment	The alleged offence(s) will have been read aloud in court, and their terms must be supplied under Rule 5.8(4)
Material disclosed under CPIA 1996	To the extent that the content is deployed at trial, it becomes public at that hearing. Otherwise, it is a criminal offence for it to be disclosed: section 18 of the 1996 Act.
Written notices, applications, replies (including any application for representation)	To the extent that evidence is introduced, or measures taken, at trial, the content becomes public at that hearing. A statutory prohibition against disclosure applies to an application for representation: sections 33, 34 and 35 of the LASPO Act 2012.
Sentencing remarks	Sentencing remarks should usually be provided to the accredited Press, if the judge was reading from a prepared script which was handed out immediately afterwards; if not, then permission for a member of the accredited Press to obtain a transcript should usually be given (see also paragraphs 26 and 29 below).
Official recordings Transcript	See Rule 5.5. See Rule 5.5.

Access by reporters

5B.26 Under Part 5 of the Rules, the same procedure applies for applications for access to information by reporters as to other members of the public. However, if the application is made by legal representatives instructed by the media, or by an accredited member of the media, who is able to produce in support of the application a valid Press Card (http://www.ukpresscardauthority.co.uk/) then there is a greater presumption in favour of providing the requested material, in recognition of the press' role as 'public watch dog' in a democratic society (*Observer and Guardian v United Kingdom* (1992) 14 EHRR 153, Times November 27, 1991). The general principle in those circumstances is that the court should supply documents and information unless there is a good reason not to in order to protect the rights or legitimate interests of others and the request will not place an undue burden on the court *R* (*Guardian News and Media Ltd*) at [87]. Subject to that, the paragraphs above relating to types of documents should be followed.

5B.27 Court staff should usually verify the authenticity of cards, checking the expiry date on the card and where necessary may consider telephoning the number on the reverse of the card to verify the card holder. Court staff may additionally request sight of other identification if necessary to ensure that the card holder has been correctly identified. The supply of information under Rule 5.8(7) is at the discretion of the court, and court staff must ensure that they have received a clear direction from the court before providing any information or material under Rule 5.8(7) to a member of the public, including to the accredited media or their legal representatives.

5B.28 Opening notes and skeleton arguments or written submissions, once they have been placed before the court, should usually be provided to the media. If there is no opening note, permission for the media to obtain a transcript of the prosecution opening should usually be given (see below). It may be convenient for copies to be provided electronically by counsel, provided that the documents are kept suitably secure. The media are expected to be aware of the limitations on the use to which such material can be put, for example that legal argument held in the absence of the jury must not be reported before the conclusion of the trial.

5B.29 The media should also be able to obtain transcripts of hearings held in open court directly from the transcription service provider, on payment of any required fee. The service providers commonly require the judge's authorisation before they will provide a transcript, as an additional verification to ensure that the correct material is released and reporting restrictions are noted. However, responsibility for compliance with any restriction always rests with the person receiving the information or material: see CPD (Preliminary proceedings) 16B.

5B.30 It is not for the judge to exercise an editorial judgment about 'the adequacy of the material already available to the paper for its journalistic purpose' (*Guardian* at 82) but the responsibility for complying with the Contempt of Court Act 1981 and any and all restrictions on the use of the material rests with the recipient.

CRIMINAL PROCEDURE RULES　PART 6　INVESTIGATION ORDERS

Section 1: understanding and applying this Part

R-40　When this Part applies

6.1　(1) Sections 2 and 3 of this Part apply where, for the purposes of a terrorist investigation—

(a) a Circuit judge can make, vary or discharge—

(i)　an order for the production of, or for giving access to, material, or for a statement of its location, under paragraphs 5 and 10 of Schedule 5 to the Terrorism Act 2000,

(ii)　an explanation order, under paragraphs 10 and 13 of Schedule 5 to the 2000 Act,

(iii)　a customer information order, under paragraphs 1 and 4 of Schedule 6 to the 2000 Act;

(b) a Circuit judge can make, and the Crown Court can vary or discharge, an account monitoring order, under paragraphs 2 and 4 of Schedule 6A to the 2000 Act.

(2) Sections 2 and 4 of this Part apply where, for the purposes of an investigation for which Part 8 of the Proceeds of Crime Act 2002 provides, a Crown Court judge can make, and the Crown Court can vary or discharge—

(a) a production order, under sections 345 and 351 of the Proceeds of Crime Act 2002;

(b) an order to grant entry, under sections 347 and 351 of the 2002 Act;

(c) a disclosure order, under sections 357 and 362 of the 2002 Act;

(d) a customer information order, under sections 363 and 369 of the 2002 Act;

(e) an account monitoring order, under sections 370 and 375 of the 2002 Act.

(3) Rule 6.5 and Section 5 of this Part apply where—

(a) a justice of the peace can make or discharge an investigation anonymity order, under sections 76 and 80(1) of the Coroners and Justice Act 2009;

(b) a Crown Court judge can determine an appeal against—

(i)　a refusal of such an order, under section 79 of the 2009 Act,

(ii)　a decision on an application to discharge such an order, under section 80(6) of the 2009 Act.

(4) Sections 2 and 6 of this Part apply where a justice of the peace can make an order approving—

(a) the grant or renewal of an authorisation, or the giving or renewal of a notice, under section 23A of the Regulation of Investigatory Powers Act 2000;

(b) the grant or renewal of an authorisation under section 32A of the 2000 Act.

(5) Rule 6.5 and Section 7 of this Part apply where a justice of the peace can issue a warrant under—

(a) section 8 of the Police and Criminal Evidence Act 1984;

(b) section 2 of the Criminal Justice Act 1987;

(c) other powers to which sections 15 and 16 of the Police and Criminal Evidence Act 1984 apply.

(6) Rules 6.4 and 6.5 and Section 8 of this Part apply where—

(a) a District Judge (Magistrates' Court) can make an order under—

(i)　section 63F(7) or 63R(6) of the Police and Criminal Evidence Act 1984, or

(ii)　paragraph 20B(5) or 20G(6) of Schedule 8 to the Terrorism Act 2000;

(b) the Crown Court can determine an appeal against an order to which paragraph (a)(i) applies, or against a refusal to make such an order, under—
    (i)   section 63F(10) of the Police and Criminal Evidence Act 1984, or
    (ii) paragraph 20B(8) of Schedule 8 to the Terrorism Act 2000.

Meaning of 'court', 'applicant' and 'respondent'   **R-41**

6.2   In this Part—
    (a) a reference to the 'court' includes a reference to any justice of the peace or judge who can exercise a power to which this Part applies;
    (b) 'applicant' means any person who, or an authority which, can apply for an order to which this Part applies; and
    (c) 'respondent' means any person—
        (i)   against whom such an order is sought or made, or
        (ii) on whom an application for such an order is served.

Section 2: general rules

Exercise of court's powers   **R-42**

6.3   (1) Subject to paragraphs (2) and (3), the court may determine an application for an order, or to vary or discharge an order—
        (a) at a hearing (which must be in private unless the court otherwise directs), or without a hearing; and
        (b) in the absence of—
            (i)   the applicant,
            (ii) the respondent (if any),
            (iii) any other person affected by the order.
    (2) The court must not determine such an application in the applicant's absence if—
        (a) the applicant asks for a hearing; or
        (b) it appears to the court that—
            (i)   the proposed order may infringe legal privilege, within the meaning of section 10 of the Police and Criminal Evidence Act 1984 or of section 348 or 361 of the Proceeds of Crime Act 2002,
            (ii) the proposed order may require the production of excluded material, within the meaning of section 11 of the 1984 Act, or
            (iii) for any other reason the application is so complex or serious as to require the court to hear the applicant.
    (3) The court must not determine such an application in the absence of any respondent or other person affected, unless—
        (a) the absentee has had at least 2 business days in which to make representations; or
        (b) the court is satisfied that—
            (i)   the applicant cannot identify or contact the absentee,
            (ii) it would prejudice the investigation if the absentee were present,
            (iii) it would prejudice the investigation to adjourn or postpone the application so as to allow the absentee to attend, or
            (iv) the absentee has waived the opportunity to attend.
    (4) The court must not make, vary or discharge an order unless the applicant states, in writing or orally, that to the best of the applicant's knowledge and belief—
        (a) the application discloses all the information that is material to what the court must decide; and
        (b) the content of the application is true.
    (5) Where the statement required by paragraph (4) is made orally—
        (a) the statement must be on oath or affirmation, unless the court otherwise directs; and
        (b) the court must arrange for a record of the making of the statement.

Court's power to vary requirements under this Part   **R-43**

6.4   (1) The court may—
        (a) shorten or extend (even after it has expired) a time limit under this Part;
        (b) dispense with a requirement for service under this Part (even after service was required); and
        (c) consider an application made orally instead of in writing.
    (2) A person who wants an extension of time must—
        (a) apply when serving the application for which it is needed; and
        (b) explain the delay.

R-44   **Documents served on the court officer**

    6.5   (1) Unless the court otherwise directs, the court officer may—

            (a) keep a written application; or

            (b) arrange for the whole or any part to be kept by some other appropriate person, subject to any conditions that the court may impose.

        (2) Where the court makes an order when the court office is closed, the applicant must, not more than 72 hours later, serve on the court officer—

            (a) a copy of the order; and

            (b) any written material that was submitted to the court.

        (3) Where the court issues a warrant—

            (a) the applicant must return it to the court officer as soon as practicable after it has been executed, and in any event not more than 3 months after it was issued (unless other legislation otherwise provides); and

            (b) the court officer must—

                (i) keep the warrant for 12 months after its return, and

                (ii) during that period, make it available for inspection by the occupier of the premises to which it relates, if that occupier asks to inspect it.

Section 3: orders under the Terrorism Act 2000

R-45   **Application for an order under the Terrorism Act 2000**

    6.6   (1) This rule applies where an applicant wants the court to make one of the orders listed in rule 6.1(1).

        (2) The applicant must—

            (a) apply in writing;

            (b) serve the application on—

                (i) the court officer, and

                (ii) the respondent (unless the court otherwise directs);

            (c) identify the respondent;

            (d) give the information required by whichever of rules 6.7 to 6.10 applies; and

            (e) serve any order made on the respondent.

R-46   **Content of application for a production etc. order**

    6.7   As well as complying with rule 6.6, an applicant who wants the court to make an order for the production of, or access to, material, or for a statement of its location, must—

            (a) describe that material;

            (b) explain why the applicant thinks the material is—

                (i) in the respondent's possession, custody or power, or

                (ii) likely to be so within 28 days of the order;

            (c) explain how the material constitutes or contains excluded material or special procedure material;

            (d) confirm that none of the material is expected to be subject to legal privilege;

            (e) explain why the material is likely to be of substantial value to the investigation;

            (f) explain why it is in the public interest for the material to be produced, or for the applicant to be given access to it, having regard to—

                (i) the benefit likely to accrue to the investigation if it is obtained, and

                (ii) the circumstances in which the respondent has the material, or is expected to have it; and

            (g) propose—

                (i) the terms of the order, and

                (ii) the period within which it should take effect.

R-47   **Content of application for an explanation order**

    6.8   As well as complying with rule 6.6, an applicant who wants the court to make an explanation order must—

            (a) identify the material that the applicant wants the respondent to explain;

            (b) confirm that the explanation is not expected to infringe legal privilege; and

            (c) propose—

                (i) the terms of the order, and

                (ii) the period within which it should take effect, if 7 days from the date of the order would not be appropriate.

Content of application for a customer information order   R-48

6.9   As well as complying with rule 6.6, an applicant who wants the court to make a customer informa-
       tion order must—
       (a) explain why it is desirable for the purposes of the investigation to trace property said to be ter-
            rorist property within the meaning of the Terrorism Act 2000;
       (b) explain why the order will enhance the effectiveness of the investigation; and
       (c) propose the terms of the order.

Content of application for an account monitoring order   R-49

6.10   As well as complying with rule 6.6, an applicant who wants the court to make an account monitor-
       ing order must—
       (a) specify—
            (i)   the information sought,
            (ii) the period during which the applicant wants the respondent to provide that information
                  (to a maximum of 90 days), and
            (iii) where, when and in what manner the applicant wants the respondent to provide that
                  information;
       (b) explain why it is desirable for the purposes of the investigation to trace property said to be ter-
            rorist property within the meaning of the Terrorism Act 2000;
       (c) explain why the order will enhance the effectiveness of the investigation; and
       (d) propose the terms of the order.

Application to vary or discharge an order   R-50

6.11   (1) This rule applies where one of the following wants the court to vary or discharge an order listed
            in rule 6.1(1)—
            (a) an applicant;
            (b) the respondent; or
            (c) a person affected by the order.
       (2) That applicant, respondent or person affected must—
            (a) apply in writing as soon as practicable after becoming aware of the grounds for doing so;
            (b) serve the application on—
                 (i)   the court officer, and
                 (ii) the respondent, applicant, or any person known to be affected, as applicable;
            (c) explain why it is appropriate for the order to be varied or discharged;
            (d) propose the terms of any variation; and
            (e) ask for a hearing, if one is wanted, and explain why it is needed.

Application containing information withheld from a respondent or other person   R-51

6.12   (1) This rule applies where—
            (a) an applicant serves on a respondent or other person an application for one of the orders
                 listed in rule 6.1(1), or for the variation or discharge of such an order; and
            (b) the application includes information that the applicant thinks ought not be revealed to
                 that recipient.
       (2) The applicant must—
            (a) omit that information from the part of the application that is served on the respondent or
                 other person;
            (b) mark the other part, to show that it is only for the court; and
            (c) in that other part, explain why the applicant has withheld it.
       (3) A hearing of an application to which this rule applies may take place, wholly or in part, in the
            absence of the respondent and any other person.
       (4) At a hearing of an application to which this rule applies—
            (a) the general rule is that the court must receive, in the following sequence—
                 (i)   representations first by the applicant and then by the respondent and any other
                       person, in the presence of them all, and then
                 (ii) further representations by the applicant, in the others' absence; but
            (b) the court may direct other arrangements for the hearing.

Application to punish for contempt of court   R-52

6.13   (1) This rule applies where a person is accused of disobeying—
            (a) a production etc. order made under paragraph 5 of Schedule 5 to the Terrorism Act 2000;
            (b) an explanation order made under paragraph 13 of that Schedule; or
            (c) an account monitoring order made under paragraph 2 of Schedule 6A to that Act.

Criminal Procedure Rules 2013 and Criminal Practice Directions

(2) An applicant who wants the court to exercise its power to punish that person for contempt of court must comply with the rules in Part 62 (Contempt of court).

Section 4: orders under the Proceeds of Crime Act 2002

R-53   **Application for an order under the Proceeds of Crime Act 2002**

6.14   (1) This rule applies where an applicant wants the court to make one of the orders listed in rule 6.1(2).

     (2) The applicant must—

       (a) apply in writing;

       (b) serve the application on—

         (i) the court officer, and

         (ii) the respondent (unless the court otherwise directs);

       (c) identify—

         (i) the respondent, and

         (ii) the person or property the subject of the confiscation or money laundering investigation;

       (d) explain why the applicant thinks the person under investigation has—

         (i) benefited from criminal conduct, in the case of a confiscation investigation, or

         (ii) committed a money laundering offence, in the case of a money laundering investigation;

       (e) give the additional information required by whichever of rules 6.15 to 6.19 applies; and

       (f) serve any order made on each respondent.

R-54   **Content of application for a production order**

6.15   As well as complying with rule 6.14, an applicant who wants the court to make an order for the production of, or access to, material, must—

     (a) describe that material;

     (b) explain why the applicant thinks the material is in the respondent's possession or control;

     (c) confirm that none of the material is—

       (i) expected to be subject to legal privilege, or

       (ii) excluded material;

     (d) explain why the material is likely to be of substantial value to the investigation;

     (e) explain why it is in the public interest for the material to be produced, or for the applicant to be given access to it, having regard to—

       (i) the benefit likely to accrue to the investigation if it is obtained, and

       (ii) the circumstances in which the respondent has the material; and

     (f) propose—

       (i) the terms of the order, and

       (ii) the period within which it should take effect, if 7 days from the date of the order would not be appropriate.

R-55   **Content of application for an order to grant entry**

6.16   An applicant who wants the court to make an order to grant entry in aid of a production order must—

     (a) specify the premises to which entry is sought;

     (b) explain why the order is needed; and

     (c) propose the terms of the order.

R-56   **Content of application for a disclosure order**

6.17   As well as complying with rule 6.14, an applicant who wants the court to make a disclosure order must—

     (a) describe in general terms the information that the applicant wants the respondent to provide;

     (b) confirm that none of the information is—

       (i) expected to be subject to legal privilege, or

       (ii) excluded material;

     (c) explain why the information is likely to be of substantial value to the investigation;

     (d) explain why it is in the public interest for the information to be provided, having regard to the benefit likely to accrue to the investigation if it is obtained; and

     (e) propose the terms of the order.

Content of application for a customer information order   R-57

6.18   As well as complying with rule 6.14, an applicant who wants the court to make a customer information order must—

    (a) explain why customer information about the person under investigation is likely to be of substantial value to that investigation;

    (b) explain why it is in the public interest for the information to be provided, having regard to the benefit likely to accrue to the investigation if it is obtained; and

    (c) propose the terms of the order.

Content of application for an account monitoring order   R-58

6.19   As well as complying with rule 6.14, an applicant who wants the court to make an account monitoring order for the provision of account information must—

    (a) specify—

        (i)   the information sought,

        (ii) the period during which the applicant wants the respondent to provide that information (to a maximum of 90 days), and

        (iii) when and in what manner the applicant wants the respondent to provide that information;

    (b) explain why the information is likely to be of substantial value to the investigation;

    (c) explain why it is in the public interest for the information to be provided, having regard to the benefit likely to accrue to the investigation if it is obtained; and

    (d) propose the terms of the order.

Application to vary or discharge an order   R-59

6.20   (1) This rule applies where one of the following wants the court to vary or discharge an order listed in rule 6.1(2)—

        (a) an applicant;

        (b) the respondent; or

        (c) a person affected by the order.

    (2) That applicant, respondent or person affected must—

        (a) apply in writing as soon as practicable after becoming aware of the grounds for doing so;

        (b) serve the application on—

            (i)   the court officer, and

            (ii) the respondent, applicant, or any person known to be affected, as applicable;

        (c) explain why it is appropriate for the order to be varied or discharged;

        (d) propose the terms of any variation; and

        (e) ask for a hearing, if one is wanted, and explain why it is needed.

Application containing information withheld from a respondent or other person   R-60

6.21   (1) This rule applies where—

        (a) an applicant serves on a respondent or other person an application for one of the orders listed in rule 6.1(2), or for the variation or discharge of such an order; and

        (b) the application includes information that the applicant thinks ought not be revealed to that recipient.

    (2) The applicant must—

        (a) omit that information from the part of the application that is served on the respondent or other person;

        (b) mark the other part, to show that it is only for the court; and

        (c) in that other part, explain why the applicant has withheld it.

    (3) A hearing of an application to which this rule applies may take place, wholly or in part, in the absence of the respondent and any other person.

    (4) At a hearing of an application to which this rule applies—

        (a) the general rule is that the court must receive, in the following sequence—

            (i)   representations first by the applicant and then by the respondent and any other person, in the presence of them all, and then

            (ii) further representations by the applicant, in the others' absence; but

        (b) the court may direct other arrangements for the hearing.

Application to punish for contempt of court   R-61

6.22   (1) This rule applies where a person is accused of disobeying—

        (a) a production order made under section 345 of the Proceeds of Crime Act 2002; or

        (b) an account monitoring order made under section 370 of that Act.

Criminal Procedure Rules 2013 and Criminal Practice Directions

(2) An applicant who wants the court to exercise its power to punish that person for contempt of court must comply with the rules in Part 62 (contempt of court).

Section 5: orders under the Coroners and Justice Act 2009

R-62　Exercise of court's powers

6.23　(1) The court may determine an application for an investigation anonymity order, and any appeal against the refusal of such an order—

(a) at a hearing (which must be in private unless the court otherwise directs); or

(b) without a hearing.

(2) The court must determine an application to discharge an investigation anonymity order, and any appeal against the decision on such an application—

(a) at a hearing (which must be in private unless the court otherwise directs); and

(b) in the presence of the person specified in the order, unless—

(i) that person applied for the discharge of the order,

(ii) that person has had an opportunity to make representations, or

(iii) the court is satisfied that it is not reasonably practicable to communicate with that person.

(3) The court may consider an application or an appeal made orally instead of in writing.

R-63　Application for an investigation anonymity order

6.24　(1) This rule applies where an applicant wants a magistrates' court to make an investigation anonymity order.

(2) The applicant must—

(a) apply in writing;

(b) serve the application on the court officer;

(c) identify the person to be specified in the order, unless—

(i) the applicant wants the court to determine the application at a hearing, or

(ii) the court otherwise directs;

(d) explain how the proposed order meets the conditions prescribed by section 78 of the Coroners and Justice Act 2009;

(e) say if the applicant intends to appeal should the court refuse the order;

(f) attach any material on which the applicant relies; and

(g) propose the terms of the order.

(3) At any hearing of the application, the applicant must—

(a) identify to the court the person to be specified in the order, unless—

(i) the applicant has done so already, or

(ii) the court otherwise directs; and

(b) unless the applicant has done so already, inform the court if the applicant intends to appeal should the court refuse the order.

R-64　Application to discharge an investigation anonymity order

6.25　(1) This rule applies where one of the following wants a magistrates' court to discharge an investigation anonymity order—

(a) an applicant; or

(b) the person specified in the order.

(2) That applicant or the specified person must—

(a) apply in writing as soon as practicable after becoming aware of the grounds for doing so;

(b) serve the application on—

(i) the court officer, and as applicable

(ii) the applicant for the order, and

(iii) the specified person;

(c) explain—

(i) what material circumstances have changed since the order was made, or since any previous application was made to discharge it, and

(ii) why it is appropriate for the order to be discharged; and

(d) attach—

(i) a copy of the order, and

(ii) any material on which the applicant relies.

(3) A party must inform the court if that party intends to appeal should the court discharge the order.

Appeal   R-65

6.26 (1) This rule applies where one of the following ('the appellant') wants to appeal to the
           Crown Court—
           (a) the applicant for an investigation anonymity order, where a magistrates' court has refused
                to make the order;
           (b) a party to an application to discharge such an order, where a magistrates' court has decided
                that application.
      (2) The appellant must—
           (a) serve on the Crown Court officer a copy of the application to the magistrates' court; and
           (b) where the appeal concerns a discharge decision, notify each other party, not more that
                21 days after the decision against which the appellant wants to appeal.
      (3) The Crown Court must hear the appeal without justices of the peace.

Section 6: orders under the Regulation of Investigatory Powers Act 2000

Application for approval for authorisation or notice   R-66

6.27 (1) This rule applies where an applicant wants a magistrates' court to make an order approving—
           (a) under sections 23A and 23B of the Regulation of Investigatory Powers Act 2000—
                (i)   an authorisation to obtain or disclose communications data, under section 22(3) of
                      the 2000 Act, or
                (ii) a notice that requires a postal or telecommunications operator if need be to obtain, and
                      in any case to disclose, communications data, under section 22(4) of the 2000 Act;
           (b) under sections 32A and 32B of the Regulation of Investigatory Powers Act 2000, an
                authorisation for—
                (i)   the carrying out of directed surveillance, under section 28 of the 2000 Act, or
                (ii) the conduct or use of a covert human intelligence source, under section 29 of the
                      2000 Act.
      (2) The applicant must—
           (a) apply in writing and serve the application on the court officer;
           (b) attach the authorisation or notice which the applicant wants the court to approve;
           (c) attach such other material (if any) on which the applicant relies to satisfy the court—
                (i)   as required by section 23A(3) and (4) of the 2000 Act, in relation to
                      communications data,
                (ii) as required by section 32A(3) and (4) of the 2000 Act, in relation to directed
                      surveillance, or
                (iii) as required by section 32A(5) and (6), and, if relevant, section 43(6A), of the 2000
                      Act, in relation to a covert human intelligence source; and
           (d) propose the terms of the order.

Exercise of court's power to quash an authorisation or notice   R-67

6.28 (1) This rule applies where, under section 23A or 32A of the Regulation of Investigatory Powers
           Act 2000, a magistrates' court refuses to approve the grant, giving or renewal of an authorisa-
           tion or notice.
      (2) The court must not exercise its power to quash that authorisation or notice unless the applicant
           has had at least 2 business days from the date of the refusal in which to make representations.

Section 7: search warrants

Exercise of court's powers   R-68

6.29 (1) The court must determine an application for a warrant—
           (a) at a hearing, which must be in private unless the court otherwise directs;
           (b) in the presence of the applicant; and
           (c) in the absence of any person affected by the warrant, including any person in occupation
                or control of premises which the applicant wants to search.
      (2) If the court so directs, the applicant may attend the hearing by live link.
      (3) The court must not determine an application unless satisfied that sufficient time has been
           allowed for it.
      (4) The court must not determine an application unless the applicant confirms, on oath or affir-
           mation, that to the best of the applicant's knowledge and belief—
           (a) the application discloses all the information that is material to what the court must decide,
                including any circumstances that might reasonably be considered capable of undermining
                any of the grounds of the application; and
           (b) the content of the application is true.

Criminal Procedure Rules 2013 and Criminal Practice Directions

(5) If the court requires the applicant to answer a question about an application—
    (a) the applicant's answer must be on oath or affirmation;
    (b) the court must arrange for a record of the gist of the question and reply; and
    (c) if the applicant cannot answer to the court's satisfaction, the court may—
        (i)   specify the information the court requires, and
        (ii) give directions for the presentation of any renewed application.
(6) Unless to do so would be inconsistent with other legislation, on an application the court may issue—
    (a) a warrant in respect of specified premises;
    (b) a warrant in respect of all premises occupied or controlled by a specified person;
    (c) a warrant in respect of all premises occupied or controlled by a specified person which specifies some of those premises; or
    (d) more than one warrant—
        (i)   each one in respect of premises specified in the warrant,
        (ii) each one in respect of all premises occupied or controlled by a person specified in the warrant (whether or not such a warrant also specifies any of those premises), or
        (iii) at least one in respect of specified premises and at least one in respect of all premises occupied or controlled by a specified person (whether or not such a warrant also specifies any of those premises).

R-69   **Application for warrant under section 8 of the Police and Criminal Evidence Act 1984**

6.30   (1) This rule applies where an applicant wants a magistrates' court to issue a warrant or warrants under section 8 of the Police and Criminal Evidence Act 1984.
    (2) The applicant must—
        (a) apply in writing;
        (b) serve the application on—
            (i)   the court officer, or
            (ii) if the court office is closed, the court;
        (c) give the court an estimate of how long the court should allow—
            (i)   to read and prepare for the application, and
            (ii) for the hearing of the application; and
        (d) tell the court when the applicant expects any warrant issued to be executed.
    (3) The application must—
        (a) specify the offence under investigation (and see paragraph (4));
        (b) so far as practicable, identify the material sought (and see paragraph (5));
        (c) specify the premises to be searched (and see paragraphs (6) and (7));
        (d) state whether the applicant wants the premises to be searched on more than one occasion (and see paragraph (8)); and
        (e) state whether the applicant wants other persons to accompany the officers executing the warrant or warrants (and see paragraph (9)).
    (4) In relation to the offence under investigation, the application must—
        (a) state whether that offence is—
            (i)   an indictable offence, or
            (ii) a relevant offence as defined in section 28D of the Immigration Act 1971; and
        (b) explain the grounds for believing that the offence has been committed.
    (5) In relation to the material sought, the application must explain the grounds for believing that that material—
        (a) is likely to be of substantial value to the investigation (whether by itself, or together with other material);
        (b) is likely to be admissible evidence at trial for the offence under investigation; and
        (c) does not consist of or include items subject to legal privilege, excluded material or special procedure material.
    (6) In relation to premises which the applicant wants to be searched and can specify, the application must—
        (a) specify each set of premises;
        (b) in respect of each set of premises, explain the grounds for believing that material sought is on those premises; and
        (c) in respect of each set of premises, explain the grounds for believing that—
            (i)   it is not practicable to communicate with any person entitled to grant entry to the premises,

      (ii) it is practicable to communicate with such a person but it is not practicable to communicate with any person entitled to grant access to the material sought,

     (iii) entry to the premises will not be granted unless a warrant is produced, or

     (iv) the purpose of a search may be frustrated or seriously prejudiced unless a constable arriving at the premises can secure immediate entry to them.

(7) In relation to premises which the applicant wants to be searched but at least some of which the applicant cannot specify, the application must—

  (a) explain the grounds for believing that—

    (i) because of the particulars of the offence under investigation it is necessary to search any premises occupied or controlled by a specified person, and

    (ii) it is not reasonably practicable to specify all the premises which that person occupies or controls which might need to be searched;

  (b) specify as many sets of premises as is reasonably practicable;

  (c) in respect of each set of premises, whether specified or not, explain the grounds for believing that material sought is on those premises; and

  (d) in respect of each specified set of premises, explain the grounds for believing that—

    (i) it is not practicable to communicate with any person entitled to grant entry to the premises,

    (ii) it is practicable to communicate with such a person but it is not practicable to communicate with any person entitled to grant access to the material sought,

    (iii) entry to the premises will not be granted unless a warrant is produced, or

    (iv) the purpose of a search may be frustrated or seriously prejudiced unless a constable arriving at the premises can secure immediate entry to them.

(8) In relation to any set of premises which the applicant wants to be searched on more than one occasion, the application must—

  (a) explain why it is necessary to search on more than one occasion in order to achieve the purpose for which the applicant wants the court to issue the warrant; and

  (b) specify any proposed maximum number of occasions.

(9) In relation to any set of premises which the applicant wants to be searched by the officers executing the warrant with other persons authorised by the court, the application must—

  (a) identify those other persons, by function or description; and

  (b) explain why those persons are required.

(10) The application must disclose anything known or reported to the applicant that might reasonably be considered capable of undermining any of the grounds of the application.

(11) Where the application includes information that the applicant thinks should be supplied only to the court, the applicant may—

  (a) set out that information in a separate document, marked accordingly; and

  (b) in that document, explain why the applicant thinks that that information ought not to be supplied to anyone other than the court.

(12) The application must include—

  (a) a declaration by the applicant that to the best of the applicant's knowledge and belief—

    (i) the application discloses all the information that is material to what the court must decide, including anything that might reasonably be considered capable of undermining any of the grounds of the application, and

    (ii) the content of the application is true; and

  (b) a declaration by an officer senior to the applicant that the senior officer has reviewed and authorised the application.

(13) The application must attach a draft warrant or warrants in the terms proposed by the applicant.

Application for warrant under section 2 of the Criminal Justice Act 1987   R-70

6.31 (1) This rule applies where an applicant wants a magistrates' court to issue a warrant or warrants under section 2 of the Criminal Justice Act 1987.

  (2) The applicant must—

    (a) apply in writing;

    (b) serve the application on—

      (i) the court officer, or

      (ii) if the court office is closed, the court;

    (c) give the court an estimate of how long the court should allow—

      (i) to read and prepare for the application, and

      (ii) for the hearing of the application; and

    (d) tell the court when the applicant expects any warrant issued to be executed.

Criminal Procedure Rules 2013 and Criminal Practice Directions

(3) The application must—

    (a) describe the investigation being conducted by the Director of the Serious Fraud Office and include—

        (i) an explanation of what is alleged and why, and

        (ii) a chronology of relevant events;

    (b) specify the document, documents or description of documents sought by the applicant (and see paragraphs (4) and (5)); and

    (c) specify the premises which the applicant wants to be searched (and see paragraph (6)).

(4) In relation to each document or description of documents sought, the application must—

    (a) explain the grounds for believing that each such document—

        (i) relates to a matter relevant to the investigation, and

        (ii) could not be withheld from disclosure or production on grounds of legal professional privilege; and

    (b) explain the grounds for believing that—

        (i) a person has failed to comply with a notice by the Director to produce the document or documents,

        (ii) it is not practicable to serve such a notice, or

        (iii) the service of such a notice might seriously impede the investigation.

(5) In relation to any document or description of documents which the applicant wants to be preserved but not seized under a warrant, the application must—

    (a) specify the steps for which the applicant wants the court's authority in order to preserve and prevent interference with the document or documents; and

    (b) explain why such steps are necessary.

(6) In respect of each set of premises which the applicant wants to be searched, the application must explain the grounds for believing that a document or description of documents sought by the applicant is on those premises.

(7) If the court so directs, the applicant must make available to the court material on which is based the information given under paragraph (3).

(8) The application must disclose anything known or reported to the applicant that might reasonably be considered capable of undermining any of the grounds of the application.

(9) Where the application includes information that the applicant thinks should be supplied only to the court, the applicant may—

    (a) set out that information in a separate document, marked accordingly; and

    (b) in that document, explain why the applicant thinks that that information ought not to be supplied to anyone other than the court.

(10) The application must include—

    (a) a declaration by the applicant that to the best of the applicant's knowledge and belief—

        (i) the application discloses all the information that is material to what the court must decide, including anything that might reasonably be considered capable of undermining any of the grounds of the application, and

        (ii) the content of the application is true; and

    (b) a declaration by an officer senior to the applicant that the senior officer has reviewed and authorised the application.

(11) The application must attach a draft warrant or warrants in the terms proposed by the applicant.

R-71   **Application for warrant under another power to which sections 15 and 16 of the Police and Criminal Evidence Act 1984 apply**

6.32 (1) This rule applies where—

    (a) an applicant wants a magistrates' court to issue a warrant or warrants under a power to which sections 15 and 16 of the Police and Criminal Evidence Act 1984 apply; and

    (b) neither rule 6.30 nor rule 6.31 applies.

(2) The applicant must—

    (a) apply in writing;

    (b) serve the application on—

        (i) the court officer, or

        (ii) if the court office is closed, the court;

    (c) give the court an estimate of how long the court should allow—

        (i) to read and prepare for the application, and

        (ii) for the hearing of the application; and

    (d) tell the court when the applicant expects any warrant issued to be executed.

(3) The application must—
- (a) state the legislation which allows the court to issue the warrant (in this rule, described as 'the main search power'; and see paragraph (4));
- (b) so far as practicable, identify the articles or persons sought (and see paragraph (5));
- (c) specify the premises to be searched (and see paragraphs (6) and (7));
- (d) state whether the applicant wants the premises to be searched on more than one occasion (and see paragraph (8)); and
- (e) state whether the applicant wants other persons to accompany the officers executing the warrant or warrants (and see paragraph (9)).

(4) The application must—
- (a) include or attach the terms of the main search power; and
- (b) explain how the circumstances satisfy any criteria prescribed by the main search power for making the application.

(5) In relation to the articles or persons sought, the application must explain how they satisfy any criteria prescribed by the main search power about such articles or persons.

(6) In relation to premises which the applicant wants to be searched and can specify, the application must—
- (a) specify each set of premises; and
- (b) in respect of each, explain how the circumstances satisfy any criteria prescribed by the main search power—
  - (i) for thinking that the articles or persons sought are on those premises, and
  - (ii) for asserting that the court can exercise its power to authorise the search of those premises.

(7) In relation to premises which the applicant wants to be searched but at least some of which the applicant cannot specify, the application must—
- (a) explain how the main search power allows the court to authorise such searching;
- (b) specify the person who occupies or controls such premises;
- (c) specify as many sets of such premises as is reasonably practicable;
- (d) explain why—
  - (i) it is necessary to search more premises than those specified, and
  - (ii) it is not reasonably practicable to specify all the premises which the applicant wants to be searched;
- (e) in respect of each set of premises, whether specified or not, explain how the circumstances satisfy any criteria prescribed by the main search power for thinking that the articles or persons sought are on those premises; and
- (f) in respect of each specified set of premises, explain how the circumstances satisfy any criteria prescribed by the main search power for asserting that the court can exercise its power to authorise the search of those premises.

(8) In relation to any set of premises which the applicant wants to be searched on more than one occasion, the application must—
- (a) explain how the main search power allows the court to authorise such searching;
- (b) explain why the applicant wants the premises to be searched more than once; and
- (c) specify any proposed maximum number of occasions.

(9) In relation to any set of premises which the applicant wants to be searched by the officers executing the warrant with other persons authorised by the court, the application must—
- (a) identify those other persons, by function or description; and
- (b) explain why those persons are required.

(10) The application must disclose anything known or reported to the applicant that might reasonably be considered capable of undermining any of the grounds of the application.

(11) Where the application includes information that the applicant thinks should be supplied only to the court, the applicant may—
- (a) set out that information in a separate document, marked accordingly; and
- (b) in that document, explain why the applicant thinks that that information ought not to be supplied to anyone other than the court.

(12) The application must include—
- (a) a declaration by the applicant that to the best of the applicant's knowledge and belief—
  - (i) the application discloses all the information that is material to what the court must decide, including anything that might reasonably be considered capable of undermining any of the grounds of the application, and
  - (ii) the content of the application is true; and

Criminal Procedure Rules 2013 and Criminal Practice Directions

　　　　(b) a declaration by an officer senior to the applicant that the senior officer has reviewed and
　　　　　　authorised the application.
　　(13) The application must attach a draft warrant or warrants in the terms proposed by the applicant.

R-72 Information to be included in a warrant

6.33 (1) A warrant must identify—
　　　　(a) the person or description of persons by whom it may be executed;
　　　　(b) any person who may accompany a person executing the warrant;
　　　　(c) so far as practicable, the material, documents, articles or persons to be sought;
　　　　(d) the legislation under which it was issued;
　　　　(e) the name of the applicant;
　　　　(f) the court that issued it, unless that is otherwise recorded by the court officer;
　　　　(g) the court office for the court that issued it; and
　　　　(h) the date on which it was issued.
　　(2) A warrant must specify—
　　　　(a) the premises to be searched, where the application specified premises;
　　　　(b) the person in occupation or control of premises to be searched, where the application
　　　　　　specified such a person; and
　　　　(c) the number of occasions on which specified premises may be searched, if more than one.
　　(3) A warrant must include, by signature, initial, or otherwise, an indication that it has been
　　　　approved by the court that issued it.
　　(4) Where a warrant comprises more than a single page, each page must include such an indication.
　　(5) A copy of a warrant must include a prominent certificate that it is such a copy.

Section 8: orders for the retention of fingerprints

R-73 Exercise of court's powers

6.34 (1) The court must determine an application under rule 6.35, and an appeal under rule 6.36—
　　　　(a) at a hearing, which must be in private unless the court otherwise directs; and
　　　　(b) in the presence of the applicant or appellant.
　　(2) The court must not determine such an application or appeal unless any person served under
　　　　those rules—
　　　　(a) is present; or
　　　　(b) has had an opportunity—
　　　　　　(i) to attend, or
　　　　　　(ii) to make representations.

R-74 Application to extend retention period

6.35 (1) This rule applies where a magistrates' court can make an order extending the period for which
　　　　there may be retained material consisting of—
　　　　(a) fingerprints taken from a person—
　　　　　　(i)   under a power conferred by Part V of the Police and Criminal Evidence Act 1984,
　　　　　　(ii) with that person's consent, in connection with the investigation of an offence by the
　　　　　　　　police, or
　　　　　　(iii) under a power conferred by Schedule 8 to the Terrorism Act 2000 in relation to a
　　　　　　　　person detained under section 41 of that Act;
　　　　(b) a DNA profile derived from a DNA sample so taken; or
　　　　(c) a sample so taken.
　　(2) A chief officer of police who wants the court to make such an order must—
　　　　(a) apply in writing—
　　　　　　(i) within the period of 3 months ending on the last day of the retention period, where
　　　　　　　　the application relates to fingerprints or a DNA profile, or
　　　　　　(ii) before the expiry of the retention period, where the application relates to a sample;
　　　　(b) in the application—
　　　　　　(i)   identify the material,
　　　　　　(ii) state when the retention period expires,
　　　　　　(iii) give details of any previous such application relating to the material, and
　　　　　　(iv) outline the circumstances in which the material was acquired;
　　　　(c) serve the application on the court officer, in every case; and
　　　　(d) serve the application on the person from whom the material was taken, where—
　　　　　　(i) the application relates to fingerprints or a DNA profile, or

    (ii) the application is for the renewal of an order extending the retention period for a sample.

(3) An application to extend the retention period for fingerprints or a DNA profile must explain why that period should be extended.

(4) An application to extend the retention period for a sample must explain why, having regard to the nature and complexity of other material that is evidence in relation to the offence, the sample is likely to be needed in any proceedings for the offence for the purposes of—

    (a) disclosure to, or use by, a defendant; or

    (b) responding to any challenge by a defendant in respect of the admissibility of material that is evidence on which the prosecution proposes to rely.

(5) On an application to extend the retention period for fingerprints or a DNA profile, the applicant must serve notice of the court's decision on any respondent where—

    (a) the court makes the order sought; and

    (b) the respondent was absent when it was made.

Appeal

R-75

6.36 (1) This rule applies where, under rule 6.35, a magistrates' court determines an application relating to fingerprints or a DNA profile and—

    (a) the person from whom the material was taken wants to appeal to the Crown Court against an order extending the retention period; or

    (b) a chief officer of police wants to appeal to the Crown Court against a refusal to make such an order.

(2) The appellant must—

    (a) serve an appeal notice—

        (i) on the Crown Court officer and on the other party, and

        (ii) not more than 21 days after the magistrates' court's decision, or, if applicable, service of notice under rule 6.35(5); and

    (b) in the appeal notice, explain, as appropriate, why the retention period should, or should not, be extended.

(3) Rule 63.10 (Constitution of the Crown Court) applies on such an appeal.

Criminal Practice Directions   Part 6   Investigation Orders and Warrants

CPD II Preliminary proceedings 6A: Investigation Orders and Warrants

PD-14

6A.1 Powers of entry, search and seizure, and powers to obtain banking and other confidential information, are among the most intrusive that investigators can exercise. Every application must be carefully scrutinised with close attention paid to what the relevant statutory provision requires of the applicant and to what it permits. Part 6 of the Rules must be followed, and the accompanying forms must be used. These are designed to prompt applicants, and the courts, to deal with all of the relevant criteria.

6A.2 The issuing of a warrant or the making of such an order is never to be treated as a formality and it is therefore essential that the judge or magistrate considering the application is given, and must take, sufficient time for the purpose. The prescribed forms require the applicant to provide a time estimate, and listing officers and justices' legal advisers should take account of these.

6A.3 Applicants for orders and warrants owe the court duties of candour and truthfulness. On any application made without notice to the respondent, and so on all applications for search warrants, the duty of frank and complete disclosure is especially onerous. The applicant must draw the court's attention to any information that is unfavourable to the application. The existence of unfavourable information will not necessarily lead to the application being refused; it will be a matter for the court what weight to place on each piece of information.

6A.4 Where an applicant supplements an application with additional oral or written information, on questioning by the court or otherwise, it is essential that the court keeps an adequate record. What is needed will depend upon the circumstances. The Rules require that a record of the 'gist' be retained. The purpose of such a record is to allow the sufficiency of the court's reasons for its decision subsequently to be assessed. The gravity of such decisions requires that their exercise should be susceptible to scrutiny and to explanation by reference to all of the information that was taken into account.

6A.5 The forms that accompany Part 6 of the Rules provide for the most frequently encountered applications. However, there are some hundreds of powers of entry, search and seizure, supplied by a corresponding number of legislative provisions. In any criminal matter, if there is no form designed for the particular warrant or order sought, the forms should still be used, as far as is practicable, and adapted as necessary. The applicant should pay particular attention to the specific legislative requirements for the granting of such an application to ensure that the court has all of the necessary information, and, if the court might be unfamiliar with the legislation, should provide a copy of the relevant provisions. Applicants must comply with the duties of candour and truthfulness, and include in their application the declarations required by the Rules and must make disclosure of any unfavourable information to the court.

CRIMINAL PROCEDURE RULES   PART 7   STARTING A PROSECUTION IN A MAGISTRATES' COURT

R-76   When this Part applies

7.1   (1)   This Part applies in a magistrates' court where—

(a)   a prosecutor wants the court to issue a summons or warrant under section 1 of the Magistrates' Courts Act 1980;

(b)   a public prosecutor—

(i)   wants the court to issue a warrant under section 1 of the Magistrates' Courts Act 1980, or

(ii)   issues a written charge and requisition under section 29 of the Criminal Justice Act 2003; or

(c)   a person who is in custody is charged with an offence.

(2)   In this Part, 'public prosecutor' means one of those public prosecutors listed in section 29 of the Criminal Justice Act 2003.

R-77   Information and written charge

7.2   (1)   A prosecutor who wants the court to issue a summons must—

(a)   serve an information in writing on the court officer; or

(b)   unless other legislation prohibits this, present an information orally to the court, with a written record of the allegation that it contains.

(2)   A prosecutor who wants the court to issue a warrant must—

(a)   serve on the court officer—

(i)   an information in writing, or

(ii)   a copy of a written charge that has been issued; or

(b)   present to the court either of those documents.

(3)   A public prosecutor who issues a written charge must notify the court officer immediately.

(4)   A single document may contain—

(a)   more than one information; or

(b)   more than one written charge.

(5)   Where an offence can be tried only in a magistrates' court, then unless other legislation otherwise provides—

(a)   a prosecutor must serve an information on the court officer or present it to the court; or

(b)   a public prosecutor must issue a written charge, not more than 6 months after the offence alleged.

(6)   Where an offence can be tried in the Crown Court then—

(a)   a prosecutor must serve an information on the court officer or present it to the court; or

(b)   a public prosecutor must issue a written charge, within any time limit that applies to that offence.

R-78   Allegation of offence in information or charge

7.3   (1)   An allegation of an offence in an information or charge must contain—

(a)   a statement of the offence that—

(i)   describes the offence in ordinary language, and

(ii)   identifies any legislation that creates it; and

(b)   such particulars of the conduct constituting the commission of the offence as to make clear what the prosecutor alleges against the defendant.

(2)   More than one incident of the commission of the offence may be included in the allegation if those incidents taken together amount to a course of conduct having regard to the time, place or purpose of commission.

Summons, warrant and requisition

7.4   (1) The court may issue or withdraw a summons or warrant—
            (a) without giving the parties an opportunity to make representations; and
            (b) without a hearing, or at a hearing in public or in private.
       (2) A summons, warrant or requisition may be issued in respect of more than one offence.
       (3) A summons or requisition must—
            (a) contain notice of when and where the defendant is required to attend the court;
            (b) specify each offence in respect of which it is issued; and
            (c) in the case of a summons, identify—
                 (i)   the court that issued it, unless that is otherwise recorded by the court officer,
                 (ii) the court office for the court that issued it; and
            (d) in the case of a requisition, identify the person under whose authority it is issued.
       (4) A summons may be contained in the same document as an information.
       (5) A requisition may be contained in the same document as a written charge.
       (6) Where the court issues a summons—
            (a) the prosecutor must—
                 (i)   serve it on the defendant, and
                 (ii) notify the court officer; or
            (b) the court officer must—
                 (i)   serve it on the defendant, and
                 (ii) notify the prosecutor.
       (7) Where a public prosecutor issues a requisition that prosecutor must—
            (a) serve on the defendant—
                 (i)   the requisition, and
                 (ii) the written charge; and
            (b) serve a copy of each on the court officer.
       (8) Unless it would be inconsistent with other legislation, a replacement summons or requisition
            may be issued without a fresh information or written charge where the one replaced—
            (a) was served by leaving or posting it under rule 4.7 (documents that must be served only by
                 handing them over, leaving or posting them); but
            (b) is shown not to have been received by the addressee.
       (9) A summons or requisition issued to a defendant under 18 may require that defendant's parent
            or guardian to attend the court with the defendant, or a separate summons or requisition may
            be issued for that purpose.

CRIMINAL PROCEDURE RULES   PART 8   DISCONTINUING A PROSECUTION

When this Part applies

8.1   (1) This Part applies where—
            (a) the Director of Public Prosecutions, or the Director of Revenue and Customs Prosecutions,
                 can discontinue a case in a magistrates' court, under section 23 of the Prosecution of
                 Offences Act 1985;
            (b) the Director of Public Prosecutions, or another public prosecutor, can discontinue a case
                 sent for trial in the Crown Court, under section 23A of the Prosecution of Offences
                 Act 1985.
       (2) In this Part, 'prosecutor' means one of those authorities.

Discontinuing a case

8.2   (1) A prosecutor exercising a power to which this Part applies must serve notice on—
            (a) the court officer;
            (b) the defendant; and
            (c) any custodian of the defendant.
       (2) Such a notice must—
            (a) identify—
                 (i)   the defendant and each offence to which the notice relates,
                 (ii) the person serving the notice, and
                 (iii) the power that that person is exercising;
            (b) explain—
                 (i)   in the copy of the notice served on the court officer, the reasons for discontinuing
                       the case,

(ii)   that the notice brings the case to an end,

(iii) if the defendant is in custody for any offence to which the notice relates, that the defendant must be released from that custody, and

(iv)   if the notice is under section 23 of the 1985 Act, that the defendant has a right to require the case to continue.

(3)   Where the defendant is on bail, the court officer must notify—

(a) any surety; and

(b) any person responsible for monitoring or securing the defendant's compliance with a condition of bail.

R-82 Defendant's notice to continue

8.3   (1) This rule applies where a prosecutor serves a notice to discontinue under section 23 of the 1985 Act.

(2) A defendant who wants the case to continue must serve notice—

(a) on the court officer; and

(b) not more than 35 days after service of the notice to discontinue.

(3) If the defendant serves such a notice, the court officer must—

(a) notify the prosecutor; and

(b) refer the case to the court.

CRIMINAL PROCEDURE RULES   PART 9   ALLOCATION AND SENDING FOR TRIAL

Section 1: general rules

R-83 When this Part applies

9.1   (1) This Part applies to the allocation and sending of cases for trial under—

(a) sections 17A to 26 of the Magistrates' Courts Act 1980; and

(b) sections 50A to 52 of the Crime and Disorder Act 1998.

(2) Section 2 of this Part applies in a magistrates' court where the court must, or can, send a defendant to the Crown Court for trial, without allocating the case for trial there.

(3) Section 3 of this Part applies in a magistrates' court where the court must allocate the case to a magistrates' court or to the Crown Court for trial.

(4) Section 4 of this Part applies in the Crown Court, where a defendant is sent for trial there.

R-84 Exercise of magistrates' court's powers

9.2   (1) This rule applies to the exercise of the powers to which Sections 2 and 3 apply.

(2) The general rule is that the court must exercise its powers at a hearing in public, but it may exercise any power it has to—

(a) withhold information from the public; or

(b) order a hearing in private.

(3) The general rule is that the court must exercise its powers in the defendant's presence, but it may exercise the powers to which the following rules apply in the defendant's absence on the conditions specified—

(a) where rule 9.8 (adult defendant: request for plea), rule 9.9 (adult defendant: guilty plea) or rule 9.13 (young defendant) applies, if—

(i)   the defendant is represented, and

(ii) the defendant's disorderly conduct makes his or her presence in the courtroom impracticable;

(b) where rule 9.10 (adult defendant: not guilty plea) or rule 9.11 (adult defendant: allocation for magistrates' court trial) applies, if—

(i)   the defendant is represented and waives the right to be present, or

(ii) the defendant's disorderly conduct makes his or her presence in the courtroom impracticable.

(4) The court may exercise its power to adjourn—

(a) if either party asks; or

(b) on its own initiative.

(5) Where the court on the same occasion deals with two or more offences offence alleged against the same defendant, the court must deal with those offences in the following sequence—

(a) any to which rule 9.6 applies (prosecutor's notice requiring Crown Court trial);

(b) any to which rule 9.7 applies (sending for Crown Court trial, without allocation there), in this sequence—

    (i) any the court must send for trial, then

    (ii) any the court can send for trial; and

(c) any to which rule 9.14 applies (allocation for Crown Court trial).

(6) Where the court on the same occasion deals with two or more defendants charged jointly with an offence that can be tried in the Crown Court then in the following sequence—

    (a) the court must explain, in terms each defendant can understand (with help, if necessary), that if the court sends one of them to the Crown Court for trial then the court must send for trial in the Crown Court, too, any other of them—

        (i) who is charged with the same offence as the defendant sent for trial, or with an offence which the court decides is related to that offence,

        (ii) who does not wish to plead guilty to each offence with which he or she is charged, and

        (iii) (if that other defendant is under 18, and the court would not otherwise have sent him or her for Crown Court trial) where the court decides that sending is necessary in the interests of justice

    even if the court by then has decided to allocate that other defendant for magistrates' court trial; and

    (b) the court may ask the defendants questions to help it decide in what order to deal with them.

(7) After following paragraph (5), if it applies, where the court on the same occasion—

    (a) deals with two or more defendants charged jointly with an offence that can be tried in the Crown Court;

    (b) allocates any of them to a magistrates' court for trial; and

    (c) then sends another one of them to the Crown Court for trial,

    the court must deal again with each one whom, on that occasion, it has allocated for magistrates' court trial.

Matters to be specified on sending for trial   R-85

9.3 (1) Where the court sends a defendant to the Crown Court for trial, it must specify—

    (a) each offence to be tried;

    (b) in respect of each, the power exercised to send the defendant for trial for that offence; and

    (c) the Crown Court centre at which the trial will take place.

(2) In a case in which the prosecutor serves a notice to which rule 9.6(1)(a) applies (notice requiring Crown Court trial in a case of serious or complex fraud), the court must specify the Crown Court centre identified by that notice.

(3) In any other case, in deciding the Crown Court centre at which the trial will take place, the court must take into account—

    (a) the convenience of the parties and witnesses;

    (b) how soon a suitable courtroom will be available; and

    (c) the directions on the allocation of Crown Court business contained in the Practice Direction.

Duty of justices' legal adviser   R-86

9.4 (1) This rule applies—

    (a) only in a magistrates' court; and

    (b) unless the court—

        (i) includes a District Judge (Magistrates' Courts), and

        (ii) otherwise directs.

(2) On the court's behalf, a justices' legal adviser may—

    (a) read the allegation of the offence to the defendant;

    (b) give any explanation and ask any question required by the rules in this Part;

    (c) make any announcement required by the rules in this Part, other than an announcement of—

        (i) the court's decisions about allocation and sending,

        (ii) any indication by the court of likely sentence, or

        (iii) sentence.

(3) A justices' legal adviser must—

    (a) assist an unrepresented defendant;

Criminal Procedure Rules 2013 and Criminal Practice Directions

    (b) give the court such advice as is required to enable it to exercise its powers;

    (c) if required, attend the members of the court outside the courtroom to give such advice, but inform the parties of any advice so given.

R-87 Duty of magistrates' court officer

9.5 (1) The magistrates' court officer must—

    (a) serve notice of a sending for Crown Court trial on—

      (i) the Crown Court officer, and

      (ii) the parties;

    (b) in that notice record—

      (i) the matters specified by the court under rule 9.3 (matters to be specified on sending for trial),

      (ii) any indication of intended guilty plea given by the defendant under rule 9.7 (sending for Crown Court trial),

      (iii) any decision by the defendant to decline magistrates' court trial under rule 9.11 (adult defendant: allocation to magistrates' court for trial), and

      (iv) the date on which any custody time limit will expire;

    (c) record any indication of likely sentence to which rule 9.11 applies; and

    (d) give the court such other assistance as it requires.

  (2) The magistrates' court officer must include with the notice served on the Crown Court officer—

    (a) the initial details of the prosecution case served by the prosecutor under rule 21.2;

    (b) a record of any—

      (i) listing or case management direction affecting the Crown Court,

      (ii) direction about reporting restrictions,

      (iii) decision about bail, for the purposes of section 5 of the Bail Act 1976,

      (iv) recognizance given by a surety, or

      (v) representation order; and

    (c) if relevant, any available details of any—

      (i) interpreter,

      (ii) intermediary, or

      (iii) other supporting adult, where the defendant is assisted by such a person.

Section 2: sending without allocation for Crown Court trial

R-88 Prosecutor's notice requiring Crown Court trial

9.6 (1) This rule applies where a prosecutor with power to do so requires a magistrates' court to send for trial in the Crown Court—

    (a) a case of serious or complex fraud; or

    (b) a case which will involve a child witness.

  (2) The prosecutor must serve written notice of that requirement—

    (a) on the magistrates' court officer and on the defendant; and

    (b) before trial in a magistrates' court begins under Part 37 (Trial and sentence in a magistrates' court).

  (3) The notice must identify—

    (a) the power on which the prosecutor relies; and

    (b) the Crown Court centre at which the prosecutor wants the trial to take place.

  (4) The prosecutor—

    (a) must, when choosing a Crown Court centre, take into account the matters listed in rule 9.3(3) (court deciding to which Crown Court centre to send a case); and

    (b) may change the centre identified before the case is sent for trial.

R-89 Sending for Crown Court trial

9.7 (1) This rule applies where a magistrates' court must, or can, send a defendant to the Crown Court for trial without first allocating the case for trial there.

  (2) The court must read the allegation of the offence to the defendant.

  (3) The court must explain, in terms the defendant can understand (with help, if necessary)—

    (a) the allegation, unless it is self-explanatory;

    (b) that the offence is one for which the court, as appropriate—

      (i) must send the defendant to the Crown Court for trial because the offence is one which can only be tried there or because the court for some other reason is required to send that offence for trial, or (ii)　may send the defendant to the Crown Court for trial if the magistrates' court decides that the offence is related to one already sent for trial there;

(c)　that reporting restrictions apply, which the defendant may ask the court to vary or remove.

(4)　In the following sequence, the court must then—

  (a)　invite the prosecutor to—

    (i)　identify the court's power to send the defendant to the Crown Court for trial for the offence, and

    (ii)　make representations about any ancillary matters, including bail and directions for the management of the case in the Crown Court;

  (b)　invite the defendant to make representations about—

    (i)　the court's power to send the defendant to the Crown Court, and

    (ii)　any ancillary matters; and

  (c)　decide whether or not to send the defendant to the Crown Court for trial.

(5)　If the court sends the defendant to the Crown Court for trial, it must—

  (a)　ask whether the defendant intends to plead guilty in the Crown Court and—

    (i)　if the answer is 'yes', make arrangements for the Crown Court to take the defendant's plea as soon as possible, or

    (ii)　if the defendant does not answer, or the answer is 'no', make arrangements for a case management hearing in the Crown Court; and

  (b)　give any other ancillary directions.

Section 3: allocation for magistrates' court or Crown Court trial

Adult defendant: request for plea　　　　　　　　　　　　　　　　　　　　　　**R-90**

9.8　(1)　This rule applies where—

  (a)　the defendant is 18 or over; and

  (b)　the court must decide whether a case is more suitable for trial in a magistrates' court or in the Crown Court.

(2)　The court must read the allegation of the offence to the defendant.

(3)　The court must explain, in terms the defendant can understand (with help, if necessary)—

  (a)　the allegation, unless it is self-explanatory;

  (b)　that the offence is one which can be tried in a magistrates' court or in the Crown Court;

  (c)　that the court is about to ask whether the defendant intends to plead guilty;

  (d)　that if the answer is 'yes', then the court must treat that as a guilty plea and must sentence the defendant, or commit the defendant to the Crown Court for sentence;

  (e)　that if the defendant does not answer, or the answer is 'no', then—

    (i)　the court must decide whether to allocate the case to a magistrates' court or to the Crown Court for trial,

    (ii)　the value involved may require the court to order trial in a magistrates' court (where the offence is one to which section 22 of the Magistrates' Courts Act 1980 applies), and

    (iii)　if the court allocates the case to a magistrates' court for trial, the defendant can nonetheless require trial in the Crown Court (unless the offence is one to which section 22 of the Magistrates' Courts Act 1980 applies and the value involved requires magistrates' court trial); and

  (f)　that reporting restrictions apply, which the defendant may ask the court to vary or remove.

(4)　The court must then ask whether the defendant intends to plead guilty.

Adult defendant: guilty plea　　　　　　　　　　　　　　　　　　　　　　　　　**R-91**

9.9　(1)　This rule applies where—

  (a)　rule 9.8 applies; and

  (b)　the defendant indicates an intention to plead guilty.

(2)　The court must exercise its power to deal with the case—

  (a)　as if the defendant had just pleaded guilty to an offence that can be tried only in a magistrates' court; and

  (b)　in accordance with rule 37.10 (procedure if the court convicts).

Adult defendant: not guilty plea　　　　　　　　　　　　　　　　　　　　　　　**R-92**

9.10　(1)　This rule applies where—

  (a)　rule 9.8 applies; and

  (b)　the defendant—

    (i)　indicates an intention to plead not guilty, or

Criminal Procedure Rules 2013 and Criminal Practice Directions

        (ii) gives no indication of intended plea.

(2) In the following sequence, the court must then—

    (a) where the offence is one to which section 22 of the Magistrates' Courts Act 1980 applies, explain in terms the defendant can understand (with help, if necessary) that—

        (i) if the court decides that the value involved clearly is less than £5,000, the court must order trial in a magistrates' court,

        (ii) if the court decides that it is not clear whether that value is more or less than £5,000, then the court will ask whether the defendant agrees to be tried in a magistrates' court, and

        (iii) if the answer to that question is 'yes', then the court must order such a trial and if the defendant is convicted then the maximum sentence is limited;

    (b) invite the prosecutor to—

        (i) identify any previous convictions of which it can take account, and

        (ii) make representations about how the court should allocate the case for trial, including representations about the value involved, if relevant;

    (c) invite the defendant to make such representations;

    (d) where the offence is one to which section 22 of the Magistrates' Courts Act 1980 applies—

        (i) if it is not clear whether the value involved is more or less than £5,000, ask whether the defendant agrees to be tried in a magistrates' court,

        (ii) if the defendant's answer to that question is 'yes', or if that value clearly is less than £5,000, order a trial in a magistrates' court,

        (iii) if the defendant does not answer that question, or the answer is 'no', or if that value clearly is more than £5,000, apply paragraph (2)(e);

    (e) exercise its power to allocate the case for trial, taking into account—

        (i) the adequacy of a magistrates' court's sentencing powers,

        (ii) any representations by the parties, and

        (iii) any allocation guidelines issued by the Sentencing Council.

R-93 Adult defendant: allocation for magistrates' court trial

9.11 (1) This rule applies where—

    (a) rule 9.10 applies; and

    (b) the court allocates the case to a magistrates' court for trial.

(2) The court must explain, in terms the defendant can understand (with help, if necessary) that—

    (a) the court considers the case more suitable for trial in a magistrates' court than in the Crown Court;

    (b) if the defendant is convicted at a magistrates' court trial, then in some circumstances the court may commit the defendant to the Crown Court for sentence;

    (c) if the defendant does not agree to a magistrates' court trial, then the court must send the defendant to the Crown Court for trial; and

    (d) before deciding whether to accept magistrates' court trial, the defendant may ask the court for an indication of whether a custodial or non-custodial sentence is more likely in the event of a guilty plea at such a trial, but the court need not give such an indication.

(3) If the defendant asks for such an indication of sentence and the court gives such an indication—

    (a) the court must then ask again whether the defendant intends to plead guilty;

    (b) if, in answer to that question, the defendant indicates an intention to plead guilty, then the court must exercise its power to deal with the case—

        (i) as if the defendant had just pleaded guilty to an offence that can be tried only in a magistrates' court, and

        (ii) in accordance with rule 37.10 (procedure if the court convicts);

    (c) if, in answer to that question, the defendant indicates an intention to plead not guilty, or gives no indication of intended plea, in the following sequence the court must then—

        (i) ask whether the defendant agrees to trial in a magistrates' court,

        (ii) if the defendant's answer to that question is 'yes', order such a trial,

        (iii) if the defendant does not answer that question, or the answer is 'no', apply rule 9.14.

(4) If the defendant asks for an indication of sentence but the court gives none, or if the defendant does not ask for such an indication, in the following sequence the court must then—

    (a) ask whether the defendant agrees to trial in a magistrates' court;

    (b) if the defendant's answer to that question is 'yes', order such a trial;

    (c) if the defendant does not answer that question, or the answer is 'no', apply rule 9.14.

Adult defendant: prosecutor's application for Crown Court trial   R-94

9.12 (1) This rule applies where—
  (a) rule 9.11 applies;
  (b) the defendant agrees to trial in a magistrates' court; but
  (c) the prosecutor wants the court to exercise its power to send the defendant to the Crown Court for trial instead.
  (2) The prosecutor must—
  (a) apply before trial in a magistrates' court begins under Part 37 (Trial and sentence in a magistrates' court); and
  (b) notify—
    (i) the defendant, and
    (ii) the magistrates' court officer.
  (3) The court must determine an application to which this rule applies before it deals with any other pre-trial application.

Young defendant   R-95

9.13 (1) This rule applies where—
  (a) the defendant is under 18; and
  (b) the court must decide whether to send the defendant for Crown Court trial instead of ordering trial in a youth court.
  (2) The court must read the allegation of the offence to the defendant.
  (3) The court must explain, in terms the defendant can understand (with help, if necessary)—
  (a) the allegation, unless it is self-explanatory;
  (b) that the offence is one which can be tried in the Crown Court instead of in a youth court;
  (c) that the court is about to ask whether the defendant intends to plead guilty;
  (d) that if the answer is 'yes', then the court must treat that as a guilty plea and must sentence the defendant, or commit the defendant to the Crown Court for sentence;
  (e) that if the defendant does not answer, or the answer is 'no', then the court must decide whether to send the defendant for Crown Court trial instead of ordering trial in a youth court; and
  (f) that reporting restrictions apply, which the defendant may ask the court to vary or remove.
  (4) The court must then ask whether the defendant intends to plead guilty.
  (5) If the defendant's answer to that question is 'yes', the court must exercise its power to deal with the case—
  (a) as if the defendant had just pleaded guilty to an offence that can be tried only in a magistrates' court; and
  (b) in accordance with rule 37.10 (procedure if the court convicts).
  (6) If the defendant does not answer that question, or the answer is 'no', in the following sequence the court must then—
  (a) invite the prosecutor to make representations about whether Crown Court or youth court trial is more appropriate;
  (b) invite the defendant to make such representations;
  (c) exercise its power to allocate the case for trial, taking into account—
    (i) the offence and the circumstances of the offence,
    (ii) the suitability of a youth court's sentencing powers,
    (iii) where the defendant is jointly charged with an adult, whether it is necessary in the interests of justice for them to be tried together in the Crown Court, and
    (iv) any representations by the parties.

Allocation and sending for Crown Court trial   R-96

9.14 (1) This rule applies where—
  (a) under rule 9.10 or rule 9.13, the court allocates the case to the Crown Court for trial;
  (b) under rule 9.11, the defendant does not agree to trial in a magistrates' court; or
  (c) under rule 9.12, the court grants the prosecutor's application for Crown Court trial.
  (2) In the following sequence, the court must—
  (a) invite the prosecutor to make representations about any ancillary matters, including bail and directions for the management of the case in the Crown Court;
  (b) invite the defendant to make any such representations; and
  (c) exercise its powers to—
    (i) send the defendant to the Crown Court for trial, and
    (ii) give any ancillary directions.

Criminal Procedure Rules 2013 and Criminal Practice Directions

Section 4: Crown Court initial procedure after sending for trial

R-97 **Service of prosecution evidence**

9.15   (1) This rule applies where—
  (a) a magistrates' court sends the defendant to the Crown Court for trial; and
  (b) the prosecutor serves on the defendant copies of the documents containing the evidence on which the prosecution case relies.
  (2) The prosecutor must at the same time serve copies of those documents on the Crown Court officer.

R-98 **Application to dismiss offence sent for Crown Court trial**

9.16   (1) This rule applies where a defendant wants the Crown Court to dismiss an offence sent for trial there.
  (2) The defendant must—
  (a) apply in writing—
    (i)   not more than 28 days after service of the prosecution evidence, and
    (ii) before the defendant's arraignment;
  (b) serve the application on—
    (i)   the Crown Court officer, and
    (ii) each other party;
  (c) in the application—
    (i)   explain why the prosecution evidence would not be sufficient for the defendant to be properly convicted,
    (ii) ask for a hearing, if the defendant wants one, and explain why it is needed,
    (iii) identify any witness whom the defendant wants to call to give evidence in person, with an indication of what evidence the witness can give,
    (iv) identify any material already served that the defendant thinks the court will need to determine the application, and
    (v)   include any material not already served on which the defendant relies.
  (3) A prosecutor who opposes the application must—
  (a) serve notice of opposition, not more than 14 days after service of the defendant's notice, on—
    (i)   the Crown Court officer, and
    (ii) each other party;
  (b) in the notice of opposition—
    (i)   explain the grounds of opposition,
    (ii) ask for a hearing, if the prosecutor wants one, and explain why it is needed,
    (iii) identify any witness whom the prosecutor wants to call to give evidence in person, with an indication of what evidence the witness can give,
    (iv) identify any material already served that the prosecutor thinks the court will need to determine the application, and
    (v)   include any material not already served on which the prosecutor relies.
  (4) The court may determine an application under this rule—
  (a) at a hearing, in public or in private, or without a hearing;
  (b) in the absence of—
    (i)   the defendant who made the application,
    (ii) the prosecutor, if the prosecutor has had at least 14 days in which to serve notice opposing the application.
  (5) The court may—
  (a) shorten or extend (even after it has expired) a time limit under this rule;
  (b) allow a witness to give evidence in person even if that witness was not identified in the defendant's application or in the prosecutor's notice.

Criminal Practice Directions   Part 9   Allocation and Sending for Trial

PD-15 **CPD II Preliminary proceedings 9A: ALLOCATION (MODE OF TRIAL)**

9A.1 Courts must follow the Sentencing Council's guideline on Allocation (mode of trial) when deciding whether or not to send defendants charged with 'either way' offences for trial in the Crown Court under section 51(1) of the Crime and Disorder Act 1998. The guideline refers to the factors to which a court must have regard in accordance with section 19 of the Magistrates' Courts Act 1980. Section 19(2) (a) permits reference to previous convictions of the defendant.

9A.2 The Allocation guideline lists four factors, a) to d), that the court must also have regard to. No examples or guidance are given, however, the following could be a consideration when applying the factors: that where cases involve complex questions of fact or difficult questions of law, including difficult issues of disclosure of sensitive material, the court should consider sending for trial.

9A.3 Certain general observations can also be made:

(a) the court should never make its decision on the grounds of convenience or expedition; and

(b) the fact that the offences are alleged to be specimens is a relevant consideration (although it has to be borne in mind that difficulties can arise in sentencing in relation to specimen counts: see *R v Clark* [1996] 2 Cr App R 282, [1996] 2 Cr App R (S) 351; *R v Canavan and others* [1998] 1 WLR 604, [1998] 1 Cr App R 79, [1998] 1 Cr App R (S) 243 and *R v Oakes* [2012] EWCA Crim 2435, [2013] 2 Cr App R (S) 22 (see case of *R v Restivo*)); the fact that the defendant will be asking for other offences to be taken into consideration, if convicted, is not.

CRIMINAL PROCEDURE RULES   PART 10   INITIAL DETAILS OF THE PROSECUTION CASE

When this Part applies   R-99

10.1 (1) This Part applies in a magistrates' court, where the offence is one that can be tried in a magistrates' court.

(2) The court may direct that, for a specified period, this Part will not apply—

(a) to any case in that court; or

(b) to any specified category of case.

Providing initial details of the prosecution case   R-100

10.2 (1) The prosecutor must serve initial details of the prosecution case on the court officer—

(a) as soon as practicable; and

(b) in any event, no later than the beginning of the day of the first hearing.

(2) Where a defendant requests those details, the prosecutor must serve them on the defendant—

(a) as soon as practicable; and

(b) in any event, no later than the beginning of the day of the first hearing.

(3) Where a defendant does not request those details, the prosecutor must make them available to the defendant at, or before, the beginning of the day of the first hearing.

Content of initial details   R-101

10.3 Initial details of the prosecution case must include—

(a) a summary of the evidence on which that case will be based; or

(b) any statement, document or extract setting out facts or other matters on which that case will be based; or

(c) any combination of such a summary, statement, document or extract; and

(d) the defendant's previous convictions.

Criminal Practice Directions   Part 10   Initial Details of the Prosecution Case

CPD II Preliminary proceedings 10A: Defendant's Record   PD-16

Copies of record

10A.1 The defendant's record (previous convictions, cautions, reprimands, etc) may be taken into account when the court decides not only on sentence but also, for example, about bail, or when allocating a case for trial. It is therefore important that up to date and accurate information is available. Previous convictions must be provided as part of the initial details of the prosecution case under Part 10 of the Rules.

10A.2 The record should usually be provided in the following format:

Personal details and summary of convictions and cautions – Police National Computer ["PNC"] Court/Defence/Probation Summary Sheet;

Previous convictions – PNC Court/Defence/Probation printout, supplemented by Form MG16 if the police force holds convictions not shown on PNC;

Recorded cautions – PNC Court/Defence/Probation printout, supplemented by Form MG17 if the police force holds cautions not shown on PNC.

10A.3 The defence representative should take instructions on the defendant's record and if the defence wish to raise any objection to the record, this should be made known to the prosecutor immediately.

10A.4 It is the responsibility of the prosecutor to ensure that a copy of the defendant's record has been provided to the Probation Service.

10A.5 Where following conviction a custodial order is made, the court must ensure that a copy is attached to the order sent to the prison.

Additional information

10A.6 In the Crown Court, the police should also provide brief details of the circumstances of the last three similar convictions and/or of convictions likely to be of interest to the court, the latter being judged on a case-by-case basis.

10A.7 Where the current alleged offence could constitute a breach of an existing sentence such as a suspended sentence, community order or conditional discharge, and it is known that that sentence is still in force then details of the circumstances of the offence leading to the sentence should be included in the antecedents. The detail should be brief and include the date of the offence.

10A.8 On occasions the PNC printout provided may not be fully up to date. It is the responsibility of the prosecutor to ensure that all of the necessary information is available to the court and the Probation Service and provided to the defence. Oral updates at the hearing will sometimes be necessary, but it is preferable if this information is available in advance.

CRIMINAL PROCEDURE RULES   PART 11
[There are no rules in this part.]

CRIMINAL PROCEDURE RULES   PART 12 DEFERRED PROSECUTION AGREEMENTS

R-101A   **When this Part applies**

12.1 (1) This Part applies to proceedings in the Crown Court under Schedule 17 to the Crime and Courts Act 2013.

(2) In this Part—

(a) 'agreement' means a deferred prosecution agreement under paragraph 1 of that Schedule;

(b) 'prosecutor' means a prosecutor designated by or under paragraph 3 of that Schedule; and

(c) 'defendant' means the corporation, partnership or association with whom the prosecutor proposes to enter, or enters, an agreement.

R-101B   **Exercise of court's powers**

12.2 (1) The court must determine an application to which this Part applies at a hearing, which—

(a) must be in private, under rule 12.3 (Application to approve a proposal to enter an agreement);

(b) may be in public or private, under rule 12.4 (Application to approve the terms of an agreement), rule 12.6 (Application to approve a variation of the terms of an agreement) or rule 12.9 (Application to postpone the publication of information by the prosecutor);

(c) must be in public, under rule 12.5 (Application on breach of agreement) or rule 12.7 (Application to lift suspension of prosecution), unless the court otherwise directs.

(2) If at a hearing in private to which rule 12.4 or rule 12.6 applies the court approves the agreement or the variation proposed, the court must announce its decision and reasons at a hearing in public.

(3) The court must not determine an application under rule 12.3, rule 12.4 or rule 12.6 unless—

(a) both parties are present;

(b) the prosecutor provides the court with a written declaration that, for the purposes of the application—

(i) the investigator enquiring into the alleged offence or offences has certified that no information has been supplied which the investigator knows to be inaccurate, misleading or incomplete, and

(ii) the prosecutor has complied with the prosecution obligation to disclose material to the defendant; and

    (c) the defendant provides the court with a written declaration that, for the purposes of the application—

        (i) the defendant has not supplied any information which the defendant knows to be inaccurate, misleading or incomplete, and

        (ii) the individual through whom the defendant makes the declaration has made reasonable enquiries and believes the defendant's declaration to be true.

(4) The court must not determine an application under rule 12.5 or rule 12.7—

    (a) in the prosecutor's absence; or

    (b) in the absence of the defendant, unless the defendant has had at least 28 days in which to make representations.

(5) If the court approves a proposal to enter an agreement—

    (a) the general rule is that any further application to which this Part applies must be made to the same judge; but

    (b) the court may direct other arrangements.

(6) The court may adjourn a hearing—

    (a) if either party asks, or on its own initiative;

    (b) in particular, if the court requires more information about—

        (i) the facts of an alleged offence,

        (ii) the terms of a proposal to enter an agreement, or of a proposed agreement or variation of an agreement, or

        (iii) the circumstances in which the prosecutor wants the court to decide whether the defendant has failed to comply with the terms of an agreement.

(7) The court may—

    (a) hear an application under rule 12.4 immediately after an application under rule 12.3, if the court approves a proposal to enter an agreement;

    (b) hear an application under rule 12.7 immediately after an application under rule 12.5, if the court terminates an agreement.

Application to approve a proposal to enter an agreement   R-101C

12.3 (1) This rule applies where a prosecutor wants the court to approve a proposal to enter an agreement.

    (2) The prosecutor must—

      (a) apply in writing after the commencement of negotiations between the parties but before the terms of agreement have been settled; and

      (b) serve the application on—

        (i) the court officer, and

        (ii) the defendant.

    (3) The application must—

      (a) identify the parties to the proposed agreement;

      (b) attach a proposed indictment setting out such of the offences listed in Part 2 of Schedule 17 to the Crime and Courts Act 2013 as the prosecutor is considering;

      (c) include or attach a statement of facts proposed for inclusion in the agreement, which must give full particulars of each alleged offence, including details of any alleged financial gain or loss;

      (d) include any information about the defendant that would be relevant to sentence in the event of conviction for the offence or offences;

      (e) specify the proposed expiry date of the agreement;

      (f) describe the proposed terms of the agreement, including details of any—

        (i) monetary penalty to be paid by the defendant, and the time within which any such penalty is to be paid,

        (ii) compensation, reparation or donation to be made by the defendant, the identity of the recipient of any such payment and the time within which any such payment is to be made,

        (iii) surrender of profits or other financial benefit by the defendant, and the time within which any such sum is to be surrendered,

        (iv) arrangement to be made in relation to the management or conduct of the defendant's business,

        (v) co-operation required of the defendant in any investigation related to the offence or offences,

        (vi) other action required of the defendant,

        (vii) arrangement to monitor the defendant's compliance with a term,

          (viii)   consequence of the defendant's failure to comply with a term, and
          (ix)   prosecution costs to be paid by the defendant, and the time within which any such costs are to be paid;

(g) in relation to those terms, explain how they comply with—
     (i)   the requirements of the code issued under paragraph 6 of Schedule 17 to the Crime and Courts Act 2013, and
     (ii) any sentencing guidelines or guideline cases which apply;

(h) contain or attach the defendant's written consent to the proposal; and

(i) explain why—
     (i)   entering into an agreement is likely to be in the interests of justice, and
     (ii) the proposed terms of the agreement are fair, reasonable and proportionate.

(4) If the proposed statement of facts includes assertions that the defendant does not admit, the application must—

(a) specify the facts that are not admitted; and

(b) explain why that is immaterial for the purposes of the proposal to enter an agreement.

R-101D   Application to approve the terms of an agreement

12.4 (1) This rule applies where—

(a) the court has approved a proposal to enter an agreement on an application under rule 12.3; and

(b) the prosecutor wants the court to approve the terms of the agreement.

(2) The prosecutor must—

(a) apply in writing as soon as practicable after the parties have settled the terms; and

(b) serve the application on—
     (i)   the court officer, and
     (ii) the defendant.

(3) The application must—

(a) attach the agreement;

(b) indicate in what respect, if any, the terms of the agreement differ from those proposed in the application under rule 12.3;

(c) contain or attach the defendant's written consent to the agreement;

(d) explain why—
     (i)   the agreement is in the interests of justice, and
     (ii) the terms of the agreement are fair, reasonable and proportionate;

(e) attach a draft indictment, charging the defendant with the offence or offences the subject of the agreement; and

(f) include any application for the hearing to be in private.

(4) If the court approves the agreement and the draft indictment, the court officer must—

(a) sign and date the indictment, as if the draft had been served under rule 14.1 (Service and signature of indictment); and

(b) treat the case as if it had been suspended by order of the court.

R-101E   Application on breach of agreement

12.5 (1) This rule applies where—

(a) the prosecutor believes that the defendant has failed to comply with the terms of an agreement; and

(b) the prosecutor wants the court to decide—
     (i)   whether the defendant has failed to comply, and
     (ii) if so, whether to terminate the agreement, or to invite the parties to agree proposals to remedy that failure.

(2) The prosecutor must—

(a) apply in writing, as soon as practicable after becoming aware of the grounds for doing so; and

(b) serve the application on—
     (i)   the court officer, and
     (ii) the defendant.

(3) The application must—

(a) specify each respect in which the prosecutor believes the defendant has failed to comply with the terms of the agreement, and explain the reasons for the prosecutor's belief; and

(b) attach a copy of any document containing evidence on which the prosecutor relies.

(4) A defendant who wants to make representations in response to the application must serve the representations on—

(a) the court officer; and

(b) the prosecutor,

not more than 28 days after service of the application.

Application to approve a variation of the terms of an agreement   R-101F

12.6 (1) This rule applies where the parties have agreed to vary the terms of an agreement because—

(a) on an application under rule 12.5 (Application on breach of agreement), the court has invited them to do so; or

(b) variation of the agreement is necessary to avoid a failure by the defendant to comply with its terms in circumstances that were not, and could not have been, foreseen by either party at the time the agreement was made.

(2) The prosecutor must—

(a) apply in writing, as soon as practicable after the parties have settled the terms of the variation; and

(b) serve the application on—

(i) the court officer, and

(ii) the defendant.

(3) The application must—

(a) specify each variation proposed;

(b) contain or attach the defendant's written consent to the variation;

(c) explain why—

(i) the variation is in the interests of justice, and

(ii) the terms of the agreement as varied are fair, reasonable and proportionate; and

(d) include any application for the hearing to be in private.

Application to lift suspension of prosecution   R-101G

12.7 (1) This rule applies where—

(a) the court terminates an agreement before its expiry date; and

(b) the prosecutor wants the court to lift the suspension of the prosecution that applied when the court approved the terms of the agreement.

(2) The prosecutor must—

(a) apply in writing, as soon as practicable after the termination of the agreement; and

(b) serve the application on—

(i) the court officer, and

(ii) the defendant.

(3) A defendant who wants to make representations in response to the application must serve the representations on—

(a) the court officer; and

(b) the prosecutor,

not more than 28 days after service of the application.

Notice to discontinue prosecution   R-101H

12.8 (1) This rule applies where an agreement expires—

(a) on its expiry date, or on a date treated as its expiry date; and

(b) without having been terminated by the court.

(2) The prosecutor must—

(a) as soon as practicable give notice in writing discontinuing the prosecution on the indictment approved by the court under rule 12.4 (Application to approve the terms of an agreement); and

(b) serve the notice on—

(i) the court officer, and

(ii) the defendant.

Application to postpone the publication of information by the prosecutor   R-101I

12.9 (1) This rule applies where the prosecutor—

(a) makes an application under rule 12.4 (Application to approve the terms of an agreement), rule 12.5 (Application on breach of agreement) or rule 12.6 (Application to approve a variation of the terms of an agreement);

    (b) decides not to make an application under rule 12.5, despite believing that the defendant has failed to comply with the terms of the agreement; or

    (c) gives a notice under rule 12.8 (Notice to discontinue prosecution).

  (2) A party who wants the court to order that the publication of information by the prosecutor about the court's or the prosecutor's decision should be postponed must—

    (a) apply in writing, as soon as practicable and in any event before such publication occurs;

    (b) serve the application on—

      (i) the court officer, and

      (ii) the other party; and

    (c) in the application—

      (i) specify the proposed terms of the order, and for how long it should last, and

      (ii) explain why an order in the terms proposed is necessary.

R-101J Duty of court officer, etc.

12.10 (1) Unless the court otherwise directs, the court officer must—

    (a) arrange for the recording of proceedings on an application to which this Part applies;

    (b) arrange for the transcription of such a recording if—

      (i) a party wants such a transcript, or

      (ii) anyone else wants such a transcript (but that is subject to the restrictions in paragraph (2)).

  (2) Unless the court otherwise directs, a person who transcribes a recording of proceedings under such arrangements—

    (a) must not supply anyone other than a party with a transcript of a recording of—

      (i) a hearing in private, or

      (ii) a hearing in public to which reporting restrictions apply;

    (b) subject to that, must supply any person with any transcript for which that person asks—

      (i) in accordance with the transcription arrangements made by the court officer, and

      (ii) on payment by that person of any fee prescribed.

  (3) The court officer must not identify either party to a hearing in private under rule 12.3 (Application to approve a proposal to enter an agreement) or rule 12.4 (Application to approve the terms of an agreement)—

    (a) in any notice displayed in the vicinity of the courtroom; or

    (b) in any other information published by the court officer.

R-101K Court's power to vary requirements under this Part

12.11 (1) The court may—

    (a) shorten or extend (even after it has expired) a time limit under this Part;

    (b) allow there to be made orally—

      (i) an application under rule 12.4 (Application to approve the terms of an agreement), or

      (ii) an application under rule 12.7 (Application to lift suspension of prosecution)

    where the court exercises its power under rule 12.2(7) to hear one application immediately after another.

  (2) A party who wants an extension of time must—

    (a) apply when serving the application or notice for which it is needed; and

    (b) explain the delay.

CRIMINAL PROCEDURE RULES PART 13

[There are no rules in this part.]

CRIMINAL PROCEDURE RULES PART 14 THE INDICTMENT

R-102 Service and signature of indictment

14.1 (1) The prosecutor must serve a draft indictment on the Crown Court officer not more than 28 days after—

    (a) service on the defendant and on the Crown Court officer of copies of the documents containing the evidence on which the charge or charges are based, in a case where the defendant is sent for trial;

    (b) a High Court judge gives permission to serve a draft indictment;

    (c) the Court of Appeal orders a retrial; or

      (d) the committal or transfer of the defendant for trial.
  (2) The Crown Court may extend the time limit, even after it has expired.
  (3) Unless the Crown Court otherwise directs, the court officer must—
      (a) sign, and add the date of receipt on, the indictment; and
      (b) serve a copy of the indictment on all parties.

Form and content of indictment   R-103

14.2 (1) An indictment must be in one of the forms set out in the Practice Direction and must contain, in a paragraph called a 'count'—
      (a) a statement of the offence charged that—
          (i)   describes the offence in ordinary language, and
          (ii) identifies any legislation that creates it; and
      (b) such particulars of the conduct constituting the commission of the offence as to make clear what the prosecutor alleges against the defendant.
  (2) More than one incident of the commission of the offence may be included in a count if those incidents taken together amount to a course of conduct having regard to the time, place or purpose of commission.
  (3) An indictment may contain more than one count if all the offences charged—
      (a) are founded on the same facts; or
      (b) form or are a part of a series of offences of the same or a similar character.
  (4) The counts must be numbered consecutively.
  (5) An indictment may contain—
      (a) any count charging substantially the same offence as one—
          (i)   specified in the notice of the offence or offences for which the defendant was sent for trial,
          (ii) on which the defendant was committed for trial, or
          (iii) specified in the notice of transfer given by the prosecutor; and
      (b) any other count based on the prosecution evidence already served which the Crown Court may try.

Criminal Practice Directions   Part 14   The Indictment

CPD II Preliminary proceedings 14A: Settling the Indictment   PD-17

14A.1 Rule 14.1 of the Criminal Procedure Rules requires the prosecutor to serve a draft indictment not more than 28 days after service of the evidence in a case sent for trial, after the sending of the defendant for trial, or after one of the other events listed in that rule. Rule 14.2(5) provides that an indictment may contain any count charging substantially the same offence as one sent for trial and any other count based on the prosecution evidence already served which the Crown Court has jurisdiction to try. Where the prosecutor intends to include in the draft indictment counts which differ materially from, or are additional to, those on which the defendant was sent for trial then the defendant should be given as much notice as possible, usually by service of a draft indictment, or a provisional draft indictment, at the earliest possible opportunity.

14A.2 There is no rule of law or practice which prohibits two indictments being in existence at the same time for the same offence against the same person and on the same facts. But the court will not allow the prosecution to proceed on both indictments. They cannot be tried together and the court will require the prosecution to elect the one on which the trial will proceed. Where different defendants have been separately sent for trial for offences which can lawfully be charged in the same indictment, then it is permissible to join in one indictment counts based on the separate sendings for trial even if an indictment based on one of them already has been signed. Where necessary the court should be invited to exercise its powers of amendment under section 5 of the Indictments Act 1915.

14A.3 Save in the special circumstances described in the following paragraphs of this Practice Direction, it is undesirable that a large number of counts should be contained in one indictment. Where defendants on trial have a variety of offences alleged against them then, in the interests of effective case management, it is the court's responsibility to exercise its powers in accordance with the overriding objective set out in Part 1 of the Criminal Procedure Rules. The prosecution may be required to identify a selection of counts on which the trial should proceed, leaving a decision to be taken later whether to try any of the remainder. Where an indictment contains substantive counts and one or more related conspiracy counts, the court will expect the prosecution to justify the joinder. Failing justification, the prosecution should be required to choose whether to proceed on the substantive counts or on the conspiracy counts. In any event, if there is a conviction on any counts that are tried, then those that have been postponed can remain on the file marked 'not to be proceeded with without the leave of the court or the Court of Appeal'. In the event that a conviction is later quashed on appeal, the remaining counts can be tried. Where necessary the court has power to order that an indictment be severed.

Multiple offending: trial by jury and then by judge alone

14A.4 Under sections 17 to 21 of the Domestic Violence, Crime and Victims Act 2004, the court may order that the trial of certain counts will be by jury in the usual way and, if the jury convicts, that other associated counts will be tried by judge alone. The use of this power is likely to be appropriate where justice cannot be done without charging a large number of separate offences and the allegations against the defendant appear to fall into distinct groups by reference to the identity of the victim, by reference to the dates of the offences, or by some other distinction in the nature of the offending conduct alleged.

14A.5 In such a case, it is essential to make clear from the outset the association asserted by the prosecutor between those counts to be tried by a jury and those counts which it is proposed should be tried by judge alone, if the jury convict on the former. A special form of indictment is prescribed for this purpose.

14A.6 An order for such a trial may be made only at a preparatory hearing. It follows that where the prosecutor intends to invite the court to order such a trial it will normally be appropriate to proceed as follows. The draft indictment served under Rule 14.1 should be in the form appropriate to such a trial. It should be accompanied by an application under Rule 15.3 for a preparatory hearing. This will ensure that the defendant is aware at the earliest possible opportunity of what the prosecution propose and of the proposed association of counts in the indictment. It is undesirable for a draft indictment in the usual form to be served where the prosecutor expects to apply for a two stage trial and hence, of necessity, for permission to amend the indictment at a later stage in order that it may be in the special form.

14A.7 On receipt of a draft two part indictment, a Crown Court officer should sign it at the end of Part Two. At the start of the preparatory hearing, the defendant should be arraigned on all counts in Part One of the indictment. Arraignment on Part Two need not take place until after there has been either a guilty plea to, or finding of guilt on, an associated count in Part One of the indictment.

14A.8 If the prosecution application is successful, the prosecutor should prepare an abstract of the indictment, containing the counts from Part One only, for use in the jury trial. Preparation of such an abstract does not involve 'amendment' of the indictment. It is akin to where a defendant pleads guilty to certain counts in an indictment and is put in the charge of the jury on the remaining counts only.

14A.9 If the prosecution application for a two stage trial is unsuccessful, the prosecutor may apply to amend the indictment to remove from it any counts in Part Two which would make jury trial on the whole indictment impracticable and to revert to a standard form of indictment. It will be a matter for the court whether arraignment on outstanding counts takes place at the preparatory hearing, or at a future date.

Multiple offending: count charging more than one incident

14A.10 Rule 14.2(2) of the Criminal Procedure Rules allows a single count to allege more than one incident of the commission of an offence in certain circumstances. Each incident must be of the same offence. The circumstances in which such a count may be appropriate include, but are not limited to, the following:

(a) the victim on each occasion was the same, or there was no identifiable individual victim as, for example, in a case of the unlawful importation of controlled drugs or of money laundering;

(b) the alleged incidents involved a marked degree of repetition in the method employed or in their location, or both;

(c) the alleged incidents took place over a clearly defined period, typically (but not necessarily) no more than about a year;

(d) in any event, the defence is such as to apply to every alleged incident without differentiation. Where what is in issue differs between different incidents, a single 'multiple incidents' count will not be appropriate, though it may be appropriate to use two or more such counts according to the circumstances and to the issues raised by the defence.

14A.11 Even in circumstances such as those set out above, there may be occasions on which a prosecutor chooses not to use such a count, in order to bring the case within section 75(3) (a) of the Proceeds of Crime Act 2002 (criminal lifestyle established by conviction of three or more offences in the same proceedings): for example, because section 75(2) (c) of that Act does not apply (criminal lifestyle established by an offence committed over a period of at least six months). Where the prosecutor proposes such a course, it is unlikely that Part 1 of the Rules (the overriding objective) will require an indictment to contain a single 'multiple incidents' count in place of a larger number of counts, subject to the general principles set out at 14A.3.

14A.12 For some offences, particularly sexual offences, the penalty for the offence may have changed during the period over which the alleged incidents took place. In such a case, additional 'multiple incidents' counts should be used so that each count only alleges incidents to which the same maximum penalty applies.

14A.13 In other cases, such as sexual or physical abuse, a complainant may be in a position only to give evidence of a series of similar incidents without being able to specify when or the precise circumstances in which they occurred. In these cases, a 'multiple incidents' count may be desirable. If on the other hand, the complainant is able to identify particular incidents of the offence by reference to a date or other specific event, but alleges that in addition there were other incidents which the complainant is unable to specify, then it may be desirable to include separate counts for the identified incidents and a 'multiple incidents' count or counts alleging that incidents of the same offence occurred 'many' times. Using a 'multiple incidents' count may be an appropriate alternative to using 'specimen' counts in some cases where repeated sexual or physical abuse is alleged. The choice of count will depend on the particular circumstances of the case and should be determined bearing in mind the implications for sentencing set out in *R v Canavan; R v Kidd; R v Shaw* [1998] 1 WLR 604, [1998] 1 Cr App R 79, [1998] 1 Cr App R (S) 243.

CPD II Preliminary proceedings 14B: Voluntary Bills of Indictment   **PD-18**

14B.1 Section 2(2) (b) of the Administration of Justice (Miscellaneous Provisions) Act 1933 and paragraph 2(6) of Schedule 3 to the Crime and Disorder Act 1998 allow the preferment of a bill of indictment by the direction or with the consent of a judge of the High Court. Bills so preferred are known as 'voluntary bills'.

14B.2 Applications for such consent must not only comply with each paragraph of the Indictments (Procedure) Rules 1971, SI 1971/2084, but must also be accompanied by:

(a) a copy of any charges on which the defendant has been sent for trial;

(b) a copy of any charges on which his or her sending for trial was refused by the magistrates' court;

(c) a copy of any existing indictment which has been preferred in consequence of his or her sending for trial;

(d) a summary of the evidence or other document which;

  (i) identifies the counts in the proposed indictment on which he or she has been sent for trial (or which are substantially the same as charges on which he or she has been so sent), and

  (ii) in relation to each other count in the proposed indictment, identifies the pages in the accompanying statements and exhibits where the essential evidence said to support that count is to be found.

14B.3 These requirements should be complied with in relation to each defendant named in the indictment for which consent is sought, whether or not it is proposed to prefer any new count against him or her.

14B.4 The preferment of a voluntary bill is an exceptional procedure. Consent should only be granted where good reason to depart from the normal procedure is clearly shown and only where the interests of justice, rather than considerations of administrative convenience, require it.

14B.5 Neither the 1933 Act, the 1998 Act nor the 1971 Rules expressly require a prosecuting authority applying for consent to the preferment of a voluntary bill to give notice of the application to the prospective defendant, nor to serve on him or her a copy of documents delivered to the judge; nor is it expressly required that the prospective defendant have any opportunity to make any submissions to the judge, whether in writing or orally.

14B.6 However, the Attorney-General previously issued guidance to prosecutors on the procedures to be adopted in seeking judicial consent to the preferment of voluntary bills. Those procedures remain applicable and prosecutors should:

(a) on making an application for consent to preferment of a voluntary bill, give notice to the prospective defendant that such application has been made;

(b) at about the same time, serve on the prospective defendant a copy of all the documents delivered to the judge (save to the extent that these have already been served on him or her);

(c) inform the prospective defendant that he or she may make submissions in writing to the judge, provided that he or she does so within nine working days of the giving of notice under (a) above.

14B.7 Prosecutors must follow these procedures unless there are good reasons for not doing so, in which case prosecutors must inform the judge that the procedures have not been followed and seek leave to dispense with all or any of them. Judges should not give leave to dispense unless good reasons are shown.

14B.8 A judge to whom application for consent to the preferment of a voluntary bill is made will, of course, wish to consider carefully the documents submitted by the prosecutor and any written submissions made by the prospective defendant, and may properly seek any necessary amplification. The judge may invite oral submissions from either party, or accede to a request for an opportunity to make oral submissions, if the judge considers it necessary or desirable to receive oral submissions in order to make a sound and fair decision on the application. Any such oral submissions should be made on notice to the other party and in open court.

CRIMINAL PROCEDURE RULES   PART 15   PREPARATORY HEARINGS IN THE CROWN COURT

R-104   **When this Part applies**

15.1   (1)   This Part applies where the Crown Court—
>   (a)   can order a preparatory hearing, under—
>>   (i)   section 7 of the Criminal Justice Act 1987 (cases of serious or complex fraud), or
>>   (ii)   section 29 of the Criminal Procedure and Investigations Act 1996 (other complex, serious or lengthy cases);
>   (b)   must order such a hearing, to determine an application for a trial without a jury, under—
>>   (i)   section 44 of the Criminal Justice Act 2003 (danger of jury tampering), or
>>   (ii)   section 17 of the Domestic Violence, Crime and Victims Act 2004 (trial of sample counts by jury, and others by judge alone);
>   (c)   must order such a hearing, under section 29 of the 1996 Act, where section 29(1B) or (1C) applies (cases in which a terrorism offence is charged, or other serious cases with a terrorist connection).

R-105   **Exercise of court's powers**

15.2   The court may decide whether to order a preparatory hearing—
>   (a)   on an application or on its own initiative;
>   (b)   at a hearing, in public or in private, or without a hearing;
>   (c)   in a party's absence, if that party—
>>   (i)   applied for the order, or
>>   (ii)   has had at least 14 days in which to make representations.

R-106   **Application for preparatory hearing**

15.3   (1)   A party who wants the court to order a preparatory hearing must—
>   (a)   apply in writing—
>>   (i)   as soon as reasonably practicable, and in any event
>>   (ii)   not more than 14 days after the defendant pleads not guilty;
>   (b)   serve the application on—
>>   (i)   the court officer, and
>>   (ii)   each other party.
   (2)   The applicant must—
>   (a)   if relevant, explain what legislation requires the court to order a preparatory hearing;
>   (b)   otherwise, explain—
>>   (i)   what makes the case complex or serious, or makes the trial likely to be long,
>>   (ii)   why a substantial benefit will accrue from a preparatory hearing, and
>>   (iii)   why the court's ordinary powers of case management are not adequate.

(3) A prosecutor who wants the court to order a trial without a jury must explain—
  (a) where the prosecutor alleges a danger of jury tampering—
    (i) what evidence there is of a real and present danger that jury tampering would take place,
    (ii) what steps, if any, reasonably might be taken to prevent jury tampering, and
    (iii) why, notwithstanding such steps, the likelihood of jury tampering is so substantial as to make it necessary in the interests of justice to order such a trial; or
  (b) where the prosecutor proposes trial without a jury on some counts on the indictment—
    (i) why a trial by jury involving all the counts would be impracticable,
    (ii) how the counts proposed for jury trial can be regarded as samples of the others, and
    (iii) why it would be in the interests of justice to order such a trial.

Application containing information withheld from a defendant   R-107

15.4 (1) This rule applies where—
  (a) the prosecutor applies for an order for a trial without a jury because of a danger of jury tampering; and
  (b) the application includes information that the prosecutor thinks ought not be revealed to a defendant.
(2) The prosecutor must—
  (a) omit that information from the part of the application that is served on that defendant;
  (b) mark the other part to show that, unless the court otherwise directs, it is only for the court; and
  (c) in that other part, explain why the prosecutor has withheld that information from that defendant.
(3) The hearing of an application to which this rule applies—
  (a) must be in private, unless the court otherwise directs; and
  (b) if the court so directs, may be, wholly or in part, in the absence of a defendant from whom information has been withheld.
(4) At the hearing of an application to which this rule applies—
  (a) the general rule is that the court must receive, in the following sequence—
    (i) representations first by the prosecutor and then by each defendant, in all the parties' presence, and then
    (ii) further representations by the prosecutor, in the absence of a defendant from whom information has been withheld; but
  (b) the court may direct other arrangements for the hearing.
(5) Where, on an application to which this rule applies, the court orders a trial without a jury—
  (a) the general rule is that the trial must be before a judge other than the judge who made the order; but
  (b) the court may direct other arrangements.

Representations in response   R-108

15.5 (1) This rule applies where a party wants to make representations about—
  (a) an application for a preparatory hearing;
  (b) an application for a trial without a jury.
(2) Such a party must—
  (a) serve the representations on—
    (i) the court officer, and
    (ii) each other party;
  (b) do so not more than 14 days after service of the application;
  (c) ask for a hearing, if that party wants one, and explain why it is needed.
(3) Where representations include information that the person making them thinks ought not be revealed to another party, that person must—
  (a) omit that information from the representations served on that other party;
  (b) mark the information to show that, unless the court otherwise directs, it is only for the court; and
  (c) with that information include an explanation of why it has been withheld from that other party.
(4) Representations against an application for an order must explain why the conditions for making it are not met.

Criminal Procedure Rules 2013 and Criminal Practice Directions

R-109   **Commencement of preparatory hearing**

     15.6   At the beginning of a preparatory hearing, the court must—

         (a) announce that it is such a hearing; and

         (b) take the defendant's plea (unless already done).

R-110   **Court's power to vary requirements**

     15.7   (1) The court may—

         (a) shorten or extend (even after it has expired) a time limit under this Part; and

         (b) allow an application or representations to be made orally.

       (2) A person who wants an extension of time must—

         (a) apply when serving the application or representations for which it is needed; and

         (b) explain the delay.

Criminal Procedure Rules   Part 16   Reporting, etc. Restrictions

Section 1: general rules

R-111   **When this Part applies**

     16.1   (1) This Part applies where the court can—

         (a) impose a restriction on—

             (i) reporting what takes place at a public hearing, or

             (ii) public access to what otherwise would be a public hearing;

         (b) vary or remove a reporting or access restriction that is imposed by legislation;

         (c) withhold information from the public during a public hearing;

         (d) order a trial in private;

         (e) allow there to take place during a hearing—

             (i) sound recording, or

             (ii) communication by electronic means.

       (2) This Part does not apply to arrangements required by legislation, or directed by the court, in connection with—

         (a) sound recording during a hearing, or the transcription of such a recording; or

         (b) measures to assist a witness or defendant to give evidence.

R-112   **Exercise of court's powers to which this Part applies**

     16.2   (1) When exercising a power to which this Part applies, as well as furthering the overriding objective, in accordance with rule 1.3, the court must have regard to the importance of—

         (a) dealing with criminal cases in public; and

         (b) allowing a public hearing to be reported to the public.

       (2) The court may determine an application or appeal under this Part—

         (a) at a hearing, in public or in private; or

         (b) without a hearing.

       (3) But the court must not exercise a power to which this Part applies unless each party and any other person directly affected—

         (a) is present; or

         (b) has had an opportunity—

             (i) to attend, or

             (ii) to make representations.

R-113   **Court's power to vary requirements under this Part**

     16.3   (1) The court may—

         (a) shorten or extend (even after it has expired) a time limit under this Part;

         (b) require an application to be made in writing instead of orally;

         (c) consider an application or representations made orally instead of in writing;

         (d) dispense with a requirement to—

             (i) give notice, or

             (ii) serve a written application.

       (2) Someone who wants an extension of time must—

         (a) apply when making the application or representations for which it is needed; and

         (b) explain the delay.

Section 2: reporting and access restrictions

Reporting and access restrictions   R-114

16.4   (1)   This rule applies where the court can—
          (a)   impose a restriction on—
              (i)   reporting what takes place at a public hearing, or
              (ii)   public access to what otherwise would be a public hearing;
          (b)   withhold information from the public during a public hearing.
     (2)   The court may do so—
          (a)   on application by a party; or
          (b)   on its own initiative.
     (3)   A party who wants the court to do so must—
          (a)   apply as soon as reasonably practicable;
          (b)   notify—
              (i)   each other party, and
              (ii)   such other person (if any) as the court directs;
          (c)   specify the proposed terms of the order, and for how long it should last;
          (d)   explain—
              (i)   what power the court has to make the order, and
              (ii)   why an order in the terms proposed is necessary;
          (e)   where the application is for a reporting direction in respect of a witness under section 46
              of the Youth Justice and Criminal Evidence Act 1999, explain—
              (i)   how the witness is eligible for assistance, and
              (ii)   why a reporting direction would be likely to improve the quality of the witness'
                    evidence, or the level of co-operation the witness gives the applicant in connection
                    with the preparation of the applicant's case.

Varying or removing restrictions   R-115

16.5   (1)   This rule applies where the court can vary or remove a reporting or access restriction.
     (2)   Unless other legislation otherwise provides, the court may do so—
          (a)   on application by a party or person directly affected; or
          (b)   on its own initiative.
     (3)   A party or person who wants the court to do so must—
          (a)   apply as soon as reasonably practicable;
          (b)   notify—
              (i)   each other party, and
              (ii)   such other person (if any) as the court directs;
          (c)   specify the restriction;
          (d)   explain, as appropriate, why it should be varied or removed.
     (4)   A person who wants to appeal to the Crown Court under section 141F of the Education Act
          2002 must—
          (a)   serve an appeal notice on—
              (i)   the Crown Court officer, and
              (ii)   each other party;
          (b)   serve on the Crown Court officer, with the appeal notice, a copy of the application to the
              magistrates' court;
          (c)   serve the appeal notice not more than 21 days after the magistrates' court's decision against
              which the appellant wants to appeal; and
          (d)   in the appeal notice, explain, as appropriate, why the restriction should be maintained,
              varied or removed.
     (5)   Rule 63.10 (Constitution of the Crown Court) applies on such an appeal.

Trial in private   R-116

16.6   (1)   This rule applies where the court can order a trial in private.
     (2)   A party who wants the court to do so must—
          (a)   apply in writing not less than 5 business days before the trial is due to begin; and
          (b)   serve the application on—
              (i)   the court officer, and
              (ii)   each other party.
     (3)   The applicant must explain—
          (a)   the reasons for the application;
          (b)   how much of the trial the applicant proposes should be in private; and

(c) why no measures other than trial in private will suffice, such as—
    (i)   reporting restrictions,
    (ii) an admission of facts,
    (iii) the introduction of hearsay evidence,
    (iv) a direction for a special measure under section 19 of the Youth Justice and Criminal Evidence Act 1999,
    (v) a witness anonymity order under section 86 of the Coroners and Justice Act 2009, or
    (vi) arrangements for the protection of a witness.

(4) Where the application includes information that the applicant thinks ought not be revealed to another party, the applicant must—
    (a) omit that information from the part of the application that is served on that other party;
    (b) mark the other part to show that, unless the court otherwise directs, it is only for the court; and
    (c) in that other part, explain why the applicant has withheld that information from that other party.

(5) The court officer must at once—
    (a) display notice of the application somewhere prominent in the vicinity of the court-room; and
    (b) give notice of the application to reporters by such other arrangements as the Lord Chancellor directs.

(6) The application must be determined at a hearing which—
    (a) must be in private, unless the court otherwise directs;
    (b) if the court so directs, may be, wholly or in part, in the absence of a party from whom information has been withheld; and
    (c) in the Crown Court, must be after the defendant is arraigned but before the jury is sworn.

(7) At the hearing of the application—
    (a) the general rule is that the court must receive, in the following sequence—
        (i)   representations first by the applicant and then by each other party, in all the parties' presence, and then
        (ii) further representations by the applicant, in the absence of a party from whom information has been withheld; but
    (b) the court may direct other arrangements for the hearing.

(8) The court must not hear a trial in private until—
    (a) the business day after the day on which it orders such a trial, or
    (b) the disposal of any appeal against, or review of, any such order, if later.

R-117 **Representations in response**

16.7 (1) This rule applies where a party, or person directly affected, wants to make representations about an application or appeal.

(2) Such a party or person must—
    (a) serve the representations on—
        (i)   the court officer,
        (ii) the applicant,
        (iii) each other party, and
        (iv) such other person (if any) as the court directs;
    (b) do so as soon as reasonably practicable after notice of the application; and
    (c) ask for a hearing, if that party or person wants one, and explain why it is needed.

(3) Representations must—
    (a) explain the reasons for any objection;
    (b) specify any alternative terms proposed.

R-118 **Order about restriction or trial in private**

16.8 (1) This rule applies where the court—
    (a) orders, varies or removes a reporting or access restriction; or
    (b) orders a trial in private.

(2) The court officer must—
    (a) record the court's reasons for the decision; and
    (b) as soon as reasonably practicable, arrange for notice of the decision to be—
        (i)   displayed somewhere prominent in the vicinity of the courtroom, and

(ii)   communicated to reporters by such other arrangements as the Lord Chancellor directs.

Section 3: sound recording and electronic communication

Sound recording and electronic communication   **R-119**

16.9   (1)   This rule applies where the court can give permission to—
     (a)   bring into a hearing for use, or use during a hearing, a device for—
         (i)   recording sound, or
         (ii)   communicating by electronic means; or
     (b)   publish a sound recording made during a hearing.
   (2)   The court may give such permission—
     (a)   on application; or
     (b)   on its own initiative.
   (3)   A person who wants the court to give such permission must—
     (a)   apply as soon as reasonably practicable;
     (b)   notify—
         (i)   each party, and
         (ii)   such other person (if any) as the court directs; and
     (c)   explain why the court should permit the use or publication proposed.
   (4)   As a condition of the applicant using such a device, the court may direct arrangements to minimise the risk of its use—
     (a)   contravening a reporting restriction;
     (b)   disrupting the hearing; or
     (c)   compromising the fairness of the hearing, for example by affecting—
         (i)   the evidence to be given by a witness, or
         (ii)   the verdict of a jury.
   (5)   Such a direction may require that the device is used only—
     (a)   in a specified part of the courtroom;
     (b)   for a specified purpose;
     (c)   for a purpose connected with the applicant's activity as a member of a specified group, for example representatives of news-gathering or reporting organisations;
     (d)   at a specified time, or in a specified way.

Forfeiture of unauthorised sound recording   **R-120**

16.10   (1)   This rule applies where someone without the court's permission—
     (a)   uses a device for recording sound during a hearing; or
     (b)   publishes a sound recording made during a hearing.
   (2)   The court may exercise its power to forfeit the device or recording—
     (a)   on application by a party, or on its own initiative;
     (b)   provisionally, despite rule 16.2(3), to allow time for representations.
   (3)   A party who wants the court to forfeit a device or recording must—
     (a)   apply as soon as reasonably practicable;
     (b)   notify—
         (i)   as appropriate, the person who used the device, or who published the recording, and
         (ii)   each other party; and
     (c)   explain why the court should exercise that power.

Criminal Practice Directions   Part 16   Reporting, etc. Restrictions

CPD II Preliminary proceedings 16A: Unofficial Sound Recording of Proceedings   **PD-19**

16A.1   Section 9 of the Contempt of Court Act 1981 contains provisions governing the unofficial use of equipment for recording sound in court.

Section 9(1) provides that it is a contempt of court:
   (a)   to use in court, or bring into court for use, any tape recorder or other instrument for recording sound, except with the permission of the court;
   (b)   to publish a recording of legal proceedings made by means of any such instrument, or any recording derived directly or indirectly from it, by playing it in the hearing of the public or any section of the public, or to dispose of it or any recording so derived, with a view to such publication;

(c) to use any such recording in contravention of any conditions of leave granted under paragraph (a).

These provisions do not apply to the making or use of sound recordings for purposes of official transcripts of the proceedings, upon which the Act imposes no restriction whatever.

16A.2 The discretion given to the court to grant, withhold or withdraw leave to use equipment for recording sound or to impose conditions as to the use of the recording is unlimited, but the following factors may be relevant to its exercise:

(a) the existence of any reasonable need on the part of the applicant for leave, whether a litigant or a person connected with the press or broadcasting, for the recording to be made;

(b) the risk that the recording could be used for the purpose of briefing witnesses out of court;

(c) any possibility that the use of the recorder would disturb the proceedings or distract or worry any witnesses or other participants.

16A.3 Consideration should always be given whether conditions as to the use of a recording made pursuant to leave should be imposed. The identity and role of the applicant for leave and the nature of the subject matter of the proceedings may be relevant to this.

16A.4 The particular restriction imposed by section 9(1) (b) applies in every case, but may not be present in the mind of every applicant to whom leave is given. It may therefore be desirable on occasion for this provision to be drawn to the attention of those to whom leave is given.

16A.5 The transcript of a permitted recording is intended for the use of the person given leave to make it and is not intended to be used as, or to compete with, the official transcript mentioned in section 9(4).

16A.6 Where a contravention of section 9(1) is alleged, the procedure in section 2 of Part 62 of the Rules should be followed. Section 9(3) of the 1981 Act permits the court to 'order the instrument, or any recording made with it, or both, to be forfeited'. The procedure at Rule 16.10 should be followed.

PD-20 **CPD II Preliminary proceedings 16B: Restrictions on Reporting Proceedings**

16B.1 Open justice is an essential principle in the criminal courts but the principle is subject to some statutory restrictions. These restrictions are either automatic or discretionary. Guidance is provided in the joint publication of the Judicial College, the Newspaper Society, the Society of Editors and Times Newspapers Limited entitled 'Reporting Restrictions in the Criminal Courts'. The current version is the second edition dated October 2009 and is available at http://www.judiciary.gov.uk/Resources/JCO/Documents/Guidance/crown_court_reporting_restrictions_021009.pdf (Note that the HMCTS protocol referred to in the guidance has since been updated.)

16B.2 Where a restriction is automatic no order can or should be made in relation to matters falling within the relevant provisions. However, the court may, if it considers it appropriate to do so, give a reminder of the existence of the automatic restriction. The court may also discuss the scope of the restriction and any particular risks in the specific case in open court with representatives of the press present. Such judicial observations cannot constitute an order binding on the editor or the reporter although it is anticipated that a responsible editor would consider them carefully before deciding what should be published. It remains the responsibility of those reporting a case to ensure that restrictions are not breached.

16B.3 Before exercising its discretion to impose a restriction the court must follow precisely the statutory provisions under which the order is to be made, paying particular regard to what has to be established, by whom and to what standard.

16B.4 Without prejudice to the above paragraph, certain general principles apply to the exercise of the court's discretion:

(a) The court must have regard to Parts 16 and 29 of the Criminal Procedure Rules.

(b) The court must keep in mind the fact that every order is a departure from the general principle that proceedings shall be open and freely reported.

(c) Before making any order the court must be satisfied that the purpose of the proposed order cannot be achieved by some lesser measure e.g., the grant of special measures, screens or the clearing of the public gallery (usually subject to a representative(s) of the media remaining).

(d) The terms of the order must be proportionate so as to comply with Article 10 ECHR (freedom of expression).

(e) No order should be made without giving other parties to the proceedings and any other interested party, including any representative of the media, an opportunity to make representations.

(f) Any order should provide for any interested party who has not been present or represented at the time of the making of the order to have permission to apply within a limited period e.g., 24 hours.

(g) The wording of the order is the responsibility of the judge or Bench making the order: it must be in precise terms and, if practicable, agreed with the advocates.

(h) The order must be in writing and must state:
   (i) the power under which it is made;
   (ii) its precise scope and purpose; and
   (iii) the time at which it shall cease to have effect, if appropriate.

(i) The order must specify, in every case, whether or not the making or terms of the order may be reported or whether this itself is prohibited. Such a report could cause the very mischief which the order was intended to prevent.

16B.5 A series of template orders have been prepared by the Judicial College and are available as an appendix to the Crown Court Bench Book Companion; these template orders should generally be used.

16B.6 A copy of the order should be provided to any person known to have an interest in reporting the proceedings and to any local or national media who regularly report proceedings in the court.

16B.7 Court staff should be prepared to answer any enquiry about a specific case; but it is and will remain the responsibility of anyone reporting a case to ensure that no breach of any order occurs and the onus rests on such person to make enquiry in case of doubt.

Criminal Procedure Rules   Part 17   Extradition

Section 1: general rules

When this Part applies   **R-121**

17.1 This Part applies to extradition under Part 1 or Part 2 of the Extradition Act 2003, but—
   (a) rules 17.8 to 17.14 do not apply to extradition under Part 1 of the Act; and
   (b) rules 17.5 to 17.7 do not apply to extradition under Part 2 of the Act.

Meaning of 'court', 'presenting officer' and 'defendant'   **R-122**

17.2 In this Part, and for the purposes of this Part in other rules—
   (a) 'court' means a District Judge (Magistrates' Courts) exercising the powers to which this Part applies;
   (b) 'presenting officer' means an officer of the National Crime Agency, a police officer, a prosecutor or other person representing an authority or territory seeking the extradition of a defendant;
   (c) 'defendant' means a person arrested under Part 1 or Part 2 of the Act.

Exercise of court's powers   **R-123**

17.3 (1) The general rule is that the court must exercise its powers at a hearing in public, but that is subject to any power it has to—
   (a) impose reporting restrictions;
   (b) withhold information from the public; or
   (c) order a hearing in private.

(2) The general rule is that the court must exercise its powers in the defendant's presence, but it may do so in the defendant's absence where—
   (a) the court discharges the defendant; or
   (b) the defendant is represented and the defendant's presence is impracticable by reason of his or her—
      (i) ill health, or
      (ii) disorderly conduct.

(3) The court may exercise its power to adjourn—
   (a) if either party asks, or on its own initiative; and
   (b) in particular—
      (i) to allow there to be obtained information that the court requires,
      (ii) following a provisional arrest under Part 1 of the Extradition Act 2003, pending receipt of the warrant,
      (iii) following a provisional arrest under Part 2 of the Act, pending receipt of the extradition request,

(iv) if the court is informed that the defendant is serving a custodial sentencing in the United Kingdom,

(v) if it appears to the court that the defendant is not fit to be extradited, unless the court discharges the defendant for that reason, or

(vi) where a court dealing with a warrant to which Part 1 of the Act applies is informed that another such warrant has been received in the United Kingdom.

(4) The court must exercise its power to adjourn if informed that the defendant has been charged with an offence in the United Kingdom.

(5) The general rule is that, before exercising a power to which this Part applies, the court must give each party an opportunity to make representations, unless that party is absent deliberately.

R-124   Duty of court officer

17.4   The court officer must—

(a) as soon as practicable, serve notice of the court's decision to extradite or discharge—

(i) on the defendant,

(ii) on the designated authority which certified the arrest warrant, where Part 1 of the Extradition Act 2003 applies,

(iii) on the Secretary of State, where Part 2 of the Act applies; and

(b) give the court such assistance as it requires.

Section 2: extradition under part 1 of the Extradition Act 2003

R-125   Preliminary hearing after arrest

17.5   (1) This rule applies where the defendant is first brought before the court after—

(a) arrest under a warrant to which Part 1 of the Extradition Act 2003 applies; or

(b) provisional arrest under Part 1 of the Act.

(2) The presenting officer must—

(a) serve on the court officer—

(i) the arrest warrant, and

(ii) a certificate, given by the authority designated by the Secretary of State, that the warrant was issued by an authority having the function of issuing such warrants in the territory to which the defendant's extradition is sought; or

(b) apply at once for an extension of time within which to serve that warrant and that certificate.

(3) An application under paragraph (2)(b) must—

(a) explain why the requirement to serve the warrant and certificate at once could not reasonably be complied with; and

(b) include—

(i) any written material in support of that explanation, and

(ii) representations about bail pending service of those documents.

(4) When the presenting officer serves the warrant and certificate, in the following sequence the court must—

(a) decide whether the defendant is the person in respect of whom the warrant was issued;

(b) explain, in terms the defendant can understand (with help, if necessary)—

(i) the allegation made in the warrant, and

(ii) that the defendant may consent to extradition, and how that may be done and with what effect;

(c) arrange for an extradition hearing to begin—

(i) no more than 21 days after the defendant's arrest, or

(ii) if either party so applies, at such a later date as the court decides is in the interests of justice;

(d) consider any ancillary application, including an application about bail pending the extradition hearing; and

(e) give any direction as is appropriate to the needs of the case about the introduction of evidence at the extradition hearing.

R-126   Extradition hearing

17.6   (1) This rule applies at the extradition hearing arranged by the court under rule 17.5.

(2) In the following sequence, the court must decide—

(a) whether the offence specified in the warrant is an extradition offence;

(b) whether a bar to extradition applies, namely—

(i) the rule against double jeopardy,

Criminal Procedure Rules 2013 and Criminal Practice Directions

      (ii) extraneous considerations,

      (iii) the passage of time,

      (iv) the defendant's age,

      (v) hostage-taking considerations,

      (vi) speciality,

      (vii) earlier extradition or transfer to the United Kingdom, or

      (viii)forum;

  (c) where the warrant alleges that the defendant is unlawfully at large after conviction, whether conviction was in the defendant's presence and if not—

      (i)   whether the defendant was absent deliberately,

      (ii) if the defendant was not absent deliberately, whether the defendant would be entitled to a retrial (or to a review of the conviction, amounting to a retrial);

  (d) whether extradition would be compatible with the defendant's human rights;

  (e) whether it would be unjust or oppressive to extradite the defendant because of his or her physical or mental condition;

  (f) after deciding each of (a) to (e) above, before progressing to the next, whether to order the defendant's discharge.

(3) If the court discharges the defendant, the court must consider any ancillary application, including an application about—

  (a) reporting restrictions; or

  (b) costs.

(4) If the court does not discharge the defendant, the court must—

  (a) exercise its power to order the defendant's extradition;

  (b) explain, in terms the defendant can understand (with help, if necessary), that the defendant may appeal to the High Court within the next 7 days; and

  (c) consider any ancillary application, including an application about—

      (i)   bail pending extradition,

      (ii) reporting restrictions, or

      (iii) costs.

Discharge where warrant withdrawn   R-127

17.7 (1) This rule applies where the authority that certified the warrant gives the court officer notice that the warrant has been withdrawn—

  (a) after the start of the hearing under rule 17.5; and

  (b) before the court orders the defendant's extradition or discharge.

(2) The court must exercise its power to discharge the defendant.

Section 3: extradition under part 2 of the Extradition Act 2003

Issue of arrest warrant   R-128

17.8 (1) This rule applies where the Secretary of State serves on the court officer—

  (a) an extradition request to which Part 2 of the Extradition Act 2003 applies;

  (b) a certificate given by the Secretary of State that the request was received in the way approved for the request; and

  (c) a copy of any Order in Council which applies to the request.

(2) In the following sequence, the court must decide—

  (a) whether the offence in respect of which extradition is requested is an extradition offence; and

  (b) whether there is sufficient evidence, or (where the Secretary of State has so ordered, for this purpose) information, to justify the issue of a warrant of arrest.

(3) The court may issue an arrest warrant—

  (a) without giving the parties an opportunity to make representations; and

  (b) without a hearing, or at a hearing in public or in private.

Preliminary hearing after arrest   R-129

17.9 (1) This rule applies where a defendant is first brought before the court after arrest under a warrant to which rule 17.8 applies.

(2) In the following sequence, the court must—

  (a) explain, in terms the defendant can understand (with help, if necessary)—

      (i)   the content of the extradition request, and

      (ii) that the defendant may consent to extradition, and how that may be done and with what effect;

(b) arrange for an extradition hearing to begin—
    (i)   no more than 2 months later, or
    (ii) if either party so applies, at such a later date as the court decides is in the interests of justice;
(c) consider any ancillary application, including an application about bail pending the extradition hearing; and
(d) give any direction as is appropriate to the needs of the case about the introduction of evidence at the extradition hearing.

R-130   **Issue of provisional arrest warrant**

17.10 (1) This rule applies where a presenting officer wants a justice of the peace to issue a provisional arrest warrant under Part 2 of the Extradition Act 2003, pending receipt of an extradition request.

    (2) The presenting officer must—
        (a) serve on the court officer an information in writing; and
        (b) verify the information on oath or affirmation.

    (3) In the following sequence, the justice must decide—
        (a) whether the alleged offence is an extradition offence; and
        (b) whether there is sufficient evidence, or (where the Secretary of State has so ordered, for this purpose) information, to justify the issue of a warrant of arrest.

R-131   **Preliminary hearing after provisional arrest**

17.11 (1) This rule applies where a defendant is first brought before the court after arrest under a provisional arrest warrant to which rule 17.10 applies.

    (2) The court must—
        (a) explain, in terms the defendant can understand (with help, if necessary)—
            (i)   the allegation in respect of which the warrant was issued, and
            (ii) that the defendant may consent to extradition, and how that may be done and with what effect; and
        (b) consider any ancillary application, including an application about bail pending receipt of the extradition request.

R-132   **Arrangement of extradition hearing after provisional arrest**

17.12 (1) This rule applies when the Secretary of State serves on the court officer—
        (a) a request for extradition in respect of which a defendant has been arrested under a provisional arrest warrant to which rule 17.10 applies;
        (b) a certificate given by the Secretary of State that the request was received in the way approved for the request; and
        (c) a copy of any Order in Council which applies to the request.

    (2) Unless a time limit for service of the request has expired, the court must—
        (a) arrange for an extradition hearing to begin—
            (i)   no more than 2 months after service of the request, or
            (ii) if either party so applies, at such a later date as the court decides is in the interests of justice;
        (b) consider any ancillary application, including an application about bail pending the extradition hearing; and
        (c) give any direction as is appropriate to the needs of the case about the introduction of evidence at the extradition hearing.

R-133   **Extradition hearing**

17.13 (1) This rule applies at the extradition hearing arranged by the court under rule 17.9 or rule 17.12.

    (2) In the following sequence, the court must decide—
        (a) whether the documents served on the court officer by the Secretary of State include—
            (i)   those listed in rule 17.8(1) or rule 17.12(1), as the case may be,
            (ii) particulars of the person whose extradition is requested,
            (iii) particulars of the offence specified in the request, and
            (iv) as the case may be, a warrant for the defendant's arrest, or a certificate of the defendant's conviction and (if applicable) sentence, issued in the requesting territory;
        (b) whether the defendant is the person whose extradition is requested;
        (c) whether the offence specified in the request is an extradition offence;
        (d) whether the documents served on the court officer by the Secretary of State have been served also on the defendant;

    (e) whether a bar to extradition applies, namely—
        (i)   the rule against double jeopardy,
        (ii) extraneous considerations,
        (iii) the passage of time,
        (iv) hostage-taking considerations, or
        (v)   forum;
    (f) where the request accuses the defendant of an offence, whether there is evidence which would be sufficient to make a case requiring an answer by the defendant if the extradition proceedings were a trial (unless the Secretary of State has otherwise ordered, for this purpose);
    (g) where the request accuses the defendant of being unlawfully at large after conviction, whether the defendant was—
        (i)   convicted in his or her presence, or
        (ii) absent deliberately;
    (h) where the request accuses the defendant of being unlawfully at large after conviction, and the defendant was absent but not deliberately—
        (i)   whether the defendant would be entitled to a retrial (or to a review of the conviction amounting to a retrial), and
        (ii) if so, whether there is evidence which would be sufficient to make a case requiring an answer by the defendant if the extradition proceedings were a trial (unless the Secretary of State has otherwise ordered, for this purpose);
    (i) whether extradition would be compatible with the defendant's human rights;
    (j) whether it would be unjust or oppressive to extradite the defendant because of his or her physical or mental condition;
    (k) after deciding each of (a) to (j) above, before progressing to the next, whether to order the defendant's discharge.
(3) If the court discharges the defendant, the court must consider any ancillary application, including an application about—
    (a) reporting restrictions; or
    (b) costs.
(4) If the court does not discharge the defendant, the court must—
    (a) exercise its power to send the case to the Secretary of State to decide whether to extradite the defendant;
    (b) explain, in terms the defendant can understand (with help, if necessary), that—
        (i)   the defendant may appeal to the High Court not more than 14 days after being informed of the Secretary of State's decision, and
        (ii) any such appeal brought before the Secretary of State's decision has been made will not be heard until after that decision; and
    (c) consider any ancillary application, including an application about—
        (i)   bail pending extradition,
        (ii) reporting restrictions, or
        (iii) costs.

Discharge where extradition request withdrawn   R-134

17.14 (1) This rule applies where the Secretary of State gives the court officer notice that the extradition request has been withdrawn—
    (a) after the start of the hearing under rule 17.9 or 17.11; and
    (b) before the court—
        (i)   sends the case to the Secretary of State to decide whether to extradite the defendant, or
        (ii) discharges the defendant.
  (2) The court must exercise its power to discharge the defendant.

Section 4: evidence at extradition hearing

Introduction of additional evidence   R-135

17.15 (1) Where a party wants to introduce evidence at an extradition hearing under the law that would apply if that hearing were a trial, the relevant Part of these Rules applies with such adaptations as the court directs.
  (2) If the court admits as evidence the written statement of a witness—
    (a) each relevant part of the statement must be read or summarised aloud; or
    (b) the court must read the statement and its gist must be summarised aloud.

(3) If a party introduces in evidence a fact admitted by another party, or the parties jointly admit a fact, a written record must be made of the admission.

Section 5: discharge after failure to comply with a time limit

R-136   **Defendant's application to be discharged**

17.16 (1) This rule applies where a defendant wants to be discharged—

   (a) because of a failure—

      (i) to give the defendant a copy of any warrant under which the defendant is arrested as soon as practicable after arrest,

      (ii) to bring the defendant before the court as soon as practicable after arrest under a warrant,

      (iii) to bring the defendant before the court no more than 48 hours after provisional arrest under Part 1 of the Extradition Act 2003;

   (b) following the expiry of a time limit for—

      (i) service of a warrant to which Part 1 of the 2003 Act applies, after provisional arrest under that Part of the Act (48 hours, under section 6 of the Act, unless the court otherwise directs),

      (ii) service of an extradition request to which Part 2 of the Act applies, after provisional arrest under that Part of the Act (45 days, under section 74 of the Act, unless the Secretary of State has otherwise ordered for this purpose),

      (iii) receipt of an undertaking that the defendant will be returned to complete a sentence in the United Kingdom, where the court required such an undertaking (21 days, under section 37 of the Act),

      (iv) making an extradition order, after the defendant has consented to extradition under Part 1 of the Act (10 days, under section 46 of the Act),

      (v) extradition, where an extradition order has been made under Part 1 of the Act and any appeal by the defendant has failed (10 days, under sections 35, 36 and 47 of the Act, unless the court otherwise directs),

      (vi) extradition, where an extradition order has been made under Part 2 of the Act and any appeal by the defendant has failed (28 days, under sections 117 and 118 of the Act),

      (vii) the resumption of extradition proceedings, where those proceedings were adjourned pending disposal of another extradition claim which has concluded (21 days, under section 180 of the Act),

      (viii) extradition, where extradition has been deferred pending the disposal of another extradition claim which has concluded (21 days, under section 181 of the Act), or

      (ix) re-extradition, where the defendant has been returned to the United Kingdom to serve a sentence before serving a sentence overseas (as soon as practicable, under section 187 of the Act); or

   (c) because an extradition hearing does not begin on the date arranged by the court.

   (2) Unless the court otherwise directs—

      (a) such a defendant must apply in writing and serve the application on—

         (i) the court officer, and

         (ii) the prosecutor;

      (b) the application must explain the grounds on which it is made; and

      (c) the court officer must arrange a hearing as soon as practicable, and in any event no later than the second business day after an application is served.

CRIMINAL PROCEDURE RULES   PART 18   WARRANTS FOR ARREST, DETENTION OR IMPRISONMENT

R-137   **When this Part applies**

18.1 (1) This Part applies where the court can issue a warrant for arrest, detention or imprisonment.

   (2) In this Part, 'defendant' means anyone against whom such a warrant is issued.

R-138   **Terms of a warrant for arrest**

18.2 A warrant for arrest must require each person to whom it is directed to arrest the defendant and—

   (a) bring the defendant to a court—

      (i) specified in the warrant, or

      (ii) required or allowed by law; or

(b) release the defendant on bail (with conditions or without) to attend court at a date, time and place—
    (i)   specified in the warrant, or
    (ii) to be notified by the court.

Terms of a warrant for detention or imprisonment

R-139

18.3 (1) A warrant for detention or imprisonment must—
    (a) require each person to whom it is directed to detain the defendant and—
        (i)   take the defendant to any place specified in the warrant or required or allowed by law, and
        (ii) deliver the defendant to the custodian of that place; and
    (b) require that custodian to detain the defendant, as ordered by the court, until in accordance with the law—
        (i)   the defendant is delivered to the appropriate court or place, or
        (ii) the defendant is released.

    (2) Where a magistrates' court remands a defendant to police detention under section 128(7) or section 136 of the Magistrates' Courts Act 1980, or to customs detention under section 152 of the Criminal Justice Act 1988, the warrant it issues must—
    (a) be directed, as appropriate, to—
        (i)   a constable, or
        (ii) an officer of Her Majesty's Revenue and Customs; and
    (b) require that constable or officer to detain the defendant—
        (i)   for a period (not exceeding the maximum permissible) specified in the warrant, or
        (ii) until in accordance with the law the defendant is delivered to the appropriate court or place.

Information to be included in a warrant

R-140

18.4 (1) A warrant must identify—
    (a) each person to whom it is directed;
    (b) the defendant against whom it was issued;
    (c) the reason for its issue;
    (d) the court that issued it, unless that is otherwise recorded by the court officer; and
    (e) the court office for the court that issued it.

    (2) A warrant for detention or imprisonment must contain a record of any decision by the court under—
    (a) section 91 of the Legal Aid, Sentencing and Punishment of Offenders Act 2012 (remands of children otherwise than on bail), including in particular—
        (i)   whether the defendant must be detained in local authority accommodation or youth detention accommodation,
        (ii) the local authority designated by the court,
        (iii) any requirement imposed by the court on that authority,
        (iv) any condition imposed by the court on the defendant, and
        (v) the reason for any such requirement or condition;
    (b) section 80 of the Magistrates' Courts Act 1980 (application of money found on defaulter to satisfy sum adjudged); or
    (c) section 82(1) or (4) of the 1980 Act (conditions for issue of a warrant).

    (3) A warrant that contains an error is not invalid, as long as—
    (a) it was issued in respect of a lawful decision by the court; and
    (b) it contains enough information to identify that decision.

Execution of a warrant

R-141

18.5 (1) A warrant may be executed—
    (a) by any person to whom it is directed; or
    (b) if the warrant was issued by a magistrates' court, by anyone authorised to do so by section 125 (warrants), 125A (civilian enforcement officers) or 125B (execution by approved enforcement agency) of the Magistrates' Courts Act 1980.

    (2) The person who executes a warrant must—
    (a) explain, in terms the defendant can understand, what the warrant requires, and why;
    (b) show the defendant the warrant, if that person has it; and
    (c) if the defendant asks—
        (i)   arrange for the defendant to see the warrant, if that person does not have it, and

          (ii) show the defendant any written statement of that person's authority required by section 125A or 125B of the 1980 Act.

(3) The person who executes a warrant of arrest that requires the defendant to be released on bail must—

    (a) make a record of—
        (i)   the defendant's name,
        (ii) the reason for the arrest,
        (iii) the defendant's release on bail, and
        (iv) when and where the warrant requires the defendant to attend court; and
    (b) serve the record on—
        (i)   the defendant, and
        (ii) the court officer.

(4) The person who executes a warrant of detention or imprisonment must—

    (a) take the defendant—
        (i)   to any place specified in the warrant, or
        (ii) if that is not immediately practicable, to any other place at which the defendant may be lawfully detained (and the warrant then has effect as if it specified that place);
    (b) obtain a receipt from the custodian; and
    (c) notify the court officer that the defendant has been taken to that place.

R-142 Warrants that cease to have effect on payment

18.6 (1) This rule applies to a warrant issued by a magistrates' court under any of the following provisions of the Magistrates' Courts Act 1980—

    (a) section 76 (enforcement of sums adjudged to be paid);
    (b) section 83 (process for securing attendance of offender);
    (c) section 86 (power of magistrates' court to fix day for appearance of offender at means inquiry, etc.);
    (d) section 136 (committal to custody overnight at police station for non-payment of sum adjudged by conviction).

(2) The warrant no longer has effect if—

    (a) the sum in respect of which the warrant was issued is paid to the person executing it;
    (b) that sum is offered to, but refused by, that person; or
    (c) that person is shown a receipt for that sum given by—
        (i)   the court officer, or
        (ii) the authority to which that sum is due.

R-143 Warrant issued when the court office is closed

18.7 (1) This rule applies where the court issues a warrant when the court office is closed.

(2) The applicant for the warrant must, not more than 72 hours later, serve on the court officer—

    (a) a copy of the warrant; and
    (b) any written material that was submitted to the court.

CRIMINAL PROCEDURE RULES   PART 19   BAIL AND CUSTODY TIME LIMITS

Section 1: general rules

R-144 When this Part applies

19.1 (1) This Part applies where a magistrates' court or the Crown Court can—

    (a) grant or withhold bail, or impose or vary a condition of bail; and
    (b) where bail has been withheld, extend a custody time limit.

(2) In this Part, 'defendant' includes a person who has been granted bail by a police officer.

R-145 Exercise of court's powers to which this Part applies

19.2 (1) The court must not make a decision to which this Part applies unless—

    (a) each party to the decision and any surety directly affected by the decision—
        (i)   is present, or
        (ii) has had an opportunity to make representations;
    (b) on an application for bail by a defendant who is absent and in custody, the court is satisfied that the defendant—
        (i)   has waived the right to attend, or

Criminal Procedure Rules 2013 and Criminal Practice Directions

> (ii) was present when a court withheld bail in the case on a previous occasion and has been in custody continuously since then;

(c) on a prosecutor's appeal against a grant of bail, application to extend a custody time limit or appeal against a refusal to extend such a time limit—

    (i) the court is satisfied that a defendant who is absent has waived the right to attend, or

    (ii) the court is satisfied that it would be just to proceed even though the defendant is absent.

(2) The court may make a decision to which this Part applies at a hearing, in public or in private.

(3) The court may determine without a hearing an application to vary a condition of bail if—

    (a) the parties to the application have agreed the terms of the variation proposed; or

    (b) on an application by a defendant, the court determines the application no sooner than the fifth business day after the application was served.

(4) The court may adjourn a determination to which this Part applies, if that is necessary to obtain information sufficient to allow the court to make the decision required.

(5) At any hearing at which the court makes one of the following decisions, the court must announce in terms the defendant can understand (with help, if necessary) its reasons for—

    (a) withholding bail, or imposing or varying a bail condition;

    (b) granting bail, where the prosecutor opposed the grant; or

    (c) where the defendant is under 18—

        (i) imposing or varying a bail condition when ordering the defendant to be detained in local authority accommodation, or

        (ii) ordering the defendant to be detained in youth detention accommodation.

(6) At any hearing at which the court grants bail, the court must—

    (a) tell the defendant where and when to surrender to custody; or

    (b) arrange for the court officer to give the defendant, as soon as practicable, notice of where and when to surrender to custody.

Duty of justices' legal adviser   R-146

19.3 (1) This rule applies—

    (a) only in a magistrates' court; and

    (b) unless the court—

        (i) includes a District Judge (Magistrates' Courts), and

        (ii) otherwise directs.

(2) A justices' legal adviser must—

    (a) assist an unrepresented defendant;

    (b) give the court such advice as is required to enable it to exercise its powers;

    (c) if required, attend the members of the court outside the courtroom to give such advice, but inform the parties of any advice so given.

General duties of court officer   R-147

19.4 (1) The court officer must arrange for a note or other record to be made of—

    (a) the parties' representations about bail; and

    (b) the court's reasons for a decision—

        (i) to withhold bail, or to impose or vary a bail condition, or

        (ii) to grant bail, where the prosecutor opposed the grant.

(2) The court officer must serve notice of a decision about bail on—

    (a) the defendant (but, in the Crown Court, only where the defendant's legal representative asks for such a notice, or where the defendant has no legal representative);

    (b) the prosecutor (but only where the court granted bail, the prosecutor opposed the grant, and the prosecutor asks for such a notice);

    (c) a party to the decision who was absent when it was made;

    (d) a surety who is directly affected by the decision;

    (e) the defendant's custodian, where the defendant is in custody and the decision requires the custodian—

        (i) to release the defendant (or will do so, if a requirement ordered by the court is met), or

        (ii) to transfer the defendant to the custody of another custodian;

    (f) the court officer for any other court at which the defendant is required by that decision to surrender to custody.

(3) Where the court postpones the date on which a defendant who is on bail must surrender to custody, the court officer must serve notice of the postponed date on—

(a) the defendant; and

(b) any surety.

(4) Where a magistrates' court withholds bail in a case to which section 5(6A) of the Bail Act 1976 applies (remand in custody after hearing full argument on an application for bail), the court officer must serve on the defendant a certificate that the court heard full argument.

Section 2: bail

R-148   **Prosecutor's representations about bail**

19.5 (1) This rule applies whenever the court can grant or withhold bail.

(2) The prosecutor must provide the court with all the information in the prosecutor's possession which is material to what the court must decide.

(3) A prosecutor who opposes the grant of bail must specify—

(a) each exception to the general right to bail on which the prosecutor relies; and

(b) each consideration that the prosecutor thinks relevant.

(4) A prosecutor who wants the court to impose a condition on any grant of bail must—

(a) specify each condition proposed; and

(b) explain what purpose would be served by such a condition.

R-149   **Reconsideration of police bail by magistrates' court**

19.6 (1) This rule applies where a party wants a magistrates' court to reconsider a bail decision by a police officer.

(2) An application under this rule must be made to—

(a) the magistrates' court to whose custody the defendant is under a duty to surrender, if any; or

(b) any magistrates' court acting for the police officer's local justice area, in any other case.

(3) The applicant party must—

(a) apply in writing; and

(b) serve the application on—

(i) the court officer,

(ii) the other party, and

(iii) any surety affected or proposed.

(4) The application must—

(a) specify—

(i) the decision that the applicant wants the court to make,

(ii) each offence charged, or for which the defendant was arrested, and

(iii) the police bail decision to be reconsidered and the reasons given for it;

(b) explain, as appropriate—

(i) why the court should grant bail itself, or withdraw it, or impose or vary a condition, and

(ii) if the applicant is the prosecutor, what material information has become available since the police bail decision was made;

(c) propose the terms of any suggested condition of bail; and

(d) if the applicant wants an earlier hearing than paragraph (7) requires, ask for that, and explain why it is needed.

(5) A prosecutor who applies under this rule must serve on the defendant, with the application, notice that the court has power to withdraw bail and, if the defendant is absent when the court makes its decision, order the defendant's arrest.

(6) A party who opposes an application must—

(a) so notify the court officer and the applicant at once; and

(b) serve on each notice of the reasons for opposition.

(7) Unless the court otherwise directs, the court officer must arrange for the court to hear the application as soon as practicable and in any event—

(a) if it is an application to withdraw bail, no later than the second business day after it was served;

(b) in any other case, no later than the fifth business day after it was served.

(8) The court may—

(a) vary or waive a time limit under this rule;

(b) allow an application to be in a different form to one set out in the Practice Direction;

(c) if rule 19.2 allows, determine without a hearing an application to vary a condition.

Notice of application to consider bail

19.7 (1) This rule applies where—

    (a) in a magistrates' court—

      (i) a prosecutor wants the court to withdraw bail granted by the court, or to impose or vary a condition of such bail, or

      (ii) a defendant wants the court to reconsider such bail before the next hearing in the case;

    (b) in the Crown Court, a party wants the court to grant bail that has been withheld, or to withdraw bail that has been granted, or to impose a new bail condition or to vary a present one.

(2) Such a party must—

    (a) apply in writing;

    (b) serve the application on—

      (i) the court officer,

      (ii) the other party, and

      (iii) any surety affected or proposed; and

    (c) serve the application not less than 2 business days before any hearing in the case at which the applicant wants the court to consider it, if such a hearing is already due.

(3) The application must—

    (a) specify—

      (i) the decision that the applicant wants the court to make,

      (ii) each offence charged, and

      (iii) each relevant previous bail decision and the reasons given for each;

    (b) if the applicant is a defendant, explain—

      (i) as appropriate, why the court should not withhold bail, or why it should vary a condition, and

      (ii) what further information or legal argument, if any, has become available since the most recent previous bail decision was made;

    (c) if the applicant is the prosecutor, explain—

      (i) as appropriate, why the court should withdraw bail, or impose or vary a condition, and

      (ii) what material information has become available since the most recent previous bail decision was made;

    (d) propose the terms of any suggested condition of bail; and

    (e) if the applicant wants an earlier hearing than paragraph (6) requires, ask for that, and explain why it is needed.

(4) A prosecutor who applies under this rule must serve on the defendant, with the application, notice that the court has power to withdraw bail and, if the defendant is absent when the court makes its decision, order the defendant's arrest.

(5) A party who opposes an application must—

    (a) so notify the court officer and the applicant at once; and

    (b) serve on each notice of the reasons for opposition.

(6) Unless the court otherwise directs, the court officer must arrange for the court to hear the application as soon as practicable and in any event—

    (a) if it is an application to grant or withdraw bail, no later than the second business day after it was served;

    (b) if it is an application to impose or vary a condition, no later than the fifth business day after it was served.

(7) The court may—

    (a) vary or waive a time limit under this rule;

    (b) allow an application to be in a different form to one set out in the Practice Direction, or to be made orally;

    (c) if rule 19.2 allows, determine without a hearing an application to vary a condition.

Defendant's application or appeal to the Crown Court after magistrates' court bail decision

19.8 (1) This rule applies where a defendant wants to—

    (a) apply to the Crown Court for bail after a magistrates' court has withheld bail; or

    (b) appeal to the Crown Court after a magistrates' court has refused to vary a bail condition as the defendant wants.

(2) The defendant must—
    (a) apply to the Crown Court in writing as soon as practicable after the magistrates' court's decision; and
    (b) serve the application on—
        (i)   the Crown Court officer,
        (ii)   the magistrates' court officer,
        (iii) the prosecutor, and
        (iv) any surety affected or proposed.
(3) The application must—
    (a) specify—
        (i)   the decision that the applicant wants the Crown Court to make, and
        (ii)   each offence charged;
    (b) explain—
        (i)   as appropriate, why the Crown Court should not withhold bail, or why it should vary the condition under appeal, and
        (ii)   what further information or legal argument, if any, has become available since the magistrates' court's decision;
    (c) propose the terms of any suggested condition of bail;
    (d) if the applicant wants an earlier hearing than paragraph (6) requires, ask for that, and explain why it is needed; and
    (e) on an application for bail, attach a copy of the certificate of full argument served on the defendant under rule 19.4(4).
(4) The magistrates' court officer must as soon as practicable serve on the Crown Court officer—
    (a) a copy of the note or record made under rule 19.4(1) in connection with the magistrates' court's decision; and
    (b) the date of the next hearing, if any, in the magistrates' court.
(5) A prosecutor who opposes the application must—
    (a) so notify the Crown Court officer and the defendant at once; and
    (b) serve on each notice of the reasons for opposition.
(6) Unless the Crown Court otherwise directs, the court officer must arrange for the court to hear the application or appeal as soon as practicable and in any event no later than the business day after it was served.
(7) The Crown Court may vary a time limit under this rule.

R-152   Prosecutor's appeal against grant of bail

19.9 (1) This rule applies where a prosecutor wants to appeal—
    (a) to the Crown Court against a grant of bail by a magistrates' court, in a case in which the defendant has been charged with, or convicted of, an offence punishable with imprisonment; or
    (b) to the High Court against a grant of bail—
        (i)   by a magistrates' court, in an extradition case, or
        (ii)   by the Crown Court, except in a case in which the Crown Court granted bail on an appeal to which paragraph (1)(a) applies.
(2) The prosecutor must tell the court which has granted bail of the decision to appeal—
    (a) at the end of the hearing during which the court granted bail; and
    (b) before the defendant is released on bail.
(3) The court which has granted bail must exercise its power to remand the defendant in custody pending determination of the appeal.
(4) The prosecutor must serve an appeal notice—
    (a) on the court officer for the court which has granted bail and on the defendant;
    (b) not more than 2 hours after telling that court of the decision to appeal.
(5) The appeal notice must specify—
    (a) each offence with which the defendant is charged;
    (b) the decision under appeal;
    (c) the reasons given for the grant of bail; and
    (d) the grounds of appeal.
(6) On an appeal to the Crown Court, the magistrates' court officer must, as soon as practicable, serve on the Crown Court officer—
    (a) the appeal notice;
    (b) a copy of the note or record made under rule 19.4(1) (record of bail decision); and
    (c) notice of the date of the next hearing in the court which has granted bail.

(7)   If the Crown Court so directs, the Crown Court officer must arrange for the defendant to be
      assisted by the Official Solicitor in a case in which the defendant—
      (a) has no legal representative; and
      (b) asks for such assistance.
(8)   On an appeal to the Crown Court, the Crown Court officer must arrange for the court to
      hear the appeal as soon as practicable and in any event no later than the second business day
      after the appeal notice was served.
(9)   The prosecutor—
      (a) may abandon an appeal to the Crown Court without the court's permission, by serving
           a notice of abandonment, signed by or on behalf of the prosecutor, on—
           (i)   the defendant,
           (ii)   the Crown Court officer, and
           (iii) the magistrates' court officer
           before the hearing of the appeal begins; but
      (b) after the hearing of the appeal begins, may only abandon the appeal with the Crown
           Court's permission.
(10) The court officer for the court which has granted bail must instruct the defendant's custo-
      dian to release the defendant on the bail granted by that court, subject to any condition or
      conditions of bail imposed, if—
      (a) the prosecutor fails to serve an appeal notice within the time to which paragraph
           (4) refers; or
      (b) the prosecutor serves a notice of abandonment under paragraph (9).

Consideration of bail in a murder case   R-153

19.10 (1) This rule applies in a case in which—
      (a) the defendant is charged with murder; and
      (b) the Crown Court has not yet considered bail.
      (2) The magistrates' court officer must arrange with the Crown Court officer for the Crown
           Court to consider bail as soon as practicable and in any event no later than the second busi-
           ness day after—
      (a) a magistrates' court sends the defendant to the Crown Court for trial; or
      (b) the first hearing in the magistrates' court, if the defendant is not at once sent for trial.

Condition of residence   R-154

19.11 (1) The defendant must notify the prosecutor of the address at which the defendant will live and
           sleep if released on bail with a condition of residence—
      (a) as soon as practicable after the institution of proceedings, unless already done; and
      (b) as soon as practicable after any change of that address.
      (2) The prosecutor must help the court to assess the suitability of an address proposed as a con-
           dition of residence.

Electronic monitoring requirements   R-155

19.12 (1) This rule applies where the court imposes electronic monitoring requirements, where avail-
           able, as a condition of bail.
      (2) The court officer must—
      (a) inform the person responsible for the monitoring ('the monitor') of—
           (i)   the defendant's name, and telephone number if available,
           (ii)   each offence with which the defendant is charged,
           (iii) details of the place at which the defendant's presence must be monitored,
           (iv)   the period or periods during which the defendant's presence at that place must be
                  monitored, and
           (v)   if fixed, the date on which the defendant must surrender to custody;
      (b) inform the defendant and, where the defendant is under 16, an appropriate adult, of the
           monitor's identity and the means by which the monitor may be contacted; and
      (c) notify the monitor of any subsequent—
           (i)   variation or termination of the electronic monitoring requirements, or
           (ii)   fixing or variation of the date on which the defendant must surrender to custody.

Accommodation or support requirements   R-156

19.13 (1) This rule applies where the court imposes as a condition of bail a requirement, where avail-
           able, that the defendant must—
      (a) reside in accommodation provided for that purpose by, or on behalf of, a public authority;
      (b) receive bail support provided by, or on behalf of, a public authority.

(2) The court officer must—

   (a) inform the person responsible for the provision of any such accommodation or support ('the service provider') of—

     (i)   the defendant's name, and telephone number if available,

     (ii)   each offence with which the defendant is charged,

     (iii)   details of the requirement,

     (iv)   any other bail condition, and

     (v)   if fixed, the date on which the defendant must surrender to custody;

   (b) inform the defendant and, where the defendant is under 16, an appropriate adult, of—

     (i)   the service provider's identity and the means by which the service provider may be contacted, and

     (ii)   the address of any accommodation in which the defendant must live and sleep; and

   (c) notify the service provider of any subsequent—

     (i)   variation or termination of the requirement,

     (ii)   variation or termination of any other bail condition, and

     (iii)   fixing or variation of the date on which the defendant must surrender to custody.

R-157   **Requirement for a surety or payment, etc.**

19.14 (1) This rule applies where the court imposes as a condition of bail a requirement for—

   (a) a surety;

   (b) a payment;

   (c) the surrender of a document or thing.

(2) The court may direct how such a condition must be met.

(3) Unless the court otherwise directs, if any such condition or direction requires a surety to enter into a recognizance—

   (a) the recognizance must specify—

     (i)   the amount that the surety will be required to pay if the purpose for which the recognizance is entered is not fulfilled, and

     (ii)   the date, or the event, upon which the recognizance will expire;

   (b) the surety must enter into the recognizance in the presence of—

     (i)   the court officer,

     (ii)   the defendant's custodian, where the defendant is in custody, or

     (iii)   someone acting with the authority of either; and

   (c) the person before whom the surety enters into the recognizance must at once serve a copy on—

     (i)   the surety, and

     (ii)   as appropriate, the court officer and the defendant's custodian.

(4) Unless the court otherwise directs, if any such condition or direction requires someone to make a payment, or surrender a document or thing—

   (a) that payment, document or thing must be made or surrendered to—

     (i)   the court officer,

     (ii)   the defendant's custodian, where the defendant is in custody, or

     (iii)   someone acting with the authority of either; and

   (b) the court officer or the custodian, as appropriate, must serve immediately on the other a statement that the payment, document or thing has been made or surrendered.

(5) The custodian must release the defendant when each requirement ordered by the court has been met.

R-158   **Forfeiture of a recognizance given by a surety**

19.15 (1) This rule applies where the court imposes as a condition of bail a requirement that a surety enter into a recognizance and, after the defendant is released on bail,—

   (a) the defendant fails to surrender to custody as required, or

   (b) it appears to the court that the surety has failed to comply with a condition or direction.

(2) The court officer must serve notice on—

   (a) the surety; and

   (b) each party to the decision to grant bail,

of the hearing at which the court will consider the forfeiture of the recognizance.

(3) The court must not forfeit the recognizance less than 5 business days after service of notice under paragraph (2).

Section 3: custody time limits

Application to extend a custody time limit   R-159

19.16 (1) This rule applies where the prosecutor gives notice of application to extend a custody time limit.

(2) The court officer must arrange for the court to hear that application as soon as practicable after the expiry of—

(a) 5 days from the giving of notice, in the Crown Court; or

(b) 2 days from the giving of notice, in a magistrates' court.

(3) The court may shorten a time limit under this rule.

Appeal against custody time limit decision   R-160

19.17 (1) This rule applies where—

(a) a defendant wants to appeal to the Crown Court against a decision by a magistrates' court to extend a custody time limit;

(b) a prosecutor wants to appeal to the Crown Court against a decision by a magistrates' court to refuse to extend a custody time limit.

(2) The appellant must serve an appeal notice—

(a) on—

(i) the other party to the decision,

(ii) the Crown Court officer, and

(iii) the magistrates' court officer;

(b) in a defendant's appeal, as soon as practicable after the decision under appeal;

(c) in a prosecutor's appeal—

(i) as soon as practicable after the decision under appeal, and

(ii) before the relevant custody time limit expires.

(3) The appeal notice must specify—

(a) each offence with which the defendant is charged;

(b) the decision under appeal;

(c) the date on which the relevant custody time limit will expire;

(d) on a defendant's appeal, the date on which the relevant custody time limit would have expired but for the decision under appeal; and

(e) the grounds of appeal.

(4) The Crown Court officer must arrange for the Crown Court to hear the appeal as soon as practicable and in any event no later than the second business day after the appeal notice was served.

(5) The appellant—

(a) may abandon an appeal without the Crown Court's permission, by serving a notice of abandonment, signed by or on behalf of the appellant, on—

(i) the other party,

(ii) the Crown Court officer, and

(iii) the magistrates' court officer

before the hearing of the appeal begins; but

(b) after the hearing of the appeal begins, may only abandon the appeal with the Crown Court's permission.

Criminal Practice Directions   Part 19   Bail and Custody Time Limits

CPD III Custody and bail 19A: Bail Before Sending for Trial   PD-21

19A.1 Before the Crown Court can deal with an application under Rule 19.8 by a defendant after a magistrates' court has withheld bail, it must be satisfied that the magistrates' court has issued a certificate, under section 5(6A) of the Bail Act 1976, that it heard full argument on the application for bail before it refused the application. The certificate of full argument is produced by the magistrates' court's computer system, Libra, as part of the GENORD (General Form of Order). Two hard copies are produced, one for the defence and one for the prosecution. (Some magistrates' courts may also produce a manual certificate which will usually be available from the justices' legal adviser at the conclusion of the hearing; the GENORD may not be produced until the following day.) Under Rule 19.4(4), the magistrates' court officer will provide the defendant with a certificate that the court heard full argument. However, it is the responsibility of the defence, as the applicant in the

Crown Court, to ensure that a copy of the certificate of full argument is provided to the Crown Court as part of the application (Rule 19.8(3)(e)). The applicant's solicitors should attach a copy of the certificate to the bail application form. If the certificate is not enclosed with the application form, it will be difficult to avoid some delay in listing.

Venue

19A.2 Applications should be made to the court to which the defendant will be, or would have been, sent for trial. In the event of an application in a purely summary case, it should be made to the Crown Court centre which normally receives Class 3 work. The hearing will be listed as a chambers matter, unless a judge has directed otherwise.

PD-22   **CPD III Custody and bail 19B: BAIL: Failure to Surrender and Trials in Absence**

19B.1 The failure of defendants to comply with the terms of their bail by not surrendering, or not doing so at the appointed time, undermines the administration of justice and disrupts proceedings. The resulting delays impact on victims, witnesses and other court users and also waste costs. A defendant's failure to surrender affects not only the case with which he or she is concerned, but also the court's ability to administer justice more generally, by damaging the confidence of victims, witnesses and the public in the effectiveness of the court system and the judiciary. It is, therefore, most important that defendants who are granted bail appreciate the significance of the obligation to surrender to custody in accordance with the terms of their bail and that courts take appropriate action, if they fail to do so.

19B.2 A defendant who will be unable for medical reasons to attend court in accordance with his or her bail must obtain a certificate from his or her general practitioner or another appropriate medical practitioner such as the doctor with care of the defendant at a hospital. This should be obtained in advance of the hearing and conveyed to the court through the defendant's legal representative. In order to minimise the disruption to the court and to others, particularly witnesses if the case is listed for trial, the defendant should notify the court through his legal representative as soon as his inability to attend court becomes known.

19B.3 Guidance has been produced by the British Medical Association and the Crown Prosecution Service on the roles and responsibilities of medical practitioners when issuing medical certificates in criminal proceedings. Judges and magistrates should seek to ensure that this guidance is followed. However, it is a matter for each individual court to decide whether, in any particular case, the issued certificate should be accepted. Without a medical certificate or if an unsatisfactory certificate is provided, the court is likely to consider that the defendant has failed to surrender to bail.

19B.4 If a defendant fails to surrender to his or her bail there are at least four courses of action for the courts to consider taking:

(a) imposing penalties for the failure to surrender;
(b) revoking bail or imposing more stringent conditions;
(c) conducting trials in the absence of the defendant; and
(d) ordering that some or all of any sums of money lodged with the court as a security or pledged by a surety as a condition on the grant of bail be forfeit.

The relevant sentencing guideline is the Definitive Guideline Fail to Surrender to Bail. Under section 125(1) of the Coroners and Justice Act 2009, for offences committed on or after 6 April 2010, the court must follow the relevant guideline unless it would be contrary to the interests of justice to do so. The guideline can be obtained from the Sentencing Council's website: http://sentencing-council.judiciary.gov.uk/guidelines/guidelines-to-download.htm/

PD-23   **CPD III Custody and bail 19C: Penalties for Failure to Surrender**

Initiating Proceedings – Bail granted by a police officer

19C.1 When a person has been granted bail by a police officer to attend court and subsequently fails to surrender to custody, the decision whether to initiate proceedings for a section 6(1) or section 6(2) offence will be for the police/prosecutor and proceedings are commenced in the usual way.

19C.2 The offence in this form is a summary offence although section 6(10) to (14) of the Bail Act 1976, inserted by section 15(3) of the Criminal Justice Act 2003, disapplies section 127 of the Magistrates' Courts Act 1980 and provides for alternative time limits for the commencement of proceedings. The offence should be dealt with on the first appearance after arrest, unless an adjournment is necessary, as it will be relevant in considering whether to grant bail again.

Initiating Proceedings – Bail granted by a court

19C.3 Where a person has been granted bail by a court and subsequently fails to surrender to custody, on arrest that person should normally be brought as soon as appropriate before the court at which the proceedings in respect of which bail was granted are to be heard. (There is no requirement to lay an information within the time limit for a Bail Act offence where bail was granted by the court).

19C.4 Given that bail was granted by a court, it is more appropriate that the court itself should initiate the proceedings by its own motion although the prosecutor may invite the court to take proceedings, if the prosecutor considers proceedings are appropriate.

Timing of disposal

19C.5 Courts should not, without good reason, adjourn the disposal of a section 6(1) or section 6(2) Bail Act 1976 offence (failure to surrender) until the conclusion of the proceedings in respect of which bail was granted but should deal with defendants as soon as is practicable. In deciding what is practicable, the court must take into account when the proceedings in respect of which bail was granted are expected to conclude, the seriousness of the offence for which the defendant is already being prosecuted, the type of penalty that might be imposed for the Bail Act offence and the original offence, as well as any other relevant circumstances.

19C.6 If the Bail Act offence is adjourned alongside the substantive proceedings, then it is still necessary to consider imposing a separate penalty at the trial. In addition, bail should usually be revoked in the meantime. Trial in the absence of the defendant is not a penalty for the Bail Act offence and a separate penalty may be imposed for the Bail Act offence.

Conduct of Proceedings

19C.7 Proceedings under section 6 of the Bail Act 1976 may be conducted either as a summary offence or as a criminal contempt of court. Where proceedings are commenced by the police or prosecutor, the prosecutor will conduct the proceedings and, if the matter is contested, call the evidence. Where the court initiates proceedings, with or without an invitation from the prosecutor, the court may expect the assistance of the prosecutor, such as in cross-examining the defendant, if required.

19C.8 The burden of proof is on the defendant to prove that he had reasonable cause for his failure to surrender to custody (section 6(3) of the Bail Act 1976).

Sentencing for a Bail Act offence

19C.9 A defendant who commits an offence under section 6(1) or section 6(2) of the Bail Act 1976 commits an offence that stands apart from the proceedings in respect of which bail was granted. The seriousness of the offence can be reflected by an appropriate and generally separate penalty being imposed for the Bail Act offence.

19C.10 As noted above, the Sentencing Council has issued a guideline on sentencing offenders for Bail Act offences and this must be followed unless it would be contrary to the interests of justice to do so. Where the appropriate penalty is a custodial sentence, consecutive sentences should be imposed unless there are circumstances that make this inappropriate.

CPD III Custody and bail 19D: Relationship between the Bail Act Offence and Further Remands on Bail or in Custody

PD-24

19D.1 The court at which the defendant is produced should, where practicable and legally permissible, arrange to have all outstanding cases brought before it (including those from different courts) for the purpose of progressing matters and dealing with the question of bail. This is likely to be practicable in the magistrates' court where cases can easily be transferred from one magistrates' court to another. Practice is likely to vary in the Crown Court. If the defendant appears before a different court, for example because he is charged with offences committed in another area, and it is not practicable for all matters to be concluded by that court then the defendant may be remanded on bail or in custody, if appropriate, to appear before the first court for the outstanding offences to be dealt with.

19D.2 When a defendant has been convicted of a Bail Act offence, the court should review the remand status of the defendant, including the conditions of that bail, in respect of all outstanding proceedings against the defendant.

19D.3 Failure by the defendant to surrender or a conviction for failing to surrender to bail in connection with the main proceedings will be significant factors weighing against the re-granting of bail.

19D.4 Whether or not an immediate custodial sentence has been imposed for the Bail Act offence, the court may, having reviewed the defendant's remand status, also remand the defendant in custody in the main proceedings.

PD-25 **CPD III Custody and bail 19E: Trials in Absence**

19E.1 A defendant has a right, in general, to be present and to be represented at his trial. However, a defendant may choose not to exercise those rights, such as by voluntarily absenting himself and failing to instruct his lawyers adequately so that they can represent him.

19E.2 The court has a discretion as to whether a trial should take place or continue in the defendant's absence and must exercise its discretion with due regard for the interests of justice. The overriding concern must be to ensure that such a trial is as fair as circumstances permit and leads to a just outcome. If the defendant's absence is due to involuntary illness or incapacity it would very rarely, if ever, be right to exercise the discretion in favour of commencing or continuing the trial.

Trials on Indictment

19E.3 Proceeding in the absence of a defendant is a step which ought normally to be taken only if it is unavoidable. The court must exercise its discretion as to whether a trial should take place or continue in the defendant's absence with the utmost care and caution. Due regard should be had to the judgment of Lord Bingham in *R v Jones* [2002] UKHL 5, [2003] 1 AC 1, [2002] 2 Cr App R 9. Circumstances to be taken into account before proceeding include:

i)   the conduct of the defendant;

ii)   the disadvantage to the defendant;

iii) the public interest, taking account of the inconvenience and hardship to witnesses, and especially to any complainant, of a delay; if the witnesses have attended court and are ready to give evidence, that will weigh in favour of continuing with the trial;

iv)   the effect of any delay;

v)   whether the attendance of the defendant could be secured at a later hearing; and

vii) the likely outcome if the defendant is found guilty.

Even if the defendant is voluntarily absent, it is still generally desirable that he or she is represented.

Trials in the Magistrates' Courts

19E.4 Section 11 of the Magistrates' Courts Act 1980 applies. If either party is absent, the court should follow the procedure at Rule 37.11. Subject to the provisions of the statute, the principles outlined above are applicable. Benches and legal advisers will note that the presumption at Rule 37.11(3) (a) does not apply if the defendant is under 18 years of age.

PD-26 **CPD III Custody and bail 19F: Forfeiture of Monies Lodged as Security or Pledged by a Surety/Estreatment of Recognisances**

19F.1 A surety undertakes to forfeit a sum of money if the defendant fails to surrender as required. Considerable care must be taken to explain that obligation and the consequences before a surety is taken. This system, in one form or another, has great antiquity. It is immensely valuable. A court concerned that a defendant will fail to surrender will not normally know that defendant personally, nor indeed much about him. When members of the community who do know the defendant say they trust him to surrender and are prepared to stake their own money on that trust, that can have a powerful influence on the decision of the court as to whether or not to grant bail. There are two important side-effects. The first is that the surety will keep an eye on the defendant, and report to the authorities if there is a concern that he will abscond. In those circumstances, the surety can withdraw. The second is that a defendant will be deterred from absconding by the knowledge that if he does so then his family or friends who provided the surety will lose their money. In the experience of the courts, it is comparatively rare for a defendant to fail to surrender when meaningful sureties are in place.

19F.2 Any surety should have the opportunity to make representations to the defendant to surrender himself, in accordance with their obligations.

19F.3 The court should not wait or adjourn a decision on estreatment of sureties or securities until such time, if any, that the bailed defendant appears before the court. It is possible that any defendant who apparently absconds may have a defence of reasonable cause to the allegation of failure to surrender. If that happens, then any surety or security estreated would be returned. The reason for proceeding is that the defendant may never surrender, or may not surrender for many years. The court should still consider the sureties' obligations if that happens. Moreover, the longer the matter is delayed the more probable it is that the personal circumstances of the sureties will change.

19F.4   The court should follow the procedure at Rule 19.15 of the Criminal Procedure Rules. Before the court makes a decision, it should give the sureties the opportunity to make representations, either in person, through counsel or by statement.

19F.5   The court has discretion to forfeit the whole sum, part only of the sum, or to remit the sum. The starting point is that the surety is forfeited in full. It would be unfortunate if this valuable method of allowing a defendant to remain at liberty were undermined. Courts would have less confidence in the efficacy of sureties. It is also important to note that a defendant who absconds without in any way forewarning his sureties does not thereby release them from any or all of their responsibilities. Even if a surety does his best, he remains liable for the full amount, except at the discretion of the court. However, all factors should be taken into account and the following are noted for guidance only:

i)   The presence or absence of culpability is a factor, but is not in itself a reason to reduce or set aside the obligations entered into by the surety.

ii)   The means of a surety, and in particular changed means, are relevant.

iii)   The court should forfeit no more than is necessary, in public policy, to maintain the integrity and confidence of the system of taking sureties.

CPD III Custody and bail 19G: Bail During Trial   PD-27

19G.1   The following should be read subject to the Bail Act 1976.

19G.2   Once a trial has begun the further grant of bail, whether during the short adjournment or overnight, is in the discretion of the trial judge or trial Bench. It may be a proper exercise of this discretion to refuse bail during the short adjournment if the accused cannot otherwise be segregated from witnesses and jurors.

19G.3   An accused who was on bail while on remand should not be refused bail during the trial unless, in the opinion of the court, there are positive reasons to justify this refusal. Such reasons might include:

(a)   that a point has been reached where there is a real danger that the accused will abscond, either because the case is going badly for him, or for any other reason;

(b)   that there is a real danger that he may interfere with witnesses, jurors or co-defendants.

19G.4   Once the jury has returned a guilty verdict or a finding of guilt has been made, a further renewal of bail should be decided in the light of the gravity of the offence, any friction between co-defendants and the likely sentence to be passed in all the circumstances of the case.

CPD III Custody and bail 19H: Crown Court Judge's Certificaton of Fitness to Appeal and Applications to the Crown Court for Bail Pending Appeal   PD-28

19H.1   The trial or sentencing judge may grant a certificate of fitness for appeal (see, for example, sections 1(2) (b) and 11(1A) of the Criminal Appeal Act 1968); the judge in the Crown Court should only certify cases in exceptional circumstances. The Crown Court judge should use the Criminal Appeal Office Form C (Crown Court Judge's Certificate of fitness for appeal) which is available to court staff on the HMCTS intranet.

19H.2   The judge may well think it right to encourage the defendant's advocate to submit to the court, and serve on the prosecutor, before the hearing of the application, a draft of the grounds of appeal which he will ask the judge to certify on Form C.

19H.3   The first question for the judge is then whether there exists a particular and cogent ground of appeal. If there is no such ground, there can be no certificate; and if there is no certificate there can be no bail. A judge should not grant a certificate with regard to sentence merely in the light of mitigation to which he has, in his opinion, given due weight, nor in regard to conviction on a ground where he considers the chance of a successful appeal is not substantial. The judge should bear in mind that, where a certificate is refused, application may be made to the Court of Appeal for leave to appeal and for bail; it is expected that certificates will only be granted in exceptional circumstances.

19H.4   Defence advocates should note that the effect of a grant of a certificate is to remove the need for leave to appeal to be granted by the Court of Appeal. It does not in itself commence the appeal. The completed Form C will be sent by the Crown Court to the Criminal Appeal Office; it is not copied to the parties. The procedures in Part 68 of the Criminal Procedure Rules should be followed.

19H.5 Bail pending appeal to the Court of Appeal (Criminal Division) may be granted by the trial or sentencing judge if they have certified the case as fit for appeal (see sections 81(1) (f) and 81(1B) of the Senior Courts Act 1981). Bail can only be granted in the Crown Court within 28 days of the conviction or sentence which is to be the subject of the appeal and may not be granted if an application for bail has already been made to the Court of Appeal. The procedure for bail to be granted by a judge of the Crown Court pending an appeal is governed by Part 19 of the Criminal Procedure Rules. The Crown Court judge should use the Criminal Appeal Office Form BC (Crown Court Judge's Order granting bail) which is available to court staff on the HMCTS intranet.

19H.6 The length of the period which might elapse before the hearing of any appeal is not relevant to the grant of a certificate; but, if the judge does decide to grant a certificate, it may be one factor in the decision whether or not to grant bail. If bail is granted, the judge should consider imposing a condition of residence in line with the practice in the Court of Appeal (Criminal Division).

CRIMINAL PROCEDURE RULES   PART 20
[There are no rules in this part.]

CRIMINAL PROCEDURE RULES   PART 21
[There no rules in this part.]

CRIMINAL PROCEDURE RULES   PART 22   DISCLOSURE

R-161   **When this Part applies**

22.1   This Part applies—

(a)   in a magistrates' court and in the Crown Court;

(b)   where Parts I and II of the Criminal Procedure and Investigations Act 1996 apply.

R-162   **Prosecution disclosure**

22.2   (1)   This rule applies in the Crown Court where, under section 3 of the Criminal Procedure and Investigations Act 1996, the prosecutor—

(a)   discloses prosecution material to the defendant; or

(b)   serves on the defendant a written statement that there is no such material to disclose.

(2)   The prosecutor must at the same time so inform the court officer.

R-163   **Prosecutor's application for public interest ruling**

22.3   (1)   This rule applies where—

(a)   without a court order, the prosecutor would have to disclose material; and

(b)   the prosecutor wants the court to decide whether it would be in the public interest to disclose it.

(2)   The prosecutor must—

(a)   apply in writing for such a decision; and

(b)   serve the application on—

(i)   the court officer,

(ii)   any person who the prosecutor thinks would be directly affected by disclosure of the material, and

(iii)   the defendant, but only to the extent that serving it on the defendant would not disclose what the prosecutor thinks ought not be disclosed.

(3)   The application must—

(a)   describe the material, and explain why the prosecutor thinks that—

(i)   it is material that the prosecutor would have to disclose,

(ii)   it would not be in the public interest to disclose that material, and

(iii)   no measure such as the prosecutor's admission of any fact, or disclosure by summary, extract or edited copy, adequately would protect both the public interest and the defendant's right to a fair trial;

(b)   omit from any part of the application that is served on the defendant anything that would disclose what the prosecutor thinks ought not be disclosed (in which case, paragraph (4) of this rule applies); and

(c)   explain why, if no part of the application is served on the defendant.

(4) Where the prosecutor serves only part of the application on the defendant, the prosecutor must—

   (a) mark the other part, to show that it is only for the court; and

   (b) in that other part, explain why the prosecutor has withheld it from the defendant.

(5) Unless already done, the court may direct the prosecutor to serve an application on—

   (a) the defendant;

   (b) any other person who the court considers would be directly affected by the disclosure of the material.

(6) The court must determine the application at a hearing which—

   (a) must be in private, unless the court otherwise directs; and

   (b) if the court so directs, may take place, wholly or in part, in the defendant's absence.

(7) At a hearing at which the defendant is present—

   (a) the general rule is that the court must receive, in the following sequence—

     (i) representations first by the prosecutor and any other person served with the application, and then by the defendant, in the presence of them all, and then

     (ii) further representations by the prosecutor and any such other person in the defendant's absence; but

   (b) the court may direct other arrangements for the hearing.

(8) The court may only determine the application if satisfied that it has been able to take adequate account of—

   (a) such rights of confidentiality as apply to the material; and

   (b) the defendant's right to a fair trial.

(9) Unless the court otherwise directs, the court officer—

   (a) must not give notice to anyone other than the prosecutor—

     (i) of the hearing of an application under this rule, unless the prosecutor served the application on that person, or

     (ii) of the court's decision on the application;

   (b) may—

     (i) keep a written application or representations, or

     (ii) arrange for the whole or any part to be kept by some other appropriate person, subject to any conditions that the court may impose.

Defence disclosure   R-164

22.4 (1) This rule applies where—

   (a) under section 5 or 6 of the Criminal Procedure and Investigations Act 1996, the defendant gives a defence statement;

   (b) under section 6C of the 1996 Act, the defendant gives a defence witness notice.

(2) The defendant must serve such a statement or notice on—

   (a) the court officer; and

   (b) the prosecutor.

Defendant's application for prosecution disclosure   R-165

22.5 (1) This rule applies where the defendant—

   (a) has served a defence statement given under the Criminal Procedure and Investigations Act 1996; and

   (b) wants the court to require the prosecutor to disclose material.

(2) The defendant must serve an application on—

   (a) the court officer; and

   (b) the prosecutor.

(3) The application must—

   (a) describe the material that the defendant wants the prosecutor to disclose;

   (b) explain why the defendant thinks there is reasonable cause to believe that—

     (i) the prosecutor has that material, and

     (ii) it is material that the Criminal Procedure and Investigations Act 1996 requires the prosecutor to disclose; and

   (c) ask for a hearing, if the defendant wants one, and explain why it is needed.

(4) The court may determine an application under this rule—

   (a) at a hearing, in public or in private; or

   (b) without a hearing.

(5) The court must not require the prosecutor to disclose material unless the prosecutor—

   (a) is present; or

   (b) has had at least 14 days in which to make representations.

R-166   **Review of public interest ruling**

22.6   (1)   This rule applies where the court has ordered that it is not in the public interest to disclose material that the prosecutor otherwise would have to disclose, and—

(a)   the defendant wants the court to review that decision; or

(b)   the Crown Court reviews that decision on its own initiative.

(2)   Where the defendant wants the court to review that decision, the defendant must—

(a)   serve an application on—

(i)   the court officer, and

(ii)   the prosecutor; and

(b)   in the application—

(i)   describe the material that the defendant wants the prosecutor to disclose, and

(ii)   explain why the defendant thinks it is no longer in the public interest for the prosecutor not to disclose it.

(3)   The prosecutor must serve any such application on any person who the prosecutor thinks would be directly affected if that material were disclosed.

(4)   The prosecutor, and any such person, must serve any representations on—

(a)   the court officer; and

(b)   the defendant, unless to do so would in effect reveal something that either thinks ought not be disclosed.

(5)   The court may direct—

(a)   the prosecutor to serve any such application on any person who the court considers would be directly affected if that material were disclosed;

(b)   the prosecutor and any such person to serve any representations on the defendant.

(6)   The court must review a decision to which this rule applies at a hearing which—

(a)   will be in private, unless the court otherwise directs; and

(b)   if the court so directs, may take place, wholly or in part, in the defendant's absence.

(7)   At a hearing at which the defendant is present—

(a)   the general rule is that the court will receive, in the following sequence—

(i)   representations first by the defendant, and then by the prosecutor and any other person served with the application, in the presence of them all, and then

(ii)   further representations by the prosecutor and any such other person in the defendant's absence; but

(b)   the court may direct other arrangements for the hearing.

(8)   The court may only conclude a review if satisfied that it has been able to take adequate account of—

(a)   such rights of confidentiality as apply to the material; and

(b)   the defendant's right to a fair trial.

R-167   **Defendant's application to use disclosed material**

22.7   (1)   This rule applies where a defendant wants the court's permission to use disclosed prosecution material—

(a)   otherwise than in connection with the case in which it was disclosed; or

(b)   beyond the extent to which it was displayed or communicated publicly at a hearing.

(2)   The defendant must serve an application on—

(a)   the court officer; and

(b)   the prosecutor.

(3)   The application must—

(a)   specify what the defendant wants to use or disclose; and

(b)   explain why.

(4)   The court may determine an application under this rule—

(a)   at a hearing, in public or in private; or

(b)   without a hearing.

(5)   The court must not permit the use of such material unless—

(a)   the prosecutor has had at least 28 days in which to make representations; and

(b)   the court is satisfied that it has been able to take adequate account of any rights of confidentiality that may apply to the material.

R-168   **Unauthorised use of disclosed material**

22.8   (1)   This rule applies where a person is accused of using disclosed prosecution material in contravention of section 17 of the Criminal Procedure and Investigations Act 1996.

(2) A party who wants the court to exercise its power to punish that person for contempt of court must comply with the rules in Part 62 (Contempt of court).

(3) The court must not exercise its power to forfeit material used in contempt of court unless—
    (a) the prosecutor; and
    (b) any other person directly affected by the disclosure of the material, is present, or has had at least 14 days in which to make representations.

Court's power to vary requirements under this Part   **R-169**

22.9   The court may—
    (a) shorten or extend (even after it has expired) a time limit under this Part;
    (b) allow a defence statement, or a defence witness notice, to be in a different written form to one set out in the Practice Direction, as long as it contains what the Criminal Procedure and Investigations Act 1996 requires;
    (c) allow an application under this Part to be in a different form to one set out in the Practice Direction, or to be presented orally; and
    (d) specify the period within which—
        (i) any application under this Part must be made, or
        (ii) any material must be disclosed, on an application to which rule 22.5 applies (defendant's application for prosecution disclosure).

Criminal Practice Directions   Part 22   Disclosure

CPD IV Disclosure 22A: Disclosure of Unused Material   **PD-29**

22A.1 Disclosure is a vital part of the preparation for trial, both in the magistrates' courts and in the Crown Court. All parties must be familiar with their obligations, in particular under the Criminal Procedure and Investigations Act 1996 as amended and the Code issued under that Act, and must comply with the relevant judicial protocol and guidelines from the Attorney-General. These documents have recently been revised and the new guidance will be issued shortly as *Judicial Protocol on the Disclosure of Unused Material in Criminal Cases* and the *Attorney-General's Guidelines on Disclosure*. The new documents should be read together as complementary, comprehensive guidance. They will be available electronically on the respective websites.

22A.2 In addition, certain procedures are prescribed under Part 22 of the Rules and these should be followed. The notes to Part 22 contain a useful summary of the requirements of the CPIA 1996 as amended.

Criminal Procedure Rules   Part 23

[There are no rules in this part.]

Criminal Procedure Rules   Part 24

[There are no rules in this part.]

Criminal Procedure Rules   Part 25

[There are no rules in this part.]

Criminal Procedure Rules   Part 26

[There are no rules in this part.]

Criminal Procedure Rules   Part 27   Witness Statements

When this Part applies   **R-170**

27.1   This Part applies where a party wants to introduce a written statement in evidence under section 9 of the Criminal Justice Act 1967.

R-171　**Content of written statement**

27.2　The statement must contain—
- (a) at the beginning—
  - (i) the witness' name, and
  - (ii) the witness' age, if under 18;
- (b) a declaration by the witness that—
  - (i) it is true to the best of the witness' knowledge and belief, and
  - (ii) the witness knows that if it is introduced in evidence, then it would be an offence wilfully to have stated in it anything that the witness knew to be false or did not believe to be true;
- (c) if the witness cannot read the statement, a signed declaration by someone else that that person read it to the witness; and
- (d) the witness' signature.

R-172　**Reference to exhibit**

27.3　Where the statement refers to a document or object as an exhibit—
- (a) the statement must contain such a description of that exhibit as to identify it clearly; and
- (b) the exhibit must be labelled or marked correspondingly, and the label or mark signed by the maker of the statement.

R-173　**Written statement in evidence**

27.4　(1) A party who wants to introduce in evidence a written statement must—
- (a) before the hearing at which that party wants to introduce it, serve a copy of the statement on—
  - (i) the court officer, and
  - (ii) each other party; and
- (b) at or before that hearing, serve on the court officer the statement or an authenticated copy.

(2) If that party relies on only part of the statement, that party must mark the copy in such a way as to make that clear.

(3) A prosecutor must serve on a defendant, with the copy of the statement, a notice—
- (a) of the right within 7 days of service to object to the introduction of the statement in evidence instead of the witness giving evidence in person; and
- (b) that if the defendant does not object in time, the court—
  - (i) can nonetheless require the witness to give evidence in person, but
  - (ii) may decide not to do so.

(4) The court may exercise its power to require the witness to give evidence in person—
- (a) on application by any party; or
- (b) on its own initiative.

(5) A party entitled to receive a copy of a statement may waive that entitlement by so informing—
- (a) the party who would have served it; and
- (b) the court.

Criminal Practice Directions　　Part 27　　Witness Statements

PD-30　**CPD V Evidence 27A: Evidence by Written Statement**

27A.1　Where the prosecution proposes to tender written statements in evidence under section 9 of the Criminal Justice Act 1967, it will frequently be necessary for certain statements to be edited. This will occur either because a witness has made more than one statement whose contents should conveniently be reduced into a single, comprehensive statement, or where a statement contains inadmissible, prejudicial or irrelevant material. Editing of statements must be done by a Crown Prosecutor (or by a legal representative, if any, of the prosecutor if the case is not being conducted by the Crown Prosecution Service) and not by a police officer.

Composite statements

27A.2　A composite statement giving the combined effect of two or more earlier statements must be prepared in compliance with the requirements of section 9 of the 1967 Act; and must then be signed by the witness.

Editing single statements

27A.3   There are two acceptable methods of editing single statements. They are:

(a)   By marking copies of the statement in a way which indicates the passages on which the prosecution will not rely. This merely indicates that the prosecution will not seek to adduce the evidence so marked. The original signed statement to be tendered to the court is not marked in any way.

The marking on the copy statement is done by lightly striking out the passages to be edited, so that what appears beneath can still be read, or by bracketing, or by a combination of both. It is not permissible to produce a photocopy with the deleted material obliterated, since this would be contrary to the requirement that the defence and the court should be served with copies of the signed original statement.

Whenever the striking out/bracketing method is used, it will assist if the following words appear at the foot of the frontispiece or index to any bundle of copy statements to be tendered:

'The prosecution does not propose to adduce evidence of those passages of the attached copy statements which have been struck out and/or bracketed (nor will it seek to do so at the trial unless a notice of further evidence is served)'.

(b)   By obtaining a fresh statement, signed by the witness, which omits the offending material, applying the procedure for composite statements above.

27A.4   In most cases where a single statement is to be edited, the striking out/bracketing method will be the more appropriate, but the taking of a fresh statement is preferable in the following circumstances:

(a)   When a police (or other investigating) officer's statement contains details of interviews with more suspects than are eventually charged, a fresh statement should be prepared and signed, omitting all details of interview with those not charged except, insofar as it is relevant, for the bald fact that a certain named person was interviewed at a particular time, date and place.

(b)   When a suspect is interviewed about more offences than are eventually made the subject of charges, a fresh statement should be prepared and signed, omitting all questions and answers about the uncharged offences unless either they might appropriately be taken into consideration, or evidence about those offences is admissible on the charges preferred. It may, however, be desirable to replace the omitted questions and answers with a phrase such as: *'After referring to some other matters, I then said, "………"'*, so as to make it clear that part of the interview has been omitted.

(c)   A fresh statement should normally be prepared and signed if the only part of the original on which the prosecution is relying is only a small proportion of the whole, although it remains desirable to use the alternative method if there is reason to believe that the defence might itself wish to rely, in mitigation or for any other purpose, on at least some of those parts which the prosecution does not propose to adduce.

(d)   When the passages contain material which the prosecution is entitled to withhold from disclosure to the defence.

27A.5   Prosecutors should also be aware that, where statements are to be tendered under section 9 of the 1967 Act in the course of summary proceedings, there will be a need to prepare fresh statements excluding inadmissible or prejudicial material, rather than using the striking out or bracketing method.

27A.6   Whenever a fresh statement is taken from a witness and served in evidence, the earlier, unedited statement(s) becomes unused material and should be scheduled and reviewed for disclosure to the defence in the usual way.

CPD V Evidence 27B: Video Recorded Evidence in Chief   PD-31

27B.1   The procedure for making an application for leave to admit into evidence video recorded evidence in chief under section 27 of the Youth Justice and Criminal Evidence Act 1999 is given in Part 29 of the Criminal Procedure Rules.

27B.2   Where a court, on application by a party to the proceedings or of its own motion, grants leave to admit a video recording in evidence under section 27(1) of the 1999 Act, it may direct that any part of the recording be excluded (section 27(2) and (3)). When such direction is given, the party who made the application to admit the video recording must edit the recording in accordance with the judge's directions and send a copy of the edited recording to the appropriate officer of the Crown Court and to every other party to the proceedings.

Criminal Procedure Rules 2013 and Criminal Practice Directions

27B.3 Where a video recording is to be adduced during proceedings before the Crown Court, it should be produced and proved by the interviewer, or any other person who was present at the interview with the witness at which the recording was made. The applicant should ensure that such a person will be available for this purpose, unless the parties have agreed to accept a written statement in lieu of attendance by that person.

27B.4 Once a trial has begun, if, by reason of faulty or inadequate preparation or for some other cause, the procedures set out above have not been properly complied with and an application is made to edit the video recording, thereby necessitating an adjournment for the work to be carried out, the court may, at its discretion, make an appropriate award of costs.

PD-32   **CPD V Evidence 27C: Evidence of Audio and Video Recorded Interviews**

27C.1 The interrogation of suspects is primarily governed by Code C, one of the Codes of Practice under the Police and Criminal Evidence Act 1984 ('PACE'). Under that Code, interviews must normally be contemporaneously recorded. Under PACE Code E, interviews conducted at a police station concerning an indictable offence must normally be audio-recorded. In practice, most interviews are audio-recorded under Code E, or video-recorded under Code F, and it is best practice to do so. The questioning of terrorism suspects is governed separately by Code H. The Codes are available electronically on the Home Office website.

27C.2 Where a record of the interview is to be prepared, this should be in accordance with the current national guidelines, as envisaged by Note 5A of Code E.

27C.3 If the prosecution wishes to rely on the defendant's interview in evidence, the prosecution should seek to agree the record with the defence. Both parties should have received a copy of the audio or video recording, and can check the record against the recording. The record should be edited (see below) if inadmissible matters are included within it and, in particular if the interview is lengthy, the prosecution should seek to shorten it by editing or summary.

27C.4 If the record is agreed there is usually no need for the audio or video recording to be played in court. It is a matter for the discretion of the trial judge, but usual practice is for edited copies of the record to be provided to the court, and to the jury if there is one, and for the prosecution advocate to read the interview with the interviewing officer or the officer in the case, as part of the officer's evidence in chief, the officer reading the interviewer and the advocate reading the defendant and defence representative. In the magistrates' court, the Bench sometimes retire to read the interview themselves, and the document is treated as if it had been read aloud in court. This is permissible, but Rule 37.5 should be followed.

27C.5 Where the prosecution intends to adduce the interview in evidence, and agreement between the parties has not been reached about the record, sufficient notice must be given to allow consideration of any amendment to the record, or the preparation of any transcript of the interview, or any editing of a recording for the purpose of playing it in court. To that end, the following practice should be followed:

(a) Where the defence is unable to agree a record of interview or transcript (where one is already available) the prosecution should be notified at latest at the Plea and Case Management Hearing ('PCMH'), with a view to securing agreement to amend. The notice should specify the part to which objection is taken, or the part omitted which the defence consider should be included. A copy of the notice should be supplied to the court within the period specified above. The PCMH form inquires about the admissibility of the defendant's interview and shortening by editing or summarising for trial.

(b) If agreement is not reached and it is proposed that the audio or video recording or part of it be played in court, notice should be given to the prosecution by the defence as ordered at the PCMH, in order that the advocates for the parties may agree those parts of the audio or video recording that should not be adduced and that arrangements may be made, by editing or in some other way, to exclude that material. A copy of the notice should be supplied to the court.

(c) Notice of any agreement reached should be supplied to the court by the prosecution, as soon as is practicable.

27C.6 Alternatively, if, the prosecution advocate proposes to play the audio or video recording or part of it, the prosecution should at latest at the PCMH, notify the defence and the court. The defence should notify the prosecution and the court within 14 days of receiving the notice, if they object to the production of the audio or video recording on the basis that a part of it should be excluded. If the objections raised by the defence are accepted, the prosecution should prepare an edited recording, or make other arrangements to exclude the material part; and should notify the court of the arrangements made.

27C.7 If the defendant wishes to have the audio or video recording or any part of it played to the court, the defence should provide notice to the prosecution and the court at latest at the PCMH. The defence should also, at that time, notify the prosecution of any proposals to edit the recording and seek the prosecution's agreement to those amendments.

27C.8 Whenever editing or amendment of a record of interview or of an audio or video recording or of a transcript takes place, the following general principles should be followed:

(i) Where a defendant has made a statement which includes an admission of one or more other offences, the portion relating to other offences should be omitted unless it is or becomes admissible in evidence;

(ii) Where the statement of one defendant contains a portion which exculpates him or her and partly implicates a co-defendant in the trial, the defendant making the statement has the right to insist that everything relevant which is exculpatory goes before the jury. In such a case the judge must be consulted about how best to protect the position of the co-defendant.

27C.9 If it becomes necessary for either party to access the master copy of the audio or video recording, they should give notice to the other party and follow the procedure in PACE Code E at section 6.

27C.10 If there is a challenge to the integrity of the master recording, notice and particulars should be given to the court and to the prosecution by the defence as soon as is practicable. The court may then, at its discretion, order a case management hearing or give such other directions as may be appropriate.

27C.11 If an audio or video recording is to be adduced during proceedings before the Crown Court, it should be produced and proved in a witness statement by the interviewing officer or any other officer who was present at the interview at which the recording was made. The prosecution should ensure that the witness is available to attend court if required by the defence in the usual way.

27C.12 It is the responsibility of the prosecution to ensure that there is a person available to operate any audio or video equipment needed during the course of the proceedings. Subject to their other responsibilities, the court staff may be able to assist.

27C.13 If either party wishes to present audio or video evidence, that party must ensure, in advance of the hearing, that the evidence is in a format that is compatible with the court's equipment, and that the material to be used does in fact function properly in the relevant court room.

27C.14 In order to avoid the necessity for the court to listen to or watch lengthy or irrelevant material before the relevant part of a recording is reached, counsel shall indicate to the equipment operator those parts of a recording which it may be necessary to play. Such an indication should, so far as possible, be expressed in terms of the time track or other identifying process used by the interviewing police force and should be given in time for the operator to have located those parts by the appropriate point in the trial.

27C.15 Once a trial has begun, if, by reason of faulty preparation or for some other cause, the procedures above have not been properly complied with, and an application is made to amend the record of interview or transcript or to edit the recording, as the case may be, thereby making necessary an adjournment for the work to be carried out, the court may make at its discretion an appropriate award of costs.

27C.16 Where a case is listed for hearing on a date which falls within the time limits set out above, it is the responsibility of the parties to ensure that all the necessary steps are taken to comply with this Practice Direction within such shorter period as is available.

CRIMINAL PROCEDURE RULES   PART 28   WITNESS SUMMONSES,
WARRANTS AND ORDERS

When this Part applies   R-174

28.1 (1) This Part applies in magistrates' courts and in the Crown Court where—

(a) a party wants the court to issue a witness summons, warrant or order under—

(i) section 97 of the Magistrates' Courts Act 1980,

(ii) section 2 of the Criminal Procedure (Attendance of Witnesses) Act 1965, or

(iii) section 7 of the Bankers' Books Evidence Act 1879;

(b) the court considers the issue of such a summons, warrant or order on its own initiative as if a party had applied; or

(c) one of those listed in rule 28.7 wants the court to withdraw such a summons, warrant or order.

(2) A reference to a 'witness' in this Part is a reference to a person to whom such a summons, warrant or order is directed.

R-175 **Issue etc. of summons, warrant or order with or without a hearing**

28.2 (1) The court may issue or withdraw a witness summons, warrant or order with or without a hearing.

(2) A hearing under this Part must be in private unless the court otherwise directs.

R-176 **Application for summons, warrant or order: general rules**

28.3 (1) A party who wants the court to issue a witness summons, warrant or order must apply as soon as practicable after becoming aware of the grounds for doing so.

(2) The party applying must—

(a) identify the proposed witness;

(b) explain—

(i) what evidence the proposed witness can give or produce,

(ii) why it is likely to be material evidence, and

(iii) why it would be in the interests of justice to issue a summons, order or warrant as appropriate.

(3) The application may be made orally unless—

(a) rule 28.5 applies; or

(b) the court otherwise directs.

R-177 **Written application: form and service**

28.4 (1) An application in writing under rule 28.3 must be in the form set out in the Practice Direction, containing the same declaration of truth as a witness statement.

(2) The party applying must serve the application—

(a) in every case, on the court officer and as directed by the court; and

(b) as required by rule 28.5, if that rule applies.

R-178 **Application for summons to produce a document, etc.: special rules**

28.5 (1) This rule applies to an application under rule 28.3 for a witness summons requiring the proposed witness—

(a) to produce in evidence a document or thing; or

(b) to give evidence about information apparently held in confidence, that relates to another person.

(2) The application must be in writing in the form required by rule 28.4.

(3) The party applying must serve the application—

(a) on the proposed witness, unless the court otherwise directs; and

(b) on one or more of the following, if the court so directs—

(i) a person to whom the proposed evidence relates,

(ii) another party.

(4) The court must not issue a witness summons where this rule applies unless—

(a) everyone served with the application has had at least 14 days in which to make representations, including representations about whether there should be a hearing of the application before the summons is issued; and

(b) the court is satisfied that it has been able to take adequate account of the duties and rights, including rights of confidentiality, of the proposed witness and of any person to whom the proposed evidence relates.

(5) This rule does not apply to an application for an order to produce in evidence a copy of an entry in a banker's book.

R-179 **Application for summons to produce a document, etc.: court's assessment of relevance and confidentiality**

28.6 (1) This rule applies where a person served with an application for a witness summons requiring the proposed witness to produce in evidence a document or thing objects to its production on the ground that—

(a) it is not likely to be material evidence; or

(b) even if it is likely to be material evidence, the duties or rights, including rights of confidentiality, of the proposed witness or of any person to whom the document or thing relates outweigh the reasons for issuing a summons.

(2) The court may require the proposed witness to make the document or thing available for the objection to be assessed.

(3) The court may invite—

    (a) the proposed witness or any representative of the proposed witness; or

    (b) a person to whom the document or thing relates or any representative of such a person, to help the court assess the objection.

Application to withdraw a summons, warrant or order   **R-180**

28.7 (1) The court may withdraw a witness summons, warrant or order if one of the following applies for it to be withdrawn—

    (a) the party who applied for it, on the ground that it no longer is needed;

    (b) the witness, on the grounds that—

        (i) he was not aware of any application for it, and

        (ii) he cannot give or produce evidence likely to be material evidence, or

        (iii) even if he can, his duties or rights, including rights of confidentiality, or those of any person to whom the evidence relates outweigh the reasons for the issue of the summons, warrant or order; or

    (c) any person to whom the proposed evidence relates, on the grounds that—

        (i) he was not aware of any application for it, and

        (ii) that evidence is not likely to be material evidence, or

        (iii) even if it is, his duties or rights, including rights of confidentiality, or those of the witness outweigh the reasons for the issue of the summons, warrant or order.

(2) A person applying under the rule must—

    (a) apply in writing as soon as practicable after becoming aware of the grounds for doing so, explaining why he wants the summons, warrant or order to be withdrawn; and

    (b) serve the application on the court officer and as appropriate on—

        (i) the witness,

        (ii) the party who applied for the summons, warrant or order, and

        (iii) any other person who he knows was served with the application for the summons, warrant or order.

(3) Rule 28.6 applies to an application under this rule that concerns a document or thing to be produced in evidence.

Court's power to vary requirements under this Part   **R-181**

28.8 (1) The court may—

    (a) shorten or extend (even after it has expired) a time limit under this Part; and

    (b) where a rule or direction requires an application under this Part to be in writing, allow that application to be made orally instead.

(2) Someone who wants the court to allow an application to be made orally under paragraph (1)(b) of this rule must—

    (a) give as much notice as the urgency of his application permits to those on whom he would otherwise have served an application in writing; and

    (b) in doing so explain the reasons for the application and for wanting the court to consider it orally.

Criminal Practice Directions   Part 28   Witness Summonses, Warrants and Orders

CPD V Evidence 28A: Wards of Court and Children Subject to Current   **PD-33**
Family Proceedings

28A.1 Where police wish to interview a child who is subject to current family proceedings, leave of the Family Court is only required where such an interview may lead to a child disclosing information confidential to those proceedings and not otherwise available to the police under Working Together to Safeguard Children (March 2013), a guide to inter-agency working to safeguard and promote the welfare of children: www.workingtogetheronline.co.uk/chapters/contents.html

28A.2 Where exceptionally the child to be interviewed or called as a witness in criminal proceedings is a Ward of Court then the leave of the court which made the wardship order will be required.

28A.3 Any application for leave in respect of any such child must be made to the court in which the relevant family proceedings are continuing and must be made on notice to the parents, any actual carer (e.g., relative or foster parent) and, in care proceedings, to the local authority and the guardian. In private proceedings the Family Court Reporter (if appointed) should be notified.

28A.4 If the police need to interview the child without the knowledge of another party (usually a parent or carer), they may make the application for leave without giving notice to that party.

28A.5 Where leave is given the order should ordinarily give leave for any number of interviews that may be required. However, anything beyond that actually authorised will require a further application.

28A.6 Exceptionally the police may have to deal with complaints by or allegations against such a child immediately without obtaining the leave of the court as, for example:

(a)　a serious offence against a child (like rape) where immediate medical examination and collection of evidence is required; or

(b)　where the child is to be interviewed as a suspect.

When any such action is necessary, the police should, in respect of each and every interview, notify the parents and other carer (if any) and the Family Court Reporter (if appointed). In care proceedings the local authority and guardian should be notified. The police must comply with all relevant Codes of Practice when conducting any such interview.

28A.7 The Family Court should be appraised of the position at the earliest reasonable opportunity by one of the notified parties and should thereafter be kept informed of any criminal proceedings.

28A.8 No evidence or document in the family proceedings or information about the proceedings should be disclosed into criminal proceedings without the leave of the Family Court.

CRIMINAL PROCEDURE RULES　PART 29　MEASURES TO ASSIST A WITNESS OR DEFENDANT TO GIVE EVIDENCE

Section 1: understanding and applying this Part

R-182　**When this Part applies**

29.1　This Part applies—

(a)　where the court can give a direction (a 'special measures direction'), under section 19 of the Youth Justice and Criminal Evidence Act 1999, on an application or on its own initiative, for any of the following measures—

    (i)　preventing a witness from seeing the defendant (section 23 of the 1999 Act),

    (ii)　allowing a witness to give evidence by live link (section 24 of the 1999 Act),

    (iii)　hearing a witness' evidence in private (section 25 of the 1999 Act),

    (iv)　dispensing with the wearing of wigs and gowns (section 26 of the 1999 Act),

    (v)　admitting video recorded evidence (sections 27 and 28 of the 1999 Act),

    (vi)　questioning a witness through an intermediary (section 29 of the 1999 Act),

    (vii)　using a device to help a witness communicate (section 30 of the 1999 Act);

(b)　where the court can vary or discharge such a direction, under section 20 of the 1999 Act;

(c)　where the court can give, vary or discharge a direction (a 'defendant's evidence direction') for a defendant to give evidence—

    (i)　by live link, under section 33A of the 1999 Act, or

    (ii)　through an intermediary, under sections 33BA and 33BB of the 1999 Act;

(d)　where the court can—

    (i)　make a witness anonymity order, under section 86 of the Coroners and Justice Act 2009, or

    (ii)　vary or discharge such an order, under section 91, 92 or 93 of the 2009 Act;

(e)　where the court can give or discharge a direction (a 'live link direction'), on an application or on its own initiative, for a witness to give evidence by live link under—

    (i)　section 32 of the Criminal Justice Act 1988, or

    (ii)　sections 51 and 52 of the Criminal Justice Act 2003;

(f)　where the court can exercise any other power it has to give, vary or discharge a direction for a measure to help a witness give evidence.

R-183　**Meaning of 'witness'**

29.2　In this Part, 'witness' means anyone (other than a defendant) for whose benefit an application, direction or order is made.

Section 2: general rules

Making an application for a direction or order   R-184

29.3   A party who wants the court to exercise its power to give or make a direction or order must—

    (a) apply in writing as soon as reasonably practicable, and in any event not more than—

        (i)   28 days after the defendant pleads not guilty, in a magistrates' court, or

        (ii) 14 days after the defendant pleads not guilty in the Crown Court; and

    (b) serve the application on—

        (i)   the court officer, and

        (ii) each other party.

Decisions and reasons   R-185

29.4   (1) A party who wants to introduce the evidence of a witness who is the subject of an application, direction or order must—

    (a) inform the witness of the court's decision as soon as reasonably practicable; and

    (b) explain to the witness the arrangements that as a result will be made for him or her to give evidence.

    (2) The court must announce, at a hearing in public before the witness gives evidence, the reasons for a decision—

    (a) to give, make, vary or discharge a direction or order; or

    (b) to refuse to do so.

Court's power to vary requirements under this Part   R-186

29.5   (1) The court may—

    (a) shorten or extend (even after it has expired) a time limit under this Part; and

    (b) allow an application or representations to be made in a different form to one set out in the Practice Direction, or to be made orally.

    (2) A person who wants an extension of time must—

    (a) apply when serving the application or representations for which it is needed; and

    (b) explain the delay.

Custody of documents   R-187

29.6   Unless the court otherwise directs, the court officer may—

    (a) keep a written application or representations; or

    (b) arrange for the whole or any part to be kept by some other appropriate person, subject to any conditions that the court may impose.

Declaration by intermediary   R-188

29.7   (1) This rule applies where—

    (a) a video recorded interview with a witness is conducted through an intermediary;

    (b) the court directs the examination of a witness or defendant through an intermediary.

    (2) An intermediary must make a declaration—

    (a) before such an interview begins;

    (b) before the examination begins (even if such an interview with the witness was conducted through the same intermediary).

    (3) The declaration must be in these terms—

    'I solemnly, sincerely and truly declare [*or* I swear by Almighty God] that I will well and faithfully communicate questions and answers and make true explanation of all matters and things as shall be required of me according to the best of my skill and understanding.'

Section 3: special measures directions

Exercise of court's powers   R-189

29.8   The court may decide whether to give, vary or discharge a special measures direction—

    (a) at a hearing, in public or in private, or without a hearing;

    (b) in a party's absence, if that party—

        (i)   applied for the direction, variation or discharge, or

        (ii) has had at least 14 days in which to make representations.

Special measures direction for a young witness   R-190

29.9   (1) This rule applies where, under section 21 or section 22 of the Youth Justice and Criminal Evidence Act 1999, the primary rule requires the court to give a direction for a special measure to assist a child witness or a qualifying witness—

(a) on an application, if one is made; or

(b) on the court's own initiative, in any other case.

(2) A party who wants to introduce the evidence of such a witness must as soon as reasonably practicable—

(a) notify the court that the witness is eligible for assistance;

(b) provide the court with any information that the court may need to assess the witness' views, if the witness does not want the primary rule to apply; and

(c) serve any video recorded evidence on—

(i) the court officer, and

(ii) each other party.

R-191 **Content of application for a special measures direction**

29.10 An applicant for a special measures direction must—

(a) explain how the witness is eligible for assistance;

(b) explain why special measures would be likely to improve the quality of the witness' evidence;

(c) propose the measure or measures that in the applicant's opinion would be likely to maximise so far as practicable the quality of that evidence;

(d) report any views that the witness has expressed about—

(i) his or her eligibility for assistance,

(ii) the likelihood that special measures would improve the quality of his or her evidence, and

(iii) the measure or measures proposed by the applicant;

(e) in a case in which a child witness or a qualifying witness does not want the primary rule to apply, provide any information that the court may need to assess the witness' views;

(f) in a case in which the applicant proposes that the witness should give evidence by live link—

(i) identify someone to accompany the witness while the witness gives evidence,

(ii) name that person, if possible, and

(iii) explain why that person would be an appropriate companion for the witness, including the witness' own views;

(g) in a case in which the applicant proposes the admission of video recorded evidence, identify—

(i) the date and duration of the recording,

(ii) which part the applicant wants the court to admit as evidence, if the applicant does not want the court to admit all of it;

(h) attach any other material on which the applicant relies; and

(i) if the applicant wants a hearing, ask for one, and explain why it is needed.

R-192 **Application to vary or discharge a special measures direction**

29.11 (1) A party who wants the court to vary or discharge a special measures direction must—

(a) apply in writing, as soon as reasonably practicable after becoming aware of the grounds for doing so; and

(b) serve the application on—

(i) the court officer, and

(ii) each other party.

(2) The applicant must—

(a) explain what material circumstances have changed since the direction was given (or last varied, if applicable);

(b) explain why the direction should be varied or discharged; and

(c) ask for a hearing, if the applicant wants one, and explain why it is needed.

R-193 **Application containing information withheld from another party**

29.12 (1) This rule applies where—

(a) an applicant serves an application for a special measures direction, or for its variation or discharge; and

(b) the application includes information that the applicant thinks ought not be revealed to another party.

(2) The applicant must—

(a) omit that information from the part of the application that is served on that other party;

(b) mark the other part to show that, unless the court otherwise directs, it is only for the court; and

(c) in that other part, explain why the applicant has withheld that information from that other party.

(3) Any hearing of an application to which this rule applies—
    (a) must be in private, unless the court otherwise directs; and
    (b) if the court so directs, may be, wholly or in part, in the absence of a party from whom information has been withheld.
(4) At any hearing of an application to which this rule applies—
    (a) the general rule is that the court must receive, in the following sequence—
        (i) representations first by the applicant and then by each other party, in all the parties' presence, and then
        (ii) further representations by the applicant, in the absence of a party from whom information has been withheld; but
    (b) the court may direct other arrangements for the hearing.

Representations in response　　　　　　　　　　　　　　　　　　　　　　　　**R-194**

29.13 (1) This rule applies where a party wants to make representations about—
    (a) an application for a special measures direction;
    (b) an application for the variation or discharge of such a direction; or
    (c) a direction, variation or discharge that the court proposes on its own initiative.
(2) Such a party must—
    (a) serve the representations on—
        (i) the court officer, and
        (ii) each other party;
    (b) do so not more than 14 days after, as applicable—
        (i) service of the application, or
        (ii) notice of the direction, variation or discharge that the court proposes; and
    (c) ask for a hearing, if that party wants one, and explain why it is needed.
(3) Where representations include information that the person making them thinks ought not be revealed to another party, that person must—
    (a) omit that information from the representations served on that other party;
    (b) mark the information to show that, unless the court otherwise directs, it is only for the court; and
    (c) with that information include an explanation of why it has been withheld from that other party.
(4) Representations against a special measures direction must explain, as appropriate—
    (a) why the witness is not eligible for assistance; or
    (b) if the witness is eligible for assistance, why—
        (i) no special measure would be likely to improve the quality of the witness' evidence,
        (ii) the proposed measure or measures would not be likely to maximise so far as practicable the quality of the witness' evidence, or
        (iii) the proposed measure or measures might tend to inhibit the effective testing of that evidence;
    (c) in a case in which the admission of video recorded evidence is proposed, why it would not be in the interests of justice for the recording, or part of it, to be admitted as evidence.
(5) Representations against the variation or discharge of a special measures direction must explain why it should not be varied or discharged.

Section 4: defendant's evidence directions

Exercise of court's powers　　　　　　　　　　　　　　　　　　　　　　　　**R-195**

29.14 The court may decide whether to give, vary or discharge a defendant's evidence direction—
    (a) at a hearing, in public or in private, or without a hearing;
    (b) in a party's absence, if that party—
        (i) applied for the direction, variation or discharge, or
        (ii) has had at least 14 days in which to make representations.

Content of application for a defendant's evidence direction　　　　　　　　　**R-196**

29.15 An applicant for a defendant's evidence direction must—
    (a) explain how the proposed direction meets the conditions prescribed by the Youth Justice and Criminal Evidence Act 1999;
    (b) in a case in which the applicant proposes that the defendant give evidence by live link—
        (i) identify a person to accompany the defendant while the defendant gives evidence, and
        (ii) explain why that person is appropriate;
    (c) ask for a hearing, if the applicant wants one, and explain why it is needed.

R-197   **Application to vary or discharge a defendant's evidence direction**

29.16 (1) A party who wants the court to vary or discharge a defendant's evidence direction must—

    (a) apply in writing, as soon as reasonably practicable after becoming aware of the grounds for doing so; and

    (b) serve the application on—

        (i) the court officer, and

        (ii) each other party.

  (2) The applicant must—

    (a) on an application to discharge a live link direction, explain why it is in the interests of justice to do so;

    (b) on an application to discharge a direction for an intermediary, explain why it is no longer necessary in order to ensure that the defendant receives a fair trial;

    (c) on an application to vary a direction for an intermediary, explain why it is necessary for the direction to be varied in order to ensure that the defendant receives a fair trial; and

    (d) ask for a hearing, if the applicant wants one, and explain why it is needed.

R-198   **Representations in response**

29.17 (1) This rule applies where a party wants to make representations about—

    (a) an application for a defendant's evidence direction;

    (b) an application for the variation or discharge of such a direction; or

    (c) a direction, variation or discharge that the court proposes on its own initiative.

  (2) Such a party must—

    (a) serve the representations on—

        (i) the court officer, and

        (ii) each other party;

    (b) do so not more than 14 days after, as applicable—

        (i) service of the application, or

        (ii) notice of the direction, variation or discharge that the court proposes; and

    (c) ask for a hearing, if that party wants one, and explain why it is needed.

  (3) Representations against a direction, variation or discharge must explain why the conditions prescribed by the Youth Justice and Criminal Evidence Act 1999 are not met.

Section 5: witness anonymity orders

R-199   **Exercise of court's powers**

29.18 (1) The court may decide whether to make, vary or discharge a witness anonymity order—

    (a) at a hearing (which must be in private, unless the court otherwise directs), or without a hearing (unless any party asks for one);

    (b) in the absence of a defendant.

  (2) The court must not exercise its power to make, vary or discharge a witness anonymity order, or to refuse to do so—

    (a) before or during the trial, unless each party has had an opportunity to make representations;

    (b) on an appeal by the defendant to which applies Part 63 (appeal to the Crown Court) or Part 68 (appeal to the Court of Appeal about conviction or sentence), unless in each party's case—

        (i) that party has had an opportunity to make representations, or

        (ii) the appeal court is satisfied that it is not reasonably practicable to communicate with that party;

    (c) after the trial and any such appeal are over, unless in the case of each party and the witness—

        (i) each has had an opportunity to make representations, or

        (ii) the court is satisfied that it is not reasonably practicable to communicate with that party or witness.

R-200   **Content and conduct of application for a witness anonymity order**

29.19 (1) An applicant for a witness anonymity order must—

    (a) include in the application nothing that might reveal the witness' identity;

    (b) describe the measures proposed by the applicant;

    (c) explain how the proposed order meets the conditions prescribed by section 88 of the Coroners and Justice Act 2009;

    (d) explain why no measures other than those proposed will suffice, such as—

        (i) an admission of the facts that would be proved by the witness,

(ii) an order restricting public access to the trial,

(iii) reporting restrictions, in particular under section 46 of the Youth Justice and Criminal Evidence Act 1999 or under section 39 of the Children and Young Persons Act 1933,

(iv) a direction for a special measure under section 19 of the Youth Justice and Criminal Evidence Act 1999,

(v) introduction of the witness' written statement as hearsay evidence, under section 116 of the Criminal Justice Act 2003, or

(vi) arrangements for the protection of the witness;

(e) attach to the application—

(i) a witness statement setting out the proposed evidence, edited in such a way as not to reveal the witness' identity,

(ii) where the prosecutor is the applicant, any further prosecution evidence to be served, and any further prosecution material to be disclosed under the Criminal Procedure and Investigations Act 1996, similarly edited, and

(iii) any defence statement that has been served, or as much information as may be available to the applicant that gives particulars of the defence; and

(f) ask for a hearing, if the applicant wants one.

(2) At any hearing of the application, the applicant must—

(a) identify the witness to the court, unless at the prosecutor's request the court otherwise directs; and

(b) present to the court, unless it otherwise directs—

(i) the unedited witness statement from which the edited version has been prepared,

(ii) where the prosecutor is the applicant, the unedited version of any further prosecution evidence or material from which an edited version has been prepared, and

(iii) such further material as the applicant relies on to establish that the proposed order meets the conditions prescribed by section 88 of the 2009 Act.

(3) At any such hearing—

(a) the general rule is that the court must receive, in the following sequence—

(i) representations first by the applicant and then by each other party, in all the parties' presence, and then

(ii) information withheld from a defendant, and further representations by the applicant, in the absence of any (or any other) defendant; but

(b) the court may direct other arrangements for the hearing.

(4) Before the witness gives evidence, the applicant must identify the witness to the court—

(a) if not already done;

(b) without revealing the witness' identity to any other party or person; and

(c) unless at the prosecutor's request the court otherwise directs.

Duty of court officer to notify the Director of Public Prosecutions   R-201

29.20 The court officer must notify the Director of Public Prosecutions of an application, unless the prosecutor is, or acts on behalf of, a public authority.

Application to vary or discharge a witness anonymity order   R-202

29.21 (1) A party who wants the court to vary or discharge a witness anonymity order, or a witness who wants the court to do so when the case is over, must—

(a) apply in writing, as soon as reasonably practicable after becoming aware of the grounds for doing so; and

(b) serve the application on—

(i) the court officer, and

(ii) each other party.

(2) The applicant must—

(a) explain what material circumstances have changed since the order was made (or last varied, if applicable);

(b) explain why the order should be varied or discharged, taking account of the conditions for making an order; and

(c) ask for a hearing, if the applicant wants one.

(3) Where an application includes information that the applicant thinks might reveal the witness' identity, the applicant must—

(a) omit that information from the application that is served on a defendant;

(b) mark the information to show that it is only for the court and the prosecutor (if the prosecutor is not the applicant); and

(c) with that information include an explanation of why it has been withheld.

(4) Where a party applies to vary or discharge a witness anonymity order after the trial and any appeal are over, the party who introduced the witness' evidence must serve the application on the witness.

R-203   Representations in response

29.22 (1) This rule applies where a party or, where the case is over, a witness, wants to make representations about—

(a) an application for a witness anonymity order;

(b) an application for the variation or discharge of such an order; or

(c) a variation or discharge that the court proposes on its own initiative.

(2) Such a party or witness must—

(a) serve the representations on—

(i)   the court officer, and

(ii) each other party;

(b) do so not more than 14 days after, as applicable—

(i)   service of the application, or

(ii) notice of the variation or discharge that the court proposes; and

(c) ask for a hearing, if that party or witness wants one.

(3) Where representations include information that the person making them thinks might reveal the witness' identity, that person must—

(a) omit that information from the representations served on a defendant;

(b) mark the information to show that it is only for the court (and for the prosecutor, if relevant); and

(c) with that information include an explanation of why it has been withheld.

(4) Representations against a witness anonymity order must explain why the conditions for making the order are not met.

(5) Representations against the variation or discharge of such an order must explain why it would not be appropriate to vary or discharge it, taking account of the conditions for making an order.

(6) A prosecutor's representations in response to an application by a defendant must include all information available to the prosecutor that is relevant to the conditions and considerations specified by sections 88 and 89 of the Coroners and Justice Act 2009.

Section 6: live link directions

R-204   Exercise of court's powers

29.23 The court may decide whether to give, vary or discharge a live link direction—

(a) at a hearing, in public or in private, or without a hearing;

(b) in a party's absence, if that party—

(i)   applied for the direction, variation or discharge, or

(ii) has had at least 14 days in which to make representations.

R-205   Content of application for a live link direction

29.24 An applicant for a live link direction must—

(a) unless the court otherwise directs, identify the place from which the witness will give evidence;

(b) if that place is in the United Kingdom, explain why it would be in the interests of the efficient or effective administration of justice for the witness to give evidence by live link;

(c) if the applicant wants the witness to be accompanied by another person while giving evidence—

(i)   name that person, if possible, and

(ii) explain why it is appropriate for the witness to be accompanied;

(d) ask for a hearing, if the applicant wants one, and explain why it is needed.

R-206   Application to discharge a live link direction

29.25 (1) A party who wants the court to discharge a live link direction must—

(a) apply in writing, as soon as reasonably practicable after becoming aware of the grounds for doing so; and

(b) serve the application on—

(i)   the court officer, and

(ii) each other party.

    (2) The applicant must—
        (a) explain what material circumstances have changed since the direction was given;
        (b) explain why it is in the interests of justice to discharge the direction; and
        (c) ask for a hearing, if the applicant wants one, and explain why it is needed.

Representations in response   R-207

29.26 (1) This rule applies where a party wants to make representations about—
        (a) an application for a live link direction;
        (b) an application for the discharge of such a direction; or
        (c) a direction or discharge that the court proposes on its own initiative.
    (2) Such a party must—
        (a) serve the representations on—
            (i) the court officer, and
            (ii) each other party;
        (b) do so not more than 14 days after, as applicable—
            (i) service of the application, or
            (ii) notice of the direction or discharge that the court proposes; and
        (c) ask for a hearing, if that party wants one, and explain why it is needed.
    (3) Representations against a direction or discharge must explain, as applicable, why the conditions prescribed by the Criminal Justice Act 1988 or the Criminal Justice Act 2003 are not met.

Criminal Practice Directions   Part 29   Measures to Assist a Witness or Defendant to give Evidence

CPD V Evidence 29A: Measures to Assist a Witness or Defendant to give Evidence   PD-34

29A.1 For special measures applications, the procedures at Part 29 should be followed. However, assisting a vulnerable witness to give evidence is not merely a matter of ordering the appropriate measure. Further directions about vulnerable people in the courts, ground rules hearings and intermediaries are given in the Practice Direction accompanying Part 3.

29A.2 Special measures need not be considered or ordered in isolation. The needs of the individual witness should be ascertained, and a combination of special measures may be appropriate. For example, if a witness who is to give evidence by live link wishes, screens can be used to shield the live link screen from the defendant and the public, as would occur if screens were being used for a witness giving evidence in the court room.

CPD V Evidence 29B: Witnesses giving Evidence by Live Link   PD-35

29B.1 A special measures direction for the witness to give evidence by live link may also provide for a specified person to accompany the witness (Rule 29.10(f)). In determining who this should be, the court must have regard to the wishes of the witness. The presence of a supporter is designed to provide emotional support to the witness, helping reduce the witness's anxiety and stress and contributing to the ability to give best evidence. It is preferable for the direction to be made well before the trial begins and to ensure that the designated person is available on the day of the witness's testimony so as to provide certainty for the witness.

29B.2 An increased degree of flexibility is appropriate as to who can act as supporter. This can be anyone known to and trusted by the witness who is not a party to the proceedings and has no detailed knowledge of the evidence in the case. The supporter may be a member of the Witness Service but need not be an usher or court official. Someone else may be appropriate.

29B.3 The usher should continue to be available both to assist the witness and the witness supporter, and to ensure that the court's requirements are properly complied with in the live link room.

29B.4 In order to be able to express an informed view about special measures, the witness is entitled to practise speaking using the live link (and to see screens in place). Simply being shown the room and equipment is inadequate for this purpose.

29B.5 If, with the agreement of the court, the witness has chosen not to give evidence by live link but to do so in the court room, it may still be appropriate for a witness supporter to be selected in the same way, and for the supporter to sit alongside the witness while the witness is giving evidence.

CPD V Evidence 29C: Visually Recorded Interviews: Memory Refreshing and Watching at a Different Time from the Jury   PD-36

29C.1 Witnesses are entitled to refresh their memory from their statement or visually recorded interview. The court should enquire at the PCMH or other case management hearing about arrangements for memory refreshing. The witness's first viewing of the visually recorded interview can be distressing or distracting. It should not be seen for the first time immediately before giving evidence. Depending upon the age and vulnerability of the witness several competing issues have to be considered and it may be that the assistance of the intermediary is needed to establish exactly how memory refreshing should be managed.

29C.2 If the interview is ruled inadmissible, the court must decide what constitutes an acceptable alternative method of memory refreshing.

29C.3 Decisions about how, when and where refreshing should take place should be court-led and made on a case-by-case basis in respect of each witness. General principles to be addressed include:

    i.   the venue for viewing. The delicate balance between combining the court familiarisation visit and watching the DVD, and having them on two separate occasions, needs to be considered in respect of each witness as combining the two may lead to 'information overload'. Refreshing need not necessarily take place within the court building but may be done, for example, at the police ABE suite;

    ii. requiring that any viewing is monitored by a person (usually the officer in the case) who will report to the court about anything said by the witness;

    iii. whether it is necessary for the witness to see the DVD more than once for the purpose of refreshing. The court will need to ask the advice of the intermediary, if any, with respect to this;

    iv. arrangements, if the witness will not watch the DVD at the same time as the trial bench or judge and jury, for the witness to watch it before attending to be cross examined, (depending upon their ability to retain information this may be the day before).

29C.4 There is no legal requirement that the witness should watch the interview at the same time as the trial bench or jury. Increasingly, this is arranged to occur at a different time, with the advantages that breaks can be taken as needed without disrupting the trial, and cross-examination starts while the witness is fresh. An intermediary may be present to facilitate communication but should not act as the independent person designated to take a note and report to the court if anything is said. Where the viewing takes place at a different time from that of the jury, the witness is sworn just before cross-examination, asked if he or she has watched the interview and if its contents are 'true' (or other words tailored to the witness's understanding).

PD-37 **CPD V Evidence 29D: Witness Anonymity Orders**

29D.1 This direction supplements Part 29 of the Rules, which governs the procedure to be followed on an application for a witness anonymity order. The court's power to make such an order is conferred by the Coroners and Justice Act 2009 (in this section, 'the Act'); section 87 of the Act provides specific relevant powers and obligations.

29D.2 As the Court of Appeal stated in *R v Mayers and Others* [2008] EWCA Crim 2989, [2009] 1 WLR 1915, [2009] 1 Cr App R 30 and emphasised again in *R v Donovan and Kafunda* [2012] EWCA Crim 2749, unreported, 'a witness anonymity order is to be regarded as a special measure of the last practicable resort': Lord Chief Justice, Lord Judge. In making such an application, the prosecution's obligations of disclosure 'go much further than the ordinary duties of disclosure' (*R v Mayers*); reference should be made to the Judicial Protocol on Disclosure, see the Practice Direction accompanying Part 22.

Case management

29D.3 Where such an application is proposed, with the parties' active assistance the court should set a realistic timetable, in accordance with the duties imposed by Rules 3.2 and 3.3. Where possible, the trial judge should determine the application, and any hearing should be attended by the parties' trial advocates.

Service of evidence and disclosure of prosecution material pending an application

29D.4 Where the prosecutor proposes an application for a witness anonymity order, it is not necessary for that application to have been determined before the proposed evidence is served. In most cases, an early indication of what that evidence will be if an order is made will be consistent with a party's duties under Rules 1.2 and 3.3. The prosecutor should serve with the other prosecution evidence a witness statement setting out the proposed evidence, redacted in such a way as to prevent disclosure of the witness' identity, as permitted by section 87(4) of the Act. Likewise the prosecutor should serve with other prosecution material disclosed under the Criminal Procedure and Investigations Act 1996 any such material appertaining to the witness, similarly redacted.

The application

29D.5 An application for a witness anonymity order should be made as early as possible and within the period for which Rule 29.3 provides. The application, and any hearing of it, must comply with the requirements of that rule and with those of Rule 29.19. In accordance with Rules 1.2 and 3.3, the applicant must provide the court with all available information relevant to the considerations to which the Act requires a court to have regard.

Response to the application

29D.6 A party upon whom an application for a witness anonymity order is served must serve a response in accordance with Rule 29.22. That period may be extended or shortened in the court's discretion: Rule 29.5.

29D.7 To avoid the risk of injustice, a respondent, whether the Prosecution or a defendant, must actively assist the court. If not already done, a respondent defendant should serve a defence statement under section 5 or 6 of the Criminal Procedure and Investigations Act 1996, so that the court is fully informed of what is in issue. When a defendant makes an application for a witness anonymity order the prosecutor should consider the continuing duty to disclose material under section 7A of the Criminal Procedure and Investigations Act 1996; therefore a prosecutor's response should include confirmation that that duty has been considered. Great care should be taken to ensure that nothing disclosed contains anything that might reveal the witness' identity. A respondent prosecutor should provide the court with all available information relevant to the considerations to which the Act requires a court to have regard, whether or not that information falls to be disclosed under the 1996 Act.

Determination of the application

29D.8 All parties must have an opportunity to make oral representations to the court on an application for a witness anonymity order: section 87(6) of the Act. However, a hearing may not be needed if none is sought: Rule 29.18(1) (a). Where, for example, the witness is an investigator who is recognisable by the defendant but known only by an assumed name, and there is no likelihood that the witness' credibility will be in issue, then the court may indicate a provisional decision and invite representations within a defined period, usually 14 days, including representations about whether there should be a hearing. In such a case, where the parties do not object the court may make an order without a hearing. Or where the court provisionally considers an application to be misconceived, an applicant may choose to withdraw it without requiring a hearing. Where the court directs a hearing of the application then it should allow adequate time for service of the representations in response.

29D.9 The hearing of an application for a witness anonymity order usually should be in private: Rule 29.18(1) (a). The court has power to hear a party in the absence of a defendant and that defendant's representatives: section 87(7) of the Act and Rule 29.18(1) (b). In the Crown Court, a recording of the proceedings will be made, in accordance with Rule 5.5. The Crown Court officer must treat such a recording in the same way as the recording of an application for a public interest ruling. It must be kept in secure conditions, and the arrangements made by the Crown Court officer for any transcription must impose restrictions that correspond with those under rule 5.5(2).

29D.10 Where confidential supporting information is presented to the court before the last stage of the hearing, the court may prefer not to read that information until that last stage.

29D.11 The court may adjourn the hearing at any stage, and should do so if its duty under rule 3.2 so requires.

29D.12 On a prosecutor's application, the court is likely to be assisted by the attendance of a senior investigator or other person of comparable authority who is familiar with the case.

29D.13 During the last stage of the hearing it is essential that the court test thoroughly the information supplied in confidence in order to satisfy itself that the conditions prescribed by the Act are met. At that stage, if the court concludes that this is the only way in which it can satisfy itself as to a relevant condition or consideration, exceptionally it may invite the applicant to present the proposed witness to be questioned by the court. Any such questioning should be carried out at such a time, and the witness brought to the court in such a way, as to prevent disclosure of his or her identity.

29D.14 The court may ask the Attorney General to appoint special counsel to assist. However, it must be kept in mind that, 'Such an appointment will always be exceptional, never automatic; a course of last and never first resort. It should not be ordered unless and until the trial judge is satisfied that no other course will adequately meet the overriding requirement of fairness to the defendant': *R v H* [2004] UKHL 3, [2004] 2 AC 134 (at paragraph 22), [2004] 2 Cr App R 10. Whether to accede to such a request is a matter for the Attorney General, and adequate time should be allowed for the consideration of such a request.

29D.15 The Court of Appeal in *R v Mayers* 'emphasise[d] that all three conditions, A, B and C, must be met before the jurisdiction to make a witness anonymity order arises. Each is mandatory. Each is distinct.' The Court also noted that if there is more than one anonymous witness in a case any link, and the nature of any link, between the witnesses should be investigated: 'questions of possible improper collusion between them, or cross-contamination of one another, should be addressed.'

29D.16 Following a hearing the court should announce its decision on an application for a witness anonymity order in the parties' presence and in public: rule 29.4(2). The court should give such reasons as it is possible to give without revealing the witness' identity. In the Crown Court, the court will be conscious that reasons given in public may be reported and reach the jury. Consequently, the court should ensure that nothing in its decision or its reasons could undermine any warning it may give jurors under section 90(2) of the Act. A record of the reasons must be kept. In the Crown Court, the announcement of those reasons will be recorded.

Order

29D.17 Where the court makes a witness anonymity order, it is essential that the measures to be taken are clearly specified in a written record of that order approved by the court and issued on its behalf. An order made in a magistrates' court must be recorded in the court register, in accordance with rule 5.4.

29D.18 Self-evidently, the written record of the order must not disclose the identity of the witness to whom it applies. However, it is essential that there be maintained some means of establishing a clear correlation between witness and order, and especially where in the same proceedings witness anonymity orders are made in respect of more than one witness, specifying different measures in respect of each. Careful preservation of the application for the order, including the confidential part, ordinarily will suffice for this purpose.

Discharge or variation of the order

29D.19 Section 91 of the Act allows the court to discharge or vary a witness anonymity order: on application, if there has been a material change of circumstances since the order was made or since any previous variation of it; or on its own initiative. Rule 29.21 allows the parties to apply for the variation of a pre-trial direction where circumstances have changed.

29D.20 The court should keep under review the question of whether the conditions for making an order are met. In addition, consistently with the parties' duties under rules 1.2 and 3.3, it is incumbent on each, and in particular on the applicant for the order, to keep the need for it under review.

29D.21 Where the court considers the discharge or variation of an order, the procedure that it adopts should be appropriate to the circumstances. As a general rule, that procedure should approximate to the procedure for determining an application for an order. The court may need to hear further representations by the applicant for the order in the absence of a respondent defendant and that defendant's representatives.

Retention of confidential material

29D.22 If retained by the court, confidential material must be stored in secure conditions by the court officer. Alternatively, subject to such directions as the court may give, such material may be committed to the safe keeping of the applicant or any other appropriate person in exercise of the powers conferred by rule 29.6. If the material is released to any such person, the court should ensure that it will be available to the court at trial.

CRIMINAL PROCEDURE RULES   PART 30

[There are no rules in this part.]

CRIMINAL PROCEDURE RULES   PART 31   RESTRICTION ON CROSS-EXAMINATION
BY A DEFENDANT ACTING IN PERSON

Restrictions on cross-examination of witness   R-208

31.1 (1) This rule and rules 31.2 and 31.3 apply where an accused is prevented from cross-examining a witness in person by virtue of section 34, 35 or 36 of the Youth Justice and Criminal Evidence Act 1999.

(2) The court shall explain to the accused as early in the proceedings as is reasonably practicable that he—

(a) is prevented from cross-examining a witness in person; and

(b) should arrange for a legal representative to act for him for the purpose of cross-examining the witness.

(3) The accused shall notify the court officer within 7 days of the court giving its explanation, or within such other period as the court may in any particular case allow, of the action, if any, he has taken.

(4) Where he has arranged for a legal representative to act for him, the notification shall include details of the name and address of the representative.

(5) The notification shall be in writing.

(6) The court officer shall notify all other parties to the proceedings of the name and address of the person, if any, appointed to act for the accused.

(7) Where the court gives its explanation under paragraph (2) to the accused either within 7 days of the day set for the commencement of any hearing at which a witness in respect of whom a prohibition under section 34, 35 or 36 of the 1999 Act applies may be cross-examined or after such a hearing has commenced, the period of 7 days shall be reduced in accordance with any directions issued by the court.

(8) Where at the end of the period of 7 days or such other period as the court has allowed, the court has received no notification from the accused it may grant the accused an extension of time, whether on its own motion or on the application of the accused.

(9) Before granting an extension of time, the court may hold a hearing at which all parties to the proceedings may attend and be heard.

(10) Any extension of time shall be of such period as the court considers appropriate in the circumstances of the case.

(11) The decision of the court as to whether to grant the accused an extension of time shall be notified to all parties to the proceedings by the court officer.

Appointment of legal representative by the court   R-209

31.2 (1) Where the court decides, in accordance with section 38(4) of the Youth Justice and Criminal Evidence Act 1999, to appoint a qualified legal representative, the court officer shall notify all parties to the proceedings of the name and address of the representative.

(2) An appointment made by the court under section 38(4) of the 1999 Act shall, except to such extent as the court may in any particular case determine, terminate at the conclusion of the cross-examination of the witness or witnesses in respect of whom a prohibition under section 34, 35 or 36 of the 1999 Act applies.

Appointment arranged by the accused   R-210

31.3 (1) The accused may arrange for the qualified legal representative, appointed by the court under section 38(4) of the Youth Justice and Criminal Evidence Act 1999, to be appointed to act for him for the purpose of cross-examining any witness in respect of whom a prohibition under section 34, 35 or 36 of the 1999 Act applies.

(2) Where such an appointment is made—

(a) both the accused and the qualified legal representative appointed shall notify the court of the appointment; and

(b) the qualified legal representative shall, from the time of his appointment, act for the accused as though the arrangement had been made under section 38(2)(a) of the 1999 Act and shall cease to be the representative of the court under section 38(4).

(3) Where the court receives notification of the appointment either from the qualified legal representative or from the accused but not from both, the court shall investigate whether the appointment has been made, and if it concludes that the appointment has not been made, paragraph (2)(b) shall not apply.

(4) An accused may, notwithstanding an appointment by the court under section 38(4) of the 1999 Act, arrange for a legal representative to act for him for the purpose of cross-examining

any witness in respect of whom a prohibition under section 34, 35 or 36 of the 1999 Act applies.

(5) Where the accused arranges for, or informs the court of his intention to arrange for, a legal representative to act for him, he shall notify the court, within such period as the court may allow, of the name and address of any person appointed to act for him.

(6) Where the court is notified within the time allowed that such an appointment has been made, any qualified legal representative appointed by the court in accordance with section 38(4) of the 1999 Act shall be discharged.

(7) The court officer shall, as soon as reasonably practicable after the court receives notification of an appointment under this rule or, where paragraph (3) applies, after the court is satisfied that the appointment has been made, notify all the parties to the proceedings—

(a) that the appointment has been made;

(b) where paragraph (4) applies, of the name and address of the person appointed; and

(c) that the person appointed by the court under section 38(4) of the 1999 Act has been discharged or has ceased to act for the court.

R-211 **Prohibition on cross-examination of witness**

31.4 (1) An application by the prosecutor for the court to give a direction under section 36 of the Youth Justice and Criminal Evidence Act 1999 in relation to any witness must be sent to the court officer and at the same time a copy thereof must be sent by the applicant to every other party to the proceedings.

(2) In his application the prosecutor must state why, in his opinion—

(a) the evidence given by the witness is likely to be diminished if cross-examination is undertaken by the accused in person;

(b) the evidence would be improved if a direction were given under section 36(2) of the 1999 Act; and

(c) it would not be contrary to the interests of justice to give such a direction.

(3) On receipt of the application the court officer must refer it—

(a) if the trial has started, to the court of trial; or

(b) if the trial has not started when the application is received—

(i) to the judge or court designated to conduct the trial, or

(ii) if no judge or court has been designated for that purpose, to such judge or court designated for the purposes of hearing that application.

(4) Where a copy of the application is received by a party to the proceedings more than 14 days before the date set for the trial to begin, that party may make observations in writing on the application to the court officer, but any such observations must be made within 14 days of the receipt of the application and be copied to the other parties to the proceedings.

(5) A party to whom an application is sent in accordance with paragraph (1) who wishes to oppose the application must give his reasons for doing so to the court officer and the other parties to the proceedings.

(6) Those reasons must be notified—

(a) within 14 days of the date the application was served on him, if that date is more than 14 days before the date set for the trial to begin;

(b) if the trial has begun, in accordance with any directions issued by the court; or

(c) if neither paragraph (6)(a) nor (b) applies, before the date set for the trial to begin.

(7) Where the application made in accordance with paragraph (1) is made before the date set for the trial to begin and—

(a) is not contested by any party to the proceedings, the court may determine the application without a hearing;

(b) is contested by a party to the proceedings, the court must direct a hearing of the application.

(8) Where the application is made after the trial has begun—

(a) the application may be made orally; and

(b) the court may give such directions as it considers appropriate to deal with the application.

(9) Where a hearing of the application is to take place, the court officer shall notify each party to the proceedings of the time and place of the hearing.

(10) A party notified in accordance with paragraph (9) may be present at the hearing and be heard.

(11) The court officer must, as soon as possible after the determination of an application made in accordance with paragraph (1), give notice of the decision and the reasons for it to all the parties to the proceedings.

(12) A person making an oral application under paragraph (8)(a) must—
    (a) give reasons why the application was not made before the trial commenced; and
    (b) provide the court with the information set out in paragraph (2).

CRIMINAL PROCEDURE RULES   PART 32   INTERNATIONAL CO-OPERATION

Notice required to accompany process served outside the United Kingdom and translations   R-212

32.1 (1) The notice which by virtue of section 3(4)(b) of the Crime (International Co-operation) Act 2003 (general requirements for service of process) must accompany any process served outside the United Kingdom must give the information specified in paragraphs (2) and (4) below.

    (2) The notice must—
      (a) state that the person required by the process to appear as a party or attend as a witness can obtain information about his rights in connection therewith from the relevant authority; and
      (b) give the particulars specified in paragraph (4) about that authority.

    (3) The relevant authority where the process is served—
      (a) at the request of the prosecuting authority, is that authority; or
      (b) at the request of the defendant or the prosecutor in the case of a private prosecution, is the court by which the process is served.

    (4) The particulars referred to in paragraph (2) are—
      (a) the name and address of the relevant authority, together with its telephone and fax numbers and e-mail address; and
      (b) the name of a person at the relevant authority who can provide the information referred to in paragraph (2)(a), together with his telephone and fax numbers and e-mail address.

    (5) The justices' clerk or Crown Court officer must send, together with any process served outside the United Kingdom—
      (a) any translation which is provided under section 3(3)(b) of the 2003 Act; and
      (b) any translation of the information required to be given by this rule which is provided to him.

    (6) In this rule 'process' has the same meaning as in section 51(3) of the 2003 Act.

Proof of service outside the United Kingdom   R-213

32.2 (1) A statement in a certificate given by or on behalf of the Secretary of State—
      (a) that process has been served on any person under section 4(1) of the Crime (International Co-operation) Act 2003 (service of process otherwise than by post);
      (b) of the manner in which service was effected; and
      (c) of the date on which process was served;
      shall be admissible as evidence of any facts so stated.

    (2) In this rule 'process' has the same meaning as in section 51(3) of the 2003 Act.

Supply of copy of notice of request for assistance abroad   R-214

32.3 Where a request for assistance under section 7 of the Crime (International Co-operation) Act 2003 is made by a justice of the peace or a judge exercising the jurisdiction of the Crown Court and is sent in accordance with section 8(1) of the 2003 Act, the justices' clerk or the Crown Court officer shall send a copy of the letter of request to the Secretary of State as soon as practicable after the request has been made.

Persons entitled to appear and take part in proceedings before a nominated court, and exclusion of public   R-215

32.4 A court nominated under section 15(1) of the Crime (International Co-operation) Act 2003 (nominating a court to receive evidence) may—
    (a) determine who may appear or take part in the proceedings under Schedule 1 to the 2003 Act before the court and whether a party to the proceedings is entitled to be legally represented; and
    (b) direct that the public be excluded from those proceedings if it thinks it necessary to do so in the interests of justice.

Record of proceedings to receive evidence before a nominated court   R-216

32.5 (1) Where a court is nominated under section 15(1) of the Crime (International Co-operation) Act 2003 the justices' clerk or Crown Court officer shall enter in an overseas record—
      (a) details of the request in respect of which the notice under section 15(1) of the 2003 Act was given;

Criminal Procedure Rules 2013 and Criminal Practice Directions

(b) the date on which, and place at which, the proceedings under Schedule 1 to the 2003 Act in respect of that request took place;

(c) the name of any witness who gave evidence at the proceedings in question;

(d) the name of any person who took part in the proceedings as a legal representative or an interpreter;

(e) whether a witness was required to give evidence on oath or (by virtue of section 5 of the Oaths Act 1978) after making a solemn affirmation; and

(f) whether the opportunity to cross-examine any witness was refused.

(2) When the court gives the evidence received by it under paragraph 6(1) of Schedule 1 to the 2003 Act to the court or authority that made the request or to the territorial authority for forwarding to the court or authority that made the request, the justices' clerk or Crown Court officer shall send to the court, authority or territorial authority (as the case may be) a copy of an extract of so much of the overseas record as relates to the proceedings in respect of that request.

R-217   **Interpreter for the purposes of proceedings involving a television or telephone link**

32.6 (1) This rule applies where a court is nominated under section 30(3) (hearing witnesses in the UK through television links) or section 31(4) (hearing witnesses in the UK by telephone) of the Crime (International Co-operation) Act 2003.

(2) Where it appears to the justices' clerk or the Crown Court officer that the witness to be heard in the proceedings under Part 1 or 2 of Schedule 2 to the 2003 Act ('the relevant proceedings') is likely to give evidence in a language other than English, he shall make arrangements for an interpreter to be present at the proceedings to translate what is said into English.

(3) Where it appears to the justices' clerk or the Crown Court officer that the witness to be heard in the relevant proceedings is likely to give evidence in a language other than that in which the proceedings of the court referred to in section 30(1) or, as the case may be, 31(1) of the 2003 Act ('the external court') will be conducted, he shall make arrangements for an interpreter to be present at the relevant proceedings to translate what is said into the language in which the proceedings of the external court will be conducted.

(4) Where the evidence in the relevant proceedings is either given in a language other than English or is not translated into English by an interpreter, the court shall adjourn the proceedings until such time as an interpreter can be present to provide a translation into English.

(5) Where a court in Wales understands Welsh—

(a) paragraph (2) does not apply where it appears to the justices' clerk or Crown Court officer that the witness in question is likely to give evidence in Welsh;

(b) paragraph (4) does not apply where the evidence is given in Welsh; and

(c) any translation which is provided pursuant to paragraph (2) or (4) may be into Welsh instead of English.

R-218   **Record of television link hearing before a nominated court**

32.7 (1) This rule applies where a court is nominated under section 30(3) of the Crime (International Co-operation) Act 2003.

(2) The justices' clerk or Crown Court officer shall enter in an overseas record—

(a) details of the request in respect of which the notice under section 30(3) of the 2003 Act was given;

(b) the date on which, and place at which, the proceedings under Part 1 of Schedule 2 to that Act in respect of that request took place;

(c) the technical conditions, such as the type of equipment used, under which the proceedings took place;

(d) the name of the witness who gave evidence;

(e) the name of any person who took part in the proceedings as a legal representative or an interpreter; and

(f) the language in which the evidence was given.

(3) As soon as practicable after the proceedings under Part 1 of Schedule 2 to the 2003 Act took place, the justices' clerk or Crown Court officer shall send to the external authority that made the request a copy of an extract of so much of the overseas record as relates to the proceedings in respect of that request.

R-219   **Record of telephone link hearing before a nominated court**

32.8 (1) This rule applies where a court is nominated under section 31(4) of the Crime (International Co-operation) Act 2003.

(2) The justices' clerk or Crown Court officer shall enter in an overseas record—
  (a) details of the request in respect of which the notice under section 31(4) of the 2003 Act was given;
  (b) the date, time and place at which the proceedings under Part 2 of Schedule 2 to the 2003 Act took place;
  (c) the name of the witness who gave evidence;
  (d) the name of any interpreter who acted at the proceedings; and
  (e) the language in which the evidence was given.

Overseas record   R-220

32.9 (1) The overseas records of a magistrates' court shall be part of the register (within the meaning of section 150(1) of the Magistrates' Courts Act 1980).
  (2) The overseas records of any court shall not be open to inspection by any person except—
  (a) as authorised by the Secretary of State; or
  (b) with the leave of the court.

Overseas freezing orders   R-221

32.10 (1) This rule applies where a court is nominated under section 21(1) of the Crime (International Co-operation) Act 2003 to give effect to an overseas freezing order.
  (2) Where the Secretary of State serves a copy of such an order on the court officer—
  (a) the general rule is that the court must consider the order no later than the next business day;
  (b) exceptionally, the court may consider the order later than that, but not more than 5 business days after service.
  (3) The court must not consider the order unless—
  (a) it is satisfied that the chief officer of police for the area in which the evidence is situated has had notice of the order; and
  (b) that chief officer of police has had an opportunity to make representations, at a hearing if that officer wants.
  (4) The court may consider the order—
  (a) without a hearing; or
  (b) at a hearing, in public or in private.

CRIMINAL PROCEDURE RULES   PART 33   EXPERT EVIDENCE

Reference to expert   R-222

33.1 A reference to an 'expert' in this Part is a reference to a person who is required to give or prepare expert evidence for the purpose of criminal proceedings, including evidence required to determine fitness to plead or for the purpose of sentencing.

Expert's duty to the court   R-223

33.2 (1) An expert must help the court to achieve the overriding objective by giving objective, unbiased opinion on matters within his expertise.
  (2) This duty overrides any obligation to the person from whom he receives instructions or by whom he is paid.
  (3) This duty includes an obligation to inform all parties and the court if the expert's opinion changes from that contained in a report served as evidence or given in a statement.

Content of expert's report   R-224

33.3 (1) An expert's report must—
  (a) give details of the expert's qualifications, relevant experience and accreditation;
  (b) give details of any literature or other information which the expert has relied on in making the report;
  (c) contain a statement setting out the substance of all facts given to the expert which are material to the opinions expressed in the report or upon which those opinions are based;
  (d) make clear which of the facts stated in the report are within the expert's own knowledge;
  (e) say who carried out any examination, measurement, test or experiment which the expert has used for the report and—
    (i) give the qualifications, relevant experience and accreditation of that person,
    (ii) say whether or not the examination, measurement, test or experiment was carried out under the expert's supervision, and
    (iii) summarise the findings on which the expert relies;

        (f) where there is a range of opinion on the matters dealt with in the report—
           (i) summarise the range of opinion, and
          (ii) give reasons for his own opinion;
        (g) if the expert is not able to give his opinion without qualification, state the qualification;
        (h) contain a summary of the conclusions reached;
        (i) contain a statement that the expert understands his duty to the court, and has complied and will continue to comply with that duty; and
        (j) contain the same declaration of truth as a witness statement.
    (2) Only sub-paragraphs (i) and (j) of rule 33.3(1) apply to a summary by an expert of his conclusions served in advance of that expert's report.

R-225   Service of expert evidence

33.4 (1) A party who wants to introduce expert evidence must—
        (a) serve it on—
           (i) the court officer, and
          (ii) each other party;
        (b) serve it—
           (i) as soon as practicable, and in any event
          (ii) with any application in support of which that party relies on that evidence; and
        (c) if another party so requires, give that party a copy of, or a reasonable opportunity to inspect—
           (i) a record of any examination, measurement, test or experiment on which the expert's findings and opinion are based, or that were carried out in the course of reaching those findings and opinion, and
          (ii) anything on which any such examination, measurement, test or experiment was carried out.
    (2) A party may not introduce expert evidence if that party has not complied with this rule, unless—
        (a) every other party agrees; or
        (b) the court gives permission.

R-226   Expert to be informed of service of report

33.5 A party who serves on another party or on the court a report by an expert must, at once, inform that expert of that fact.

R-227   Pre-hearing discussion of expert evidence

33.6 (1) This rule applies where more than one party wants to introduce expert evidence.
    (2) The court may direct the experts to—
        (a) discuss the expert issues in the proceedings; and
        (b) prepare a statement for the court of the matters on which they agree and disagree, giving their reasons.
    (3) Except for that statement, the content of that discussion must not be referred to without the court's permission.

R-228   Failure to comply with directions

[The former r. 33.7 was not reproduced in the new part 33 having effect from 5 October 2009.]

R-229   Court's power to direct that evidence is to be given by a single joint expert

33.7 (1) Where more than one defendant wants to introduce expert evidence on an issue at trial, the court may direct that the evidence on that issue is to be given by one expert only.
    (2) Where the co-defendants cannot agree who should be the expert, the court may—
        (a) select the expert from a list prepared or identified by them; or
        (b) direct that the expert be selected in another way.

R-230   Instructions to a single joint expert

33.8 (1) Where the court gives a direction under rule 33.7 for a single joint expert to be used, each of the co-defendants may give instructions to the expert.
    (2) When a co-defendant gives instructions to the expert he must, at the same time, send a copy of the instructions to the other co-defendant(s).
    (3) The court may give directions about—
        (a) the payment of the expert's fees and expenses; and
        (b) any examination, measurement, test or experiment which the expert wishes to carry out.

(4) The court may, before an expert is instructed, limit the amount that can be paid by way of fees and expenses to the expert.

(5) Unless the court otherwise directs, the instructing co-defendants are jointly and severally liable for the payment of the expert's fees and expenses.

Court's power to vary requirements under this Part   R-231

33.9 (1) The court may—

    (a) extend (even after it has expired) a time limit under this Part;

    (b) allow the introduction of expert evidence which omits a detail required by this Part.

(2) A party who wants an extension of time must—

    (a) apply when serving the expert evidence for which it is required; and

    (b) explain the delay.

CRIMINAL PROCEDURE RULES   PART 34   HEARSAY EVIDENCE

When this Part applies   R-232

34.1 This Part applies—

    (a) in a magistrates' court and in the Crown Court;

    (b) where a party wants to introduce hearsay evidence, within the meaning of section 114 of the Criminal Justice Act 2003.

Notice to introduce hearsay evidence   R-233

34.2 (1) This rule applies where a party wants to introduce hearsay evidence for admission under any of the following sections of the Criminal Justice Act 2003—

    (a) section 114(1)(d) (evidence admissible in the interests of justice);

    (b) section 116 (evidence where a witness is unavailable);

    (c) section 117(1)(c) (evidence in a statement prepared for the purposes of criminal proceedings);

    (d) section 121 (multiple hearsay).

(2) That party must—

    (a) serve notice on—

        (i) the court officer, and

        (ii) each other party;

    (b) in the notice—

        (i) identify the evidence that is hearsay,

        (ii) set out any facts on which that party relies to make the evidence admissible,

        (iii) explain how that party will prove those facts if another party disputes them, and

        (iv) explain why the evidence is admissible; and

    (c) attach to the notice any statement or other document containing the evidence that has not already been served.

(3) A prosecutor who wants to introduce such evidence must serve the notice not more than—

    (a) 28 days after the defendant pleads not guilty, in a magistrates' court; or

    (b) 14 days after the defendant pleads not guilty, in the Crown Court.

(4) A defendant who wants to introduce such evidence must serve the notice as soon as reasonably practicable.

(5) A party entitled to receive a notice under this rule may waive that entitlement by so informing—

    (a) the party who would have served it; and

    (b) the court.

Opposing the introduction of hearsay evidence   R-234

34.3 (1) This rule applies where a party objects to the introduction of hearsay evidence.

(2) That party must—

    (a) apply to the court to determine the objection;

    (b) serve the application on—

        (i) the court officer, and

        (ii) each other party;

    (c) serve the application as soon as reasonably practicable, and in any event not more than 14 days after—

        (i) service of notice to introduce the evidence under rule 34.2,

        (ii) service of the evidence to which that party objects, if no notice is required by that rule, or

          (iii) the defendant pleads not guilty whichever of those events happens last; and

    (d) in the application, explain—

          (i)   which, if any, facts set out in a notice under rule 34.2 that party disputes,

          (ii) why the evidence is not admissible,

          (iii) any other objection to the evidence.

  (3) The court—

    (a) may determine an application—

          (i)   at a hearing, in public or in private, or

          (ii) without a hearing;

    (b) must not determine the application unless the party who served the notice—

          (i)   is present, or

          (ii) has had a reasonable opportunity to respond;

    (c) may adjourn the application; and

    (d) may discharge or vary a determination where it can do so under—

          (i)   section 8B of the Magistrates' Courts Act 1980 (ruling at pre-trial hearing in a magistrates' court), or

          (ii) section 9 of the Criminal Justice Act 1987, or section 31 or 40 of the Criminal Procedure and Investigations Act 1996 (ruling at preparatory or other pre-trial hearing in the Crown Court).

R-235   Unopposed hearsay evidence

  34.4 (1) This rule applies where—

    (a) a party has served notice to introduce hearsay evidence under rule 34.2; and

    (b) no other party has applied to the court to determine an objection to the introduction of the evidence.

    (2) The court must treat the evidence as if it were admissible by agreement.

R-236   Court's power to vary requirements under this Part

  34.5 (1) The court may—

    (a) shorten or extend (even after it has expired) a time limit under this Part;

    (b) allow an application or notice to be given in a different form to one set out in the Practice Direction, or to be made or given orally; or

    (c) dispense with the requirement for notice to introduce hearsay evidence.

    (2) A party who wants an extension of time must—

    (a) apply when serving the application or notice for which it is needed; and

    (b) explain the delay.

CRIMINAL PROCEDURE RULES   PART 35   EVIDENCE OF BAD CHARACTER

R-237   When this Part applies

  35.1 This Part applies—

    (a) in a magistrates' court and in the Crown Court;

    (b) where a party wants to introduce evidence of bad character, within the meaning of section 98 of the Criminal Justice Act 2003.

R-238   Content of application or notice

  35.2 (1) A party who wants to introduce evidence of bad character must—

    (a) make an application under rule 35.3, where it is evidence of a non-defendant's bad character;

    (b) give notice under rule 35.4, where it is evidence of a defendant's bad character.

    (2) An application or notice must—

    (a) set out the facts of the misconduct on which that party relies;

    (b) explain how that party will prove those facts (whether by certificate of conviction, other official record, or other evidence), if another party disputes them; and

    (c) explain why the evidence is admissible.

R-239   Application to introduce evidence of a non-defendant's bad character

  35.3 (1) This rule applies where a party wants to introduce evidence of the bad character of a person other than the defendant.

    (2) That party must serve an application to do so on—

    (a) the court officer; and

    (b) each other party.

(3) The applicant must serve the application—

    (a) as soon as reasonably practicable; and in any event

    (b) not more than 14 days after the prosecutor discloses material on which the application is based (if the prosecutor is not the applicant).

(4) A party who objects to the introduction of the evidence must—

    (a) serve notice on—

       (i) the court officer, and

       (ii) each other party not more than 14 days after service of the application; and

    (b) in the notice explain, as applicable—

       (i) which, if any, facts of the misconduct set out in the application that party disputes,

       (ii) what, if any, facts of the misconduct that party admits instead,

       (iii) why the evidence is not admissible, and

       (iv) any other objection to the application.

(5) The court—

    (a) may determine an application—

       (i) at a hearing, in public or in private, or

       (ii) without a hearing;

    (b) must not determine the application unless each party other than the applicant—

       (i) is present, or

       (ii) has had at least 14 days in which to serve a notice of objection;

    (c) may adjourn the application; and

    (d) may discharge or vary a determination where it can do so under—

       (i) section 8B of the Magistrates' Courts Act 1980 (ruling at pre-trial hearing in a magistrates' court), or

       (ii) section 9 of the Criminal Justice Act 1987, or section 31 or 40 of the Criminal Procedure and Investigations Act 1996 (ruling at preparatory or other pre-trial hearing in the Crown Court).

Notice to introduce evidence of a defendant's bad character

R-240

35.4 (1) This rule applies where a party wants to introduce evidence of a defendant's bad character.

(2) That party must serve notice on—

    (a) the court officer; and

    (b) each other party.

(3) A prosecutor who wants to introduce such evidence must serve the notice not more than—

    (a) 28 days after the defendant pleads not guilty, in a magistrates' court; or

    (b) 14 days after the defendant pleads not guilty, in the Crown Court.

(4) A co-defendant who wants to introduce such evidence must serve the notice—

    (a) as soon as reasonably practicable; and in any event

    (b) not more than 14 days after the prosecutor discloses material on which the notice is based.

(5) A party who objects to the introduction of the evidence must—

    (a) apply to the court to determine the objection;

    (b) serve the application on—

       (i) the court officer, and

       (ii) each other party not more than 14 days after service of the notice; and

    (c) in the application explain, as applicable—

       (i) which, if any, facts of the misconduct set out in the notice that party disputes,

       (ii) what, if any, facts of the misconduct that party admits instead,

       (iii) why the evidence is not admissible,

       (iv) why it would be unfair to admit the evidence, and

       (v) any other objection to the notice.

(6) The court—

    (a) may determine an application—

       (i) at a hearing, in public or in private, or

       (ii) without a hearing;

    (b) must not determine the application unless the party who served the notice—

       (i) is present, or

       (ii) has had a reasonable opportunity to respond;

    (c) may adjourn the application; and

    (d) may discharge or vary a determination where it can do so under—

       (i) section 8B of the Magistrates' Courts Act 1980 (ruling at pre-trial hearing in a magistrates' court), or

Criminal Procedure Rules 2013 and Criminal Practice Directions

(ii) section 9 of the Criminal Justice Act 1987, or section 31 or 40 of the Criminal Procedure and Investigations Act 1996 (ruling at preparatory or other pre-trial hearing in the Crown Court).

(7) A party entitled to receive a notice may waive that entitlement by so informing—

(a) the party who would have served it; and

(b) the court.

R-241   Reasons for decisions

35.5 The court must announce at a hearing in public (but in the absence of the jury, if there is one) the reasons for a decision—

(a) to admit evidence as evidence of bad character, or to refuse to do so; or

(b) to direct an acquittal or a retrial under section 107 of the Criminal Justice Act 2003.

R-242   Court's power to vary requirements under this Part

35.6 (1) The court may—

(a) shorten or extend (even after it has expired) a time limit under this Part;

(b) allow an application or notice to be in a different form to one set out in the Practice Direction, or to be made or given orally;

(c) dispense with a requirement for notice to introduce evidence of a defendant's bad character.

(2) A party who wants an extension of time must—

(a) apply when serving the application or notice for which it is needed; and

(b) explain the delay.

Criminal Practice Directions   Part 35   Evidence of Bad Character

PD-38   CPD V Evidence 35A: Spent Convictions

35A.1 The effect of section 4(1) of the Rehabilitation of Offenders Act 1974 is that a person who has become a rehabilitated person for the purpose of the Act in respect of a conviction (known as a 'spent' conviction) shall be treated for all purposes in law as a person who has not committed, or been charged with or prosecuted for, or convicted of or sentenced for, the offence or offences which were the subject of that conviction.

35A.2 Section 4(1) of the 1974 Act does not apply, however, to evidence given in criminal proceedings: section 7(2) (a). During the trial of a criminal charge, reference to previous convictions (and therefore to spent convictions) can arise in a number of ways. The most common is when a bad character application is made under the Criminal Justice Act 2003. When considering bad character applications under the 2003 Act, regard should always be had to the general principles of the Rehabilitation of Offenders Act 1974.

35A.3 On conviction, the court must be provided with a statement of the defendant's record for the purposes of sentence. The record supplied should contain all previous convictions, but those which are spent should, so far as practicable, be marked as such. No one should refer in open court to a spent conviction without the authority of the judge, which authority should not be given unless the interests of justice so require. When passing sentence the judge should make no reference to a spent conviction unless it is necessary to do so for the purpose of explaining the sentence to be passed.

CRIMINAL PROCEDURE RULES   PART 36   EVIDENCE OF A COMPLAINANT'S PREVIOUS SEXUAL BEHAVIOUR

R-243   When this Part applies

36.1 This Part applies in magistrates' courts and in the Crown Court where a defendant wants to—

(a) introduce evidence; or

(b) cross-examine a witness about a complainant's sexual behaviour despite the prohibition in section 41 of the Youth Justice and Criminal Evidence Act 1999.

R-244   Application for permission to introduce evidence or cross-examine

36.2 The defendant must apply for permission to do so—

(a) in writing; and

(b) not more than 28 days after the prosecutor has complied or purported to comply with section 3 of the Criminal Procedure and Investigations Act 1996 (disclosure by prosecutor).

Content of application   R-245

36.3   The application must—
  (a) identify the issue to which the defendant says the complainant's sexual behaviour is relevant;
  (b) give particulars of—
      (i) any evidence that the defendant wants to introduce, and
      (ii) any questions that the defendant wants to ask;
  (c) identify the exception to the prohibition in section 41 of the Youth Justice and Criminal Evidence Act 1999 on which the defendant relies; and
  (d) give the name and date of birth of any witness whose evidence about the complainant's sexual behaviour the defendant wants to introduce.

Service of application   R-246

36.4   The defendant must serve the application on the court officer and all other parties.

Reply to application   R-247

36.5   A party who wants to make representations about an application under rule 36.2 must—
  (a) do so in writing not more than 14 days after receiving it; and
  (b) serve those representations on the court officer and all other parties.

Application for special measures   R-248

36.6   If the court allows an application under rule 36.2 then—
  (a) a party may apply not more than 14 days later for a special measures direction or for the variation of an existing special measures direction; and
  (b) the court may shorten the time for opposing that application.

Court's power to vary requirements under this Part   R-249

36.7   The court may shorten or extend (even after it has expired) a time limit under this Part.

CRIMINAL PROCEDURE RULES   PART 37   TRIAL AND SENTENCE IN A
MAGISTRATES' COURT

When this Part applies   R-250

37.1   (1) This Part applies in a magistrates' court where—
      (a) the court tries a case; or
      (b) the defendant pleads guilty.
  (2) Where the defendant is under 18, in this Part—
      (a) a reference to convicting the defendant includes a reference to finding the defendant guilty of an offence; and
      (b) a reference to sentence includes a reference to an order made on a finding of guilt.

General rules   R-251

37.2   (1) Where this Part applies—
      (a) the general rule is that the hearing must be in public; but
      (b) the court may exercise any power it has to—
          (i)   impose reporting restrictions,
          (ii) withhold information from the public, or
          (iii) order a hearing in private; and
      (c) unless the court otherwise directs, only the following may attend a hearing in a youth court—
          (i)   the parties and their legal representatives,
          (ii) a defendant's parents, guardian or other supporting adult,
          (iii) a witness,
          (iv) anyone else directly concerned in the case, and
          (v)   a representative of a news-gathering or reporting organisation.
  (2) Unless already done, the justices' legal adviser or the court must—
      (a) read the allegation of the offence to the defendant;
      (b) explain, in terms the defendant can understand (with help, if necessary)—
          (i) the allegation, and
          (ii) what the procedure at the hearing will be;
      (c) ask whether the defendant has been advised about the potential effect on sentence of a guilty plea;

(d) ask whether the defendant pleads guilty or not guilty; and

(e) take the defendant's plea.

(3) The court may adjourn the hearing—

(a) at any stage, to the same or to another magistrates' court; or

(b) to a youth court, where the court is not itself a youth court and the defendant is under 18.

R-252 Procedure on plea of not guilty

37.3 (1) This rule applies—

(a) if the defendant has—

(i) entered a plea of not guilty, or

(ii) not entered a plea; or

(b) if, in either case, it appears to the court that there may be grounds for making a hospital order without convicting the defendant.

(2) If a not guilty plea was taken on a previous occasion, the justices' legal adviser or the court must ask the defendant to confirm that plea.

(3) In the following sequence—

(a) the prosecutor may summarise the prosecution case, identifying the relevant law and facts;

(b) the prosecutor must introduce the evidence on which the prosecution case relies;

(c) at the conclusion of the prosecution case, on the defendant's application or on its own initiative, the court—

(i) may acquit on the ground that the prosecution evidence is insufficient for any reasonable court properly to convict, but

(ii) must not do so unless the prosecutor has had an opportunity to make representations;

(d) the justices' legal adviser or the court must explain, in terms the defendant can understand (with help, if necessary)—

(i) the right to give evidence, and

(ii) the potential effect of not doing so at all, or of refusing to answer a question while doing so;

(e) the defendant may introduce evidence;

(f) a party may introduce further evidence if it is then admissible (for example, because it is in rebuttal of evidence already introduced);

(g) the prosecutor may make final representations in support of the prosecution case, where—

(i) the defendant is represented by a legal representative, or

(ii) whether represented or not, the defendant has introduced evidence other than his or her own; and

(h) the defendant may make final representations in support of the defence case.

(4) Where a party wants to introduce evidence or make representations after that party's opportunity to do so under paragraph (3), the court—

(a) may refuse to receive any such evidence or representations; and

(b) must not receive any such evidence or representations after it has announced its verdict.

(5) If the court—

(a) convicts the defendant; or

(b) makes a hospital order instead of doing so,

it must give sufficient reasons to explain its decision.

(6) If the court acquits the defendant, it may—

(a) give an explanation of its decision; and

(b) exercise any power it has to make—

(i) a civil behaviour order,

(ii) a costs order.

R-253 Evidence of a witness in person

37.4 (1) This rule applies where a party wants to introduce evidence by calling a witness to give that evidence in person.

(2) Unless the court otherwise directs—

(a) a witness waiting to give evidence must not wait inside the courtroom, unless that witness is—

(i) a party, or

(ii) an expert witness;

(b) a witness who gives evidence in the courtroom must do so from the place provided for that purpose; and

(c) a witness' address must not be announced unless it is relevant to an issue in the case.

(3) Unless other legislation otherwise provides, before giving evidence a witness must take an oath or affirm.

(4) In the following sequence—

    (a) the party who calls a witness must ask questions in examination-in-chief;

    (b) every other party may ask questions in cross-examination;

    (c) the party who called the witness may ask questions in re-examination.

(5) If other legislation so permits, at any time while giving evidence a witness may refer to a record of that witness' recollection of events.

(6) The justices' legal adviser or the court may—

    (a) ask a witness questions; and in particular

    (b) where the defendant is not represented, ask any question necessary in the defendant's interests.

Evidence of a witness in writing

R-254

37.5 (1) This rule applies where a party wants to introduce in evidence the written statement of a witness to which applies—

    (a) Part 27 (Witness statements);

    (b) Part 33 (Expert evidence); or

    (c) Part 34 (Hearsay evidence).

(2) If the court admits such evidence—

    (a) each relevant part of the statement must be read or summarised aloud; or

    (b) the court must read the statement and its gist must be summarised aloud.

Evidence by admission

R-255

37.6 (1) This rule applies where—

    (a) a party introduces in evidence a fact admitted by another party; or

    (b) parties jointly admit a fact.

(2) Unless the court otherwise directs, a written record must be made of the admission.

Procedure on plea of guilty

R-256

37.7 (1) This rule applies if—

    (a) the defendant pleads guilty; and

    (b) the court is satisfied that the plea represents a clear acknowledgement of guilt.

(2) The court may convict the defendant without receiving evidence.

Written guilty plea: special rules

R-257

37.8 (1) This rule applies where—

    (a) the offence alleged—

        (i) can be tried only in a magistrates' court, and

        (ii) is not one specified under section 12(1)(a) of the Magistrates' Courts Act 1980;

    (b) the defendant is at least 16 years old;

    (c) the prosecutor has served on the defendant—

        (i) the summons or requisition,

        (ii) the material on which the prosecutor relies to set out the facts of the offence and to provide information relevant to sentence,

        (iii) a notice that the procedure set out in this rule applies, and

        (iv) a notice for the defendant's use if the defendant wants to plead guilty without attending court; and

    (d) the prosecutor has served on the court officer—

        (i) copies of those documents, and

        (ii) a certificate of service of those documents on the defendant.

(2) A defendant who wants to plead guilty without attending court must, before the hearing date specified in the summons or requisition—

    (a) serve a notice of guilty plea on the court officer; and

    (b) include with that notice any representations that the defendant wants the court to consider on that date.

(3) A defendant who wants to withdraw such a notice must notify the court officer in writing before the hearing date.

(4) If the defendant does not withdraw the notice before the hearing date, then on or after that date—

    (a) to establish the facts of the offence and other information about the defendant, the court may take account only of the material and any representations served under this rule (and rule 37.10(3) to (9) inclusive must be read accordingly);

       (b) unless the court otherwise directs, the prosecutor need not attend; and

       (c) the court may accept such a guilty plea and pass sentence in the defendant's absence.

  (5) With the defendant's agreement, the court may deal with the case in the same way as under paragraph (4) where the defendant—

       (a) is present; and

       (b) has served a notice of guilty plea under paragraph (2); or

       (c) pleads guilty there and then.

R-258 Application to withdraw a guilty plea

37.9 (1) This rule applies where the defendant wants to withdraw a guilty plea.

  (2) The defendant must apply to do so—

       (a) as soon as practicable after becoming aware of the reasons for doing so; and

       (b) before sentence.

  (3) Unless the court otherwise directs, the application must be in writing and the defendant must serve it on—

       (a) the court officer; and

       (b) the prosecutor.

  (4) The application must—

       (a) explain why it would be unjust not to allow the defendant to withdraw the guilty plea;

       (b) identify—

           (i) any witness that the defendant wants to call, and

          (ii) any other proposed evidence; and

       (c) say whether the defendant waives legal professional privilege, giving any relevant name and date.

R-259 Procedure if the court convicts

37.10 (1) This rule applies if the court convicts the defendant.

  (2) The court—

       (a) may exercise its power to require—

           (i) a statement of the defendant's financial circumstances,

          (ii) a pre-sentence report; and

       (b) may (and in some circumstances must) remit the defendant to a youth court for sentence where—

           (i) the defendant is under 18, and

          (ii) the convicting court is not itself a youth court.

  (3) The prosecutor must—

       (a) summarise the prosecution case, if the sentencing court has not heard evidence;

       (b) identify any offence to be taken into consideration in sentencing;

       (c) provide information relevant to sentence, including any statement of the effect of the offence on the victim, the victim's family and others; and

       (d) where it is likely to assist the court, identify any other matter relevant to sentence, including—

           (i) aggravating and mitigating factors,

          (ii) the legislation applicable, and

         (iii) any sentencing guidelines or guideline cases.

  (4) The defendant must provide details of financial circumstances—

       (a) in any form required by the court officer;

       (b) by any date directed by the court or by the court officer.

  (5) Where the defendant pleads guilty but wants to be sentenced on a different basis to that disclosed by the prosecution case—

       (a) the defendant must set out that basis in writing, identifying what is in dispute;

       (b) the court may invite the parties to make representations about whether the dispute is material to sentence; and

       (c) if the court decides that it is a material dispute, the court must—

           (i) invite such further representations or evidence as it may require, and

          (ii) decide the dispute.

  (6) Where the court has power to order the endorsement of the defendant's driving licence, or power to order the disqualification of the defendant from holding or obtaining one—

       (a) if other legislation so permits, a defendant who wants the court not to exercise that power must introduce the evidence or information on which the defendant relies;

       (b) the prosecutor may introduce evidence; and

       (c) the parties may make representations about that evidence or information.

(7) Before the court passes sentence—
    (a) the court must—
        (i)   give the defendant an opportunity to make representations and introduce evidence relevant to sentence, and
        (ii) where the defendant is under 18, give the defendant's parents, guardian or other supporting adult, if present, such an opportunity as well; and
    (b) the justices' legal adviser or the court must elicit any further information relevant to sentence that the court may require.
(8) If the court requires more information, it may exercise its power to adjourn the hearing for not more than—
    (a) 3 weeks at a time, if the defendant will be in custody; or
    (b) 4 weeks at a time.
(9) When the court has taken into account all the evidence, information and any report available, the court must—
    (a) as a general rule, pass sentence there and then;
    (b) when passing sentence, explain the reasons for deciding on that sentence, unless neither the defendant nor any member of the public is present;
    (c) when passing sentence, explain to the defendant its effect, the consequences of failing to comply with any order or pay any fine, and any power that the court has to vary or review the sentence, unless—
        (i)   the defendant is absent, or
        (ii) the defendant's ill-health or disorderly conduct makes such an explanation impracticable;
    (d) give any such explanation in terms the defendant, if present, can understand (with help, if necessary); and
    (e) consider exercising any power it has to make a costs or other order.
(10) Despite the general rule—
    (a) the court must adjourn the hearing if the defendant is absent, the case started with a summons or requisition, and either—
        (i)   the court considers passing a custodial sentence, or
        (ii) the court considers imposing a disqualification (unless it has already adjourned the hearing to give the defendant an opportunity to attend);
    (b) the court may exercise any power it has to—
        (i)   commit the defendant to the Crown Court for sentence (and in some cases it must do so), or
        (ii) defer sentence for up to 6 months.

Procedure where a party is absent

R-260

37.11 (1) This rule—
    (a) applies where a party is absent; but
    (b) does not apply where the defendant has served a notice of guilty plea under rule 37.8 (written guilty plea: special rules).
(2) Where the prosecutor is absent, the court may—
    (a) if it has received evidence, deal with the case as if the prosecutor were present; and
    (b) in any other case—
        (i)   enquire into the reasons for the prosecutor's absence, and
        (ii) if satisfied there is no good reason, exercise its power to dismiss the allegation.
(3) Where the defendant is absent—
    (a) the general rule is that the court must proceed as if the defendant—
        (i)   were present, and
        (ii) had pleaded not guilty (unless a plea already has been taken)
    and the court must give reasons if it does not do so; but
    (b) the general rule does not apply if the defendant is under 18;
    (c) the general rule is subject to the court being satisfied that—
        (i)   any summons or requisition was served on the defendant a reasonable time before the hearing, or
        (ii) in a case in which the hearing has been adjourned, the defendant had reasonable notice of where and when it would resume;

       (d) the general rule is subject also to rule 37.10(10)(a) (restrictions on passing sentence in the defendant's absence); and

       (e) the hearing must be treated as if it had not taken place at all if—

           (i)   the case started with a summons or requisition,

           (ii) the defendant makes a statutory declaration of not having found out about the case until after the hearing began, and

           (iii) the defendant serves that declaration on the court officer not more than 21 days after the date of finding out about the case, unless the court extends that time limit.

   (4) Where the defendant is absent, the court—

       (a) must exercise its power to issue a warrant for the defendant's arrest, if it passes a custodial sentence; and

       (b) may exercise its power to do so in any other case, if it does not apply the general rule in paragraph (3)(a) of this rule about proceeding in the defendant's absence.

R-261   Provision of documents for the court

37.12 (1) A party who introduces a document in evidence, or who otherwise uses a document in presenting that party's case, must provide a copy for—

       (a) each other party;

       (b) any witness that party wants to refer to that document;

       (c) the court; and

       (d) the justices' legal adviser.

   (2) Unless the court otherwise directs, on application or on its own initiative, the court officer must provide for the court—

       (a) any copy received under paragraph (1) before the hearing begins; and

       (b) a copy of the court officer's record of—

           (i)   information supplied by each party for the purposes of case management, including any revision of information previously supplied,

           (ii) each pre-trial direction for the management of the case,

           (iii) any pre-trial decision to admit evidence,

           (iv) any pre-trial direction about the giving of evidence, and

           (v) any admission to which rule 37.6 applies.

R-262   Place of trial

37.13 (1) Unless the court otherwise directs, the hearing must take place in a courtroom provided by the Lord Chancellor.

   (2) Where the hearing takes place in Wales—

       (a) any party or witness may use the Welsh language; and

       (b) if practicable, at least one member of the court must be Welsh-speaking.

R-263   Duty of justices' legal adviser

37.14 (1) A justices' legal adviser must attend, unless the court—

       (a) includes a District Judge (Magistrates' Courts); and

       (b) otherwise directs.

   (2) A justices' legal adviser must—

       (a) before the hearing begins, by reference to what is provided for the court under rule 37.12 draw the court's attention to—

           (i)   what the prosecutor alleges,

           (ii) what the parties say is agreed,

           (iii) what the parties say is in dispute, and

           (iv) what the parties say about how each expects to present the case, especially where that may affect its duration and timetabling;

       (b) whenever necessary, give the court legal advice and—

           (i)   if necessary, attend the members of the court outside the courtroom to give such advice, but

           (ii) inform the parties of any such advice given outside the courtroom; and

       (c) assist the court, where appropriate, in the formulation of its reasons and the recording of those reasons.

(3) A justices' legal adviser must—
    (a) assist an unrepresented defendant;
    (b) assist the court by—
        (i) making a note of the substance of any oral evidence or representations, to help the court recall that information,
        (ii) if the court rules inadmissible part of a written statement introduced in evidence, marking that statement in such a way as to make that clear,
        (iii) ensuring that an adequate record is kept of the court's decisions and the reasons for them, and
        (iv) making any announcement, other than of the verdict or sentence.
(4) Where the defendant has served a notice of guilty plea to which rule 37.8 (written guilty plea: special rules) applies, a justices' legal adviser must read aloud to the court—
    (a) the material on which the prosecutor relies to set out the facts of the offence and to provide information relevant to sentence (or summarise any written statement included in that material, if the court so directs); and
    (b) any written representations by the defendant.

Duty of court officer

R-264

37.15 The court officer must—
    (a) serve on each party notice of where and when an adjourned hearing will resume, unless—
        (i) the party was present when that was arranged, or
        (ii) the defendant has served a notice of guilty plea to which rule 37.8 applies, and the adjournment is for not more than 4 weeks;
    (b) if the reason for the adjournment was to postpone sentence, include that reason in any such notice to the defendant;
    (c) unless the court otherwise directs, make available to the parties any written report to which rule 37.10 applies;
    (d) where the court has ordered a defendant to provide information under section 25 of the Road Traffic Offenders Act 1988, serve on the defendant notice of that order unless the defendant was present when it was made;
    (e) serve on the prosecutor—
        (i) any notice of guilty plea to which rule 37.8 applies, and
        (ii) any declaration served under rule 37.11(3)(e) that the defendant did not know about the case;
    (f) record in the magistrates' court register the court's reasons for not proceeding in the defendant's absence where rule 37.11(3)(a) applies; and
    (g) give the court such other assistance as it requires.

Criminal Practice Directions   Part 37   Trial and Sentence in a Magistrates' Court

CPD VI Trial 37A: Role of the Justices' Clerk/Legal Adviser

PD-39

37A.1 The role of the justices' clerk/legal adviser is a unique one, which carries with it independence from direction when undertaking a judicial function and when advising magistrates. These functions must be carried out in accordance with the Bangalore Principles of Judicial Conduct (judicial independence, impartiality, integrity, propriety, ensuring fair treatment and competence and diligence). More specifically, duties must be discharged in accordance with the relevant professional Code of Conduct and the Legal Adviser Competence Framework.

37A.2 A justices' clerk is responsible for:
    (a) the legal advice tendered to the justices within the area;
    (b) the performance of any of the functions set out below by any member of his staff acting as justices' legal adviser;
    (c) ensuring that competent advice is available to justices when the justices' clerk is not personally present in court; and
    (d) ensuring that advice given at all stages of proceedings and powers exercised (including those delegated to justices' legal advisers) take into account the court's duty to deal with cases justly and actively to manage the case.

37A.3 Where a person other than the justices' clerk (a justices' legal adviser), who is authorised to do so, performs any of the functions referred to in this direction, he or she will have the same duties, powers and responsibilities as the justices' clerk. The justices' legal adviser may consult the justices' clerk, or other person authorised by the justices' clerk for that purpose, before tendering advice to the bench. If the justices' clerk or that person gives any advice directly to the bench, he or she should give the parties or their advocates an opportunity of repeating any relevant submissions, prior to the advice being given.

37A.4 When exercising judicial powers, a justices' clerk or legal adviser is acting in exactly the same capacity as a magistrate. The justices' clerk may delegate powers to a justices' legal adviser in accordance with the relevant statutory authority. The scheme of delegation must be clear and in writing, so that all justices' legal advisers are certain of the extent of their powers. Once a power is delegated, judicial discretion in an individual case lies with the justices' legal adviser exercising the power. When exercise of a power does not require the consent of the parties, a justices' clerk or legal adviser may deal with and decide a contested issue or may refer that issue to the court.

37A.5 It shall be the responsibility of the justices' clerk or legal adviser to provide the justices with any advice they require to perform their functions justly, whether or not the advice has been requested, on:

(a) questions of law;
(b) questions of mixed law and fact;
(c) matters of practice and procedure;
(d) the process to be followed at sentence and the matters to be taken into account, together with the range of penalties and ancillary orders available, in accordance with the relevant sentencing guidelines;
(e) any relevant decisions of the superior courts or other guidelines;
(f) the appropriate decision-making structure to be applied in any given case; and
(g) other issues relevant to the matter before the court.

37A.6 In addition to advising the justices, it shall be the justices' legal adviser's responsibility to assist the court, where appropriate, as to the formulation of reasons and the recording of those reasons.

37A.7 The justices' legal adviser has a duty to assist an unrepresented defendant, see Rule 9.4(3) (a), in particular when the court is making a decision on allocation, bail, at trial and on sentence.

37A.8 Where the court must determine allocation, the legal adviser may deal with any aspect of the allocation hearing save for the decision on allocation, indication of sentence and sentence.

37A.9 When a defendant acting in person indicates a guilty plea, the legal adviser must explain the procedure and inform the defendant of their right to address the court on the facts and to provide details of their personal circumstances in order that the court can decide the appropriate sentence.

37A.10 When a defendant indicates a not guilty plea but has not completed the relevant sections of the Magistrates' Courts Trial Preparation Form, the legal adviser must either ensure that the Form is completed or, in appropriate cases, assist the court to obtain and record the essential information on the form.

37A.11 Immediately prior to the commencement of a trial, the legal adviser must summarise for the court the agreed and disputed issues, together with the way in which the parties propose to present their cases. If this is done by way of pre-court briefing, it should be confirmed in court or agreed with the parties.

37A.12 A justices' clerk or legal adviser must not play any part in making findings of fact, but may assist the bench by reminding them of the evidence, using any notes of the proceedings for this purpose, and clarifying the issues which are agreed and those which are to be determined.

37A.13 A justices' clerk or legal adviser may ask questions of witnesses and the parties in order to clarify the evidence and any issues in the case. A legal adviser has a duty to ensure that every case is conducted justly.

37A.14 When advising the justices, the justices' clerk or legal adviser, whether or not previously in court, should:

(a) ensure that he is aware of the relevant facts; and
(b) provide the parties with an opportunity to respond to any advice given.

37A.15 At any time, justices are entitled to receive advice to assist them in discharging their responsibilities. If they are in any doubt as to the evidence which has been given, they should seek the aid of their legal adviser, referring to his notes as appropriate. This should ordinarily be done in open court. Where the justices request their adviser to join them in the retiring room, this request should be made in the presence of the parties in court. Any legal advice given to the justices other than in open court should be clearly stated to be provisional; and the adviser should subsequently repeat the substance of the advice in open court and give the parties the opportunity to make any representations they wish on that provisional advice. The legal adviser should then state in open court whether the provisional advice is confirmed or, if it is varied, the nature of the variation.

37A.16 The legal adviser is under a duty to assist unrepresented parties, whether defendants or not, to present their case, but must do so without appearing to become an advocate for the party concerned. The legal adviser should also ensure that members of the court are aware of obligations under the Victims' Code.

37A.17 The role of legal advisers in fine default proceedings, or any other proceedings for the enforcement of financial orders, obligations or penalties, is to assist the court. They must not act in an adversarial or partisan manner, such as by attempting to establish wilful refusal or neglect or any other type of culpable behaviour, to offer an opinion on the facts, or to urge a particular course of action upon the justices. The expectation is that a legal adviser will ask questions of the defaulter to elicit information which the justices will require to make an adjudication, such as the explanation for the default. A legal adviser may also advise the justices as to the options open to them in dealing with the case.

37A.18 The performance of a legal adviser is subject to regular appraisal. For that purpose the appraiser may be present in the justices' retiring room. The content of the appraisal is confidential, but the fact that an appraisal has taken place, and the presence of the appraiser in the retiring room, should be briefly explained in open court.

CRIMINAL PROCEDURE RULES   PART 38

[There are no rules in this part.]

CRIMINAL PROCEDURE RULES   PART 39   TRIAL ON INDICTMENT

Time limits for beginning of trials   R-265

39.1   The periods set out for the purposes of section 77(2)(a) and (b) of the Senior Courts Act 1981 shall be 14 days and 8 weeks respectively and accordingly the trial of a person committed by a magistrates' court—

    (a) shall not begin until the expiration of 14 days beginning with the date of his committal, except with his consent and the consent of the prosecution; and

    (b) shall, unless the Crown Court has otherwise ordered, begin not later than the expiration of 8 weeks beginning with the date of his committal.

Appeal against refusal to excuse from jury service or to defer attendance   R-266

39.2   (1) A person summoned under the Juries Act 1974 for jury service may appeal in accordance with the provisions of this rule against any refusal of the appropriate court officer to excuse him under section 9(2), or to defer his attendance under section 9A(1), of that Act.

    (2) Subject to paragraph (3), an appeal under this rule shall be heard by the Crown Court.

    (3) Where the appellant is summoned under the 1974 Act to attend before the High Court in Greater London the appeal shall be heard by a judge of the High Court and where the appellant is summoned under that Act to attend before the High Court outside Greater London or before a county court and the appeal has not been decided by the Crown Court before the day on which the appellant is required by the summons to attend, the appeal shall be heard by the court before which he is summoned to attend.

    (4) An appeal under this rule shall be commenced by the appellant's giving notice of appeal to the appropriate court officer of the Crown Court or the High Court in Greater London, as the case may be, and such notice shall be in writing and shall specify the matters upon which the appellant relies as providing good reason why he should be excused from attending in pursuance of the summons or why his attendance should be deferred.

    (5) The court shall not dismiss an appeal under this rule unless the appellant has been given an opportunity of making representations.

    (6) Where an appeal under this rule is decided in the absence of the appellant, the appropriate court officer of the Crown Court or the High Court in Greater London, as the case may be, shall notify him of the decision without delay.

R-267   **Application to change a plea of guilty**

39.3   (1)   The defendant must apply as soon as practicable after becoming aware of the grounds for making an application to change a plea of guilty, and may only do so before the final disposal of the case, by sentence or otherwise.

(2)   Unless the court otherwise directs, the application must be in writing and it must—

(a)   set out the reasons why it would be unjust for the guilty plea to remain unchanged;

(b)   indicate what, if any, evidence the defendant wishes to call;

(c)   identify any proposed witness; and

(d)   indicate whether legal professional privilege is waived, specifying any material name and date.

(3)   The defendant must serve the written application on—

(a)   the court officer; and

(b)   the prosecutor.

Criminal Practice Directions   Part 39   Trial on Indictment

PD-40   **CPD VI Trial 39A: Juries: Introduction**

39A.1   Jury service is an important public duty which individual members of the public are chosen at random to undertake. As the Court has acknowledged: 'Jury service is not easy; it never has been. It involves a major civic responsibility' (*R v Thompson* [2010] EWCA Crim 1623, [9] per Lord Judge CJ, [2011] 1 WLR 200, [2010] 2 Cr App R 27.)

Provision of information to prospective jurors

39A.2   HMCTS provide every person summoned as a juror with information about the role and responsibilities of a juror. Prospective jurors are provided with a pamphlet, 'Your Guide to Jury Service', and may also view the film 'Your Role as a Juror' online at any time on the Ministry of Justice YouTube site

www.youtube.com/watch?v=JP7slp-X9Pc There is also information at https://www.gov.uk/jury-service/overview

PD-41   **CPD VI Trial 39B: Juries: Preliminary Matters Arising before Jury Service Commences**

39B.1   The effect of section 321 of the Criminal Justice Act 2003 was to remove certain categories of persons from those previously ineligible for jury service (the judiciary and others concerned with the administration of justice) and certain other categories ceased to be eligible for excusal as of right, (such as members of Parliament and medical professionals). The normal presumption is that everyone, unless ineligible or disqualified, will be required to serve when summoned to do so.

Excusal and deferral

39B.2   The jury summoning officer is empowered to defer or excuse individuals in appropriate circumstances and in accordance with the HMCTS *Guidance for summoning officers when considering deferral and excusal applications* (2009): http://www.official-documents.gov.uk/document/other/9780108508400/9780108508400.pdf

Appeals from officer's refusal to excuse or postpone jury service

39B.3   Rule 39.2 governs the procedure for a person's appeal against a summoning officer's decision in relation to excusal or deferral of jury service.

Provision of information at court

39B.4   The court officer is expected to provide relevant further information to jurors on their arrival in the court centre.

PD-42   **CPD VI Trial 39C: Juries: Eligibility**

English language ability

39C.1   Under the Juries Act 1974 section 10, a person summoned for jury service who applies for excusal on the grounds of insufficient understanding of English may, where necessary, be brought before the judge.

39C.2   The court may exercise its power to excuse any person from jury service for lack of capacity to act effectively as a juror because of an insufficient understanding of English.

39C.3   The judge has the discretion to stand down jurors who are not competent to serve by reason of a personal disability: *R v Mason* [1981] QB 881, (1980) 71 Cr App R 157; *R v Jalil* [2008] EWCA Crim 2910, [2009] 2 Cr App R (S) 40.

Jurors with professional and public service commitments

39C.4 The legislative change in the Criminal Justice Act 2003 means that more individuals are eligible to serve as jurors, including those previously excused as of right or ineligible. Judges need to be vigilant to the need to exercise their discretion to adjourn a trial, excuse or discharge a juror should the need arise.

39C.5 Whether or not an application has already been made to the jury summoning officer for deferral or excusal, it is also open to the person summoned to apply to the court to be excused. Such applications must be considered with common sense and according to the interests of justice. An explanation should be required for an application being much later than necessary.

Serving police officers, prison officers or employees of prosecuting agencies

39C.6 A judge should always be made aware at the stage of jury selection if any juror in waiting is in these categories. The juror summons warns jurors in these categories that they will need to alert court staff.

39C.7 In the case of police officers an inquiry by the judge will have to be made to assess whether a police officer may serve as a juror. Regard should be had to: whether evidence from the police is in dispute in the case and the extent to which that dispute involves allegations made against the police; whether the potential juror knows or has worked with the officers involved in the case; whether the potential juror has served or continues to serve in the same police units within the force as those dealing with the investigation of the case or is likely to have a shared local service background with police witnesses in a trial.

39C.8 In the case of a serving prison officer summoned to a court, the judge will need to inquire whether the individual is employed at a prison linked to that court or is likely to have special knowledge of any person involved in a trial.

39C.9 The judge will need to ensure that employees of prosecuting authorities do not serve on a trial prosecuted by the prosecuting authority by which they are employed. They can serve on a trial prosecuted by another prosecuting authority: *R v Abdroikov* [2007] UKHL 37, [2007] 1 WLR 2679, [2008] 1 Cr App R 21; *Hanif v UK* [2011] ECHR 2247, (2012) 55 EHRR 16; *R v L* [2011] EWCA Crim 65, [2011] 1 Cr App R 27. Similarly, a serving police officer can serve where there is no particular link between the court and the station where the police officer serves.

39C.10 Potential jurors falling into these categories should be excused from jury service unless there is a suitable alternative court/trial to which they can be transferred.

CPD VI Trial 39D: Juries: Precautionary Measures before Swearing   PD-43

39D.1 There should be a consultation with the advocates as to the questions, if any, it may be appropriate to ask potential jurors. Topics to be considered include:

a.   the availability of jurors for the duration of a trial that is likely to run beyond the usual period for which jurors are summoned;
b.   whether any juror knows the defendant or parties to the case;
c.   whether potential jurors are so familiar with any locations that feature in the case that they may have, or come to have, access to information not in evidence;
d.   in cases where there has been any significant local or national publicity, whether any questions should be asked of potential jurors.

39D.2 Judges should however exercise caution. At common law a judge has a residual discretion to discharge a particular juror who ought not to be serving, but this discretion can only be exercised to prevent an individual juror who is not competent from serving. It does not include a discretion to discharge a jury drawn from particular sections of the community or otherwise to influence the overall composition of the jury. However, if there is a risk that there is widespread local knowledge of the defendant or a witness in a particular case, the judge may, after hearing submissions from the advocates, decide to exclude jurors from particular areas to avoid the risk of jurors having or acquiring personal knowledge of the defendant or a witness.

Length of trial

39D.3 Where the length of the trial is estimated to be significantly longer than the normal period of jury service, it is good practice for the trial judge to enquire whether the potential jurors on the jury panel foresee any difficulties with the length and if the judge is satisfied that the jurors' concerns are justified, he may say that they are not required for that particular jury. This does not mean that the judge must excuse the juror from sitting at that court altogether, as it may well be possible for the juror to sit on a shorter trial at the same court.

Juror with potential connection to the case or parties

39D.4 Where a juror appears on a jury panel, it will be appropriate for a judge to excuse the juror from that particular case where the potential juror is personally concerned with the facts of the particular case, or is closely connected with a prospective witness. Judges need to exercise due caution as noted above.

PD-44   **CPD VI Trial 39E: Juries: Swearing in Jurors**

Swearing Jury for trial

39E.1 All jurors shall be sworn or affirm. All jurors shall take the oath or affirmation in open court in the presence of one another. If, as a result of the juror's delivery of the oath or affirmation, a judge has concerns that a juror has such difficulties with language comprehension or reading ability that might affect that juror's capacity to undertake his or her duties, bearing in mind the likely evidence in the trial, the judge should make appropriate inquiry of that juror.

Form of oath or affirmation

39E.2 Each juror should have the opportunity to indicate to the court the Holy Book on which he or she wishes to swear. The precise wording will depend on his or her faith as indicated to the court.

39E.3 Any person who prefers to affirm shall be permitted to make a solemn affirmation instead. The wording of the affirmation is: 'I do solemnly, sincerely and truly declare and affirm that I will faithfully try the defendant and give a true verdict according to the evidence'.

PD-45   **CPD VI Trial 39F: Juries: Ensuring an Effective Jury Panel**

Adequacy of numbers

39F.1 By section 6 of the Juries Act 1974, if it appears to the court that a jury to try any issue before the court will be, or probably will be, incomplete, the court may, if the court thinks fit, require any persons who are in, or in the vicinity of, the court, to be summoned (without any written notice) for jury service up to the number needed (after allowing for any who may not be qualified under section 1 of the Act, and for excusals and challenges) to make up a full jury.

PD-46   **CPD VI Trial 39G: Juries: Preliminary Instructions to Jurors**

39G.1 After the jury has been sworn and the defendant has been put in charge the judge will want to give directions to the jury on a number of matters.

39G.2 Jurors can be expected to follow the instructions diligently. As the Privy Council stated in *Taylor* [2013] UKPC 8, [2013] 1 WLR 1144:

> The assumption must be that the jury understood and followed the direction that they were given: ... the experience of trial judges is that juries perform their duty according to law. ... [T]he law proceeds on the footing that the jury, acting in accordance with the instructions given to them by the trial judge, will render a true verdict in accordance with the evidence. To conclude otherwise would be to underrate the integrity of the system of trial by jury and the effect on the jury of the instructions by the trial judge.

At the start of the trial

39G.3 Trial judges should instruct the jury on general matters which will include the time estimate for the trial and normal sitting hours. The jury will always need clear guidance on the following:

i.   The need to try the case only on the evidence and remain faithful to their oath or affirmation;

ii. The prohibition on internet searches for matters related to the trial, issues arising or the parties;

iii. The importance of not discussing any aspect of the case with anyone outside their own number or allowing anyone to talk to them about it, whether directly, by telephone, through internet facilities such as Facebook or Twitter or in any other way;

iv. The importance of taking no account of any media reports about the case;

v.   The collective responsibility of the jury. As the Lord Chief Justice made clear in *R v Thompson and Others* [2010] EWCA Crim 1623, [2011] 1 WLR 200, [2010] 2 Cr App R 27:

> [T]here is a collective responsibility for ensuring that the conduct of each member is consistent with the jury oath and that the directions of the trial judge about the discharge of their responsibilities are followed. ... The collective responsibility of the jury for its own conduct must be regarded as an integral part of the trial itself.

vi. The need to bring any concerns, including concerns about the conduct of other jurors, to the attention of the judge at the time, and not to wait until the case is concluded. The point should be made that, unless that is done while the case is continuing, it may not be possible to deal with the problem at all.

Subsequent reminder of the jury instructions

39G.4 Judges should consider reminding jurors of these instructions as appropriate at the end of each day and in particular when they separate after retirement.

CPD VI Trial 39H: Juries: Discharge of a Juror for Personal Reasons   PD-47

39H.1 Where a juror unexpectedly finds him or herself in difficult professional or personal circumstances during the course of the trial, jurors should be encouraged to raise such problems with the trial judge. This might apply, for example, to a parent whose childcare arrangements unexpectedly fail, or a worker who is engaged in the provision of services the need for which can be critical, or a Member of Parliament who has deferred their jury service to an apparently more convenient time, but is unexpectedly called back to work for a very important reason. Such difficulties would normally be raised through a jury note in the normal manner.

39H.2 In such circumstances, the judge must exercise his or her discretion according to the interests of justice and the requirements of each individual case. The judge must decide for him or herself whether the juror has presented a sufficient reason to interfere with the course of the trial. If the juror has presented a sufficient reason, in longer trials it may well be possible to adjourn for a short period in order to allow the juror to overcome the difficulty.

39H.3 In shorter cases, it may be more appropriate to discharge the juror and to continue the trial with a reduced number of jurors. The power to do this is implicit in section 16(1) of the Juries Act 1974. In unusual cases (such as an unexpected emergency arising overnight) a juror need not be discharged in open court. The good administration of justice depends on the co-operation of jurors, who perform an essential public service. All such applications should be dealt with sensitively and sympathetically and the trial judge should always seek to meet the interests of justice without unduly inconveniencing any juror.

CPD VI Trial 39J: Juries: Views   PD-48

39J.1 In each case in which it is necessary for the jury to view a location, the judge should produce ground rules for the view, after discussion with the advocates. The rules should contain details of what the jury will be shown and in what order and who, if anyone, will be permitted to speak and what will be said. The rules should also make provision for the jury to ask questions and receive a response from the judge, following submissions from the advocates, while the view is taking place.

CPD VI Trial 39K: Juries: Directions to Jury before Retirement   PD-49

39K.1 At the conclusion of the summing up, a number of directions are required. In particular it is important that judges direct the jury:
  i.   That their verdict must be unanimous in respect of each count and each defendant.
  ii.   Not to think about 'majority verdicts' unless and until given further directions.
  iii. That they will need to select one of their number to chair their discussions and speak on their behalf.

CPD VI Trial 39L: Juries: Jury Access to Exhibits and Evidence in Retirement   PD-50

39L.1 At the end of the summing up it is also important that the judge informs the jury that any exhibits they wish to have will be made available to them.

39L.2 Judges should invite submissions from the advocates as to what material the jury should retire with and what material before them should be removed, such as the transcript of an ABE interview (which should usually be removed from the jury as soon as the recording has been played.)

39L.3 Judges will also need to inform the jury of the opportunity to view certain audio, DVD or CCTV evidence that has been played (excluding, for example ABE interviews). If possible, it may be appropriate for the jury to be able to view any such material in the jury room alone, such as on a sterile laptop, so that they can discuss it freely; this will be a matter for the judge's discretion, following discussion with counsel.

CPD VI Trial 39M: Juries: Jury Irregularities   PD-51

39M.1 This section consolidates the protocol issued by the President of the Queen's Bench Division in November 2012: Protocol in relation to Jury Irregularities at the Crown Court.

39M.2 A jury irregularity is anything that may prevent a juror, or the whole jury, from remaining faithful to their oath or affirmation as jurors to 'faithfully try the defendant and give a true verdict according to the evidence.' Anything that compromises the jury's independence, or introduces into the jury's deliberations material or considerations extraneous to the evidence in the case, may impact on the jurors' ability to remain faithful to their oath or affirmation.

During the course of the trial

39M.3 Any irregularity relating to the jury should be drawn to the attention of the trial judge in the absence of the jury as soon as it is known.

39M.4 Irregularities take many forms: some may clearly appear to be contempt by a juror, for example, searching for material about the defendant on the internet; others may appear to be an attempt to intimidate or suborn a juror; on other occasions, for example, where there has been contact between a juror and a defendant, it may not be clear whether it may be a contempt or an attempt at intimidation. The judge may also be made aware of friction between individual jurors.

39M.5 Difficult situations do arise and, although the trial process must not be delayed unduly, the trial judge may wish to consult with the Registrar of Criminal Appeals. Contact details for the Registrar and the Criminal Appeal Office are given at the end of this section.

39M.6 When an irregularity is drawn to the attention of the trial judge, the judge should consider whether the juror(s) concerned should be isolated from the rest of the jury if that has not already been done by the usher. If it appears that a juror has improperly obtained information, consideration should be given as to the risk that the information has already been shared with other members of the jury or that the information could be shared if the jury remain together.

39M.7 The judge should consult with the advocates and invite submissions. This should be in open court in the presence of the defendant(s) unless there is good reason not to do so.

39M.8 The trial judge should try to establish the basic facts of what has occurred. This may involve questioning individually the juror(s) involved. Unless there is good reason, again this should be in open court in the presence of the defendant(s). However, if there is suspicion about the defendant's conduct in the irregularity then the hearing should take place with all parties represented, but in the defendant's absence. The hearing should be held in court sitting in chambers, not in the judge's room. If there is any suspicion of tampering, the defendant, if not already in custody, ought to be taken into custody.

39M.9 The judge's inquiries should be directed towards ascertaining whether the juror(s) can remain faithful to their oath or affirmation; the trial judge should not inquire into the deliberations of the jury. The inquiry should only be to ascertain what has occurred and what steps should be taken next. It may be appropriate for the judge to ask the juror(s) whether they feel able to continue and remain faithful to their oath or affirmation.

39M.10 In the light of the basic facts as they appear to be, the trial judge may invite further submissions from the advocates, including on what should be said to the jurors, and take time to reflect on the appropriate course of action. The judge may consider the stage the trial has reached and in cases of potential bias whether a fair minded and informed observer would conclude that there was a real possibility that the juror or jury would be biased. Judges should be alert to attempts by defendants or others to obstruct or thwart the trial process.

39M.11 In relation to the conduct of the trial, the trial judge may:

    i.   Take no action and continue the trial. If so, the judge should consider giving some explanation to the jurors to reassure them that nothing untoward has happened that need concern them.

    ii.   Continue the trial but, if appropriate, give a reminder to the jury, tailored to the requirements of the case, that their verdict is a decision of the whole jury as a body and that they should give and take and try to work together. It is, in every case, essential that no undue pressure is exerted on the jury.

    iii.   Discharge the juror(s) concerned and continue the trial if sufficient jurors remain. The minimum number required to continue is nine: Juries Act 1974, section 16(1). Consideration must be given as to what to say to the remaining jury members when one or more have been discharged and to the juror(s) on discharge. The juror(s) must be warned not to discuss the circumstances with anyone and it may be necessary to discharge the juror(s) from current jury service.

    iv.   Discharge the whole jury and re-list the trial. Again the jury should be warned not to discuss the circumstances with anyone. Consideration should be given to discharging them from current jury service. If the jury has been discharged and there is a danger of jury tampering in the new trial, the Crown may make an application under section 44 of the Criminal Justice

Act 2003 at a preliminary hearing for a trial without a jury if jury protection measures would be insufficient.

v.   If the judge is satisfied that jury tampering has taken place, discharge the jury and continue the trial without a jury: section 46(3) of the Criminal Justice Act 2003, or discharge the jury and order that a new trial take place without a jury: section 46(5) of the Criminal Justice Act 2003.

39M.12   Contempt by jurors should generally be dealt with by the Attorney General; however it may be appropriate for the trial judge to deal with a very minor and clear contempt in the face of the court admitted by the juror. The procedure in such a case is provided for in Section 2 of Part 62 of the Criminal Procedure Rules. If, after the preliminary inquiry, it appears to the trial judge that someone may be in contempt and it is not appropriate for the trial judge to deal with it, or that a criminal offence may have been committed, an investigation by the police may be appropriate to clarify the factual position or to gather evidence.

39M.13   Before the name(s) and address(es) of any juror(s) are provided to the police or the police are requested to take any action, the approval of the Court of Appeal (Criminal Division) (the 'CA (CD)') to the release of information must be obtained. The court manager, on behalf of the trial judge, should contact the Registrar of Criminal Appeals setting out the position neutrally and seeking the approval of the CA (CD) to release the name(s) and address(es) of the juror(s) to the police. The initial approach may be by telephone, but the information must be provided in writing; e-mail is acceptable.

39M.14   The Registrar will put the application before the Vice-President of the CA (CD) or a judge of the CA (CD) nominated by the Vice-President to consider approval. The Court of Appeal judge will consider the application and, if approval is granted, may also give directions as to the scope of the investigation. It may be that any investigation is made in stages. The Registrar will also inform the Attorney General's Office, who may allocate a lawyer and assist the police in the direction of the investigation.

39M.15   Where there is to be an investigation by the police, it will be necessary to act expeditiously to obtain witness statements whilst memories are still fresh. Such statements may be required for criminal or contempt proceedings. Police investigating the matter must pay scrupulous regard to section 8 Contempt of Court Act 1981.

39M.16   When the investigation is complete, the police should report to the Attorney General through the allocated AGO lawyer. If it appears that a criminal offence may have been committed, the Attorney General will hand the file to the Crown Prosecution Service; if a contempt may have taken place, the Attorney General will decide whether or not to instigate proceedings in the Divisional Court.

39M.17   In the event that such an incident does occur, trial judges should have regard to the remarks of Lord Hope in *R v Connors and Mirza* [2004] UKHL 2, [2004] 1 AC 1118, [2004] 2 Cr App R 8 at [127] and [128] and consider the desirability of preparing a statement that could be used in connection with any appeal arising from the incident to the CA (CD). Members of the CA (CD) should also remind themselves of the power to request the judge to furnish them with any information or assistance under rule 22 of the Criminal Appeal Rules 1968 (SI 1968/1262) and section 87(4) of the Senior Courts Act 1981.

After verdicts have been returned

39M.18   A trial judge has no jurisdiction in relation to enquiries about jury irregularities that come to light after the end of the trial. A trial will be considered to have concluded for these purposes when a jury has delivered all verdicts or has been discharged from giving all verdicts on all defendants in the trial. In *R v Thompson and others* [2010] EWCA Crim 1623, [2011] 1 WLR 200, [2010] 2 Cr App R 27, the Lord Chief Justice, Lord Judge said:

> Much more difficult problems arise when after the verdict has been returned, attention is drawn to alleged irregularities. This may take the form of a complaint from a defendant, or his solicitors, or in a very few cases it may emerge from one or more jurors, or indeed from information revealed by the jury bailiff. It is then beyond the jurisdiction of the trial judge to intervene. Responsibility for investigating any irregularity must be assumed by this court. In performing its responsibilities, it is bound to apply the principle that the deliberations of the jury are confidential. Except with the authority of the trial judge during the trial, or this court after the verdict, inquiries into jury deliberations are "forbidden territory" (per Gage LJ in *R v Adams* [2007] EWCA Crim 1, [2007] 1 Cr App R 34).

39M.19 If information about a jury irregularity comes to light during an adjournment after verdict but before sentence, then the trial judge should be considered functus officio in relation to the jury matter, not least because the jury will have been discharged. The trial judge should inform the Registrar of Criminal Appeals about the information. Unless there is a good reason not to do so, the trial judge should proceed to sentence.

39M.20 If at any stage after trial, a juror contacts the trial judge about the trial, that communication should be referred to the Registrar of Criminal Appeals to consider what steps may be appropriate. The Registrar may seek the direction of the Vice-President of the CA (CD) or a judge of the CA (CD) nominated by the Vice-President.

39M.21 If the communication suggests any issue of contempt or criminal offence, the Registrar will inform the Attorney General. If it appears to suggest a possible ground of appeal, the defendant's legal representatives will be informed. Where it raises no issues of legal significance (for example, a general complaint about the verdict from a dissenting juror or expressions of doubt or second thoughts), the Registrar will respond to the communication explaining that no action is required.

39M.22 If the prosecution become aware of an irregularity which might form a basis for an appeal then they should notify the defence in accordance with their duties to act fairly and assist in the administration of justice: *R v Makin* [2004] EWCA Crim 1607, (2004) 148 SJ LB 821.

39M.23 If the defence become aware of an irregularity which would found an arguable ground of appeal, whether they are informed directly or via the prosecution or the Registrar of Criminal Appeals, they may wish to lodge a notice and grounds of appeal. The defence should be mindful of the provisions of section 8 Contempt of Court Act 1981.

39M.24 If an application for leave to appeal is received with grounds relating to a jury irregularity then the Registrar may refer the case to the Full Court to consider whether the Court would wish to direct the Criminal Cases Review Commission (CCRC) to conduct an investigation into the irregularity under section 23A of the Criminal Appeal Act 1968 and section 5(1) of the Criminal Appeal Act 1995.

39M.25 An investigation may be directed before or after leave is granted: section 23A and section 23A(1)(a) Criminal Appeal Act 1968.

39M.26 If the Court directs that an investigation should take place, directions will be given as to the scope of the investigation. The CCRC will report back to the Court. Copies of the report or other appropriate information will be provided to the parties and the Court will either refuse leave or grant leave and subsequently hear the appeal.

Contact details

Master Egan QC
The Registrar of Criminal Appeals
Royal Courts of Justice
Strand
London
WC2A 2LL

Secretary to the Registrar:
Penny Donnelly
Tel: 0207 947 6103
E-mail: penny.donnelly@hmcts.x.gsi.gov.uk

Criminal Appeal Office, General Office
Tel: 0207 947 6011
E-mail: criminalappealoffice.generaloffice@hmcts.x.gsi.gov.uk

PD-52   **CPD VI Trial 39N: Open Justice**

39N.1 There must be freedom of access between advocate and judge. Any discussion must, however, be between the judge and the advocates on both sides. If an advocate is instructed by a solicitor who is in court, he or she, too, should be allowed to attend the discussion. This freedom of access is important because there may be matters calling for communication or discussion of such a nature that the advocate cannot, in the client's interest, mention them in open court, e.g., the advocate, by way of mitigation, may wish to tell the judge that reliable medical evidence shows that the defendant is suffering from a terminal illness and may not have long to live. It is imperative that, so far as possible, justice must be administered in open court. Advocates should, therefore, only ask to see the judge when it is felt to be really necessary. The judge must be careful only to treat such communications as private where, in the interests of justice, this is necessary. Where any such discussion takes place it should be recorded, preferably by audio recording.

CPD VI Trial 39P: DEFENDANT'S RIGHT TO GIVE OR NOT TO GIVE EVIDENCE   PD-53

39P.1 At the conclusion of the evidence for the prosecution, section 35(2) of the Criminal Justice and Public Order Act 1994 requires the court to satisfy itself that the defendant is aware that the stage has been reached at which evidence can be given for the defence and that the defendant's failure to give evidence, or if he does so his failure to answer questions, without a good reason, may lead to inferences being drawn against him.

If the defendant is legally represented

39P.2 After the close of the prosecution case, if the defendant's representative requests a brief adjournment to advise his client on this issue the request should, ordinarily, be granted. When appropriate the judge should, in the presence of the jury, inquire of the representative in these terms:

> 'Have you advised your client that the stage has now been reached at which he may give evidence and, if he chooses not to do so or, having been sworn, without good cause refuses to answer any question, the jury may draw such inferences as appear proper from his failure to do so?'

39P.3 If the representative replies to the judge that the defendant has been so advised, then the case shall proceed. If counsel replies that the defendant has not been so advised, then the judge shall direct the representative to advise his client of the consequences and should adjourn briefly for this purpose, before proceeding further.

If the defendant is not legally represented

39P.4 If the defendant is not represented, the judge shall, at the conclusion of the evidence for the prosecution, in the absence of the jury, indicate what he will say to him in the presence of the jury and ask if he understands and whether he would like a brief adjournment to consider his position.

39P.5 When appropriate, and in the presence of the jury, the judge should say to the defendant:

> 'You have heard the evidence against you. Now is the time for you to make your defence. You may give evidence on oath, and be cross-examined like any other witness. If you do not give evidence or, having been sworn, without good cause refuse to answer any question, the jury may draw such inferences as appear proper. That means they may hold it against you. You may also call any witness or witnesses whom you have arranged to attend court or lead any agreed evidence. Afterwards you may also, if you wish, address the jury. But you cannot at that stage give evidence. Do you now intend to give evidence?'

CPD VI Trial 39Q: Majority Verdicts   PD-54

39Q.1 It is very important that all those trying indictable offences should, so far as possible, adopt a uniform practice when complying with section 17 of the Juries Act 1974, both in directing the jury in summing-up and also in receiving the verdict or giving further directions after retirement. So far as the summing-up is concerned, it is inadvisable for the judge, and indeed for advocates, to attempt an explanation of the section for fear that the jury will be confused.

Before the jury retires, however, the judge should direct the jury in some such words as the following:

> 'As you may know, the law permits me, in certain circumstances, to accept a verdict which is not the verdict of you all. Those circumstances have not as yet arisen, so that when you retire I must ask you to reach a verdict upon which each one of you is agreed. Should, however, the time come when it is possible for me to accept a majority verdict, I will give you a further direction.'

39Q.2 Thereafter, the practice should be as follows:

Should the jury return before two hours and ten minutes has elapsed since the last member of the jury left the jury box to go to the jury room (or such longer time as the judge thinks reasonable) (see section 17(4)), they should be asked:

(a) 'Have you reached a verdict upon which you are all agreed? Please answer "Yes" or "No".';

(b) (i) If unanimous, 'What is your verdict?';

    (ii) If not unanimous, the jury should be sent out again for further deliberation, with a further direction to arrive if possible at a unanimous verdict.

39Q.3 Should the jury return (whether for the first time or subsequently) or be sent for after the two hours and ten minutes (or the longer period) has elapsed, questions (a) and (b)(i) in the paragraph above should be put to them and, if it appears that they are not unanimous, they should be asked to retire once more and told they should continue to endeavour to reach a unanimous verdict but that, if they cannot, the judge will accept a majority verdict as in section 17(1).

39Q.4 When the jury finally return, they should be asked:

    (a) 'Have at least ten (or nine as the case may be) of you agreed on your verdict?';

    (b) If 'Yes', 'What is your verdict? Please only answer "Guilty" or "Not Guilty".';

    (c) (i) If 'Not Guilty', accept the verdict without more ado;

        (ii) If 'Guilty', 'Is that the verdict of you all, or by a majority?';

    (d) If 'Guilty' by a majority, 'How many of you agreed to the verdict and how many dissented?'

39Q.5 At whatever stage the jury return, before question (a) is asked, the senior officer of the court present shall state in open court, for each period when the jury was out of court for the purpose of considering their verdict(s), the time at which the last member of the jury left the jury box to go to the jury room and the time of their return to the jury box; and will additionally state in open court the total of such periods.

39Q.6 The reason why section 17(3) is confined to a majority verdict of 'Guilty', and for the somewhat complicated procedure set out above, is to prevent it being known that a verdict of 'Not Guilty' is a majority verdict. If the final direction continues to require the jury to arrive, if possible, at a unanimous verdict and the verdict is received as specified, it will not be known for certain that the acquittal is not unanimous.

39Q.7 Where there are several counts (or alternative verdicts) left to the jury the above practice will, of course, need to be adapted to the circumstances. The procedure will have to be repeated in respect of each count (or alternative verdict), the verdict being accepted in those cases where the jury are unanimous and the further direction being given in cases in which they are not unanimous.

39Q.8 Should the jury in the end be unable to agree on a verdict by the required majority, the judge in his discretion will either ask them to deliberate further, or discharge them.

39Q.9 Section 17 will, of course, apply also to verdicts other than 'Guilty' or 'Not Guilty', e.g., to special verdicts under the Criminal Procedure (Insanity) Act 1964, following a finding by the judge that the defendant is unfit to be tried, and special verdicts on findings of fact. Accordingly, in such cases the questions to jurors will have to be suitably adjusted.

CRIMINAL PROCEDURE RULES   PART 40   TAINTED ACQUITTALS

R-268 **Time of certification**

40.1 Where a person is convicted of an offence as referred to in section 54(1)(b) of the Criminal Procedure and Investigations Act 1996 and it appears to the court before which the conviction has taken place that the provisions of section 54(2) are satisfied, the court shall make the certification referred to in section 54(2) at any time following conviction but no later than—

    (a) immediately after the court sentences or otherwise deals with that person in respect of the offence; or

    (b) where the court, being a magistrates' court, commits that person to the Crown Court, or remits him to another magistrates' court, to be dealt with in respect of the offence, immediately after he is so committed or remitted, as the case may be; or

    (c) where that person is a child or young person and the court, being the Crown Court, remits him to a youth court to be dealt with in respect of the offence, immediately after he is so remitted.

R-269 **Form of certification in the Crown Court**

40.2 A certification referred to in section 54(2) of the Criminal Procedure and Investigations Act 1996 by the Crown Court shall be drawn up in the form set out in the Practice Direction.

R-270 **Service of a copy of the certification**

40.3 Where a magistrates' court or the Crown Court makes a certification as referred to in section 54(2) of the Criminal Procedure and Investigations Act 1996, the court officer shall, as soon as practicable after the drawing up of the form, serve a copy on the acquitted person referred to in the certification, on the prosecutor in the proceedings which led to the acquittal, and, where the acquittal has taken place before a court other than, or at a different place to, the court where the certification has been made, on—

    (a) the clerk of the magistrates' court before which the acquittal has taken place; or

    (b) the Crown Court officer at the place where the acquittal has taken place.

Entry in register or records in relation to the conviction which occasioned certification   R-271

40.4   A clerk of a magistrates' court or an officer of a Crown Court which has made a certification under section 54(2) of the Criminal Procedure and Investigations Act 1996 shall enter in the register or records, in relation to the conviction which occasioned the certification, a note of the fact that certification has been made, the date of certification, the name of the acquitted person referred to in the certification, a description of the offence of which the acquitted person has been acquitted, the date of the acquittal, and the name of the court before which the acquittal has taken place.

Entry in the register or records in relation to the acquittal   R-272

40.5   The court officer of the court before which an acquittal has taken place shall, as soon as practicable after receipt of a copy of a form recording a certification under section 54(2) of the Criminal Procedure and Investigations Act 1996 relating to the acquittal, enter in the register or records a note that the certification has been made, the date of the certification, the name of the court which has made the certification, the name of the person whose conviction occasioned the making of the certification, and a description of the offence of which that person has been convicted. Where the certification has been made by the same court as the court before which the acquittal has occurred, sitting at the same place, the entry shall be made as soon as practicable after the making of the certification. In the case of an acquittal before a magistrates' court the entry in the register shall be signed by the clerk of the court.

Display of copy certification form   R-273

40.6   (1)   Where a court makes a certification as referred to in section 54(2) of the Criminal Procedure and Investigations Act 1996, the court officer shall, as soon as practicable after the drawing up of the form, display a copy of that form at a prominent place within court premises to which place the public has access.

(2)   Where an acquittal has taken place before a court other than, or at a different place to, the court which has made the certification under section 54(2) of the 1996 Act in relation to the acquittal, the court officer at the court where the acquittal has taken place shall, as soon as practicable after receipt of a copy of the form recording the certification, display a copy of it at a prominent place within court premises to which place the public has access.

(3)   The copy of the form referred to in paragraph (1), or the copy referred to in paragraph (2), shall continue to be displayed as referred to, respectively, in those paragraphs at least until the expiry of 28 days from, in the case of paragraph (1), the day on which the certification was made, or, in the case of paragraph (2), the day on which the copy form was received at the court.

Entry in the register or records in relation to decision of High Court   R-274

40.7   (1)   The court officer at the court where an acquittal has taken place shall, on receipt from the Administrative Court Office of notice of an order made under section 54(3) of the Criminal Procedure and Investigations Act 1996 quashing the acquittal, or of a decision not to make such an order, enter in the register or records, in relation to the acquittal, a note of the fact that the acquittal has been quashed by the said order, or that a decision has been made not to make such an order, as the case may be.

(2)   The court officer of the court which has made a certification under section 54(2) of the 1996 Act shall, on receipt from the Administrative Court Office of notice of an order made under section 54(3) of that Act quashing the acquittal referred to in the certification, or of a decision not to make such an order, enter in the register or records, in relation to the conviction which occasioned the certification, a note that the acquittal has been quashed by the said order, or that a decision has been made not to make such an order, as the case may be.

(3)   The entries in the register of a magistrates' court referred to, respectively, in paragraphs (1) and (2) above shall be signed by the magistrates' court officer.

Display of copy of notice received from High Court   R-275

40.8   (1)   Where the court officer of a court which has made a certification under section 54(2) of the Criminal Procedure and Investigations Act 1996 or before which an acquittal has occurred to which such a certification refers, receives from the Administrative Court Office notice of an order quashing the acquittal concerned, or notice of a decision not to make such an order, he shall, as soon as practicable after receiving the notice, display a copy of it at a prominent place within court premises to which place the public has access.

(2)   The copy notice referred to in paragraph (1) shall continue to be displayed as referred to in that paragraph at least until the expiry of 28 days from the day on which the notice was received at the court.

Criminal Procedure Rules 2013 and Criminal Practice Directions

CRIMINAL PROCEDURE RULES   PART 41   RETRIAL FOLLOWING
ACQUITTAL FOR SERIOUS OFFENCE

R-276   **Interpretation**

41.1   In this Part:

'business day' means any day other than a Saturday, Sunday, Christmas Day, Good Friday or a bank holiday under the Banking and Financial Dealings Act 1971, in England and Wales; and

'section 76 application' means an application made by a prosecutor under section 76(1) or (2) of the Criminal Justice Act 2003.

R-277   **Notice of a section 76 application**

41.2   (1)   A prosecutor who wants to make a section 76 application must serve notice of that application in the form set out in the Practice Direction on the Registrar and the acquitted person.

(2)   That notice shall, where practicable, be accompanied by—

(a)   relevant witness statements which are relied upon as forming new and compelling evidence of guilt of the acquitted person as well as any relevant witness statements from the original trial;

(b)   any unused statements which might reasonably be considered capable of undermining the section 76 application or of assisting an acquitted person's application to oppose that application under rule 41.3;

(c)   a copy of the indictment and paper exhibits from the original trial;

(d)   copies of the transcript of the summing up and any other relevant transcripts from the original trial; and

(e)   any other documents relied upon to support the section 76 application.

(3)   The prosecutor must, as soon as practicable after service of that notice on the acquitted person, file with the Registrar a witness statement or certificate of service which exhibits a copy of that notice.

R-278   **Response of the acquitted person**

41.3   (1)   An acquitted person who wants to oppose a section 76 application must serve a response in the form set out in the Practice Direction on the Registrar and the prosecutor which—

(a)   indicates if he is also seeking an order under section 80(6) of the Criminal Justice Act 2003 for—

(i)   the production of any document, exhibit or other thing, or

(ii)   a witness to attend for examination and to be examined before the Court of Appeal; and

(b)   exhibits any relevant documents.

(2)   The acquitted person must serve that response not more than 28 days after receiving notice under rule 41.2.

(3)   The Court of Appeal may extend the period for service under paragraph (2), either before or after that period expires.

R-279   **Examination of witnesses or evidence by the Court of Appeal**

41.4   (1)   Prior to the hearing of a section 76 application, a party may apply to the Court of Appeal for an order under section 80(6) of the Criminal Justice Act 2003 for—

(a)   the production of any document, exhibit or other thing; or

(b)   a witness to attend for examination and to be examined before the Court of Appeal.

(2)   An application under paragraph (1) must be in the form set out in the Practice Direction and must be sent to the Registrar and a copy sent to each party to the section 76 application.

(3)   An application must set out the reasons why the order was not sought from the Court when—

(a)   the notice was served on the Registrar under rule 41.2, if the application is made by the prosecutor; or

(b)   the response was served on the Registrar under rule 41.3, if the application is made by the acquitted person.

(4)   An application must be made at least 14 days before the day of the hearing of the section 76 application.

(5)   If the Court of Appeal makes an order under section 80(6) of the 2003 Act on its own motion or on application from the prosecutor, it must serve notice and reasons for that order on all parties to the section 76 application.

Bail or custody hearings in the Crown Court   R-280

41.5   (1)   Part 19 (Bail and custody time limits) shall apply where a person is to appear or be brought before the Crown Court pursuant to section 88 or 89 of the Criminal Justice Act 2003 as it applies to other proceedings in the Crown Court but with the modification set out in paragraph (2).

(2)   For rule 19.7 substitute:
'Where a person is to appear or be brought before the Crown Court pursuant to sections 88 or 89 of the Criminal Justice Act 2003, the prosecutor must serve notice of the need for such a hearing on the court officer.'

(3)   Where a person is to appear or be brought before the Crown Court pursuant to sections 88 or 89 of the 2003 Act the Crown Court may order that the person shall be released from custody on entering into a recognizance, with or without sureties, or giving other security before—

(a)   the Crown Court officer; or

(b)   any other person authorised by virtue of section 119(1) of the Magistrates' Courts Act 1980 to take a recognizance where a magistrates' court having power to take the recognizance has, instead of taking it, fixed the amount in which the principal and his sureties, if any, are to be bound.

(4)   The court officer shall forward to the Registrar a copy of any record made in pursuance of section 5(1) of the Bail Act 1976.

Further provisions regarding bail and custody in the Crown Court   R-281

41.6   (1)   The prosecutor may only apply to extend or further extend the relevant period before it expires and that application must be served on the Crown Court officer and the acquitted person.

(2)   A prosecutor's application for a summons or a warrant under section 89(3)(a) or (b) of the Criminal Justice Act 2003 must be served on the court officer and the acquitted person.

Bail or custody orders in the Court of Appeal   R-282

41.7   Rules 68.8 and 68.9 shall apply to bail or custody orders made in the Court of Appeal under section 90 of the Criminal Justice Act 2003 as if they were orders made pursuant to an application under rule 68.7.

Application for restrictions on publication   R-283

41.8   (1)   An application by the Director of Public Prosecutions, under section 82 of the Criminal Justice Act 2003, for restrictions on publication must be in the form set out in the Practice Direction and be served on the Registrar and the acquitted person.

(2)   If notice of a section 76 application has not been given and the Director of Public Prosecution has indicated that there are reasons why the acquitted person should not be notified of the application for restrictions on publication, the Court of Appeal may order that service on the acquitted person is not to be effected until notice of a section 76 application is served on that person.

(3)   If the Court of Appeal makes an order for restrictions on publication of its own motion or on application of the Director of Public Prosecutions, the Registrar must serve notice and reasons for that order on all parties, unless paragraph (2) applies.

Variation or revocation of restrictions on publication   R-284

41.9   (1)   A party who wants to vary or revoke an order for restrictions on publication, under section 82(7) of the Criminal Justice Act 2003, may apply to the Court of Appeal in writing at any time after that order was made.

(2)   A copy of the application to vary or revoke shall be sent to all parties to the section 76 application unless paragraph (3) applies.

(3)   If the application to vary or revoke is made by the Director of Public Prosecutions and—

(a)   the notice of a section 76 application has not been given under rule 41.2; and

(b)   the Director of Public Prosecutions has indicated that there are reasons why the acquitted person should not be notified of an application for restrictions on publication, the Court of Appeal may order that service on the acquitted person is not to be effected until notice of a section 76 application is served on that person.

(4)   If the Court of Appeal varies or revokes an order for restrictions on publication of its own motion or on application, it must serve notice and reasons for that order on all parties, unless paragraph (3) applies.

Criminal Procedure Rules 2013 and Criminal Practice Directions

R-285   **Powers exercisable by a single judge of the Court of Appeal**

     41.10 (1)   The following powers under the Criminal Justice Act 2003 and under this Part may be exercised by a single judge in the same manner as they may be exercised by the Court of Appeal and subject to the same provisions, namely to—

           (a)   order the production of any document, exhibit or thing under section 80(6)(a) of the 2003 Act;

           (b)   order any witness who would be a compellable witness in proceedings pursuant to an order or declaration made on the application to attend for examination and be examined before the Court of Appeal under section 80(6)(b) of the 2003 Act;

           (c)   extend the time for service under rule 41.3(2); and

           (d)   delay the requirement of service on the acquitted person of an application for restrictions on publication under rules 41.8(2) and 41.9(3).

       (2)   A single judge may, for the purposes of exercising any of the powers specified in paragraph (1), sit in such place as he appoints and may sit otherwise than in open court.

       (3)   Where a single judge exercises one of the powers set out in paragraph (1), the Registrar must serve notice of the single judge's decision on all parties to the section 76 application.

R-286   **Powers exercisable by the Registrar**

     41.11 (1)   The Registrar may require the Crown Court at the place of original trial to provide the Court of Appeal with any assistance or information which it may require for the purposes of exercising its jurisdiction under Part 10 of the Criminal Justice Act 2003 or this Part.

       (2)   The following powers may be exercised by the Registrar in the same manner as the Court of Appeal and subject to the same provisions

           (a)   order the production of any document, exhibit or thing under section 80(6)(a) of the 2003 Act;

           (b)   order any witness who would be a compellable witness in proceedings pursuant to an order or declaration made on the application to attend for examination and be examined before the Court of Appeal under section 80(6)(b) of the 2003 Act; and

           (c)   extend the time for service under rule 41.3(2).

       (3)   Where the Registrar exercises one of the powers set out in paragraph (2) the Registrar must serve notice of that decision on all parties to the section 76 application.

       (4)   Where the Registrar has refused an application to exercise any of the powers referred to in paragraph (2), the party making the application may have it determined by a single judge by serving a notice of renewal within 14 days of the day on which notice of the Registrar's decision is served on the party making the application, unless that period is extended by the Court of Appeal.

R-287   **Determination by full court**

     41.12 (1)   Where a single judge has refused an application to exercise any of the powers referred to in rule 41.10, the applicant may have that application determined by the Court of Appeal by serving a notice of renewal.

       (2)   A notice under paragraph (1) must be served on the Registrar within 14 days of the day on which notice of the single judge's decision is served on the party making the application, unless that period is extended by the Court of Appeal.

       (3)   If a notice under paragraph (1) is not served on the Registrar within the period specified in paragraph (2) or such extended period as the Court of Appeal has allowed, the application shall be treating as having been refused by the Court of Appeal.

R-288   **Notice of the determination of the application**

     41.13 (1)   The Court of Appeal may give its determination of the section 76 application at the conclusion of the hearing.

       (2)   If determination is reserved, the Registrar shall as soon as practicable, serve notice of the determination on the parties to the section 76 application.

       (3)   If the Court of Appeal orders under section 77 of the Criminal Justice Act 2003 that a retrial take place, the Registrar must as soon as practicable, serve notice on the Crown Court officer at the appropriate place of retrial.

R-289   **Notice of application to set aside order for retrial**

     41.14 (1)   If an acquitted person has not been arraigned before the end of 2 months after the date of an order under section 77 of the Criminal Justice Act 2003 he may apply in the form set out in the Practice Direction to the Court of Appeal to set aside the order.

       (2)   An application under paragraph (1) must be served on the Registrar and the prosecutor.

Leave to arraign R-290

41.15 (1) If the acquitted person has not been arraigned before the end of 2 months after the date of an order under section 77 of the Criminal Justice Act 2003, the prosecutor may apply in the form set out in the Practice Direction to the Court of Appeal for leave to arraign.

(2) An application under paragraph (1) must be served on the Registrar and the acquitted person.

Abandonment of the application R-291

41.16 (1) A section 76 application may be abandoned by the prosecutor before the hearing of that application by serving a notice in the form set out in the Practice Direction on the Registrar and the acquitted person.

(2) The Registrar must, as soon as practicable, after receiving a notice under paragraph (1) send a copy of it endorsed with the date of receipt to the prosecutor and acquitted person.

Criminal Practice Directions: Sentencing

CPD VII Sentencing A: Pleas of Guilty in the Crown Court PD-55

A.1 Prosecutors and Prosecution Advocates should be familiar with and follow the Attorney-General's Guidelines on the Acceptance of Pleas and the Prosecutor's Role in the Sentencing Exercise.

CPD VII Sentencing B: Determining the Factual Basis of Sentence PD-56

'Where a guilty plea is offered to less than the whole indictment and the prosecution is minded to accept pleas tendered to some counts or to lesser alternative counts.'

B.1 In some cases, defendants wishing to plead guilty will simply plead guilty to all charges on the basis of the facts as alleged and opened by the prosecution, with no dispute as to the factual basis or the extent of offending. Alternatively a defendant may plead guilty to some of the charges brought; in such a case, the judge will consider whether that plea represents a proper plea on the basis of the facts set out by the papers.

B.2 Where the prosecution advocate is considering whether to accept a plea to a lesser charge, the advocate may invite the judge to approve the proposed course of action. In such circumstances, the advocate must abide by the decision of the judge.

B.3 If the prosecution advocate does not invite the judge to approve the acceptance by the prosecution of a lesser charge, it is open to the judge to express his or her dissent with the course proposed and invite the advocate to reconsider the matter with those instructing him or her.

B.4 In any proceedings where the judge is of the opinion that the course proposed by the advocate may lead to serious injustice, the proceedings may be adjourned to allow the following procedure to be followed:

(a) as a preliminary step, the prosecution advocate must discuss the judge's observations with the Chief Crown Prosecutor or the senior prosecutor of the relevant prosecuting authority as appropriate, in an attempt to resolve the issue;

(b) where the issue remains unresolved, the Director of Public Prosecutions or the Director of the relevant prosecuting authority should be consulted;

(c) in extreme circumstances the judge may decline to proceed with the case until the prosecuting authority has consulted with the Attorney General, as may be appropriate.

B.5 Prior to entering a plea of guilty, a defendant may seek an indication of sentence under the procedure set out in *R v Goodyear* [2005] EWCA Crim 888, [2005] 1 WLR 2532, [2005] 2 Cr App R 20; see below.

Where a guilty plea is offered on a limited basis

B.6 A defendant may put forward a plea of guilty without accepting all of the facts as alleged by the prosecution. The basis of plea offered may seek to limit the facts or the extent of the offending for which the defendant is to be sentenced. Depending on the view taken by the prosecution, and the content of the offered basis, the case will fall into one of the following categories:

(a) a plea of guilty upon a basis of plea agreed by the prosecution and defence;

(b) a plea of guilty on a basis signed by the defendant but in respect of which there is no or only partial agreement by the prosecution;

(c) a plea of guilty on a basis that contains within it matters that are purely mitigation and which do not amount to a contradiction of the prosecution case; or

(d) in cases involving serious or complex fraud, a plea of guilty upon a basis of plea agreed by the prosecution and defence accompanied by joint submissions as to sentence.

(a) A plea of guilty upon a basis of plea agreed by the prosecution and defence

B.7   The prosecution may reach an agreement with the defendant as to the factual basis on which the defendant will plead guilty, often known as an 'agreed basis of plea'. It is always subject to the approval of the court, which will consider whether it adequately and appropriately reflects the evidence as disclosed on the papers, whether it is fair and whether it is in the interests of justice.

B.8   *R v Underwood* [2004] EWCA Crim 2256, [2005] 1 Cr App R 13, [2005] 1 Cr App R (S) 90 outlines the principles to be applied where the defendant admits that he or she is guilty, but disputes the basis of offending alleged by the prosecution:

(a) The prosecution may accept and agree the defendant's account of the disputed facts or reject it in its entirety, or in part. If the prosecution accepts the defendant's basis of plea, it must ensure that the basis of plea is factually accurate and enables the sentencing judge to impose a sentence appropriate to reflect the justice of the case;

(b) In resolving any disputed factual matters, the prosecution must consider its primary duty to the court and must not agree with or acquiesce in an agreement which contains material factual disputes;

(c) If the prosecution does accept the defendant's basis of plea, it must be reduced to writing, be signed by advocates for both sides, and made available to the judge prior to the prosecution's opening;

(d) An agreed basis of plea that has been reached between the parties should not contain matters which are in dispute and any aspects upon which there is not agreement should be clearly identified;

(e) On occasion, the prosecution may lack the evidence positively to dispute the defendant's account, for example, where the defendant asserts a matter outside the knowledge of the prosecution. Simply because the prosecution does not have evidence to contradict the defendant's assertions does not mean those assertions should be agreed. In such a case, the prosecution should test the defendant's evidence and submissions by requesting a *Newton* hearing (*R v Newton* (1982) 77 Cr App R 13, (1982) 4 Cr App R (S) 388), following the procedure set out below;

(f) If it is not possible for the parties to resolve a factual dispute when attempting to reach a plea agreement under this part, it is the responsibility of the prosecution to consider whether the matter should proceed to trial, or to invite the court to hold a *Newton* hearing as necessary.

B.9   *R v Underwood* emphasises that, whether or not pleas have been 'agreed', the judge is not bound by any such agreement and is entitled of his or her own motion to insist that any evidence relevant to the facts in dispute (or upon which the judge requires further evidence for whatever reason) should be called. Any view formed by the prosecution on a proposed basis of plea is deemed to be conditional on the judge's acceptance of the basis of plea.

B.10   A judge is not entitled to reject a defendant's basis of plea absent a *Newton* hearing unless it is determined by the court that the basis is manifestly false and as such does not merit examination by way of the calling of evidence or alternatively the defendant declines the opportunity to engage in the process of the *Newton* hearing whether by giving evidence on his own behalf or otherwise.

(b) A plea of guilty on a basis signed by the defendant but in respect of which there is no or only partial agreement by the prosecution

B.11   Where the defendant pleads guilty, but disputes the basis of offending alleged by the prosecution and agreement as to that has not been reached, the following procedure should be followed:

(a) The defendant's basis of plea must be set out in writing, identifying what is in dispute and must be signed by the defendant;

(b) The prosecution must respond in writing setting out their alternative contentions and indicating whether or not they submit that a *Newton* hearing is necessary;

(c) The court may invite the parties to make representations about whether the dispute is material to sentence; and

(d) If the court decides that it is a material dispute, the court will invite such further representations or evidence as it may require and resolve the dispute in accordance with the principles set out in *R v Newton*.

B.12   Where the disputed issue arises from facts which are within the exclusive knowledge of the defendant and the defendant is willing to give evidence in support of his case, the defence advocate should be prepared to call the defendant. If the defendant is not willing to testify, and subject to any explanation which may be given, the judge may draw such inferences as appear appropriate.

B.13   The decision whether or not a *Newton* hearing is required is one for the judge. Once the decision has been taken that there will be a *Newton* hearing, evidence is called by the parties in the usual way and the criminal burden and standard of proof applies. Whatever view has been taken by the prosecution, the prosecutor should not leave the questioning to the judge, but should assist the court by exploring the issues which the court wishes to have explored. The rules of evidence should be followed as during a trial, and the judge should direct himself appropriately as the tribunal of fact. Paragraphs 6 to 10 of *Underwood* provide additional guidance regarding the *Newton* hearing procedure.

(c) A plea of guilty on a basis that contains within it matters that are purely mitigation and which do not amount to a contradiction of the prosecution case

B.14 A basis of plea should not normally set out matters of mitigation but there may be circumstances where it is convenient and sensible for the document outlining a basis to deal with facts closely aligned to the circumstances of the offending which amount to mitigation and which may need to be resolved prior to sentence. The resolution of these matters does not amount to a *Newton* hearing properly so defined and in so far as facts fall to be established the defence will have to discharge the civil burden in order to do so. The scope of the evidence required to resolve issues that are purely matters of mitigation is for the court to determine.

(d) Cases involving serious fraud – a plea of guilty upon a basis of plea agreed by the prosecution and defence accompanied by joint submissions as to sentence

B.15 This section applies when the prosecution and the defendant(s) to a matter before the Crown Court involving allegations of serious or complex fraud have agreed a basis of plea and seek to make submissions to the court regarding sentence.

B.16 Guidance for prosecutors regarding the operation of this procedure is set out in the 'Attorney General's Guidelines on Plea Discussions in Cases of Serious or Complex Fraud', which came into force on 5 May 2009 and is referred to in this direction as the 'Attorney General's Plea Discussion Guidelines'.

B.17 In this part –

(a) 'a plea agreement' means a written basis of plea agreed between the prosecution and defendant(s) in accordance with the principles set out in *R v Underwood*, supported by admissible documentary evidence or admissions under section 10 of the Criminal Justice Act 1967;

(b) 'a sentencing submission' means sentencing submissions made jointly by the prosecution and defence as to the appropriate sentencing authorities and applicable sentencing range in the relevant sentencing guideline relating to the plea agreement;

(c) 'serious or complex fraud' includes, but is not limited to, allegations of fraud where two or more of the following are present:

    (i) the amount obtained or intended to be obtained exceeded £500,000;

    (ii) there is a significant international dimension;

    (iii) the case requires specialised knowledge of financial, commercial, fiscal or regulatory matters such as the operation of markets, banking systems, trusts or tax regimes;

    (iv) the case involves allegations of fraudulent activity against numerous victims;

    (v) the case involves an allegation of substantial and significant fraud on a public body;

    (vi) the case is likely to be of widespread public concern;

    (vii) the alleged misconduct endangered the economic well-being of the United Kingdom, for example by undermining confidence in financial markets.

Procedure

B.18 The procedure regarding agreed bases of plea outlined above, applies with equal rigour to the acceptance of pleas under this procedure. However, because under this procedure the parties will have been discussing the plea agreement and the charges from a much earlier stage, it is vital that the judge is fully informed of all relevant background to the discussions, charges and the eventual basis of plea.

B.19 Where the defendant has not yet appeared before the Crown Court, the prosecutor must send full details of the plea agreement and sentencing submission(s) to the court, at least 7 days in advance of the defendant's first appearance. Where the defendant has already appeared before the Crown Court, the prosecutor must notify the court as soon as is reasonably practicable that a plea agreement and sentencing submissions under the Attorney General's Plea Discussion Guidelines are to be submitted. The court should set a date for the matter to be heard, and the prosecutor must send full details of the plea agreement and sentencing submission(s) to the court as soon as practicable, or in accordance with the directions of the court.

B.20 The provision to the judge of full details of the plea agreement requires sufficient information to be provided to allow the judge to understand the facts of the case and the history of the plea discussions, to assess whether the plea agreement is fair and in the interests of justice, and to decide the appropriate sentence. This will include, but is not limited to:

(i)   the plea agreement;

(ii) the sentencing submission(s);

(iii) all of the material provided by the prosecution to the defendant in the course of the plea discussions;

(iv) relevant material provided by the defendant, for example documents relating to personal mitigation; and

(v)   the minutes of any meetings between the parties and any correspondence generated in the plea discussions.

The parties should be prepared to provide additional material at the request of the court.

B.21 The court should at all times have regard to the length of time that has elapsed since the date of the occurrence of the events giving rise to the plea discussions, the time taken to interview the defendant, the date of charge and the prospective trial date (if the matter were to proceed to trial) so as to ensure that its consideration of the plea agreement and sentencing submissions does not cause any unnecessary further delay.

Status of plea agreement and joint sentencing submissions

B.22 Where a plea agreement and joint sentencing submissions are submitted, it remains entirely a matter for the court to decide how to deal with the case. The judge retains the absolute discretion to refuse to accept the plea agreement and to sentence otherwise than in accordance with the sentencing submissions made under the Attorney General's Plea Discussion Guidelines.

B.23 Sentencing submissions should draw the court's attention to any applicable range in any relevant guideline, and to any ancillary orders that may be applicable. Sentencing submissions should not include a specific sentence or agreed range other than the ranges set out in sentencing guidelines or authorities.

B.24 Prior to pleading guilty in accordance with the plea agreement, the defendant(s) may apply to the court for an indication of the likely maximum sentence under the procedure set out below (a '*Goodyear* indication').

B.25 In the event that the judge indicates a sentence or passes a sentence which is not within the submissions made on sentencing, the plea agreement remains binding.

B.26 If the defendant does not plead guilty in accordance with the plea agreement, or if a defendant who has pleaded guilty in accordance with a plea agreement, successfully applies to withdraw his plea under Rule 39.3 of the Criminal Procedure Rules, the signed plea agreement may be treated as confession evidence, and may be used against the defendant at a later stage in these or any other proceedings. Any credit for a timely guilty plea may be lost. The court may exercise its discretion under section 78 of the Police and Criminal Evidence Act 1984 to exclude any such evidence if it appears to the court that, having regard to all the circumstances, including the circumstances in which the evidence was obtained, the admission of the evidence would have such an adverse effect on the fairness of the proceedings that the court ought not to admit it.

B.27 Where a defendant has failed to plead guilty in accordance with a plea agreement, the case is unlikely to be ready for trial immediately. The prosecution may have been commenced earlier than it otherwise would have been, in reliance upon the defendant's agreement to plead guilty. This is likely to be a relevant consideration for the court in deciding whether or not to grant an application to adjourn or stay the proceedings to allow the matter to be prepared for trial in accordance with the protocol on the 'Control and Management of Heavy Fraud and other Complex Criminal Cases', or as required.

PD-57   **CPD VII Sentencing C: INDICATIONS OF SENTENCE: *R v Goodyear***

C.1 Prior to pleading guilty, it is open to a defendant in the Crown Court to request from the judge an indication of the maximum sentence that would be imposed if a guilty plea were to be tendered at that stage in the proceedings, in accordance with the guidance in *R v Goodyear* [2005] EWCA Crim 888, [2005] 1 WLR 2532, [2005] 2 Cr App R 20. The defence should notify the court and the prosecution of the intention to seek an indication in advance of any hearing.

C.2 Attention is drawn to the guidance set out in paragraphs 53 and following of *R v Goodyear*. The objective of the *Goodyear* guidelines is to safeguard against the creation or appearance of judicial pressure on a defendant. Any advance indication given should be the maximum sentence if a guilty plea were to be tendered at that stage of the proceedings only; the judge should not indicate the maximum possible sentence following conviction by a jury after trial. The judge should only give a *Goodyear* indication if one is requested by the defendant, although the judge can, in an appropriate case, remind the defence advocate of the defendant's entitlement to seek an advance indication of sentence.

C.3 Whether to give a *Goodyear* indication, and whether to give reasons for a refusal, is a matter for the discretion of the judge, to be exercised in accordance with the principles outlined by the Court of Appeal in that case. Such indications should normally not be given if there is a dispute as to the basis of plea unless the judge concludes that he or she can properly deal with the case without the need for a *Newton* hearing. If there is a basis of plea agreed by the prosecution and defence, it must be reduced into writing and a copy provided to the judge. As always, any basis of plea will be subject to the approval of the court. In cases where a dispute arises, the procedure in *R v Underwood* should be followed prior to the court considering a sentence indication further, as set out above. The judge should not become involved in negotiations about the acceptance of pleas or any agreed basis of plea, nor should a request be made for an indication of the different sentences that might be imposed if various different pleas were to be offered.

C.4 There should be no prosecution opening nor should the judge hear mitigation. However, during the sentence indication process the prosecution advocate is expected to assist the court by ensuring that the court has received all of the prosecution evidence, any statement from the victim about the impact of the offence, and any relevant previous convictions. Further, where appropriate, the prosecution should provide references to the relevant statutory powers of the court, relevant sentencing guidelines and authorities, and such other assistance as the court requires.

C.5 Attention is drawn to paragraph 70(d) of *Goodyear* which emphasises that the prosecution 'should not say anything which may create the impression that the sentence indication has the support or approval of the Crown.' This prohibition against the Crown indicating its approval of a particular sentence applies in all circumstances when a defendant is being sentenced, including when joint sentencing submissions are made.

C.6 An indication, once given, is, save in exceptional circumstances (such as arose in *R v Newman* [2010] EWCA Crim 1566, [2011] 1 Cr App R (S) 68), binding on the judge who gave it, and any other judge, subject to overriding statutory obligations such as those following a finding of 'dangerousness'. In circumstances where a judge proposes to depart from a *Goodyear* indication this must only be done in a way that does not give rise to unfairness (see *Newman*). However, if the defendant does not plead guilty, the indication will not thereafter bind the court.

C.7 If the offence is a specified offence such that the defendant might be liable to an assessment of 'dangerousness' in accordance with the Criminal Justice Act 2003 it is unlikely that the necessary material for such an assessment will be available.. The court can still proceed to give an indication of sentence, but should state clearly the limitations of the indication that can be given.

C.8 A *Goodyear* indication should be given in open court in the presence of the defendant but any reference to the hearing is not admissible in any subsequent trial; and reporting restrictions should normally be imposed.

CPD VII Sentencing D: Facts to be Stated on Pleas of Guilty   PD-58

D.1 To enable the press and the public to know the circumstances of an offence of which an accused has been convicted and for which he is to be sentenced, in relation to each offence to which an accused has pleaded guilty the prosecution shall state those facts in open court, before sentence is imposed.

CPD VII Sentencing E: Concurrent and Consecutive Sentences   PD-59

E.1 Where a court passes on a defendant more than one term of imprisonment, the court should state in the presence of the defendant whether the terms are to be concurrent or consecutive. Should this not be done, the court clerk should ask the court, before the defendant leaves court, to do so.

E.2 If a defendant is, at the time of sentence, already serving two or more consecutive terms of imprisonment and the court intends to increase the total period of imprisonment, it should use the expression 'consecutive to the total period of imprisonment to which you are already subject' rather than 'at the expiration of the term of imprisonment you are now serving', as the defendant may not then be serving the last of the terms to which he is already subject.

E.3 The Sentencing Council has issued a definitive guideline on Totality which should be consulted. Under section 125(1) of the Coroners and Justice Act 2009, for offences committed after 6 April 2010, the guideline must be followed unless it would be contrary to the interests of justice to do so.

CPD VII Sentencing F: Victim Personal Statements   PD-60

F.1 Victims of crime are invited to make a statement, known as a Victim Personal Statement ('VPS'). The statement gives victims a formal opportunity to say how a crime has affected them. It may help to identify whether they have a particular need for information, support and protection. The court will take the statement into account when determining sentence. In some circumstances, it may be appropriate for relatives of a victim to make a VPS, for example where the victim has died as a result of the relevant criminal conduct. The revised Code of Practice for Victims of Crime, published on 29 October 2013 gives further information about victims' entitlements within the criminal justice system, and the duties placed on criminal justice agencies when dealing with victims of crime.

F.2   When a police officer takes a statement from a victim, the victim should be told about the scheme and given the chance to make a VPS. The decision about whether or not to make a VPS is entirely a matter for the victim; no pressure should be brought to bear on their decision, and no conclusion should be drawn if they choose not to make such a statement. A VPS or a further VPS may be made (in proper s.9 form, see below) at any time prior to the disposal of the case. It will not normally be appropriate for a VPS to be made after the disposal of the case; there may be rare occasions between sentence and appeal when a further VPS may be necessary, for example, when the victim was injured and the final prognosis was not available at the date of sentence. However, VPS after disposal should be confined to presenting up to date factual material, such as medical information, and should be used sparingly.

F.3   If the court is presented with a VPS the following approach, subject to the further guidance given by the Court of Appeal in *R v Perkins; Bennett; Hall* [2013] EWCA Crim 323, [2013] Crim L.R. 533, should be adopted:

   a)   The VPS and any evidence in support should be considered and taken into account by the court, prior to passing sentence.

   b)   Evidence of the effects of an offence on the victim contained in the VPS or other statement, must be in proper form, that is a witness statement made under section 9 of the Criminal Justice Act 1967 or an expert's report; and served in good time upon the defendant's solicitor or the defendant, if he or she is not represented. Except where inferences can properly be drawn from the nature of or circumstances surrounding the offence, a sentencing court must not make assumptions unsupported by evidence about the effects of an offence on the victim. The maker of a VPS may be cross-examined on its content.

   c)   At the discretion of the court, the VPS may also be read aloud or played in open court, in whole or in part, or it may be summarised. If the VPS is to be read aloud, the court should also determine who should do so. In making these decisions, the court should take account of the victim's preferences, and follow them unless there is good reason not to do so; examples of this include the inadmissibility of the content or the potentially harmful consequences for the victim or others. Court hearings should not be adjourned solely to allow the victim to attend court to read the VPS. For the purposes of CPD I General matters 5B: Access to information held by the court, a VPS that is read aloud or played in open court in whole or in part should be considered as such, and no longer treated as a confidential document.

   d)   In all cases it will be appropriate for a VPS to be referred to in the course of the sentencing hearing and/or in the sentencing remarks.

   e)   The court must pass what it judges to be the appropriate sentence having regard to the circumstances of the offence and of the offender, taking into account, so far as the court considers it appropriate, the impact on the victim. The opinions of the victim or the victim's close relatives as to what the sentence should be are therefore not relevant, unlike the consequences of the offence on them. Victims should be advised of this. If, despite the advice, opinions as to sentence are included in the statement, the court should pay no attention to them.

PD-61   CPD VII Sentencing G: Families Bereaved by Homicide and other Criminal Conduct

G.1   In cases in which the victim has died as a result of the relevant criminal conduct, the victim's family is not a party to the proceedings, but does have an interest in the case. Bereaved families have particular entitlements under the Code of Practice for Victims of Crime. All parties should have regard to the needs of the victim's family and ensure that the trial process does not expose bereaved families to avoidable intimidation, humiliation or distress.

G.2   In so far as it is compatible with family members' roles as witnesses, the court should consider the following measures:

   a)   Practical arrangements being discussed with the family and made in good time before the trial, such as seating for family members in the courtroom; if appropriate, in an alternative area, away from the public gallery;

   b)   Warning being given to families if the evidence on a certain day is expected to be particularly distressing;

c) Ensuring that appropriate use is made of the scheme for Victim Personal Statements, in accordance with the paragraphs above.

G.3   The sentencer should consider providing a written copy of the sentencing remarks to the family after sentence has been passed. Sentencers should tend in favour of providing such a copy, unless there is good reason not to do so, and the copy should be provided as soon as is reasonably practicable after the sentencing hearing.

CPD VII Sentencing H: Community Impact Statements

PD-62

H.1   A community impact statement may be prepared by the police to make the court aware of particular crime trends in the local area and the impact of these on the local community.

H.2   Such statements must be in proper form, that is a witness statement made under section 9 of the Criminal Justice Act 1967 or an expert's report; and served in good time upon the defendant's solicitor or the defendant, if he is not represented.

H.3   The community impact statement and any evidence in support should be considered and taken into account by the court, prior to passing sentence. The statement should be referred to in the course of the sentencing hearing and/or in the sentencing remarks. Subject to the court's discretion, the contents of the statement may be summarised or read out in open court.

H.4   The court must pass what it judges to be the appropriate sentence having regard to the circumstances of the offence and of the offender, taking into account, so far as the court considers it appropriate, the impact on the local community. Opinions as to what the sentence should be are therefore not relevant. If, despite the advice, opinions as to sentence are included in the statement, the court should pay no attention to them.

H.5   Except where inferences can properly be drawn from the nature of or circumstances surrounding the offence, a sentencing court must not make assumptions unsupported by evidence about the effects of an offence on the local community.

H.6   It will not be appropriate for a Community Impact Statement to be made after disposal of the case but before an appeal.

CPD VII Sentencing I: Impact Statements for Businesses

PD-63

I.1   Individual victims of crime are invited to make a statement, known as a Victim Personal Statement ('VPS'), see CPD VII Sentencing F. If the victim, or one of the victims, is a business or enterprise (including charities but excluding public sector bodies), of any size, a nominated representative may make an Impact Statement for Business ('ISB'). The ISB gives a formal opportunity for the court to be informed how a crime has affected a business. The court will take the statement into account when determining sentence. This does not prevent individual employees from making a VPS about the impact of the same crime on them as individuals. Indeed the ISB should be about the impact on the business exclusively, and the impact on any individual included within a VPS.

I.2   When a police officer takes statements about the alleged offence, he or she should also inform the business about the scheme. An ISB may be made to the police at that time, or the ISB template may be downloaded from www.police.uk, completed and emailed or posted to the relevant police contact. Guidance on how to complete the form is available on www.police.uk and on the CPS website. There is no obligation on any business to make an ISB.

I.3   An ISB or an updated ISB may be made (in proper s.9 form, see below) at any time prior to the disposal of the case. It will not be appropriate for an ISB to be made after disposal of the case but before an appeal.

I.4   A business wishing to make an ISB should consider carefully who to nominate as the representative to make the statement on its behalf. A person making an ISB on behalf of a business, the nominated representative, must be authorised to do so on behalf of the business, either by nature of their position within the business, such as a director or owner, or by having been suitably authorised, such as by the owner or Board of Directors. The nominated representative must also be in a position to give admissible evidence about the impact of the crime on the business. This will usually be through first hand personal knowledge, or using business documents (as defined in section 117 of the Criminal Justice Act 2003). The most appropriate person will vary depending on the nature of the crime, and the size and structure of the business and may for example include a manager, director, chief executive or shop owner.

I.5   If the nominated representative leaves the business before the case comes to court, he or she will usually remain the representative, as the ISB made by him or her will still provide the best evidence of the impact of the crime, and he or she could still be asked to attend court. Nominated representatives should be made aware of the on-going nature of the role at the time of making the ISB.

Criminal Procedure Rules 2013 and Criminal Practice Directions

I.6   If necessary a further ISB may be provided to the police if there is a change in circumstances. This could be made by an alternative nominated representative. However, the new ISB will usually supplement, not replace, the original ISB and again must contain admissible evidence. The prosecutor will decide which ISB to serve on the defence as evidence, and any ISB that is not served in evidence will be included in the unused material and considered for disclosure to the defence.

I.7   The ISB must be made in proper form, that is as a witness statement made under section 9 of the Criminal Justice Act 1967 or an expert's report; and served in good time upon the defendant's solicitor or the defendant, if he or she is not represented. The maker of an ISB can be cross-examined on its content.

I.8   The ISB and any evidence in support should be considered and taken into account by the court, prior to passing sentence. The statement should be referred to in the course of the sentencing hearing and/or in the sentencing remarks. Subject to the court's discretion, the contents of the statement may be summarised or read out in open court; the views of the business should be taken into account in reaching a decision.

I.9   The court must pass what it judges to be the appropriate sentence having regard to the circumstances of the offence and of the offender, taking into account, so far as the court considers it appropriate, the impact on the victims, including any business victim. Opinions as to what the sentence should be are therefore not relevant. If, despite the advice, opinions as to sentence are included in the statement, the court should pay no attention to them.

I.10   Except where inferences can properly be drawn from the nature of or circumstances surrounding the offence, a sentencing court must not make assumptions unsupported by evidence about the effects of an offence on a business.

PD-64 CPD VII Sentencing J: Binding Over Orders and Conditional Discharges

J.1   This direction takes into account the judgments of the European Court of Human Rights in *Steel v United Kingdom* (1999) 28 EHRR 603, [1998] Crim LR 893 and in *Hashman and Harrup v United Kingdom* (2000) 30 EHRR 241, [2000] Crim LR 185. Its purpose is to give practical guidance, in the light of those two judgments, on the practice of imposing binding over orders. The direction applies to orders made under the court's common law powers, under the Justices of the Peace Act 1361, under section 1(7) of the Justices of the Peace Act 1968 and under section 115 of the Magistrates' Courts Act 1980. This direction also gives guidance concerning the court's power to bind over parents or guardians under section 150 of the Powers of Criminal Courts (Sentencing) Act 2000 and the Crown Court's power to bind over to come up for judgment. The court's power to impose a conditional discharge under section 12 of the Powers of Criminal Courts (Sentencing) Act 2000 is also covered by this direction.

Binding over to keep the peace

J.2   Before imposing a binding over order, the court must be satisfied so that it is sure that a breach of the peace involving violence, or an imminent threat of violence, has occurred or that there is a real risk of violence in the future. Such violence may be perpetrated by the individual who will be subject to the order or by a third party as a natural consequence of the individual's conduct.

J.3   In light of the judgment in *Hashman*, courts should no longer bind an individual over 'to be of good behaviour'. Rather than binding an individual over to 'keep the peace' in general terms, the court should identify the specific conduct or activity from which the individual must refrain.

Written order

J.4   When making an order binding an individual over to refrain from specified types of conduct or activities, the details of that conduct or those activities should be specified by the court in a written order, served on all relevant parties. The court should state its reasons for the making of the order, its length and the amount of the recognisance. The length of the order should be proportionate to the harm sought to be avoided and should not generally exceed 12 months.

Evidence

J.5   Sections 51 to 57 of the Magistrates' Courts Act 1980 set out the jurisdiction of the magistrates' court to hear an application made on complaint and the procedure which is to be followed. This includes a requirement under section 53 to hear evidence and the parties, before making any order. This practice should be applied to all cases in the magistrates' court and the Crown Court where the court is considering imposing a binding over order. The court should give the individual who would be subject to the order and the prosecutor the opportunity to make representations, both as to the making of the order and as to its terms. The court should also hear any admissible evidence the parties wish to call and which has not already been heard in the proceedings. Particularly careful consideration may be required where the individual who would be subject to the order is a witness in the proceedings.

J.6   Where there is an admission which is sufficient to found the making of a binding over order and/or the individual consents to the making of the order, the court should nevertheless hear sufficient representations and, if appropriate, evidence, to satisfy itself that an order is appropriate in all the circumstances and to be clear about the terms of the order.

J.7   Where there is an allegation of breach of a binding over order and this is contested, the court should hear representations and evidence, including oral evidence, from the parties before making a finding. If unrepresented and no opportunity has been given previously the court should give a reasonable period for the person said to have breached the binding over order to find representation.

Burden and standard of proof

J.8   The court should be satisfied so that it is sure of the matters complained of before a binding over order may be imposed. Where the procedure has been commenced on complaint, the burden of proof rests on the complainant. In all other circumstances, the burden of proof rests upon the prosecution.

J.9   Where there is an allegation of breach of a binding over order, the court should be satisfied on the balance of probabilities that the defendant is in breach before making any order for forfeiture of a recognisance. The burden of proof shall rest on the prosecution.

Recognisance

J.10   The court must be satisfied on the merits of the case that an order for binding over is appropriate and should announce that decision before considering the amount of the recognisance. If unrepresented, the individual who is made subject to the binding over order should be told he has a right of appeal from the decision.

J.11   When fixing the amount of recognisance, courts should have regard to the individual's financial resources and should hear representations from the individual or his legal representatives regarding finances.

J.12   A recognisance is made in the form of a bond giving rise to a civil debt on breach of the order.

Refusal to enter into a recognisance

J.13   If there is any possibility that an individual will refuse to enter a recognisance, the court should consider whether there are any appropriate alternatives to a binding over order (for example, continuing with a prosecution). Where there are no appropriate alternatives and the individual continues to refuse to enter into the recognisance, the court may commit the individual to custody. In the magistrates' court, the power to do so will derive from section 1(7) of the Justices of the Peace Act 1968 or, more rarely, from section 115(3) of the Magistrates' Courts Act 1980, and the court should state which power it is acting under; in the Crown Court, this is a common law power.

J.14   Before the court exercises a power to commit the individual to custody, the individual should be given the opportunity to see a duty solicitor or another legal representative and be represented in proceedings if the individual so wishes. Public funding should generally be granted to cover representation. In the Crown Court this rests with the Judge who may grant a Representation Order.

J.15   In the event that the individual does not take the opportunity to seek legal advice, the court shall give the individual a final opportunity to comply with the request and shall explain the consequences of a failure to do so.

Antecedents

J.16   Courts are reminded of the provisions of section 7(5) of the Rehabilitation of Offenders Act 1974 which excludes from a person's antecedents any order of the court 'with respect to any person otherwise than on a conviction'.

Binding over to come up for judgment

J.17   If the Crown Court is considering binding over an individual to come up for judgment, the court should specify any conditions with which the individual is to comply in the meantime and not specify that the individual is to be of good behaviour.

J.18   The Crown Court should, if the individual is unrepresented, explain the consequences of a breach of the binding over order in these circumstances.

Binding over of parent or guardian

J.19 Where a court is considering binding over a parent or guardian under section 150 of the Powers of Criminal Courts (Sentencing) Act 2000 to enter into a recognisance to take proper care of and exercise proper control over a child or young person, the court should specify the actions which the parent or guardian is to take.

Security for good behaviour

J.20 Where a court is imposing a conditional discharge under section 12 of the Powers of Criminal Courts (Sentencing) Act 2000, it has the power, under section 12(6) to make an order that a person who consents to do so give security for the good behaviour of the offender. When making such an order, the court should specify the type of conduct from which the offender is to refrain.

PD-65   **CPD VII Sentencing K: Committal for Sentence**

K.1 Rule 42.10 applies when a case is committed to the Crown Court for sentence and specifies the information and documentation that must be provided by the magistrates' court. On a committal for sentence any reasons given by the magistrates for their decision should be included with the documents. All of these documents should be made available to the judge in the Crown Court if the judge requires them, in order to decide before the hearing questions of listing or representation or the like. They will also be available to the court during the hearing if it becomes necessary or desirable for the court to see what happened in the lower court.

PD-66   **CPD VII Sentencing L: Imposition of Life Sentences**

L.1 Section 82A of the Powers of Criminal Courts (Sentencing) Act 2000 empowers a judge when passing a sentence of life imprisonment, where such a sentence is not fixed by law, to specify by order such part of the sentence ('the relevant part') as shall be served before the prisoner may require the Secretary of State to refer his case to the Parole Board. This is applicable to defendants under the age of 18 years as well as to adult defendants.

L.2 Thus the life sentence falls into two parts:

    (a) the relevant part, which consists of the period of detention imposed for punishment and deterrence, taking into account the seriousness of the offence; and

    (b) the remaining part of the sentence, during which the prisoner's detention will be governed by consideration of risk to the public.

L.3 The judge is not obliged by statute to make use of the provisions of section 82A when passing a life sentence. However, the judge should do so, save in the very exceptional case where the judge considers that the offence is so serious that detention for life is justified by the seriousness of the offence alone, irrespective of the risk to the public. In such a case, the judge should state this in open court when passing sentence.

L.4 In cases where the judge is to specify the relevant part of the sentence under section 82A, the judge should permit the advocate for the defendant to address the court as to the appropriate length of the relevant part. Where no relevant part is to be specified, the advocate for the defendant should be permitted to address the court as to the appropriateness of this course of action.

L.5 In specifying the relevant part of the sentence, the judge should have regard to the specific terms of section 82A and should indicate the reasons for reaching his decision as to the length of the relevant part.

PD-67   **CPD VII Sentencing M: Mandatory Life Sentences**

M.1 The purpose of this section is to give practical guidance as to the procedure for passing a mandatory life sentence under section 269 and schedule 21 of the Criminal Justice Act 2003 ('the Act'). This direction also gives guidance as to the transitional arrangements under section 276 and schedule 22 of the Act. It clarifies the correct approach to looking at the practice of the Secretary of State prior to December 2002 for the purposes of schedule 22 of the Act, in the light of the judgment in *R v Sullivan, Gibbs, Elener and Elener* [2004] EWCA Crim 1762, [2005] 1 Cr App R 3, [2005] 1 Cr App R (S) 67.

M.2 Section 269 came into force on 18 December 2003. Under section 269, all courts passing a mandatory life sentence must either announce in open court the minimum term the prisoner must serve before the Parole Board can consider release on licence under the provisions of section 28 of the Crime (Sentences) Act 1997 (as amended by section 275 of the Act), or announce that the seriousness of the offence is so exceptionally high that the early release provisions should not apply at all (a 'whole life order').

M.3 In setting the minimum term, the court must set the term it considers appropriate taking into account the seriousness of the offence. In considering the seriousness of the offence, the court must have regard to the general principles set out in Schedule 21 of the Act as amended and any guidelines relating to offences in general which are relevant to the case and not incompatible with the provisions of Schedule 21. Although it is necessary to have regard to such guidance, it is always permissible not to apply the guidance if a judge considers there are reasons for not following it. It is always necessary to have regard to the need to do justice in the particular case. However, if a court departs from any of the starting points given in Schedule 21, the court is under a duty to state its reasons for doing so (section 270(2) (b) of the Act).

M.4 Schedule 21 states that the first step is to choose one of five starting points: 'whole life', 30 years, 25 years, 15 years or 12 years. Where the 15 year starting point has been chosen, judges should have in mind that this starting point encompasses a very broad range of murders. At paragraph 35 of *Sullivan*, the court found it should not be assumed that Parliament intended to raise all minimum terms that would previously have had a lower starting point, to 15 years.

M.5 Where the offender was 21 or over at the time of the offence, and the court takes the view that the murder is so grave that the offender ought to spend the rest of his life in prison, the appropriate starting point is a 'whole life order' (paragraph 4(1) of Schedule 21). The effect of such an order is that the early release provisions in section 28 of the Crime (Sentences) Act 1997 will not apply. Such an order should only be specified where the court considers that the seriousness of the offence (or the combination of the offence and one or more other offences associated with it) is exceptionally high. Paragraph 4(2) sets out examples of cases where it would normally be appropriate to take the 'whole life order' as the appropriate starting point.

M.6 Where the offender is aged 18 to 20 and commits a murder that is so serious that it would require a whole life order if committed by an offender aged 21 or over, the appropriate starting point will be 30 years. (Paragraph 5(2) (h) of Schedule 21).

M.7 Where a case is not so serious as to require a 'whole life order' but where the seriousness of the offence is particularly high and the offender was aged 18 or over when he committed the offence, the appropriate starting point is 30 years (paragraph 5(1) of Schedule 21). Paragraph 5(2) sets out examples of cases where a 30 year starting point would normally be appropriate (if they do not require a 'whole life order').

M.8 Where the offender was aged 18 or over when he committed the offence, took a knife or other weapon to the scene intending to commit any offence or have it available to use as a weapon, and used it in committing the murder, the offence is normally to be regarded as sufficiently serious for an appropriate starting point of 25 years (paragraph 5A of Schedule 21).

M.9 Where the offender was aged 18 or over when he committed the offence and the case does not fall within paragraph 4 (1), 5 (1) or 5A (1) of Schedule 21, the appropriate starting point is 15 years (see paragraph 6).

M.10 18 to 20 year olds are only the subject of the 30-year, 25-year and 15-year starting points.

M.11 The appropriate starting point when setting a sentence of detention during Her Majesty's pleasure for offenders aged under 18 when they committed the offence is always 12 years (paragraph 7 of Schedule 21).

M.12 The second step after choosing a starting point is to take account of any aggravating or mitigating factors which would justify a departure from the starting point. Additional aggravating factors (other than those specified in paragraphs 4(2), 5(2) and 5A) are listed at paragraph 10 of Schedule 21. Examples of mitigating factors are listed at paragraph 11 of Schedule 21. Taking into account the aggravating and mitigating features, the court may add to or subtract from the starting point to arrive at the appropriate punitive period.

M.13 The third step is that the court should consider the effect of section 143(2) of the Act in relation to previous convictions; section 143(3) of the Act where the offence was committed whilst the offender was on bail; and section 144 of the Act where the offender has pleaded guilty (paragraph 12 of Schedule 21). The court should then take into account what credit the offender would have received for a remand in custody under section 240 or 240ZA of the Act and/or for a remand on bail subject to a qualifying curfew condition under section 240A, but for the fact that the mandatory sentence is one of life imprisonment. Where the offender has been thus remanded in connection with the offence or a related offence, the court should have in mind that no credit will otherwise be given for this time when the prisoner is considered for early release. The appropriate time to take it into account is when setting the minimum term. The court should make any appropriate subtraction from the punitive period it would otherwise impose, in order to reach the minimum term.

M.14 Following these calculations, the court should have arrived at the appropriate minimum term to be announced in open court. As paragraph 9 of Schedule 21 makes clear, the judge retains ultimate discretion and the court may arrive at any minimum term from any starting point. The minimum term is subject to appeal by the offender under section 271 of the Act and subject to review on a reference by the Attorney-General under section 272 of the Act.

PD-68   **CPD VII Sentencing N: Transitional Arrangements for Sentences where the Offence was Committed before 18 December 2003**

N.1 Where the court is passing a sentence of mandatory life imprisonment for an offence committed before 18 December 2003, the court should take a fourth step in determining the minimum term in accordance with section 276 and Schedule 22 of the Act.

N.2 The purpose of those provisions is to ensure that the sentence does not breach the principle of non-retroactivity, by ensuring that a lower minimum term would not have been imposed for the offence when it was committed. Before setting the minimum term, the court must check whether the proposed term is greater than that which the Secretary of State would probably have notified under the practice followed by the Secretary of State before December 2002.

N.3 The decision in *Sullivan, Gibbs, Elener and Elener* [2004] EWCA Crim 1762, [2005] 1 Cr App R 3, [2005] 1 Cr App R (S) 67 gives detailed guidance as to the correct approach to this practice and judges passing mandatory life sentences where the murder was committed prior to 18 December 2003 are well advised to read that judgment before proceeding.

N.4 The practical result of that judgment is that in sentences where the murder was committed before 31 May 2002, the best guide to what would have been the practice of the Secretary of State is the letter sent to judges by Lord Bingham CJ on 10th February 1997, the relevant parts of which are set out below.

N.5 The practice of Lord Bingham, as set out in his letter of 10 February 1997, was to take 14 years as the period actually to be served for the 'average', 'normal' or 'unexceptional' murder. Examples of factors he outlined as capable, in appropriate cases, of mitigating the normal penalty were:

(1) Youth;

(2) Age (where relevant to physical capacity on release or the likelihood of the defendant dying in prison);

(3) [Intellectual disability or mental disorder];

(4) Provocation (in a non-technical sense), or an excessive response to a personal threat;

(5) The absence of an intention to kill;

(6) Spontaneity and lack of premeditation (beyond that necessary to constitute the offence: e.g., a sudden response to family pressure or to prolonged and eventually insupportable stress);

(7) Mercy killing;

(8) A plea of guilty, or hard evidence of remorse or contrition.

N.6 Lord Bingham then listed the following factors as likely to call for a sentence more severe than the norm:

(1) Evidence of planned, professional, revenge or contract killing;

(2) The killing of a child or a very old or otherwise vulnerable victim;

(3) Evidence of sadism, gratuitous violence, or sexual maltreatment, humiliation or degradation before the killing;

(4) Killing for gain (in the course of burglary, robbery, blackmail, insurance fraud, etc.);

(5) Multiple killings;

(6) The killing of a witness, or potential witness, to defeat the ends of justice;

(7) The killing of those doing their public duty (policemen, prison officers, postmasters, firemen, judges, etc.);

(8) Terrorist or politically motivated killings;

(9) The use of firearms or other dangerous weapons, whether carried for defensive or offensive reasons;

(10) A substantial record of serious violence;

(11) Macabre attempts to dismember or conceal the body.

N.7 Lord Bingham further stated that the fact that a defendant was under the influence of drink or drugs at the time of the killing is so common he would be inclined to treat it as neutral. But in the not unfamiliar case in which a couple, inflamed by drink, indulge in a violent quarrel in which one dies, often against a background of longstanding drunken violence, then he would tend to recommend a term somewhat below the norm.

N.8 Lord Bingham went on to say that given the intent necessary for proof of murder, the consequences of taking life and the understandable reaction of relatives to the deceased, a substantial term will almost always be called for, save perhaps in a truly venial case of mercy killing. While a recommendation of a punitive term longer than, say, 30 years will be very rare indeed, there should not be any upper limit. Some crimes will certainly call for terms very well in excess of the norm.

N.9 For the purposes of sentences where the murder was committed after 31 May 2002 and before 18 December 2003, the judge should apply the Practice Statement handed down on 31 May 2002 reproduced at paragraphs N.10 to N.20 below.

N.10 This Statement replaces the previous single normal tariff of 14 years by substituting a higher and a normal starting point of respectively 16 (comparable to 32 years) and 12 years (comparable to 24 years). These starting points have then to be increased or reduced because of aggravating or mitigating factors such as those referred to below. It is emphasised that they are no more than starting points.

The normal starting point of 12 years

N.11 Cases falling within this starting point will normally involve the killing of an adult victim, arising from a quarrel or loss of temper between two people known to each other. It will not have the characteristics referred to in paragraph N.13. Exceptionally, the starting point may be reduced because of the sort of circumstances described in the next paragraph.

N.12 The normal starting point can be reduced because the murder is one where the offender's culpability is significantly reduced, for example, because:

(a) the case came close to the borderline between murder and manslaughter; or

(b) the offender suffered from mental disorder, or from a mental disability which lowered the degree of his criminal responsibility for the killing, although not affording a defence of diminished responsibility; or

(c) the offender was provoked (in a non-technical sense) such as by prolonged and eventually unsupportable stress; or

(d) the case involved an over-reaction in self-defence; or

(e) the offence was a mercy killing.

These factors could justify a reduction to 8/9 years (equivalent to 16/18 years).

The higher starting point of 15/16 years

N.13 The higher starting point will apply to cases where the offender's culpability was exceptionally high, or the victim was in a particularly vulnerable position. Such cases will be characterised by a feature which makes the crime especially serious, such as:

(a) the killing was 'professional' or a contract killing;

(b) the killing was politically motivated;

(c) the killing was done for gain (in the course of a burglary, robbery etc.);

(d) the killing was intended to defeat the ends of justice (as in the killing of a witness or potential witness);

(e) the victim was providing a public service;

(f) the victim was a child or was otherwise vulnerable;

(g) the killing was racially aggravated;

(h) the victim was deliberately targeted because of his or her religion or sexual orientation;

(i) there was evidence of sadism, gratuitous violence or sexual maltreatment, humiliation or degradation of the victim before the killing;

(j) extensive and/or multiple injuries were inflicted on the victim before death;

(k) the offender committed multiple murders.

Variation of the starting point

N.14 Whichever starting point is selected in a particular case, it may be appropriate for the trial judge to vary the starting point upwards or downwards, to take account of aggravating or mitigating factors, which relate to either the offence or the offender, in the particular case.

N.15 Aggravating factors relating to the offence can include:

(a) the fact that the killing was planned;

(b) the use of a firearm;

(c) arming with a weapon in advance;

(d) concealment of the body, destruction of the crime scene and/or dismemberment of the body;

(e) particularly in domestic violence cases, the fact that the murder was the culmination of cruel and violent behaviour by the offender over a period of time.

N.16 Aggravating factors relating to the offender will include the offender's previous record and failures to respond to previous sentences, to the extent that this is relevant to culpability rather than to risk.

N.17 Mitigating factors relating to the offence will include:

(a) an intention to cause grievous bodily harm, rather than to kill;

(b) spontaneity and lack of pre-meditation.

N.18 Mitigating factors relating to the offender may include:

(a) the offender's age;

(b) clear evidence of remorse or contrition;

(c) a timely plea of guilty.

Very serious cases

N.19 A substantial upward adjustment may be appropriate in the most serious cases, for example, those involving a substantial number of murders, or if there are several factors identified as attracting the higher starting point present. In suitable cases, the result might even be a minimum term of 30 years (equivalent to 60 years) which would offer little or no hope of the offender's eventual release. In cases of exceptional gravity, the judge, rather than setting a whole life minimum term, can state that there is no minimum period which could properly be set in that particular case.

N.20 Among the categories of case referred to in paragraph N.13, some offences may be especially grave. These include cases in which the victim was performing his duties as a prison officer at the time of the crime, or the offence was a terrorist or sexual or sadistic murder, or involved a young child. In such a case, a term of 20 years and upwards could be appropriate.

N.21 In following this guidance, judges should bear in mind the conclusion of the Court in *Sullivan* that the general effect of both these statements is the same. While Lord Bingham does not identify as many starting points, it is open to the judge to come to exactly the same decision irrespective of which was followed. Both pieces of guidance give the judge a considerable degree of discretion.

PD-69   CPD VII Sentencing P: Procedure for Announcing the Minimum Term in Open Court

P.1 Having gone through the three or four steps outlined above, the court is then under a duty, under section 270 of the Act, to state in open court, in ordinary language, its reasons for deciding on the minimum term or for passing a whole life order.

P.2 In order to comply with this duty, the court should state clearly the minimum term it has determined. In doing so, it should state which of the starting points it has chosen and its reasons for doing so. Where the court has departed from that starting point due to mitigating or aggravating features, it must state the reasons for that departure and any aggravating or mitigating features which have led to that departure. At that point, the court should also declare how much, if any, time is being deducted for time spent in custody and/or on bail subject to a qualifying curfew condition. The court must then explain that the minimum term is the minimum amount of time the prisoner will spend in prison, from the date of sentence, before the Parole Board can order early release. If it remains necessary for the protection of the public, the prisoner will continue to be detained after that date. The court should also state that where the prisoner has served the minimum term and the Parole Board has decided to direct release, the prisoner will remain on licence for the rest of his life and may be recalled to prison at any time.

P.3 Where the offender was 21 or over when he committed the offence and the court considers that the seriousness of the offence is so exceptionally high that a 'whole life order' is appropriate, the court should state clearly its reasons for reaching this conclusion. It should also explain that the early release provisions will not apply.

CRIMINAL PROCEDURE RULES   PART 42   SENTENCING PROCEDURES IN SPECIAL CASES

R-292   Reasons for not following usual sentencing requirements

42.1 (1) This rule applies where the court decides—

(a) not to follow a relevant sentencing guideline;

(b) not to make, where it could—

(i) a reparation order (unless it passes a custodial or community sentence),

(ii) a compensation order, or

(iii) a travel restriction order;

(c) not to order, where it could—

(i) that a suspended sentence of imprisonment is to take effect,

(ii) the endorsement of the defendant's driving record, or

(iii) the defendant's disqualification from driving, for the usual minimum period or at all;

(d) to pass a lesser sentence than it otherwise would have passed because the defendant has assisted, or has agreed to assist, an investigator or prosecutor in relation to an offence.

(2) The court must explain why it has so decided, when it explains the sentence that it has passed.

(3) Where paragraph (1)(d) applies, the court must arrange for such an explanation to be given to the defendant and to the prosecutor in writing, if the court thinks that it would not be in the public interest to explain in public.

Notice of requirements of suspended sentence and community, etc. orders

R-293

42.2 (1) This rule applies where the court—

(a) makes a suspended sentence order

(b) imposes a requirement under—

(i) a community sentence,

(ii) a youth rehabilitation order, or

(iii) a suspended sentence order; or

(c) orders the defendant to attend meetings with a supervisor.

(2) The court officer must notify—

(a) the defendant of—

(i) the length of the sentence suspended by a suspended sentence order, and

(ii) the period of the suspension;

(b) the defendant and, where the defendant is under 14, an appropriate adult, of—

(i) any requirement or requirements imposed, and

(ii) the identity of any responsible officer or supervisor, and the means by which that person may be contacted;

(c) any responsible officer or supervisor, and, where the defendant is under 14, the appropriate qualifying officer (if that is not the responsible officer), of—

(i) the defendant's name, address and telephone number (if available),

(ii) the offence or offences of which the defendant was convicted, and

(iii) the requirement or requirements imposed; and

(d) the person affected, where the court imposes a requirement—

(i) for the protection of that person from the defendant, or

(ii) requiring the defendant to reside with that person.

(3) If the court imposes an electronic monitoring requirement, the monitor of which is not the responsible officer, the court officer must—

(a) notify the defendant and, where the defendant is under 16, an appropriate adult, of the monitor's name, and the means by which the monitor may be contacted; and

(b) notify the monitor of—

(i) the defendant's name, address and telephone number (if available),

(ii) the offence or offences of which the defendant was convicted,

(iii) the place or places at which the defendant's presence must be monitored,

(iv) the period or periods during which the defendant's presence there must be monitored, and

(v) the identity of the responsible officer, and the means by which that officer may be contacted.

Notification requirements

R-294

42.3 (1) This rule applies where, on a conviction, sentence or order, legislation requires the defendant—

(a) to notify information to the police; or

(b) to be included in a barred list.

(2) The court must tell the defendant that notification requirements apply, and under what legislation.

Variation of sentence

R-295

42.4 (1) This rule—

(a) applies where a magistrates' court or the Crown Court can vary or rescind a sentence or order; and

(b) authorises the Crown Court, in addition to its other powers, to do so within the period of 56 days beginning with another defendant's acquittal or sentencing where—

(i)   defendants are tried separately in the Crown Court on the same or related facts alleged in one or more indictments, and

(ii) one is sentenced before another is acquitted or sentenced.

(2) The court may exercise its power—

(a) on application by a party; or

(b) on its own initiative.

(3) A party who wants the court to exercise that power must—

(a) apply in writing as soon as reasonably practicable after—

(i)   the sentence or order that that party wants the court to vary or rescind, or

(ii) where paragraph (1)(b) applies, the other defendant's acquittal or sentencing;

(b) serve the application on—

(i)   the court officer, and

(ii) each other party; and

(c) in the application—

(i)   explain why the sentence should be varied or rescinded,

(ii) specify the variation that the applicant proposes, and

(iii) if the application is late, explain why.

(4) The court must not exercise its power in the defendant's absence unless—

(a) the court makes a variation proposed by the defendant; or

(b) the defendant has had an opportunity to make representations at a hearing (whether or not the defendant in fact attends).

(5) The court may—

(a) extend (even after it has expired) the time limit under paragraph (3), unless the court's power to vary or rescind the sentence cannot be exercised; and

(b) allow an application to be made orally.

R-296   **Application to vary or discharge a compensation order**

42.5 (1) This rule applies where a magistrates' court can vary or discharge a compensation order on application by the defendant.

(2) A defendant who wants the court to exercise that power must—

(a) apply in writing as soon as practicable after becoming aware of the grounds for doing so;

(b) serve the application on the magistrates' court officer;

(c) where the compensation order was made in the Crown Court, serve a copy of the application on the Crown Court officer; and

(d) in the application, specify the compensation order that the defendant wants the court to vary or discharge and explain (as applicable)—

(i)   what civil court finding shows that the injury, loss or damage was less than it had appeared to be when the order was made,

(ii) in what circumstances the person for whose benefit the order was made has recovered the property for the loss of which it was made,

(iii) why a confiscation order makes the defendant now unable to pay compensation in full, or

(iv) in what circumstances the defendant's means have been reduced substantially and unexpectedly, and why they seem unlikely to increase for a considerable period.

(3) The court officer must serve a copy of the application on the person for whose benefit the compensation order was made.

(4) The court must not vary or discharge the compensation order unless—

(a) the defendant, and the person for whose benefit it was made, each has had an opportunity to make representations at a hearing (whether or not either in fact attends); and

(b) where the order was made in the Crown Court, the Crown Court has notified its consent.

R-297   **Application to remove, revoke or suspend a disqualification or restriction**

42.6 (1) This rule applies where, on application by the defendant, the court can remove, revoke or suspend a disqualification or restriction included in a sentence (except a disqualification from driving).

(2) A defendant who wants the court to exercise such a power must—

(a) apply in writing, no earlier than the date on which the court can exercise the power;

(b) serve the application on the court officer; and

(c) in the application—

(i)   specify the disqualification or restriction, and

(ii) explain why the defendant wants the court to remove, revoke or suspend it.

(3) The court officer must serve a copy of the application on the chief officer of police for the local justice area.

Application for a restitution order by the victim of a theft   R-298

42.7 (1) This rule applies where, on application by the victim of a theft, the court can order a defendant to give that person goods obtained with the proceeds of goods stolen in that theft.

(2) A person who wants the court to exercise that power if the defendant is convicted must—
   (a) apply in writing as soon as practicable (without waiting for the verdict);
   (b) serve the application on the court officer; and
   (c) in the application—
      (i) identify the goods, and
      (ii) explain why the applicant is entitled to them.

(3) The court officer must serve a copy of the application on each party.

(4) The court must not determine the application unless the applicant and each party has had an opportunity to make representations at a hearing (whether or not each in fact attends).

(5) The court may—
   (a) extend (even after it has expired) the time limit under paragraph (2); and
   (b) allow an application to be made orally.

Requests for medical reports, etc.   R-299

42.8 (1) This rule applies where the court—
   (a) requests a medical examination of the defendant and a report; or
   (b) requires information about the arrangements that could be made for the defendant where the court is considering—
      (i) a hospital order, or
      (ii) a guardianship order.

(2) Unless the court otherwise directs, the court officer must, as soon as practicable, serve on each person from whom a report or information is sought a note that—
   (a) specifies the power exercised by the court;
   (b) explains why the court seeks a report or information from that person; and
   (c) sets out or summarises any relevant information available to the court.

Information to be supplied on admission to hospital or guardianship   R-300

42.9 (1) This rule applies where the court—
   (a) orders the defendant's detention and treatment in hospital; or
   (b) makes a guardianship order.

(2) Unless the court otherwise directs, the court officer must, as soon as practicable, serve on (as applicable) the hospital or the guardian—
   (a) a record of the court's order;
   (b) such information as the court has received that appears likely to assist in treating or otherwise dealing with the defendant, including information about—
      (i) the defendant's mental condition,
      (ii) the defendant's other circumstances, and
      (iii) the circumstances of the offence.

Information to be supplied on committal for sentence, etc.   R-301

42.10 (1) This rule applies where a magistrates' court or the Crown Court convicts the defendant and—
   (a) commits or adjourns the case to another court—
      (i) for sentence, or
      (ii) for the defendant to be dealt with for breach of a deferred sentence, a conditional discharge, or a suspended sentence of imprisonment, imposed by that other court;
   (b) deals with a deferred sentence, a conditional discharge, or a suspended sentence of imprisonment, imposed by another court; or
   (c) makes an order that another court is, or may be, required to enforce.

(2) Unless the convicting court otherwise directs, the court officer must, as soon as practicable—
   (a) where paragraph (1)(a) applies, arrange the transmission from the convicting to the other court of relevant copy court records and other relevant documents, including any—
      (i) certificate of conviction,
      (ii) magistrates' court register entry,
      (iii) record relating to bail,

          (iv)   note of evidence,

          (v)   statement or other document introduced in evidence,

          (vi)   medical or other report,

          (vii)   representation order or application for such order, and

          (viii) interim driving disqualification;

    (b) where paragraph (1)(b) or (c) applies, arrange—

          (i)   the transmission from the convicting to the other court of notice of the convicting court's order, and

          (ii)   the recording of that order at the other court;

    (c) in every case, notify the defendant and, where the defendant is under 14, an appropriate adult, of the location of the other court.

R-302   Application to review sentence because of assistance given or withheld

42.11 (1) This rule applies where the Crown Court can reduce or increase a sentence on application by a prosecutor in a case in which—

    (a) since being sentenced, the defendant has assisted, or has agreed to assist, an investigator or prosecutor in relation to an offence; or

    (b) since receiving a reduced sentence for agreeing to give such assistance, the defendant has failed to do so.

  (2) A prosecutor who wants the court to exercise that power must—

    (a) apply in writing as soon as practicable after becoming aware of the grounds for doing so;

    (b) serve the application on—

          (i)   the court officer, and

          (ii)   the defendant; and

    (c) in the application—

          (i)   explain why the sentence should be reduced, or increased, as appropriate, and

          (ii)   identify any other matter relevant to the court's decision, including any sentencing guideline or guideline case.

  (3) The general rule is that the application must be determined by the judge who passed the sentence, unless that judge is unavailable.

  (4) The court must not determine the application in the defendant's absence unless the defendant has had an opportunity to make representations at a hearing (whether or not the defendant in fact attends).

CRIMINAL PROCEDURE   RULES PART 43

[There are no rules in this part.]

CRIMINAL PROCEDURE RULES   PART 44   BREACH, REVOCATION AND AMENDMENT OF COMMUNITY AND OTHER ORDERS

R-303   When this Part applies

44.1 This Part applies where—

    (a) the person responsible for a defendant's compliance with an order to which applies—

          (i)   Schedule 3, 5, 7 or 8 to the Powers of Criminal Courts (Sentencing) Act 2000,

          (ii)   Schedule 8 or 12 to the Criminal Justice Act 2003,

          (iii) Schedule 2 to the Criminal Justice and Immigration Act 2008,

          (iv) or the Schedule to the Street Offences Act 1959

      wants the court to deal with that defendant for failure to comply;

    (b) one of the following wants the court to exercise any power it has to revoke or amend such an order—

          (i)   the responsible officer or supervisor,

          (ii)   the defendant, or

          (iii) where the legislation allows, a person affected by the order; or

    (c) the court considers exercising on its own initiative any power it has to revoke or amend such an order.

Application by responsible officer or supervisor   R-304

44.2 (1) This rule applies where—
    (a) the responsible officer wants the court to—
        (i) deal with a defendant for failure to comply with an order to which this Part applies, or
        (ii) revoke or amend such an order; or
    (b) the court considers exercising on its own initiative any power it has to—
        (i) revoke or amend such an order, and
        (ii) summon the defendant to attend for that purpose.
    (2) Rules 7.2 to 7.4, which deal, among other things, with starting a prosecution in a magistrates' court by information and summons, apply—
    (a) as if—
        (i) a reference in those rules to an allegation of an offence included a reference to an allegation of failure to comply with an order to which this Part applies, and
        (ii) a reference to the prosecutor included a reference to the responsible officer or supervisor; and
    (b) with the necessary consequential modifications.

Application by defendant or person affected   R-305

44.3 (1) This rule applies where—
    (a) the defendant wants the court to exercise any power it has to revoke or amend an order to which this Part applies; or
    (b) where the legislation allows, a person affected by such an order wants the court to exercise any such power.
    (2) That defendant, or person affected, must—
    (a) apply in writing, explaining why the order should be revoked or amended; and
    (b) serve the application on—
        (i) the court officer,
        (ii) the responsible officer or supervisor, and
        (iii) as appropriate, the defendant or the person affected.

Procedure on application by responsible officer or supervisor   R-306

44.4 (1) Except for rule 37.8, the rules in Part 37, which deal with the procedure at a trial in a magistrates' court, apply—
    (a) as if—
        (i) a reference in those rules to an allegation of an offence included a reference to an allegation of failure to comply with an order to which this Part applies,
        (ii) a reference to the court's verdict included a reference to the court's decision to revoke or amend such an order, or to exercise any other power it has to deal with the defendant, and
        (iii) a reference to the court's sentence included a reference to the exercise of any such power; and
    (b) with the necessary consequential modifications.
    (2) The court officer must serve on each party any order revoking or amending an order to which this Part applies.

CRIMINAL PROCEDURE RULES   PART 45

[There are no rules in this part.]

CRIMINAL PROCEDURE RULES   PART 46

[There are no rules in this part.]

CRIMINAL PROCEDURE RULES   PART 47

[There are no rules in this part.]

CRIMINAL PROCEDURE RULES   PART 48

[There are no rules in this part.]

CRIMINAL PROCEDURE RULES   PART 49

[There are no rules in this part.]

CRIMINAL PROCEDURE RULES   PART 50   CIVIL BEHAVIOUR ORDERS
AFTER VERDICT OR FINDING

R-307   **When this Part applies**

50.1   (1)   This Part applies in magistrates' courts and in the Crown Court where the court could decide to make, vary or revoke a civil order—

    (a)   under a power that the court can exercise after reaching a verdict or making a finding, and

    (b)   that requires someone to do, or not do, something.

(2)   A reference to a 'behaviour order' in this Part is a reference to any such order.

(3)   A reference to 'hearsay evidence' in this Part is a reference to evidence consisting of hearsay within the meaning of section 1(2) of the Civil Evidence Act 1995.

R-308   **Behaviour orders: general rules**

50.2   (1)   The court must not make a behaviour order unless the person to whom it is directed has had an opportunity—

    (a)   to consider—

        (i)   what order is proposed and why,

        (ii)   the evidence in support, and

    (b)   to make representations at a hearing (whether or not that person in fact attends).

(2)   That restriction does not apply to making an interim behaviour order, but such an order has no effect unless the person to whom it is directed—

    (a)   is present when it is made; or

    (b)   is handed a document recording the order not more than 7 days after it is made.

(3)   Where the court decides not to make, where it could—

    (a)   a football banning order;

    (b)   a parenting order, after a person under 16 is convicted of an offence; or

    (c)   a drinking banning order,

the court must announce, at a hearing in public, the reasons for its decision.

R-309   **Application for behaviour order: special rules**

50.3   (1)   This rule applies where—

    (a)   a prosecutor wants the court to make—

        (i)   an anti-social behaviour order, or

        (ii)   a serious crime prevention order; or

    (b)   a prosecutor proposes a sexual offences prevention order, on the prosecutor's initiative or at the court's request,

if the defendant is convicted.

(2)   Where paragraph (1)(a) applies, the prosecutor must serve a notice of intention to apply for such an order on—

    (a)   the court officer;

    (b)   the defendant against whom the prosecutor wants the court to make the order; and

    (c)   any person on whom the order would be likely to have a significant adverse effect, as soon as practicable (without waiting for the verdict).

(3)   A notice under paragraph (2) must—

    (a)   summarise the relevant facts;

    (b)   identify the evidence on which the prosecutor relies in support;

    (c)   attach any written statement that the prosecutor has not already served; and

    (d)   specify the order that the prosecutor wants the court to make.

(4)   A defendant served with a notice under paragraph (2) must—

    (a)   serve written notice of any evidence on which the defendant relies on—

        (i)   the court officer, and

        (ii)   the prosecutor, as soon as practicable (without waiting for the verdict); and

    (b)   in the notice, identify that evidence and attach any written statement that has not already been served.

(5) Where paragraph (1)(b) applies, the prosecutor must—

    (a) serve a draft order on the court officer and on the defendant not less than 2 business days before the hearing at which the order may be made; and

    (b) in the draft order, specify those prohibitions which the prosecutor proposes as necessary for the purpose of protecting the public or any particular members of the public from serious sexual harm from the defendant.

(6) This rule does not apply to an application for an interim anti-social behaviour order.

Evidence to assist the court: special rules   **R-310**

50.4 (1) This rule applies where the court can make on its own initiative—

    (a) a football banning order;

    (b) a restraining order;

    (c) an anti-social behaviour order; or

    (d) a drinking banning order.

(2) A party who wants the court to take account of evidence not already introduced must—

    (a) serve notice in writing on—

        (i) the court officer, and

        (ii) every other party, as soon as practicable (without waiting for the verdict); and

    (b) in the notice, identify that evidence; and

    (c) attach any written statement containing such evidence.

Application to vary or revoke behaviour order   **R-311**

50.5 (1) The court may vary or revoke a behaviour order if—

    (a) the legislation under which it is made allows the court to do so; and

    (b) one of the following applies—

        (i) the prosecutor,

        (ii) the person to whom the order is directed,

        (iii) any other person mentioned in the order,

        (iv) the relevant authority or responsible officer,

        (v) the relevant Chief Officer of Police, or

        (vi) the Director of Public Prosecutions.

(2) A person applying under this rule must—

    (a) apply in writing as soon as practicable after becoming aware of the grounds for doing so, explaining—

        (i) what material circumstances have changed since the order was made, and

        (ii) why the order should be varied or revoked as a result;

    (b) serve the application on—

        (i) the court officer,

        (ii) as appropriate, the prosecutor or defendant,

        (iii) any other person listed in paragraph (1)(b), if the court so directs.

(3) A party who wants the court to take account of any particular evidence before making its decision must, as soon as practicable—

    (a) serve notice in writing on—

        (i) the court officer,

        (ii) as appropriate, the prosecutor or defendant, and

        (iii) as appropriate, anyone listed in paragraph (1)(b) on whom the court directed the application to be served; and

    (b) in that notice identify the evidence and attach any written statement that has not already been served.

(4) The court may decide an application under this rule with or without a hearing.

(5) But the court must not—

    (a) dismiss an application under this rule unless the applicant has had an opportunity to make representations at a hearing (whether or not the applicant in fact attends); or

    (b) allow an application under this rule unless everyone required to be served, by this rule or by the court, has had at least 14 days in which to make representations, including representations about whether there should be a hearing.

(6) The court officer must—

    (a) serve the application on any person, if the court so directs; and

    (b) give notice of any hearing to—

        (i) the applicant, and

        (ii) any person required to be served, by this rule or by the court.

R-312   **Notice of hearsay evidence**

50.6 (1) A party who wants to introduce hearsay evidence must—
    (a) serve notice in writing on—
        (i)   the court officer, and
        (ii) every other party directly affected; and
    (b) in that notice—
        (i)   explain that it is a notice of hearsay evidence,
        (ii) identify that evidence,
        (iii) identify the person who made the statement which is hearsay, or explain why if that person is not identified, and
        (iv) explain why that person will not be called to give oral evidence.
  (2) A party may serve one notice under this rule in respect of more than one statement and more than one witness.

R-313   **Cross-examination of maker of hearsay statement**

50.7 (1) This rule applies where a party wants the court's permission to cross-examine a person who made a statement which another party wants to introduce as hearsay.
  (2) The party who wants to cross-examine that person must—
    (a) apply in writing, with reasons, not more than 7 days after service of the notice of *hearsay* evidence; and
    (b) serve the application on—
        (i)   the court officer,
        (ii) the party who served the hearsay evidence notice, and
        (iii) every party on whom the hearsay evidence notice was served.
  (3) The court may decide an application under this rule with or without a hearing.
  (4) But the court must not—
    (a) dismiss an application under this rule unless the applicant has had an opportunity to make representations at a hearing (whether or not the applicant in fact attends); or
    (b) allow an application under this rule unless everyone served with the application has had at least 7 days in which to make representations, including representations about whether there should be a hearing.

R-314   **Credibility and consistency of maker of hearsay statement**

50.8 (1) This rule applies where a party wants to challenge the credibility or consistency of a person who made a statement which another party wants to introduce as hearsay.
  (2) The party who wants to challenge the credibility or consistency of that person must—
    (a) serve a written notice of intention to do so on—
        (i)   the court officer, and
        (ii) the party who served the notice of hearsay evidence
    not more than 7 days after service of that hearsay evidence notice; and
    (b) in the notice, identify any statement or other material on which that party relies.
  (3) The party who served the hearsay notice—
    (a) may call that person to give oral evidence instead; and
    (b) if so, must serve a notice of intention to do so on—
        (i)   the court officer, and
        (ii) every party on whom he served the hearsay notice
    not more than 7 days after service of the notice under paragraph (2).

R-315   **Court's power to vary requirements under this Part**

50.9 The court may—
    (a) shorten a time limit or extend it (even after it has expired);
    (b) allow a notice or application to be given in a different form, or presented orally.

CRIMINAL PROCEDURE RULES   PART 51

[There are no rules in this part.]

CRIMINAL PROCEDURE RULES   PART 52   ENFORCEMENT OF FINES
AND OTHER ORDERS FOR PAYMENT

When this Part applies   R-316

52.1 (1) This Part applies where a magistrates' court can enforce payment of—
           (a) a fine, or a sum that legislation requires the court to treat as a fine; or
           (b) any other sum that a court has ordered to be paid—
                (i)   on a conviction, or
                (ii) on the forfeiture of a surety.
      (2) Rules 52.7 to 52.9 apply where the court, or a fines officer, issues a warrant that requires some-
           one to—
           (a) take control of goods or money belonging to the defendant;
           (b) remove and sell any such goods; and
           (c) pay any such money, and any proceeds of such a sale, to the court officer towards payment
                of a sum to which this Part applies.
      (3) In this Part—
           (a) 'defendant' means anyone liable to pay a sum to which this Part applies;
           (b) 'payment terms' means by when, and by what (if any) instalments, such a sum must
                be paid.

Exercise of court's powers   R-317

52.2 The court must not exercise its enforcement powers unless—
      (a) the court officer has served on the defendant any collection order or other notice of—
           (i)   the obligation to pay,
           (ii)   the payment terms, and
           (iii) how and where the defendant must pay; and
      (b) the defendant has failed to comply with the payment terms.

Duty to give receipt   R-318

52.3 (1) This rule applies where the defendant makes a payment to—
           (a) the court officer specified in an order or notice served under rule 52.2;
           (b) another court officer;
           (c) any—
                (i)   custodian of the defendant,
                (ii)   supervisor appointed to encourage the defendant to pay, or
                (iii) responsible officer appointed under a community sentence or a suspended sentence
                       of imprisonment; or
           (d) a person executing a warrant to which rule 18.6 (warrants for arrest, detention or impris-
                onment that cease to have effect on payment) or this Part applies.
      (2) The person receiving the payment must—
           (a) give the defendant a receipt; and
           (b) as soon as practicable transmit the payment to the court officer specified in an order or
                notice served under rule 52.2, if the recipient is not that court officer.

Appeal against decision of fines officer   R-319

52.4 (1) This rule applies where—
           (a) a collection order is in force;
           (b) a fines officer makes a decision under one of these paragraphs of Schedule 5 to the Courts
                Act 2003—
                (i)   paragraph 22 (Application to fines officer for variation of order or attachment of
                       earnings order, etc.),
                (ii)   paragraph 31 (Application to fines officer for variation of reserve terms), or
                (iii) paragraph 37 (Functions of fines officer in relation to defaulters: referral or further
                       steps notice); and
           (c) the defendant wants to appeal against that decision.
      (2) Unless the court otherwise directs, the defendant must—
           (a) appeal in writing not more than 10 business days after the decision;
           (b) serve the appeal on the court officer; and
           (c) in the appeal—
                (i)   explain why a different decision should be made, and
                (ii)   specify the decision that the defendant proposes.

(3) Where the court determines an appeal—
    (a) the general rule is that it must do so at a hearing; but
    (b) it may do so without a hearing.

R-320   **Application to reduce a fine or vary payment terms**

52.5 (1) This rule applies where—
    (a) no collection order is in force; and
    (b) the defendant wants the court to—
        (i)   reduce the amount of a fine, or
        (ii) vary payment terms.
  (2) Unless the court otherwise directs, the defendant must—
    (a) apply in writing;
    (b) serve the application on the court officer; and
    (c) in the application, explain—
        (i)   what relevant circumstances have not yet been considered by the court, and
        (ii) why the fine should be reduced, or the payment terms varied.

R-321   **Claim to avoid fine after penalty notice**

52.6 (1) This rule applies where—
    (a) a chief officer of police serves on the magistrates' court officer a certificate registering, for enforcement as a fine, a sum payable by a defendant after failure to comply with a penalty notice; and
    (b) the court or a fines officer enforces the fine.
  (2) A defendant who claims not to be the person to whom the penalty notice was issued must, unless the court otherwise directs—
    (a) make that claim in writing; and
    (b) serve it on the court officer.
  (3) The court officer must—
    (a) notify the chief officer of police by whom the certificate was registered; and
    (b) refer the case to the court.
  (4) Where such a claim is made—
    (a) the general rule is that the court must adjourn the enforcement for 28 days and fix a hearing; but
    (b) the court may make a different order.
  (5) At any such hearing, the chief officer of police must introduce any evidence to contradict the defendant's claim.

R-322   **Information to be included in a warrant to take goods, etc.**

52.7 (1) A warrant must identify—
    (a) each person to whom it is directed;
    (b) the defendant against whom it was issued;
    (c) the sum for which it was issued and the reason that sum is owed;
    (d) the court or fines officer who issued it, unless that is otherwise recorded by the court officer; and
    (e) the court office for the court or fines officer who issued it.
  (2) A person to whom a warrant is directed must record on it the date and time at which it is received.
  (3) A warrant that contains an error is not invalid, as long as—
    (a) it was issued in respect of a lawful decision by the court or fines officer; and
    (b) it contains enough information to identify that decision.

R-323   **Execution of a warrant to take goods, etc.**

52.8 (1) A warrant may be executed by—
    (a) any person to whom it is directed; or
    (b) anyone authorised to do so by section 125 (warrants), 125A (civilian enforcement officers) or 125B (execution by approved enforcement agency) of the Magistrates' Courts Act 1980.
  (2) The person who executes a warrant must—
    (a) explain, in terms the defendant can understand—
        (i)   the order or decision that the warrant was issued to enforce,
        (ii) the sum for which the warrant was issued, and
        (iii) any extra sum payable in connection with the execution of the warrant;
    (b) show the defendant the warrant, if that person has it;

    (c) if the defendant asks—
       (i) arrange for the defendant to see the warrant, if that person does not have it, and
       (ii) show the defendant any written statement of that person's authority required by section 125A or 125B of the 1980 Act; and
    (d) clearly mark any goods that are taken under the warrant, unless that person removes those goods at once.
(3) These goods must not be taken under the warrant—
    (a) clothes or bedding used by the defendant or by anyone living with the defendant;
    (b) tools, books, vehicles or other equipment that the defendant needs to use in the defendant's employment, business or vocation, unless the defendant is a corporation.
(4) Unless the court otherwise directs, or the defendant otherwise agrees, if the person who executes the warrant takes household goods they must not be removed until the day of sale.
(5) The warrant no longer has effect if—
    (a) there is paid to the person executing it the sum for which it was issued and any extra sum payable in connection with its execution;
    (b) those sums are offered to, but refused by, that person; or
    (c) that person—
       (i) is shown a receipt given under rule 52.3 for the sum for which the warrant was issued, and
       (ii) is paid any extra sum payable in connection with its execution.

Sale of goods taken under a warrant   **R-324**

52.9 (1) Unless the court otherwise directs or the defendant otherwise agrees, goods taken under a warrant must be sold—
    (a) at public auction; and
    (b) as soon as reasonably practicable after the expiry of 5 business days from the date of execution of the warrant.
(2) After a sale, the person who executed the warrant must, as soon as reasonably practicable—
    (a) collect the proceeds of sale;
    (b) deduct any sum payable in connection with the execution of the warrant;
    (c) pay the court officer specified in an order or notice served under rule 52.2 the sum for which the warrant was issued;
    (d) pay any balance remaining to the defendant; and
    (e) deliver an account of those deductions and payments to the court officer.

Financial penalties imposed in other European Union member States   **R-325**

52.10 (1) This rule applies where the Lord Chancellor gives the court officer a request to enforce a financial penalty imposed in another European Union member State.
(2) The court officer must serve on the defendant—
    (a) notice of the request for enforcement, and of its effect;
    (b) a copy of—
       (i) the certificate requesting enforcement, and
       (ii) the decision requiring payment to which that certificate relates; and
    (c) notice that the procedure set out in this rule applies.
(3) A defendant who wants the court to refuse enforcement must—
    (a) serve notice of objection on the court officer;
    (b) unless the court otherwise directs, serve that notice not more than 14 days after service of notice of the request; and
    (c) in the notice of objection—
       (i) identify each ground for refusal on which the defendant relies,
       (ii) summarise any relevant facts not already included in the certificate and decision served with the notice of the request, and
       (iii) identify any other document that the defendant thinks the court will need to determine the request (and serve any such document with the notice).
(4) The court—
    (a) may determine a request for enforcement—
       (i) at a hearing, which must be in public unless the court otherwise directs, or
       (ii) without a hearing; but
    (b) must not allow enforcement unless the defendant has had at least 14 days in which to serve notice of objection.
(5) Paragraphs (2) and (3) do not apply if, on receipt of the request, the court decides that a ground for refusal applies.
(6) The court officer must serve on the Lord Chancellor notice of the court's decision.

CRIMINAL PROCEDURE RULES   PART 53

[There are no rules in this part.]

CRIMINAL PROCEDURE RULES   PART 54

[There are no rules in this part.]

CRIMINAL PROCEDURE RULES   PART 55   ROAD TRAFFIC PENALTIES

R-326   **Application to remove a disqualification from driving**

55.1 (1) This rule applies where, on application by the defendant, the court can remove a disqualification from driving.

     (2) A defendant who wants the court to exercise that power must—

       (a) apply in writing, no earlier than the date on which the court can exercise the power;

       (b) serve the application on the court officer; and

       (c) in the application—

          (i) specify the disqualification that the defendant wants the court to remove, and

          (ii) explain why.

     (3) The court officer must serve a copy of the application on the chief officer of police for the local justice area.

R-327   **Information to be supplied on order for endorsement of driving record, etc.**

55.2 (1) This rule applies where the court—

       (a) convicts the defendant of an offence involving obligatory endorsement, and orders there to be endorsed on the defendant's driving record and on any counterpart licence—

          (i) particulars of the conviction,

          (ii) particulars of any disqualification from driving that the court imposes, and

          (iii) the penalty points to be attributed to the offence;

       (b) disqualifies the defendant from driving for any other offence; or

       (c) suspends or removes a disqualification from driving.

     (2) The court officer must, as soon as practicable, serve on the Secretary of State notice that includes details of—

       (a) where paragraph (1)(a) applies—

          (i) the local justice area in which the court is acting,

          (ii) the dates of conviction and sentence,

          (iii) the offence, and the date on which it was committed,

          (iv) the sentence, and

          (v) the date of birth, and sex, of the defendant, where those details are available;

       (b) where paragraph (1)(b) applies—

          (i) the date and period of the disqualification,

          (ii) the power exercised by the court;

       (c) where paragraph (1)(c) applies—

          (i) the date and period of the disqualification,

          (ii) the date and terms of the order for its suspension or removal,

          (iii) the power exercised by the court, and

          (iv) where the court suspends the disqualification pending appeal, the court to which the defendant has appealed.

R-328   **Statutory declaration to avoid fine after fixed penalty notice**

55.3 (1) This rule applies where—

       (a) a chief officer of police, or the Secretary of State, serves on the magistrates' court officer a certificate registering, for enforcement as a fine, a sum payable by a defendant after failure to comply with a fixed penalty notice;

       (b) the court officer notifies the defendant of the registration; and

       (c) the defendant makes a statutory declaration with the effect that—

          (i) the fixed penalty notice, or any associated notice sent to the defendant as owner of the vehicle concerned, and

          (ii) the registration and any enforcement proceedings become void.

     (2) The defendant must serve that statutory declaration not more than 21 days after service of notice of the registration, unless the court extends that time limit.

(3) The court officer must—

    (a) serve a copy of the statutory declaration on the person by whom the certificate was registered,

    (b) cancel any endorsement on the defendant's driving record and on any counterpart licence, and

    (c) notify the Secretary of State of any such cancellation.

Application for declaration about a course or programme certificate decision   R-329

55.4 (1) This rule applies where the court can declare unjustified—

    (a) a course provider's failure or refusal to give a certificate of the defendant's satisfactory completion of an approved course; or

    (b) a programme provider's giving of a certificate of the defendant's failure fully to participate in an approved programme.

  (2) A defendant who wants the court to exercise that power must—

    (a) apply in writing, not more than 28 days after—

      (i) the date by which the defendant was required to complete the course, or

      (ii) the giving of the certificate of failure fully to participate in the programme;

    (b) serve the application on the court officer; and

    (c) in the application, specify the course or programme and explain (as applicable)—

      (i) that the course provider has failed to give a certificate,

      (ii) where the course provider has refused to give a certificate, why the defendant disagrees with the reasons for that decision, or

      (iii) where the programme provider has given a certificate, why the defendant disagrees with the reasons for that decision.

  (3) The court officer must serve a copy of the application on the course or programme provider.

  (4) The court must not determine the application unless the defendant, and the course or programme provider, each has had an opportunity to make representations at a hearing (whether or not either in fact attends).

Appeal against recognition of foreign driving disqualification   R-330

55.5 (1) This rule applies where—

    (a) a minister gives a disqualification notice under section 57 of the Crime (International Co-operation) Act 2003 (159); and

    (b) the person to whom it is given wants to appeal under section 59 of the Act to a magistrates' court.

  (2) That person ('the appellant') must serve an appeal notice on—

    (a) the court officer, at a magistrates' court in the local justice area in which the appellant lives; and

    (b) the minister, at the address given in the disqualification notice.

  (3) The appellant must serve the appeal notice within the period for which section 59 of the 2003 Act provides.

  (4) The appeal notice must—

    (a) attach a copy of the disqualification notice;

    (b) explain which of the conditions in section 56 of the 2003 Act is not met, and why section 57 of the Act therefore does not apply; and

    (c) include any application to suspend the disqualification, under section 60 of the Act.

  (5) The minister may serve a respondent's notice, and must do so if—

    (a) the minister wants to make representations to the court; or

    (b) the court so directs.

  (6) The minister must—

    (a) unless the court otherwise directs, serve any such respondent's notice not more than 14 days after—

      (i) the appellant serves the appeal notice, or

      (ii) a direction to do so;

    (b) in any such respondent's notice—

      (i) identify the grounds of opposition on which the minister relies,

      (ii) summarise any relevant facts not already included in the disqualification and appeal notices, and

      (iii) identify any other document that the minister thinks the court will need to decide the appeal (and serve any such document with the notice).

(7) Where the court determines an appeal—
   (a) the general rule is that it must do so at a hearing (which will be in public, unless the court otherwise directs); but
   (b) it may do so without a hearing.
(8) The court officer must serve on the minister—
   (a) notice of the outcome of the appeal; and
   (b) notice of any suspension of the disqualification; and
   (c) the appellant's driving licence, if surrendered to the court officer.

CRIMINAL PROCEDURE RULES   PART 56   CONFISCATION PROCEEDINGS UNDER THE CRIMINAL JUSTICE ACT 1988 AND THE DRUG TRAFFICKING ACT 1994

R-331   **Statements etc., relevant to making confiscation orders**

56.1   (1) Where a prosecutor or defendant—
   (a) tenders to a magistrates' court any statement or other document under section 73 of the Criminal Justice Act 1988 in any proceedings in respect of an offence listed in Schedule 4 to that Act; or
   (b) tenders to the Crown Court any statement or other document under section 11 of the Drug Trafficking Act 1994 or section 73 of the 1988 Act in any proceedings in respect of a drug trafficking offence or in respect of an offence to which Part VI of the 1988 Act applies,
   he must serve a copy as soon as practicable on the defendant or the prosecutor, as the case may be.
   (2) Any statement tendered by the prosecutor to the magistrates' court under section 73 of the 1988 Act or to the Crown Court under section 11(1) of the 1994 Act or section 73(1A) of the 1988 Act shall include the following particulars—
   (a) the name of the defendant;
   (b) the name of the person by whom the statement is made and the date on which it was made;
   (c) where the statement is not tendered immediately after the defendant has been convicted, the date on which and the place where the relevant conviction occurred; and
   (d) such information known to the prosecutor as is relevant to the determination as to whether or not the defendant has benefited from drug trafficking or relevant criminal conduct and to the assessment of the value of his proceeds of drug trafficking or, as the case may be, benefit from relevant criminal conduct.
   (3) Where, in accordance with section 11(7) of the 1994 Act or section 73(1C) of the 1988 Act, the defendant indicates the extent to which he accepts any allegation contained within the prosecutor's statement, if he indicates the same in writing to the prosecutor, he must serve a copy of that reply on the court officer.
   (4) Expressions used in this rule shall have the same meanings as in the 1994 Act or, where appropriate, the 1988 Act.

R-332   **Postponed determinations**

56.2   (1) Where an application is made by the defendant or the prosecutor—
   (a) to a magistrates' court under section 72A(5)(a) of the Criminal Justice Act 1988 asking the court to exercise its powers under section 72A(4) of that Act; or
   (b) to the Crown Court under section 3(5)(a) of the Drug Trafficking Act 1994 asking the Court to exercise its powers under section 3(4) of that Act, or under section 72A(5)(a) of the 1988 Act asking the court to exercise its powers under section 72A(4) of the 1988 Act, the application must be made in writing and a copy must be served on the prosecutor or the defendant, as the case may be.
   (2) A party served with a copy of an application under paragraph (1) shall, within 28 days of the date of service, notify the applicant and the court officer, in writing, whether or not he proposes to oppose the application, giving his reasons for any opposition.
   (3) After the expiry of the period referred to in paragraph (2), the court shall determine whether an application under paragraph (1) is to be dealt with—
   (a) without a hearing; or
   (b) at a hearing at which the parties may be represented.

R-333   **Confiscation orders—revised assessments**

56.3   (1) Where the prosecutor makes an application under section 13, 14 or 15 of the Drug Trafficking Act 1994 or section 74A, 74B or 74C of the Criminal Justice Act 1988, the application must be in writing and a copy must be served on the defendant.

(2) The application must include the following particulars—
  (a) the name of the defendant;
  (b) the date on which and the place where any relevant conviction occurred;
  (c) the date on which and the place where any relevant confiscation order was made or, as the case may be, varied;
  (d) the grounds on which the application is made; and
  (e) an indication of the evidence available to support the application.

Application to the Crown Court to discharge or vary order to make material available   **R-334**

56.4 (1) Where an order under section 93H of the Criminal Justice Act 1988 (order to make material available) or section 55 of the Drug Trafficking Act 1994 (order to make material available) has been made by the Crown Court, any person affected by it may apply in writing to the court officer for the order to be discharged or varied, and on hearing such an application a circuit judge may discharge the order or make such variations to it as he thinks fit.
  (2) Subject to paragraph (3), where a person proposes to make an application under paragraph (1) for the discharge or variation of an order, he shall give a copy of the application, not later than 48 hours before the making of the application—
  (a) to a constable at the police station specified in the order; or
  (b) to the office of the appropriate officer who made the application, as specified in the order, in either case together with a notice indicating the time and place at which the application for discharge or variation is to be made.
  (3) A circuit judge may direct that paragraph (2) need not be complied with if he is satisfied that the person making the application has good reason to seek a discharge or variation of the order as soon as possible and it is not practicable to comply with that paragraph.
  (4) In this rule:
    'constable' includes a person commissioned by the Commissioners for Her Majesty's Revenue and Customs;
    'police station' includes a place for the time being occupied by Her Majesty's Revenue and Customs.

Application to the Crown Court for increase in term of imprisonment in default of payment   **R-335**

56.5 (1) This rule applies to applications made, or that have effect as made, to the Crown Court under section 10 of the Drug Trafficking Act 1994 and section 75A of the Criminal Justice Act 1988 (interest on sums unpaid under confiscation orders).
  (2) Notice of an application to which this rule applies to increase the term of imprisonment or detention fixed in default of payment of a confiscation order by a person ('the defendant') shall be made by the prosecutor in writing to the court officer.
  (3) A notice under paragraph (2) shall—
  (a) state the name and address of the defendant;
  (b) specify the grounds for the application;
  (c) give details of the enforcement measures taken, if any; and
  (d) include a copy of the confiscation order.
  (4) On receiving a notice under paragraph (2), the court officer shall—
  (a) forthwith send to the defendant and the magistrates' court required to enforce payment of the confiscation order under section 140(1) of the Powers of Criminal Courts (Sentencing) Act 2000, a copy of the said notice; and
  (b) notify in writing the applicant and the defendant of the date, time and place appointed for the hearing of the application.
  (5) Where the Crown Court makes an order pursuant to an application mentioned in paragraph (1) above, the court officer shall send forthwith a copy of the order—
  (a) to the applicant;
  (b) to the defendant;
  (c) where the defendant is at the time of the making of the order in custody, to the person having custody of him; and
  (d) to the magistrates' court mentioned in paragraph (4)(a).

Drug trafficking—compensation on acquittal in the Crown Court   **R-336**

56.6 Where a Crown Court cancels a confiscation order under section 22(2) of the Drug Trafficking Act 1994, the court officer shall serve notice to that effect on the High Court and on the magistrates' court which has responsibility for enforcing the order.

CRIMINAL PROCEDURE RULES   PART 57   PROCEEDS OF CRIME ACT 2002: RULES
APPLICABLE TO ALL PROCEEDINGS

R-337 **Interpretation**

57.1   In this Part and in Parts 58, 59, 60 and 61:

'document' means anything in which information of any description is recorded;

'hearsay evidence' means evidence consisting of hearsay within the meaning of section 1(2) of the Civil Evidence Act 1995;

'restraint proceedings' means proceedings under sections 42 and 58(2) and (3) of the Proceeds of Crime Act 2002;

'receivership proceedings' means proceedings under sections 48, 49, 50, 51, 54(4), 59(2) and (3), 62 and 63 of the 2002 Act;

'witness statement' means a written statement signed by a person which contains the evidence, and only that evidence, which that person would be allowed to give orally; and

words and expressions used have the same meaning as in Part 2 of the 2002 Act.

R-338 **Calculation of time**

57.2   (1) This rule shows how to calculate any period of time for doing any act which is specified by this Part and Parts 58, 59, 60 and 61 for the purposes of any proceedings under Part 2 of the Proceeds of Crime Act 2002 or by an order of the Crown Court in restraint proceedings or receivership proceedings.

(2) A period of time expressed as a number of days shall be computed as clear days.

(3) In this rule 'clear days' means that in computing the number of days—

(a) the day on which the period begins; and

(b) if the end of the period is defined by reference to an event, the day on which that event occurs are not included.

(4) Where the specified period is five days or less and includes a day which is not a business day that day does not count.

R-339 **Court office closed**

57.3   When the period specified by this Part or Parts 58, 59, 60 and 61, or by an order of the Crown Court under Part 2 of the Proceeds of Crime Act 2002, for doing any act at the court office falls on a day on which the office is closed, that act shall be in time if done on the next day on which the court office is open.

R-340 **Application for registration of Scottish or Northern Ireland Order**

57.4   (1) This rule applies to an application for registration of an order under article 6 of the Proceeds of Crime Act 2002 (Enforcement in different parts of the United Kingdom) Order 2002.

(2) The application may be made without notice.

(3) The application must be in writing and may be supported by a witness statement which must—

(a) exhibit the order or a certified copy of the order; and

(b) to the best of the witness's ability, give full details of the realisable property located in England and Wales in respect of which the order was made and specify the person holding that realisable property.

(4) If the court registers the order, the applicant must serve notice of the registration on—

(a) any person who holds realisable property to which the order applies; and

(b) any other person whom the applicant knows to be affected by the order.

(5) The permission of the Crown Court under rule 57.13 is not required to serve the notice outside England and Wales.

R-341 **Application to vary or set aside registration**

57.5   (1) An application to vary or set aside registration of an order under article 6 of the Proceeds of Crime Act 2002 (Enforcement in different parts of the United Kingdom) Order 2002 may be made to the Crown Court by—

(a) any person who holds realisable property to which the order applies; and

(b) any other person affected by the order.

(2) The application must be in writing and may be supported by a witness statement.

(3) The application and any witness statement must be lodged with the Crown Court.

(4) The application must be served on the person who applied for registration at least seven days before the date fixed by the court for hearing the application, unless the Crown Court specifies a shorter period.

(5) No property in England and Wales may be realised in pursuance of the order before the Crown Court has decided the application.

Register of orders   R-342

57.6 (1) The Crown Court must keep, under the direction of the Lord Chancellor, a register of the orders registered under article 6 of the Proceeds of Crime Act 2002 (Enforcement in different parts of the United Kingdom) Order 2002.

(2) The register must include details of any variation or setting aside of a registration under rule 57.5 and of any execution issued on a registered order.

(3) If the person who applied for registration of an order which is subsequently registered notifies the Crown Court that the court which made the order has varied or discharged the order, details of the variation or discharge, as the case may be, must be entered in the register.

Statements of truth   R-343

57.7 (1) Any witness statement required to be served by this Part or by Parts 58, 59, 60 or 61 must be verified by a statement of truth contained in the witness statement.

(2) A statement of truth is a declaration by the person making the witness statement to the effect that the witness statement is true to the best of his knowledge and belief and that he made the statement knowing that, if it were tendered in evidence, he would be liable to prosecution if he wilfully stated in it anything which he knew to be false or did not believe to be true.

(3) The statement of truth must be signed by the person making the witness statement.

(4) If the person making the witness statement fails to verify the witness statement by a statement of truth, the Crown Court may direct that it shall not be admissible as evidence.

Use of witness statements for other purposes   R-344

57.8 (1) Except as provided by this rule, a witness statement served in proceedings under Part 2 of the Proceeds of Crime Act 2002 may be used only for the purpose of the proceedings in which it is served.

(2) Paragraph (1) does not apply if and to the extent that—

(a) the witness gives consent in writing to some other use of it;

(b) the Crown Court gives permission for some other use; or

(c) the witness statement has been put in evidence at a hearing held in public.

Expert evidence   R-345

57.9 (1) A party to proceedings under Part 2 of the Proceeds of Crime Act 2002 who wishes to adduce expert evidence (whether of fact or opinion) in the proceedings must, as soon as practicable—

(a) serve on the other parties a statement in writing of any finding or opinion which he proposes to adduce by way of such evidence; and

(b) serve on any party who requests it in writing, a copy of (or if it appears to the party proposing to adduce the evidence to be more practicable, give the requesting party a reasonable opportunity to examine)—

(i) the record of any observation, test, calculation or other procedure on which the finding or opinion is based, and

(ii) any document or other thing or substance in respect of which the observation, test, calculation or other procedure mentioned in paragraph (1)(b)(i) has been carried out.

(2) A party may serve notice in writing waiving his right to be served with or given any of the matters mentioned in paragraph (1) and, in particular, may agree that the statement mentioned in paragraph (1)(a) may be given to him orally and not served in writing.

(3) If a party who wishes to adduce expert evidence in proceedings under Part 2 of the 2002 Act fails to comply with this rule he may not adduce that evidence in those proceedings without the leave of the court, except where rule 57.10 applies.

Exceptions to procedure for expert evidence   R-346

57.10 (1) If a party has reasonable grounds for believing that the disclosure of any evidence in compliance with rule 57.9 might lead to the intimidation, or attempted intimidation, of any person on whose evidence he intends to rely in the proceedings, or otherwise to the course of justice being interfered with, he shall not be obliged to comply with those requirements in relation to that evidence, unless the Crown Court orders otherwise.

(2) Where, in accordance with paragraph (1), a party considers that he is not obliged to comply with the requirements imposed by rule 57.9 with regard to any evidence in relation to any other party, he must serve notice in writing on that party stating—

      (a) that the evidence is being withheld; and

      (b) the reasons for withholding the evidence.

R-347 **Service of documents**

57.11 (1) Rule 32.1 (notice required to accompany process served outside the United Kingdom and translations) shall not apply in restraint proceedings and receivership proceedings.

     (2) An order made in restraint proceedings or receivership proceedings may be enforced against the defendant or any other person affected by it notwithstanding that service of a copy of the order has not been effected in accordance with Part 4 of these rules if the Crown Court is satisfied that the person had notice of the order by being present when the order was made.

R-348 **Service outside the jurisdiction**

57.12 (1) Where this Part requires a document to be served on someone who is outside England and Wales, it may be served outside England and Wales with the permission of the Crown Court.

     (2) Where a document is to be served outside England and Wales it may be served by any method permitted by the law of the country in which it is to be served.

     (3) Nothing in this rule or in any court order shall authorise or require any person to do anything in the country where the document is to be served which is against the law of that country.

     (4) Where this Part requires a document to be served a certain period of time before the date of a hearing and the recipient does not appear at the hearing, the hearing must not take place unless the Crown Court is satisfied that the document has been duly served.

R-349 **Certificates of service**

57.13 (1) Where this Part requires that the applicant for an order in restraint proceedings or receivership proceedings serve a document on another person, the applicant must lodge a certificate of service with the Crown Court within seven days of service of the document.

     (2) The certificate must state—

        (a) the method of service;

        (b) the date of service; and

        (c) if the document is served under rule 4.9, such other information as the court may require when making the order permitting service by an alternative method.

     (3) Where a document is to be served by the Crown Court in restraint proceedings and receivership proceedings and the court is unable to serve it, the court must send a notice of non-service stating the method attempted to the party who requested service.

R-350 **External requests and orders**

57.14 (1) The rules in this Part and in Parts 59 to 61 and 71 to 73 apply with the necessary modifications to proceedings under the Proceeds of Crime Act 2002 (External Requests and Orders) Order 2005 in the same way that they apply to corresponding proceedings under Part 2 of the Proceeds of Crime Act 2002.

     (2) This table shows how provisions of the 2005 Order correspond with provisions of the 2002 Act.

Article of the Proceeds of Crime Act 2002 (External Requests and Orders) Order 2005	Section of the Proceeds of Crime Act 2002
8	41
9	42
10	43
11	44
15	48
16	49
17	58
23	31
27	50
28	51
41	62
42	63
44	65
45	66

CRIMINAL PROCEDURE RULES   PART 58   PROCEEDS OF CRIME ACT 2002: RULES
APPLICABLE ONLY TO CONFISCATION PROCEEDINGS

Statements in connection with confiscation orders   R-351

58.1   (1)   When the prosecutor or the Director is required, under section 16 of the Proceeds of Crime
Act 2002, to give a statement to the Crown Court, the prosecutor or the Director, as the case
may be, must also, as soon as practicable, serve a copy of the statement on the defendant.

(2)   Any statement given to the Crown Court by the prosecutor under section 16 of the 2002
Act must, in addition to the information required by the 2002 Act, include the following information—

(a)   the name of the defendant;

(b)   the name of the person by whom the statement is made and the date on which it is
made; and

(c)   where the statement is not given to the Crown Court immediately after the defendant has
been convicted, the date on which and the place where the relevant conviction occurred.

(3)   Where, under section 17 of the 2002 Act, the Crown Court orders the defendant to indicate the
extent to which he accepts each allegation in a statement given by the prosecutor, the defendant
must indicate this in writing to the prosecutor and must give a copy to the Crown Court.

(4)   Where the Crown Court orders the defendant to give to it any information under section 18
of the 2002 Act, the defendant must provide the information in writing and must, as soon as
practicable, serve a copy of it on the prosecutor.

Postponement of confiscation proceedings   R-352

58.2   The Crown Court may grant a postponement under section 14(1)(b) of the Proceeds of Crime Act
2002 without a hearing.

Application for reconsideration   R-353

58.3   (1)   This rule applies where the prosecutor makes an application under section 19, 20 or 21 of the
Proceeds of Crime Act 2002.

(2)   The application must be in writing and give details of—

(a)   the name of the defendant;

(b)   the date on which and the place where any relevant conviction occurred;

(c)   the date on which and the place where any relevant confiscation order was made or varied;

(d)   the grounds for the application; and

(e)   an indication of the evidence available to support the application.

(3)   The application must be lodged with the Crown Court.

(4)   The application must be served on the defendant at least seven days before the date fixed by the
court for hearing the application, unless the Crown Court specifies a shorter period.

Application for new calculation of available amount   R-354

58.4   (1)   This rule applies where the prosecutor or a receiver makes an application under section 22 of
the Proceeds of Crime Act 2002 for a new calculation of the available amount.

(2)   The application must be in writing and may be supported by a witness statement.

(3)   The application and any witness statement must be lodged with the Crown Court.

(4)   The application and any witness statement must be served on—

(a)   the defendant;

(b)   the receiver, if the prosecutor is making the application and a receiver has been appointed
under section 50 of the 2002 Act; and

(c)   the prosecutor, if the receiver is making the application,

at least seven days before the date fixed by the court for hearing the application, unless the
Crown Court specifies a shorter period.

Variation of confiscation order due to inadequacy of available amount   R-355

58.5   (1)   This rule applies where the defendant or a receiver makes an application under section 23 of
the Proceeds of Crime Act 2002 for the variation of a confiscation order.

(2)   The application must be in writing and may be supported by a witness statement.

(3)   The application and any witness statement must be lodged with the Crown Court.

(4)   The application and any witness statement must be served on—

(a)   the prosecutor;

(b)   the defendant, if the receiver is making the application; and

(c)   the receiver, if the defendant is making the application and a receiver has been appointed
under section 50 of the 2002 Act,

at least seven days before the date fixed by the court for hearing the application, unless the Crown Court specifies a shorter period.

R-356   Application by magistrates' court officer to discharge confiscation order

58.6   (1) This rule applies where a magistrates' court officer makes an application under section 24 or 25 of the Proceeds of Crime Act 2002 for the discharge of a confiscation order.

(2) The application must be in writing and give details of—
   (a) the confiscation order;
   (b) the amount outstanding under the order; and
   (c) the grounds for the application.

(3) The application must be served on—
   (a) the defendant;
   (b) the prosecutor; and
   (c) any receiver appointed under section 50 of the 2002 Act.

(4) The Crown Court may determine the application without a hearing unless a person listed in paragraph (3) indicates, within seven days after the application was served on him, that he would like to make representations.

(5) If the Crown Court makes an order discharging the confiscation order, the court must, at once, send a copy of the order to—
   (a) the magistrates' court officer who applied for the order;
   (b) the defendant;
   (c) the prosecutor; and
   (d) any receiver appointed under section 50 of the 2002 Act.

R-357   Application for variation of confiscation order made against an absconder

58.7   (1) This rule applies where the defendant makes an application under section 29 of the Proceeds of Crime Act 2002 for the variation of a confiscation order made against an absconder.

(2) The application must be in writing and supported by a witness statement which must give details of—
   (a) the confiscation order made against an absconder under section 6 of the 2002 Act as applied by section 28 of the 2002 Act;
   (b) the circumstances in which the defendant ceased to be an absconder;
   (c) the defendant's conviction of the offence or offences concerned; and
   (d) the reason why he believes the amount required to be paid under the confiscation order was too large.

(3) The application and witness statement must be lodged with the Crown Court.

(4) The application and witness statement must be served on the prosecutor at least seven days before the date fixed by the court for hearing the application, unless the Crown Court specifies a shorter period.

R-358   Application for discharge of confiscation order made against an absconder

58.8   (1) This rule applies if the defendant makes an application under section 30 of the Proceeds of Crime Act 2002 for the discharge of a confiscation order.

(2) The application must be in writing and supported by a witness statement which must give details of—
   (a) the confiscation order made under section 28 of the 2002 Act;
   (b) the date on which the defendant ceased to be an absconder;
   (c) the acquittal of the defendant if he has been acquitted of the offence concerned; and
   (d) if the defendant has not been acquitted of the offence concerned—
      (i)   the date on which the defendant ceased to be an absconder,
      (ii) the date on which the proceedings taken against the defendant were instituted and a summary of steps taken in the proceedings since then, and
      (iii) any indication given by the prosecutor that he does not intend to proceed against the defendant.

(3) The application and witness statement must be lodged with the Crown Court.

(4) The application and witness statement must be served on the prosecutor at least seven days before the date fixed by the court for hearing the application, unless the Crown Court specifies a shorter period.

(5) If the Crown Court orders the discharge of the confiscation order, the court must serve notice on the magistrates' court responsible for enforcing the order.

Application for increase in term of imprisonment in default   **R-359**

58.9　(1)　This rule applies where the prosecutor makes an application under section 39(5) of the Proceeds of Crime Act 2002 to increase the term of imprisonment in default of payment of a confiscation order.

　　　(2)　The application must be made in writing and give details of—
　　　　　(a)　the name and address of the defendant;
　　　　　(b)　the confiscation order;
　　　　　(c)　the grounds for the application; and
　　　　　(d)　the enforcement measures taken, if any.

　　　(3)　On receipt of the application, the court must—
　　　　　(a)　at once, send to the defendant and the magistrates' court responsible for enforcing the order, a copy of the application; and
　　　　　(b)　fix a time, date and place for the hearing and notify the applicant and the defendant of that time, date and place.

　　　(4)　If the Crown Court makes an order increasing the term of imprisonment in default, the court must, at once, send a copy of the order to—
　　　　　(a)　the applicant;
　　　　　(b)　the defendant;
　　　　　(c)　where the defendant is in custody at the time of the making of the order, the person having custody of the defendant; and
　　　　　(d)　the magistrates' court responsible for enforcing the order.

Compensation—general   **R-360**

58.10　(1)　This rule applies to an application for compensation under section 72 of the Proceeds of Crime Act 2002.

　　　(2)　The application must be in writing and may be supported by a witness statement.

　　　(3)　The application and any witness statement must be lodged with the Crown Court.

　　　(4)　The application and any witness statement must be served on—
　　　　　(a)　the person alleged to be in default; and
　　　　　(b)　the person or authority by whom the compensation would be payable under section 72(9) or 302(7A) of the 2002 Act (or if the compensation is payable out of a police fund under section 72(9)(a) or 302(7A), the chief officer of the police force concerned),

　　　at least seven days before the date fixed by the court for hearing the application, unless the Crown Court directs otherwise.

Compensation—confiscation order made against absconder   **R-361**

58.11　(1)　This rule applies to an application for compensation under section 73 of the Proceeds of Crime Act 2002.

　　　(2)　The application must be in writing and supported by a witness statement which must give details of—
　　　　　(a)　the confiscation order made under section 28 of the 2002 Act;
　　　　　(b)　the variation or discharge of the confiscation order under section 29 or 30 of the 2002 Act;
　　　　　(c)　the realisable property to which the application relates; and
　　　　　(d)　the loss suffered by the applicant as a result of the confiscation order.

　　　(3)　The application and witness statement must be lodged with the Crown Court.

　　　(4)　The application and witness statement must be served on the prosecutor at least seven days before the date fixed by the court for hearing the application, unless the Crown Court specifies a shorter period.

Payment of money in bank or building society account in satisfaction of confiscation order   **R-362**

58.12　(1)　An order under section 67 of the Proceeds of Crime Act 2002 requiring a bank or building society to pay money to a magistrates' court officer ('a payment order') shall—
　　　　　(a)　be directed to the bank or building society in respect of which the payment order is made;
　　　　　(b)　name the person against whom the confiscation order has been made;
　　　　　(c)　state the amount which remains to be paid under the confiscation order;
　　　　　(d)　state the name and address of the branch at which the account in which the money ordered to be paid is held and the sort code of that branch, if the sort code is known;
　　　　　(e)　state the name in which the account in which the money ordered to be paid is held and the account number of that account, if the account number is known;
　　　　　(f)　state the amount which the bank or building society is required to pay to the court officer under the payment order;

(g) give the name and address of the court officer to whom payment is to be made; and

(h) require the bank or building society to make payment within a period of seven days beginning on the day on which the payment order is made, unless it appears to the court that a longer or shorter period would be appropriate in the particular circumstances.

(2) In this rule 'confiscation order' has the meaning given to it by section 88(6) of the Proceeds of Crime Act 2002.

CRIMINAL PROCEDURE RULES   PART 59   PROCEEDS OF CRIME ACT 2002: RULES APPLICABLE ONLY TO RESTRAINT PROCEEDINGS

R-363 **Application for restraint order or ancillary order**

59.1 (1) This rule applies where the prosecutor, or an accredited financial investigator, makes an application for a restraint order under section 42 of the Proceeds of Crime Act 2002 for—

(a) a restraint order, under section 41(1) of the 2002 Act; or

(b) an ancillary order, under section 41(7) of that Act, for the purpose of ensuring that a restraint order is effective.

(2) The application may be made without notice if the application is urgent or if there are reasonable grounds for believing that giving notice would cause the dissipation of realisable property which is the subject of the application.

(3) An application for a restraint order must be in writing and supported by a witness statement which must—

(a) give the grounds for the application;

(b) to the best of the witness's ability, give full details of the realisable property in respect of which the applicant is seeking the order and specify the person holding that realisable property;

(c) include the proposed terms of the order.

(4) An application for an ancillary order must be in writing and supported by a witness statement which must—

(a) give the grounds for, and details of, the application;

(b) include, if appropriate—

(i) any request for an order for disclosure of documents to which rule 61.9 applies (rules applicable to restraint and receivership proceedings: disclosure and inspection of documents),

(ii) the identity of any person whom the applicant wants the court to examine about the extent or whereabouts of realisable property,

(iii) a list of the main questions that the applicant wants to ask any such person, and

(iv) a list of any documents to which the applicant wants to refer such a person; and

(c) include the proposed terms of the order.

(5) An application for a restraint order and an application for an ancillary order may (but need not) be made at the same time and contained in the same documents.

(6) An application by an accredited financial investigator must include a statement that, under section 68 of the 2002 Act, the applicant has authority to apply.

R-364 **Restraint and ancillary orders**

59.2 (1) The Crown Court may make a restraint order subject to exceptions, including, but not limited to, exceptions for reasonable living expenses and reasonable legal expenses, and for the purpose of enabling any person to carry on any trade, business or occupation.

(2) But the Crown Court must not make an exception for legal expenses where this is prohibited by section 41(4) of the Proceeds of Crime Act 2002.

(3) An exception to a restraint order may be made subject to conditions.

(4) The Crown Court must not require the applicant for a restraint order to give any undertaking relating to damages sustained as a result of the restraint order by a person who is prohibited from dealing with realisable property by the restraint order.

(5) The Crown Court may require the applicant for a restraint order to give an undertaking to pay the reasonable expenses of any person, other than a person who is prohibited from dealing with realisable property by the restraint order, which are incurred in complying with the restraint order.

(6) An order must include a statement that disobedience of the order, either by a person to whom the order is addressed, or by another person, may be contempt of court and the order must include details of the possible consequences of being held in contempt of court.

(7) Unless the Crown Court otherwise directs, an order made without notice has effect until the court makes an order varying or discharging it.

(8) The applicant for an order must—

    (a) serve copies of the order and of the witness statement made in support of the application on the defendant and any person who is prohibited by the order from dealing with realisable property; and

    (b) notify any person whom the applicant knows to be affected by the order of its terms.

Application for discharge or variation of restraint or ancillary order by a person affected by the order   R-365

59.3 (1) This rule applies where a person affected by a restraint order makes an application to the Crown Court under section 42(3) of the Proceeds of Crime Act 2002 to discharge or vary the restraint order or any ancillary order made under section 41(7) of the Act.

    (2) The application must be in writing and may be supported by a witness statement.

    (3) The application and any witness statement must be lodged with the Crown Court.

    (4) The application and any witness statement must be served on the person who applied for the restraint order and any person who is prohibited from dealing with realisable property by the restraint order (if he is not the person making the application) at least two days before the date fixed by the court for hearing the application, unless the Crown Court specifies a shorter period.

Application for variation of restraint or ancillary order by the person who applied for the order   R-366

59.4 (1) This rule applies where the applicant for a restraint order makes an application under section 42(3) of the Proceeds of Crime Act 2002 to the Crown Court to vary the restraint order or any ancillary order made under section 41(7) of the 2002 Act (including where the court has already made a restraint order and the applicant is seeking to vary the order in order to restrain further realisable property).

    (2) The application may be made without notice if the application is urgent or if there are reasonable grounds for believing that giving notice would cause the dissipation of realisable property which is the subject of the application.

    (3) The application must be in writing and must be supported by a witness statement which must—

        (a) give the grounds for the application;

        (b) where the application is for the inclusion of further realisable property in a restraint order give full details, to the best of the witness's ability, of the realisable property in respect of which the applicant is seeking the order and specify the person holding that realisable property;

        (c) where the application is to vary an ancillary order, include, if appropriate—

            (i) any request for an order for disclosure of documents to which rule 61.9 applies (rules applicable to restraint and receivership proceedings: disclosure and inspection of documents),

            (ii) the identity of any person whom the applicant wants the court to examine about the extent or whereabouts of realisable property,

            (iii) a list of the main questions that the applicant wants to ask any such person, and

            (iv) a list of any documents to which the applicant wants to refer such a person; and

        (d) include the proposed terms of the variation.

    (4) An application by an accredited financial investigator must include a statement that, under section 68 of the 2002 Act, the applicant has authority to apply.

    (5) The application and witness statement must be lodged with the Crown Court.

    (6) Except where, under paragraph (2), notice of the application is not required to be served, the application and witness statement must be served on any person who is prohibited from dealing with realisable property by the restraint order at least 2 days before the date fixed by the court for hearing the application, unless the Crown Court specifies a shorter period.

    (7) If the court makes an order for the variation of a restraint or ancillary order, the applicant must serve copies of the order and of the witness statement made in support of the application on—

        (a) the defendant;

        (b) any person who is prohibited from dealing with realisable property by the restraint order (whether before or after the variation); and

        (c) any other person whom the applicant knows to be affected by the order.

Criminal Procedure Rules 2013 and Criminal Practice Directions

R-367 **Application for discharge of restraint or ancillary order by the person who applied for the order**

59.5 (1) This rule applies where the applicant for a restraint order makes an application under section 42(3) of the Proceeds of Crime Act 2002 to discharge the order or any ancillary order made under section 41(7) of the 2002 Act.

(2) The application may be made without notice.

(3) The application must be in writing and must state the grounds for the application.

(4) If the court makes an order for the discharge of a restraint order, the applicant must serve copies of the order on—

    (a) the defendant;

    (b) any person who is prohibited from dealing with realisable property by the restraint order (whether before or after the discharge); and

    (c) any other person whom the applicant knows to be affected by the order.

R-368 **Application to punish for contempt of court**

59.6 (1) This rule applies where a person is accused of disobeying—

    (a) a restraint order; or

    (b) an ancillary order made for the purpose of ensuring that a restraint order is effective.

(2) An applicant who wants the Crown Court to exercise its power to punish that person for contempt of court must comply with the rules in Part 62 (Contempt of court).

CRIMINAL PROCEDURE RULES   PART 60   PROCEEDS OF CRIME ACT 2002: RULES APPLICABLE ONLY TO RECEIVERSHIP PROCEEDINGS

R-369 **Application for appointment of a management or an enforcement receiver**

60.1 (1) This rule applies to an application for the appointment of a management receiver under section 48(1) of the Proceeds of Crime Act 2002 and an application for the appointment of an enforcement receiver under section 50(1) of the 2002 Act.

(2) The application may be made without notice if—

    (a) the application is joined with an application for a restraint order under rule 59.1;

    (b) the application is urgent; or

    (c) there are reasonable grounds for believing that giving notice would cause the dissipation of realisable property which is the subject of the application.

(3) The application must be in writing and must be supported by a witness statement which must—

    (a) give the grounds for the application;

    (b) give full details of the proposed receiver;

    (c) to the best of the witness's ability, give full details of the realisable property in respect of which the applicant is seeking the order and specify the person holding that realisable property;

    (d) where the application is made by an accredited financial investigator, include a statement that, under section 68 of the 2002 Act, the applicant has authority to apply; and

    (e) if the proposed receiver is not a person falling within section 55(8) of the 2002 Act and the applicant is asking the court to allow the receiver to act—

      (i) without giving security, or

      (ii) before he has given security or satisfied the court that he has security in place, explain the reasons why that is necessary.

(4) Where the application is for the appointment of an enforcement receiver, the applicant must provide the Crown Court with a copy of the confiscation order made against the defendant.

(5) The application and witness statement must be lodged with the Crown Court.

(6) Except where, under paragraph (2), notice of the application is not required to be served, the application and witness statement must be lodged with the Crown Court and served on—

    (a) the defendant;

    (b) any person who holds realisable property to which the application relates; and

    (c) any other person whom the applicant knows to be affected by the application,

at least seven days before the date fixed by the court for hearing the application, unless the Crown Court specifies a shorter period.

(7) If the court makes an order for the appointment of a receiver, the applicant must serve copies of the order and of the witness statement made in support of the application on—

    (a) the defendant;

    (b) any person who holds realisable property to which the order applies; and

    (c) any other person whom the applicant knows to be affected by the order.

Application for conferral of powers on a management receiver or an enforcement receiver   R-370

60.2   (1)   This rule applies to an application for the conferral of powers on a management receiver under section 49(1) of the Proceeds of Crime Act 2002 or an enforcement receiver under section 51(1) of the 2002 Act.

(2)   The application may be made without notice if the application is to give the receiver power to take possession of property and—

(a)   the application is joined with an application for a restraint order under rule 59.1;

(b)   the application is urgent; or

(c)   there are reasonable grounds for believing that giving notice would cause the dissipation of the property which is the subject of the application.

(3)   The application must be made in writing and supported by a witness statement which must—

(a)   give the grounds for the application;

(b)   give full details of the realisable property in respect of which the applicant is seeking the order and specify the person holding that realisable property; and

(c)   where the application is made by an accredited financial investigator, include a statement that, under section 68 of the 2002 Act, the applicant has authority to apply;

(d)   where the application is for power to start, carry on or defend legal proceedings in respect of the property, explain—

(i)   what proceedings are concerned, in what court, and

(ii)   what powers the receiver will ask that court to exercise.

(4)   Where the application is for the conferral of powers on an enforcement receiver or Director's receiver, the applicant must provide the Crown Court with a copy of the confiscation order made against the defendant.

(5)   The application and witness statement must be lodged with the Crown Court.

(6)   Except where, under paragraph (2), notice of the application is not required to be served, the application and witness statement must be served on—

(a)   the defendant;

(b)   any person who holds realisable property in respect of which a receiver has been appointed or in respect of which an application for a receiver has been made;

(c)   any other person whom the applicant knows to be affected by the application; and

(d)   the receiver (if one has already been appointed), at least seven days before the date fixed by the court for hearing the application, unless the Crown Court specifies a shorter period.

(7)   If the court makes an order for the conferral of powers on a receiver, the applicant must serve copies of the order on—

(a)   the defendant;

(b)   any person who holds realisable property in respect of which the receiver has been appointed; and

(c)   any other person whom the applicant knows to be affected by the order.

Applications for discharge or variation of receivership orders, and applications for other orders   R-371

60.3   (1)   This rule applies to applications under section 62(3) of the Proceeds of Crime Act 2002 for orders (by persons affected by the action of receivers) and applications under section 63(1) of the 2002 Act for the discharge or variation of orders relating to receivers.

(2)   The application must be made in writing and lodged with the Crown Court.

(3)   The application must be served on the following persons (except where they are the person making the application)—

(a)   the person who applied for appointment of the receiver;

(b)   the defendant;

(c)   any person who holds realisable property in respect of which the receiver has been appointed;

(d)   the receiver; and

(e)   any other person whom the applicant knows to be affected by the application, at least seven days before the date fixed by the court for hearing the application, unless the Crown Court specifies a shorter period.

(4)   If the court makes an order for the discharge or variation of an order relating to a receiver under section 63(2) of the 2002 Act, the applicant must serve copies of the order on any persons whom he knows to be affected by the order.

Sums in the hands of receivers   R-372

60.4   (1)   This rule applies where the amount payable under a confiscation order has been fully paid and any sums remain in the hands of an enforcement receiver or Director's receiver.

(2) The receiver must make an application to the Crown Court for directions as to the distribution of the sums in his hands.

(3) The application and any evidence which the receiver intends to rely on in support of the application must be served on—

(a) the defendant; and

(b) any other person who held (or holds) interests in any property realised by the receiver, at least seven days before the date fixed by the court for hearing the application, unless the Crown Court specifies a shorter period.

(4) If any of the provisions listed in paragraph (5) (provisions as to the vesting of funds in a trustee in bankruptcy) apply, then the Crown Court must make a declaration to that effect.

(5) These are the provisions—

(a) section 31B of the Bankruptcy (Scotland) Act 1985;

(b) section 306B of the Insolvency Act 1986; and

(c) article 279B of the Insolvency (Northern Ireland) Order 1989.

R-373   Security

60.5 (1) This rule applies where the Crown Court appoints a receiver under section 48, 50 or 52 of the Proceeds of Crime Act 2002 and the receiver is not a person falling within section 55(8) of the 2002 Act (and it is immaterial whether the receiver is a permanent or temporary member of staff or on secondment).

(2) The Crown Court may direct that before the receiver begins to act, or within a specified time, he must either—

(a) give such security as the Crown Court may determine; or

(b) file with the Crown Court and serve on all parties to any receivership proceedings evidence that he already has in force sufficient security,

to cover his liability for his acts and omissions as a receiver.

(3) The Crown Court may terminate the appointment of a receiver if he fails to—

(a) give the security; or

(b) satisfy the court as to the security he has in force, by the date specified.

R-374   Remuneration

60.6 (1) This rule applies where the Crown Court appoints a receiver under section 48, 50 or 52 of the Proceeds of Crime Act 2002 and the receiver is not a person falling within section 55(8) of the 2002 Act (and it is immaterial whether the receiver is a permanent or temporary member or he is on secondment from elsewhere).

(2) The receiver may only charge for his services if the Crown Court—

(a) so directs; and

(b) specifies the basis on which the receiver is to be remunerated.

(3) Unless the Crown Court orders otherwise, in determining the remuneration of the receiver, the Crown Court shall award such sum as is reasonable and proportionate in all the circumstances and which takes into account—

(a) the time properly given by him and his staff to the receivership;

(b) the complexity of the receivership;

(c) any responsibility of an exceptional kind or degree which falls on the receiver in consequence of the receivership;

(d) the effectiveness with which the receiver appears to be carrying out, or to have carried out, his duties; and

(e) the value and nature of the subject matter of the receivership.

(4) The Crown Court may refer the determination of a receiver's remuneration to be ascertained by the taxing authority of the Crown Court and rules 76.11 to 76.14 shall have effect as if the taxing authority was ascertaining costs.

(5) A receiver appointed under section 48 of the 2002 Act is to receive his remuneration by realising property in respect of which he is appointed, in accordance with section 49(2)(d) of the 2002 Act.

(6) A receiver appointed under section 50 of the 2002 Act is to receive his remuneration by applying to the magistrates' court officer for payment under section 55(4)(b) of the 2002 Act.

(7) A receiver appointed under section 52 of the 2002 Act is to receive his remuneration by applying to the Director for payment under section 57(4)(b) of the 2002 Act.

R-375   Accounts

60.7 (1) The Crown Court may order a receiver appointed under section 48, 50 or 52 of the Proceeds of Crime Act 2002 to prepare and serve accounts.

(2) A party to receivership proceedings served with such accounts may apply for an order permitting him to inspect any document in the possession of the receiver relevant to those accounts.

(3) Any party to receivership proceedings may, within 14 days of being served with the accounts, serve notice on the receiver—

(a) specifying any item in the accounts to which he objects;

(b) giving the reason for such objection; and

(c) requiring the receiver within 14 days of receipt of the notice, either—

(i) to notify all the parties who were served with the accounts that he accepts the objection, or

(ii) if he does not accept the objection, to apply for an examination of the accounts in relation to the contested item.

(4) When the receiver applies for the examination of the accounts he must at the same time lodge with the Crown Court—

(a) the accounts; and

(b) a copy of the notice served on him under this section of the rule.

(5) If the receiver fails to comply with paragraph (3)(c) of this rule, any party to receivership proceedings may apply to the Crown Court for an examination of the accounts in relation to the contested item.

(6) At the conclusion of its examination of the accounts the court must certify the result.

Non-compliance by receiver   R-376

60.8 (1) If a receiver appointed under section 48, 50 or 52 of the Proceeds of Crime Act 2002 fails to comply with any rule, practice direction or direction of the Crown Court, the Crown Court may order him to attend a hearing to explain his non-compliance.

(2) At the hearing, the Crown Court may make any order it considers appropriate, including—

(a) terminating the appointment of the receiver;

(b) reducing the receiver's remuneration or disallowing it altogether; and

(c) ordering the receiver to pay the costs of any party.

CRIMINAL PROCEDURE RULES   PART 61   PROCEEDS OF CRIME ACT 2002: RULES APPLICABLE TO RESTRAINT AND RECEIVERSHIP PROCEEDINGS

Distress and forfeiture   R-377

61.1 (1) This rule applies to applications under sections 58(2) and (3) and 59(2) and (3) of the Proceeds of Crime Act 2002 for leave of the Crown Court to levy distress against property or exercise a right of forfeiture by peaceable re-entry in relation to a tenancy, in circumstances where the property or tenancy is the subject of a restraint order or a receiver has been appointed in respect of the property or tenancy.

(2) The application must be made in writing to the Crown Court.

(3) The application must be served on—

(a) the person who applied for the restraint order or the order appointing the receiver; and

(b) any receiver appointed in respect of the property or tenancy,

at least seven days before the date fixed by the court for hearing the application, unless the Crown Court specifies a shorter period.

Joining of applications   R-378

61.2 An application for the appointment of a management receiver or enforcement receiver under rule 60.1 may be joined with—

(a) an application for a restraint order under rule 59.1; and

(b) an application for the conferral of powers on the receiver under rule 60.2.

Applications to be dealt with in writing   R-379

61.3 Applications in restraint proceedings and receivership proceedings are to be dealt with without a hearing, unless the Crown Court orders otherwise.

Business in chambers   R-380

61.4 Restraint proceedings and receivership proceedings may be heard in chambers.

R-381 **Power of court to control evidence**

    61.5 (1) When hearing restraint proceedings and receivership proceedings, the Crown Court may control the evidence by giving directions as to—

          (a) the issues on which it requires evidence;

          (b) the nature of the evidence which it requires to decide those issues; and

          (c) the way in which the evidence is to be placed before the court.

      (2) The court may use its power under this rule to exclude evidence that would otherwise be admissible.

      (3) The court may limit cross-examination in restraint proceedings and receivership proceedings.

R-382 **Evidence of witnesses**

    61.6 (1) The general rule is that, unless the Crown Court orders otherwise, any fact which needs to be proved in restraint proceedings or receivership proceedings by the evidence of a witness is to be proved by their evidence in writing.

      (2) Where evidence is to be given in writing under this rule, any party may apply to the Crown Court for permission to cross-examine the person giving the evidence.

      (3) If the Crown Court gives permission under paragraph (2) but the person in question does not attend as required by the order, his evidence may not be used unless the court gives permission.

R-383 **Witness summons**

    61.7 (1) Any party to restraint proceedings or receivership proceedings may apply to the Crown Court to issue a witness summons requiring a witness to—

          (a) attend court to give evidence; or

          (b) produce documents to the court.

      (2) Rule 28.3 applies to an application under this rule as it applies to an application under section 2 of the Criminal Procedure (Attendance of Witnesses) Act 1965.

R-384 **Hearsay evidence**

    61.8 Section 2(1) of the Civil Evidence Act 1995 (duty to give notice of intention to rely on hearsay evidence) does not apply to evidence in restraint proceedings and receivership proceedings.

R-385 **Disclosure and inspection of documents**

    61.9 (1) This rule applies where, in the course of restraint proceedings or receivership proceedings, an issue arises as to whether property is realisable property.

      (2) The Crown Court may make an order for disclosure of documents.

      (3) Part 31 of the Civil Procedure Rules 1998 as amended from time to time shall have effect as if the proceedings were proceedings in the High Court.

R-386 **Court documents**

    61.10 (1) Any order which the Crown Court issues in restraint proceedings or receivership proceedings must—

          (a) state the name and judicial title of the person who made it;

          (b) bear the date on which it is made; and

          (c) be sealed by the Crown Court.

      (2) The Crown Court may place the seal on the order—

          (a) by hand; or

          (b) by printing a facsimile of the seal on the order whether electronically or otherwise.

      (3) A document purporting to bear the court's seal shall be admissible in evidence without further proof.

R-387 **Consent orders**

    61.11 (1) This rule applies where all the parties to restraint proceedings or receivership proceedings agree the terms in which an order should be made.

      (2) Any party may apply for a judgment or order in the terms agreed.

      (3) The Crown Court may deal with an application under paragraph (2) without a hearing.

      (4) Where this rule applies—

          (a) the order which is agreed by the parties must be drawn up in the terms agreed;

          (b) it must be expressed as being 'By Consent'; and

          (c) it must be signed by the legal representative acting for each of the parties to whom the order relates or by the party if he is a litigant in person.

      (5) Where an application is made under this rule, then the requirements of any other rule as to the procedure for making an application do not apply.

Slips and omissions   R-388

61.12 (1) The Crown Court may at any time correct an accidental slip or omission in an order made in restraint proceedings or receivership proceedings.

(2) A party may apply for a correction without notice.

Supply of documents from court records   R-389

61.13 (1) No document relating to restraint proceedings or receivership proceedings may be supplied from the records of the Crown Court for any person to inspect or copy unless the Crown Court grants permission.

(2) An application for permission under paragraph (1) must be made on notice to the parties to the proceedings.

Disclosure of documents in criminal proceedings   R-390

61.14 (1) This rule applies where—

(a) proceedings for an offence have been started in the Crown Court and the defendant has not been either convicted or acquitted on all counts; and

(b) an application for a restraint order under section 42(1) of the Proceeds of Crime Act 2002 has been made.

(2) The judge presiding at the proceedings for the offence may be supplied from the records of the Crown Court with documents relating to restraint proceedings and any receivership proceedings.

(3) Such documents must not otherwise be disclosed in the proceedings for the offence.

Preparation of documents   R-391

61.15 (1) Every order in restraint proceedings or receivership proceedings must be drawn up by the Crown Court unless—

(a) the Crown Court orders a party to draw it up;

(b) a party, with the permission of the Crown Court, agrees to draw it up; or

(c) the order is made by consent under rule 61.10.

(2) The Crown Court may direct that—

(a) an order drawn up by a party must be checked by the Crown Court before it is sealed; or

(b) before an order is drawn up by the Crown Court, the parties must lodge an agreed statement of its terms.

(3) Where an order is to be drawn up by a party—

(a) he must lodge it with the Crown Court no later than seven days after the date on which the court ordered or permitted him to draw it up so that it can be sealed by the Crown Court; and

(b) if he fails to lodge it within that period, any other party may draw it up and lodge it.

(4) Nothing in this rule shall require the Crown Court to accept a document which is illegible, has not been duly authorised, or is unsatisfactory for some other similar reason.

Change of solicitor   R-392

61.16 (1) This rule applies where—

(a) a party for whom a solicitor is acting in restraint proceedings or receivership proceedings wants to change his solicitor;

(b) a party, after having represented himself in such proceedings, appoints a solicitor to act on his behalf (except where the solicitor is appointed only to act as an advocate for a hearing); or

(c) a party, after having been represented by a solicitor in such proceedings, intends to act in person.

(2) Where this rule applies, the party or his solicitor (where one is acting) must—

(a) lodge notice of the change at the Crown Court; and

(b) serve notice of the change on every other party and, where paragraph (1)(a) or (c) applies, on the former solicitor.

(3) The notice lodged at the Crown Court must state that notice has been served as required by paragraph (2)(b).

Application by solicitor for declaration that solicitor has ceased to act   R-393

61.17 (1) A solicitor may apply to the Crown Court for an order declaring that he has ceased to be the solicitor acting for a party to restraint proceedings or receivership proceedings.

(2) Where an application is made under this rule—

    (a) notice of the application must be given to the party for whom the solicitor is acting, unless the Crown Court directs otherwise; and

    (b) the application must be supported by evidence.

(3) Where the Crown Court makes an order that a solicitor has ceased to act, the solicitor must serve a copy of the order on every party to the proceedings.

R-394 Application by other party for declaration that solicitor has ceased to act

61.18 (1) Where—

    (a) a solicitor who has acted for a party to restraint proceedings or receivership proceedings—

        (i) has died,

        (ii) has become bankrupt,

        (iii) has ceased to practise, or

        (iv) cannot be found, and

    (b) the party has not given notice of a change of solicitor or notice of intention to act in person as required by rule 61.16,

any other party may apply to the Crown Court for an order declaring that the solicitor has ceased to be the solicitor acting for the other party in the proceedings.

(2) Where an application is made under this rule, notice of the application must be given to the party to whose solicitor the application relates unless the Crown Court directs otherwise.

(3) Where the Crown Court makes an order under this rule, the applicant must serve a copy of the order on every other party to the proceedings.

R-395 Order for costs

61.19 (1) This rule applies where the Crown Court is deciding whether to make an order for costs in restraint proceedings or receivership proceedings.

(2) The court has discretion as to—

    (a) whether costs are payable by one party to another;

    (b) the amount of those costs; and

    (c) when they are to be paid.

(3) If the court decides to make an order about costs—

    (a) the general rule is that the unsuccessful party must be ordered to pay the costs of the successful party; but

    (b) the court may make a different order.

(4) In deciding what order (if any) to make about costs, the court must have regard to all of the circumstances, including—

    (a) the conduct of all the parties; and

    (b) whether a party has succeeded on part of an application, even if he has not been wholly successful.

(5) The orders which the court may make include an order that a party must pay—

    (a) a proportion of another party's costs;

    (b) a stated amount in respect of another party's costs;

    (c) costs from or until a certain date only;

    (d) costs incurred before proceedings have begun;

    (e) costs relating to particular steps taken in the proceedings;

    (f) costs relating only to a distinct part of the proceedings; and

    (g) interest on costs from or until a certain date, including a date before the making of an order.

(6) Where the court would otherwise consider making an order under paragraph (5)(f), it must instead, if practicable, make an order under paragraph (5)(a) or (c).

(7) Where the court has ordered a party to pay costs, it may order an amount to be paid on account before the costs are assessed.

R-396 Assessment of costs

61.20 (1) Where the Crown Court has made an order for costs in restraint proceedings or receivership proceedings it may either—

    (a) make an assessment of the costs itself; or

    (b) order assessment of the costs under rule 76.11.

(2) In either case, the Crown Court or the assessing authority, as the case may be, must—

    (a) only allow costs which are proportionate to the matters in issue; and

    (b) resolve any doubt which it may have as to whether the costs were reasonably incurred or reasonable and proportionate in favour of the paying party.

(3) The Crown Court or the assessing authority, as the case may be, is to have regard to all the circumstances in deciding whether costs were proportionately or reasonably incurred or proportionate and reasonable in amount.

(4) In particular, the Crown Court or the assessing authority must give effect to any orders which have already been made.

(5) The Crown Court or the assessing authority must also have regard to—
   (a) the conduct of all the parties, including in particular, conduct before, as well as during, the proceedings;
   (b) the amount or value of the property involved;
   (c) the importance of the matter to all the parties;
   (d) the particular complexity of the matter or the difficulty or novelty of the questions raised;
   (e) the skill, effort, specialised knowledge and responsibility involved;
   (f) the time spent on the application; and
   (g) the place where and the circumstances in which work or any part of it was done.

Time for complying with an order for costs   R-397

61.21 A party to restraint proceedings or receivership proceedings must comply with an order for the payment of costs within 14 days of—
   (a) the date of the order if it states the amount of those costs;
   (b) if the amount of those costs is decided later under rule 76.11, the date of the assessing authority's decision; or
   (c) in either case, such later date as the Crown Court may specify.

Application of costs rules   R-398

61.22 Rules 61.19, 61.20 and 61.21 do not apply to the assessment of costs in proceedings to the extent that section 11 of the Access to Justice Act 1999 applies and provisions made under that Act make different provision.

CRIMINAL PROCEDURE RULES   PART 62   CONTEMPT OF COURT

Section 1: general rules

When this Part applies   R-399

62.1 (1) This Part applies where the court can deal with a person for conduct—
   (a) in contempt of court; or
   (b) in contravention of the legislation to which rules 62.5 and 62.9 refer.
(2) In this Part, 'respondent' means any such accused person.

Exercise of court's power to deal with contempt of court   R-400

62.2 (1) The court must determine at a hearing—
   (a) an enquiry under rule 62.8;
   (b) an allegation under rule 62.9.
(2) The court must not proceed in the respondent's absence unless—
   (a) the respondent's behaviour makes it impracticable to proceed otherwise; or
   (b) the respondent has had at least 14 days' notice of the hearing, or was present when it was arranged.
(3) If the court hears part of an enquiry or allegation in private, it must announce at a hearing in public—
   (a) the respondent's name;
   (b) in general terms, the nature of any conduct that the respondent admits, or the court finds proved; and
   (c) any punishment imposed.

Notice of suspension of imprisonment by Court of Appeal or Crown Court   R-401

62.3 (1) This rule applies where—
   (a) the Court of Appeal or the Crown Court suspends an order of imprisonment for contempt of court; and
   (b) the respondent is absent when the court does so.
(2) The respondent must be served with notice of the terms of the court's order—
   (a) by any applicant under rule 62.9; or
   (b) by the court officer, in any other case.

R-402   **Application to discharge an order for imprisonment**

62.4   (1)   This rule applies where the court can discharge an order for a respondent's imprisonment for contempt of court.

     (2)   A respondent who wants the court to discharge such an order must—

       (a)   apply in writing, unless the court otherwise directs, and serve any written application on—

          (i)   the court officer, and

          (ii)   any applicant under rule 62.9 on whose application the respondent was imprisoned;

       (b)   in the application—

          (i)   explain why it is appropriate for the order for imprisonment to be discharged, and

          (ii)   give details of any appeal, and its outcome; and

       (c)   ask for a hearing, if the respondent wants one.

Section 2: contempt of court by obstruction, disruption, etc.

R-403   **Initial procedure on obstruction, disruption etc.**

62.5   (1)   This rule applies where the court observes, or someone reports to the court—

       (a)   in the Court of Appeal or the Crown Court, obstructive, disruptive, insulting or intimidating conduct, in the courtroom or in its vicinity, or otherwise immediately affecting the proceedings;

       (b)   in the Crown Court, a contravention of—

          (i)   section 3 of the Criminal Procedure (Attendance of Witnesses) Act 1965 (disobeying a witness summons);

          (ii)   section 20 of the Juries Act 1974 (disobeying a jury summons);

          (iii)   section 8 of the Contempt of Court Act 1981 (obtaining details of a jury's deliberations, etc.);

       (c)   in a magistrates' court, a contravention of—

          (i)   section 97(4) of the Magistrates' Courts Act 1980 (refusing to give evidence), or

          (ii)   section 12 of the Contempt of Court Act 1981 (insulting or interrupting the court, etc.);

       (d)   a contravention of section 9 of the Contempt of Court Act 1981 (without the court's permission, recording the proceedings, etc.);

       (e)   any other conduct with which the court can deal as, or as if it were, a criminal contempt of court, except failure to surrender to bail under section 6 of the Bail Act 1976.

     (2)   Unless the respondent's behaviour makes it impracticable to do so, the court must—

       (a)   explain, in terms the respondent can understand (with help, if necessary)—

          (i)   the conduct that is in question,

          (ii)   that the court can impose imprisonment, or a fine, or both, for such conduct,

          (iii)   (where relevant) that the court has power to order the respondent's immediate temporary detention, if in the court's opinion that is required,

          (iv)   that the respondent may explain the conduct,

          (v)   that the respondent may apologise, if he or she so wishes, and that this may persuade the court to take no further action, and

          (vi)   that the respondent may take legal advice; and

       (b)   allow the respondent a reasonable opportunity to reflect, take advice, explain and, if he or she so wishes, apologise.

     (3)   The court may then—

       (a)   take no further action in respect of that conduct;

       (b)   enquire into the conduct there and then; or

       (c)   postpone that enquiry (if a magistrates' court, only until later the same day).

R-404   **Review after temporary detention**

62.6   (1)   This rule applies in a case in which the court has ordered the respondent's immediate temporary detention for conduct to which rule 62.5 applies.

     (2)   The court must review the case—

       (a)   if a magistrates' court, later the same day;

       (b)   in the Court of Appeal or the Crown Court, no later than the next business day.

     (3)   On the review, the court must—

       (a)   unless the respondent is absent, repeat the explanations required by rule 62.5(2)(a); and

       (b)   allow the respondent a reasonable opportunity to reflect, take advice, explain and, if he or she so wishes, apologise.

(4) The court may then—

    (a) take no further action in respect of the conduct;

    (b) if a magistrates' court, enquire into the conduct there and then; or

    (c) if the Court of Appeal or the Crown Court—

        (i) enquire into the conduct there and then, or

        (ii) postpone the enquiry, and order the respondent's release from such detention in the meantime.

Postponement of enquiry   **R-405**

62.7 (1) This rule applies where the Court of Appeal or the Crown Court postpones the enquiry.

    (2) The court must arrange for the preparation of a written statement containing such particulars of the conduct in question as to make clear what the respondent appears to have done.

    (3) The court officer must serve on the respondent—

        (a) that written statement;

        (b) notice of where and when the postponed enquiry will take place; and

        (c) a notice that—

            (i) reminds the respondent that the court can impose imprisonment, or a fine, or both, for contempt of court, and

            (ii) warns the respondent that the court may pursue the postponed enquiry in the respondent's absence, if the respondent does not attend.

Procedure on enquiry   **R-406**

62.8 (1) At an enquiry, the court must—

        (a) ensure that the respondent understands (with help, if necessary) what is alleged, if the enquiry has been postponed from a previous occasion;

        (b) explain what the procedure at the enquiry will be; and

        (c) ask whether the respondent admits the conduct in question.

    (2) If the respondent admits the conduct, the court need not receive evidence.

    (3) If the respondent does not admit the conduct, the court must receive—

        (a) any statement served under rule 62.7;

        (b) any other evidence of the conduct;

        (c) any evidence introduced by the respondent; and

        (d) any representations by the respondent about the conduct.

    (4) If the respondent admits the conduct, or the court finds it proved, the court must—

        (a) before imposing any punishment for contempt of court, give the respondent an opportunity to make representations relevant to punishment;

        (b) explain, in terms the respondent can understand (with help, if necessary)—

            (i) the reasons for its decision, including its findings of fact, and

            (ii) the punishment it imposes, and its effect; and

        (c) if a magistrates' court, arrange for the preparation of a written record of those findings.

    (5) The court that conducts an enquiry—

        (a) need not include the same member or members as the court that observed the conduct; but

        (b) may do so, unless that would be unfair to the respondent.

Section 3: contempt of court by failure to comply with court order

Initial procedure on failure to comply with court order, etc.   **R-407**

62.9 (1) This rule applies where—

    (a) a party, or other person directly affected, alleges—

        (i) in the Crown Court, a failure to comply with an order to which rule 6.13 or 6.22 (certain investigation orders), or rule 59.6 (restraint order or ancillary order), applies,

        (ii) in the Court of Appeal or the Crown Court, any other conduct with which that court can deal as a civil contempt of court, or

        (iii) in the Crown Court or a magistrates' court, unauthorised use of disclosed prosecution material under section 17 of the Criminal Procedure and Investigations Act 1996;

    (b) the court deals on its own initiative with conduct to which paragraph (1)(a) applies.

    (2) Such a party or person must—

        (a) apply in writing and serve the application on the court officer; and

        (b) serve on the respondent—

            (i) the application, and

(ii) notice of where and when the court will consider the allegation (not less than 14 days after service).

(3) The application must—

(a) identify the respondent;

(b) explain that it is an application for the respondent to be dealt with for contempt of court;

(c) contain such particulars of the conduct in question as to make clear what is alleged against the respondent; and

(d) include a notice warning the respondent that the court—

(i) can impose imprisonment, or a fine, or both, for contempt of court, and

(ii) may deal with the application in the respondent's absence, if the respondent does not attend the hearing.

(4) A court which acts on its own initiative under paragraph (1)(b) must—

(a) arrange for the preparation of a written statement containing the same information as an application; and

(b) arrange for the service on the respondent of—

(i) that written statement, and

(ii) notice of where and when the court will consider the allegation (not less than 14 days after service).

R-408 Procedure on hearing

62.10 (1) At the hearing of an allegation under rule 62.9, the court must—

(a) ensure that the respondent understands (with help, if necessary) what is alleged;

(b) explain what the procedure at the hearing will be; and

(c) ask whether the respondent admits the conduct in question.

(2) If the respondent admits the conduct, the court need not receive evidence.

(3) If the respondent does not admit the conduct, the court must receive—

(a) the application or written statement served under rule 62.9;

(b) any other evidence of the conduct;

(c) any evidence introduced by the respondent; and

(d) any representations by the respondent about the conduct.

(4) If the respondent admits the conduct, or the court finds it proved, the court must—

(a) before imposing any punishment for contempt of court, give the respondent an opportunity to make representations relevant to punishment;

(b) explain, in terms the respondent can understand (with help, if necessary)—

(i) the reasons for its decision, including its findings of fact, and

(ii) the punishment it imposes, and its effect; and

(c) in a magistrates' court, arrange for the preparation of a written record of those findings.

R-409 Introduction of written witness statement or other hearsay

62.11 (1) Where rule 62.9 applies, an applicant or respondent who wants to introduce in evidence the written statement of a witness, or other hearsay, must—

(a) serve a copy of the statement, or notice of other hearsay, on—

(i) the court officer, and

(ii) the other party; and

(b) serve the copy or notice—

(i) when serving the application under rule 62.9, in the case of an applicant, or

(ii) not more than 7 days after service of that application or of the court's written statement, in the case of the respondent.

(2) Such service is notice of that party's intention to introduce in evidence that written witness statement, or other hearsay, unless that party otherwise indicates when serving it.

(3) A party entitled to receive such notice may waive that entitlement.

R-410 Content of written witness statement

62.12 (1) This rule applies to a written witness statement served under rule 62.11.

(2) Such a written witness statement must contain a declaration by the person making it that it is true to the best of that person's knowledge and belief.

R-411 Content of notice of other hearsay

62.13 (1) This rule applies to a notice of hearsay, other than a written witness statement, served under rule 62.6.

(2) Such a notice must—

(a) set out the evidence, or attach the document that contains it; and

(b) identify the person who made the statement that is hearsay.

Cross-examination of maker of written witness statement or other hearsay   R-412

62.14 (1) This rule applies where a party wants the court's permission to cross-examine a person who made a statement which another person wants to introduce as hearsay.

(2) The party who wants to cross-examine that person must—

   (a) apply in writing, with reasons; and

   (b) serve the application on—

      (i) the court officer, and

      (ii) the party who served the hearsay.

(3) A respondent who wants to cross-examine such a person must apply to do so not more than 7 days after service of the hearsay by the applicant.

(4) An applicant who wants to cross-examine such a person must apply to do so not more than 3 days after service of the hearsay by the respondent.

(5) The court—

   (a) may decide an application under this rule without a hearing; but

   (b) must not dismiss such an application unless the person making it has had an opportunity to make representations at a hearing.

Credibility and consistency of maker of written witness statement or other hearsay   R-413

62.15 (1) This rule applies where a party wants to challenge the credibility or consistency of a person who made a statement which another party wants to introduce as hearsay.

(2) The party who wants to challenge the credibility or consistency of that person must—

   (a) serve a written notice of intention to do so on—

      (i) the court officer, and

      (ii) the party who served the hearsay; and

   (b) in it, identify any statement or other material on which that party relies.

(3) A respondent who wants to challenge such a person's credibility or consistency must serve such a notice not more than 7 days after service of the hearsay by the applicant.

(4) An applicant who wants to challenge such a person's credibility or consistency must serve such a notice not more than 3 days after service of the hearsay by the respondent.

(5) The party who served the hearsay—

   (a) may call that person to give oral evidence instead; and

   (b) if so, must serve a notice of intention to do so on—

      (i) the court officer, and

      (ii) the other party

as soon as practicable after service of the notice under paragraph (2).

Magistrates' courts' powers to adjourn   R-414

62.16 (1) This rule applies where a magistrates' court deals with unauthorised disclosure of prosecution material under sections 17 and 18 of the Criminal Procedure and Investigations Act 1996.

(2) The sections of the Magistrates' Courts Act 1980 listed in paragraph (3) apply as if in those sections—

   (a) 'complaint' and 'summons' each referred to an application or written statement under rule 62.9;

   (b) 'complainant' meant an applicant; and

   (c) 'defendant' meant the respondent.

(3) Those sections are—

   (a) section 51 (issue of summons on complaint);

   (b) section 54 (adjournment);

   (c) section 55 (non-appearance of defendant);

   (d) section 97(1) (summons to witness);

   (e) section 121(1) (constitution and place of sitting of court);

   (f) section 123 (defect in process).

(4) Section 127 of the 1980 Act (limitation of time) does not apply.

Court's power to vary requirements under Section 3   R-415

62.17 (1) The court may shorten or extend (even after it has expired) a time limit under rule 62.11, 62.14 or 62.15.

(2) A person who wants an extension of time must—

   (a) apply when serving the statement, notice or application for which it is needed; and

   (b) explain the delay.

Criminal Practice Directions   Part 62   Contempt of Court

PD-70   CPD IX Contempt of court 62A: CONTEMPT IN THE FACE OF THE MAGISTRATES' COURT

General

62A.1   The procedure to be followed in cases of contempt of court is given in Part 62 of the Rules. The magistrates' courts' power to deal with contempt in the face of the court is contained within section 12 of the Contempt of Court Act 1981. Magistrates' courts also have the power to punish a witness who refuses to be sworn or give evidence under section 97(4) of the Magistrates' Courts Act 1980.

Contempt consisting of wilfully insulting anyone specified in section 12 or interrupting proceedings

62A.2   In the majority of cases, an apology and a promise as to future conduct should be sufficient for the court to order a person's release. However, there are likely to be certain cases where the nature and seriousness of the misconduct requires the court to consider using its powers, under section 12(2) of the Contempt of Court Act 1981, either to fine or to order the person's committal to custody.

Imposing a penalty for contempt

62A.3   The court should allow the person a further opportunity to apologise for his or her contempt, and should follow the procedure at r.62.8(4). The court should consider whether it is appropriate to release the person or whether it must exercise its powers to fine the person or to commit the person to custody under section 12(2) of the 1981 Act. In deciding how to deal with the person, the court should have regard to the period for which he or she has been detained, whether the conduct was admitted and the seriousness of the contempt. Any period of committal to custody should be for the shortest period of time commensurate with the interests of preserving good order in the administration of justice.

CRIMINAL PROCEDURE RULES   PART 63   APPEAL TO THE CROWN COURT

R-416   **When this Part applies**

63.1   (1)   This part applies where—

    (a)   a defendant wants to appeal under—

        (i)   section 108 of the Magistrates' Courts Act 1980,

        (ii)   section 45 of the Mental Health Act 1983,

        (iii)   paragraph 10 of Schedule 3 to the Powers of Criminal Courts (Sentencing) Act 2000, or paragraphs 9(8) or 13(5) of Schedule 8 to the Criminal Justice Act 2003;

    (b)   the Criminal Cases Review Commission refers a defendant's case to the Crown Court under section 11 of the Criminal Appeal Act 1995;

    (c)   a prosecutor wants to appeal under—

        (i)   section 14A(5A) of the Football Spectators Act 1989, or

        (ii)   section 147(3) of the Customs and Excise Management Act 1979; or

    (d)   a person wants to appeal under—

        (i)   section 1 of the Magistrates' Courts (Appeals from Binding Over Orders) Act 1956,

        (ii)   section 12(5) of the Contempt of Court Act 1981,

        (iii)   regulation 3C or 3H of the Costs in Criminal Cases (General) Regulations 1986,

        (iv)   section 22 of the Football Spectators Act 1989,

        (v)   section 10(4) or (5) of the Crime and Disorder Act 1998.

    (2)   A reference to an 'appellant' in this part is a reference to such a party or person.

R-417   **Service of appeal notice**

63.2   (1)   An appellant must serve an appeal notice on—

    (a)   the magistrates' court officer; and

    (b)   every other party.

    (2)   The appellant must serve the appeal notice—

    (a)   as soon after the decision appealed against as the appellant wants; but

    (b)   not more than 21 days after—

        (i)   sentence or the date sentence is deferred, whichever is earlier, if the appeal is against conviction or against a finding of guilt,

        (ii)   sentence, if the appeal is against sentence, or

        (iii)   the order or failure to make an order about which the appellant wants to appeal, in any other case.

(3) The appellant must serve with the appeal notice any application for the following, with reasons—
   (a) an extension of the time limit under this rule, if the appeal notice is late;
   (b) bail pending appeal, if the appellant is in custody;
   (c) the suspension of any disqualification imposed in the case, where the magistrates' court or the Crown Court can order such a suspension pending appeal.
(4) Where both the magistrates' court and the Crown Court can suspend a disqualification pending appeal, an application for its suspension must indicate by which court the appellant wants the application determined.

Form of appeal notice   R-418

63.3 The appeal notice must be in writing and must—
   (a) specify—
      (i) the conviction or finding of guilt,
      (ii) the sentence, or
      (iii) the order, or the failure to make an order
      about which the appellant wants to appeal;
   (b) summarise the issues;
   (c) in an appeal against conviction—
      (i) identify the prosecution witnesses whom the appellant will want to question if they are called to give oral evidence, and
      (ii) say how long the trial lasted in the magistrates' court and how long the appeal is likely to last in the Crown Court;
   (d) in an appeal against a finding that the appellant insulted someone or interrupted proceedings in the magistrates' court, attach—
      (i) the magistrates' court's written findings of fact, and
      (ii) the appellant's response to those findings;
   (e) say whether the appellant has asked the magistrates' court to reconsider the case; and
   (f) include a list of those on whom the appellant has served the appeal notice.

Duty of magistrates' court officer   R-419

63.4 The magistrates' court officer must—
   (a) as soon as practicable serve on the Crown Court officer—
      (i) the appeal notice and any accompanying application served by the appellant,
      (ii) details of the parties including their addresses,
      (iii) a copy of each magistrates' court register entry relating to the decision under appeal and to any application for bail pending appeal, and
      (iv) any report received for the purposes of sentencing;
   (b) keep any document or object exhibited in the proceedings in the magistrates' court, or arrange for it to be kept by some other appropriate person, until—
      (i) 6 weeks after the conclusion of those proceedings, or
      (ii) the conclusion of any proceedings in the Crown Court that begin within that 6 weeks;
   (c) provide the Crown Court with any document, object or information for which the Crown Court officer asks, within such period as the Crown Court officer may require; and
   (d) arrange for the magistrates' court to hear as soon as practicable any application to that court under rule 63.2(3) (suspension of disqualification pending appeal).

Duty of person keeping exhibit   R-420

63.5 A person who, under arrangements made by the magistrates' court officer, keeps a document or object exhibited in the proceedings in the magistrates' court must—
   (a) keep that exhibit until—
      (i) 6 weeks after the conclusion of those proceedings, or
      (ii) the conclusion of any proceedings in the Crown Court that begin within that 6 weeks, unless the magistrates' court or the Crown Court otherwise directs; and
   (b) provide the Crown Court with any such document or object for which the Crown Court officer asks, within such period as the Crown Court officer may require.

Reference by the Criminal Cases Review Commission   R-421

63.6 (1) The Crown Court officer must, as soon as practicable, serve a reference by the Criminal Cases Review Commission on—
   (a) the appellant;
   (b) every other party; and
   (c) the magistrates' court officer.

Criminal Procedure Rules 2013 and Criminal Practice Directions

(2) The appellant may serve an appeal notice on—
   (a) the Crown Court officer; and
   (b) every other party,
   not more than 21 days later.
(3) The Crown Court must treat the reference as the appeal notice if the appellant does not serve an appeal notice.

R-422 **Hearings and decisions**

63.7 (1) The Crown Court as a general rule must hear in public an appeal or reference to which this part applies, but—
   (a) may order any hearing to be in private; and
   (b) where a hearing is about a public interest ruling, must hold that hearing in private.
(2) The Crown Court officer must give as much notice as reasonably practicable of every hearing to—
   (a) the parties;
   (b) any party's custodian; and
   (c) any other person whom the Crown Court requires to be notified.
(3) The Crown Court officer must serve every decision on—
   (a) the parties;
   (b) any other person whom the Crown Court requires to be served; and
   (c) the magistrates' court officer and any party's custodian, where the decision determines an appeal.
(4) But where a hearing or decision is about a public interest ruling, the Crown Court officer must not—
   (a) give notice of that hearing to; or
   (b) serve that decision on,
   anyone other than the prosecutor who applied for that ruling, unless the court otherwise directs.

R-423 **Abandoning an appeal**

63.8 (1) The appellant—
   (a) may abandon an appeal without the Crown Court's permission, by serving a notice of abandonment on—
      (i) the magistrates' court officer,
      (ii) the Crown Court officer, and
      (iii) every other party
      before the hearing of the appeal begins; but
   (b) after the hearing of the appeal begins, may only abandon the appeal with the Crown Court's permission.
(2) A notice of abandonment must be signed by or on behalf of the appellant.
(3) Where an appellant who is on bail pending appeal abandons an appeal—
   (a) the appellant must surrender to custody as directed by the magistrates' court officer; and
   (b) any conditions of bail apply until then.

R-424 **Court's power to vary requirements under this Part**

63.9 The Crown Court may—
   (a) shorten or extend (even after it has expired) a time limit under this Part;
   (b) allow an appellant to vary an appeal notice that that appellant has served;
   (c) direct that an appeal notice be served on any person;
   (d) allow an appeal notice or a notice of abandonment to be in a different form to one set out in the Practice Direction, or to be presented orally.

R-425 **Constitution of the Crown Court**

63.10 On the hearing of an appeal—
   (a) the general rule is that the Crown Court must comprise—
      (i) a judge of the High Court, a Circuit judge, a Recorder or a qualifying judge advocate, and
      (ii) no less than two and no more than four justices of the peace, none of whom took part in the decision under appeal; and
   (b) if the appeal is from a youth court—
      (i) each justice of the peace must be qualified to sit as a member of a youth court, and
      (ii) the Crown Court must include a man and a woman; but

(c) the Crown Court may include only one justice of the peace and need not include both a man and a woman if—

    (i) the presiding judge decides that otherwise the start of the appeal hearing will be delayed unreasonably, or

    (ii) one or more of the justices of the peace who started hearing the appeal is absent.

Criminal Practice Directions   Part 63   Appeal to the Crown Court

CPD X Appeal 63A: APPEALS TO THE CROWN COURT   PD-71

63A.1 Rule 63.4 applies when a defendant appeals to the Crown Court against conviction or sentence and specifies the information and documentation that must be provided by the magistrates' court.

63A.2 On an appeal against conviction, the reasons given by the magistrates for their decision should not be included with the documents; the appeal hearing is not a review of the magistrates' court's decision but a re-hearing.

63A.3 On an appeal against sentence, the magistrates' court's reasons and factual finding leading to the finding of guilt should be included, but any reasons for the sentence imposed should be omitted as the Crown Court will be conducting a fresh sentencing exercise.

Criminal Procedure Rules   Part 64   Appeal to the High Court by Case Stated

When this Part applies   R-426

64.1 This Part applies where a person wants to appeal to the High Court by case stated—

    (a) under section 111 of the Magistrates' Courts Act 1980, against a decision of a magistrates' court; or

    (b) under section 28 of the Senior Courts Act 1981, against a decision of the Crown Court.

Application to state a case   R-427

64.2 (1) A party who wants the court to state a case for the opinion of the High Court must—

    (a) apply in writing, not more than 21 days after the decision against which the applicant wants to appeal; and

    (b) serve the application on—

        (i) the court officer, and

        (ii) each other party.

(2) The application must—

    (a) specify the decision in issue;

    (b) specify the proposed question or questions of law or jurisdiction on which the opinion of the High Court will be asked;

    (c) indicate the proposed grounds of appeal; and

    (d) include or attach any application for the following, with reasons—

        (i) if the application is to the Crown Court, an extension of time within which to apply to state a case,

        (ii) bail pending appeal,

        (iii) the suspension of any disqualification imposed in the case, where the court can order such a suspension pending appeal.

(3) A party who wants to make representations about the application must—

    (a) serve the representations on—

        (i) the court officer, and

        (ii) each other party; and

    (b) do so not more than 14 days after service of the application.

(4) The court may determine the application without a hearing.

(5) If the court decides not to state a case, the court officer must serve on each party—

    (a) notice of that decision; and

    (b) the court's written reasons for that decision, if not more than 21 days later the applicant asks for those reasons.

R-428 **Preparation of case stated**

64.3 (1) This rule applies where the court decides to state a case for the opinion of the High Court.

    (2) The court officer must serve on each party notice of—

        (a) the decision to state a case, and

        (b) any recognizance ordered by the court.

    (3) Unless the court otherwise directs, not more than 21 days after the court's decision to state a case—

        (a) in a magistrates court, the court officer must serve a draft case on each party;

        (b) in the Crown Court, the applicant must serve a draft case on the court officer and each other party.

    (4) The draft case must—

        (a) specify the decision in issue;

        (b) specify the question(s) of law or jurisdiction on which the opinion of the High Court will be asked;

        (c) include a succinct summary of—

            (i)   the nature and history of the proceedings,

            (ii) the court's relevant findings of fact, and

            (iii) the relevant contentions of the parties;

        (d) if a question is whether there was sufficient evidence on which the court reasonably could reach a finding of fact—

            (i)   specify that finding, and

            (ii) include a summary of the evidence on which the court reached that finding.

    (5) Except to the extent that paragraph (4)(d) requires, the draft case must not include an account of the evidence received by the court.

    (6) A party who wants to make representations about the content of the draft case, or to propose a revised draft, must—

        (a) serve the representations, or revised draft, on—

            (i)   the court officer, and

            (ii) each other party; and

        (b) do so not more than 21 days after service of the draft case.

    (7) The court must state the case not more than 21 days after the time for service of representations under paragraph (6) has expired.

    (8) A case stated for the opinion of the High Court must—

        (a) comply with paragraphs (4) and (5); and

        (b) identify—

            (i)   the court that stated it, and

            (ii) the court office for that court.

    (9) The court officer must serve the case stated on each party.

R-429 **Duty of justices' legal adviser**

64.4 (1) This rule applies—

        (a) only in a magistrates' court; and

        (b) unless the court—

            (i)   includes a District Judge (Magistrates' Courts), and

            (ii) otherwise directs.

    (2) A justices' legal adviser must—

        (a) give the court legal advice; and

        (b) if the court so requires, assist it by—

            (i)   preparing and amending the draft case, and

            (ii) completing the case stated.

R-430 **Court's power to vary requirements under this Part**

64.5 (1) The court may shorten or extend (even after it has expired) a time limit under this Part.

    (2) A person who wants an extension of time must—

        (a) apply when serving the application, representations or draft case for which it is needed; and

        (b) explain the delay.

CRIMINAL PROCEDURE RULES   PART 65   APPEAL TO THE COURT OF APPEAL: GENERAL RULES

When this Part applies

R-431

65.1 (1) This Part applies to all applications, appeals and references to the Court of Appeal to which Parts 66, 67, 68, 69, 70 and 74 apply.

(2) In this Part and in those, unless the context makes it clear that something different is meant, 'court' means the Court of Appeal or any judge of that court.

Case management in the Court of Appeal

R-432

65.2 (1) The court and the parties have the same duties and powers as under Part 3 (case management).

(2) The Registrar—

(a) must fulfil the duty of active case management under rule 3.2; and

(b) in fulfilling that duty may exercise any of the powers of case management under—

(i) rule 3.5 (the court's general powers of case management),

(ii) rule 3.9(3) (requiring a certificate of readiness), and

(iii) rule 3.10 (requiring a party to identify intentions and anticipated requirements) subject to the directions of the court.

(3) The Registrar must nominate a case progression officer under rule 3.4.

Power to vary requirements

R-433

65.3 The court or the Registrar may—

(a) shorten a time limit or extend it (even after it has expired) unless that is inconsistent with other legislation;

(b) allow a party to vary any notice that that party has served;

(c) direct that a notice or application be served on any person;

(d) allow a notice or application to be in a different form, or presented orally.

Application for extension of time

R-434

65.4 A person who wants an extension of time within which to serve a notice or make an application must—

(a) apply for that extension of time when serving that notice or making that application; and

(b) give the reasons for the application for an extension of time.

Renewing an application refused by a judge or the Registrar

R-435

65.5 (1) This rule applies where a party with the right to do so wants to renew—

(a) to a judge of the Court of Appeal an application refused by the Registrar; or

(b) to the Court of Appeal an application refused by a judge of that court.

(2) That party must—

(a) renew the application in the form set out in the Practice Direction, signed by or on behalf of the applicant;

(b) serve the renewed application on the Registrar not more than 14 days after—

(i) the refusal of the application that the applicant wants to renew; or

(ii) the Registrar serves that refusal on the applicant, if the applicant was not present in person or by live link when the original application was refused.

Hearings

R-436

65.6 (1) The general rule is that the Court of Appeal must hear in public—

(a) an application, including an application for permission to appeal; and

(b) an appeal or reference,

but it may order any hearing to be in private.

(2) Where a hearing is about a public interest ruling that hearing must be in private unless the court otherwise directs.

(3) Where the appellant wants to appeal against an order restricting public access to a trial, the court—

(a) may decide without a hearing—

(i) an application, including an application for permission to appeal, and

(ii) an appeal; but

(b) must announce its decision on such an appeal at a hearing in public.

(4) Where the appellant wants to appeal or to refer a case to the Supreme Court the court—

(a) may decide without a hearing an application—

(i) for permission to appeal or to refer a sentencing case, or

      (ii) to refer a point of law; but

  (b) must announce its decision on such an application at a hearing in public.

(5) A judge of the Court of Appeal and the Registrar may exercise any of their powers—

  (a) at a hearing in public or in private; or

  (b) without a hearing.

R-437   **Notice of hearings and decisions**

65.7 (1) The Registrar must give as much notice as reasonably practicable of every hearing to—

  (a) the parties;

  (b) any party's custodian;

  (c) any other person whom the court requires to be notified; and

  (d) the Crown Court officer, where Parts 66, 67 or 69 apply.

(2) The Registrar must serve every decision on—

  (a) the parties;

  (b) any other person whom the court requires to be served; and

  (c) the Crown Court officer and any party's custodian, where the decision determines an appeal or application for permission to appeal.

(3) But where a hearing or decision is about a public interest ruling, the Registrar must not—

  (a) give notice of that hearing to; or

  (b) serve that decision on,

anyone other than the prosecutor who applied for that ruling, unless the court otherwise directs.

R-438   **Duty of Crown Court officer**

65.8 (1) The Crown Court officer must provide the Registrar with any document, object or information for which the Registrar asks within such period as the Registrar may require.

(2) Where someone may appeal to the Court of Appeal, the Crown Court officer must keep any document or object exhibited in the proceedings in the Crown Court, or arrange for it to be kept by some other appropriate person, until—

  (a) 6 weeks after the conclusion of those proceedings; or

  (b) the conclusion of any appeal proceedings that begin within that 6 weeks,

unless the court, the Registrar or the Crown Court otherwise directs.

(3) Where Part 66 applies (appeal to the Court of Appeal against ruling at preparatory hearing), the Crown Court officer must as soon as practicable serve on the appellant a transcript or note of—

  (a) each order or ruling against which the appellant wants to appeal; and

  (b) the decision by the Crown Court judge on any application for permission to appeal.

(4) Where Part 67 applies (appeal to the Court of Appeal against ruling adverse to prosecution), the Crown Court officer must as soon as practicable serve on the appellant a transcript or note of—

  (a) each ruling against which the appellant wants to appeal;

  (b) the decision by the Crown Court judge on any application for permission to appeal; and

  (c) the decision by the Crown Court judge on any request to expedite the appeal.

(5) Where Part 68 applies (appeal to the Court of Appeal about conviction or sentence), the Crown Court officer must as soon as practicable serve on the Registrar—

  (a) the appeal notice and any accompanying application that the appellant serves on the Crown Court officer;

  (b) any Crown Court judge's certificate that the case is fit for appeal;

  (c) the decision on any application at the Crown Court centre for bail pending appeal;

  (d) such of the Crown Court case papers as the Registrar requires; and

  (e) such transcript of the Crown Court proceedings as the Registrar requires.

(6) Where Part 69 applies (appeal to the Court of Appeal regarding reporting or public access) and an order is made restricting public access to a trial, the Crown Court officer must—

  (a) immediately notify the Registrar of that order, if the appellant has given advance notice of intention to appeal; and

  (b) as soon as practicable provide the applicant for that order with a transcript or note of the application.

R-439   **Duty of person transcribing proceedings in the Crown Court**

65.9 A person who transcribes a recording of proceedings in the Crown Court under arrangements made by the Crown Court officer must provide the Registrar with any transcript for which the Registrar asks, within such period as the Registrar may require.

Duty of person keeping exhibit   R-440

65.10 A person who under arrangements made by the Crown Court officer keeps a document or object exhibited in the proceedings in the Crown Court must—

  (a) keep that exhibit until—
    (i) 6 weeks after the conclusion of the Crown Court proceedings, or
    (ii) the conclusion of any appeal proceedings that begin within that 6 weeks,
    unless the court, the Registrar or the Crown Court otherwise directs; and
  (b) provide the Registrar with any such document or object for which the Registrar asks within such period as the Registrar may require.

Registrar's duty to provide copy documents for appeal or reference   R-441

65.11 Unless the court otherwise directs, for the purposes of an appeal or reference—

  (a) the Registrar must—
    (i) provide a party with a copy of any document or transcript held by the Registrar for such purposes, or
    (ii) allow a party to inspect such a document or transcript,
  on payment by that party of any charge fixed by the Treasury; but
  (b) the Registrar must not provide a copy or allow the inspection of—
    (i) a document provided only for the court and the Registrar, or
    (ii) a transcript of a public interest ruling or of an application for such a ruling.

Declaration of incompatibility with a Convention right   R-442

65.12 (1) This rule applies where a party—

  (a) wants the court to make a declaration of incompatibility with a Convention right under section 4 of the Human Rights Act 1998; or
  (b) raises an issue that the Registrar thinks may lead the court to make such a declaration.

  (2) The Registrar must serve notice on—
  (a) the relevant person named in the list published under section 17(1) of the Crown Proceedings Act 1947; or
  (b) the Treasury Solicitor, if it is not clear who is the relevant person.

  (3) That notice must include or attach details of—
  (a) the legislation affected and the Convention right concerned;
  (b) the parties to the appeal; and
  (c) any other information or document that the Registrar thinks relevant.

  (4) A person who has a right under the 1998 Act to become a party to the appeal must—
  (a) serve notice on—
    (i) the Registrar, and
    (ii) the other parties, if that person wants to exercise that right; and
  (b) in that notice—
    (i) indicate the conclusion that that person invites the court to reach on the question of incompatibility, and
    (ii) identify each ground for that invitation, concisely outlining the arguments in support.

  (5) The court must not make a declaration of incompatibility—
  (a) less than 21 days after the Registrar serves notice under paragraph (2); and
  (b) without giving any person who serves a notice under paragraph (4) an opportunity to make representations at a hearing.

Abandoning an appeal   R-443

65.13 (1) This rule applies where an appellant wants to—

  (a) abandon—
    (i) an application to the court for permission to appeal, or
    (ii) an appeal; or
  (b) reinstate such an application or appeal after abandoning it.

  (2) The appellant—
  (a) may abandon such an application or appeal without the court's permission by serving a notice of abandonment on—
    (i) the Registrar, and
    (ii) any respondent
  before any hearing of the application or appeal; but

(b) at any such hearing, may only abandon that application or appeal with the court's permission.

(3) A notice of abandonment must be in the form set out in the Practice Direction, signed by or on behalf of the appellant.

(4) On receiving a notice of abandonment the Registrar must—
  (a) date it;
  (b) serve a dated copy on—
    (i) the appellant,
    (ii) the appellant's custodian, if any,
    (iii) the Crown Court officer, and
    (iv) any other person on whom the appellant or the Registrar served the appeal notice; and
  (c) treat the application or appeal as if it had been refused or dismissed by the Court of Appeal.

(5) An appellant who wants to reinstate an application or appeal after abandoning it must—
  (a) apply in writing, with reasons; and
  (b) serve the application on the Registrar.

R-444   Abandoning a ground of appeal or opposition

65.14 (1) This rule applies where a party wants to abandon—
  (a) a ground of appeal identified in an appeal notice; or
  (b) a ground of opposition identified in a respondent's notice.

(2) Such a party must give written notice to—
  (a) the Registrar; and
  (b) every other party,
before any hearing at which that ground will be considered by the court.

CRIMINAL PROCEDURE RULES   PART 66   APPEAL TO THE COURT OF
APPEAL AGAINST RULING AT PREPARATORY HEARING

R-445   When this Part applies

66.1 (1) This Part applies where a party wants to appeal under—
  (a) section 9(11) of the Criminal Justice Act 1987 or section 35(1) of the Criminal Procedure and Investigations Act 1996; or
  (b) section 47(1) of the Criminal Justice Act 2003.

(2) A reference to an 'appellant' in this Part is a reference to such a party.

R-446   Service of appeal notice

66.2 (1) An appellant must serve an appeal notice on—
  (a) the Crown Court officer;
  (b) the Registrar; and
  (c) every party directly affected by the order or ruling against which the appellant wants to appeal.

(2) The appellant must serve the appeal notice not more than 5 business days after—
  (a) the order or ruling against which the appellant wants to appeal; or
  (b) the Crown Court judge gives or refuses permission to appeal.

R-447   Form of appeal notice

66.3 (1) An appeal notice must be in the form set out in the Practice Direction.

(2) The appeal notice must—
  (a) specify each order or ruling against which the appellant wants to appeal;
  (b) identify each ground of appeal on which the appellant relies, numbering them consecutively (if there is more than one) and concisely outlining each argument in support;
  (c) summarise the relevant facts;
  (d) identify any relevant authorities;
  (e) include or attach any application for the following, with reasons—
    (i) permission to appeal, if the appellant needs the court's permission,
    (ii) an extension of time within which to serve the appeal notice,
    (iii) a direction to attend in person a hearing that the appellant could attend by live link, if the appellant is in custody;
  (f) include a list of those on whom the appellant has served the appeal notice; and

> (g) attach—
>> (i) a transcript or note of each order or ruling against which the appellant wants to appeal,
>> (ii) all relevant skeleton arguments considered by the Crown Court judge,
>> (iii) any written application for permission to appeal that the appellant made to the Crown Court judge,
>> (iv) a transcript or note of the decision by the Crown Court judge on any application for permission to appeal, and
>> (v) any other document or thing that the appellant thinks the court will need to decide the appeal.

Crown Court judge's permission to appeal   R-448

66.4 (1) An appellant who wants the Crown Court judge to give permission to appeal must—
> (a) apply orally, with reasons, immediately after the order or ruling against which the appellant wants to appeal; or
> (b) apply in writing and serve the application on—
>> (i) the Crown Court officer, and
>> (ii) every party directly affected by the order or ruling not more than 2 business days after that order or ruling.

(2) A written application must include the same information (with the necessary adaptations) as an appeal notice.

Respondent's notice   R-449

66.5 (1) A party on whom an appellant serves an appeal notice may serve a respondent's notice, and must do so if—
> (a) that party wants to make representations to the court; or
> (b) the court so directs.

(2) Such a party must serve the respondent's notice on—
> (a) the appellant;
> (b) the Crown Court officer;
> (c) the Registrar; and
> (d) any other party on whom the appellant served the appeal notice.

(3) Such a party must serve the respondent's notice not more than 5 business days after—
> (a) the appellant serves the appeal notice; or
> (b) a direction to do so.

(4) The respondent's notice must be in the form set out in the Practice Direction.

(5) The respondent's notice must—
> (a) give the date on which the respondent was served with the appeal notice;
> (b) identify each ground of opposition on which the respondent relies, numbering them consecutively (if there is more than one), concisely outlining each argument in support and identifying the ground of appeal to which each relates;
> (c) summarise any relevant facts not already summarised in the appeal notice;
> (d) identify any relevant authorities;
> (e) include or attach any application for the following, with reasons—
>> (i) an extension of time within which to serve the respondent's notice,
>> (ii) a direction to attend in person any hearing that the respondent could attend by live link, if the respondent is in custody;
> (f) identify any other document or thing that the respondent thinks the court will need to decide the appeal.

Powers of Court of Appeal judge   R-450

66.6 A judge of the Court of Appeal may give permission to appeal as well as exercising the powers given by other legislation (including these Rules).

Renewing applications   R-451

66.7 Rule 65.5 (renewing an application refused by a judge or the Registrar) applies with a time limit of 5 business days.

Right to attend hearing   R-452

66.8 (1) A party who is in custody has a right to attend a hearing in public.

(2) The court or the Registrar may direct that such a party is to attend a hearing by live link.

CRIMINAL PROCEDURE RULES   PART 67   APPEAL TO THE COURT OF APPEAL AGAINST RULING ADVERSE TO THE PROSECUTION

R-453   **When this Part applies**

     67.1   (1)   This Part applies where a prosecutor wants to appeal under section 58(2) of the Criminal Justice Act 2003.

           (2)   A reference to an 'appellant' in this Part is a reference to such a prosecutor.

R-454   **Decision to appeal**

     67.2   (1)   An appellant must tell the Crown Court judge of any decision to appeal—

               (a)   immediately after the ruling against which the appellant wants to appeal; or

               (b)   on the expiry of the time to decide whether to appeal allowed under paragraph (2).

           (2)   If an appellant wants time to decide whether to appeal—

               (a)   the appellant must ask the Crown Court judge immediately after the ruling; and

               (b)   the general rule is that the judge must not require the appellant to decide there and then but instead must allow until the next business day.

R-455   **Service of appeal notice**

     67.3   (1)   An appellant must serve an appeal notice on—

               (a)   the Crown Court officer;

               (b)   the Registrar; and

               (c)   every defendant directly affected by the ruling against which the appellant wants to appeal.

           (2)   The appellant must serve the appeal notice not later than—

               (a)   the next business day after telling the Crown Court judge of the decision to appeal, if the judge expedites the appeal; or

               (b)   5 business days after telling the Crown Court judge of that decision, if the judge does not expedite the appeal.

R-456   **Form of appeal notice**

     67.4   (1)   An appeal notice must be in the form set out in the Practice Direction.

           (2)   The appeal notice must—

               (a)   specify each ruling against which the appellant wants to appeal;

               (b)   identify each ground of appeal on which the appellant relies, numbering them consecutively (if there is more than one) and concisely outlining each argument in support;

               (c)   summarise the relevant facts;

               (d)   identify any relevant authorities;

               (e)   include or attach any application for the following, with reasons—

                   (i)   permission to appeal, if the appellant needs the court's permission,

                   (ii)   an extension of time within which to serve the appeal notice,

                   (iii)   expedition of the appeal, or revocation of a direction expediting the appeal;

               (f)   include a list of those on whom the appellant has served the appeal notice;

               (g)   attach—

                   (i)   a transcript or note of each ruling against which the appellant wants to appeal,

                   (ii)   all relevant skeleton arguments considered by the Crown Court judge,

                   (iii)   any written application for permission to appeal that the appellant made to the Crown Court judge,

                   (iv)   a transcript or note of the decision by the Crown Court judge on any application for permission to appeal,

                   (v)   a transcript or note of the decision by the Crown Court judge on any request to expedite the appeal, and

                   (vi)   any other document or thing that the appellant thinks the court will need to decide the appeal; and

               (h)   attach a form of respondent's notice for any defendant served with the appeal notice to complete if that defendant wants to do so.

R-457   **Crown Court judge's permission to appeal**

     67.5   (1)   An appellant who wants the Crown Court judge to give permission to appeal must—

               (a)   apply orally, with reasons, immediately after the ruling against which the appellant wants to appeal; or

               (b)   apply in writing and serve the application on—

                   (i)   the Crown Court officer, and

(ii)   every defendant directly affected by the ruling

on the expiry of the time allowed under rule 67.2 to decide whether to appeal.

(2) A written application must include the same information (with the necessary adaptations) as an appeal notice.

(3) The Crown Court judge must allow every defendant directly affected by the ruling an opportunity to make representations.

(4) The general rule is that the Crown Court judge must decide whether or not to give permission to appeal on the day that the application for permission is made.

Expediting an appeal

R-458

67.6 (1) An appellant who wants the Crown Court judge to expedite an appeal must ask, giving reasons, on telling the judge of the decision to appeal.

(2) The Crown Court judge must allow every defendant directly affected by the ruling an opportunity to make representations.

(3) The Crown Court judge may revoke a direction expediting the appeal unless the appellant has served the appeal notice.

Respondent's notice

R-459

67.7 (1) A defendant on whom an appellant serves an appeal notice may serve a respondent's notice, and must do so if—

(a) the defendant wants to make representations to the court; or

(b) the court so directs.

(2) Such a defendant must serve the respondent's notice on—

(a) the appellant;

(b) the Crown Court officer;

(c) the Registrar; and

(d) any other defendant on whom the appellant served the appeal notice.

(3) Such a defendant must serve the respondent's notice—

(a) not later than the next business day after—

(i)   the appellant serves the appeal notice, or

(ii) a direction to do so if the Crown Court judge expedites the appeal; or

(b) not more than 5 business days after—

(i)   the appellant serves the appeal notice, or

(ii) a direction to do so if the Crown Court judge does not expedite the appeal.

(4) The respondent's notice must be in the form set out in the Practice Direction.

(5) The respondent's notice must—

(a) give the date on which the respondent was served with the appeal notice;

(b) identify each ground of opposition on which the respondent relies, numbering them consecutively (if there is more than one), concisely outlining each argument in support and identifying the ground of appeal to which each relates;

(c) summarise any relevant facts not already summarised in the appeal notice;

(d) identify any relevant authorities;

(e) include or attach any application for the following, with reasons—

(i)   an extension of time within which to serve the respondent's notice,

(ii) a direction to attend in person any hearing that the respondent could attend by live link, if the respondent is in custody;

(f) identify any other document or thing that the respondent thinks the court will need to decide the appeal.

Public interest ruling

R-460

67.8 (1) This rule applies where the appellant wants to appeal against a public interest ruling.

(2) The appellant must not serve on any defendant directly affected by the ruling—

(a) any written application to the Crown Court judge for permission to appeal; or

(b) an appeal notice

if the appellant thinks that to do so in effect would reveal something that the appellant thinks ought not be disclosed.

(3) The appellant must not include in an appeal notice—

(a) the material that was the subject of the ruling; or

(b) any indication of what sort of material it is if the appellant thinks that to do so in effect would reveal something that the appellant thinks ought not be disclosed.

(4) The appellant must serve on the Registrar with the appeal notice an annex—

    (a) marked to show that its contents are only for the court and the Registrar;

    (b) containing whatever the appellant has omitted from the appeal notice, with reasons; and

    (c) if relevant, explaining why the appellant has not served the appeal notice.

(5) Rules 67.5(3) and 67.6(2) do not apply.

R-461   Powers of Court of Appeal judge

67.9 A judge of the Court of Appeal may—

    (a) give permission to appeal;

    (b) revoke a Crown Court judge's direction expediting an appeal; and

    (c) where an appellant abandons an appeal, order a defendant's acquittal, his release from custody and the payment of his costs,

as well as exercising the powers given by other legislation (including these Rules).

R-462   Renewing applications

67.10 Rule 65.5 (renewing an application refused by a judge or the Registrar) applies with a time limit of 5 business days.

R-463   Right to attend hearing

67.11 (1) A respondent who is in custody has a right to attend a hearing in public.

    (2) The court or the Registrar may direct that such a respondent is to attend a hearing by live link.

CRIMINAL PROCEDURE RULES   PART 68   APPEAL TO THE COURT OF APPEAL ABOUT CONVICTION OR SENTENCE

R-464   When this Part applies

68.1 (1) This Part applies where—

    (a) a defendant wants to appeal under—

        (i) Part 1 of the Criminal Appeal Act 1968,

        (ii) section 274(3) of the Criminal Justice Act 2003,

        (iii) paragraph 14 of Schedule 22 to the Criminal Justice Act 2003, or

        (iv) section 42 of the Counter-Terrorism Act 2008;

    (b) the Criminal Cases Review Commission refers a case to the Court of Appeal under section 9 of the Criminal Appeal Act 1995;

    (c) a prosecutor wants to appeal to the Court of Appeal under section 14A(5A) of the Football Spectators Act 1989;

    (d) a party wants to appeal under section 74(8) of the Serious Organised Crime and Police Act 2005;

    (e) a person found to be in contempt of court wants to appeal under section 13 of the Administration of Justice Act 1960 and section 18A of the Criminal Appeal Act 1968; or

    (f) a person wants to appeal to the Court of Appeal under—

        (i) section 24 of the Serious Crime Act 2007, or

        (ii) regulation 3C or 3H of the Costs in Criminal Cases (General) Regulations 1986.

    (2) A reference to an 'appellant' in this Part is a reference to such a party or person.

R-465   Service of appeal notice

68.2 (1) The general rule is that an appellant must serve an appeal notice—

    (a) on the Crown Court officer at the Crown Court centre where there occurred—

        (i) the conviction, verdict, or finding,

        (ii) the sentence, or

        (iii) the order, or the failure to make an order

    about which the appellant wants to appeal; and

    (b) not more than—

        (i) 28 days after that occurred, or

        (ii) 21 days after the order, in a case in which the appellant appeals against a wasted or third party costs order.

(2) But an appellant must serve an appeal notice—
    (a) on the Registrar instead where—
        (i) the appeal is against a minimum term review decision under section 274(3) of, or paragraph 14 of Schedule 22 to, the Criminal Justice Act 2003, or
        (ii) the Criminal Cases Review Commission refers the case to the court; and
    (b) not more than 28 days after—
        (i) the minimum term review decision about which the appellant wants to appeal, or
        (ii) the Registrar serves notice that the Commission has referred a conviction.

Form of appeal notice
R-466

68.3 (1) An appeal notice must be in the form set out in the Practice Direction.
    (2) The appeal notice must—
    (a) specify—
        (i) the conviction, verdict, or finding,
        (ii) the sentence, or
        (iii) the order, or the failure to make an order about which the appellant wants to appeal;
    (b) identify each ground of appeal on which the appellant relies, numbering them consecutively (if there is more than one) and concisely outlining each argument in support;
    (c) identify the transcript that the appellant thinks the court will need, if the appellant wants to appeal against a conviction;
    (d) identify the relevant sentencing powers of the Crown Court, if sentence is in issue;
    (e) where the Criminal Cases Review Commission refers a case to the court, explain how each ground of appeal relates (if it does) to the reasons for the reference;
    (f) summarise the relevant facts;
    (g) identify any relevant authorities;
    (h) include or attach any application for the following, with reasons—
        (i) permission to appeal, if the appellant needs the court's permission,
        (ii) an extension of time within which to serve the appeal notice,
        (iii) bail pending appeal,
        (iv) a direction to attend in person a hearing that the appellant could attend by live link, if the appellant is in custody,
        (v) the introduction of evidence, including hearsay evidence and evidence of bad character,
        (vi) an order requiring a witness to attend court,
        (vii) a direction for special measures for a witness,
        (viii) a direction for special measures for the giving of evidence by the appellant;
        (ix) identify any other document or thing that the appellant thinks the court will need to decide the appeal.

Crown Court judge's certificate that case is fit for appeal
R-467

68.4 (1) An appellant who wants the Crown Court judge to certify that a case is fit for appeal must—
    (a) apply orally, with reasons, immediately after there occurs—
        (i) the conviction, verdict, or finding,
        (ii) the sentence, or
        (iii) the order, or the failure to make an order about which the appellant wants to appeal; or
    (b) apply in writing and serve the application on the Crown Court officer not more than 14 days after that occurred.
    (2) A written application must include the same information (with the necessary adaptations) as an appeal notice.

Reference by Criminal Cases Review Commission
R-468

68.5 (1) The Registrar must serve on the appellant a reference by the Criminal Cases Review Commission.
    (2) The court must treat that reference as the appeal notice if the appellant does not serve such a notice under rule 68.2.

Respondent's notice
R-469

68.6 (1) The Registrar—
    (a) may serve an appeal notice on any party directly affected by the appeal; and
    (b) must do so if the Criminal Cases Review Commission refers a conviction, verdict, finding or sentence to the court.

(2) Such a party may serve a respondent's notice, and must do so if—

    (a) that party wants to make representations to the court; or

    (b) the court or the Registrar so directs.

(3) Such a party must serve the respondent's notice on—

    (a) the appellant;

    (b) the Registrar; and

    (c) any other party on whom the Registrar served the appeal notice.

(4) Such a party must serve the respondent's notice—

    (a) not more than 14 days after the Registrar serves—

        (i) the appeal notice, or

        (ii) a direction to do so; or

    (b) not more than 28 days after the Registrar serves notice that the Commission has referred a conviction.

(5) The respondent's notice must be in the form set out in the Practice Direction.

(6) The respondent's notice must—

    (a) give the date on which the respondent was served with the appeal notice;

    (b) identify each ground of opposition on which the respondent relies, numbering them consecutively (if there is more than one), concisely outlining each argument in support and identifying the ground of appeal to which each relates;

    (c) identify the relevant sentencing powers of the Crown Court, if sentence is in issue;

    (d) summarise any relevant facts not already summarised in the appeal notice;

    (e) identify any relevant authorities;

    (f) include or attach any application for the following, with reasons—

        (i) an extension of time within which to serve the respondent's notice,

        (ii) bail pending appeal,

        (iii) a direction to attend in person a hearing that the respondent could attend by live link, if the respondent is in custody,

        (iv) the introduction of evidence, including hearsay evidence and evidence of bad character,

        (v) an order requiring a witness to attend court,

        (vi) a direction for special measures for a witness; and

    (g) identify any other document or thing that the respondent thinks the court will need to decide the appeal.

R-470   Adaptation of rules about introducing evidence

68.7 (1) The following Parts apply with such adaptations as the court or the Registrar may direct—

    (a) Part 29 (measures to assist a witness or defendant to give evidence);

    (b) Part 34 (hearsay evidence);

    (c) Part 35 (evidence of bad character); and

    (d) Part 36 (evidence of a complainant's previous sexual behaviour).

(2) But the general rule is that—

    (a) a respondent who opposes an appellant's application to which one of those Parts applies must do so in the respondent's notice, with reasons;

    (b) an appellant who opposes a respondent's application to which one of those Parts applies must serve notice, with reasons, on—

        (i) the Registrar, and

        (ii) the respondent not more than 14 days after service of the respondent's notice; and

    (c) the court or the Registrar may give directions with or without a hearing.

R-471   Application for bail pending appeal or retrial

68.8 (1) This rule applies where a party wants to make an application to the court about bail pending appeal or retrial.

(2) That party must serve an application in the form set out in the Practice Direction on—

    (a) the Registrar, unless the application is with the appeal notice; and

    (b) the other party.

(3) The court must not decide such an application without giving the other party an opportunity to make representations, including representations about any condition or surety proposed by the applicant.

R-472   Conditions of bail pending appeal or retrial

68.9 (1) This rule applies where the court grants a party bail pending appeal or retrial subject to any condition that must be met before that party is released.

(2) The court may direct how such a condition must be met.

(3) The Registrar must serve a certificate in the form set out in the Practice Direction recording any such condition and direction on—

    (a) that party;

    (b) that party's custodian; and

    (c) any other person directly affected by any such direction.

(4) A person directly affected by any such direction need not comply with it until the Registrar serves that person with that certificate.

(5) Unless the court otherwise directs, if any such condition or direction requires someone to enter into a recognizance it must be—

    (a) in the form set out in the Practice Direction and signed before—

        (i) the Registrar,

        (ii) the custodian, or

        (iii) someone acting with the authority of the Registrar or custodian;

    (b) copied immediately to the person who enters into it; and

    (c) served immediately by the Registrar on the appellant's custodian or vice versa, as appropriate.

(6) Unless the court otherwise directs, if any such condition or direction requires someone to make a payment, surrender a document or take some other step—

    (a) that payment, document or step must be made, surrendered or taken to or before—

        (i) the Registrar,

        (ii) the custodian, or

        (iii) someone acting with the authority of the Registrar or custodian;

    (b) the Registrar or the custodian, as appropriate, must serve immediately on the other a statement that the payment, document or step has been made, surrendered or taken, as appropriate.

(7) The custodian must release the appellant where it appears that any condition ordered by the court has been met.

(8) For the purposes of section 5 of the Bail Act 1976 (record of decision about bail), the Registrar must keep a copy of—

    (a) any certificate served under paragraph (3);

    (b) a notice of hearing given under rule 65.7(1); and

    (c) a notice of the court's decision served under rule 65.7(2).

(9) Where the court grants bail pending retrial the Registrar must serve on the Crown Court officer copies of the documents kept under paragraph (8).

Forfeiture of a recognizance given as a condition of bail   R-473

68.10 (1) This rule applies where—

    (a) the court grants a party bail pending appeal or retrial; and

    (b) the bail is subject to a condition that that party provides a surety to guarantee that he will surrender to custody as required; but

    (c) that party does not surrender to custody as required.

(2) The Registrar must serve notice on—

    (a) the surety; and

    (b) the prosecutor of the hearing at which the court may order the forfeiture of the recognizance given by that surety.

(3) The court must not forfeit a surety's recognizance—

    (a) less than 7 days after the Registrar serves notice under paragraph (2); and

    (b) without giving the surety an opportunity to make representations at a hearing.

Right to attend hearing   R-474

68.11 A party who is in custody has a right to attend a hearing in public unless—

    (a) it is a hearing preliminary or incidental to an appeal, including the hearing of an application for permission to appeal; or

    (b) that party is in custody in consequence of—

        (i) a verdict of not guilty by reason of insanity, or

        (ii) a finding of disability.

Power to vary determination of appeal against sentence   R-475

68.12 (1) This rule applies where the court decides an appeal affecting sentence in a party's absence.

(2) The court may vary such a decision if it did not take account of something relevant because that party was absent.

(3) A party who wants the court to vary such a decision must—

    (a) apply in writing, with reasons;

    (b) serve the application on the Registrar not more than 7 days after—

        (i) the decision, if that party was represented at the appeal hearing, or

        (ii) the Registrar serves the decision, if that party was not represented at that hearing.

R-476 **Directions about re-admission to hospital on dismissal of appeal**

68.13 (1) This rule applies where—

    (a) an appellant subject to—

        (i) an order under section 37(1) of the Mental Health Act 1983 (detention in hospital on conviction), or

        (ii) an order under section 5(2) of the Criminal Procedure (Insanity) Act 1964 (detention in hospital on finding of insanity or disability)

        has been released on bail pending appeal; and

    (b) the court—

        (i) refuses permission to appeal,

        (ii) dismisses the appeal, or

        (iii) affirms the order under appeal.

(2) The court must give appropriate directions for the appellant's—

    (a) re-admission to hospital; and

    (b) if necessary, temporary detention pending re-admission.

R-477 **Renewal or setting aside of order for retrial**

68.14 (1) This rule applies where—

    (a) a prosecutor wants a defendant to be arraigned more than 2 months after the court ordered a retrial under section 7 of the Criminal Appeal Act 1968; or

    (b) a defendant wants such an order set aside after 2 months have passed since it was made.

(2) That party must apply in writing, with reasons, and serve the application on—

    (a) the Registrar;

    (b) the other party.

Criminal Practice Directions   Part 68   Appeal to the Court of Appeal about Conviction or Sentence

PD-72 **CPD X Appeal 68A: Appeals Against Conviction and Sentence – The Provision of Notice to the Prosecution**

68A.1 When an appeal notice served under Rule 68.2 is received by the Registrar of Criminal Appeals, the Registrar will notify the relevant prosecution authority, giving the case name, reference number and the trial or sentencing court.

68A.2 If the court or the Registrar directs, or invites, the prosecution authority to serve a respondent's notice under Rule 68.6, prior to the consideration of leave, the Registrar will also at that time serve on the prosecution authority the appeal notice containing the grounds of appeal and the transcripts, if available. If the prosecution authority is not directed or invited to serve a respondent's notice but wishes to do so, the authority should request the grounds of appeal and any existing transcript from the Criminal Appeal Office. Any respondent's notice received prior to the consideration of leave will be made available to the single judge.

68A.3 The Registrar of Criminal Appeals will notify the relevant prosecution authority in the event that:

    (a) leave to appeal against conviction or sentence is granted by the single Judge; or

    (b) the single Judge or the Registrar refers an application for leave to appeal against conviction or sentence to the Full Court for determination; or

    (c) there is to be a renewed application for leave to appeal against sentence only.

If the prosecution authority has not yet been served with the appeal notice and transcript, the Registrar will serve these with the notification, and if leave is granted, the Registrar will also serve the authority with the comments of the single judge.

68A.4 The prosecution should notify the Registrar without delay if they wish to be represented at the hearing. The prosecution should note that the Registrar will not delay listing to await a response from the Prosecution as to whether they wish to attend. Prosecutors should note that occasionally, for example, where the single Judge fixes a hearing date at short notice, the case may be listed very quickly.

68A.5 If the prosecution wishes to be represented at any hearing, the notification should include details of Counsel instructed and a time estimate. An application by the prosecution to remove a case from the list for Counsel's convenience, or to allow further preparation time, will rarely be granted.

68A.6 There may be occasions when the Court of Appeal Criminal Division will grant leave to appeal to an unrepresented applicant and proceed forthwith with the appeal in the absence of the appellant and Counsel. The prosecution should not attend any hearing at which the appellant is unrepresented. *Nasteska v The former Yugoslav Republic of Macedonia (Application No.23152/05)* As a Court of Review, the Court of Appeal Criminal Division would expect the prosecution to have raised any specific matters of relevance with the sentencing Judge in the first instance.

CPD X Appeal 68B: Listing of Appeals against Conviction and Sentence in the Court of Appeal Criminal Division (CACD)   PD-73

68B.1 Arrangements for the fixing of dates for the hearing of appeals will be made by the Criminal Appeal Office Listing Officer, under the superintendence of the Registrar of Criminal Appeals who may give such directions as he deems necessary.

68B.2 Where possible, regard will be had to an advocate's existing commitments. However, in relation to the listing of appeals, the Court of Appeal takes precedence over all lower courts, including the Crown Court. Wherever practicable, a lower court will have regard to this principle when making arrangements to release an advocate to appear in the Court of Appeal. In case of difficulty the lower court should communicate with the Registrar. In general an advocate's commitment in a lower court will not be regarded as a good reason for failing to accept a date proposed for a hearing in the Court of Appeal.

68B.3 Similarly when the Registrar directs that an appellant should appear by video link, the prison must give precedence to video-links to the Court of Appeal over video-links to the lower courts, including the Crown Court.

68B.4 The copy of the Criminal Appeal Office summary provided to advocates will contain the summary writer's time estimate for the whole hearing including delivery of judgment. It will also contain a time estimate for the judges' reading time of the core material. The Listing Officer will rely on those estimates, unless the advocate for the appellant or the Crown provides different time estimates to the Listing Officer, in writing, within 7 days of the receipt of the summary by the advocate. Where the time estimates are considered by an advocate to be inadequate, or where the estimates have been altered because, for example, a ground of appeal has been abandoned, it is the duty of the advocate to inform the Court promptly, in which event the Registrar will reconsider the time estimates and inform the parties accordingly.

68B.5 The following target times are set for the hearing of appeals. Target times will run from the receipt of the appeal by the Listing Officer, as being ready for hearing.

68B.6

Nature of Appeal:	From Receipt by Listing Officer to Fixing of Hearing Date:	From Fixing of Hearing Date to Hearing:	Total Time From Receipt by Listing Officer to Hearing:
Sentence Appeal	14 days	14 days	28 days
Conviction Appeal	21 days	42 days	63 days
Conviction Appeal where witness to attend	28 days	52 days	80 days

68B.7 Where legal vacations impinge, these periods may be extended. Where expedition is required, the Registrar may direct that these periods be abridged.

68B.8 'Appeal' includes an application for leave to appeal which requires an oral hearing.

CPD X Appeal 68C: Appeal Notices Containing Grounds of Appeal   PD-74

68C.1 The requirements for the service of notices of appeal and the time limits for doing so are as set out in Part 68 of the Criminal Procedure Rules. The Court must be provided with an appeal notice as a single document which sets out the grounds of appeal. Advocates should not provide the Court with an advice addressed to lay or professional clients. Any appeal notice or grounds of appeal served on the Court will usually be provided to the respondent.

68C.2 Advocates should not settle grounds unless they consider that they are properly arguable. Grounds should be carefully drafted; the Court is not assisted by grounds of appeal which are not properly set out and particularised. Should leave to amend the grounds be granted, it is most unlikely that further grounds will be entertained.

PD-75 **CPD X Appeal 68D: Respondents' Notices**

68D.1 The requirements for the service of respondents' notices and the time limits for doing so are as set out in Part 68 of the Criminal Procedure Rules. Any respondent's notice served should be in accordance with Rule 68.6. The Court does not require a response to the respondent's notice.

PD-76 **CPD X Appeal 68E: Loss of Time**

68E.1 Both the Court and the single judge have power, in their discretion, under the Criminal Appeal Act 1968 sections 29 and 31, to direct that part of the time during which an applicant is in custody after lodging his notice of application for leave to appeal should not count towards sentence. Those contemplating an appeal should seek advice and should remember that a notice of appeal without grounds is ineffective and that grounds should be substantial and particularised and not a mere formula. When leave to appeal has been refused by the single judge, it is often of assistance to consider the reasons given by the single judge before making a decision whether to renew the application. Where an application devoid of merit has been refused by the single judge he may indicate that the Full Court should consider making a direction for loss of time on renewal of the application. However the Full Court may make such a direction whether or not such an indication has been given by the single judge.

68E.2 Applicants and counsel are reminded of the warning given by the Court of Appeal in *R v Hart and Others* [2006] EWCA Crim 3239, [2007] 1 Cr App R 31, [2007] 2 Cr App R (S) 34 and should 'heed the fact that this court is prepared to exercise its power…The mere fact that counsel has advised that there are grounds of appeal will not always be a sufficient answer to the question as to whether or not an application has indeed been brought which was totally without merit.'

PD-77 **CPD X Appeal 68F: Skeleton Arguments**

68F.1 Skeleton arguments are not required, but may be provided. Advocates intending to serve a skeleton argument should consider carefully whether a skeleton argument is necessary, or whether the appeal notice or the respondent's notice will suffice. In most cases, if the appeal notice and respondent's notice have been prepared in compliance with Part 68, a skeleton argument will be unnecessary. Advocates should always ensure that the Court, and any other party as appropriate, has a single document containing all of the points that are to be argued.

68F.2 The appellant's skeleton argument, if any, must be served no later than 21 days before the hearing date, and the respondent's skeleton argument, if any, no later than 14 days before the hearing date, unless otherwise directed by the Court.

68F.3 A skeleton argument, if provided, should contain a numbered list of the points the advocate intends to argue, grouped under each ground of appeal, and stated in no more than one or two sentences. It should be as succinct as possible. Advocates should ensure that the correct Criminal Appeal Office number appears at the beginning of the respondent's notice and any skeleton argument and that their names are at the end.

PD-78 **CPD X Appeal 68G: Criminal Appeal Office Summaries**

68G.1 To assist the Court, the Criminal Appeal Office prepares summaries of the cases coming before it. These are entirely objective and do not contain any advice about how the Court should deal with the case or any view about its merits. They consist of two Parts.

68G.2 Part I, which is provided to all of the advocates in the case, generally contains:

(a) particulars of the proceedings in the Crown Court, including representation and details of any co-accused;

(b) particulars of the proceedings in the Court of Appeal (Criminal Division);

(c) the facts of the case, as drawn from the transcripts, appeal notice, respondent's notice, witness statements and/or the exhibits;

(d) the submissions and rulings, summing up and sentencing remarks.

68G.3 The contents of the summary are a matter for the professional judgment of the writer, but an advocate wishing to suggest any significant alteration to Part I should write to the Registrar of Criminal Appeals. If the Registrar does not agree, the summary and the letter will be put to the Court for decision. The Court will not generally be willing to hear oral argument about the content of the summary.

68G.4 Advocates may show Part I of the summary to their professional or lay clients (but to no one else) if they believe it would help to check facts or formulate arguments, but summaries are not to be copied or reproduced without the permission of the Criminal Appeal Office; permission for this will not normally be given in cases involving children, or sexual offences, or where the Crown Court has made an order restricting reporting.

68G.5 Unless a judge of the High Court or the Registrar of Criminal Appeals gives a direction to the contrary, in any particular case involving material of an explicitly salacious or sadistic nature, Part I will also be supplied to appellants who seek to represent themselves before the Full Court, or who renew to the full court their applications for leave to appeal against conviction or sentence.

68G.6 Part II, which is supplied to the Court alone, contains:

(a) a summary of the grounds of appeal; and

(b) in appeals against sentence (and applications for such leave), summaries of the antecedent histories of the parties and of any relevant pre-sentence, medical or other reports.

68G.7 All of the source material is provided to the Court and advocates are able to draw attention to anything in it which may be of particular relevance.

CRIMINAL PROCEDURE RULES   PART 69   APPEAL TO THE COURT OF APPEAL REGARDING REPORTING OR PUBLIC ACCESS RESTRICTION

When this Part applies

R-478

69.1 (1) This Part applies where a person directly affected by an order to which section 159(1) of the Criminal Justice Act 1988 applies wants to appeal against that order.

(2) A reference to an 'appellant' in this Part is a reference to such a party.

Service of appeal notice

R-479

69.2 (1) An appellant must serve an appeal notice on—

(a) the Crown Court officer;

(b) the Registrar;

(c) the parties; and

(d) any other person directly affected by the order against which the appellant wants to appeal.

(2) The appellant must serve the appeal notice not later than—

(a) the next business day after an order restricting public access to the trial;

(b) 10 business days after an order restricting reporting of the trial.

Form of appeal notice

R-480

69.3 (1) An appeal notice must be in the form set out in the Practice Direction.

(2) The appeal notice must—

(a) specify the order against which the appellant wants to appeal;

(b) identify each ground of appeal on which the appellant relies, numbering them consecutively (if there is more than one) and concisely outlining each argument in support;

(c) summarise the relevant facts;

(d) identify any relevant authorities;

(e) include or attach, with reasons—

(i) an application for permission to appeal,

(ii) any application for an extension of time within which to serve the appeal notice,

(iii) any application for a direction to attend in person a hearing that the appellant could attend by live link, if the appellant is in custody,

(iv) any application for permission to introduce evidence, and

(v) a list of those on whom the appellant has served the appeal notice; and

(f) attach any document or thing that the appellant thinks the court will need to decide the appeal.

Advance notice of appeal against order restricting public access

R-481

69.4 (1) This rule applies where the appellant wants to appeal against an order restricting public access to a trial.

(2) The appellant may serve advance written notice of intention to appeal against any such order that may be made.

    (3) The appellant must serve any such advance notice—
       (a) on—
          (i)   the Crown Court officer,
          (ii) the Registrar,
          (iii) the parties, and
          (iv) any other person who will be directly affected by the order against which the appellant intends to appeal, if it is made; and
       (b) not more than 5 business days after the Crown Court officer displays notice of the application for the order.
    (4) The advance notice must include the same information (with the necessary adaptations) as an appeal notice.
    (5) The court must treat that advance notice as the appeal notice if the order is made.

R-482 Duty of applicant for order restricting public access

69.5 (1) This rule applies where the appellant wants to appeal against an order restricting public access to a trial.
    (2) The party who applied for the order must serve on the Registrar—
       (a) a transcript or note of the application for the order; and
       (b) any other document or thing that that party thinks the court will need to decide the appeal.
    (3) That party must serve that transcript or note and any such other document or thing as soon as practicable after—
       (a) the appellant serves the appeal notice; or
       (b) the order, where the appellant served advance notice of intention to appeal.

R-483 Respondent's notice on appeal against reporting restriction

69.6 (1) This rule applies where the appellant wants to appeal against an order restricting the reporting of a trial.
    (2) A person on whom an appellant serves an appeal notice may serve a respondent's notice, and must do so if—
       (a) that person wants to make representations to the court; or
       (b) the court so directs.
    (3) Such a person must serve the respondent's notice on—
       (a) the appellant;
       (b) the Crown Court officer;
       (c) the Registrar;
       (d) the parties; and
       (e) any other person on whom the appellant served the appeal notice.
    (4) Such a person must serve the respondent's notice not more than 3 business days after—
       (a) the appellant serves the appeal notice; or
       (b) a direction to do so.
    (5) The respondent's notice must be in the form set out in the Practice Direction.
    (6) The respondent's notice must—
       (a) give the date on which the respondent was served with the appeal notice;
       (b) identify each ground of opposition on which the respondent relies, numbering them consecutively (if there is more than one), concisely outlining each argument in support and identifying the ground of appeal to which each relates;
       (c) summarise any relevant facts not already summarised in the appeal notice;
       (d) identify any relevant authorities;
       (e) include or attach any application for the following, with reasons—
          (i)   an extension of time within which to serve the respondent's notice,
          (ii) a direction to attend in person any hearing that the respondent could attend by live link, if the respondent is in custody,
          (iii) permission to introduce evidence; and
       (f) identify any other document or thing that the respondent thinks the court will need to decide the appeal.

R-484 Renewing applications

69.7 Rule 65.5 (renewing an application refused by a judge or the Registrar) applies with a time limit of 5 business days.

Right to introduce evidence   R-485

69.8   No person may introduce evidence without the court's permission.

Right to attend hearing   R-486

69.9   (1)   A party who is in custody has a right to attend a hearing in public of an appeal against an order restricting the reporting of a trial.

(2)   The court or the Registrar may direct that such a party is to attend a hearing by live link.

CRIMINAL PROCEDURE RULES   PART 70   REFERENCE TO THE COURT OF APPEAL OF POINT OF LAW OR UNDULY LENIENT SENTENCING

When this Part applies   R-487

70.1   This Part applies where the Attorney General wants to—
(a)   refer a point of law to the Court of Appeal under section 36 of the Criminal Justice Act 1972; or
(b)   refer a sentencing case to the Court of Appeal under section 36 of the Criminal Justice Act 1988.

Service of notice of reference and application for permission   R-488

70.2   (1)   The Attorney General must—
(a)   serve on the Registrar—
(i)   any notice of reference, and
(ii)   any application for permission to refer a sentencing case; and
(b)   with a notice of reference of a point of law, give the Registrar details of—
(i)   the defendant affected,
(ii)   the date and place of the relevant Crown Court decision, and
(iii) the relevant verdict and sentencing.

(2)   The Attorney General must serve an application for permission to refer a sentencing case not more than 28 days after the last of the sentences in that case.

Form of notice of reference and application for permission   R-489

70.3   (1)   A notice of reference and an application for permission to refer a sentencing case must be in the appropriate form set out in the Practice Direction, giving the year and number.

(2)   A notice of reference of a point of law must—
(a)   specify the point of law in issue and indicate the opinion that the Attorney General invites the court to give;
(b)   identify each ground for that invitation, numbering them consecutively (if there is more than one) and concisely outlining each argument in support;
(c)   exclude any reference to the defendant's name and any other reference that may identify the defendant;
(d)   summarise the relevant facts; and
(e)   identify any relevant authorities.

(3)   An application for permission to refer a sentencing case must—
(a)   give details of—
(i)   the defendant affected,
(ii)   the date and place of the relevant Crown Court decision, and
(iii) the relevant verdict and sentencing;
(b)   explain why that sentencing appears to the Attorney General unduly lenient, concisely outlining each argument in support; and
(c)   include the application for permission to refer the case to the court.

(4)   A notice of reference of a sentencing case must—
(a)   include the same details and explanation as the application for permission to refer the case;
(b)   summarise the relevant facts; and
(c)   identify any relevant authorities.

(5)   Where the court gives the Attorney General permission to refer a sentencing case, it may treat the application for permission as the notice of reference.

Registrar's notice to defendant   R-490

70.4   (1)   The Registrar must serve on the defendant—
(a)   a notice of reference;
(b)   an application for permission to refer a sentencing case.

(2) Where the Attorney General refers a point of law, the Registrar must give the defendant notice that—

    (a) the outcome of the reference will not make any difference to the outcome of the trial; and

    (b) the defendant may serve a respondent's notice.

(3) Where the Attorney General applies for permission to refer a sentencing case, the Registrar must give the defendant notice that—

    (a) the outcome of the reference may make a difference to that sentencing, and in particular may result in a more severe sentence; and

    (b) the defendant may serve a respondent's notice.

R-491   Respondent's notice

70.5 (1) A defendant on whom the Registrar serves a reference or an application for permission to refer a sentencing case may serve a respondent's notice, and must do so if—

    (a) the defendant wants to make representations to the court; or

    (b) the court so directs.

(2) Such a defendant must serve the respondent's notice on—

    (a) the Attorney General; and

    (b) the Registrar.

(3) Such a defendant must serve the respondent's notice—

    (a) where the Attorney General refers a point of law, not more than 28 days after—

        (i) the Registrar serves the reference, or

        (ii) a direction to do so;

    (b) where the Attorney General applies for permission to refer a sentencing case, not more than 14 days after—

        (i) the Registrar serves the application, or

        (ii) a direction to do so.

(4) Where the Attorney General refers a point of law, the respondent's notice must—

    (a) identify each ground of opposition on which the respondent relies, numbering them consecutively (if there is more than one), concisely outlining each argument in support and identifying the Attorney General's ground or reason to which each relates;

    (b) summarise any relevant facts not already summarised in the reference;

    (c) identify any relevant authorities; and

    (d) include or attach any application for the following, with reasons—

        (i) an extension of time within which to serve the respondent's notice,

        (ii) permission to attend a hearing that the respondent does not have a right to attend,

        (iii) a direction to attend in person a hearing that the respondent could attend by live link, if the respondent is in custody.

(5) Where the Attorney General applies for permission to refer a sentencing case, the respondent's notice must—

    (a) say if the respondent wants to make representations at the hearing of the application or reference; and

    (b) include or attach any application for the following, with reasons—

        (i) an extension of time within which to serve the respondent's notice,

        (ii) permission to attend a hearing that the respondent does not have a right to attend,

        (iii) a direction to attend in person a hearing that the respondent could attend by live link, if the respondent is in custody.

R-492   Variation or withdrawal of notice of reference or application for permission

70.6 (1) This rule applies where the Attorney General wants to vary or withdraw—

    (a) a notice of reference; or

    (b) an application for permission to refer a sentencing case.

(2) The Attorney General—

    (a) may vary or withdraw the notice or application without the court's permission by serving notice on—

        (i) the Registrar, and

        (ii) the defendant

    before any hearing of the reference or application; but

    (b) at any such hearing, may only vary or withdraw that notice or application with the court's permission.

Right to attend hearing
R-493

70.7 (1) A respondent who is in custody has a right to attend a hearing in public unless it is a hearing preliminary or incidental to a reference, including the hearing of an application for permission to refer a sentencing case.

(2) The court or the Registrar may direct that such a respondent is to attend a hearing by live link.

Anonymity of defendant on reference of point of law
R-494

70.8 Where the Attorney General refers a point of law, the court must not allow anyone to identify the defendant during the proceedings unless the defendant gives permission.

CRIMINAL PROCEDURE RULES   PART 71   APPEAL TO THE COURT OF APPEAL UNDER THE PROCEEDS OF CRIME ACT 2002: GENERAL RULES

Extension of time
R-495

71.1 (1) An application to extend the time limit for giving notice of application for leave to appeal under Part 2 of the Proceeds of Crime Act 2002 must—

(a) be included in the notice of appeal; and

(b) state the grounds for the application.

(2) The parties may not agree to extend any date or time limit set by this Part, Part 72 or Part 73, or by the Proceeds of Crime Act 2002 (Appeals under Part 2) Order 2003.

Other applications
R-496

71.2 Rules 68.3(2)(h) (form of appeal notice) shall apply in relation to an application—

(a) by a party to an appeal under Part 2 of the Proceeds of Crime Act 2002 that, under article 7 of the Proceeds of Crime Act 2002 (Appeals under Part 2) Order 2003, a witness be ordered to attend or that the evidence of a witness be received by the Court of Appeal; or

(b) by the defendant to be given leave by the court to be present at proceedings for which leave is required under article 6 of the 2003 Order,

as they apply in relation to applications under Part I of the Criminal Appeal Act 1968 and the form in which rules 68.15 and 68.26 require notice to be given may be modified as necessary.

Examination of witness by court
R-497

71.3 Rule 65.7 (notice of hearings and decisions) shall apply in relation to an order of the court under article 7 of the Proceeds of Crime Act 2002 (Appeals under Part 2) Order 2003 to require a person to attend for examination as it applies in relation to such an order of the court under Part I of the Criminal Appeal Act 1968.

Supply of documentary and other exhibits
R-498

71.4 Rule 65.11 (supply of documentary and other exhibits) shall apply in relation to an appellant or respondent under Part 2 of the Proceeds of Crime Act 2002 as it applies in relation to an appellant and respondent under Part I of the Criminal Appeal Act 1968.

Registrar's power to require information from court of trial
R-499

71.5 The Registrar may require the Crown Court to provide the Court of Appeal with any assistance or information which they may require for the purposes of exercising their jurisdiction under Part 2 of the Proceeds of Crime Act 2002, the Proceeds of Crime Act 2002 (Appeals under Part 2) Order 2003, this Part or Parts 72 and 73.

Hearing by single judge
R-500

71.6 Rule 65.6(5) (hearings) applies in relation to a judge exercising any of the powers referred to in article 8 of the Proceeds of Crime Act 2002 (Appeals under Part 2) Order 2003 or the powers in rules 72.2(3) and (4) (respondent's notice), 73.2(2) (notice of appeal) and 73.3(6) (respondent's notice), as it applies in relation to a judge exercising the powers referred to in section 31(2) of the Criminal Appeal Act 1968.

Determination by full court
R-501

71.7 Rule 65.5 (renewing an application refused by a single judge or the registrar) shall apply where a single judge has refused an application by a party to exercise in his favour any of the powers listed in article 8 of the Proceeds of Crime Act 2002 (Appeals under Part 2) Order 2003 or the power in rule 72.2(3) or (4) as it applies where the judge has refused to exercise the powers referred to in section 31(2) of the Criminal Appeal Act 1968.

Criminal Procedure Rules 2013 and Criminal Practice Directions

R-502 **Notice of determination**

71.8 (1) This rule applies where a single judge or the Court of Appeal has determined an application or appeal under the Proceeds of Crime Act 2002 (Appeals under Part 2) Order 2003 or under Part 2 of the Proceeds of Crime Act 2002.

(2) The Registrar must, as soon as practicable, serve notice of the determination on all of the parties to the proceedings.

(3) Where a single judge or the Court of Appeal has disposed of an application for leave to appeal or an appeal under section 31 of the 2002 Act, the registrar must also, as soon as practicable, serve the order on a court officer of the court of trial and any magistrates' court responsible for enforcing any confiscation order which the Crown Court has made.

R-503 **Record of proceedings and transcripts**

71.9 Rule 65.8(2)(a) and (b) (duty of Crown Court officer—arranging recording of proceedings in Crown Court and arranging transcription) and rule 65.9 (duty of person transcribing proceedings in the Crown Court) apply in relation to proceedings in respect of which an appeal lies to the Court of Appeal under Part 2 of the Proceeds of Crime Act 2002 as they apply in relation to proceedings in respect of which an appeal lies to the Court of Appeal under Part I of the Criminal Appeal Act 1968.

R-504 **Appeal to Supreme Court**

71.10 (1) An application to the Court of Appeal for leave to appeal to the Supreme Court under Part 2 of the Proceeds of Crime Act 2002 must be made—

(a) orally after the decision of the Court of Appeal from which an appeal lies to the Supreme Court; or

(b) in the form set out in the Practice Direction, in accordance with article 12 of the Proceeds of Crime Act 2002 (Appeals under Part 2) Order 2003 and served on the Registrar.

(2) The application may be abandoned at any time before it is heard by the Court of Appeal by serving notice in writing on the Registrar.

(3) Rule 65.6(5) (hearings) applies in relation to a single judge exercising any of the powers referred to in article 15 of the 2003 Order, as it applies in relation to a single judge exercising the powers referred to in section 31(2) of the Criminal Appeal Act 1968.

(4) Rules 65.5 (renewing an application refused by a judge or the registrar) applies where a single judge has refused an application by a party to exercise in his favour any of the powers listed in article 15 of the 2003 Order as they apply where the judge has refused to exercise the powers referred to in section 31(2) of the 1968 Act.

(5) The form in which rule 65.5(2) requires an application to be made may be modified as necessary.

CRIMINAL PROCEDURE RULES   PART 72   APPEAL TO THE COURT OF APPEAL UNDER PROCEEDS OF CRIME ACT 2002: PROSECUTOR'S APPEAL REGARDING CONFISCATION

R-505 **Notice of appeal**

72.1 (1) Where an appellant wishes to apply to the Court of Appeal for leave to appeal under section 31 of the Proceeds of Crime Act 2002, he must serve a notice of appeal in the form set out in the Practice Direction on—

(a) the Crown Court officer; and

(b) the defendant.

(2) When the notice of the appeal is served on the defendant, it must be accompanied by a respondent's notice in the form set out in the Practice Direction for the defendant to complete and a notice which—

(a) informs the defendant that the result of an appeal could be that the Court of Appeal would increase a confiscation order already imposed on him, make a confiscation order itself or direct the Crown Court to hold another confiscation hearing;

(b) informs the defendant of any right he has under article 6 of the Proceeds of Crime Act 2002 (Appeals under Part 2) Order 2003 to be present at the hearing of the appeal, although he may be in custody;

(c) invites the defendant to serve notice on the registrar if he wishes—

(i) to apply to the Court of Appeal for leave to be present at proceedings for which leave is required under article 6 of the 2003 Order, or

(ii) to present any argument to the Court of Appeal on the hearing of the application or, if leave is given, the appeal, and whether he wishes to present it in person or by means of a legal representative;

(d) draws to the defendant's attention the effect of rule 71.4 (supply of documentary and other exhibits); and

(e) advises the defendant to consult a solicitor as soon as possible.

(3) The appellant must provide a Crown Court officer with a certificate of service stating that he has served the notice of appeal on the defendant in accordance with paragraph (1) or explaining why he has been unable to effect service.

Respondent's notice
R-506

72.2 (1) This rule applies where a defendant is served with a notice of appeal under rule 72.1.

(2) If the defendant wishes to oppose the application for leave to appeal, he must, not later than 14 days after the date on which he received the notice of appeal, serve on the Registrar and on the appellant a notice in the form set out in the Practice Direction—

(a) stating the date on which he received the notice of appeal;

(b) summarising his response to the arguments of the appellant; and

(c) specifying the authorities which he intends to cite.

(3) The time for giving notice under this rule may be extended by the Registrar, a single judge or by the Court of Appeal.

(4) Where the Registrar refuses an application under paragraph (3) for the extension of time, the defendant shall be entitled to have his application determined by a single judge.

(5) Where a single judge refuses an application under paragraph (3) or (4) for the extension of time, the defendant shall be entitled to have his application determined by the Court of Appeal.

Amendment and abandonment of appeal
R-507

72.3 (1) The appellant may amend a notice of appeal served under rule 72.1 or abandon an appeal under section 31 of the Proceeds of Crime Act 2002—

(a) without the permission of the Court at any time before the Court of Appeal have begun hearing the appeal; and

(b) with the permission of the Court after the Court of Appeal have begun hearing the appeal, by serving notice in writing on the Registrar.

(2) Where the appellant serves a notice abandoning an appeal under paragraph (1), he must send a copy of it to—

(a) the defendant;

(b) a court officer of the court of trial; and

(c) the magistrates' court responsible for enforcing any confiscation order which the Crown Court has made.

(3) Where the appellant serves a notice amending a notice of appeal under paragraph (1), he must send a copy of it to the defendant.

(4) Where an appeal is abandoned under paragraph (1), the application for leave to appeal or appeal shall be treated, for the purposes of section 85 of the 2002 Act (conclusion of proceedings), as having been refused or dismissed by the Court of Appeal.

CRIMINAL PROCEDURE RULES PART 73 APPEAL TO THE COURT OF APPEAL UNDER POCA 2002: RESTRAINT OR RECEIVERSHIP ORDERS

Leave to appeal
R-508

73.1 (1) Leave to appeal to the Court of Appeal under section 43 or section 65 of the Proceeds of Crime Act 2002 will only be given where—

(a) the Court of Appeal considers that the appeal would have a real prospect of success; or

(b) there is some other compelling reason why the appeal should be heard.

(2) An order giving leave may limit the issues to be heard and be made subject to conditions.

Notice of appeal
R-509

73.2 (1) Where an appellant wishes to apply to the Court of Appeal for leave to appeal under section 43 or 65 of the Proceeds of Crime Act 2002 Act, he must serve a notice of appeal in the form set out in the Practice Direction on the Crown Court officer.

(2) Unless the Registrar, a single judge or the Court of Appeal directs otherwise, the appellant must serve the notice of appeal, accompanied by a respondent's notice in the form set out in the Practice Direction for the respondent to complete, on—

(a) each respondent;

(b) any person who holds realisable property to which the appeal relates; and

    (c) any other person affected by the appeal, as soon as practicable and in any event not later than 7 days after the notice of appeal is served on a Crown Court officer.

(3) The appellant must serve the following documents with his notice of appeal—

    (a) four additional copies of the notice of appeal for the Court of Appeal;

    (b) four copies of any skeleton argument;

    (c) one sealed copy and four unsealed copies of any order being appealed;

    (d) four copies of any witness statement or affidavit in support of the application for leave to appeal;

    (e) four copies of a suitable record of the reasons for judgment of the Crown Court; and

    (f) four copies of the bundle of documents used in the Crown Court proceedings from which the appeal lies.

(4) Where it is not possible to serve all of the documents referred to in paragraph (3), the appellant must indicate which documents have not yet been served and the reasons why they are not currently available.

(5) The appellant must provide a Crown Court officer with a certificate of service stating that he has served the notice of appeal on each respondent in accordance with paragraph (2) and including full details of each respondent or explaining why he has been unable to effect service.

R-510 Respondent's notice

73.3 (1) This rule applies to an appeal under section 43 or 65 of the Proceeds of Crime Act 2002.

(2) A respondent may serve a respondent's notice on the Registrar.

(3) A respondent who—

    (a) is seeking leave to appeal from the Court of Appeal; or

    (b) wishes to ask the Court of Appeal to uphold the decision of the Crown Court for reasons different from or additional to those given by the Crown Court,

must serve a respondent's notice on the Registrar.

(4) A respondent's notice must be in the form set out in the Practice Direction and where the respondent seeks leave to appeal to the Court of Appeal it must be requested in the respondent's notice.

(5) A respondent's notice must be served on the Registrar not later than 14 days after—

    (a) the date the respondent is served with notification that the Court of Appeal has given the appellant leave to appeal; or

    (b) the date the respondent is served with notification that the application for leave to appeal and the appeal itself are to be heard together.

(6) Unless the Registrar, a single judge or the Court of Appeal directs otherwise, the respondent serving a respondent's notice must serve the notice on the appellant and any other respondent—

    (a) as soon as practicable; and

    (b) in any event not later than seven days,

after it is served on the Registrar.

R-511 Amendment and abandonment of appeal

73.4 (1) The appellant may amend a notice of appeal served under rule 73.2 or abandon an appeal under section 43 or 65 of the Proceeds of Crime Act 2002—

    (a) without the permission of the Court at any time before the Court of Appeal have begun hearing the appeal; and

    (b) with the permission of the Court after the Court of Appeal have begun hearing the appeal, by serving notice in writing on the Registrar.

(2) Where the appellant serves a notice under paragraph (1), he must send a copy of it to each respondent.

R-512 Stay

73.5 Unless the Court of Appeal or the Crown Court orders otherwise, an appeal under section 43 or 65 of the Proceeds of Crime Act 2002 shall not operate as a stay of any order or decision of the Crown Court.

R-513 Striking out appeal notices and setting aside or imposing conditions on leave to appeal

73.6 (1) The Court of Appeal may—

    (a) strike out the whole or part of a notice of appeal served under rule 73.2; or

    (b) impose or vary conditions upon which an appeal under section 43 or 65 of the Proceeds of Crime Act 2002 may be brought.

(2) The Court of Appeal will only exercise its powers under paragraph (1) where there is a compelling reason for doing so.

(3) Where a party is present at the hearing at which leave to appeal was given, he may not subsequently apply for an order that the Court of Appeal exercise its powers under paragraph (1)(b).

Hearing of appeals

R-514

73.7 (1) This rule applies to appeals under section 43 or 65 of the Proceeds of Crime Act 2002.

(2) Every appeal will be limited to a review of the decision of the Crown Court unless the Court of Appeal considers that in the circumstances of an individual appeal it would be in the interests of justice to hold a re-hearing.

(3) The Court of Appeal will allow an appeal where the decision of the Crown Court was—
  (a) wrong; or
  (b) unjust because of a serious procedural or other irregularity in the proceedings in the Crown Court.

(4) The Court of Appeal may draw any inference of fact which it considers justified on the evidence.

(5) At the hearing of the appeal a party may not rely on a matter not contained in his notice of appeal unless the Court of Appeal gives permission.

CRIMINAL PROCEDURE RULES   PART 74   APPEAL OR REFERENCE TO THE SUPREME COURT

When this Part applies

R-515

74.1 (1) This Part applies where—
  (a) a party wants to appeal to the Supreme Court after—
    (i) an application to the Court of Appeal to which Part 41 applies (retrial following acquittal for serious offence), or
    (ii) an appeal to the Court of Appeal to which applies Part 66 (appeal to the Court of Appeal against ruling at preparatory hearing), Part 67 (appeal to the Court of Appeal against ruling adverse to prosecution), or Part 68 (appeal to the Court of Appeal about conviction or sentence); or
  (b) a party wants to refer a case to the Supreme Court after a reference to the Court of Appeal to which Part 70 applies (reference to the Court of Appeal of point of law or unduly lenient sentencing).

(2) A reference to an 'appellant' in this Part is a reference to such a party.

Application for permission or reference

R-516

74.2 (1) An appellant must—
  (a) apply orally to the Court of Appeal—
    (i) for permission to appeal or to refer a sentencing case, or
    (ii) to refer a point of law immediately after the court gives the reasons for its decision; or
  (b) apply in writing and serve the application on the Registrar and every other party not more than—
    (i) 14 days after the court gives the reasons for its decision if that decision was on a sentencing reference to which Part 70 applies (Attorney General's reference of sentencing case), or
    (ii) 28 days after the court gives those reasons in any other case.

(2) An application for permission to appeal or to refer a sentencing case must—
  (a) identify the point of law of general public importance that the appellant wants the court to certify is involved in the decision; and
  (b) give reasons why—
    (i) that point of law ought to be considered by the Supreme Court, and
    (ii) the court ought to give permission to appeal.

(3) An application to refer a point of law must give reasons why that point ought to be considered by the Supreme Court.

(4) An application must include or attach any application for the following, with reasons—
  (a) an extension of time within which to make the application for permission or for a reference,
  (b) bail pending appeal,
  (c) permission to attend any hearing in the Supreme Court, if the appellant is in custody.

(5) A written application must be in the form set out in the Practice Direction.

R-517 **Determination of detention pending appeal, etc.**

  74.3 On an application for permission to appeal the Court of Appeal must—

    (a) decide whether to order the detention of a defendant who would have been liable to be detained but for the decision of the court; and

    (b) determine any application for—

      (i) bail pending appeal,

      (ii) permission to attend any hearing in the Supreme Court, or

      (iii) a representation order.

R-518 **Bail pending appeal**

  74.4 Rules 68.8 (Application for bail pending appeal or retrial), 68.9 (Conditions of bail pending appeal or re-trial) and 68.10 (Forfeiture of a recognizance given as a condition of bail) apply.

CRIMINAL PROCEDURE RULES PART 75 REQUEST TO THE EUROPEAN
COURT FOR A PRELIMINARY RULING

R-519 **When this Part applies**

  75.1 This Part applies where the court can request the Court of Justice of the European Union ('the European Court') to give a preliminary ruling, under Article 267 of the Treaty on the Functioning of the European Union.

R-520 **Preparation of request**

  75.2 (1) The court may—

    (a) make an order for the submission of a request—

      (i) on application by a party, or

      (ii) on its own initiative;

    (b) give directions for the preparation of the terms of such a request.

    (2) The court must—

    (a) include in such a request—

      (i) the identity of the court making the request,

      (ii) the parties' identities,

      (iii) a statement of whether a party is in custody,

      (iv) a succinct statement of the question on which the court seeks the ruling of the European Court,

      (v) a succinct statement of any opinion on the answer that the court may have expressed in any judgment that it has delivered,

      (vi) a summary of the nature and history of the proceedings, including the salient facts and an indication of whether those facts are proved, admitted or assumed,

      (vii) the relevant rules of national law,

      (viii) a summary of the relevant contentions of the parties,

      (ix) an indication of the provisions of European Union law that the European Court is asked to interpret, and

      (x) an explanation of why a ruling of the European Court is requested;

    (b) express the request in terms that can be translated readily into other languages; and

    (c) set out the request in a schedule to the order.

R-521 **Submission of request**

  75.3 (1) The court officer must serve the order for the submission of the request on the Senior Master of the Queen's Bench Division of the High Court.

    (2) The Senior Master must—

    (a) submit the request to the European Court; but

    (b) unless the court otherwise directs, postpone the submission of the request until—

      (i) the time for any appeal against the order has expired, and

      (ii) any appeal against the order has been determined.

**Criminal Practice Directions Part 75 Request to the European
Court for a Preliminary Ruling**

PD-79 **CPD X Appeal 75A: References to the European Court of Justice**

  75A.1 Further to rule 75.3 of the Criminal Procedure Rules, the order containing the reference shall be filed with the Senior Master of the Queen's Bench Division of the High Court for onward transmission to the Court of Justice of the European Union. The order should be marked for the attention of Mrs Isaac and sent to the Senior Master:

c/o Queen's Bench Division Associates Dept
Room WG03
Royal Courts of Justice
Strand
London
WC2A 2LL

75A.2 There is no longer a requirement that the relevant court file be sent to the Senior Master. The parties should ensure that all appropriate documentation is sent directly to the European Court at the following address:

The Registrar
Court of Justice of the European Union
Kirchberg
L-2925 Luxemburg

75A.3 There is no prescribed form for use but the following details must be included in the back sheet to the order:

i.   Solicitor's full address;
ii. Solicitor's and Court references;
iii. Solicitor's e-mail address.

75A.4 The European Court of Justice regularly updates its Recommendation to national courts and tribunals in relation to the initiation of preliminary ruling proceedings. The current Recommendation is 2012/ C 338/01: http://eurlex.europa.eu/LexUriServ/LexUriServ.do?uri=OJ:C:2012:338:0001 :0006:EN:PDF

75A.5 The referring court may request the Court of Justice of the European Union to apply its urgent preliminary ruling procedure where the referring court's proceedings relate to a person in custody. For further information see Council Decision 2008/79/EC [2008] OJ L24/42: http://eurlex. europa.eu/LexUriServ/LexUriServ.do?uri=OJ:L:2008:024:0042:0043:EN:PDF

75A.6 Any such request must be made in a document separate from the order or in a covering letter and must set out:

iv. The matters of fact and law which establish the urgency;
v. The reasons why the urgent preliminary ruling procedure applies; and
vi. In so far as possible, the court's view on the answer to the question referred to the Court of Justice of the European Union for a preliminary ruling.

75A.7 Any request to apply the urgent preliminary ruling procedure should be filed with the Senior Master as described above.

CRIMINAL PROCEDURE RULES   PART 76   COSTS

Section 1: general

When this Part applies   R-522

76.1 (1) This Part applies where the court can make an order about costs under—
    (a) Part II of the Prosecution of Offences Act 1985 and Part II, IIA or IIB of The Costs in Criminal Cases (General) Regulations 1986;
    (b) section 109 of the Magistrates' Courts Act 1980;
    (c) section 52 of the Senior Courts Act 1981 and rule 76.6 or rule 76.7;
    (d) section 8 of the Bankers Books Evidence Act 1879;
    (e) section 2C(8) of the Criminal Procedure (Attendance of Witnesses) Act 1965;
    (f) section 36(5) of the Criminal Justice Act 1972;
    (g) section 159(5) and Schedule 3, paragraph 11, of the Criminal Justice Act 1988;
    (h) section 14H(5) of the Football Spectators Act 1989;
    (i) section 4(7) of the Dangerous Dogs Act 1991;
    (j) Part 3 of The Serious Crime Act 2007 (Appeals under Section 24) Order 2008; or
    (k) Part 1 or 2 of the Extradition Act 2003.
  (2) In this Part, 'costs' means—
    (a) the fees payable to a legal representative;
    (b) the disbursements paid by a legal representative; and
    (c) any other expenses incurred in connection with the case.

R-523   **Costs orders: general rules**

76.2   (1)   The court must not make an order about costs unless each party and any other person directly affected—

     (a)   is present; or

     (b)   has had an opportunity—

         (i)   to attend, or

         (ii)   to make representations.

   (2)   The court may make an order about costs—

     (a)   at a hearing in public or in private; or

     (b)   without a hearing.

   (3)   In deciding what order, if any, to make about costs, the court must have regard to all the circumstances, including—

     (a)   the conduct of all the parties; and

     (b)   any costs order already made.

   (4)   If the court makes an order about costs, it must—

     (a)   specify who must, or must not, pay what, to whom; and

     (b)   identify the legislation under which the order is made, where there is a choice of powers.

   (5)   The court must give reasons if it—

     (a)   refuses an application for a costs order; or

     (b)   rejects representations opposing a costs order.

   (6)   If the court makes an order for the payment of costs—

     (a)   the general rule is that it must be for an amount that is sufficient reasonably to compensate the recipient for costs—

         (i)   actually, reasonably and properly incurred, and

         (ii)   reasonable in amount; but

     (b)   the court may order the payment of—

         (i)   a proportion of that amount,

         (ii)   a stated amount less than that amount,

         (iii)   costs from or until a certain date only,

         (iv)   costs relating only to particular steps taken, or

         (v)   costs relating only to a distinct part of the case.

   (7)   On an assessment of the amount of costs, relevant factors include—

     (a)   the conduct of all the parties;

     (b)   the particular complexity of the matter or the difficulty or novelty of the questions raised;

     (c)   the skill, effort, specialised knowledge and responsibility involved;

     (d)   the time spent on the case;

     (e)   the place where and the circumstances in which work or any part of it was done; and

     (f)   any direction or observations by the court that made the costs order.

   (8)   If the court orders a party to pay costs to be assessed under rule 76.11, it may order that party to pay an amount on account.

   (9)   An order for the payment of costs takes effect when the amount is assessed, unless the court exercises any power it has to order otherwise.

R-524   **Court's power to vary requirements under Sections 2, 3 and 4**

76.3   (1)   The court may—

     (a)   extend a time limit for serving an application or representations under section 2, 3 or 4 of this Part, even after it has expired; and

     (b)   consider an application or representations—

         (i)   made in a different form to one set out in the Practice Direction, or

         (ii)   made orally instead of in writing.

   (2)   A person who wants an extension of time must—

     (a)   apply when serving the application or representations for which it is needed; and

     (b)   explain the delay.

Section 2: costs out of central funds

R-525   **Costs out of central funds**

76.4   (1)   This rule applies where the court can order the payment of costs out of central funds.

   (2)   In this rule, costs—

     (a)   include—

         (i)   on an appeal, costs incurred in the court that made the decision under appeal, and

         (ii)   at a retrial, costs incurred at the initial trial and on any appeal; but

     (b)   do not include costs met by legal aid.

(3) The court may make an order—
   (a) on application by the person who incurred the costs; or
   (b) on its own initiative.
(4) Where a person wants the court to make an order that person must—
   (a) apply as soon as practicable; and
   (b) outline the type of costs and the amount claimed, if that person wants the court to direct an assessment; or
   (c) specify the amount claimed, if that person wants the court to assess the amount itself.
(5) The general rule is that the court must make an order, but—
   (a) the court may decline to make a defendant's costs order if, for example—
      (i) the defendant is convicted of at least one offence, or
      (ii) the defendant's conduct led the prosecutor reasonably to think the prosecution case stronger than it was; and
   (b) the court may decline to make a prosecutor's costs order if, for example, the prosecution was started or continued unreasonably.
(6) If the court makes an order—
   (a) the court may direct an assessment under, as applicable—
      (i) Part III of The Costs in Criminal Cases (General) Regulations 1986, or
      (ii) Part 3 of The Serious Crime Act 2007 (Appeals under Section 24) Order 2008;
   (b) the court may assess the amount itself in a case in which either—
      (i) the recipient agrees the amount, or
      (ii) the court decides to allow a lesser sum than that which is reasonably sufficient to compensate the recipient for expenses properly incurred in the proceedings;
   (c) an order for the payment of a defendant's costs which includes an amount in respect of fees payable to a legal representative, or disbursements paid by a legal representative, must include a statement to that effect.
(7) If the court directs an assessment, the order must specify any restriction on the amount to be paid that the court considers appropriate.
(8) If the court assesses the amount itself, it must do so subject to any restriction on the amount to be paid that is imposed by regulations made by the Lord Chancellor.

Section 3: payment of costs by one party to another

Costs on conviction and sentence R-526

76.5 (1) This rule applies where the court can order a defendant to pay the prosecutor's costs if the defendant is—
   (a) convicted or found guilty;
   (b) dealt with in the Crown Court after committal for sentence there;
   (c) dealt with for breach of a sentence; or
   (d) in an extradition case—
      (i) ordered to be extradited, under Part 1 of the Extradition Act 2003, or
      (ii) sent for extradition to the Secretary of State, under Part 2 of that Act.
(2) The court may make an order—
   (a) on application by the prosecutor; or
   (b) on its own initiative.
(3) Where the prosecutor wants the court to make an order—
   (a) the prosecutor must—
      (i) apply as soon as practicable, and
      (ii) specify the amount claimed; and
   (b) the general rule is that the court must make an order if it is satisfied that the defendant can pay; but
   (c) the court may decline to do so.
(4) A defendant who wants to oppose an order must make representations as soon as practicable.
(5) If the court makes an order, it must assess the amount itself.

Costs on appeal R-527

76.6 (1) This rule—
   (a) applies where a magistrates' court, the Crown Court or the Court of Appeal can order a party to pay another person's costs on an appeal, or an application for permission to appeal;
   (b) authorises the Crown Court, in addition to its other powers, to order a party to pay another party's costs on an appeal to that court, except on an appeal under—
      (i) section 108 of the Magistrates' Courts Act 1980, or

      (ii)   section 45 of the Mental Health Act 1983.

(2) In this rule, costs include—

    (a) costs incurred in the court that made the decision under appeal; and

    (b) costs met by legal aid.

(3) The court may make an order—

    (a) on application by the person who incurred the costs; or

    (b) on its own initiative.

(4) A person who wants the court to make an order must—

    (a) apply as soon as practicable;

    (b) notify each other party;

    (c) specify—

        (i)   the amount claimed, and

        (ii) against whom; and

    (d) where an appellant abandons an appeal to the Crown Court by serving a notice of abandonment—

        (i)   apply in writing not more than 14 days later, and

        (ii) serve the application on the appellant and on the Crown Court officer.

(5) A party who wants to oppose an order must—

    (a) make representations as soon as practicable; and

    (b) where the application was under paragraph (4)(d), serve written representations on the applicant, and on the Crown Court officer, not more than 7 days after it was served.

(6) Where the application was under paragraph (4)(d), the Crown Court officer may—

    (a) submit it to the Crown Court; or

    (b) serve it on the magistrates' court officer, for submission to the magistrates' court.

(7) If the court makes an order, it may direct an assessment under rule 76.11, or assess the amount itself where—

    (a) the appellant abandons an appeal to the Crown Court;

    (b) the Crown Court decides an appeal, except an appeal under—

        (i)   section 108 of the Magistrates' Courts Act 1980, or

        (ii) section 45 of the Mental Health Act 1983; or

    (c) the Court of Appeal decides an appeal to which Part 69 applies (appeal to the Court of Appeal regarding reporting or public access restriction).

(8) If the court makes an order in any other case, it must assess the amount itself.

R-528   Costs on an application

76.7 (1) This rule—

    (a) applies where the court can order a party to pay another person's costs in a case in which—

        (i)   the court decides an application for the production in evidence of a copy of a bank record,

        (ii) a magistrates' court or the Crown Court decides an application to terminate a football banning order,

        (iii) a magistrates' court or the Crown Court decides an application to terminate a disqualification for having custody of a dog, or

        (iv) the Crown Court allows an application to withdraw a witness summons, or

        (v) the Crown Court decides an application relating to a deferred prosecution agreement under rule 12.5 (breach), rule 12.6 (variation) or rule 12.7 (lifting suspension of prosecution);

    (b) authorises the Crown Court, in addition to its other powers, to order a party to pay another party's costs on an application to that court under rule 12.5, 12.6 or 12.7.

(2) The court may make an order—

    (a) on application by the person who incurred the costs; or

    (b) on its own initiative.

(3) A person who wants the court to make an order must—

    (a) apply as soon as practicable;

    (b) notify each other party; and

    (c) specify—

        (i)   the amount claimed, and

        (ii) against whom.

(4) A party who wants to oppose an order must make representations as soon as practicable.

(5) If the court makes an order, it may direct an assessment under rule 76.11, or assess the amount itself.

Costs resulting from unnecessary or improper act, etc.   **R-529**

76.8   (1)   This rule applies where the court can order a party to pay another party's costs incurred as a result of an unnecessary or improper act or omission by or on behalf of the first party.

(2)   In this rule, costs include costs met by legal aid.

(3)   The court may make an order—
    (a)   on application by the party who incurred such costs; or
    (b)   on its own initiative.

(4)   A party who wants the court to make an order must—
    (a)   apply in writing as soon as practicable after becoming aware of the grounds for doing so;
    (b)   serve the application on—
        (i)   the court officer (or, in the Court of Appeal, the Registrar), and
        (ii)   each other party;
    (c)   in that application specify—
        (i)   the party by whom costs should be paid,
        (ii)   the relevant act or omission,
        (iii)   the reasons why that act or omission meets the criteria for making an order,
        (iv)   the amount claimed, and
        (v)   those on whom the application has been served.

(5)   Where the court considers making an order on its own initiative, it must—
    (a)   identify the party against whom it proposes making the order; and
    (b)   specify—
        (i)   the relevant act or omission,
        (ii)   the reasons why that act or omission meets the criteria for making an order, and
        (iii)   with the assistance of the party who incurred the costs, the amount involved.

(6)   A party who wants to oppose an order must—
    (a)   make representations as soon as practicable; and
    (b)   in reply to an application, serve written representations on the applicant and on the court officer (or Registrar) not more than 7 days after it was served.

(7)   If the court makes an order, it must assess the amount itself.

Section 4: other costs orders

Costs against a legal representative   **R-530**

76.9   (1)   This rule applies where—
    (a)   a party has incurred costs—
        (i)   as a result of an improper, unreasonable or negligent act or omission by a legal or other representative or representative's employee, or
        (ii)   which it has become unreasonable for that party to have to pay because of such an act or omission occurring after those costs were incurred; and
    (b)   the court can—
        (i)   order the representative responsible to pay such costs, or
        (ii)   prohibit the payment of costs to that representative.

(2)   In this rule, costs include costs met by legal aid.

(3)   The court may make an order—
    (a)   on application by the party who incurred such costs; or
    (b)   on its own initiative.

(4)   A party who wants the court to make an order must—
    (a)   apply in writing as soon as practicable after becoming aware of the grounds for doing so;
    (b)   serve the application on—
        (i)   the court officer (or, in the Court of Appeal, the Registrar),
        (ii)   the representative responsible,
        (iii)   each other party, and
        (iv)   any other person directly affected;
    (c)   in that application specify—
        (i)   the representative responsible,
        (ii)   the relevant act or omission,
        (iii)   the reasons why that act or omission meets the criteria for making an order,
        (iv)   the amount claimed, and
        (v)   those on whom the application has been served.

(5) Where the court considers making an order on its own initiative, it must—
  (a) identify the representative against whom it proposes making that order; and
  (b) specify—
    (i) the relevant act or omission,
    (ii) the reasons why that act or omission meets the criteria for making an order, and
    (iii) with the assistance of the party who incurred the costs, the amount involved.
(6) A representative who wants to oppose an order must—
  (a) make representations as soon as practicable; and
  (b) in reply to an application, serve written representations on the applicant and on the court officer (or Registrar) not more than 7 days after it was served.
(7) If the court makes an order—
  (a) the general rule is that it must do so without waiting until the end of the case, but it may postpone making the order; and
  (b) it must assess the amount itself.
(8) Instead of making an order, the court may make adverse observations about the representative's conduct for use in an assessment where—
  (a) a party's costs are—
    (i) to be met by legal aid, or
    (ii) to be paid out of central funds; or
  (b) there is to be an assessment under rule 76.11.

R-531 Costs against a third party

76.10 (1) This rule applies where—
  (a) there has been serious misconduct by a person who is not a party; and
  (b) the court can order that person to pay a party's costs.
(2) In this rule, costs include costs met by legal aid.
(3) The court may make an order—
  (a) on application by the party who incurred the costs; or
  (b) on its own initiative.
(4) A party who wants the court to make an order must—
  (a) apply in writing as soon as practicable after becoming aware of the grounds for doing so;
  (b) serve the application on—
    (i) the court officer (or, in the Court of Appeal, the Registrar),
    (ii) the person responsible,
    (iii) each other party, and
    (iv) any other person directly affected;
  (c) in that application specify—
    (i) the person responsible,
    (ii) the relevant misconduct,
    (iii) the reasons why the criteria for making an order are met,
    (iv) the amount claimed, and
    (v) those on whom the application has been served.
(5) Where the court considers making an order on its own initiative, it must—
  (a) identify the person against whom it proposes making that order; and
  (b) specify—
    (i) the relevant misconduct,
    (ii) the reasons why the criteria for making an order are met, and
    (iii) with the assistance of the party who incurred the costs, the amount involved.
(6) A person who wants to oppose an order must—
  (a) make representations as soon as practicable; and
  (b) in reply to an application, serve written representations on the applicant and on the court officer (or Registrar) not more than 7 days after it was served.
(7) If the court makes an order—
  (a) the general rule is that it must do so at the end of the case, but it may do so earlier; and
  (b) it must assess the amount itself.

Section 5: assessment of costs

R-532 Assessment and re-assessment

76.11 (1) This rule applies where the court directs an assessment under—
  (a) rule 61.20 (Proceeds of Crime Act 2002—rules applicable to restraint and receivership proceedings, assessment of costs);

   (b) rule 76.6 (costs on appeal); or
   (c) rule 76.7 (costs on an application).
(2) The assessment must be carried out by the relevant assessing authority, namely—
   (a) the court officer, where the direction was given by a magistrates' court or by the Crown Court; or
   (b) the Registrar of Criminal Appeals, where the direction was given by the Court of Appeal.
(3) The party in whose favour the court made the costs order ('the applicant') must—
   (a) apply for an assessment—
      (i)   in writing, in any form required by the assessing authority, and
      (ii) not more than 3 months after the costs order; and
   (b) serve the application on—
      (i)   the assessing authority, and
      (ii) the party against whom the court made the costs order ('the respondent').
(4) The applicant must—
   (a) summarise the work done;
   (b) specify—
      (i)   each item of work done, giving the date, time taken and amount claimed,
      (ii) any disbursements or expenses, including the fees of any advocate, and
      (iii) any circumstances of which the applicant wants the assessing authority to take particular account; and
   (c) supply—
      (i)   receipts or other evidence of the amount claimed, and
      (ii) any other information or document for which the assessing authority asks, within such period as that authority may require.
(5) A respondent who wants to make representations about the amount claimed must—
   (a) do so in writing; and
   (b) serve the representations on the assessing authority, and on the applicant, not more than 21 days after service of the application.
(6) The assessing authority must—
   (a) if it seems likely to help with the assessment, obtain any other information or document;
   (b) resolve in favour of the respondent any doubt about what should be allowed; and
   (c) serve the assessment on the parties.
(7) Where either party wants the amount allowed re-assessed—
   (a) that party must—
      (i)   apply to the assessing authority, in writing and in any form required by that authority,
      (ii) serve the application on the assessing authority, and on the other party, not more than 21 days after service of the assessment,
      (iii) explain the objections to the assessment,
      (iv) supply any additional supporting information or document, and
      (v)   ask for a hearing, if that party wants one; and
   (b) a party who wants to make representations about an application for re-assessment must—
      (i)   do so in writing,
      (ii) serve the representations on the assessing authority, and on the other party, not more than 21 days after service of the application, and
      (iii) ask for a hearing, if that party wants one;
   (c) the assessing authority—
      (i)   must arrange a hearing, in public or in private, if either party asks for one,
      (ii) subject to that, may re-assess the amount allowed with or without a hearing,
      (iii) must re-assess the amount allowed on the initial assessment, taking into account the reasons for disagreement with that amount and any other representations,
      (iv) may maintain, increase or decrease the amount allowed on the assessment,
      (v)   must serve the re-assessment on the parties, and
      (vi) must serve written reasons on the parties, if not more than 21 days later either party asks for such reasons.
(8) A time limit under this rule may be extended even after it has expired—
   (a) by the assessing authority, or
   (b) by the Senior Costs Judge, if the assessing authority declines to do so.

Criminal Procedure Rules 2013 and Criminal Practice Directions

R-533   **Appeal to a costs judge**

76.12 (1)   This rule applies where—

     (a)   the assessing authority has re-assessed the amount allowed under rule 76.11; and

     (b)   either party wants to appeal against that amount.

(2)   That party must—

     (a)   serve an appeal notice on—

         (i)   the Senior Costs Judge,

         (ii)   the other party, and

         (iii)   the assessing authority

     not more than 21 days after service of the written reasons for the re-assessment;

     (b)   explain the objections to the re-assessment;

     (c)   serve on the Senior Costs Judge with the appeal notice—

         (i)   the applications for assessment and re-assessment,

         (ii)   any other information or document considered by the assessing authority,

         (iii)   the assessing authority's written reasons for the re-assessment, and

         (iv)   any other information or document for which a costs judge asks, within such period as the judge may require; and

     (d)   ask for a hearing, if that party wants one.

(3)   A party who wants to make representations about an appeal must—

     (a)   serve representations in writing on—

         (i)   the Senior Costs Judge, and

         (ii)   the applicant

     not more than 21 days after service of the appeal notice; and

     (b)   ask for a hearing, if that party wants one.

(4)   Unless a costs judge otherwise directs, the parties may rely only on—

     (a)   the objections to the amount allowed on the initial assessment; and

     (b)   any other representations and material considered by the assessing authority.

(5)   A costs judge—

     (a)   must arrange a hearing, in public or in private, if either party asks for one;

     (b)   subject to that, may determine an appeal with or without a hearing;

     (c)   may—

         (i)   consult the assessing authority,

         (ii)   consult the court which made the costs order, and

         (iii)   obtain any other information or document;

     (d)   must reconsider the amount allowed by the assessing authority, taking into account the objections to the re-assessment and any other representations;

     (e)   may maintain, increase or decrease the amount allowed on the re-assessment;

     (f)   may provide for the costs incurred by either party to the appeal; and

     (g)   must serve reasons for the decision on—

         (i)   the parties, and

         (ii)   the assessing authority.

(6)   A costs judge may extend a time limit under this rule, even after it has expired.

R-534   **Appeal to a High Court judge**

76.13 (1)   This rule applies where—

     (a)   a costs judge has determined an appeal under rule 76.12; and

     (b)   either party wants to appeal against the amount allowed.

(2)   A party who wants to appeal—

     (a)   may do so only if a costs judge certifies that a point of principle of general importance was involved in the decision on the review; and

     (b)   must apply in writing for such a certificate and serve the application on—

         (i)   the costs judge,

         (ii)   the other party

     not more than 21 days after service of the decision on the review.

(3)   That party must—

     (a)   appeal to a judge of the High Court attached to the Queen's Bench Division as if it were an appeal from the decision of a master under Part 52 of the Civil Procedure Rules 1998 ; and

     (b)   serve the appeal not more than 21 days after service of the costs judge's certificate under paragraph (2).

(4) A High Court judge—
    (a) may extend a time limit under this rule even after it has expired;
    (b) has the same powers and duties as a costs judge under rule 76.12; and
    (c) may hear the appeal with one or more assessors.

Application for an extension of time under Section 5   R-535

76.14 A party who wants an extension of time under rule 76.11, 76.12 or 76.13 must—
    (a) apply in writing;
    (b) explain the delay; and
    (c) attach the application, representations or appeal for which the extension of time is needed.

Criminal Practice Directions General
Application

CPD XII General application A: Court Dress   PD-80

A.1   In magistrates' courts, advocates appear without robes or wigs. In all other courts, Queen's Counsel wear a short wig and a silk (or stuff) gown over a court coat with bands, junior counsel wear a short wig and stuff gown with bands. Solicitors and other advocates authorised under the Courts and Legal Services Act 1990 wear a black solicitor's gown with bands; they may wear short wigs in circumstances where they would be worn by Queen's Counsel or junior counsel.

A.2   High Court Judges hearing criminal cases may wear the winter criminal robe year-round. However, scarlet summer robes may be worn.

CPD XII General application B: Modes of Address and Titles of Judges   PD-81
and Magistrates

Modes of Address

B.1   The following judges, when sitting in court, should be addressed as 'My Lord' or 'My Lady', as the case may be, whatever their personal status:
    (a) Judges of the Court of Appeal and of the High Court;
    (b) any Circuit Judge sitting as a judge of the Court of Appeal (Criminal Division) or the High Court under section 9(1) of the Senior Courts Act 1981;
    (c) any judge sitting at the Central Criminal Court
    (d) any Senior Circuit Judge who is an Honorary Recorder

B.2   Subject to the paragraph above, Circuit Judges, qualifying judge advocates, Recorders and Deputy Circuit Judges should be addressed as 'Your Honour' when sitting in court.

District Judges (Magistrates' Courts) should be addressed as 'Sir [or Madam]' or 'Judge' when sitting in Court.

Magistrates in court should be addressed through the Chairperson as 'Sir[or Madam]' or collectively as 'Your Worships'.

Description

B.3   In cause lists, forms and orders members of the judiciary should be described as follows:
    (a) Circuit Judges, as 'His [or Her] Honour Judge A'.
       When the judge is sitting as a judge of the High Court under section 9(1) of the Senior Courts Act 1981, the words 'sitting as a judge of the High Court' should be added;
    (b) Recorders, as 'Mr [or Mrs, Ms or Miss] Recorder B'.
       This style is appropriate irrespective of any honour or title which the recorder might possess, but if in any case it is desired to include an honour or title, the alternative description, 'Sir CD, Recorder' or 'The Lord D, Recorder' may be used;
    (c) Deputy Circuit Judges, as 'His [or Her] Honour EF, sitting as a Deputy Circuit Judge';
    (d) qualifying judges advocates, as 'His [or Her] Honour GH, sitting as a qualifying judge advocate.';
    (e) District Judges (Magistrates' Courts), as 'District Judge (Magistrates' Courts) J'.

CPD XII General application C: Availability of Judgments given in the Court of Appeal and the   PD-82
High Court

C.1   For cases in the High Court, reference should be made to Practice Direction 40E, the supplementary Practice Direction to the Civil Procedure Rules Part 40.

C.2   For cases in the Court of Appeal (Criminal Division), the following provisions apply.

Criminal Procedure Rules 2013 and Criminal Practice Directions

Availability of reserved judgments before handing down, corrections and applications consequential on judgment

C.3 Where judgment is to be reserved the Presiding Judge may, at the conclusion of the hearing, invite the views of the parties' legal representatives as to the arrangements to be made for the handing down of the judgment.

C.4 Unless the court directs otherwise, the following provisions apply where the Presiding Judge is satisfied that the judgment will attract no special degree of confidentiality or sensitivity.

C.5 The court will provide a copy of the draft judgment to the parties' legal representatives about three working days before handing down, or at such other time as the court may direct. Every page of every judgment which is made available in this way will be marked 'Unapproved judgment: No permission is granted to copy or use in court.' The draft is supplied in confidence and on the conditions that:

  (a) neither the draft judgment nor its substance will be disclosed to any other person or used in the public domain; and

  (b) no action will be taken (other than internally) in response to the draft judgment, before the judgment is handed down.

C.6 Unless the parties' legal representatives are told otherwise when the draft judgment is circulated, any proposed corrections to the draft judgment should be sent to the clerk of the judge who prepared the draft (or to the associate, if the judge has no clerk) with a copy to any other party's legal representatives, by 12 noon on the day before judgment is handed down.

C.7 If, having considered the draft judgment, the prosecution will be applying to the Court for a retrial or either party wishes to make any other application consequent on the judgment, the judge's clerk should be informed with a time estimate for the application by 12 noon on the day before judgment is handed down. This will enable the court to make appropriate listing arrangements and notify advocates to attend if the court so requires. There is no fee payable to advocates who attend the hand down hearing if not required to do so by the court. If either party is considering applying to the Court to certify a point for appeal to the Supreme Court, it would assist if the judge's clerk could be informed at the same time, although this is not obligatory as under section 34 of the Criminal Appeal Act 1968, the time limit for such applications is 28 days.

Communication to the parties including the defendant or the victim

C.8 The contents are not to be communicated to the parties, including to the defendant, respondent or the victim (defined as a person entitled to receive services under the Code of Practice for Victims of Crime) until two hours before the listed time for pronouncement of judgment.

C.9 Judges may permit more information about the result of a case to be communicated on a confidential basis to the parties including to the defendant, respondent or the victim at an earlier stage if good reason is shown for making such a direction.

C.10 If, for any reason, the parties' legal representatives have special grounds for seeking a relaxation of the usual condition restricting disclosure to the parties, a request for relaxation of the condition may be made informally through the judge's clerk (or through the associate, if the judge has no clerk).

C.11 If the parties or their legal representatives are in any doubt about the persons to whom copies of the draft judgment may be distributed they should enquire of the judge or Presiding Judge.

C.12 Any breach of the obligations or restrictions in this section or failure to take reasonable steps to ensure compliance may be treated as contempt of court.

Restrictions on disclosure or reporting

C.13 Anyone who is supplied with a copy of the handed-down judgment, or who reads it in court, will be bound by any direction which the court may have given in a child case under section 39 of the Children and Young Persons Act 1933, or any other form of restriction on disclosure, or reporting, of information in the judgment.

C.14 Copies of the approved judgment can be ordered from the official shorthand writers, on payment of the appropriate fee. Judgments identified as of legal or public interest will generally be made available on the website managed by BAILLI: http://www.bailii.org/

PD-83 CPD XII General Application D: Citation of Authority and Provision of Copies of Judgments to the Court

D.1 This Practice Direction applies to all criminal matters before the Court of Appeal (Criminal Division), the Crown Court and the magistrates' courts. In relation to those matters only, Practice Direction (Citation of Authorities) [2012] 1 WLR 780 is hereby revoked.

Citation of authority

D.2 In *R v Erskine; R v Williams* [2009] EWCA Crim 1425, [2010] 1 WLR 183, (2009) 2 Cr App R 29 the Lord Chief Justice stated:

> 75. The essential starting point, relevant to any appeal against conviction or sentence, is that, adapting the well known aphorism of Viscount Falkland in 1641: if it is not necessary to refer to a previous decision of the court, it is necessary not to refer to it. Similarly, if it is not necessary to include a previous decision in the bundle of authorities, it is necessary to exclude it. That approach will be rigidly enforced.
>
> 76. It follows that when the advocate is considering what authority, if any, to cite for a proposition, only an authority which establishes the principle should be cited. Reference should not be made to authorities which do no more than either (a) illustrate the principle or (b) restate it.
>
> 78. Advocates must expect to be required to justify the citation of each authority relied on or included in the bundle. The court is most unlikely to be prepared to look at an authority which does no more than illustrate or restate an established proposition.
>
> 80. ...In particular, in sentencing appeals, where a definitive Sentencing Guidelines Council guideline is available there will rarely be any advantage in citing an authority reached before the issue of the guideline, and authorities after its issue which do not refer to it will rarely be of assistance. In any event, where the authority does no more than uphold a sentence imposed at the Crown Court, the advocate must be ready to explain how it can assist the court to decide that a sentence is manifestly excessive or wrong in principle.

D.3 Advocates should only cite cases when it is necessary to do so; when the case identifies or represents a principle or the development of a principle. In sentencing appeals, other cases are rarely helpful, providing only an illustration, and this is especially true if there is a sentencing guideline. Unreported cases should only be cited in exceptional circumstances, and the advocate must expect to explain why such a case has been cited.

D.4 Advocates should not assume that because a case cited to the court is not referred to in the judgment the court has not considered it; it is more likely that the court was not assisted by it.

D.5 When an authority is to be cited, whether in written or oral submissions, the advocate should always provide the neutral citation followed by the law report reference.

D.6 The following practice should be followed:

i) Where a judgment is reported in the Official Law Reports (Q.Ch Fam) published by the Incorporated Council of Law Reporting for England and Wales or the Criminal Appeal Reports or the Criminal Appeal Reports (Sentencing) one of those two series of reports must be cited; either is equally acceptable. However, where a judgment is reported in the Criminal Appeal Reports or the Criminal Appeal Reports (Sentencing) that reference must be given in addition to any other reference. Other series of reports and official transcripts of judgment may only be used when a case is not reported, or not yet reported, in the Official Law Reports or the Criminal Appeal Reports or the Criminal Appeal Reports (Sentencing).

ii) If a judgment is not reported in the Official Law Reports, the Criminal Appeal Reports or the Criminal Appeal Reports (Sentencing), but it is reported in an authoritative series of reports which contains a headnote and is made by individuals holding a Senior Courts qualification (for the purposes of section 115 of the Courts and Legal Services Act 1990), that report should be cited.

iii) Where a judgment is not reported in any of the reports referred to above, but is reported in other reports, they may be cited.

iv) Where a judgment has not been reported, reference may be made to the official transcript if that is available, not the handed-down text of the judgment, as this may have been subject to late revision after the text was handed down. Official transcripts may be obtained from, for instance, BAILII (http://www.bailii.org/).

D.7 In the majority of cases, it is expected that all references will be to the Official Law Reports and the Criminal Appeal Reports or the Criminal Appeal Reports (Sentencing); it will be rare for there to be a need to refer to any other reports. An unreported case should not be cited unless it contains a relevant statement of legal principle not found in reported authority, and it is expected that this will only occur in exceptional circumstances.

Provision of copies of judgments to the Court

D.8 The paragraphs below specify whether or not copies should be provided to the court. Authorities should not be included for propositions not in dispute. If more than one authority is to be provided, the copies should be presented in paginated and tagged bundles.

D.9 If required, copies of judgments should be provided either by way of a photocopy of the published report or by way of a copy of a reproduction of the judgment in electronic form that has been authorised by the publisher of the relevant series, but in any event:

    i)   the report must be presented to the court in an easily legible form (a 12-point font is preferred but a 10 or 11-point font is acceptable); and

    ii)   the advocate presenting the report must be satisfied that it has not been reproduced in a garbled form from the data source.

In any case of doubt the court will rely on the printed text of the report (unless the editor of the report has certified that an electronic version is more accurate because it corrects an error contained in an earlier printed text of the report).

D.10 If such a copy is unavailable, a printed transcript such as from BAILLI may be included.

Provision of copies to the Court of Appeal (Criminal Division)

D.11 Advocates must provide to the Registrar of Criminal Appeals, with their appeal notice, respondent's notice or skeleton argument, a list of authorities upon which they wish to rely in their written or oral submissions. The list of authorities should contain the name of the applicant, appellant or respondent and the Criminal Appeal Office number where known. The list should include reference to the relevant paragraph numbers in each authority. An updated list can be provided if a new authority is issued, or in response to a respondent's notice or skeleton argument. From time to time, the Registrar may issue guidance as to the style or content of lists of authorities, including a suggested format; this guidance should be followed by all parties. The latest guidance is available from the Criminal Appeal Office.

D.12 If the case cited is reported in the Official Law Reports, the Criminal Appeal Reports or the Criminal Appeal Reports (Sentencing), the law report reference must be given after the neutral citation, and the relevant paragraphs listed, but copies should not be provided to the court.

D.13 If, exceptionally, reference is made to a case that is not reported in the Official Law Reports, the Criminal Appeal Reports or the Criminal Appeal Reports (Sentencing), three copies must be provided to the Registrar with the list of authorities and the relevant appeal notice or respondent's notice (or skeleton argument, if provided). The relevant passages of the authorities should be marked or sidelined.

Provision of copies to the Crown Court and the magistrates' courts

D.14 When the court is considering routine applications, it may be sufficient for the court to be referred to the applicable legislation or to one of the practitioner texts. However, it is the responsibility of the advocate to ensure that the court is provided with the material that it needs properly to consider any matter.

D.15 If it would assist the court to consider any authority, the directions at paragraphs D.2 to D.7 above relating to citation will apply and a list of authorities should be provided.

D.16 Copies should be provided by the party seeking to rely upon the authority in accordance with Rule 37.12. This Rule is applicable in the magistrates' courts, and in relation to the provision of authorities, should also be followed in the Crown Court since courts often do not hold library stock. Advocates should comply with paragraphs D.8 to D.10 relating to the provision of copies to the court.

PD-84 **CPD XII General application E: Preparation of Judgments: Neutral Citation**

E.1 Since 11 January 2001 every judgment of the Court of Appeal, and of the Administrative Court, and since 14 January 2002 every judgment of the High Court, has been prepared and issued as approved with single spacing, paragraph numbering (in the margins) and no page numbers. In courts with more than one judge, the paragraph numbering continues sequentially through each judgment and does not start again at the beginning of each judgment. Indented paragraphs are not numbered. A unique reference number is given to each judgment. For judgments of the Court of Appeal, this number is given by the official shorthand writers, Merrill Legal Solutions (Tel: 020 7421 4000 ext.4036). For judgments of the High Court, it is provided by the Courts Recording and Transcription Unit at the Royal Courts of Justice. Such a number will also be furnished, on request to the Courts Recording and Transcription Unit, Royal Courts of Justice, Strand, London WC2A 2LL (Tel: 020 7947 7820), (e-mail: rcj.cratu@hmcts.gsi.gov.uk) for High Court judgments delivered outside London.

E.2 Each Court of Appeal judgment starts with the year, followed by EW (for England and Wales), then CA (for Court of Appeal), followed by Civ or Crim and finally the sequential number. For example, '*Smith v Jones* [2001] EWCA Civ 10'.

E.3 In the High Court, represented by HC, the number comes before the divisional abbreviation and, unlike Court of Appeal judgments, the latter is bracketed: (Ch), (Pat), (QB), (Admin), (Comm), (Admlty), (TCC) or (Fam), as appropriate. For example, '[2002] EWHC 123 (Fam)', or '[2002] EWHC 124 (QB)', or '[2002] EWHC 125 (Ch)'.

E.4 This 'neutral citation', as it is called, is the official number attributed to the judgment and must always be used at least once when the judgment is cited in a later judgment. Once the judgment is reported, this neutral citation appears in front of the familiar citation from the law reports series. Thus: '*Smith v Jones* [2001] EWCA Civ 10; [2001] QB 124; [2001] 2 All ER 364', etc.

E.5 Paragraph numbers are referred to in square brackets. When citing a paragraph from a High Court judgment, it is unnecessary to include the descriptive word in brackets: (Admin), (QB), or whatever. When citing a paragraph from a Court of Appeal judgment, however, 'Civ' or 'Crim' is included. If it is desired to cite more than one paragraph of a judgment, each numbered paragraph should be enclosed with a square bracket. Thus paragraph 59 in *Green v White* [2002] EWHC 124 (QB) would be cited: '*Green v White* [2002] EWHC 124 at [59]'; paragraphs 30 – 35 in *Smith v Jones* would be '*Smith v Jones* [2001] EWCA Civ 10 at [30] – [35]'; similarly, where a number of paragraphs are cited: '*Smith v Jones* [2001] EWCA Civ 10 at [30], [35] and [40 – 43]'.

E.6 If a judgment is cited more than once in a later judgment, it is helpful if only one abbreviation is used, e.g., '*Smith v Jones*' or '*Smith's case*', but preferably not both (in the same judgment).

CPD XII General application F: Citation of Hansard

PD-85

F.1 Where any party intends to refer to the reports of Parliamentary proceedings as reported in the Official Reports of either House of Parliament ("Hansard") in support of any such argument as is permitted by the decisions in *Pepper v Hart* [1993] AC 593 and *Pickstone v Freemans PLC* [1989] AC 66, or otherwise, he must, unless the court otherwise directs, serve upon all other parties and the court copies of any such extract, together with a brief summary of the argument intended to be based upon such extract. No other report of Parliamentary proceedings may be cited.

F.2 Unless the court otherwise directs, service of the extract and summary of the argument shall be effected not less than 5 clear working days before the first day of the hearing, whether or not it has a fixed date. Advocates must keep themselves informed as to the state of the lists where no fixed date has been given. Service on the court shall be effected by sending three copies to the Registrar of Criminal Appeals, Royal Courts of Justice, Strand, London, WC2A 2LL or to the court manager of the relevant Crown Court centre, as appropriate. If any party fails to do so, the court may make such order (relating to costs or otherwise) as is, in all the circumstances, appropriate.

Criminal Practice Directions Listing

SAVED PROVISIONS

PD-86

From the Consolidated Criminal Practice Direction of 8 July 2002 ([2002] 1 WLR 2870; [2002] 3 All ER 904; [2002] 2 Cr App R 35), as amended

III.21. Classification of Crown Court business and allocation to Crown Court Centres

PD-87

Classification

III.21.1 For the purposes of trial in the Crown Court offences are classified as follows:

Class 1: (a) Misprision of treason and treason felony; (b) Murder; (c) Genocide; (d) Torture, hostage-taking and offences under the War Crimes Act 1991; (e) An offence under the Official Secrets Acts; (f) Manslaughter; (g) Infanticide; (h) Child destruction; (i) Abortion (section 58 of the Offences against the Person Act 1861); (j) Sedition; (k) An offence under section 1 of the Geneva Conventions Act 1957; (l) Mutiny; (m) Piracy; (n) Soliciting, incitement, attempt or conspiracy to commit any of the above offences.

Class 2: (a) Rape; (b) Sexual intercourse with a girl under 13; (c) Incest with a girl under 13; (d) Assault by penetration; (e) Causing a person to engage in sexual activity, where penetration is involved; (f) Rape of a child under 13; (g) Assault of a child under 13 by penetration; (h) Causing or inciting a child under 13 to engage in sexual activity, where penetration is involved; (i) Sexual activity with a person with a mental disorder, where penetration is involved; (j) Inducement to procure sexual activity with a mentally disordered person where penetration is involved; (k) Paying for sexual services of a child where child is under 13 and penetration is involved; (l) Committing an offence with intent to commit a sexual offence, where the offence is kidnapping or false imprisonment; (m) Soliciting, incitement, attempt or conspiracy to commit any of the above offences.

Class 3: All other offences not listed in classes 1 or 2.

III.21.2 The magistrates' court, upon either committing a person for trial under section 6 of the Magistrates' Courts Act 1980, or sending a person under section 51 of the Crime and Disorder Act 1998, shall:

(a) if the offence or any of the offences is included in Class 1, specify the most convenient location of the Crown Court where a High Court Judge, or, where a Circuit Judge duly authorised by the Lord Chief Justice to try class 1 cases, regularly sits.

(b) if the offence or any of the offences is included in Class 2, specify the most convenient location of the Crown Court where a Judge duly authorised to try Class 2 regularly sits. These courts on each Circuit will be identified by the Presiding Judges, with the concurrence of the Lord Chief Justice.

(c) where an offence is in Class 3 the magistrates' court shall specify the most convenient location of the Crown Court.

Where a case is transferred under section 4 of the Criminal Justice Act 1987 or section 53 of the Criminal Justice Act 1991, the authority shall, in specifying the proposed place of trial in the notice of transfer, comply with the provisions of this paragraph.

III.21.3 In selecting the most convenient location of the Crown Court the justices shall have regard to the considerations referred to in section 7 of the Magistrates' Courts Act 1980 and section 51(10) of the Crime and Disorder Act 1998 and the location or locations of the Crown Court designated by a Presiding Judge as the location to which cases should normally be committed from their court.

III.21.4 Where on one occasion a person is committed in respect of a number of offences all the committals shall be to the same location of the Crown Court and that location shall be the one where a High Court Judge regularly sits if such a location is appropriate for any of the offences.

Committals following breach

III.21.5 Where, in the Crown Court, a community order or an order for conditional discharge has been made, or a suspended sentence has been passed, and the offender is subsequently found or alleged to be in breach before a magistrates' court which decides to commit the offender to the Crown Court, he shall be committed in accordance with paragraphs III.21.6, III.21.7 or III.21.8

III.21.6 He shall be committed to the location of the Crown Court where the order was made or the suspended sentence was passed, unless it is inconvenient, impracticable or inappropriate to do so in all the circumstances.

III.21.7 If, for whatever reason, he is not so committed and the order was made or sentence passed by a High Court Judge, he shall be committed to the most convenient location of the Crown Court where a High Court Judge regularly sits.

III.21.8 In all other cases he shall be committed to the most convenient location of the Crown Court.

III.21.9 In selecting the most convenient location of the Crown Court, the justices shall have regard to the locations of the Crown Court designated by a Presiding Judge as the locations to which cases should normally be committed from their court.

Notice of transfer in cases of serious or complex fraud

III.21.10 Where a notice of transfer is served under section 4 of the Criminal Justice Act 1987 the proposed place of trial to be specified in the notice shall be one of the Crown Court centres designated by the Senior Presiding Judge.

Notice of transfer in child witness cases

III.21.11 Where a notice of transfer is served under section 53 of the Criminal Justice Act 1991 (child witness cases) the proposed place of trial to be specified in accordance with paragraph 1(1) of schedule 6 to the Act shall be a Crown Court centre which is equipped with live television link facilities.

PD-88   **IV.31. Transfer of cases from one circuit to another**

IV.31.1 An application that a case be transferred from one Circuit to another should not be granted unless the judge is satisfied that:

(a) the approval of the Presiding Judges and Regional Director for each Region/Circuit has been obtained, or

(b) the case may be transferred under general arrangements approved by the Presiding Judges and Regional Directors.

IV.32. Transfer of proceedings between locations of the Crown Court **PD-89**

IV.32.1 Without prejudice to the provisions of section 76 of the Supreme Court Act 1981 (committal for trial: alteration of place of trial) directions may be given for the transfer from one location of the Crown Court to another of: (a) appeals; (b) proceedings on committal for sentence or to be dealt with.

IV.32.2 Such directions may be given in a particular case by an officer of the Crown Court, or generally, in relation to a class or classes of case, by the Presiding Judge or a judge acting on his behalf.

IV.32.3 If dissatisfied with such directions given by an officer of the Crown Court, any party to the proceedings may apply to a judge of the Crown Court who may hear the application in chambers.

IV.33. Allocation of business within the Crown Court **PD-90**

General

IV.33.1 Cases in Class 1 may only be tried by:

    (1) a High Court Judge, or

    (2) a Circuit Judge or Deputy High Court Judge or Deputy Circuit Judge provided (a) that, in all cases save attempted murder, such judge is authorised by the Lord Chief Justice to try murder cases, or in the case of attempted murder, to try murder or attempted murder, and (b) the Presiding Judge has released the case for trial by such a judge.

IV.33.2 Cases in Class 2 may be tried by:

    (1) a High Court Judge

    (2) a Circuit Judge or Deputy High Court Judge or Deputy Circuit Judge or a Recorder, provided that in all cases such judge is authorised to try class 2 cases by the Lord Chief Justice and the case has been assigned to the judge by or under the direction of either the Presiding Judge or Resident Judge in accordance with guidance given by the Presiding Judges.

IV.33.3 Cases in Class 3 may be tried by a High Court Judge, or in accordance with guidance given by the Presiding Judges, a Circuit Judge, a Deputy Circuit Judge or a Recorder. A case in Class 3 shall not be listed for trial by a High Court Judge except with the consent of a Presiding Judge.

IV.33.4 Appeals from decisions of magistrates shall be heard by:

    (a) a Resident Judge, or

    (b) a Circuit Judge, nominated by the Resident Judge, who regularly sits at the Crown Court centre, or

    (c) an experienced Recorder or Deputy Circuit Judge specifically approved by or under the direction of the Presiding Judges for the purpose, or

    (d) where no Circuit Judge or Recorder satisfying the requirements above is available and it is not practicable to obtain the approval of the Presiding Judges, by a Circuit Judge, Recorder or Deputy Circuit Judge selected by the Resident Judge to hear a specific case or cases listed on a specific day.

IV.33.5 Committals following breach (such as a matter in which a community order has been made, or a suspended sentence passed) should, where possible, be listed before the judge who originally dealt with the matter, or, if not, before a judge of the same or higher level.

Applications for removal of a driving disqualification

IV.33.6 Application should be made to the location of the Crown Court where the order of disqualification was made.

Absence of Resident Judge

IV.33.7 A Resident Judge must appoint a deputy to exercise his functions when he is absent from his centre.

Guidance issued by the Senior Presiding Judge and the Presiding Judges

IV.33.8 For the just, speedy and economical disposal of the business of the Circuits or a Circuit, the Senior Presiding Judge or the Presiding Judges, with the approval of the Senior Presiding Judge, may issue guidance to Resident Judges in relation to the allocation and management of the work at their court.

IV.33.9 With the approval of the Senior Presiding Judge, general directions may be given by the Presiding Judges of the South Eastern Circuit concerning the distribution and allocation of business of all classes of case at the Central Criminal Court.

IV.38. Applications for representation orders **PD-91**

IV.38.1 Applications for representation by a Queen's Counsel alone or by more than one advocate under Part IV of the Criminal Defence Service (General) (No 2) Regulations 2001 SI 2001/1437 made to the Crown Court shall be placed before the Resident Judge of that Crown Court (or, in his absence, a judge nominated for that purpose by a Presiding Judge of the circuit) who shall determine the application, save that, where the application relates to a case which is to be heard before a named High Court judge or a named Circuit Judge, he should refer the application to the named judge for determination.

IV.38.2 This does not apply where an application is made in the course of a trial or of a preliminary hearing, pre-trial review, or plea and directions hearing by the judge presiding at that trial or hearing.

IV.38.3 In the event of any doubt as to the proper application of this direction, reference shall be made by the judge concerned to a Presiding Judge of the circuit, who shall give such directions as he thinks fit.

PD-92   **IV.41 Management of cases to be heard in the Crown Court (paragraph 9 only)**

IV.41.9 In Class 1 and Class 2 cases, and in all cases involving a serious sexual offence against a child, the PCMH must be conducted by a High Court judge; by a circuit judge or by a recorder to whom the case has been assigned in accordance with paragraph IV.33 (allocation of business within the Crown Court); or by a judge authorised by the Presiding Judges to conduct such hearings. In the event of a guilty plea before such an authorised judge, the case will be adjourned for sentencing by a High Court judge or by a circuit judge or recorder to whom the case has been assigned.

PD-93   Annex F

[This annex contains the listing practice direction and is omitted].

Criminal Practice Directions Case Management Forms

PD-94   Annex E forms

[This annex contains the forms to be used to facilitate case management and is omitted.]

Criminal Practice Directions Forms other than Case Management Forms

PD-95   Annex D forms

[This annex contains a list of forms to be used in criminal proceedings and is omitted.]

Criminal Practice Directions Index and Destination Table

CPD	Division	New CPD ref	Title of CPD, if applicable	Related Rule	Derived from CCPD ref
CPD	General matters	A			New
CPD	General matters	1A		Part 1 The overriding objective	New
CPD	General matters	3A	Case management	Part 3 Case management	V.56 Case management in magistrates' courts IV.41 Management of cases to be heard in the Crown Court
CPD	General matters	3B	Pagination and indexing of served evidence	Part 3 Case management	IV.41.12-16 Management of cases to be heard in the Crown Court
CPD	General matters	3C	Abuse of process stay applications	Part 3 Case management	IV.36 Abuse of process stay applications
CPD	General matters	3D	Vulnerable people in the Courts	Part 3 Case management	III.30 Treatment of Vulnerable Defendants
CPD	General matters	3E	Ground rules hearings to plan the questioning of a vulnerable witness or defendant	Part 3 Case management	New
CPD	General matters	3F	Intermediaries	Part 3 Case management	New
CPD	General matters	3G	Vulnerable defendants	Part 3 Case management	III.30 Treatment of Vulnerable Defendants
CPD	General matters	3H	Wales and the Welsh Language: Devolution issues	Part 3 Case management	I.11 Devolution Issues
CPD	General matters	3J	Wales and the Welsh Language: Applications for evidence to be given in Welsh	Part 3 Case management	III.22 Applications for Evidence to be Given in Welsh
CPD	General matters	3K	Wales and the Welsh Language: Use of the Welsh Language in Courts in Wales	Part 3 Case management	III.23 Use of the Welsh Language in Court in Wales
CPD	General matters	5A	Forms	Part 5 Forms and court records	I.14 Forms
CPD	General matters	5B	Access to information held by the Court	Part 5 Forms and court records	New
CPD	Preliminary proceedings	6A	Investigation orders and search warrants	Part 6 Investigation orders and warrants	New
CPD	Preliminary proceedings	9A	Allocation (mode of trial)	Part 9 Allocation and sending for trial	V.51 Mode of trial
CPD	Preliminary proceedings	10A	Defendant's record	Part 10 Sending for trial	III.27 Antecedents
CPD	Preliminary proceedings	14A	Settling the indictment	Part 14 The indictment	IV.34 Settling the Indictment
CPD	Preliminary proceedings	14B	Voluntary bills of indictment	Part 14 The indictment	IV.35 Voluntary Bills of Indictment
CPD	Preliminary proceedings	16A	Unofficial sound recording of proceedings	Part 16 Reporting, etc. restrictions	I.2 Unofficial tape recording of proceedings

CPD	Division	New CPD ref	Title of CPD, if applicable	Related Rule	Derived from CCPD ref
CPD	Preliminary proceedings	16B	Restrictions on reporting proceedings	Part 16 Reporting, etc. restrictions	I.3 Restrictions on reporting proceedings
CPS	Custody and bail	19A	Bail before sending for trial	Part 19 Bail and custody time limits	V.53 Bail before committal for trial
CPD	Custody and bail	19B	Bail: Failure to surrender and trials in absence	Part 19 Bail and custody time limits	I.13 Bail: failure to surrender to bail and trials in absence
CPD	Custody and bail	19C	Penalties for failure to surrender	Part 19 Bail and custody time limits	I.13 Bail: failure to surrender to bail and trials in absence
CPD	Custody and bail	19D	Relationship between the Bail Act offence and further remands on bail or in custody	Part 19 Bail and custody time limits	I.13 Bail: failure to surrender to bail and trials in absence
CPD	Custody and bail	19E	Trials in absence	Part 19 Bail and custody time limits	I.13 Bail: failure to surrender to bail and trials in absence
CPD	Custody and bail	19F	Forfeiture of monies lodged as security or pledged by a surety/ estreatment of recognizances	Part 19 Bail and custody time limits	New
CPD	Custody and bail	19G	Bail during trial	Part 19 Bail and custody time limits	III.25 Bail during trial
CPD	Custody and bail	19H	Crown Court judge's certification of fitness to appeal and applications to the Crown Court for bail pending appeal	Part 19 Bail and custody time limits	IV.50 Bail pending appeal
CPD	Disclosure	22A	Disclosure of unused material	Part 22 Disclosure	New
CPD	Evidence	27A	Evidence by written statement	Part 27 Witness statements	III.24 Evidence by written statement
CPD	Evidence	27B	Video recorded evidence in chief	Part 27 Witness statements	IV.40 Video recorded evidence in chief
CPD	Evidence	27C	Evidence of audio and video recorded interviews	Part 27 Witness statements	IV.43 Evidence of tape recorded interviews
CPD	Evidence	28A	Wards of Court and children subject to current Family proceedings	Part 28 Witness summonses, warrants and orders	I.5 Wards of court
CPD	Evidence	29A	Measures to assist a witness or defendant to give evidence	Part 29 Measures to assist a witness or defendant to give evidence	New
CPD	Evidence	29B	Witnesses giving evidence by live link	Part 29 Measures to assist a witness or defendant to give evidence	III.29 Support for witnesses giving evidence by live television link/New
CPD	Evidence	29C	Visually recorded interviews: memory refreshing and watching at a different time from the jury	Part 29 Measures to assist a witness or defendant to give evidence	New

CPD	Division	New CPD ref	Title of CPD, if applicable	Related Rule	Derived from CCPD ref
CPD	Evidence	29D	Witness anonymity orders	Part 29 Measures to assist a witness or defendant to give evidence	I.15 Witness anonymity orders
CPD	Evidence	35A	Spent convictions	Part 35 Evidence of bad character	I.6 Spent convictions
CPD	Trial	37A	Role of the justices' clerk/legal adviser	Part 37 Trial and sentence in a magistrates' court	V.55 Clerk retiring with justices
CPD	Trial	39A	Juries: introduction	Part 39 Trial on indictment	IV.42 Juries and New
CPD	Trial	39B	Juries: preliminary matters arising before jury service commences	Part 39 Trial on indictment	IV.42 Juries and New
CPD	Trial	39C	Juries: eligibility	Part 39 Trial on indictment	IV.42 Juries and New
CPD	Trial	39D	Juries: precautionary measures before swearing	Part 39 Trial on indictment	IV.42 Juries and New
CPD	Trial	39E	Juries: swearing in jurors	Part 39 Trial on indictment	IV.42 Juries and New
CPD	Trial	39F	Juries: ensuring an effective jury panel	Part 39 Trial on indictment	IV.42 Juries and New
CPD	Trial	39G	Juries: preliminary instructions to jurors	Part 39 Trial on indictment	IV.42 Juries and New
CPD	Trial	39H	Juries: discharge of a juror for personal reasons	Part 39 Trial on indictment	IV.42 Juries and New
CPD	Trial	39J	Juries: views	Part 39 Trial on indictment	IV.42 Juries and New
CPD	Trial	39K	Juries: directions to jury before retirement	Part 39 Trial on indictment	IV.42 Juries and New
CPD	Trial	39L	Juries: jury access to exhibits and evidence in retirement	Part 39 Trial on indictment	IV.42 Juries and New
CPD	Trial	39M	Jury irregularities	Part 39 Trial on indictment	Consolidation of protocol issued by the PQBD in November 2012
CPD	Trial	39N	Open justice	Part 39 Trial on indictment	IV.45.3 (Pleas of guilty in the Crown Court)
CPD	Trial	39P	Defendant's right to give or not to give evidence	Part 39 Trial on indictment	IV.44 Defendant's right to give or not to give evidence
CPD	Trial	39Q	Majority verdicts	Part 39 Trial on indictment	IV.46 Majority verdicts
CPD	Sentencing	A	Pleas of guilty in the Crown Court		IV.45 Pleas of guilty in the Crown Court
CPD	Sentencing	B	Determining the factual basis of sentence		IV.45 Pleas of guilty in the Crown Court
CPD	Sentencing	C	Indications of sentence: *R v Goodyear*		IV.45 Pleas of guilty in the Crown Court
CPD	Sentencing	D	Facts to be stated on pleas of guilty		III.26 Facts to be stated on pleas of guilty
CPD	Sentencing	E	Concurrent and consecutive sentences		I.8 Words to be used when passing sentence

CPD	Division	New CPD ref	Title of CPD, if applicable	Related Rule	Derived from CCPD ref
CPD	Sentencing	F	Victim Personal Statements		III.28 Victim Personal Statements
CPD	Sentencing	G	Families bereaved by homicide and other criminal conduct		New
CPD	Sentencing	H	Community Impact Statements		New
CPD	Sentencing	J	Binding over orders and conditional discharges		III.31 Binding over orders and conditional discharges
CPD	Sentencing	K	Committal for sentence		V.52 Committal for sentence and appeals to the Crown Court
CPD	Sentencing	L	Imposition of life sentences		IV.47 Imposition of discretionary life sentences
CPD	Sentencing	M	Mandatory life sentences		IV.49 Life sentences
CPD	Sentencing	N	Transitional arrangements for sentences where the offence was committed before 18 December 2003		IV.49 Life sentences
CPD	Sentencing	P	Procedure for announcing the minimum term in open court		IV.49 Life sentences
CPD	Contempt of court	62A	Contempt in the face of the magistrates' court	Part 62 Contempt of court	V.54 Contempt in the face of the magistrates' court
CPD	Appeal	63A	Appeals to the Crown Court	Part 63 Appeal to the Crown Court	V.52 Committal for sentence and appeals to the Crown Court
CPD	Appeal	68A	Appeals against conviction and sentence – the provision of notice to the prosecution	Part 68 Appeal to the Court of Appeal about conviction or sentence	II.1 Appeals against sentence – the provision of notice to the prosecution
CPD	Appeal	68B	Listing of appeals against conviction and sentence in the Court of Appeal Criminal Division (CACD)	Part 68 Appeal to the Court of Appeal about conviction or sentence	II.2 Listing of Appeals against conviction and sentence in the CACD
CPD	Appeal	68C	Appeal notices containing grounds of appeal	Part 68 Appeal to the Court of Appeal about conviction or sentence	II.15 Grounds of appeal
CPD	Appeal	68D	Respondents' notices	Part 68 Appeal to the Court of Appeal about conviction or sentence	II.17 Skeleton arguments
CPD	Appeal	68E	Loss of time	Part 68 Appeal to the Court of Appeal about conviction or sentence	II.16 Loss of time
CPD	Appeal	68F	Skeleton arguments	Part 68 Appeal to the Court of Appeal about conviction or sentence	II.17 Skeleton arguments

CPD	Division	New CPD ref	Title of CPD, if applicable	Related Rule	Derived from CCPD ref
CPD	Appeal	68G	Criminal Appeal Office summaries	Part 68 Appeal to the Court of Appeal about conviction or sentence	II.18 Criminal Appeal Office summaries
CPD	Appeal	75A	References to the European Court of Justice	Part 75 Request to the European Court for a preliminary ruling	I.10 References to the European Court of Justice
CPD	Costs			Part 76 Costs	Refer to the separate PD on Costs in Criminal Proceedings
CPD	General application	A	Court dress		I.1 Court dress
CPD	General application	B	Modes of address and titles of judges and magistrates		II.13 Mode of addressing the court and IV.30 Modes of address and titles of judges
CPD	General application	C	Availability of judgments given in the Court of Appeal and the High Court		I.4 Availability of judgments given in the Court of Appeal and the High Court and Practice Direction (Court of Appeal (Civil Division)) [1999] 1 WLR 1027 section 9, reserved judgments of the Court of Appeal
CPD	General application	D	Citation of authority and provision of copies of judgments to the Court		II.19 Citation of judgments in Court
CPD	General application	E	Preparation of judgments: neutral citation		I.12 Preparation of judgments: neutral citation
CPD	General application	F	Citation of Hansard		II.20 Citation of Hansard and IV.37 Citation of Hansard
	Retained				III.21 Classification of Crown Court business and allocation to Crown Court centres
	Retained				IV.31 Transfer of cases from one circuit to another
	Retained				IV.32 Transfer of cases between locations to the Crown Court
	Retained				IV.33 Allocation of business within the Crown Court
	Retained				IV.38 Applications for representation orders
	Retained				IV.41.9 Management of cases to be heard in the Crown Court
	Retained				Annex D
	Retained				Annex E
	Retained				Annex F

Criminal Procedure Rules 2013 and Criminal Practice Directions

CPD	Division	New CPD ref	Title of CPD, if applicable	Related Rule	Derived from CCPD ref
	Deleted				I.7 Explanations for the imposition of custodial sentences
	Deleted				I.9 Substitution of suspended sentences for immediate custodial sentences
	Deleted				II.14 Notices of appeal and application for leave to appeal
	Deleted				IV.48 Life sentences for juveniles convicted of murder
	Deleted				Annex A
	Deleted				Annex B
	Deleted				Annex C

SENTENCING GUIDELINES

Sentencing Guidelines

This is an edited version of the various definitive sentencing guidelines, both those originally issued by the Sentencing Guidelines Council and those issued by the Sentencing Council for England and Wales. It contains all of the essential guideline material relevant to offences in *Blackstone's Criminal Practice*. Fuller versions are available on the Sentencing Council website via http://sentencingcouncil.judiciary.gov.uk/sentencing-guidelines.htm. By virtue of the Coroners and Justice Act 2009 (Commencement No. 4, Transitional and Saving Provisions) Order 2010 (SI 2010 No. 816), art. 7, guidelines issued by the SGC 'are to be treated as guidelines issued by the Sentencing Council'. For more on the status of guidelines and the duty of courts to follow them, see **E1.3** in the main work.

PART 1   REDUCTION IN SENTENCE FOR A GUILTY PLEA   SG-1

[Introductory material and declaration that the guideline applies to all cases sentenced on or after *23 July 2007*.]

A. Statutory Provision
[Sets out the CJA 2003, ss. 144 (reduction in sentence for guilty plea: see **E1.8** in the main work) and 174(2)(d) (duty to give reasons and explain effect of sentence: see **E1.23**).]

1.1 This guideline applies whether a case is dealt with in a magistrates' court or in the Crown Court and whenever practicable in the youth court (taking into account legislative restrictions such as those relevant to the length of Detention and Training orders).

1.2 The application of this guideline to sentencers when arriving at the appropriate minimum term for the offence of murder is set out in Section F.

...

B. Statement of Purpose   SG-2

2.1 When imposing a custodial sentence, statute requires that a court must impose the shortest term that is commensurate with the seriousness of the offence(s).[1] Similarly, when imposing a community order, the restrictions on liberty must be commensurate with the seriousness of the offence(s).[2] Once that decision is made, a court is required to give consideration to the reduction for any guilty plea. As a result, the final sentence after the reduction for a guilty plea will be less than the seriousness of the offence requires.

2.2 A reduction in sentence is appropriate because a guilty plea avoids the need for a trial (thus enabling other cases to be disposed of more expeditiously), shortens the gap between charge and sentence, saves considerable cost, and, in the case of an early plea, saves victims and witnesses from the concern about having to give evidence. The reduction principle derives from the need for the effective administration of justice and not as an aspect of mitigation.

2.3 Where a sentencer is in doubt as to whether a custodial sentence is appropriate, the reduction attributable to a guilty plea will be a relevant consideration. Where this is amongst the factors leading to the imposition of a non-custodial sentence, there will be no need to apply a further reduction on account of the guilty plea. A similar approach is appropriate where the reduction for a guilty plea is amongst the factors leading to the imposition of a financial penalty or discharge instead of a community order.

2.4 When deciding the most appropriate length of sentence, the sentencer should address separately the issue of remorse, together with any other mitigating features, before calculating the reduction for the guilty plea. Similarly, assistance to the prosecuting or enforcement authorities is a separate issue which may attract a reduction in sentence under other procedures; care will need to be taken to ensure that there is no 'double counting'.

2.5 The implications of other offences that an offender has asked to be taken into consideration should be reflected in the sentence before the reduction for guilty plea has been applied.

2.6 A reduction in sentence should only be applied to the *punitive elements* of a penalty.[3] The guilty plea reduction has no impact on sentencing decisions in relation to ancillary orders, including orders of disqualification from driving.

---

[1] Criminal Justice Act 2003, s.153(2)

[2] Criminal Justice Act 2003, s.148(2)

[3] Where a court imposes an indeterminate sentence for public protection, the reduction principle applies in the normal way to the determination of the minimum term (see para. 5.1, footnote and para. 7 below) but release from custody requires the authorisation of the Parole Board once that minimum term has been served.

SG-3 C. **Application of the Reduction Principle**

3.1 Recommended Approach

> The court decides sentence for the offences taking into account other offences
> that have been formally admitted (TICs),
>
> ↓
>
> The court selects the amount of the reduction by reference to the sliding scale,
>
> ↓
>
> The court applies the reduction,
>
> ↓
>
> When pronouncing sentence the court should usually state what the sentence would
> have been if there had been no reduction as a result of the guilty plea.

SG-4 D. **Determining the Level of Reduction**

4.1 The level of reduction should be *a proportion of the total sentence* imposed, with the proportion calculated by reference to the circumstances in which the guilty plea was indicated, in particular the stage in the proceedings. The greatest reduction will be given where the plea was indicated at the 'first reasonable opportunity'.

4.2 Save where section 144(2) of the 2003 Act[4] applies, the level of the reduction will be gauged on a *sliding scale* ranging from a recommended *one third* (where the guilty plea was entered at the first reasonable opportunity in relation to the offence for which sentence is being imposed), reducing to a recommended *one quarter* (where a trial date has been set) and to a recommended *one tenth* (for a guilty plea entered at the 'door of the court' or after the trial has begun). See diagram below.

4.3 The level of reduction should reflect the stage at which the offender indicated a *willingness to admit guilt* to the offence for which he is eventually sentenced:

   (i)   the largest recommended reduction will not normally be given unless the offender indicated willingness to admit guilt at the *first reasonable opportunity*; when this occurs will vary from case to case. (*see Annex 1 for illustrative examples*);

   (ii)   where the admission of guilt comes later than the first reasonable opportunity, the reduction for guilty plea will be less than one third;

   (iii) where the plea of guilty comes very late, it is still appropriate to give some reduction;

   (iv)   if after pleading guilty there is a *Newton* hearing and the offender's version of the circumstances of the offence is rejected, this should be taken into account in determining the level of reduction;

   (v)   if the not guilty plea was entered and maintained for tactical reasons (such as to retain privileges whilst on remand), a late guilty plea should attract very little, if any, discount.

> **In each category, there is a presumption that the recommended reduction
> will be given unless there are good reasons for a lower amount.**

First reasonable opportunity	After trial date is set	Door of the court/ after trial has begun
=========	===============	================
recommended 1/3	recommended 1/4	recommended 1/10

SG-5 E. **Withholding a Reduction**

On the basis of dangerousness

5.1 Where a sentence for a 'dangerous offender' is imposed under the provisions in the Criminal Justice Act 2003, whether the sentence requires the calculation of a minimum term or is an extended sentence, the approach will be the same as for any other determinate sentence (see also section G below).[5]

---

[4] See section A above.

[5] There will be some cases arising from offences committed before the commencement of the relevant provisions of the Criminal Justice Act 2003 in which a court will determine that a longer than commensurate, extended, or indeterminate sentence is required for the protection of the public. In such a case, the minimum custodial term (but not the protection of public element of the sentence) should be reduced to reflect the plea.

Where the prosecution case is overwhelming

5.2   The purpose of giving credit is to encourage those who are guilty to plead at the earliest opportunity. Any defendant is entitled to put the prosecution to proof and so every defendant who is guilty should be encouraged to indicate that guilt at the first reasonable opportunity.

5.3   Where the prosecution case is overwhelming, it may not be appropriate to give the full reduction that would otherwise be given. Whilst there is a presumption in favour of the full reduction being given where a plea has been indicated at the first reasonable opportunity, the fact that the prosecution case is overwhelming without relying on admissions from the defendant may be a reason justifying departure from the guideline.

5.4   Where a court is satisfied that a lower reduction should be given for this reason, a recommended reduction of 20% is likely to be appropriate where the guilty plea was indicated at the first reasonable opportunity.

5.5   A Court departing from a guideline must state the reasons for doing so.[6]

Where the maximum penalty for the offence is thought to be too low

5.6   The sentencer is bound to sentence for the offence with which the offender has been charged, and to which he has pleaded guilty. The sentencer cannot remedy perceived defects (for example an inadequate charge or maximum penalty) by refusal of the appropriate discount.

Where jurisdictional issues arise

(i)   Where sentencing powers are limited to 6 months imprisonment despite multiple offences

5.7   When the total sentence for both or all of the offences is 6 months imprisonment, a court may determine to impose consecutive sentences which, even allowing for a reduction for a guilty plea where appropriate on each offence, would still result in the imposition of the maximum sentence available. In such circumstances, in order to achieve the purpose for which the reduction principle has been established,[7] some modest allowance should normally be given against the total sentence for the entry of a guilty plea.

(ii)   Where a maximum sentence might still be imposed

5.8   Despite a guilty plea being entered which would normally attract a reduction in sentence, a magistrates' court may impose a sentence of imprisonment of 6 months for a single either-way offence where, but for the plea, that offence would have been committed to the Crown Court for sentence.

5.9   Similarly, a detention and training order of 24 months may be imposed on an offender aged under 18 if the offence is one which would but for the plea have attracted a sentence of long-term detention in excess of 24 months under the Powers of Criminal Courts (Sentencing) Act 2000, section 91.

F. Application to Sentencing for Murder   SG-6

6.1   Murder has always been regarded as the most serious criminal offence and the sentence prescribed is different from other sentences. By law, the sentence for murder is imprisonment (detention) for life and an offender will remain subject to the sentence for the rest of his/her life.

6.2   The decision whether to release the offender from custody during this sentence will be taken by the Parole Board which will consider whether it is safe to release the offender on licence. The Court that imposes the sentence is required by law to set a minimum term that has to be served before the Parole Board may start to consider whether to authorise release on licence. If an offender is released, the licence continues for the rest of the offender's life and recall to prison is possible at any time.

6.3   Uniquely, Parliament has set starting points[8] (based on the circumstances of the killing) which a Court will apply when it fixes the minimum term. Parliament has further prescribed that, having identified the appropriate starting point, the Court must then consider whether to increase or reduce it in the light of aggravating or mitigating factors, some of which are listed in statute. Finally, Parliament specifically provides[9] that the obligation to have regard to any guilty plea applies to the fixing of the minimum term, by making the same statutory provisions that apply to other offences apply to murder without limiting the courts discretion (as it did with other sentences under the Powers of Criminal Courts (Sentencing) Act 2000).

6.4   There are important differences between the usual fixed term sentence and the minimum term set following the imposition of the mandatory life sentence for murder. The most significant of these,

---

[6] Criminal Justice Act 2003, s. 174(2)(a)
[7] See section B above.
[8] Criminal Justice Act 2003, schedule 21
[9] Criminal Justice Act 2003, schedule 1 para. 12(c)

from the sentencer's point of view, is that a reduction for a plea of guilty in the case of murder will have double the effect on time served in custody when compared with a determinate sentence. This is because a determinate sentence will provide (in most circumstances) for the release of the offender[10] on licence half way through the total sentence whereas in the case of murder a minimum term is the period in custody before consideration is given by the Parole Board to whether release is appropriate.

6.5   Given this difference, the special characteristic of the offence of murder and the unique statutory provision of starting points, careful consideration will need to be given to the extent of any reduction and to the need to ensure that the minimum term properly reflects the seriousness of the offence. Whilst the general principles continue to apply (both that a guilty plea should be encouraged and that the extent of any reduction should reduce if the indication of plea is later than the first reasonable opportunity), the process of determining the level of reduction will be different.

6.6   *Approach*

    1. Where a Court determines that there should be a *whole life* minimum term, there will be no reduction for a guilty plea.

    2. In other circumstances,

        a) the Court will weigh carefully the overall length of the minimum term taking into account other reductions for which offenders may be eligible so as to avoid a combination leading to an inappropriately short sentence;

        b) where it is appropriate to reduce the minimum term having regard to a plea of guilty, the reduction will not exceed one sixth and will never exceed 5 years;

        c) the sliding scale will apply so that, where it is appropriate to reduce the minimum term on account of a guilty plea, the maximum reduction (one sixth or five years whichever is the less) is only available where there has been an indication of willingness to plead guilty at the first reasonable opportunity, with a recommended 5% for a late guilty plea;

        d) the Court should then review the sentence to ensure that the minimum term accurately reflects the seriousness of the offence taking account of the statutory starting point, all aggravating and mitigating factors and any guilty plea entered.

SG-7   **G. Application to other Indeterminate Sentences**

7.1   There are other circumstances in which an indeterminate sentence will be imposed. This may be a discretionary life sentence or imprisonment for public protection.

7.2   As with the mandatory life sentence imposed following conviction for murder, the Court will be obliged to fix a minimum term to be served before the Parole Board is able to consider whether the offender can be safely released.

7.3   However, the process by which that minimum term is fixed is different from that followed in relation to the mandatory life sentence and requires the Court first to determine what the equivalent determinate sentence would have been. Accordingly, the approach to the calculation of the reduction for any guilty plea should follow the process and scale adopted in relation to determinate sentences, as set out in section D above.

SG-8   ANNEX 1

FIRST REASONABLE OPPORTUNITY

1. The critical time for determining the reduction for a guilty plea is the first reasonable opportunity for the defendant to have indicated a willingness to plead guilty. This opportunity will vary with a wide range of factors and the Court will need to make a judgement on the particular facts of the case before it.

2. The key principle is that the purpose of giving a reduction is to recognise the benefits that come from a guilty plea both for those directly involved in the case in question but also in enabling Courts more quickly to deal with other outstanding cases.

3. This Annex seeks to help Courts to adopt a consistent approach by giving examples of circumstances where a determination will have to be made.

    (a) the first reasonable opportunity may be the first time that a defendant appears before the court and has the opportunity to plead guilty;

    (b) but the court may consider that it would be reasonable to have expected an indication of willingness even earlier, perhaps whilst under interview;

Note: For a) and b) to apply, the Court will need to be satisfied that the defendant (and any legal adviser) would have had sufficient information about the allegations.

---

[10] In accordance with the provisions of the Criminal Justice Act 2003

(c) where an offence triable either way is committed to the Crown Court for trial and the defendant pleads guilty at the first hearing in that Court, the reduction will be less than if there had been an indication of a guilty plea given to the magistrates' court (recommended reduction of one third) but more than if the plea had been entered after a trial date had been set (recommended reduction of one quarter), and is likely to be in the region of 30%;

(d) where an offence is triable only on indictment, it may well be that the first reasonable opportunity would have been during the police station stage; where that is not the case, the first reasonable opportunity is likely to be at the first hearing in the Crown Court;

(e) where a defendant is convicted after pleading guilty to an alternative (lesser) charge to that to which he/she had originally pleaded not guilty, the extent of any reduction will be determined by the stage at which the defendant first formally indicated to the court willingness to plead guilty to the lesser charge, and the reason why that lesser charge was proceeded with in preference to the original charge.

PART 2   NEW SENTENCES: CRIMINAL JUSTICE ACT 2003   SG-9

Foreword

[Introductory material which is not reproduced.]

This guideline applies only to sentences passed under the sentencing framework applicable to those aged 18 or over.

The guideline is divided into two sections:

- Section 1 covers the practical aspects of implementing the non-custodial powers namely the new community sentence and the new form of deferred sentence;
- Section 2 deals with the new custodial sentence provisions relating to suspended sentences, prison sentences of 12 months or more, and intermittent custody.[11]

The Act also contains an extensive range of provisions to protect the public from dangerous offenders. These will be dealt with separately.

…

Section 1

Part 1—Community Sentences   SG-10

A. Statutory Provisions

(i) The Thresholds for Community Sentences

1.1.1   Seriousness—Section 148 Criminal Justice Act 2003:
[Sets out the CJA 2003, s. 148(1) (restrictions on imposing community sentence: see **E8.2** in the main work).]

1.1.2   Persistent Offenders—Section 151 Criminal Justice Act 2003:
[Sets out the CJA 2003, s. 151(1) and (2) (community order for persistent offender previously fined – not yet in force: see **E8.6** in the main work).]

(ii) The Sentences Available

1.1.3   Meaning of Community Sentence—Section 147 Criminal Justice Act 2003
　　(1) In this Part 'community sentence' means a sentence which consists of or includes—
　　　　(a) a community order (as defined by section 177), or
　　　　(b) one or more youth community orders.

1.1.4   Offenders aged 16 or over—Section 177 Criminal Justice Act 2003:
[Sets out the CJA 2003, s. 177(1) to (4) (community order requirements: see **E8.9** *et seq* in the main work).]

---

[11] References to the Probation Service reflect current roles and responsibilities. By the time these provisions come into force, some or all of those roles and responsibilities may be those of the National Offender Management Service (NOMS).

(iii) Determining Which Orders to make & Requirements to Include

1.1.5   Suitability—Section 148 Criminal Justice Act 2003:
[Sets out the CJA 2003, s. 148(2) (restrictions on imposing community sentence: see **E8.2** in the main work).]
1.1.6   Restrictions on liberty—Section 149 Criminal Justice Act 2003:
[Sets out the CJA 2003, s. 149(1) (passing of community sentence on offender remanded in custody: see **E8.3** in the main work).]
1.1.7   Compatibility—Section 177 Criminal Justice Act 2003:
[Sets out the CJA 2003, s. 177(6) (community orders requirements: see **E8.10** in the main work).]

(iv) Electronic Monitoring

1.1.8   [Sets out the CJA 2003, s. 177(3) and (4) (electronic monitoring requirements: see **E8.28** in the main work).]

SG-11 **B. Imposing a Community Sentence—The Approach**

1.1.9   In the Seriousness guideline [at **SG-26**)] the two thresholds for the imposition of a community sentence are considered. Sentencers must consider all of the disposals available (within or below the threshold passed) at the time of sentence, and reject them before reaching the provisional decision to make a community sentence, so that even where the threshold for a community sentence has been passed a financial penalty or discharge may still be an appropriate penalty. Where an offender has a low risk of reoffending, particular care needs to be taken in the light of evidence that indicates that there are circumstances where inappropriate intervention can increase the risk of re-offending rather than decrease it. In addition, recent improvements in enforcement of financial penalties make them a more viable sentence in a wider range of cases.
1.1.10 Where an offender is being sentenced for a non-imprisonable offence or offences, great care will be needed in assessing whether a community sentence is appropriate since failure to comply could result in a custodial sentence.
1.1.11 Having decided (in consultation with the Probation Service where appropriate) that a community sentence is justified, the court must decide which requirements should be included in the community order. The requirements or orders imposed will have the effect of restricting the offender's liberty, whilst providing punishment in the community, rehabilitation for the offender, and/or ensuring that the offender engages in reparative activities.
The key issues arising are:
(i)   which requirements to impose;
(ii) how to make allowance for time spent on remand; and
(iii) how to deal with breaches.

(i) Requirements

1.1.12 When deciding which requirements to include, the court must be satisfied on three matters—
(i)   that the *restriction on liberty is commensurate with the seriousness* of the offence(s);[12]
(ii) that the *requirements are the most suitable* for the offender;[13] and
(iii) that, where there are two or more requirements included, they are *compatible with each other*.[14]
1.1.13 Sentencers should have the possibility of breach firmly in mind when passing sentence for the original offence. If a court is to reflect the seriousness of an offence, there is little value in setting requirements as part of a community sentence that are not demanding enough for an offender. On the other hand, there is equally little value in imposing requirements that would 'set an offender up to fail' and almost inevitably lead to sanctions for a breach.
In community sentences, the guiding principles are proportionality and suitability. Once a court has decided that the offence has crossed the community sentence threshold and that a community sentence is justified, the *initial* factor in defining which requirements to include in a community sentence should be the seriousness of the offence committed.
1.1.14 This means that 'seriousness' is an important factor in deciding whether the Court chooses the low, medium or high range (see below) but, having taken that decision, selection of the content of the order within the range will be determined by a much wider range of factors.
• **Sentencing ranges must remain flexible enough to take account of the suitability of the offender, his or her ability to comply with particular requirements and their availability in the local area.**

---

[12] Criminal Justice Act 2003 section 148(2)(b)
[13] ibid section 148(2)(a)
[14] ibid section 177(6)

- **The justification for imposing a community sentence in response to persistent petty offending is the persistence of the offending behaviour rather than the seriousness of the offences being committed. The requirements imposed should ensure that the restriction on liberty is proportionate to the seriousness of the offending, to reflect the fact that the offences, of themselves, are not sufficiently serious to merit a community sentence.**

(a) Information for Sentencers

1.1.15   In many cases, a pre-sentence report[15] will be pivotal in helping a sentencer decide whether to impose a custodial sentence or whether to impose a community sentence and, if so, whether particular requirements, or combinations of requirements, are suitable for an individual offender. The court must always ensure (especially where there are multiple requirements) that the restriction on liberty placed on the offender is proportionate to the seriousness of the offence committed.[16] The court must also consider the likely effect of one requirement on another, and that they do not place conflicting demands upon the offender.[17]

1.1.16   The Council supports the approach proposed by the Panel at paragraph 78 of its Advice that, having reached the provisional view that a community sentence is the most appropriate disposal, the sentencer should request a pre-sentence report, indicating which of the three sentencing ranges is relevant and the purpose(s) of sentencing that the package of requirements is required to fulfil. Usually the most helpful way for the court to do this would be to produce a written note for the report writer, copied on the court file. If it is known that the same tribunal and defence advocate will be present at the sentencing hearing and a probation officer is present in court when the request for a report is made, it may not be necessary to commit details of the request to writing. However, events may change during the period of an adjournment and it is good practice to ensure that there is a clear record of the request for the court. These two factors will guide the Probation Service in determining the nature and combination of requirements that may be appropriate and the onerousness and intensity of those requirements. A similar procedure should apply when ordering a pre-sentence report when a custodial sentence is being considered.

1.1.17   There will be occasions when any type of report may be unnecessary despite the intention to pass a community sentence though this is likely to be infrequent. A court could consider dispensing with the need to obtain a pre-sentence report for adult offenders—
- where the offence falls within the **LOW** range of seriousness (see [below]) and
- where the sentencer was minded to impose a single requirement, such as an exclusion requirement (where the circumstances of the case mean that this would be an appropriate disposal without electronic monitoring) and
- where the sentence will not require the involvement of the Probation Service, for example an electronically monitored curfew (subject to the court being satisfied that there is an appropriate address at which the curfew can operate).

(b) Ranges of Sentence Within the Community Sentence Band

1.1.18   To enable the court to benefit from the flexibility that community sentences provide and also to meet its statutory obligations, any structure governing the use of community requirements must allow the courts to choose the most appropriate sentence for each individual offender.

1.1.19   Sentencers have a statutory obligation to pass sentences that are commensurate with the seriousness of an offence. However, within the range of sentence justified by the seriousness of the offence(s), courts will quite properly consider those factors that heighten the risk of the offender committing further offences or causing further harm with a view to lessening that risk. The extent to which requirements are imposed must be capable of being varied to ensure that the restriction on liberty is commensurate with the seriousness of the offence.

1.1.20   The Council recognises that it would be helpful for sentencers to have a framework to help them decide on the most appropriate use of the new community sentence. While there is no single guiding principle, the seriousness of the offence that has been committed is an important factor. Three sentencing ranges (low, medium and high) within the community sentence band can be identified. It is not possible to position particular types of offence at firm points within the three ranges because the seriousness level of an offence is largely dependent upon the culpability of

---

[15] Under the Act, a pre-sentence report includes a full report following adjournment, a specific sentence report, a short format report or an oral report. The type of report supplied will depend on the level of information requested. Wherever it appears, the term 'pre-sentence report' includes all these types of report.

[16] Criminal Justice Act 2003 section 148(2)

[17] ibid section 177(6)

the offender and this is uniquely variable. The difficulty is particularly acute in relation to the medium range where it is clear that requirements will need to be tailored across a relatively wide range of offending behaviour.

1.1.21 In general terms, the lowest range of community sentence would be for those offenders whose offence was relatively minor within the community sentence band and would include persistent petty offenders whose offences only merit a community sentence by virtue of failing to respond to the previous imposition of fines. Such offenders would merit a 'light touch' approach, for example, normally a single requirement such as a short period of unpaid work, or a curfew, or a prohibited activity requirement or an exclusion requirement (where the circumstances of the case mean that this would be an appropriate disposal without electronic monitoring).

1.1.22 The top range would be for those offenders who have only just fallen short of a custodial sentence and for those who have passed the threshold but for whom a community sentence is deemed appropriate.

1.1.23 In all three ranges there must be sufficient flexibility to allow the sentence to be varied to take account of the suitability of particular requirements for the individual offender and whether a particular requirement or package of requirements might be more effective at reducing any identified risk of re-offending. It will fall to the sentencer to ensure that the sentence strikes the right balance between proportionality and suitability.

There should be three sentencing ranges (low medium and high) within the community sentence band based upon seriousness.

It is not intended that an offender necessarily progress from one range to the next on each sentencing occasion. The decision as to the appropriate range each time is based upon the seriousness of the new offence(s).

The decision on the nature and severity of the requirements to be included in a community sentence should be guided by:

(i)   **the assessment of offence seriousness (LOW, MEDIUM OR HIGH);**

(ii) **the purpose(s) of sentencing the court wishes to achieve;**

(iii) **the risk of re-offending;**

(iv) **the ability of the offender to comply; and**

(v)   **the availability of requirements in the local area.**

The resulting restrictions on liberty must be a proportionate response to the offence that was committed.

1.1.24 Below we set out a non-exhaustive description of examples of requirements that might be appropriate in the three sentencing ranges. These examples focus on punishment in the community, although it is recognised that not all packages will necessarily need to include a punitive requirement. There will clearly be other requirements of a rehabilitative nature, such as a treatment requirement or an accredited programme, which may be appropriate depending on the specific needs of the offender and assessment of suitability. Given the intensity of such interventions, it is expected that these would normally only be appropriate at medium and high levels of seriousness, and where assessed as having a medium or high risk of re-offending. In addition, when passing sentence in any one of the three ranges, the court should consider whether a rehabilitative intervention such as a programme requirement, or a restorative justice intervention might be suitable as an additional or alternative part of the sentence.

LOW

1.1.25 For offences only just crossing the community sentence threshold (such as persistent petty offending, some public order offences, some thefts from shops, or interference with a motor vehicle, where the seriousness of the offence or the nature of the offender's record means that a discharge or fine is inappropriate).

1.1.26 Suitable requirements might include:

- 40 to 80 hours of unpaid work or
- a curfew requirement within the lowest range (e.g. up to 12 hours per day for a few weeks) or
- an exclusion requirement (where the circumstances of the case mean that this would be an appropriate disposal without electronic monitoring) lasting a few months or
- a prohibited activity requirement or
- an attendance centre requirement (where available).

1.1.27 Since the restriction on liberty must be commensurate with the seriousness of the offence, particular care needs to be taken with this band to ensure that this obligation is complied with.

In most cases, only one requirement will be appropriate and the length may be curtailed if additional requirements are necessary.

MEDIUM

1.1.28   For offences that obviously fall within the community sentence band such as handling stolen goods worth less than £1000 acquired for resale or somewhat more valuable goods acquired for the handlers own use, some cases of burglary in commercial premises, some cases of taking a motor vehicle without consent, or some cases of obtaining property by deception.

1.1.29   Suitable requirements might include:
- a greater number (e.g. 80 to 150) of hours of unpaid work or
- an activity requirement in the middle range (20 to 30 days) or
- a curfew requirement within the middle range (e.g. up to 12 hours for 2–3 months) or
- an exclusion requirement lasting in the region of 6 months or
- a prohibited activity requirement.

1.1.30   Since the restriction on liberty must be commensurate with the seriousness of the offence, particular care needs to be taken with this band to ensure that this obligation is complied with.

HIGH

1.1.31   For offences that only just fall below the custody threshold or where the custody threshold is crossed but a community sentence is more appropriate in all the circumstances, for example some cases displaying the features of a standard domestic burglary committed by a first-time offender.

1.1.32   More intensive sentences which combine two or more requirements may be appropriate at this level. Suitable requirements might include an unpaid work order of between 150 and 300 hours; an activity requirement up to the maximum 60 days; an exclusion order lasting in the region of 12 months; a curfew requirement of up to 12 hours a day for 4–6 months.

(c) Electronic Monitoring

1.1.33   The court must also consider whether an electronic monitoring requirement[18] should be imposed which is mandatory[19] in some circumstances.
Electronic monitoring should be used with the primary purpose of promoting and monitoring compliance with other requirements, in circumstances where the punishment of the offender and/or the need to safeguard the public and prevent re-offending are the most important concerns.

(d) Recording the Sentence Imposed

1.1.34   Under the new framework there is only one (generic) community sentence provided by statute. This does not mean that offenders who have completed a community sentence and have then re-offended should be regarded as ineligible for a second community sentence on the basis that this has been tried and failed. Further community sentences, perhaps with different requirements, may well be justified.

1.1.35   Those imposing sentence will wish to be clear about the 'purposes' that the community sentence is designed to achieve when setting the requirements. Sharing those purposes with the offender and Probation Service will enable them to be clear about the goals that are to be achieved.

1.1.36   Any future sentencer must have full information about the requirements that were inserted by the court into the previous community sentence imposed on the offender (including whether it was a low/medium/high level order) and also about the offender's response. This will enable the court to consider the merits of imposing the same or different requirements as part of another community sentence. The requirements should be recorded in such a way as to ensure that they can be made available to another court if another offence is committed.
When an offender is required to serve a community sentence, the court records should be clearly annotated to show which particular requirements have been imposed.

(ii) Time Spent on Remand

1.1.37   The court will need to consider whether to give any credit for time spent in custody on remand.[20] (For further detail from the Panel's Advice, see Annex A)
The court should seek to give credit for time spent on remand (in custody or equivalent status) in all cases. It should make clear, when announcing sentence, whether or not credit for time on

---

[18] ibid section 177(3) and (4)
[19] Unless the necessary facilities are not available or, in the particular circumstances of the case, the court considers it inappropriate.
[20] Criminal Justice Act 2003 section 149

Sentencing Guidelines

remand has been given (bearing in mind that there will be no automatic reduction in sentence once section 67 of the Criminal Justice Act 1967 is repealed) and should explain its reasons for not giving credit when it considers either that this is not justified, would not be practical, or would not be in the best interests of the offender.

1.1.38 Where an offender has spent a period of time in custody on remand, there will be occasions where a custodial sentence is warranted but the length of the sentence justified by the seriousness of the offence would mean that the offender would be released immediately. Under the present framework, it may be more appropriate to pass a community sentence since that will ensure supervision on release.

1.1.39 However, given the changes in the content of the second part of a custodial sentence of 12 months or longer, a court in this situation where the custodial sentence would be 12 months or more should, under the new framework, pass a custodial sentence in the knowledge that licence requirements will be imposed on release from custody. This will ensure that the sentence imposed properly reflects the seriousness of the offence.

1.1.40 Recommendations made by the court at the point of sentence will be of particular importance in influencing the content of the licence. This will properly reflect the gravity of the offence(s) committed.

(iii) Breaches

1.1.41 Where an offender fails, without reasonable excuse, to comply with one or more requirements, the 'responsible officer'[21] can either give a warning or initiate breach proceedings. Where the offender fails to comply without reasonable excuse for the second time within a 12-month period, the 'responsible officer' must initiate proceedings.

1.1.42 In such proceedings the court must[22] either *increase the severity of the existing sentence* (i.e. impose more onerous conditions including requirements aimed at enforcement, such as a curfew or supervision requirement) or *revoke the existing sentence and proceed as though sentencing for the original offence*. The court is required to take account of the circumstances of the breach,[23] which will inevitably have an impact on its response.

1.1.43 In certain circumstances (where an offender has wilfully and persistently failed to comply with an order made in respect of an offence that is not itself punishable by imprisonment), the court can *impose a maximum of 51 weeks custody.*[24]

1.1.44 When increasing the onerousness of requirements, the court must consider the impact on the offender's ability to comply and the possibility of precipitating a custodial sentence for further breach. For that reason, and particularly where the breach occurs towards the end of the sentence, the court should take account of compliance to date and may consider that extending the supervision or operational periods will be more sensible; in other cases it might choose to add punitive or rehabilitative requirements instead. In making these changes the court must be mindful of the legislative restrictions on the overall length of community sentences and on the supervision and operational periods allowed for each type of requirement.

1.1.45 The court dealing with breach of a community sentence should have as its primary objective ensuring that the requirements of the sentence are finished, and this is important if the court is to have regard to the statutory purposes of sentencing. A court that imposes a custodial sentence for breach without giving adequate consideration to alternatives is in danger of imposing a sentence that is not commensurate with the seriousness of the original offence and is solely a punishment for breach. This risks undermining the purposes it has identified as being important. Nonetheless, courts will need to be vigilant to ensure that there is a realistic prospect of the purposes of the order being achieved.

Having decided that a community sentence is commensurate with the seriousness of the offence, the *primary* objective when sentencing for breach of requirements is to ensure that those requirements are completed.

1.1.46 A court sentencing for breach must take account of the extent to which the offender has complied with the requirements of the community order, the reasons for breach and the point at which the breach has occurred. Where a breach takes place towards the end of the operational period and the court is satisfied that the offender's appearance before the court is likely to be sufficient in itself to ensure future compliance, then given that it is not open to the court to make no order, an

---

[21] Criminal Justice Act 2003 schedule 8, paragraphs 5–6
[22] ibid paragraphs 9–10
[23] ibid paragraph 9(2)
[24] ibid paragraph 9(1)(c)

approach that the court might wish to adopt could be to re-sentence in a way that enables the original order to be completed properly—for example, a differently constructed community sentence that aims to secure compliance with the purposes of the original sentence.

1.1.47   If the court decides to increase the onerousness of an order, it must give careful consideration, with advice from the Probation Service, to the offender's ability to comply. A custodial sentence should be the last resort, where all reasonable efforts to ensure that an offender completes a community sentence have failed.

- The Act allows for a custodial sentence to be imposed in response to breach of a community sentence. Custody should be the last resort, reserved for those cases of deliberate and repeated breach where all reasonable efforts to ensure that the offender complies have failed.
- Before increasing the onerousness of requirements, sentencers should take account of the offender's ability to comply and should avoid precipitating further breach by overloading the offender with too many or conflicting requirements.
- There may be cases where the court will need to consider re-sentencing to a differently constructed community sentence in order to secure compliance with the purposes of the original sentence, perhaps where there has already been partial compliance or where events since the sentence was imposed have shown that a different course of action is likely to be effective.

Section i
Part 2—Deferred Sentences   SG-12

A. Statutory Provisions

1.2.1   Under the existing legislation,[25] a court can defer a sentence for up to six months, provided the offender consents and the court considers that deferring the sentence is in the interests of justice.

1.2.2   The new provisions[26] continue to require the consent of the offender and that the court be satisfied that the making of such a decision is in the interests of justice. However, it is also stated that the power to defer sentence can only be exercised where:
'the offender undertakes to comply with any requirements as to his conduct during the period of the deferment that the court considers it appropriate to impose'.[27]

1.2.3   This enables the court to impose a wide variety of conditions (including a residence requirement).[28] The Act allows the court to appoint the probation service or other responsible person to oversee the offender's conduct during this period and prepare a report for the court at the point of sentence i.e. the end of the deferment period.

1.2.4   As under the existing legislation, if the offender commits another offence during the deferment period the court may have the power to sentence for both the original and the new offence at once. Sentence cannot be deferred for more than six months and, in most circumstances, no more than one period of deferment can be granted.[29]

1.2.5   A significant change is the provision enabling a court to deal with an offender before the end of the period of deferment.[30] For example if the court is satisfied that the offender has failed to comply with one or more requirements imposed in connection with the deferment, the offender can be brought back before the court and the court can proceed to sentence.

B. Use of Deferred Sentences   SG-13

1.2.6   Under the new framework, there is a wider range of sentencing options open to the courts, including the increased availability of suspended sentences, and deferred sentences are likely to be used in very limited circumstances. A deferred sentence enables the court to review the conduct of the defendant before passing sentence, having first prescribed certain requirements. It also provides several opportunities for an offender to have some influence as to the sentence passed—
   a)   it tests the commitment of the offender not to re-offend;

---

[25]   Powers of Criminal Courts (Sentencing) Act 2000 sections 1 and 2
[26]   Criminal Justice Act 2003 schedule 23 repealing and replacing sections 1 and 2 of the 2000 Act
[27]   ibid new section 1(3)(b) as inserted by schedule 23 to the Criminal Justice Act 2003
[28]   ibid new section 1A(1)
[29]   ibid new section 1(4)
[30]   ibid new section 1B

    b) it gives the offender an opportunity to do something where progress can be shown within a short period;

    c) it provides the offender with an opportunity to behave or refrain from behaving in a particular way that will be relevant to sentence.

1.2.7   Given the new power to require undertakings and the ability to enforce those undertakings before the end of the period of deferral, the decision to defer sentence should be predominantly for a small group of cases at either the custody threshold or the community sentence threshold where the sentencer feels that there would be particular value in giving the offender the opportunities listed because, if the offender complies with the requirements, a different sentence will be justified at the end of the deferment period. This could be a community sentence instead of a custodial sentence or a fine or discharge instead of a community sentence. It may, rarely, enable a custodial sentence to be suspended rather than imposed immediately.

The use of deferred sentences should be predominantly for a small group of cases close to a significant threshold where, should the defendant be prepared to adapt his behaviour in a way clearly specified by the sentencer, the court may be prepared to impose a lesser sentence.

1.2.8   A court may impose any conditions during the period of deferment that it considers appropriate.[31] These could be specific requirements as set out in the provisions for community sentences,[32] or requirements that are drawn more widely. These should be specific, measurable conditions so that the offender knows exactly what is required and the court can assess compliance; the restriction on liberty should be limited to ensure that the offender has a reasonable expectation of being able to comply whilst maintaining his or her social responsibilities.

1.2.9   Given the need for clarity in the mind of the offender and the possibility of sentence by another court, the court should give a clear indication (and make a written record) of the type of sentence it would be minded to impose if it had not decided to defer and ensure that the offender understands the consequences of failure to comply with the court's wishes during the deferral period.

When deferring sentence, the sentencer must make clear the consequence of not complying with any requirements and should indicate the type of sentence it would be minded to impose. Sentencers should impose specific, measurable conditions that do not involve a serious restriction on liberty.

Section 2 —Custodial Sentences

SG-14

Part 1—Custodial Sentences of 12 Months or More

A. Statutory Provisions

2.1.1   Under existing legislation:

- an adult offender receiving a custodial sentence of at least 12 months and below 4 years will automatically be released at the halfway point and will then be supervised under licence until the three-quarter point of the sentence. [For some, the actual release date may be earlier as a result of release on Home Detention Curfew (HDC).]

- an adult offender receiving a determinate sentence of 4 years or above will be eligible for release from the halfway point and, if not released before, will automatically be released at the two-thirds point. After release, the offender will be supervised under licence until the three-quarter point of the sentence.

2.1.2   Under the new framework, the impact of a custodial sentence will be more severe since the period in custody and under supervision will be for the whole of the sentence term set by the court. Additionally, separate provisions for the protection of the public will be introduced for those offenders designated as 'dangerous' under the Act which are designed to ensure that release only occurs when it is considered safe to do so.

2.1.3   Where a prison sentence of 12 months or more is imposed on an offender who is not classified as 'dangerous', that offender will be entitled to be released from custody after completing half of the sentence. The whole of the second half of the sentence will be subject to licence requirements. These requirements will be set shortly before release by the Secretary of State (with advice from the Governor responsible for authorising the prisoner's release in consultation with the Probation Service) but a court will be able to make recommendations at the sentencing stage on the content

---

[31] ibid new section 1 (3)(b) as inserted by schedule 23 to the Criminal Justice Act 2003
[32] Criminal Justice Act 2003 section 177

of those requirements.[33] The conditions that the Secretary of State may attach to a licence are to be prescribed by order.[34]

2.1.4   The Act requires that a custodial sentence for a fixed term should be for the shortest term that is commensurate with the seriousness of the offence.[35]

B. Imposition of Custodial Sentences of 12 Months or More   SG-15

(i) Length of Sentence

2.1.5   The requirement that the second half of a prison sentence will be served in the community subject to conditions imposed prior to release is a major new development and will require offenders to be under supervision for the full duration of the sentence prescribed by the court. The Probation Service will be able to impose a number of complementary requirements on the offender during the second half of a custodial sentence and these are expected to be more demanding and involve a greater restriction on liberty than current licence conditions.

2.1.6   As well as restricting liberty to a greater extent, the new requirements will last until the very end of the sentence, rather than to the three-quarter point as at present, potentially making a custodial sentence significantly more demanding than under existing legislation. Breach of these requirements at any stage is likely to result in the offender being returned to custody and this risk continues, therefore, for longer under the new framework than under the existing legislation.

Transitional arrangements

2.1.7   In general, a fixed term custodial sentence of 12 months or more under the new framework will increase the sentence actually served (whether in custody or in the community) since it continues to the end of the term imposed. Existing guidelines issued since 1991 have been based on a different framework and so, in order to maintain consistency between the lengths of sentence under the current and the new framework, there will need to be some adjustment to the starting points for custodial sentences contained in those guidelines (subject to the special sentences under the 2003 Act where the offender is a 'dangerous' offender).

2.1.8   This aspect of the guideline will be temporary to overcome the short-term situation where sentencing guidelines (issued since implementation of the reforms to custodial sentences introduced by the Criminal Justice Act 1991) are based on a different framework and the new framework has made those sentences more demanding. As new guidelines are issued they will take into account the new framework in providing starting points and ranges of appropriate sentence lengths for offences and an adjustment will not be necessary.

2.1.9   Since there are so many factors that will vary, it is difficult to calculate precisely how much more demanding a sentence under the new framework will be. The Council's conclusion is that the sentencer should seek to achieve the best match between a sentence under the new framework and its equivalent under the old framework so as to maintain the same level of punishment. As a guide, the Council suggests the sentence length should be reduced by in the region of 15%.

2.1.10 The changes in the nature of a custodial sentence will require changes in the way the sentence is announced. Sentencers will need to continue[36] to spell out the practical implications of the sentence being imposed so that offenders, victims and the public alike all understand that the sentence does not end when the offender is released from custody. The fact that a breach of the requirements imposed in the second half of the sentence is likely to result in a return to custody should also be made very clear at the point of sentence.

* When imposing a fixed term custodial sentence of 12 months or more under the new provisions, courts should consider reducing the overall length of the sentence that would have been imposed under the current provisions by in the region of 15%.

* When announcing sentence, sentencers should explain the way in which the sentence has been calculated, how it will be served and the implications of non-compliance with licence requirements. In particular, it needs to be stated clearly that the sentence is in two parts, one in custody and one under supervision in the community.

* This proposal does not apply to sentences for dangerous offenders, for which separate provision has been made in the Act.

---

[33] Criminal Justice Act 2003 section 238(1)
[34] ibid section 250
[35] ibid section 153(2)
[36] Having reference to the Consolidated Criminal Practice Direction [see appendix 5], Annex C, as suitably amended.

(ii) Licence conditions

2.1.11   Under the Act, a court imposing a prison sentence of 12 months or more may recommend conditions that should be imposed by the Secretary of State (with advice from the Governor responsible for authorising the prisoner's release in consultation with the Probation Service) on release from custody.[37] Recommendations do not form part of the sentence and they are not binding on the Secretary of State.[38]

2.1.12   When passing such a sentence, the court will not know with any certainty to what extent the offender's behaviour may have been addressed in custody or what the offender's health and other personal circumstances might be on release and so it will be extremely difficult, especially in the case of longer custodial sentences, for sentencers to make an informed judgement about the most appropriate licence conditions to be imposed on release. However, in most cases, it would be extremely helpful for sentencers to indicate areas of an offender's behaviour about which they have the most concern and to make suggestions about the types of intervention whether this, in practice, takes place in prison or in the community.

2.1.13   The involvement of the Probation Service at the pre-sentence stage will clearly be pivotal. A recommendation on the likely post-release requirements included in a presentence report will assist the court with the decision on overall sentence length, although any recommendation would still have to be open to review when release is being considered. A curfew, exclusion requirement or prohibited activity requirement might be suitable conditions to recommend for the licence period. A court might also wish to suggest that the offender should complete a rehabilitation programme, for example for drug abuse, anger management, or improving skills such as literacy and could recommend that this should be considered as a licence requirement if the programme has not been undertaken or completed in custody.

2.1.14   The Governor responsible for authorising the prisoner's release, in consultation with the Probation Service, is best placed to make recommendations at the point of release; this is the case at present and continues to be provided for in the Act. *Specific* court recommendations will only generally be appropriate in the context of relatively short sentences, where it would not be unreasonable for the sentencer to anticipate the relevance of particular requirements at the point of release. Making recommendations in relation to longer sentences (other than suggestions about the types of intervention that might be appropriate at some point during the sentence) would be unrealistic. The Governor and Probation Service should have due regard to any recommendations made by the sentencing court and the final recommendation to the Secretary of State on licence conditions will need to build upon any interventions during the custodial period and any other changes in the offender's circumstances.

- **A court may sensibly suggest interventions that could be useful when passing sentence, but should only make *specific* recommendations about the requirements to be imposed on licence when announcing short sentences and where it is reasonable to anticipate their relevance at the point of release. The Governor and Probation Service should have due regard to any recommendations made by the sentencing court but its decision should be contingent upon any changed circumstances during the custodial period.**
- **The court should make it clear, at the point of sentence, that the requirements to be imposed on licence will ultimately be the responsibility of the Governor and Probation Service and that they are entitled to review any recommendations made by the court in the light of any changed circumstances.**

Section 2 —Custodial Sentences

Part 2—Suspended Sentences of Imprisonment

A. Statutory Provisions

2.2.1   *Section 189 Criminal Justice Act 2003*

[Sets out the CJA 2003, s. 189(1) to (7) (suspended sentences of imprisonment: see **E6.2** to **E6.6** in the main work).]

2.2.2   *Imposition of requirements*—Section 190 Criminal Justice Act 2003:

[Sets out the CJA 2003, s. 190(1) to (5) (imposition of requirements by suspended sentence order: see **E6.7** in the main work).]

2.2.3   *Power to provide for review*—Section 191 Criminal Justice Act 2003:

---

[37] Criminal Justice Act 2003 section 238(1)
[38] ibid section 250

[Sets out the CJA 2003, s. 191(1) to (5) (power to provide for review of suspended sentence order: see **E6.10** in the main work).]

2.2.4   *Periodic reviews*—Section 192 Criminal Justice Act 2003:

[Sets out the CJA 2003, s. 192(1) to (8) (periodic review of suspended sentence order: see **E6.10** in the main work).]

2.2.5   *Breach, revocation or amendment of orders, and effect of further conviction—Section 193 Criminal Justice Act 2003*

Schedule 12 (which relates to the breach, revocation or amendment of the community requirements of suspended sentence orders, and to the effect of any further conviction) shall have effect.

B. Imposing a Suspended Sentence

2.2.6   A suspended sentence is a sentence of imprisonment. It is subject to the same criteria as a sentence of imprisonment which is to commence immediately. In particular, this requires a court to be satisfied that the custody threshold has been passed and that the length of the term is the shortest term commensurate with the seriousness of the offence.

2.2.7   A court which passes a prison sentence of less than 12 months may suspend it for between 6 months and 2 years (the operational period).[39] During that period, the court can impose one or more requirements for the offender to undertake in the community. The requirements are identical to those available for the new community sentence.

2.2.8   The period during which the offender undertakes community requirements is 'the supervision period' when the offender will be under the supervision of a 'responsible officer'; this period may be shorter than the operational period. The court may periodically review the progress of the offender in complying with the requirements and the reviews will be informed by a report from the responsible officer.

2.2.9   If the offender fails to comply with a requirement during the supervision period, or commits a further offence during the operational period, the suspended sentence can be activated in full or in part or the terms of the supervision made more onerous. There is a presumption that the suspended sentence will be activated either in full or in part.

(i) The decision to suspend

2.2.10   There are many similarities between the suspended sentence and the community sentence. In both cases, requirements can be imposed during the supervision period and the court can respond to breach by sending the offender to custody. The crucial difference is that the suspended sentence is a prison sentence and is appropriate only for an offence that passes the custody threshold and for which imprisonment is the only option. A community sentence may also be imposed for an offence that passes the custody threshold where the court considers that to be appropriate.

2.2.11   The full decision making process for imposition of custodial sentences under the new framework (including the custody threshold test) is set out in paragraphs 1.31–1.33 of the Seriousness guideline. For the purposes of suspended sentences the relevant steps are:

(a) has the custody threshold been passed?

(b) if so, is it unavoidable that a custodial sentence be imposed?

(c) if so, can that sentence be suspended? (sentencers should be clear that they would have imposed a custodial sentence if the power to suspend had not been available)

(d) if not, can the sentence be served intermittently?

(e) if not, impose a sentence which takes immediate effect for the term commensurate with the seriousness of the offence.

(ii) Length of sentence

2.2.12   Before making the decision to suspend sentence, the court must already have decided that a prison sentence is justified and should also have decided the length of sentence that would be the shortest term commensurate with the seriousness of the offence if it were to be imposed immediately. The decision to suspend the sentence should not lead to a longer term being imposed than if the sentence were to take effect immediately.

A prison sentence that is suspended should be for the same term that would have applied if the offender were being sentenced to immediate custody.

2.2.13   When assessing the length of the operational period of a suspended sentence, the court should have in mind the relatively short length of the sentence being suspended and the advantages to be gained by retaining the opportunity to extend the operational period at a later stage (see below).

---

[39] The power to suspend a sentence is expected to come into force earlier than the provisions implementing 'custody plus' and transitional provisions are expected to enable any sentence of imprisonment of under 12 months to be suspended. This guideline therefore is written in the language of the expected transitional provisions.

Sentencing Guidelines

The operational period of a suspended sentence should reflect the length of the sentence being suspended. As an approximate guide, an operational period of up to 12 months might normally be appropriate for a suspended sentence of up to 6 months and an operational period of up to 18 months might normally be appropriate for a suspended sentence of up to 12 months.

(iii) Requirements

2.2.14 The court will set the requirements to be complied with during the supervision period. Whilst the offence for which a suspended sentence is imposed is generally likely to be more serious than one for which a community sentence is imposed, the imposition of the custodial sentence is a clear punishment and deterrent. In order to ensure that the overall terms of the sentence are commensurate with the seriousness of the offence, it is likely that the requirements to be undertaken during the supervision period would be less onerous than if a community sentence had been imposed. These requirements will need to ensure that they properly address those factors that are most likely to reduce the risk of re-offending.

Because of the very clear deterrent threat involved in a suspended sentence, requirements imposed as part of that sentence should generally be less onerous than those imposed as part of a community sentence. A court wishing to impose onerous or intensive requirements on an offender should reconsider its decision to suspend sentence and consider whether a community sentence might be more appropriate.

SG-18 ## C. Breaches

2.2.15 The essence of a suspended sentence is to make it abundantly clear to an offender that failure to comply with the requirements of the order or commission of another offence will almost certainly result in a custodial sentence. Where an offender has breached any of the requirements without reasonable excuse for the first time, the responsible officer must either give a warning or initiate breach proceedings.[40] Where there is a further breach within a twelve-month period, breach proceedings must be initiated.[41]

2.2.16 Where proceedings are brought the court has several options, including extending the operational period. However, the presumption (which also applies where breach is by virtue of the commission of a further offence) is that the suspended prison sentence will be activated (either with its original custodial term or a lesser term) unless the court takes the view that this would, in all the circumstances, be unjust. In reaching that decision, the court may take into account both the extent to which the offender has complied with the requirements and the facts of the new offence.[42]

2.2.17 Where a court considers that the sentence needs to be activated, it may activate it in full or with a reduced term. Again, the extent to which the requirements have been complied with will be very relevant to this decision.

2.2.18 If a court amends the order rather than activating the suspended prison sentence, it must either make the requirements more onerous, or extend the supervision or operational periods (provided that these remain within the limits defined by the Act).[43] In such cases, the court must state its reasons for not activating the prison sentence,[44] which could include the extent to which the offender has complied with requirements or the facts of the subsequent offence.

2.2.19 If an offender near the end of an operational period (having complied with the requirements imposed) commits another offence, it may be more appropriate to amend the order rather than activate it.

2.2.20 If a new offence committed is of a less serious nature than the offence for which the suspended sentence was passed, it may justify activating the sentence with a reduced term or amending the terms of the order.

2.2.21 It is expected that any activated suspended sentence will be consecutive to the sentence imposed for the new offence.

2.2.22 If the new offence is non-imprisonable, the sentencer should consider whether it is appropriate to activate the suspended sentence at all.

---

[40] Criminal Justice Act 2003 schedule 12, para 4
[41] ibid para. 5
[42] ibid para. 8(4)
[43] ibid section 189 (3) and (4)
[44] ibid schedule 12, para. 8(3)

Where the court decides to amend a suspended sentence order rather than activate the custodial sentence, it should give serious consideration to extending the supervision or operational periods (within statutory limits) rather than making the requirements more onerous.

Section 2 Custodial Sentences

Part 3—Intermittent Custody   SG-19

[The relevant guidelines on intermittent custody are not reproduced in light of the Home Office announcement of November 2006 that the provisions are not to be implemented.]

Annex A   SG-20

Time Spent on Remand—Sentencing Advisory Panel's Advice

The Act makes provision for a sentencer to give credit for time spent on remand in custody where a custodial sentence is passed.[45] It also empowers the court to have regard to time spent on remand in custody when determining the restrictions on liberty to be imposed by a community order or youth community order.[46] Where an offender has spent several weeks in custody, this may affect the nature of the sentence that is passed. For example, where the court decides that a custodial sentence is justified some sentencers may decide to pass a community sentence instead, on the basis that the offender has already completed the equivalent of a punitive element in a sentence. The Panel takes the view that, given the changes in the content of the second part of a custodial sentence, in such cases it will be more appropriate to pass a custodial sentence knowing that licence requirements will be imposed on release from custody (which may be immediate). Recommendations made by the court at the point of sentence will then be of particular importance in influencing the content of the licence. This will help to ensure that the record clearly shows the assessment of seriousness of the offending behaviour.

Whereas the Act clearly states that time spent on remand is to be regarded as part of a custodial sentence unless the Court considers it unjust,[47] it states that sentencers passing a community sentence *may* have regard to time spent on remand, but no further information is given on how this discretion should be exercised. The Panel recognises that giving credit for time spent on remand is likely to be easier to apply in relation to punitive requirements rather than the rehabilitative elements of a community sentence. For example, reducing the number of unpaid work hours could be fairly easy, whereas reducing the length of a rehabilitation programme might not be appropriate as it could undermine its effectiveness. Where an offender has been kept on remand, one could take the view that this action was justified by the bail provisions and that the sentencer should not, therefore, feel obliged to adjust the terms of the community sentence. However, in principle, the Panel recommends that the court should seek to give credit for time spent on remand in all cases and should explain its reasons for not doing so when it considers either that this is not justified, would not be practical, or would not be in the best interests of the offender.

The court should seek to give credit for time spent on remand in all cases. It should make clear, when announcing sentence, whether or not credit for time on remand has been given and should explain its reasons for not giving credit when it considers either that this is not justified, would not be practical, or would not be in the best interests of the offender.

Where, following a period of time spent in custody on remand, the court decides that a custodial sentence is justified then, given the changes in the content of the second part of a custodial sentence, the court should pass a custodial sentence in the knowledge that licence requirements will be imposed on release from custody. Recommendations made by the court at the point of sentence will be of particular importance in influencing the content of the licence.[48]

---

[45] Criminal Justice Act 2003 section 240
[46] ibid section 149
[47] ibid section 240 (which will, at a future date, replace Criminal Justice Act 1967, section 67, by which such period is now deducted automatically).
[48] This recommendation only applies to sentences of 12 months and above pending the implementation of 'custody plus'.

SG-21   PART 3   OVERARCHING PRINCIPLES: SERIOUSNESS

FOREWORD

Following the planned implementation of many of the sentencing provisions in the 2003 Act in April 2005, this guideline deals with the general concept of seriousness in the light of those provisions and considers how sentencers should determine when the respective sentencing thresholds have been crossed when applying the provisions of the Act.

This guideline applies only to sentences passed under the sentencing framework applicable to those aged 18 or over although there are some aspects that will assist courts assessing the seriousness of offences committed by those under 18.

. . .

SG-22   SERIOUSNESS

A. Statutory provisions

1.1 In every case where the offender is aged 18 or over at the time of conviction, the court must have regard to the five purposes of sentencing contained in section 142(1) Criminal Justice Act 2003:

(a) the punishment of offenders

(b) the reduction of crime (including its reduction by deterrence)

(c) the reform and rehabilitation of offenders

(d) the protection of the public

(e) the making of reparation by offenders to persons affected by their offence.

1.2 The Act does not indicate that any one purpose should be more important than any other and in practice they may all be relevant to a greater or lesser degree in any individual case—the sentencer has the task of determining the manner in which they apply.

1.3 The sentencer must start by considering the *seriousness* of the offence, the assessment of which will:

• determine which of the sentencing thresholds has been crossed;

• indicate whether a custodial, community or other sentence is the most appropriate;

• be the key factor in deciding the length of a custodial sentence, the onerousness of requirements to be incorporated in a community sentence and the amount of any fine imposed.

1.4 A court is required to pass a sentence that is commensurate with the seriousness of the offence. The *seriousness* of an offence is determined by two main parameters; the *culpability* of the offender and the *harm* caused or risked being caused by the offence.

1.5 Section 143(1) Criminal Justice Act 2003 provides:

'In considering the seriousness of any offence, the court must consider the offender's culpability in committing the offence and any harm which the offence caused, was intended to cause or might foreseeably have caused.'

SG-23   B. Culpability

1.6 Four levels of criminal culpability can be identified for sentencing purposes:

1.7 Where the offender;

(i) has the *intention* to cause harm, with the highest culpability when an offence is planned. The worse the harm intended, the greater the seriousness.

(ii) is *reckless* as to whether harm is caused, that is, where the offender appreciates at least some harm would be caused but proceeds giving no thought to the consequences even though the extent of the risk would be obvious to most people.

(iii) has *knowledge* of the specific risks entailed by his actions even though he does not intend to cause the harm that results.

(iv) is guilty of *negligence*.

Note: *There are offences where liability is strict and no culpability need be proved for the purposes of obtaining a conviction, but the degree of culpability is still important when deciding sentence. The extent to which recklessness, knowledge or negligence are involved in a particular offence will vary.*

SG-24   C. Harm

1.8 The relevant provision is widely drafted so that it encompasses those offences where harm is caused but also those where neither individuals nor the community suffer harm but a risk of harm is present.

To Individual Victims

1.9   The types of harm caused or risked by different types of criminal activity are diverse and victims may suffer physical injury, sexual violation, financial loss, damage to health or psychological distress. There are gradations of harm within all of these categories.

1.10   The nature of harm will depend on personal characteristics and circumstances of the victim and the court's assessment of harm will be an effective and important way of taking into consideration the impact of a particular crime on the victim.

1.11   In some cases no actual harm may have resulted and the court will be concerned with assessing the relative dangerousness of the offender's conduct; it will consider the likelihood of harm occurring and the gravity of the harm that could have resulted.

To the Community

1.12   Some offences cause harm to the community at large (instead of or as well as to an individual victim) and may include economic loss, harm to public health, or interference with the administration of justice.

Other Types of harm

1.13   There are other types of harm that are more difficult to define or categorise. For example, cruelty to animals certainly causes significant harm to the animal but there may also be a human victim who also suffers psychological distress and/or financial loss.

1.14   Some conduct is criminalised purely by reference to public feeling or social mores. In addition, public concern about the damage caused by some behaviour, both to individuals and to society as a whole, can influence public perception of the harm caused, for example, by the supply of prohibited drugs.

D.   The Assessment of Culpability and Harm

1.15   Section 143(1) makes clear that the assessment of the seriousness of any individual offence must take account not only of any harm actually caused by the offence, but also of any harm that was intended to be caused or might foreseeably be caused by the offence.

1.16   Assessing seriousness is a difficult task, particularly where there is an imbalance between culpability and harm:
* sometimes the harm that actually results is greater than the harm intended by the offender;
* in other circumstances, the offender's culpability may be at a higher level than the harm resulting from the offence.

1.17   Harm must always be judged in the light of culpability. The precise level of culpability will be determined by such factors as motivation, whether the offence was planned or spontaneous or whether the offender was in a position of trust.

Culpability will be greater if:
* an offender deliberately causes more harm than is necessary for the commission of the offence, or
* where an offender targets a vulnerable victim (because of their old age or youth, disability or by virtue of the job they do).

1.18   Where unusually serious harm results and was unintended and beyond the control of the offender, culpability will be significantly influenced by the extent to which the harm could have been foreseen.

1.19   If much *more* harm, or much *less* harm has been caused by the offence than the offender intended or foresaw, the culpability of the offender, depending on the circumstances, may be regarded as carrying greater or lesser weight as appropriate.

The culpability of the offender in the particular circumstances of an individual case should be the initial factor in determining the seriousness of an offence.

(i)   Aggravating Factors

1.20   Sentencing guidelines for a particular offence will normally include a list of aggravating features which, if present in an individual instance of the offence, would indicate *either* a higher than usual level of culpability on the part of the offender, *or* a greater than usual degree of harm caused by the offence (or sometimes both).

1.21   The lists below bring together the most important aggravating features with potential application to more than one offence or class of offences. They include some factors (such as the vulnerability of victims or abuse of trust) which are integral features of certain offences; in such cases, the presence of the aggravating factor is already reflected in the penalty for the offence and *cannot be used as justification for increasing the sentence further*. The lists are not intended to be comprehensive and the aggravating factors are not listed in any particular order of priority. On occasions, two or more of the factors listed will describe the same feature of the offence and care needs to be taken to avoid 'doublecounting'. Those factors starred with an asterisk are statutory aggravating factors where the statutory provisions are in force. Those marked with a hash are yet to be brought into force but as factors in an individual case are still relevant and should be taken into account.

1.22   *Factors indicating higher culpability:*
- Offence committed whilst on bail for other offences*
- Failure to respond to previous sentences
- Offence was racially or religiously aggravated*
- Offence motivated by, or demonstrating, hostility to the victim based on his or her sexual orientation (or presumed sexual orientation)
- Offence motivated by, or demonstrating, hostility based on the victims disability (or presumed disability)
- Previous conviction(s), particularly where a pattern of repeat offending is disclosed
- Planning of an offence
- An intention to commit more serious harm than actually resulted from the offence
- Offenders operating in groups or gangs
- 'Professional' offending
- Commission of the offence for financial gain (where this is not inherent in the offence itself)
- High level of profit from the offence
- An attempt to conceal or dispose of evidence
- Failure to respond to warnings or concerns expressed by others about the offender's behaviour
- Offence committed whilst on licence
- Offence motivated by hostility towards a minority group, or a member or members of it
- Deliberate targeting of vulnerable victim(s)
- Commission of an offence while under the influence of alcohol or drugs
- Use of a weapon to frighten or injure victim
- Deliberate and gratuitous violence or damage to property, over and above what is needed to carry out the offence
- Abuse of power
- Abuse of a position of trust

1.23   *Factors indicating a more than usually serious degree of harm:*
- Multiple victims
- An especially serious physical or psychological effect on the victim, even if unintended
- A sustained assault or repeated assaults on the same victim
- Victim is particularly vulnerable
- Location of the offence (for example, in an isolated place)
- Offence is committed against those working in the public sector or providing a service to the public
- Presence of others e.g. relatives, especially children or partner of the victim
- Additional degradation of the victim (e.g. taking photographs of a victim as part of a sexual offence)
- In property offences, high value (including sentimental value) of property to the victim, or substantial consequential loss (e.g. where the theft of equipment causes serious disruption to a victim's life or business)

(ii) Mitigating factors

1.24   Some factors may indicate that an offender's culpability is *unusually* low, or that the harm caused by an offence is less than usually serious.

1.25   **Factors indicating significantly lower culpability:**
- A greater degree of provocation than normally expected
- Mental illness or disability
- Youth or age, where it affects the responsibility of the individual defendant
- The fact that the offender played only a minor role in the offence

(iii) Personal mitigation

1.26   Section 166(1) Criminal Justice Act 2003 makes provision for a sentencer to take account of any matters that 'in the opinion of the court, are relevant in mitigation of sentence'.

1.27   When the court has formed an initial assessment of the seriousness of the offence, then it should consider any offender mitigation. The issue of remorse should be taken into account at this point along with other mitigating features such as admissions to the police in interview.

(iv) Reduction for a guilty plea

1.28   Sentencers will normally reduce the severity of a sentence to reflect an early guilty plea. This subject is covered by a separate guideline and provides a sliding scale reduction with a normal maximum one-third reduction being given to offenders who enter a guilty plea at the first reasonable opportunity.

1.29   Credit may also be given for ready co-operation with the authorities. This will depend on the particular circumstances of the individual case.

E. The Sentencing Thresholds

SG-26

1.30   Assessing the seriousness of an offence is only the first step in the process of determining the appropriate sentence in an individual case. Matching the offence to a type and level of sentence is a separate and complex exercise assisted by the application of the respective threshold tests for custodial and community sentences.

The Custody Threshold

1.31   Section 152(2) Criminal Justice Act 2003 provides:
The court must not pass a custodial sentence unless it is of the opinion that the offence, or the combination of the offence and one or more offences associated with it, was so serious that neither a fine alone nor a community sentence can be justified for the offence.'

1.32   In applying the threshold test, sentencers should note:
* the clear intention of the threshold test is to reserve prison as a punishment for the most serious offences;
* it is impossible to determine definitively which features of a particular offence make it serious enough to merit a custodial sentence;
* passing the custody threshold does *not* mean that a custodial sentence should be deemed inevitable, and custody can still be avoided in the light of personal mitigation or where there is a suitable intervention in the community which provides sufficient restriction (by way of punishment) while addressing the rehabilitation of the offender to prevent future crime. For example, a prolific offender who currently could expect a short custodial sentence (which, in advance of custody plus, would have no provision for supervision on release) might more appropriately receive a suitable community sentence.

1.33   The approach to the imposition of a custodial sentence under the new framework should be as follows:
(a) has the custody threshold been passed?
(b) if so, is it unavoidable that a custodial sentence be imposed?
(c) if so, can that sentence be suspended? (sentencers should be clear that they would have imposed a custodial sentence if the power to suspend had not been available)
(d) if not, can the sentence be served intermittently?
(e) if not, impose a sentence which takes immediate effect for the term commensurate with the seriousness of the offence.

The Threshold for Community Sentences

1.34   Section 148(1) Criminal Justice Act 2003 provides:
'A court must not pass a community sentence on an offender unless it is of the opinion that the offence, or the combination of the offence and one or more offences associated with it, was serious enough to warrant such a sentence.'

1.35   In addition, the threshold for a community sentence can be crossed even though the seriousness criterion is not met. Section 151 Criminal Justice Act 2003 provides that, in relation to an offender aged 16 or over on whom, on 3 or more previous occasions, sentences had been passed consisting only of a fine, a community sentence may be imposed (if it is in the interests of justice) despite the fact that the seriousness of the current offence (and others associated with it) might not warrant such a sentence.

1.36   Sentencers should consider all of the disposals available (within or below the threshold passed) at the time of sentence before reaching the provisional decision to make a community sentence, so that, even where the threshold for a community sentence has been passed, a financial penalty or discharge may still be an appropriate penalty.

Summary

1.37　It would not be feasible to provide a form of words or to devise any formula that would provide a general solution to the problem of where the custody threshold lies. Factors vary too widely between offences for this to be done. It is the task of *guidelines for individual offences* to provide more detailed guidance on what features within that offence point to a custodial sentence, and also to deal with issues such as sentence length, the appropriate requirements for a community sentence or the use of appropriate ancillary orders.

Having assessed the seriousness of an individual offence, sentencers must consult the sentencing guidelines for an offence of that type for guidance on the factors that are likely to indicate whether a custodial sentence or other disposal is most likely to be appropriate.

SG-27　**F. Prevalence**

1.38　The seriousness of an individual case should be judged on its own dimensions of harm and culpability rather than as part of a collective social harm. It is legitimate for the overall approach to sentencing levels for particular offences to be guided by their cumulative effect. However, it would be wrong to further penalise individual offenders by increasing sentence length for committing an individual offence of that type.

1.39　There may be exceptional local circumstances that arise which may lead a court to decide that prevalence should influence sentencing levels. The pivotal issue in such cases will be the harm being caused to the community. It is essential that sentencers both have supporting evidence from an external source (for example the local Criminal Justice Board) to justify claims that a particular crime is prevalent in their area and are satisfied that there is a compelling need to treat the offence more seriously than elsewhere.

The key factor in determining whether sentencing levels should be enhanced in response to prevalence will be the level of harm being caused in the locality. Enhanced sentences should be exceptional and in response to exceptional circumstances. Sentencers must sentence within the sentencing guidelines once the prevalence has been addressed.

SG-28　**PART 4　MANSLAUGHTER BY REASON OF PROVOCATION**

FOREWORD

…This guideline stems from a reference from the Home Secretary for consideration of the issue of sentencing where provocation is argued in cases of homicide, and, in particular, domestic violence homicides. For the purpose of describing 'domestic violence', the Home Secretary adopted the Crown Prosecution Service definition.[49] The guideline applies to sentencing of an adult offender for this offence in whatever circumstances it occurs. It identifies the widely varying features of both the provocation and the act of retaliation and sets out the approach to be adopted in deciding both the sentencing range and the starting point within that range.

This guideline is for use where the conviction for manslaughter is clearly founded on provocation alone. There will be additional, different and more complicated matters to be taken into account where the other main partial defence, diminished responsibility, is a factor.

The Council's Guideline *New Sentences: Criminal Justice Act 2003* recognised the potentially more demanding nature of custodial sentences of 12 months or longer imposed under the new framework introduced by the Criminal Justice Act 2003. Consequently the sentencing ranges and starting points in this guideline take that principle into account.

…

---

[49] 'Any criminal offence arising out of physical, sexual, psychological, emotional or financial abuse by one person against a current or former partner in a close relationship, or against a current or former family member.' A new definition of domestic violence was agreed in 2004 (and appears in the CPS Policy on Prosecuting cases of Domestic Violence, 2005) 'any incident of threatening behaviour, violence or abuse [psychological, physical, sexual, financial or emotional] between adults who are or have been intimate partners or family members, regardless of gender or sexuality'.

Manslaughter by Reason of Provocation

A. Statutory Provision

SG-29

1.1 Murder and manslaughter are common law offences and there is no complete statutory definition of either. 'Provocation' is one of the partial defences by which an offence that would otherwise be murder may be reduced to manslaughter.

1.2 Before the issue of provocation can be considered, the Crown must have proved beyond reasonable doubt that all the elements of murder were present, including the necessary intent (i.e. the offender must have intended either to kill the victim or to cause grievous bodily harm). The court must then consider section 3 of the Homicide Act 1957, which provides:

Where on a charge of murder there is evidence on which the jury can find that the person charged was provoked (whether by things done or by things said or by both together) to lose his self-control, the question whether the provocation was enough to make a reasonable man do as he did shall be left to be determined by the jury; and in determining that question the jury shall take into account everything both done and said according to the effect which, in their opinion, it would have on a reasonable man.

Although both murder and manslaughter result in death, the difference in the level of culpability creates offences of a distinctively different character. Therefore the approach to sentencing in each should start from a different basis.

B. Establishing the Basis for Sentencing

SG-30

2.1 The Court of Appeal in *Attorney General's Reference (Nos. 74, 95 and 118 of 2002) (Suratan and others)*,[50] set out a number of assumptions that a judge must make in favour of an offender found not guilty of murder but guilty of manslaughter by reason of provocation. The assumptions are required in order to be faithful to the verdict and should be applied equally in all cases whether conviction follows a trial or whether the Crown has accepted a plea of guilty to manslaughter by reason of provocation:

- first, that the offender had, at the time of the killing, lost self-control; mere loss of temper or jealous rage is not sufficient
- second, that the offender was caused to lose self-control by things said or done, normally by the person killed
- third, that the offender's loss of control was reasonable in all the circumstances, even bearing in mind that people are expected to exercise reasonable control over their emotions and that, as society advances, it ought to call for a higher measure of self control
- fourth, that the circumstances were such as to make the loss of self-control sufficiently excusable to reduce the gravity of the offence from murder to manslaughter.

Bearing in mind the loss of life caused by manslaughter by reason of provocation, the starting point for sentencing should be a custodial sentence. Only in a very small number of cases involving very exceptional mitigating factors should a judge consider that a non-custodial sentence is justified.

The same general sentencing principles should apply in all cases of manslaughter by reason of provocation irrespective of whether or not the killing takes place in a domestic context.

C. Factors Influencing Sentence

SG-31

3.1 A number of elements must be considered and balanced by the sentencer. Some of these are common to all types of manslaughter by reason of provocation; others have a particular relevance in cases of manslaughter in a domestic context.

3.2 *The degree of provocation as shown by its nature and duration*—An assessment of the *degree* of the provocation as shown by its nature and duration is the critical factor in the sentencing decision.

(a)   In assessing the degree of provocation, account should be taken of the following factors:
- if the provocation (which does not have to be a wrongful act) involves gross and extreme conduct on the part of the victim, it is a more significant mitigating factor than conduct which, although significant, is not as extreme
- the fact that the victim presented a threat not only to the offender, but also to children in his or her care
- the offender's previous experiences of abuse and/or domestic violence either by the victim or by other people

---

[50]   [2003] 2 Cr App R (S) 42

- any mental condition which may affect the offender's perception of what amounts to provocation
- the nature of the conduct, the period of time over which it took place and its cumulative effect
- discovery or knowledge of the fact of infidelity on the part of a partner does not necessarily amount to *high* provocation. The gravity of such provocation depends entirely on all attendant circumstances.

(b) *Whether the provocation was suffered over a long or short period is important to the assessment of gravity. The following factors should be considered:*
- the impact of provocative behaviour on an offender can build up over a period of time
- consideration should not be limited to acts of provocation that occurred immediately before the victim was killed. For example, in domestic violence cases, cumulative provocation may eventually become intolerable, the latest incident seeming all the worse because of what went before.

(c) *When looking at the nature of the provocation the court should consider both the type of provocation and whether, in the particular case, the actions of the victim would have had a particularly marked effect on the offender:*
- actual (or anticipated) violence from the victim will generally be regarded as involving a higher degree of provocation than provocation arising from abuse, infidelity or offensive words unless that amounts to psychological bullying
- in cases involving actual or anticipated violence, the culpability of the offender will therefore generally be less than in cases involving verbal provocation
- where the offender's actions were motivated by fear or desperation, rather than by anger, frustration, resentment or a desire for revenge, the offender's culpability will generally be lower.

3.3 **The extent and timing of the retaliation**—It is implicit in the verdict of manslaughter by reason of provocation that the killing was the result of a loss of self-control because of things said and/or done. The intensity, extent and nature of that loss of control must be assessed in the context of the provocation that preceded it.

3.4 The *circumstances of the killing* itself will be relevant to the offender's culpability, and hence to the appropriate sentence:
- in general, the offender's violent response to provocation is likely to be less culpable the shorter the time gap between the provocation (or the last provocation) and the killing—as evidenced, for example, by the use of a weapon that happened to be available rather than by one that was carried for that purpose or prepared for use in advance
- conversely, it is not necessarily the case that greater culpability will be found where there has been a significant lapse of time between the provocation (or the last provocation) and the killing. Where the provocation is cumulative, and particularly in those circumstances where the offender is found to have suffered domestic violence from the victim over a significant period of time, the required loss of self-control may not be sudden as some experience a 'slow-burn' reaction and appear calm
- choosing or taking advantage of favourable circumstances for carrying out the killing (so that the victim was unable to resist, such as where the victim was not on guard, or was asleep) may well be an aggravating factor—unless this is mitigated by the circumstances of the offender, resulting in the offender being the weaker or vulnerable party.

3.5 The *context of the relationship* between the offender and the victim must be borne in mind when assessing the nature and degree of the provocation offered by the victim before the crime and the length of time over which the provocation existed. In cases where the parties were still in a relationship at the time of the killing, it will be necessary to examine the balance of power between one party and the other and to consider other family members who may have been drawn into, or been victims of, the provocative behaviour.

Although there will usually be less culpability when the retaliation to provocation is sudden, it is not always the case that greater culpability will be found where there has been a significant lapse of time between the provocation and the killing.

It is for the sentencer to consider the impact on an offender of provocative behaviour that has built up over a period of time.

An offence should be regarded as aggravated where it is committed in the presence of a child or children or other vulnerable family member, whether or not the offence takes place in a domestic setting.

3.6 *Post-offence behaviour*—The behaviour of the offender after the killing can be relevant to sentence:
- immediate and genuine remorse may be demonstrated by the summoning of medical assistance, remaining at the scene, and co-operation with the authorities
- concealment or attempts to dispose of evidence or dismemberment of the body may aggravate the offence.

Post-offence behaviour is relevant to the sentence. It may be an aggravating or mitigating factor. When sentencing, the judge should consider the motivation behind the offender's actions.

3.7 *Use of a weapon*
- (a) In relation to this offence, as in relation to many different types of offence, the carrying and use of a weapon is an aggravating factor. Courts must consider the type of weapon used and, importantly, whether it was to hand or carried to the scene and who introduced it to the incident.
- (b) The use or not of a weapon is a factor heavily influenced by the gender of the offender. Whereas men can and do kill using physical strength alone, women often cannot and thus resort to using a weapon. The issue of key importance is whether the weapon was to hand or carried deliberately to the scene, although the circumstances in which the weapon was brought to the scene will need to be considered carefully.

Although there will usually be less culpability when the retaliation to provocation is sudden, it is not always the case that greater culpability will be found where there has been a significant lapse of time between the provocation and the killing.

It is for the sentencer to consider the impact on an offender of provocative behaviour that has built up over a period of time.

An offence should be regarded as aggravated where it is committed in the presence of a child or children or other vulnerable family member, whether or not the offence takes place in a domestic setting.

The use of a weapon should not necessarily move a case into another sentencing bracket.

In cases of manslaughter by reason of provocation, use of a weapon may reflect the imbalance in strength between the offender and the victim and how that weapon came to hand is likely to be far more important than the use of the weapon itself.

It will be an aggravating factor where the weapon is brought to the scene in contemplation of use *before* the loss of self-control (which may occur some time before the fatal incident).

D. Sentence Ranges and Starting Points   SG-32

4.1 **Manslaughter is a 'serious offence' for the purposes of the provisions in the Criminal Justice Act 2003[51] for dealing with dangerous offenders. It is possible that a court will be required to use the sentences for public protection prescribed in the Act when sentencing an offender convicted of the offence of manslaughter by reason of provocation. An alternative is a discretionary life sentence. In accordance with normal practice, when setting the minimum term to be served within an indeterminate sentence under these provisions, that term will usually be half the equivalent determinate sentence.**

4.2 *Identifying sentence ranges*—The key factor that will be relevant in every case is the nature and the duration of the provocation.
- (a) The process to be followed by the court will be:
  - identify the sentence range by reference to the degree of provocation
  - adjust the starting point within the range by reference to the length of time over which the provocation took place
  - take into consideration the circumstances of the killing (e.g. the length of time that had elapsed between the provocation and the retaliation and the circumstances in which any weapon was used).
- (b) This guideline establishes that:
  - there are three sentencing ranges defined by the degree of provocation—low, substantial and high
  - within the three ranges, the starting point is based on provocation taking place over a short period of time
  - the court will move from the starting point (based upon the degree of provocation) by considering the length of time over which the provocation has taken place, and by reference to any aggravating and mitigating factors.

---

[51] Sections 224–230

Manslaughter by Reason of Provocation

Factors to take into consideration

1. The sentences for public protection must be considered in all cases of manslaughter.
2. The presence of any of the general aggravating factors identified in the Council's Guideline *Overarching Principles: Seriousness* or any of the additional factors identified in this Guideline will indicate a sentence above the normal starting point.
3. This offence will not be an initial charge but will arise following a charge of murder. The Council Guideline *Reduction in Sentence for a Guilty Plea* will need to be applied with this in mind. In particular, consideration will need to be given to the time at which it was indicated that the defendant would plead guilty to manslaughter by reason of provocation.
4. An assessment of the *degree* of the provocation as shown by its nature and duration is the critical factor in the sentencing decision.
5. The intensity, extent and nature of the loss of control must be assessed in the context of the pro-vocation that preceded it.
6. Although there will usually be less culpability when the retaliation to provocation is sudden, it is not always the case that greater culpability will be found where there has been a significant lapse of time between the provocation and the killing.
7. It is for the sentencer to consider the impact on an offender of provocative behaviour that has built up over a period of time.
8. The use of a weapon should not necessarily move a case into another sentencing bracket.
9. Use of a weapon may reflect the imbalance in strength between the offender and the victim and how that weapon came to hand is likely to be far more important than the use of the weapon itself.
10. It will be an aggravating factor where the weapon is brought to the scene in contemplation of use *before* the loss of self-control (which may occur some time before the fatal incident).
11. Post-offence behaviour is relevant to the sentence. It may be an aggravating or mitigating factor. When sentencing, the judge should consider the motivation behind the offender's actions.

This is a serious offence for the purposes of section 224 of the Criminal Justice Act 2003

Maximum penalty: Life imprisonment

Type/Nature of Activity	Sentence Ranges & Starting Points
Low degree of provocation: A low degree of provocation occurring over a short period	Sentence Range: 10 years–life Starting Point—12 years custody
Substantial degree of provocation: A substantial degree of provocation occurring over a short period	Sentence Range: 4–9 years Starting Point—8 years custody
High degree of provocation: A high degree of provocation occurring over a short period	Sentence Range: if custody is necessary, up to 4 years Starting Point—3 years custody

Additional aggravating factors	Additional mitigating factors
1. Concealment or attempts to dispose of evidence* 2. Dismemberment or mutilation of the body* 3. Offence committed in the presence of a child/children or other vulnerable family member	1. The offender was acting to protect another 2. Spontaneity and lack of premeditation 3. Previous experiences of abuse and/or domestic violence 4. Evidence that the victim presented an ongoing danger to the offender or another 5. Actual (or reasonably anticipated) violence from the victim
*subject to para 3.6 above.	

The Council Guideline New Sentences: Criminal Justice Act 2003 recognised the potentially more demanding nature of custodial sentences of 12 months or longer imposed under the new framework introduced by the Criminal Justice Act 2003. The sentencing ranges and starting points in the above guideline take account of this.

PART 5   ROBBERY

SG-34

...This guideline applies to the sentencing of offenders convicted of robbery who are sentenced on or after 1 August 2006.

Part 1 of this guideline provides starting points and sentencing ranges that are applicable to three types of robbery; street robbery or 'mugging', robberies of small businesses and less sophisticated commercial robberies. For other types of robbery, relevant guidance from the Court of Appeal should be applied; this is summarised in Part 2 of this guideline.

The guideline makes clear that robbery will usually merit a custodial sentence but that exceptional circumstances may justify a non-custodial penalty for an adult and, more frequently, for a young offender. In this way it is not intended to make a significant change to current practice. Over the past ten years the majority of young offenders sentenced for robbery have been given a non-custodial sentence. This contrasts with adult offenders where the majority sentenced for robbery have been given a custodial sentence.[52]

The Council Guideline *New Sentences: Criminal Justice Act 2003* recognised the potentially more demanding nature of custodial sentences of 12 months or longer imposed under the new framework introduced by the Criminal Justice Act 2003. Consequently the sentencing ranges and starting points in this guideline take that principle into account...

A. Statutory Provision

SG-35

Section 8(1) Theft Act 1968 provides:
A person is guilty of robbery if he steals, and immediately before or at the time of doing so, and in order to do so, he uses force on any person or puts or seeks to put any person in fear of being then and there subjected to force.

B. Forms of Robbery and Structure of the Guideline

SG-36

For the purposes of this guideline, five categories of robbery have been identified and established from sentencing ranges and previous guidance. They are:
1. Street robbery or 'mugging'
2. Robberies of small businesses
3. Less sophisticated commercial robberies
4. Violent personal robberies in the home
5. Professionally planned commercial robberies

The guideline is divided into two parts.

Part 1—This part covers categories 1–3 above.

For each of the three categories, three levels of seriousness have been identified based on the extent of force used or threatened.

For each level of seriousness a sentencing range and a starting point within that range have been identified.

Adult and youth offenders are distinguished and the guideline provides for them as separate groups.

Part 2—No guideline is provided for categories 4 and 5. Violent personal robberies are often accompanied by other serious offences which affect sentencing decisions. For professionally planned commercial robberies, existing case authority is still valid and this is summarised in Part 2.

C. Part 1

SG-37

Street robbery or 'mugging'
Street robberies will usually involve some physical force (or threat) to steal modest sums, although in some cases there is significant intimidation or violence. The victim may or may not be physically injured.

Robberies of small businesses
This category covers robberies of businesses such as a small shop or post office, petrol station or public transport/taxi facility which may well lack the physical and electronic security devices available to banks or building societies and larger businesses.

---

[52] In 2004 37% of youths and 87% of adults sentenced for robbery were given custodial sentences.

Less sophisticated commercial robberies

This category covers a wide range of locations, extent of planning and degree of violence including less sophisticated bank robberies or where larger commercial establishments are the target but without detailed planning or high levels of organisation.

SG-38　**D.　Assessing Seriousness**

(i)　Levels of Seriousness

Three levels of seriousness are identified by reference to the features or type of activity that characterise an offence at each level and the degree of force or threat present. The levels apply to all three categories of robbery but it will be very rare for robberies of small businesses or less sophisticated commercial robberies to have the features of the lowest level of seriousness.

Level 1—Threat and/or use of minimal force

The offence includes the threat or use of force and removal of property such as snatching from a persons grasp causing bruising/pain and discomfort.

The relative seriousness of a level 1 offence depends on:
(a)　the nature and duration of any force, threat or intimidation
(b)　the extent of injury (if any) to the victim
(c)　the value of the property taken
(d)　the number and degree of aggravating factors

Level 2—Use of weapon to threaten and/or use of significant force

A weapon is produced and used to threaten, and/or force is used which results in injury to the victim.

The relative seriousness of a level 2 offence depends on:
(a)　the nature and duration of the threat or intimidation
(b)　the extent of injury (if any) to the victim
(c)　the nature of the weapon used, whether it was real and, if it was a real firearm, whether it was loaded
(d)　the value of the property taken
(e)　the number and degree of aggravating factors

Level 3—Use of weapon and/or significant force and serious injury caused

The victim is caused serious physical injury, such as a broken limb, stab wound or internal injury, by the use of significant force and/or use of a weapon. Offences at this level are often accompanied by the presence of additional aggravating factors such as a degree of planning or the targeting of large sums of money or valuable goods.

The relative seriousness of a level 3 offence depends on:
(a)　the extent of injury (if any) to the victim
(b)　the nature of the weapon used
(c)　the value of the property taken
(d)　the number and degree of aggravating factors

(ii)　Aggravating & Mitigating Factors

The presence of one or more aggravating features will indicate a more severe sentence within the suggested range. If the aggravating feature(s) are exceptionally serious, the case may move to the next level of seriousness.

Aggravating factors particularly relevant to robbery

(a)　Degree of force or violence
- Use of a particular degree of force is more serious than the threat (which is not carried into effect) to use that same degree of force.
- Depending on the facts, however, a threat to use a high degree of force might properly be regarded as more serious than actual use of a lesser degree of force.

(b)　Use of a weapon
- Possession of a weapon during the course of an offence will be an aggravating factor, even if it is not used, because it indicates planning.
- Possession of a firearm which is loaded is more serious than possession of a firearm which is unloaded.
- Whether the weapon is real or imitation is not a major factor in determining sentence because the amount of fear created in the victim is likely to be the same.

- In cases of robbery in which a firearm is carried by the offender, a separate offence of possession of a firearm may be charged. In such circumstances, sentencers should consider, where appropriate, the use of consecutive sentences which properly reflect the totality of the offending.

(c) **Vulnerability of the victim**

- Targeting the elderly, the young, those with disabilities and persons performing a service to the public, especially outside normal working hours, will aggravate an offence.

(d) **Number involved in the offence and roles of offenders**

- Group offending will aggravate an offence because the level of intimidation and fear caused to the victim is likely to be greater.
- It may also indicate planning or 'gang' activity.
- The precise role of each offender will be important. Being the ringleader in a group is an aggravating factor. However, an offender may have played a peripheral role in the offence and, rather than having planned to take part, may have become involved spontaneously through the influence of others (see Mitigating Factors below).

(e) **Value of items taken**

- Property value may be more important in planned/sophisticated robberies.
- The value of the property capable of being taken should be taken into account as well as the amount/value of the property actually taken.

(f) **Offence committed at night/in hours of darkness**

- A victim is more vulnerable while in darkness than during daylight, all other things being equal.
- The degree of fear experienced by the victim is likely to be greater if an offence is committed at night or during hours of darkness.

(g) **Wearing of a disguise**

- The wearing of a disguise in order to commit an offence of robbery usually indicates a degree of planning on the part of the offender.
- The deliberate selection of a particular type of disguise in advance of the offence, for example, a balaclava or a mask, will be more serious than the improvised use of items of clothing such as a hat or hood.

Mitigating factors particularly relevant to robbery:

(a) **Unplanned/opportunistic**

- Many street robberies are unplanned or opportunistic by their nature so the extent of the mitigation in such cases may be limited.

(b) **Peripheral Involvement**

- Where, as part of a group robbery, the offender has played a peripheral role in the offence this should be treated as a mitigating factor although it should be borne in mind that by participating as part of a group, even in a minor role, the offender is likely to have increased the degree of fear caused to the victim (see Aggravating Factors above).

(c) **Voluntary return of property taken**

- The point at which the property is returned will be important and, in general, the earlier the property is returned the greater the degree of mitigation the offender should receive.

The court will also take account of the presence or absence of other factors including:
- **Personal mitigation**
- **First offence of violence**
- **Clear evidence of remorse**
- **Ready co-operation with the police**
- **Response to previous sentences**

A list of the most important general aggravating and mitigating factors can be found in the Guideline *Overarching Principles: Seriousness.*[53] These factors are reproduced at Annex A for ease of reference.

---

[53] Paragraphs 1.22–1.25

Young Offenders

- Young offenders may have characteristics relevant to their offending behaviour which are different from adult offenders. Also, by statute, the youth justice system has the principal aim of preventing offending by children and young persons.[54] Because of this, there may be factors which are of greater significance in cases involving young offenders including:
- Age of the offender
- Immaturity of the offender
- Group Pressure

Sentencers should recognise the varying significance of these factors for different ages.

(iii) Reduction in Sentence for Guilty Plea

Having taking account of aggravating and mitigating factors the court should consider whether the sentence should be reduced to take account of a guilty plea and by how much, in accordance with the Guideline: *Reduction in Sentence for a Guilty Plea*.

SG-39   **E. Public Protection Sentences—Dangerous Offenders**

Robbery is a serious offence for the purposes of section 225 of the Criminal Justice Act 2003 and sentencers should consider whether a life sentence or sentence for public protection should be imposed.

SG-40   **F. Ancillary Orders**

In all cases, courts should consider making the following orders:
- Restitution Order[55]—requiring the return of property
- Compensation Order[56]—for injury, loss or damage suffered.

Where a non-custodial sentence is imposed, courts may also consider making:
- Anti-social behaviour order[57]—to protect the public from behaviour causing harassment, alarm or distress. This order may be particularly appropriate where the offence of robbery forms part of a pattern of behaviour but such an order may be unnecessary if it will simply prohibit what is already criminal conduct. It may be used to prevent some offenders associating with other offenders with whom offences of robbery have been committed.

SG-41   **G. Factors to take into consideration—Adult Offenders**

1. Robbery is a serious offence for the purposes of section 225 of the Criminal Justice Act 2003 and sentencers should consider whether a life sentence or sentence for public protection should be imposed. The following guidelines apply to offenders who have not been assessed as dangerous.
2. The sentencing ranges and presumptive starting points apply to all three categories of robbery detailed above:
    - **Street robbery or 'mugging'**
    - **Robberies of small businesses**
    - **Less sophisticated commercial robberies**
3. The 'starting points' are based upon a first time offender who pleaded not guilty.
4. A reduction to the appropriate sentence, taking account of seriousness and aggravating and mitigating factors, will need to be made if an offender has pleaded guilty. The effect of applying the reduction may be that the sentence imposed for an offence at one level of seriousness may fall within the range suggested for the next lowest level of seriousness.
5. The relative seriousness of each offence will be determined by the following factors:
    - **Degree of force and/or nature and duration of threats**
    - **Degree of injury to the victim**
    - **Degree of fear experienced by the victim**
    - Value of property taken
6. Use of a particular degree of force is more serious than the threat (which is not carried into effect) to use that same degree of force. Depending on the facts, however, a threat to use a high degree of force might properly be regarded as more serious than actual use of a lesser degree of force.
7. If a weapon is involved in the use or threat of force, the offence will be more serious. Possession of a weapon during the course of an offence will be an aggravating factor, even if it is not used, because it

---

[54] Crime and Disorder Act 1998, s. 37
[55] Powers of Criminal Courts (Sentencing) Act 2000, ss. 148–149
[56] ibid s. 130
[57] Crime and Disorder Act 1998, s. 1 as amended

indicates planning. If the offence involves a real firearm it will be more serious if that firearm is loaded. Whether the weapon is real or imitation is not a major factor in determining sentence because the amount of fear created in the victim is likely to be the same.

8. The value of the property capable of being taken as well as the actual amount taken is important.

9. The presence of one or more aggravating features will indicate a more severe sentence within the suggested range and, if the aggravating feature(s) are exceptionally serious, the case will move up to the next level.

10. In all cases, courts should consider making a restitution order and/or a compensation order. Where a non-custodial sentence is imposed, the court may also consider making an anti-social behaviour order.

11. Passing the custody threshold does not mean that a custodial sentence should be deemed inevitable.[58]

Street Robbery or 'Mugging' Robberies of Small Businesses   SG-42
Less Sophisticated Commercial Robberies

Robbery is a serious offence for the purposes of sections 225 and 227 Criminal Justice Act 2003

Maximum Penalty: **Life imprisonment**

ADULT OFFENDERS

Type/nature of activity	Starting point	Sentencing Range
The offence includes the threat or use of minimal force and removal of property.	12 months custody	Up to 3 years
A weapon is produced and used to threaten, and/or force is used which results in injury to the victim.	4 years custody	2–7 years custody
The victim is caused serious physical injury by the use of significant force and/or use of a weapon.	8 years custody	7–12 years custody

Additional aggravating factors	Additional mitigating factors
1. More than one offender involved. 2. Being the ringleader of a group of offenders. 3. Restraint, detention or additional degradation, taken. 4. Offence was pre-planned. 5. Wearing a disguise. 6. Offence committed at night. 7. Vulnerable victim targeted. 8. Targeting of large sums of money or valuable goods. 9. Possession of a weapon that was not used.	1. Unplanned/opportunistic. 2. Peripheral involvement. 3. Voluntary return of property of the victim. 4. Clear evidence of remorse. 5. Ready co-operation with the police.

H. Factors to take into consideration—Young Offenders   SG-43

1. A youth court cannot impose a custodial sentence on an offender aged 10 or 11. If the offender is aged 12, 13 or 14, a detention and training order can only be imposed by a youth court in the case of persistent young offenders. In the Crown Court, however, long term detention in accordance with the Powers of Criminal Courts (Sentencing) Act 2000 can be ordered on any young offender without the requirement of persistence. The Crown Court may also impose an extended sentence, detention for public protection or detention for life where the young offender meets the criteria for being a 'dangerous offender.' **The following guidelines apply to offenders who have *not* been assessed as dangerous.**

---

[58] Guideline *Overarching Principles: Seriousness*, para 1.32

2. If a youth court is considering sending a case to the Crown Court, the court must be of the view that it is such a serious case that detention above two years is required, or that the appropriate sentence is a custodial sentence approaching the two year limit which is normally applicable to older offenders.[59]

3. The sentencing ranges and presumptive starting points apply to all three categories of robbery detailed above:
   • **Street robbery or 'mugging'**
   • **Robberies of small businesses**
   • **Less sophisticated commercial robberies**

4. The 'starting points' are based upon a first-time offender, aged 17 years old, who pleaded not guilty. For younger offenders sentencers should consider whether a lower starting point is justified in recognition of the offender's age or immaturity.

5. Young offenders may have characteristics relevant to their offending behaviour which are different from adult offenders. Also, by statute, the youth justice system has the principal aim of preventing offending by children and young persons.[60] Because of this, there may be factors which are of greater significance in cases involving young offenders. Sentencers should recognise the varying significance of such factors for different ages.

6. A reduction to the appropriate sentence, taking account of seriousness, and aggravating and mitigating factors, will need to be made if an offender has pleaded guilty. The effect of applying the reduction may be that the sentence imposed for an offence at one level of seriousness may fall within the range suggested for the next lowest level of seriousness.

7. The relative seriousness of each offence will be determined by the following factors:
   • **Degree of force and/or nature and duration of threats**
   • **Degree of injury to the victim**
   • **Degree of fear experienced by the victim**
   • **Value of property taken**

8. Use of a particular degree of force is more serious than the threat (which is not carried into effect) to use that same degree of force. Depending on the facts, however, a threat to use a high degree of force might properly be regarded as more serious than actual use of a lesser degree of force.

9. If a weapon is involved in the use or threat of force, the offence will be more serious. Possession of a weapon during the course of an offence will be an aggravating factor, even if it is not used, because it indicates planning. If the offence involves a real firearm it will be more serious if that firearm is loaded. Whether the weapon is real or imitation is not a major factor in determining sentence because the amount of fear created in the victim is likely to be the same.

10. The value of the property capable of being taken as well as the actual amount taken is important.

11. The presence of one or more aggravating features will indicate a more severe sentence within the suggested range and, if the aggravating feature(s) are exceptionally serious, the case will move up to the next level.

12. In all cases, courts should consider making a restitution order and/or a compensation order. Where a non-custodial sentence is imposed, the court may also consider making an anti-social behaviour order.

13. Courts are required by section 44(1) of the Children and Young Persons Act 1933 to have regard to the welfare of the child, and under section 37 of the Crime and Disorder Act 1998 to have regard to the overall aim of the youth justice system of preventing re-offending.

14. Passing the custody threshold does not mean that a custodial sentence should be deemed inevitable.[61]

15. Where there is evidence that the offence has been committed to fund a drug habit and that treatment for this could help tackle the offender's offending behaviour, sentencers should consider a drug treatment requirement as part of a supervision order or action plan order.

---

[59] *W v Southampton Youth Court, K v Wirral Borough Magistrates' Court* [2003] 1 Cr App R (S) 87
[60] Crime and Disorder Act 1998, s. 37
[61] Guideline *Overarching Principles: Seriousness*, para 1.32

STREET ROBBERY OR 'MUGGING' ROBBERIES OF SMALL BUSINESSES LESS SOPHISTICATED COMMERCIAL ROBBERIES

Robbery is a serious offence for the purposes of sections 226 and 228 Criminal Justice Act 2003

YOUNG OFFENDERS*

Type/nature of activity	Starting point	Sentencing Range
The offence includes the threat or use of minimal force and removal of property.	Community Order	Community Order–12 months detention and training order
A weapon is produced and used to threaten, and/or force is used which results in injury to the victim.	3 years detention	1–6 years detention
The victim is caused serious physical injury by the use of significant force and/or use of a weapon.	7 years detention	6–10 years detention

* The 'starting points' are based upon a first-time offender aged 17 years old who pleaded not guilty. For younger offenders, sentencers should consider whether a lower starting point is justified in recognition of the offender's age or immaturity.

Maximum Penalty: **Life imprisonment**

Additional aggravating factors	Additional mitigating factors
1. More than one offender involved. 2. Being the ringleader of a group of offenders. 3. Restraint, detention or additional degradation, taken. 4. Offence was pre-planned. 5. Wearing a disguise. 6. Offence committed at night. 7. Vulnerable victim targeted. 8. Targeting of large sums of money or valuable goods. 9. Possession of a weapon that was not used.	1. Unplanned/opportunistic. 2. Peripheral involvement. 3. Voluntary return of property of the victim. 4. Clear evidence of remorse. 5. Ready co-operation with the police. 6. Age of the offender. 7. Immaturity of the offender. 8. Peer group pressure.

I. Part 2

Relevant guidance from the Court of Appeal (which is summarised below for ease of reference) should apply to cases falling within the final two categories of robbery.

Violent personal robberies in the home

The sentencing range for robbery in the home involving physical violence is 13–16 years for a first time offender pleading not guilty. In this type of case, the starting point reflects the high level of violence, although it is clear that longer terms will be appropriate where extreme violence is used.[62]

This category overlaps with some cases of aggravated burglary (an offence which also carries a maximum of life imprisonment) where comparable sentences are passed. Consideration will need to be given as to whether the offender is a 'dangerous offender' for the purposes of the Criminal Justice Act 2003.

---

[62] *O'Driscoll* (1986) 8 Cr App R (S) 121

Professionally planned commercial robberies

The leading Court of Appeal decision on sentencing for robbery is the 1975 case of *Turner*.[63] This focuses on serious commercial robberies at the upper end of the sentencing range but just below the top level— planned professional robberies of banks and security vehicles, involving firearms and high value theft, but without the additional elements that characterise the most serious cases. The Court of Appeal said it had 'come to the conclusion that the normal sentence for anyone taking part in a bank robbery or in the holdup of a security or a Post Office van should be 15 years if firearms were carried and no serious injury done.'

The Court also said that 18 years should be about the maximum for crimes which are not 'wholly abnormal' (such as the Great Train Robbery).[64]

In cases involving the most serious commercial robberies the Court has imposed 20–30 years (15–20 years after a plea of guilty).

Consideration will need to be given as to whether the offender is a 'dangerous offender' for the purposes of the Criminal Justice Act 2003.

SG-44

ANNEX A

[Annex A consists of extracts from the SGC Guideline, *Overarching Principles: Seriousness*, which is reproduced in full in **part 3**.]

SG-45

PART 6   BREACH OF A PROTECTIVE ORDER

FOREWORD

…This guideline applies to offenders convicted of breach of an order who are sentenced on or after 18 December 2006.

This guideline deals specifically with the sentencing of offenders who have breached either a restraining order imposed in order to prevent future conduct causing harassment or fear of violence, or a non-molestation order which prohibits a person from molesting another person.

It highlights the particular factors that courts should take into account when dealing with the criminal offence of breaching an order and includes starting points based on the different types of activity which can constitute a breach. It also identifies relevant aggravating and mitigating factors.

…

SG-46   **A. Statutory Provisions**

1.1 For the purposes of this guideline, two protective orders are considered:

(i) Restraining Order

1.2 It is an offence contrary to the Protection from Harassment Act 1997 to behave in a way which a person knows (or ought to know) causes someone else harassment (section 2) or fear of violence (section 4). When imposing sentence on an offender, a court may also impose a restraining order to prevent future conduct causing harassment or fear of violence.

1.3 An offence under these provisions may have occurred in a domestic context or may have occurred in other contexts. The Domestic Violence, Crime and Victims Act 2004 provides for such orders also to be made on conviction for any offence or following acquittal.[65]

1.4 It is an offence contrary to section 5(5) of the Act to fail to comply with the restraining order without reasonable excuse. That offence is punishable with a maximum of five years imprisonment.

(ii) Non-Molestation Order

1.5 Section 42 of the Family Law Act 1996 provides that, during family proceedings, a court may make a non-molestation order containing either or both of the following provisions:

   (a) provision prohibiting a person ('the respondent') from molesting another person who is associated with the respondent;

   (b) provision prohibiting the respondent from molesting a relevant child.

---

[63] (1975) 61 Cr App R 67
[64] *Wilson and others* (1964) 48 Cr App R 329
[65] When in force, s. 12 of the 2004 Act amends s. 5 of the 1997 Act and inserts a new s. 5A to that Act.

1.6 Section 1 of the Domestic Violence, Crime and Victims Act 2004[66] inserts a new section 42A into the 1996 Act. Section 42A (1) will provide that it is an offence to fail to comply with the order without reasonable excuse. That offence is punishable with a maximum of five years imprisonment.

1.7 In addition, breach of a non-molestation order may be dealt with as a contempt of court.

B. Sentencing for Breach

SG-47

2.1 The facts that constitute a breach of a protective order may or may not also constitute a substantive offence. Where they do constitute a substantive offence, it is desirable that the substantive offence and the breach of the order should be charged as separate counts. Where necessary, consecutive sentences should be considered to reflect the seriousness of the counts and achieve the appropriate totality.

2.2 Sometimes, however, only the substantive offence or only the breach of the order will be charged. The basic principle is that the sentence should reflect all relevant aspects of the offence so that, provided the facts are not in issue, the result should be the same, regardless of whether one count or two has been charged. For example:

   (i)   **if the substantive offence only has been charged, the fact that it constitutes breach of a protective order should be treated as an aggravating factor;**

   (ii) **if breach of the protective order only has been charged, the sentence should reflect the nature of the breach, namely, the conduct that amounts to the substantive offence, aggravated by the fact that it is also breach of an order.**

2.3 If breach of a protective order has been charged where no substantive offence was involved, the sentence should reflect the circumstances of the breach, including whether it was an isolated breach, or part of a course of conduct in breach of the order; whether it was planned or unpre-meditated; and any consequences of the breach, including psychiatric injury or distress to the person protected by the order.

C. Factors Influencing Sentencing

SG-48

3.1 **In order to ensure that a protective order achieves the purpose it is intended for—protecting the victim from harm—it is important that the terms of the order are necessary and proportionate.**

3.2 The circumstances leading to the making of one of the protective orders will vary widely. Whilst a restraining order will be made in criminal proceedings, it will almost certainly result from offences of markedly different levels of seriousness or even acquittal. A nonmolestation order will have been made in civil proceedings and, again, may follow a wide variety of conduct by the subject of the order.

3.3 **In all cases the order will have been made to protect an individual from harm and action in response to breach should have as its primary aim the importance of ensuring that the order is complied with and that it achieves the protection that it was intended to achieve.**

3.4 **When sentencing for a breach of an order, the main aim should be to achieve future compliance with that order where that is realistic.**

The nature and context of the originating conduct or offence

3.5 The nature of the original conduct or offence is relevant in so far as it allows a judgement to be made on the level of harm caused to the victim by the breach and the extent to which that harm was intended by the offender.

3.6 If the original offence was serious, conduct which breaches the order might have a severe effect on the victim where in other contexts such conduct might appear minor. Even indirect contact, such as telephone calls, can cause significant harm or anxiety for a victim.

3.7 However, sentence following a breach is for the breach alone and must avoid punishing the offender again for the offence or conduct as a result of which the order was made.

The nature and context of the conduct that caused the breach

3.8 **The protective orders are designed to protect a victim. When dealing with a breach, a court will need to consider the extent to which the conduct amounting to breach put the victim at risk of harm.**

3.9 There may be exceptional cases where the nature of the breach is particularly serious but has not been dealt with by a separate offence being charged. In these cases, the risk posed by the offender and the nature of the breach will be particularly significant in determining the response. Where the order is breached by the use of physical violence, the starting point should normally be a custodial sentence.

---

[66] When in force.

Sentencing Guidelines

3.10   Non-violent behaviour and/or indirect contact can also cause (or be intended to cause) a high degree of harm and anxiety. In such circumstances, it is likely that the custody threshold will have been crossed.

3.11   Where an order was made in civil proceedings, its purpose may have been to cause the subject of the order to modify behaviour rather than to imply that the conduct was especially serious. If so, it is likely to be disproportionate to impose a custodial sentence for a breach of the order if the breach did not involve threats or violence.

3.12   In some cases where a breach might result in a short custodial sentence but the court is satisfied that the offender genuinely intends to reform his or her behaviour and there is a real prospect of rehabilitation, the court may consider it appropriate to impose a sentence that will allow this. This may mean imposing a suspended sentence order or a community order (where appropriate with a requirement to attend an accredited domestic violence programme).

3.13   **Breach of a protective order will generally be more serious than breach of a conditional discharge.** Not only is a breach of a protective order an offence in its own right but it also undermines a specific prohibition imposed by the court. Breach of a conditional discharge amounts to an offender failing to take a chance that has been provided by the court.

SG-49   **D. Aggravating and Mitigating Factors**

4.1   Many of the aggravating factors which apply to an offence of violence in a domestic context will apply also to an offence arising from breach of a protective order.

Aggravating Factors

(i) Victim is particularly vulnerable

4.2   For cultural, religious, language, financial or any other reasons, some victims may be more vulnerable than others. This vulnerability means that the terms of a protective order are particularly important and a violation of those terms will warrant a higher penalty than usual.

4.3   Age, disability or the fact that the victim was pregnant or had recently given birth at the time of the offence may make a victim particularly vulnerable.

4.4   Any steps taken to prevent the victim reporting an incident or obtaining assistance will usually aggravate the offence.

(ii) Impact on children

4.5   If a protective order is imposed in order to protect children, either solely or in addition to another victim, then a breach of that order will generally be more serious.[67]

(iii) A proven history of violence or threats by the offender

4.6   Of necessity, a breach of a protective order will not be the first time an offender has caused fear or harassment towards a victim. However, the offence will be more serious if the breach is part of a series of prolonged violence or harassment towards the victim or the offender has a history of disobedience to court orders.

4.7   Where an offender has previously been convicted of an offence involving domestic violence, either against the same or a different person, or has been convicted for a breach of an order, this is likely to be a statutory aggravating factor.[68]

(iv) Using contact arrangements with a child to instigate an offence

4.8   An offence will be aggravated where an offender exploits contact arrangements with a child in order to commit an offence.

(v) Victim is forced to leave home

4.9   A breach will be aggravated if, as a consequence, the victim is forced to leave home.

(vi) Additional aggravating factors

4.10   In addition to the factors listed above, the following will aggravate a breach of an order:
   • the offence is a further breach, following earlier breach proceedings;
   • the breach was committed immediately or shortly after the order was made.

---

[67] The definition of 'harm' in s. 31(9) of the Children Act 1989 as amended by s. 120 of the Adoption and Children Act 2002 includes 'impairment suffered from seeing or hearing the ill-treatment of another'.
[68] Criminal Justice Act 2003, s. 143(2)

Mitigating Factors

(i) Breach was committed after a long period of compliance

4.11   If the court is satisfied that the offender has complied with a protective order for a substantial period before a breach is committed, the court should take this into account when imposing sentence for the breach. The history of the relationship and the specific nature of the contact will be relevant in determining its significance as a mitigating factor.

(ii) Victim initiated contact

4.12   If the conditions of an order are breached following contact from the victim, this should be considered as mitigation. It is important to consider the history of the relationship and the specific nature of the contact in determining its significance as a mitigating factor.

4.13   Nonetheless it is important for the court to make clear that it is the responsibility of the offender and not the victim to ensure that the order is complied with.

E. Factors to take into Consideration   SG-50

Aims of sentencing

(a)   When sentencing for a breach of a protective order (which would have been imposed to protect a victim from further harm), the main aim should be to achieve future compliance with that order.

(b)   A court will need to assess the level of risk posed by the offender. If the offender requires treatment or assistance for mental health or other issues, willingness to undergo treatment or accept help may influence sentence.

1. *Key Factors*

(a)   The nature of the conduct that caused the breach of the order, in particular, whether the contact was direct or indirect, although it is important to recognise that indirect contact is capable of causing significant harm or anxiety.

(b)   **There may be exceptional cases where the nature of the breach is particularly serious but has not been dealt with by a separate offence being charged. In these cases the risk posed by the offender and the nature of the breach will be particularly significant in determining the response.**

(c)   The nature of the original conduct or offence is relevant to sentencing for the breach in so far as it allows a judgement to be made on the level of harm caused to the victim by the breach, and the extent to which that harm was intended by the offender.

(d)   The sentence following a breach is for the breach alone and must avoid punishing the offender again for the offence or conduct as a result of which the order was made.

(e)   Where violence is used to breach a restraining order or a molestation order, custody is the starting point for sentence.

(f)   Non-violent conduct in breach may cross the custody threshold where a high degree of harm or anxiety has been caused to the victim.

(g)   Where an order was made in civil proceedings, its purpose may have been to cause the subject of the order to modify behaviour rather than to imply that the conduct was especially serious. If so, it is likely to be disproportionate to impose a custodial sentence for a breach of the order if the breach did not involve threats or violence.

(h)   In some cases where a breach might result in a short custodial sentence but the court is satisfied that the offender genuinely intends to reform his or her behaviour and there is a real prospect of rehabilitation, the court may consider it appropriate to impose a sentence that will allow this. This may mean imposing a suspended sentence order or a community order (where appropriate with a requirement to attend an accredited domestic violence programme).

(i)   While, in principle, consecutive sentences may be imposed for each breach of which the offender is convicted, the overall sentence should reflect the totality principle.

2. *General*

(a)   Breach of a protective order should be considered more serious than a breach of a conditional discharge.

(b)   The principle of reduction in sentence for a guilty plea should be applied as set out in the Council guideline *Reduction in Sentence for a Guilty Plea*.

3. *Non-custodial sentences*

(a)   It is likely that all breaches of protective orders will pass the threshold for a community sentence. The reference in the starting points to medium and low range community orders refers to the Council guideline *New Sentences: Criminal Justice Act 2003* paragraphs 1.1.18–1.1.32.

(b) In accordance with general principle, the fact that the seriousness of an offence crosses a particular threshold does not preclude the court from imposing another type of sentence of a lower level where appropriate.

BREACH OF A PROTECTIVE ORDER

Breach of a Restraining Order
Section 5(5) Protection from Harassment Act 1997

Breach of a Non-Molestation Order
Section 42A Family Law Act 1996*

Maximum Penalty: **5 years imprisonment**

Where the conduct is particularly serious, it would normally be charged as a separate offence. These starting points are based on the premise that the activity has either been prosecuted separately as an offence or is not of a character sufficient to justify prosecution of it as an offence in its own right.

Nature of activity	Starting points
	Custodial Sentence
Breach (whether one or more) involving significant physical violence and significant physical or psychological harm to the victim	**More than 12 months** The length of the custodial sentence imposed will depend on the nature and seriousness of the breach(es).
More than one breach involving some violence and/or significant physical or psychological harm to the victim	**26–39 weeks custody** [Medium/High Custody Plus order]**
Single breach involving some violence and/or significant physical or psychological harm to the victim	**13–26 weeks custody** [Low/Medium Custody Plus order]**
	Non-Custodial Sentence
More than one breach involving no/minimal contact or some direct contact	MEDIUM range community order
Single breach involving no/minimal direct contact	**LOW range community order**

Additional aggravating factors	Additional mitigating factors
1. Victim is particularly vulnerable. 2. Impact on children. 3. A proven history of violence or threats by the offender. 4. Using contact arrangements with a child to instigate an offence. 5. Victim is forced to leave home. 6. Offence is a further breach, following earlier breach proceedings. 7. Offender has a history of disobedience to court orders. 8. Breach was committed immediately or shortly after the order was made.	1. Breach occurred after a long period of compliance. 2. Victim initiated contact.

* When in force.
** When the relevant provisions of the Criminal Justice Act 2003 are in force.

SG-51   PART 7   OVERARCHING PRINCIPLES: DOMESTIC VIOLENCE

FOREWORD

…This guideline applies to offences sentenced on or after 18 December 2006.

This guideline stems from a reference from the Home Secretary for consideration of sentencing in cases of domestic violence. The referral suggested that 'domestic violence' should be described in terms of the Crown Prosecution Service definition (described on page 3) and this suggestion was adopted by the Council.

Consequently this guideline is for use for all cases that fall within the Crown Prosecution Service definition of domestic violence.

There is no specific offence of domestic violence. The definition covers a broad set of circumstances and allows conduct amounting to domestic violence to be covered by a wide range of offences. The guideline identifies the principles relevant to the sentencing of cases involving violence that has occurred in a domestic context and includes details of particular aggravating and mitigating factors.

This guideline makes clear that offences committed in a domestic context should be regarded as being no less serious than offences committed in a non-domestic context. Indeed, because an offence has been committed in a domestic context, there are likely to be aggravating factors present that make it more serious.

In many situations of domestic violence, the circumstances require the sentence to demonstrate clearly that the conduct is unacceptable. However, there will be some situations where all parties genuinely and realistically wish the relationship to continue as long as the violence stops. In those situations, and where the violence is towards the lower end of the scale of seriousness, it is likely to be appropriate for the court to impose a sentence that provides the support necessary.

...

A. Definition of Domestic Violence   SG-52

1.1   There is no specific offence of domestic violence and conduct amounting to domestic violence is covered by a number of statutory provisions. For the purposes of this guideline, wherever such offending occurs, domestic violence is:

> 'Any incident of threatening behaviour, violence or abuse [psychological, physical, sexual, financial or emotional] between adults who are or have been intimate partners or family members, regardless of gender or sexuality.'[69]

1.2   Most incidents of domestic violence can be charged as one of a wide range of offences including physical assault (with or without a weapon), harassment, threats to cause injury or to kill, destroying or damaging property, false imprisonment (locking the victim in a room or preventing that person from leaving the house), and sexual offences.

1.3   This guideline covers issues which are relevant across the range of offences that might be committed in a domestic context. Under the above definition, the domestic context includes relationships involving intimate partners who are living together, intimate partners who do not live together and former intimate partners. It is also wide enough to include relationships between family members, for example between a father and a daughter, or a mother and a daughter, perhaps where the daughter is the mother's carer.

B. Assessing Seriousness   SG-53

2.1   **As a starting point for sentence, offences committed in a domestic context should be regarded as being no less serious than offences committed in a non-domestic context.**

2.2   Thus, the starting point for sentencing should be the same irrespective of whether the offender and the victim are known to each other (whether by virtue of being current or former intimate partners, family members, friends or acquaintances) or unknown to each other.

2.3   A number of aggravating factors may commonly arise by virtue of the offence being committed in a domestic context and these will increase the seriousness of such offences. These are described in more detail in C below.

C. Aggravating and Mitigating Factors   SG-54

3.1   Since domestic violence takes place within the context of a current or past relationship, the history of the relationship will often be relevant in assessing the gravity of the offence. Therefore, a court is entitled to take into account anything occurring within the relationship as a whole, which may reveal relevant aggravating or mitigating factors.

---

[69] This is the Government definition of domestic violence agreed in 2004. It is taken from Policy on Prosecuting cases of Domestic Violence, Crown Prosecution Service, 2005.

3.2 The following aggravating and mitigating factors (which are not intended to be exhaustive) are of particular relevance to offences committed in a domestic context, and should be read alongside the general factors set out in the Council guideline *Overarching Principles: Seriousness*.[70]

Aggravating Factors

(i) Abuse of trust and abuse of power

3.3 The guideline *Overarching Principles: Seriousness* identifies abuse of a position of trust and abuse of power as factors that indicate higher culpability. Within the nature of relationship required to meet the definition of domestic violence set out above, trust implies a mutual expectation of conduct that shows consideration, honesty, care and responsibility. In some such relationships, one of the parties will have the power to exert considerable control over the other.

3.4 In the context of domestic violence:
- an *abuse of trust*, whether through direct violence or emotional abuse, represents a violation of this understanding;
- an *abuse of power* in a relationship involves restricting another individual's autonomy which is sometimes a specific characteristic of domestic violence. This involves the exercise of control over an individual by means which may be psychological, physical, sexual, financial or emotional.

3.5 Where an abuse of trust or abuse of power is present, it will aggravate the seriousness of an offence. These factors are likely to exist in many offences of violence within a domestic context.

3.6 However, the breadth of the definition of domestic violence (set out in 1.1 above) encompasses offences committed by a former spouse or partner. Accordingly, there will be circumstances where the abuse of trust or abuse of power may be a very minor feature of an offence or may be deemed no longer to exist—for example, where the offender and victim have been separated for a long period of time.

(ii) Victim is particularly vulnerable

3.7 For cultural, religious, language, financial or any other reasons, some victims of domestic violence may be more vulnerable than others, not least because these issues may make it almost impossible for the victim to leave a violent relationship.

3.8 Where a perpetrator has exploited a victim's vulnerability (for instance, when the circumstances have been used by the perpetrator to prevent the victim from seeking and obtaining help), an offence will warrant a higher penalty.

3.9 Age, disability or the fact that the victim was pregnant or had recently given birth at the time of the offence may make a victim particularly vulnerable.

3.10 Any steps taken to prevent the victim reporting an incident or obtaining assistance will usually aggravate the offence.

(iii) Impact on children

3.11 Exposure of children to an offence (either directly or indirectly) is an aggravating factor.

3.12 Children are likely to be adversely affected by directly witnessing violence or other abuse and by being aware of it taking place while they are elsewhere in the home.[71]

(iv) Using contact arrangements with a child to instigate an offence

3.13 An offence will be aggravated where an offender exploits contact arrangements with a child in order to commit an offence.

(v) A proven history of violence or threats by the offender in a domestic setting

3.14 It is important that an assessment of the seriousness of an offence recognises the cumulative effect of a series of violent incidents or threats over a prolonged period, where such conduct has been proved or accepted.

3.15 Where an offender has previously been convicted of an offence involving domestic violence either against the same or a different partner, this is likely to be a statutory aggravating factor.[72]

---

[70] Published December 2004. The lists of aggravating factors from the guideline are reproduced at Annex A for ease of reference. See also www.sentencing-guidelines.gov.uk

[71] The definition of 'harm' in s. 31(9) of the Children Act 1989 as amended by s. 120 of the Adoption and Children Act 2002 includes 'impairment suffered from seeing or hearing the ill-treatment of another'.

[72] Criminal Justice Act 2003, s. 143(2)

(vi) A history of disobedience to court orders

3.16   A breach of an order that has been imposed for the purpose of protecting a victim can cause significant harm or anxiety. Where an offender's history of disobedience has had this effect, it will be an aggravating factor.

3.17   Commission of the offence in breach of a non-molestation order imposed in civil proceedings, in breach of a sentence (such as a conditional discharge) imposed for similar offending, or while subject to an ancillary order, such as a restraining order, will aggravate the seriousness of the offence.

3.18   The appropriate response to breach of a civil order is dealt with in a separate guideline *Breach of a Protective Order*.

(vii) Victim forced to leave home

3.19   An offence will be aggravated if, as a consequence, the victim is forced to leave home.

Mitigating Factors

(i) Positive good character

3.20   As a general principle of sentencing, a court will take account of an offender's positive good character. However, it is recognised that one of the factors that can allow domestic violence to continue unnoticed for lengthy periods is the ability of the perpetrator to have two personae. In respect of an offence of violence in a domestic context, an offender's good character in relation to conduct outside the home should generally be of no relevance where there is a proven pattern of behaviour.

3.21   Positive good character is of greater relevance in the rare case where the court is satisfied that the offence was an isolated incident.

(ii) Provocation

3.22   It may be asserted that the offence, at least in part, has been provoked by the conduct of the victim. Such assertions need to be treated with great care, both in determining whether they have a factual basis and in considering whether in the circumstances the alleged conduct amounts to provocation sufficient to mitigate the seriousness of the offence.

3.23   For provocation to be a mitigating factor, it will usually involve actual or anticipated violence including psychological bullying. Provocation is likely to have more of an effect as mitigation if it has taken place over a significant period of time.

D. Other factors influencing sentence   SG-55

Wishes of the victim and effect of the sentence

4.1   As a matter of general principle, a sentence imposed for an offence of violence should be determined by the seriousness of the offence, not by the expressed wishes of the victim.

4.2   There are a number of reasons why it may be particularly important that this principle is observed in a case of domestic violence:
- it is undesirable that a victim should feel a responsibility for the sentence imposed;
- there is a risk that a plea for mercy made by a victim will be induced by threats made by, or by a fear of, the offender;
- the risk of such threats will be increased if it is generally believed that the severity of the sentence may be affected by the wishes of the victim.

4.3   Nonetheless, there may be circumstances in which the court can properly mitigate a sentence to give effect to the expressed wish of the victim that the relationship be permitted to continue. The court must, however, be confident that such a wish is genuine, and that giving effect to it will not expose the victim to a real risk of further violence. Critical conditions are likely to be the seriousness of the offence and the history of the relationship. It is vitally important that the court has up-to-date information in a pre-sentence report and victim personal statement.

4.4   Either the offender or the victim (or both) may ask the court to take into consideration the interests of any children and to impose a less severe sentence. The court will wish to have regard not only to the effect on the children if the relationship is disrupted but also to the likely effect on the children of any further incidents of domestic violence.

E. Factors to Take into Consideration   SG-56

The following points of principle should be considered by a court when imposing sentence for any offence of violence committed in a domestic context.

1.   Offences committed in a domestic context should be regarded as being no less serious than offences committed in a non-domestic context.

Sentencing Guidelines

2. Many offences of violence in a domestic context are dealt with in a magistrates' court as an offence of common assault or assault occasioning actual bodily harm because the injuries sustained are relatively minor. Offences involving serious violence will warrant a custodial sentence in the majority of cases.

3. Some offences will be specified offences for the purposes of the dangerous offender provisions.[73] In such circumstances, consideration will need to be given to whether there is a significant risk of serious harm to members of the public, which include, of course, family members. If so, the court will be required to impose a life sentence, imprisonment for public protection or an extended sentence.

4. Where the custody threshold is only just crossed, so that if a custodial sentence is imposed it will be a short sentence, the court will wish to consider whether the better option is a suspended sentence order or a community order, including in either case a requirement to attend an accredited domestic violence programme. Such an option will only be appropriate where the court is satisfied that the offender genuinely intends to reform his or her behaviour and that there is a real prospect of rehabilitation being successful. Such a situation is unlikely to arise where there has been a pattern of abuse.

Annex A
Extracts from Guideline *Overarching Principles: Seriousness*

[Omitted: the relevant Guideline is set out in full in part 3.]

PART 8   SEXUAL OFFENCES ACT 2003

[Guidelines issued in April 2007 apply to the sentencing of offenders convicted of certain sexual offences who are sentenced between 14 May 2007 and 31 March 2014. For adult offenders convicted of sexual offences and sentenced after that date, the guidelines in Part 26 apply: see **SG-528** *et seq*. In view of the replacement of the 2007 guidelines, they are no longer reproduced here (but see Supplement 1 for the full text) and thus there is no **SG-58** to **SG-129**. The list below shows the paragraph number for the new sexual offences guidelines where an equivalent is available in the new guidelines. Because these are structured quite differently to those applying before 1 April 2014, it is often the case that no true equivalent exists. Part 7 of the 2007 guidelines has no equivalent and sentencers must refer to *Overarching Principles — Sentencing Youths* at **SG-433**.]

SG-57   See now the new sentencing guidelines at **SG-528**.

SG-58   Replaced by the new sentencing guidelines available at **SG-528** *et seq*.

SG-59   Replaced by the new sentencing guidelines available at **SG-528** *et seq*.

SG-60   Replaced by the new sentencing guidelines available at **SG-528** *et seq*.

SG-61   Replaced by the new sentencing guidelines available at **SG-528** *et seq*.

SG-62   Replaced by the new sentencing guidelines available at **SG-528** *et seq*.

SG-63   Replaced by the new sentencing guidelines available at **SG-528** *et seq*.

SG-64   Replaced by the new sentencing guidelines available at **SG-528** *et seq*.

SG-65   Replaced by the new sentencing guidelines available at **SG-528** *et seq*.

SG-66   Replaced by the new sentencing guidelines available at **SG-528** *et seq*.

SG-67   Replaced by the new sentencing guidelines available at **SG-528** *et seq*.

SG-68   Replaced by the new sentencing guidelines available at **SG-528** *et seq*.

SG-69   Replaced by the new sentencing guidelines available at **SG-528** *et seq*.

SG-70   Replaced by the new sentencing guidelines available at **SG-528** *et seq*.

SG-71   See now the new sentencing guidelines at SG-530.

SG-72   Replaced by the new sentencing guidelines available at **SG-528** *et seq*.

SG-73   See now the new sentencing guidelines at SG-530.

SG-74   Replaced by the new sentencing guidelines available at **SG-528** *et seq*.

---

[73] Criminal Justice Act 2003, part 12, chapter 5

Replaced by the new sentencing guidelines available at SG-528 *et seq.*	**SG-75**
Replaced by the new sentencing guidelines available at SG-528 *et seq.*	**SG-76**
See now the new sentencing guidelines at SG-531, SG-532 and SG-546.	**SG-77**
See now the new sentencing guidelines at SG-534 and SG-550.	**SG-78**
See now the new sentencing guidelines at SG-538.	**SG-79**
See now the new sentencing guidelines at SG-538 and SG-554.	**SG-80**
See now the new sentencing guidelines at SG-542 and SG-558.	**SG-81**
See now the new sentencing guidelines at SG-542 and SG-558.	**SG-82**
No equivalent.	**SG-83**
See now the new sentencing guidelines at SG-570.	**SG-84**
See now the new sentencing guidelines at SG-570.	**SG-85**
No equivalent.	**SG-86**
See now the new sentencing guidelines at SG-562.	**SG-87**
See now the new sentencing guidelines at SG-566.	**SG-88**
See now the new sentencing guidelines at SG-579.	**SG-89**
See now the new sentencing guidelines at SG-562.	**SG-90**
See now the new sentencing guidelines at SG-562.	**SG-91**
See now the new sentencing guidelines at SG-656.	**SG-92**
See now the new sentencing guidelines at SG-579.	**SG-93**
See now the new sentencing guidelines at SG-583.	**SG-94**
See now the new sentencing guidelines at SG-583.	**SG-95**
See now the new sentencing guidelines at SG-574.	**SG-96**
No equivalent.	**SG-97**
See now the new sentencing guidelines at SG-611 and SG-619.	**SG-98**
See now the new sentencing guidelines at SG-627.	**SG-99**
See now the new sentencing guidelines at SG-615 and SG-623.	**SG-100**
See now the new sentencing guidelines at SG-615, SG-623 and SG-631.	**SG-101**
No equivalent.	**SG-102**
See now the new sentencing guidelines at SG-575.	**SG-103**
See now the new sentencing guidelines at SG-651.	**SG-104**
See now the new sentencing guidelines at SG-652.	**SG-105**
See now the new sentencing guidelines at SG-647.	**SG-106**
No equivalent.	**SG-107**
See now the new sentencing guidelines at SG-643.	**SG-108**
No equivalent but see the Magistrates' Court Sentencing Guidelines at SG-255.	**SG-109**
See now the new sentencing guidelines at SG-635.	**SG-110**
See now the new sentencing guidelines at SG-639.	**SG-111**
No equivalent but see Part 26 at SG-661.	**SG-112**
No equivalent but see Part 26 at SG-661.	**SG-113**

Sentencing Guidelines

SG-114   No equivalent.

SG-115   No equivalent.

SG-116   No equivalent.

SG-117   No equivalent.

SG-118   No equivalent.

SG-119   See now the new sentencing guidelines at SG-587.

SG-120   See now the new sentencing guidelines at SG-587.

SG-121   See now the new sentencing guidelines at SG-587.

SG-122   See now the new sentencing guidelines at SG-587.

SG-123   No equivalent.

SG-124   See now the new sentencing guidelines at SG-603.

SG-125   See now the new sentencing guidelines at SG-599.

SG-126   No equivalent.

SG-127   See now the new sentencing guidelines at SG-591.

SG-128   See now the new sentencing guidelines at SG-595.

SG-129   No equivalent.

SG-130   PART 7: SENTENCING YOUNG OFFENDERS—OFFENCES
WITH A LOWER STATUTORY MAXIMUM

7.1 The SOA 2003 makes special provision in respect of the maximum sentence that can be imposed for certain offences where committed by a person under the age of 18 (a young offender). The sentencing framework that applies to the sentencing of young offenders is also different.

7.2 This section deals with those offences within the context of the framework that currently applies. Many cases will be sentenced in the youth court, but a significant proportion may also be dealt with in the Crown Court. The essential elements of each offence, relevant charging standards and any other general issues pertaining to the offence are set out in the offence guidelines....

7.3 The offences with which Part 7 is concerned are:
   (i)   Sexual activity with a child
   (ii)   Causing or inciting a child to engage in sexual activity
   (iii)   Engaging in sexual activity in the presence of a child
   (iv)   Causing a child to watch a sexual act
   (v)   Sexual activity with a child family member
   (vi)   Inciting a child family member to engage in sexual activity

7.4 In relation to each offence, the maximum sentence for an offence committed by a young offender is 5 years' custody compared with a maximum of 14 years or 10 years for an offender aged 18 or over. Offences under (i), (ii), (v) and (vi) above can be committed to the Crown Court where it is considered that sentencing powers greater than those available in a magistrates' court may be needed.[74]

7.5 The provisions relating to the sentencing of dangerous offenders apply to young offenders with some variation and, where appropriate, cases should be sent for trial or committed for sentence in the Crown Court. The offences in this section are 'serious' offences for the purposes of the provisions. Where the significant harm criterion is met, the court is required[75] to impose one of the sentences for public protection, which in the case of those under 18 are discretionary detention for life, indeterminate detention for public protection or an extended sentence.

7.6 The following guidelines are for those offences where the court considers that the facts found by the court justify the involvement of the criminal law—these findings may be different from those on which the decision to prosecute was made.

---

[74] Powers of Criminal Courts (Sentencing) Act 2000, s. 91
[75] Criminal Justice Act 2003, ss. 226 and 228

7.7   The sentencing framework that applies to young offenders is different from that for adult offenders. The significant factors are set out below.

7.8   For each offence, the circumstances that would suggest that a custodial sentence should be passed where it is available to the court and those that would suggest that a case should be dealt with in the Crown Court (as 'grave crimes') are set out. As for adult offenders, these guidelines relate to sentencing on conviction for a first-time offender after a plea of not guilty.

7.9   The principal aim for all involved in the youth justice system is to prevent offending by children and young persons.[76]

7.10 A court imposing sentence on a youth must have regard to the welfare,[77] maturity, sexual development and intelligence of the youth. These are always important factors.

7.11 Where a young offender pleads guilty to one of these offences and it is the first offence of which they are convicted, a youth court may impose an absolute discharge, a mental health disposal, a custodial sentence, or make a referral order.

7.12 Except where the dangerous offender provisions apply:
   (i)   Where the young offender is aged 12, 13 or 14, a custodial sentence may only be imposed if the youth is a 'persistent offender' or has committed a 'grave crime' warranting detention for a period in excess of 2 years.[78]
   (ii) Where a young offender is aged 10 or 11, no custodial sentence is available in the youth court.
   (iii) Where a custodial sentence is imposed in the youth court, it must be a Detention and Training Order (DTO), which can only be for 4/6/8/10/12/18 or 24 months.
   (iv) Where a custodial sentence is imposed in the Crown Court, it may be a DTO or it may be detention for a period up to the maximum for the offence.

Sexual activity with a child

(when committed by a person under the age of 18)

SG-131

THIS IS A SPECIFIED OFFENCE FOR THE PURPOSES OF SECTION 224 CJA 2003

Intentional sexual touching of a person under 16 (sections 9 and 13)

Maximum penalty: **5 years** (**14 years** if offender is 18 or over)

The starting points below are based upon a first-time offender aged 17 years old who pleaded not guilty. For younger offenders, sentencers should consider whether a lower starting point is justified in recognition of the offender's age or immaturity.

Type/nature of activity	Starting points	Sentencing ranges
Offence involving penetration where one or more aggravating factors exist or where there is a substantial age gap between the parties	**Detention and Training Order 12 months**	**Detention and Training Order 6–24 months**
CUSTODY THRESHOLD		
Any form of sexual activity that does not involve any aggravating factors	**Community order**	**An appropriate non-custodial sentence**[*]

[*] 'Non-custodial sentence' in this context suggests a youth community order (as defined in the Criminal Justice Act 2003, section 147(2)) or a fine. In most instances, an offence will have crossed the threshold for a community order. However, in accordance with normal sentencing practice, a court is not precluded from imposing a financial penalty where that is determined to be the appropriate sentence.

---

[76] Crime and Disorder Act 1998, s. 37
[77] Children and Young Persons Act 1933, s. 44
[78] Powers of Criminal Courts (Sentencing) Act 2000, s. 100

Aggravating factors	Mitigating factors
1. Background of intimidation or coercion 2. Use of drugs, alcohol or other substance to facilitate the offence 3. Threats to prevent victim reporting the incident 4. Abduction or detention 5. Offender aware that he or she is suffering from a sexually transmitted infection	1. Relationship of genuine affection 2. Youth and immaturity of offender

An offender convicted of this offence is automatically subject to notification requirements when sentenced to imprisonment for a term of at least 12 months.[79]

SG-132   **Causing or inciting a child to engage in sexual activity**

(when committed by a person under the age of 18)

THIS IS A SPECIFIED OFFENCE FOR THE PURPOSES OF SECTION 224 CJA 2003

Intentional causing/inciting of person under 16 to engage in sexual activity (sections 10 and 13)

Maximum penalty: **5 years** (**14 years** if offender is 18 or over)

The same starting points apply whether the activity was caused or incited and whether or not the incited activity took place.

The starting points below are based upon a first-time offender aged 17 years old who pleaded not guilty. For younger offenders, sentencers should consider whether a lower starting point is justified in recognition of the offender's age or immaturity

Type/nature of activity	Starting points	Sentencing ranges
Sexual activity involving penetration where one or more aggravating factors exist	Detention and Training Order 12 months	Detention and Training Order 6–24 months
CUSTODY THRESHOLD		
Any form of sexual activity (non-penetrative or penetrative) not involving any aggravating factors	Community order	An appropriate non-custodial sentence*

*   'Non-custodial sentence' in this context suggests a youth community order (as defined in the Criminal Justice Act 2003, section 147(2)) or a fine. In most instances, an offence will have crossed the threshold for a community order. However, in accordance with normal sentencing practice, a court is not precluded from imposing a financial penalty where that is determined to be the appropriate sentence.

Aggravating factors	Mitigating factors
1. Background of intimidation or coercion 2. Use of drugs, alcohol or other substance to facilitate the offence 3. Threats to prevent victim reporting the incident 4. Abduction or detention 5. Offender aware that he or she is suffering from a sexually transmitted infection	1. Relationship of genuine affection 2. Offender intervenes to prevent incited offence from taking place 3. Youth and immaturity of offender

An offender convicted of this offence is automatically subject to notification requirements when sentenced to imprisonment for a term of at least 12 months.[80]

SG-133   **Engaging in sexual activity in the presence of a child**

(when committed by a person under the age of 18)

THIS IS A SPECIFIED OFFENCE FOR THE PURPOSES OF SECTION 224 CJA 2003

Intentionally and for the purpose of obtaining sexual gratification, engaging in sexual activity in the presence of a person under 16, knowing or believing that the child is aware of the activity (sections 11 and 13)

Maximum penalty: **5 years** (**10 years** if offender is 18 or over)

---

[79] In accordance with the SOA 2003, s. 80 and schedule 3
[80] In accordance with the SOA 2003, s. 80 and schedule 3

The starting points below are based upon a first-time offender aged 17 years old who pleaded not guilty. For younger offenders, sentencers should consider whether a lower starting point is justified in recognition of the offender's age or immaturity.

Type/nature of activity	Starting points	Sentencing ranges
Sexual activity involving penetration where one or more aggravating factors exist	Detention and Training Order 12 months	Detention and Training Order 6–24 months
CUSTODY THRESHOLD		
Any form of sexual activity (non-penetrative or penetrative) not involving any aggravating factors	Community order	An appropriate non-custodial sentence*

* 'Non-custodial sentence' in this context suggests a youth community order (as defined in the Criminal Justice Act 2003, section 147(2)) or a fine. In most instances, an offence will have crossed the threshold for a community order. However, in accordance with normal sentencing practice, a court is not precluded from imposing a financial penalty where that is determined to be the appropriate sentence.

Aggravating factors	Mitigating factors
1. Background of intimidation or coercion 2. Use of drugs, alcohol or other substance to facilitate the offence 3. Threats to prevent victim reporting the incident 4. Abduction or detention	1. Youth and immaturity of offender

An offender convicted of this offence is automatically subject to notification requirements when sentenced to imprisonment for a term of at least 12 months.[81]

Causing a child to watch a sexual act
(when committed by a person under the age of 18)

SG-134

THIS IS A SPECIFIED OFFENCE FOR THE PURPOSES OF SECTION 224 CJA 2003

Intentionally causing a person under 16 to watch sexual activity or look at a photograph or pseudo-photograph of sexual activity for the purpose of obtaining sexual gratification (sections 12 and 13)

Maximum penalty: **5 years** (**10 years** if offender is 18 or over)

The starting points below are based upon a first-time offender aged 17 years old who pleaded not guilty. For younger offenders, sentencers should consider whether a lower starting point is justified in recognition of the offender's age or immaturity.

Type/nature of activity	Starting points	Sentencing ranges
Live sexual activity	Detention and Training Order 8 months	Detention and Training Order 6–12 months
CUSTODY THRESHOLD		
Moving or still images of people engaged in sexual acts involving penetration	Community order	An appropriate non-custodial sentence*
Moving or still images of people engaged in sexual acts other than penetration	Community order	An appropriate non-custodial sentence*

* 'Non-custodial sentence' in this context suggests a youth community order (as defined in the Criminal Justice Act 2003, section 147(2)) or a fine. In most instances, an offence will have crossed the threshold for a community order. However, in accordance with normal sentencing practice, a court is not precluded from imposing a financial penalty where that is determined to be the appropriate sentence.

---

[81] In accordance with the SOA 2003, s. 80 and schedule 3

Sentencing Guidelines

Aggravating factors	Mitigating factors
1. Background of intimidation or coercion 2. Use of drugs, alcohol or other substance to facilitate the offence 3. Threats to prevent victim reporting the incident 4. Abduction or detention 5. Images of violent activity	1. Youth and immaturity of offender

An offender convicted of this offence is automatically subject to notification requirements when sentenced to imprisonment for a term of at least 12 months.[82]

SG-135 **Sexual activity with a child family member and Inciting a child family member to engage in sexual activity**

(when committed by a person under the age of 18)

THIS IS A SERIOUS OFFENCE FOR THE PURPOSES OF SECTION 224 CJA 2003

Intentional sexual touching with a child family member (section 25)

Intentionally inciting sexual touching by a child family member (section 26)

Maximum penalty for both offences: **5 years** (**14 years** if offender is 18 or over)

The starting points below are based upon a first-time offender aged 17 years old who pleaded not guilty. For younger offenders, sentencers should consider whether a lower starting point is justified in recognition of the offender's age or immaturity.

Type/nature of activity	Starting points	Sentencing ranges
Offence involving penetration where one or more aggravating factors exist or where there is a substantial age gap between the parties	Detention and Training Order 18 months	Detention and Training Order 6–24 months
CUSTODY THRESHOLD		
Any form of sexual activity (non-penetrative or penetrative) not involving any aggravating factors	Community order	An appropriate non-custodial sentence[*]

[*] 'Non-custodial sentence' in this context suggests a youth community order (as defined in the Criminal Justice Act 2003, section 147(2)) or a fine. In most instances, an offence will have crossed the threshold for a community order. However, in accordance with normal sentencing practice, a court is not precluded from imposing a financial penalty where that is determined to be the appropriate sentence.

Aggravating factors	Mitigating factors
1. Background of intimidation or coercion 2. Use of drugs, alcohol or other substance 3. Threats deterring the victim from reporting the incident 4. Offender aware that he or she is suffering from a sexually transmitted infection	1. Small disparity in age between victim and offender 2. Relationship of genuine affection 3. Youth and immaturity of offender

An offender convicted of this offence is automatically subject to notification requirements when sentenced to imprisonment for a term of at least 12 months.[83]

SG-136   PART 9   FAIL TO SURRENDER TO BAIL

FOREWORD

This guideline applies to the sentencing of offenders convicted of failing to surrender to bail who are sentenced on or after **10 December 2007**. Bail Act offences are committed in significant numbers each year and are a major cause of disruption, delay and unnecessary cost for the criminal justice system. A prime

---

[82] In accordance with the SOA 2003, s. 80 and schedule 3
[83] In accordance with the SOA 2003, s. 80 and schedule 3

objective of courts is to bring criminal proceedings to a conclusion as soon as practicable, and a rigorous and consistent response when offenders fail to answer bail is needed to help achieve this. This, in turn, may help to discourage future offending. Where it is not possible to dispose of the original offence, sentencing for a Bail Act offence should normally be undertaken separately and carried out as soon as appropriate in light of the circumstances of an individual case.

When a Bail Act offence has been committed, the sentence must be commensurate with the seriousness of the offence and must take into account both the reason why the offender failed to surrender and the degree of harm intended or caused. For these purposes, 'harm' is not only that caused to individual victims and witnesses but includes the consequential effect on police and court resources and the wider negative impact on public confidence in the criminal justice system.

As the considerations for offences committed by youths will differ markedly from those relevant for adult offenders, this guideline relates to the sentencing of adult offenders only.

FAIL TO SURRENDER TO BAIL   SG-137

A. Statutory provision

1. [Sets out the Bail Act 1976, s. 6 (see **D7.136** in the main work.)]
2. An offence under subsection (1) or (2) is punishable either on summary conviction or, in the Crown Court, as if it were a criminal contempt of court. The maximum sentence in a magistrates' court is 3 months imprisonment.[84] If the matter is committed to the Crown Court for sentence, or dealt with there, the maximum sentence is 12 months custody and the sentence is subject to the usual appellate procedures.[85]

B. **Assessing Seriousness**   SG-138

3. When assessing the seriousness of an offence, the court must consider the offender's culpability and any harm which the offence caused, was intended to cause or might foreseeably have caused.[86]
4. In assessing **culpability**, a court will need to consider whether the failure to surrender was intended to cause harm and, if so, what level of harm. In assessing **harm**, a court will need to consider to what extent the failure to surrender impeded the course of justice. When applied to Bail Act offences, 'harm' includes not only the harm caused to individual victims and witnesses but the consequential drain on police and court resources and the wider negative impact on public confidence in the criminal justice system.
5. The same *approach* to sentencing should be adopted whether the offence is committed contrary to section 6(1) or to section 6(2). However, the offence contrary to section 6(2) requires that there had been a reasonable excuse not to attend on the original date and so the degree of harm arising from the failure to attend as soon as reasonably practicable after that date is likely to be less. Accordingly, the seriousness of the offence is likely to be less also.

(i) Culpability

6. The obligation on a person who is granted bail is to surrender to custody at the court or the police station as required. The assessment of culpability requires consideration of the immediate reason why the defendant failed to appear. This can range from forgetfulness (comparable to the category of culpability described as 'negligence' in the Council guideline on seriousness[87]) or fear of the outcome of the hearing through to a deliberate act. Where the failure to surrender was deliberate, it will be relevant whether it was designed to disrupt the system to the defendant's advantage or whether the defendant simply gave no thought at all to the consequences.

(ii) Harm

7. Some degree of harm, even if only a minor delay or inconvenience to the authorities, will always be caused when a defendant fails to surrender. The degree of harm *actually* caused will vary considerably depending on the particular circumstances of the offence. The harm that the offence might foresee-ably have caused[88] must also be taken into account.

---

[84] Police and Justice Act 2006, s.34 amends various sections of the Criminal Justice Act 2003 so that this maximum sentence is not affected by the general provisions relating to custodial sentences of less than 12 months when in force.
[85] Administration of Justice Act 1960, s.13
[86] Criminal Justice Act 2003, s.143(1)
[87] *Overarching Principles: Seriousness*, page 4, www.sentencing-guidelines.gov.uk
[88] Criminal Justice Act, s.143(1)

8. **Failure to surrender to a court** for any reason (whether bail is granted by the police or by a court) inevitably delays justice. Potentially, it will result in additional distress to victims and witnesses. It will almost always waste public money in the form of court time and the resources of the prosecution, the police and the defence.

   (a) Where a defendant fails to appear for a first court hearing but attends shortly afterwards, the only harm caused is likely to be the financial cost to the system. Procedural delays may also be caused by the prosecution, the defence or the Courts Service at various stages of the process and, where a case could not have proceeded even if the defendant had surrendered to bail, this should be taken into account when assessing the harm actually caused.

   (b) Where a defendant appears for trial on the wrong day but enters a late guilty plea enabling the case to be disposed of to some degree at least (albeit with some delay and disruption), the harm caused by the delay may be offset by the benefits stemming from the change of plea.

   (c) The most serious harm is likely to result when a defendant fails to appear for trial, especially if this results in witnesses being sent away. A lengthy aborted trial in the Crown Court will be more harmful than a short hearing in a magistrates' court though each situation has the potential to affect public confidence in the system.

   (d) Where a court decides not to proceed to trial in the absence of the defendant (see paragraphs 34–39), interference with the course of justice may be particularly acute. Memories may become less certain with the passage of time. Victims and witnesses, many of whom find the prospect of preparing for and attending court daunting, are likely to be caused distress and/or inconvenience. They may find it more difficult to attend court on the second or subsequent occasion, to the extent that they may not even appear at all. In such circumstances the harm is very high because justice will be prevented. Victims of violent or sexual offences are particularly likely to be distressed to learn that the accused is 'at large' in defiance of the court.

   (e) The level of harm is likely to be assessed as high where an offender fails to appear for sentence and is also seen to be flouting the authority of the court, such as where the avoidance of sentence results in the consequential avoidance of ancillary orders such as disqualification from driving or from working with children or vulnerable adults, the payment of compensation or registration as a sex offender. This may increase the level of harm whenever the offender continues to present a risk to public safety.

9. In general terms, the same approach to sentencing should be adopted whether the offence involves a failure to surrender to a court or to a police station since the legal obligation is the same. However, the harm that results from failure to surrender to a court will usually be greater than that resulting from failure to surrender to a police station and this will affect the assessment of the seriousness of an individual offence.

10. **Failure to surrender to a police station** results in police time being wasted and the course of justice being impeded; potentially, it can also result in victims and witnesses being distressed and concerned about their safety and the ability of the system to protect the public and deliver justice. However, the circumstances in which such bail is granted are less formal than the grant of court bail and the history of the individual case should be examined. There may be less culpability where bail has been enlarged on a number of occasions and less harm if *court* proceedings are not significantly delayed.

(iii) Nature and seriousness of original offence

11. Failure to surrender to custody is an offence in its own right and the sentence imposed should be proportionate to the seriousness of the offending behaviour itself. Where the Bail Act offence is sentenced in advance of the offence in relation to which bail was granted the assessment of seriousness will take place without reference to the seriousness of, or likely sentence for, the original offence.

12. However, the specific nature of the original offence may significantly affect the harm or likelihood of harm caused by the failure to surrender. Particular types of offence (such as violent or sexual offences) may have implications for public protection and safety and the offender's failure to surrender might cause fear and distress to witnesses.

13. Seriousness is not reduced automatically by subsequent acquittal of the original offence. Whilst it may seem harsh that a defendant before the court for an offence of which he is not guilty should be punished for the ancillary offence of failure to surrender during the course of the prosecution of that offence, both the culpability and the likely harm – delay, distress and inconvenience to witnesses, and additional costs—are the same. Moreover, one of the most serious effects of a Bail Act offence can be that a trial cannot take place because of the failure to surrender and it will often be invidious to expect a court to identify genuinely innocent defendants.

(iv) Aggravating and mitigating factors

14. Since 'recent and relevant' previous convictions aggravate the seriousness of an offence,[89] defendants who repeatedly fail to attend court are likely to receive more severe sentences.

15. The period of time for which a defendant absconds is also likely to influence the court when considering sentence. Whilst being absent for a long period of time will aggravate an offence, the fact that a defendant arrives at court only a few days, or even only a few hours, late, is not a factor that will necessarily mitigate sentence; in many cases, the harm will already have been done (for example, the trial may have been put back, witnesses may have been inconvenienced and there may be an increased likelihood that witnesses will fail to attend at a future hearing).

16. Leaving the jurisdiction is an aggravating factor as are other actions designed to avoid the jurisdiction of the court such as changing identity and appearance.

17. **The following aggravating factors are particularly relevant to an offence of failing to surrender to bail:**
    - Repeat offending
    - Offender's absence causes a lengthy delay to the administration of justice
    - Determined attempt to avoid the jurisdiction of the court

18. Prompt voluntary surrender might mitigate sentence where it saves police time in tracing and arresting an offender. It may also be an indication of remorse. This must be weighed against the degree of harm caused by the offence, which may still be significant. Surrender initiated by the offender merits consideration as a mitigating factor. Surrender in response to follow up action has no significance.

19. The fact that an offender has a disorganised or chaotic lifestyle, which may be due to a dependency on drugs or alcohol, does not of itself reduce the seriousness of the offence. Depending on the particular facts, it may be regarded as personal mitigation.

20. A misunderstanding (which does not amount to a defence) may be a mitigating factor but must be differentiated from a mistake on the part of the defendant, where the error must be regarded as his or her own responsibility.[90]

21. Where an offender has literacy or language difficulties, steps should normally be taken by the police or the court to address this when bail is granted. Such difficulties may be mitigation (where they do not amount to a defence but contribute to the offender failing to surrender to bail) where potential problems were not identified and/or appropriate steps were not taken to mitigate the risk in the circumstances as known at the time that bail is granted.

22. An offender's position as the sole or primary carer of dependant relatives may be personal mitigation when it is the reason why the offender has failed to surrender to custody.

23. **The following mitigating factors are particularly relevant to an offence of failing to surrender:**
    - prompt voluntary surrender;
    and, where they are not sufficient to amount to a defence:
    - misunderstanding;
    - a failure to comprehend the requirements or significance of bail;
    - caring responsibilities.

C. Procedural issues

SG-139

(i) When to sentence

24. The key principle is that a court should *deal* with a defendant who fails to surrender *as soon as is practicable* even if the trial or other hearing for the offence that led to the grant of bail is adjourned.[91] The following factors are relevant to the decision as to what is practicable:
    - when the proceedings in respect of which bail was granted are expected to conclude;
    - the seriousness of the offence for which the defendant is already being prosecuted;
    - the type of penalty that might be imposed for the breach of bail and for the original offence;
    - any other relevant circumstances.

25. Whether or not the defendant is guilty of a Bail Act offence should be determined as soon as possible. It will be central to the issue of whether bail should now be granted or refused. Even where the offence is denied, a trial is normally short; it should be held on the first appearance after arrest or surrender, unless an adjournment is necessary (for example, for the defence to obtain medical evidence).

26. When there is a plea or finding of guilt, sentence should be imposed *as soon as practicable*. The point at which it becomes possible to sentence an offence and the point at which it is practicable to do so will vary widely from case to case; a decision about timing is best made according to individual circumstances.

---

[89] ibid. s.143(2)
[90] See, for example, *Laidlaw v Atkinson* Queen's Bench Division CO/275/86
[91] See Consolidated Criminal Practice Direction last revised April 2007— www.hmcourtsservice.gov.uk/cms/pds.htm

27. A key relevant circumstance is whether the substantive offence is to be adjourned, either for a pre-sentence report or for trial, and whether the remand is to be on bail or in custody.

28. Where the defendant is remanded in custody, the sentencing options for the Bail Act offence are limited.

29. Where the defendant is to regain his or her liberty, there is the possibility of a noncustodial sentence. A community order, including an electronically monitored curfew requirement and, perhaps, a supervision requirement or an activity requirement may be helpful in ensuring attendance at future court hearings.

30. In more serious cases in which the custody threshold has been passed, a suspended sentence order could serve the same purpose.

31. These factors support sentencing without delay or with a short delay for a presentence report. On the other hand, there will be occasions when it is more appropriate that all outstanding matters should be dealt with on one sentencing occasion. This may be where the totality of offending may affect sentence type (for example where two or more offences together pass the custody threshold, but individually do not) or where the harm caused by the failure to surrender cannot be assessed at an early stage (for example, where witnesses may no longer be available).

32. A magistrates' court will be constrained by the maximum sentence available. In certain circumstances, Bail Act offences that would normally be dealt with in a magistrates' court may be committed to the Crown Court to be dealt with.[92]

(ii) Consecutive and concurrent custodial sentences

33. Where a custodial sentence is imposed for the original offence and a custodial sentence is also deemed appropriate for a Bail Act offence, a court should normally impose a consecutive sentence. However, a concurrent sentence will be appropriate where otherwise the overall sentence would be disproportionate to the combined seriousness of the offences.

(iii) Conducting trials in the absence of the defendant

34. A defendant has a duty to surrender to bail and a right to be present at his or her trial. However, where a defendant is absent voluntarily, having breached the duty to surrender, a court may proceed to hear a case in the defendant's absence. In a magistrates' court this is a statutory power.[93] While some sentences may be imposed in a defendant's absence, it is not possible to impose a custodial sentence or a community order, and it is undesirable to impose a disqualification from driving.

35. The Consolidated Criminal Practice Direction[94] reinforces the encouragement to courts to proceed in absence and identifies factors to be taken into account before so doing which include:
    - the conduct of the defendant;
    - the disadvantage to the defendant;
    - the public interest;
    - the effect of any delay; and
    - whether the attendance of the defendant could be secured at a later hearing.

36. Additional factors for a magistrates' court to consider include:
    - there is less risk of either a magistrate or a district judge drawing an impermissible inference from a defendant's absence than would be the case with a jury; and
    - in a magistrates' court the finder of fact may ask questions and test the evidence of prosecution witnesses.

37. The overriding concern of the court is to ensure that a trial conducted in the absence of the defendant is as fair as circumstances permit and, in particular, that the defendant's rights under Article 6 of the European Convention on Human Rights (ECHR)[95] are not infringed.

38. Proceeding to trial in the absence of the defendant may reduce the harm arising from a Bail Act offence. When considering the degree to which this should influence sentence, it must be borne in mind that the position in a magistrates' court is different from that in the Crown Court. An appeal against conviction from a magistrates' court can result in a re-hearing, whereas that is not the case after a jury trial. There is also the discretionary power under section 142 of the Magistrates' Courts Act 1980 to set aside a conviction and order a re-hearing in a magistrates' court. If an application to set aside a conviction is successful, witnesses will be required to give evidence again at a later date. It will be relevant to an assessment of harm whether either of those provisions has been used.

---

[92] Bail Act 1976, s.6(6)
[93] Magistrates' Courts Act 1980, s.11
[94] Last revised April 2007—www.hmcourts-service.gov.uk/cms/pds.htm
[95] Right to a fair trial

39. Where it has proved possible to proceed to trial or conclude proceedings in the absence of the defendant, this should have no bearing on *culpability* for a Bail Act offence as the intention of the defendant remains unchanged. It may, however, be relevant to the assessment of *harm* as this may have been reduced or avoided because of the decision to proceed in absence.

D.   Sentencing ranges and starting points   SG-140

(i)   This guideline applies to a first time offender who has been convicted after a trial. A first time offender is a person who does not have a conviction which, by virtue of section 143(2) of the Criminal Justice Act 2003, must be treated as an aggravating factor.

(ii)   The guideline establishes levels of seriousness based upon both offender culpability and the resulting consequences. These are set out in the column headed 'nature of failure and harm'.

(iii) A court will identify the description that most nearly matches the particular facts of the offence and this will identify a starting point from which the sentencer can depart to reflect any aggravating or mitigating factors affecting the *seriousness of the offence* to reach a provisional sentence.

(iv)   The sentencing range is the bracket into which the provisional sentence will normally fall. The particular circumstances may, however, make it appropriate that the provisional sentence falls outside the range.

(v)   Where the offender has previous convictions which aggravate the seriousness of the current offence, that may take the provisional sentence beyond the range given particularly where there are significant other aggravating factors present.

(vi)   Once the provisional sentence has been identified by reference to those factors affecting the seriousness of the offence, the court will take into account any relevant factors of personal mitigation, which may take the sentence beyond the range given.

(vii) Where there has been a guilty plea, any reduction attributable to that plea will be applied to the sentence at this stage. Again, this reduction may take the sentence below the range provided.

(viii) A court must give its reasons for imposing a sentence of a different kind or outside the range provided in the guidelines.[96]

The Decision Making Process

[Sets out the standard sequential decision making process: identify starting point, consider aggravating factors, consider mitigating factors, apply reduction for guilty plea, review in light of the totality principle and give reasons.]

E.   Factors to take into consideration   SG-141

1. Whilst the approach to sentencing should generally be the same whether the defendant failed to surrender to a court or to a police station and whether the offence is contrary to section 6(1) or 6(2), the court must examine all the relevant circumstances.

2. Whilst the seriousness of the original offence does not of itself aggravate or mitigate the seriousness of the offence of failing to surrender, the circumstances surrounding the original offence may be relevant in assessing the harm arising from this offence.

3. Where it has proved possible to conclude proceedings in the absence of the defendant, this may be relevant to the assessment of harm caused.

4. Where the failure to surrender to custody was 'deliberate';
    - at or near the bottom of the range will be cases where the defendant gave no thought at all to the consequences, or other mitigating factors are present, and the degree of delay or interference with the progress of the case was not significant in all the circumstances;
    - at or near the top of the range will be cases where any of aggravating factors 1–3 are present if there is also a significant delay and/or interference with the progress of the case.

5. Only the most common aggravating and mitigating factors specifically relevant to Bail Act offences are included in the guideline. When assessing the seriousness of an offence, the courts must always have regard to the full list of aggravating and mitigating factors in the Council guideline on Seriousness.[97]

6. A previous conviction that is likely to be 'relevant' for the purposes of this offence is one which demonstrates failure to comply with an order of a court.

7. Acquittal of the original offence does not automatically mitigate this offence.

8. The fact that an offender has a disorganised or chaotic lifestyle should not normally be treated as mitigation of the offence, but may be regarded as personal mitigation depending on the particular facts of a case.

---

[96] Criminal Justice Act 2003, s.174(2)(a)
[97] *Overarching Principles: Seriousness*, pages 6–7, published 16 December 2004, www.sentencing-guidelines.gov.uk

9. Once the provisional sentence has been identified by reference to factors affecting the seriousness of the offence, the court will take into account any relevant factors of personal mitigation, and any reduction where a guilty plea was entered.[98]

10. The sentence for this offence should normally be in addition to any sentence for the original offence. Where custodial sentences are being imposed for a Bail Act offence and the original offence at the same time, the normal approach should be for the sentences to be consecutive. The length of any custodial sentence imposed must be commensurate with the seriousness of the offence(s).[99]

11. If an offence is serious enough to justify imposition of a community order, a curfew requirement with an electronic monitoring requirement may be a particularly appropriate part of such an order in any of the three sentencing ranges.

12. Power exists for magistrates' courts to impose one day's detention in appropriate cases.[100]

SG-142   BAIL ACT 1976, ss. 6(1) & 6(2)

Maximum penalty: 12 months imprisonment in the Crown Court
3 months imprisonment in a magistrates' court

The following starting points and sentencing ranges are for a first time offender aged 18 or over who pleaded not guilty. They should be applied as set out above.

Nature of failure & harm	Starting point	Sentencing range
Deliberate failure to attend causing delay and/or interference with the administration of justice. *The type and degree of harm actually caused will affect where in the range the case falls. See guidance…*	14 days custody	*Crown Court* **Community order (medium)— 40 weeks custody** *Magistrates' court* **Community order (low)— 10 weeks custody**
Negligent or non-deliberate failure to attend causing delay and/or interference with the administration of justice	**Fine**	**Fine—Community order (medium)**
Surrenders late on day but case proceeds as planned	**Fine**	**Fine**

Additional aggravating factors	Additional mitigating factors
1. Lengthy absence 2. Serious attempts to evade justice 3. Determined attempt seriously to undermine the course of justice 4. Previous relevant convictions and/or repeated breach of court orders or police bail	1. Prompt voluntary surrender *When not amounting to a defence* 2. Misunderstanding 3. A failure to comprehend bail significance or requirements 4. Caring responsibilities [see para. 22 for further detail.]

SG-143   PART 10   ASSAULT DEFINITIVE GUIDELINE
                                        (CROWN COURT)

[Note: This definitive guideline was the first to be issued by the Sentencing Council: see **E1.2** in the main work.]

SG-144   **Applicability of Guideline**

In accordance with section 120 of the Coroners and Justice Act 2009, the Sentencing Council issues this definitive guideline. It applies to all offenders aged 18 and older, who are sentenced on or after 13 June 2011, regardless of the date of the offence.

---

[98] Reduction in sentence for a guilty plea (revised), published July 2007, www.sentencing-guidelines.gov.uk
[99] Criminal Justice Act 2003, s.152(2)
[100] Magistrates' Courts Act 1980, s.135

Section 125(1) of the Coroners and Justice Act 2009 provides that when sentencing offences committed after 6 April 2010:

'Every court—

(a) must, in sentencing an offender, follow any sentencing guideline which is relevant to the offender's case, and

(b) must, in exercising any other function relating to the sentencing of offenders, follow any sentencing guidelines which are relevant to the exercise of the function,

unless the court is satisfied that it would be contrary to the interests of justice to do so.'

This guideline applies only to offenders aged 18 and older. General principles to be considered in the sentencing of youths are in the Sentencing Guidelines Council's definitive guideline, *Overarching Principles—Sentencing Youths* [see **SG-433**].

Structure, ranges and starting points   **SG-145**

For the purposes of section 125(3)–(4) of the Coroners and Justice Act 2009, the guideline specifies *offence ranges*—the range of sentences appropriate for each type of offence. Within each offence, the Council has specified three *categories* which reflect varying degrees of seriousness. The offence range is split into *category ranges*—sentences appropriate for each level of seriousness. The Council has also identified a starting point within each category.

Starting points define the position within a category range from which to start calculating the provisional sentence. **Starting points apply to all offences within the corresponding category and are applicable to all offenders in all cases irrespective of plea or previous convictions.** Once the starting point is established the court should consider further aggravating and mitigating factors and previous convictions so as to adjust the sentence within the range. Credit for a guilty plea is taken into consideration only at step 4 in the process, after the appropriate sentence has been identified.

Information on community orders and fine bands is [available at **SG-306**].

CAUSING GRIEVOUS BODILY HARM WITH INTENT TO DO GRIEVOUS BODILY HARM/   **SG-146**
WOUNDING WITH INTENT TO DO GRIEVOUS BODILY HARM
Offences against the Person Act 1861 (section 18)

This is a serious specified offence for the purposes of section 224 of the Criminal Justice Act 2003

Triable only on indictment
Maximum: Life imprisonment

Offence range: 3–16 years' custody

STEP ONE   Determining the offence category
The court should determine the offence category using the table below.

Category 1	Greater harm (serious injury must normally be present) and higher culpability
Category 2	Greater harm (serious injury must normally be present) **and** lower culpability; **or** lesser harm **and** higher culpability
Category 3	Lesser harm **and** lower culpability

The court should determine the offender's culpability and the harm caused, or intended, by reference only to the factors below (as demonstrated by the presence of one or more). These factors comprise the principal factual elements of the offence and should determine the category.

Factors indicating greater harm	Factors indicating higher culpability
Injury (which includes disease transmission and/or psychological harm) which is serious in the context of the offence (must normally be present)	*Statutory aggravating factors:*
	Offence racially or religiously aggravated
	Offence motivated by, or demonstrating, hostility to the victim based on his or her sexual orientation (or presumed sexual orientation)
	Offence motivated by, or demonstrating, hostility to the victim based on the victim's disability (or presumed disability)
Victim is particularly vulnerable because of personal circumstances	*Other aggravating factors:*
	A significant degree of premeditation
	Use of weapon or weapon equivalent (for example, shod foot, headbutting, use of acid, use of animal)
Sustained or repeated assault on the same victim	Intention to commit more serious harm than actually resulted from the offence
	Deliberately causes more harm than is necessary for commission of offence
	Deliberate targeting of vulnerable victim
Factors indicating lesser harm	Leading role in group or gang
	Offence motivated by, or demonstrating, hostility based on the victim's age, sex, gender identity (or presumed gender identity)
Injury which is less serious in the context of the offence	**Factors indicating lower culpability**
	Subordinate role in a group or gang
	A greater degree of provocation than normally expected
	Lack of premeditation
	Mental disorder or learning disability, where linked to commission of the offence
	Excessive self defence

STEP TWO Starting point and category range

Having determined the category, the court should use the corresponding starting points to reach a sentence within the category range below. The starting point applies to all offenders irrespective of plea or previous convictions. A case of particular gravity, reflected by multiple features of culpability in step one, could merit upward adjustment from the starting point before further adjustment for aggravating or mitigating features, set out below.

Offence category	Starting Point (*Applicable to all Offenders*)	Category Range (*Applicable to all Offenders*)
Category 1	12 years custody	9–16 years custody
Category 2	6 years custody	5–9 years custody
Category 3	4 years custody	3–5 years custody

The table below contains a non-exhaustive list of additional factual elements providing the context of the offence and factors relating to the offender. Identify whether any combination of these, or other relevant factors, should result in an upward or downward adjustment from the starting point. In some cases, having considered these factors, it may be appropriate to move outside the identified category range.

Factors increasing seriousness	
Statutory aggravating factors:	Exploiting contact arrangements with a child to commit an offence
Previous convictions, having regard to a) the nature of the offence to which the conviction relates and its relevance to the current offence; and b) the time that has elapsed since the conviction	Previous violence or threats to the same victim
	Established evidence of community impact
	Any steps taken to prevent the victim reporting an incident, obtaining assistance and/or from assisting or supporting the prosecution
Offence committed whilst on bail	Offences taken into consideration (TICs)
Other aggravating factors include:	**Factors reducing seriousness or reflecting personal mitigation**
Location of the offence	No previous convictions or no relevant/recent convictions
Timing of the offence	
Ongoing effect upon the victim	Single blow
Offence committed against those working in the public sector or providing a service to the public	Remorse
	Good character and/or exemplary conduct
Presence of others including relatives, especially children or partner of the victim	Determination, and/or demonstration of steps taken to address addiction or offending behaviour
Gratuitous degradation of victim	Serious medical conditions requiring urgent, intensive or long-term treatment
In domestic violence cases, victim forced to leave their home	Isolated incident
Failure to comply with current court orders	
Offence committed whilst on licence	

(*Continued*)

An attempt to conceal or dispose of evidence Failure to respond to warnings or concerns expressed by others about the offender's behaviour Commission of offence whilst under the influence of alcohol or drugs Abuse of power and/or position of trust	Age and/or lack of maturity where it affects the responsibility of the offender Lapse of time since the offence where this is not the fault of the offender Mental disorder or learning disability, where not linked to the commission of the offence Sole or primary carer for dependent relatives

STEP THREE   Consider any other factors which indicate a reduction, such as assistance to the prosecution

The court should take into account sections 73 and 74 of the Serious Organised Crime and Police Act 2005 (assistance by defendants: reduction or review of sentence) and any other rule of law by virtue of which an offender may receive a discounted sentence in consequence of assistance given (or offered) to the prosecutor or investigator.

STEP FOUR   Reduction for Guilty Pleas

The court should take account of any potential reduction for a guilty plea in accordance with section 144 of the Criminal Justice Act 2003 and the *Guilty Plea* guideline.

STEP FIVE   Dangerousness

Causing grievous bodily harm with intent to do grievous bodily harm/wounding with intent to do grievous bodily harm is a serious offence within the meaning of Chapter 5 of the Criminal Justice Act 2003 and at this stage the court should consider whether having regard to the criteria contained in that Chapter it would be appropriate to award a life sentence, imprisonment for public protection or an extended sentence. Where offenders meet the dangerousness criteria, the notional determinate sentence should be used as the basis for the setting of a minimum term.

STEP SIX   Totality Principle

If sentencing an offender for more than one offence, or where the offender is already serving a sentence, consider whether the total sentence is just and proportionate to the offending behaviour.

STEP SEVEN   Compensation and ancillary orders

In all cases, the court should consider whether to make compensation and/or other ancillary orders.

STEP EIGHT   Reasons

Section 174 of the Criminal Justice Act 2003 imposes a duty to give reasons for, and explain the effect of, the sentence.

STEP NINE   Consideration for remand time

Sentencers should take into consideration any remand time served in relation to the final sentence. The court should consider whether to give credit for time spent on remand in custody or on bail in accordance with sections 240 and 240A of the Criminal Justice Act 2003.

Inflicting Grievous Bodily Harm/Unlawful Wounding   **SG-147**

Offences against the Person Act 1861 (section 20)

Racially/Religiously Aggravated GBH/Unlawful Wounding

Crime and Disorder Act 1998 (section 29)

These are specified offences for the purposes of section 224 of the Criminal Justice Act 2003

Triable either way
Maximum (section 20): 5 years
Maximum (section 29): 7 years

Offence range: Community order—4 years custody

STEP ONE Determining the offence category

Category 1	Greater harm (serious injury must normally be present) and higher culpability
Category 2	Greater harm (serious injury must normally be present) and lower culpability; or lesser harm and higher culpability
Category 3	Lesser harm and lower culpability

The court should determine the offender's culpability and the harm caused, or intended, by reference only to the factors below (as demonstrated by the presence of one or more). These factors comprise the principal factual elements of the offence and should determine the category.

Factors indicating greater harm Injury (which includes disease transmission and/or psychological harm) which is serious in the context of the offence (must normally be present) Victim is particularly vulnerable because of personal circumstances Sustained or repeated assault on the same victim	Factors indicating lesser harm Injury which is less serious in the context of the offence
Factors indicating higher culpability *Statutory aggravating factors:* Offence motivated by, or demonstrating, hostility to the victim based on his or her sexual orientation (or presumed sexual orientation) Offence motivated by, or demonstrating, hostility to the victim based on the victim's disability (or presumed disability) *Other aggravating factors:* A significant degree of premeditation Use of weapon or weapon equivalent (for example, shod foot, headbutting, use of acid, use of animal) Intention to commit more serious harm than actually resulted from the offence Deliberately causes more harm than is necessary for commission of offence Deliberate targeting of vulnerable victim Leading role in group or gang Offence motivated by, or demonstrating, hostility based on the victim's age, sex, gender identity (or presumed gender identity)	Factors indicating lower culpability Subordinate role in group or gang A greater degree of provocation than normally expected Lack of premeditation Mental disorder or learning disability, where linked to commission of the offence Excessive self defence

STEP TWO Starting Point and Category Range

Having determined the category, the court should use the corresponding starting points to reach a sentence within the category range below. The starting point applies to all offenders irrespective of plea or previous convictions. A case of particular gravity, reflected by multiple features of culpability in step one, could merit upward adjustment from the starting point before further adjustment for aggravating or mitigating features, set out below.

Offence Category	Starting Point (*Applicable to all offenders*)	Category Range (*Applicable to all offenders*)
Category 1	3 years custody	2 years 6 months—4 years custody
Category 2	1 year 6 months custody	1–3 years custody
Category 3	High level community order	Low level community order—51 weeks custody

The table below contains a **non-exhaustive** list of additional factual elements providing the context of the offence and factors relating to the offender. Identify whether any combination of these, or other relevant factors, should result in an upward or downward adjustment from the starting point. In some cases, having considered these factors, it may be appropriate to move outside the identified category range.

When sentencing **category 3 offences**, the court should also consider the custody threshold as follows:

- has the custody threshold been passed?
- if so, is it unavoidable that a custodial sentence be imposed?
- if so, can that sentence be suspended?

Factors increasing seriousness	Factors reducing seriousness or reflecting personal mitigation
Statutory aggravating factors: Previous convictions, having regard to a) the nature of the offence to which the conviction relates and its relevance to the current offence; and b) the time that has elapsed since the conviction Offence committed whilst on bail *Other aggravating factors include:* Location of the offence Timing of the offence Ongoing effect upon the victim Offence committed against those working in the public sector or providing a service to the public Presence of others including relatives, especially children or partner of the victim Gratuitous degradation of victim In domestic violence cases, victim forced to leave their home Failure to comply with current court orders Offence committed whilst on licence An attempt to conceal or dispose of evidence Failure to respond to warnings or concerns expressed by others about the offender's behaviour Commission of offence whilst under the influence of alcohol or drugs Abuse of power and/or position of trust Exploiting contact arrangements with a child to commit an offence Previous violence or threats to the same victim Established evidence of community impact Any steps taken to prevent the victim reporting an incident, obtaining assistance and/or from assisting or supporting the prosecution Offences taken into consideration (TICs)	No previous convictions **or** no relevant/recent convictions Single blow Remorse Good character and/or exemplary conduct Determination and/or demonstration of steps taken to address addiction or offending behaviour Serious medical conditions requiring urgent, intensive or long-term treatment Isolated incident Age and/or lack of maturity where it affects the responsibility of the offender Lapse of time since the offence where this is not the fault of the offender Mental disorder or learning disability, where **not** linked to the commission of the offence Sole or primary carer for dependent relatives

Section 29 offences only: The court should determine the appropriate sentence for the offence without taking account of the element of aggravation and then make an addition to the sentence, considering the level of aggravation involved. It may be appropriate to move outside the identified category range, taking into account the increased statutory maximum.

STEP THREE   Consider any other factors which indicate a reduction, such as assistance to the prosecution

The court should take into account sections 73 and 74 of the Serious Organised Crime and Police Act 2005 (assistance by defendants: reduction or review of sentence) and any other rule of law by virtue of which an offender may receive a discounted sentence in consequence of assistance given (or offered) to the prosecutor or investigator.

STEP FOUR   Reduction for guilty pleas

The court should take account of any potential reduction for a guilty plea in accordance with section 144 of the Criminal Justice Act 2003 and the *Guilty Plea* guideline.

STEP FIVE   Dangerousness

Inflicting grievous bodily harm/Unlawful wounding and racially/religiously aggravated GBH/Unlawful wounding are specified offences within the meaning of Chapter 5 of the Criminal Justice Act 2003 and at this stage the court should consider whether having regard to the criteria contained in that Chapter it would be appropriate to award an extended sentence.

[Steps Six to Nine are almost identical to those which apply for causing grievous bodily harm with intent: see **SG-146**.]

Assault Occasioning Actual Bodily Harm
Offences against the Person Act 1861 (section 47)

Racially/Religiously Aggravated ABH
Crime and Disorder Act 1998 (section 29)

These are specified offences for the purposes of section 224 of the Criminal Justice Act 2003

Triable either way
Maximum (section 47): 5 years' custody
Maximum (section 29): 7 years' custody

Offence range: Fine—3 years' custody

STEP ONE Determining the offence category
The court should determine the offence category using the table below.

Category 1	Greater harm (serious injury must normally be present) **and** higher culpability
Category 2	Greater harm (serious injury must normally be present) **and** lower culpability; **or** lesser harm **and** higher culpability
Category 3	Lesser harm **and** lower culpability

The court should determine the offender's culpability and the harm caused, or intended, by reference **only** to the factors identified in the table below (as demonstrated by the presence of one or more). These factors comprise the principal factual elements of the offence and should determine the category.

Factors indicating greater harm	Factors indicating lesser harm
Injury (which includes disease transmission and/or psychological harm) which is serious in the context the offence (must normally be present)	Injury which is less serious in the context of the offence
Victim is particularly vulnerable because of personal circumstances	
Sustained or repeated assault on the same victim	
Factors indicating higher culpability	**Factors indicating lower culpability**
Statutory aggravating factors:	Subordinate role in a group or gang
Offence motivated by, or demonstrating, hostility to the victim based on his or her sexual orientation (or presumed sexual orientation)	A greater degree of provocation than normally expected
	Lack of premeditation
Offence motivated by, or demonstrating, hostility to the victim based on the victim's disability (or presumed disability)	Mental disorder or learning disability, where linked to commission of the offence
	Excessive self defence
Other aggravating factors:	
A significant degree of premeditation	
Use of weapon or weapon equivalent (for example, shod foot, headbutting, use of acid, use of animal)	
Intention to commit more serious harm than actually resulted from the offence	
Deliberately causes more harm than is necessary for commission of offence	
Deliberate targeting of vulnerable victim	
Leading role in group or gang	
Offence motivated by, or demonstrating, hostility based on the victim's age, sex, gender identity (or presumed gender identity)	

STEP TWO Starting Point and Category Range
Having determined the category, the court should use the corresponding starting points to reach a sentence within the category range below. The starting point applies to all offenders irrespective of plea or previous convictions. A case of particular gravity, reflected by multiple features of culpability in step one, could merit upward adjustment from the starting point before further adjustment for aggravating or mitigating features, set out below.

Offence category	Starting Point _(Applicable to all offenders)_	Category Range _(Applicable to all offenders)_
Category 1	1 year 6 months custody	1–3 years custody
Category 2	26 weeks custody	Low level community order—51 weeks custody
Category 3	Medium level community order	Band A fine—High level community order

The table below contains a **non-exhaustive** list of additional factual elements providing the context of the offence and factors relating to the offender. Identify whether any combination of these, or other relevant factors, should result in an upward or downward adjustment from the starting point. In some cases, having considered these factors, it may be appropriate to move outside the identified category range.

When sentencing **category 2** offences, the court should also consider the custody threshold as follows:

- has the custody threshold been passed?
- if so, is it unavoidable that a custodial sentence be imposed?
- if so, can that sentence be suspended?

When sentencing **category 3** offences, the court should also consider the community order threshold as follows:

- has the community order threshold been passed?

Factors increasing seriousness	Factors reducing seriousness or reflecting personal mitigation
Statutory aggravating factors: Previous convictions, having regard to a) the nature of the offence to which the conviction relates and its relevance to the current offence; and b) the time that has elapsed since the conviction Offence committed whilst on bail _Other aggravating factors include:_ Location of the offence Timing of the offence Ongoing effect upon the victim Offence committed against those working in the public sector or providing a service to the public Presence of others including relatives, especially children or partner of the victim Gratuitous degradation of victim In domestic violence cases, victim forced to leave their home Failure to comply with current court orders Offence committed whilst on licence An attempt to conceal or dispose of evidence Failure to respond to warnings or concerns expressed by others about the offender's behaviour Commission of offence whilst under the influence of alcohol or drugs Abuse of power and/or position of trust Exploiting contact arrangements with a child to commit an offence Established evidence of community impact Any steps taken to prevent the victim reporting an incident, obtaining assistance and/or from assisting or supporting the prosecution Offences taken into consideration (TICs)	No previous convictions or no relevant/recent convictions Single blow Remorse Good character and/or exemplary conduct Determination and/or demonstration of steps taken to address addiction or offending behaviour Serious medical conditions requiring urgent, intensive or long-term treatment Isolated incident Age and/or lack of maturity where it affects the responsibility of the offender Lapse of time since the offence where this is not the fault of the offender Mental disorder or learning disability, where not linked to the commission of the offence Sole or primary carer for dependent relatives

Section 29 offences only: The court should determine the appropriate sentence for the offence without taking account of the element of aggravation and then make an addition to the sentence, considering the level of aggravation involved. It may be appropriate to move outside the identified category range, taking into account the increased statutory maximum.

[Steps Three to Nine are almost identical to those for inflicting grievous bodily harm: see **SG-146**.]

ASSAULT WITH INTENT TO RESIST ARREST

Offences against the Person Act 1861 (section 38)

This is a specified offence for the purposes of section 224 of the Criminal Justice Act 2003

Triable either way
Maximum 2 years custody

Offence range: Fine—51 weeks custody

STEP ONE Determining the offence category

The court should determine the offence category using the table below.

Category 1	Greater harm **and** higher culpability
Category 2	Greater harm **and** lower culpability; **or** lesser harm **and** higher culpability
Category 3	Lesser harm **and** lower culpability

The court should determine the offender's culpability and the harm caused, or intended, by reference **only** to the factors identified in the table below (as demonstrated by the presence of one or more). These factors comprise the principal factual elements of the offence and should determine the category.

Factors indicating greater harm Sustained or repeated assault on the same victim	**Factors indicating lesser harm** Injury which is less serious in the context of the offence
Factors indicating higher culpability *Statutory aggravating factors:* Offence racially or religiously aggravated Offence motivated by, or demonstrating, hostility to the victim based on his or her sexual orientation (or presumed sexual orientation) Offence motivated by, or demonstrating, hostility to the victim based on the victim's disability (or presumed disability) *Other aggravating factors:* A significant degree of premeditation Use of weapon or weapon equivalent (for example, shod foot, headbutting, use of acid, use of animal) Intention to commit more serious harm than actually resulted from the offence Deliberately causes more harm than is necessary for commission of offence Leading role in group or gang Offence motivated by, or demonstrating, hostility based on the victim's age, sex, gender identity (or presumed gender identity)	**Factors indicating lower culpability** Subordinate role in group or gang Lack of premeditation Mental disorder or learning disability, where linked to commission of the offence

STEP TWO Starting Point and Category Range

Having determined the category, the court should use the corresponding starting points to reach a sentence within the category range below. The starting point applies to all offenders irrespective of plea or previous convictions. A case of particular gravity, reflected by multiple features of culpability in step one, could merit upward adjustment from the starting point before further adjustment for aggravating or mitigating features, set out below.

Offence Category	Starting Point *(Applicable to all offenders)*	Category Range *(Applicable to all offenders)*
Category 1	26 weeks custody	12 weeks—51 weeks custody
Category 2	Medium level community order	Low level community order—High level community order
Category 3	Band B fine	Band A fine—Band C fine

The table below contains a **non-exhaustive** list of additional factual elements providing the context of the offence and factors relating to the offender. Identify whether any combination of these, or other relevant factors, should result in an upward or downward adjustment from the starting point. In some cases, having considered these factors, it may be appropriate to move outside the identified category range.

When sentencing **category 1** offences, the court should consider whether the sentence can be suspended.

Factors increasing seriousness	Factors reducing seriousness or reflecting personal mitigation
Statutory aggravating factors: Previous convictions, having regard to a) the nature of the offence to which the conviction relates and its relevance to the current offence; and b) the time that has elapsed since the conviction Offence committed whilst on bail *Other aggravating factors include:* Location of the offence Timing of the offence Ongoing effect upon the victim Gratuitous degradation of victim Failure to comply with current court orders Offence committed whilst on licence An attempt to conceal or dispose of evidence Failure to respond to warnings or concerns expressed by others about the offender's behaviour Commission of offence whilst under the influence of alcohol or drugs Established evidence of community impact Any steps taken to prevent the victim reporting an incident, obtaining assistance and/or from assisting or supporting the prosecution Offences taken into consideration (TICs)	No previous convictions **or** no relevant/recent convictions Single blow Remorse Good character and/or exemplary conduct Determination and/or demonstration of steps taken to address addiction or offending behaviour Serious medical conditions requiring urgent, intensive or long-term treatment Isolated incident Age and/or lack of maturity where it affects the responsibility of the offender Lapse of time since the offence where this is not the fault of the offender Mental disorder or learning disability, where **not** linked to the commission of the offence Sole or primary carer for dependent relatives

[Steps Three to Nine are almost identical to those for inflicting grievous bodily harm: see **SG-146**.]

Assault on a Police Constable in Execution of his Duty   SG-150
Police Act 1996 (section 89)

Triable only summarily
Maximum: 26 weeks custody

Offence range: Fine—26 weeks custody

STEP ONE   Determining the offence category
The court should determine the offence category using the table below.

Category 1	Greater harm **and** higher culpability
Category 2	Greater harm **and** lower culpability; **or** lesser harm **and** higher culpability
Category 3	Lesser harm **and** lower culpability

The court should determine the offender's culpability and the harm caused, or intended, by reference **only** to the factors below (as demonstrated by the presence of one or more). These factors comprise the principal factual elements of the offence and should determine the category.

Factors indicating greater harm	Factors indicating lesser harm
Sustained or repeated assault on the same victim	Injury which is less serious in the context of the offence

Factors indicating higher culpability	Factors indicating lower culpability
Statutory aggravating factors:	Subordinate role in group or gang
Offence racially or religiously aggravated	Lack of premeditation
Offence motivated by, or demonstrating, hostility to the victim based on his or her sexual orientation (or presumed sexual orientation)	Mental disorder or learning disability, where linked to commission of the offence
Offence motivated by, or demonstrating, hostility to the victim based on the victim's disability (or presumed disability)	
Other aggravating factors:	
A significant degree of premeditation	
Use of weapon or weapon equivalent (for example, shod foot, headbutting, use of acid, use of animal)	
Intention to commit more serious harm than actually resulted from the offence	
Deliberately causes more harm than is necessary for commission of offence	
Leading role in group or gang	
Offence motivated by, or demonstrating, hostility based on the victim's age, sex, gender identity (or presumed gender identity)	

STEP TWO Starting point and category range

Having determined the category, the court should use the corresponding starting points to reach a sentence within the category range below. The starting point applies to all offenders irrespective of plea or previous convictions. A case of particular gravity, reflected by multiple features of culpability in step one, could merit upward adjustment from the starting point before further adjustment for aggravating or mitigating features, set out below.

Offence Category	Starting Point *(Applicable to all offenders)*	Category Range *(Applicable to all offenders)*
Category 1	12 weeks custody	Low level community order—26 weeks custody
Category 2	Medium level community order	Low level community order—High level community order
Category 3	Band B fine	Band A fine—Band C fine

The table below contains a **non-exhaustive** list of additional factual elements providing the context of the offence and factors relating to the offender. Identify whether any combination of these, or other relevant factors, should result in an upward or downward adjustment from the starting point. In some cases, having considered these factors, it may be appropriate to move outside the identified category range.

When sentencing **category 1** offences, the court should also consider the custody threshold as follows:

- has the custody threshold been passed?
- if so, is it unavoidable that a custodial sentence be imposed?
- if so, can that sentence be suspended?

Factors increasing seriousness	Factors reducing seriousness or reflecting personal mitigation
Statutory aggravating factors: Previous convictions, having regard to a) the nature of the offence to which the conviction relates and its relevance to the current offence; and b) the time that has elapsed since the conviction Offence committed whilst on bail *Other aggravating factors include:* Location of the offence Timing of the offence Ongoing effect upon the victim Gratuitous degradation of victim Failure to comply with current court orders Offence committed whilst on licence An attempt to conceal or dispose of evidence Failure to respond to warnings or concerns expressed by others about the offender's behaviour Commission of offence whilst under the influence of alcohol or drugs Established evidence of community impact Any steps taken to prevent the victim reporting an incident, obtaining assistance and/or from assisting or supporting the prosecution Offences taken into consideration (TICs)	No previous convictions **or** no relevant/recent convictions Single blow Remorse Good character and/or exemplary conduct Determination and/or demonstration of steps taken to address addiction or offending behaviour Serious medical conditions requiring urgent, intensive or long-term treatment Isolated incident Age and/or lack of maturity where it affects the responsibility of the defendant Mental disorder or learning disability, where **not** linked to the commission of the offence Sole or primary carer for dependent relatives

[Steps Three to Eight are almost identical to those for inflicting grievous bodily harm (see **SG-146**) but with the omission of Step Five (Dangerousness).]

Common Assault

Criminal Justice Act 1988 (section 39)

Racially/Religiously Aggravated Common Assault

Crime and Disorder Act 1998 (section 29)

SG-151

Racially/religiously aggravated assault is a specified offence for the purposes of section 224 of the Criminal Justice Act 2003

Triable only summarily
Maximum (section 39): 26 weeks custody

Triable either way
Maximum (section 29): 2 years custody

Offence range: Discharge—26 weeks custody

STEP ONE Determining the Offence Category

The court should determine the offence category using the table below.

Category 1	Greater harm (injury or fear of injury must normally be present) **and** higher culpability
Category 2	Greater harm (injury or fear of injury must normally be present) **and** lower culpability; **or** lesser harm and higher culpability
Category 3	Lesser harm **and** lower culpability

The court should determine the offender's culpability and the harm caused, or intended, by reference **only** to the factors below (as demonstrated by the presence of one or more). These factors comprise the principal factual elements of the offence and should determine the category.

Factors indicating greater harm	Factors indicating lesser harm
Injury or fear of injury which is serious in the context of the offence (must normally be present) Victim is particularly vulnerable because of personal circumstances Sustained or repeated assault on the same victim	Injury which is less serious in the context of the offence
Factors indicating higher culpability *Statutory aggravating factors:* Offence motivated by, or demonstrating, hostility to the victim based on his or her sexual orientation (or presumed sexual orientation) Offence motivated by, or demonstrating, hostility to the victim based on the victim's disability (or presumed disability) *Other aggravating factors:* A significant degree of premeditation Threatened or actual use of weapon or weapon equivalent (for example, shod foot, headbutting, use of acid, use of animal) Intention to commit more serious harm than actually resulted from the offence Deliberately causes more harm than is necessary for commission of offence Deliberate targeting of vulnerable victim Leading role in group or gang Offence motivated by, or demonstrating, hostility based on the victim's age, sex, gender identity (or presumed gender identity)	**Factors indicating lower culpability** Subordinate role in group or gang A greater degree of provocation than normally expected Lack of premeditation Mental disorder or learning disability, where linked to commission of the offence Excessive self defence

STEP TWO   Starting point and category range

Having determined the category, the court should use the corresponding starting points to reach a sentence within the category range below. The starting point applies to all offenders irrespective of plea or previous convictions. A case of particular gravity, reflected by multiple features of culpability in step one, could merit upward adjustment from the starting point before further adjustment for aggravating or mitigating features, set out below.

Offence Category	Starting Point (*Applicable to all offenders*)	Category Range (*Applicable to all offenders*)
Category 1	High level community order	Low level community order—26 weeks custody
Category 2	Medium level community order	Band A fine—High level community order
Category 3	Band A fine	Discharge—Band C fine

The table below contains a **non-exhaustive** list of additional factual elements providing the context of the offence and factors relating to the offender. Identify whether any combination of these, or other relevant factors, should result in an upward or downward adjustment from the starting point. In some cases, having considered these factors, it may be appropriate to move outside the identified category range.

When sentencing **category 1** offences, the court should also consider the custody threshold as follows:

- has the custody threshold been passed?
- if so, is it unavoidable that a custodial sentence be imposed?
- if so, can that sentence be suspended?

When sentencing **category 2** offences, the court should also consider the community order threshold as follows:

- has the community order threshold been passed?

Factors increasing seriousness	Factors reducing seriousness or reflecting personal mitigation
Statutory aggravating factors: Previous convictions, having regard to a) the nature of the offence to which the conviction relates and its relevance to the current offence; and b) the time that has elapsed since the conviction	No previous convictions **or** no relevant/recent convictions Single blow Remorse
Offence committed whilst on bail	Good character and/or exemplary conduct Determination and/or demonstration of steps taken to address addiction or offending behaviour
Other aggravating factors include: Location of the offence Timing of the offence Ongoing effect upon the victim Offence committed against those working in the public sector or providing a service to the public Presence of others including relatives, especially children or partner of the victim Gratuitous degradation of victim In domestic violence cases, victim forced to leave their home Failure to comply with current court orders Offence committed whilst on licence An attempt to conceal or dispose of evidence Failure to respond to warnings or concerns expressed by others about the offender's behaviour Commission of offence whilst under the influence of alcohol or drugs Abuse of power and/or position of trust Exploiting contact arrangements with a child to commit an offence Established evidence of community impact Any steps taken to prevent the victim reporting an incident, obtaining assistance and/or from assisting or supporting the prosecution Offences taken into consideration (TICs)	Serious medical conditions requiring urgent, intensive or long-term treatment Isolated incident Age and/or lack of maturity where it affects the responsibility of the offender Lapse of time since the offence where this is not the fault of the offender Mental disorder or learning disability, where **not** linked to the commission of the offence Sole or primary carer for dependent relatives

Section 29 offences only: The court should determine the appropriate sentence for the offence without taking account of the element of aggravation and then make an addition to the sentence, considering the level of aggravation involved. It may be appropriate to move outside the identified category range, taking into account the increased statutory maximum.

[Steps Three to Nine are almost identical to those for inflicting grievous bodily harm: see **SG-146**.]

ANNEX: FINE BANDS AND COMMUNITY ORDERS

[The tables set out here are also set out in the Magistrates' Court Sentencing Guidelines, which includes further guidance on fines and community orders: see **SG-306** and **SG-330**.]

SG-153 PART 11 OVERARCHING PRINCIPLES: ASSAULTS ON CHILDREN AND CRUELTY TO A CHILD

FOREWORD

…This guideline applies to the sentencing of offenders on or after 3 March 2008.

In a separate guideline the Council has set out the principles and guidance relevant to the sentencing of assault offences ranging from common assault at the lowest end of the seriousness scale, up to wounding or causing grievous bodily harm with intent.

This guideline details additional relevant principles for sentencing where the assault was on a child.

In addition, this guideline defines sentencing principles, starting points and ranges for the offence of cruelty to a child which may involve a variety of types of conduct and stem from a pattern of offending behaviour against a child rather than an isolated assault.…

SG-154 **Introduction and structure of the guideline**[101]

1. The Council has produced a separate guideline covering offences of assault which do not result in the death of the victim, ranging in seriousness from common assault to wounding or causing grievous bodily harm with intent. Those offences involve the infliction of permanent or temporary harm on a victim by direct action, or an intention to cause harm to a victim even if harm does not in fact result.

2. That guideline applies only to the sentencing of offenders aged 18 and older convicted of assault, primarily where the victim of the assault is aged 16 or over. It covers:
   - assessing the culpability of the offender and the harm caused;
   - relevant aggravating and mitigating factors;
   - use of a weapon and particular parts of the body;
   - aggravated assaults;
   - provocation as mitigation;
   - compensating victims, and
   - ancillary orders.

3. In **Part 1** of this guideline additional principles are set out which should be considered when the victim of an assault is a child (aged 15 years and under).

4. **Part 2** provides guidance in relation to the offence of cruelty to a child[102] which has a wide-ranging definition that can include assault but also other forms of conduct likely to cause a child under 16 years of age unnecessary suffering or injury to health.

Part 1: Assaults on children: General principles

SG-155 **A. Assessing seriousness**

5. The primary factor in considering sentence is the seriousness of the offence committed; that is determined by assessing the culpability of the offender and the harm caused, intended or reasonably foreseeable.[103] A community sentence can be imposed only if the court considers that the offence is serious enough to justify it[104] and a custodial sentence can be imposed only if the court considers that a community sentence or a fine alone cannot be justified in view of the seriousness of the offence.[105] The Council has published a definitive guideline that guides sentencers determining whether the respective thresholds have been crossed.[106]

6. In considering the seriousness of an offence committed by an offender who has one or more previous convictions, the court must consider whether it should treat any of them as an aggravating factor hav-

---

[101] Assault and other offences against the person; www.sentencing-guidelines.gov.uk
[102] Children and Young Persons Act 1933, s.1(1)
[103] Criminal Justice Act 2003, s.152(2)
[104] ibid, s.148(1)
[105] ibid, s.152(2)
[106] *Overarching Principles: Seriousness* published on 16 December 2004; www.sentencing-guidelines.gov.uk

ing regard to the nature of the offence to which each conviction relates and its relevance to the current offence, and the time that has elapsed since the conviction.[107]

7. When dealing with cases involving assaults committed by adults against children, many of which involved some of the aggravating factors described below, the Court of Appeal has given a consistent message that an assault against a child will normally merit a custodial sentence. The Council's view is that such a presumption will not always be appropriate, but in all cases, the fact that the victim is a child is likely to aggravate the seriousness of the offence where the offender is an adult.

(i) Aggravation

8. The fact that the victim of an assault is a child will often mean that the offence involves a particularly vulnerable victim.

9. For all offences of assault, where the offence has been committed by an adult offender and the victim is a child under 16 years, the most relevant aggravating factors, as listed in the Council guideline *Overarching Principles: Seriousness*, are likely to be those set out below. Many of those are most likely to be present where the defendant has caring responsibilities for the child:

- victim is particularly vulnerable;
- abuse of power;
- abuse of position of trust;
- an especially serious physical or psychological effect on the victim, even if unintended;
- presence of others e.g. relatives, especially other children;
- additional degradation of the victim.

Additional aggravating factors are:

- sadistic behaviour;
- threats to prevent the victim reporting the offence;
- deliberate concealment of the victim from the authorities; and
- failure to seek medical help.

10. Many offences committed by adults against children will involve an abuse of power and many also will include an abuse of a position of trust. The Education Act 1996 abolished the right of teachers and other school staff to administer corporal punishment.[108]

11. The location of the offence, for example the fact that an offence takes place in the child's home, and the particular circumstances, such as the fact that the victim is isolated—common aggravating factors in cases of child cruelty—may also be present in relation to individual offences of assault against children.

(ii) Mitigation

12. An offender might seek to argue that any harm caused to the child amounted to lawful chastisement and a court might form the view that the offender held a genuine belief that his or her actions amounted to no more than a legitimate form of physical punishment. The defence of lawful chastisement is available only in relation to a charge of common assault. Where that defence is not available, or, in relation to a charge of common assault, such a defence has failed, sentence for the offence would normally be approached in the same way as any other assault.

13. There will be circumstances where the defendant has been charged with an assault occasioning actual bodily harm and the court finds as fact that the defendant only intended to administer lawful chastisement to the child, and the injury that was inflicted was neither intended nor foreseen by the defendant.

14. Although the defendant would have intended nothing more than lawful chastisement (as currently allowed by the law), he or she would have no defence to such a charge because an assault occasioning actual bodily harm does not require the offender to intend or even foresee that his act will result in any physical harm; it is sufficient that it did. Such a finding of fact should result in a substantial reduction in sentence and should not normally result in a custodial sentence. Where not only was the injury neither intended nor foreseen, but was not even reasonably foreseeable, then a discharge might be appropriate.

B. Other factors relevant to sentencing

SG-156

(i) The adverse effect of the sentence on the victim

15. In many circumstances, an offence of assault on a child will cause the court to conclude that only a custodial sentence can be justified. Imposition of such a sentence will often protect a victim from

---

[107] Criminal Justice Act 2003, s.143(2)
[108] s. 548

further harm and anguish; some children will be less traumatised once they are no longer living with an abusive carer.

16. However, where imprisonment of the offender deprives a child victim of his or her sole or main carer (and may result in the child being taken into care), it may punish and re-victimise the child.

17. In view of the seriousness of the offence committed and the risk of further harm to the victim or other children, even though a child may be distressed by separation from a parent or carer, imposing a custodial sentence on the offender may be the only option. However, where sentencing options remain more open, the court should take into account the impact that a custodial sentence for the offender might have on the victim.

18. There will be cases where the child victim is the subject of concurrent care proceedings and, indeed, the child's future care arrangements may well have been determined by the time the offender is sentenced. Both the sentencing court and the Family Court need to be aware of the progress of any concurrent proceedings.

19. **In considering whether a custodial sentence is the most appropriate disposal for an offence of assault on a child the court should take into account any available information concerning the future care of the child.**

(ii) Offenders who have primary care responsibilities

20. The gender of an offender is irrelevant for sentencing purposes. The important factor for consideration is the offender's role as sole or primary carer of the victim or other children or dependants.

21. In cases where an immediate custodial sentence of less than 12 months is justified, it is possible that a suspended sentence order (where available) might be the most appropriate sentence. This could enable the offender, subject to the necessary risk assessment being made, to resume care for, or at least have regular contact with, the child and could also open up opportunities for imposing requirements to rehabilitate and support an offender in need. In practice, this principle is likely to benefit more women than men, firstly because women commit the larger proportion of offences and secondly because men are less likely to be the sole or primary carers of children but the principle is established on the grounds of carer status and not gender.

22. **Where the offender is the sole or primary carer of the victim or other dependants, this potentially should be taken into account for sentencing purposes, regardless of whether the offender is male or female. In such cases, an immediate custodial sentence may not be appropriate and, subject to a risk assessment, the offender may be able to resume care for or have contact with the victim.**

Part 2: Cruelty to a child

SG-157 A. **Statutory provision**

23. [Sets out the CYPA 1933, s. 1(1) (see **B2.130** in the main work).][109]

SG-158 B. **Forms of cruelty to a child**

24. As is clear from the definition, the offence covers a variety of types of conduct that can compendiously or separately amount to child cruelty. The four generally accepted categories are:
    (i)   assault and ill-treatment;
    (ii) failure to protect;
    (iii) neglect; and
    (iv) abandonment.

25. With regard to assaults, the CPS Charging Standard[110] suggests that an assault charged as child cruelty will differ in nature from that which is generally charged as an offence against the person and notes that 'the offence is particularly relevant in cases of cruelty over a period of time.' As such, it is more likely to apply to offences where there is evidence that a child was assaulted by someone with caring responsibility during a certain period but where there is no clear evidence of any particular incidents, the extent of those incidents or the specific time of the incidents.

26. Where a serious assault has been committed, the CPS Charging Standard advises that a charge of child cruelty will not be appropriate and that the most appropriate offence against the person should be charged in such circumstances.[111]

---

[109] In addition to the Children and Young Persons Act 1933 the UN Convention on the Rights of the Child may be particularly relevant when dealing with this offence. Article 19 obliges States Parties to take all appropriate legislative, administrative, social and educational measures to protect the child from all forms of physical or mental violence, injury or abuse, neglect or negligent treatment, maltreatment or exploitation, including sexual abuse, while in the care of parent(s), legal guardian(s) or any other person who has the care of the child.

[110] The Charging Standard on Offences Against the Person; www.cps.gov.uk

[111] *Child Cruelty: Charging Practice*; www.cps.gov.uk/legal/section7

27. For the purposes of the offence, 'neglect' can mean physical and/or emotional neglect.

C. Assessing seriousness

28. It is not appropriate to identify one category of child cruelty as being automatically more serious than another; there will be a multitude of scenarios, some of which will involve more than one type of cruelty, in which the seriousness of the types of cruelty judged one against another will vary markedly. A long period of neglect, for example, could, in some circumstances, be more harmful to a child than a short period of violence.

29. In order to assess properly the seriousness of an offence, the precise nature of the offence must be established before consideration is given to a range of contingent factors, including the defendants intent, the length of time over which the cruelty took place, and the degree of physical and psychological harm suffered by the victim.

(i) Culpability

30. Although the nature and degree of harm that was caused, was intended or was reasonably foreseeable will impact on the seriousness of an offence of child cruelty, the Council guideline[112] clearly establishes that culpability should be the initial factor in determining the seriousness of an offence. In child cruelty offences, where there is such a wide variation in the nature and degree of harm that can be caused to a victim, there will similarly be a considerable variation in levels of culpability.

31. Child cruelty may be the consequence of a wide range of factors including:
    - sadism
    - violence resulting from any number of causes
    - a reduced ability to protect a child in the face of aggression from an overbearing partner
    - indifference or apathy resulting from low intelligence or induced by alcohol or drug dependence
    - immaturity or social deprivation resulting in an inability to cope with the pressures of caring for children
    - psychiatric illness

32. In the short term, an offence might arise as the result of a momentary lack of control by an otherwise responsible and loving carer. The extent to which any of these factors might have contributed to the commission of an offence will be important in determining the culpability of the offender.

33. A court must strike a balance between the need to reflect the serious view which society takes of the ill-treatment of very young children and the need to protect those children, and also the pressures upon immature and inadequate parents attempting to cope with the problems of infancy.

34. The extent to which remorse should influence sentence will always have to be judged in the light of all the circumstances surrounding the case.

35. In view of the seriousness with which society as a whole regards child cruelty, the normal sentencing starting point for an offence of child cruelty should be a custodial sentence. The length of that sentence will be influenced, however, by the circumstances in which the offence took place.

(ii) Harm

36. In order to assist a court in assessing the exact nature and seriousness of an offence of child cruelty, the CPS Charging Standard[113] advises that 'it may be preferable to have two or more alternative allegations in order that conduct complained of is appropriately described' and this certainly seems to be of benefit to sentencers. Where an offender has been convicted of an offence of child cruelty and the indictment clearly states the nature of the offender's conduct—neglect for example—the sentencer can be clear about the nature of the conduct for which the offender is to be sentenced.

37. However, even if the nature of the offending behaviour can be identified, statute is silent as to the relative seriousness of the different types of child cruelty identified above, creating obvious difficulties for the sentencing court.

38. There is a significant distinction between cases of wilful ill-treatment which usually involve positive acts of abuse and physical violence, and cases of neglect which are typified by the absence of actions.

39. In some cases there will be physical injury, whether resulting directly from an assault or ill-treatment or resulting from a period of abandonment or neglect. In other cases the harm occasioned may be lack of proper care, attention or supervision or exposure to the risk of harm.

40. As to whether one form of cruelty is worse than another will depend not only on the degree to which the victim suffers as a result but also on the motivation and culpability of the offender, which can range from inadequate parenting skills and an inability to cope, or constantly prioritising the needs of the offender or the offender's partner over those of the child, through to purposeful, sadistic and systematic abuse.

---

[112] *Overarching Principles: Seriousness*, page 5, published on 16 December 2004; www.sentencing-guidelines.gov.uk
[113] The Charging Standard on Offences Against the Person; www.cps.gov.uk

(iii) Aggravating and mitigating factors

41. The *Seriousness* guideline[114] sets out aggravating and mitigating factors that are applicable to a wide range of cases. Not all will be relevant to the offence of cruelty to a child. Care needs to be taken to ensure that there is no double counting where an essential element of the offence charged might, in other circumstances, be an aggravating factor. The sentencing starting points for the offence of child cruelty have been calculated to reflect the inherent abuse of trust or power and these cannot be treated as aggravating factors.

42. The following additional factors will aggravate offences of child cruelty:
   - targeting one particular child from the family
   - sadistic behaviour
   - threats to prevent the victim from reporting the offence
   - deliberate concealment of the victim from the authorities
   - failure to seek medical help

43. The following additional factor will mitigate offences of child cruelty:
   - seeking medical help or bringing the situation to the notice of the authorities

SG-160   D. **Other factors relevant to sentencing**

(i) Long-term psychological harm

44. There is no immediately predictable link between a type of offending behaviour and the impact it may have on the victim, either in the immediate or long term. The innate resilience of children and the presence of protection from another adult or the wider environment are also important factors that will influence the impact of the offence upon the child.

45. However, victims of child cruelty will frequently suffer psychological as well as physical harm. The evidence of emotional and behavioural consequences of child abuse is frequently presented by the following characteristics:[115]
   - impaired capacity to enjoy life—abused children often appear sad, preoccupied and listless;
   - psychiatric or psychosomatic stress symptoms, for example, bed-wetting, tantrums, bizarre behaviour, eating problems etc;
   - low self-esteem—children who have been abused often think they must be worthless to deserve such treatment;
   - school learning problems, such as lack of concentration;
   - withdrawal—many abused children withdraw from relationships with other children and become isolated and depressed;
   - opposition/defiance—a generally negative, uncooperative attitude;
   - hyper-vigilance—typified in the 'frozen watchfulness' expression;
   - compulsivity—abused children sometimes compulsively carry out certain activities or rituals;
   - pseudo-mature behaviour—a false appearance of independence or being excessively 'good' all the time or offering indiscriminate affection to any adult who takes an interest.

46. Abuse can also be evidenced by 'learned behaviour aggression' and a tendency for a victim of child cruelty to inflict violence on others. Victims may also mature into adults with poor parenting skills who perpetrate similar acts of cruelty on their own children.

47. There is an established general principle that the sentence imposed for an offence can be based both on what is known about the harm caused to an individual victim and, in some cases, what is known about the harm caused to society as a whole.

48. Whilst objective evidence about the degree of physical harm should be available at the point of sentence, psychological harm, especially that which may or may not manifest itself in the future, will be extremely difficult, and often impossible, to assess at the point of sentence. Where there is objective expert evidence about the particularly severe psychological trauma suffered by an individual victim, which indicates a more than usually serious degree of harm, this would be captured by the generic aggravating factor in the Council guideline—*An especially serious physical or psychological effect on the victim, even if unintended.*[116]

49. **The sentencing starting points for the offence of child cruelty have been calculated to reflect the likelihood of psychological harm and this cannot be treated as aggravating factors. Where there is an especially serious physical or psychological effect on the victim, even if unintended, this should increase sentence.**

---

[114] *Overarching Principles: Seriousness*, paragraphs 1.20–1.27, published on 16 December 2004; www.sentencing-guidelines. gov.uk
[115] 'The Effects of Physical Abuse and Neglect' in Wendy Stanton Rogers et al ed, *Child Abuse and Neglect*, The Open University 1992 page 206, citing a study by Martin, H.P. and Beezley P., 'Behavioural observations of abused children', *Developmental Medicine and Child Neurology*, Vol 19 (1977), pages 373–87
[116] *Overarching Principles: Seriousness*, page 7, published on 16 December 2004; www.sentencing-guidelines.gov.uk

(ii) The adverse effect of the sentence on the victim

50. Imposing a custodial sentence for an offence of child cruelty is the most appropriate outcome in most cases in that it properly reflects society's view of the seriousness of this type of offending behaviour and protects victims from further harm and anguish. In addition, it is not unreasonable to suppose that some children will be less traumatised once they are no longer living with an abusive carer.

51. However, there is a counter argument that, as the imprisonment of the offender may deprive a child victim of his or her sole or main carer and may result in the child being taken into care, a custodial sentence effectively punishes and re-victimises the child and, it is argued, should only be considered in the most serious of cases.

52. In some cases, even though a child may be distressed by separation from a parent or carer, imposing a custodial sentence on the offender may be the only option in view of the seriousness of the offence committed and the risk of further harm to the victim or other children. However, where sentencing options remain open, the court should take into account the impact that a custodial sentence for the offender might have on the victim.

53. In many cases the child victim will be the subject of concurrent care proceedings and, indeed, the child's future care arrangements may well have been determined by the time the offender is sentenced. Both the sentencing court and the Family Court need to be aware of the progress of any concurrent proceedings.

54. **In considering whether a custodial sentence is the most appropriate disposal for an offence of child cruelty, the court should take into account any available information concerning the future care of the child.**

(iii) Offenders who have primary care responsibilities

55. The gender of an offender is irrelevant for sentencing purposes. The important factor for consideration is the offender's role as sole or primary carer of the victim or other children or dependants.

56. In cases where an immediate custodial sentence of less than 12 months is justified, it is possible that a suspended sentence order might be the most appropriate sentence. This could enable the offender, subject to the necessary risk assessment being made, to resume care for, or at least have regular contact with, the child and could also open up opportunities for imposing requirements to rehabilitate and support an offender in need. In practice, this principle is likely to benefit more women than men, firstly because women commit the larger proportion of offences and secondly because men are less likely to be the sole or primary carers of children but the principle is established on the grounds of carer status and not gender.

57. **Where the offender is the sole or primary carer of the victim or other dependants, this potentially should be taken into account for sentencing purposes, regardless of whether the offender is male or female. In such cases, an immediate custodial sentence may not be appropriate and, subject to a risk assessment, the offender may be able to resume care for or have contact with the victim.**

(iv) Personal mitigation

58. There may be other factors that impact on an offender's behaviour towards children in his or her care and should legitimately influence the nature and length of the sentence passed in child cruelty cases.

59. In relation to the offence of cruelty to a child, the most relevant areas of personal mitigation are likely to be:
  • Mental illness/depression
  • Inability to cope with the pressures of parenthood
  • Lack of support
  • Sleep deprivation
  • Offender dominated by an abusive or stronger partner
  • Extreme behavioural difficulties in the child, often coupled with a lack of support
  • Inability to secure assistance or support services in spite of every effort having been made by the offender

60. It must be noted, however, that some of the factors identified above, in particular sleep deprivation, lack of support and an inability to cope could be regarded as an inherent part of caring for children, especially when a child is very young. Thus, such factors could be put forward in mitigation by most carers charged with an offence of child cruelty. It follows that, before being accepted in mitigation, there must be evidence that these factors were present to a high degree and had an identifiable and significant impact on the offender's behaviour.

E. Starting points and sentencing ranges   **SG-161**

1. Typically, a guideline will apply to an offence that can be committed in a variety of circumstances with different levels of seriousness. It will apply to a first-time offender who has been convicted after

a trial. Within the guidelines, a first-time offender is a person who does not have a conviction which, by virtue of section 143(2) of the CJA 2003, must be treated as an aggravating factor.

2. As an aid to consistency of approach, the guidelines describe a number of types of activity which would fall within the broad definition of the offence. These are set out in a column headed 'Type/ nature of activity'.

3. The expected approach is for a court to identify the description that most nearly matches the particular facts of the offence for which sentence is being imposed. This will identify a starting point from which the sentencer can depart to reflect aggravating or mitigating factors affecting the seriousness of the offence (beyond those contained within the column describing the type or nature of offence activity) to reach a provisional sentence.

4. The *sentencing range* is the bracket into which the provisional sentence will normally fall after having regard to factors which aggravate or mitigate the seriousness of the offence. The particular circumstances may, however, make it appropriate that the provisional sentence falls outside the range.

5. Where the offender has previous convictions which aggravate the seriousness of the current offence, that may take the provisional sentence beyond the range given, particularly where there are significant other aggravating factors present.

6. Once the provisional sentence has been identified by reference to those factors affecting the seriousness of the offence, the court will take into account any relevant factors of personal mitigation, which may take the sentence outside the range indicated in the guideline.

7. Where there has been a guilty plea, any reduction attributable to that plea will be applied to the sentence at this stage. This reduction may take the sentence below the range provided.

8. A court must give its reasons for imposing a sentence of a different kind or outside the range provided in the guidelines.[117]

SG-162   The Decision Making Process

The process ... is intended to show that the sentencing approach for the offence of cruelty to a child is fluid and requires the structured exercise of discretion.

[Sets out the standard sequential decision making process: identify dangerous offenders, identify starting point, consider aggravating factors, consider mitigating factors, apply reduction for guilty plea, consider ancillary orders, review in light of the totality principle and give reasons.]

SG-163   F. Factors to take into consideration

1. Cruelty to a child is a specified offence for the purposes of section 224 of the Criminal Justice Act 2003 and sentencers should consider whether a sentence for public protection should be imposed. **The following guideline applies to offenders who have *not* been assessed as dangerous.**

2. The suggested starting points and sentencing ranges in the guideline are based upon a first-time adult offender convicted after a trial (see ... above).

3. The same starting point and sentencing range is proposed for offences which might fall into the four categories (assault; ill-treatment or neglect; and abandonment). These are designed to take into account the fact that the victim is particularly vulnerable, assuming an abuse of trust or power and the likelihood of psychological harm, and designed to reflect the seriousness with which society as a whole regards these offences, is proposed for an offence in each.

4. Only additional aggravating and mitigating factors specifically relevant to this offence are included in the guideline. When assessing the seriousness of any offence, the courts must always refer to the full list of aggravating and mitigating factors in the Council guideline on Seriousness.[118]

5. Where there is an especially serious physical or psychological effect on the victim, even if unintended, this should increase sentence.

6. In considering whether a custodial sentence is the most appropriate disposal for an offence of child cruelty, the court should take into account any available information concerning the future care of the child.

7. Where the offender is the sole or primary carer of the victim or other dependants, this potentially should be taken into account for sentencing purposes, regardless of whether the offender is male or female. In such cases, an immediate custodial sentence may not be appropriate.

8. Sentencers should take into account relevant matters of personal mitigation such as those suggested at paragraph 59 above.

---

[117] Criminal Justice Act 2003, s. 174(2)(a)
[118] *Overarching Principles: Seriousness*, published on 16 December 2004; www.sentencing-guidelines.gov.uk

Cruelty to a child   **SG-164**

Children and Young Persons Act 1933 (section 1(1))

THIS IS A SERIOUS OFFENCE FOR THE PURPOSES OF SECTION 224 CRIMINAL JUSTICE ACT 2003.

Maximum penalty: 10 years imprisonment

Nature of failure & harm	Starting point	Sentencing range
(i) Serious cruelty over a period of time. (ii) Serious long-term neglect. (iii) Failure to protect a child from either of the above.	6 years custody	5–9 years custody
(i) Series of assaults (the more serious the individual assaults and the longer the period over which they are perpetrated, the more serious the offence). (ii) Protracted neglect or ill-treatment (the longer the period of ill-treatment or neglect and the longer the period over which it takes place, the more serious the offence). (iii) Failure to protect a child from either of the above.	3 years custody	2–5 years custody
(i) Assault(s) resulting in injuries consistent with ABH. (ii) More than one incident of neglect or ill-treatment (but not amounting to long-term behaviour). (iii) Single incident of long-term abandonment OR regular incidents of short-term abandonment (the longer the period of long-term abandonment or the greater the number of incidents of short-term abandonment) the more serious the offence). (iv) Failure to protect a child from any of the above.	36 weeks custody	26 weeks–2 years custody
(i) Short-term neglect or ill-treatment. (ii) Single incident of short-term abandonment. (iii) Failure to protect a child from any of the above.	12 weeks custody	Community Order (LOW)—26 weeks custody

Additional aggravating factors	Additional mitigating factors
1. Targeting one particular child from the family. 2. Sadistic behaviour. 3. Threats to prevent the victim from reporting the offence. 4. Deliberate concealment of the victim from the authorities. 5. Failure to seek medical help.	1. Seeking medical help or bringing the situation to the notice of the authorities.

PART 12   MAGISTRATES' COURT SENTENCING GUIDELINES   **SG-165**

What's included in the Magistrates' Court Sentencing Guidelines

- Overarching guidelines issued by the Sentencing Council...
- Guidelines and guidance issued by the Sentencing Guidelines Council:
  - offence guidelines...
  - motoring offence guidelines... and
  - explanatory material...
- Offence specific guidelines issued by the Sentencing Council....
- In some instances, the guidelines previously issued by the Sentencing Guidelines Council and Court of Appeal have been necessarily summarised; the original guideline or Court of Appeal judgment should be consulted for comprehensive guidance.

Following these guidelines

When sentencing offences committed after 6 April 2010, every court is under a statutory obligation to follow any relevant Council guideline unless it would be contrary to the interests of justice to do so.[119] If a court imposes a sentence outside the range indicated in an offence specific guideline, it is obliged to state its reasons for doing so.[120]

When to use these guidelines

- These guidelines apply to sentencing in a magistrates' court whatever the composition of the court. They cover offences for which sentences are frequently imposed in a magistrates' court when dealing with adult offenders.
- They also apply to allocation (mode of trial) decisions. When dealing with an either way offence for which there is no plea or an indication of a not guilty plea, these guidelines will be relevant to the allocation decision and should be consulted at this stage.

In general, either way offences should be tried summarily unless it is likely that the court's sentencing powers will be insufficient and reference should be made to the definitive offence guidelines to assess the likely sentence. Reference should be made to the allocation guideline [at SG-508] which replaces the relevant sections of the Mode of Trial guidelines in Part V.51 of the *Consolidated Criminal Practice Direction*.

- These guidelines apply also to the Crown Court when dealing with appeals against sentences imposed in a magistrates' court and when sentencing for summary only offences.

...

SG-166   Uᴜsᴇʀ Gᴜɪᴅᴇ

[The User Guide briefly explains that the Magistrates' Court Sentencing Guidelines include two structures requiring different approaches by the user. Where offence guidelines (and motoring offence guidelines) were originally issued by the Sentencing Guidelines Council, one approach is to be followed; where offence guidelines have been issued by the Sentencing Council, another must be followed. The offence guidelines are set out below in accordance with the alphabetical order originally adopted on the issue of the Magistrates' Court Sentencing Guidelines, integrating guidelines from the Sentencing Council into that format. However, it should be noted that the guidelines for assault offences, burglary offences, most drugs offences, offences relating to dangerous dogs, sexual offences and environmental offences were issued by the Sentencing Council and are thus subject to the second approach mentioned above (see SG-173).]

[User Guide applicable where offence guidelines issued by the Sentencing Guidelines Council]

1. Assess offence seriousness (culpability and harm)

Offence seriousness is the starting point for sentencing under the Criminal Justice Act 2003. The court's assessment of offence seriousness will:

- determine which of the sentencing thresholds has been crossed;
- indicate whether a custodial, community or other sentence is the most appropriate;
- be the key factor in deciding the length of a custodial sentence, the onerousness of requirements to be incorporated in a community sentence and the amount of any fine

When considering the seriousness of any offence, the court must consider the offender's *culpability* in committing the offence and any *harm* which the offence caused, was intended to cause, or might forseeably have caused.[121] In using these guidelines, this assessment should be approached in two stages:

SG-167   **1. Offence seriousness (culpability and harm)**

A. Identify the appropriate starting point

The guidelines set out *examples* of the nature of activity which may constitute the offence, progressing from less to more serious conduct, and provide a *starting point* based on a *first time offender pleading not guilty*. The guidelines also specify a sentencing *range for* each example of activity. Refer [below] for further guidance on the meaning of the terms 'starting point', 'range' and 'first time offender'.

---

[119] Coroners and Justice Act 2009, s.125(1)
[120] Criminal Justice Act 2003, s.174(2)(a)
[121] Criminal Justice Act 2003, s.143(1)

Sentencers should begin by considering which of the examples of offence activity corresponds most closely to the circumstances of the particular case in order to identify the appropriate *starting point:*
- where the starting point is a fine, this is indicated as band A, B or C. The approach to assessing fines is set out [below];
- where the community sentence threshold is passed, the guideline sets out whether the starting point should be a low, medium or high level community order. Refer [below] for further guidance;
- where the starting point is a custodial sentence, refer [below] for further guidance.

The Council's definitive guideline *Overarching Principles: Seriousness*, published 16 December 2004 [see *SG-21*], identifies four levels of culpability for sentencing purposes (intention, recklessness, knowledge and negligence). The starting points in the individual offence guidelines assume that culpability is at the highest level applicable to the offence (often, but not always, intention). *Where a lower level of culpability is present, this should be taken into account.*

1. Offence seriousness (culpability and harm)

SG-168

B. Consider the effect of aggravating and mitigating factors

Once the starting point has been identified, the court can add to or reduce this to reflect any aggravating or mitigating factors that impact on the *culpability* of the offender and/or *harm* caused by the offence to reach a provisional sentence. Any factors contained in the description of the activity used to reach the starting point must not be counted again.

The *range* is the bracket into which the provisional sentence will normally fall after having regard to factors which aggravate or mitigate the seriousness of the offence.

However:
- the court is not precluded from going outside the range where the facts justify it;
- previous convictions which aggravate the seriousness of the current offence may take the provisional sentence beyond the range, especially where there are significant other aggravating factors present.

In addition, where an offender is being sentenced for multiple offences, the courts assessment of the totality of the offending may result in a sentence above the range indicated for the individual offences, including a sentence of a different type. Refer [below] for further guidance.

The guidelines identify aggravating and mitigating factors which may be particularly relevant to each individual offence. These include some factors drawn from the general list of aggravating and mitigating factors in the Council's definitive guideline *Overarching Principles: Seriousness*. In each case, sentencers should have regard to the full list, which includes the factors that, by statute, make an offence more serious:
- offence committed while on bail for other offences;
- offence was racially or religiously aggravated;
- offence was motivated by, or demonstrates, hostility based on the victim's sexual orientation (or presumed sexual orientation);
- offence was motivated by, or demonstrates, hostility based on the victim's disability (or presumed disability);
- offender has previous convictions that the court considers can reasonably be treated as aggravating factors having regard to their relevance to the current offence and the time that has elapsed since conviction.

While the lists...aim to identify the most common aggravating and mitigating factors, *they are not intended to be exhaustive*. Sentencers should always consider whether there are any other factors that make the offence more or less serious.

2. Form a preliminary view of the appropriate sentence, then consider offender mitigation

SG-169

When the court has reached a provisional sentence based on its assessment of offence seriousness, it should take into account matters of offender mitigation. The Council guideline *Overarching Principles: Seriousness* states that the issue of remorse should be taken into account at this point along with other mitigating features such as admissions to the police in interview.

3. Consider a reduction for a guilty plea

SG-170

The Council guideline *Reduction in Sentence for a Guilty Plea* [set out in full in **part 1**] states that the *punitive* elements of the sentence should be reduced to recognise an offender's guilty plea. The reduction has no impact on sentencing decisions in relation to ancillary orders, including disqualification.

The level of the reduction should reflect the stage at which the offender indicated a willingness to admit guilt and will be gauged on a sliding scale, ranging from a *recommended* one third (where the guilty plea was entered at the first reasonable opportunity), reducing to a *recommended* one quarter (where a trial date has been set) and to a *recommended* one tenth (for a guilty plea entered at the 'door of the court' or after the trial has begun). There is a presumption that the recommended reduction will be given unless there are good reasons for a lower amount.

The application of the reduction may affect the type, as well as the severity, of the sentence. It may also take the sentence below the *range* in some cases.

The court must state that it has reduced a sentence to reflect a guilty plea.[122] It should usually indicate what the sentence would have been if there had been no reduction as a result of the plea.

SG-171   **4. Consider ancillary orders, including compensation**

Ancillary orders of particular relevance to individual offences are identified in the relevant guidelines.

The court must *always* consider making a compensation order where the offending has resulted in personal injury, loss or damage.[123] The court is required to give reasons if it decides not to make such an order.[124]

SG-172   **5. Decide sentence: Give reasons**

Sentencers must state reasons for the sentence passed in every case, including for any ancillary orders imposed.[125] It is particularly important to identify any aggravating or mitigating factors, or matters of offender mitigation, that have resulted in a sentence more or less severe than the suggested starting point.

If a court imposes a sentence of a different kind or outside the *range* indicated in the guidelines, *it must state its reasons for doing so*.[126]

The court should also give its reasons for not making an order that has been canvassed before it or that it might have been expected to make.

SG-173   **[User Guide applicable where offence guidelines issued by the Sentencing Council]**

Step One: Determining the offence category

The decision making process includes a two step approach to assessing seriousness. The first step is to determine the offence category by means of an assessment of the offender's culpability and the harm caused, or intended, by reference *only* to the factors set out at step one in each guideline. The contents are tailored for each offence and comprise the principal factual elements of the offence.

Step Two: Starting point and category range

The guidelines provide a *starting point* which applies to all offenders irrespective of plea or previous convictions. The guidelines also specify a *category range* for each offence category.

The guidelines provide non-exhaustive lists of aggravating and mitigating factors relating to the context of the offence and to the offender. Sentencers should identify whether any combination of these, or other relevant factors, should result in an upward or downward adjustment from the starting point.

In some cases, it may be appropriate to move outside the identified category range when reaching a provisional sentence.

Further Steps

Having reached a provisional sentence, there are a number of further steps within the guidelines. These steps are clearly set out within each guideline and are tailored specifically for each offence in order to ensure that only the most appropriate guidance is included within each offence specific guideline.

The further steps include:

- reduction for assistance to the prosecution;
- reduction for guilty pleas (courts should refer to the *Guilty Plea* guideline [at **SG-1**]);
- where an offender is being sentenced for multiple offences — the court's assessment of the totality of the offending may result in a sentence above the range indicated for the individual offences,

---

[122] Criminal Justice Act 2003, s.174(2)(d)
[123] Powers of Criminal Courts (Sentencing) Act 2000, s.130(1)
[124] ibid s.130(3)
[125] Criminal Justice Act 2003, s.174(1)
[126] ibid s.174(2)(a)

including a sentence of a different type (refer to [the Totality Guideline at **SG-496**] for further
guidance);
- compensation orders and/or ancillary orders appropriate to the case; and
- reasons for, and explain the effect of, the sentence.

Allocation Guideline   **SG-174**
[Not reproduced here: see **SG-508**.]

Offences Taken into Consideration Guideline   **SG-175**
[Not reproduced here: see **SG-490**.]

Totality Guideline   **SG-176**
[Not reproduced here: see **SG-496**.]

OFFENCES   **SG-177**

ALCOHOL SALE OFFENCES

*Licensing Act 2003, s. 141 (sale of alcohol to drunk person); s. 146 (sale of alcohol to children); s. 147
(allowing sale of alcohol to children)*

Triable only summarily:

Examples of nature of activity	Starting point	Range
Sale to a child (i.e. person under 18)/to a drunk person	Band B fine	Band A fine to band C fine

Maximum: Level 3 fine (s.141); Level 5 fine (ss.146 and 147)

Offence seriousness (culpability and harm)

A. Identify the appropriate starting point
Starting points based on first time offender pleading not guilty

Note: refer to [below] for approach to fines for offences committed for commercial purposes

B. Consider the effect of aggravating and mitigating factors (other than those within examples above)

Common aggravating and mitigating factors are identified [elsewhere]—the following may be particularly
relevant but these lists are not exhaustive

Factors indicating higher culpability	Factors indicating greater degree of harm
1. No attempt made to establish age 2. Spirits/high alcohol level of drink 3. Drunk person highly intoxicated 4. Large quantity of alcohol supplied 5. Sale intended for consumption by group of children/drunk people 6. Offender in senior or management position	1. Younger child/children 2. Drunk person causing distress to others 3. Drunk person aggressive

[Sets out the standard sequential sentencing procedure but specifies the need to consider the forfeiture or
suspension of a personal liquor licence.]

Note: Section 23 of the Violent Crime Reduction Act 2006 created a new offence of persistently selling
alcohol to children, which came into force on 6 April 2007. This is committed if, on three or more different
occasions within a period of three consecutive months, alcohol is unlawfully sold on the same
premises to a person under 18. The offence is summary only and the maximum penalty is a £10,000 fine.
*Consult your legal adviser for guidance on the approach to sentencing and the court's powers in relation to
liquor licences.*

SG-178

Alcohol/Tobacco, Fraudulently Evade Duty
Customs and Excise Management Act 1979, s. 170

Triable either way:
Maximum when tried summarily: Level 5 fine or three times the value of the goods (whichever is greater) and/or 6 months
Maximum when tried on indictment: 7 years

Refer to guideline *Fraud—banking and insurance fraud and obtaining credit through fraud, benefit fraud and revenue fraud* [see **SG-230** *et seq.*].

SG-179

Animal Cruelty
Animal Welfare Act 2006, s. 4 (unnecessary suffering); s. 8 (fighting etc.); s. 9 (breach of duty of person responsible for animal to ensure welfare)

Triable only summarily:
Maximum: £20,000 fine and/or 6 months (ss. 4 and 8) Level 5 fine and/or 6 months (s. 9)

Offence seriousness (culpability and harm)

A. Identify the appropriate starting point

Starting points based on first time offender pleading not guilty

Examples of nature of activity	Starting point	Range
One impulsive act causing little or no injury; short term neglect	Band C fine	Band B fine to medium level community order
Several incidents of deliberate ill-treatment/frightening animal(s); medium term neglect	High level community order	Medium level community order to 12 weeks custody
Attempt to kill/torture; animal baiting/conducting or permitting cock-fighting etc.; prolonged neglect	18 weeks custody	12 to 26 weeks custody

Offence seriousness (culpability and harm)

B. Consider the effect of aggravating and mitigating factors (other than those within examples above)

Common aggravating and mitigating factors are identified [elsewhere]—the following may be particularly relevant but these lists are not exhaustive

Factors indicating higher culpability	Factors indicating greater degree of harm
1. Offender in position of special responsibility 2. Adult involves children in offending 3. Animal(s) kept for livelihood 4. Use of weapon 5. Offender ignored advice/warnings 6. Offence committed for commercial gain	1. Serious injury or death 2. Several animals affected **Factors indicating lower culpability** 1. Offender induced by others 2. Ignorance of appropriate care 3. Offender with limited capacity

[Sets out the standard sequential sentencing procedure but also mentions the need to consider disqualification from ownership of animal.]

SG-180

Anti-social Behaviour Order, Breach Of

Factors to take into consideration

This guideline and accompanying notes are taken from the Sentencing Guidelines Council's definitive guideline *Breach of an Anti-Social Behaviour Order*, published 9 December 2008 [see **SG-406**].

Key factors

(a) An ASBO may be breached in a very wide range of circumstances and may involve one or more terms not being complied with. The examples given below are intended to illustrate how the scale of the conduct that led to the breach, taken as a whole, might come within the three levels of seriousness:

- No harm caused or intended—in the absence of intimidation or the causing of fear of violence, breaches involving being drunk or begging may be at this level, as may prohibited use of public transport or entry into a prohibited area, where there is no evidence that harassment, alarm or distress was caused or intended.
- Lesser degree of harm intended or likely—examples may include lesser degrees of threats or intimidation, the use of seriously abusive language, or causing more than minor damage to property.
- Serious harm caused or intended—breach at this level of seriousness will involve the use of violence, significant threats or intimidation or the targeting of individuals or groups of people in a manner that leads to a fear of violence.

(b) The suggested starting points are based on the assumption that the offender had the highest level of culpability.

(c) In the most serious cases, involving repeat offending and a breach causing serious harassment together with the presence of several aggravating factors, such as the use of violence, a sentence beyond the highest range will be justified.

(d) When imposing a community order, the court must ensure that the requirements imposed are proportionate to the seriousness of the breach, compatible with each other, and also with the prohibitions of the ASBO if the latter is to remain in force. Even where the threshold for a custodial sentence is crossed, a custodial sentence is not inevitable.

(e) An offender may be sentenced for more than one offence of breach, which occurred on different days. While consecutive sentences may be imposed in such cases, the overall sentence should reflect the totality principle.

Crime and Disorder Act 1988, s.1(10)

Triable either way:
Maximum when tried summarily: Level 5 fine and/or 6 months
Maximum when tried on indictment: 5 years

Note: A conditional discharge is not available as a sentence for this offence

Offence seriousness (culpability and harm)

A. Identify the appropriate starting point

Starting points based on first time offender* pleading not guilty

Examples of nature of activity	Starting point	Range
Breach where no harassment, alarm or distress was caused or intended	Low level community order	Band B fine to medium level community order
Breach involving a lesser degree of actual or intended harassment, alarm or distress than in the box below, or where such harm would have been likely had the offender not been apprehended	6 weeks custody	Medium level community order to 26 weeks custody
Breach involving serious actual or intended harassment, alarm or distress	26 weeks custody	Custody threshold to Crown Court

* *For the purposes of this guideline a "first time offender" is one who does not have a previous conviction for breach of an ASBO*

Offence seriousness (culpability and harm)

B. Consider the effect of aggravating and mitigating factors (other than those within examples above)

Common aggravating and mitigating factors are identified [elsewhere]—the following may be particularly relevant but these lists are not exhaustive

Factors indicating higher culpability	Factors indicating lower culpability
1. Offender has a history of disobedience to court orders 2. Breach was committed immediately or shortly after the order was made 3. Breach was committed subsequent to earlier breach proceedings arising from the same order 4. Targeting of a person the order was made to protect or a witness in the original proceedings	1. Breach occurred after a long period of compliance 2. The prohibition(s) breached was not fully understood, especially where an interim order was made without notice

[Sets out the standard sequential sentencing procedure.]

SG-181

ARSON (CRIMINAL DAMAGE BY FIRE)
Criminal Damage Act 1971, s. 1

Triable either way:
Maximum when tried summarily: Level 5 fine and/or 6 months
Maximum when tried on indictment: Life

Where offence committed in domestic context, refer [below] for guidance.

Offence seriousness (culpability and harm)

A. Identify the appropriate starting point

Starting points based on first time offender pleading not guilty

Examples of nature of activity	Starting point	Range
Minor damage by fire	High level community order	Medium level community order to 12 weeks custody
Moderate damage by fire	12 weeks custody	6 to 26 weeks custody
Significant damage by fire	Crown Court	Crown Court

Offence seriousness (culpability and harm)

B. Consider the effect of aggravating and mitigating factors
(other than those within examples above)

Common aggravating and mitigating factors are identified [elsewhere]—the following may be particularly relevant but these lists are not exhaustive

Factors indicating higher culpability	Factor indicating lower culpability
1. Revenge attack **Factors indicating greater degree of harm** 1. Damage to emergency equipment 2. Damage to public amenity 3. Significant public or private fear caused e.g. in domestic context	1. Damage caused recklessly

[Sets out the standard sequential sentencing procedure.]

ASSAULT OCCASIONING ACTUAL BODILY HARM   **SG-182**
Offences against the Person Act 1861 (section 47)
RACIALLY/RELIGIOUSLY AGGRAVATED ABH
Crime and Disorder Act 1998 (section 29)

[This guideline was published by the Sentencing Council and has effect in respect of all sentences passed after 13 June 2011 on offenders aged 18 or older. It replaces the guideline which previously applied and which continued to have effect until that date.]

These are specified offences for the purposes of section 224 of the Criminal Justice Act 2003

Triable either way

Section 47
Maximum when tried summarily: Level 5 fine and/or 26 weeks custody
Maximum when tried on indictment: 5 years custody

Section 29
Maximum when tried summarily: Level 5 fine and/or 26 weeks custody
Maximum when tried on indictment: 7 years custody

Offence range: Fine—3 years custody

This guideline applies to all offenders aged 18 and older, who are sentenced on or after 13 June 2011. The definitions [at **SG-297**] of 'starting point' and 'first time offender' do not apply for this guideline. Starting point and category ranges apply to all offenders in all cases, irrespective of plea or previous convictions.

STEP ONE Determining the offence category
The court should determine the offence category using the table below.

Category 1	Greater harm (serious injury must normally be present) **and** higher culpability
Category 2	Greater harm (serious injury must normally be present) **and** lower culpability; **or** lesser harm and higher culpability
Category 3	Lesser harm and lower culpability

The court should determine the offender's culpability and the harm caused, or intended, by reference only to the factors identified in the table below (as demonstrated by the presence of one or more). These factors comprise the principal factual elements of the offence and should determine the category.

Factors indicating greater harm Injury (which includes disease transmission and/or psychological harm) which is serious in the context of the offence (must normally be present) Victim is particularly vulnerable because of personal circumstances Sustained or repeated assault on the same victim	**Factors indicating lesser harm** Injury which is less serious in the context of the offence
Factors indicating higher culpability *Statutory aggravating factors:* Offence motivated by, or demonstrating, hostility to the victim based on his or her sexual orientation (or presumed sexual orientation) Offence motivated by, or demonstrating, hostility to the victim based on the victim's disability (or presumed disability) *Other aggravating factors:* A significant degree of premeditation Use of weapon or weapon equivalent (for example, shod foot, headbutting, use of acid, use of animal) Intention to commit more serious harm than actually resulted from the offence Deliberately causes more harm than is necessary for commission of offence Deliberate targeting of vulnerable victim Leading role in group or gang Offence motivated by, or demonstrating, hostility based on the victim's age, sex, gender identity (or presumed gender identity)	**Factors indicating lower culpability** Subordinate role in group or gang A greater degree of provocation than normally expected Lack of premeditation Mental disorder or learning disability, where linked to commission of the offence Excessive self defence

STEP TWO Starting point and category range

Having determined the category, the court should use the corresponding starting points to reach a sentence within the category range below. The starting point applies to all offenders irrespective of plea or previous convictions. A case of particular gravity, reflected by multiple features of culpability in step one, could merit upward adjustment from the starting point before further adjustment for aggravating or mitigating features, set out below.

Offence Category	Starting Point *(Applicable to all offenders)*	Category Range *(Applicable to all offenders)*
Category 1	Crown Court	Crown Court
Category 2	26 weeks custody	Low level community order – Crown Court (51 weeks custody)
Category 3	Medium level community order	Band A fine—High level community order

The table below contains a **non-exhaustive** list of additional factual elements providing the context of the offence and factors relating to the offender. Identify whether any combination of these, or other relevant factors, should result in an upward or downward adjustment from the starting point. In some cases, having considered these factors, it may be appropriate to move outside the identified category range.

When sentencing **category 2** offences, the court should also consider the custody threshold as follows:

- has the custody threshold been passed?
- if so, is it unavoidable that a custodial sentence be imposed?
- if so, can that sentence be suspended?

When sentencing **category 3** offences, the court should also consider the community order threshold as follows:

- has the community order threshold been passed?

Factors increasing seriousness	Factors reducing seriousness or reflecting personal mitigation
Statutory aggravating factors: Previous convictions, having regard to a) the nature of the offence to which the conviction relates and its relevance to the current offence; and b) the time that has elapsed since the conviction	No previous convictions **or** no relevant/recent convictions Single blow Remorse
Offence committed whilst on bail	Good character and/or exemplary conduct
Other aggravating factors include: Location of the offence	Determination and/or demonstration of steps taken to address addiction or offending behaviour
Timing of the offence	Serious medical conditions requiring urgent, intensive or long-term treatment
Ongoing effect upon the victim	Isolated incident
Offence committed against those working in the public sector or providing a service to the public	Age and/or lack of maturity where it affects the responsibility of the offender
Presence of others including relatives, especially children or partner of the victim	Lapse of time since the offence where this is not the fault of the offender
Gratuitous degradation of victim	Mental disorder or learning disability, where **not** linked to the commission of the offence
In domestic violence cases, victim forced to leave their home	Sole or primary carer for dependent relatives
Failure to comply with current court orders	
Offence committed whilst on licence	
An attempt to conceal or dispose of evidence	
Failure to respond to warnings or concerns expressed by others about the offender's behaviour	
Commission of offence whilst under the influence of alcohol or drugs	
Abuse of power and/or position of trust	
Exploiting contact arrangements with a child to commit an offence	
Established evidence of community impact	
Any steps taken to prevent the victim reporting an incident, obtaining assistance and/or from assisting or supporting the prosecution	
Offences taken into consideration (TICs)	

Section 29 offences only: The court should determine the appropriate sentence for the offence without taking account of the element of aggravation and then make an addition to the sentence, considering the level of aggravation involved. It may be appropriate to move outside the identified category range, taking into account the increased statutory maximum.

STEP THREE Consider any other factors which indicate a reduction, such as assistance to the prosecution

The court should take into account any rule of law by virtue of which an offender may receive a discounted sentence in consequence of assistance given (or offered) to the prosecutor or investigator.

STEP FOUR Reduction for guilty pleas

The court should take account of any potential reduction for a guilty plea in accordance with section 144 of the Criminal Justice Act 2003 and the Guilty Plea guideline.

STEP FIVE Dangerousness

Inflicting grievous bodily harm/Unlawful wounding and racially/religiously aggravated GBH/Unlawful wounding are specified offences within the meaning of Chapter 5 of the Criminal Justice Act 2003 and at this stage the court should consider whether having regard to the criteria contained in that Chapter it would be appropriate to award an extended sentence.

STEP SIX Totality principle

If sentencing an offender for more than one offence, or where the offender is already serving a sentence, consider whether the total sentence is just and proportionate to the offending behaviour.

STEP SEVEN Compensation and ancillary orders

In all cases, the court should consider whether to make compensation and/or other ancillary orders.

STEP EIGHT Reasons

Section 174 of the Criminal Justice Act 2003 imposes a duty to give reasons for, and explain the effect of, the sentence.

STEP NINE Consideration for remand time

Sentencers should take into consideration any remand time served in relation to the final sentence. The court should consider whether to give credit for time spent on remand in custody or on bail in accordance with sections 240 and 240A of the Criminal Justice Act 2003.

ASSAULT WITH INTENT TO RESIST ARREST   SG-183

Offences against the Person Act 1861 (section 38)

[This guideline was published by the Sentencing Council and has effect in respect of all sentences passed after 13 June 2011 on offenders aged 18 or older. It replaces the guideline which previously applied and which continued to have effect until that date.]

This is a specified offence for the purposes of section 224 of the Criminal Justice Act 2003

Triable either way
Maximum when tried summarily: Level 5 fine and/or 26 weeks custody
Maximum when tried on indictment: 2 years custody

Offence range: Fine—51 weeks custody

This guideline applies to all offenders aged 18 and older, who are sentenced on or after 13 June 2011. The definitions [at **SG-297**] of 'starting point' and 'first time offender' do not apply for this guideline. Starting point and category ranges apply to all offenders in all cases, irrespective of plea or previous convictions.

STEP ONE Determining the offence category

The court should determine the offence category using the table below.

Category 1	Greater harm **and** higher culpability
Category 2	Greater harm **and** lower culpability; or lesser harm **and** higher culpability
Category 3	Lesser harm **and** lower culpability

The court should determine the offender's culpability and the harm caused, or intended, by reference only to the factors identified in the table below (as demonstrated by the presence of one or more). These factors comprise the principal factual elements of the offence and should determine the category.

Factors indicating greater harm Sustained or repeated assault on the same victim	**Factors indicating lesser harm** Injury which is less serious in the context of the offence
Factors indicating higher culpability *Statutory aggravating factors:* Offence racially or religiously aggravated Offence motivated by, or demonstrating, hostility to the victim based on his or her sexual orientation(or presumed sexual orientation) Offence motivated by, or demonstrating, hostility to the victim based on the victim's disability (or presumed disability) *Other aggravating factors:* A significant degree of premeditation Use of weapon or weapon equivalent (for example, shod foot, headbutting, use of acid, use of animal) Intention to commit more serious harm than actually resulted from the offence Deliberately causes more harm than is necessary for commission of offence Leading role in group or gang Offence motivated by, or demonstrating, hostility based on the victim's age, sex, gender identity (or presumed gender identity)	**Factors indicating lower culpability** Subordinate role in group or gang Lack of premeditation Mental disorder or learning disability, where linked to commission of the offence

STEP TWO Starting point and category range

Having determined the category, the court should use the corresponding starting points to reach a sentence within the category range below. The starting point applies to all offenders irrespective of plea or previous convictions. A case of particular gravity, reflected by multiple features of culpability in step one, could merit upward adjustment from the starting point before further adjustment for aggravating or mitigating features, set out below.

Offence Category	Starting Point *(Applicable to all offenders)*	Category Range *(Applicable to all offenders)*
Category 1	26 weeks custody	12 weeks custody—Crown Court (51 weeks custody)
Category 2	Medium level community order	Low level community order—High level community order
Category 3	Band B fine	Band A fine—Band C fine

The table below contains a **non-exhaustive** list of additional factual elements providing the context of the offence and factors relating to the offender. Identify whether any combination of these, or other relevant factors, should result in an upward or downward adjustment from the starting point. In some cases, having considered these factors, it may be appropriate to move outside the identified category range.

When sentencing **category 1** offences, the court should consider whether the sentence can be suspended.

Factors increasing seriousness	Factors reducing seriousness or reflecting personal mitigation
Statutory aggravating factors: Previous convictions, having regard to a) the nature of the offence to which the conviction relates and its relevance to the current offence; and b) the time that has elapsed since the conviction Offence committed whilst on bail *Other aggravating factors include:* Location of the offence Timing of the offence Ongoing effect upon the victim Gratuitous degradation of victim Failure to comply with current court orders Offence committed whilst on licence An attempt to conceal or dispose of evidence Failure to respond to warnings or concerns expressed by others about the offender's behaviour Commission of offence whilst under the influence of alcohol or drugs Established evidence of community impact Any steps taken to prevent the victim reporting an incident, obtaining assistance and/or from assisting or supporting the prosecution Offences taken into consideration (TICs)	No previous convictions or no relevant/recent convictions Single blow Remorse Good character and/or exemplary conduct Determination and/or demonstration of steps taken to address addiction or offending behaviour Serious medical conditions requiring urgent, intensive or long-term treatment Isolated incident Age and/or lack of maturity where it affects the responsibility of the defendant Mental disorder or learning disability, where not linked to the commission of the offence Sole or primary carer for dependent relatives

[Steps Three to Nine are almost identical to those which apply to assault occasioning actual bodily harm: see **SG-182**.]

ASSAULT ON A POLICE CONSTABLE IN EXECUTION OF HIS DUTY   **SG-184**
Police Act 1996 (section 89)

[This guideline was published by the Sentencing Council and has effect in respect of all sentences passed after 13 June 2011 on offenders aged 18 or older. It replaces the guideline which previously applied and which continued to have effect until that date.]

Triable only summarily
Maximum: Level 5 fine and/or 26 weeks custody

Offence range: Fine—26 weeks custody

This guideline applies to all offenders aged 18 and older, who are sentenced on or after 13 June 2011. The definitions [at **SG-297**] of 'starting point' and 'first time offender' do not apply for this guideline. Starting point and category ranges apply to all offenders in all cases, irrespective of plea or previous convictions.

STEP ONE   Determining the offence category

The court should determine the offence category using the table below.

Category 1	Greater harm **and** higher culpability
Category 2	Greater harm **and** lower culpability; or lesser harm **and** higher culpability
Category 3	Lesser harm **and** lower culpability

The court should determine the offender's culpability and the harm caused, or intended, by reference only to the factors below (as demonstrated by the presence of one or more). These factors comprise the principal factual elements of the offence and should determine the category.

Factors indicating greater harm Sustained or repeated assault on the same victim	**Factors indicating lesser harm** Injury which is less serious in the context of the offence
Factors indicating higher culpability *Statutory aggravating factors:* Offence racially or religiously aggravated Offence motivated by, or demonstrating, hostility to the victim based on his or her sexual orientation (or presumed sexual orientation) Offence motivated by, or demonstrating, hostility to the victim based on the victim's disability (or presumed disability) *Other aggravating factors:* A significant degree of premeditation Use of weapon or weapon equivalent (for example, shod foot, headbutting, use of acid, use of animal) Intention to commit more serious harm than actually resulted from the offence Deliberately causes more harm than is necessary for commission of offence Leading role in group or gang Offence motivated by, or demonstrating, hostility based on the victim's age, sex, gender identity (or presumed gender identity)	**Factors indicating lower culpability** Subordinate role in group or gang Lack of premeditation Mental disorder or learning disability, where linked to commission of the offence

STEP TWO   Starting point and category range

Having determined the category, the court should use the corresponding starting points to reach a sentence within the category range below. The starting point applies to all offenders irrespective of plea or previous convictions. A case of particular gravity, reflected by multiple features of culpability in step one, could merit upward adjustment from the starting point before further adjustment for aggravating or mitigating features, set out below.

Offence Category	Starting Point (*Applicable to all offenders*)	Category Range (*Applicable to all offenders*)
Category 1	12 weeks custody	Low level community order—26 weeks custody
Category 2	Medium level community order	Low level community order—High level community order
Category 3	Band B fine	Band A fine—Band C fine

The table below contains a **non-exhaustive** list of additional factual elements providing the context of the offence and factors relating to the offender. Identify whether any combination of these, or other relevant factors, should result in an upward or downward adjustment from the starting point. In some cases, having considered these factors, it may be appropriate to move outside the identified category range.

When sentencing **category 1** offences, the court should also consider the custody threshold as follows:

- has the custody threshold been passed?
- if so, is it unavoidable that a custodial sentence be imposed?
- if so, can that sentence be suspended?

Factors increasing seriousness	Factors reducing seriousness or reflecting personal mitigation
Statutory aggravating factors: Previous convictions, having regard to a) the nature of the offence to which the conviction relates and its relevance to the current offence; and b) the time that has elapsed since the conviction Offence committed whilst on bail *Other aggravating factors include:* Location of the offence Timing of the offence Ongoing effect upon the victim Gratuitous degradation of victim Failure to comply with current court orders Offence committed whilst on licence An attempt to conceal or dispose of evidence Failure to respond to warnings or concerns expressed by others about the offender's behaviour Commission of offence whilst under the influence of alcohol or drugs Established evidence of community impact Any steps taken to prevent the victim reporting an incident, obtaining assistance and/or from assisting or supporting the prosecution Offences taken into consideration (TICs)	No previous convictions or no relevant/recent convictions Single blow Remorse Good character and/or exemplary conduct Determination and/or demonstration of steps taken to address addiction or offending behaviour Serious medical conditions requiring urgent, intensive or long-term treatment Isolated incident Age and/or lack of maturity where it affects the responsibility of the offender Lapse of time since the offence where this is not the fault of the offender Mental disorder or learning disability, where not linked to the commission of the offence Sole or primary carer for dependent relatives

[Steps Three to Eight are almost identical to Steps Three to Nine which apply to assault occasioning actual bodily harm (see **SG-182**) but Step Five (Dangerousness) is omitted.]

Bail, Failure to Surrender   SG-185

Factors to take into consideration

This guideline and accompanying notes are taken from the Sentencing Guidelines Council's definitive guideline *Fail to Surrender to Bail*, published 29 November 2007 [see **SG-136**]

Key factors

(a)   Whilst the approach to sentencing should generally be the same whether the offender failed to surrender to a court or to a police station *and* whether the offence is contrary to ss. 6(1) or 6(2), the court must examine all the relevant circumstances.

(b)   The following factors may be relevant when assessing the harm caused by the offence:

- Where an offender fails to appear for a first court hearing but attends shortly afterwards, the only harm caused is likely to be the financial cost to the system. Where a case could not have proceeded even if the offender had surrendered to bail, this should be taken into account.
- Where an offender appears for trial on the wrong day but enters a late guilty plea enabling the case to be disposed of to some degree at least, the harm caused by the delay may be offset by the benefits stemming from the change of plea.
- The most serious harm is likely to result when an offender fails to appear for trial, especially if this results in witnesses being sent away. Where it has been possible to conclude proceedings in the absence of the offender, this may be relevant to the assessment of harm caused.
- The level of harm is likely to be assessed as high where an offender fails to appear for sentence and is also seen to be flouting the authority of the court, such as where the avoidance of sentence results in the consequential avoidance of ancillary orders such as disqualification from driving, the payment of compensation or registration as a sex offender. This may increase the level of harm whenever the offender continues to present a risk to public safety.
- Whilst the seriousness of the original offence does not of itself aggravate or mitigate the seriousness of the offence of failing to surrender, the circumstances surrounding the original offence may be relevant in assessing the harm arising from the Bail Act offence.

- The circumstances in which bail to return to a police station is granted are less formal than the grant of court bail and the history of the individual case should be examined. There may be less culpability where bail has been enlarged on a number of occasions and less harm if court proceedings are not significantly delayed.

(c) Where the failure to surrender to custody was 'deliberate':
- at or near the bottom of the sentencing range will be cases where the offender gave no thought at all to the consequences, or other mitigating factors are present, and the degree of delay or interference with the progress of the case was not significant in all the circumstances;
- at or near the top of the range will be cases where aggravating factors 1, 2 or 4 [below] are present if there is also a significant delay and/or interference with the progress of the case.

(d) A previous conviction that is likely to be 'relevant' for the purposes of this offence is one which demonstrates failure to comply with an order of a court.

(e) Acquittal of the original offence does not automatically mitigate the Bail Act offence.

(f) The fact that an offender has a disorganised or chaotic lifestyle should not normally be treated as offence mitigation, but may be regarded as offender mitigation depending on the particular facts.

(g) A misunderstanding which does not amount to a defence may be a mitigating factor whereas a mistake on the part of the offender is his or her own responsibility.

(h) Where an offender has literacy or language difficulties, these may be mitigation (where they do not amount to a defence) where potential problems were not identified and/or appropriate steps were not taken to mitigate the risk in the circumstances as known at the time that bail was granted.

(i) An offender's position as the sole or primary carer of dependent relatives may be offender mitigation when it is the reason why the offender failed to surrender to custody.

(j) The sentence for this offence should usually be in addition to any sentence for the original offence. Where custodial sentences are being imposed for a Bail Act offence and the original offence at the same time, the normal approach should be for the sentences to be consecutive. The length of any custodial sentence imposed must be commensurate with the seriousness of the offence(s).

(k) If an offence is serious enough to justify the imposition of a community order, a curfew requirement with an electronic monitoring requirement may be particularly appropriate—see [below].

Guidelines

Bail Act 1976, ss. 6(1) and 6(2)

Triable either way:
Maximum when tried summarily: Level 5 fine and/or 3 months
Maximum when tried on indictment: 12 months

In certain circumstances, a magistrates' court may commit to the Crown Court for sentence. *Consult your legal adviser for guidance.*

Offence seriousness (culpability and harm)

A. Identify the appropriate starting point

Starting points based on first time offender pleading not guilty

Examples of nature of activity	Starting point	Range
Surrenders late on day but case proceeds as planned	Band A fine	Band A fine to Band B fine
Negligent or non-deliberate failure to attend causing delay and/or interference with the administration of justice	Band C fine	Band B fine to medium level community order
Deliberate failure to attend causing delay and/or interference with the administration of justice	14 days custody	Low level community order to 10 weeks custody

B. Consider the effect of aggravating and mitigating factors (other than those within examples above)

Common aggravating and mitigating factors are identified [elsewhere]—the following may be particularly relevant but these lists are not exhaustive

Factors indicating higher culpability	Factors indicating lower culpability
1. Serious attempts to evade justice 2. Determined attempt seriously to undermine the course of justice 3. Previous relevant convictions and/or breach of court orders or police bail	Where not amounting to a defence: 1. Misunderstanding 2. Failure to comprehend bail significance or requirements 3. Caring responsibilities
Factor indicating greater degree of harm 4. Lengthy absence	**Factor indicating lesser degree of harm** 4. Prompt voluntary surrender

[Sets out the standard sequential sentencing procedure.]

In appropriate cases, a magistrates' court may impose one day's detention: Magistrates' Courts Act 1980, s. 135

BLADED ARTICLE/OFFENSIVE WEAPON, POSSESSION OF

SG-186

Factors to take into consideration

These guidelines and accompanying notes are drawn from the Court of Appeal's decision in *R v Celaire and Poulton* [2003] 1 Cr App R (S) 116. [But see the note issued as to the effect of *Povey* [2009] 1 Cr App R (S) 228, discussed at **B12.140** in the main work.]

Key factors

(a) Concurrent sentences may be appropriate if the weapons offence is ancillary to a more serious offence; consecutive sentences may be appropriate if the offences are distinct and independent.

(b) When assessing offence seriousness, consider the offender's intention, the circumstances of the offence and the nature of the weapon involved.

(c) Some weapons are inherently more dangerous than others but the nature of the weapon is not the primary determinant of offence seriousness. A relatively less dangerous weapon, such as a billiard cue or knuckle-duster, may be used to create fear and such an offence may be at least as serious as one in which a more obviously dangerous weapon, such as a knife or an acid spray, is being carried for self-defence or no actual attempt has been made by the offender to use it.

(d) Nevertheless, the fact that the offender was carrying a weapon which is offensive per se may shed light on his or her intentions.

Guidelines

Triable either way:
Maximum when tried summarily: Level 5 fine and/or 6 months
Maximum when tried on indictment: 4 years

Offence seriousness (culpability and harm)

A. Identify the appropriate starting point

Starting points based on first time offender pleading not guilty

Examples of nature of activity	Starting point	Range
Weapon not used to threaten or cause fear	High level community order	Band C fine to 12 weeks custody
Weapon not used to threaten or cause fear but offence committed in dangerous circumstances	6 weeks custody	High level community order to Crown Court
Weapon used to threaten or cause fear and offence committed in dangerous circumstances	Crown Court	Crown Court

B. Consider the effect of aggravating and mitigating factors (other than those within examples above)

Common aggravating and mitigating factors are identified [elsewhere]—the following may be particularly relevant but these lists are not exhaustive

Sentencing Guidelines

Factors indicating higher culpability	Factors indicating greater degree of harm
1. Particularly dangerous weapon 2. Specifically planned use of weapon to commit violence, threaten violence or intimidate 3. Offence motivated by hostility towards minority individual or group 4. Offender under influence of drink or drugs 5. Offender operating in group or gang	1. Offence committed at school, hospital or other place where vulnerable persons may be present 2. Offence committed on premises where people carrying out public services 3. Offence committed on or outside licensed premises 4. Offence committed on public transport 5. Offence committed at large public gathering, especially where there may be risk of disorder
	Factors indicating lower culpability 1. Weapon carried only on temporary basis 2. Original possession legitimate e.g. in course of trade or business

[Sets out the standard sequential sentencing procedure and mentions need to consider deprivation of property (including weapon).]

SG-187   BURGLARY: DOMESTIC BURGLARY

[The Guidelines apply to all offenders aged 18 and older, who are sentenced on or after 16 January 2012, regardless of the date of the offence.]

Theft Act 1968 (section 9)

This is a serious specified offence for the purposes of section 224 Criminal Justice Act 2003 if it was committed with intent to:

(a)   inflict grievous bodily harm on a person, or
(b)   do unlawful damage to a building or anything in it.

Triable either way:
Maximum when tried summarily: Level 5 fine and/or 26 weeks custody
Maximum when tried on indictment: 14 years custody

Offence range: Community order — 6 years custody

Where sentencing an offender for a qualifying **third domestic burglary**, the Court must apply section 111 of the Powers of the Criminal Courts (Sentencing) Act 2000 and impose a custodial term of at least three years, unless it is satisfied that there are particular circumstances which relate to any of the offences or to the offender which would make it unjust to do so.

This guideline applies to all offenders aged 18 and older, who are sentenced on or after 16 January 2012. The definitions... of 'starting point' and 'first time offender' do not apply for this guideline. Starting point and category ranges apply to all offenders in all cases, irrespective of plea or previous convictions.

STEP ONE Determining the offence category
The court should determine the offence category using the table below.

Category 1	Greater harm **and** higher culpability
Category 2	Greater harm **and** lower culpability or lesser harm **and** higher culpability
Category 3	Lesser harm **and** lower culpability

The court should determine culpability and harm caused or intended, by reference only to the factors below, which comprise the principal factual elements of the offence. Where an offence does not fall squarely into a category, individual factors may require a degree of weighting before making an overall assessment and determining the appropriate offence category.

Factors indicating greater harm	Factors indicating higher culpability
Theft of/damage to property causing a significant degree of loss to the victim (whether economic, commercial or personal value)	Premises or victim deliberately targeted (to include pharmacy or doctor's surgery and targeting due to vulnerability of victim or hostility based on disability, race, sexual orientation and so forth)
Soiling, ransacking or vandalism of property	
Victim on the premises (or returns) while offender present	A significant degree of planning or organisation
Trauma to the victim, beyond the normal inevitable consequence of intrusion and theft	Knife or other weapon carried (where not charged separately)
Violence used or threatened against victim	Equipped for burglary (for example, implements carried and/or use of vehicle)
Context of general public disorder	Member of a group or gang
Factors indicating lesser harm	**Factors indicating lower culpability**
Nothing stolen or only property of very low value to the victim (whether economic, commercial or personal)	Offence committed on impulse, with limited intrusion into property
	Offender exploited by others
Limited damage or disturbance to property	Mental disorder or learning disability, where linked to the commission of the offence

STEP TWO   Starting point and category range

Having determined the category, the court should use the corresponding starting points to reach a sentence within the category range below. The starting point applies to all offenders irrespective of plea or previous convictions.

Where the defendant is dependent on or has a propensity to misuse drugs and there is sufficient prospect of success, a community order with a drug rehabilitation requirement under section 209 of the Criminal Justice Act 2003 may be a proper alternative to a short or moderate custodial sentence.

A case of particular gravity, reflected by multiple features of culpability or harm in step 1, could merit upward adjustment from the starting point before further adjustment for aggravating or mitigating features, set out [below].

Offence Category	Starting Point (*Applicable to all offenders*)	Category Range (*Applicable to all offenders*)
Category 1	Crown Court	Crown Court
Category 2	1 years custody	High level community order — Crown Court (2 years custody)
Category 3	High level community order	Low level community order — 26 weeks custody

The table below contains a **non-exhaustive** list of additional factual elements providing the context of the offence and factors relating to the offender. Identify whether any combination of these, or other relevant factors, should result in an upward or downward adjustment from the starting point. **In particular, relevant recent convictions are likely to result in an upward adjustment.** In some cases, having considered these factors, it may be appropriate to move outside the identified category range.

When sentencing **category 2 or 3** offences, the court should also consider the custody threshold as follows:

- has the custody threshold been passed?
- if so, is it unavoidable that a custodial sentence be imposed?
- if so, can that sentence be suspended?

Sentencing Guidelines

Factors increasing seriousness	Factors reducing seriousness or reflecting personal mitigation
Statutory aggravating factors	Offender has made voluntary reparation to the victim
Previous convictions, having regard to a) the nature of the offence to which the conviction relates and its relevance to the current offence; and b) the time that has elapsed since the conviction*	Subordinate role in a group or gang
	No previous convictions or no relevant/recent convictions
	Remorse
Offence committed whilst on bail	Good character and/or exemplary conduct
Other aggravating factors include:	Determination, and/or demonstration of steps taken to address addiction or offending behaviour
Child at home (or returns home) when offence committed	Serious medical conditions requiring urgent, intensive or long-term treatment
Offence committed at night	Age and/or lack of maturity where it affects the responsibility of the offender
Gratuitous degradation of the victim	
Any steps taken to prevent the victim reporting the incident or obtaining assistance and/or from assisting or supporting the prosecution	Lapse of time since the offence where this is not the fault of the offender
Established evidence of community impact	Mental disorder or learning disability, where not linked to the commission of the offence
Commission of offence whilst under the influence of alcohol or drugs	Sole or primary carer for dependent relatives
Failure to comply with current court orders	
Offence committed whilst on licence	
Offences Taken Into Consideration (TICs)	

* Where sentencing an offender for a qualifying third domestic burglary, the Court must apply section 111 of the Powers of the Criminal Courts (Sentencing) Act 2000 and impose a custodial term of at least three years, unless it is satisfied that there are particular circumstances which relate to any of the offences or to the offender which would make it unjust to do so.

STEP THREE Consider any factors which indicate a reduction, such as assistance to the prosecution

The court should take into account any rule of law by virtue of which an offender may receive a discounted sentence in consequence of assistance given (or offered) to the prosecutor or investigator.

STEP FOUR Reduction for guilty pleas

The court should take account of any potential reduction for a guilty plea in accordance with section 144 of the Criminal Justice Act 2003 and the *Guilty Plea* guideline.

Where a minimum mandatory sentence is imposed under section 111 Powers of Criminal Courts (Sentencing) Act, the discount for an early guilty plea must not exceed 20 per cent.

STEP FIVE Dangerousness

A burglary offence under section 9 Theft Act 1986 is a serious specified offence within the meaning of chapter 5 of the Criminal Justice Act 2003 if it was committed with the intent to (a) inflict grievous bodily harm on a person, or (b) do unlawful damage to a building or anything in it. The court should consider whether having regard to the criteria contained in that chapter it would be appropriate to award imprisonment for public protection or an extended sentence. Where offenders meet the dangerousness criteria, the notional determinate sentence should be used as the basis for the setting of a minimum term.

[Steps Six to Nine follow the standard sequential sentencing procedure: see **SG-182**.]

SG-188

Burglary: Non-Domestic Burglary

[The Guidelines apply to all offenders aged 18 and older, who are sentenced on or after 16 January 2012, regardless of the date of the offence.]

Theft Act 1968 (section 9)

This is a serious specified offence for the purposes of section 224 Criminal Justice Act 2003 if it was committed with intent to:

(a) inflict grievous bodily harm on a person, or
(b) do unlawful damage to a building or anything in it.

Triable either way:
Maximum when tried summarily: Level 5 fine and/or 26 weeks custody

Maximum when tried on indictment: 10 years custody

Offence range: Fine — 5 years custody

This guideline applies to all offenders aged 18 and older, who are sentenced on or after 16 January 2012. The definitions . . . of 'starting point' and 'first time offender' do not apply for this guideline. Starting point and category ranges apply to all offenders in all cases, irrespective of plea or previous convictions.

STEP ONE   Determining the offence category

The court should determine the offence category using the table below.

Category 1	Greater harm **and** higher culpability
Category 2	Greater harm **and** lower culpability or lesser harm **and** higher culpability
Category 3	Lesser harm **and** lower culpability

The court should determine culpability and harm caused or intended, by reference only to the factors below, which comprise the principal factual elements of the offence. Where an offence does not fall squarely into a category, individual factors may require a degree of weighting before making an overall assessment and determining the appropriate offence category.

Factors indicating greater harm	Factors indicating higher culpability
Theft of/damage to property causing a significant degree of loss to the victim (whether economic, commercial or personal value) Soiling, ransacking or vandalism of property Victim on the premises (or returns) while offender present Trauma to the victim, beyond the normal inevitable consequence of intrusion and theft Violence used or threatened against victim Context of general public disorder	Premises or victim deliberately targeted (to include pharmacy or doctor's surgery and targeting due to vulnerability of victim or hostility based on disability, race, sexual orientation and so forth) A significant degree of planning or organisation Knife or other weapon carried (where not charged separately) Equipped for burglary (for example, implements carried and/or use of vehicle) Member of a group or gang
Factors indicating lesser harm Nothing stolen or only property of very low value to the victim (whether economic, commercial or personal) Limited damage or disturbance to property	**Factors indicating lower culpability** Offence committed on impulse, with limited intrusion into property Offender exploited by others Mental disorder or learning disability, where linked to the commission of the offence

STEP TWO   Starting point and category range

Having determined the category, the court should use the corresponding starting points to reach a sentence within the category range below. The starting point applies to all offenders irrespective of plea or previous convictions.

Where the defendant is dependent on or has a propensity to misuse drugs and there is sufficient prospect of success, a community order with a drug rehabilitation requirement under section 209 of the Criminal Justice Act 2003 may be a proper alternative to a short or moderate custodial sentence.

A case of particular gravity, reflected by multiple features of culpability or harm in step 1, could merit upward adjustment from the starting point before further adjustment for aggravating or mitigating features, set out below.

Offence Category	Starting Point *(Applicable to all offenders)*	Category Range *(Applicable to all offenders)*
Category 1	Crown Court	Crown Court
Category 2	18 weeks custody	Low level community order — Crown Court (51 weeks custody)
Category 3	Medium level community order	Band B fine — 18 weeks custody

The table below contains a **non-exhaustive** list of additional factual elements providing the context of the offence and factors relating to the offender. Identify whether any combination of these, or other relevant factors, should result in an upward or downward adjustment from the starting point. **In particular, relevant recent convictions are likely to result in an upward adjustment**. In some cases, having considered these factors, it may be appropriate to move outside the identified category range.

When sentencing **category 2 or 3** offences, the court should also consider the custody threshold as follows:

- has the custody threshold been passed?
- if so, is it unavoidable that a custodial sentence be imposed?
- if so, can that sentence be suspended?

When sentencing category 3 offences, the court should also consider the community order threshold as follows:

- has the community order threshold been passed?

Factors increasing seriousness	Factors reducing seriousness or reflecting personal mitigation
Statutory aggravating factors: Previous convictions, having regard to a) the nature of the offence to which the conviction relates and its relevance to the current offence; and b) the time that has elapsed since the conviction Offence committed whilst on bail *Other aggravating factors include:* Offence committed at night, particularly where staff present or likely to be present Abuse of a position of trust Gratuitous degradation of the victim Any steps taken to prevent the victim reporting the incident or obtaining assistance and/or from assisting or supporting the prosecution Established evidence of community impact Commission of offence whilst under the influence of alcohol or drugs Failure to comply with current court orders Offence committed whilst on licence Offences Taken Into Consideration (TICs)	Offender has made voluntary reparation to the victim Subordinate role in a group or gang No previous convictions **or** no relevant/recent convictions Remorse Good character and/or exemplary conduct Determination, and/or demonstration of steps taken to address addiction or offending behaviour Serious medical conditions requiring urgent, intensive or long-term treatment Age and/or lack of maturity where it affects the responsibility of the offender Lapse of time since the offence where this is not the fault of the offender Mental disorder or learning disability, where not linked to the commission of the offence Sole or primary carer for dependent relatives

STEP THREE Consider any factors which indicate a reduction, such as assistance to the prosecution

The court should take into account any rule of law by virtue of which an offender may receive a discounted sentence in consequence of assistance given (or offered) to the prosecutor or investigator.

STEP FOUR Reduction for guilty pleas

The court should take account of any potential reduction for a guilty plea in accordance with section 144 of the Criminal Justice Act 2003 and the *Guilty Plea* guideline.

[Steps Five to Nine are the same as for domestic burglary: see **SG-187–8**.]

SG-189

CHILD PROSTITUTION AND PORNOGRAPHY

Factors to take into consideration

This guideline is taken from the Sentencing Guidelines Council's definitive guideline Sexual Offences Act 2003, published 30 April 2007 [see **SG-125**]

Key factors

(a) Few cases will be suitable to be dealt with in a magistrates' court for the following reasons:
- The courts should consider making an order confiscating any profits stemming from the offender's criminal life-style or forfeiting any possessions (e.g. cameras, computers, property) used in connection with the commission of the offence. Only the Crown Court can make a confiscation order.
- The starting point for the child prostitution and pornography offences will always be a custodial sentence.
- In cases where a number of children are involved, consecutive sentences may be appropriate, leading to cumulative sentences significantly higher than the starting points for individual offences.

(b) In accordance with s. 80 [of] and sch. 3 [to] the Sexual Offences Act 2003, automatic notification requirements apply upon conviction to an offender aged 18 or over.

Guidelines

Sexual Offences Act 2003, s. 48 (causing or inciting child prostitution or pornography);
s. 49 (controlling a child prostitute or a child involved in pornography);
s. 50 (arranging or facilitating child prostitution or pornography)

Triable either way:
Maximum when tried summarily: Level 5 fine and/or 6 months
Maximum when tried on indictment: 14 years

Offence seriousness (culpability and harm)

A. Identify the appropriate starting point

> *These offences should normally be dealt with in the Crown Court.* However, there may be rare cases of non-penetrative activity involving a victim aged 16 or 17 where the offender's involvement is minimal and not perpetrated for gain in which a custodial sentence within the jurisdiction of a magistrates' court may be appropriate.
> *Consult your legal adviser for further guidance.*

Starting points based on first time offender pleading not guilty

B. Consider the effect of aggravating and mitigating factors (other than those within examples above)

Common aggravating and mitigating factors are identified [elsewhere]—the following may be particularly relevant but these lists are not exhaustive

Factors indicating higher culpability	Factor indicating lower culpability
1. Background of threats or intimidation	1. Offender also being controlled in prostitution or pornography and subject to threats or intimidation
2. Large-scale commercial operation	
3. Use of drugs, alcohol or other substance to secure the victim's compliance	
4. Forcing a victim to violate another person	
5. Abduction or detention	
6. Threats to prevent the victim reporting the activity	
7. Threats to disclose victim's activity to friends/relatives	
8. Images distributed to other children or persons known to the victim	
9. Financial or other gain	
Factors indicating greater degree of harm	
1. Induced dependency on drugs	
2. Victim has been manipulated into physical and emotional dependence on the offender	
3. Storing, making available or distributing images in such a way that they can be inadvertently accessed by others	

[Sets out the standard sequential sentencing procedure.]

COMMON ASSAULT   **SG-190**
Criminal Justice Act 1988 (section 39)
RACIALLY/RELIGIOUSLY AGGRAVATED COMMON ASSAULT
Crime and Disorder Act 1998 (section 29)

[This guideline was published by the Sentencing Council and has effect in respect of all sentences passed after 13 June 2011 on offenders aged 18 or older. It replaces the guideline which previously applied and which continued to have effect until that date.]

Racially/religiously aggravated assault is a specified offence for the purposes of section 224 of the Criminal Justice Act 2003

Section 39
Triable only summarily
Maximum when tried summarily: Level 5 fine and/or 26 weeks' custody

Section 29
Triable either way
Maximum when tried summarily: Level 5 fine and/or 26 weeks' custody
Maximum when tried on indictment: 2 years' custody

Offence range: Discharge—26 weeks' custody

This guideline applies to all offenders aged 18 and older, who are sentenced on or after 13 June 2011. The definitions [at **SG-297**] of 'starting point' and 'first time offender' do not apply for this guideline. Starting point and category ranges apply to all offenders in all cases, irrespective of plea or previous convictions.

STEP ONE Determining the offence category

The court should determine the offence category using the table below.

Category 1	Greater harm (injury or fear of injury must normally be present) **and** higher culpability
Category 2	Greater harm (injury or fear of injury must normally be present) **and** lower culpability;**or** lesser harm and higher culpability
Category 3	Lesser harm **and** lower culpability

The court should determine the offender's culpability and the harm caused, or intended, by reference only to the factors below (as demonstrated by the presence of one or more). These factors comprise the principal factual elements of the offence and should determine the category.

Factors indicating greater harm	**Factors indicating lesser harm**
Injury or fear of injury which is serious in the context of the offence (must normally be present)	Injury which is less serious in the context of the offence
Victim is particularly vulnerable because of personal circumstances	**Factors indicating lower culpability**
Sustained or repeated assault on the same victim	Subordinate role in group or gang
	A greater degree of provocation than normally expected
Factors indicating higher culpability	Lack of premeditation
Statutory aggravating factors:	Mental disorder or learning disability, where linked to commission of the offence
Offence motivated by, or demonstrating, hostility to the victim based on his or her sexual orientation (or presumed sexual orientation)	Excessive self defence
Offence motivated by, or demonstrating, hostility to the victim based on the victim's disability (or presumed disability)	
Other aggravating factors:	
A significant degree of premeditation	
Threatened or actual use of weapon or weapon equivalent (for example, shod foot, headbutting, use of acid, use of animal)	
Intention to commit more serious harm than actually resulted from the offence	
Deliberately causes more harm than is necessary for commission of offence	
Deliberate targeting of vulnerable victim	
Leading role in group or gang	
Offence motivated by, or demonstrating, hostility based on the victim's age, sex, gender identity (or presumed gender identity)	

STEP TWO Starting point and category range

Having determined the category, the court should use the corresponding starting points to reach a sentence within the category range below. The starting point applies to all offenders irrespective of plea or previous convictions. A case of particular gravity, reflected by multiple features of culpability in step one, could merit upward adjustment from the starting point before further adjustment for aggravating or mitigating features, set out below.

Offence Category	Starting Point (*Applicable to all offenders*)	Category Range (*Applicable to all offenders*)
Category 1	High level community order	Low level community order—26 weeks custody
Category 2	Medium level community order	Band A fine—High level community order
Category 3	Band A fine	Discharge—Band C fine

The table below contains a **non-exhaustive** list of additional factual elements providing the context of the offence and factors relating to the offender. Identify whether any combination of these, or other relevant factors, should result in an upward or downward adjustment from the starting point. In some cases, having considered these factors, it may be appropriate to move outside the identified category range.

When sentencing **category 1** offences, the court should also consider the custody threshold as follows:

- has the custody threshold been passed?
- if so, is it unavoidable that a custodial sentence be imposed?
- if so, can that sentence be suspended?

When sentencing **category 2** offences, the court should also consider the community order threshold as follows:

- has the community order threshold been passed?

Sentencing Guidelines

Factors increasing seriousness	Factors reducing seriousness or reflecting personal mitigation
Statutory aggravating factors: Previous convictions, having regard to a) the nature of the offence to which the conviction relates and its relevance to the current offence; and b) the time that has elapsed since the conviction Offence committed whilst on bail *Other aggravating factors include:* Location of the offence Timing of the offence Ongoing effect upon the victim Offence committed against those working in the public sector or providing a service to the public Presence of others including relatives, especially children or partner of the victim Gratuitous degradation of victim In domestic violence cases, victim forced to leave their home Failure to comply with current court orders Offence committed whilst on licence An attempt to conceal or dispose of evidence Failure to respond to warnings or concerns expressed by others about the offender's behaviour Commission of offence whilst under the influence of alcohol or drugs Abuse of power and/or position of trust Exploiting contact arrangements with a child to commit an offence Established evidence of community impact Any steps taken to prevent the victim reporting an incident, obtaining assistance and/or from assisting or supporting the prosecution Offences taken into consideration (TICs)	No previous convictions or no relevant/recent convictions Single blow Remorse Good character and/or exemplary conduct Determination and/or demonstration of steps taken to address addiction or offending behaviour Serious medical conditions requiring urgent, intensive or long-term treatment Isolated incident Age and/or lack of maturity where it affects the responsibility of the offender Lapse of time since the offence where this is not the fault of the offender Mental disorder or learning disability, where not linked to the commission of the offence Sole or primary carer for dependent relatives

Section 29 offences only: The court should determine the appropriate sentence for the offence without taking account of the element of aggravation and then make an addition to the sentence, considering the level of aggravation involved. It may be appropriate to move outside the identified category range, taking into account the increased statutory maximum.

[Steps Three to Nine are almost identical to those which apply to assault occasioning actual bodily harm: see **SG-182**.]

SG-191

COMMUNICATION NETWORK OFFENCES
Communications Act 2003, ss. 127(1) and 127(2)

Triable only summarily:
Maximum: Level 5 fine and/or 6 months

Offence seriousness (culpability and harm)

A. Identify the appropriate starting point

Starting points based on first time offender pleading not guilty

Sending grossly offensive, indecent, obscene or menacing messages (s.127(1))		
Examples of nature of activity	Starting point	Range
Single offensive, indecent, obscene or menacing call of short duration, having no significant impact on receiver	Band B fine	Band A fine to band C fine
Single call where extreme language used, having only moderate impact on receiver	Medium level community order	Low level community order to high level community order
Single call where extreme language used and substantial distress or fear caused to receiver; OR One of a series of similar calls as described in box above	6 weeks custody	High level community order to 12 weeks custody

Sending false message/persistent use of communications network for purpose of causing annoyance, inconvenience or needless anxiety (s.127(2))		
Examples of nature of activity	Starting point	Range
Persistent silent calls over short period to private individual, causing inconvenience or annoyance	Band B fine	Band A fine to band C fine
Single hoax call to public or private organisation resulting in moderate disruption or anxiety	Medium level community order	Low level community order to high level community order
Single hoax call resulting in major disruption or substantial public fear or distress; OR One of a series of similar calls as described in box above	12 weeks custody	High level community order to 18 weeks custody

B. Consider the effect of aggravating and mitigating factors (other than those within examples above)

Common aggravating and mitigating factors are identified [elsewhere]

[Sets out the standard sequential sentencing procedure.]

SG-192

COMMUNITY ORDER, BREACH OF
Criminal Justice Act 2003, sch. 8

These notes are taken from the Sentencing Guidelines Council's definitive guideline *New Sentences: Criminal Justice Act 2003*, published 16 December 2004[127] [see **SG-11**]

Options in breach proceedings:
When dealing with breaches of community orders for offences committed after 4 April 2005, the court must either: • amend the terms of the original order so as to impose more onerous requirements. The court may extend the duration of particular requirements within the order, but it cannot extend the overall length of the original order; or • revoke the original order and proceed to sentence for the original offence. Where an offender has wilfully and persistently failed to comply with an order made in respect of an offence that is not punishable by imprisonment, the court can impose up to six months' custody.

---

[127] Criminal Justice Act 2003, sch.8, para. 9(1)(c)

Approach:
- having decided that a community order is commensurate with the seriousness of the offence, the primary objective when sentencing for breach of requirements is to ensure that those requirements are completed;
- a court sentencing for breach must take account of the extent to which the offender has complied with the requirements of the original order, the reasons for the breach, and the point at which the breach has occurred;
- if increasing the onerousness of requirements, sentencers should take account of the offender's ability to comply and should avoid precipitating further breach by overloading the offender with too many or conflicting requirements;
- there may be cases where the court will need to consider re-sentencing to a differently constructed community order in order to secure compliance with the purposes of the original sentence, perhaps where there has already been partial compliance or where events since the sentence was imposed have shown that a different course of action is likely to be effective;
- where available, custody should be the last resort, reserved for those cases of deliberate and repeated breach where all reasonable efforts to ensure that the offender complies have failed.

Where the original order was made by the Crown Court, breach proceedings must be commenced in that court unless the order provided that any failure to comply with its requirements may be dealt with in a magistrates' court.

Criminal Damage (other than by Fire)
Racially Or Religiously Aggravated Criminal Damage
Criminal Damage Act 1971, s. 1(1)
Crime and Disorder Act 1998, s. 30

SG-193

Criminal damage: triable only summarily if value involved does not exceed £5,000:
Maximum: Level 4 fine and/or 3 months
Triable either way if value involved exceeds £5,000:
Maximum when tried summarily: Level 5 fine and/or 6 months
Maximum when tried on indictment: 10 years

Racially or religiously aggravated criminal damage: triable either way
Maximum when tried summarily: Level 5 fine and/or 6 months
Maximum when tried on indictment: 14 years

Where offence committed in domestic context, refer [below] for guidance

Offence seriousness (culpability and harm)

A. Identify the appropriate starting point

Starting points based on first time offender pleading not guilty

Examples of nature of activity	Starting point	Range
Minor damage e.g. breaking small window; small amount of graffiti	Band B fine	Conditional discharge to band C fine
Moderate damage e.g. breaking large plate-glass or shop window; widespread graffiti	Low level community order	Band C fine to medium level community order
Significant damage up to £5,000 e.g. damage caused as part of a spree	High level community order	Medium level community order to 12 weeks custody
Damage between £5,000 and £10,000	12 weeks custody	6 to 26 weeks custody
Damage over £10,000	Crown Court	Crown Court

B. Consider the effect of aggravating and mitigating factors (other than those within examples above)

Common aggravating and mitigating factors are identified [elsewhere]—the following may be particularly relevant but these lists are not exhaustive

Factors indicating higher culpability	Factors indicating lower culpability
1. Revenge attack	1. Damage caused recklessly
2. Targeting vulnerable victim	2. Provocation
Factors indicating greater degree of harm	
1. Damage to emergency equipment	
2. Damage to public amenity	
3. Significant public or private fear caused e.g. in domestic context	

[Sets out the standard sequential sentencing procedure. Notes that 'If offender charged and convicted of the racially or religiously aggravated offence, increase the sentence to reflect this element']

SG-194   CRUELTY TO A CHILD

Factors to take into consideration

This guideline and accompanying notes are taken from the Sentencing Guidelines Council's definitive guidelines *Overarching Principles: Assaults on children and Cruelty to a child*, published 20 February 2008 [see **SG-153**]

Key factors

(a)   The same starting point and sentencing range is proposed for offences which might fall into the four categories (assault; ill-treatment or neglect; abandonment; and failure to protect). These are designed to take into account the fact that the victim is particularly vulnerable, assuming an abuse of trust or power and the likelihood of psychological harm, and designed to reflect the seriousness with which society as a whole regards these offences.

(b)   As noted above, the starting points have been calculated to reflect the likelihood of psychological harm and this cannot be treated as an aggravating factor. Where there is an especially serious physical or psychological effect on the victim, even if unintended, this should increase sentence.

(c)   The normal sentencing starting point for an offence of child cruelty should be a custodial sentence. The length of that sentence will be influenced by the circumstances in which the offence took place.

(d)   However, in considering whether a custodial sentence is the most appropriate disposal, the court should take into account any available information concerning the future care of the child.

(e)   Where the offender is the sole or primary carer of the victim or other dependants, this potentially should be taken into account for sentencing purposes, regardless of whether the offender is male or female. In such cases, an immediate custodial sentence may not be appropriate.

(f)   The most relevant areas of personal mitigation are likely to be:
  • Mental illness/depression
  • Inability to cope with the pressures of parenthood
  • Lack of support
  • Sleep deprivation
  • Offender dominated by an abusive or stronger partner
  • Extreme behavioural difficulties in the child, often coupled with a lack of support
  • Inability to secure assistance or support services in spite of every effort having been made by the offender.

Some of the factors identified above, in particular sleep deprivation, lack of support and an inability to cope, could be regarded as an inherent part of caring for children, especially when a child is very young and could be put forward as mitigation by most carers charged with an offence of child cruelty. It follows that, before being accepted as mitigation, there must be evidence that these factors were present to a high degree and had an identifiable and significant impact on the offender's behaviour.

Guidelines

Children and Young Persons Act 1933, s.1(1)

Triable either way:
Maximum when tried summarily: Level 5 fine and/or 6 months
Maximum when tried on indictment: 10 years

Offence seriousness (culpability and harm)

A. Identify the appropriate starting point

Starting points based on first time offender pleading not guilty

Examples of nature of activity	Starting point	Range
(i) Short term neglect or ill-treatment (ii) Single incident of short-term abandonment (iii) Failure to protect a child from any of the above	12 weeks custody	Low level community order to 26 weeks custody
(i) Assault(s) resulting in injuries consistent with ABH (ii) More than one incident of neglect or ill-treatment (but not amounting to long-term behaviour) (iii) Single incident of long-term abandonment OR regular incidents of short-term abandonment (the longer the period of long-term abandonment or the greater the number of incidents of short-term abandonment, the more serious the offence) (iv) Failure to protect a child from any of the above	Crown Court	26 weeks custody to Crown Court
(i) Series of assaults (ii) Protracted neglect or ill-treatment (iii) Serious cruelty over a period of time (iv) Failure to protect a child from any of the above	Crown Court	Crown Court

B. Consider the effect of aggravating and mitigating factors (other than those within examples above)

Common aggravating and mitigating factors are identified [elsewhere]—the following may be particularly relevant but these lists are not exhaustive

1. Targeting one particular child from the family 2. Sadistic behaviour 3. Threats to prevent the victim from reporting the offence 4. Deliberate concealment of the victim from the authorities 5. Failure to seek medical help
1. Seeking medical help or bringing the situation to the notice of the authorities

[Sets out the standard sequential sentencing procedure.]

Dangerous Dogs Act Offences and Related Offences   SG-195

[The guidelines for the magistrates' court are identical to the general guidelines: see **SG-513**.]

Drugs—Class A—Fail to Attend/Remain for Initial Assessment   SG-196
Drugs Act 2005, s. 12

Triable only summarily:
Maximum: Level 4 fine and/or 3 months
Offence seriousness (culpability and harm)

A. Identify the appropriate starting point

Starting points based on first time offender pleading not guilty

Examples of nature of activity	Starting point	Range
Refusal to provide sample without good cause when required by police officer	**Medium level community order**	Band C fine to high level community order

B. Consider the effect of aggravating and mitigating factors (other than those within examples above)

Common aggravating and mitigating factors are identified [elsewhere]—the following may be particularly relevant but these lists are not exhaustive

Factor indicating greater degree of harm	Factors indicating lower culpability
1. Threats or abuse to staff	1. Subsequent voluntary contact with drug workers 2. Subsequent compliance with testing on arrest/charge

[Sets out the standard sequential sentencing procedure.]

SG-197   DRUGS—CLASS A—FAIL/REFUSE TO PROVIDE A SAMPLE
                            Police and Criminal Evidence Act 1984, s. 63B

Triable only summarily:
Maximum: Level 4 fine and/or 3 months

Offence seriousness (culpability and harm)

A. Identify the appropriate starting point

Starting points based on first time offender pleading not guilty

Examples of nature of activity	Starting point	Range
Failure to attend at the appointed place and time	Medium level community order	Band C fine to high level community order

B. Consider the effect of aggravating and mitigating factors (other than those within examples above)

Common aggravating and mitigating factors are identified [elsewhere]—the following may be particularly relevant but these lists are not exhaustive

Factors indicating greater degree of harm	Factors indicating lower culpability
1. Threats or abuse to assessor or other staff	1. Offender turns up but at wrong place or time or fails to remain for duration of appointment 2. Subsequent voluntary contact to rearrange appointment

[Sets out the standard sequential sentencing procedure.]

SG-198   DRUGS—FRAUDULENT EVASION OF A PROHIBITION BY BRINGING
                    INTO OR TAKING OUT OF THE UK A CONTROLLED DRUG
                          Misuse of Drugs Act 1971 (section 3)
                    Customs and Excise Management Act 1979 (section 170(2))

Triable either way unless the defendant could receive the minimum sentence of seven years for a third drug trafficking offence under section 110 Powers of Criminal Courts (Sentencing) Act 2000 in which case the offence is triable only on indictment.

CLASS A

Maximum: Life imprisonment

Offence range: 3 years 6 months' — 16 years' custody

A Class A offence is a drug trafficking offence for the purpose of imposing a minimum sentence under section 110 Powers of Criminal Courts (Sentencing) Act 2000

CLASS B

Maximum: 14 years' custody and/or unlimited fine

Offence range: 12 weeks' — 10 years' custody

CLASS C

Maximum: 14 years' custody and/or unlimited fine

Offence range: Community order — 8 years' custody

SG-199   **STEP ONE Determining the offence category**

The court should determine the offender's culpability (role) and the harm caused (quantity) with reference to the tables below.

In assessing culpability, the sentencer should weigh up all the factors of the case to determine role. Where there are characteristics present which fall under different role categories, the court should balance these characteristics to reach a fair assessment of the offender's culpability.

In assessing harm, quantity is determined by the weight of the product. Purity is not taken into account at step 1 but is dealt with at step 2.

Where the operation is on the most serious and commercial scale, involving a quantity of drugs significantly higher than category 1, sentences of 20 years and above may be appropriate, depending on the role of the offender.

Culpability demonstrated by offender's role One or more of these characteristics may demonstrate the offender's role. These lists are not exhaustive.	Category of harm Indicative quantity of drug concerned (upon which the starting point is based):
LEADING role: • Directing or organising buying and selling on a commercial scale; • Substantial links to, and influence on, others in a chain; • Close links to original source; • Expectation of substantial financial gain; • Uses business as cover; • Abuses a position of trust or responsibility.	**Category 1:** • Heroin, cocaine – 5kg; • Ecstasy – 10,000 tablets; • LSD – 250,000 squares; • Amphetamine – 20kg; • Cannabis – 200kg; • Ketamine – 5kg.
SIGNIFICANT role: • Operational or management function within a chain; • involves others in the operation whether by pressure, influence, intimidation or reward; • Motivated by financial or other advantage, whether or not operating alone; • Some awareness and understanding of scale of operation.	**Category 2:** • Heroin, cocaine – 1kg; • Ecstasy – 2,000 tablets; • LSD – 25,000 squares; • Amphetamine – 4kg; • Cannabis – 40kg; • Ketamine – 1kg.
LESSER role: • Performs a limited function under direction; • Engaged by pressure, coercion, intimidation; • Involvement through naivety/exploitation; • No influence on those above in a chain; • Very little, if any, awareness or understanding of the scale of operation; • If own operation, solely for own use (considering reasonableness of account in all the circumstances).	**Category 3:** • Heroin, cocaine – 150g; • Ecstasy – 300 tablets; • LSD – 2,500 squares; • Amphetamine – 750g; • Cannabis – 6kg; • Ketamine – 150g. **Category 4:** • Heroin, cocaine – 5g; • Ecstasy – 20 tablets; • LSD – 170 squares; • Amphetamine – 20g; • Cannabis – 100g; • Ketamine – 5g.

STEP TWO Starting point and category range   **SG-200**

Having determined the category, the court should use the corresponding starting point to reach a sentence within the category range below. The starting point applies to all offenders irrespective of plea or previous convictions. The court should then consider further adjustment within the category range for aggravating or mitigating features, set out [at **SG-201**]. In cases where the offender is regarded as being at the very top of the 'leading' role it may be justifiable for the court to depart from the guideline.

Where the defendant is dependent on or has a propensity to misuse drugs and there is sufficient prospect of success, a community order with a drug rehabilitation requirement under section 209 of the Criminal Justice Act 2003 can be a proper alternative to a short or moderate length custodial sentence.

*For **class A** cases, section 110 of the Powers of Criminal Courts (Sentencing) Act 2000 provides that a court should impose a minimum sentence of at least seven years' imprisonment for a third class A trafficking offence except where the court is of the opinion that there are particular circumstances which (a) relate to any of the offences or to the offender; and (b) would make it unjust to do so in all the circumstances.*

Sentencing Guidelines

CLASS A	Leading role	Significant role	Lesser role
Category 1	**Starting point** 14 years' custody **Category range** 12 – 16 years' custody	**Starting point** 10 years' custody **Category range** 9 – 12 years' custody	**Starting point** 8 years' custody **Category range** 6 – 9 years' custody
Category 2	**Starting point** 11 years' custody **Category range** 9 – 13 years' custody	**Starting point** 8 years' custody **Category range** 6 years 6 months' – 10 years' custody	**Starting point** 6 years' custody **Category range** 5 – 7 years' custody
Category 3	**Starting point** 8 years 6 months' custody **Category range** 6 years 6 months' – 10 years' custody	**Starting point** 6 years' custody **Category range** 5 – 7 years' custody	**Starting point** 4 years 6 months' custody **Category range** 3 years 6 months' – 5 years' custody
Category 4	Where the quantity falls below the indicative amount set out for category 4 [at **SG-199**], first identify the role for the importation offence, then refer to the starting point and ranges for possession or supply offences, depending on intent. Where the quantity is significantly larger than the indicative amounts for category 4 but below category 3 amounts, refer to the category 3 ranges above.		

CLASS B	Leading role	Significant role	Lesser role
Category 1	**Starting point** 8 years' custody **Category range** 7 – 10 years' custody	**Starting point** 5 years 6 months' custody **Category range** 5 – 7 years' custody	**Starting point** 4 years' custody **Category range** 2 years 6 months' – 5 years' custody
Category 2	**Starting point** 6 years' custody **Category range** 4 years 6 months' – 8 years' custody	**Starting point** 4 years' custody **Category range** 2 years 6 months' – 5 years' custody	**Starting point** 2 years' custody **Category range** 18 months' – 3 years' custody
Category 3	**Starting point** 4 years' custody **Category range** 2 years 6 months' – 5 years' custody	**Starting point** 2 years' custody **Category range** 18 months' – 3 years' custody	**Starting point** 1 years' custody **Category range** 12 weeks – 18 months' custody
Category 4	Where the quantity falls below the indicative amount set out for category 4 [at **SG-199**], first identify the role for the importation offence, then refer to the starting point and ranges for possession or supply offences, depending on intent. Where the quantity is significantly larger than the indicative amounts for category 4 but below category 3 amounts, refer to the category 3 ranges above		

CLASS C	Leading role	Significant role	Lesser role
Category 1	**Starting point** 5 years' custody **Category range** 4 – 8 years' custody	**Starting point** 3 years' custody **Category range** 2 – 5 years' custody	**Starting point** 18 months' custody **Category range** 1 – 3 years' custody
Category 2	**Starting point** 3 years 6 months' custody **Category range** 2 years' – 5 years' custody	**Starting point** 18 months' custody **Category range** 1 – 3 years' custody	**Starting point** 26 weeks' custody **Category range** 12 weeks – 18 months' custody

Category 3	Starting point 18 months' custody	Starting point 26 weeks' custody	Starting point High level community order
	Category range 1 – 3 years' custody	Category range 12 weeks – 18 months' custody	Category range Medium level community order – 12 weeks' custody
Category 4	Where the quantity falls below the indicative amount set out for category 4 [at SG-199], first identify the role for the importation offence, then refer to the starting point and ranges for possession or supply offences, depending on intent. Where the quantity is significantly larger than the indicative amounts for category 4 but below category 3 amounts, refer to the category 3 ranges above.		

The table below contains a **non-exhaustive** list of additional factual elements providing the context of the offence and factors relating to the offender. Identify whether any combination of these, or other relevant factors, should result in an upward or downward adjustment from the starting point. In some cases, having considered these factors, it may be appropriate to move outside the identified category range.   **SG-201**

For appropriate **class C** ranges, consider the custody threshold as follows:

- has the custody threshold been passed?
- if so, is it unavoidable that a custodial sentence be imposed?
- if so, can that sentence be suspended?

Factors increasing seriousness	Factors reducing seriousness or reflecting personal mitigation
Statutory aggravating factors: Previous convictions, having regard to a) nature of the offence to which conviction relates and relevance to current offence; and b) time elapsed since conviction (see [italicised text at SG-200] if third drug trafficking conviction) Offender used or permitted a person under 18 to deliver a controlled drug to a third person Offence committed on bail *Other aggravating factors include:* Sophisticated nature of concealment and/or attempts to avoid detection Attempts to conceal or dispose of evidence, where not charged separately Exposure of others to more than usual danger, for example drugs cut with harmful substances Presence of weapon, where not charged separately High purity Failure to comply with current court orders Offence committed on licence	Lack of sophistication as to nature of concealment Involvement due to pressure, intimidation or coercion falling short of duress, except where already taken into account at step 1 Mistaken belief of the offender regarding the type of drug, taking into account the reasonableness of such belief in all the circumstances Isolated incident Low purity No previous convictions or no relevant or recent convictions Offender's vulnerability was exploited Remorse Good character and/or exemplary conduct Determination and/or demonstration of steps having been taken to address addiction or offending behaviour Serious medical conditions requiring urgent, intensive or long-term treatment Age and/or lack of maturity where it affects the responsibility of the offender Mental disorder or learning disability Sole or primary carer for dependent relatives

STEP THREE Consider any factors which indicate a reduction, such as assistance to the prosecution   **SG-202**

The court should take into account sections 73 and 74 of the Serious Organised Crime and Police Act 2005 (assistance by defendants: reduction or review of sentence) and any other rule of law by virtue of which an offender may receive a discounted sentence in consequence of assistance given (or offered) to the prosecutor or investigator.

STEP FOUR Reduction for guilty pleas

The court should take account of any potential reduction for a guilty plea in accordance with section 144 of the Criminal Justice Act 2003 and the *Guilty Plea* guideline [see **SG-1**].

For class A offences, where a minimum mandatory sentence is imposed under section 110 Powers of Criminal Courts (Sentencing) Act, the discount for an early guilty plea must not exceed 20 per cent.

STEP FIVE   Totality principle

If sentencing an offender for more than one offence, or where the offender is already serving a sentence, consider whether the total sentence is just and proportionate to the offending behaviour.

STEP SIX   Confiscation and ancillary orders

In all cases, the court is required to consider confiscation where the Crown invokes the process or where the court considers it appropriate. It should also consider whether to make ancillary orders.

STEP SEVEN   Reasons

Section 174 of the Criminal Justice Act 2003 imposes a duty to give reasons for, and explain the effect of, the sentence.

STEP EIGHT   Consideration for remand time

Sentencers should take into consideration any remand time served in relation to the final sentence at this final step. The court should consider whether to give credit for time spent on remand in custody or on bail in accordance with sections 240 and 240A of the Criminal Justice Act 2003.

SG-203

Drugs - Supplying or Offering to Supply a Controlled Drug
Misuse of Drugs Act 1971 (section 4(3))

Possession of a Controlled Drug with Intent to Supply it to Another
Misuse of Drugs Act 1971 (section 5(3))

Triable either way unless the defendant could receive the minimum sentence of seven years for a third drug trafficking offence under section 110 Powers of Criminal Courts (Sentencing) Act 2000 in which case the offence is triable only on indictment.

Class A

Maximum: Life imprisonment

Offence range: Community order—16 years' custody

A class A offence is a drug trafficking offence for the purpose of imposing a minimum sentence under section 110 Powers of Criminal Courts (Sentencing) Act 2000

Class B

Maximum: 14 years' custody and/or unlimited fine

Offence range: Fine—10 years' custody

Class C

Maximum: 14 years' custody and/or unlimited fine

Offence range: Fine—8 years' custody

SG-204   **STEP ONE   Determining the offence category**

The court should determine the offender's culpability (role) and the harm caused (quantity/type of offender) with reference to the tables below.

In assessing culpability, the sentencer should weigh up all the factors of the case to determine role. Where there are characteristics present which fall under different role categories, the court should balance these characteristics to reach a fair assessment of the offender's culpability.

*In assessing harm, quantity is determined by the weight of the product. Purity is not taken into account at step 1 but is dealt with at step 2. Where the offence is **street dealing** or **supply of drugs in prison by a prison employee**, the quantity of the product is less indicative of the harm caused and therefore **the starting point is not based on quantity**.*

Where the operation is on the most serious and commercial scale, involving a quantity of drugs significantly higher than category 1, sentences of 20 years and above may be appropriate, depending on the role of the offender.

Culpability demonstrated by offender's role One or more of these characteristics may demonstrate the offender's role. These lists are not exhaustive.	Category of harm Indicative quantity of drug concerned (upon which the starting point is based):
LEADING role: • Directing or organising buying and selling on a commercial scale; • Substantial links to, and influence on, others in a chain; • Close links to original source; • Expectation of substantial financial gain; • Uses business as cover; • Abuses a position of trust or responsibility, for example prison employee, medical professional. **SIGNIFICANT role:** • Operational or management function within a chain; • Involves others in the operation whether by pressure, influence, intimidation or reward; • Motivated by financial or other advantage, whether or not operating alone; • Some awareness and understanding of scale of operation; • Supply, other than by a person in position of responsibility, to a prisoner for gain without coercion. **LESSER role:** • Performs a limited function under direction; • Engaged by pressure, coercion, intimidation; • Involvement through naivety/exploitation; • No influence on those above in a chain; • Very little, if any, awareness or understanding of the scale of operation; • If own operation, absence of financial gain, for example joint purchase for no profit, or sharing minimal quantity between peers on non-commercial basis.	**Category 1** • Heroin, cocaine – 5kg; • Ecstasy – 10,000 tablets; • LSD – 250,000 squares; • Amphetamine – 20kg; • Cannabis – 200kg; • Ketamine – 5kg. **Category 2** • Heroin, cocaine – 1kg; • Ecstasy – 2,000 tablets; • LSD – 25,000 squares; • Amphetamine – 4kg; • Cannabis – 40kg; • Ketamine – 1kg. **Category 3** Where the offence is selling direct to users [footnote indicates that this includes test purchase officers] ('street-dealing'), the starting point is not based on a quantity OR Where the offence is supply of drugs in prison by a prison employee, the starting point is not based on a quantity – see [italicised text above]. OR • Heroin, cocaine – 150g; • Ecstasy – 300 tablets; • LSD – 2,500 squares; • Amphetamine – 750g; • Cannabis – 6kg; • Ketamine – 150g. **Category 4** • Heroin, cocaine – 5g; • Ecstasy – 20 tablets; • LSD – 170 squares; • Amphetamine – 20g; • Cannabis – 100g; • Ketamine – 5g; OR Where the offence is selling directly to users [footnote indicates that this includes test purchase officers] ('street-dealing'), the starting point is not based on quantity – go to category 3.

STEP TWO   Starting point and category range   SG-205

Having determined the category, the court should use the corresponding starting point to reach a sentence within the category range below. The starting point applies to all offenders irrespective of plea or previous convictions. The court should then consider further adjustment within the category range for aggravating or mitigating features, set out [at **SG-206**]. In cases where the offender is regarded as being at the very top of the 'leading' role it may be justifiable for the court to depart from the guideline.

Where the defendant is dependent on or has a propensity to misuse drugs and there is sufficient prospect of success, a community order with a drug rehabilitation requirement under section 209 of the Criminal Justice Act 2003 can be a proper alternative to a short or moderate length custodial sentence.

*For **class A** cases, section 110 of the Powers of Criminal Courts (Sentencing) Act 2000 provides that a court should impose a minimum sentence of at least seven years' imprisonment for a third class A trafficking offence* *except where the court is of the opinion that there are particular circumstances which (a) relate to any of the offences or to the offender; and (b) would make it unjust to do so in all the circumstances.*

CLASS A	Leading role	Significant role	Lesser role
Category 1	**Starting point** 14 years' custody **Category range** 12 – 16 years' custody	**Starting point** 10 years' custody **Category range** 9 – 12 years' custody	**Starting point** 7 years' custody **Category range** 6 – 9 years' custody
Category 2	**Starting point** 11 years' custody **Category range** 9 – 13 years' custody	**Starting point** 8 years' custody **Category range** 6 years 6 months' – 10 years' custody	**Starting point** 5 years' custody **Category range** 3 years 6 months' – 7 years' custody
Category 3	**Starting point** 8 years 6 months' custody **Category range** 6 years 6 months' – 10 years' custody	**Starting point** 4 years 6 months' custody **Category range** 3 years 6 months' – 7 years' custody	**Starting point** 3 years' custody **Category range** 2 – 4 years 6 months' custody
Category 4	**Starting point** 5 years 6 months' custody **Category range** 4 years 6 months' – 7 years 6 months' custody	**Starting point** 3 years 6 months' custody **Category range** 2 – 5 years' custody	**Starting point** 18 months' custody **Category range** High level community order – 3 years' custody

CLASS B	Leading role	Significant role	Lesser role
Category 1	**Starting point** 8 years' custody **Category range** 7 – 10 years' custody	**Starting point** 5 years 6 months' custody **Category range** 5 – 7 years' custody	**Starting point** 3 years' custody **Category range** 2 years 6 months' – 5 years' custody
Category 2	**Starting point** 6 years' custody **Category range** 4 years 6 months' – 8 years' custody	**Starting point** 4 years' custody **Category range** 2 years 6 months' – 5 years' custody	**Starting point** 1 years' custody **Category range** 26 weeks' – 3 years' custody
Category 3	**Starting point** 4 years' custody **Category range** 2 years 6 months' – 5 years' custody	**Starting point** 1 year's custody **Category range** 26 weeks' – 3 years' custody	**Starting point** High level community order **Category range** Low level community order – 26 weeks' custody
Category 4	**Starting point** 18 months' custody **Category range** 26 weeks' – 3 years' custody	**Starting point** High level community order **Category range** Medium level community order – 26 weeks' custody	**Starting point** Low level community order **Category range** Band B fine – medium level community order

CLASS C	Leading role	Significant role	Lesser role
Category 1	**Starting point** 5 years' custody	**Starting point** 3 years' custody	**Starting point** 18 months' custody
	Category range 4 – 8 years' custody	**Category range** 2 – 5 years' custody	**Category range** 1 – 3 years' custody
Category 2	**Starting point** 3 years 6 months' custody	**Starting point** 18 months' custody	**Starting point** 26 weeks' custody
	Category range 2 years' – 5 years' custody	**Category range** 1 – 3 years' custody	**Category range** 12 weeks – 18 months' custody
Category 3	**Starting point** 18 months' custody	**Starting point** 26 weeks' custody	**Starting point** High level community order
	Category range 1 – 3 years' custody	**Category range** 12 weeks – 18 months' custody	**Category range** Low level community order – 12 weeks' custody
Category 4	**Starting point** 26 weeks' custody	**Starting point** High level community order	**Starting point** Low level community order
	Category range High level community order – 18 months' custody	**Category range** Low level community order – 12 weeks' custody	**Category range** Band A fine – medium level community order

The table below contains a **non-exhaustive** list of additional factual elements providing the context of the **SG-206** offence and factors relating to the offender. Identify whether any combination of these, or other relevant factors, should result in an upward or downward adjustment from the starting point. In some cases, having considered these factors, it may be appropriate to move outside the identified category range.

For appropriate **class B** and **C** ranges, consider the custody threshold as follows:

- has the custody threshold been passed?
- if so, is it unavoidable that a custodial sentence be imposed?
- if so, can that sentence be suspended?

For appropriate **class B** and **C** ranges, the court should also consider the community threshold as follows:

- has the community threshold been passed?

Factors increasing seriousness	Factors reducing seriousness or reflecting personal mitigation
Statutory aggravating factors: Previous convictions, having regard to a) nature of the offence to which conviction relates and relevance to current offence; and b) time elapsed since conviction (see [italicised text at **SG-205**] if third drug trafficking conviction) Offender used or permitted a person under 18 to deliver a controlled drug to a third person Offender 18 or over supplies or offers to supply a drug on, or in the vicinity of, school premises either when school in use as such or at a time between one hour before and one hour after they are to be used Offence committed on bail	Involvement due to pressure, intimidation or coercion falling short of duress, except where already taken into account at step 1 Supply only of drug to which offender addicted Mistaken belief of the offender regarding the type of drug, taking into account the reasonableness of such belief in all the circumstances Isolated incident Low purity No previous convictions **or** no relevant or recent convictions Offender's vulnerability was exploited

(Continued)

Other aggravating factors include:	Remorse
Targeting of any premises intended to locate vulnerable individuals or supply to such individuals and/or supply to those under 18	Good character and/or exemplary conduct
	Determination and/or demonstration of steps having been taken to address addiction or offending behaviour
Exposure of others to more than usual danger, for example drugs cut with harmful substances	Serious medical conditions requiring urgent, intensive or long-term treatment
Attempts to conceal or dispose of evidence, where not charged separately	Age and/or lack of maturity where it affects the responsibility of the offender
Presence of others, especially children and/or non-users	Mental disorder or learning disability
Presence of weapon, where not charged separately	Sole or primary carer for dependent relatives
Charged as importation of a very small amount	
High purity	
Failure to comply with current court orders	
Offence committed on licence	
Established evidence of community impact	

SG-207 [Steps Three to Eight are identical to those applicable to Fraudulent evasion of a prohibition by bringing into or taking out of the UK a controlled drug: see **SG-202**.]

SG-208 PRODUCTION OF A CONTROLLED DRUG

Misuse of Drugs Act 1971 (section 4(2)(a) or (b))

Triable either way unless the defendant could receive the minimum sentence of seven years for a third drug trafficking offence under section 110 Powers of Criminal Courts (Sentencing) Act 2000 in which case the offence is triable only on indictment.

CLASS A

Maximum: Life imprisonment

Offence range: Community order—16 years' custody

A class A offence is a drug trafficking offence for the purpose of imposing a minimum sentence under section 110 Powers of Criminal Courts (Sentencing) Act 2000

CLASS B

Maximum: 14 years' custody

Offence range: Discharge—10 years' custody

CLASS C

Maximum: 14 years' custody

Offence range: Discharge—8 years' custody

SG-209 CULTIVATION OF CANNABIS PLANT

Misuse of Drugs Act 1971 (section 6(2))

Maximum: 14 years' custody

Offence range: Discharge—10 years' custody

STEP ONE Determining the offence category

The court should determine the offender's culpability (role) and the harm caused (output or potential output) with reference to the tables below.

In assessing culpability, the sentencer should weigh up all of the factors of the case to determine role. Where there are characteristics present which fall under different role categories, the court should balance these characteristics to reach a fair assessment of the offender's culpability.

In assessing harm, output or potential output is determined by the weight of the product or number of plants/scale of operation. For production offences, purity is not taken into account at step 1 but is dealt with at step 2.

Where the operation is on the most serious and commercial scale, involving a quantity of drugs significantly higher than category 1, sentences of 20 years and above may be appropriate, depending on the role of the offender.

Culpability demonstrated by offender's role One or more of these characteristics may demonstrate the offender's role. These lists are not exhaustive.	Category of harm Indicative quantity of drug concerned (upon which the starting point is based):
LEADING role: • Directing or organising buying and selling on a commercial scale; • Substantial links to, and influence on, others in a chain; • Expectation of substantial financial gain; • Uses business as cover; • Abuses a position of trust or responsibility	**Category 1** • Heroin, cocaine – 5kg; • Ecstasy – 10,000 tablets; • LSD – 250,000 squares; • Amphetamine – 20kg; • Cannabis—operation capable of producing industrial quantities for commercial use; • Ketamine – 5kg.
SIGNIFICANT role: • Operational or management function within a chain; • Involves others in the operation whether by pressure, influence, intimidation or reward; • Motivated by financial or other advantage, whether or not operating alone; • Some awareness and understanding of scale of operation;	**Category 2** • Heroin, cocaine – 1kg; • Ecstasy – 2,000 tablets; • LSD – 25,000 squares; • Amphetamine – 4kg; • Cannabis—operation capable of producing significant quantities for commercial use; • Ketamine – 1kg.
LESSER role: • Performs a limited function under direction; • Engaged by pressure, coercion, intimidation; • Involvement through naivety/exploitation; • No influence on those above in a chain; • Very little, if any, awareness or understanding of the scale of operation; • If own operation, solely for own use (considering reasonableness of account in all the circumstances).	**Category 3** • Heroin, cocaine – 150g; • Ecstasy – 300 tablets; • LSD – 2,500 squares; • Amphetamine – 750g; • Cannabis—28 plants; [footnote indicates 'With assumed yield of 40g per plant'] • Ketamine – 150g. **Category 4** • Heroin, cocaine – 5g; • Ecstasy – 20 tablets; • LSD – 170 squares; • Amphetamine – 20g; • Cannabis – 9 plants (domestic operation); [footnote indicates 'With assumed yield of 40g per plant'] • Ketamine – 5g.

SG-210 **STEP TWO** **Starting point and category range**

Having determined the category, the court should use the corresponding starting point to reach a sentence within the category range below. The starting point applies to all offenders irrespective of plea or previous convictions. The court should then consider further adjustment within the category range for aggravating or mitigating features, set out [at **SG-211**]. In cases where the offender is regarded as being at the very top of the 'leading' role it may be justifiable for the court to depart from the guideline.

Where the defendant is dependent on or has a propensity to misuse drugs and there is sufficient prospect of success, a community order with a drug rehabilitation requirement under section 209 of the Criminal Justice Act 2003 can be a proper alternative to a short or moderate length custodial sentence.

*For **class A** cases, section 110 of the Powers of Criminal Courts (Sentencing) Act 2000 provides that a court should impose a minimum sentence of at least seven years' imprisonment for a third class A trafficking offence except where the court is of the opinion that there are particular circumstances which (a) relate to any of the offences or to the offender; and (b) would make it unjust to do so in all the circumstances.*

CLASS A	Leading role	Significant role	Lesser role
Category 1	**Starting point** 14 years' custody	**Starting point** 10 years' custody	**Starting point** 7 years' custody
	Category range 12 – 16 years' custody	**Category range** 9 – 12 years' custody	**Category range** 6 – 9 years' custody
Category 2	**Starting point** 11 years' custody	**Starting point** 8 years' custody	**Starting point** 5 years' custody
	Category range 9 – 13 years' custody	**Category range** 6 years 6 months'– 10 years' custody	**Category range** 3 years 6 months'– 7 years' custody
Category 3	**Starting point** 8 years 6 months' custody	**Starting point** 5 years 'custody	**Starting point** 3 years 6 months' custody
	Category range 6 years 6 months'– 10 years' custody	**Category range** 3 years 6 months'– 7 years' custody	**Category range** 2 – 5 years' custody
Category 4	**Starting point** 5 years 6 months' custody	**Starting point** 13 years 6 months' custody	**Starting point** 18 months' custody
	Category range 4 years 6 months'– 7 years 6 months' custody	**Category range** 2 – 5 years' custody	**Category range** High level community order – 3 years' custody

CLASS B	Leading role	Significant role	Lesser role
Category 1	**Starting point** 8 years' custody	**Starting point** 5 years 6 months' custody	**Starting point** 3 years' custody
	Category range 7 – 10 years' custody	**Category range** 5 – 7 years' custody	**Category range** 2 years 6 months' – 5 years' custody
Category 2	**Starting point** 6 years' custody	**Starting point** 4 years' custody	**Starting point** 1 years' custody
	Category range 4 years 6 months' – 8 years' custody	**Category range** 2 years 6 months' – 5 years' custody	**Category range** 26 weeks' – 3 years' custody
Category 3	**Starting point** 4 years' custody	**Starting point** 1 year's custody	**Starting point** High level community order
	Category range 2 years 6 months' – 5 years' custody	**Category range** 26 weeks' – 3 years' custody	**Category range** Low level community order – 26 weeks' custody
Category 4	**Starting point** 1 years' custody	**Starting point** High level community order	**Starting point** Band C fine
	Category range High level community order – 3 years' custody	**Category range** Medium level community order – 26 weeks' custody	**Category range** Discharge – medium level community order

CLASS C	Leading role	Significant role	Lesser role
Category 1	**Starting point** 5 years' custody **Category range** 4 – 8 years' custody	**Starting point** 3 years' custody **Category range** 2 – 5 years' custody	**Starting point** 18 months' custody **Category range** 1 – 3 years' custody
Category 2	**Starting point** 3 years 6 months' custody **Category range** 2 – 5 years' custody	**Starting point** 18 months' custody **Category range** 1 – 3 years' custody	**Starting point** 26 weeks' custody **Category range** High level community order – 18 months' custody
Category 3	**Starting point** 18 months' custody **Category range** 1 – 3 years' custody	**Starting point** 26 weeks' custody **Category range** High level community order – 18 months' custody	**Starting point** High level community order **Category range** Low level community order – 12 weeks' custody
Category 4	**Starting point** 26 weeks' custody **Category range** High level community order – 18 months' custody	**Starting point** High level community order **Category range** Low level community order – 12 weeks' custody	**Starting point** Band C fine **Category range** Discharge – medium level community order

The table below contains a **non-exhaustive** list of additional factual elements providing the context of the offence and factors relating to the offender. Identify whether any combination of these, or other relevant factors, should result in an upward or downward adjustment from the starting point. In some cases, having considered these factors, it may be appropriate to move outside the identified category range.

Where appropriate, consider the custody threshold as follows:

- has the custody threshold been passed?
- if so, is it unavoidable that a custodial sentence be imposed?
- if so, can that sentence be suspended?

Where appropriate, the court should also consider the community threshold as follows:

- has the community threshold been passed?

SG-211

Factors increasing seriousness	Factors reducing seriousness or reflecting personal mitigation
Statutory aggravating factors: Previous convictions, having regard to a) nature of the offence to which conviction relates and relevance to current offence; and b) time elapsed since conviction (see [italicised text at **SG-210**] if third drug trafficking conviction) Offence committed on bail *Other aggravating factors include:* Nature of any likely supply Level of any profit element Use of premises accompanied by unlawful access to electricity/other utility supply of others Ongoing/large scale operation as evidenced by presence and nature of specialist equipment Exposure of others to more than usual danger, for example drugs cut with harmful substances Attempts to conceal or dispose of evidence, where not charged separately Presence of others, especially children and/or non-users Presence of weapon, where not charged separately High purity or high potential yield Failure to comply with current court orders Offence committed on licence Established evidence of community impact	Involvement due to pressure, intimidation or coercion falling short of duress, except where already taken into account at step 1 Isolated incident Low purity No previous convictions **or** no relevant or recent convictions Offender's vulnerability was exploited Remorse Good character and/or exemplary conduct Determination and/or demonstration of steps having been taken to address addiction or offending behaviour Serious medical conditions requiring urgent, intensive or long-term treatment Age and/or lack of maturity where it affects the responsibility of the offender Mental disorder or learning disability Sole or primary carer for dependent relatives

SG-212 [Steps Three to Eight are identical to those applicable to Fraudulent evasion of a prohibition by bringing into or taking out of the UK a controlled drug: see **SG-202**.]

SG-213   PERMITTING PREMISES TO BE USED
                              Misuse of Drugs Act 1971 (section 8)

Triable either way unless the defendant could receive the minimum sentence of seven years for a third drug trafficking offence under section 110 Powers of Criminal Courts (Sentencing) Act 2000 in which case the offence is triable only on indictment.

                                      CLASS A

Maximum: 14 years' custody

Offence range: Community order – 4 years' custody

A class A offence is a drug trafficking offence for the purpose of imposing a minimum sentence under section 110 Powers of Criminal Courts (Sentencing) Act 2000

                                      CLASS B

Maximum: 14 years' custody

Offence range: Fine – 18 months' custody

                                      CLASS C

Maximum: 14 years' custody

Offence range: Discharge – 26 weeks' custody

SG-214 STEP ONE **Determining the offence category**

The court should determine the offender's culpability and the harm caused (extent of the activity and/or the quantity of drugs) with reference to the table below.

In assessing harm, quantity is determined by the weight of the product. Purity is not taken into account at step 1 but is dealt with at step 2

Category 1	Higher culpability **and** greater harm
Category 2	Lower culpability **and** greater harm; **or** higher culpability **and** lesser harm
Category 3	Lower culpability **and** lesser harm

Factors indicating culpability (non-exhaustive)	Factors indicating harm (non-exhaustive)
Higher culpability: Permits premises to be used primarily for drug activity, for example crack house Permits use in expectation of substantial financial gain Uses legitimate business premises to aid and/or conceal illegal activity, for example public house or club *Lower culpability*: Permits use for limited or no financial gain No active role in any supply taking place Involvement through naivety	*Greater harm*: Regular drug-related activity Higher quantity of drugs, for example: • Heroin, cocaine – more than 5g; • Cannabis – more than 50g. *Lesser harm:* Infrequent drug-related activity Lower quantity of drugs, for example: • Heroin, cocaine – up to 5g; • Cannabis – up to 50g.

SG-215 STEP TWO **Starting point and category range**

Having determined the category, the court should use the table below to identify the corresponding starting point to reach a sentence within the category range. The starting point applies to all offenders irrespective of plea or previous convictions. The court should then consider further adjustment within the category range for aggravating or mitigating features, set out [at **SG-216**].

Where the defendant is dependent on or has a propensity to misuse drugs and there is sufficient prospect of success, a community order with a drug rehabilitation requirement under section 209 of the Criminal Justice Act 2003 can be a proper alternative to a short or moderate length custodial sentence.

*For **class A** cases, section 110 of the Powers of Criminal Courts (Sentencing) Act 2000 provides that a court should impose a minimum sentence of at least seven years' imprisonment for a third class A trafficking offence except where the court is of the opinion that there are particular circumstances which (a) relate to any of the offences or to the offender; and (b) would make it unjust to do so in all the circumstances.*

CLASS A

Offence category	Starting point *(applicable to all offenders)*	Category range *(applicable to all offenders)*
Category 1	2 years 6 months' custody	18 months' – 4 years' custody
Category 2	36 weeks' custody	High level community order – 18 months' custody
Category 3	Medium level community order	Low level community order – high level community order

CLASS B

Offence category	Starting point *(applicable to all offenders)*	Category range *(applicable to all offenders)*
Category 1	1 year's custody	26 weeks' – 18 months' custody
Category 2	High level community order	Low level community order – 26 weeks' custody
Category 3	Band C fine	Band A fine – low level community order

CLASS C

Offence category	Starting point *(applicable to all offenders)*	Category range *(applicable to all offenders)*
Category 1	12 weeks' custody	High level community order – 26 weeks' custody [footnote indicates that 'when tried summarily, the maximum penalty is 12 weeks' custody']
Category 2	Low level community order	Band C fine – high level community order
Category 3	Band A fine	Discharge – band C fine

The table below contains a **non-exhaustive** list of additional factual elements providing the context of the offence and factors relating to the offender. Identify whether any combination of these, or other relevant factors, should result in an upward or downward adjustment from the starting point. In some cases, having considered these factors, it may be appropriate to move outside the identified category range.   **SG-216**

Where appropriate, consider the custody threshold as follows:

- has the custody threshold been passed?
- if so, is it unavoidable that a custodial sentence be imposed?
- if so, can that sentence be suspended?

Where appropriate, the court should also consider the community threshold as follows:

- has the community threshold been passed?

Factors increasing seriousness	Factors reducing seriousness or reflecting personal mitigation
Statutory aggravating factors: Previous convictions, having regard to a) nature of the offence to which conviction relates and relevance to current offence; and b) time elapsed since conviction (see italicised text at **SG-215** if third drug trafficking conviction) Offence committed on bail *Other aggravating factors include:* Length of time over which premises used for drug activity Volume of drug activity permitted Premises adapted to facilitate drug activity Location of premises, for example proximity to school Attempts to conceal or dispose of evidence, where not charged separately Presence of others, especially children and/or non-users High purity Presence of weapons, where not charged separately Failure to comply with current court orders Offence committed on licence Established evidence of community impact	Involvement due to pressure, intimidation or coercion falling short of duress Isolated incident Low purity No previous convictions **or** no relevant or recent convictions Offender's vulnerability was exploited Remorse Good character and/or exemplary conduct Determination and/or demonstration of steps having been taken to address addiction or offending behaviour Serious medical conditions requiring urgent, intensive or long-term treatment Age and/or lack of maturity where it affects the responsibility of the offender Mental disorder or learning disability Sole or primary carer for dependent relatives

SG-217 [Steps Three to Eight are identical to those applicable to Fraudulent evasion of a prohibition by bringing into or taking out of the UK a controlled drug: see **SG-202**.]

SG-218

Possession of a Controlled Drug

Misuse of Drugs Act 1971 (section 5(2))

Triable either way

Class A

Maximum: 7 years' custody

Offence range: Fine—51 weeks' custody

Class B

Maximum: 5 years' custody

Offence range: Discharge—26 weeks' custody

Class C

Maximum: 2 years' custody

Offence range: Discharge—Community order

SG-219 STEP ONE Determining the offence category

The court should identify the offence category based on the class of drug involved.

Category 1	Class A drug
Category 2	Class B drug
Category 3	Class C drug

STEP TWO Starting point and category range   SG-220

The court should use the table below to identify the corresponding starting point. The starting point applies to all offenders irrespective of plea or previous convictions. The court should then consider further adjustment within the category range for aggravating or mitigating features, set out [at **SG-221**].

Where the defendant is dependent on or has a propensity to misuse drugs and there is sufficient prospect of success, a community order with a drug rehabilitation requirement under section 209 of the Criminal Justice Act 2003 can be a proper alternative to a short or moderate length custodial sentence.

Offence category	Starting point (*applicable to all offenders*)	Category range (*applicable to all offenders*)
Category 1 (class A)	Band C fine	Band A fine – 51 weeks' custody
Category 2 (class B)	Band B fine	Discharge – 26 weeks' custody
Category 3 (class C)	Band A fine	Discharge – medium level community order

The table below contains a **non-exhaustive** list of additional factual elements providing the context of the   SG-221
offence and factors relating to the offender. Identify whether any combination of these, or other relevant factors, should result in an upward or downward adjustment from the starting point. **In particular, possession of drugs in prison is likely to result in an upward adjustment**. In some cases, having considered these factors, it may be appropriate to move outside the identified category range.

Where appropriate, consider the custody threshold as follows:

- has the custody threshold been passed?
- if so, is it unavoidable that a custodial sentence be imposed?
- if so, can that sentence be suspended?

Where appropriate, the court should also consider the community threshold as follows:

- has the community threshold been passed?

Factors increasing seriousness	Factors reducing seriousness or reflecting personal mitigation
Statutory aggravating factors: Previous convictions, having regard to a) nature of the offence to which conviction relates and relevance to current offence; and b) time elapsed since conviction Offence committed on bail	No previous convictions **or** no relevant or recent convictions Remorse Good character and/or exemplary conduct Offender is using cannabis to help with a diagnosed medical condition Determination and/or demonstration of steps having been taken to address addiction or offending behaviour Serious medical conditions requiring urgent, intensive or long-term treatment Isolated incident Age and/or lack of maturity where it affects the responsibility of the offender Mental disorder or learning disability Sole or primary carer for dependent relatives
Other aggravating factors include: Possession of drug in prison Presence of others, especially children and/or non-users Possession of drug in a school or licensed premises Failure to comply with current court orders Offence committed on licence Attempts to conceal or dispose of evidence, where not charged separately Charged as importation of a very small amount Established evidence of community impact	

[Steps Three to Eight are similar to those applicable to Fraudulent evasion of a prohibition by bringing   SG-222
into or taking out of the UK a controlled drug (see **SG-202**) but the reference at Step Four to minimum mandatory sentences does not apply and Step Six merely states 'In all cases, the court should consider whether to make ancillary orders'.]

SG-223

DRUNK AND DISORDERLY IN A PUBLIC PLACE

Criminal Justice Act 1967, s. 91

Triable only summarily
Maximum: Level 3 fine

Offence seriousness (culpability and harm)

A. Identify the appropriate starting point

Starting points based on first time offender pleading not guilty

Examples of nature of activity	Starting point	Range
Shouting, causing disturbance for some minutes	Band A fine	Conditional discharge to band B fine
Substantial disturbance caused	Band B fine	Band A fine to band C fine

B. Consider the effect of aggravating and mitigating factors (other than those within examples above)

Common aggravating and mitigating factors are identified [elsewhere]—the following may be particularly relevant but these lists are not exhaustive

Factors indicating higher culpability	Factors indicating lower culpability
1. Offensive words or behaviour involved 2. Lengthy incident 3. Group action	1. Minor and non-threatening 2. Stopped as soon as police arrived
Factors indicating greater degree of harm 1. Offence committed at school, hospital or other place where vulnerable persons may be present 2. Offence committed on public transport 3. Victim providing public service	

[Sets out the standard sequential sentencing procedure and includes mention of need to consider football banning order.]

SG-224

ELECTRICITY, ABSTRACT/USE WITHOUT AUTHORITY

Factors to take into consideration
Key factors

(a) The starting points and sentencing ranges in this guideline are based on the assumption that the offender was motivated by greed or a desire to live beyond his or her means. To avoid double counting, such a motivation should not be treated as a factor that increases culpability.

(b) When assessing the harm caused by this offence, the starting point should be the loss suffered by the victim. In general, the greater the loss, the more serious the offence. However, the monetary value of the loss may not reflect the full extent of the harm caused by the offence. The court should also take into account the impact of the offence on the victim, any harm to persons other than the direct victim, and any harm in the form of public alarm or erosion of public confidence.

(c) The following matters of offender mitigation may be relevant to this offence:

    (i) *Offender motivated by desperation or need*
        The fact that an offence has been committed in desperation or need arising from particular hardship may count as offender mitigation in exceptional circumstances.

    (ii) *Voluntary restitution*
        Whether and the degree to which payment for stolen electricity constitutes a matter of offender mitigation will depend on an assessment of the circumstances and, in particular, the voluntariness and timeliness of the payment.

    (iii) *Impact on sentence of offender's dependency*
        Many offenders convicted of acquisitive crimes are motivated by an addiction, often to drugs, alcohol or gambling. This does not mitigate the seriousness of the offence, but an offender's dependency may properly influence the type of sentence imposed. In particular, it may sometimes be appropriate to impose a drug rehabilitation requirement or an alcohol treatment requirement as part of a community order or a suspended sentence order in an attempt to break

the cycle of addiction and offending, even if an immediate custodial sentence would otherwise be warranted.[128]

Guidelines

Theft Act 1968, s. 13

Triable either way:

Maximum when tried summarily: Level 5 fine and/or 6 months

Maximum when tried on indictment: 5 years

Offence seriousness (culpability and harm)

A. Identify the appropriate starting point

Starting points based on first time offender pleading not guilty

Examples of nature of activity	Starting point	Range
Where the offence results in substantial commercial gain, a custodial sentence may be appropriate		
Offence involving evidence of planning and indication that the offending was intended to be continuing, such as using a device to interfere with the electricity meter or re-wiring to by-pass the meter	Medium level community order	Band A fine to high level community order

B. Consider the effect of aggravating and mitigating factors (other than those within examples above)

Common aggravating and mitigating factors are identified [elsewhere]—the following may be particularly relevant but these lists are not exhaustive

Factor indicating greater degree of harm
1. Risk of danger caused to property and/or life

[Sets out the standard sequential sentencing procedure.]

ENVIRONMENTAL OFFENCES

SG-224A

[The guidelines applicable in magistrates' courts are identical to those set out in part 28 of the Sentencing Guidelines, see **SG-674**.]

EXPLOITATION OF PROSTITUTION

SG-225

[The *guidelines* set out below are applicable to adult offenders sentenced after 1 April 2014.]

CAUSING OR INCITING PROSTITUTION FOR GAIN
Sexual Offences Act 2003 (section 52)

CONTROLLING PROSTITUTION FOR GAIN
Sexual Offences Act 2003 (section 53)

Triable either way:

Maximum: 7 years' custody

Offence range: Community order — 6 years' custody

For convictions on or after 3 December 2012 (irrespective of the date of commission of the offence), these are specified offences for the purposes of section 226A (extended sentence for certain violent or sexual offences) of the Criminal Justice Act 2003.

The terms 'prostitute' and 'prostitution' are used in this guideline in accordance with the statutory language contained in the Sexual Offences Act 2003.

STEP ONE Determining the offence category

The court should determine which categories of harm and culpability the offence falls into by reference **only** to the tables below.

---

[128] See para.2 on p.163. The Court of Appeal gave guidance on the approach to making drug treatment and testing orders, which also applies to imposing a drug rehabilitation requirement in *Attorney General's Reference No. 64 of 2003* (*Boujettif and Harrison*) [2003] EWCA Crim 3514 and *Woods and Collins* [2005] EWCA Crim 2065 summarised in the Sentencing Guidelines Council *Guideline Judgments Case Compendium* (section (A) Generic Sentencing Principles) available at: www.sentencing-guidelines.gov.uk

HARM	
Category 1	• Abduction/detention • Violence or threats of violence • Sustained and systematic psychological abuse • Individual(s) forced or coerced to participate in unsafe/degrading sexual activity • Individual(s) forced or coerced into seeing many "customers" • Individual(s) forced/coerced/deceived into prostitution
Category 2	Factor(s) in category 1 not present

CULPABILITY		
A	**B**	**C**
• Causing, inciting or controlling prostitution on significant commercial basis • Expectation of significant financial or other gain • Abuse of trust • Exploitation of those known to be trafficked • Significant involvement in limiting the freedom of prostitute(s) • Grooming of individual(s) to enter prostitution including through cultivation of a dependency on drugs or alcohol	• Close involvement with prostitute(s) for example control of finances, choice of clients, working conditions, etc (where offender's involvement is not as a result of coercion)	• Performs limited function under direction • Close involvement but engaged by coercion/intimidation/exploitation

STEP TWO Starting point and category range

Having determined the category, the court should use the corresponding starting points to reach a sentence within the category range below. The starting point applies to all offenders irrespective of plea or previous convictions. Having determined the starting point, step two allows further adjustment for aggravating or mitigating features, set out [below].

A case of particular gravity, reflected by multiple features of culpability or harm in step one, could merit upward adjustment from the starting point before further adjustment for aggravating or mitigating features, set out [below].

Where there is a sufficient prospect of rehabilitation, a community order with a sex offender treatment programme requirement under section 202 of the Criminal Justice Act 2003 can be a proper alternative to a short or moderate length custodial sentence.

Category 1	**Starting point** 4 years' custody **Category range** 3 – 6 years' custody	**Starting point** 2 years 6 months' custody **Category range** 2 – 4 years' custody	**Starting point** 1 year's custody **Category range** 26 weeks' – 2 years' custody
Category 2	**Starting point** 2 years' 6 months' custody **Category range** 2 – 5 years' custody	**Starting point** 1 year's custody **Category range** High level community order – 2 years' custody	**Starting point** Medium level community Order **Category range** Low level community order – High level community order

The table below contains a **non-exhaustive** list of additional factual elements providing the context of the offence and factors relating to the offender. Identify whether any combination of these, or other relevant factors, should result in an upward or downward adjustment from the starting point. **In particular, relevant recent convictions are likely to result in an upward adjustment**. In some cases, having considered these factors, it may be appropriate to move outside the identified category range.

When sentencing appropriate **category 2 offences**, the court should also consider the custody threshold as follows:

- has the custody threshold been passed?
- if so, is it unavoidable that a custodial sentence be imposed?
- if so, can that sentence be suspended?

Aggravating factors

Statutory aggravating factors

- Previous convictions, having regard to a) the nature of the offence to which the conviction relates and its relevance to the current offence; and b) the time that has elapsed since the conviction
- Offence committed whilst on bail

Other aggravating factors

- Failure to comply with current court orders
- Offence committed whilst on licence
- Deliberate isolation of prostitute(s)
- Threats made to expose prostitute(s) to the authorities (for example, immigration or police), family/friends or others
- Harm threatened against the family/friends of prostitute(s)
- Passport/identity documents removed
- Prostitute(s) prevented from seeking medical treatment
- Food withheld
- Earnings withheld/kept by offender or evidence of excessive wage reduction or debt bondage, inflated travel or living expenses or unreasonable interest rates
- Any steps taken to prevent the reporting of an incident, obtaining assistance and/or from assisting or supporting the prosecution
- Attempts to dispose of or conceal evidence
- Prostitute(s) forced or coerced into pornography
- Timescale over which operation has been run

Mitigating factors

- No previous convictions **or** no relevant/recent convictions
- Remorse
- Previous good character and/or exemplary conduct*
- Age and/or lack of maturity where it affects the responsibility of the offender
- Mental disorder or learning disability, particularly where linked to the commission of the offence
- Demonstration of steps taken to address offending behaviour

* Previous good character/exemplary conduct is different from having no previous convictions. The more serious the offence, the less the weight which should normally be attributed to this factor. Where previous good character/exemplary conduct has been used to facilitate the offence, this mitigation should not normally be allowed and such conduct may constitute an aggravating factor.

[Sets out the standard sequential sentencing procedure.]

EXPOSURE   SG-226

[The guidelines set out below are applicable to adult offenders sentenced after 1 April 2014.]

Sexual Offences Act 2003 (section 66)

Triable either way:
Maximum: 2 years' custody
Offence range: Fine - 1 year's custody

For convictions on or after 3 December 2012 (irrespective of the date of commission of the offence), this is a specified offence for the purposes of section 226A (extended sentence for certain violent or sexual offences) of the Criminal Justice Act 2003.

STEP ONE Determining the offence category

The court should determine the offence category using the table below.

Category 1	Raised harm **and** raised culpability
Category 2	Raised harm **or** raised culpability
Category 3	Exposure **without** raised harm or culpability factors present

The court should determine culpability and harm caused or intended, by reference **only** to the factors below, which comprise the principal factual elements of the offence. Where an offence does not fall squarely into a category, individual factors may require a degree of weighting before making an overall assessment and determining the appropriate offence category.

Factors indicating raised harm
• Victim followed/pursued • Offender masturbated

Factors indicating raised culpability
• Specific or previous targeting of a particularly vulnerable victim • Abuse of trust • Use of threats (including blackmail) • Offence racially or religiously aggravated • Offence motivated by, or demonstrating, hostility to the victim based on his or her sexual orientation (or presumed sexual orientation) or transgender identity (or presumed transgender identity) • Offence motivated by, or demonstrating, hostility to the victim based on his or her disability (or presumed disability)

STEP TWO Starting point and category range

Having determined the category, the court should use the corresponding starting points to reach a sentence within the category range [below]. The starting point applies to all offenders irrespective of plea or previous convictions. Having determined the starting point, step two allows further adjustment for aggravating or mitigating features, set out [below].

A case of particular gravity, reflected by multiple features of culpability or harm in step one, could merit upward adjustment from the starting point before further adjustment for aggravating or mitigating features, set out [below].

Where there is a sufficient prospect of rehabilitation, a community order with a sex offender treatment programme requirement under section 202 of the Criminal Justice Act 2003 can be a proper alternative to a short or moderate length custodial sentence.

Category 1	**Starting point** 26 weeks' custody **Category range** 12 weeks' – 1 year's custody
Category 2	**Starting point** High level community order **Category range** Medium level community order – 26 weeks' custody
Category 3	**Starting point** Medium level community order **Category range** Band A fine - High level community order

The table below contains a **non-exhaustive** list of additional factual elements providing the context of the offence and factors relating to the offender. Identify whether any combination of these, or other relevant factors, should result in an upward or downward adjustment from the starting point. **In particular, relevant recent convictions are likely to result in an upward adjustment**. In some cases, having considered these factors, it may be appropriate to move outside the identified category range.

When sentencing **category 2 offences**, the court should also consider the custody threshold as follows:

• has the custody threshold been passed?
• if so, is it unavoidable that a custodial sentence be imposed?
• if so, can that sentence be suspended?

When sentencing **category 3 offences**, the court should also consider the community order threshold as follows:

• has the community order threshold been passed?

Aggravating factors

Statutory aggravating factors

- Previous convictions, having regard to a) the nature of the offence to which the conviction relates and its relevance to the current offence; and b) the time that has elapsed since the conviction
- Offence committed whilst on bail

Other aggravating factors

- Location of the offence
- Timing of the offence
- Any steps taken to prevent the victim reporting an incident, obtaining assistance and/or from assisting or supporting the prosecution
- Failure to comply with current court orders
- Offence committed whilst on licence
- Commission of offence whilst under the influence of alcohol or drugs
- Presence of others, especially children

Mitigating factors

- No previous convictions **or** no relevant/recent convictions
- Remorse
- Previous good character and/or exemplary conduct*
- Age and/or lack of maturity where it affects the responsibility of the offender
- Mental disorder or learning disability, particularly where linked to the commission of the offence
- Demonstration of steps taken to address offending behaviour

*   Previous good character/exemplary conduct is different from having no previous convictions. The more serious the offence, the less the weight which should normally be attributed to this factor. Where previous good character/ exemplary conduct has been used to facilitate the offence, this mitigation should not normally be allowed and such conduct may constitute an aggravating factor.

[Sets out the standard sequential sentencing procedure.]

False Accounting   SG-227
Theft Act 1968, s. 17

Triable either way:
Maximum when tried summarily: Level 5 fine and/or 6 months
Maximum when tried on indictment: 7 years

Refer to guideline *Fraud — banking and insurance fraud and obtaining credit through fraud, benefit fraud and revenue fraud* [see **SG-230** *et seq.*].

Firearm, Carrying in Public Place   SG-228
Firearms Act 1968, s. 19

Triable either way (but triable only summarily if the firearm is an air weapon):
Maximum when tried summarily: Level 5 fine and/or 6 months
Maximum when tried on indictment: 7 years (12 months for imitation firearms)

Offence seriousness (culpability and harm)

A. Identify the appropriate starting point

Starting points based on first time offender pleading not guilty

Examples of nature of activity	Starting point	Range
Carrying an unloaded air weapon	Low level community order	Band B fine to medium level community order
Carrying loaded air weapon/imitation firearm/unloaded shot gun without ammunition	High level community order	Medium level community order to 26 weeks custody (air weapon) Medium level community order to Crown Court (imitation firearm, unloaded shot gun)
Carrying loaded shot gun/carrying shot gun or any other firearm together with ammunition for it	Crown Court	Crown Court

Sentencing Guidelines

B. Consider the effect of aggravating and mitigating factors (other than those within examples above)

Common aggravating and mitigating factors are identified [elsewhere]—the following may be particularly relevant but these lists are not exhaustive

Factors indicating higher culpability	Factors indicating lower culpability
1. Brandishing the firearm	1. Firearm not in sight
2. Carrying firearm in a busy place	2. No intention to use firearm
3. Planned illegal use	3. Firearm to be used for lawful purpose (not amounting to a defence)
Factors indicating greater degree of harm	
1. Person or people put in fear	
2. Offender participating in violent incident	

[Sets out the standard sequential sentencing procedure, ancillary orders to be considered include compensation, forfeiture or suspension of personal liquor licence and football banning order (where appropriate).]

SG-229

FOOTBALL RELATED OFFENCES

Sporting Events (Control of Alcohol etc.) Act 1985: s. 2(1) (possession of alcohol whilst entering or trying to enter ground); s.2(2) (being drunk in, or whilst trying to enter, ground) Football Offences Act 1991: s. 2 (throwing missile); s. 3 (indecent or racist chanting); s. 4 (going onto prohibited areas)

Criminal Justice and Public Order Act 1994: s. 166 (unauthorised sale or attempted sale of tickets)

Triable only summarily:
Maximum: Level 2 fine (being drunk in ground) Level 3 fine (throwing missile; indecent or racist chanting; going onto prohibited areas) Level 5 fine (unauthorised sale of tickets) Level 3 fine and/or 3 months (possession of alcohol)

Offence seriousness (culpability and harm)

A. Identify the appropriate starting point

Starting points based on first time offender pleading not guilty

Examples of nature of activity	Starting point	Range
Being drunk in, or whilst trying to enter, ground	Band A fine	Conditional discharge to band B fine
Going onto playing or other prohibited area; Unauthorised sale or attempted sale of tickets	Band B fine	Band A fine to band C fine
Throwing missile; Indecent or racist chanting	Band C fine	Band C fine
Possession of alcohol whilst entering or trying to enter ground	Band C fine	Band B fine to high level community order

B. Consider the effect of aggravating and mitigating factors (other than those within examples above)

Common aggravating and mitigating factors are identified [elsewhere]—the following may be particularly relevant but these lists are not exhaustive

Factors indicating higher culpability
1. Commercial ticket operation; potential high cash value; counterfeit tickets
2. Inciting others to misbehave
3. Possession of large quantity of alcohol
4. Offensive language or behaviour (where not an element of the offence)
Factors indicating greater degree of harm
1. Missile likely to cause serious injury e.g. coin, glass, bottle, stone

[Sets out the standard sequential sentencing procedure and mentions need to consider a football banning order.]

FRAUD—BANKING AND INSURANCE FRAUD, AND OBTAINING CREDIT THROUGH FRAUD, BENEFIT FRAUD, AND REVENUE FRAUD

SG-230

Factors to take into consideration

This guideline and accompanying notes are taken from the Sentencing Guidelines Council's definitive guideline *Sentencing for Fraud — Statutory offences*, published 26 October 2009 [see **SG-420**]. The starting points and ranges for fraud against HM Revenue and Customs, for benefit fraud and for banking and insurance and obtaining credit through fraud are the same since the seriousness of all offences of organisational fraud derives from the extent of the fraudulent activity (culpability) and the financial loss caused or likely to be caused (harm).

Key factors common to these types of fraud

(a) As the determinants of seriousness include the 'value of property or consequential loss involved', the table provides both a fixed amount (on which the starting point is based) and a band (on which the sentencing range is based). Where the value is larger or smaller than the amount on which the starting point is based, this should lead to upward or downward movement from the starting point as appropriate. Where the amount the offender intended to obtain cannot be established, the appropriate measure will be the amount that was likely to be achieved in all the circumstances. Where the offender was entitled to part or all of the amount obtained, the starting point should be based on the amount to which they were not entitled.

(b) A further determinant of seriousness is whether the fraud was a single fraudulent transaction or a multiple fraud. Where one false declaration or a failure to disclose a change in circumstances results in multiple payments, this should be regarded as multiple fraud.

(c) In general terms, the greater the loss, the more serious will be the offence. However, the financial value of the loss may not reflect the full extent of the harm caused. The court should also take into account; the impact of the offence on the victim (particularly where the loss may be significantly greater than the monetary value); harm to persons other than the direct victim (including the aggravation and stress of unscrambling the consequences of an offence); erosion of public confidence; and the difference between the loss intended and that which results (which may involve adjusting the assessment of seriousness to reflect the degree of loss caused).

(d) When the offending involves a number of people acting co-operatively, this will aggravate an offence as it indicates planning or professional activity, and may also increase the degree of loss caused or intended. The role of each offender is important in determining the appropriate level of seriousness and movement above or below the starting point within the applicable level.

(e) Use of another person's identity is an aggravating factor; the extent to which it aggravates an offence will be based on the degree of planning and the impact that the offence has had on the living victim or relatives of the deceased—whether the identity belongs to a living or deceased person is neutral for this purpose.

(f) Matters of offender mitigation which may be particularly relevant to these types of fraud include:

- *Voluntary cessation of offending* — a claim, supported by objective evidence, that an offender stopped offending before being apprehended should be treated as mitigation, particularly where accompanied by a genuine expression of remorse. The lapse of time since commission of the last offence is relevant to whether the claim is genuine, and reasons for the cessation will assist the court in determining whether it amounts to mitigation and if so, to what degree.

- *Complete and unprompted disclosure of the extent of the fraud* — an admission that a greater sum has been obtained than that known to the authorities ensures that an offender is sentenced for the complete extent of the fraud. This is ready co-operation with the authorities and should be treated as mitigation. Provision of information about others involved in the fraud should also be treated as mitigation. Generally, the earlier the disclosure is given and the higher the degree of assistance, the greater the allowance for mitigation.

- *Voluntary restitution* — the timing of the voluntary restitution will indicate the degree to which it reflects genuine remorse. Generally, the earlier the property or money is returned the greater the degree of mitigation the offender should receive. If circumstances beyond the control of the offender prevent return of defrauded items, the degree of mitigation will depend on the point in time at which, and the determination with which the offender tried to return the items.

- *Financial pressure* — financial pressure neither increases nor diminishes an offender's culpability. However, where such pressure is **exceptional** and not of the offender's own making, it may in very rare circumstances constitute mitigation.

(g) A court should be aware that a confiscation order is an important sanction. Such an order may only be made in the Crown Court. The court must commit the offender to the Crown Court where this is requested by the prosecution with a view to an order being considered.

(h) Ancillary orders should be considered in all cases, principally compensation, deprivation and disqualification from driving, as well as other powers particular to the type of offending behaviour.

Additional notes:

Banking and insurance fraud and obtaining credit through fraud:

(i) A payment card or bank account fraud is unlikely to be committed in circumstances where the offender's intention was not fraudulent from the outset.

(ii) Use of another person's identity is a feature of nearly all payment card and bank account frauds since in most cases the offender claims to be the account holder or a person authorised to deal with the account. Courts should therefore increase the starting point to reflect the presence of this aggravating factor.

Benefit fraud:

(i) This guideline is based on an understanding that the prosecutor will generally seek summary trial for appropriate benefit fraud cases involving sums up to £35,000.

(ii) The fact that defrauded sums may have been recovered is not relevant to the choice of the type of sentence to be imposed.

(iii) The court should have regard to personal and family circumstances of offenders which will vary greatly and may be particularly significant to sentencing this type of fraud.

Revenue fraud:

(i) The proposals for the sentencing of revenue fraud take as a starting point an offender who acts intentionally. Where the offender has acted recklessly (relevant only to offences under the Value Added Tax Act 1994), courts should adjust the assessment of seriousness to take account of this lower level of culpability.

(ii) Payments to HMRC may be evaded in order to increase the profitability of a legitimate business or the level of an individual's legitimate remuneration; payments may be fraudulently obtained from HMRC without any underlying legitimate activity at all as in a Carousel Fraud. Although the type of harm is the same since both result in a loss to HMRC, where payment is sought from HMRC in such circumstances, culpability is likely to be higher. Accordingly, such offences are likely to be regarded as more serious.

Guidelines

Fraud Act 2006, s.1

Theft Act 1968, s.17

Social Security Administration Act 1992, ss.111A(1), 111A(1A), 111A(1B), 111A(1D) and 111(1E)

Tax Credits Act 2002, s.35

Value Added Tax Act 1994, ss.72(1), (3) and (8)

Finance Act 2000, s.144

Customs and Excise Management Act 1979, ss.170(1)(a)(i) and (ii), 170(1)(b), 170(2)(a), 170B, 50(1)(a) and 50(2)

All offences: Triable either way
Maximum when tried summarily: Level 5 fine and/or 6 months
Maximum when tried on indictment: Fraud, 10 years; other offences, 7 years

Offences under s.112, Social Security Administration Act 1992 are not covered by this guideline.

This guideline does not apply to offences under s.50 or s.170, Customs and Excise Management Act 1979 which involve prohibited weapons and have a maximum penalty of 10 years.

Offence seriousness (culpability and harm)

A. Identify the appropriate starting point

Starting points based on first time offender pleading not guilty

Examples of nature of activity	Starting point	Range
Single fraudulent transaction, not fraudulent from the outset	Value £2,500* – **Band B fine** Value £12,500* – **Medium level community order** Value £60,000* – **12 weeks custody**	Value less than £5,000 – **Band A fine to low level community order** Value £5,000 to less than £20,000 – **Band B fine to 6 weeks custody** Value £20,000 to less than £100,000 – **Medium level community order to Crown Court**
Single fraudulent transaction, fraudulent from the outset	Value £2,500* – **Low level community order** Value £12,500* – **High level community order** Value £60,000* – **26 weeks custody**	Value less than £5,000 – **Band A fine to medium level community order** Value £5,000 to less than £20,000 – **Band C fine to 18 weeks custody** Value £20,000 to less than £100,000 – **6 weeks custody to Crown Court**
Not fraudulent from the outset, and either • fraud carried out over a significant period of time or • multiple frauds **Where value exceeds £100,000**	Value £2,500* – **Medium level community order** Value £12,500* – **6 weeks custody** Value £60,000* – **Crown Court** **Crown Court**	Value less than £5,000 – **Band B fine to high level community order** Value £5,000 to less than £20,000 – **Medium level community order to 26 weeks custody** Value £20,000 to less than £100,000 – **12 weeks custody to Crown Court** **Crown Court**
Fraudulent from the outset, and either • fraud carried out over a significant period of time or • multiple frauds **Where value £100,000 or more or fraud was professionally planned**	Value £2,500* – **High level community order** Value £12,500* – **12 weeks custody** Value £60,000* – **Crown Court** **Crown Court**	Value less than £5,000 – **Low level community order to 6 weeks custody** Value £5,000 to less than £20,000 – **High level community order to Crown Court** Value £20,000 to less than £100,000 – **18 weeks custody to Crown Court** **Crown Court**

* Where the actual amount is greater or smaller than the value on which the starting point is based, that is likely to be one of the factors that will move the sentence within the range (see (a) [under Key Factors above])

B. Consider the effect of aggravating and mitigating factors (other than those within examples above)

Common aggravating and mitigating factors are identified [elsewhere] - the following may be particularly relevant but **these lists are not exhaustive**

Factors indicating higher culpability	Factors indicating lower culpability
1. Number involved in the offence and role of the offender 2. Making repeated importations, particularly in the face of warnings from the authorities 3. Dealing in goods with an additional health risk **Factors indicating greater degree of harm** 1. Use of another person's identity 2. Disposing of goods to under-aged purchasers	1. Peripheral involvement 2. Misleading or incomplete advice

[Sets out the standard sequential sentencing procedure.]

Sentencing Guidelines

FRAUD – CONFIDENCE

Factors to take into consideration

This guideline and accompanying notes are taken from the Sentencing Guidelines Council's definitive guideline *Sentencing for Fraud—Statutory offences*, published 26 October 2009 [see **SG-420**].

Key factors

(a) This type of offending involves a victim transferring money and/or property as a result of being deceived or misled by the offender. An example of a simple confidence fraud is a person claiming to be collecting money for charity when, in fact, he or she intends to keep the money. Other examples of common confidence frauds are *Advance fee frauds* (such as lottery/prize draw scams and foreign money-making frauds) and *Fraudulent sales of goods and services* (where goods or services are never received/performed or are worth less than represented.

(b) As the determinants of seriousness include the 'value of property or consequential loss involved', the table provides both a fixed amount (on which the starting point is based) and a band (on which the sentencing range is based). Where the value is larger or smaller than the amount on which the starting point is based, this should lead to upward or downward movement as appropriate. Where the amount the offender intended to obtain cannot be established, the appropriate measure will be the amount that was likely to be achieved in all the circumstances.

(c) A further determinant of seriousness is whether the fraud was a single fraudulent transaction or a multiple fraud. Most confidence frauds will by their nature involve many actual or potential victims and multiple transactions and should be regarded as multiple fraud.

(d) Targeting a vulnerable victim is also a determinant of seriousness. A victim might be vulnerable as a result of old age, youth or disability. In addition, some victims of advance fee frauds may have personalities which make them 'vulnerable in a way and to a degree not typical of the general population' because they fall for scams many times and may be targeted using 'sucker lists' of people who have previously fallen victim to scams. Care should be taken to ensure that where targeting a vulnerable victim is used to determine the appropriate level of seriousness and starting point, that it is not used again as an aggravating factor to move within the sentencing range.

(e) In general terms, the greater the loss, the more serious will be the offence. However, the financial value of the loss may not reflect the full extent of the harm caused. The court should also take into account; the impact of the offence on the victim (particularly where the loss may be significantly greater than the monetary value); harm to persons other than the direct victim (including the aggravation and stress of unscrambling the consequences of an offence); erosion of public confidence; and the difference between the loss intended and that which results (which may involve adjusting the assessment of seriousness to reflect the degree of loss caused).

(f) When the offending involves a number of people acting co-operatively, this will aggravate an offence as it indicates planning or professional activity, and may also increase the degree of loss caused or intended. The role of each offender is important in determining the appropriate level of seriousness and movement above or below the starting point within the applicable level.

(g) Use of another person's identity is an aggravating factor; the extent to which it aggravates an offence will be based on the degree of planning and the impact that the offence has had on the living victim or relatives of the deceased—whether the identity belongs to a living or deceased person is neutral for this purpose.

(h) Matters of offender mitigation which may be particularly relevant to this type of fraud include:
  • *Voluntary cessation of offending* — a claim, supported by objective evidence, that an offender stopped offending before being apprehended should be treated as mitigation, particularly where accompanied by a genuine expression of remorse. The lapse of time since commission of the last offence is relevant to whether the claim is genuine, and reasons for the cessation will assist the court in determining whether it amounts to mitigation and if so, to what degree.
  • *Complete and unprompted disclosure of the extent of the fraud* — an admission that a greater sum has been obtained than that known to the authorities ensures that an offender is sentenced for the complete extent of the fraud. This amounts to ready co-operation with the authorities and should be treated as mitigation. Provision of information about others involved in the fraud should also be treated as mitigation. Generally, the earlier the disclosure is given and the higher the degree of assistance, the greater the allowance for mitigation.
  • *Voluntary restitution* — the timing of the voluntary restitution will indicate the degree to which it reflects genuine remorse. Generally, the earlier the property or money is returned the greater the degree of mitigation the offender should receive. If circumstances beyond the control of the

offender prevent return of defrauded items, the degree of mitigation will depend on the point in time at which, and the determination with which the offender tried to return the items.

- *Financial pressure* — financial pressure neither increases nor diminishes an offender's culpability. However, where such pressure is **exceptional** and not of the offender's own making, it may in very rare circumstances constitute mitigation.

(i)   A court should be aware that a confiscation order is an important sanction. Such an order may only be made in the Crown Court. The court must commit the offender to the Crown Court where this is requested by the prosecution with a view to an order being considered.

(j)   Ancillary orders should be considered in all cases, principally compensation and deprivation.

Guidelines

Fraud Act 2006, s.1

Theft Act 1968, s.17

All offences: Triable either way
Maximum when tried summarily: Level 5 fine and/or 6 months
Maximum when tried on indictment: Fraud, 10 years; other offences, 7 years

Offence seriousness (culpability and harm)

A. Identify the appropriate starting point

Starting points based on first time offender pleading not guilty

Examples of nature of activity	Starting point	Range
Single fraudulent transaction confidence fraud not targeting a vulnerable victim, and involving no or limited planning	Value £10,000* – **Medium level community order** Value £60,000* – **12 weeks custody**	Value less than £20,000 – **Band B fine to 6 weeks custody** Value £20,000 to less than £100,000 – **Medium level community order to Crown Court**
Single fraudulent transaction confidence fraud involving targeting of a vulnerable victim	Value £10,000* – **6 weeks custody** Value £60,000* – **26 weeks custody**	Value less than £20,000 – **Medium level community order to 26 weeks custody** Value £20,000 to less than £100,000 – **High level community order to Crown Court**
Lower scale advance fee fraud **or** other confidence fraud characterised by a degree of planning and/ or multiple transactions	Value £10,000* – **Crown Court** Value £60,000* – **Crown Court**	Value less than £20,000 – **26 weeks custody to Crown Court** Value £20,000 to less than £100,000 – **Crown Court**
Large scale advance fee fraud **or** other confidence fraud involving the deliberate targeting of a large number of vulnerable victims	Value £10,000* – **Crown Court** Value £60,000* – **Crown Court**	Value less than £20,000 – **Crown Court** Value £20,000 to less than £100,000 – **Crown Court**

* Where the actual amount is greater or smaller than the value on which the starting point is based, that is likely to be one of the factors that will move the sentence within the range (see (b) [under Key Factors above])

B. Consider the effect of aggravating and mitigating factors (other than those within examples above)

Common aggravating and mitigating factors are identified [elsewhere] — the following may be particularly relevant but **these lists are not exhaustive**

Factors indicating higher culpability	Factors indicating lower culpability
1. Number involved in the offence and role of the offender 2. Offending carried out over a significant period of time	1. Peripheral involvement 2. Behaviour not fraudulent from the outset 3. Misleading or inaccurate advice
Factors indicating greater degree of harm 1. Use of another person's identity 2. Offence has lasting effect on the victim	

[Sets out the standard sequential sentencing procedure.]

SG-232   FRAUD — POSSESSING, MAKING OR SUPPLYING ARTICLES FOR USE IN FRAUD

Factors to take into consideration

This guideline and accompanying notes are taken from the Sentencing Guidelines Council's definitive guideline *Sentencing for Fraud — Statutory offences*, published 26 October 2009 [see **SG-420**].

Key factors

(a) There are many ways in which offenders may commit this group of offences. 'Articles' will include any electronic programs or data stored electronically false fronts for cash machines, computer programs for generating credit card numbers, lists of credit card or bank account details, 'sucker lists' and draft letters or emails for use in advance fee frauds.

(b) Offenders who possess, make or supply articles for use in fraud intend their actions to lead to a fraud, and therefore have the highest level of culpability. The three offences in this group all involve an element of planning (whether by the offender or by another person) which indicates a higher level of culpability; this has been incorporated into the proposed starting points.

(c) In relation to harm, the value of the fraud (either that intended by the offender where that can be ascertained, or that which was likely to be achieved) is not a determinant of seriousness for these offences but is a factor that should be taken into account in determining the appropriate sentence within the sentencing range.

(d) Whilst in many cases no financial harm will have been caused, in some cases, particularly where the 'article' is a list of credit card or bank account details, the victim(s) may have been inconvenienced despite not suffering any financial loss. In all cases, the harm must be judged in light of the offender's culpability.

(e) When the offending involves a number of people acting co-operatively, this will aggravate an offence as it indicates planning or professional activity, and may also increase the degree of loss caused or intended. The role of each offender is important in determining the appropriate level of seriousness and movement above or below the starting point within the applicable level.

(f) Matters of offender mitigation which may be particularly relevant to this type of fraud include:

- *Voluntary cessation of offending* — a claim, supported by objective evidence, that an offender stopped offending before being apprehended should be treated as mitigation, particularly where accompanied by a genuine expression of remorse. The lapse of time since commission of the last offence is relevant to whether the claim is genuine, and reasons for the cessation will assist the court in determining whether it amounts to mitigation and if so, to what degree.

- *Complete and unprompted disclosure of the extent of the fraud* — an admission that a greater sum has been obtained than that known to the authorities ensures that an offender is sentenced for the complete extent of the fraud. This amounts to ready co-operation with the authorities and should be treated as mitigation. Provision of information about others involved in the fraud should also be treated as mitigation. Generally, the earlier the disclosure is given and the higher the degree of assistance, the greater the allowance for mitigation.

- *Voluntary restitution* — the timing of the voluntary restitution will indicate the degree to which it reflects genuine remorse. Generally, the earlier the property or money is returned the greater the degree of mitigation the offender should receive. If circumstances beyond the control of the offender prevent return of defrauded items, the degree of mitigation will depend on the point in time at which, and the determination with which the offender tried to return the items.

- *Financial pressure* — financial pressure neither increases nor diminishes an offender's culpability. However, where such pressure is exceptional and not of the offender's own making, it may in very rare circumstances constitute mitigation.

(g) A court should be aware that a confiscation order is an important sanction. Such an order may only be made in the Crown Court. The court must commit the offender to the Crown Court where this is requested by the prosecution with a view to an order being considered.

(h) Ancillary orders should be considered in all cases, principally compensation and deprivation.

Guidelines

Fraud Act 2006, s.6

Fraud Act 2006, s.7

Fraud Act 2006, s.1

Possession of articles: Triable either way

Maximum when tried summarily: Level 5 fine and/or 6 months

Maximum when tried on indictment: 5 years

Making or supplying articles, and Fraud (s.1): Triable either way

Maximum when tried summarily: Level 5 fine and/or 6 months
Maximum when tried on indictment: 10 years

Offence seriousness (culpability and harm)

A. Identify the appropriate starting point

Starting points based on first time offender pleading not guilty

Examples of nature of activity	Starting point	Range
Possessing articles intended for use in a less extensive and less skilfully planned fraud	Medium level community order	Low level community order to 26 weeks custody
Possessing articles for use in an extensive and skilfully planned fraud	Crown Court	6 weeks custody to Crown Court
Making or adapting, supplying or offering to supply articles intended for use in a less extensive and less skilfully planned fraud	26 weeks custody	High level community order to Crown Court
Making or adapting, supplying or offering to supply articles for use in an extensive and skilfully planned fraud	Crown Court	Crown Court

B. Consider the effect of aggravating and mitigating factors (other than those within examples above)

Common aggravating and mitigating factors are identified [elsewhere] — the following may be particularly relevant but **these lists are not exhaustive**

Factors indicating higher culpability	Factor indicating lower culpability
1. Number involved in the offence and role of the offender 2. Offending carried out over a significant period of time	1. Peripheral involvement
Factors indicating greater degree of harm 1. Use of another person's identity 2. Offence has lasting effect on the victim	

[Sets out the standard sequential sentencing procedure.]

GOING EQUIPPED, FOR THEFT
SG-233
Theft Act 1968, s. 25

Triable either way:
Maximum when tried summarily: Level 5 fine and/or 6 months
Maximum when tried on indictment: 3 years

May disqualify if offence committed with reference to theft or taking of motor vehicles (no points available)

Offence seriousness (culpability and harm)

A. Identify the appropriate starting point

Starting points based on first time offender pleading not guilty

Examples of nature of activity	Starting point	Range
Possession of items for theft from shop or of vehicle	Medium level community order	Band C fine to high level community order
Possession of items for burglary, robbery	High level community order	Medium level community order to Crown Court

B. Consider the effect of aggravating and mitigating factors (other than those within examples above)

Common aggravating and mitigating factors are identified [elsewhere]—the following may be particularly relevant but these lists are not exhaustive

> **Factors indicating higher culpability**
> 1. Circumstances suggest offender equipped for particularly serious offence
> 2. Items to conceal identity

[Sets out the standard sequential sentencing procedure and notes need to consider disqualification from driving and deprivation of property.]

SG-234 GRIEVOUS BODILY HARM/UNLAWFUL WOUNDING & RACIALLY OR RELIGIOUSLY AGGRAVATED GRIEVOUS BODILY HARM/UNLAWFUL WOUNDING

[See now 'Inflicting Grievous Bodily Harm/Unlawful Wounding' at **SG-241**, the new Guideline from the Sentencing Council which has effect from 13 June 2011.]

SG-235 HANDLING STOLEN GOODS
Theft Act 1968, s. 22

Triable either way:
Maximum when tried summarily: Level 5 fine and/or 6 months
Maximum when tried on indictment: 14 years

These guidelines are drawn from the Court of Appeal's decision in *R v Webbe and others* [2001] EWCA Crim 1217

Offence seriousness (culpability and harm)

A. Identify the appropriate starting point

Starting points based on first time offender pleading not guilty

Examples of nature of activity	Starting point	Range
Property worth £1,000 or less acquired for offender's own use	Band B fine	Band B fine to low level community order
Property worth £1,000 or less acquired for re-sale; or Property worth more than £1,000 acquired for offender's own use; or Presence of at least one aggravating factor listed below—regardless of value	Medium level community order	Low level community order to 12 weeks custody **Note:** the custody threshold is likely to be passed if the offender has a record of dishonesty offences
Sophisticated offending; or Presence of at least two aggravating factors listed below	12 weeks custody	6 weeks custody to Crown Court
Offence committed in context of a business; or Offender acts as organiser/distributor of proceeds of crime; or Offender makes self available to other criminals as willing to handle the proceeds of thefts or burglaries; or Offending highly organised, professional; or Particularly serious original offence, such as armed robbery	Crown Court	Crown Court

B. Consider the effect of aggravating and mitigating factors (other than those within examples above)

Common aggravating and mitigating factors are identified [elsewhere]—the following may be particularly relevant but these lists are not exhaustive

Factors indicating higher culpability	Factors indicating lower culpability
1. Closeness of offender to primary offence. Closeness may be geographical, arising from presence at or near the primary offence when it was committed, or temporal, where the handler instigated or encouraged the primary offence beforehand, or, soon after, provided a safe haven or route for disposal 2. High level of profit made or expected by offender	1. Little or no benefit to offender 2. Voluntary restitution to victim
Factors indicating greater degree of harm 1. Seriousness of the primary offence, including domestic burglary 2. High value of goods to victim, including sentimental value 3. Threats of violence or abuse of power by offender over others, such as an adult commissioning criminal activity by children, or a drug dealer pressurising addicts to steal in order to pay for their habit	**Factor indicating lower degree of harm** 1. Low value of goods

[Sets out the standard sequential sentencing procedure and mentions need to consider deprivation of property.]

SG-236

HARASSMENT—PUTTING PEOPLE IN FEAR OF VIOLENCE
RACIALLY OR RELIGIOUSLY AGGRAVATED HARASSMENT—PUTTING PEOPLE
IN FEAR OF VIOLENCE

Protection from Harassment Act 1997, s. 4
Crime and Disorder Act 1998, s. 32

Harassment: triable either way
Maximum when tried summarily: Level 5 fine and/or 6 months
Maximum when tried on indictment: 5 years

Racially or religiously aggravated harassment: triable either way
Maximum when tried summarily: Level 5 fine and/or 6 months
Maximum when tried on indictment: 7 years

Where offence committed in domestic context, refer [below] for guidance

Offence seriousness (culpability and harm)

A. Identify the appropriate starting point

Starting points based on first time offender pleading not guilty

Examples of nature of activity	Starting point	Range
A pattern of two or more incidents of unwanted contact	6 weeks custody	High level community order to 18 weeks custody
Deliberate threats, persistent action over a longer period; or Intention to cause fear of violence	18 weeks custody	12 weeks custody to Crown Court
Sexual threats, vulnerable person targeted	Crown Court	Crown Court

B. Consider the effect of aggravating and mitigating factors (other than those within examples above)

Common aggravating and mitigating factors are identified [elsewhere]—the following may be particularly relevant but these lists are not exhaustive

Factors indicating higher culpability	Factors indicating lower culpability
1. Planning 2. Offender ignores obvious distress 3. Visits in person to victim's home or workplace 4. Offender involves others 5. Using contact arrangements with a child to instigate offence	1. Limited understanding of effect on victim 2. Initial provocation
Factors indicating greater degree of harm 1. Victim needs medical help/counselling 2. Physical violence used 3. Victim aware that offender has history of using violence 4. Grossly violent or offensive material sent 5. Children frightened 6. Evidence that victim changed lifestyle to avoid contact	

[Sets out the standard sequential sentencing procedure. Notes that 'If offender charged and convicted of the racially or religiously aggravated offence, increase the sentence to reflect this element'.]

SG-237

HARASSMENT (WITHOUT VIOLENCE)
RACIALLY OR RELIGIOUSLY AGGRAVATED HARASSMENT (NON VIOLENT)

Protection from Harassment Act 1997, s.2
Crime and Disorder Act 1998, s.32

Harassment: triable only summarily
Maximum: Level 5 fine and/or 6 months

Racially or religiously aggravated harassment: triable either way
Maximum when tried summarily: Level 5 fine and/or 6 months
Maximum when tried on indictment: 2 years

Where offence committed in domestic context, refer [below] for guidance

Offence seriousness (culpability and harm)

A. Identify the appropriate starting point

Examples of nature of activity	Starting point	Range
Small number of incidents	**Medium level community order**	**Band C fine to high level community order**
Constant contact at night, trying to come into workplace or home, involving others	**6 weeks custody**	**Medium level community order to 12 weeks custody**
Threatening violence, taking personal photographs, sending offensive material	**18 weeks custody**	**12 to 26 weeks custody**

Starting points based on first time offender pleading not guilty

B. Consider the effect of aggravating and mitigating factors (other than those within examples above)

Common aggravating and mitigating factors are identified [elsewhere]—the following may be particularly relevant but these lists are not exhaustive

Factors indicating higher culpability	Factors indicating lower culpability
1. Planning 2. Offender ignores obvious distress 3. Offender involves others 4. Using contact arrangements with a child to instigate offence	1. Limited understanding of effect on victim 2. Initial provocation
Factors indicating greater degree of harm 1. Victim needs medical help/counselling 2. Action over long period 3. Children frightened 4. Use or distribution of photographs	

[Sets out the standard sequential sentencing procedure. Notes that 'If offender charged and convicted of the racially or religiously aggravated offence, increase the sentence to reflect this element'.]

IDENTITY DOCUMENTS—POSSESS FALSE/ANOTHER'S/IMPROPERLY OBTAINED   **SG-238**

Identity Cards Act 2006, s. 25(5)
(possession of a false identity document (as defined in s. 26—includes a passport))

Triable either way:
Maximum when tried summarily: Level 5 fine and/or 6 months
Maximum when tried on indictment: 2 years (s.25(5))

Note: possession of a false identity document with the intention of using it is an indictable-only offence (Identity Cards Act 2006, s. 25(1)). The maximum penalty is 10 years imprisonment.

Offence seriousness (culpability and harm)

A. Identify the appropriate starting point

Starting points based on first time offender pleading not guilty

Examples of nature of activity	Starting point	Range
Single document possessed	Medium level community order	Band C fine to high level community order
Small number of documents, no evidence of dealing	12 weeks custody	6 weeks custody to Crown Court
Considerable number of documents possessed, evidence of involvement in larger operation	Crown Court	Crown Court

B. Consider the effect of aggravating and mitigating factors (other than those within examples above)

Common aggravating and mitigating factors are identified [elsewhere]—the following may be particularly relevant but these lists are not exhaustive

Factors indicating higher culpability	Factor indicating lower culpability
1. Clear knowledge that documents false	1. Genuine mistake or ignorance
2. Number of documents possessed (where not in offence descriptions above)	
Factors indicating greater degree of harm	
1. Group activity	
2. Potential impact of use (where not in offence descriptions above)	

[Sets out the standard sequential sentencing procedure.]

INCOME TAX EVASION   **SG-239**
Finance Act 2000, s. 144

Triable either way:
Maximum when tried summarily: Level 5 fine and/or 6 months
Maximum when tried on indictment: 7 years

Refer to guideline *Fraud — banking and insurance fraud and obtaining credit through fraud, benefit fraud and revenue fraud* [see **SG-230** *et seq.*].

INDECENT PHOTOGRAPHS OF CHILDREN [, POSSESSION OF]   **SG-240**
[The guidelines set out below are applicable to adult offenders sentenced after 1 April 2014.]
Criminal Justice Act 1988 (section 160)

Triable either way:
Maximum: 5 years' custody
Offence range: Community order – 3 years' custody

INDECENT PHOTOGRAPHS OF CHILDREN
Protection of Children Act 1978 (section 1)

Triable either way
Maximum: 10 years' custody
Offence range: Community order – 9 years' custody

For section 1 offences committed on or after 3 December 2012, this is an offence listed in Part 1 of Schedule 15B for the purposes of section 224A (life sentence for second listed offence) of the Criminal Justice Act 2003.

For convictions on or after 3 December 2012 (irrespective of the date of commission of the offence), these are specified offences for the purposes of section 226A (extended sentence for certain violent or sexual offences) of the Criminal Justice Act 2003.

STEP ONE Determining the offence category
The court should determine the offence category using the table below.

	Possession	Distribution*	Production**
Category A	Possession of images involving penetrative sexual activity	Sharing images involving penetrative sexual activity	Creating images involving penetrative sexual activity
	Possession of images involving sexual activity with an animal or sadism	Sharing images involving sexual activity with an animal or sadism	Creating images involving sexual activity with an animal or sadism
Category B	Possession of images involving non-penetrative sexual activity	Sharing of images involving non-penetrative sexual activity	Creating images involving non-penetrative sexual activity
Category C	Possession of other indecent images not falling within categories A or B	Sharing of other indecent images not falling within categories A or B	Creating other indecent images not falling within categories A or B

* Distribution includes possession with a view to distributing or sharing images.
** Production includes the taking or making of any image at source, for instance the original image. Making an image by simple downloading should be treated as possession for the purposes of sentencing.

In most cases the intrinsic character of the most serious of the offending images will initially determine the appropriate category. If, however, the most serious images are unrepresentative of the offender's conduct a lower category may be appropriate. A lower category will not, however, be appropriate if the offender has produced or taken (for example photographed) images of a higher category.

STEP TWO Starting point and category range
Having determined the category, the court should use the corresponding starting points to reach a sentence within the category range below. The starting point applies to all offenders irrespective of plea or previous convictions. Having determined the starting point, step two allows further adjustment for aggravating or mitigating features, set out [below].

Where there is a sufficient prospect of rehabilitation, a community order with a sex offender treatment programme requirement under section 202 of the Criminal Justice Act 2003 can be a proper alternative to a short or moderate length custodial sentence.

	Possession	Distribution	Production
Category A	**Starting point** 1 year's custody **Category range** 26 weeks – 3 years' custody	**Starting point** 3 years' custody **Category range** 2 – 5 years' custody	**Starting point** 6 years' custody **Category range** 4 – 9 years' custody
Category B	**Starting point** 26 weeks' custody **Category range** High level community order – 18 months' custody	**Starting point** 1 year's custody **Category range** 26 weeks' – 2 years' custody	**Starting point** 2 years' custody **Category range** 1 – 4 years' custody
Category C	**Starting point** High level community order **Category range** Medium level community order – 26 weeks' custody	**Starting point** 13 weeks' custody **Category range** High level community order – 26 weeks' custody	**Starting point** 18 months' custody **Category range** 1 – 3 years' custody

The table below contains a **non-exhaustive** list of additional factual elements providing the context of the offence and factors relating to the offender. Identify whether any combination of these, or other relevant factors, should result in an upward or downward adjustment from the starting point. **In particular, relevant recent convictions are likely to result in an upward adjustment.** In some cases, having considered these factors, it may be appropriate to move outside the identified category range.

When sentencing appropriate **category 2 or 3 offences**, the court should also consider the custody threshold as follows:

- has the custody threshold been passed?
- if so, is it unavoidable that a custodial sentence be imposed?
- if so, can that sentence be suspended?

Aggravating factors
Statutory aggravating factors
• Previous convictions, having regard to a) the nature of the offence to which the conviction relates and its relevance to the current offence; and b) the time that has elapsed since the conviction • Offence committed whilst on bail
Other aggravating factors
• Failure to comply with current court orders • Offence committed whilst on licence • Age and/or vulnerability of the child depicted[+] • Discernable pain or distress suffered by child depicted • Period over which images were possessed, distributed or produced • High volume of images possessed, distributed or produced • Placing images where there is the potential for a high volume of viewers • Collection includes moving images • Attempts to dispose of or conceal evidence • Abuse of trust • Child depicted known to the offender • Active involvement in a network or process that facilitates or commissions the creation or sharing of indecent images of children • Commercial exploitation and/or motivation • Deliberate or systematic searching for images portraying young children, category A images or the portrayal of familial sexual abuse • Large number of different victims • Child depicted intoxicated or drugged

[+] Age and/or vulnerability of the child should be given significant weight. In cases where the actual age of the victim is difficult to determine sentencers should consider the development of the child (infant, pre-pubescent, post-pubescent)

Mitigating factors
• No previous convictions **or** no relevant/recent convictions • Remorse • Previous good character and/or exemplary conduct* • Age and/or lack of maturity where it affects the responsibility of the offender • Mental disorder or learning disability, particularly where linked to the commission of the offence • Demonstration of steps taken to address offending behaviour

* Previous good character/exemplary conduct is different from having no previous convictions. The more serious the offence, the less the weight which should normally be attributed to this factor. Where previous good character/ exemplary conduct has been used to facilitate the offence, this mitigation should not normally be allowed and such conduct may constitute an aggravating factor.

[Sets out the standard sequential sentencing procedure.]

SG-241

Inflicting Grievous Bodily Harm/Unlawful Wounding
Offences against the Person Act 1861 (section 20)

Racially/Religiously Aggravated GBH/Unlawful Wounding
Crime and Disorder Act 1998 (section 29)

[This guideline was published by the Sentencing Council and has effect in respect of all sentences passed after 13 June 2011 on offenders aged 18 or older. It replaces the guideline which previously applied and which continued to have effect until that date.]

These are specified offences for the purposes of section 224 of the Criminal Justice Act 2003

Triable either way

Section 20
Maximum when tried summarily: Level 5 fine and/or 26 weeks' custody
Maximum when tried on indictment: 5 years' custody

Section 29
Maximum when tried summarily: Level 5 fine and/or 26 weeks' custody
Maximum when tried on indictment: 7 years' custody

Offence range: Community order—4 years' custody

This guideline applies to all offenders aged 18 and older, who are sentenced on or after 13 June 2011. The definitions at [**SG-297**] of 'starting point' and 'first time offender' do not apply for this guideline. Starting point and category ranges apply to all offenders in all cases, irrespective of plea or previous convictions.

STEP ONE Determining the offence category
The court should determine the offence category using the table below:

Category 1	Greater harm (serious injury must normally be present) **and** higher culpability
Category 2	Greater harm (serious injury must normally be present) **and** lower culpability; **or** lesser harm and higher culpability
Category 3	Lesser harm and lower culpability

The court should determine the offender's culpability and the harm caused, or intended, by reference only to the factors below (as demonstrated by the presence of one or more). These factors comprise the principal factual elements of the offence and should determine the category.

Factors indicating greater harm	Factors indicating lesser harm
Injury (which includes disease transmission and/or psychological harm) which is serious in the context of the offence (must normally be present)	Injury which is less serious in the context of the offence
Victim is particularly vulnerable because of personal circumstances	**Factors indicating lower culpability**
	Subordinate role in a group or gang
Sustained or repeated assault on the same victim	A greater degree of provocation than normally expected
Factors indicating higher culpability	Lack of premeditation
Statutory aggravating factors:	Mental disorder or learning disability, where linked to commission of the offence
Offence motivated by, or demonstrating, hostility to the victim based on his or her sexual orientation (or presumed sexual orientation)	Excessive self defence
Offence motivated by, or demonstrating, hostility to the victim based on the victim's disability (or presumed disability)	
Other aggravating factors:	
A significant degree of premeditation	
Use of weapon or weapon equivalent (for example, shod foot, headbutting, use of acid, use of animal)	
Intention to commit more serious harm than actually resulted from the offence	
Deliberately causes more harm than is necessary for commission of offence	
Deliberate targeting of vulnerable victim	
Leading role in group or gang	
Offence motivated by, or demonstrating, hostility based on the victim's age, sex, gender identity (or presumed gender identity)	

STEP TWO Starting point and category range

Having determined the category, the court should use the corresponding starting points to reach a sentence within the category range below. The starting point applies to all offenders irrespective of plea or previous convictions.

A case of particular gravity, reflected by multiple features of culpability in step one, could merit upward adjustment from the starting point before further adjustment for aggravating or mitigating features, set out below.

Offence Category	Starting Point (*Applicable to all offenders*)	Category Range (*Applicable to all offenders*)
Category 1	Crown Court	Crown Court
Category 2	Crown Court	Crown Court
Category 3	High level community order	Low level community order—Crown Court (51 weeks' custody)

The table below contains a **non-exhaustive** list of additional factual elements providing the context of the offence and factors relating to the offender. Identify whether any combination of these, or other relevant factors, should result in an upward or downward adjustment from the starting point. In some cases, having considered these factors, it may be appropriate to move outside the identified category range.

When sentencing **category 3** offences, the court should also consider the custody threshold as follows:

- has the custody threshold been passed?
- if so, is it unavoidable that a custodial sentence be imposed?
- if so, can that sentence be suspended?

Factors increasing seriousness	Factors reducing seriousness or reflecting personal mitigation
Statutory aggravating factors: Previous convictions, having regard to a) the nature of the offence to which the conviction relates and its relevance to the current offence; and b) the time that has elapsed since the conviction Offence committed whilst on bail	No previous convictions or no relevant/recent convictions Single blow Remorse Good character and/or exemplary conduct
Other aggravating factors include: Location of the offence Timing of the offence Ongoing effect upon the victim Offence committed against those working in the public sector or providing a service to the public Presence of others including relatives, especially children or partner of the victim Gratuitous degradation of victim In domestic violence cases, victim forced to leave their home Failure to comply with current court orders Offence committed whilst on licence An attempt to conceal or dispose of evidence Failure to respond to warnings or concerns expressed by others about the offender's behaviour Commission of offence whilst under the influence of alcohol or drugs Abuse of power and/or position of trust Exploiting contact arrangements with a child to commit an offence Established evidence of community impact Any steps taken to prevent the victim reporting an incident, obtaining assistance and/or from assisting or supporting the prosecution Offences taken into consideration (TICs)	Determination and/or demonstration of steps taken to address addiction or offending behaviour Serious medical conditions requiring urgent, intensive or long-term treatment Isolated incident Age and/or lack of maturity where it affects the responsibility of the offender Lapse of time since the offence where this is not the fault of the offender Mental disorder or learning disability, where not linked to the commission of the offence Sole or primary carer for dependent relatives

Section 29 offences only: The court should determine the appropriate sentence for the offence without taking account of the element of aggravation and then make an addition to the sentence, considering the level of aggravation involved. It may be appropriate to move outside the identified category range, taking into account the increased statutory maximum.

[Steps Three to Nine are almost identical to those which apply to assault occasioning actual bodily harm: see **SG-182**.]

SG-242   KEEPING A BROTHEL USED FOR PROSTITUTION

[The guidelines set out below are applicable to adult offenders sentenced after 1 April 2014.]

Sexual Offences Act 1956 (section 33A)

Triable either way
Maximum: 7 years' custody
Offence range: Community order - 6 years' custody

The terms 'prostitute' and 'prostitution' are used in this guideline in accordance with the statutory language contained in the Sexual Offences Act 2003.

STEP ONE   Determining the offence category

The court should determine which categories of harm and culpability the offence falls into by reference **only** to the tables below.

Harm	
Category 1	• Under 18 year olds working in brothel • Abduction/detention • Violence or threats of violence • Sustained and systematic psychological abuse • Those working in brothel forced or coerced to participate in unsafe/degrading sexual activity • Those working in brothel forced or coerced into seeing many 'customers' • Those working in brothel forced/coerced/deceived into prostitution • Established evidence of community impact
Category 2	Factor(s) in category 1 not present.

Culpability		
A	B	C
• Keeping brothel on significant commercial basis • Involvement in keeping a number of brothels • Expectation of significant financial or other gain • Abuse of trust • Exploitation of those known to be trafficked • Significant involvement in limiting freedom of those working in brothel • Grooming of a person to work in the brothel including through cultivation of a dependency on drugs or alcohol	• Keeping/managing premises • Close involvement with those working in brothel e.g. control of finances, choice of clients, working conditions, etc. (where offender's involvement is not as a result of coercion)	• Performs limited function under direction • Close involvement but engaged by coercion/intimidation/exploitation

STEP TWO Starting point and category range

Having determined the category, the court should use the corresponding starting points to reach a sentence within the category range [below]. The starting point applies to all offenders irrespective of plea or previous convictions. Having determined the starting point, step two allows further adjustment for aggravating or mitigating features, set out [below].

A case of particular gravity, reflected by multiple features of culpability or harm in step one, could merit upward adjustment from the starting point before further adjustment for aggravating or mitigating features, set out [below].

Where there is a sufficient prospect of rehabilitation, a community order with a sex offender treatment programme requirement under section 202 of the Criminal Justice Act 2003 can be a proper alternative to a short or moderate length custodial sentence.

	A	B	C
Category 1	**Starting point** 5 years' custody **Category range** 3 – 6 years' custody	**Starting point** 3 years' custody **Category range** 2 – 5 years' custody	**Starting point** 1 year's custody **Category range** High level community order – 18 months' custody
Category 2	**Starting point** 3 years' custody **Category range** 2 – 5 years' custody	**Starting point** 12 months' custody **Category range** 26 weeks' – 2 years' custody	**Starting point** Medium level community order **Category range** Low level community order – High level community order

The table below contains a **non-exhaustive** list of additional factual elements providing the context of the offence and factors relating to the offender. Identify whether any combination of these, or other relevant factors, should result in an upward or downward adjustment from the starting point. **In particular, relevant recent convictions are likely to result in an upward adjustment**. In some cases, having considered these factors, it may be appropriate to move outside the identified category range.

When sentencing appropriate **category 1 offences**, the court should also consider the custody threshold as follows:

- has the custody threshold been passed?
- if so, is it unavoidable that a custodial sentence be imposed?
- if so, can that sentence be suspended?

Aggravating factors

Statutory aggravating factors

- Previous convictions, having regard to a) the nature of the offence to which the conviction relates and its relevance to the current offence; and b) the time that has elapsed since the conviction
- Offence committed whilst on bail

Other aggravating factors

- Failure to comply with current court orders
- Offence committed whilst on licence
- Deliberate isolation of those working in brothel
- Threats made to expose those working in brothel to the authorities (for example, immigration or police), family/friends or others
- Harm threatened against the family/friends of those working in brothel
- Passport/identity documents removed
- Those working in brothel prevented from seeking medical treatment
- Food withheld
- Those working in brothel passed around by offender and moved to other brothels
- Earnings of those working in brothel withheld/kept by offender or evidence of excessive wage reduction or debt bondage, inflated travel or living expenses or unreasonable interest rates
- Any steps taken to prevent those working in brothel reporting an incident, obtaining assistance and/or from assisting or supporting the prosecution
- Attempts to dispose of or conceal evidence
- Those working in brothel forced or coerced into pornography
- Timescale over which operation has been run

Mitigating factors

- No previous convictions **or** no relevant/recent convictions
- Remorse
- Previous good character and/or exemplary conduct*
- Age and/or lack of maturity where it affects the responsibility of the offender
- Mental disorder or learning disability, particularly where linked to the commission of the offence
- Demonstration of steps taken to address offending behaviour

---

* Previous good character/exemplary conduct is different from having no previous convictions. The more serious the offence, the less the weight which should normally be attributed to this factor. Where previous good character/exemplary conduct has been used to facilitate the offence, this mitigation should not normally be allowed and such conduct may constitute an aggravating factor.

[Sets out the standard sequential sentencing procedure.]

SG-243   MAKING OFF WITHOUT PAYMENT

Factors to take into consideration

Key factors
(a) The starting points and sentencing ranges in this guideline are based on the assumption that the offender was motivated by greed or a desire to live beyond his or her means. To avoid double counting, such a motivation should not be treated as a factor that increases culpability.
(b) When assessing the harm caused by this offence, the starting point should be the loss suffered by the victim. In general, the greater the loss, the more serious the offence. However, the monetary value of the loss may not reflect the full extent of the harm caused by the offence. The court should also take into account the impact of the offence on the victim, any harm to persons other than the direct victim, and any harm in the form of public alarm or erosion of public confidence.

(c)   The following matters of offender mitigation may be relevant to this offence:
   (i)   Offender motivated by desperation or need
         The fact that an offence has been committed in desperation or need arising from particular hardship may count as offender mitigation in exceptional circumstances.
   (ii) Voluntary return of stolen property
         Whether and the degree to which the return of stolen property constitutes a matter of offender mitigation will depend on an assessment of the circumstances and, in particular, the voluntariness and timeliness of the return.
   (iii) Impact on sentence of offender's dependency
         Many offenders convicted of acquisitive crimes are motivated by an addiction, often to drugs, alcohol or gambling. This does not mitigate the seriousness of the offence, but an offender's dependency may properly influence the type of sentence imposed. In particular, it may sometimes be appropriate to impose a drug rehabilitation requirement or an alcohol treatment requirement as part of a community order or a suspended sentence order in an attempt to break the cycle of addiction and offending, even if an immediate custodial sentence would otherwise be warranted.[129]

Guidelines

Theft Act 1978, s. 3

Triable either way:
Maximum when tried summarily: Level 5 fine and/or 6 months
Maximum when tried on indictment: 2 years

Offence seriousness (culpability and harm)

A. Identify the appropriate starting point

Starting points based on first time offender pleading not guilty

Examples of nature of activity	Starting point	Range
Single offence committed by an offender acting alone with evidence of little or no planning, goods or services worth less than £200	Band C fine	Band A fine to high level community order
Offence displaying one or more of the following: – offender acting in unison with others – evidence of planning – offence part of a 'spree' – intimidation of victim – goods or services worth £200 or more	Medium level community order	Low level community order to 12 weeks custody

B. Consider the effect of aggravating and mitigating factors (other than those within examples above)

Common aggravating and mitigating factors are identified [elsewhere]—the following may be particularly relevant but these lists are not exhaustive

[Sets out the standard sequential sentencing procedure.]

OBSTRUCT/RESIST A POLICE CONSTABLE IN EXECUTION OF DUTY   **SG-244**
Police Act 1996, s. 89(2)

Triable only summarily:
Maximum: Level 3 fine and/or one month

Offence seriousness (culpability and harm)

A. Identify the appropriate starting point

Starting points based on first time offender pleading not guilty

[129]   See para.2 on p.163. The Court of Appeal gave guidance on the approach to making drug treatment and testing orders, which also applies to imposing a drug rehabilitation requirement in *Attorney General's Reference No. 64 of 2003 (Boujettif and Harrison)* [2003] EWCA Crim 2514 and *Woods and Collins* [2005] EWCA Crim 2065 summarised in the Sentencing Guidelines Council *Guideline Judgments Case Compendium* (section (A) Generic Sentencing Principles) available at: www.sentencing-guidelines.gov.uk

Examples of nature of activity	Starting point	Range
Failure to move when required to do so	Band A fine	Conditional discharge to band B fine
Attempt to prevent arrest or other lawful police action; or giving false details	Band B fine	Band A fine to band C fine
Several people attempting to prevent arrest or other lawful police action	Low level community order	Band C fine to medium level community order

B. Consider the effect of aggravating and mitigating factors (other than those within examples above)

Common aggravating and mitigating factors are identified [elsewhere]—the following may be particularly relevant but these lists are not exhaustive

Factors indicating higher culpability	Factors indicating lower culpability
1. Premeditated action 2. Aggressive words/threats 3. Aggressive group action	1. Genuine mistake or misjudgement 2. Brief incident

[Sets out the standard sequential sentencing procedure.]

SG-245

Obtaining Services Dishonestly

Fraud Act 2006, s. 11

Triable either way:
Maximum when tried summarily: Level 5 fine and/or 6 months
Maximum when tried on indictment: 5 years

The offence of obtaining services dishonestly may be committed in circumstances that otherwise could be charged as an offence contrary to section 1 of the Fraud Act 2006 or may be more akin to making off without payment, contrary to section 3 of the Theft Act 1978. For this reason, it has not been included specifically within any of the guidelines for fraud, and one of the following approaches should be used:
- where it involves conduct which can be characterised as a fraud offence (such as obtaining credit through fraud or payment card fraud), the court should apply the guideline for the relevant type of fraud (see [above]); or
- where the conduct could be characterised as making off without payment (that is, where an offender, knowing that payment on the spot for any goods supplied or service done is required or expected, dishonestly makes off without having paid and with intent to avoid payment), the guideline for that offence should be used (see [above]).

SG-246

Protective Order, Breach Of

Factors to take into consideration

This guideline and accompanying notes are taken from the Sentencing Guidelines Council's definitive guideline *Breach of a Protective Order*, published 7 December 2006 [see **SG-45**]

Aims of sentencing

(a) The main aim of sentencing for breach of a protective order (which would have been imposed to protect a victim from future harm) should be to achieve future compliance with that order.
(b) The court will need to assess the level of risk posed by the offender. Willingness to undergo treatment or accept help may influence sentence.

Key factors

(i) The nature of the conduct that caused the breach of the order. In particular, whether the contact was direct or indirect, although it is important to recognise that indirect contact is capable of causing significant harm or anxiety.
(ii) There may be exceptional cases where the nature of the breach is particularly serious but has not been dealt with by a separate offence being charged. In these cases the risk posed by the offender and the nature of the breach will be particularly significant in determining the response.

(iii) The nature of the original conduct or offence is relevant in so far as it allows a judgement to be made on the level of harm caused to the victim by the breach, and the extent to which that harm was intended.

(iv) The sentence following a breach is for the breach alone and must avoid punishing the offender again for the offence or conduct as a result of which the order was made.

(v) It is likely that all breaches of protective orders will pass the threshold for a community sentence. Custody is the starting point where violence is used. Non-violent conduct may also cross the custody threshold where a high degree of harm or anxiety has been caused.

(vi) Where an order was made in civil proceedings, its purpose may have been to cause the subject of the order to modify behaviour rather than to imply that the conduct was especially serious. If so, it is likely to be disproportionate to impose a custodial sentence if the breach of the order did not involve threats or violence.

(vii) In some cases where a breach might result in a short custodial sentence but the court is satisfied that the offender genuinely intends to reform his or her behaviour and there is a real prospect of rehabilitation, the court may consider it appropriate to impose a sentence that will allow this. This may mean imposing a suspended sentence order or a community order (where appropriate with a requirement to attend an accredited domestic violence programme).

Guidelines

Protection from Harassment Act 1997, s. 5(5) (breach of restraining order)

Family Law Act 1996, s. 42A (breach of non-molestation order)

Triable either way:
Maximum when tried summarily: Level 5 fine and/or 6 months
Maximum when tried on indictment: 5 years

Where the conduct is particularly serious, it would normally be charged as a separate offence. These starting points are based on the premise that the activity has either been prosecuted separately as an offence or is not of a character sufficient to justify prosecution of it as an offence in its own right.

Where offence committed in domestic context, refer [below] for guidance

Offence seriousness (culpability and harm)

A. Identify the appropriate starting point

Starting points based on first time offender pleading not guilty

Examples of nature of activity	Starting point	Range
Single breach involving no/minimal direct contact	Low level community order	Band C fine to medium level community order
More than one breach involving no/minimal contact or some direct contact	Medium level community order	Low level community order to high level community order
Single breach involving some violence and/or significant physical or psychological harm to the victim	18 weeks custody	13 to 26 weeks custody
More than one breach involving some violence and/or significant physical or psychological harm to the victim	Crown Court	26 weeks custody to Crown Court
Breach (whether one or more) involving significant physical violence and significant physical or psychological harm to the victim	Crown Court	Crown Court

B. Consider the effect of aggravating and mitigating factors (other than those within examples above)

Common aggravating and mitigating factors are identified [elsewhere]—the following may be particularly relevant but these lists are not exhaustive

Factors indicating higher culpability	Factors indicating greater degree of harm
1. Proven history of violence or threats by the offender	1. Victim is particularly vulnerable
2. Using contact arrangements with a child to instigate offence	2. Impact on children
3. Offence is a further breach, following earlier breach proceedings	3. Victim is forced to leave home
4. Offender has history of disobedience to court orders	**Factors indicating lower culpability**
5. Breach committed immediately or shortly after order made	1. Breach occurred after long period of compliance
	2. Victim initiated contact

[Sets out the standard sequential sentencing procedure.]

SG-247

PUBLIC ORDER ACT, S. 2—VIOLENT DISORDER

Public Order Act 1986, s. 2

Triable either way:
Maximum when tried summarily: Level 5 fine and/or 6 months
Maximum when tried on indictment: 5 years

Offence seriousness (culpability and harm)

A. Identify the appropriate starting point

Starting points based on first time offender pleading not guilty

> *These offences should normally be dealt with in the Crown Court.* However, there may be rare cases involving minor violence or threats of violence leading to no or minor injury, with few people involved and no weapon or missiles, in which a custodial sentence within the jurisdiction of a magistrates' court may be appropriate.

SG-248

PUBLIC ORDER ACT, S. 3—AFFRAY

Public Order Act 1986, s. 3

Triable either way:
Maximum when tried summarily: Level 5 fine and/or 6 months
Maximum when tried on indictment: 3 years

Offence seriousness (culpability and harm)

A. Identify the appropriate starting point

Starting points based on first time offender pleading not guilty

Examples of nature of activity	Starting point	Range
Brief offence involving low-level violence, no substantial fear created	Low level community order	Band C fine to medium level community order
Degree of fighting or violence that causes substantial fear	High level community order	Medium level community order to 12 weeks custody
Fight involving a weapon/throwing objects, or conduct causing risk of serious injury	18 weeks custody	12 weeks custody to Crown Court

B. Consider the effect of aggravating and mitigating factors (other than those within examples above)

Common aggravating and mitigating factors are identified [elsewhere]—the following may be particularly relevant but these lists are not exhaustive

Factors indicating higher culpability	Factors indicating lower culpability
1. Group action	1. Did not start the trouble
2. Threats	2. Provocation
3. Lengthy incident	3. Stopped as soon as police arrived
Factors indicating greater degree of harm	
1. Vulnerable person(s) present	
2. Injuries caused	
3. Damage to property	

[Sets out the standard sequential sentencing procedure and mentions the need to consider a football banning order.]

PUBLIC ORDER ACT, S. 4—THREATENING BEHAVIOUR—FEAR OR PROVOCATION OF VIOLENCE RACIALLY OR RELIGIOUSLY AGGRAVATED THREATENING BEHAVIOUR   SG-249

Public Order Act 1986, s. 4

Crime and Disorder Act 1998, s. 31

Threatening behaviour: triable only summarily
Maximum: Level 5 fine and/or 6 months

Racially or religiously aggravated threatening behaviour: triable either way
Maximum when tried summarily: Level 5 fine and/or 6 months
Maximum when tried on indictment: 2 years

Where offence committed in domestic context, refer [below] for guidance

Offence seriousness (culpability and harm)

A. Identify the appropriate starting point

Starting points based on first time offender pleading not guilty

Examples of nature of activity	Starting point	Range
Fear or threat of low level immediate unlawful violence such as push, shove or spit	Low level community order	Band B fine to medium level community order
Fear or threat of medium level immediate unlawful violence such as punch	High level community order	Low level community order to 12 weeks custody
Fear or threat of high level immediate unlawful violence such as use of weapon; missile thrown; gang involvement	12 weeks custody	6 to 26 weeks custody

B. Consider the effect of aggravating and mitigating factors (other than those within examples above)

Common aggravating and mitigating factors are identified [elsewhere]—the following may be particularly relevant but these lists are not exhaustive

| **Factors indicating higher culpability**
1. Planning
2. Offender deliberately isolates victim
3. Group action
4. Threat directed at victim because of job
5. History of antagonism towards victim

Factors indicating greater degree of harm
1. Offence committed at school, hospital or other place where vulnerable persons may be present
2. Offence committed on enclosed premises such as public transport
3. Vulnerable victim(s)
4. Victim needs medical help/counselling | **Factors indicating lower culpability**
1. Impulsive action
2. Short duration
3. Provocation |

[Sets out the standard sequential sentencing procedure and mentions the need to consider a football banning order. Notes that 'If offender charged and convicted of the racially or religiously aggravated offence, increase the sentence to reflect this element'.]

SG-250   Public Order Act, s. 4A—Disorderly Behaviour with Intent to Cause
Harassment, Alarm or Distress

Racially Or Religiously Aggravated Disorderly Behaviour With Intent To Cause Harassment, Alarm Or Distress

Public Order Act 1986, s. 4A

Crime and Disorder Act 1998, s. 31

Disorderly behaviour with intent to cause harassment, alarm or distress: triable only summarily
Maximum: Level 5 fine and/or 6 months

Racially or religiously aggravated disorderly behaviour with intent to cause harassment etc.: triable either way

Maximum when tried summarily: Level 5 fine and/or 6 months
Maximum when tried on indictment: 2 years

Offence seriousness (culpability and harm)

A. Identify the appropriate starting point

Starting points based on first time offender pleading not guilty

Examples of nature of activity	Starting point	Range
Threats, abuse or insults made more than once but on same occasion against the same person e.g. while following down the street	Band C fine	Band B fine to low level community order
Group action or deliberately planned action against targeted victim	Medium level community order	Low level community order to 12 weeks custody
Weapon brandished or used or threats against vulnerable victim—course of conduct over longer period	12 weeks custody	High level community order to 26 weeks custody

B. Consider the effect of aggravating and mitigating factors (other than those within examples above)

Common aggravating and mitigating factors are identified [elsewhere]—the following may be particularly relevant but these lists are not exhaustive

Factors indicating higher culpability	Factors indicating lower culpability
1. High degree of planning	1. Very short period
2. Offender deliberately isolates victim	2. Provocation
Factors indicating greater degree of harm	
1. Offence committed in vicinity of victim's home	
2. Large number of people in vicinity	
3. Actual or potential escalation into violence	
4. Particularly serious impact on victim	

[Sets out the standard sequential sentencing procedure and mentions the need to consider a football banning order. Notes that 'If offender charged and convicted of the racially or religiously aggravated offence, increase the sentence to reflect this element'.]

SG-251   Public Order Act, s. 5—Disorderly Behaviour (Harassment, Alarm or
Distress) Racially or Religiously Aggravated Disorderly Behaviour

Public Order Act 1986, s. 5

Crime and Disorder Act 1998, s. 31

Disorderly behaviour: triable only summarily
Maximum: Level 3 fine

Racially or religiously aggravated disorderly behaviour: triable only summarily
Maximum: Level 4 fine

Offence seriousness (culpability and harm)

A. Identify the appropriate starting point

Starting points based on first time offender pleading not guilty

Examples of nature of activity	Starting point	Range
Shouting, causing disturbance for some minutes	Band A fine	Conditional discharge to band B fine
Substantial disturbance caused	Band B fine	Band A fine to band C fine

B. Consider the effect of aggravating and mitigating factors (other than those within examples above)

Common aggravating and mitigating factors are identified [elsewhere]—the following may be particularly relevant but these lists are not exhaustive

Factors indicating higher culpability	Factors indicating lower culpability
1. Group action 2. Lengthy incident **Factors indicating greater degree of harm** 1. Vulnerable person(s) present 2. Offence committed at school, hospital or other place where vulnerable persons may be present 3. Victim providing public service	1. Stopped as soon as police arrived 2. Brief/minor incident 3. Provocation

[Sets out the standard sequential sentencing procedure and mentions the need to consider a football banning order. Notes that 'If offender charged and convicted of the racially or religiously aggravated offence, increase the sentence to reflect this element'.]

RAILWAY FARE EVASION   SG-252

Regulation of Railways Act 1889, s. 5(3) (travelling on railway without paying fare, with intent to avoid payment); s. 5(1) (failing to produce ticket)

Triable only summarily:
Maximum: Level 3 fine or 3 months (s. 5(3)); level 2 fine (s. 5(1))

Offence seriousness (culpability and harm)

A. Identify the appropriate starting point

Starting points based on first time offender pleading not guilty

Examples of nature of activity	Starting point	Range
Failing to produce ticket or pay fare on request	Band A fine	Conditional discharge to band B fine
Travelling on railway without having paid the fare or knowingly and wilfully travelling beyond the distance paid for, with intent to avoid payment	Band B fine	Band A fine to band C fine

B. Consider the effect of aggravating and mitigating factors (other than those within examples above)

Common aggravating and mitigating factors are identified [elsewhere]—the following may be particularly relevant but these lists are not exhaustive

Factor indicating higher culpability	Factor indicating greater degree of harm
1. Offensive or intimidating language or behaviour towards railway staff	1. High level of loss caused or intended to be caused

[Sets out the standard sequential sentencing procedure.]

SG-253   School Non-attendance

Education Act 1996, s. 444(1) (parent fails to secure regular attendance at school of registered pupil);
s. 444(1A) (parent knowingly fails to secure regular attendance at school of registered pupil)

Triable only summarily

Maximum: Level 3 fine (s. 444(1)); level 4 fine and/or 3 months (s. 444(1A))

Offence seriousness (culpability and harm)

A. Identify the appropriate starting point

Starting points based on first time offender pleading not guilty

Examples of nature of activity	Starting point	Range
Short period following previous good attendance (s.444(1))	Band A fine	Conditional discharge to band A fine
Erratic attendance for long period (s. 444(1))	Band B fine	Band B fine to Band C fine
Colluding in and condoning non-attendance or deliberately instigating non-attendance (s. 444(1A))	Medium level community order	Low level community order to high level community order

B. Consider the effect of aggravating and mitigating factors (other than those within examples above)

Common aggravating and mitigating factors are identified [elsewhere]—the following may be particularly relevant but these lists are not exhaustive

Factors indicating higher culpability	Factors indicating lower culpability
1. Parental collusion (s.444(1) only) 2. Lack of parental effort to ensure attendance (s.444(1) only) 3. Threats to teachers and/or officials 4. Refusal to co-operate with school and/or officials **Factors indicating greater degree of harm** 1. More than one child 2. Harmful effect on other children in family	1. Parent unaware of child's whereabouts 2. Parent tried to ensure attendance 3. Parent concerned by child's allegations of bullying/unable to get school to address bullying

[Sets out the standard sequential sentencing procedure and mentions need to consider a parenting order.]

SG-254   Sex Offenders Register—Fail to Comply with Notification Requirements

Sexual Offences Act 2003, s. 91(1)(a) (fail to comply with notification requirements);
s. 91(1)(b) (supply false information)

Triable either way:
Maximum when tried summarily: Level 5 fine and/or 6 months
Maximum when tried on indictment: 5 years

Offence seriousness (culpability and harm)

A. Identify the appropriate starting point

Starting points based on first time offender pleading not guilty

Examples of nature of activity	Starting point	Range
Negligent or inadvertent failure to comply with requirements	Medium level community order	Band C fine to high level community order
Deliberate failure to comply with requirements OR Supply of information known to be false	6 weeks custody	High level community order to 26 weeks custody
Conduct as described in box above AND Long period of non-compliance OR Attempts to avoid detection	18 weeks custody	6 weeks custody to Crown Court

B. Consider the effect of aggravating and mitigating factors (other than those within examples above)

Common aggravating and mitigating factors are identified [elsewhere]—the following may be particularly relevant but these lists are not exhaustive

Factor indicating higher culpability	Factor indicating lower culpability
1. Long period of non-compliance (where not in the examples above)	1. Genuine misunderstanding
Factor indicating greater degree of harm	
1. Alarm or distress caused to victim	
2. Particularly serious original offence	

[Sets out the standard sequential sentencing procedure.]

Note:

An offender convicted of this offence will always have at least one relevant previous conviction for the offence that resulted in the notification requirements being imposed. The starting points and ranges take this into account; any other previous convictions should be considered in the usual way.

SEXUAL ACTIVITY IN A PUBLIC LAVATORY

Sexual Offences Act 2003, s. 71

SG-255

Triable only summarily
Maximum: Level 5 fine and/or 6 months

This guideline and accompanying notes are taken from the Sentencing Guidelines Council's definitive guideline *Sexual Offences Act 2003*, published 30 April 2007 [see **SG-109**]

Key factors

(a) This offence is committed where an offender intentionally engages in sexual activity in a public lavatory. It was introduced to give adults and children the freedom to use public lavatories for the purpose for which they are designed, without the fear of being an unwilling witness to overtly sexual behaviour of a kind that most people would not expect to be conducted in public. It is primarily a public order offence rather than a sexual offence.

(b) When dealing with a repeat offender, the starting point should be a low level community order with a range of Band C fine to medium level community order. The presence of aggravating factors may suggest that a sentence above the range is appropriate.

(c) This guideline may be relevant by way of analogy to conduct charged as the common law offence of outraging public decency; the offence is triable either way and has a maximum penalty of a level 5 fine and/or 6 months imprisonment when tried summarily.

Offence seriousness (culpability and harm)

A. Identify the appropriate starting point

Starting points based on first time offender pleading not guilty

Examples of nature of activity	Starting point	Range
Basic offence as defined in the Act, assuming no aggravating or mitigating factors	Band C fine	Band C fine
Offence with aggravating factors	Low level community order	Band C fine to medium level community order

B. Consider the effect of aggravating and mitigating factors (other than those within examples above)

Common aggravating and mitigating factors are identified [elsewhere]—the following may be particularly relevant but these lists are not exhaustive

Factors indicating higher culpability	
1. Intimidating behaviour/threats of violence to member(s) of the public	
2. Blatant behaviour	

[Sets out the standard sequential sentencing procedure.]

Sentencing Guidelines

Sexual Assault

[The guidelines set out below are applicable to adult offenders sentenced after 1 April 2014.]

Sexual Offences Act 2003 (section 3)

Triable either way
Maximum: 10 years' custody

Offence range: Community order–7 years' custody

For convictions on or after 3 December 2012 (irrespective of the date of commission of the offence), this is a specified offence for the purposes of section 226A (extended sentence for certain violent or sexual offences) of the Criminal Justice Act 2003.

STEP ONE Determining the offence category

The court should determine which categories of harm and culpability the offence falls into by reference only to the tables below.

Harm	
Category 1	• Severe psychological or physical harm • Abduction • Violence or threats of violence • Forced/uninvited entry into victim's home
Category 2	• Touching of naked genitalia or naked breasts • Prolonged detention/sustained incident • Additional degradation/humiliation • Victim is particularly vulnerable due to personal circumstances* * for children under 13 please refer to the guideline [at **SG-256A**]
Category 3	Factor(s) in categories 1 and 2 not present

Culpability	
A	**B**
• Significant degree of planning • Offender acts together with others to commit the offence • Use of alcohol/drugs on victim to facilitate the offence • Abuse of trust • Previous violence against victim • Offence committed in course of burglary • Recording of offence • Commercial exploitation and/or motivation • Offence racially or religiously aggravated • Offence motivated by, or demonstrating, hostility to the victim based on his or her sexual orientation (or presumed sexual orientation) or transgender identity (or presumed transgender identity) • Offence motivated by, or demonstrating, hostility to the victim based on his or her disability (or presumed disability)	Factor(s) in category A not present

STEP TWO Starting point and category range

Having determined the category, the court should use the corresponding starting points to reach a sentence within the category range [below]. The starting point applies to all offenders irrespective of plea or previous convictions. Having determined the starting point, step two allows further adjustment for aggravating or mitigating features, set out [below].

A case of particular gravity, reflected by multiple features of culpability or harm in step one, could merit upward adjustment from the starting point before further adjustment for aggravating or mitigating features, set out [below].

Where there is a sufficient prospect of rehabilitation, a community order with a sex offender treatment programme requirement under section 202 of the Criminal Justice Act 2003 can be a proper alternative to a short or moderate length custodial sentence.

	A	**B**
Category 1	**Starting point** 4 years' custody **Category range** 3 – 7 years' custody	**Starting point** 2 years 6 months' custody **Category range** 2 – 4 years' custody
Category 2	**Starting point** 2 years' custody **Category range** 1 – 4 years' custody	**Starting point** 1 year's custody **Category range** High level community order – 2 years' custody
Category 3	**Starting point** 26 weeks' custody **Category range** High level community order – 1 year's custody	**Starting point** High level community order **Category range** Medium level community order – 26 weeks' custody

The table below contains a **non-exhaustive** list of additional factual elements providing the context of the offence and factors relating to the offender. Identify whether any combination of these, or other relevant factors, should result in an upward or downward adjustment from the starting point. **In particular, relevant recent convictions are likely to result in an upward adjustment**. In some cases, having considered these factors, it may be appropriate to move outside the identified category range.

When sentencing appropriate **category 2 or 3 offences**, the court should also consider the custody threshold as follows:

- has the custody threshold been passed?
- if so, is it unavoidable that a custodial sentence be imposed?
- if so, can that sentence be suspended?

Aggravating factors
Statutory aggravating factors
• Previous convictions, having regard to a) the nature of the offence to which the conviction relates and its relevance to the current offence; and b) the time that has elapsed since the conviction • Offence committed whilst on bail

Other aggravating factors
• Specific targeting of a particularly vulnerable victim • Blackmail or other threats made (where not taken into account at step one) • Location of offence • Timing of offence • Use of weapon or other item to frighten or injure • Victim compelled to leave their home (including victims of domestic violence) • Failure to comply with current court orders • Offence committed whilst on licence • Exploiting contact arrangements with a child to commit an offence • Presence of others, especially children • Any steps taken to prevent the victim reporting an incident, obtaining assistance and/or from assisting or supporting the prosecution • Attempts to dispose of or conceal evidence • Commission of offence whilst under the influence of alcohol or drugs

Mitigating factors
• No previous convictions **or** no relevant/recent convictions • Remorse • Previous good character and/or exemplary conduct* • Age and/or lack of maturity where it affects the responsibility of the offender • Mental disorder or learning disability, particularly where linked to the commission of the offence • Demonstration of steps taken to address offending behaviour

*   Previous good character/exemplary conduct is different from having no previous convictions. The more serious the offence, the less the weight which should normally be attributed to this factor. Where previous good character/ exemplary conduct has been used to facilitate the offence, this mitigation should not normally be allowed and such conduct may constitute an aggravating factor.

[Sets out the standard sequential sentencing procedure.]

Sentencing Guidelines

Sexual Assault of a Child Under 13

[The guidelines set out below are applicable to adult offenders sentenced after 1 April 2014.]

Sexual Offences Act 2003 (section 7)

Triable either way
Maximum: 14 years' custody

Offence range: Community order–9 years' custody

For offences committed on or after 3 December 2012, this is an offence listed in Part 1 of Schedule 15B for the purposes of section 224A (life sentence for second listed offence) of the Criminal Justice Act 2003.

For convictions on or after 3 December 2012 (irrespective of the date of commission of the offence), this is a specified offence for the purposes of section 226A (extended sentence for certain violent or sexual offences) of the Criminal Justice Act 2003.

STEP ONE Determining the offence category

The court should determine which categories of harm and culpability the offence falls into by reference **only** to the tables below.

Harm	
Category 1	• Severe psychological or physical harm • Abduction • Violence or threats of violence • Forced/uninvited entry into victim's home
Category 2	• Touching of naked genitalia or naked breast area • Prolonged detention/sustained incident • Additional degradation/humiliation • Child is particularly vulnerable due to extreme youth and/or personal circumstances
Category 3	Factor(s) in categories 1 and 2 not present

Culpability	
A	**B**
• Significant degree of planning • Offender acts together with others to commit the offence • Use of alcohol/drugs on victim to facilitate the offence • Grooming behaviour used against victim • Abuse of trust • Previous violence against victim • Offence committed in course of burglary • Sexual images of victim recorded, retained, solicited or shared • Deliberate isolation of victim • Commercial exploitation and/or motivation • Offence racially or religiously aggravated • Offence motivated by, or demonstrating, hostility to the victim based on his or her sexual orientation (or presumed sexual orientation) or transgender identity (or presumed transgender identity) • Offence motivated by, or demonstrating, hostility to the victim based on his or her disability (or presumed disability)	Factor(s) in category A not present

STEP TWO Starting point and category range

Having determined the category, the court should use the corresponding starting points to reach a sentence within the category range [below]. The starting point applies to all offenders irrespective of plea or previous convictions. Having determined the starting point, step two allows further adjustment for aggravating or mitigating features, set out [below].

A case of particular gravity, reflected by multiple features of culpability or harm in step one, could merit upward adjustment from the starting point before further adjustment for aggravating or mitigating features, set out [below].

Where there is a sufficient prospect of rehabilitation, a community order with a sex offender treatment programme requirement under section 202 of the Criminal Justice Act 2003 can be a proper alternative to a short or moderate length custodial sentence.

	A	B
Category 1	**Starting point** 6 years' custody **Category range** 4 – 9 years' custody	**Starting point** 4 years' custody **Category range** 3 – 7 years' custody
Category 2	**Starting point** 4 years' custody **Category range** 3 – 7 years' custody	**Starting point** 2 years' custody **Category range** 1 – 4 years' custody
Category 3	**Starting point** 1 year's custody **Category range** 26 weeks' – 2 years' custody	**Starting point** 26 weeks' custody **Category range** High level community order – 1 year's custody

The table below contains **a non-exhaustive** list of additional factual elements providing the context of the offence and factors relating to the offender. Identify whether any combination of these, or other relevant factors, should result in an upward or downward adjustment from the starting point. **In particular, relevant recent convictions are likely to result in an upward adjustment.** In some cases, having considered these factors, it may be appropriate to move outside the identified category range.

Aggravating factors
Statutory aggravating factors
• Previous convictions, having regard to a) the nature of the offence to which the conviction relates and its relevance to the current offence; and b) the time that has elapsed since the conviction • Offence committed whilst on bail

Other aggravating factors
• Specific targeting of a particularly vulnerable child • Blackmail or other threats made (where not taken into account at step one) • Location of offence • Timing of offence • Use of weapon or other item to frighten or injure • Victim compelled to leave their home, school, etc • Failure to comply with current court orders • Offence committed whilst on licence • Exploiting contact arrangements with a child to commit an offence • Presence of others, especially other children • Any steps taken to prevent the victim reporting an incident, obtaining assistance and/or from assisting or supporting the prosecution • Attempts to dispose of or conceal evidence • Commission of offence whilst under the influence of alcohol or drugs • Victim encouraged to recruit others

Mitigating factors
• No previous convictions **or** no relevant/recent convictions • Remorse • Previous good character and/or exemplary conduct* • Age and/or lack of maturity where it affects the responsibility of the offender • Mental disorder or learning disability, particularly where linked to the commission of the offence

* Previous good character/exemplary conduct is different from having no previous convictions. The more serious the offence, the less the weight which should normally be attributed to this factor. Where previous good character/exemplary conduct has been used to facilitate the offence, this mitigation should not normally be allowed and such conduct may constitute an aggravating factor.

Sentencing Guidelines

In the context of this offence, previous good character/exemplary conduct should not normally be given any significant weight and will not normally justify a reduction in what would otherwise be the appropriate sentence.

[Sets out the standard sequential sentencing procedure.]

SG-257   SOCIAL SECURITY BENEFIT, FALSE STATEMENT/REPRESENTATION TO OBTAIN

Social Security Administration Act 1992, s. 112
(makes statement/representation known to be false)

Triable only summarily
Maximum: Level 5 fine and/or 3 months

For offences under s. 111A, refer to guideline *Fraud — banking and insurance fraud and obtaining credit through fraud, benefit fraud and revenue fraud* [see **SG-230** *et seq.*].

Offence seriousness (culpability and harm)

A. Identify the appropriate starting point

Starting points based on first time offender pleading not guilty

Examples of nature of activity	Starting point	Range
Claim fraudulent from the start, up to £5,000 obtained	Medium level community order	Band B fine to high level community order

B. Consider the effect of aggravating and mitigating factors (other than those within examples above)

Common aggravating and mitigating factors are identified [elsewhere]—the following may be particularly relevant but these lists are not exhaustive

Factors indicating higher culpability	Factors indicating lower culpability
1. Offending carried out over a long period 2. Offender acting in unison with one or more others 3. Planning 4. Offender motivated by greed or desire to live beyond his/her means 5. False identities or other personal details used 6. False or forged documents used 7. Official documents altered or falsified	1. Pressurised by others 2. Claim initially legitimate **Factor indicating lesser degree of harm** 1. Voluntary repayment of amounts overpaid

[Sets out the standard sequential sentencing procedure.]

Note: A maximum of £5,000 compensation may be imposed for each offence of which the offender has been convicted. The above guidelines have been drafted on the assumption that, in most cases, the Department for Work and Pensions will take separate steps to recover the overpayment.

SG-258   TAX CREDIT FRAUD

Tax Credits Act 2002, s. 35

Triable either way:
Maximum when tried summarily: Level 5 fine and/or 6 months
Maximum when tried on indictment: 7 years

Refer to guideline *Fraud — banking and insurance fraud and obtaining credit through fraud, benefit fraud and revenue fraud* [see **SG-230** *et seq.*].

TAXI TOUTING/SOLICITING FOR HIRE   **SG-259**
Criminal Justice and Public Order Act 1994, s. 167

Triable only summarily:
Maximum: Level 4 fine
Offence seriousness (culpability and harm)

A. Identify the appropriate starting point

Starting points based on first time offender pleading not guilty

Examples of nature of activity	Starting point	Range
Licensed taxi-driver touting for trade (i.e. making approach rather than waiting for a person to initiate hiring)	**Band A fine**	**Conditional discharge to band A fine and consider disqualification 1–3 months**
PHV licence held but touting for trade rather than being booked through an operator; an accomplice to touting	**Band B fine**	**Band A fine to band C fine and consider disqualification 3–6 months**
No PHV licence held	**Band C fine**	**Band B fine to Band C fine and disqualification 6–12 months**

Note: refer [below] for approach to fines for offences committed for commercial purposes

B. Consider the effect of aggravating and mitigating factors (other than those within examples above)

Common aggravating and mitigating factors are identified [elsewhere]—the following may be particularly relevant but these lists are not exhaustive

Factors indicating higher culpability	Factor indicating lower culpability
1. Commercial business/large scale operation 2. No insurance/invalid insurance 3. No driving licence and/or no MOT 4. Vehicle not roadworthy **Factors indicating greater degree of harm** 1. Deliberately diverting trade from taxi rank 2. PHV licence had been refused/offender ineligible for licence	1. Providing a service when no licensed taxi available

[Sets out the standard sequential sentencing procedure and mentions need to consider disqualification from driving and deprivation of property.]

THEFT—GENERAL PRINCIPLES   **SG-260**

1. The guideline *Theft and Burglary in a building other than a dwelling*, published by the Sentencing Guidelines Council 9 December 2008 [see **SG-395**] covers four forms of theft. However, the principles relating to the assessment of seriousness in the guideline are of general application and are likely to be of assistance where a court is sentencing for a form of theft not covered by a specific guideline. These are summarised below for ease of reference.

Assessing seriousness

(i) Culpability and harm

2. As it is an essential element of the offence of theft that the offender acted dishonestly, an offender convicted of theft will have a high level of culpability. Even so, the precise level of culpability will vary according to factors such as the offender's motivation, whether the offence was planned or spontaneous and whether the offender was in a position of trust. An offence will be aggravated where there is evidence of planning.

3. When assessing the harm caused by a theft offence, the starting point is normally based on the loss suffered by the victim. Whilst, in general, the greater the loss, the more serious the offence, the monetary value of the loss may not reflect the full extent of the harm caused by the offence. The court should also take into account the impact of the offence on the victim (which may be significantly greater than the monetary value of the loss; this may be particularly important where the value of the loss is high in proportion to the victim's financial circumstances even though relatively low in absolute terms), any harm to persons other than the direct victim, and any harm in the form of public concern or erosion of public confidence.

(ii) Aggravating and mitigating factors

4.　The most common factors that are likely to aggravate an offence of theft are:

　　factors indicating higher culpability: planning of an offence, offenders operating in groups or gangs, and deliberate targeting of vulnerable victims.

　　factors indicating a more than usually serious degree of harm: victim is particularly vulnerable, high level of gain from the offence, and high value (including sentimental value) of property to the victim or substantial consequential loss.

(iii) Offender mitigation

5.　The Council has identified the following matters of offender mitigation that might apply to offences of theft:

　　(a)　Return of stolen property—depending on the circumstances and in particular, the voluntariness and timeliness of the return.

　　(b)　Impact on sentence of offender's dependency—where an offence is motivated by an addiction (often to drugs, alcohol or gambling) this does not mitigate the seriousness of the offence, but a dependency may properly influence the type of sentence imposed. In particular, it may some-times be appropriate to impose a drug rehabilitation requirement, an alcohol treatment requirement (for dependent drinkers) or an activity or supervision requirement including alcohol specific information, advice and support (for harmful and hazardous drinkers) as part of a community order or a suspended sentence order in an attempt to break the cycle of addic-tion and offending, even if an immediate custodial sentence would otherwise be warranted.

　　(c)　Offender motivated by desperation or need—the fact that an offence has been committed in desperation or need arising from particular hardship may count as offender mitigation in **exceptional circumstances**.

SG-261　　　　　　　Theft—breach of trust—factors to take into consideration

This guideline and accompanying notes are taken from the Sentencing Guidelines Council's definitive guideline *Theft and Burglary in a building other than a dwelling*, published 9 December 2008 [see SG-395]

Key factors

(a)　When assessing the harm caused by this offence, the starting point should be the loss suffered by the victim. In general, the greater the loss, the more serious the offence. However, the monetary value of the loss may not reflect the full extent of the harm caused by the offence. The court should also take into account the impact of the offence on the victim (which may be significant and disproportionate to the value of the loss having regard to their financial circumstances), any harm to persons other than the direct victim, and any harm in the form of public concern or erosion of public confidence.

(b)　In general terms, the seriousness of the offence will increase in line with the level of trust breached. The extent to which the nature and degree of trust placed in an offender should be regarded as increas-ing seriousness will depend on a careful assessment of the circumstances of each individual case, including the type and terms of the relationship between the offender and victim.

(c)　The concept of breach of trust for the purposes of the offence of theft includes employer/employee relationships and those between a professional adviser and client. It also extends to relationships in which a person is in a position of authority in relation to the victim or would be expected to have a duty to protect the interests of the victim, such as medical, social or care workers. The targeting of a vulnerable victim by an offender through a relationship or position of trust will indicate a higher level of culpability.

(d)　The Council has identified the following matters of offender mitigation which may be relevant to this offence:

　　(i)　*Return of stolen property*

　　　　Whether and the degree to which the return of stolen property constitutes a matter of offender mitigation will depend on an assessment of the circumstances and, in particular, the voluntari-ness and timeliness of the return.

　　(ii)　*Impact on sentence of offender's dependency*

　　　　Where an offence is motivated by an addiction (often to drugs, alcohol or gambling) this does not mitigate the seriousness of the offence, but a dependency may properly influence the type of sentence imposed. In particular, it may sometimes be appropriate to impose a drug rehabilita-tion requirement, an alcohol treatment requirement (for dependent drinkers) or an activity or supervision requirement including alcohol specific information, advice and support (for harm-ful and hazardous drinkers) as part of a community order or a suspended sentence order in an attempt to break the cycle of addiction and offending, even if an immediate custodial sentence would otherwise be warranted.

(iii) *Offender motivated by desperation or need*

The fact that an offence has been committed in desperation or need arising from particular hardship may count as offender mitigation in exceptional circumstances.

(iv) *Inappropriate degree of trust or responsibility*

The fact that an offender succumbed to temptation having been placed in a position of trust or given responsibility to an inappropriate degree may be regarded as offender mitigation.

(v) *Voluntary cessation of offending*

The fact that an offender voluntarily ceased offending before being discovered does not reduce the seriousness of the offence. However, if the claim to have stopped offending is genuine, it may constitute offender mitigation, particularly if it is evidence of remorse.

(vi) *Reporting an undiscovered offence*

Where an offender brings the offending to the attention of his or her employer or the authorities, this may be treated as offender mitigation.

(f) In many cases of theft in breach of trust, termination of an offender's employment will be a natural consequence of committing the offence. Other than in the most exceptional of circumstances, loss of employment and any consequential hardship should not constitute offender mitigation.

(g) Where a court is satisfied that a custodial sentence is appropriate for an offence of theft in breach of trust, consideration should be given to whether that sentence can be suspended in accordance with the criteria in the Council guideline *New Sentences: Criminal Justice Act 2003*. A suspended sentence may be particularly appropriate where this would allow for reparation to be made either to the victim or to the community at large.

THEFT—BREACH OF TRUST

Theft Act 1968, s. 1

SG-262

Triable either way:
Maximum when tried summarily: Level 5 fine and/or 6 months
Maximum when tried on indictment: 7 years

Offence seriousness (culpability and harm)

A. Identify the appropriate starting point

Starting points based on first time offender pleading not guilty

Examples of nature of activity	Starting point	Range
Theft of less than £2,000	Medium level community order	Band B fine to 26 weeks custody
Theft of £2,000 or more but less than £20,000 OR Theft of less than £2,000 in breach of a high degree of trust	18 weeks custody	High level community order to Crown Court
Theft of £20,000 or more OR Theft of £2,000 or more in breach of a high degree of trust	Crown Court	Crown Court

B. Consider the effect of aggravating and mitigating factors (other than those within examples above)

Common aggravating and mitigating factors are identified [elsewhere]—the following may be particularly relevant but these lists are not exhaustive

Factors indicating higher culpability
1. Long course of offending
2. Suspicion deliberately thrown on others
3. Offender motivated by intention to cause harm or out of revenge

THEFT—DWELLING

Factors to take into consideration

This guideline and accompanying notes are taken from the Sentencing Guidelines Council's definitive guideline *Theft and Burglary in a building other than a dwelling*, published 9 December 2008 [see **SG-395**]

Key factors

(a)　The category of theft in a dwelling covers the situation where a theft is committed by an offender who is present in a dwelling with the authority of the owner or occupier. Examples include thefts by lodgers or visitors to the victim's residence, such as friends, relatives or salespeople. Such offences involve a violation of the privacy of the victim's home and constitute an abuse of the victim's trust. Where an offender enters a dwelling as a trespasser in order to commit theft, his or her conduct will generally constitute the more serious offence of burglary; this guideline does not apply where the offender has been convicted of burglary—see [above] for guidance.

(b)　The starting points and sentencing ranges in this guideline are based on the assumption that the offender was motivated by greed or a desire to live beyond his or her means. To avoid double counting, such a motivation should not be treated as a factor that increases culpability.

(c)　For the purpose of this guideline, a 'vulnerable victim' is a person targeted by the offender because it is anticipated that he or she is unlikely or unable to resist the theft. The exploitation of a vulnerable victim indicates a high level of culpability and will influence the category of seriousness into which the offence falls.

(d)　The guideline is based on the assumption that most thefts in a dwelling do not involve property of high monetary value or of high value to the victim. Where the property stolen is of high monetary value or of high value (including sentimental value) to the victim, the appropriate sentence may be beyond the range into which the offence otherwise would fall. For the purpose of this form of theft, property worth more than £2,000 should generally be regarded as being of 'high monetary value', although this will depend on an assessment of all the circumstances of the particular case.

(e)　A sentence beyond the range into which the offence otherwise would fall may also be appropriate where the effect on the victim is particularly severe or where substantial consequential loss results (such as where the theft of equipment causes serious disruption to the victim's life or business).

(f)　The Council has identified the following matters of offender mitigation which may be relevant to this offence:

　(i)　*Return of stolen property*

　　Whether and the degree to which the return of stolen property constitutes a matter of offender mitigation will depend on an assessment of the circumstances and, in particular, the voluntariness and timeliness of the return.

　(ii)　*Impact on sentence of offender's dependency*

　　Where an offence is motivated by an addiction (often to drugs, alcohol or gambling) this does not mitigate the seriousness of the offence, but a dependency may properly influence the type of sentence imposed. In particular, it may sometimes be appropriate to impose a drug rehabilitation requirement, an alcohol treatment requirement (for dependent drinkers) or an activity or supervision requirement including alcohol specific information, advice and support (for harmful and hazardous drinkers) as part of a community order or a suspended sentence order in an attempt to break the cycle of addiction and offending, even if an immediate custodial sentence would otherwise be warranted.

　(iii)　*Offender motivated by desperation or need*

　　The fact that an offence has been committed in desperation or need arising from particular hardship may count as offender mitigation in exceptional circumstances.

Guidelines

Theft Act 1968, s. 1

Triable either way:
Maximum when tried summarily: Level 5 fine and/or 6 months
Maximum when tried on indictment: 7 years

Offence seriousness (culpability and harm)

A. Identify the appropriate starting point

Starting points based on first time offender pleading not guilty

Examples of nature of activity	Starting point	Range
Where the effect on the victim is particularly severe, the stolen property is of high value (as defined in note (d) [above]), or substantial consequential loss results, a sentence higher than the range into which the offence otherwise would fall may be appropriate		
Theft in a dwelling not involving vulnerable victim	Medium level community order	Band B fine to 18 weeks custody
Theft from a vulnerable victim (as defined in note (c) [above])	18 weeks custody	High level community order to Crown Court
Theft from a vulnerable victim (as defined in note (c) [above]) involving intimidation or the use or threat of force (falling short of robbery) or the use of deception	Crown Court	Crown Court

B. Consider the effect of aggravating and mitigating factors (other than those within examples above)

Common aggravating and mitigating factors are identified [elsewhere]—the following may be particularly relevant but these lists are not exhaustive

Factors indicating higher culpability 1. Offender motivated by intention to cause harm or out of revenge **Factors indicating greater degree of harm** 1. Intimidation or face-to-face confrontation with victim [except where this raises the offence into a higher sentencing range] 2. Use of force, or threat of force, against victim (not amounting to robbery) [except where this raises the offence into a higher sentencing range] 3. Use of deception [except where this raises the offence into a higher sentencing range] 4. Offender takes steps to prevent the victim from reporting the crime or seeking help	

[Sets out the standard sequential sentencing procedure.]

THEFT—PERSON

SG-264

Factors to take into consideration

This guideline and accompanying notes are taken from the Sentencing Guidelines Council's definitive guideline *Theft and Burglary in a building other than a dwelling*, published 9 December 2008 [see **SG-395**]

Key factors

(a) Theft from the person may encompass conduct such as 'pick-pocketing', where the victim is unaware that the property is being stolen, as well as the snatching of handbags, wallets, jewellery and mobile telephones from the victim's possession or from the vicinity of the victim. The offence constitutes an invasion of the victim's privacy and may cause the victim to experience distress, fear and inconvenience either during or after the event. While in some cases the conduct may be similar, this guideline does not apply where the offender has been convicted of robbery; sentencers should instead refer to the Council guideline on robbery.

(b) The starting points and sentencing ranges in this guideline are based on the assumption that the offender was motivated by greed or a desire to live beyond his or her means. To avoid double counting, such a motivation should not be treated as a factor that increases culpability.

(c) For the purpose of this guideline, a 'vulnerable victim' is a person targeted by the offender because it is anticipated that he or she is unlikely or unable to resist the theft. Young or elderly persons, or those with disabilities may fall into this category. The exploitation of a vulnerable victim indicates a high level of culpability and will influence the category of seriousness into which the offence falls.

(d) Offences of this type will be aggravated where there is evidence of planning, such as where tourists are targeted because of their unfamiliarity with an area and a perception that they will not be available to give evidence.

(e) The guideline is based on the assumption that most thefts from the person do not involve property of high monetary value or of high value to the victim. Where the stolen property is of high monetary value or of high value (including sentimental value) to the victim, the appropriate sentence may be beyond the range into which the offence otherwise would fall. For the purposes of this form of theft, 'high monetary value' is defined as more than £2,000.

(f) A sentence beyond the range into which the offence otherwise would fall may also be appropriate where the effect on the victim is particularly severe or where substantial consequential loss results (such as where the theft of equipment causes serious disruption to the victim's life or business).

(g) The Council has identified the following matters of offender mitigation which may be relevant to this offence:

   (i) *Return of stolen property*
      Whether and the degree to which the return of stolen property constitutes a matter of offender mitigation will depend on an assessment of the circumstances and, in particular, the voluntariness and timeliness of the return.

   (ii) *Impact on sentence of offender's dependency*
      Where an offence is motivated by an addiction (often to drugs, alcohol or gambling) this does not mitigate the seriousness of the offence, but a dependency may properly influence the type of sentence imposed. In particular, it may sometimes be appropriate to impose a drug rehabilitation requirement, an alcohol treatment requirement (for dependent drinkers) or an activity or supervision requirement including alcohol specific information, advice and support (for harmful and hazardous drinkers) as part of a community order or a suspended sentence order in an attempt to break the cycle of addiction and offending, even if an immediate custodial sentence would otherwise be warranted.

   (iii) *Offender motivated by desperation or need*
      The fact that an offence has been committed in desperation or need arising from particular hardship may count as offender mitigation in exceptional circumstances.

Guidelines

Theft Act 1968, s. 1

Triable either way:
Maximum when tried summarily: Level 5 fine and/or 6 months
Maximum when tried on indictment: 7 years

Offence seriousness (culpability and harm)

A. Identify the appropriate starting point

Starting points based on first time offender pleading not guilty

Examples of nature of activity	Starting point	Range
Where the effect on the victim is particularly severe, the stolen property is of high value (as defined in note (e) [above]), or substantial consequential loss results, a sentence higher than the range into which the offence otherwise would fall may be appropriate		
Theft from the person not involving vulnerable victim	Medium level community order	Band B fine to 18 weeks custody
Theft from a vulnerable victim (as defined in note (c) [above])	18 weeks custody	High level community order to Crown Court
Theft involving the use or threat of force (falling short of robbery) against a vulnerable victim (as defined in note (c) [above])	Crown Court	Crown Court

B. Consider the effect of aggravating and mitigating factors (other than those within examples above)

Common aggravating and mitigating factors are identified [elsewhere]—the following may be particularly relevant but these lists are not exhaustive

Factors indicating higher culpability 1. Offender motivated by intention to cause harm or out of revenge **Factors indicating greater degree of harm** 1. Intimidation or face-to-face confrontation with victim [except where this raises the offence into a higher sentencing range] 2. Use of force, or threat of force, against victim (not amounting to robbery) [except where this raises the offence into a higher sentencing range] 3. High level of inconvenience caused to victim, e.g. replacing house keys, credit cards etc

[Sets out the standard sequential sentencing procedure.]

THEFT—SHOP   **SG-265**

Factors to take into consideration

This guideline and accompanying notes are taken from the Sentencing Guidelines Council's definitive guideline *Theft and Burglary in a building other than a dwelling*, published 9 December 2008 [see **SG-395**]

Key factors

(a)   The circumstances of this offence can vary significantly. At the least serious end of the scale are thefts involving low value goods, no (or little) planning and no violence or damage; a non-custodial sentence will usually be appropriate for a first time offender. At the higher end of the spectrum are thefts involving organised gangs or groups or the threat or use of force and a custodial starting point will usually be appropriate.

(b)   The starting points and sentencing ranges in this guideline are based on the assumption that the offender was motivated by greed or a desire to live beyond his or her means. To avoid double counting, such a motivation should not be treated as a factor that increases culpability.

(c)   When assessing the level of harm, the circumstances of the retailer are a proper consideration; a greater level of harm may be caused where the theft is against a small retailer.

(d)   Retailers may suffer additional loss as a result of this type of offending such as the cost of preventative security measures, higher insurance premiums and time spent by staff dealing with the prosecution of offenders. However, the seriousness of an individual case must be judged on its own dimension of harm and culpability and the sentence on an individual offender should not be increased to reflect the harm caused to retailers in general by the totality of this type of offending.

(e)   Any recent previous convictions for theft and dishonesty offences will need to be taken into account in sentencing. Where an offender demonstrates a level of 'persistent' or 'seriously persistent' offending, the community and custody thresholds may be crossed even though the other characteristics of the offence would otherwise warrant a lesser sentence.

(f)   The list of aggravating and mitigating factors on the pullout card identifies high value as an aggravating factor in property offences. In cases of theft from a shop, theft of high value goods may be associated with other aggravating factors such as the degree of planning, professionalism and/or operating in a group, and care will need to be taken to avoid double counting. Deliberately targeting high value goods will always make an offence more serious.

(g)   The Council has identified the following matters of offender mitigation which may be relevant to this offence:

  (i)   *Return of stolen property*
        Whether and the degree to which the return of stolen property constitutes a matter of offender mitigation will depend on an assessment of the circumstances and, in particular, the voluntariness and timeliness of the return.

  (ii) *Impact on sentence of offender's dependency*
        Where an offence is motivated by an addiction (often to drugs, alcohol or gambling) this does not mitigate the seriousness of the offence, but a dependency may properly influence the type of sentence imposed. In particular, it may sometimes be appropriate to impose a drug rehabilitation requirement, an alcohol treatment requirement (for dependent drinkers) or an activity or supervision requirement including alcohol specific information, advice and support (for harmful and hazardous drinkers) as part of a community order or a suspended sentence order in an attempt to break the cycle of addiction and offending, even if an immediate custodial sentence would otherwise be warranted.

  (iii) *Offender motivated by desperation or need*
        The fact that an offence has been committed in desperation or need arising from particular hardship may count as offender mitigation in exceptional circumstances.

Guidelines

Theft Act 1968, s. 1

Triable either way:
Maximum when tried summarily: Level 5 fine and/or 6 months
Maximum when tried on indictment: 7 years

Offence seriousness (culpability and harm)

A. Identify the appropriate starting point

Starting points based on first time offender pleading not guilty

Examples of nature of activity	Starting point	Range
Little or no planning or sophistication and Goods stolen of low value	Band B fine	Conditional discharge to low level community order
Low level intimidation or threats or Some planning e.g. a session of stealing on the same day or going equipped or Some related damage	Low level community order	Band B fine to medium level community order
Significant intimidation or threats or Use of force resulting in slight injury or Very high level of planning or Significant related damage	6 weeks custody	High level community order to Crown Court
Organised gang/group and Intimidation or the use or threat of force (short of robbery)	Crown Court	Crown Court

B. Consider the effect of aggravating and mitigating factors (other than those within examples above)

Common aggravating and mitigating factors are identified [elsewhere]—the following may be particularly relevant but these lists are not exhaustive

Factors indicating higher culpability 1. Child accompanying offender is involved or aware of theft 2. Offender is subject to a banning order that includes the store targeted 3. Offender motivated by intention to cause harm or out of revenge 4. Professional offending **Factors indicating greater degree of harm** 1. Victim particularly vulnerable (e.g. small independent shop) 2. Offender targeted high value goods	

[Sets out the standard sequential sentencing procedure.]

SG-266

THREATS TO KILL

Offences Against the Person Act 1861, s. 16

Triable either way:
Maximum when tried summarily: Level 5 fine and/or 6 months
Maximum when tried on indictment: 10 years

Where offence committed in domestic context, refer [below] for guidance

Offence seriousness (culpability and harm)

A. Identify the appropriate starting point

Starting points based on first time offender pleading not guilty

Examples of nature of activity	Starting point	Range
One threat uttered in the heat of the moment, no more than fleeting impact on victim	Medium level community order	Low level community order to high level community order
Single calculated threat or victim fears that threat will be carried out	12 weeks custody	6 to 26 weeks custody
Repeated threats or visible weapon	Crown Court	Crown Court

B. Consider the effect of aggravating and mitigating factors (other than those within examples above)

Common aggravating and mitigating factors are identified [elsewhere]—the following may be particularly relevant but these lists are not exhaustive

Factors indicating higher culpability	Factor indicating lower culpability
1. Planning	1. Provocation
2. Offender deliberately isolates victim	
3. Group action	
4. Threat directed at victim because of job	
5. History of antagonism towards victim	
Factors indicating greater degree of harm	
1. Vulnerable victim	
2. Victim needs medical help/counselling	

[Sets out the standard sequential sentencing procedure and mentions need to consider football banning order.]

TRADE MARK, UNAUTHORISED USE OF ETC.

Trade Marks Act 1994, s. 92

SG-267

Triable either way:
Maximum when tried summarily: Level 5 fine and/or 6 months
Maximum when tried on indictment: 10 years

Offence seriousness (culpability and harm)

A. Identify the appropriate starting point

Starting points based on first time offender pleading not guilty

Examples of nature of activity	Starting point	Range
Small number of counterfeit items	**Band C fine**	**Band B fine to low level community order**
Larger number of counterfeit items but no involvement in wider operation	**Medium level community order, plus fine***	**Low level community order to 12 weeks custody, plus fine***
High number of counterfeit items or involvement in wider operation e.g. manufacture or distribution	**12 weeks custody**	**6 weeks custody to Crown Court**
Central role in large-scale operation	**Crown Court**	**Crown Court**

* This may be an offence for which it is appropriate to combine a fine with a community order. Consult your legal adviser for further guidance.

B. Consider the effect of aggravating and mitigating factors (other than those within examples above)

Common aggravating and mitigating factors are identified [elsewhere]—the following may be particularly relevant but these lists are not exhaustive

Factors indicating higher culpability	Factor indicating lower culpability
1. High degree of professionalism	1. Mistake or ignorance about provenance of goods
2. High level of profit	
Factor indicating greater degree of harm	
1. Purchasers at risk of harm e.g. from counterfeit drugs	

[Sets out the standard sequential sentencing procedure and mentions need to consider ordering forfeiture and destruction of the goods.]

SG-268   TV LICENCE PAYMENT EVASION
Communications Act 2003, s. 363

Triable only summarily:
Maximum: Level 3 fine

Offence seriousness (culpability and harm)

A. Identify the appropriate starting point

Starting points based on first time offender pleading not guilty

B. Consider the effect of aggravating and mitigating factors (other than those within examples above)

Examples of nature of activity	Starting point	Range
Up to 6 months unlicensed use	Band A fine	Band A fine
Over 6 months unlicensed use	Band B Fine	Band A fine to band B fine

Common aggravating and mitigating factors are identified [elsewhere]—the following may be particularly relevant but these lists are not exhaustive

	Factors indicating lower culpability
	1. Accidental oversight or belief licence held 2. Confusion of responsibility 3. Licence immediately obtained

[Sets out the standard sequential sentencing procedure.]

SG-269   VAT EVASION
Value Added Tax Act 1994, s. 72

Triable either way:
Maximum when tried summarily: Level 5 fine and/or 6 months
Maximum when tried on indictment: 7 years

Refer to guideline *Fraud — banking and insurance fraud and obtaining credit through fraud, benefit fraud and revenue fraud* [see **SG-230** *et seq.*].

SG-270   VEHICLE INTERFERENCE
Criminal Attempts Act 1981, s. 9

Triable only summarily:
Maximum: Level 4 fine and/or 3 months

Offence seriousness (culpability and harm)

A. Identify the appropriate starting point

Starting points based on first time offender pleading not guilty

B. Consider the effect of aggravating and mitigating factors (other than those within examples above)

Examples of nature of activity	Starting point	Range
Trying door handles; no entry gained to vehicle; no damage caused	Band C fine	Band A fine to low level community order
Entering vehicle, little or no damage caused	Medium level community order	Band C fine to high level community order
Entering vehicle, with damage caused	High level community order	Medium level community order to 12 weeks custody

Common aggravating and mitigating factors are identified [elsewhere]—the following may be particularly relevant but these lists are not exhaustive

| Factor indicating higher culpability
1. Targeting vehicle in dark/isolated location

Factors indicating greater degree of harm
1. Emergency services vehicle
2. Disabled driver's vehicle
3. Part of series | |

[Sets out the standard sequential sentencing procedure.]

Vehicle Licence/Registration Fraud

SG-271

Vehicle Excise and Registration Act 1994, s.44

Triable either way:
Maximum when tried summarily: Level 5 fine
Maximum when tried on indictment: 2 years

Offence seriousness (culpability and harm)

A. Identify the appropriate starting point

Starting points based on first time offender pleading not guilty

Examples of nature of activity	Starting point	Range
Use of unaltered licence from another vehicle	Band B fine	Band B fine
Forged licence bought for own use, or forged/altered for own use	Band C fine	Band C fine
Use of number plates from another vehicle; or Licence/number plates forged or altered for sale to another	High level community order (in Crown Court)	Medium level community order to Crown Court (Note: community order and custody available only in Crown Court)

B. Consider the effect of aggravating and mitigating factors (other than those within examples above)

Common aggravating and mitigating factors are identified [elsewhere]—the following may be particularly relevant but these lists are not exhaustive

| Factors indicating higher culpability
1. LGV, PSV, taxi etc.
2. Long-term fraudulent use

Factors indicating greater degree of harm
1. High financial gain
2. Innocent victim deceived
3. Legitimate owner inconvenienced | Factors indicating lower culpability
1. Licence/registration mark from another vehicle owned by defendant
2. Short-term use |

[Sets out the standard sequential sentencing procedure and mentions the need to consider disqualification from driving and deprivation of property (including vehicle).]

Vehicle Taking, without Consent

SG-272

Theft Act 1968, s. 12

Triable only summarily:
Maximum: Level 5 fine and/or 6 months
May disqualify (no points available)

Offence seriousness (culpability and harm)

A. Identify the appropriate starting point

Starting points based on first time offender pleading not guilty

Examples of nature of activity	Starting point	Range
Exceeding authorised use of e.g. employer's or relative's vehicle; retention of hire car beyond return date	Low level community order	Band B fine to medium level community order
As above with damage caused to lock/ignition; OR Stranger's vehicle involved but no damage caused	Medium level community order	Low level community order to high level community order
Taking vehicle from private premises; OR Causing damage to e.g. lock/ignition of stranger's vehicle	High level community order	Medium level community order to 26 weeks custody

B. Consider the effect of aggravating and mitigating factors (other than those within examples above)

Common aggravating and mitigating factors are identified [elsewhere]—the following may be particularly relevant but these lists are not exhaustive

Factors indicating greater degree of harm	Factor indicating lower culpability
1. Vehicle later burnt	1. Misunderstanding with owner
2. Vehicle belonging to elderly/disabled person	
3. Emergency services vehicle	**Factor indicating lesser degree of harm**
4. Medium to large goods vehicle	1. Offender voluntarily returned vehicle to owner
5. Passengers carried	

[Sets out the standard sequential sentencing procedure and mentions need to consider disqualification from driving.]

SG-273

Vehicle Taking (Aggravated)

Damage caused to Property other than the Vehicle in Accident or damage Caused to the Vehicle

Theft Act 1968, ss. 12A(2)(c) and (d)

Triable either way (triable only summarily if damage under £5,000):
Maximum when tried summarily: Level 5 fine and/or 6 months
Maximum when tried on indictment: 2 years
• Must endorse and disqualify for at least 12 months
• Must disqualify for *at least* 2 years if offender has had two or more disqualifications for periods of 56 days or more in preceding 3 years...
If there is a delay in sentencing after conviction, consider interim disqualification

Offence seriousness (culpability and harm)

A. Identify the appropriate starting point

Starting points based on first time offender pleading not guilty

Examples of nature of activity	Starting point	Range
Exceeding authorised use of e.g. employer's or relative's vehicle; retention of hire car beyond return date; minor damage to taken vehicle	Medium level community order	Low level community order to high level community order
Greater damage to taken vehicle and/or moderate damage to another vehicle and/or property	High level community order	Medium level community order to 12 weeks custody
Vehicle taken as part of burglary or from private premises; severe damage	18 weeks custody	12 to 26 weeks custody (Crown Court if damage over £5,000)

B. Consider the effect of aggravating and mitigating factors (other than those within examples above)

Common aggravating and mitigating factors are identified [elsewhere]—the following may be particularly relevant but these lists are not exhaustive

Factors indicating higher culpability	Factors indicating lower culpability
1. Vehicle deliberately damaged/destroyed 2. Offender under influence of alcohol/drugs **Factors indicating greater degree of harm** 1. Passenger(s) carried 2. Vehicle belonging to elderly or disabled person 3. Emergency services vehicle 4. Medium to large goods vehicle 5. Damage caused in moving traffic accident	1. Misunderstanding with owner 2. Damage resulting from actions of another (where this does not provide a defence)

[Sets out the standard sequential sentencing procedure.]

VEHICLE TAKING (AGGRAVATED)
DANGEROUS DRIVING OR ACCIDENT CAUSING INJURY
Theft Act 1968, ss. 12A(2)(a) and (b)

SG-274

Triable either way:
Maximum when tried summarily: Level 5 fine and/or 6 months
Maximum when tried on indictment: 2 years; 14 years if accident caused death
- Must endorse and disqualify for at least 12 months
- Must disqualify for *at least* 2 years if offender has had two or more disqualifications for periods of 56 days or more in preceding 3 years...

If there is a delay in sentencing after conviction, consider interim disqualification

Offence seriousness (culpability and harm)

A. Identify the appropriate starting point

Starting points based on first time offender pleading not guilty

Examples of nature of activity	Starting point	Range
Taken vehicle involved in single incident of bad driving where little or no damage or risk of personal injury	High level community order	Medium level community order to 12 weeks custody
Taken vehicle involved in incident(s) involving excessive speed or showing off, especially on busy roads or in built-up area	18 weeks custody	12 to 26 weeks custody
Taken vehicle involved in prolonged bad driving involving deliberate disregard for safety of others	Crown Court	Crown Court

B. Consider the effect of aggravating and mitigating factors (other than those within examples above)

Common aggravating and mitigating factors are identified [elsewhere]—the following may be particularly relevant but these lists are not exhaustive

Factors indicating higher culpability	Factors indicating greater degree of harm
1. Disregarding warnings of others 2. Evidence of alcohol or drugs 3. Carrying out other tasks while driving 4. Carrying passengers or heavy load 5. Tiredness 6. Trying to avoid arrest 7. Aggressive driving, such as driving much too close to vehicle in front, inappropriate attempts to overtake, or cutting in after overtaking	1. Injury to others 2. Damage to other vehicles or property

[Sets out the standard sequential sentencing procedure and mentions the need to consider ordering disqualification until appropriate driving test passed.]

SG-275   Voyeurism

[The guidelines set out below are applicable to adult offenders sentenced after 1 April 2014.]

Sexual Offences Act 2003 (section 67)

Triable either way
Maximum: 2 years' custody

Offence range: Fine–18 months' custody

For convictions on or after such date (irrespective of the date of commission of the offence), these are specified offences for the purposes of section 226A (extended sentence for certain violent or sexual offences) of the Criminal Justice Act 2003.

STEP ONE Determining the offence category

The court should determine the offence category using the table below.

Category 1	Raised harm **and** raised culpability
Category 2	Raised harm **or** raised culpability
Category 3	Voyeurism **without** raised harm or culpability factors present

The court should determine culpability and harm caused or intended, by reference only to the factors below, which comprise the principal factual elements of the offence. Where an offence does not fall squarely into a category, individual factors may require a degree of weighting before making an overall assessment and determining the appropriate offence category.

Factors indicating raised harm
• Image(s) available to be viewed by others • Victim observed or recorded in their own home or residence

Factors indicating raised culpability
• Significant degree of planning • Image(s) recorded • Abuse of trust • Specific or previous targeting of a particularly vulnerable victim • Commercial exploitation and/or motivation • Offence racially or religiously aggravated • Offence motivated by, or demonstrating, hostility to the victim based on his or her sexual orientation (or presumed sexual orientation) or transgender identity (or presumed transgender identity) • Offence motivated by, or demonstrating, hostility to the victim based on his or her disability (or presumed disability)

STEP TWO Starting point and category range

Having determined the category, the court should use the corresponding starting points to reach a sentence within the category range [below]. The starting point applies to all offenders irrespective of plea or previous convictions. Having determined the starting point, step two allows further adjustment for aggravating or mitigating features, set out [below].

A case of particular gravity, reflected by multiple features of culpability or harm in step one, could merit upward adjustment from the starting point before further adjustment for aggravating or mitigating features, set out [below].

Where there is a sufficient prospect of rehabilitation, a community order with a sex offender treatment programme requirement under section 202 of the Criminal Justice Act 2003 can be a proper alternative to a short or moderate length custodial sentence.

Category 1	**Starting point** 26 weeks' custody
	Category range 12 weeks' – 18 months' custody
Category 2	**Starting point** High level community order
	Category range Medium level community order – 26 weeks' custody
Category 3	**Starting point** Medium level community order
	Category range Band A fine - High level community order

The table below contains a **non-exhaustive** list of additional factual elements providing the context of the offence and factors relating to the offender. Identify whether any combination of these, or other relevant factors, should result in an upward or downward adjustment from the starting point. **In particular, relevant recent convictions are likely to result in an upward adjustment**. In some cases, having considered these factors, it may be appropriate to move outside the identified category range.

When sentencing **category 2 offences**, the court should also consider the custody threshold as follows:

- has the custody threshold been passed?
- if so, is it unavoidable that a custodial sentence be imposed?
- if so, can that sentence be suspended?

When sentencing **category 3 offences**, the court should also consider the community order threshold as follows:

- has the community order threshold been passed?

Aggravating factors
Statutory aggravating factors
• Previous convictions, having regard to a) the nature of the offence to which the conviction relates and its relevance to the current offence; and b) the time that has elapsed since the conviction • Offence committed whilst on bail
Other aggravating factors
• Location of offence • Timing of offence • Failure to comply with current court orders • Offence committed whilst on licence • Distribution of images, whether or not for gain • Placing images where there is the potential for a high volume of viewers • Period over which victim observed • Period over which images were made or distributed • Any steps taken to prevent victim reporting an incident, obtaining assistance and/or from assisting or supporting the prosecution • Attempts to dispose of or conceal evidence

Mitigating factors
• No previous convictions **or** no relevant/recent convictions • Remorse • Previous good character and/or exemplary conduct* • Age and/or lack of maturity where it affects the responsibility of the offender • Mental disorder or learning disability, particularly where linked to the commission of the offence • Demonstration of steps taken to address offending behaviour

* Previous good character/exemplary conduct is different from having no previous convictions. The more serious the offence, the less the weight which should normally be attributed to this factor. Where previous good character/ exemplary conduct has been used to facilitate the offence, this mitigation should not normally be allowed and such conduct may constitute an aggravating factor.

[Sets out the standard sequential sentencing procedure.]

WITNESS INTIMIDATION

Criminal Justice and Public Order Act 1994, s. 51

Triable either way:
Maximum when tried summarily: 6 months or level 5 fine
Maximum when tried on indictment: 5 years

Where offence committed in domestic context, refer [below] for guidance

Offence seriousness (culpability and harm)

A. Identify the appropriate starting point

Starting points based on first time offender pleading not guilty

Examples of nature of activity	Starting point	Range
Sudden outburst in chance encounter	6 weeks custody	Medium level community order to 18 weeks custody
Conduct amounting to a threat; staring at, approaching or following witnesses; talking about the case; trying to alter or stop evidence	18 weeks custody	12 weeks custody to Crown Court
Threats of violence to witnesses and/or their families; deliberately seeking out witnesses	**Crown Court**	**Crown Court**

B. Consider the effect of aggravating and mitigating factors (other than those within examples above)

Common aggravating and mitigating factors are identified [elsewhere]—the following may be particularly relevant but these lists are not exhaustive

Factors indicating higher culpability	
1. Breach of bail conditions	
2. Offender involves others	
Factors indicating greater degree of harm	
1. Detrimental impact on administration of justice	
2. Contact made at or in vicinity of victim's home	

[Sets out the standard sequential sentencing procedure.]

MOTORING OFFENCES

CARELESS DRIVING (DRIVE WITHOUT DUE CARE AND ATTENTION)

Road Traffic Act 1988, s. 3

Triable only summarily: Maximum: Level 5 fine
Must endorse and may disqualify. If no disqualification, impose 3–9 points

Offence seriousness (culpability and harm)

A. Identify the appropriate starting point

Starting points based on first time offender pleading not guilty

Examples of nature of activity	Starting point	Range
Momentary lapse of concentration or misjudgement at low speed	**Band A fine**	**Band A fine** 3–4 points
Loss of control due to speed, mishandling or insufficient attention to road conditions, or carelessly turning right across on-coming traffic	**Band B fine**	**Band B fine** 5–6 points
Overtaking manoeuvre at speed resulting in collision of vehicles, or driving bordering on the dangerous	**Band C fine**	**Band C fine** Consider disqualification OR 7–9 points

B. Consider the effect of aggravating and mitigating factors (other than those within examples above)

Common aggravating and mitigating factors are identified [elsewhere]—the following may be particularly relevant but these lists are not exhaustive

Factors indicating higher culpability	Factors indicating lower culpability
1. Excessive speed	1. Minor risk
2. Carrying out other tasks while driving	2. Inexperience of driver
3. Carrying passengers or heavy load	3. Sudden change in road or weather conditions
4. Tiredness	
Factors indicating greater degree of harm	
1. Injury to others	
2. Damage to other vehicles or property	
3. High level of traffic or pedestrians in vicinity	
4. Location e.g. near school when children are likely to be present	

[Sets out the standard sequential sentencing procedure and mentions need to consider ordering disqualification until appropriate driving test passed.]

Causing Death by Careless or Inconsiderate Driving

SG-278

Factors to take into consideration

This guideline and accompanying notes are taken from the Sentencing Guidelines Council's definitive guideline *Causing Death by Driving*, published 15 July 2008 [see **SG-392**].

Key factors

(a) It is unavoidable that some cases will be on the borderline between *dangerous* and *careless* driving, or may involve a number of factors that significantly increase the seriousness of an offence. As a result, the guideline for this offence identifies three levels of seriousness, the range for the highest of which overlaps with ranges for the lower levels of seriousness for *causing death by dangerous driving*.

(b) The three levels of seriousness are defined by the degree of carelessness involved in the standard of driving:
  • the most serious level for this offence is where the offender's driving fell *not that far short of dangerous*;
  • the least serious group of offences relates to those cases where the level of culpability is low—for example in a case involving an offender who misjudges the speed of another vehicle, or turns without seeing an oncoming vehicle because of restricted visibility;
  • other cases will fall into the intermediate level.

(c) Where the level of carelessness is low and there are no aggravating factors, even the fact that death was caused is not sufficient to justify a prison sentence.

(d) A fine is unlikely to be an appropriate sentence for this offence; where a non-custodial sentence is considered appropriate, this should be a community order. The nature of the requirements will be determined by the purpose identified by the court as of primary importance. Requirements most likely to be relevant include unpaid work requirement, activity requirement, programme requirement and curfew requirement.

(e) Offender mitigation particularly relevant to this offence includes conduct after the offence such as where the offender gave direct, positive, assistance at the scene of a collision to victim(s). It may also include remorse—whilst it can be expected that anyone who has caused a death by driving would be remorseful, this cannot undermine its importance for sentencing purposes. It is for the court to determine whether an expression of remorse is genuine.

(f) Where an offender has a good driving record, this is not a factor that automatically should be treated as mitigation, especially now that the presence of previous convictions is a statutory aggravating factor. However, any evidence to show that an offender has previously been an exemplary driver, for example having driven an ambulance, police vehicle, bus, taxi or similar vehicle conscientiously and without incident for many years, is a fact that the courts may well wish to take into account by way of offender mitigation. This is likely to have even greater effect where the driver is driving on public duty (for example, on ambulance, fire services or police duties) and was responding to an emergency.

(g) Disqualification of the offender from driving and endorsement of the offender's driving licence are mandatory, and the offence carries between 3 and 11 penalty points when the court finds special reasons for not imposing disqualification. There is a discretionary power to order an extended driving test/re-test where a person is convicted of this offence.

Guidelines

Road Traffic Act 1988, s. 2B

Triable either way:

Maximum when tried summarily: Level 5 fine and/or 6 months

Maximum when tried on indictment: 5 years

Offence seriousness (culpability and harm)

A. Identify the appropriate starting point

Starting points based on first time offender pleading not guilty

Examples of nature of activity	Starting point	Range
Careless or inconsiderate driving arising from momentary inattention with no aggravating factors	Medium level community order	Low level community order to high level community order
Other cases of careless or inconsiderate driving	Crown Court	High level community order to Crown Court
Careless or inconsiderate driving falling not far short of dangerous driving	Crown Court	Crown Court

B. Consider the effect of aggravating and mitigating factors (other than those within examples above)

Common aggravating and mitigating factors are identified [elsewhere]—the following may be particularly relevant but these lists are not exhaustive

Factors indicating higher culpability	Factors indicating lower culpability
1. Other offences committed at the same time, such as driving other than in accordance with the terms of a valid licence; driving while disqualified; driving without insurance; taking a vehicle without consent; driving a stolen vehicle 2. Previous convictions for motoring offences, particularly offences that involve bad driving 3. Irresponsible behaviour, such as failing to stop or falsely claiming that one of the victims was responsible for the collision	1. Offender seriously injured in the collision 2. The victim was a close friend or relative 3. The actions of the victim or a third party contributed to the commission of the offence 4. The offender's lack of driving experience contributed significantly to the likelihood of a collision occurring and/or death resulting 5. The driving was in response to a proven and genuine emergency falling short of a defence
Factors indicating greater degree of harm 1. More than one person was killed as a result of the offence 2. Serious injury to one or more persons in addition to the death(s)	

[Sets out the standard sequential sentencing procedure and mentions need to consider ordering disqualification and deprivation of property.]

SG-279 CAUSING DEATH BY DRIVING: UNLICENSED, DISQUALIFIED OR UNINSURED DRIVERS

Factors to take into consideration

Key factors

(a) Culpability arises from the offender driving a vehicle on a road or other public place when, by law, not allowed to do so; the offence does not involve any fault in the standard of driving.

(b) Since driving whilst disqualified is more culpable than driving whilst unlicensed or uninsured, a higher starting point is proposed when the offender was disqualified from driving at the time of the offence.

(c) Being uninsured, unlicensed or disqualified are the only determinants of seriousness for this offence, as there are no factors relating to the standard of driving. The list of aggravating factors identified is slightly different as the emphasis is on the decision to drive by an offender who is not permitted by law to do so.

(d) A fine is unlikely to be an appropriate sentence for this offence; where a non-custodial sentence is considered appropriate, this should be a community order.

(e) Where the *decision to drive was brought about by a genuine and proven emergency*, that may mitigate offence seriousness and so it is included as an additional mitigating factor.

(f) An additional mitigating factor covers those situations where an offender genuinely believed that there was valid insurance or a valid licence.

(g) Offender mitigation particularly relevant to this offence includes conduct after the offence such as where the offender gave direct, positive, assistance at the scene of a collision to victim(s). It may also include remorse—whilst it can be expected that anyone who has caused a death by driving would be remorseful, this cannot undermine its importance for sentencing purposes. It is for the court to determine whether an expression of remorse is genuine.

(h) Where an offender has a good driving record, this is not a factor that automatically should be treated as mitigation, especially now that the presence of previous convictions is a statutory aggravating factor. However, any evidence to show that an offender has previously been an exemplary driver, for example having driven an ambulance, police vehicle, bus, taxi or similar vehicle conscientiously and without incident for many years, is a fact that the courts may well wish to take into account by way of offender mitigation. This is likely to have even greater effect where the driver is driving on public duty (for example, on ambulance, fire services or police duties) and was responding to an emergency.

(i) Disqualification of the offender from driving and endorsement of the offender's driving licence are mandatory, and the offence carries between 3 and 11 penalty points when the court finds special reasons for not imposing disqualification. There is a discretionary power[130] to order an extended driving test/re-test where a person is convicted of this offence.

Guidelines

Road Traffic Act 1988, s. 3ZB

Triable either way:
Maximum when tried summarily: Level 5 fine and/or 6 months
Maximum when tried on indictment: 2 years

Offence seriousness (culpability and harm)

A. Identify the appropriate starting point

Starting points based on first time offender pleading not guilty

Examples of nature of activity	Starting point	Range
The offender was unlicensed or uninsured—no aggravating factors	Medium level community order	Low level community order to high level community order
The offender was unlicensed or uninsured plus at least 1 aggravating factor from the list below	26 weeks custody	High level community order to Crown Court
The offender was disqualified from driving OR The offender was unlicensed or uninsured plus 2 or more aggravating factors from the list below	Crown Court	Crown Court

B. Consider the effect of aggravating and mitigating factors (other than those within examples above)

Common aggravating and mitigating factors are identified [elsewhere]—the following may be particularly relevant but these lists are not exhaustive

Factors indicating higher culpability	Factors indicating lower culpability
1. Previous convictions for motoring offences, whether involving bad driving or involving an offence of the same kind that forms part of the present conviction (i.e. unlicensed, disqualified or uninsured driving) 2. Irresponsible behaviour such as failing to stop or falsely claiming that someone else was driving **Factors indicating greater degree of harm** 1. More than one person was killed as a result of the offence 2. Serious injury to one or more persons in addition to the death(s)	1. The decision to drive was brought about by a proven and genuine emergency falling short of a defence 2. The offender genuinely believed that he or she was insured or licensed to drive 3. The offender was seriously injured as a result of the collision 4. The victim was a close friend or relative

---

[130]   Road Traffic Offenders Act 1988, s.36(4)

[Sets out the standard sequential sentencing procedure and mentions need to consider ordering disqualification and deprivation of property.]

SG-280

DANGEROUS DRIVING

Road Traffic Act 1988, s. 2

Triable either way:

Maximum when tried summarily: Level 5 fine and/or 6 months

Maximum when tried on indictment: 2 years

- Must endorse and disqualify for *at least* 12 months. Must order extended re-test
- Must disqualify for *at least* 2 years if offender has had two or more disqualifications for periods of 56 days or more in preceding 3 years. If there is a delay in sentencing after conviction, consider interim disqualification

Offence seriousness (culpability and harm)

A. Identify the appropriate starting point

Starting points based on first time offender pleading not guilty

Examples of nature of activity	Starting point	Range
Single incident where little or no damage or risk of personal injury	Medium level community order	Low level community order to high level community order Disqualify 12–15 months
Incident(s) involving excessive speed or showing off, especially on busy roads or in built-up area; OR Single incident where little or no damage or risk of personal injury but offender was disqualified driver	12 weeks custody	High level community order to 26 weeks custody Disqualify 15–24 months
Prolonged bad driving involving deliberate disregard for safety of others; OR Incident(s) involving excessive speed or showing off, especially on busy roads or in built-up area, by disqualified driver; OR Driving as described in box above while being pursued by police	Crown Court	Crown Court

B. Consider the effect of aggravating and mitigating factors (other than those within examples above)

Common aggravating and mitigating factors are identified [elsewhere]—the following may be particularly relevant but these lists are not exhaustive

Factors indicating higher culpability	Factors indicating lower culpability
1. Disregarding warnings of others	1. Genuine emergency
2. Evidence of alcohol or drugs	2. Speed not excessive
3. Carrying out other tasks while driving	3. Offence due to inexperience rather
4. Carrying passengers or heavy load	than irresponsibility of driver
5. Tiredness	
6. Aggressive driving, such as driving much too close to vehicle in front, racing, inappropriate attempts to overtake, or cutting in after overtaking	
7. Driving when knowingly suffering from a medical condition which significantly impairs the offender's driving skills	
8. Driving a poorly maintained or dangerously loaded vehicle, especially where motivated by commercial concerns	
Factors indicating greater degree of harm	
1. Injury to others	
2. Damage to other vehicles or property	

[Sets out the standard sequential sentencing procedure and mentions need to consider order for deprivation of property.]

DRIVE WHILST DISQUALIFIED

Road Traffic Act 1988, s. 103

SG-281

Triable only summarily: Maximum: Level 5 fine and/or 6 months
Must endorse and may disqualify. If no disqualification, impose 6 points

Offence seriousness (culpability and harm)

A. Identify the appropriate starting point

Starting points based on first time offender pleading not guilty

Examples of nature of activity	Starting point	Range
Full period expired but retest not taken	Low level community order	Band C fine to medium level community order 6 points or disqualify for 3–6 months
Lengthy period of ban already served	High level community order	Medium level community order to 12 weeks custody Lengthen disqualification for 6–12 months beyond expiry of current ban
Recently imposed ban	12 weeks custody	High level community order to 26 weeks custody Lengthen disqualification for 12–18 months beyond expiry of current ban

B. Consider the effect of aggravating and mitigating factors (other than those within examples above)

Common aggravating and mitigating factors are identified [elsewhere]—the following may be particularly relevant but these lists are not exhaustive

Factors indicating higher culpability	Factors indicating lower culpability
1. Never passed test 2. Planned long-term evasion 3. Vehicle obtained during ban 4. Driving for remuneration	1. Defendant not present when disqualification imposed and genuine reason why unaware of ban 2. Genuine emergency established
Factors indicating greater degree of harm 1. Distance driven 2. Evidence of associated bad driving 3. Offender caused accident	

[Sets out the standard sequential sentencing procedure and mentions need to consider order for deprivation of property.]

Note: An offender convicted of this offence will always have at least one relevant previous conviction for the offence that resulted in disqualification. The starting points and ranges take this into account; any other previous convictions should be considered in the usual way…

EXCESS ALCOHOL (DRIVE/ATTEMPT TO DRIVE)

Road Traffic Act 1988, s. 5(1)(a)

SG-282

Triable only summarily: Maximum: Level 5 fine and/or 6 months

- Must endorse and disqualify for at least 12 months
- Must disqualify for *at least* 2 years if offender has had two or more disqualifications for periods of 56 days or more in preceding 3 years—refer [below]…
- Must disqualify for *at least* 3 years if offender has been convicted of a relevant offence in preceding 10 years—refer [below]…

If there is a delay in sentencing after conviction, consider interim disqualification

Note: the final column below provides guidance regarding the length of disqualification that may be appropriate in cases to which the 3 year minimum applies. The period to be imposed in any individual case will depend on an assessment of all the relevant circumstances, including the length of time since the earlier ban was imposed and the gravity of the current offence.

Offence seriousness (culpability and harm)

A. Identify the appropriate starting point

Starting points based on first time offender pleading not guilty

Level of alcohol			Starting point	Range	Disqualification	Disqual. 2nd offence in 10 years—see note above
Breath (mg)	Blood (ml)	Urine (ml)				
36–59	81–137	108–183	Band C fine	Band C fine	12–16 months	36–40 months
60–89	138–206	184–274	Band C fine	Band C fine	17–22 months	36–46 months
90–119	207–275	275–366	Medium level community order	Low level community order to high level community order	23–28 months	36–52 months
120–150 and above	276–345 and above	367–459 and above	12 weeks custody	High level community order to 26 weeks custody	29–36 months	36–60 months

B. Consider the effect of aggravating and mitigating factors (other than those within examples above)

Common aggravating and mitigating factors are identified [elsewhere]—the following may be particularly relevant but these lists are not exhaustive

Factors indicating higher culpability	Factors indicating lower culpability
1. LGV, HGV, PSV etc.	1. Genuine emergency established*
2. Poor road or weather conditions	2. Spiked drinks*
3. Carrying passengers	3. Very short distance driven*
4. Driving for hire or reward	
5. Evidence of unacceptable standard of driving	
Factors indicating greater degree of harm	
1. Involved in accident	
2. Location e.g. near school	
3. High level of traffic or pedestrians in the vicinity	

*   even where not amounting to special reasons

[Sets out the standard sequential sentencing procedure and mentions need to consider offering drink/drive rehabilitation course and forfeiture or suspension of personal liquor licence.]

SG-283

Excess Alcohol (In Charge)

Road Traffic Act 1988, s. 5(1)(b)

Triable only summarily: Maximum: Level 4 fine and/or 3 months
Must endorse and may disqualify. If no disqualification, impose 10 points

Offence seriousness (culpability and harm)

A. Identify the appropriate starting point

Starting points based on first time offender pleading not guilty

Level of alcohol			Starting point	Range
Breath (mg)	Blood (ml)	Urine (ml)		
36–59	81–137	108–183	Band B fine	Band B fine 10 points
60–89	138–206	184–274	Band B fine	Band B fine 10 points OR consider disqualification
90–119	207–275	275–366	Band C fine	Band C fine to medium level community order Consider disqualification up to 6 months OR 10 points
120–150 and above	276–345 and above	367–459 and above	Medium level community order	Low level community order to 6 weeks custody Disqualify 6–12 months

B. Consider the effect of aggravating and mitigating factors (other than those within examples above)

Common aggravating and mitigating factors are identified [elsewhere]—the following may be particularly relevant but these lists are not exhaustive

Factors indicating higher culpability	Factor indicating lower culpability
1. LGV, HGV, PSV etc. 2. Ability to drive seriously impaired 3. High likelihood of driving 4. Driving for hire or reward	1. Low likelihood of driving

[Sets out the standard sequential sentencing procedure and mentions need to consider forfeiture or suspension of personal liquor licence.]

FAIL TO STOP/REPORT ROAD ACCIDENT   **SG-284**

Road Traffic Act 1988, s. 170(4)

Triable only summarily: Maximum: Level 5 fine and/or 6 months

Must endorse and may disqualify. If no disqualification, impose 5–10 points

Offence seriousness (culpability and harm)

A. Identify the appropriate starting point

Starting points based on first time offender pleading not guilty

Examples of nature of activity	Starting point	Range
Minor damage/injury or stopped at scene but failed to exchange particulars or report	Band B fine	Band B fine 5–6 points
Moderate damage/injury or failed to stop and failed to report	Band C fine	Band C fine 7–8 points Consider disqualification
Serious damage/injury and/or evidence of bad driving	High level community order	Band C fine to 26 weeks custody Disqualify 6–12 months OR 9–10 points

B. Consider the effect of aggravating and mitigating factors (other than those within examples above)

Common aggravating and mitigating factors are identified [elsewhere]—the following may be particularly relevant but these lists are not exhaustive

Factors indicating higher culpability	Factors indicating lower culpability
1. Evidence of drink or drugs/evasion of test 2. Knowledge/suspicion that personal injury caused (where not an element of the offence) 3. Leaving injured party at scene 4. Giving false details	1. Believed identity known 2. Genuine fear of retribution 3. Subsequently reported

[Sets out the standard sequential sentencing procedure.]

Fail to Provide Specimen for Analysis (Drive/Attempt to Drive)
Road Traffic Act 1988, s. 7(6)

Triable only summarily: Maximum: Level 5 fine and/or 6 months
- Must endorse and disqualify for at least 12 months
- Must disqualify for *at least* 2 years if offender has had two or more disqualifications for periods of 56 days or more in preceding 3 years—refer [below] . . .
- Must disqualify for *at least* 3 years if offender has been convicted of a relevant offence in preceding 10 years—refer [below] . . .

If there is a delay in sentencing after conviction, consider interim disqualification

Note: the final column below provides guidance regarding the length of disqualification that may be appropriate in cases to which the 3 year minimum applies. The period to be imposed in any individual case will depend on an assessment of all the relevant circumstances, including the length of time since the earlier ban was imposed and the gravity of the current offence.

Offence seriousness (culpability and harm)

A. Identify the appropriate starting point

Starting points based on first time offender pleading not guilty

Examples of nature of activity	Starting point	Range	Disqualification	Disqual. 2nd offence in 10 years
Defendant refused test when had honestly held but unreasonable excuse	Band C fine	Band C fine	12–16 months	36–40 months
Deliberate refusal or deliberate failure	Low level community order	Band C fine to high level community order	17–28 months	36–52 months
Deliberate refusal or deliberate failure where evidence of serious impairment	12 weeks custody	High level community order to 26 weeks custody	29–36 months	36–60 months

B. Consider the effect of aggravating and mitigating factors (other than those within examples above)

Common aggravating and mitigating factors are identified [elsewhere]—the following may be particularly relevant but these lists are not exhaustive

Factors indicating higher culpability	Factor indicating lower culpability
1. Evidence of unacceptable standard of driving 2. LGV, HGV, PSV etc. 3. Obvious state of intoxication 4. Driving for hire or reward **Factor indicating greater degree of harm** 1. Involved in accident	1. Genuine but unsuccessful attempt to provide specimen

[Sets out the standard sequential sentencing procedure and mentions need to consider offering drink/drive rehabilitation course.]

Fail to Provide Specimen for Analysis (In Charge)
Road Traffic Act 1988, s. 7(6)

Triable only summarily: Maximum: Level 4 fine and/or 3 months
Must endorse and may disqualify. If no disqualification, impose 10 points

Offence seriousness (culpability and harm)

A. Identify the appropriate starting point

Starting points based on first time offender pleading not guilty

Examples of nature of activity	Starting point	Range
Defendant refused test when had honestly held but unreasonable excuse	Band B fine	Band B fine 10 points
Deliberate refusal or deliberate failure	Band C fine	Band C fine to medium level community order Consider disqualification OR 10 points
Deliberate refusal or deliberate failure where evidence of serious impairment	Medium level community order	Low level community order to 6 weeks custody Disqualify 6–12 months

B. Consider the effect of aggravating and mitigating factors (other than those within examples above)

Common aggravating and mitigating factors are identified [elsewhere]—the following may be particularly relevant but these lists are not exhaustive

Factors indicating higher culpability	Factors indicating lower culpability
1. Obvious state of intoxication 2. LGV, HGV, PSV etc. 3. High likelihood of driving 4. Driving for hire or reward	1. Genuine but unsuccessful attempt to provide specimen 2. Low likelihood of driving

[Sets out the standard sequential sentencing procedure.]

No Insurance

Road Traffic Act 1988, s. 143

Triable only summarily: Maximum: Level 5 fine
Must endorse and may disqualify. If no disqualification, impose 6–8 points—see notes below

Offence seriousness (culpability and harm)

A. Identify the appropriate starting point

Starting points based on first time offender pleading not guilty

Examples of nature of activity	Starting point	Range
Using a motor vehicle on a road or other public place without insurance	Band C fine	Band C fine 6 points—12 months disqualification—-see notes below

B. Consider the effect of aggravating and mitigating factors (other than those within examples above)

Common aggravating and mitigating factors are identified [elsewhere]—the following may be particularly relevant but these lists are not exhaustive

Factors indicating higher culpability	Factors indicating lower culpability
1. Never passed test 2. Gave false details 3. Driving LGV, HGV, PSV etc. 4. Driving for hire or reward 5. Evidence of sustained uninsured use **Factor indicating greater degree of harm** 1. Involved in accident 2. Accident resulting in injury	1. Responsibility for providing insurance rests with another 2. Genuine misunderstanding 3. Recent failure to renew or failure to transfer vehicle details where insurance was in existence 4. Vehicle not being driven

[Sets out the standard sequential sentencing procedure.]

Note: Consider range from 7 points–2 months disqualification where vehicle was being driven and no evidence that the offender has held insurance. Consider disqualification of 6–12 months if evidence of sustained uninsured use and/or involvement in accident.

SPEEDING
Road Traffic Regulation Act 1984, s. 89(10)

Triable only summarily: Maximum: Level 3 fine (level 4 if motorway)
Must endorse and may disqualify. If no disqualification, impose 3–6 points

Offence seriousness (culpability and harm)

A. Identify the appropriate starting point

Starting points based on first time offender pleading not guilty

Speed limit (mph)	Recorded speed (mph)		
20	21–30	31–40	41–50
30	31–40	41–50	51–60
40	41–55	56–65	66–75
50	51–65	66–75	76–85
60	61–80	81–90	91–100
70	71–90	91–100	101–110
Starting point	Band A fine	Band B fine	Band B fine
Range	Band A fine	Band B fine	Band B fine
Points/disqualification	3 points	4–6 points OR Disqualify 7–28 days	Disqualify 7–56 days OR 6 points

B. Consider the effect of aggravating and mitigating factors (other than those within examples above)

Common aggravating and mitigating factors are identified [elsewhere]—the following may be particularly relevant but these lists are not exhaustive

Factors indicating higher culpability	Factor indicating lower culpability
1. Poor road or weather conditions 2. LGV, HGV, PSV etc. 3. Towing caravan/trailer 4. Carrying passengers or heavy load 5. Driving for hire or reward 6. Evidence of unacceptable standard of driving over and above speed limit **Factors indicating greater degree of harm** 1. Location e.g. near school 2. High level of traffic or pedestrians in the vicinity	1. Genuine emergency established

[Sets out the standard sequential sentencing procedure.]

UNFIT THROUGH DRINK OR DRUGS (DRIVE/ATTEMPT TO DRIVE)
Road Traffic Act 1988, s. 4(1)

Triable only summarily: Maximum: Level 5 fine and/or 6 months
- Must endorse and disqualify for at least 12 months
- Must disqualify for *at least* 2 years if offender has had two or more disqualifications for periods of 56 days or more in preceding 3 years—refer [below] ...
- Must disqualify for *at least* 3 years if offender has been convicted of a relevant offence in preceding 10 years—refer [below] ...

If there is a delay in sentencing after conviction, consider interim disqualification

Note: the final column below provides guidance regarding the length of disqualification that may be appropriate in cases to which the 3 year minimum applies. The period to be imposed in any individual case will depend on an assessment of all the relevant circumstances, including the length of time since the earlier ban was imposed and the gravity of the current offence.

Offence seriousness (culpability and harm)

A. Identify the appropriate starting point

Starting points based on first time offender pleading not guilty

Examples of nature of activity	Starting point	Range	Disqualification	Disqual. 2nd offence in 10 years
Evidence of moderate level of impairment and no aggravating factors	Band C fine	Band C fine	12–16 months	36–40 months
Evidence of moderate level of impairment and presence of one or more aggravating factors listed below	Band C fine	Band C fine	17–22 months	36–46 months
Evidence of high level of impairment and no aggravating factors	Medium level community order	Low level community order to high level community order	23–28 months	36–52 months
Evidence of high level of impairment and presence of one or more aggravating factors listed below	12 weeks custody	High level community order to 26 weeks custody	29–36 months	36–60 months

B. Consider the effect of aggravating and mitigating factors (other than those within examples above)

Common aggravating and mitigating factors are identified [elsewhere]—the following may be particularly relevant but these lists are not exhaustive

Factors indicating higher culpability	Factors indicating lower culpability
1. LGV, HGV, PSV etc. 2. Poor road or weather conditions 3. Carrying passengers 4. Driving for hire or reward 5. Evidence of unacceptable standard of driving **Factors indicating greater degree of harm** 1. Involved in accident 2. Location e.g. near school 3. High level of traffic or pedestrians in the vicinity	1. Genuine emergency established* 2. Spiked drinks* 3. Very short distance driven*

* even where not amounting to special reasons

[Sets out the standard sequential sentencing procedure and mentions need to consider offering a drink/drive rehabilitation course.]

UNFIT THROUGH DRINK OR DRUGS (IN CHARGE)   **SG-290**

Road Traffic Act 1988, s. 4(2)

Triable only summarily: Maximum: Level 4 fine and/or 3 months

Must endorse and may disqualify. If no disqualification, impose 10 points

Offence seriousness (culpability and harm)

A. Identify the appropriate starting point

Starting points based on first time offender pleading not guilty

Examples of nature of activity	Starting point	Range
Evidence of moderate level of impairment and no aggravating factors	Band B fine	Band B fine 10 points
Evidence of moderate level of impairment and presence of one or more aggravating factors listed below	Band B fine	Band B fine 10 points or consider disqualification
Evidence of high level of impairment and no aggravating factors	Band C fine	Band C fine to medium level community order 10 points or consider disqualification
Evidence of high level of impairment and presence of one or more aggravating factors listed below	High level community order	Medium level community order to 12 weeks custody Consider disqualification OR 10 points

Sentencing Guidelines

B. Consider the effect of aggravating and mitigating factors (other than those within examples above)

Common aggravating and mitigating factors are identified [elsewhere]—the following may be particularly relevant but these lists are not exhaustive

Factors indicating higher culpability	Factor indicating lower culpability
1. LGV, HGV, PSV etc. 2. High likelihood of driving 3. Driving for hire or reward	1. Low likelihood of driving

[Sets out the standard sequential sentencing procedure and mentions need to consider offering a drink/drive rehabilitation course.]

SG-291   OFFENCES APPROPRIATE FOR IMPOSITION OF FINE OR DISCHARGE

SG-292   **Part 1: Offences concerning the driver**

Offence	Maximum	Points	Starting point	Special considerations
Fail to co-operate with preliminary (roadside) breath test	L3	4	B	
Fail to give information of driver's identity as required	L3	6	C	For limited companies, endorsement is not available; a fine is the only available penalty
Fail to produce insurance certificate	L4	–	A	Fine per offence, not per document
Fail to produce test certificate	L3	–	A	
Drive otherwise than in accordance with licence (where could be covered)	L3	–	A	
Drive otherwise than in accordance with licence	L3	3–6	A	Aggravating factor if no licence ever held

SG-293   **Part 2: Offences concerning the vehicle**

*The guidelines for some of the offences below differentiate between three types of offender when the offence is committed in the course of business: driver, owner-driver and owner-company. **For owner-driver, the starting point is the same as for driver; however, the court should consider an uplift of at least 25%.***

Offence	Maximum	Points	Starting point	Special considerations
No excise licence	L3 or 5 times annual duty, whichever is greater	–	A (1–3 months unpaid) B (4–6 months unpaid) C (7–12 months unpaid)	Add duty lost
Fail to notify change of ownership to DVLA	L3	–	A	If offence committed in course of business: A (driver) A* (owner-driver) B (owner-company)
No test certificate	L3	–	A	If offence committed in course of business: A (driver) A* (owner-driver) B (owner-company)
Brakes defective	L4	3	B	If offence committed in course of business: B (driver) B* (owner-driver) C (owner-company) L5 if goods vehicle—see Part 5 below
Steering defective	L4	3	B	If offence committed in course of business: B (driver) B* (owner-driver) C (owner-company) L5 if goods vehicle—see Part 5 below

Tyres defective	L4	3	B	If offence committed in course of business: B (driver) B* (owner-driver) C (owner-company) L5 if goods vehicle—see Part 5 below Penalty per tyre
Condition of vehicle/accessories/ Equipment involving danger of injury (Road Traffic Act 1988, s.40A)	L4	3	B	Must disqualify for at least 6 months if offender has one or more previous convictions for same offence within three years If offence committed in course of business: B (driver) B* (owner-driver) C (owner-company) L5 if goods vehicle—see Part 5 below
Exhaust defective	L3	–	A	If offence committed in course of business: A (driver) A* (owner-driver) B (owner-company)
Lights defective	L3	–	A	If offence committed in course of business: A (driver) A* (owner-driver) B (owner-company)

Part 3: Offences concerning use of vehicle

SG-294

*The guidelines for some of the offences below differentiate between three types of offender when the offence is committed in the course of business: driver, owner-driver and owner-company. **For owner-driver, the starting point is the same as for driver; however, the court should consider an uplift of at least 25%.**

Offence	Maximum	Points	Starting point	Special considerations
Weight, position or distribution of load or manner in which load secured involving danger of injury (Road Traffic Act 1988, s.40A)	L4	3	B	Must disqualify for at least 6 months if offender has one or more previous convictions for same offence within three years. If offence committed in course of business: A (driver) A* (owner-driver) B (owner-company) L5 if goods vehicle—see Part 5 below
Number of passengers or way carried involving danger of injury (Road Traffic Act 1988, s.40A)	L4	3	B	If offence committed in course of business: A (driver) A* (owner-driver) B (owner-company) L5 if goods vehicle—see Part 5 below
Position or manner in which load secured (not involving danger) (Road Traffic Act 1988, s.42)	L3	–	A	L4 if goods vehicle—see Part 5 below
Overloading/exceeding axle weight	L5	–	A	Starting point caters for cases where the overload is up to and including 10%. Thereafter, 10% should be added to the penalty for each additional 1% of overload Penalty per axle If offence committed in course of business: A (driver) A* (owner-driver) B (owner-company) If goods vehicle—see Part 5 below
Dangerous parking	L3	3	A	
Pelican/zebra crossing contravention	L3	3	A	
Fail to comply with traffic sign (e.g. red traffic light, stop sign, double white lines, no entry sign)	L3	3	A	

Fail to comply with traffic sign (e.g. give way sign, keep left sign, temporary signs)	L3	–	A	
Fail to comply with police constable directing traffic	L3	3	A	
Fail to stop when required by police constable	L5 (mechanically propelled vehicle) L3 (cycle)	–	B	
Use of mobile telephone	L3	3	A	
Seat belt offences	L2 (adult or child in front) L2 (child in rear)	–	A	
Fail to use appropriate child car seat	L2	–	A	

SG-295   Part 4: Motorway offences

Offence	Maximum	Points	Starting point	Special considerations
Drive in reverse or wrong way on slip road	L4	3	B	
Drive in reverse or wrong way on motorway	L4	3	C	
Drive off carriageway (central reservation or hard shoulder)	L4	3	B	
Make U turn	L4	3	C	
Learner driver or excluded vehicle	L4	3	B	
Stop on hard shoulder	L4	–	A	
Vehicle in prohibited lane	L4	3	A	
Walk on motorway, slip road or hard shoulder	L4	–	A	

SG-296   **Part 5: Offences re buses/goods vehicles over 3.5 tonnes (GVW)**

* The guidelines for these offences differentiate between three types of offender: driver; owner-driver; and owner-company. **For owner-driver, the starting point is the same as for driver; however, the court should consider an uplift of at least 25%.**

** In all cases, take safety, damage to roads and commercial gain into account. Refer [below] for approach to fines for 'commercially motivated' offences.

Offence	Maximum	Points	Starting point	Special considerations
No goods vehicle plating certificate	L3	–	A (driver) A* (owner-driver) B (owner-company)	
No goods vehicle test certificate	L4	–	B (driver) B* (owner-driver) C (owner-company)	
Brakes defective	L5	3	B (driver) B* (owner-driver) C (owner-company)	
Steering defective	L5	3	B (driver) B* (owner-driver) C (owner-company)	
Tyres defective	L5	3	B (driver) B* (owner-driver) C (owner-company)	Penalty per tyre

Offence	Maximum	Points	Starting point	Special considerations
Exhaust emission	L4	–	B (driver) B* (owner-driver) C (owner-company)	
Condition of vehicle/ accessories/equipment involving danger of injury (Road Traffic Act 1988, s.40A)	L5	3	B (driver) B* (owner-driver) C (owner-company)	Must disqualify for at least 6 months if offender has one or more previous convictions for same offence within three years
Number of passengers or way carried involving danger of injury (Road Traffic Act 1988, s.40A)	L5	3	B (driver) B* (owner-driver) C (owner-company)	Must disqualify for at least 6 months if offender has one or more previous convictions for same offence within three years
Weight, position or distribution of load or manner in which load secured involving danger of injury (Road Traffic Act 1988, s.40A)	L5	3	B (driver) B* (owner-driver) C (owner-company)	Must disqualify for at least 6 months if offender has one or more previous convictions for same offence within three years
Position or manner in which load secured (not involving danger) (Road Traffic Act 1988, s.42)	L4	–	B (driver) B* (owner-driver) C (owner-company)	
Overloading/exceeding axle weight	L5	–	B (driver) B* (owner-driver) C (owner-company)	Starting points cater for cases where the overload is up to and including 10%. Thereafter, 10% should be added to the penalty for each additional 1% of overload Penalty per axle
No operators licence	L4	–	B (driver) B* (owner-driver) C (owner-company)	
Speed limiter not used or incorrectly calibrated	L4	–	B (driver) B* (owner-driver) C (owner-company)	
Tachograph not used/not working	L5	–	B (driver) B* (owner-driver) C (owner-company)	
Exceed permitted driving time/periods of duty	L4	–	B (driver) B* (owner-driver) C (owner-company)	
Fail to keep/return written record sheets	L4	–	B (driver) B* (owner-driver) C (owner-company)	
Falsify or alter records with intent to deceive	L5/2 years	–	B (driver) B* (owner-driver) C (owner-company)	Either way offence

EXPLANATORY MATERIAL

Meaning of 'range', 'starting point' and 'first time offender'   SG-297

…, these guidelines are for *a first time offender* convicted after a trial. They provide a *starting point* based on an assessment of the seriousness of the offence and a *range* within which the sentence will normally fall in most cases.

A clear, consistent understanding of each of these terms is essential and the Council and the Sentencing Advisory Panel have agreed the meanings set out in paragraphs 1(a)–(d) below.

They are explained in a format that follows the structured approach to the sentencing decision which identifies first those aspects that affect the assessment of the seriousness of the offence, then those aspects that form part of personal mitigation and, finally, any reduction for a guilty plea.

In practice, the boundaries between these stages will not always be as clear cut but the underlying principles will remain the same.

In accordance with section 174 of the Criminal Justice Act 2003, a court is obliged to '*state in open court, in ordinary language and in general terms, its reasons for deciding on the sentence passed*'. In particular, '*where guidelines indicate that a sentence of a particular kind, or within a particular range, would normally be appropriate and the sentence is of a different kind, or is outside that range*' the court must give its reasons for imposing a sentence of a different kind or outside the range.

SG-298　　**Assessing the seriousness of the offence**

1.　a)　These guidelines apply to an offence that can be committed in a variety of circumstances with different levels of seriousness. They apply to a *first time offender* who has been convicted after a trial.[131] Within the guidelines, a *first time offender* is a person who does not have a conviction which, by virtue of section 143(2) of the Criminal Justice Act 2003, must be treated as an aggravating factor.

　　b)　As an aid to consistency of approach, a guideline will describe a number of types of activity falling within the broad definition of the offence. These are set out in a column headed 'examples of nature of activity'.

　　c)　The expected approach is for a court to identify the description that most nearly matches the particular facts of the offence for which sentence is being imposed. This will identify a *starting point* from which the sentencer can depart to reflect aggravating or mitigating factors affecting the seriousness of the *offence* (beyond those contained in the description itself) to reach a *provisional sentence*.

　　d)　The range is the bracket into which the *provisional sentence* will normally fall after having regard to factors which aggravate or mitigate the seriousness of the offence. The particular circumstances may, however, make it appropriate that the *provisional sentence* falls outside the *range*.

2.　Where the offender has previous convictions which aggravate the seriousness of the current offence, that may take the *provisional sentence* beyond the *range* given particularly where there are significant other aggravating factors present.

SG-299　　**Offender Mitigation**

3.　Once the *provisional sentence* has been identified (by reference to the factors affecting the seriousness of the *offence*), the court will take into account any relevant factors of *offender* mitigation. Again, this may take the provisional sentence outside the range.

SG-300　　**Reduction for Guilty Plea**

4.　Where there has been a guilty plea, any reduction attributable to that plea will be applied to the sentence at this stage. This reduction may take the sentence below the range provided.

SG-301　　**Fine band starting points and ranges**

In these guidelines, where the starting point or range for an offence is or includes a fine, it is expressed as one of three fine bands (A, B or C). As detailed . . . below, each fine band has both a starting point and a range.

On some offence guidelines, both the starting point and the range are expressed as a single fine band; see for example careless driving . . . where the starting point and range for the first level of offence activity are 'band A fine'. This means that the starting point will be the starting point for fine band A (50% of the offender's relevant weekly income) and the range will be the range for fine band A (25–75% of relevant weekly income). On other guidelines, the range encompasses more than one fine band; see for example drunk and disorderly in a public place . . . where the starting point for the second level of offence activity is 'band B fine' and the range is 'band A fine to band C fine'. This means that the starting point will be the starting point for fine band B (100% of relevant weekly income) and the range will be the lowest point of the range for fine band A to the highest point of the range for fine band C (25%–175% of relevant weekly income).

---

[131] This means any case in which there is no guilty plea including, e.g., where an offender is convicted in absence after evidence has been heard

Sentencing for multiple offences   SG-302

Courts should refer to the Totality Guidelines at [**SG-496**].

Offences not included in the guidelines   SG-303

A number of offences are currently under consideration by the Council and will be included in the MCSG by way of an update when agreed. In the interim, the relevant guideline from the previous version of the MCSG has been included for ease of reference—*these do not constitute formal guidelines issued by the Council.*

Where there is no guideline for an offence, it may assist in determining sentence to consider the starting points and ranges indicated for offences that are of a similar level of seriousness. When sentencing for the breach of any order for which there is not a specific guideline, the primary objective will be to ensure compliance.

Reference to existing guidelines in respect of breaches of orders may provide a helpful point of comparison (see in particular . . . (breach of community order) and . . . (breach of protective order)). . . .

APPROACH TO THE ASSESSMENT OF FINES   SG-304

Introduction   SG-305

1.   The amount of a fine must reflect the *seriousness* of the offence.[132]
2.   The court must also take into account the *financial circumstances* of the offender; this applies whether it has the effect of increasing or reducing the fine.[133] Normally a fine should be of an amount that is capable of being paid within 12 months.
3.   The aim is for the fine to have an equal impact on offenders with different financial circumstances; it should be a hardship but should not force the offender below a reasonable 'subsistence' level.
4.   The guidance below aims to establish a clear, consistent and principled approach to the assessment of fines that will apply fairly in the majority of cases. However, it is impossible to anticipate every situation that may be encountered and in each case the court will need to exercise its judgement to ensure that the fine properly reflects the *seriousness of the offence* and takes into account the *financial circumstances* of the offender.

Fine bands   SG-306

5.   For the purpose of the offence guidelines, a fine is based on one of three bands (A, B or C).[134] The selection of the relevant fine band, and the position of the individual offence within that band, is determined by the seriousness of the offence.
6.   For an explanation of the meaning of starting point and range, both generally and in relation to fines, see [above].

	Starting point	Range
Fine Band A	50% of relevant weekly income	25–75% of relevant weekly income
Fine Band B	100% of relevant weekly income	75–125% of relevant weekly income
Fine Band C	150% of relevant weekly income	125–175% of relevant weekly income

Definition of relevant weekly income   SG-307

7.   The *seriousness* of an offence determines the choice of fine band and the position of the offence within the range for that band. The offender's *financial circumstances* are taken into account by expressing that position as a proportion of the offender's *relevant weekly income.*
8.   Where an offender is in receipt of income from employment or is self-employed *and* that income is more than £110 per week after deduction of tax and national insurance (or equivalent where the offender is self-employed), the actual income is the *relevant weekly income.*

---

[132]   Criminal Justice Act 2003, s.164(2)
[133]   ibid., ss.164(1) and 164(4)
[134]   As detailed in paras. 34–36 below, two further bands are provided which apply where the offence has passed the threshold for a community order (Band D) or a custodial sentence (Band E) but the court decides that it need not impose such a sentence and that a financial penalty is appropriate.

9. Where an offender's only source of income is state benefit (including where there is relatively low additional income as permitted by the benefit regulations) or the offender is in receipt of income from employment or is self-employed but the amount of income after deduction of tax and national insurance is £110 or less, the *relevant weekly income is deemed to be £110*. Additional information about the basis for this approach is set out [below].

10. In calculating relevant weekly income, no account should be taken of tax credits, housing benefit, child benefit or similar.

SG-308   No reliable information

11. Where an offender has failed to provide information, or the court is not satisfied that it has been given sufficient reliable information, it is entitled to make such determination as it thinks fit regarding the financial circumstances of the offender.[135] Any determination should be clearly stated on the court records for use in any subsequent variation or enforcement proceedings. In such cases, a record should also be made of the applicable fine band and the court's assessment of the position of the offence within that band based on the seriousness of the offence.

12. Where there is no information on which a determination can be made, the court should proceed on the basis of an *assumed relevant weekly income of £400*. This is derived from national median pre-tax earnings; a gross figure is used as, in the absence of financial information from the offender, it is not possible to calculate appropriate deductions.[136]

13. Where there is some information that tends to suggest a significantly lower or higher income than the recommended £400 default sum, the court should make a determination based on that information.

14. A court is empowered to remit a fine in whole or part if the offender subsequently provides information as to means.[137] The assessment of offence seriousness and, therefore, the appropriate fine band and the position of the offence within that band is not affected by the provision of this information.

SG-309   Assessment of financial circumstances

15. While the initial consideration for the assessment of a fine is the offender's relevant weekly income, the court is required to take account of the offender's *financial circumstances* more broadly. Guidance on important parts of this assessment is set out below.

16. An offender's financial circumstances may have the effect of increasing or reducing the amount of the fine; however, they are not relevant to the assessment of offence seriousness. They should be considered separately from the selection of the appropriate fine band and the court's assessment of the position of the offence within the range for that band.

SG-310   Out of the ordinary expenses

17. In deciding the proportions of relevant weekly income that are the starting points and ranges for each fine band, account has been taken of reasonable living expenses. Accordingly, no further allowance should normally be made for these. In addition, no allowance should normally be made where the offender has dependants.

18. Outgoings will be relevant to the amount of the fine only where the expenditure is *out of the ordinary* and *substantially* reduces the ability to pay a financial penalty so that the requirement to pay a fine based on the standard approach would lead to *undue* hardship.

SG-311   Unusually low outgoings

19. Where the offender's living expenses are substantially lower than would normally be expected, it may be appropriate to adjust the amount of the fine to reflect this. This may apply, for example, where an offender does not make any financial contribution towards his or her living costs.

SG-312   Savings

20. Where an offender has savings these will not normally be relevant to the assessment of the amount of a fine although they may influence the decision on time to pay.

21. However, where an offender has little or no income but has substantial savings, the court may consider it appropriate to adjust the amount of the fine to reflect this.

SG-313   Household has more than one source of income

22. Where the household of which the offender is a part has more than one source of income, the fine should normally be based on the income of the offender alone.

---

[135] Criminal Justice Act 2003, s.164(5)

[136] For 2009–10, the median pre-tax income was £377 per week (http://www.hmrc.gov.uk/stats/income_distribution/3-2table-feb2012.pdf). This figure has been increased to take account of earnings growth.

[137] Criminal Justice Act 2003, s.165(2)

23. However, where the offender's part of the income is very small (or the offender is wholly dependent on the income of another), the court may have regard to the extent of the household's income and assets which will be available to meet any fine imposed on the offender.[138]

Potential earning capacity   SG-314

24. Where there is reason to believe that an offender's potential earning capacity is greater than his or her current income, the court may wish to adjust the amount of the fine to reflect this.[139] This may apply, for example, where an unemployed offender states an expectation to gain paid employment within a short time. The basis for the calculation of fine should be recorded in order to ensure that there is a clear record for use in variation or enforcement proceedings.

High income offenders   SG-315

25. Where the offender is in receipt of very high income, a fine based on a proportion of relevant weekly income may be disproportionately high when compared with the seriousness of the offence. In such cases, the court should adjust the fine to an appropriate level; as a general indication, in most cases the fine for a first time offender pleading not guilty should not exceed 75% of the maximum fine.

Offence committed for 'commercial' purposes   SG-316

26. Some offences are committed with the intention of gaining a significant commercial benefit. These often occur where, in order to carry out an activity lawfully, a person has to comply with certain processes which may be expensive. They include, for example, 'taxi-touting' (where unauthorised persons seek to operate as taxi drivers) and 'fly-tipping' (where the cost of lawful disposal is considerable).

27. In some of these cases, a fine based on the standard approach set out above may not reflect the level of financial gain achieved or sought through the offending. Accordingly:

    a. where the offender has generated income or avoided expenditure to a level that can be calculated or estimated, the court may wish to consider that amount when determining the financial penalty;

    b. where it is not possible to calculate or estimate that amount, the court may wish to draw on information from the enforcing authorities about the general costs of operating within the law.

Reduction for a guilty plea   SG-317

28. Where a guilty plea has been entered, the amount of the fine should be reduced by the appropriate proportion. Courts should refer to the Guilty Plea guidelines [at **SG-1**].

Other considerations   SG-318

Maximum fines

29. A fine must not exceed the statutory limit. Where this is expressed in terms of a 'level', the maxima are:

Level 1	£200
Level 2	£500
Level 3	£1,000
Level 4	£2,500
Level 5	£5,000

Victim surcharge

30. See [below] for guidance on the approach to the Victim Surcharge. Where the offender does not have sufficient means to pay the total financial penalty considered appropriate by the court, the order of priority is compensation, surcharge, fine, costs.

---

[138] *R v Engen* [2004] EWCA Crim 1536 (CA)
[139] *R v Little* (unreported) 14 April 1976 (CA)

Costs

31. See [below] for guidance on the approach to costs. Where the offender does not have sufficient means to pay the total financial penalty considered appropriate by the court, the order of priority is compensation, surcharge, fine, costs.

Multiple offences

32. Where an offender is to be fined for two or more offences that arose out of the same incident, it will often be appropriate to impose on the most serious offence a fine which reflects the totality of the offending where this can be achieved within the maximum penalty for that offence. 'No separate penalty' should be imposed for the other offences.

33. Where compensation is being ordered, that will need to be attributed to the relevant offence as will any necessary ancillary orders.

Fine Bands D and E

34. Two further fine bands are provided to assist a court in calculating a fine where the offence and general circumstances would otherwise warrant a community order (band D) or a custodial sentence (band E) but the court has decided that it need not impose such a sentence and that a financial penalty is appropriate. [See [below] for further guidance.]

35. The following starting points and ranges apply:

	Starting point	Range
Fine Band D	250% of relevant weekly income	200–300% of relevant weekly income
Fine Band E	400% of relevant weekly income	300–500% of relevant weekly income

36. In cases where these fine bands apply, it may be appropriate for the fine to be of an amount that is larger than can be repaid within 12 months. See paragraph 41 below.

Imposition of fines with custodial sentences

37. A fine and a custodial sentence may be imposed for the same offence although there will be few circumstances in which this is appropriate, particularly where the custodial sentence is to be served immediately. One example might be where an offender has profited financially from an offence but there is no obvious victim to whom compensation can be awarded. Combining these sentences is most likely to be appropriate only where the custodial sentence is short and/or the offender clearly has, or will have, the means to pay.

38. Care must be taken to ensure that the overall sentence is proportionate to the seriousness of the offence and that better off offenders are not able to 'buy themselves out of custody'.

Consult your legal adviser in any case in which you are considering combining a fine with a custodial sentence.

Payment

39. A fine is payable in full on the day on which it is imposed. The offender should always be asked for immediate payment when present in court and some payment on the day should be required wherever possible.

40. Where that is not possible, the court may, in certain circumstances, require the offender to be detained. More commonly, a court will allow payments to be made over a period set by the court:

    a.   if periodic payments are allowed, the fine should normally be payable within a maximum of 12 months. However, it may be unrealistic to expect those on very low incomes to maintain payments for as long as a year;

    b.   compensation should normally be payable within 12 months. However, in exceptional circumstances it may be appropriate to allow it to be paid over a period of up to 3 years.

41. Where fine bands D and E apply (see paragraphs 34–36 above), it may be appropriate for the fine to be of an amount that is larger than can be repaid within 12 months. In such cases, the fine should normally be payable within a maximum of 18 months (band D) or 2 years (band E).

42. It is generally recognised that the maximum weekly payment by a person in receipt of state benefit should rarely exceed £5.

43. When allowing payment by instalments by an offender in receipt of earned income, the following approach may be useful. If the offender has dependants or larger than usual commitments, the weekly payment is likely to be decreased.

Net weekly income	Starting point for weekly payment
£60	£5
£120	£10
£200	£25
£250	£30
£300	£50
£400	£80

44. The payment terms must be included in any collection order made in respect of the amount imposed; see [below].

Assessment of fines: sentencing structure

SG-319

1. Decide that a fine is appropriate

2. Offence seriousness A. Identify the appropriate fine band

- In the offence guidelines, the starting point for a fine is identified as fine band A, B or C
- Each fine band provides a **starting point** and a **range** related to the **seriousness** of the offence expressed as a proportion of the offender's **relevant weekly income**...

2. Offence seriousness B. Consider the effect of aggravating and mitigating factors

- **Move up or down from the starting point** to reflect aggravating or mitigating factors that affect the **seriousness** of the offence—this will usually be within the indicated **range** for the fine band but the court is not precluded from going outside the range where the facts justify it...

3. Consider offender mitigation

- The court may consider it appropriate to make a further adjustment to the starting point in light of any matters of offender mitigation...

4. Form a view of the position of the offence within the range for the fine band then take into account the offenders financial circumstances

- Require the offender to provide a statement of **financial circumstances**. Obtain further information through questioning if necessary. Failure to provide the information when required is an offence
- The provision of financial information does not affect the seriousness of the offence or, therefore, the position of the offence within the range for the applicable fine band
- The initial consideration for the assessment of the fine is the offender's **relevant weekly income**...
- However, the court must take account of the offender's financial circumstances more broadly. These may have the effect of **increasing or reducing** the amount of the fine...
- Where the court has **insufficient information** to make a proper determination of the offender's financial circumstances, it may make such determination as it thinks fit...

5. Consider a reduction for a guilty plea

- Reduce the fine by the appropriate proportion...

6. Consider ancillary orders, including compensation

- Consider compensation in every case where the offending has resulted in personal injury, loss or damage—give reasons if order not made.... Compensation takes priority over a fine where there are insufficient resources to pay both...

7. Decide sentence Give reasons

- The resulting fine must reflect the seriousness of the offence and must take into account the offender's financial circumstances
- Consider the proposed total financial penalty, including compensation, victims surcharge and costs. Where there are insufficient resources to pay the total amount, the order of priority is compensation, surcharge, fine, costs
- Give reasons for the sentence passed, including any ancillary orders
- State if the sentence has been reduced to reflect a guilty plea; indicate what the sentence would otherwise have been
- Explain if the sentence is of a different kind or outside the range indicated in the guidelines
- Expect immediate payment. If payment by instalments allowed, the court must make a collection order unless this would be impracticable or inappropriate...

SG-320   **Additional information: approach to offenders on low income**

1. An offender whose primary source of income is state benefit will generally receive a base level of benefit (e.g. job seekers' allowance, a relevant disability benefit or income support) and may also be eligible for supplementary benefits depending on his or her individual circumstances (such as child tax credits, housing benefit, council tax benefit and similar).
2. If relevant weekly income were defined as the amount of benefit received, this would usually result in higher fines being imposed on offenders with a higher level of need; in most circumstances that would not properly balance the seriousness of the offence with the financial circumstances of the offender. While it might be possible to exclude from the calculation any allowance above the basic entitlement of a single person, that could be complicated and time consuming.
3. Similar issues can arise where an offender is in receipt of a low earned income since this may trigger eligibility for means related benefits such as working tax credits and housing benefit depending on the particular circumstances. It will not always be possible to determine with any confidence whether such a person's financial circumstances are significantly different from those of a person whose primary source of income is state benefit.
4. For these reasons, a simpler and fairer approach to cases involving offenders in receipt of low income (whether primarily earned or as a result of benefit) is to identify an amount that is deemed to represent the offender's relevant weekly income.
5. While a precise calculation is neither possible nor desirable, it is considered that an amount that is approximately half-way between the base rate for job seekers' allowance and the net weekly income of an adult earning the minimum wage for 30 hours per week represents a starting point that is both realistic and appropriate; *this is currently £110*.[140] The calculation is based on a 30 hour working week in recognition of the fact that many of those on minimum wage do not work a full 37 hour week and that lower minimum wage rates apply to younger people.
6. It is expected that this figure will remain in use until 31 March 2015. Future revisions of the guideline will update the amount in accordance with current benefit and minimum wage levels.

SG-321   ENFORCEMENT OF FINES

1. The Courts Act 2003 created a new fines collection scheme which provides for greater administrative enforcement of fines. The main features are set out below....

SG-322   **Attachment of earnings orders/applications for benefit deductions**

2. Unless it would be impracticable or inappropriate to do so, the court must make an attachment of earnings order (AEO) or application for benefit deductions (ABD) whenever:
   - compensation is imposed;[141] or
   - the court concludes that the offender is an existing defaulter and that the existing default cannot be disregarded.[142]
3. In other cases, the court may make an AEO or ABD with the offender's consent.[143]

---

[140] With effect from 1 October 2011, the minimum wage is £6.08 per hour for an adult aged 22 or over. Based on a 30 hour week, this equates to approximately £173 after deductions for tax and national insurance. To ensure equivalence of approach, the level of job seekers' allowance for a single person aged 22 has been used for the purpose of calculating the mid point; this is currently £53.45

[141] Courts Act 2003, sch.5, para.7A

[142] ibid., para.8

[143] ibid., para.9

Collection orders

SG-323

4. The court must make a collection order in every case in which a fine or compensation order is imposed unless this would be impracticable or inappropriate.[144] The collection order must state:
   - the amount of the sum due, including the amount of any fine, compensation order or other sum;
   - whether the court considers the offender to be an existing defaulter;
   - whether an AEO or ABD has been made and information about the effect of the order;
   - if the court has not made an AEO or ABD, the payment terms;
   - if an AEO or ABD has been made, the reserve terms (i.e. the payment terms that will apply if the AEO or ABD fails). It will often be appropriate to set a reserve term of payment in full within 14 days.

5. If an offender defaults on a collection order and is not already subject to an AEO or ABD, a fines officer must make an AEO or ABD.[145] Where this would be impracticable or inappropriate, or where the offender is already subject to an AEO or ABD, a fines officer must either:[146]
   - issue a 'further steps' notice advising that the officer intends to take any of the enforcement action listed below; or
   - refer the case to a magistrates' court.

6. The following enforcement action is available to a fines officer:[147]
   - making an AEO or ABD;
   - issuing a distress warrant;
   - registering the sum in the register of judgments and orders;
   - making a clamping order. A magistrates' court may order the sale of the vehicle if the sum remains unpaid one month after the vehicle was clamped;[148]
   - taking enforcement proceedings in the High Court or county court.

7. Where a fines officer refers the case to a magistrates' court, the court may:[149]
   - vary the payment terms or reserve terms;
   - take any of the enforcement steps available to fines officers listed above;
   - where the court is satisfied that the default is due to wilful refusal or culpable neglect, increase the fine by up to 50 per cent;[150]
   - discharge the collection order and exercise any of the court's standard fine enforcement powers.

8. The case may also be referred to a magistrates' court if an offender appeals against a 'further steps' notice issued by a fines officer.[151]

Standard fine enforcement powers

SG-324

9. These powers are normally available if:
   - a collection order is not made; or
   - a case is referred to a magistrates' court by a fines officer; or
   - an offender appeals against a 'further steps' notice issued by a fines officer.

Remission of fine

SG-325

10. The court can remit a fine 'if it thinks it just to do so having regard to a change of circumstances since the date of conviction'.[152] This requirement may be satisfied where:
    - the defaulter's means have changed since the fine was imposed;
    - arrears have accumulated by the imposition of additional fines to a level which makes repayment of the total amount within a reasonable time unlikely;
    - the defaulter is serving a term of imprisonment; remission may be more practical than lodging concurrent warrants of imprisonment.

11. There is no power to remit excise penalties (which include fines and back duty for using an untaxed vehicle).[153]

---

[144] ibid., para.12
[145] ibid., para.26
[146] ibid., para.37
[147] ibid., para.38
[148] Courts Act 2003, sch.5, para.41
[149] ibid., para.39
[150] ibid., para.42A
[151] ibid., para.37
[152] Magistrates' Courts Act 1980, s.85
[153] Criminal Justice Act 2003, s.165

Sentencing Guidelines

12. Compensation and costs cannot be remitted but, where payment is unlikely or impractical due to the defaulter's means or circumstances, the sum may be discharged or reduced. Victims and claimants should be consulted and given an opportunity to attend the hearing.

13. The court is also empowered to remit a fine that was imposed in the absence of information about the offender's means.

SG-326 Imprisonment in default of payment

14. A court may issue a warrant of commitment if the defaulter is already serving a custodial sentence.[154]

15. If a means inquiry establishes that the defaulter has the ability to pay immediately, and the offence was punishable by imprisonment, the court can commit him or her to prison.[155]

16. Otherwise, the court may issue a warrant of commitment only if there has been a means inquiry and the court:[156]
    • is satisfied that the default is due to wilful refusal or culpable neglect; and
    • has considered or tried all other methods of enforcing payment and concluded that they are inappropriate or unsuccessful.

17. The other methods that the court is required to have considered or tried are:
    • money payment supervision order;[157]
    • application for deductions from benefit;
    • attachment of earnings order;
    • distress warrant;
    • taking enforcement proceedings in the High Court or county court;
    • if the offender is aged under 25, an attendance centre order (where available).[158]

18. The period of commitment should be the shortest which is likely to succeed in obtaining payment; the periods prescribed in schedule 4 of the Magistrates' Courts Act 1980 ... should be regarded as maxima rather than the norm. The period of imprisonment may be suspended on condition that regular payments are made. Where such payments are not made, the defaulter should be brought back before the court for consideration of whether the period of imprisonment should be implemented.

Maximum periods of imprisonment in default of payment	
Amount not exceeding £200	7 days
Amount exceeding £200 but not exceeding £500	14 days
Amount exceeding £500 but not exceeding £1,000	28 days
Amount exceeding £1,000 but not exceeding £2,500	45 days
Amount exceeding £2,500 but not exceeding £5,000	3 months
Amount exceeding £5,000 but not exceeding £10,000	6 months
Amount exceeding £10,000	12 months

SG-327 Detention in the precincts of the court or at a police station

19. The court may order that an offender be detained for a specified period ending no later than 8pm on the day on which the order is made:[159] this is available both as a sentence in its own right and as an order in respect of unpaid fines where it can be used as an alternative to remission. No means inquiry is required.

---

[154] Magistrates' Courts Act 1980, s.82(3)
[155] Magistrates' Courts Act 1980, s.82(4)(a)
[156] ibid., s.82(4)(b)
[157] ibid., s.88
[158] Powers of Criminal Courts (Sentencing) Act 2000, s.60
[159] Magistrates' Courts Act 1980, s.135

Warrant for detention in police station overnight

20. The court may issue a warrant for the overnight detention of a defaulter in a police station.[160] The defaulter must be released at 8am the following day, or the same day if arrested after midnight.

[Material on discharge of fines by unpaid work — no longer included in the Guideline.]

COMMUNITY ORDERS

1. Community orders have the effect of restricting the offender's liberty while providing punishment in the community, rehabilitation for the offender, and/or ensuring that the offender engages in reparative activities. They are available in respect of all offences, including those for which the maximum penalty is a fine.

2. A community order must not be imposed unless the offence is 'serious enough to warrant such a sentence'.[161] For detailed guidance regarding this threshold and the approach to community orders, sentencers should refer to the Sentencing Guidelines Council's definitive guideline *New Sentences: Criminal Justice Act 2003*, published 16 December 2004 [see **SG-9**], and the National Standards for the Probation Service. The Council guideline emphasises that:
   - sentencers must consider all available disposals at the time of sentence; even where the threshold for a community sentence has been passed, a fine or discharge may be an appropriate penalty;
   - where an offender is being sentenced for a non-imprisonable offence, great care is needed in assessing whether a community sentence is appropriate since failure to comply could result in a custodial sentence (see above).[162]

3. Community orders consist of one or more of the following requirements:
   - unpaid work requirement;
   - activity requirement;
   - programme requirement;
   - prohibited activity requirement;
   - curfew requirement;
   - exclusion requirement;
   - residence requirement;
   - foreign travel prohibition requirement (when in force);[163]
   - mental health treatment requirement;
   - drug rehabilitation requirement;
   - alcohol treatment requirement;
   - alcohol abstinence and monitoring requirement (in pilot areas);[164]
   - supervision requirement;
   - in a case where the offender is aged under 25, attendance centre requirement (where available).

4. The court must ensure that the restriction on the offender's liberty is commensurate with the seriousness of the offence and that the requirements are the most suitable for the offender.[165] Where two or more requirements are included, they must be compatible with each other.[166]

5. The Council guideline provides that the seriousness of the offence should be the *initial* factor in determining which requirements to include in a community order. It establishes three sentencing ranges within the community order band based on offence seriousness (low, medium and high), and identifies non-exhaustive examples of requirements that might be appropriate in each. These are set out below. The examples focus on punishment in the community; other requirements of a rehabilitative nature may be more appropriate in some cases.

---

[160] ibid., s.136
[161] Criminal Justice Act 2003, s.148
[162] ibid., s. 150A(1) as amended by the Criminal Justice and Immigration Act 2008, s. 11(1)
[163] ibid., s. 206A as amended by the Legal Aid, Sentencing and Punishment of Offenders Act 2012, s. 72
[164] Legal Aid, Sentencing and Punishment of Offenders Act 2012, s. 77
[165] Criminal Justice Act 2003, ss.148(2)(a) and 148(2)(b)
[166] ibid., s.177(6)

Low	Medium	High
Offences only just cross community order threshold, where the seriousness of the offence or the nature of the offender's record means that a discharge or fine is inappropriate	Offences that obviously fall within the community order band	Offences only just fall below the custody threshold or the custody threshold is crossed but a community order is more appropriate in the circumstances
In general, only one requirement will be appropriate and the length may be curtailed if additional requirements are necessary		More intensive sentences which combine two or more requirements may be appropriate
Suitable requirements might include: • 40–80 hours unpaid work • Curfew requirement within the lowest range (e.g. up to 16 hours per day for a few weeks) • Exclusion requirement, without electronic monitoring, for a few months • Prohibited activity requirement • Attendance centre requirement (where available)	Suitable requirements might include: • Greater number of hours of unpaid work (e.g. 80–150 hours) • Curfew requirement within the middle range (e.g. up to 16 hours for 2–3 months) • Exclusion requirement lasting in the region of 6 months • Prohibited activity requirement	Suitable requirements might include: • 150–300 hours unpaid work • Activity requirement up to the maximum of 60 days • Curfew requirement up to 16 hours per day for 4–6 months • Exclusion order lasting in the region of 12 months

6. The particular requirements imposed within the range must be suitable for the individual offender and will be influenced by a wide range of factors including the stated purpose(s) of the sentence, the risk of re-offending, the ability of the offender to comply, and the availability of the requirements in the local area. Sentencers must ensure that the sentence strikes the right balance between proportionality and suitability. The resulting restriction on liberty must be a proportionate response to the offence that was committed.

7. In many cases, a pre-sentence report will be pivotal in helping the court decide whether to impose a community order and, if so, whether particular requirements or combinations of requirements are suitable for an individual offender. Whenever the court reaches the provisional view that a community order may be appropriate, it should usually request a pre-sentence report. It will be helpful to indicate the court's preliminary opinion as to which of the three sentencing ranges is relevant and the purpose(s) of sentencing that the package of requirements is expected to fulfil. Ideally this should be provided to the Probation Service in written form, with a copy retained on the court file for the benefit of the sentencing bench.

SG-331   Electronic monitoring

8. Subject to limited exceptions, the court must impose an electronic monitoring requirement where it makes a community order with a curfew or exclusion requirement, and may do so in all other cases.[167] Electronic monitoring should be used with the primary purpose of promoting and monitoring compliance with other requirements, in circumstances where the punishment of the offender and/or the need to safeguard the public and prevent re-offending are the most important concerns.

SG-332   Breach of Community Order

9. Refer to [the specific guideline above] for guidance on the approach to sentencing for breaches of community orders.

---

[167] Criminal Justice Act 2003, ss.177(3) and 177(4)

Custodial Sentences

1. A custodial sentence must not be imposed unless the offence 'was so serious that neither a fine alone nor a community sentence can be justified for the offence'.[168] Guidance regarding this threshold and the approach to the imposition of custodial sentences is set out in the Sentencing Guidelines Council's definitive guideline *Overarching Principles: Seriousness*, published 16 December 2004 [see **SG-21**].

2. The guideline emphasises that:
    *   the clear intention of the threshold test is to reserve prison as a punishment for the most serious offences;
    *   passing the custody threshold does not mean that a custodial sentence should be deemed inevitable; custody can still be avoided in light of offender mitigation or where there is a suitable intervention in the community which provides sufficient restriction (by way of punishment) while addressing the rehabilitation of the offender to prevent future crime. However, where the offence would otherwise appear to warrant a term of imprisonment within the Crown Court's jurisdiction, it is for the Crown Court to make that judgement;
    *   the approach to the imposition of a custodial sentence should be as follows:
        (a) Has the custody threshold been passed?
        (b) If so, is it unavoidable that a custodial sentence be imposed?
        (c) If so, can that sentence be suspended? (Sentencers should be clear that they would have imposed a custodial sentence if the power to suspend had not been available.)
        (d) If not, impose a sentence which takes immediate effect for the shortest term commensurate with the seriousness of the offence.[169]

Suspended sentences

3. If the court imposes a term of imprisonment between 14 days and six months,[170] it may suspend the sentence for between 6 months and 2 years (the 'operational period').[171]
    Before s.68 of the Legal Aid, Sentencing and Punishment of Offenders Act 2012 is in force
    *   Where the court imposes two or more sentences to be served consecutively, the court may only suspend the sentence where the aggregate of the terms does not exceed 6 months.[172]
    *   When the court suspends a sentence, it must impose one or more requirements for the offender to undertake in the community. The requirements are identical to those available for community orders.
    After s.68 of the Legal Aid, Sentencing and Punishment of Offenders Act 2012 is in force
    *   Where the court imposes two or more sentences to be served consecutively, the court may suspend the sentence where the aggregate of the terms is between 14 days and 12 months.[173]
    *   When the court suspends a sentence, it may impose one or more requirements for the offender to undertake in the community.[174] The requirements are identical to those available for community orders.

4. If the offender fails to comply with a community requirement or commits a further offence, the court must *either* activate the suspended sentence in full *or* in part or amend the order so as to:[175]
    a) extend the period during which the offender is subject to community requirements;
    b) make the community requirements more onerous; or
    c) extend the operational period.

5. There are many similarities between suspended sentences and community orders: requirements can be imposed on the offender and the court can respond to breach by sending him or her to custody. The crucial difference is that a suspended sentence is a prison sentence; *it may be imposed only where the court is satisfied both that the custodial threshold has been passed and that it is not appropriate to impose a community order, fine or other non-custodial sentence.*

6. A further difference is the approach to any breach; when sentencing for breach of a community order, the primary objective is to ensure that the requirements of the order are complied with. When responding to breach of a suspended sentence, the statutory presumption is that the custodial sentence will be activated.[176]

---

[168] Criminal Justice Act 2003, s.152(2)
[169] ibid., s.153(2)
[170] ibid., s. 189(1) as amended by art. 2(2)(a) of the Criminal Justice Act 2003 (Sentencing) (Transitory Provisions) Order 2005
[171] ibid, s.189(3)
[172] ibid., s.189(2) as amended by art.2(2)(b) of the Criminal Justice Act 2003 (Sentencing) (Transitory Provisions) Order 2005
[173] ibid., s. 189(2) as amended by the Legal Aid, Sentencing and Punishment of Offenders Act 2012, s.68(2)
[174] ibid., s. 189(1A) as amended by the Legal Aid, Sentencing and Punishment of Offenders Act 2012, s.68(1)
[175] ibid., sch.12, para.8; after s.69 of the Legal Aid, Sentencing and Punishment of Offenders Act 2012 is in force, as an alternative to the options set out in paragraph 4, courts will be able to order the offender to pay a fine of up to £2,500
[176] ibid., sch.12, para.8(3)

7. Detailed guidance regarding suspended sentences and the appropriate response to breaches is set out in the Sentencing Guidelines Council's definitive guideline *New Sentences: Criminal Justice Act 2003*, published 16 December 2004 [see **SG-9**]. The guideline emphasises that:

    - *a custodial sentence that is suspended should be for the same term that would have applied if the sentence was to be served immediately*;
    - the time for which a sentence is suspended should reflect the length of the sentence; up to 12 months might normally be appropriate for a suspended sentence of up to 6 months;
    - the imposition of a custodial sentence is both punishment and a deterrent; to ensure that the over-all terms of the sentence are commensurate with offence seriousness, requirements imposed as part of the sentence should generally be less onerous than if a community order had been imposed;
    - a court wishing to impose onerous or intensive requirements should reconsider whether a community sentence might be more appropriate [see **SG-330**];
    - where an offender has breached a suspended sentence, there is a presumption that the suspended prison term will be activated in full or in part. Relevant considerations will include the extent to which (if any) the offender complied with the requirements, and the circumstances of the breach.

8. When the court imposes a suspended sentence, it may also order that the sentence be reviewed periodically at a review hearing.[177]

SG-334   COMPENSATION

1. The court *must* consider making a compensation order in any case where personal injury, loss or damage has resulted from the offence.[178] It can either be a sentence in its own right or an ancillary order. The court must give reasons if it decides not to order compensation.

2. Up to £5,000 compensation may be imposed in respect of each offence of which the offender has been convicted.[179] Compensation may also be ordered in respect of offences taken into consideration. The total amount of compensation must not exceed the maximum available for the offence(s) of which the offender has been convicted so that, e.g., where an offender has been convicted of two offences, the maximum amount of compensation able to be awarded is £10,000 regardless of the number of offences taken into consideration.

3. Where the personal injury, loss or damage arises from a road accident, a compensation order may be made only if there is a conviction for an offence under the Theft Act 1968, or the offender is uninsured and the Motor Insurers' Bureau will not cover the loss.[180] Compensation paid by the Motor Insurers' Bureau is subject to an excess of £300.

4. Subject to consideration of the victim's views (see paragraph 6 below), the court must order compensation wherever possible and should not have regard to the availability of other sources such as civil litigation or the Criminal Injuries Compensation Scheme. Any amount paid by an offender under a compensation order will generally be deducted from a subsequent civil award or payment under the Scheme to avoid double compensation.[181]

5. Compensation may be ordered for such amount as the court considers appropriate having regard to any evidence and any representations made by the offender or prosecutor.[182] The court must also take into account the offender's means (see also paragraphs 11–13 below).[183]

6. Compensation should benefit, not inflict further harm on, the victim. Any financial recompense from the offender may cause distress. A victim may or may not want compensation from the offender and assumptions should not be made either way. The victim's views are properly obtained through sensitive discussion by the police or witness care unit, when it can be explained that the offender's ability to pay will ultimately determine whether, and how much, compensation is ordered and whether the compensation will be paid in one lump sum or by instalments. If the victim does not want compensation, this should be made known to the court and respected.

7. In cases where it is difficult to ascertain the full amount of the loss suffered by the victim, consideration should be given to making a compensation order for an amount representing the agreed or likely loss. Where relevant information is not immediately available, it may be appropriate to grant an adjournment for it to be obtained.

8. The court should consider two types of loss:

    - financial loss sustained as a result of the offence such as the cost of repairing damage or, in case of injury, any loss of earnings or medical expenses;

---

[177] ibid., s.191; after s.68(6) of the Legal Aid, Sentencing and Punishment of Offenders Act 2012 is in force, the power to provide reviews will only be available for suspended sentences that impose community requirements

[178] Powers of Criminal Courts (Sentencing) Act 2000, s.130

[179] ibid., s.131(1)

[180] ibid., s.130(6)

[181] The minimum amount payable under the Criminal Injuries Compensation Scheme is £1,000

[182] Powers of Criminal Courts (Sentencing) Act 2000, s.130(4)

[183] ibid., s.130(11)

- pain and suffering caused by the injury (including terror, shock or distress) and any loss of facility. This should be assessed in light of all factors that appear to the court to be relevant, including any medical evidence, the victim's age and personal circumstances.

9. The tables below suggest starting points for compensating physical and mental injuries commonly encountered in a magistrates' court. They have been developed to be consistent with the approach in the Criminal Injuries Compensation Authority tariff (revised 2001), available at: www.cica.gov.uk.

Physical injury   SG-335

Type of injury	Description	Starting point
Graze	Depending on size	Up to £75
Bruise	Depending on size	Up to £100
Cut: no permanent scar	Depending on size and whether stitched	£100 – 500
Black eye		£125
Eye	Blurred or double vision lasting up to 6 weeks Blurred or double vision lasting for 6 to 13 weeks Blurred or double vision lasting for more than 13 weeks (recovery expected)	Up to £1,000 £1,000 £1,750
Brain	Concussion lasting one week	£1,500
Nose	Undisplaced fracture of nasal bone Displaced fracture requiring manipulation Deviated nasal septum requiring septoplasty	£1,000 £2,000 £2,000
Loss of non-front tooth Loss of front tooth	Depending on cosmetic effect	£1,250 £1,750
Facial scar	Minor disfigurement (permanent)	£1,500
Arm	Fractured humerus, radius, ulna (substantial recovery)	£3,300
Shoulder	Dislocated (substantial recovery)	£1,750
Wrist	Dislocated/fractured—including scaphoid fracture (substantial recovery) Fractured—colles type (substantial recovery)	£3,300 £4,400
Sprained wrist, ankle	Disabling for up to 6 weeks Disabling for 6 to 13 weeks Disabling for more than 13 weeks	Up to £1,000 £1,000 £2,500
Finger	Fractured finger other than index finger (substantial recovery) Fractured index finger (substantial recovery) Fractured thumb (substantial recovery)	£1,000 £1,750 £2,000
Leg	Fractured fibula (substantial recovery) Fractured femur, tibia (substantial recovery)	£2,500 £3,800
Abdomen	Injury requiring laparotomy	£3,800

Mental injury   SG-336

Description	Starting point
Temporary mental anxiety (including terror, shock, distress), not medically verified	Up to £1,000
Disabling mental anxiety, lasting more than 6 weeks, medically verified*	£1,000
Disability mental illness, lasting up to 28 weeks, confirmed by psychiatric diagnosis*	£2,500

* In this context, 'disabling' means a person's functioning is significantly impaired in some important aspect of his or her life, such as impaired work or school performance or significant adverse effects on social relationships.

10. The following table, which is also based on the Criminal Injuries Compensation Authority tariff, sets out suggested starting points for compensating physical and sexual abuse. It will be rare for cases involving this type of harm to be dealt with in a magistrates' court and it will be important to consult your legal adviser for guidance in these situations.

Sentencing Guidelines

SG-337 Physical and sexual abuse

Type of abuse	Description	Starting point
Physical abuse of adult	Intermittent physical assaults resulting in accumulation of healed wounds, burns or scalds, but with no appreciable disfigurement	£2,000
Physical abuse of child	Isolated or intermittent assault(s) resulting in weals, hair pulled from scalp etc. Intermittent physical assaults resulting in accumulation of healed wounds, burns or scalds, but with no appreciable disfigurement	£1,000 £2,000
Sexual abuse of adult	Non-penetrative indecent physical acts over clothing Non-penetrative indecent act(s) under clothing	£1,000 £2,000
Sexual abuse of child (under 18)	Non-penetrative indecent physical act(s) over clothing Non-penetrative frequent assaults over clothing or non-penetrative indecent act under clothing Repetitive indecent acts under clothing	£1,000 £2,000 £3,300

11. Once the court has formed a preliminary view of the appropriate level of compensation, it must have regard to the means of the offender so far as they are known. Where the offender has little money, the order may have to be scaled down or additional time allowed to pay; the court may allow compensation to be paid over a period of up to three years in appropriate cases.

12. The fact that a custodial sentence is imposed does not, in itself, make it inappropriate to order compensation; however, it may be relevant to whether the offender has the means to satisfy the order.

13. Where the court considers that it would be appropriate to impose a fine and a compensation order but the offender has insufficient means to pay both, priority should be given to compensation. Compensation also takes priority over the victim surcharge where the offender's means are an issue.

SG-338

Victim Surcharge

1. A court must order the Victim Surcharge when it deals with an offender in respect of an offence committed on or after 1 October 2012 in the following ways:[184]

Offenders aged 18 and older at the date of the offence

Disposal type	Victim Surcharge
Conditional discharge	£15
Fine	At 10% of the fine value with a £20 minimum and a £120 maximum *(Surcharge should be rounded up or down to the nearest pound)*
Community order	£60
Suspended sentence order	6 months and below — £80 Over 6 months and up to and including 1 year — £100
Immediate custody	N/A*

Offenders aged under 18 at the date of the offence

Disposal type	Victim Surcharge
Conditional discharge	£10
Fine, Youth Rehabilitation Order or Referral Order	£15
Immediate custody	N/A*

* Magistrates cannot order an offender sentenced to immediate custody to pay the Victim Surcharge.

---

[184] Criminal Justice Act 2003, s.161A; Criminal Justice Act 2003 (Surcharge) Order 2012

Person who is not an individual (for example, a company or other legal person)

Disposal type	Victim Surcharge
Conditional discharge	£15
Fine	At 10% of the fine value with a £20 minimum and a £120 maximum *(Surcharge should be rounded up or down to the nearest pound)*

2. Where the court dealing with an offender imposes more than one disposal, for example, a fine in conjunction with a community order, the Surcharge amount should be whichever amount payable is greatest.

3. Transitional provision is made for cases: **SG-339**
    a) where the court deals with an offender for more than one offence, and at least one of these offences was committed before, and at least one other after, 1 October 2012, a Surcharge is payable only if the offender is dealt with by way of a fine, at a flat rate of £15;[185] and
    b) where a court deals with an adult offender for more than one offence, each of which was committed after 1 October 2012, and at least one of those offences was committed when under 18, the Surcharge should be ordered at the rate for under 18s.[186]

4. The Criminal Justice Act 2003 (Surcharge) (No. 2) Order 2007 continues to apply where the court deals with a person for one or more offences, all of which were committed before 1 October 2012. In such cases, the Surcharge will continue to be payable only if the person is dealt with by way of a fine, at a flat rate of £15.

5. Where the offender has the means to pay the financial impositions of the court, there should be no   **SG-340** reduction in compensation or fines whenever the Surcharge is ordered.
    However, when the court:
    • orders the offender to pay both a Surcharge and compensation, but the offender is unable to pay both, the court must reduce the amount of the Surcharge (if necessary to nil);[187] or
    • orders the offender to pay both a fine and a Surcharge, but the offender is unable to pay both, the court may only reduce the amount of the fine.[188]

6. Where the offender does not have sufficient means to pay the total financial penalty considered appropriate by the court, the order of priority is compensation, surcharge, fine, costs.

ANCILLARY ORDERS   **SG-341**

1. There are several ancillary orders available in a magistrates' court which should be considered in appropriate cases. Annex A lists the offences in respect of which certain orders are available [not reproduced]. The individual offence guidelines above also identify ancillary orders particularly likely to be relevant to the offence. In all cases, consult your legal adviser regarding available orders and their specific requirements and effects.

2. Ancillary orders should be taken into account when assessing whether the overall penalty is commensurate with offence seriousness.

Anti-social behaviour orders   **SG-342**

• The court may make an anti-social behaviour order (ASBO) in respect of any person convicted of an offence.[189]
• Before making an order, the court must find that the offender acted in an anti-social manner, i.e. in a manner likely to cause harassment, alarm or distress.
• The court must also consider that the order is necessary to protect the public from further anti-social acts by the offender.
• The order must have effect for at least two years. If the offender is sentenced to custody, the provisions of the order may be suspended until release.
• An ASBO may include only prohibitions; there is no power to impose positive obligations.
• The following is a summary of principles and other considerations relevant to the making of an ASBO in relation to adults and youths taken from the Sentencing Guidelines Council's definitive guideline *Breach of an Anti-Social Behaviour Order* [see **SG-406**]:

---

[185] Criminal Justice Act 2003 (Surcharge) Order 2012, art.7(2)
[186] ibid., art.5(3)
[187] ibid., s.161A(3)
[188] ibid., s.164(4A)
[189] Crime and Disorder Act 1998, s.1C

(1) Proceedings for the imposition of an ASBO are civil in nature, so that hearsay evidence is admissible, but a court must be satisfied to a criminal standard that the individual has acted in the anti-social manner alleged.

(2) The test of 'necessity' requires the exercise of judgement or evaluation; it does not require proof beyond reasonable doubt that the order is 'necessary'.

(3) It is particularly important that the findings of fact giving rise to the making of the order are recorded by the court.

(4) As the ASBO is a preventative order it is unlawful to use it as a punishment; so, when sentencing an offender, a court must not allow itself to be diverted into making an ASBO as an alternative or additional sanction.

(5) The police have powers to arrest an individual for any criminal offence, and the court should not impose an order which prohibits the subject from committing an offence if it will not add significantly to the existing powers of the police to protect others from anti-social behaviour by the subject. An order must not prohibit a criminal offence merely to increase the sentence range available for that offence.

(6) The terms of the order made must be precise and capable of being understood by the subject. Where the subject is aged under 18, it is important for both the subject and the parent or guardian to confirm their understanding of the order and its terms. The prohibitions must be enforceable in the sense that they should allow a breach to be readily identified and capable of being proved.

(7) An order should not impose a 'standard list' of prohibitions, but should identify and prohibit the particular type of anti-social behaviour that gives rise to the necessity of an ASBO. Each separate prohibition must be necessary to protect persons from anti-social behaviour by the subject, and each order must be specifically fashioned to deal with the individual concerned.

(8) The order must be proportionate to the legitimate aim pursued and commensurate with the risk guarded against. The court should avoid making compliance very difficult through the imposition of numerous prohibitions, and those that will cause great disruption to the subject should be considered with particular care. It is advisable to make an order for a specific period; when considering the duration of an order imposed on a youth, the potential for the subject to mature may be a relevant factor.

(9) Not all prohibitions set out in an ASBO have to run for the full term of the ASBO itself. The test must always be what is necessary to deal with the particular anti-social behaviour of the offender and what is proportionate in the circumstances. At least one of the prohibitions must last for the duration of the order but not all are required to last for the 2 years that is the minimum length of an order. The court can vary the terms of an order at any time upon application by the subject (or the applicant in the case of an order made upon application).

(10) When making an order upon conviction, the court has the power to suspend its terms until the offender has been released from a custodial sentence. However, where a custodial sentence of 12 months or more is imposed and the offender is liable to be released on licence and thus subject to recall, an order will not generally be necessary. There might be cases where geographical restraints could supplement licence conditions.

(11) Other considerations:
  (i) Where an ASBO is imposed on a subject aged 10–17, the court must consider whether a Parenting order would be desirable in the interests of preventing repetition of the anti-social behaviour.[190] Such an order *must* be made where the offender is aged under 16 and the condition is met, but is discretionary where the offender is aged 16 or 17.
  (ii) Where a magistrates' court imposes a stand-alone ASBO, it must also consider whether an Individual support order (ISO) would be desirable to tackle the underlying causes of the behaviour.[191]
  (iii) In the case of an adult, the court may make an Intervention order if the underlying causes of the anti-social behaviour are drug-related and appropriate treatment is available.[192]

(12) Interim orders:
  Where a decision to impose an order (either upon application or conviction) is pending, the court may make an interim order if it considers it just to do so.[193] The court must balance the seriousness

[190] Crime and Disorder Act 1998, s.8. The Anti-social Behaviour Act 2003 now provides for a court to impose stand-alone Parenting Orders, if it is satisfied that the child has engaged in criminal or anti-social behaviour. The ASBA also provides for certain agencies to enter into Parenting Contracts which, as an alternative to legal action, have much in common with the nonstatutory Acceptable Behaviour Contracts
[191] ibid., s.1A
[192] ibid., s.1G
[193] ibid., s.1D

of the behaviour and the urgency with which it is necessary to take steps to control it, with the likely impact of an interim order upon the potential subject.[194]

- Further guidance is set out in A Guide for the Judiciary (third edition) January 2007 (supplement January 2008) published by the Judicial Studies Board.[195] Refer also to Anti-Social Behaviour Orders—A Guide to Law and Procedure in the Magistrates' Court published by the Justices' Clerks' Society.[196]

Binding over orders   SG-343

- The court has the power to bind an individual over to keep the peace.[197]
- The order is designed to prevent future misconduct and requires the individual to promise to pay a specified sum if the terms of the order are breached. Exercise of the power does not depend upon conviction.
- Guidance on the making of binding over orders is set out in part III.31 of the Consolidated Criminal Practice Direction, as amended in March 2007. Key principles include:
  (1) before imposing the order, the court must be satisfied beyond reasonable doubt that a breach of the peace involving violence or an imminent threat of violence has occurred, or that there is a real risk of violence in the future. The court should hear evidence and the parties before making any order;
  (2) the court should state its reasons for making the order;
  (3) the order should identify the specific conduct or activity from which the individual must refrain, the length of the order and the amount of the recognisance;
  (4) the length of the order should be proportionate to the harm sought to be avoided and should not generally exceed 12 months;
  (5) when fixing the amount of the recognisance, the court should have regard to the individual's financial resources.

Confiscation orders   SG-344

- Confiscation orders under the Proceeds of Crime Act 2002 may only be made by the Crown Court.
- An offender convicted of an offence in a magistrates' court must be committed to the Crown Court where this is requested by the prosecution with a view to a confiscation order being considered.[198]
- If the committal is made in respect of an either way offence, the court must state whether it would have committed the offender to the Crown Court for sentencing had the issue of a confiscation order not arisen.

Deprivation orders   SG-345

- The court has the power to deprive an offender of property used for the purpose of committing or facilitating the commission of an offence, whether or not it deals with the offender in any other way.[199]
- Before making the order, the court must have regard to the value of the property and the likely financial and other effects on the offender.
- Without limiting the circumstances in which the court may exercise the power, a vehicle is deemed to have been used for the purpose of committing the offence where the offence is punishable by imprisonment and consists of:
  (1) driving, attempting to drive, or being in charge of a motor vehicle;
  (2) failing to provide a specimen; or
  (3) failing to stop and/or report an accident.[200]

Deprivation of ownership of animal   SG-346

- Where an offender is convicted of one of the following offences under the Animal Welfare Act 2006, the court may make an order depriving him or her of ownership of the animal and for its disposal:[201]
  (1) causing unnecessary suffering (s. 4);
  (2) mutilation (s. 5);
  (3) docking of dogs' tails (ss. 6(1) and 6(2));

---

[194] *Leeds Magistrates Court, ex parte Kenny; Secretary of State for Constitutional Affairs and another, ex parte M* [2004] EWCA Civ 312
[195] www.jsboard.co.uk
[196] www.jc-society.com/File/ASBO_updated_GPG_May_2006.pdf
[197] Justices of the Peace Act 1361, Magistrates Court Act 1980, s.115
[198] Proceeds of Crime Act 2002, s.70
[199] Powers of Criminal Courts (Sentencing) Act 2000, s.143
[200] ibid., ss.143(6) and 143(7)
[201] Animal Welfare Act 2006, s.33

(4) fighting etc. (s. 8);

(5) breach of duty to ensure welfare (s. 9);

(6) breach of disqualification order (s. 36(9)).

- The court is required to give reasons if it decides not to make such an order.
- Deprivation of ownership may be ordered instead of or in addition to dealing with the offender in any other way.

SG-347   **Disqualification from ownership of animals**

- Where an offender is convicted of one of the following offences under the Animal Welfare Act 2006, the court may disqualify him or her from owning or keeping animals, dealing in animals, and/or transporting animals:[202]

  (1) causing unnecessary suffering (s. 4);

  (2) mutilation (s. 5);

  (3) docking of dogs' tails (ss. 6(1) and 6(2));

  (4) administration of poisons etc. (s. 7);

  (5) fighting etc. (s. 8);

  (6) breach of duty to ensure welfare (s. 9);

  (7) breach of licensing or registration requirements (s. 13(6));

  (8) breach of disqualification order (s. 36(9)).

- The court is required to give reasons if it decides not to make such an order.
- The court may specify a period during which an offender may not apply for termination of the order under section 43 of the Animal Welfare Act 2006; if no period is specified, an offender may not apply for termination of the order until one year after the order was made.
- Disqualification may be imposed instead of or in addition to dealing with the offender in any other way.

SG-348   **Disqualification orders**

- The court may disqualify any person convicted of an offence from driving for such period as it thinks fit.[203] This may be instead of or in addition to dealing with the offender in any other way.
- The section does not require the offence to be connected to the use of a vehicle. The Court of Appeal has held that the power is available as part of the overall punitive element of a sentence, and the only restrictions on the exercise of the power are those in the statutory provision.[204]

SG-349   **Disqualification of company directors**

- The Company Directors Disqualification Act 1986 empowers the court to disqualify an offender from being a director or taking part in the promotion, formation or management of a company for up to five years.
- An order may be made in two situations:

  (1) where an offender has been convicted of an indictable offence in connection with the promotion, formation, management, liquidation or striking off of a company;[205] or

  (2) where an offender has been convicted of an offence involving a failure to file documents with, or give notice to, the registrar of companies. If the offence is triable only summarily, disqualification can be ordered only where the offender has been the subject of three default orders or convictions in the preceding five years.[206]

SG-350   **Drinking banning orders (when in force)**

- Where an offender is convicted of an offence which was committed while under the influence of alcohol, the court must consider whether a drinking banning order is necessary for the purpose of protecting others from further criminal or disorderly conduct by the offender while he or she is under the influence of alcohol.[207] If the court decides not to make such an order, it must state its reasons.
- A drinking banning order may impose any prohibition on the offender which is necessary for the purpose identified above, and must include such prohibition as the court considers necessary on the offender's entering licensed premises.[208]

---

[202] ibid., s.34

[203] Powers of Criminal Courts (Sentencing) Act 2000, s.146

[204] *R v Sofekun* [2008] EWCA Crim 2035

[205] Company Directors Disqualification Act 1988, s.2

[206] ibid., s.5

[207] Violent Crime Reduction Act 2006, s.6

[208] ibid., s.1

- The court must specify the duration of the order, which must be between two months and two years.[209]
- The court may direct that the order will cease to have effect before the end of the specified period if the offender completes an approved course;[210] consult your legal adviser for guidance on this provision. The court is required to give reasons if it does not include such a direction in the order.

Exclusion orders   SG-351

- The court may make an exclusion order where an offender has been convicted of an offence committed on licensed premises involving the use or threat of violence.
- The order prohibits the offender from entering specified licensed premises without the consent of the licensee.[211]
- The term of the order must be between three months and two years.
- Note that the provisions regarding exclusion orders will be repealed when the power to impose drinking banning orders is brought into force.

Football banning orders   SG-352

- The court must make a football banning order where an offender has been convicted of a relevant offence and it is satisfied that there are reasonable grounds to believe that making a banning order would help to prevent violence or disorder.[212] If the court is not so satisfied, it must state that fact and give its reasons.
- Relevant offences are those set out in schedule 1 [to] the Football Spectators Act 1989…
- The order requires the offender to report to a police station within five days, may require the offender to surrender his or her passport, and may impose requirements on the offender in relation to any regulated football matches.
- Where the order is imposed in addition to a sentence of immediate imprisonment, the term of the order must be between six and ten years. In other cases, the term of the order must be between three and five years.

Forfeiture and destruction of drugs   SG-353

- Where an offender is convicted of an offence under the Misuse of Drugs Act 1971, the court may order forfeiture and destruction of anything shown to the satisfaction of the court to relate to the offence.[213]

Forfeiture and destruction of goods bearing unauthorised trade mark   SG-354

- Where the court is satisfied that an offence under section 92 of the Trade Marks Act 1994 has been committed, it must (on the application of a person who has come into possession of the goods in connection with the investigation or prosecution of the offence) order forfeiture of the goods.[214]
- If it considers it appropriate, instead of ordering destruction of the goods, the court may direct that they be released to a specified person on condition that the offending sign is erased, removed or obliterated.

Forfeiture or suspension of liquor licence   SG-355

- Where an offender who holds a personal licence to supply alcohol is charged with a 'relevant offence', he or she is required to produce the licence to the court, or inform the court of its existence, no later than his or her first appearance.
- 'Relevant offences' are listed in schedule 4 of the Licensing Act 2003…
- Where the offender is convicted, the court may order forfeiture of the licence or suspend it for up to six months.[215] When deciding whether to order forfeiture or suspension, the court may take account of the offender's previous convictions for 'relevant offences'.[216]
- Whether or not forfeiture or suspension is ordered, the court is required to notify the licensing authority of the offender's conviction and the sentence imposed.

Parenting orders   SG-356

- The court may make a parenting order where an offender has been convicted of an offence under section 444 of the Education Act 1996 (failing to secure regular attendance at school) and the court is

---

[209] ibid., s.2
[210] ibid., ss.2(3)–(8)
[211] Licensed Premises (Exclusion of Certain Persons) Act 1980, s.1
[212] Football Spectators Act 1989, s.14A
[213] Misuse of Drugs Act 1971, s.27(1)
[214] Trade Marks Act 1994, s.97
[215] Licensing Act 2003, s.129(2)
[216] ibid., s.129(3)

satisfied that the order would be desirable in the interests of preventing the commission of any further offence under that section.[217]

- The order may impose such requirements that the court considers desirable in the interests of preventing the commission of a further offence under section 444.
- A requirement to attend a counselling or guidance programme may be included only if the offender has been the subject of a parenting order on a previous occasion.
- The term of the order must not exceed 12 months.

SG-357   Restitution orders

- Where goods have been stolen and an offender is convicted of any offence with reference to theft of those goods, the court may make a restitution order.[218]
- The court may:
  (1) order anyone in possession or control of the stolen goods to restore them to the victim;
  (2) on the application of the victim, order that goods directly or indirectly representing the stolen goods (as being the proceeds of any disposal or realisation of the stolen goods) be transferred to the victim; or
  (3) order that a sum not exceeding the value of the stolen goods be paid to the victim out of any money taken out of the offender's possession on his or her apprehension.

SG-358   Restraining orders

- Where an offender is convicted of harassment or conduct causing fear of violence, the court may make a restraining order.[219]
- The order may prohibit the offender from doing anything for the purpose of protecting the victim of the offence, or any other person mentioned in the order, from further conduct which amounts to harassment or will cause a fear of violence.[220]
- The order may have effect for a specified period or until further order.[221]
- When in force, section 5A of the Protection from Harassment Act 1997 will enable the court to make a restraining order in respect of an offender who has been acquitted of an offence if the court considers that it is necessary to protect a person from harassment. Consult your legal adviser for guidance.

SG-359   Sexual offences prevention orders

- The court may make a sexual offences prevention order where it deals with an offender in respect of an offence listed in schedules 3 or 5 [to] the Sexual Offences Act 2003...
- The court must be satisfied that the order is necessary to protect others from 'serious sexual harm' from the offender; the prohibitions in the order must also be necessary for this purpose.
- 'Serious sexual harm' means serious physical or psychological harm caused by the offender committing an offence listed in schedule 3 [to] the Sexual Offences Act 2003.
- The order may include only negative prohibitions; there is no power to impose positive obligations.
- The order must have effect for at least five years.

SG-360   Costs

1. Where an offender is convicted of an offence, the court has discretion to make such order as to costs as it considers just and reasonable.[222]
2. The Court of Appeal has given the following guidance:[223]
   - an order for costs should never exceed the sum which, having regard to the offender's means and any other financial order imposed, he or she is able to pay and which it is reasonable to order him or her to pay;
   - an order for costs should never exceed the sum which the prosecutor actually and reasonably incurred;
   - the purpose of the order is to compensate the prosecutor. Where the conduct of the defence has put the prosecutor to avoidable expense, the offender may be ordered to pay some or all of that sum to the prosecutor but the offender must not be punished for exercising the right to defend himself or herself;

---

[217] Crime and Disorder Act 1998, s.8
[218] Powers of Criminal Courts (Sentencing) Act 2000, s.148
[219] Protection from Harassment Act 1997, s.5
[220] ibid., s.5(2)
[221] ibid., s.5(3)
[222] Prosecution of Offences Act 1985, s.18
[223] *R v Northallerton Magistrates' Court, ex parte Dove* [2000] 1 Cr App R (S) 136 (CA)

- the costs ordered to be paid should not be grossly disproportionate to any fine imposed for the offence. This principle was affirmed in *BPS Advertising Limited v London Borough of Barnet*[224] in which the Court held that, while there is no question of an arithmetical relationship, the question of costs should be viewed in the context of the maximum penalty considered by Parliament to be appropriate for the seriousness of the offence;
- if the combined total of the proposed fine and the costs sought by the prosecutor exceeds the sum which the offender could reasonably be ordered to pay, the costs order should be reduced rather than the fine;
- it is for the offender to provide details of his or her financial position so as to enable the court to assess what he or she can reasonably afford to pay. If the offender fails to do so, the court is entitled to draw reasonable inferences as to means from all the circumstances of the case;
- if the court proposes to make any financial order against the offender, it must give him or her fair opportunity to adduce any relevant financial information and to make appropriate submissions.

3. A costs award may cover the costs of investigation as well as prosecution. However, where the investigation was carried out as part of a council officer's routine duties, for which he or she would have been paid in the normal way, this is a relevant factor to be taken into account when deciding the appropriate amount of any costs order.[225]

4. Where the court wishes to impose costs in addition to a fine, compensation and/or the victim surcharge but the offender has insufficient resources to pay the total amount, the order of priority is:
   i)   compensation;
   ii) victim surcharge;
   iii) fine;
   iv) costs.

Deferred Sentences   SG-361

1. The court is empowered to defer passing sentence for up to six months.[226] The court may impose any conditions during the period of deferment that it considers appropriate. These could be specific requirements as set out in the provisions for community sentences, or requirements that are drawn more widely. The purpose of deferment is to enable the court to have regard to the offender's conduct after conviction or any change in his or her circumstances, including the extent to which the offender has complied with any requirements imposed by the court.

2. Three conditions must be satisfied before sentence can be deferred:
   - the offender must consent;
   - the offender must undertake to comply with requirements imposed by the court; and
   - the court must be satisfied that deferment is in the interests of justice.

3. Guidance regarding deferred sentences is set out in the Sentencing Guidelines Council's definitive guideline *New Sentences: Criminal Justice Act 2003*, published 16 December 2004 [see **part 2**]. The guideline emphasises that:
   - deferred sentences will be appropriate in very limited circumstances;
   - deferred sentences are likely to be relevant predominantly in a small group of cases close to either the community or custodial sentence threshold where, should the offender be prepared to adapt his behaviour in a way clearly specified by the sentencer, the court may be prepared to impose a lesser sentence;
   - sentencers should impose specific and measurable conditions that do not involve a serious restriction on liberty;
   - the court should give a clear indication of the type of sentence it would have imposed if it had decided not to defer;
   - the court should also ensure that the offender understands the consequences of failure to comply with the court's wishes during the deferment period.

4. If the offender fails to comply with any requirement imposed in connection with the deferment, or commits another offence, he or she can be brought back to court before the end of the deferment period and the court can proceed to sentence.

---

[224] [2006] EWCA 3335 (Admin) QBD
[225] ibid.
[226] Powers of Criminal Courts (Sentencing) Act 2000, s.1 as amended by Criminal Justice Act 2003, s.278 and sch.23, para.1

SG-362   Offences Committed in a Domestic Context

1. When sentencing an offence committed in a domestic context, refer to the Sentencing Guidelines Council's definitive guideline *Overarching Principles: Domestic Violence*, published 7 December 2006 [see **SG-51**]. The guideline emphasises that:
   - as a starting point for sentence, offences committed in a domestic context should be regarded as no less serious than offences committed in a non-domestic context;
   - many offences of violence in a domestic context are dealt with in a magistrates' court as an offence of common assault or assault occasioning actual bodily harm because the injuries sustained are relatively minor. Offences involving serious violence will warrant a custodial sentence in the majority of cases;
   - a number of aggravating factors may commonly arise by virtue of the offence being committed in a domestic context (see list below);
   - since domestic violence takes place within the context of a current or past relationship, the history of the relationship will often be relevant in assessing the gravity of the offence. A court is entitled to take into account anything occurring within the relationship as a whole, which may reveal relevant aggravating or mitigating factors;
   - in respect of an offence of violence in a domestic context, an offender's good character in relation to conduct outside the home should generally be of no relevance where there is a proven pattern of behaviour;
   - assertions that the offence has been provoked by conduct of the victim need to be treated with great care, both in determining whether they have a factual basis and in considering whether the circumstances of the alleged conduct amounts to provocation sufficient to mitigate the seriousness of the offence;
   - where the custody threshold is only just crossed, so that if a custodial sentence is imposed it will be a short sentence, the court will wish to consider whether the better option is a suspended sentence order or a community order, including in either case a requirement to attend an accredited domestic violence programme. Such an option will only be appropriate where the court is satisfied that the offender genuinely intends to reform his or her behaviour and that there is a real prospect of rehabilitation being successful. Such a situation is unlikely to arise where there has been a pattern of abuse.

   Refer to paragraphs 4.1 to 4.4 of the Council guideline [at **SG-55**] for guidance regarding the relevance of the victim's wishes [as] to sentence.

Aggravating factors

2. The following aggravating factors may be of particular relevance to offences committed in a domestic context and should be read alongside the general factors set out [elsewhere]:
   Factors indicating higher culpability
   1. Abuse of trust and abuse of power
   2. Using contact arrangements with a child to instigate an offence
   3. Proven history of violence or threats by the offender in a domestic setting
   4. History of disobedience to court orders
   Factors indicating a greater degree of harm
   1. Victim is particularly vulnerable
   2. Impact on children

SG-363   Aggravation Related To Race, Religion, Disability, Sexual Orientation, or Transgender Identity[227]

SG-364   **Racial or religious aggravation—statutory provisions**

1. Sections 29 to 32 of the Crime and Disorder Act 1998 create specific racially or religiously aggravated offences, which have higher maximum penalties than the non-aggravated versions of those offences. The individual offence guidelines indicate whether there is a specifically aggravated form of the offence.

2. An offence is racially or religiously aggravated for the purposes of sections 29–32 of the Act if the offender demonstrates hostility towards the victim based on his or her membership (or presumed membership) of a racial or religious group, or if the offence is racially or religiously motivated.[228]

---

[227] In respect of the guidance in paragraphs 5–9 below, courts must treat transgender identity as an aggravating factor under s.146 of the Criminal Justice Act 2003 only upon implementation of s.65 of the Legal Aid, Sentencing and Punishment of Offenders Act 2012

[228] Crime and Disorder Act 1988, s.28

3. For all other offences, section 145 of the Criminal Justice Act 2003 provides that the court must regard racial or religious aggravation as an aggravating factor.

4. The court should not treat an offence as racially or religiously aggravated for the purposes of section 145 where a racially or religiously aggravated form of the offence was charged but resulted in an acquittal.[229] The court should not normally treat an offence as racially or religiously aggravated if a racially or religiously aggravated form of the offence was available but was not charged.[230] Consult your legal adviser for further guidance in these situations.

Aggravation related to disability, sexual orientation or transgender identity—statutory provisions   SG-365

5. Under section 146 of the Criminal Justice Act 2003, the court must treat as an aggravating factor the fact that:
   - an offender demonstrated hostility towards the victim based on his or her disability, sexual orientation or transgender identity (or presumed disability, sexual orientation or transgender identity); or
   - the offence was motivated by hostility towards persons who have a particular disability, who are of a particular sexual orientation or who are transgender.

Approach to sentencing   SG-366

6. A court should not conclude that offending involved aggravation related to race, religion, disability, sexual orientation or transgender identity without first putting the offender on notice and allowing him or her to challenge the allegation.

7. When sentencing any offence where such aggravation is found to be present, the following approach should be followed. This applies both to the specific racially or religiously aggravated offences under the Crime and Disorder Act 1998 and to offences which are regarded as aggravated under section 145 or 146 of the Criminal Justice Act 2003:[231]
   - sentencers should first determine the appropriate sentence, leaving aside the element of aggravation related to race, religion, disability, sexual orientation or transgender identity but taking into account all other aggravating or mitigating factors;
   - the sentence should then be increased to take account of the aggravation related to race, religion, disability, sexual orientation or transgender identity;
   - the increase may mean that a more onerous penalty of the same type is appropriate, or that the threshold for a more severe type of sentence is passed;
   - the sentencer must state in open court that the offence was aggravated by reason of race, religion, disability, sexual orientation or transgender identity;
   - the sentencer should state what the sentence would have been without that element of aggravation.

8. The extent to which the sentence is increased will depend on the seriousness of the aggravation. The following factors could be taken as indicating a high level of aggravation:

Offender's intention   SG-367

   - The element of aggravation based on race, religion, disability, sexual orientation or transgender identity was planned
   - The offence was part of a pattern of offending by the offender
   - The offender was a member of, or was associated with, a group promoting hostility based on race, religion, disability, sexual orientation or transgender identity
   - The incident was deliberately set up to be offensive or humiliating to the victim or to the group of which the victim is a member

Impact on the victim or others   SG-368

   - The offence was committed in the victim's home
   - The victim was providing a service to the public
   - The timing or location of the offence was calculated to maximise the harm or distress it caused
   - The expressions of hostility were repeated or prolonged
   - The offence caused fear and distress throughout a local community or more widely
   - The offence caused particular distress to the victim and/or the victim's family.

9. At the lower end of the scale, the aggravation may be regarded as less serious if:
   - It was limited in scope or duration
   - The offence was not motivated by hostility on the basis of race, religion, disability, sexual orientation or transgender identity, and the element of hostility or abuse was minor or incidental

---

[229]   Refer to *R v McGillivray* [2005] EWCA Crim 604 (CA)
[230]   Refer to *R v O'Callaghan* [2005] EWCA Crim 317 (CA)
[231]   Refer to *R v Kelly and Donnelly* [2001] EWCA Crim 170 in which the Court considered the approach to sentencing in cases involving racial or religious aggravation

Sentencing Guidelines

10. In these guidelines, the specific racially or religiously aggravated offences under the Crime and Disorder Act 1998 are addressed on the same page as the 'basic offence'; the starting points and ranges indicated on the guideline relate to the 'basic' (i.e. non-aggravated) offence. The increase for the element of racial or religious aggravation may result in a sentence above the range; this will not constitute a departure from the guideline for which reasons must be given.

SG-369

ENVIRONMENTAL/HEALTH AND SAFETY OFFENCES

[Omitted.]

SG-370

ROAD TRAFFIC OFFENCES

SG-371 **Disqualification**

Obligatory disqualification

1. Some offences carry obligatory disqualification for a minimum of 12 months.[232] The minimum period is automatically increased where there have been certain previous convictions and disqualifications.

2. An offender must be disqualified for *at least two years* if he or she has been disqualified two or more times for a period of at least 56 days in the three years preceding the commission of the offence.[233] The following disqualifications are to be disregarded for the purposes of this provision:
   • interim disqualification;
   • disqualification where vehicle used for the purpose of crime;
   • disqualification for stealing or taking a vehicle or going equipped to steal or take a vehicle.

3. An offender must be disqualified for *at least three years* if he or she is convicted of one of the following offences *and* has within the ten years preceding the commission of the offence been convicted of any of these offences:[234]
   • causing death by careless driving when under the influence of drink or drugs;
   • driving or attempting to drive while unfit;
   • driving or attempting to drive with excess alcohol;
   • failing to provide a specimen (drive/attempting to drive).

4. The individual offence guidelines above indicate whether disqualification is mandatory for the offence and the applicable minimum period. Consult your legal adviser for further guidance.

5. The period of disqualification may be reduced or avoided if there are special reasons.[235] These must relate to the offence; circumstances peculiar to the offender cannot constitute special reasons.[236] The Court of Appeal has established that, to constitute a special reason, a matter must:[237]
   • be a mitigating or extenuating circumstance;
   • not amount in law to a defence to the charge;
   • be directly connected with the commission of the offence;
   • be one which the court ought properly to take into consideration when imposing sentence.

6. Consult your legal adviser for further guidance on special reasons applications.

'Totting up' disqualification

7. Disqualification for a *minimum* of six months must be ordered if an offender incurs 12 penalty points or more within a three-year period.[238] The minimum period may be automatically increased if the offender has been disqualified within the preceding three years. Totting up disqualifications, unlike other disqualifications, erase all penalty points.

8. The period of a totting up disqualification can be reduced or avoided for exceptional hardship or other mitigating circumstances. No account is to be taken of hardship that is not exceptional hardship or circumstances alleged to make the offence not serious. Any circumstances taken into account in the preceding three years to reduce or avoid a totting disqualification must be disregarded.[239]

9. Consult your legal adviser for further guidance on exceptional hardship applications.

---

[232] Road Traffic Offenders Act 1988, s.34
[233] ibid., s.34(4)
[234] ibid., s.34(3)
[235] ibid., s.34(1)
[236] *Whittal v Kirby* [1946] 2 All ER 552 (CA)
[237] *R v Wickens* (1958) 42 Cr App R 436 (CA)
[238] Road Traffic Offenders Act 1988, s.35
[239] ibid.

Discretionary disqualification

10. Whenever an offender is convicted of an endorsable offence or of taking a vehicle without consent, the court has a discretionary power to disqualify instead of imposing penalty points. The individual offence guidelines above indicate whether the offence is endorsable and the number or range of penalty points it carries.

11. The number of variable points or the period of disqualification should reflect the seriousness of the offence. Some of the individual offence guidelines above include penalty points and/or periods of disqualification in the sentence starting points and ranges; however, the court is not precluded from sentencing outside the range where the facts justify it. Where a disqualification is for less than 56 days, there are some differences in effect compared with disqualification for a longer period; in particular, the licence will automatically come back into effect at the end of the disqualification period (instead of requiring application by the driver) and the disqualification is not taken into account for the purpose of increasing subsequent obligatory periods of disqualification.[240]

12. In some cases in which the court is considering discretionary disqualification, the offender may already have sufficient penalty points on his or her licence that he or she would be liable to a 'totting up' disqualification if further points were imposed. In these circumstances, the court should impose penalty points rather than discretionary disqualification so that the minimum totting up disqualification period applies (see paragraph 7 above).

Disqualification until a test is passed

13. Where an offender is convicted of dangerous driving, the court must order disqualification until an extended driving test is passed.

14. The court has discretion to disqualify until a test is passed where an offender is convicted of any endorsable offence.[241] Where disqualification is obligatory, the extended test applies. In other cases, it will be the ordinary test.

15. An offender disqualified as a 'totter' under the penalty points provisions may also be ordered to re-take a driving test; in this case, the extended test applies.

16. The discretion to order a re-test is likely to be exercised where there is evidence of inexperience, incompetence or infirmity, or the disqualification period is lengthy (that is, the offender is going to be 'off the road' for a considerable time).

Reduced period of disqualification for completion of rehabilitation course

17. Where an offender is disqualified for 12 months or more in respect of an alcohol-related driving offence, the court may order that the period of disqualification will be reduced if the offender satisfactorily completes an approved rehabilitation course.[242]

18. Before offering an offender the opportunity to attend a course, the court must be satisfied that an approved course is available and must inform the offender of the effect of the order, the fees that the offender is required to pay, and when he or she must pay them.

19. The court should also explain that the offender may be required to satisfy the Secretary of State that he or she does not have a drink problem and is fit to drive before the offender's licence will be returned at the end of the disqualification period.[243]

20. In general, a court should consider offering the opportunity to attend a course to all offenders convicted of a relevant offence for the first time. The court should be willing to consider offering an offender the opportunity to attend a second course where it considers there are good reasons. It will not usually be appropriate to give an offender the opportunity to attend a third course.

21. The reduction must be at least three months but cannot be more than one quarter of the total period of disqualification:
    - a period of 12 months disqualification must be reduced to nine months;
    - in other cases, a reduction of one week should be made for every month of the disqualification so that, for example, a disqualification of 24 months will be reduced by 24 weeks.

22. When it makes the order, the court must specify a date for completion of the course which is at least two months before the end of the reduced period of disqualification.

---

[240] ibid., ss.34(4), 35(2), 37(1A)
[241] ibid., s.36(4)
[242] Road Traffic Offenders Act 1988, s.34A
[243] Road Traffic Act 1988, s.94 and Motor Vehicles (Driving Licences) Regulations 1999, reg.74

Disqualification in the offender's absence

23. When considering disqualification in absence the starting point should be that disqualification in absence should be imposed if there is no reason to believe the defendant is not aware of the proceedings, and after the statutory notice has been served pursuant to section 11(4) of the 1980 Act[244] where appropriate. Disqualification should not be imposed in absence where there is evidence that the defendant has an acceptable reason for not attending or where there are reasons to believe it would be contrary to the interests of justice to do so.

SG-372 New drivers

24. Drivers who incur six points or more during the two-year probationary period after passing the driving test will have their licence revoked automatically by the Secretary of State; they will be able to drive only after application for a provisional licence pending the passing of a further test.[245]

25. An offender liable for an endorsement which will cause the licence to be revoked under the new drivers' provisions may ask the court to disqualify rather than impose points. This will avoid the requirement to take a further test. Generally, this would be inappropriate since it would circumvent the clear intention of Parliament.

SG-373 [Material on dangerous offenders — no longer included in the Guideline.]

SG-374 INFORMAL WARNINGS, CANNABIS WARNINGS AND SIMPLE CAUTIONS

1. There are several alternatives to formal charges available to police, including informal warnings, cannabis warnings and simple cautions.

2. A cannabis warning may be given where the offender is found in possession of a small amount of cannabis consistent with personal use and the offender admits the elements of the offence.

3. A simple caution may be issued where there is evidence that the offender has committed an offence, the offender admits to the offence, and the offender agrees to being given the caution.

4. When sentencing an offender who has received a warning or simple caution on a previous occasion:
   - the warning or simple caution is not a previous conviction and, therefore, is not a statutory aggravating factor;
   - the earlier warning or simple caution does not increase the seriousness of the current offence.

SG-375 CONDITIONAL CAUTIONS

1. The Criminal Justice Act 2003 empowers the Crown Prosecution Service to issue a conditional caution, which requires an offender to comply with rehabilitative and/or reparative conditions, as an alternative to prosecution. Before the caution can be given, the offender must admit the offence and consent to the conditions.

Approach to sentencing for offence for which offender was cautioned but failed to comply with conditions

2. If the offender fails, without reasonable cause, to comply with the conditional caution, he or she may be prosecuted for the original offence. When sentencing in such a case:
   - the offender's non-compliance with the conditional caution does not increase the seriousness of the original offence and must not be regarded as an aggravating factor;
   - the offender's non-compliance may be relevant to selection of the type of sentence. For example, it may indicate that it is inappropriate to include certain requirements as part of a community order. The circumstances of the offender's failure to satisfy the conditions, and any partial compliance, will be relevant to this assessment.

Approach to sentencing for later offence where offender has had a previous conditional caution

3. When sentencing an offender who has received a conditional caution in respect of an earlier offence:
   - a conditional caution is not a previous conviction and, therefore, is not a statutory aggravating factor;
   - the earlier conditional caution does not increase the level of seriousness of the current offence;
   - nevertheless, the offender's response to the caution may properly influence the court's assessment of the offender's suitability for a particular sentence, so long as it remains within the limits established by the seriousness of the current offence.

---

[244] Magistrates' Courts Act 1980, s.11(4)
[245] Road Traffic (New Drivers) Act 1995

PENALTY NOTICES—FIXED PENALTY NOTICES AND PENALTY NOTICES FOR DISORDER   **SG-376**

1.   Penalty notices may be issued as an alternative to prosecution in respect of a range of offences. Unlike conditional cautions, an admission of guilt is not a prerequisite to issuing a penalty notice.

2.   An offender who is issued with a penalty notice may nevertheless be prosecuted for the offence if he or she:
   • asks to be tried for the offence;
   • fails to pay the penalty within the period stipulated in the notice and the prosecutor decides to proceed with charges.[246]

Approach to sentencing for offence for which penalty notice was available

3.   When sentencing in cases in which a penalty notice was available:
   • the fact that the offender did not take advantage of the penalty (whether that was by requesting a hearing or failing to pay within the specified timeframe) does not increase the seriousness of the offence and must not be regarded as an aggravating factor. The appropriate sentence must be determined in accordance with the sentencing principles set out above (including the amount of any fine, which must take an offender's financial circumstances into account), disregarding the availability of the penalty;
   • where a penalty notice was not offered or taken up for reasons unconnected with the offence itself, such as administrative difficulties, the starting point should be a fine equivalent to the amount of the penalty and no order of costs should be imposed. The offender should not be disadvantaged by the unavailability of the penalty notice in these circumstances. A list of offences for which penalty notices are available, and the amount of the penalty, is set out in Annex B.

Approach to sentencing for later offence where offender has had previous penalty notices

4.   The fact that an offender has previously been issued with a penalty notice does not increase the seriousness of the current offence and must not be regarded as an aggravating factor. It may, however, properly influence the court's assessment of the offender's suitability for a particular sentence, so long as it remains within the limits established by the seriousness of the current offence.

PRE-SENTENCE REPORTS   **SG-377**

1.   The purpose of a pre-sentence report ('PSR') is to provide information to help the court decide on the most suitable sentence. In relation to an offender aged 18 or over, unless the court considers a report to be unnecessary, it is required to request a report before deciding:
   • that the community or custody threshold is passed;
   • what is the shortest term of a custodial sentence that is commensurate with the seriousness of the offence;
   • whether the restrictions on liberty within a community order are commensurate with the seriousness of the offence; and
   • whether the requirements are suitable for the offender.[247]

2.   A report should not normally be requested where the court considers that it is appropriate to impose a fine.

3.   A report may be oral or written.

4.   Written reports may be either:

Fast delivery reports ('FDR')   **SG-378**
   • Completed without a full OASys assessment.
   • Where community orders are being considered, generally appropriate for low or medium seriousness cases and may be appropriate in some high seriousness cases.
   • Should normally be available within 24 hours.

Standard delivery reports ('SDR')   **SG-379**
   • Based on a full OASys assessment.
   • Generally appropriate where a custodial sentence is being considered, although in some straightforward cases a fast delivery PSR may be sufficient.
   • Where community orders are being considered, generally appropriate for high seriousness cases.
   • Should normally be available within 15 working days; 10 working days if the offender is in custody.

---

[246] In some cases of non-payment, the penalty is automatically registered and enforceable as a fine without need for recourse to the courts. This procedure applies to penalty notices for disorder and fixed penalty notices issued in respect of certain road traffic offences but not to fixed penalty notices issued for most other criminal offences

[247] Criminal Justice Act 2003, ss.156(3) and 156(4)

Probation staff are able to determine the most appropriate type of report based on the circumstances of the case and the requirements of the court.

5. Every report should contain:[248]
    - basic facts about the offender and the sources used to prepare the report;
    - an offence analysis;
    - an assessment of the offender;
    - an assessment of the risk of harm to the public and the likelihood of re-offending;
    - a sentencing proposal.

SG-380   VICTIM PERSONAL STATEMENTS

1. Victim personal statements give victims a formal opportunity to say how a crime has affected them. Where the victim has chosen to make such a statement, a court should consider and take it into account prior to passing sentence.

2. The Consolidated Criminal Practice Direction (as amended March 2007) emphasises that:
    - evidence of the effects of an offence on the victim must be in the form of a witness statement under section 9 of the Criminal Justice Act 1967 or an expert's report;
    - the statement must be served on the defence prior to sentence;
    - except where inferences can properly be drawn from the nature of or circumstances surrounding the offence, the court must not make assumptions unsupported by evidence about the effects of an offence on the victim;
    - the court must pass what it judges to be the appropriate sentence having regard to the circumstances of the offence and the offender, taking into account, so far as the court considers it appropriate, the consequences to the victim;
    - the opinions of the victim or the victim's close relatives as to what the sentence should be are not relevant.

3. For cases involving sexual offences, see also page 165 regarding the relevance of the victim's views to any compensation order that may be imposed.

SG-381   ANNEX A: AVAILABILITY OF ANCILLARY ORDERS

[Annex A consists of a list of offences covered in the MCSG for which particular ancillary orders are available and is omitted. For guidance on the various available ancillary orders, see the relevant material in the main work.]

SG-382   ANNEX B: OFFENCES FOR WHICH PENALTY NOTICES ARE AVAILABLE

The tables below list the offences covered in the MCSG for which penalty notices are available and the amount of the penalty. Consult your legal adviser for further guidance.

SG-383   **Penalty notices for disorder**

Offence	Legislation	Amount
Criminal damage (where damage under £500 in value, and not normally where damage over £300)	Criminal Damage Act 1971, s.1	£80
Disorderly behaviour	Public Order Act 1986, s.5	£80
Drunk and disorderly	Criminal Justice Act 1967, s.91	£80
Sale of alcohol to drunk person on relevant premises (not including off-licenses)	Licensing Act 2003, s.141	£80
Sale of alcohol to person under 18 (staff only; licensees should be subject of a summons)	Licensing Act 2003, s.146	£80
Theft from a shop (where goods under £200 in value, and not normally where goods over £100)	Theft Act 1968, s.1	£80

---

[248] Probation Bench Handbook (2005)

Fixed penalty notices

Offence	Legislation	Amount	Penalty points
Brakes, steering or tyres defective	Road Traffic Act 1988, s.41A	£60	3
Breach of other construction and use requirements	Road Traffic Act 1988, s.42	£60	3
Driving other than in accordance with licence	Road Traffic Act 1988, s.87(1)	£60	3
Failing to comply with police officer signal	Road Traffic Act 1988, s.35	£30	3
Failing to comply with traffic sign	Road Traffic Act 1988, s.36	£60	3
Failing to supply details of driver's identity	Road Traffic Act 1988, s.172	£120	6
No insurance	Road Traffic Act 1988, s.143	£200	6
No test certificate	Road Traffic Act 1988, s.47	£30	–
Overloading/exceeding axle weight	Road Traffic Act 1988, s.41B	£30	–
Pelican/zebra crossing contravention	Road Traffic Regulation Act 1984, s.25(5)	£60	3
Railway fare evasion (where penalty notice scheme in operation by train operator)	Railways (Penalty Fares) Regulations 1994	£20 or twice the full single fare to next stop, whichever is greater	–
Seat belt offences	Road Traffic Act 1988, s.14	£30	–
School non-attendance	Education Act 1996, s.444(1)	£50 if paid within 28 days; £100 if paid within 42 days	–
Speeding	Road Traffic Regulation Act 1984, s.89(1)	£60	3
Using hand-held mobile phone while driving	Road Traffic Act 1988, s.41D	£60	3
Using vehicle in dangerous condition	Road Traffic Act 1988, s.40A	£60	3

PART 13   CAUSING DEATH BY DRIVING

FOREWORD

…This guideline applies to the sentencing of offenders convicted of any of the offences dealt with herein who are sentenced on or after **4 August 2008**.

This guideline applies only to the sentencing of offenders aged 18 and older. The legislative provisions relating to the sentencing of youths are different; the younger the age, the greater the difference. A separate guideline setting out general principles relating to the sentencing of youths is planned.

…

Introduction

1. This guideline applies to the four offences of *causing death by dangerous driving, causing death by driving under the influence of alcohol or drugs, causing death by careless driving and causing death by driving: unlicensed, disqualified or uninsured drivers.*
2. The Crown Prosecution Service's *Policy for Prosecuting Cases of Bad Driving* sets out the approach for prosecutors when considering the appropriate charge based on an assessment of the standard of the offender's driving. This has been taken into account when formulating this guideline. Annex A sets out the statutory definitions for dangerous, careless and inconsiderate driving together with examples of the types of driving behaviour likely to result in the charge of one offence rather than another.

3. Because the principal harm done by these offences (the death of a person) is an element of the offence, the factor that primarily determines the starting point for sentence is the culpability of the offender. Accordingly, for all offences other than *causing death by driving: unlicensed, disqualified or uninsured drivers*, the central feature should be an evaluation of the quality of the driving involved and the degree of danger that it foreseeably created. These guidelines draw a distinction between those factors of an offence that are intrinsic to the quality of driving (referred to as 'determinants of seriousness') and those which, while they aggravate the offence, are not.

4. The levels of seriousness in the guidelines for those offences based on dangerous or careless driving alone have been determined by reference *only* to determinants of seriousness. Aggravating factors will have the effect of either increasing the starting point within the sentencing range provided or, in certain circumstances, of moving the offence up to the next sentencing range. The outcome will depend on both the number of aggravating factors present and the potency of those factors. Thus, the same outcome could follow from the presence of one particularly bad aggravating factor or two or more less serious factors.

5. The determinants of seriousness likely to be relevant in relation to *causing death by careless driving under the influence* are both the degree of carelessness and the level of intoxication. The guideline sets out an approach to assessing both those aspects but giving greater weight to the degree of intoxication since Parliament has provided for a maximum of 14 years imprisonment rather than the maximum of 5 years where the death is caused by careless driving only.

6. Since there will be no allegation of bad driving, the guideline for *causing death by driving; unlicensed, disqualified or uninsured drivers* links the assessment of offender culpability to the nature of the prohibition on the offender's driving and includes a list of factors that may aggravate an offence.

7. The degree to which an aggravating factor is present (and its interaction with any other aggravating and mitigating factors) will be immensely variable and the court is best placed to judge the appropriate impact on sentence. Clear identification of those factors relating to the standard of driving as the initial determinants of offence seriousness is intended to assist the adoption of a common approach.

SG-387   **A. Assessing seriousness**

(i) Determinants of seriousness

8. There are five factors that may be regarded as determinants of offence seriousness, each of which can be demonstrated in a number of ways. Common examples of each of the determinants are set out below and key issues are discussed in the text that follows…

Examples of the determinants are:
- *Awareness of risk*
  - (a) a prolonged, persistent and deliberate course of very bad driving

- *Effect of alcohol or drugs*
  - (b) consumption of alcohol above the legal limit
  - (c) consumption of alcohol at or below the legal limit where this impaired the offender's ability to drive
  - (d) failure to supply a specimen for analysis
  - (e) consumption of illegal drugs, where this impaired the offender's ability to drive
  - (f) consumption of legal drugs or medication where this impaired the offender's ability to drive (including legal medication known to cause drowsiness) where the driver knew, or should have known, about the likelihood of impairment

- *Inappropriate speed of vehicle*
  - (g) greatly excessive speed; racing; competitive driving against another vehicle
  - (h) driving above the speed limit
  - (i) driving at a speed that is inappropriate for the prevailing road or weather conditions
  - (j) driving a PSV, HGV or other goods vehicle at a speed that is inappropriate either because of the nature of the vehicle or its load, especially when carrying passengers

- *Seriously culpable behaviour of offender*
  - (k) aggressive driving (such as driving much too close to the vehicle in front, persistent inappropriate attempts to overtake, or cutting in after overtaking)
  - (l) driving while using a hand-held mobile phone
  - (m) driving whilst the driver's attention is avoidably distracted, for example by reading or adjusting the controls of electronic equipment such as a radio, hands-free mobile phone or satellite navigation equipment
  - (n) driving when knowingly suffering from a medical or physical condition that significantly impairs the offender's driving skills, including failure to take prescribed medication

     (o) driving when knowingly deprived of adequate sleep or rest, especially where commercial concerns had a bearing on the commission of the offence

     (p) driving a poorly maintained or dangerously loaded vehicle, especially where commercial concerns had a bearing on the commission of the offence

  • *Victim*

     (q) failing to have proper regard to vulnerable road users

9. Issues relating to the determinants of seriousness are considered below.

(a) Alcohol/drugs

10. For those offences where the presence of alcohol or drugs is not an element of the offence, where there is sufficient evidence of driving impairment attributable to alcohol or drugs, the consumption of alcohol or drugs prior to driving will make an offence more serious. Where the drugs were legally purchased or prescribed, the offence will only be regarded as more serious if the offender knew or should have known that the drugs were likely to impair driving ability.

11. Unless inherent in the offence or charged separately, failure to provide a specimen for analysis (or to allow a blood specimen taken without consent to be analysed) should be regarded as a determinant of offence seriousness.

12. Where it is established to the satisfaction of the court that an offender had consumed alcohol or drugs unwittingly before driving, that may be regarded as a mitigating factor. However, consideration should be given to the circumstances in which the offender decided to drive or continue to drive when driving ability was impaired.

(b) Avoidable distractions

13. A distinction has been drawn between **ordinary** avoidable distractions and those that are more significant because they divert the attention of the driver for longer periods or to a greater extent; in this guideline these are referred to as a **gross** avoidable distraction. The guideline for causing *death by dangerous driving* provides for a gross avoidable distraction to place the offence in a higher level of seriousness.

14. Any avoidable distraction will make an offence more serious but the degree to which an offender's driving will be impaired will vary. Where the reaction to the distraction is significant, it may be the factor that determines whether the offence is based on *dangerous* driving or on *careless* driving; in those circumstances, care must be taken to avoid 'double counting'.

15. Using a hand-held mobile phone when driving is, in itself, an unlawful act; the fact that an offender was avoidably distracted by using a hand-held mobile phone when a causing death by driving offence was committed will always make an offence more serious. Reading or composing text messages *over a period of time will be a gross* avoidable distraction and is likely to result in an offence of causing death by dangerous driving being in a higher level of seriousness.

16. Where it is proved that an offender was briefly distracted by reading a text message or adjusting a hands-free set or its controls at the time of the collision, this would be on a par with consulting a map or adjusting a radio or satellite navigation equipment, activities that would be considered an avoidable distraction.

(c) Vulnerable road users

17. Cyclists, motorbike riders, horse riders, pedestrians and those working in the road are vulnerable road users and a driver is expected to take extra care when driving near them. Driving too close to a bike or horse; allowing a vehicle to mount the pavement; driving into a cycle lane; and driving without the care needed in the vicinity of a pedestrian crossing, hospital, school or residential home, are all examples of factors that should be taken into account when determining the seriousness of an offence. See paragraph 24 below for the approach where the actions of another person contributed to the collision.

18. The fact that the victim of a causing death by driving offence was a particularly vulnerable road user is a factor that should be taken into account when determining the seriousness of an offence.

(ii) Aggravating and mitigating factors

(a) More than one person killed

19. The seriousness of any offence included in these guidelines will generally be greater where more than one person is killed since it is inevitable that the degree of harm will be greater. In relation to the assessment of culpability, whilst there will be circumstances in which a driver could reasonably anticipate the possible death of more than one person (for example, the driver of a vehicle with passengers (whether that is a bus, taxi or private car) or a person driving badly in an area where there are many people), there will be many circumstances where the driver could not anticipate the number of people who would be killed.

20. The greater obligation on those responsible for driving other people is not an element essential to the quality of the driving and so has not been included amongst the determinants of seriousness that affect the choice of sentencing range. In practical terms, separate charges are likely to be brought in relation to each death caused. Although concurrent sentences are likely to be imposed (in recognition of the fact that the charges relate to one episode of offending behaviour), each individual sentence is likely to be higher because the offence is aggravated by the fact that more than one death has been caused.

21. Where more than one person is killed, that will aggravate the seriousness of the offence because of the increase in harm. Where the number of people killed is high *and* that was reasonably foreseeable, the number of deaths is likely to provide sufficient justification for moving an offence into the next highest sentencing band.

(b) Effect on offender

22. Injury to the offender may be a mitigating factor when the offender has suffered very serious injuries. In most circumstances, the weighting it is given will be dictated by the circumstances of the offence and the effect should bear a direct relationship to the extent to which the offender's driving was at fault—the greater the fault, the less the effect on mitigation; this distinction will be of particular relevance where an offence did not involve any fault in the offender's standard of driving.

23. Where one or more of the victims was in a close personal or family relationship with the offender, this may be a mitigating factor. In line with the approach where the offender is very seriously injured, the degree to which the relationship influences the sentence should be linked to offender culpability in relation to the commission of the offence; mitigation for this reason is likely to have less effect where the culpability of the driver is particularly high.

(c) Actions of others

24. Where the actions of the victim or a third party contributed to the commission of an offence, this should be acknowledged and taken into account as a mitigating factor.

(d) Offender's age/lack of driving experience

25. The Council guideline *Overarching Principles: Seriousness* [see **SG-21**] includes a generic mitigating factor '*youth or age, where it affects the responsibility of the individual defendant*'. There is a great deal of difference between recklessness or irresponsibility—which may be due to youth—and inexperience in dealing with prevailing conditions or an unexpected or unusual situation that presents itself— which may be present regardless of the age of the offender. The fact that an offender's lack of driving experience contributed to the commission of an offence should be treated as a mitigating factor; in this regard, the age of the offender is not relevant.

(iii) Personal mitigation

(a) Good driving record

26. This is not a factor that automatically should be treated as a mitigating factor, especially now that the presence of previous convictions is a statutory aggravating factor. However, any evidence to show that an offender has previously been an exemplary driver, for example having driven an ambulance, police vehicle, bus, taxi or similar vehicle conscientiously and without incident for many years, is a fact that the courts may well wish to take into account by way of personal mitigation. This is likely to have even greater effect where the driver is driving on public duty (for example, on ambulance, fire services or police duties) and was responding to an emergency.

(b) Conduct after the offence

—Giving assistance at the scene

27. There may be many reasons why an offender does not offer help to the victims at the scene—the offender may be injured, traumatised by shock, afraid of causing further injury or simply have no idea what action to take—and it would be inappropriate to assess the offence as more serious on this ground (and so increase the level of sentence). However, where an offender gave direct, positive, assistance to victim(s) at the scene of a collision, this should be regarded as personal mitigation.

—Remorse

28. Whilst it can be expected that anyone who has caused death by driving would be expected to feel remorseful, this cannot undermine its importance for sentencing purposes. Remorse is identified as personal mitigation in [*Overarching Principles: Seriousness*: see **SG-21**] and the Council can see no reason for it to be treated differently for this group of offences. It is for the court to determine whether an expression of remorse is genuine; where it is, this should be taken into account as personal mitigation.

(c) Summary

29. Evidence that an offender is normally a careful and conscientious driver, giving direct, positive assistance to a victim and genuine remorse may be taken into account as personal mitigation and may justify a reduction in sentence.

B. Ancillary orders   SG-388

(i) Disqualification for driving

30. For each offence, disqualification is a mandatory part of the sentence (subject to the usual (very limited) exceptions), and therefore an important element of the overall punishment for the offence. In addition, an order that the disqualification continues until the offender passes an extended driving test order is compulsory[249] for those convicted of causing death by dangerous driving or by careless driving when under the influence, and discretionary[250] in relation to the two other offences.

31. Any disqualification is effective from the date on which it is imposed. When ordering disqualification from driving, the duration of the order should allow for the length of any custodial period in order to ensure that the disqualification has the desired impact. In principle, the minimum period of disqualification should either equate to the length of the custodial sentence imposed (in the knowledge that the offender is likely to be released having served half of that term), or the relevant statutory minimum disqualification period, whichever results in the longer period of disqualification.

(ii) Deprivation order

32. A general sentencing power exists which enables courts to deprive an offender of property used for the purposes of committing an offence.[251] A vehicle used to commit an offence included in this guideline can be regarded as being used for the purposes of committing the offence.

C. Sentencing ranges and starting points   SG-389

1. Typically, a guideline will apply to an offence that can be committed in a variety of circumstances with different levels of seriousness. It will apply to a first-time offender who has been convicted after a trial. Within the guidelines, a first-time offender is a person who does not have a conviction which, by virtue of section 143(2) of the CJA 2003, must be treated as an aggravating factor.

2. As an aid to consistency of approach, the guidelines describe a number of types of activity which would fall within the broad definition of the offence. These are set out in a column headed 'Type/nature of activity'.

3. The expected approach is for a court to identify the description that most nearly matches the particular facts of the offence for which sentence is being imposed. This will identify a starting point from which the sentencer can depart to reflect aggravating or mitigating factors affecting the seriousness of the offence (beyond those contained within the column describing the type or nature of offence activity) to reach a provisional sentence.

4. The *sentencing range* is the bracket into which the provisional sentence will normally fall after having regard to factors which aggravate or mitigate the seriousness of the offence. The particular circumstances may, however, make it appropriate that the provisional sentence falls outside the range.

5. Where the offender has previous convictions which aggravate the seriousness of the current offence, that may take the provisional sentence beyond the range given, particularly where there are significant other aggravating factors present.

6. Once the provisional sentence has been identified by reference to those factors affecting the seriousness of the offence, the court will take into account any relevant factors of personal mitigation, which may take the sentence outside the range indicated in the guideline.

7. Where there has been a guilty plea, any reduction attributable to that plea will be applied to the sentence at this stage. This reduction may take the sentence below the range provided.

8. A court must give its reasons for imposing a sentence of a different kind or outside the range provided in the guidelines.[252]

The decision making process

The process set out below is intended to show that the sentencing approach for offences of causing death by driving is fluid and requires the structured exercise of discretion.

---

[249] Road Traffic Offenders Act 1988, s. 36(1)
[250] ibid., s. 36(4)
[251] Powers of Criminal Courts (Sentencing) Act 2000, s. 143
[252] Criminal Justice Act 2003, s. 174(2)(a)

[Sets out the standard decision making process: identify dangerous offenders, identify starting point, consider aggravating factors, consider mitigating factors, apply reduction for guilty plea, consider ancillary orders, review in light of totality principle and give reasons.]

SG-390 **D. Offence guidelines**
Causing death by dangerous driving
Factors to take into consideration

1. The following guideline applies to a 'first-time offender' aged 18 or over convicted after trial (see... above), who has not been assessed as a dangerous offender requiring a sentence under ss. 224–228 Criminal Justice Act 2003 (as amended).
2. When assessing the seriousness of any offence, the court must always refer to the full list of aggravating and mitigating factors in the Council guideline on Seriousness[253] as well as those set out in the adjacent table as being particularly relevant to this type of offending behaviour.

3. Levels of seriousness

The 3 levels are distinguished by factors related predominantly to the standard of driving; the general description of the degree of risk is complemented by examples of the type of bad driving arising. The presence of aggravating factors or combinations of a small number of determinants of seriousness will increase the starting point within the range. Where there is a larger group of determinants of seriousness and/or aggravating factors, this may justify moving the starting point to the next level.

Level 1—The most serious offences encompassing driving that involved a deliberate decision to ignore (or a flagrant disregard for) the rules of the road and an apparent disregard for the great danger being caused to others. Such offences are likely to be characterised by:
- *A prolonged, persistent and deliberate course of very bad driving AND/OR*
- *Consumption of substantial amounts of alcohol or drugs leading to gross impairment AND/OR*
- *A group of determinants of seriousness which in isolation or smaller number would place the offence in level 2*

Level 1 is that for which the increase in maximum penalty was aimed primarily. Where an offence involves both of the determinants of seriousness identified, particularly if accompanied by aggravating factors such as multiple deaths or injuries, or a very bad driving record, this may move an offence towards the top of the sentencing range.

Level 2—This is driving that created a substantial risk of danger and is likely to be characterised by:
- *Greatly excessive speed, racing or competitive driving against another driver OR*
- *Gross avoidable distraction such as reading or composing text messages over a period of time OR*
- *Driving whilst ability to drive is impaired as a result of consumption of alcohol or drugs, failing to take prescribed medication or as a result of a known medical condition OR*
- *A group of determinants of seriousness which in isolation or smaller number would place the offence in level 3*

Level 3 – This is driving that created a significant risk of danger and is likely to be characterised by:
- *Driving above the speed limit/at a speed that is inappropriate for the prevailing conditions OR*
- *Driving when knowingly deprived of adequate sleep or rest or knowing that the vehicle has a dangerous defect or is poorly maintained or is dangerously loaded OR*
- *A brief but obvious danger arising from a seriously dangerous manoeuvre OR*
- *Driving whilst avoidably distracted OR*
- *Failing to have proper regard to vulnerable road users*

The starting point and range overlap with Level 2 is to allow the breadth of discretion necessary to accommodate circumstances where there are significant aggravating factors.

4. Sentencers should take into account relevant matters of personal mitigation; see in particular guidance on **good driving record, giving assistance at the scene** and **remorse**... above.

CAUSING DEATH BY DANGEROUS DRIVING
Road Traffic Act 1988 (section 1)

This is a serious offence for the purposes of section 224 Criminal Justice Act 2003

Maximum penalty: 14 years imprisonment;
minimum disqualification of 2 years with compulsory extended re-test

---

[253] *Overarching Principles: Seriousness*, published 16 December 2004, www.sentencing-guidelines.gov.uk

Nature of offence	Starting point	Sentencing range
Level 1 The most serious offences encompassing driving that involved a deliberate decision to ignore (or a flagrant disregard for) the rules of the road and an apparent disregard for the great danger being caused to others	8 years custody	7–14 years custody
Level 2 Driving that created a *substantial* risk of danger	5 years custody	4–7 years custody
Level 3 Driving that created a *significant* risk of danger *[Where the driving is markedly less culpable than for this level, reference should be made to the starting point and range for the most serious level of causing death by careless driving]*	3 years custody	2–5 years custody

Additional aggravating factors	Additional mitigating factors
1. Previous convictions for motoring offences, particularly offences that involve bad driving or the consumption of excessive alcohol or drugs before driving 2. More than one person killed as a result of the offence 3. Serious injury to one or more victims, in addition to the death(s) 4. Disregard of warnings 5. Other offences committed at the same time, such as driving other than in accordance with the terms of a valid licence; driving while disqualified; driving without insurance; taking a vehicle without consent; driving a stolen vehicle 6. The offender's irresponsible behaviour such as failing to stop, falsely claiming that one of the victims was responsible for the collision, or trying to throw the victim off the car by swerving in order to escape 7. Driving off in an attempt to avoid detection or apprehension	1. Alcohol or drugs consumed unwittingly 2. Offender was seriously injured in the collision 3. The victim was a close friend or relative 4. Actions of the victim or a third party contributed significantly to the likelihood of a collision occurring and/or death resulting 5. The offender's lack of driving experience contributed to the commission of the offence 6. The driving was in response to a proven and genuine emergency falling short of a defence

Causing death by careless driving when under the influence of drink or drugs or having failed without reasonable excuse either to provide a specimen for analysis or to permit the analysis of a blood sample   **SG-391**

Factors to take into consideration

1. The following guideline applies to a 'first-time offender' aged 18 or over convicted after trial (see . . . above), who has not been assessed as a dangerous offender requiring a sentence under ss. 224–228 Criminal Justice Act 2003 (as amended).

2. When assessing the seriousness of any offence, the court must always refer to the full list of aggravating and mitigating factors in the Council guideline on Seriousness[254] as well as those set out in the adjacent table as being particularly relevant to this type of offending behaviour.

3. This offence can be committed through:
   (i) being unfit to drive through drink or drugs;
   (ii) having consumed so much alcohol as to be over the prescribed limit;
   (iii) failing without reasonable excuse to provide a specimen for analysis within the timescale allowed; or
   (iv) failing without reasonable excuse to permit the analysis of a blood sample taken when incapable of giving consent.

---

[254] *Overarching Principles: Seriousness*, published 16 December 2004, www.sentencing-guidelines.gov.uk

4. In comparison with *causing death by dangerous driving*, the level of culpability in the actual manner of driving is lower but that culpability is increased in all cases by the fact that the offender has driven after consuming drugs or an excessive amount of alcohol. Accordingly, there is considerable parity in the levels of seriousness with the deliberate decision to drive after consuming alcohol or drugs aggravating the *careless* standard of driving onto a par with *dangerous* driving.

5. The fact that the offender was under the influence of drink or drugs is an inherent element of this offence. For discussion on the significance of driving after having consumed drink or drugs, see...above.

6. The guideline is based both on the level of alcohol or drug consumption and on the degree of carelessness.

7. The increase in sentence is more marked where there is an increase in the level of intoxication than where there is an increase in the degree of carelessness reflecting the 14 year imprisonment maximum for this offence compared with a 5 year maximum for causing death by careless or inconsiderate driving alone.

8. A refusal to supply a specimen for analysis may be a calculated step by an offender to avoid prosecution for driving when having consumed in excess of the prescribed amount of alcohol, with a view to seeking to persuade the court that the amount consumed was relatively small. A court is entitled to draw adverse inferences from a refusal to supply a specimen without reasonable excuse and should treat with caution any attempt to persuade the court that only a limited amount of alcohol had been consumed.[255] The three levels of seriousness where the offence has been committed in this way derive from the classification in the Magistrates' Court Sentencing Guidelines.

9. Sentencers should take into account relevant matters of personal mitigation; see in particular guidance on **good driving record, giving assistance at the scene** and **remorse**...above.

CAUSING DEATH BY CARELESS DRIVING WHEN UNDER THE INFLUENCE OF DRINK OR DRUGS OR HAVING FAILED EITHER TO PROVIDE A SPECIMEN FOR ANALYSIS OR TO PERMIT ANALYSIS OF A BLOOD SAMPLE

Road Traffic Act 1988 (section 3A)

This is a serious offence for the purposes of section 224 Criminal Justice Act 2003

Maximum penalty: 14 years imprisonment;
minimum disqualification of 2 years with compulsory extended re-test

The legal limit of alcohol is 35 μg breath (80 mg in blood and 107 mg in urine)	Careless/inconsiderate driving arising from momentary inattention with no aggravating factors	Other cases of careless/inconsiderate driving	Careless/inconsiderate driving falling not far short of dangerousness
71 μ or above of alcohol/high quantity of drugs OR deliberate non-provision of specimen where evidence of serious impairment	**Starting point:** 6 years custody **Sentencing range:** 5–10 years custody	**Starting point:** 7 years custody **Sentencing range:** 6–12 years custody	**Starting point:** 8 years custody **Sentencing range:** 7–14 years custody
51–70 μg of alcohol/moderate quantity of drugs OR deliberate non-provision of specimen	**Starting point:** 4 years custody **Sentencing range:** 3–7 years custody	**Starting point:** 5 years custody **Sentencing range:** 4–8 years custody	**Starting point:** 6 years custody **Sentencing range:** 5–9 years custody
35–50 μg of alcohol/minimum quantity of drugs OR test refused because of honestly held but unreasonable belief	**Starting point:** 18 months custody **Sentencing range:** 26 weeks–4 years custody	**Starting point:** 3 years custody **Sentencing range:** 2–5 years custody	**Starting point:** 4 years custody **Sentencing range:** 3–6 years custody

---

[255] *Attorney-General's Reference No. 21 of 2000* [2001] 1 Cr App R (S) 173

Additional aggravating factors	Additional mitigating factors
1. Other offences committed at the same time, such as driving other than in accordance with the terms of a valid licence; driving while disqualified; driving without insurance; taking a vehicle without consent; driving a stolen vehicle 2. Previous convictions for motoring offences, particularly offences that involve bad driving or the consumption of excessive alcohol before driving 3. More than one person was killed as a result of the offence 4. Serious injury to one or more persons in addition to the death(s) 5. Irresponsible behaviour such as failing to stop or falsely claiming that one of the victims was responsible for the collision	1. Alcohol or drugs consumed unwittingly 2. Offender was seriously injured in the collision 3. The victim was a close friend or relative 4. The actions of the victim or a third party contributed significantly to the likelihood of a collision occurring and/or death resulting 5. The driving was in response to a proven and genuine emergency falling short of a defence

Causing death by careless or inconsiderate driving

SG-392

Factors to take into consideration

1. The following guideline applies to a 'first-time offender' aged 18 or over convicted after trial (see...above), who has not been assessed as a dangerous offender requiring a sentence under ss. 224–228 Criminal Justice Act 2003 (as amended).

2. When assessing the seriousness of any offence, the court must always refer to the full list of aggravating and mitigating factors in the Council guideline on Seriousness[256] as well as those set out in the adjacent table as being particularly relevant to this type of offending behaviour.

3. The maximum penalty on indictment is 5 years imprisonment. The offence is triable either way and, in a magistrates' court, statute provides that the maximum sentence is 12 months imprisonment; this will be revised to 6 months imprisonment until such time as the statutory provisions increasing the sentencing powers of a magistrates' court are implemented.[257]

4. Disqualification of the offender from driving and endorsement of the offender's driving licence are mandatory, and the offence carries between 3 and 11 penalty points when the court finds special reasons for not imposing disqualification. There is a discretionary power[258] to order an extended driving test where a person is convicted of this offence.

5. Since the maximum sentence has been set at 5 years imprisonment, the sentence ranges are generally lower for this offence than for the offences of *causing death by dangerous driving* or *causing death by careless driving under the influence*, for which the maximum sentence is 14 years imprisonment. However, it is unavoidable that some cases will be on the borderline between *dangerous* and *careless* driving, or may involve a number of factors that significantly increase the seriousness of an offence. As a result, the guideline for this offence identifies three levels of seriousness, the range for the highest of which overlaps with ranges for the lowest level of seriousness for *causing death by dangerous driving*.

6. The three levels of seriousness are defined by the degree of carelessness involved in the standard of driving. The most serious level for this offence is where the offender's driving fell *not that far short of dangerous*. The least serious group of offences relates to those cases where the level of culpability is low—for example in a case involving an offender who misjudges the speed of another vehicle, or turns without seeing an oncoming vehicle because of restricted visibility. Other cases will fall into the intermediate level.

7. The starting point for the most serious offence of *causing death by careless driving* is lower than that for the least serious offence of *causing death by dangerous driving* in recognition of the different standards of driving behaviour. However, the range still leaves scope, within the 5 year maximum, to impose longer sentences where the case is particularly serious.

8. Where the level of carelessness is low and there are no aggravating factors, even the fact that death was caused is not sufficient to justify a prison sentence.

9. A fine is unlikely to be an appropriate sentence for this offence; where a non-custodial sentence is considered appropriate, this should be a community order. The nature of the requirements will be determined by the purpose[259] identified by the court as of primary importance. Requirements most likely to be relevant include unpaid work requirement, activity requirement, programme requirement and curfew requirement.

---

[256] *Overarching Principles: Seriousness*, published 16 December 2004, www.sentencing-guidelines.gov.uk
[257] Criminal Justice Act 2003, ss. 154(1) and 282; Road Safety Act 2006, s. 61(5)
[258] Road Traffic Offenders Act 1988, s. 36(4)
[259] Criminal Justice Act 2003, s. 142(1)

10. Sentencers should take into account relevant matters of personal mitigation; see in particular guidance on **good driving record, giving assistance at the scene** and **remorse**... above.

CAUSING DEATH BY CARELESS OR INCONSIDERATE DRIVING
Road Traffic Act 1988 (section 2B)

Maximum penalty: 5 years imprisonment;
minimum disqualification of 12 months, discretionary re-test

Nature of offence	Starting point	Sentencing range
Careless or inconsiderate driving falling not far short of dangerous driving	15 months custody	36 weeks–3 years custody
Other cases of careless or inconsiderate driving	36 weeks custody	Community order (HIGH)—2 years custody
Careless or inconsiderate driving arising from momentary inattention with no aggravating factors	Community order (MEDIUM)	Community order (LOW)— Community order (HIGH)

Additional aggravating factors	Additional mitigating factors
1. Other offences committed at the same time, such as driving other than in accordance with the terms of a valid licence; driving while disqualified; driving without insurance; taking a vehicle without consent; driving a stolen vehicle 2. Previous convictions for motoring offences, particularly offences that involve bad driving 3. More than one person was killed as a result of the offence 4. Serious injury to one or more persons in addition to the death(s) 5. Irresponsible behaviour, such as failing to stop or falsely claiming that one of the victims was responsible for the collision	1. Offender was seriously injured in the collision 2. The victim was a close friend or relative 3. The actions of the victim or a third party contributed to the commission of the offence 4. The offender's lack of driving experience contributed significantly to the likelihood of a collision occurring and/or death resulting 5. The driving was in response to a proven and genuine emergency falling short of a defence

SG-393 **Causing death by driving: unlicensed, disqualified or uninsured drivers**

Factors to take into consideration

1. The following guideline applies to a 'first-time offender' aged 18 or over convicted after trial (see... above), who has not been assessed as a dangerous offender requiring a sentence under ss. 224–228 Criminal Justice Act 2003 (as amended).
2. When assessing the seriousness of any offence, the court must always refer to the full list of aggravating and mitigating factors in the Council guideline on Seriousness[260] as well as those set out in the adjacent table as being particularly relevant to this type of offending behaviour.
3. This offence has a maximum penalty of 2 years imprisonment and is triable either way. In a magistrates' court, statute provides that the maximum sentence is 12 months imprisonment; this will be revised to 6 months imprisonment until such time as the statutory provisions increasing the sentencing powers of a magistrates' court are implemented.[261]
4. Disqualification of the offender from driving and endorsement of the offender's driving licence are mandatory, and the offence carries between 3 and 11 penalty points when the court finds special reasons for not imposing disqualification. There is a discretionary power[262] to order an extended driving test where a person is convicted of this offence.
5. Culpability arises from the offender driving a vehicle on a road or other public place when, by law, not allowed to do so; the offence does not require proof of any fault in the standard of driving.
6. Because of the significantly lower maximum penalty, the sentencing ranges are considerably lower than for the other three offences covered in this guideline; many cases may be sentenced in a magistrates' court, particularly where there is an early guilty plea.
7. A fine is unlikely to be an appropriate sentence for this offence; where a noncustodial sentence is considered appropriate, this should be a community order.

---

[260] *Overarching Principles: Seriousness*, published 16 December 2004, www.sentencing-guidelines.gov.uk
[261] Criminal Justice Act 2003, ss. 154(1) and 282; Road Safety Act 2006, s. 61(5)
[262] Road Traffic Offenders Act 1988, s. 36(4)

8. Since driving whilst disqualified is more culpable than driving whilst unlicensed or uninsured, a higher starting point is proposed when the offender was disqualified from driving at the time of the offence.

9. Being uninsured, unlicensed or disqualified are the only determinants of seriousness for this offence, as there are no factors relating to the standard of driving. The list of aggravating factors identified is slightly different as the emphasis is on the decision to drive by an offender who is not permitted by law to do so.

10. In some cases, the extreme circumstances that led an offender to drive whilst unlicensed, disqualified or uninsured may result in a successful defence of 'duress of circumstances'.[263] In less extreme circumstances, where the *decision to drive was brought about by a genuine and proven emergency*, that may mitigate offence seriousness and so it is included as an additional mitigating factor.

11. A driver may hold a reasonable belief in relation to the validity of insurance (for example having just missed a renewal date or relied on a third party to make an application) and also the validity of a licence (for example incorrectly believing that a licence covered a particular category of vehicle). In light of this, an additional mitigating factor covers those situations where an offender genuinely believed that there was valid insurance or a valid licence.

12. Sentencers should take into account relevant matters of personal mitigation; see in particular guidance on **good driving record, giving assistance at the scene** and **remorse**...above.

CAUSING DEATH BY DRIVING: UNLICENSED, DISQUALIFIED OR UNINSURED DRIVERS
Road Traffic Act 1988 (section 3ZB)

Maximum penalty: 2 years imprisonment;
minimum disqualification of 12 months, discretionary re-test

Nature of offence	Starting point	Sentencing range
The offender was disqualified from driving **OR** The offender was unlicensed or uninsured plus 2 or more aggravating factors from the list below	**12 months custody**	**36 weeks–2 years custody**
The offender was unlicensed or uninsured plus at least 1 aggravating factor from the list below	**26 weeks custody**	**Community order (HIGH)— 36 weeks custody**
The offender was unlicensed or uninsured—no aggravating factors	**Community order (MEDIUM)**	**Community order (LOW)— Community order (HIGH)**

Additional aggravating factors	Additional mitigating factors
1. Previous convictions for motoring offences, whether involving bad driving or involving an offence of the same kind that forms part of the present conviction (i.e. unlicensed, disqualified or uninsured driving) 2. More than one person was killed as a result of the offence 3. Serious injury to one or more persons in addition to the death(s) 4. Irresponsible behaviour such as failing to stop or falsely claiming that someone else was driving	1. The decision to drive was brought about by a proven and genuine emergency falling short of a defence 2. The offender genuinely believed that he or she was insured or licensed to drive 3. The offender was seriously injured as a result of the collision 4. The victim was a close friend or relative

ANNEX A: DANGEROUS AND CARELESS DRIVING
Statutory definitions and examples

SG-394

[Omitted—see the relevant material in part C]

---

[263] In *DPP v Mullally* [2006] EWHC 3448 (Admin) the Divisional Court held that the defence of necessity must be strictly controlled and that it must be proved that the actions of the defendant were reasonable in the given circumstances. See also *Hasan* [2005] UKHL 22

SG-395

PART 14　THEFT

…This guideline applies to the sentencing of offenders convicted of theft…who are sentenced on or after 5 January 2009. [This guideline originally covered burglary in a building other than a dwelling in addition to theft, but has been superseded to that extent. For burglary offences sentenced after 16 January 2012, see Part 20 at **SG-457**.]

…

This guideline applies only to the sentencing of offenders aged 18 and over.…

SG-396　　**A. Statutory provisions**

1. The forms of theft…covered by this guideline are:
   - theft in breach of trust;
   - theft in a dwelling;
   - theft from the person;
   - theft from a shop.
2. [Sets out the Theft Act 1968, s. 1.]
   Although this guideline covers four particular forms of theft, the principles covered in paragraphs 5 to 30 are of general application and are likely to be of assistance where a court is sentencing for a form of theft not covered by a specific guideline.
3. [Related to burglary and is now superseded.]
4. Offences under section 1 …of the Theft Act are punishable either on summary conviction or on indictment. The maximum sentence in a magistrates' court is 6 months imprisonment. In the Crown Court, the maximum sentence is 7 years custody for theft…

SG-397　　**B. Assessing seriousness**

5. The primary factor in considering sentence is the seriousness of the offence; that is determined by assessing the culpability of the offender and any harm which the offence caused, was intended to cause or might foreseeably have caused.[264] A community sentence can be imposed only if a court considers that the offence is serious enough to justify it,[265] and a custodial sentence can be imposed only if a court considers that a community order or a fine alone cannot be justified in view of the seriousness of the offence.[266] The Council has published a definitive guideline on seriousness that guides sentencers through the process of determining whether the respective sentencing thresholds have been crossed.[267]

(i) Culpability and harm

6. The culpability of the offender is the initial factor in determining offence seriousness. It is an essential element of the offences addressed in this guideline that the offender acted dishonestly. This requires that:[268]
   - the conduct was dishonest according to ordinary standards of reasonable and honest people and
   - the offender knew that the conduct was by those standards dishonest.
     Accordingly, an offender convicted of these offences will have demonstrated a high level of culpability.
7. Even so, the precise level of culpability will vary according to factors such as the offender's motivation, whether the offence was planned or spontaneous and whether the offender was in a position of trust.[269] An offence will be aggravated where there is evidence of planning.
8. The starting points and sentencing ranges in this guideline are based on the assumption that the offender was motivated by greed or a desire to live beyond his or her means. To avoid double counting, such a motivation should not be treated as a factor that increases culpability. Where an offence of theft is motivated by an intention to cause harm, or out of revenge, this will aggravate the offence.

---

[264] Criminal Justice Act 2003, s.143(1)
[265] ibid., s.148(1)
[266] ibid., s.152(2)
[267] *Overarching Principles: Seriousness*, published 16 December 2004, www.sentencing-guidelines.gov.uk
[268] *R v Ghosh* [1982] QB 1053
[269] *Overarching Principles: Seriousness*, published 16 December 2004, www.sentencing-guidelines.gov.uk

9. When assessing the harm caused by theft ... offences, the starting point should be the loss suffered by the victim. In general, the greater the loss, the more serious the offence. However, the monetary value of the loss may not reflect the full extent of the harm caused by the offence. The court should also take into account the impact of the offence on the victim (which may be significantly greater than the monetary value of the loss; this may be particularly important where the value of the loss is high in proportion to the victim's financial circumstances even though relatively low in absolute terms), any harm to persons other than the direct victim, and any harm in the form of public concern or erosion of public confidence.

10. In some theft ... cases, the harm that results from an offence may be greater than the harm intended by the offender. In others, the offender may have intended more harm than actually results.[270]

(ii) Aggravating and mitigating factors

11. The Council guideline *Overarching Principles: Seriousness* identifies a number of factors that might increase or mitigate the seriousness of an offence. For ease of reference, the factors are set out in Annex A.

12. The most common factors that are likely to aggravate an offence of theft ... are:
    Factors indicating higher culpability
    - planning of an offence;
    - offenders operating in groups or gangs; and
    - deliberate targeting of vulnerable victims.

    Factors indicating a more than usually serious degree of harm
    - victim is particularly vulnerable;
    - high level of gain from the offence; and
    - high value (including sentimental value) of property to the victim or substantial consequential loss.

13. In the offence guidelines that follow, the Council has identified aggravating factors in addition to those from the general list that may be of particular relevance to the individual offences. The Council has not identified any additional offence mitigating factors pertinent to the offences in this guideline.

(iii) Personal mitigation

14. The Council has identified the following matters of personal mitigation that might apply to the offences contained in this guideline.

(a) Return of stolen property

15. Whether and the degree to which the return of stolen property constitutes a matter of personal mitigation will depend on an assessment of the circumstances and, in particular, the voluntariness and timeliness of the return.

(b) Impact on sentence of offender's dependency

16. Many offenders convicted of acquisitive crimes are motivated by an addiction, often to drugs, alcohol or gambling. This does not mitigate the seriousness of the offence, but an offender's dependency may properly influence the type of sentence imposed. In particular, it may sometimes be appropriate to impose:
    - a drug rehabilitation requirement (which can be part of a community order within all the community sentencing bands from low to high seriousness), or
    - an alcohol treatment requirement (for dependent drinkers), or
    - an activity or supervision requirement including alcohol specific information, advice and support (for harmful and hazardous drinkers)

    as part of a community order or a suspended sentence order in an attempt to break the cycle of addiction and offending, even if an immediate custodial sentence would otherwise be warranted.[271]

---

[270] See *Overarching Principles: Seriousness*, para.1.17, published 16 December 2004, www.sentencing-guidelines.gov.uk

[271] *New Sentences: Criminal Justice Act 2003*, published 16 December 2004, www.sentencing-guidelines.gov.uk. The Court of Appeal gave guidance on the approach to making drug treatment and testing orders, which also applies to imposing a drug rehabilitation requirement, in *Attorney General's Reference No. 64 of 2003 (Boujettif and Harrison)* [2003] EWCA Crim 3514 and Woods and Collins [2005] EWCA Crim 2065 summarised in the Sentencing Guidelines Council *Guideline Judgments Case Compendium* (section (A) Generic Sentencing Principles) available at www.sentencing-guidelines.gov.uk

(c) Offender motivated by desperation or need

17. The fact that an offence has been committed in desperation or need arising from particular hardship may count as personal mitigation in exceptional circumstances.

SG-398 **C. Ancillary and other orders**

(i) Restitution order

18. Under section 148 of the Powers of Criminal Courts (Sentencing) Act 2000, a court may order that stolen goods be restored to the victim or that a sum not exceeding the value of the goods be paid to the victim from money taken out of the offender's possession at the time of apprehension. Further, on the application of the victim, the court may order that other goods representing the proceeds of disposal or realisation of the stolen goods be transferred to the victim. Where the stolen property cannot be traced or the offender is not in possession of sufficient money at the time of apprehension, a restitution order will not be available and a compensation order should be considered instead.

19. A restitution order should not normally impact on or influence the choice of sentence as the offender has no control over the making of the order.

(ii) Compensation order

20. Under section 130 of the Powers of Criminal Courts (Sentencing) Act 2000, the court must consider making a compensation order in any case where an offence has resulted in personal injury, loss or damage. Compensation can either be a sentence in its own right or an ancillary order.

21. Compensation should benefit, not inflict further harm on, the victim. A victim may or may not want compensation from the offender and assumptions should not be made either way. The victim's views are properly obtained through sensitive discussion with the police when it can be explained that the offender's ability to pay will ultimately determine whether, and how much, compensation is ordered and whether the compensation will be paid in one lump sum or by instalments. If the victim does not want compensation, this should be made known to the court and respected.

22. In cases where it is difficult to ascertain the full amount of the loss suffered by the victim, consideration should be given to making a compensation order for an amount representing the agreed or likely loss. Where relevant information is not immediately available, it may be appropriate to grant an adjournment for it to be obtained.

23. When imposed as an ancillary order, a compensation order normally should not impact on or influence the choice of sentence. However, in cases where the court considers that it is appropriate to impose both a fine and compensation order and the offender has insufficient means to pay both, priority must be given to the compensation order.[272]

24. Where an offender has acted (as opposed to offered) to free assets in order to pay compensation, this is akin to making voluntary restitution and may be regarded as personal mitigation.

(iii) Confiscation order

25. Where there is evidence in a case before the Crown Court that the offender has benefited financially from his or her offending, the court must, in accordance with the Proceeds of Crime Act 2002, consider whether to make a confiscation order. A magistrates' court may commit the offender to the Crown Court for sentence with a view to such an order being made.

26. If the court makes a confiscation order, it must take account of the order before it imposes a fine or a deprivation order.[273]

27. Except as provided in paragraph 26 above, the court must not take account of the confiscation order in deciding the appropriate sentence.[274]

28. Where a court makes both a compensation order and a confiscation order and it believes that the offender does not have sufficient means to satisfy both orders, it must direct that the compensation is paid from the confiscated assets.[275]

(iv) Deprivation order

29. Under section 143 of the Powers of Criminal Courts (Sentencing) Act 2000, a court may deprive an offender of property used or intended to be used to commit or facilitate the commission of an offence.

---

[272] Powers of Criminal Courts (Sentencing) Act 2000, s.130(12). The court must also impose a surcharge of £15 in any case in which a fine is imposed. Where there are insufficient means, compensation will take priority over the surcharge but the surcharge will take priority over a fine.

[273] Proceeds of Crime Act 2002, ss.13(2) and (3)

[274] ibid., s.13(4)

[275] ibid., ss.13(5) and (6)

30. Where the property has an 'innocent use' but can also be used to commit or facilitate the commission of an offence, a deprivation order must be taken into account when considering whether the overall penalty is commensurate with the seriousness of the offence.[276] However, where the property can be used only for the purpose of crime, a deprivation order should not be taken into account when determining the appropriate sentence.

D. Sentencing ranges and starting points

SG-399

1. Typically, a guideline will apply to an offence that can be committed in a variety of circumstances with different levels of seriousness. It will apply to a first time offender who has been convicted after a trial. Within the guidelines, a "first time offender" is a person who does not have a conviction which, by virtue of section 143(2) of the Criminal Justice Act 2003, must be treated as an aggravating factor.
2. As an aid to consistency of approach, the guidelines describe a number of types of activity which would fall within the broad definition of the offence. These are set out in a column headed 'type/ nature of activity'.
3. The expected approach is for a court to identify the description that most nearly matches the particular facts of the offence for which sentence is being imposed. This will identify a starting point from which the sentencer can depart to reflect aggravating or mitigating factors affecting the seriousness of the offence (beyond those contained within the column describing the type or nature of offence activity) to reach a **provisional sentence**.
4. The **sentencing range** is the bracket into which the provisional sentence will normally fall after having regard to factors which aggravate or mitigate the seriousness of the offence. The particular circumstances may, however, make it appropriate that the provisional sentence falls outside the range.
5. Where the offender has previous convictions which aggravate the seriousness of the current offence, that may take the provisional sentence beyond the range given particularly where there are significant other aggravating factors present.
6. Once the provisional sentence has been identified by reference to those factors affecting the seriousness of the offence, the court will take into account any relevant factors of personal mitigation, which may take the sentence beyond the range given.
7. Where there has been a guilty plea, any reduction attributable to that plea will be applied to the sentence at this stage. Again, this reduction may take the sentence below the range provided.
8. A court must give its reasons for imposing a sentence of a different kind or outside the range provided in the guidelines.[277]

The decision making process

[Sets out the standard sequential decision making process: identify starting point, consider aggravating factors, consider mitigating factors, apply reduction for guilty plea, consider ancillary orders, review in light of the totality principle and give reasons.]

E. Offence guidelines

SG-400

Theft in breach of trust

SG-401

Factors to take into consideration

1. The following starting points and sentencing ranges are for a first time offender aged 18 or over who pleaded not guilty. They should be applied as set out...above.
2. In relation to harm, in general, the greater the loss, the more serious the offence. However, this is subject to the considerations set out in the rest of this paragraph. The guideline is based on the monetary value of the amount involved but, the monetary value may not reflect the full extent of the harm caused by the offence. The court should also take into account the impact of the offence on the victim (which may be significantly greater than the monetary value of the loss; this may be particularly important where the value of the loss is high in proportion to the victim's financial circumstances even though relatively low in absolute terms), any harm to persons other than the direct victim, and any harm in the form of public concern or erosion of public confidence.
3. In general terms, the seriousness of the offence will increase in line with the level of trust breached. The extent to which the nature and degree of trust placed in an offender should be regarded as increas-

---

[276] *R v Buddo* (1982) 4 Cr App R (S) 268, *R v Joyce and others* (1989) 11 Cr App R (S) 253, *R v Priestley* [1996] 2 Cr App R (S) 144
[277] Criminal Justice Act 2003, s.174(2)(a)

Sentencing Guidelines

ing seriousness will depend on a careful assessment of the circumstances of each individual case, including the type and terms of the relationship between the offender and victim.

4. The concept of breach of trust for the purposes of the offence of theft is wide. It includes not only employer/employee relationships and those between a professional adviser and client, but also extends more generally to relationships in which the offender was in a position of authority in relation to the victim, or one whereby they would be expected to have a duty to protect the interests of the victim, such as medical, social or care workers.

5. Thefts by offenders in whom a high degree of trust has been placed should generally attract higher sentences than thefts of similar amounts by offenders in whom a lower degree of trust is vested. The targeting of a vulnerable victim by an offender through a relationship or position of trust will indicate a higher level of culpability.

6. When assessing the seriousness of an offence, a court must always have regard to the full list of aggravating and mitigating factors in the Council guideline *Overarching Principles: Seriousness* (reproduced in Annex A [but not set out below: see **SG-25**]). Identified below are additional aggravating factors likely to be particularly relevant to this type of theft:

(i) Long course of offending

Offending carried out over a period of months or years represents a sustained and deliberate course of conduct and should be regarded as increasing an offender's culpability. Offending over an extended period may also result in greater harm to the victim in terms of financial loss and/or distress.

(ii) Suspicion deliberately thrown on others

Where an offender has taken positive steps to incriminate another, either at the time of committing the offence or subsequently, this should be regarded as an aggravating factor.

7. The Council has identified the following matters of personal mitigation which may be relevant in addition to those set out [in part B] above:

(i) Inappropriate degree of trust or responsibility

The fact that an offender succumbed to temptation having been placed in a position of trust or given responsibility to an inappropriate degree may be regarded as personal mitigation.

(ii) Cessation of offending

The fact that an offender voluntarily ceased offending before being discovered does not reduce the seriousness of the offence. However, if the claim to have stopped offending is genuine, it may constitute personal mitigation, particularly if it is evidence of remorse.[278]

(iii) Reporting an undiscovered offence

Where an offender brings the offending to the attention of his or her employer or the authorities, this may be treated as personal mitigation.[279]

8. In many cases of theft in breach of trust, termination of an offender's employment will be a natural consequence of committing the offence. Other than in the most exceptional of circumstances, loss of employment and any consequential hardship should not constitute personal mitigation.

9. Where a court is satisfied that a custodial sentence of 12 months or less is appropriate for an offence of theft in breach of trust, consideration should be given to whether that sentence can be suspended in accordance with the criteria in the Council guideline *New Sentences: Criminal Justice Act 2003*.[280] A suspended sentence order may be particularly appropriate where this would allow for reparation to be made either to the victim or to the community at large.

THEFT IN BREACH OF TRUST
Theft Act 1968 (section 1)

Maximum penalty: 7 years imprisonment

---

[278] *Overarching Principles: Seriousness*, published 16 December 2004, www.sentencing-guidelines.gov.uk
[279] ibid., para.1.29
[280] See pages 20–25

Type/nature of activity	Starting point	Sentencing range
Theft of £125,000 or more or Theft of £20,000 or more in breach of a high degree of trust	3 years custody	2–6 years custody
Theft of £20,000 or more but less than £125,000 or Theft of £2,000 or more but less than £20,000 in breach of a high degree of trust	2 years custody	12 months–3 years custody
Theft of £2,000 or more but less than £20,000 or Theft of less than £2,000 in breach of a high degree of trust	18 weeks custody	Community order (HIGH)—12 months custody
Theft of less than £2,000	Community order (MEDIUM)	Fine—26 weeks custody

Additional aggravating factors:
1. Long course of offending
2. Suspicion deliberately thrown on others
3. Offender motivated by intention to cause harm or out of revenge

Theft in a dwelling

SG-402

Factors to take into consideration

1. The following starting points and sentencing ranges are for a first time offender aged 18 or over who pleaded not guilty. They should be applied as set out . . . above.
2. The category of theft in a dwelling covers the situation where a theft is committed by an offender who is present in a dwelling with the authority of the owner or occupier. Examples include thefts by lodgers or visitors to the victim's residence, such as friends, relatives or salespeople. Such offences involve a violation of the privacy of the victim's home and constitute an abuse of the victim's trust. Where an offender enters a dwelling as a trespasser in order to commit theft, his or her conduct will generally constitute the more serious offence of burglary; **this guideline does not apply where the offender has been convicted of burglary.**[281]
3. For the purpose of this guideline, a 'vulnerable victim' is a person targeted by the offender because it is anticipated that he or she is unlikely or unable to resist the theft. The exploitation of a vulnerable victim indicates a high level of culpability and will influence the category of seriousness into which the offence falls.
4. The guideline is based on the assumption that most thefts in a dwelling do not involve property of high monetary value or of high value to the victim. Where the property stolen is of high monetary value or of high value (including sentimental value) to the victim, the appropriate sentence may be beyond the range into which the offence otherwise would fall. For the purpose of this form of theft, property worth more than £2,000 should generally be regarded as being of 'high monetary value', although this will depend on an assessment of all the circumstances of the particular case.
5. A sentence beyond the range into which the offence otherwise would fall may also be appropriate where the effect on the victim is particularly severe or where substantial consequential loss results (such as where the theft of equipment causes serious disruption to the victim's life or business).
6. When assessing the seriousness of an offence, a court must always have regard to the full list of aggravating and mitigating factors in the Council guideline *Overarching Principles: Seriousness* (reproduced in Annex A [not set out below: see **SG-25**]). Identified below are additional aggravating factors likely to be particularly relevant to this type of theft:

(i) Confrontation with the victim

Where there is intimidation and/or a face-to-face confrontation between the offender and victim, this should be regarded as an aggravating factor. Where the victim is a 'vulnerable victim' (as defined in para. 3 above), the use of intimidation will influence the category of seriousness into which the offence falls.

---

[281] [See now **SG-457**.]

(ii) Use of force, or threat of force

Generally, where theft in a dwelling is accompanied by force or the threat of force, it will constitute the more serious offence of robbery. However, there may be some cases involving force which are charged as theft in a dwelling, perhaps where the force was used after the theft had taken place. In such cases, an offender can be sentenced only for the offence of which he or she is convicted and the court is bound by the maximum penalty for that offence. At the same time, the court must have regard to all the circumstances of the case when determining the appropriate sentence. Where the victim is a 'vulnerable victim' (as defined in para. 3 [above]), the use or threat of force will influence the category of seriousness into which the offence falls. In other cases, it may be an aggravating factor.

(iii) Use of deception

Where an offender has deceived or tricked the victim in order to gain entry, for example by falsely claiming to be a meter reader, this should be regarded as an aggravating factor. Where the victim is a 'vulnerable victim' (as defined in para. 3 [above]), the use of deception will influence the category of seriousness into which the offence falls.

(iv) Taking steps to prevent the victim reporting the crime or seeking help

Where an offender takes steps to prevent the victim from reporting the offence or seeking help, such as by damaging a telephone, this should be regarded as increasing offence seriousness.

THEFT IN A DWELLING
Theft Act 1968 (section 1)

Maximum penalty: 7 years imprisonment

Type/nature of activity	Starting point	Range
Where the effect on the victim is particularly severe, the stolen property is of high value (as defined in para. 4 [above]), or substantial consequential loss results, a sentence higher than the range into which the offence otherwise would fall may be appropriate		
Theft from a vulnerable victim (as defined in para. 3 [above]) involving intimidation or the use or threat of force (falling short of robbery) or the use of deception	18 months custody	12 months–3 years custody
Theft from a vulnerable victim (as defined in para. 3 [above])	18 weeks custody	Community order (HIGH)— 12 months custody
Theft in a dwelling not involving vulnerable victim	Community order (MEDIUM)	Fine—18 weeks custody

Additional aggravating factors:
1. Offender motivated by intention to cause harm or out of revenge
2. Intimidation or face-to-face confrontation with victim [except where this raises the offence into a higher sentencing range]
3. Use of force, or threat of force, against victim (not amounting to robbery) [except where this raises the offence into a higher sentencing range]
4. Use of deception [except where this raises the offence into a higher sentencing range]
5. Offender takes steps to prevent the victim from reporting the crime or seeking help

SG-403   Theft from the person

Factors to take into consideration

1. The following starting points and sentencing ranges are for a first time offender aged 18 or over who pleaded not guilty. They should be applied as set out . . . above. While in some cases the conduct may be similar, **this guideline does not apply where the offender has been convicted of robbery; sentencers should instead refer to the Council guideline on robbery (see also para 6(ii) below).**

2. Theft from the person may encompass conduct such as 'pick-pocketing', where the victim is unaware that the property is being stolen, as well as the snatching of handbags, wallets, jewellery and mobile telephones from the victim's possession or from the vicinity of the victim. Where there is evidence of

planning, that will be an aggravating factor. This may, for example, be demonstrated where tourists are targeted because of their unfamiliarity with an area or because of a perception that they will not be available to give evidence if a case proceeds to trial. The offence constitutes an invasion of the victim's privacy and may cause the victim to experience distress, fear and inconvenience either during or after the event.

3. For the purpose of this guideline, a 'vulnerable victim' is a person targeted by the offender because it is anticipated that he or she is unlikely or unable to resist the theft. Young or elderly persons or those with disabilities may fall into this category. The exploitation of a vulnerable victim indicates a high level of culpability and will influence the category of seriousness into which the offence falls.

4. The guideline is based on the assumption that most thefts from the person do not involve property of high monetary value or of high value to the victim. Where the property stolen is of high monetary value or of high value (including sentimental value) to the victim, the appropriate sentence may be beyond the range into which the offence otherwise would fall. For the purpose of this form of theft, 'high monetary value' is defined as more than £2,000.

5. A sentence beyond the range into which the offence otherwise would fall may also be appropriate where the effect on the victim is particularly severe or where substantial consequential loss results (such as where the theft of equipment causes serious disruption to the victim's life or business).

6. When assessing the seriousness of an offence, a court must always have regard to the full list of aggravating and mitigating factors in the Council guideline *Overarching Principles: Seriousness* (reproduced in Annex A [not set out below: see **SG-25**]). Identified below are additional aggravating factors likely to be particularly relevant to this type of theft:

(i) Confrontation with the victim

Where there is intimidation and/or a face-to-face confrontation between the offender and victim, this should be regarded as an aggravating factor. Where the victim is a 'vulnerable victim' (as defined in para. 3 above), the use of intimidation will influence the category of seriousness into which the offence falls.

(ii) Use of force, or threat of force

Where the offender uses or threatens to use force to commit the theft, the conduct may constitute the more serious offence of robbery.[282] However, there may be some cases involving force which are charged as theft from the person. In such cases, an offender can be sentenced only for the offence of which he or she is convicted and the court is bound by the maximum penalty for that offence. At the same time, the court must have regard to all the circumstances of the case when determining the appropriate sentence. Where the victim is a 'vulnerable victim' (as defined in para. 3 above), the use or threat of force will influence the category of seriousness into which the offence falls. In other cases, it may be an aggravating factor.

(iii) High level of inconvenience caused to victim

The theft of some items, such as house keys and credit cards, may cause a particularly high level of distress and inconvenience to victims and this should be regarded as an aggravating factor. Tourists are vulnerable as a target for thefts from the person (not least because it may be perceived that they will not be available to give evidence) and may experience greater distress and inconvenience than others in arranging the replacement of documents, cash and cards. Such factors should be taken into account as increasing the seriousness of the offence.

7. Previous authorities have expressed concern about the prevalence of theft against the person and the associated need for deterrence, particularly in relation to pick-pocketing. The Council guideline *Overarching Principles: Seriousness* sets out the approach which should be adopted when considering issues of local prevalence. Further, national prevalence should not be used by sentencers to justify including a deterrent element in sentences as this is already taken into account in Council guidelines.

Theft from the Person
Theft Act 1968 (section 1)

Maximum penalty: 7 years imprisonment

---

[282] Theft Act 1968, s.8(1)

Sentencing Guidelines

Type/nature of activity	Starting point	Sentencing range
Where the effect on the victim is particularly severe, the stolen property is of high value (as defined in para. 4 [above]), or substantial consequential loss results, a sentence higher than the range into which the offence otherwise would fall may be appropriate.		
Theft from a vulnerable victim (as defined in para. 3 [above]) involving intimidation or the use or threat of force (falling short of robbery)	18 months custody	12 months–3 years custody
Theft from a vulnerable victim (as defined in para. 3 [above])	18 weeks custody	Community order (HIGH)— 12 months custody
Theft from the person not involving vulnerable victim	Community order (MEDIUM)	Fine—18 weeks custody

Additional aggravating factors:
1. Offender motivated by intention to cause harm or out of revenge
2. Intimidation or face-to-face confrontation with victim [except where this raises the offence into a higher sentencing range]
3. Use of force, or threat of force, against victim (not amounting to robbery) [except where this raises the offence into a higher sentencing range]
4. High level of inconvenience caused to victim, e.g. replacing house keys, credit cards etc.

SG-404   **Theft from a shop**

Factors to take into consideration

1. The following starting points and sentencing ranges are for a first time offender aged 18 or over who pleaded not guilty. They should be applied as set out . . . above.

2. The circumstances of this offence can vary significantly. At the least serious end of the scale are thefts involving low value goods, no (or little) planning and no violence or damage; a non-custodial sentence will usually be appropriate for a first time offender. At the higher end of the spectrum are thefts involving organised gangs or groups or the threat or use of force and a custodial starting point will usually be appropriate.

3. When assessing the level of harm, the circumstances of the retailer are a proper consideration; a greater level of harm may be caused where the theft is against a small retailer.

4. Retailers may suffer additional loss as a result of this type of offending such as the cost of preventative security measures, higher insurance premiums and time spent by staff dealing with the prosecution of offenders. However, the seriousness of an individual case must be judged on its own dimension of harm and culpability and the sentence on an individual offender should not be increased to reflect the harm caused to retailers in general by the totality of this type of offending.

5. In accordance with section 143(2) of the Criminal Justice Act 2003, any recent previous convictions for theft and dishonesty offences will need to be taken into account in sentencing. Where an offender demonstrates a level of 'persistent' or 'seriously persistent' offending, the community and custody thresholds may be crossed even though the other characteristics of the offence would otherwise warrant a lesser sentence.

6. When assessing the seriousness of an offence, a court must always have regard to the full list of aggravating and mitigating factors in the Council guideline *Overarching Principles: Seriousness* (reproduced in Annex A [not set out below]).

7. The Council guideline on Seriousness identifies high value as an aggravating factor in property offences. In cases of theft from a shop, theft of high value goods may be associated with other aggravating factors such as the degree of planning, professionalism and/or operating in a group, and care will need to be taken to avoid double counting. Deliberately targeting high value goods will always make an offence more serious.

8. Additional aggravating factors particularly relevant to this type of theft include:

    (i) Involving a child

    Where a child accompanies an offender during the offence, it will be an aggravating factor if the child is involved in, or is likely to be aware of, the theft or could be influenced or distressed by it. However, the mere presence of a child does not make the offence more serious.

(ii) Offender subject to a banning order

The fact that an offender is subject to a banning order that includes the store in which the offence is committed is an aggravating factor. Breach of any type of order (for example a civil banning order or a shop imposed ban) will aggravate to the same degree. However, where an offender is being sentenced also for breach, care must be taken to ensure that there is no double counting.

(iii) Intimidation, threat or use of force and additional damage to property

Generally, where theft from a shop is accompanied by force or the threat of force, it will be appropriate to charge the offender with the more serious offence of robbery. However, there may be some cases involving force which are charged as theft from a shop. In such cases, an offender can be sentenced only for the offence of which he or she is convicted and the court is bound by the maximum penalty for that offence. At the same time, the court must have regard to all the circumstances of the case when determining the appropriate sentence. This may result in sentencers concluding that the offending was aggravated by the use or threat of force and that a more severe sentence is warranted. Any additional damage to property (for example caused when an offender is tackled or detained) also aggravates the seriousness of the offence.

THEFT FROM A SHOP
Theft Act 1968 (section 1)

Maximum penalty: 7 years imprisonment

Type/nature of activity	Starting point	Sentencing range
Organised gang/group **and** Intimidation or the use or threat of force (short of robbery)	12 months custody	36 weeks–4 years custody
Significant intimidation or threats **or** Use of force resulting in slight injury **or** Very high level of planning **or** Significant related damage	6 weeks custody	Community order (HIGH)—36 weeks custody
Low level intimidation or threats **or** Some planning e.g. a session of stealing on the same day or going equipped **or** Some related damage	Community order (LOW)	Fine-Community order (MEDIUM)
Little or no planning or sophistication and Goods stolen of low value	Fine	Conditional discharge—Community order (LOW)

Additional aggravating factors:
1. Child accompanying offender is involved in or aware of theft
2. Offender is subject to a banning order that includes the store targeted
3. Offender motivated by intention to cause harm or out of revenge
4. Professional offending
5. Victim particularly vulnerable (e.g. small independent shop)
6. Offender targeted high value goods

Burglary in a building other than a dwelling   **SG-405**

[Superseded in respect of Sentences after 16 January 2012: See now SG-457.]
ANNEX A: AGGRAVATING AND MITIGATING FACTORS IDENTIFIED IN THE COUNCIL
GUIDELINE *OVERARCHING PRINCIPLES: SERIOUSNESS*

[Not reproduced – see **SG-25**.]

SG-406   PART 15   BREACH OF AN ANTI-SOCIAL BEHAVIOUR ORDER

...This guideline applies to the sentencing of offenders convicted of breaching an anti-social behaviour order (ASBO) who are sentenced on or after 5 January 2009.

The Council has previously set out the approach to dealing with breaches of orders in its guidelines on New Sentences: Criminal Justice Act 2003 and Breach of Protective Orders. The main aim of sentencing for breach of a court order is to achieve the purpose of the order; in the case of an ASBO that is to protect the public from behaviour that is likely to cause harassment, alarm or distress.

Any perception that the courts do not treat seriously a failure to comply with a court order can undermine public confidence and is therefore an important additional consideration.

Since the ability of a court to deal appropriately with an order that has been breached depends on how it was made, Annex A to the guideline summarises the key principles and considerations applicable to the making of an ASBO.

This guideline applies to the sentencing of adult and young offenders. It is recognised that a large proportion of orders are imposed on persons under 18 years of age. Although the sentencing framework for youths is very different from that for adults, and a guideline for sentencing young offenders will follow in due course, the Council considered that sentencers would find it helpful to have guiding principles for sentencing young offenders for breach of an ASBO...

SG-407   A. Statutory provision

1. [Sets out the CDA 1998, s. 1(10).]
2. Where a person is convicted of an offence of breach of an anti-social behaviour order (ASBO), it is not open to the court to make an order discharging the offender conditionally.[283]

SG-408   B. Introduction

3. An ASBO is a preventative order that can be made in either civil or criminal proceedings; its aim is to protect the public from behaviour that causes, or is likely to cause, harassment, alarm or distress. An order may be made on application to a magistrates' court, on conviction, or in conjunction with other proceedings in the County Court.
4. Since the ability of a court to deal appropriately with an order that has been breached depends on how it was made, Annex A summarises the key principles and considerations applicable to the making of an ASBO.
5. This guideline relates to the sentencing of both adult and young offenders. As the sentencing framework that applies to offenders aged under 18 is significantly different from that for older offenders, the guidance for young offenders is in the form of principles particularly regarding the circumstances in which a custodial sentence might be justified. The maximum penalty in the case of a young offender is detention for 24 months.
6. Breach of this type of order is different from breach of a community order or failure to surrender to custody because it has the potential to affect a community or the public at large in a way that causes direct harm.

The main aim of sentencing for breach of a court order is to achieve the purpose of the order. Therefore, the sentence for breach of an ASBO should primarily reflect the harassment, alarm or distress involved; the fact that it constituted breach of a court order is a secondary consideration.

SG-409   C. Assessing seriousness

7. The sentence for breach of an ASBO must be commensurate with the seriousness of the offence; that is determined by assessing the culpability of the offender and any harm which the offence caused, was intended to cause or might foreseeably have caused.[284]
8. A community sentence can be imposed only if a court considers that the offence is serious enough to justify it,[285] and a custodial sentence can be imposed only if a court considers that a community sentence or a fine alone cannot be justified in view of the seriousness of the offence.[286] The Council

---

[283] Crime and Disorder Act 1998, s.1(11)
[284] Criminal Justice Act 2003, s.143(1)
[285] Criminal Justice Act 2003, s.148(1)
[286] ibid., s.152(2)

has published a definitive guideline on seriousness that guides sentencers through the process of determining whether the respective sentencing thresholds have been crossed.[287]

9. A wide range of prohibitions can be attached to an order; consequently the degree of harm resulting from a breach will vary greatly and may be experienced by the wider community as well as by individuals.

10. In order properly to assess the seriousness of a breach of an ASBO, a court needs to be aware of the purpose of the order and the context in which it was made. A breach may be of one or more prohibitions in an order; the approach to sentencing is based on an assessment of the seriousness of the harm arising from the breach (or intended by the offender) rather than the number of prohibitions not complied with.

(i) Culpability and harm

11. When a court is considering the seriousness of breach of an order such as an ASBO, it will need to consider two aspects of culpability:

(a)   **The degree to which the offender intended to breach the order.**

Culpability is variable and an offender may have:

- intended the breach;
- been reckless as to whether the order was breached;
- been aware of the risk of breach; or
- been unaware of this risk due to an incomplete understanding of the terms of the order.

(b)   **The degree to which the offender intended to cause the harm that resulted (or could have resulted).**

Culpability will be higher where the offender foresaw the harm likely to be caused by the breach and will be at its highest where such harm was intended.

12. There are also two dimensions to the harm involved in breach of an ASBO:

(a)   the breach may itself cause harassment, alarm or distress, which can reduce the quality of life in a community.

(b)   breach of an ASBO contravenes an order of the court, and this can undermine public confidence in the effective administration of justice.

13. The assessment of the seriousness of an individual offence must take into account not only the harm actually caused by an offence but also any harm that was intended or might foreseeably have been caused.[288]

14. The test of foreseeability is objective[289] but as the prohibitions imposed must have been considered by a court to be necessary to prevent anti-social behaviour, some degree of harm must always be foreseeable whenever an order is breached. Where a breach causes harm that was not readily foreseeable, the level of culpability should carry more weight than harm when assessing offence seriousness.[290]

(ii) Relevance of the originating conduct

15. The **original conduct** that led to the making of an order is a relevant consideration in so far as it indicates the level of harm caused and whether this was intended.[291]

16. High culpability and/or harm may be indicated if the breach continues a pattern of behaviour against an identifiable victim. Conversely, where there is little connection between the breach and the behaviour that the order was aimed at, this may indicate a less serious offence.

17. The court should examine the prohibitions of the order itself (particularly those in older orders which may have been made without the benefit of the guidance summarised in Annex A), their necessity and reasonableness in all the circumstances.[292]

---

[287] *Overarching Principles: Seriousness*, published 16 December 2004, www.sentencing-guidelines.gov.uk

[288] Criminal Justice Act 2003, s.143(1)

[289] Harm must have been foreseeable by 'a reasonable person'

[290] *Overarching Principles: Seriousness*, published 16 December 2004, www.sentencing-guidelines.gov.uk

[291] *Breach of a Protective Order*, published 7 December 2006, www.sentencing-guidelines.gov.uk

[292] Where appropriate, an application may be made separately for the order to be varied: Crime and Disorder Act 1998, ss.1(8) or 1CA. See also the Magistrates' Courts (Anti-Social Behaviour Orders) Rules 2002. Where the subject/offender is aged under 18, Practice Direction (Magistrates' Courts: Anti-Social Behaviour Orders: Composition of Benches) [2006] 1 AER 886 provides for the constitution of the court.

(iii) Breach of an interim order

18. Breach of an interim order or a final order is equally serious and the same approach to sentencing should be taken.

19. Sentence for a breach of an interim order should be imposed as soon as possible. If the hearing regarding the final order can be brought forward, this should be done so that the two issues can be considered together. However, sentencing for the breach of the interim order should not be delayed for this purpose.

20. Where an interim order is breached the court should consider the extent to which an urgent need for specific interim prohibitions was demonstrated, or if the interim order was sought principally to obtain additional time to prepare a case for the full hearing.[293]

21. Where an interim order has been made without notice to the subject, the order does not take effect until it has been served. If doubts arise about the extent to which the subject has understood the prohibitions but the defence of reasonable excuse is not made out, a lack of understanding of the terms of the order may still mitigate the seriousness of the offence through reducing culpability.

(iv) A breach that also constitutes another criminal offence

22. Whether one offence or two has been charged, the sentence should reflect all relevant aspects of the offence so that, provided the facts are not in issue, the result should be the same.[294]

   (a) if the substantive offence only has been charged, the fact that it constitutes breach of an ASBO should be treated as an aggravating factor;

   (b) if breach of the order only has been charged, the sentence should reflect the full circumstances of the breach, which will include the conduct that could have been charged as a substantive offence.

23. Where breach of an ASBO also constitutes another offence with a lower maximum penalty than that for breach of the order, this penalty is an element to be considered in the interests of proportionality, although the court is not limited by it when sentencing an adult or youth for breach.

(v) Aggravating and mitigating factors

24. The Council guideline *Overarching Principles: Seriousness* identifies a number of factors that might increase or mitigate the seriousness of an offence. For ease of reference, the factors are set out in Annex B.

(vi) Personal mitigation

25. Offender mitigation is particularly relevant to breach of an ASBO as compliance with the order depends on the ability to understand its terms and make rational decisions in relation to these. Sentence may be mitigated where:

   • the offender has a lower level of understanding due to mental health issues or learning difficulties;
   • the offender was acting under the influence of an older or more experienced offender; or
   • there has been compliance with an Individual Support Order or Intervention Order imposed when the ASBO was made.

SG-410   ## D. Sentencing guideline—Adult offenders

Sentencing ranges and starting points

1. This guideline applies to a *"first time offender"* who has been **convicted after a trial**. In common with other proceedings based on breach of a court order,[295] it is likely that an offender in breach of an ASBO will have previous convictions. That has been taken into account in determining the starting points and ranges. Therefore, within this guideline, a "first time offender" is a person who does not have a conviction for breach of an ASBO rather than the usual approach which is based on the existence of any conviction which, by virtue of section 143(2) of the Criminal Justice Act 2003, must be treated as an aggravating factor.

---

[293] A report commissioned by the YJB concluded that there may be grounds for interim ASBOs only where there is an urgent need for specific prohibitions: Aikta-Reena Solanki, Tim Bateman, Gwyneth Boswell and Emily Hill, Anti-social Behaviour Orders, YJB (2006).

[294] *Breach of a Protective Order*, published 7 December 2006, www.sentencing-guidelines.gov.uk

[295] for example, failing to surrender to bail

2. As an aid to consistency of approach, the guideline describes a number of types of activity which would fall within the broad definition of the offence. These are set out in a column headed 'Nature of failure & harm'.

3. The expected approach is for a court to identify the description that most nearly matches the particular facts of the offence for which sentence is being imposed. This will identify a starting point from which the sentencer can depart to reflect aggravating or mitigating factors affecting the seriousness of the offence (beyond those contained within the column describing the nature of the failure or of the harm) to reach a **provisional sentence**.

4. The **sentencing range** is the bracket into which the provisional sentence will normally fall after having regard to factors which aggravate or mitigate the seriousness of the offence. The particular circumstances may, however, make it appropriate that the provisional sentence falls outside the range.

5. Where the offender has previous convictions which aggravate the seriousness of the current offence, that may take the provisional sentence beyond the range given particularly where there are significant other aggravating factors present.

6. Once the provisional sentence has been identified by reference to those factors affecting the seriousness of the offence, the court will take into account any relevant factors of personal mitigation, which may take the sentence beyond the range given.

7. Where there has been a guilty plea, any reduction attributable to that plea will be applied to the sentence at this stage. Again, this reduction may take the sentence below the range provided.

8. A court must give its reasons for imposing a sentence of a different kind or outside the range provided in the guidelines.[296]

The decision making process

[Sets out the standard sequential decision making process: identify starting point, consider aggravating factors, consider mitigating factors, apply reduction for guilty plea, consider ancillary orders, review in light of the totality principle and give reasons.]

Factors to take into consideration

1. The starting points and sentencing ranges are for a *"first time offender"* who pleaded not guilty. In this guideline, a *"first time offender"* is one who does not have a previous conviction for breach of an ASBO.

2. Where a court determines that there are other convictions which it is reasonable to treat as a factor aggravating the seriousness of the breach,[297] that factor will be taken into account at stage 2 of the sentencing process set out on page 7.

3. An ASBO may be breached in a wide range of circumstances and may involve one or more prohibitions not being complied with. The examples given below are intended to illustrate how the scale of the conduct that led to the breach, taken as a whole, might come within the three levels of seriousness:

   • Serious harm caused or intended—breach at this level of seriousness will involve the use of violence, significant threats or intimidation or the targeting of individuals or groups of people in a manner that leads to a fear of violence.

   • Lesser degree of harm intended or likely—examples may include lesser degrees of threats or intimidation, the use of seriously abusive language, or causing more than minor damage to property.

   • No harm caused or intended—in the absence of intimidation or the causing of fear of violence, breaches involving being drunk or begging may be at this level, as may prohibited use of public transport or entry into a prohibited area, where there is no evidence that harassment, alarm or distress was caused or intended.

4. The suggested starting points are based on the assumption that the offender had the highest level of culpability.

5. Aggravating and mitigating factors specifically relevant to sentencing for breach of an ASBO are included in the guideline. Care needs to be taken to ensure that there is no double counting where an element of the breach determines the level of seriousness where it might in other circumstances be an aggravating factor. When assessing the seriousness of an offence, the court must always refer to the full list of aggravating and mitigating factors in the Council guideline on Seriousness (see Annex B).[298]

---

[296] Criminal Justice Act 2003, s.174(2)(a)
[297] in accordance with Criminal Justice Act 2003, s.143(2)
[298] *Overarching Principles: Seriousness*, published 16 December 2004, www.sentencing-guidelines.gov.uk

6. In the most serious cases, involving repeat offending and a breach causing serious harassment together with the presence of several aggravating factors, such as the use of violence, a sentence beyond the highest range will be justified.

7. Once the provisional sentence has been identified by reference to factors affecting the seriousness of the offence, the court will take into account any relevant factors of personal mitigation (see paragraph 25 above), and, in accordance with the Council guideline[299] consider reducing the sentence where a guilty plea was entered.

8. When imposing a community order, the court must ensure that the requirements imposed are proportionate to the seriousness of the breach, compatible with each other,[300] and also with the prohibitions of the ASBO if the latter is to remain in force. Even where the threshold for a custodial sentence is crossed, a custodial sentence is not inevitable.[301]

9. An offender may be sentenced for more than one offence of breach, which occurred on different days. While consecutive sentences may be imposed in such cases, the overall sentence should reflect the totality principle.

BREACH OF AN ANTI-SOCIAL BEHAVIOUR ORDER
Crime and Disorder Act 1998 (section 1(10))

Maximum Penalty: 5 years imprisonment

Note: A conditional discharge is not available as a sentence for this offence

Nature of failure & harm	Starting point	Sentencing range
Serious harassment, alarm or distress has been caused or where such harm was intended	26 weeks custody	Custody threshold—2 years custody
Lesser degree of harassment, alarm or distress, where such harm was intended, or where it would have been likely if the offender had not been apprehended	6 weeks custody	Community Order (MEDIUM)—26 weeks custody
No harassment, alarm or distress was actually caused by the breach and none was intended by the offender	Community Order (LOW)	Fine Band B—Community Order (MEDIUM)

Aggravating factors	Mitigating factors
1. Offender has a history of disobedience to court orders. 2. Breach was committed immediately or shortly after the order was made. 3. Breach was committed subsequent to earlier breach proceedings arising from the same order. 4. Targeting of a person the order was made to protect or a witness in the original proceedings.	1. Breach occurred after a long period of compliance. 2. The prohibition(s) breached was not fully understood, especially where an interim order was made without notice.

SG-411 **E. Sentencing principles: Young Offenders**

1. The approach to assessing the seriousness of a breach outlined above at paragraphs 7 to 25 applies equally to youths. A court must impose a community or custodial sentence only if such a sentence is warranted by the seriousness of the offence and no lesser sentence can be justified.

2. When sentencing a young offender, the normal approach is for the penalty to reflect both the reduction in culpability (for example, due to a lesser ability to foresee the consequences of actions) and the more onerous effects of punishments on education and personal development in comparison with an adult offender.

3. The sentencing framework that applies to offenders aged under 18 is significantly different from that for adult offenders and key principles are set out in Annex C. The maximum penalty for this offence when committed by a young offender is a 24 month detention and training order (DTO). With the

---

[299] *Reduction in Sentence for a Guilty Plea*, published 20 July 2007, www.sentencing-guidelines.gov.uk
[300] *New Sentences: Criminal Justice Act 2003*, published 16 December 2004, www.sentencing-guidelines.gov.uk
[301] ibid.

exception of a conditional discharge,[302] the full range of disposals of the youth court is available, and these are also outlined in Annex C.[303]

4. In most cases of breach by a young offender convicted after a trial, the appropriate sentence will be a community sentence.[304] Within the sentence(s) available, a range of requirements can be attached; the court will consider the seriousness of the breach, which requirement(s) will best prevent further offending and the individual circumstances of the offender.

5. The court must ensure that the requirements imposed are compatible both with each other and with the prohibitions of the ASBO if the latter is to remain in force, and that the combination of both is not so onerous as to make further breaches likely.

6. The particular stage of intellectual or emotional maturity of the individual (which may not correspond with actual age) will also influence sentence. A young offender is likely to perceive a particular time period as being longer in comparison with an adult, and this may be of relevance when considering how much time has elapsed between imposition and breach of the order.

7. The principles to be followed when sentencing a youth for breach of an ASBO are as follows:
"**First time offender**"[305] **pleading guilty**: the court[306] must make a referral order unless it imposes an absolute discharge, a custodial sentence or a hospital order;

In all other cases:

(i)   in some less serious cases, such as where the breach has not involved any harassment, alarm or distress, a fine may be appropriate if it will be paid by the offender, or otherwise a reparation order;

(ii)   in most cases, the appropriate sentence will be a community sentence;

(iii) the custody threshold should be set at a significantly higher level than the threshold applicable to adult offenders;

(iv)   the custody threshold usually will not be crossed unless the breach involved serious harassment, alarm or distress through either the use of violence, threats or intimidation or the targeting of individuals/groups in a manner that led to a fear of violence;

(v)   exceptionally, the custody threshold may also be crossed where a youth is being sentenced for more than one offence of breach (committed on separate occasions within a short period) involving a lesser but substantial degree of harassment, alarm or distress;

(vi)   even where the custody threshold is crossed, the court should normally impose a community sentence in preference to a DTO, as custody should be used only as a measure of last resort; and

(vii) where the court considers a custodial sentence to be unavoidable, the starting point for sentencing should be 4 months detention, with a range of up to 12 months. Where a youth is being sentenced for more than one breach involving serious harassment, alarm or distress, sentence may go beyond that range.

Aggravating and mitigating factors

8. As with adult offenders, factors that are likely to <u>aggravate</u> an offence of breach of an anti-social behaviour order are:
   • history of disobedience of court orders;
   • the breach was committed immediately or shortly after the order was made;
   • the breach was committed subsequent to earlier breach proceedings arising from the same order;
   • targeting of a person the order was made to protect or of a witness in the original proceedings.

9. Factors that are likely to <u>mitigate</u> the seriousness of the breach are:
   • the breach occurred after a long period of compliance;
   • the prohibition(s) breached was not fully understood, especially where an interim order was made without notice.

Personal mitigation

10. Offender mitigation is particularly relevant to breach of an ASBO as compliance with the order depends on the ability to understand its terms and make rational decisions in relation to these. Sentence may be mitigated where:

---

[302] Crime and Disorder Act 1998, s.1(11) and s.1C(9)

[303] If the young offender has also been charged with a grave crime under s.91 Powers of Criminal Courts (Sentencing) Act 2000, the case may be committed to the Crown Court. Similarly, where the young offender is committed to the Crown Court for sentence under the dangerous offender provisions.

[304] though see paragraph 7 below

[305] For the purpose of this requirement, a "first time offender" is an offender who has never been convicted by or before a court in the United Kingdom of any offence other than the offence and any connected offence, or been bound over in criminal proceedings; Powers of Criminal Court (Sentencing) Act 2000, s.17(1)(b) and (c)

[306] A referral order may be made by a youth court or other magistrates' court; Powers of Criminal Courts (Sentencing) Act 2000, s.16(1)

- the offender has a lower level of understanding due to mental health issues or learning difficulties;
- the offender was acting under the influence of an older or more experienced offender; or
- there has been compliance with an Individual Support Order or Intervention Order imposed when the ASBO was made.

11. Other offender mitigating factors that may be particularly relevant to young offenders include peer pressure and a lack of parental support.

SG-412   PART 16   ATTEMPTED MURDER

…This guideline applies to the sentencing of offenders convicted of any of the offences dealt with herein who are sentenced on or after 27 July 2009.

This guideline applies only to the sentencing of offenders aged 18 and older. The legislative provisions relating to the sentencing of youths are different; the younger the age, the greater the difference. A separate guideline setting out general principles relating to the sentencing of youths is planned.

…

SG-413   Introduction

1. This guideline covers the single offence of attempted murder. The Council has published a separate definitive guideline for offences of assault which do not result in the death of the victim.[307]
2. There are critical differences between murder and attempted murder; not only is the intended result not achieved but also, for attempted murder, there must have been an intention to kill whereas a charge of murder may arise where the intention was to inflict grievous bodily harm. These differences are reflected in the approach set out below which supersedes previous guidance from the Court of Appeal in *Ford*[308] and other judgments.

SG-414   A. Assessing seriousness

(i) *Culpability and harm*

3. The culpability of the offender is the initial factor in determining the seriousness of an offence. It is an essential element of the offence of attempted murder that the offender had an intention to kill; accordingly an offender convicted of this offence will have demonstrated a high level of culpability. Even so, the precise level of culpability will vary in line with the circumstances of the offence and whether the offence was planned or spontaneous. The use of a weapon may influence this assessment.
4. In common with all offences against the person, this offence has the potential to contain an imbalance between culpability and harm.[309]
5. Where the degree of harm actually caused to the victim of an attempted murder is negligible, it is inevitable that this will impact on the overall assessment of offence seriousness.
6. However, although the degree of (or lack of) physical or psychological harm suffered by a victim may generally influence sentence, the statutory definition of harm encompasses not only the harm actually caused by an offence but also any harm that the offence was intended to cause or might foreseeably have caused; since the offence can only be committed where there is an intention to kill, an offence of attempted murder will always involve, in principle, the most serious level of harm.

(ii) *Aggravating and mitigating factors*

7. The most serious offences of attempted murder will include those which encompass the factors set out in schedule 21 to the Criminal Justice Act 2003, paragraphs 4 and 5 that, had the offence been murder, would make the seriousness of the offence 'exceptionally high' or 'particularly high'. [See **E3.2** in the main work.]
8. The particular facts of the offence will identify the appropriate level. In all cases, the aggravating and mitigating factors that will influence the identification of the provisional sentence within the range follow those set out in schedule 21 with suitable adjustments. These factors are included in the guideline [below].
9. The *Seriousness* guideline[310] sets out aggravating and mitigating factors that are applicable to a wide range of cases; [see **SG-21**]. Some are already reflected in the factors referred to above. Care needs to be taken to ensure that there is no double counting where an essential element of the offence charged

---

[307] *Assault and other offences against the person*, published 20 February 2008, www.sentencing-guidelines.gov.uk
[308] [2005] EWCA Crim 1358
[309] See *Overarching Principles: Seriousness*, para. 1.17, published 16 December 2004, www.sentencing-guidelines.gov.uk
[310] *Overarching Principles: Seriousness*, paras. 1.20–1.27 published on 16 December 2004; www.sentencing-guidelines.gov.uk

might, in other circumstances, be an aggravating factor. An additional statutory aggravating factor has been introduced by the Counter-Terrorism Act 2008 for prescribed offences which include attempted murder.[311]

10. This guideline is not intended to provide for an offence found to be based on a genuine belief that the murder would have been an act of mercy. Whilst the approach to assessing the seriousness of the offence may be similar, there are likely to be other factors present (relating to the offence and the offender) that would have to be taken into account and reflected in the sentence.

B. Ancillary orders   SG-415

Compensation orders

11. A court must consider making a compensation order in respect of any personal injury, loss or damage occasioned. There is no limit to the amount of compensation that may be awarded in the Crown Court.

C. Sentencing ranges and starting points   SG-416

12. Typically, a guideline will apply to an offence that can be committed in a variety of circumstances with different levels of seriousness. The starting points and ranges are based upon an adult '*first time offender*' who has been **convicted after a trial**. Within the guidelines, a '*first time offender*' is a person who does not have a conviction which, by virtue of section 143(2) of the Criminal Justice Act 2003, must be treated as an aggravating factor.

13. As an aid to consistency of approach, the guideline describes a number of levels or types of activity which would fall within the broad definition of the offence.

14. The expected approach is for a court to identify the description that most nearly matches the particular facts of the offence for which sentence is being imposed. This will identify a **starting point** from which the sentencer can depart to reflect aggravating or mitigating factors affecting the seriousness of the offence (beyond those contained within the column describing the nature of the offence) to reach a **provisional sentence**.

15. The **sentencing range** is the bracket into which the provisional sentence will normally fall after having regard to factors which aggravate or mitigate the seriousness of the offence. The particular circumstances may, however, make it appropriate that the provisional sentence falls outside the range.

16. Where the offender has previous convictions which aggravate the seriousness of the current offence, that may take the provisional sentence beyond the range given particularly where there are significant other aggravating factors present.

17. Once the provisional sentence has been identified by reference to those factors affecting the seriousness of the offence, the court will take into account any relevant factors of personal mitigation, which may take the sentence below the range given.

18. Where there has been a guilty plea, any reduction attributable to that plea will be applied to the sentence at this stage. This reduction may take the sentence below the range provided.

19. A court must give its reasons for imposing a sentence of a different kind or outside the range provided in the guidelines.

D. Factors to take into consideration   SG-417

1. Attempted murder is a serious offence for the purposes of the provisions in the Criminal Justice Act 2003[312] for dealing with dangerous offenders. When sentencing an offender convicted of this offence, in many circumstances a court may need to consider imposing a discretionary life sentence or one of the sentences for public protection prescribed in the Act.

2. The starting points and ranges are based upon a first time adult offender convicted after a trial (see paragraphs 12–19 above). They will be relevant when imposing a determinate sentence and when fixing any minimum term that may be necessary. When setting the minimum term to be served within an indeterminate sentence, in accordance with normal practice that term will usually be half the equivalent determinate sentence.[313]

3. Attempted murder requires an intention to kill. Accordingly, an offender convicted of this offence will have demonstrated a high level of culpability. Even so, the precise level of culpability will vary in line with the circumstances of the offence and whether the offence was planned or spontaneous. The use of a weapon may influence this assessment.

---

[311] s. 30 and schedule 2. If a court determines that the offence has a terrorist connection, it must treat that as an aggravating factor, and state in open court that the offence was so aggravated.

[312] Sections 224–230 as amended

[313] *R v Szczerba* [2002] 2 Cr App R (S) 86

4. The level of injury or harm sustained by the victim as well as any harm that the offence was intended to cause or might foreseeably have caused, must be taken into account and reflected in the sentence imposed.

5. The degree of harm will vary greatly. Where there is low harm and high culpability, culpability is more significant.[314] Even in cases where a low level of injury (or no injury) has been caused, an offence of attempted murder will be extremely serious.

6. The most serious offences will include those which encompass the factors set out in schedule 21 to the Criminal Justice Act 2003, paragraphs 4 and 5 that, had the offence been murder, would make the seriousness of the offence 'exceptionally high' or 'particularly high': see [E3.2 in the main work].

7. The particular facts of the offence will identify the appropriate level. In all cases, the aggravating and mitigating factors that will influence the identification of the provisional sentence within the range follow those set out in schedule 21 with suitable adjustments. This guideline is not intended to provide for an offence found to be based on a genuine belief that the murder would have been an act of mercy.

8. When assessing the seriousness of an offence, the court should also refer to the list of general aggravating and mitigating factors in the Council guideline on *Seriousness* (see [SG-21]). Care should be taken to ensure there is no double counting where an essential element of the offence charged might, in other circumstances, be an aggravating factor.

SG-418

ATTEMPTED MURDER
Criminal Attempts Act 1981 (section 1(1))

THIS IS A SERIOUS OFFENCE FOR THE PURPOSES OF SECTION 224 CRIMINAL JUSTICE ACT 2003

Maximum penalty: Life imprisonment

Nature of offence	Starting point	Sentencing range
Level 1 *The most serious offences including those which (if the charge had been murder) would come within para. 4 or para. 5 of schedule 21 to the Criminal Justice Act 2003*		
• Serious and long term physical or psychological harm	30 years custody	27–35 years custody
• Some physical or psychological harm	20 years custody	17–25 years custody
• Little or no physical or psychological harm	15 years custody	12–20 years custody
Level 2 *Other planned attempt to kill*		
• Serious and long term physical or psychological harm	20 years custody	17–25 years custody
• Some physical or psychological harm	15 years custody	12–20 years custody
• Little or no physical or psychological harm	10 years custody	7–15 years custody
Level 3 *Other spontaneous attempt to kill*		
• Serious and long term physical or psychological harm	15 years custody	12–20 years custody
• Some physical or psychological harm	12 years custody	9–17 years custody
• Little or no physical or psychological harm	9 years custody	6–14 years custody

Specific aggravating factors	Specific mitigating factors
(a) the fact that the victim was particularly vulnerable, for example, because of age or disability (b) mental or physical suffering inflicted on the victim (c) the abuse of a position of trust (d) the use of duress or threats against another person to facilitate the commission of the offence (e) the fact that the victim was providing a public service or performing a public duty	(a) the fact that the offender suffered from any mental disorder or mental disability which lowered his degree of culpability (b) the fact that the offender was provoked (for example, by prolonged stress) (c) the fact that the offender acted to any extent in self-defence (d) the age of the offender

---

[314] *Overarching Principles: Seriousness*, para. 1.19, published on 16 December 2004; www.sentencing.guidelines.gov.uk

The presence of one or more aggravating features will indicate a more severe sentence within the suggested range and, if the aggravating feature(s) are exceptionally serious, the case will move up to the next level.

[Annex A is an extract from the CJA 2003, sch. 21. It is not reproduced here. For the relevant text, see **E3.4** in the main work.   **SG-419**

Annex B reproduces the elements indicating higher culpability, a more than usually serious degree of harm and lower culpability and factors which may be relevant personal mitigation from the Council guideline *Overarching Principles: Seriousness*. See **SG-21** for the full guideline.]

PART 17   SENTENCING FOR FRAUD—STATUTORY OFFENCES   **SG-420**

…This guideline applies to the sentencing of offenders convicted of statutory offences of fraud who are sentenced on or after 26 October 2009.

This guideline does not cover the common law offence of **cheating the public revenue**, or **conspiracy to defraud**. Judges should continue to refer to existing guidance from the Court of Appeal (Criminal Division) when sentencing these offences.

This guideline applies only to the sentencing of offenders aged 18 and over. The legislative provisions relating to the sentencing of youths are different; the younger the age, the greater the difference. A separate guideline setting out general principles relating to the sentencing of youths is planned.

…

A. Statutory provisions and Introduction   **SG-421**

1. Fraud offences involve offenders dishonestly intending to make a gain by exposing someone else to a risk of loss; the gain may be financial and/or involve other property. Fraud offences are diverse and there is an ever-increasing number of ways in which they can be committed.
2. This guideline applies to sentencing for statutory offences of fraud. This guideline does not cover the common law offence of **cheating the public revenue, or conspiracy to defraud**. The common law offence of cheating the public revenue is generally reserved for the most serious and unusual offences[315] and where a sentence 'in excess of the statutory maximum for other offences…would be…proper.'[316] As such cases are unusual, no proposals are made for sentencing offenders convicted of this offence. It would be open to a court to have regard to the principles expressed in the guideline for fraud against HMRC when sentencing an offender convicted of cheating the public revenue, but it should be used only as a point of reference as higher starting points are likely to be necessary. Sentencers should continue to refer to existing guidance from the Court of Appeal (Criminal Division) when sentencing these offences.
3. The statutory offences included in this guideline are set out in paragraph 5 (statutory definitions and maximum penalties are set out in **Annex A**). The generic fraud offence introduced by section 1 of the Fraud Act 2006 was designed to capture all forms of fraudulent activity committed by individual offenders, including minor offences. However, other offences will continue to be prosecuted, thus the proposed guidelines include related offences.
4. Since many of the offences are defined broadly (in order to encapsulate a wide range of behaviour), some types of fraudulent activity are capable of leading to conviction for more than one offence; accordingly, the guidelines focus on the type of fraud,[317] rather than the specific conviction offence, in order to establish appropriate sentence levels which take account of the interrelationship between the offences. The guideline aims to produce a coherent and consistent approach to sentencing all forms of fraudulent behaviour; it supersedes previous guideline (and other significant) cases which have been reviewed in the light of subsequent changes to the sentencing framework, particularly those in the Criminal Justice Act 2003.
5. In this guideline, the offences are grouped by type as follows:

   • *Confidence fraud*
   Fraud Act 2006, s. 1
   Theft Act 1968, s. 17

---

[315] *Mavji* (1987) 84 Cr App R 34
[316] *Ward* [2005] EWCA Crim 1926
[317] The types of fraud are based on those used in *Current Sentencing Practice*, published by Sweet & Maxwell. However, the category 'mortgage fraud' has been expanded to include obtaining other forms of credit and is labelled 'obtaining credit through fraud'. Similarly, the category 'cheque fraud' has been expanded to include other forms of bank account and payment method fraud and is labelled 'payment card and bank account fraud'.

- *Possessing, making or supplying articles for use in fraud*
Fraud Act 2006, ss. 1, 6 and 7

- *Banking and insurance fraud, and obtaining credit through fraud*
Fraud Act 2006, s. 1
Theft Act 1968, s. 17

- *Benefit fraud*
Fraud Act 2000, s. 1
Theft Act 1968, s. 17
Tax Credits Act 2002, s. 35
Social Security Administration Act 1992, ss. 111A(1), 111(1A), 111(1B), 111(1D) and 111(1E)

- *Revenue fraud (against HM Revenue and Customs)*
Fraud Act 2006, s. 1
Theft Act 1968, s. 17
Value Added Tax Act 1994, ss. 72(1), 72(3), and 72(8)
Finance Act 2000, s. 144
Customs and Excise Management Act 1979, ss. 170(1)(a)(i) and (ii), 170(1)(b), 170(2)(a), 170B, 50(1)(a), and 50(2)

6. The offence of **obtaining services dishonestly** (contrary to section 11 of the Fraud Act 2006) may be committed in circumstances that otherwise could be charged as an offence contrary to section 1 of the Act or may be more akin to *making off without payment*. For this reason, it has not been included specifically within any of these guidelines, and one of the following approaches should be used:
   - *where it involves conduct which can be characterised as a fraud offence (such as obtaining credit through fraud or payment card fraud), the court should apply the guideline for the relevant type of fraud; or*
   - *where the conduct could be characterised as making off without payment (that is, where an offender, knowing that payment on the spot for any goods supplied or service done is required or expected, dishonestly makes off without having paid and with intent to avoid payment),[318] the guideline for that offence[319] should be used.*

7. The primary consideration when sentencing fraud offences is the seriousness of the offending behaviour. Sentencers must also have regard to the five purposes of sentencing set out in section 142(1) of the Criminal Justice Act 2003; as a general principle, the approach to sentencing types of fraud offence should be the same, regardless of the context within which the offence was committed.

8. The approach to sentencing, starting points and ranges has taken account of the other sanctions and ancillary orders likely to be applied (some of which are mandatory and others discretionary), which may have a significant impact on an offender.

9. The guideline applies to the sentencing of adult offenders only; separate legislative provisions and sentencing principles apply to young offenders.

SG-422 **B. Assessing seriousness**

10. When assessing offence seriousness, the court must consider the offender's culpability in committing the offence and any harm that the offence caused, was intended to cause, or might foreseeably have caused.[320] Key considerations are the degree of planning, the determination with which the offender carried out the offence and the value of the money or property involved.

(i) Culpability and harm

11. The Council guideline *Overarching Principles: Seriousness*[321] sets out four levels of culpability, the highest of which is an intention to cause harm. It is a general feature of fraud offences (with one exception)[322] that an offender intended to bring about a gain (whether for the offender or for another person) or to cause a loss, or risk of loss, to another. Generally, therefore, fraud offences involve the highest level of culpability. Within that level, culpability will vary according to the offender's motivation, whether the offence was planned or spontaneous and whether the offender was in a position of trust.[323]

---

[318] Theft Act 1978, s. 3
[319] *Magistrates' Court Sentencing Guidelines*, page 79, www.sentencing-guidelines.gov.uk
[320] Criminal Justice Act 2003, s. 143(1)
[321] at para. 1.7, published 16 December 2004, www.sentencing-guidelines.gov.uk
[322] VAT fraud can be committed by recklessly making a statement that contains a false detail (Value Added Tax Act 1994, s. 72(3) (b))
[323] *Overarching Principles: Seriousness*, para. 1.17, published 16 December 2004, www.sentencing-guidelines.gov.uk

12. Some of the forms of fraud covered by this guideline will, at times, involve offending by a number of people acting co-operatively. This will aggravate an offence of fraud because it will indicate planning or professional activity; it may also increase the degree of loss caused or intended. As a result, it is likely to cause an offence to be in a higher level of seriousness. The role of each offender will be important in determining movement above or below the starting point within the range applicable to that level (see aggravating and mitigating factors below).

13. Fraud is not a victimless crime. The monetary cost is significant, but fraud offences also cause considerable social and economic harm beyond their immediate financial impact. Fraud can be used to fund organised crime that may target vulnerable victims (drug and people trafficking, for example) and fraud offences that target individuals can ruin lives, close businesses or take life savings.

14. In assessing the harm caused by fraud offences, the primary consideration is the loss to the victim or to the community at large. In some fraud cases, the harm that results from an offence may be greater than the harm intended by the offender. In others, the offender may have intended more harm than actually results. In these situations, the harm caused by the offence should be judged in light of the offender's culpability.[324]

15. In general terms, the greater the loss, the more serious will be the offence. However, the financial value of the loss may not reflect the full extent of the harm caused by the offence. The court should also take into account:

(a) The impact of the offence on the victim

16. Whilst an offender who obtains a particular sum will benefit to the same extent regardless of the circumstances of the victim, the impact may vary considerably. Where the loss is significantly greater than the monetary value (for example, where, although relatively low in absolute terms, the value is high in proportion to the victim's financial circumstances or resources or the property has considerable sentimental value) the court should take into account the impact of the offence on the victim; this is likely to apply whether the victim is an individual, a small business or a large company.

(b) Harm to persons other than the direct victim

17. Some fraud offences will have a varying impact on different victims. For example, fraudulently using the credit or debit card details of another person will have a direct financial impact on the card issuer, who normally will be expected to absorb the loss, but it may also have an impact on the cardholder. The aggravation and stress of unscrambling the consequences of the offender's criminal activities often far outweighs the impact of the financial loss suffered by the card issuer.

(c) Erosion of public confidence

18. Frauds using credit and debit cards may undermine the integrity of those payment methods.

(d) Any physical harm or risk of physical harm to the direct victim or another person

19. As part of committing a fraud, a risk may be created of physical injury either to the victim or to some other person not directly involved. For example, where a person deliberately sets fire to premises owned by them or causes an innocent driver to crash into his or her vehicle, in order that an insurance claim may be made, the risk of injury and the impact on the innocent driver will increase the harm caused by the fraud on the insurance company.

(e) Difference between loss intended and resulting

20. In the guidelines that follow, where the amount of money obtained is used as a determinant of seriousness, a court should take the starting point corresponding to the amount that the offender dishonestly intended to obtain and adjust the assessment of seriousness to reflect the degree of loss actually caused by the offence. Common situations include:

no loss intended: in obtaining credit through fraud, an offender may not intend to cause any loss but to repay any sums advanced or to keep the bank account in credit. Indeed, an application that was not fraudulent may have been successful. Whilst, in such a case, the offender does not intend to cause any harm, nonetheless a loss may result.

A court should use the starting point corresponding to no financial loss and, where a loss occurs, adjust the assessment of seriousness to reflect the degree of loss.

Gain intended but no actual loss results: in some insurance fraud cases, an offender may present a fraudulent claim to an insurer but the insurer, suspecting fraud, does not pay out any money. In these cases, although the insurer suffers no actual financial loss, it is possible to calculate the amount of money which the offender dishonestly intended to obtain.

---

[324] ibid.

In such cases a court should use the starting point corresponding to the amount which the offender intended to obtain and adjust the assessment of seriousness to reflect the fact that no loss has resulted.

(f)   Legitimate entitlement to part or all of the amount obtained

21.   In some cases an offender may be entitled honestly to all or part of the money that is obtained following the fraudulent activity. This is a feature of all exaggerated claims but may arise in other cases.

In such cases, the starting point should be based on the amount to which the offender was not legitimately entitled.

(ii)   Aggravating factors

22.   The Council guideline *Overarching Principles: Seriousness* sets out a number of factors that indicate a higher than usual level of culpability on the part of the offender or a greater than usual degree of harm to the victim.[325] The complete list is set out in <u>Annex B</u> [not reproduced here: see **SG-25**]. Those factors most likely to be present in offences of fraud are:

Factors indicating higher culpability
- Planning of an offence
- An intention to commit more serious harm than actually resulted from the offence (including any physical harm or risk of physical harm)
- Offenders operating in groups or gangs
- 'Professional offending'
- High level of profit from the offence
- An attempt to conceal or dispose of evidence
- Deliberate targeting of vulnerable victim(s)
- Abuse of a position of trust

Factors indicating a more than usually serious degree of harm
- Multiple victims
- Victim is particularly vulnerable
- High value (including sentimental value) of property to the victim, or substantial consequential loss

23.   The Council has identified four factors that are particularly relevant to this type of offending behaviour:

(a)   Number involved in the offence and role of offender

24.   Where an offender was an organiser, planner or prime mover in a fraudulent enterprise carried out by a number of individuals acting together, this is likely to be an aggravating factor which will tend to move the sentence above the appropriate starting point.

(b)   Offending carried out over a significant period of time

25.   Where a fraud is committed by obtaining money or property on several occasions over a long period[326] (for example, in some benefit frauds where each payment is relatively low but the fraud continues over a period), the seriousness of the offence will be assessed both on the amount of money or property involved and on the period of time over which it was obtained.

(c)   Use of another person's identity

26.   Use of another person's identity may increase the harm caused; this may vary depending on the origins of the stolen identity:
- *using the identity of a living person is likely to cause emotional distress for that individual who will also have the practical and potentially stressful problem of untangling the financial consequences of the fraud;*
- *using the identity of a deceased person is likely to indicate a higher degree of planning (as it can be an attempt to make the fraud more difficult to uncover) and is likely to cause considerable distress to the relatives of the deceased, especially if that person has only recently died.*

27.   Using the identity of another person is an aggravating factor; the extent to which it aggravates an offence will be based on the degree of planning and the impact that the offence has had on the living

---

[325]   *Overarching Principles: Seriousness*, paras. 1.22 and 1.23, published 16 December 2004, www.sentencing-guidelines.gov.uk
[326]   Due to changes in the rules governing indictments, frauds undertaken over a significant period of time may now be charged in one count where previously multiple counts were required: Criminal Procedure Rules 2005, r.14.2(2), inserted by the Criminal Procedure (Amendment) Rules 2007. However, where multiple counts are charged and a trial of all those counts by jury would be impractical, a representative sample of counts can be tried by a jury with the remaining counts tried, if the defendant is convicted of the sample counts, by a judge sitting alone: Domestic Violence, Crime and Victims Act 2004, s. 17

victim or the relatives of the deceased. Accordingly, in itself, whether the identity belongs to a living or deceased person should be neutral for this purpose.

(d) Offence has a lasting effect on the victim

28. The lives of individual victims may be severely affected by fraud offences. Individual victims may lose most or all of their savings, be unable to make mortgage and loan repayments, or have to work beyond retirement age. Where the fraud was perpetrated by someone entrusted with the victim's financial affairs, the victim's ability to trust future advice may be permanently damaged. Such lasting impacts will aggravate an offence.

(iii) Mitigating factors

29. The Council guideline *Overarching Principles: Seriousness* sets out factors which indicate that an offender's culpability is unusually low or that the harm caused by an offence is less than usually serious.[327] These are set out in <u>Annex B</u> [not reproduced here: see **SG-25**]. Those factors most likely to be present in offences of fraud are:

Factors indicating significantly lower culpability:
- Mental illness or disability
- Youth or age, where it affects the responsibility of the individual defendant
- The fact that the offender played only a minor role in the offence.

30. The Council has identified three mitigating factors that are particularly relevant to this type of offending:

(a) Peripheral involvement

31. Where an offender played a minor or peripheral role in an offence of fraud or, rather than having planned to take part, became involved through the influence of others and not as an organiser or prime mover, this is likely to be a mitigating factor which will tend to move the sentence below the appropriate starting point.

(b) Behaviour not fraudulent from the outset

32. Where an offender originally had a legitimate entitlement to financial benefits but continued to claim following a change in circumstances that affected entitlement, the initial intention was not dishonest but it became so at the point when the changed circumstances were not disclosed to the financial authority and the offender made the decision to continue to claim.

33. In principle, continuing to claim monies to which there is no longer entitlement may in certain circumstances be less culpable than claiming monies to which there had never been a legitimate entitlement; therefore, this is likely to influence the assessment of the seriousness of the offence.

34. However, the degree to which this difference has an effect on the sentence imposed will depend on the circumstances that led to the failure to disclose, the effort that was involved in commencing or perpetuating the fraud, the length of time over which the sums were defrauded and the amount of money defrauded.

35. Where applicable, a guideline is based on an offence where the offender's initial intention is dishonest; accordingly, conduct that was not fraudulent from the outset is capable of being a mitigating factor. The degree of mitigation is likely to be greater where there is evidence that the customer service of the financial authority was inadequate and it proved difficult for the offender to understand the rules or to properly explain his or her position.

(c) Misleading or incomplete advice

36. Even where the behaviour was fraudulent from the outset, the fact that an offender can demonstrate that he or she was given misleading or incomplete advice may in certain circumstances be treated as a mitigating factor.

(iv) Personal mitigation

37. Having formed an initial assessment of the seriousness of an offence, the court should then take account of any offender mitigation. A number of factors may be present in relation to fraud offences and may influence the choice or severity of sentence in an individual case. These are considered below.

(a) Voluntary cessation of offending

38. In some cases, particularly those where a fraud has been carried out over a significant period of time, offenders may stop offending (or claim to have stopped offending) before they are apprehended.

---

[327] *Overarching Principles: Seriousness*, para. 1.25, published 16 December 2004, www.sentencing-guidelines.gov.uk

Where there is objective evidence to support such a claim, particularly where it is accompanied by a genuine expression of remorse,[328] this usually should be treated as offender mitigation.

39. The time that has elapsed since the commission of the last offence will be an important factor in determining whether the cessation of offending is genuine and was likely to have lasted even if the offending had not come to notice. In addition, the court will want to consider the reasons why an offender stopped offending; where that was because of a heightened fear of discovery or the fact that the additional funds were no longer needed, a court may conclude that the degree of mitigation is negligible or that this factor should not be taken into account at all.

(b) Complete and unprompted disclosure of the extent of the fraud

40. Some offenders voluntarily disclose offences of which the authorities were previously unaware. Others, when apprehended, make a complete and unprompted disclosure to the authorities of the extent of the fraud.

41. Where an offender admits to obtaining fraudulently a greater sum than that known to the authorities, this increases the likelihood that victims will be able to recover some of the money and ensures that the offender is sentenced for the complete extent of the fraud, rather than according to what would otherwise have been known to the prosecutor. This amounts to ready co-operation with the authorities, which the Council has recognised as offender mitigation.[329]

42. Where an offender provides information about other individuals who were involved in committing the fraud, the court will normally treat this as offender mitigation. In addition, the practice of reducing the sentence is now permitted by statute in some circumstances where the offender enters into a written agreement with a specified prosecutor.[330]

43. The point at which the disclosure is made, and the degree of assistance given to the authorities, should determine the amount of mitigation. In order to promote complete disclosure at the earliest possible time, generally the earlier the disclosure is given and the higher the degree of assistance, the greater the allowance for offender mitigation.

(c) Voluntary restitution

44. The point at which an offender voluntarily returns property or money obtained through fraud will be important and, in general, the earlier the property or money is returned the greater the degree of mitigation the offender should receive.[331] Providing an incentive to return property or money is particularly important as it may be difficult for a victim to recover his or her losses in any other way.[332] The timing of the voluntary restitution may be an indicator of the degree to which it reflects genuine remorse or is a calculated step designed to reduce the severity of the sentence that is likely to be imposed.

45. If an offender has been temporarily or permanently prevented by circumstances beyond his or her control from returning defrauded items, the degree of mitigation should depend on the point in time at which, and the determination with which, the offender tried to return the items.

(d) Financial pressure

46. Whilst many fraud offences are motivated by greed or a desire to live beyond legitimate means, others may be motivated by financial pressure. In principle, financial pressure is a factor that neither increases nor diminishes an offender's culpability in relation to any type of dishonesty offence, including fraud. However, where financial pressure is *exceptional* and not of the offender's own making, it may in very rare circumstances constitute offender mitigation.

SG-423 **C. Other sentencing matters**

Combining custodial sentences and fines

47. The issue whether to impose a fine alongside a custodial sentence may arise when sentencing for fraud offences. If a fine is imposed, further issues arise concerning the impact of the fine on the length of the custodial sentence. Some guideline judgments relating to tax fraud[333] have indicated that a fine should be imposed alongside a custodial sentence and such an approach has been used as a means of

---

[328] *Overarching Principles: Seriousness*, para. 1.27, published 16 December 2004, www.sentencing-guidelines.gov.uk

[329] ibid., para. 1.29

[330] Serious Organised Crime and Police Act 2005, s. 73

[331] *Robbery*, page 7, published 25 July 2006, www.sentencing-guidelines.gov.uk

[332] This is because the scope of restitution orders under the Powers of Criminal Courts (Sentencing) Act 2000 is tightly circumscribed and the courts traditionally have been reluctant to impose compensation orders in conjunction with custodial sentences.

[333] *Ford* (1981) 3 Cr App R (S) 15; *Attorney General's Reference Nos. 87 and 86 of 1999 (Webb and Simpson)* [2001] 1 Cr App R (S) 505

confiscation.[334] However, these cases largely were decided before the creation of the extensive powers relating to confiscation and to seizure of assets or the proceeds of crime.

48. In the light of those additional powers and the general powers relating to compensation, forfeiture and confiscation, a court normally *should not* impose a fine alongside a custodial sentence. However, exceptionally, it may be appropriate to impose a fine in addition to a custodial sentence where:

   (i)   a confiscation order is not being contemplated; **and**

   (ii) there is no obvious victim to whom compensation can be awarded; **and**

   (iii) the offender has, or will have, resources from which a fine can be paid.

49. A court must ensure that the overall sentence remains commensurate with the seriousness of the offence and that the size of the fine does not enable wealthier offenders to 'buy themselves out of custody'.

D. Ancillary and other orders

SG-424

50. Ancillary orders may aim to minimise the harm caused by the offender (either to the victim or, through the risk of re-offending, to society), may aim to achieve reparation or may aim to punish the offender.

51. Orders relating to property that either must be considered or are most likely to be imposed in relation to fraud offences are:

[Paragraphs 52 to 63 reproduce standard guidance on the use of (i) compensation orders, (ii) confiscation orders and (iii) deprivation orders, which mirrors in all but the most trivial ways the guidance found in the guidelines on theft (see **SG-398**)].

(iv) Restitution order[335]

64. A court may order that stolen goods be restored to the victim or that a sum not exceeding the value of the goods be paid to the victim from money taken out of the offender's possession at the time of apprehension. Further, on the application of the victim, the court may order that other goods representing the proceeds of disposal or realisation of the stolen goods be transferred to the victim. Where the stolen property cannot be traced or the offender is not in possession of sufficient money at the time of apprehension, a restitution order will not be available and a compensation order should be considered instead.

65. A restitution order should not normally impact on or influence the choice of sentence as the offender has no control over the making of the order.

66. Orders relating to the future conduct of the offender include:

(v) Disqualification from acting as a company director[336]

67. The general power to disqualify may be used where an offender is convicted of an indictable offence committed in connection with the management or general conduct of a company. The disqualification term may be for a maximum of 15 years if made by the Crown Court or 5 years if made by a magistrates' court.

68. A disqualification order should not normally impact on or influence the choice of sentence as its purpose is to protect the public from the risk of re-offending.

(vi) Disqualification from driving[337]

69. A court may disqualify any person convicted of an offence from driving for such period as it considers appropriate. This may be instead of or in addition to dealing with the offender in any other way.

70. Disqualification under this provision is a punitive sanction and should be taken into account in ensuring that the overall sentence is commensurate with the seriousness of the offence.

(vii) Financial reporting order[338]

71. Where there is a sufficiently high risk of the offender committing a further offence of fraud or dishonesty, an order may be made requiring a report of the offender's financial affairs to be made as directed, for a period of up to 15 years where the order is made in the Crown Court or 5 years if made by a magistrates' court.

---

[334] See, for example, *Garner and others* (1985) 7 Cr App R (S) 285

[335] Powers of Criminal Courts (Sentencing) Act 2000, s. 148

[336] Company Directors Disqualification Act 1986, s. 2

[337] Powers of Criminal Courts (Sentencing) Act 2000, ss. 146 and 147

[338] Serious Organised Crime and Police Act 2005, s. 76

72. As the purpose of the order is to minimise the risk of re-offending by those likely to commit financial crime, a financial reporting order should not be taken into account when deciding the appropriate sentence.

(viii) Serious crime prevention order[339]

73. On application by the Crown, where an offender is convicted by the Crown Court of a *serious offence* (or is committed to the Crown Court following conviction in a magistrates' court) an order may be made if the court has reasonable grounds to believe that it would protect the public by preventing, restricting or disrupting involvement by the person in serious crime. The order may contain such prohibitions, restrictions, requirements or terms as the court considers necessary to achieve the purpose of the order.

74. The order must be of a specified duration, not exceeding five years. Commencement of the order can be delayed, for example to commence upon the offender's release from custody.

75. A serious crime prevention order should not normally impact on or influence the choice of sentence as the purpose of the order is to provide protection to the public from future involvement of the offender in serious crime.

SG-425   E. Sentencing ranges and starting points

1. Typically, a guideline will apply to an offence that can be committed in a variety of circumstances with different levels of seriousness. It will apply to a *'first time offender'* who has been **convicted after a trial**. Within the guidelines, a *'first time offender'* is a person who does not have a conviction which, by virtue of section 143(2) of the Criminal Justice Act 2003, must be treated as an aggravating factor.

2. As an aid to consistency of approach, the guidelines describe a number of types of conduct which would fall within the broad definition of the offences. These are set out in a column headed 'Nature of offence'. Additionally, the top row provides financial bands relating to the amount that the offender intended to obtain or was likely to be achieved from the fraudulent conduct.

3. The expected approach is for a court to identify the description and financial band that most nearly matches the particular facts of the offence for which sentence is being imposed. This will identify a **starting point** from which the sentencer can depart to reflect aggravating or mitigating factors affecting the seriousness of the offence (beyond those contained within the column describing the nature of the failure or of the harm) to reach a **provisional sentence**.

4. The **sentencing range** is the bracket into which the provisional sentence will normally fall after having regard to factors which aggravate or mitigate the seriousness of the offence. The particular circumstances may, however, make it appropriate that the provisional sentence falls outside the range.

5. Where the offender has previous convictions which aggravate the seriousness of the current offence, that may take the provisional sentence beyond the range given particularly where there are significant other aggravating factors present.

6. Once the provisional sentence has been identified by reference to those factors affecting the seriousness of the offence, the court will take into account any relevant factors of personal mitigation, which may take the sentence below the range given.

7. Where there has been a guilty plea, any reduction attributable to that plea will be applied to the sentence at this stage. Again, this reduction may take the sentence below the range provided.

8. A court must give its reasons for imposing a sentence of a different kind or outside the range provided in the guidelines.[340]

The decision making process

[Sets out the standard sequential decision making process: identify starting point, consider aggravating factors, consider mitigating factors, apply reduction for guilty plea, consider ancillary orders, review in light of the totality principle and give reasons.]

SG-426   F. Guidelines and approach to sentencing

1. The guidelines are based on types of conduct reflecting common fraudulent behaviour. Confidence frauds are dealt with as a separate category as is the possession, making or supply of articles for use in fraud.

2. A further group includes those offences committed against an organisation in either the private or public sector; most commonly, in the public sector these will arise in relation to the tax and benefit system and, in the private sector, in relation to banking and insurance.

---

[339] Serious Crime Act 2007, s. 1 and 19
[340] Criminal Justice Act 2003, s. 174(2)(a)

3. Although not intended to be exclusive, each guideline includes examples of the fraudulent activity likely to have taken place. In addition, the guideline refers to the offences under which the activity might be charged and the related legislative provisions.

4. The starting points and sentencing ranges for *banking and insurance fraud*, for *benefit fraud*, and for *fraud against HM Revenue and Customs (revenue fraud)* are the same since the seriousness of all offences of organisational fraud derives from the extent of the fraudulent activity (culpability) and the financial loss caused or likely to be caused (harm).

   (i) For ease of use, separate guidelines have been provided for banking, insurance and credit fraud, benefit fraud and revenue fraud, which has allowed greater detail of the types of activity and the aggravating or mitigating factors likely to be particularly relevant to be included.

   (ii) In relation to these types of fraud, the Council considers that there will be few cases where £100,000 or more is obtained in a single fraudulent transaction. Similarly, it is likely that there will be few cases where less than £20,000 is obtained in a professionally planned fraud carried out over a significant period of time or multiple professionally planned frauds. Accordingly, the Council has not proposed starting points and ranges for such frauds.

Confidence fraud   SG-427

Factors to take into consideration

1. The principal offences likely to be used to prosecute confidence frauds are **fraud under the Fraud Act 2006, section 1 and false accounting contrary to the Theft Act 1968, section 17**.

2. The following starting points and sentencing ranges are for a '*first time offender*' aged 18 or over who pleaded not guilty. They should be applied as set out [above].

3. This type of offending involves a victim transferring money and/or property as a result of being deceived or misled by the offender. An example of a simple confidence fraud is a person claiming to be collecting money for charity when, in fact, he or she intends to keep the money.[341] Other examples of common confidence frauds are:

   Advance fee frauds - Common advance fee frauds include *lottery/prize draw scams* where, in order to claim a 'prize', a processing or administration fee (or a customs levy in foreign lottery scams) must be paid and, after the fee is paid, the prize never materialises and *foreign money-making frauds* where persons claim to need assistance in transferring money overseas and offer a share of the money for help, or ask for money to be sent to cover customs levies, bribes and/or other fees.

   Fraudulent sales of goods and services - These include goods that are never received by the purchaser or are worth less than the seller represents; services that are unnecessary, overpriced or not performed; and investments that are never obtained for the investor or are worth less than the seller represents.

4. A factor common to many confidence frauds, is that the offender targets a vulnerable victim; it is therefore a determinant of seriousness for this type of fraud. An offender is more culpable if he or she deliberately targets a victim who is vulnerable as a result of old age, youth or disability and there is a more than usually serious degree of harm where the victim is particularly vulnerable.[342]

5. Some victims of advance fee frauds may have personalities which make them 'vulnerable in a way and to a degree not typical of the general population'[343] because they fall for scams many times. It is a feature of some advance fee frauds that victims are targeted using 'sucker lists' of people who have previously fallen victim to scams. An offender who uses a 'sucker list' will have planned the offence and deliberately targeted vulnerable victims; therefore he or she has a higher level of culpability.[344]

6. As the determinants of seriousness include the 'value of property or consequential loss involved', the table provides both a fixed amount (on which the starting point is based) and a band (on which the sentencing range is based). Where the value is larger or smaller than the amount on which the starting point is based, this should lead to upward or downward movement as appropriate. Where the amount the offender intended to obtain cannot be established, the appropriate measure will be the amount that was likely to be achieved in all the circumstances.

7. A further determinant of seriousness is whether the fraud was a single fraudulent transaction or a multiple fraud. Most confidence frauds will by their nature involve many actual or potential victims and multiple transactions and should be regarded as multiple fraud.

8. When assessing the seriousness of an offence, a court must always have regard to the full list of aggravating and mitigating factors in the Council guideline *Overarching Principles: Seriousness* (reproduced

---

[341] See, for example, *Pippard and Harris* [2001] EWCA Crim 2925 and *Day and O'Leary* [2002] EWCA Crim 503

[342] *Overarching Principles: Seriousness*, paras. 1.17, 1.22 and 1.23, published 16 December 2004, www.sentencing-guidelines.gov.uk

[343] M. Levi, *Sentencing Frauds: A Review*, p. 58

[344] *Overarching Principles: Seriousness*, para. 1.22, published 16 December 2004, www.sentencing-guidelines.gov.uk

in <u>Annex B</u> [not reproduced here: see **SG-25**]); those most likely to be present in offences of fraud are set out at paragraphs 22 and 29 above. Additional aggravating and mitigating factors likely to be particularly relevant to this type of fraud are considered at paragraphs 24–28 and 31–36 above.

9. The Council has identified matters of personal mitigation which may be relevant, which are set out in paragraphs 38 to 46 above.

10. In all cases sentencers should consider whether to make ancillary orders, particularly compensation, confiscation and/or deprivation (see paragraphs 50–75 above).

CONFIDENCE FRAUD

Fraud: Fraud Act 2006 (section 1)
False accounting: Theft Act 1968 (section 17)

Maximum penalty: Fraud, 10 years custody
                     False accounting, 7 years custody

Value of property or consequential loss				
Nature of offence	**£500,000 or more** *Starting point based on: £750,000**	**£100,000 or more and less than £500,000** *Starting point based on: £300,000**	**£20,000 or more and less than £100,000** *Starting point based on: £60,000**	**Less than £20,000** *Starting point based on: £10,000**
Large scale advance fee fraud or other confidence fraud involving the deliberate targeting of a large number of vulnerable victims	**Starting point:** 6 years custody **Range:** 5–8 years custody	**Starting point:** 5 years custody **Range:** 4–7 years custody	**Starting point:** 4 years custody **Range:** 3–6 years custody	**Starting point:** 3 years custody **Range:** 2–5 years custody
Lower scale advance fee fraud or other confidence fraud characterised by a degree of planning and/or multiple transactions	**Starting point:** 5 years custody **Range:** 4–7 years custody	**Starting point:** 4 years custody **Range:** 3–6 years custody	**Starting point:** 3 years custody **Range:** 2–5 years custody	**Starting point:** 18 months custody **Range:** 26 weeks–3 years custody
Single fraudulent transaction confidence fraud involving targeting of a vulnerable victim			**Starting point:** 26 weeks custody **Range:** Community order (HIGH)–18 months custody	**Starting point:** 6 weeks custody **Range:** Community order (MEDIUM)–26 weeks custody
Single fraudulent transaction confidence fraud not targeting a vulnerable victim, and involving no or limited planning			**Starting point:** 12 weeks custody **Range:** Community order (MEDIUM)–36 weeks custody	**Starting point:** Community order (MEDIUM) **Range:** Fine–6 weeks custody

* Where the actual amount is greater or smaller than the figure on which the starting point is based, that is likely to be one of the factors that will move the sentence within the range (see paragraph 6 [above]).

Additional aggravating factors	Additional mitigating factors
1. Number involved in the offence and role of the offender 2. Offending carried out over a significant period of time 3. Use of another person's identity 4. Offence has a lasting effect on the victim	1. Peripheral involvement 2. Behaviour not fraudulent from the outset 3. Misleading or inaccurate advice

The presence of one or more aggravating factors may indicate a more severe sentence within the suggested range while the presence of one or more mitigating factors may indicate a less severe sentence within the suggested range.

The presence of aggravating or mitigating factors of exceptional significance may indicate that the case should move to a higher or lower level of seriousness.

Possessing, making or supplying articles for use in fraud   **SG-428**

Factors to take into consideration

1. The principal offences are contrary to the Fraud Act 2006 and are **possession of articles for use in frauds (section 6), making or supplying articles for use in frauds (section 7) and the general offence of fraud (section 1)**.

2. The following starting points and sentencing ranges are for a '*first time offender*' aged 18 or over who pleaded not guilty. They should be applied as set out [above].

3. There are many ways in which offenders may commit this group of offences but, with the constant improvements in technology, computers have become a common and increasingly effective tool for both creating and disseminating *articles* for use in fraud. Thus, 'articles' will include any electronic programs or data stored electronically.[345] Examples of articles for use in frauds include false fronts for cash machines, computer programs for generating credit card numbers, lists of credit card or bank account details, 'sucker lists' and draft letters or emails for use in advance fee frauds.

4. As lists of credit card and bank account details constitute 'articles', the making of such lists through certain electronic programmes, which contravenes section 1 of the Fraud Act 2006, is also criminalised by section 7 of the same Act. The Council considers that carrying out the following activities should be treated as making articles for use in fraud and sentenced using this guideline, regardless of whether the offence is charged under section 1 or section 7:

    Phishing - where an offender sends an email purporting to come from a financial institution, which asks victims to follow a hyperlink to a (false) website and induces them to enter their card or account details (which may include their PIN);

    Vishing - where an offender uses an automated telephone system, purporting to be the telephone system of a financial institution, to induce victims to disclose their card or account details (which may include their PIN);

    Pharming - where victims intend to visit a financial institution's website but are redirected to the offender's website (which purports to be the financial institution's website) and induced to enter their card or account details (which may include their PIN); and

    Use of a 'Trojan' - where an offender installs a virus on victims' computers (often a 'keystroke logger', which captures all of the keystrokes entered into a computer keyboard) in order to gain access to their card or account details. Often the offender will send an email inducing victims to visit a website, where the virus is automatically downloaded onto their computers.

5. Making, adapting, supplying or offering to supply computer programmes, emails or websites for the above activities amounts to an offence under section 7 of the Fraud Act 2006.

6. Offenders who possess, make or supply articles for use in fraud intend their actions to lead to a fraud. Such offenders therefore have the highest level of culpability.[346] Whilst in many cases no financial harm will have been caused, in some cases, particularly where the 'article' is a list of credit card or bank account details, the victim(s) may have been inconvenienced despite not suffering any financial loss.[347]

7. There are three types of activity relating to articles for use in fraud: making or adapting, supplying or offering to supply and possession. The guideline does not distinguish between the first two categories; they carry the same maximum penalty and, depending on the sophistication and planning involved and the harm resulting from an offence, they may be equally serious.

---

[345] Fraud Act 2006, s. 8
[346] See *Overarching Principles: Seriousness*, para. 1.7, published 16 December 2004, www.sentencing-guidelines.gov.uk
[347] Where the article is a list of credit card or bank account details, the victims will need to cancel their cards and obtain new ones and/or change their bank accounts. See *Overarching Principles: Seriousness*, para. 1.17, published 16 December 2004, www.sentencing-guidelines.gov.uk

Sentencing Guidelines

8. The three offences in this group all involve an element of planning (whether by the offender or by another person); the planning of an offence has been identified by the Council as a factor indicating a higher level of culpability[348] and the proposed starting points incorporate this aggravating factor.

9. In relation to harm, the value of the fraud (either that intended by the offender where that can be ascertained, or that which was likely to be achieved) is not a determinant of seriousness for these offences in the way that it is for other offences of fraud. However, it is a factor that should be taken into account in determining the appropriate sentence within the sentencing range.

10. When assessing the seriousness of an offence, a court must always have regard to the full list of aggravating and mitigating factors in the Council guideline *Overarching Principles: Seriousness* (reproduced in Annex B [not reproduced here: see **SG-25**]); those most likely to be present in offences of fraud are set out at paragraphs 22 and 29 above. Additional aggravating and mitigating factors likely to be particularly relevant to this type of fraud are considered at paragraphs 24–28 and 31 above.

11. The Council has identified matters of personal mitigation which may be relevant, which are set out in paragraphs 38–46 above.

12. The sentencing range for the most serious category of offences is deliberately wide; most offences will be at the lower end of the range but there are likely to be some offences, possibly but not exclusively those with an international dimension, that will justify a sentence at the top end of the suggested range or even higher.

13. In all cases sentencers should consider whether to make ancillary orders, particularly compensation, confiscation and/or deprivation orders (see paragraphs 50–75 above).

POSSESSING, MAKING OR SUPPLYING ARTICLES FOR USE IN FRAUD
Possession of articles for use in frauds: Fraud Act 2006 (section 6)
Making or supplying articles for use in frauds: Fraud Act 2006 (section 7)
Fraud: Fraud Act 2006 (section 1)

Maximum penalty: Possession of articles for use in frauds, 5 years custody
For both other offences, 10 years custody

Nature of offence	Type of offence	
	Making or adapting (ss. 1 or 7) **or** Supplying or offering to supply (s. 7)	Possessing (s. 6)
Article(s) intended for use in an extensive and skilfully planned fraud	**Starting point:** 4 years custody **Range:** 2–7 years custody	**Starting point:** 36 weeks custody **Range:** 6 weeks–2 years custody
Article(s) intended for use in a less extensive and less skilfully planned fraud	**Starting point:** 26 weeks custody **Range:** Community order (HIGH)–2 years custody	**Starting point:** Community order (MEDIUM) **Range:** Community order (LOW)–26 weeks custody

Additional aggravating factors	Additional mitigating factors
1. Number involved in the offence and role of the offender	1. Peripheral involvement
2. Offending carried out over a significant period of time	
3. Use of another person's identity	
4. Offence has a lasting effect on the victim	

The presence of one or more aggravating factors may indicate a more severe sentence within the suggested range while the presence of one or more mitigating factors may indicate a less severe sentence within the suggested range.

The presence of aggravating or mitigating factors of exceptional significance may indicate that the case should move to a higher or lower level of seriousness.

---

[348] ibid., para. 1.22

Banking and insurance fraud, and obtaining credit through fraud

Factors to take into consideration

1. In relation to each of these types of fraud, the principal offences likely to be used to prosecute are **fraud under the Fraud Act 2006, section 1 and false accounting contrary to the Theft Act 1968, section 17**.

2. The following starting points and sentencing ranges are for a '*first time offender*' aged 18 or over who pleaded not guilty. They should be applied as set out [above].

3. Types of offending behaviour include:

   Payment card and bank account fraud - Frauds involving the use of payment cards and bank accounts include use of another person's card, cloning another person's card, taking over or sending instructions relating to another person's bank or card account, and use of another person's cheque.

   Insurance fraud - Fraudulent claims by or against the insurer (claims that are entirely fraudulent and those that are exaggerated through either claiming for injury, loss or damage that did not occur or increasing the value of a genuine claim for injury, loss or damage) and supplier fraud (whereby builders, motor repairers and other trades-people engaged by insurers to repair insured property charge for work that they have not done or inflate the cost of their work).

   Obtaining credit through fraud - Obtaining credit through fraud includes the fraudulent obtaining of mortgages, loans, interest free credit, in-store credit, goods or services on a 'buy now pay later' basis, car finance, credit cards, store cards, and bank accounts (with overdrafts).

4. A payment card or bank account fraud is unlikely to be committed in circumstances where the offender's intention was not fraudulent from the outset.

5. As the determinants of seriousness include the 'value of property or consequential loss involved', the table provides both a fixed amount (on which the starting point is based) and a band (on which the sentencing range is based). Where the value is larger or smaller than the amount on which the starting point is based, this should lead to upward or downward movement as appropriate. Where the amount the offender intended to obtain cannot be established, the appropriate measure will be the amount that was likely to be achieved in all the circumstances.

6. A further determinant of seriousness is whether the fraud was a single fraudulent transaction or a multiple fraud. Where one false declaration or a failure to disclose a change in circumstances results in multiple payments, this should be regarded as multiple fraud.

7. The maximum penalty for most of the offences covered by this guideline is 7 years imprisonment. Where fraud under the 2006 Act is charged and the maximum penalty is 10 years, the proposed sentencing ranges leave headroom for offences involving the most serious frauds to be sentenced outside the range and up to the maximum.

8. When assessing the seriousness of an offence, a court must always have regard to the full list of aggravating and mitigating factors in the Council guideline *Overarching Principles: Seriousness* (reproduced in Annex B [not reproduced here: see **SG-25**]); those most likely to be present in offences of fraud are set out at paragraphs 22 and 29 above. Additional aggravating and mitigating factors likely to be particularly relevant to this type of fraud are considered at paragraphs 24 and 26–27, 31 and 36 above.

9. Use of another person's identity is an aggravating factor (see paragraphs 26–27 above). Whilst this factor may be present in any fraud, it is a feature of nearly all payment card and bank account frauds.[349] Courts should therefore depart from the suggested starting points in all cases of payment card and bank account fraud (and any other case in which it arises) to reflect the presence of this aggravating factor.

10. The Council has identified matters of personal mitigation which may be relevant, which are set out in paragraphs 38–46 above.

11. In all cases sentencers should consider whether to make ancillary orders, particularly confiscation and compensation (see paragraphs 50–75 above).

BANKING AND INSURANCE FRAUD, AND OBTAINING CREDIT THROUGH FRAUD

Maximum penalty: Fraud (prosecuted under the Fraud Act 2006), 10 years custody
           For all other offences, 7 years custody

---

[349] In most cases the offender claims to be the account holder or a person authorised to deal with the account.

Nature of offence	Amount obtained or intended to be obtained				
	£500,000 or more *Starting point based on: £750,000**	£100,000 or more and less than £500,000 *Starting point based on: £300,000**	£20,000 or more and less than £100,000 *Starting point based on: £60,000**	£5,000 or more and less than £20,000 *Starting point based on: £12,500**	Less than £5,000 *Starting point based on: £2,500**
Fraudulent from the outset, professionally planned **and either** fraud carried out over a significant period of time **or** multiple frauds	**Starting point:** 5 years custody **Range:** 4–7 years custody	**Starting point:** 4 years custody **Range:** 3–5 years custody	**Starting point:** 2 years custody **Range:** 18 months– 3 years custody		
Fraudulent from the outset **and either** fraud carried out over a significant period of time **or** multiple frauds	**Starting point:** 4 years custody **Range:** 3–7 years custody	**Starting point:** 3 years custody **Range:** 2–4 years custody	**Starting point:** 15 months custody **Range:** 18 weeks– 30 months custody	**Starting point:** 12 weeks custody **Range:** Community order (HIGH)– 12 months custody	**Starting point:** Community order (HIGH) **Range:** Community order (LOW)– 6 weeks custody
Not fraudulent from the outset **and either** fraud carried out over a significant period of time **or** multiple frauds	**Starting point:** 3 years custody **Range:** 2–6 years custody	**Starting point:** 2 years custody **Range:** 12 months– 3 years custody	**Starting point:** 36 weeks custody **Range:** 12 weeks– 18 months custody	**Starting point:** 6 weeks custody **Range:** Community order (MEDIUM)– 26 weeks custody	**Starting point:** Community order (MEDIUM) **Range:** Fine– Community order (HIGH)
Single fraudulent transaction, fraudulent from the outset			**Starting point:** 26 weeks custody **Range:** 6 weeks– 12 months custody	**Starting point:** Community order (HIGH) **Range:** Fine– 18 weeks custody	**Starting point:** Community order (LOW) **Range:** Fine– Community order (MEDIUM)
Single fraudulent transaction, not fraudulent from the outset			**Starting point:** 12 weeks custody **Range:** Community order (MEDIUM)– 36 weeks custody	**Starting point:** Community order (MEDIUM) **Range:** Fine– 6 weeks custody	**Starting point:** Fine **Range:** Fine– Community order (LOW)

* Where the actual amount is greater or smaller than the figure on which the starting point is based, that is likely to be one of the factors that will move the sentence within the range (see paragraph 4 [above]).

Additional aggravating factors	Additional mitigating factors
1. Number involved in the offence and role of the offender	1. Peripheral involvement
2. Use of another person's identity	2. Misleading or incomplete advice

The presence of one or more aggravating factors may indicate a more severe sentence within the suggested range while the presence of one or more mitigating factors may indicate a less severe sentence within the suggested range.

The presence of aggravating or mitigating factors of exceptional significance may indicate that the case should move to a higher or lower level of seriousness.

Benefit fraud   SG-430
Factors to take into consideration
The principal offences likely to be used to prosecute benefit frauds are:

- *Fraud (Fraud Act 2006, section 1)*
- *False accounting (Theft Act 1968, section 17)*
- *False representation to obtain benefit (Social Security Administration Act 1992, section 111A(1))*
- *Failing to disclose a change in circumstances (Social Security Administration Act 1992, section 111A(1A), (1B), (1D) or (1E))*
- *Tax credit fraud (Tax Credits Act 2002, section 35)*

1. The following starting points and sentencing ranges are for a '*first time offender*' aged 18 or over who pleaded not guilty. They should be applied as set out [above].
2. This guideline is based on an understanding that the prosecutor will generally seek summary trial for appropriate benefit fraud cases involving sums up to £35,000; the Council does not consider that the starting points proposed would interfere with that practice.
3. The Council's proposals are governed by bands based on amounts of money. The starting point defined at the top of each column relates to the midpoint of each financial band.
4. As the determinants of seriousness include the 'value of property or consequential loss involved', the table provides both a fixed amount (on which the starting point is based) and a band (on which the sentencing range is based). Where the value is larger or smaller than the amount on which the starting point is based, this should lead to upward or downward movement as appropriate. Where the amount the offender intended to obtain cannot be established, the appropriate measure will be the amount that was likely to be achieved in all the circumstances.
5. A further determinant of seriousness is whether the fraud was a single fraudulent transaction or a multiple fraud. Where one false declaration or a failure to disclose a change in circumstances results in multiple payments, this should be regarded as multiple fraud.
6. The Council considers it unlikely that more than £100,000 could be obtained in a benefit fraud, unless the offence was professionally planned and either carried out over a significant period of time or through multiple frauds. In addition, it is unlikely that more than £20,000 could be obtained in a single fraudulent transaction benefit fraud. Consequently, the guideline does not provide separately for such circumstances.
7. The maximum penalty for most of the offences covered by this guideline is 7 years imprisonment. Where fraud under the 2006 Act is charged and the maximum penalty is 10 years, the proposed sentencing ranges leave headroom for offences involving the largest scale frauds to be sentenced outside the range and up to the maximum.
8. When assessing the seriousness of an offence, a court must always have regard to the full list of aggravating and mitigating factors in the Council guideline *Overarching Principles: Seriousness* (reproduced in <u>Annex B</u> [not reproduced here: see **SG-25**]); those most likely to be present in offences of fraud are set out at paragraphs 22 and 29 above. Additional aggravating and mitigating factors likely to be particularly relevant to this type of fraud are considered at paragraphs 24 and 26–27, 31 and 36 above.
9. The Council has identified matters of personal mitigation which may be relevant, which are set out in paragraphs 38–46 above. The court should have specific regard to personal and family circumstances of offenders which will vary greatly and may be particularly significant to sentencing for this type of fraud.
10. Generally, those who commit benefit fraud are asked to repay the sums defrauded, although the process of recovery may be spread over a significant period and may not be possible in every case. As recovery of defrauded benefits is not guaranteed and operates quite separately from civil or

criminal sanctions, this has not been taken into account in the Council's proposals. The fact that defrauded sums may have been recovered is not relevant to the choice of the type of sentence to be imposed.

BENEFIT FRAUD

Maximum penalty: Fraud (prosecuted under Fraud Act 2006), 10 years custody
For all other offences, 7 years custody

Nature of offence	Amount obtained or intended to be obtained				
	£500,000 or more *Starting point based on: £750,000**	£100,000 or more and less than £500,000 *Starting point based on: £300,000**	£20,000 or more and less than £100,000 *Starting point based on: £60,000**	£5,000 or more and less than £20,000 *Starting point based on: £12,500**	Less than £5,000 *Starting point based on: £2,500**
Fraudulent from the outset, professionally planned **and either** fraud carried out over a significant period of time **or** multiple frauds	**Starting point:** 5 years custody **Range:** 4–7 years custody	**Starting point:** 4 years custody **Range:** 3–5 years custody	**Starting point:** 2 years custody **Range:** 18 months– 3 years custody		
Fraudulent from the outset **and either** fraud carried out over a significant period of time **or** multiple frauds	**Starting point:** 4 years custody **Range:** 3–7 years custody	**Starting point:** 3 years custody **Range:** 2–4 years custody	**Starting point:** 15 months custody **Range:** 18 weeks– 30 months custody	**Starting point:** 12 weeks custody **Range:** Community order (HIGH)– 12 months custody	**Starting point:** Community order (HIGH) **Range:** Community order (LOW)– 6 weeks custody
Not fraudulent from the outset **and either** fraud carried out over a significant period of time **or** multiple frauds	**Starting point:** 3 years custody **Range:** 2–6 years custody	**Starting point:** 2 years custody **Range:** 12 months– 3 years custody	**Starting point:** 36 weeks custody **Range:** 12 weeks– 18 months custody	**Starting point:** 6 weeks custody **Range:** Community order (MEDIUM)– 26 weeks custody	**Starting point:** Community order (MEDIUM) **Range:** Fine– Community order (HIGH)
Single fraudulent transaction, fraudulent from the outset			**Starting point:** 26 weeks custody **Range:** 6 weeks– 12 months custody	**Starting point:** Community order (HIGH) **Range:** Fine– 18 weeks custody	**Starting point:** Community order (LOW) **Range:** Fine– Community order (MEDIUM)
Single fraudulent transaction, not fraudulent from the outset			**Starting point:** 12 weeks custody **Range:** Community order (MEDIUM)– 36 weeks custody	**Starting point:** Community order (MEDIUM) **Range:** Fine– 6 weeks custody	**Starting point:** Fine **Range:** Fine– Community order (LOW)

* Where the actual amount is greater or smaller than the figure on which the starting point is based, that is likely to be one of the factors that will move the sentence within the range (see paragraph 5 [above]).

Additional aggravating factors	Additional mitigating factors
1. Number involved in the offence and role of the offender	1. Peripheral involvement
2. Use of another person's identity	2. Misleading or incomplete advice

The presence of one or more aggravating factors may indicate a more severe sentence within the suggested range while the presence of one or more mitigating factors may indicate a less severe sentence within the suggested range.

The presence of aggravating or mitigating factors of exceptional significance may indicate that the case should move to a higher or lower level of seriousness.

Revenue fraud (against HM Revenue and Customs (HMRC))   **SG-431**

Factors to take into consideration

The principal offences likely to be used to prosecute these frauds are:

- *Fraud (Fraud Act 2006, s. 1)*
- *False accounting (Theft Act 1968, s. 17)*
- *Fraudulent evasion of VAT (Value Added Tax Act 1994, s. 72(1))*
- *False statement for VAT purposes (Value Added Tax Act 1994, s. 72(3))*
- *Conduct amounting to an offence (Value Added Tax Act 1994, s. 72(8))*
- *Fraudulent evasion of income tax (Finance Act 2000, s. 144)*
- *Evasion of excise duty (Customs and Excise Management Act 1979, s. 170(1)(a)(i), (ii), (b))*
- *Fraudulent evasion of excise duty (Customs and Excise Management Act 1979, s. 170(2)(a), 170B)*
- *Improper importation of goods (Customs and Excise Management Act 1979, s. 50(1) (a), (2))*

1. The following starting points and sentencing ranges are for a *'first time offender'* aged 18 or over who pleaded not guilty. They should be applied as set out [above].

2. This type of offending may take many forms, including:

    Fraudulent evasion of VAT - this includes situations where a trader does not charge VAT to the customer, situations where a customer pays VAT to the trader but the trader does not pay it to HM Revenue and Customs (HMRC), and so-called 'Missing Trader Intra-Community Frauds' (MTIC Frauds) or 'Carousel Frauds'.

    MTIC Frauds involve traders importing goods from the European Union free from VAT, charging VAT when they sell the goods and then keeping the money rather than paying it to HMRC. *Carousel Frauds* are MTIC Frauds where the trader sells the goods to another trader who re-exports them and claims back the VAT paid to the first trader from HMRC. Usually the goods are passed along a chain of traders between the missing trader and the broker known as 'buffers', in order to disguise the fraudulent nature of the activity. Having been exported by the broker, the goods are typically re-imported by the missing trader and pass through the same circle of transactions again and again in rapid succession.

    Fraudulent evasion of income tax - this may be committed by failing to declare earnings in a tax return or by an employer keeping the tax collected from employees rather than paying it to HMRC.

    Fraudulent evasion of excise duty - this includes alcohol and tobacco smuggling and the laundering of 'red diesel' into diesel engine road fuel.[350]

3. For the purposes of this guideline the Council considers it unlikely that more than £20,000 could be obtained in a single fraudulent transaction against HMRC in circumstances where the offender's intention was not fraudulent from the outset or where the claim was exaggerated. In addition, it is

---

[350] *Offences under the Customs and Excise Management Act 1979*, ss. 50 and 170 involving smuggling of prohibited weapons covered by minimum sentence provisions (carrying a maximum penalty of 10 years custody) are not covered by this guideline.

unlikely that more than £100,000 could be obtained in a fraud against HMRC in circumstances where the offender's intention was not fraudulent from the outset.

4. In most VAT frauds the offender intends to evade VAT. However, it is possible to commit the offence in section 72(3) of the VAT Act (and accordingly also the offence in section 72(8) of the same Act) by recklessly making a false statement for the purposes of VAT. The Council guideline *Overarching Principles: Seriousness*[351] states that an offender who acts recklessly is less culpable than an offender who acts intentionally. The proposals for the sentencing of frauds against HMRC take as a starting point an offender who acts intentionally. Where the offender has acted recklessly (relevant only to offences under the Value Added Tax Act 1994), courts should adjust the assessment of seriousness to take account of this lower level of culpability.

5. As in other types of fraud, the fact that the behaviour was not fraudulent from the outset may be a mitigating factor. Payments *to* HMRC may be evaded in order to increase the profitability of a legitimate business or the level of an individual's legitimate remuneration; payments may be fraudulently obtained *from* HMRC without any underlying legitimate activity at all as in a Carousel Fraud. Although the type of harm is the same since both result in a loss to HMRC, where payment is sought *from* HMRC in such circumstances, culpability is likely to be higher. Accordingly, such offences are likely to be regarded as more serious.

6. As the determinants of seriousness include the 'value of property or consequential loss involved', the table provides both a fixed amount (on which the starting point is based) and a band (on which the sentencing range is based). Where the value is larger or smaller than the amount on which the starting point is based, this should lead to upward or downward movement as appropriate. Where the amount the offender intended to obtain cannot be established, the appropriate measure will be the amount that was likely to be achieved in all the circumstances.

7. A further determinant of seriousness is whether the fraud was a single fraudulent transaction or a multiple fraud. Where one false declaration or a failure to disclose a change in circumstances results in multiple payments, this should be regarded as multiple fraud.

8. The maximum penalty for most of the offences covered by this guideline is 7 years imprisonment. Where fraud under the 2006 Act is charged and the maximum penalty is 10 years, the proposed sentencing ranges leave headroom for offences involving multi-million pound frauds to be sentenced outside the range and up to the maximum.

9. When assessing the seriousness of an offence, a court must always have regard to the full list of aggravating and mitigating factors in the Council guideline *Overarching Principles: Seriousness* (reproduced in Annex B [not reproduced here: see **SG-25**]); those most likely to be present in offences of fraud are set out at paragraphs 22 and 29 above. Additional aggravating and mitigating factors likely to be relevant generally to this type of fraud are considered at paragraphs 24, 26–27 and 31 and 36 above. Other additional aggravating factors specific to evasion of duty[352] are also included in the guideline.

10. The Council has identified matters of personal mitigation which may be relevant, which are set out in paragraphs 38–46 above.

11. In all cases sentencers should consider whether to make ancillary orders, particularly confiscation (see paragraphs 50–75 above).

Revenue Fraud (Against HM Revenue and Customs (HMRC))

Maximum penalty: Fraud (prosecuted under Fraud Act 2006), 10 years custody
                   For all other offences, 7 years custody

---

[351] *Overarching Principles: Seriousness*, para. 1.7, published 16 December 2004, www.sentencing-guidelines.gov.uk
[352] *Czyzewski* [2003] EWCA Crim 2139

Amount obtained or intended to be obtained					
Nature of offence	**£500,000 or more** *Starting point based on: £750,000**	**£100,000 or more and less than £500,000** *Starting point based on: £300,000**	**£20,000 or more and less than £100,000** *Starting point based on: £60,000**	**£5,000 or more and less than £20,000** *Starting point based on: £12,500**	**Less than £5,000** *Starting point based on: £2,500**
Fraudulent from the outset, professionally planned **and either** fraud carried out over a significant period of time **or** multiple frauds	**Starting point:** 5 years custody **Range:** 4–7 years custody	**Starting point:** 4 years custody **Range:** 3–5 years custody	**Starting point:** 2 years custody **Range:** 18 months–3 years custody		
Fraudulent from the outset **and either** fraud carried out over a significant period of time **or** multiple frauds	**Starting point:** 4 years custody **Range:** 3–7 years custody	**Starting point:** 3 years custody **Range:** 2–4 years custody	**Starting point:** 15 months custody **Range:** 18 weeks–30 months custody	**Starting point:** 12 weeks custody **Range:** Community order (HIGH)–12 months custody	**Starting point:** Community order (HIGH) **Range:** Community order (LOW)–6 weeks custody
Not fraudulent from the outset **and either** fraud carried out over a significant period of time **or** multiple frauds	**Starting point:** 3 years custody **Range:** 2–6 years custody	**Starting point:** 2 years custody **Range:** 12 months–3 years custody	**Starting point:** 36 weeks custody **Range:** 12 weeks–18 months custody	**Starting point:** 6 weeks custody **Range:** Community order (MEDIUM)–26 weeks custody	**Starting point:** Community order (MEDIUM) **Range:** Fine–Community order (HIGH)
Single fraudulent transaction, fraudulent from the outset			**Starting point:** 26 weeks custody **Range:** 6 weeks–12 months custody	**Starting point:** Community order (HIGH) **Range:** Fine–18 weeks custody	**Starting point:** Community order (LOW) **Range:** Fine–Community order (MEDIUM)
Single fraudulent transaction, not fraudulent from the outset			**Starting point:** 12 weeks custody **Range:** Community order (MEDIUM)–36 weeks custody	**Starting point:** Community order (MEDIUM) **Range:** Fine–6 weeks custody	**Starting point:** Fine **Range:** Fine–Community order (LOW)

* Where the actual amount is greater or smaller than the figure on which the starting point is based, that is likely to be one of the factors that will move the sentence within the range (see paragraph 6 [above]).

Sentencing Guidelines

Additional aggravating factors	Additional mitigating factors
1. Number involved in the offence and role of the offender 2. Use of another person's identity 3. Making repeated importations, particularly in the face of warnings from the authorities 4. Dealing in goods with an additional health risk 5. Disposing of goods to under-aged purchasers	1. Peripheral involvement 2. Misleading or incomplete advice

The presence of one or more aggravating factors may indicate a more severe sentence within the suggested range while the presence of one or more mitigating factors may indicate a less severe sentence within the suggested range.

The presence of aggravating or mitigating factors of exceptional significance may indicate that the case should move to a higher or lower level of seriousness.

SG-432   ANNEX A: STATUTORY DEFINITIONS AND MAXIMUM PENALTIES FOR

FRAUDOFFENCES INCLUDED IN THIS GUIDELINE

Offence	Statutory provision	Definition	Maximum custodial term in the Crown Court	Maximum custodial term in a Magistrates' Court	Financial reporting order available?
Fraud	Fraud Act 2006, s. 1	Dishonestly: – making a false representation; – failing to disclose information; or – abusing a position, – intending to make a gain for any person or cause a loss, or risk of loss, to another person.	10 years	6 months	Yes
Obtaining services dishonestly	Fraud Act 2006, s. 11	Dishonestly obtaining a service for any person by a dishonest act: – where the services are available on the basis that payment is made before, during or after receiving them, – knowing that the services are or might be being made available on that basis, – not paying in full, and – intending not to pay in full.	5 years	6 months	Yes
False accounting	Theft Act 1968, s. 17	Dishonestly: – destroying, defacing, concealing or falsifying any account, record or document made or required for any accounting purpose; or – when providing information for any purpose, producing or using any account, record or document made or required for any accounting purpose, knowing it is misleading, false or deceptive, with a view to creating a gain for oneself or another person or with intent to cause loss to another person.	7 years	6 months	Yes

Offence	Statutory provision	Definition	Maximum custodial term in the Crown Court	Maximum custodial term in a Magistrates' Court	Financial reporting order available?
Possession of articles for use in fraud	Fraud Act 2006, s. 6	Possessing or having under one's control any article for use in the course of or in connection with any fraud.	5 years	6 months	No
Making or supplying articles for use in frauds	Fraud Act 2006, s. 7	Making, adapting, supplying or offering to supply any article: – knowing that it is designed or adapted for use in the course of or in connection with any fraud; or – intending it to be used to commit, or assist in the commission of, fraud.	10 years	6 months	No
VAT evasion	Value Added Tax Act 1994, s. 72	Being knowingly concerned in or, in the taking of steps with a view to, the fraudulent evasion of VAT by any person. OR Producing, furnishing, sending or otherwise making use of any document which is false in a material particular for VAT purposes, or In furnishing any information for VAT purposes making any statement knowing it to be false in a material particular or making a statement that is false in a material particular. OR Where a person's conduct during any specified period must have involved the commission by him/her of one or more offences under this section.	7 years	6 months	Yes
Income tax evasion	Finance Act 2000, s. 144	Being knowingly concerned in the fraudulent evasion of income tax by any person.	7 years	6 months	Yes
Excise duty evasion	Customs and Excise Management Act 1979, s. 170	Knowingly acquiring possession of goods which have been unlawfully removed from a warehouse or Queen's warehouse or goods which are chargeable with a duty which has not been paid, or being in any way knowingly concerned in carrying, removing, depositing, harbouring, keeping or concealing or in any manner dealing with any such goods with intent to defraud Her Majesty of any duty payable on the goods. OR Being knowingly concerned in any fraudulent evasion or attempt at evasion of any duty chargeable on any goods.	7 years*	6 months	Yes

Offence	Statutory provision	Definition	Maximum custodial term in the Crown Court	Maximum custodial term in a Magistrates' Court	Financial reporting order available?
Taking preparatory steps for evasion of excise duty	Customs and Excise Management Act 1979, s. 170B	Being knowingly concerned in the taking of any steps with a view to the fraudulent evasion, by any person, of any duty of excise on any goods.	7 years	6 months	No
Improper importation of goods	Customs and Excise Management Act 1979, s. 50	With intent to defraud Her Majesty of any duty: – unshipping or landing in any port or unloading from any aircraft in the United Kingdom or from any vehicle in Northern Ireland any goods chargeable with a duty which has not been paid, or assisting or being otherwise concerned in such unshipping, landing or unloading; OR – removing from their place of importation or from any approved wharf, examination station, transit shed or customs and excise station any goods chargeable with a duty which has not been paid, or assisting or being otherwise concerned in such removal.	7 years*	6 months	No
Benefit fraud offences	Social Security Administration Act 1992, s. 111A	Dishonestly making a false statement or representation or producing or furnishing or allowing to be produced or furnished any document or information which is false in a material particular with a view to obtaining any benefit or other payment or advantage for any person. OR Dishonestly failing to give a prompt notification or causing or allowing another person to fail to give a prompt notification of a change in circumstances affecting the entitlement of any person to any benefit or other payment or advantage, knowing that the change affects an entitlement to such a benefit or other payment or advantage. OR Where there has been a change of circumstances affecting any person's claim to any benefit or other payment or advantage under which the 'recipient' has a right to receive payments:	7 years	6 months	No

Offence	Statutory provision	Definition	Maximum custodial term in the Crown Court	Maximum custodial term in a Magistrates' Court	Financial reporting order available?
		– the recipient dishonestly fails to give prompt notification of the change in circumstances; OR – causing or allowing the recipient to fail to give a prompt notification of the change in circumstances.			
Tax credit fraud	Tax Credits Act 2002, s. 35	Being knowingly concerned in any fraudulent activity undertaken with a view to obtaining payment of a tax credit by any person.	7 years	6 months	Yes

* 10 years if goods are prohibited weapons covered by minimum sentence provisions (Criminal Justice Act 2003, s. 293) in relation to which this guideline does not apply.

PART 18   OVERARCHING PRINCIPLES— SENTENCING YOUTHS

SG-433

Foreword

…This guideline applies to the sentencing of offenders on or after **30 November 2009**.

Generally, the Sentencing Guidelines Council has not produced offence specific guidelines for those under the age of 18 years. However, guidelines have been produced for those offences under the Sexual Offences Act 2003 which have a lower maximum penalty when committed by a person under 18 and for Robbery. These continue to provide the relevant starting points and ranges for all youths convicted of those offences and are not superseded by this guideline.

OVERARCHING PRINCIPLES—SENTENCING YOUTHS

SG-434

General Approach

1. Statutory provisions

1.1 Offence seriousness is the starting point for sentencing. In considering the seriousness of any offence, the court must consider the offender's culpability in committing the offence and any harm which the offence caused, was intended to cause or might foreseeably have caused.[353] In imposing sentence, the restrictions on liberty must be commensurate with the seriousness of the offence.

1.2 When sentencing an offender aged under 18, a court must[354] have regard to:
   a) the principal aim of the youth justice system (to prevent offending by children and young persons);[355] and
   b) the welfare of the offender.[356]

1.3 In addition to the statutory provisions,[357] a court sentencing a young offender must be aware of obligations under a range of international conventions which emphasise the importance of avoiding 'criminalisation' of young people whilst ensuring that they are held responsible for their actions and, where possible, take part in repairing the damage that they have caused. This includes recognition of the damage caused to the victims and understanding by the young person that the deed was not acceptable. Within a system that provides for both the acknowledgement of guilt and sanctions

---

[353] Criminal Justice Act 2003, s.143(1)

[354] This section does not apply when imposing a mandatory life sentence, when imposing a statutory minimum custodial sentence, when imposing detention for life under the dangerous offender provisions or when making certain orders under the Mental Health Act 1983.

[355] Crime and Disorder Act 1998, s. 37(1), see para. 2.6 below

[356] Children and Young Persons Act 1933, s. 44(1), see para. 2.7

[357] Criminal Justice and Immigration Act 2008, s. 9 (inserting s.142A into the Criminal Justice Act 2003) has not been brought into force.

which rehabilitate, the intention is to establish responsibility and, at the same time, to promote re-integration rather than to impose retribution.

SG-435 **2. Sentencing principles**

2.1 **The approach to sentence will be individualistic**.

2.2 The youth of the offender is widely recognised as requiring a different approach from that which would be adopted in relation to an adult. Even within the category of 'youth', the response to an offence is likely to be very different depending on whether the offender is at the lower end of the age bracket, in the middle or towards the top end; in many instances, the maturity of the offender will be at least as important as the chronological age.

2.3 However, the sentence must remain proportionate to the seriousness of the present offence (except in the rare circumstances where the criteria for a sentence under the dangerous offender provisions are met) and should not impose greater restrictions on liberty than the seriousness of the offence justifies simply to deal with the risk of re-offending. Particular care will need to be taken where a young person has committed a relatively less serious offence but there is a high risk of re-offending.

2.4 Whilst a court is required to aggravate the seriousness of an offence where there are previous convictions (if the court considers that to be reasonable taking account both of the offence and the time that had elapsed since the previous conviction[358]), **a sentence that follows re-offending does not need to be more severe than the previous sentence solely because there had been a previous conviction**.

(i) Approach to determining sentence

2.5 When determining sentence, the court will:

(1) **Assess the culpability of the offender and the harm caused (or intended or foreseeable) taking into account aggravating and mitigating factors relating to the offence**.

    The assessment of offence seriousness will fix the most severe penalty that can be imposed and will determine whether an offence has crossed the necessary threshold to enable the court to impose a community or custodial sentence.

    Even where the custody threshold has been crossed, a court is not required to impose a custodial sentence; similarly with the community sentence threshold.[359]

    Harm may be to individual victims or to the community or society at large. Of the four levels of culpability for sentencing purposes, intention is the highest followed by recklessness, knowledge and negligence. Even within those levels there will be gradations of seriousness.

    Statutory aggravating factors (including previous convictions) will be relevant in assessing the seriousness of an offence.

(2) **Consider any mitigating factors that apply to the offender and any reduction for a guilty plea**.

    When considering the maturity of the offender and its relevance to the sentence, it will only be in the most exceptional case that this will require more information than is available to the court through the representations of the advocates and any pre-sentence report.

(3) **Having taken account of all these factors, a court must then determine sentence including any relevant ancillary orders**.

    The overall impact of the sentence and the ancillary orders must be considered to ensure that the restrictions on liberty are no more than is commensurate with the seriousness of the offence.

(ii) The principal aim of the youth justice system

2.6 By section 37 of the Crime and Disorder Act 1998, the principal aim of the youth justice system is to prevent offending by children and young people. For the offender, it incorporates the need to demonstrate that such conduct is not acceptable in a way that makes an impact on the offender whilst also identifying and seeking to address any other factors that make offending more likely. For any victim of the offence and society as a whole, it incorporates the need to demonstrate that the law is being effectively enforced and to sustain confidence in the rule of law.

(iii) The welfare of the offender

2.7 By section 44 of the Children and Young Persons Act 1933, 'Every court in dealing with a child or young person who is brought before it, either as an offender or otherwise, shall have regard to the *welfare* of the child or young person, and shall in a proper case take steps for removing him from undesirable surroundings, and for securing that proper provision is made for his education and training'.

2.8 In other requirements or obligations, different terminology—*best interests*, *well-being* or *welfare*—may be used. Generally, although there are shades of difference between the meanings, it is unlikely that different decisions will arise solely from those differences.

---

[358] Criminal Justice Act 2003, s.174(2)
[359] ibid., s.148(5)

2.9   Accordingly, since 'welfare' is the term used in the legislation applicable to England and Wales, that is the term used in this guideline. Welfare includes the obligation to secure proper provision for education and training,[360] where appropriate to remove from undesirable surroundings[361] and the need to choose the best option for the young person taking account of the circumstances of the offence.

In having regard to the 'welfare' of the young person, a court should ensure that it is alert to:

- the high incidence of mental health problems amongst young people in the criminal justice system;
- the high incidence of those with learning difficulties or learning disabilities amongst young people in the criminal justice system;
- the effect that speech and language difficulties might have on the ability of the young person (or any adult with them) to communicate with the court, to understand the sanction imposed or to fulfil the obligations resulting from that sanction;
- the extent to which young people anticipate that they will be discriminated against by those in authority and the effect that it has on the way that they conduct themselves during court proceedings;
- the vulnerability of young people to self harm, particularly within a custodial environment;
- the extent to which changes taking place during adolescence can lead to experimentation;
- the effect on young people of experiences of loss or of abuse.

2.10   In the light of the high incidence of these impairments amongst young people in custody or subject to a community sentence, and taking account of the fact that the principal aim of the youth justice system is preventing offending, a court should always seek to ensure that it has access to information about how best to identify and respond to those impairments and, where necessary, that a proper assessment has taken place in order to enable the most appropriate sentence to be imposed.

(iv)   The purpose of sentencing

2.11   As set out in paragraph 1 above, a court sentencing a person under the age of 18 is obliged to have regard to the principal aim of the youth justice system (to prevent offending by children and young persons) and to the welfare of the offender. As the principal aim of the youth justice system[362] is the prevention of offending by children and young people, the emphasis should be on approaches that seem most likely to be effective with young people.

3.   Effect on sentence of the offender being a young person

3.1   In addition to the distinctive range of penalties available for youths, there is an expectation that, generally, a young person will be dealt with less severely than an adult offender, although this distinction diminishes as the offender approaches age 18 (subject to an assessment of maturity and criminal sophistication). In part, this is because young people are unlikely to have the same experience and capacity as an adult to realise the effect of their actions on other people or to appreciate the pain and distress caused and because a young person is likely to be less able to resist temptation, especially where peer pressure is exerted.

3.2   Additionally, in most cases a young person is likely to benefit from being given greater opportunity to learn from mistakes without undue penalisation or stigma, especially as a court sanction might have a significant effect on the prospects and opportunities of the young person, and, therefore, on the likelihood of effective integration into society.

3.3   When sentencing a young offender whose offence involves sexual activity but there is no evidence of a coercive or abusive relationship or of anything other than consensual activity, a court will need to be aware that a desire to explore gender identity or sexual orientation may result in offending behaviour. Depending on the seriousness of the offending behaviour, offender mitigation may arise where that behaviour stems from sexual immaturity or confusion.[363]

3.4   Individual sanctions are likely to have a greater impact on a youth than on an adult, especially lengths of time spent in a custodial establishment, not least because of the exposure to influences likely to entrench criminal conduct (to which a young person may be more susceptible than an adult) and the greater risk of self harm than exists in relation to an adult.

SG-436

Sentencing Guidelines

---

[360] Children and Young Persons Act 1933, s. 44
[361] ibid.
[362] See para. 2.6 above
[363] The Sentencing Advisory Panel has previously stated that Crown Prosecutors and the court should take account of an offender's immaturity and normal juvenile experimentation: *Sexual Offences Act 2003 – the Panel's Advice to the Council –* page 4, para. 21, www.sentencing-guidelines.gov.uk

3.5 It is also important to consider whether the young offender lacks the maturity fully to appreciate the consequences of his conduct and the extent to which the offender has been acting on an impulsive basis and the offender's conduct has been affected by inexperience, emotional volatility or negative influences.

3.6 Factors regularly present in the background of those juveniles who commit offences include: low family income, poor housing, poor employment records, low educational attainment, early experience of offending by other family members or of violence or abuse (often accompanied by harsh and erratic discipline within the home) and the misuse of drugs.[364] There is also evidence that those young people who are 'looked after' have been more at risk of being drawn into the criminal justice system than other young people acting *in similar ways*.[365]

3.7 It is clear that these factors do not cause delinquency (since many who have experienced them do not commit crime); nonetheless, there is a strong association and any response to criminal activity amongst young people will need to recognise the presence of such factors if it is to be effective.

The following factors have led to a different approach to the sentencing of young people who offend (compared with the approach for adult offenders) and will affect the sentence imposed in an individual case:

- offending by a young person is frequently a phase which passes fairly rapidly and therefore the reaction to it needs to be kept well balanced in order to avoid alienating the young person from society;
- a criminal conviction at this stage of a person's life may have a disproportionate impact on the ability of the young person to gain meaningful employment and play a worthwhile role in society;
- the impact of punishment is felt more heavily by young people in the sense that any sentence will seem to be far longer in comparison with their relative age compared with adult offenders;
- young people may be more receptive to changing the way they conduct themselves and be able to respond more quickly to interventions;
- young people should be given greater opportunity to learn from their mistakes;
- young people will be no less vulnerable than adults to the contaminating influences that can be expected within a custodial context and probably more so.

SG-437 **4. The relevant considerations**

4.1 This guideline sets out a process that will enable the various obligations and requirements to be applied consistently. It is, however, only a framework and is intended to apply to the generality of cases.

In determining the sentence, the key elements are:
- the age of the offender (chronological and emotional),
- the seriousness of the offence,
- the likelihood of further offences being committed, and
- the extent of harm likely to result from those further offences.

The approach to sentence will be individualistic.

Proper regard should be had to the mental health and capability of the young person, and to any learning disability, learning difficulty, speech and language difficulty or other disorder, any of which is likely to affect the likelihood of those purposes being achieved.

4.2 The younger an offender (taking account of maturity and not just chronological age) the more likely it is that considering the welfare of the young person will be of greater significance. Since many young people 'grow out of' crime, the obligation to have regard to the welfare of a young person who has offended might in some circumstances be best manifested by protecting that person from the adverse effects of intervention in his or her life rather than by providing for some positive action.

4.3 The requirement to have regard to the welfare of a young person is subject to the obligation to impose only those restrictions on liberty that are commensurate with the seriousness of the offence; accordingly, a court should not impose greater restrictions because of other factors in the young person's life.

4.4 In relation to custodial sentences, the reconviction rate is high and there are concerns about the effect on vulnerable young people of being in closed conditions. Risks commonly found are those of self harm and suicide and, in relation to female offenders, the additional impact on the offender herself

---

[364] See, for example, the range of approaches in the *Youth Crime Action Plan 2008* Chapter 5: www.homeoffice.gov.uk
[365] See, for example, *Care experience and criminalisation* The Adolescent and Childcare Trust, September 2008 www.tactcare.org.uk *Sentencing Guidelines Council*

and on the child if the offender is the primary carer of a child or is pregnant.[366] Since a court is obliged to have regard to the welfare of the young person, it must have regard to these issues when considering sentence.

4.5   Particular care should be taken where an offender has mental health problems, learning disabilities, learning difficulties or other disabilities. Research shows that there is a high incidence of these issues in young people in the youth justice system and, in particular, in custody.

4.6   These issues are not always able to be identified at an early stage in the proceedings leading to sentence. As a result, a court needs to be alert to the possibility that the conduct of the young person (and that of any adult accompanying them in court) might be affected by issues relating to mental health, learning or communication, or some other form of disability that has not previously been identified.

4.7   In such circumstances, care needs to be taken in ensuring that the young person is able to take a proper part in the court proceedings, is able to understand what the court requires as a result of the sentence imposed and that that sentence properly takes account of difficulties in compliance that may arise from those issues.

4.8   Some young people may attend court believing that they will be discriminated against or otherwise unfairly treated; this might be for any of a wide range of reasons including ethnicity and sexuality. However unjustified that belief is, a court will need to be alert to the fact that the young persons behaviour in court might be affected by it.

4.9   The obligations to treat the prevention of offending by children and young persons as the principal aim of sentencing and to have regard to their welfare both require a court to consider the impairments and life experiences noted above, not only in determining the sentence to be imposed, but also in determining the length or content of that sentence.

The proper approach for the Crown Court, a magistrates' court or a youth court when sentencing a young offender is for the court, within a sentence that is no more restrictive on liberty than is proportionate to the seriousness of the offence(s), to seek to impose a sentence that takes proper account of the matters to which the court must have regard (see paragraph 1 above) by:

- confronting the young offender with the consequences of the offending and helping the young offender to develop a sense of personal responsibility—these consequences may be experienced by the offender himself or herself, by the family of the offender, by the victim(s) of the offence and/ or by the community;
- tackling the particular factors (personal, family, social, educational or health) that put the young person at risk of offending;
- strengthening those factors that reduce the risk that the young person will continue to offend;
- encouraging reparation to victims;
- defining, agreeing and reinforcing the responsibilities of parents.

5.   Crossing a significant age threshold between commission of an offence and sentence

SG-438

5.1   There will be occasions when an increase in the age of an offender[367] will result in the maximum sentence on the date of *conviction* being greater than that available on the date on which the offence was *committed*.

5.2   In such circumstances, the approach should be:

- where an offender crosses a relevant age threshold between the date on which the offence was committed and the date of conviction or sentence, a court should take as its starting point the sentence likely to have been imposed on the date on which the offence was committed;
- where an offender attains the age of 18 after committing the offence but before conviction, section 142 of the Criminal Justice Act 2003 applies (whilst section 37 of the 1998 Act and section 44 of the 1933 Act (see 2.6–2.10 above) apply to those aged under 18) and the sentencing disposal has to take account of the matters set out in that section;[368]
- it will be rare for a court to have to consider passing a sentence more severe than the maximum it would have had jurisdiction to pass at the time the offence was committed even where an offender has subsequently attained the age of 18;
- however, a sentence at or close to that maximum may be appropriate, especially where a serious offence was committed by an offender close to the age threshold.

---

[366] *The Corston Report – a review of women with particular vulnerabilities in the Criminal Justice System*, March 2007, www. homeoffice.gov.uk

[367] Primarily attaining the age of 12, 15 or 18.

[368] Accordingly, when sentencing those convicted when aged 18 and above who have committed an offence whilst under that age, more general public policy considerations may play a greater part.

SG-439 **6. Persistent offenders**

6.1 Certain sentences are available only where the offender is a 'persistent offender' – in particular, a youth rehabilitation order with intensive supervision and surveillance or with fostering in relation to an offender aged between 10 and 14[369] and a detention and training order in relation to an offender aged between 12 and 14.[370] This criterion does not have to be met before the Crown Court imposes long term detention (see paragraph 12 below) or detention for life.

6.2 Similarly, additional powers may be available to a court where a youth rehabilitation order has been breached 'wilfully and persistently'.

6.3 'Persistent offender' is not defined in legislation but has been considered by the Court of Appeal on a number of occasions. However, following the implementation of the 2008 Act, the sentencing framework is different from that when the definition was judicially developed, particularly the greater emphasis on the requirement to use a custodial sentence as 'a measure of last resort'.

6.4 A dictionary definition of 'persistent offender' is 'persisting or having a tendency to persist'; 'persist' is defined as 'to continue firmly or obstinately in a course of action in spite of difficulty or opposition'.

6.5 In determining whether an offender is a persistent offender for these purposes, a court should consider the simple test of whether the young person is one who persists in offending:

    i) in most circumstances, the normal expectation is that the offender will have had some contact with authority in which the offending conduct was challenged before being classed as 'persistent'; a finding of persistence in offending may be derived from information about previous convictions but may also arise from orders which require an admission or finding of guilt – these include reprimands, final warnings, restorative justice disposals and conditional cautions; since they do not require such an admission, penalty notices for disorder are unlikely to be sufficiently reliable;

    ii) a young offender is certainly likely to be found to be persistent (and, in relation to a custodial sentence, the test of being a measure of last resort is most likely to be satisfied) where the offender has been convicted of, or made subject to a pre-court disposal that involves an admission or finding of guilt in relation to, imprisonable offences on at least 3 occasions in the past 12 months.

6.6 Even where a young person is found to be a persistent offender, a court is not obliged to impose the custodial sentence or youth rehabilitation order with intensive supervision and surveillance or fostering that becomes available as a result of that finding. The other tests continue to apply and it is clear that Parliament expects custodial sentences to be imposed only rarely on those aged 14 or less.

SG-440 **7. Enforcing the responsibilities of parents and guardians**

7.1 A significant difference arising from the procedures for dealing with young people who commit criminal offences is the importance attached to the presence of a parent, carer or appropriate adult at key stages, especially when sentence is imposed. In addition, specific provisions exist to enable a court to reinforce the responsibilities of a parent or guardian.

7.2 The statutory framework clearly envisages the attendance of an adult with a degree of responsibility for the young person; this obligation reflects the principal aim of reducing offending, recognising that that is unlikely to be achieved by the young person alone. A court must be aware of a risk that a young person will seek to avoid this requirement either by urging the court to proceed in the absence of an adult or in arranging for a person to come to court who purports to have (but in reality does not have) the necessary degree of responsibility.

7.3 Insistence on attendance may produce a delay in the case before the court; however, it is important that this obligation is maintained and that it is widely recognised that a court will require such attendance, especially when imposing sentence. If a court proceeds in the absence of a responsible adult, it should ensure that the outcome of the hearing is properly communicated.

7.4 Where a person under the age of 18 is convicted of an offence, the court is under a duty to **bind over a parent or guardian** if satisfied that such a course of action would be desirable in the interest of preventing the commission of further offences.[371] Such an order may not be made where the court imposes a referral order. Similarly, the court has the power to make a **parenting order** where it would be desirable in the interest of preventing the commission of any further offence.[372] Where the offender is aged 16 or less and the court considers that a parenting order would be desirable, there is a presumption in favour of the order being made and reasons must be given if it is not made.[373]

---

[369] Criminal Justice and Immigration Act 2008, s.1(4)(c)
[370] Powers of Criminal Courts (Sentencing) Act 2000, s.100(2)
[371] Powers of Criminal Courts (Sentencing) Act 2000, s.150
[372] Crime and Disorder Act 1998, s. 8(6)
[373] ibid., s. 9(1)

In most circumstances where an order is necessary, it is more likely that a parenting order will be appropriate.

7.5   When considering whether to impose a parenting order, the court should give careful consideration to the strength of the familial relationships and to any diversity issues that might impact on the achievement of the purposes of the order. Such factors and issues arising may be documented in a pre-sentence report.

7.6   Particular issues may arise in relation to an offender who is, or who runs the risk of, experiencing familial abuse or rejection on the grounds of sexual orientation. In considering such factors, which may be documented in a pre-sentence report the court must take care not to disclose facts about an offender's sexual orientation without his or her consent. Similar issues might arise in a family where racial tensions exist.

Sentences   SG-441

8. Referral orders

8.1   Where an offender is being sentenced in a youth court or a magistrates' court, a referral order is a mandatory sentence in many circumstances in which a young person is to be sentenced for the first time and is discretionary in a wider range of situations. In particular, it is possible to make an order on a second conviction where a referral order was not made following the first conviction.

8.2   When an order is made, the court determines the length of the order (between 3 months and 12 months) but the action taken during that order is decided by a Youth Offender Panel consisting of members of the community supported by a member of a Youth Offending Team. Any victim of the offence may be invited to attend the meeting of the Panel at which the terms are agreed.

8.3   When determining the length of an order, although the needs of the offender are a factor, the primary consideration in most circumstances is the relative seriousness of the offence. Given the mandatory nature of the order in many circumstances, it is less likely that the needs of the offender will be considered in a pre-sentence report. This consideration is more likely to take place once the order has been made and in preparation for the Panel meeting since, within the period of the order, the Youth Offender Panel will agree what needs to be undertaken by the young person both in the light of the nature of the offence and of the young person's needs.

8.4   **A court should be prepared to use the whole range of periods allowed; in general, orders of 10–12 months should be made only for the more serious offences.**

8.5   Typically, the length of an order should be between 3–5 months for offences where the court assesses seriousness to be relatively low, between 5–7 months for an offence of medium level seriousness and between 7–9 months for an offence where the court considers seriousness to be relatively high. In determining which level applies, a court may find assistance in Section 2 of the Youth Court Bench Book issued by the Judicial Studies Board which provides indications of the level of seriousness of an average offence of the types described.[374]

9. Financial orders   SG-442

9.1   A court may impose a fine for any offence. In accordance with statutory requirements, where financial orders are being considered, priority must be given to compensation orders and, where an order for costs is to be made alongside a fine, the amount of the costs must not exceed the amount of the fine.

9.2   In practice, many young people who offend have few financial resources. Where a young person is in receipt of the *Education Maintenance Allowance* or a similar provision which is related to the means of the offender or those with whom the offender lives, a court will need to consider the extent to which making a deduction from the allowance would prejudice the access of the young person to education or training.

9.3   **As a general rule, it will rarely be appropriate to take the allowance into account as a resource from which a financial penalty may be paid, especially where the recipient is a young person who is living independently or as part of a household primarily dependent on state benefit.**

10. Youth Rehabilitation Orders   SG-443

10.1   The Criminal Justice and Immigration Act 2008 provides for a single community sentence (the youth rehabilitation order) within which a court may include one or more requirements variously designed to provide for punishment, for protection of the public, for reducing reoffending and for reparation.

Sentencing Guidelines

---

[374] www.jsboard.co.uk/downloads/ycbb/ycbb_section2.pdf

10.2 A youth rehabilitation order with intensive supervision and surveillance or with fostering is also provided but may be imposed only where a custodial sentence otherwise would have been appropriate (see 10.23 below).[375]

(i) Threshold and availability

10.3 In order for a court to be able to impose a youth rehabilitation order, it must be satisfied that the offence is 'serious enough'.[376] Even where an offence crosses this threshold, a court is not obliged to make a youth rehabilitation order.[377]

10.4 In determining the content and length of an order, the guiding principles are proportionality and suitability since statute provides that the restrictions on liberty within such an order must be commensurate with the seriousness of the offence[378] and that, taken together, the requirements within the order are the most suitable for the offender.[379]

10.5 In contrast to the provisions relating to adult offenders, a court may impose a youth rehabilitation order (other than one with intensive supervision and surveillance or fostering[380]) for an offence that is not imprisonable.

10.6 A youth rehabilitation order is not an available sentence where the 'compulsory referral conditions' are found to exist; accordingly, the order will not be available in a youth court or other magistrates' court for a first time offender who has pleaded guilty to an imprisonable offence.

(ii) Effect of a guilty plea

10.7 Where a court is considering sentence for an offence for which a custodial sentence is justified, a guilty plea may be one of the factors that persuades a court that it can properly impose a youth rehabilitation order instead and no further adjustment to the sentence needs to be made to fulfil the obligation to give credit for that plea.

10.8 Where the provisional sentence is already a youth rehabilitation order, the necessary reduction for a guilty plea should apply to those requirements within the order that are primarily punitive rather than to those which are primarily rehabilitative.

(iii) Approach to determining nature and extent of requirements

10.9 In determining the nature and extent of requirements to be included within an order and the length of that order, the key factors are the assessment of the seriousness of the offence, the objective(s) the court wishes to achieve, the risk of re-offending, the ability of the offender to comply, and the availability of requirements in the local area.

10.10 Since a court must determine that the offence (or combination of offences) is 'serious enough' to justify such an order, a court will be able to determine the nature and extent of the requirements within the order primarily by reference to the likelihood of the young person re-offending and to the risk of the young person causing serious harm. This is in accordance with the principal aim of the youth justice system and the welfare principle.

10.11 Before making an order a court will consider a pre-sentence report. In preparing that report, (following national standards and practice guidance) the Youth Offending Team (YOT) will be seeking to identify an appropriate balance between the seriousness of the offence, the risk of harm in the future from any further offences the young person might commit and the needs of the young person.

10.12 In most cases, the assessment by the YOT will be undertaken by use of *Asset*[381] supported by professional judgement. An initial assessment will calculate the risk of re-offending; where necessary, an additional assessment will assess the risk of serious harm likely to be involved in further offending.

10.13 Those assessments will be reviewed by the YOT in the context of all other available information and the report will identify a level of intervention for the court to consider. There are three intervention levels:

---

[375] Criminal Justice and Immigration Act 2008, ss.1(3) and 1(4); Criminal Justice Act 2003, s.174(2)(ca) and (cb) as inserted by Criminal Justice and Immigration Act 2008, sched. 4, para. 80(2); however, it may be imposed in other circumstances following 'wilful and persistent' breach of a youth rehabilitation order: see para. 10.41 below

[376] Criminal Justice Act 2003, s.148(1)

[377] ibid., s.148(5)

[378] ibid., s.148(3)(b)

[379] ibid., s.148(3)(a)

[380] Such an order may be imposed following wilful and persistent failure to comply with a youth rehabilitation order imposed for a non-imprisonable offence: Criminal Justice and Immigration Act 2008, sched. 2, para. 6(13) and para. 8(12)

[381] A 'common, structured framework for the assessment of all young people involved in the criminal justice system' which is designed to 'identify a multitude of factors and circumstances...which may have contributed' to the offending behaviour: see www.yjb.gov.uk

- **Standard level** – for those who show a low likelihood of reoffending and a low risk of serious harm; in those circumstances, the order primarily will seek to repair the harm caused by the offence – typically, this will involve interventions to meet the requirements of the order and the engagement of parents in those interventions and/or in supporting the young person;
- **Enhanced level** – for those who show a medium likelihood of reoffending or a medium risk of serious harm; in those circumstances, the order will, in addition, seek to enable help or change as appropriate – typically, this will involve greater activity in motivating the young person and in addressing the reasons for non-compliance with the law and may involve external interventions;
- **Intensive level** – for those with a high likelihood of reoffending or a high or very high risk of serious harm; in those circumstances, the order will, in addition, seek to ensure control of the young person as necessary to minimise the risk of further offending or of serious harm—typically this will involve additional controls, restrictions and monitoring.[382]

10.14 For the broad generality of offences where a youth rehabilitation order is to be imposed, this approach will enable the writer of a pre-sentence report to make proposals that match the obligations on the court to balance the various statutory obligations that apply.

10.15 Where a young person is assessed as presenting a **high risk of re-offending or of causing serious harm** despite having committed a relatively less serious offence, the emphasis is likely to be on requirements that are primarily rehabilitative or for the protection of the public. Care will need to be taken to ensure both that the requirements are 'those most suitable for the offender' and that the restrictions on liberty are commensurate with the seriousness of the offence.

10.16 Where a young person is assessed as presenting a **low risk despite having committed a relatively high seriousness offence**, the emphasis is likely to be on requirements that are primarily punitive, again ensuring that restrictions on liberty are commensurate with the seriousness of the offence. In relation to young offenders, the primary purpose of punitive sanctions is to achieve acknowledgement by the young person of responsibility for his or her actions and, where possible, to take a proper part in repairing the damage caused.

(iv) Length of order

10.17 When imposing a youth rehabilitation order, the court must fix a period within which the requirements of the order are to be completed; this must not be more than 3 years from the date on which the order comes into effect.[383] Where the order contains two or more requirements, the order may specify an earlier date for any of those requirements.[384]

10.18 The period specified as the overall period for the order will normally commence on the day the order is made but, where the young person is already subject to a detention and training order, the court may specify that the youth rehabilitation order will take effect either on the day that supervision begins in relation to the detention and training order or on the expiry of the term of that order.[385]

10.19 It is not possible to make a youth rehabilitation order when the young person is already subject to another youth rehabilitation order or to a reparation order unless the court revokes those orders.[386]

10.20 The overall length of an order has three main consequences:
- where a supervision requirement is included, the obligation to attend appointments as directed by the responsible officer continues for the whole period;
- where a young person is in breach of a youth rehabilitation order, one of the sanctions available to a court is to amend the order by including within it any requirement that it would have had power to include when the order was made;[387] however, that new requirement must be capable of being complied with before the expiry of the overall period;[388]
- a young person is liable to re-sentence for the offence(s) for which the order was made if convicted of another offence whilst the order is in force.[389]

10.21 In determining the length of an order, a court should allow sufficient time for the order as a whole to be complied with, recognising that the young person is at risk of further sanction throughout

[382] YOUTH JUSTICE: The Scaled Approach, YJB 2009 www.yjb.gov.uk/scaledapproach
[383] Criminal Justice and Immigration Act 2008, sched. 1, para. 32(1)
[384] ibid., para. 32(2)
[385] ibid., para. 30
[386] ibid., para. 30(4)
[387] Criminal Justice and Immigration Act 2008, sched. 2, para. 6(2) (magistrates' court) and para. 8(2) (Crown Court)
[388] ibid., para. 6(6) and para. 8(6)
[389] ibid., para. 18 and para. 19

the whole of the period, but allowing sufficient flexibility should a sanction need to be imposed for breach of the order. Where appropriate, an application for early discharge may be made.

(v) Determining the requirements and the length of an order—summary

10.22 As set out in paragraph 2.1 above, the approach to the sentencing of a youth will be individualistic. Where a court is satisfied that an offence has crossed the community sentence threshold and that such a sentence is necessary or has crossed the custody threshold but is an offence for which a youth rehabilitation order is nonetheless considered to be appropriate, taking account of the assessment in the pre-sentence report, the consideration process that the court should follow is:

i) *what requirements are most suitable for the offender?*
ii) *what overall period is necessary to ensure that all requirements may be satisfactorily completed?*
iii) *are the restrictions on liberty that result from those requirements commensurate with the seriousness of the offence?*

(vi) Orders with intensive supervision and surveillance or with fostering

10.23 Such orders may be made where:[390]
- the court is dealing with a young person for an offence punishable with imprisonment;
- that offence (or combination of offences) crosses the custody threshold; and
- custody would be an appropriate sentence.
  If the offender was under 15 at the time of conviction, such an order may be imposed only where the offender is a 'persistent offender'.

10.24 When imposing such an order, the court must give its reasons for concluding that the offence(s) cross(es) the community sentence threshold and that the requirements set out above have been met.[391]

(a) With intensive supervision and surveillance

10.25 A youth rehabilitation order with intensive supervision and surveillance is an order that contains an 'extended activity requirement', that is, an activity requirement with a maximum of 180 days. As a result, there are further obligations to include a supervision requirement[392] and a curfew requirement.[393]

10.26 Where appropriate, a youth rehabilitation order with intensive supervision and surveillance may also include additional requirements, although the order as a whole must comply with the obligation that the requirements must be those most suitable for the offender and that any restrictions on liberty must be commensurate with the seriousness of the offence.

10.27 When imposing such an order, a court must ensure that the requirements are not so onerous as to make the likelihood of breach almost inevitable.

(b) With fostering

10.28 Where a fostering requirement is included within a youth rehabilitation order, it will require the offender to reside with a local authority foster parent for a specified period; that period must not exceed 12 months.[394] The court must be satisfied that a significant factor in the offence was the circumstances in which the young person was living and that the imposition of a fostering requirement would assist in the rehabilitation of the young person. It is likely that other rights will be engaged (such as those under Article 8 of the European Convention on Human Rights[395]) and any interference with such rights must be proportionate.

10.29 Before including this requirement, the court must consult both the young person's parent or guardian (unless impracticable) and the local authority; it cannot be included unless the offender was legally represented in court when the court was considering whether or not to impose the requirement or, having had the opportunity to be represented, the offender has not applied for representation or that right was withdrawn because of the offender's conduct.[396] This requirement may be

---

[390] Though see the additional powers where an offender has 'wilfully and persistently' failed to comply with a youth rehabilitation order; para. 10.41 below

[391] Criminal Justice Act 2003, s.174(2)(ca) and (cb)

[392] A requirement to attend appointments with the responsible officer (or any other person determined by the responsible officer): Criminal Justice and Immigration Act 2008, sched. 1, para. 9

[393] A minimum of 2 hours and a maximum of 12 hours on any one day which must fall within the period of 6 months from the day on which the requirement first takes effect: ibid., para. 14; it is likely that this curfew will be electronically monitored: ibid., para. 3(4)(b) and para. 2

[394] Criminal Justice and Immigration Act 2008, sched. 1, para. 18

[395] Right to respect for family and private life

[396] Criminal Justice and Immigration Act 2008, sched. 1, para. 19

included only where the court has been notified that arrangements are available in the area of the relevant local authority.

10.30   A fostering requirement cannot be included with intensive supervision and surveillance and it cannot be included in a youth rehabilitation order unless the higher criteria described above have been met. Where appropriate, a youth rehabilitation order with fostering may also include other requirements (and must include supervision) although the order as a whole must comply with the obligation that the requirements must be those most suitable for the offender and that any restrictions on liberty must be commensurate with the seriousness of the offence.

10.31   It is unlikely that the statutory criteria will be met in many cases; where they are met and the court is considering making an order, care should be taken to ensure that there is a well developed plan for the care and support of the young person throughout the period of the order and following conclusion of the order. A court will need to be provided with sufficient information, including proposals for education and training during the order and plans for the offender on completion of the order.

(vii)   Breaches

10.32   Where a young person fails to comply with a youth rehabilitation order, the 'responsible officer' must consider whether there was a reasonable excuse. If the officer considers that there was no reasonable excuse and this is the first failure to comply with the order without reasonable excuse, the officer must issue a 'warning'.[397]

10.33   The warning will describe the circumstances of the failure to comply, a statement that the failure is not acceptable and a warning that a further failure to comply may lead to the order being referred back to the court. In most circumstances, two warnings will be permitted within a 12 month period before the matter is referred back to court.

10.34   There is a presumption in favour of referring the matter back to court after a third failure to comply and a discretionary power to do so after the second failure to comply.[398]

10.35   Breach of an order brought before a court may arise from a failure to keep an appointment or otherwise co-operate with the responsible officer or may arise from a failure to comply with one or more of the other requirements of the order.

10.36   Even where a breach has been proved, a court is not obliged to make any order but may allow the youth rehabilitation order to continue as imposed. In contrast with the powers in relation to an adult offender, there is no obligation on the court to make an order more onerous. Where a court determines that a sanction is necessary, it has the power to:

- impose a fine (in which case the order continues in its original form);
- amend the terms of the order; or
- revoke the order and re-sentence the offender.[399]

10.37   If amending the terms of the order, the court may impose any requirement that it could have imposed when making the order and this may be in addition to, or in substitution for, any requirements contained in the order. If the youth rehabilitation order did not contain an unpaid work requirement and the court includes such a requirement using this power, the minimum period of unpaid work is 20 hours; this will give greater flexibility when responding to less serious breaches or where there are significant other requirements to be complied with.[400]

10.38   A court may not amend the terms of a youth rehabilitation order that did not include an extended activity requirement or a fostering requirement by inserting them at this stage; should these requirements be considered appropriate following breach, the offender must be re-sentenced and the original youth rehabilitation order revoked.[401]

10.39   Before imposing a custodial sentence as a result of re-sentencing following breach, a court should be satisfied that the YOT and other local authority services have taken all steps necessary to ensure that the young person has been given appropriate opportunity and support necessary for compliance.[402]

10.40   Where the failure arises primarily from non-compliance with reporting or other similar obligations and a sanction is necessary, the most appropriate response is likely to be the inclusion of

---

[397] Criminal Justice and Immigration Act 2008, sched. 2, para. 3
[398] ibid., para. 4; where a young person has attained the age of 18 since the order was made, except where the order was made in the Crown Court and no direction was made permitting breach proceedings to be dealt with in the youth court or a magistrates' court, breach proceedings will be dealt with in a magistrates' court other than a youth court: ibid., para. 5(3); however, the powers of a magistrates' court are the same as those of a youth court: ibid., para. 6
[399] ibid., para. 6 and para. 8
[400] Criminal Justice and Immigration Act 2008, sched. 2, para. 6(7) and para. 8(7)
[401] ibid., para. 6(8) and para. 8(8)
[402] cp Education and Skills Act 2008, s.45(5)

(or increase in) a primarily punitive requirement such as the curfew requirement, unpaid work, the exclusion requirement and the prohibited activity requirement or . . . the imposition of a fine. However, continuing failure to comply with the order is likely to lead to revocation of the order and re-sentencing for the original offence.

10.41 Where the offender has 'wilfully and persistently' failed to comply with the order, and the court proposes to sentence again for the offence(s) in respect of which the order was made, additional powers are available.[403] These additional powers include:

- the making of a youth rehabilitation order with intensive supervision and surveillance even though the offence is not imprisonable or a custodial sentence would not have been imposed if the order had not been available;
- even though the offence is not imprisonable, the imposition of a detention and training order for 4 months for breach of a youth rehabilitation order with intensive supervision and surveillance imposed following wilful and persistent breach of an order made for a non-imprisonable offence.

10.42 In considering whether the failure to comply is 'persistent', account should be taken of the principles set out in paragraph 6 above.

The primary objective when sentencing for breach of a youth rehabilitation order is to ensure that the young person completes the requirements imposed by the court.

Where the failure arises primarily from non-compliance with reporting or other similar obligations, where a sanction is necessary, the most appropriate is likely to be the inclusion of (or increase in) a primarily punitive requirement.

A court must ensure that it has sufficient information to enable it to understand why the order has been breached and that all steps have been taken by the YOT and other local authority services to give the young person appropriate opportunity and support. This will be particularly important if the court is considering imposing a custodial sentence as a result of the breach.

Where a court is determining whether the young person has 'wilfully and persistently breached an order, it should apply the same approach as when determining whether an offender is a 'persistent offender'. In particular, almost certainly a young person will have 'persistently breached a youth rehabilitation order where there have been three breaches (each resulting in an appearance before a court) demonstrating a lack of willingness to comply with the order.

SG-444 11. Custodial sentences

11.1 There is a statutory presumption that a person aged under 18 will be dealt with summarily, usually in a youth court; in such circumstances, the maximum custodial sentence will be a detention and training order of no more than 24 months. Such an order may be made only for the periods prescribed—4, 6, 8, 10, 12, 18 or 24 months.[404]

11.2 The custodial sentences available in the Crown Court are:

- detention and training order of up to 24 months;
- long term detention—in relation to a young person convicted[405] in the Crown Court, under section 91 of the Powers of Criminal Courts (Sentencing) Act 2000;
- extended sentence of detention or detention for public protection – where a young person is sent for trial or committed for sentence to the Crown Court to be dealt with under the dangerous offender provisions; in each case, the minimum period to be spent in custody under the sentence must be two years;
- detention at Her Majesty's pleasure—for offences of murder.

11.3 A detention and training order may not be imposed on an offender aged 10 or 11 years at the time of conviction; an order may be imposed in relation to an offender aged between 12 and 14 at the time of conviction only if the offender is a 'persistent offender' (see paragraph 6 above).[406] However, the persistent offender criterion does not have to be met before the Crown Court imposes long term detention or detention for life in relation to offenders who are under 15 years of age.

11.4 A pre-sentence report must be considered before a custodial sentence is imposed.

---

[403] In accordance with para. 6 and para. 8 of sched. 2 to the Criminal Justice and Immigration Act 2008
[404] Although consecutive sentences may lead to different periods being imposed in total.
[405] On the implementation of provisions contained in Criminal Justice Act 2003, sched. 3, this sentence is likely to be able to be imposed following conviction in a youth court also subsequent to an indication to plead guilty.
[406] Powers of Criminal Courts (Sentencing) Act 2000, s.100(2)

(i) Threshold and approach

11.5   Under both domestic law and international convention, a custodial sentence must be imposed only as a 'measure of last resort'; statute provides that such a sentence may be imposed only where an offence is 'so serious that neither a community sentence nor a fine alone can be justified'.[407]

11.6   For a first time offender who has pleaded guilty to an imprisonable offence, in most circumstances a referral order will be the most appropriate sentence.

11.7   Since the minimum length of a custodial sentence in the youth court is 4 months (significantly in excess of the minimum available in relation to an adult offender) and since the term of a custodial sentence must be the shortest commensurate with the seriousness of the offence, it is inevitable that the custody threshold is higher in the case of a young person than in the case of an adult—any case that warrants a detention and training order of less than four months must result in a non-custodial sentence.

11.8   In relation to a person under the age of 18, in determining whether an offence has crossed the custody threshold a court will need to consider whether the offence has resulted (or could reasonably have resulted) in serious harm. In determining whether a custodial sentence is unavoidable, generally, a court will need to take account both of the seriousness of the offence (particularly the extent to which it caused (or was likely to cause) serious harm) and of the risk of serious harm in the future. A custodial sentence is most likely to be unavoidable where it is necessary to protect the public from serious harm.

11.9   In addition, a court must take account of:
i)   the requirement to have regard to the principal aim of the youth justice system;[408]
ii)   the requirement to have regard to the welfare of the offender and the evidence that the risks associated with young offenders in a custodial setting are high.[409]

11.10 Even where the threshold is crossed, a court is not required to impose a custodial sentence.

11.11 Before deciding to impose a custodial sentence on a young offender, the court must ensure that all the statutory tests are satisfied—namely:
i)   that the offender cannot properly be dealt with by a fine alone or by a youth rehabilitation order,
ii)   that a youth rehabilitation order with intensive supervision and surveillance or with fostering cannot be justified, and
iii) that custody is the last resort and in doing so should take account of the circumstances, age and maturity of the young offender.

11.12 When a custodial sentence is imposed, a court must state its reasons for being satisfied that the offence(s) is (are) so serious that no other sanction is appropriate and, in particular, why a youth rehabilitation order with intensive supervision and surveillance or with fostering cannot be justified.[410] This justification will need to be based on the principles set out in the statutory framework.

Where the offence(s) has crossed the custody threshold, the statutory tests are likely to be satisfied only where a custodial sentence will be more effective in preventing offending by children and young persons. The obligation to have regard to the welfare of the offender will require a court to take account of a wide range of issues including those relating to mental health, capability and maturity.

(ii) Length of sentence

11.13 A court imposing a custodial sentence is required to set the shortest term commensurate with the seriousness of the offence(s).[411] Offence specific guidelines do not generally provide starting points or ranges for offenders aged under 18 because of the wide range of issues that are likely to arise and the marked differences in the sentencing framework depending on the age of the offender. Where they are provided,[412] they are for offenders aged 17 with a provision that, for younger offenders, a court should consider whether a lower starting point is justified in recognition of the offender's age and maturity.

---

[407] Criminal Justice Act 2003, s.152(2)
[408] The prevention of offending; see para. 2.6 above
[409] See para. 2 above
[410] Criminal Justice Act 2003, s.174(4B) as inserted by Criminal Justice and Immigration Act 2008, sched. 4, para. 80(3)
[411] Criminal Justice Act 2003, s.153(2)
[412] Robbery pages 12–14; *Sexual Offences Act 2003* pages 133–139; *Breach of an Anti-Social Behaviour Order* pages 10–12: www.sentencing-guidelines.gov.uk

11.14 Any approach needs to take account of the general sentencing rules that apply where there is more than one offence or more than one defendant. Where the offence has been committed by offender(s) aged 18 or over and by offender(s) aged under 18, the court will need to consider the role of each offender and the number of offenders involved.

11.15 Where the primary offender is under the age of 18, a court is likely to determine sentence for that offender first giving proper weight to the offender's age and maturity; that will provide a framework within which sentence for the offender(s) over 18 can be determined. Where the primary offender is over 18, a court is likely to determine sentence for that offender first; that will provide a framework within which sentence for the offender(s) under 18 can be determined giving proper weight to age and maturity.

11.16 Where an offence crosses the custodial threshold and the court determines that a custodial sentence is unavoidable:
- where the offender is aged 15, 16 or 17, the court will need to consider the maturity of the offender as well as chronological age. Where there is no offence specific guideline, it may be appropriate, depending on maturity, to consider a starting point from <u>half to three quarters of that which would have been identified for an adult offender</u>.
  It will be particularly important to consider maturity when the court has to sentence more than one offender. When the offenders are of different ages, including when one or more is over 18, the court will also need to have proper regard to parity between their sentences.
  The closer an offender was to age 18 when the offence was committed and the greater the maturity of the offender or the sophistication of the offence, the closer the starting point is likely to be to that appropriate for an adult. Some offenders will be extremely mature, more so than some offenders who are over 18, whilst others will be significantly less mature.
  For younger offenders, greater flexibility will be required to reflect the potentially wide range of culpability.
  Where an offence shows considerable planning or sophistication, a court may need to adjust the approach upwards.
  Where the offender is particularly immature, the court may need to adjust the approach downwards.
- where the offender is aged 14 or less, sentence should normally be imposed in a youth court (except in cases of homicide or where the young person comes within the 'dangerous offender' criteria); the length of a custodial sentence will normally be shorter than for an offender aged 15–17 convicted of the same offence.
- an offender aged 14 years or less should be sentenced to long term detention[413] only where that is necessary for the protection of the public either because of the risk of serious harm from future offending or because of the persistence of offending behaviour; exceptionally, such a sentence may be appropriate where an offender aged 14 years or less has committed a very serious offence but is not a persistent offender and there is no risk of serious harm from future offending.

11.17 In determining the term of a detention and training order, the court must take account of any period for which the offender has been remanded in custody or on bail subject to a qualifying curfew condition and electronic monitoring.[414] As the available terms are specified, the proper approach in taking a remand period into account is to reduce, if possible, the sentence otherwise appropriate to reflect that period.[415] Where a short custodial sentence was being considered, the court might conclude that a non-custodial sentence was appropriate.

11.18 On the implementation of the relevant parts of schedule 3 to the Criminal Justice Act 2003, a 'plea before venue' procedure will be introduced for offenders under the age of 18 and will include a general power to commit for sentence where a court accepts jurisdiction following indication of a guilty plea. As with adult offenders, where a young person could have been dealt with in the Crown Court but the youth court has retained jurisdiction, where appropriate the maximum period of 24 months may be imposed following a guilty plea at the first reasonable opportunity where that plea was a factor in retaining a case for sentence in the youth court.

---

[413] Powers of Criminal Courts (Sentencing) Act 2000, s. 91

[414] Powers of Criminal Courts (Sentencing) Act 2000, s.101(8) and (9); for these purpose, 'remanded in custody' includes periods held in police detention and certain remands or committals to local authority accommodation: ibid., s.101(11)

[415] Such a period must be set against the part of the sentence that is to be served in custody, not the whole sentence: *Eagles* [2006] EWCA Crim 2368; *Joyce* [2007] EWCA Crim 3374

12. Trial and Sentencing of Cases in the Crown Court

12.1 There is a clear principle (established both in statute and in domestic and European case law) that cases involving young offenders should be tried and sentenced in the youth court wherever possible. This section summarises the relevant statutory provisions and case law.[416]

12.2 It has long been recognised that the Crown Court should be reserved for the most serious cases, noting the greater formality of the proceedings and the increased number of people likely to be present.[417] These factors present additional obstacles in ensuring that proceedings in the Crown Court involving young offenders are conducted in accordance with international obligations.[418]

12.3 Accordingly, it is rare for a young offender to be tried or sentenced in the Crown Court and for a sentence beyond the powers of the youth court to be imposed, except where that sentence is substantially beyond those powers.

12.4 A youth will appear in the Crown Court for trial and sentence only:

   i) when charged with 'homicide';

   ii) when subject to a minimum statutory sentence;

   iii) when charged with a 'grave crime' and a youth court has determined that, if convicted, a sentence beyond its powers should be available; or

   iv) when charged together with an adult offender who has been sent to the Crown Court and it has been determined that the cases should be kept together.

12.5 Where a sentence under the 'dangerous offender' provisions is likely to be needed the youth may be committed for trial or for sentence.

(i) Homicide

12.6 An exception to the presumption that a person aged under 18 should be tried summarily arises where the young person is charged with an offence of 'homicide'. For a case falling within this description, there is no discretion and it must be sent to the Crown Court for trial. The meaning of 'homicide' is not defined in statute.

(ii) Statutory minimum sentences

12.7 A further exception to the presumption in favour of summary trial arises where a young person is charged with an offence which has a statutory minimum custodial sentence and the criteria for that sentence would be likely to be satisfied if the young person were convicted.[419] A sentence of long term detention[420] may be imposed following committal where these mandatory sentence provisions apply; before there can be a departure from the minimum sentence prescribed, a court must find that there are 'exceptional circumstances'.

(iii) 'Grave crimes'

12.8 A further exception to the statutory presumption in favour of summary trial arises where a young person is charged with a 'grave crime' and a youth court has determined that, if convicted, a sentence beyond its powers should be available. In such circumstances, a young person may be sentenced by the Crown Court to long term detention under section 91 of the Powers of Criminal Courts (Sentencing) Act 2000. At present, such a sentence may be imposed only by the Crown Court and only where the offender was convicted in the Crown Court, and that court considers that neither a community order nor a detention and training order is suitable.

12.9 An offence comes within section 91 where:

   • it is punishable with 14 years imprisonment or more for an adult (but is not a sentence fixed by law), or

   • is an offence contrary to sections 3, 13, 25 or 26 of the Sexual Offences Act 2003,[421] or

   • is one of a number of specified offences in relation to firearms, ammunition and weapons which are subject to a minimum term but in respect of which a court has found exceptional circumstances justifying a lesser sentence.

12.10 This general power should be used rarely since:

   i) it is the general policy of Parliament that those under 18 should be tried in the youth court wherever possible;

---

[416] See in particular *R (H, A, and O) v Southampton Youth Court* [2004] EWHC 2912 (Admin)

[417] ibid., [33]

[418] See, for example, *S.C. v United Kingdom* (2005) 40 EHRR 10

[419] Magistrates' Courts Act 1980, s. 24

[420] Under Powers of Criminal Courts (Sentencing) Act 2000, s. 91

[421] Sexual assault, child sex offences committed by a child or young person, sexual activity with a child family member, inciting a child family member to engage in sexual activity

> ii) trial in the Crown Court under this provision should be reserved for the most serious cases, recognising the greater formality of the proceedings and the greatly increased number of people involved;
>
> iii) offenders aged under 15 will rarely attract a period of detention under this provision and those under 12 even more rarely.[422]

12.11 Accordingly,

> i) a young person aged 10 or 11 (or aged 12–14 but not a persistent offender) should be committed to the Crown Court under this provision only where charged with an offence of such gravity that, despite the normal prohibition on a custodial sentence for a person of that age, a sentence exceeding two years is a realistic possibility[423]
>
> ii) a young person aged 12–17 (for which a detention and training order could be imposed) should be committed to the Crown Court under this provision only where charged with an offence of such gravity that a sentence substantially beyond the 2 year maximum for a detention and training order is a realistic possibility[424]

(iv) Dangerous offenders

12.12 There are rigorous statutory tests which must be satisfied before a court may conclude that a youth is a 'dangerous offender' and requires sentence under the dangerous offender provisions in the Criminal Justice Act 2003 (as amended).[425] Such a sentence may be imposed only where an equivalent determinate sentence of at least 4 years would have been imposed. Criteria relating to future offending and the risk of serious harm must be assessed in the light of the maturity of the offender, the possibility of change in a much shorter time than would apply for an adult and the wider circumstances of the young person.

12.13 At present, the provisions by which a potentially 'dangerous' young offender reaches the Crown Court are overlapping to some extent as a result of the only partial implementation of the provisions of the Criminal Justice Act 2003, which introduce a new section 51A to the Crime and Disorder Act 1998. This new section requires a young offender to be sent for trial where it appears that the criteria for imposition of a sentence under the dangerous offender provisions will be met on conviction. However, the power to commit for sentence following conviction in a youth court or magistrates' court is preserved.[426]

12.14 The nature of the offence is likely to be very significant in determining both whether the offender meets the risk and harm criteria and, even if so, whether a sentence under the provisions is necessary (given that there is now wide discretion).

Since a young offender should normally be dealt with in a youth court, where a young person charged with a specified offence would not otherwise be committed or sent to the Crown Court for trial, generally it is preferable for the decision whether to commit under these provisions to be made after conviction.[427]

(v) Jointly charged with an adult

12.15 A further exception to the presumption in favour of summary trial arises where a young person is charged jointly with a person aged 18 or over; if the court considers it necessary to commit them both for trial it will have the power to commit the young person to the Crown Court for trial.[428]

12.16 Any presumption in favour of sending a youth to the Crown Court to be tried jointly with an adult must be balanced with the general presumption that young offenders should be dealt with in a youth court.

12.17 When deciding whether to separate the youth and adult defendants, a court must consider:

- the young age of the offender, particularly where the age gap between the adult and youth is substantial,
- the immaturity and intellect of the youth,

---

[422] See footnote [402]; those who meet the criteria for "dangerous offenders" will be dealt with under separate provisions: see below

[423] See *R(D) v Manchester City Youth Court* [2001] EWHC Admin 860

[424] See *C & D v Sheffield Youth Court* [2003] EWHC Admin 35 confirming the relevance of undisputed personal mitigation

[425] See the review of statutory provisions and case law authority in *Dangerous Offenders: A Guide for Sentencers and Practitioners* at p.18 www.sentencing-guidelines.gov.uk

[426] Powers of Criminal Courts (Sentencing) Act 2000, s.3C; where an offence falls within s. 91 (see para. 12.9) and, following committal under this section, the Crown Court does not impose a sentence under the dangerous offender provisions, it may impose a sentence of long term detention: ibid., s. 5A

[427] See, for example, the statement that there is a strong presumption against sending young offenders to the Crown Court unless clearly required: *R(W) v Southampton Youth Court* [2002] EWHC 1640 per Lord Woolf CJ

[428] The procedures around the transfer to the Crown Court of a young person charged with an offence will change on the implementation of the relevant provisions in the Criminal Justice Act 2003, sched. 3

- the relative culpability of the youth compared with the adult and whether or not the role played by the youth was minor, and
- any lack of previous convictions on the part of the youth compared with the adult offender.

12.18 A very significant factor will be whether the trial of the adult and youth could be severed without inconvenience to witnesses or injustice to the case as a whole, including whether there are benefits in the same tribunal sentencing all offenders. In most circumstances, a single trial of all issues is likely to be most in the interests of justice.

(vi) Remittal from the Crown Court

12.19 Where a young person is convicted before the Crown Court of an offence other than homicide, there is an obligation to remit the young person to a youth court for sentence unless that is 'undesirable'.[429] In considering whether remittal is 'undesirable', a court should balance the need for expertise in the sentencing of young offenders with the benefits of sentence being imposed by the court which had determined guilt.

12.20 Particular attention should be given to the presumption where a young person appears before the Crown Court only because he or she is jointly charged with an adult offender. A referral order is not available in the Crown Court for a first-time offender and such orders may now be made following a second conviction in certain circumstances.

PART 19   CORPORATE MANSLAUGHTER AND HEALTH AND SAFETY OFFENCES CAUSING DEATH

SG-446

DEFINITIVE GUIDELINE

FOREWORD

…This guideline applies to the sentencing of organisations on or after 15 February 2010.

This is the first offence guideline relating to sentencing organisations rather than individuals, and concerns sentencing for offences where the most serious form of harm was caused, the death of one or more persons.

The guideline takes a different form from that used for most other offences. It sets out the key principles relevant to assessing the seriousness of the range of offences covered which may involve a wide variation in culpability. Principles concerning the assessment of financial penalties are also provided and consideration is given to the additional powers available to a court imposing sentence for these offences.

CORPORATE MANSLAUGHTER AND HEALTH AND SAFETY OFFENCES CAUSING DEATH

A. Elements of the offences

SG-447

1. Corporate manslaughter is created by the Corporate Manslaughter and Corporate Homicide Act 2007 (CMCHA). The offence:
    - (a) can be committed only by organisations and not by individuals. The organisations which can commit the offence are exhaustively defined by section 1(2) and Schedule 1;
    - (b) has as its root element *a breach of a duty of care* under the law of negligence (s. 2(1));
    - (c) requires that the breach be a *gross* breach, that is to say one where the conduct falls *far below* what can reasonably be expected of the organisation (s.1(4));
    - (d) further requires that a substantial element in the breach is the way in which the organisation's activities are managed or organised by its *senior management* (s.1(3));
    - (e) is committed only where death is shown to have been caused by the gross breach of duty (s.1(1)(a)).

    An obligation is imposed upon the prosecution to prove each of these elements to the criminal standard.

2. Health and safety offences, typically (but not exclusively) those contrary to sections 2 and 3 of the Health and Safety at Work Act 1974 (HSWA):
    - (a) can be committed by both organisations and individuals; **this guideline relates only to organisations;**

---

[429] Powers of Criminal Courts (Sentencing) Act 2000, s. 8(2)

(b) do not depend on the law of negligence; the root element is a breach of a duty to *ensure* the health and safety of other persons, or absence of risk to them, whether employees or members of the public affected by the activity of the defendant;

(c) once an absence of safety, or at least a risk to the health or safety of others, is proved by the prosecution, involve a statutory reverse burden of proof placed upon the defendant to show that it was *not* reasonably practicable to do more than was done to comply with the duty;

(d) do not involve the proof of any particular injury or consequence; whilst prosecutions will very often ensue where there has been injury or death, the offence does not require proof that that injury or death was caused by the breach; this may well be in dispute even if a breach is proved or admitted;

(e) thus embrace a very wide spread of culpability from the minimal to the very grave.

3. Where death occurs, there may therefore be a significant overlap between the offences, and it is to be expected that some cases will be prosecuted in the alternative despite the increased complexity that that will entail for a jury.

4. However, there are considerable differences between the two offences:

(a) because corporate manslaughter involves both a *gross* breach of duty of care and senior management failings as a substantial element in that breach, those cases will generally involve systemic failures; by contrast health and safety offences are committed whenever the defendant cannot show that it was not reasonably practicable to avoid a risk of injury or lack of safety; that may mean that the failing is at an operational rather than systemic level and can mean in some cases that there has been only a very limited falling below the standard of reasonable practicability;

(b) in corporate manslaughter the burden of proof remains on the prosecution throughout; in particular this will ordinarily involve the prosecution identifying the acts or omissions which it relies upon as constituting the breach, and then proving them; by contrast, in a prosecution for a health and safety offence the prosecutor need only prove that there has been a failure to ensure safety or absence of risk, which it may often be able to do simply by pointing to the injury; once it has done so the burden of proof shifts to the defendant; the prosecution need not identify the precautions which it says ought to have been taken, nor need it prove how the accident happened;[430] usually however it will do so;

(c) in corporate manslaughter the prosecution must prove that the breach was a significant (but not necessarily *the only*) cause of death; by contrast health and safety offences can be proved without demonstrating that any injury was caused by the failure to ensure safety; **this guideline is for cases where it is proved that the offence was a significant cause of death, not simply that death occurred.**

SG-448   **B. Factors likely to affect seriousness**

5. This guideline applies only to corporate manslaughter and to those health and safety offences where the offence is shown to have been a significant cause of the death. By definition, the harm involved is very serious.

6. Beyond that, the possible range of factors affecting the seriousness of the offence will be very wide indeed. Seriousness should ordinarily be assessed first by asking:

(a) **How foreseeable was serious injury?**
    The more foreseeable it was, the graver usually will be the offence.

(b) **How far short of the applicable standard did the defendant fall?**

(c) **How common is this kind of breach in this organisation?**
    How widespread was the non-compliance? Was it isolated in extent or indicative of a systematic departure from good practice across the defendant's operations?

(d) **How far up the organisation does the breach go?**
    Usually, the higher up the responsibility for the breach, the more serious the offence.[431]

7. In addition, other factors are likely, if present, to aggravate the offence (the list is not exhaustive):

(a) **more than one death, or very grave personal injury in addition to death;**

(b) **failure to heed warnings or advice, whether from officials such as the Inspectorate, or by employees (especially health and safety representatives) or other persons, or to respond appropriately to 'near misses' arising in similar circumstances;**

(c) **cost-cutting at the expense of safety;**

(d) **deliberate failure to obtain or comply with relevant licences, at least where the process of licensing involves some degree of control, assessment or observation by independent authorities with a health and safety responsibility;**

---

[430] *Chargot* [2008] UKHL 73 at paragraph 30, *Electric Gate Services Ltd* [2009] EWCA Crim 1942

[431] For corporate manslaughter the involvement of senior management is a necessary element in the offence.

   (e) **injury to vulnerable persons.**
     In this context, vulnerable persons would include those whose personal circumstances make them susceptible to exploitation.

8. Conversely, the following factors, which are similarly non-exhaustive, are likely, if present, to afford mitigation:
   (a) **a prompt acceptance of responsibility;**
   (b) **a high level of co-operation with the investigation, beyond that which will always be expected;**
   (c) **genuine efforts to remedy the defect;**
   (d) **a good health and safety record;**
   (e) **a responsible attitude to health and safety, such as the commissioning of expert advice or the consultation of employees or others affected by the organisation's activities.**

9. Since corporate manslaughter requires proof of gross breach of duty and the substantial involvement of senior management, it is unlikely that the unauthorised act of an employee will significantly reduce the culpability of the defendant in that offence.

10. Commission of a health and safety offence may in some cases be established solely by the unauthorised act of an employee. In such a case the responsibility of the organisation must be assessed, for example for inadequate supervision or training. There may be some cases where there is very little culpability in the organisation itself.

11. It will generally be appropriate to require the prosecution to set out in writing the facts of the case relied upon and any aggravating or mitigating features which it identifies;[432] the defence may conveniently be required similarly to set out in writing any points on which it differs. If sentence is to proceed upon agreed facts, they should be set out in writing.[433]

C. Financial information; size and nature of organisation   **SG-449**

12. The law must expect the same standard of behaviour from a large and a small organisation. Smallness does not by itself mitigate, and largeness does not by itself aggravate, these offences. Size may affect the approach to safety, whether because a small organisation is careless or because a large one is bureaucratic, but these considerations affect the seriousness of the offence via the assessment set out in paragraphs 6–8 above, rather than demonstrating a direct correlation between size and culpability.

13. A large organisation may be more at risk of committing an offence than a small one simply because it conducts very many more operations. Some large corporate groups operate as a single company whereas others are structured as separate companies for separate operations. A large organisation may be operating upon a budget as tight (or tighter) than a small one because of the demands placed upon it—large local authorities, hospital trusts or police forces may be examples, but so might commercial companies with large turnover but small profit margins. However, in some instances, a large organisation may have less excuse for not dealing properly with matters affecting health and safety, since it may have greater access to expertise, advice and training resources, whether in-house or otherwise.

14. Size is, however, relevant. The means of any defendant are relevant to a fine, which is the principal available penalty for organisations. The court should require information about the financial circumstances of the defendant before it. The best practice will usually be to call for the relevant information for a three year period including the year of the offence, so as to avoid any risk of atypical figures in a single year.

15. **A fixed correlation between the fine and either turnover or profit is not appropriate.** The circumstances of defendant organisations and the financial consequences of the fine will vary too much; similar offences committed by companies structured in differing ways ought not to attract fines which are vastly different; a fixed correlation might provide a perverse incentive to manipulation of corporate structure.

16. The court should, however, look carefully at both turnover and profit, and also at assets, in order to gauge the resources of the defendant. When taking account of financial circumstances, statute[434] provides for that to either increase or decrease the amount of the fine and it is just that a wealthy defendant should pay a larger fine than a poor one; whilst a fine is intended to inflict painful punishment, it should be one which the defendant is capable of paying, if appropriate over a period which may be up to a number of years.

17. **Annex A** sets out the kind of financial information with which, in the ordinary way, a court should expect to be provided in relation to a defendant. The primary obligation to provide it lies on the

---

[432] In accordance with the Attorney General's guidelines on the acceptance of pleas and the prosecutor's role in the sentencing exercise, published November 2009.

[433] See *Friskies Petcare (UK) Ltd* [2000] EWCA Crim 95; [2000] 2 Cr App Rep (S) 401

[434] Criminal Justice Act 2003, ss.164(1) and 164(4)

defendant. As a matter of practice it would be helpful if the prosecution takes the preliminary step of calling upon the defendant to provide it to the court and prosecution and, if the defendant does not do so, of assembling what can be obtained from public records and furnishing that to the court. If a defendant fails to provide relevant information, the court is justified in making adverse assumptions as to its means, and may be obliged to do so.

18. It will not ordinarily be necessary for the prosecution to embark upon analysis of the figures, as distinct from ensuring that the raw material is available to the court, and it may not in any event normally have the expertise to do so. In a few complex cases of relevant dispute the prosecution can if genuinely necessary undertake such analysis either in-house or by the instruction of an accountant and if it can justify the expense as part of its necessary costs those costs will ordinarily be recoverable from the defendant.[435]

19. In assessing the financial consequences of a fine, the court should consider (inter alia) the following factors:

    (i)   the effect on the employment of the innocent may be relevant;
    (ii)   any effect upon shareholders will, however, not normally be relevant; those who invest in and finance a company take the risk that its management will result in financial loss;
    (iii) the effect on directors will not, likewise, normally be relevant;
    (iv)   nor would it ordinarily be relevant that the prices charged by the defendant might in consequence be raised, at least unless the defendant is a monopoly supplier of public services;
    (v)   the effect upon the provision of services to the public will be relevant; although a public organisation such as a local authority, hospital trust or police force must be treated the same as a commercial company where the standards of behaviour to be expected are concerned, and must suffer a punitive fine for breach of them, a different approach to determining the level of fine may well be justified;
    'The Judge has to consider how any financial penalty will be paid. If a very substantial financial penalty will inhibit the proper performance by a statutory body of the public function that it has been set up to perform, that is not something to be disregarded.'[436]

    The same considerations will be likely to apply to non-statutory bodies or charities if providing public services.

    (vi)   the liability to pay civil compensation will ordinarily not be relevant; normally this will be provided by insurance or the resources of the defendant will be large enough to meet it from its own resources (for compensation generally see paragraphs 27–28 below);
    (vii) the cost of meeting any remedial order will not ordinarily be relevant, except to the overall financial position of the defendant; such an order requires no more than should already have been done;
    (viii) whether the fine will have the effect of putting the defendant out of business will be relevant; in some bad cases this may be an acceptable consequence.

20. In the case of a large organisation the fine should be payable within twenty eight days. In the case of a smaller or financially stretched organisation, it is permissible to require payment to be spread over a much longer period. There is no limitation to payment within twelve months, but the first payment should be required within a short time of sentencing. An extended period for the payment of further instalments may be particularly appropriate for an organisation of limited means which has committed a serious offence, and where it is undesirable that the fine should cause it to be put out of business.

21. In some cases it may be apparent that a broadly quantifiable saving has been made by the defendant by committing the offence. In such cases it will normally be the proper approach to ensure that the fine removes the profit and imposes an appropriate additional penalty.

SG-450 **D. Level of fines**

22. There will inevitably be a broad range of fines because of the range of seriousness involved and the differences in the circumstances of the defendants. Fines must be punitive and sufficient to have an impact on the defendant.

23. Fines cannot and do not attempt to value a human life in money. Civil compensation will be payable separately. The fine is designed to punish the defendant and is therefore tailored not only to what it has done but also to its individual circumstances.

[435] Criminal Justice Act 2003, s.164(5)(b)(iii)
[436] *Milford Haven Port Authority* [2000] 2 Cr App R(S) 423 per Lord Bingham CJ at 433–4 *Sentencing*

24. The offence of corporate manslaughter, because it requires gross breach at a senior level, will ordinarily involve a level of seriousness significantly greater than a health and safety offence. The appropriate fine will seldom be less than **£500,000** and may be measured in **millions of pounds**.[437]

25. The range of seriousness involved in health and safety offences is greater than for corporate manslaughter. However, where the offence is shown to have caused death, the appropriate fine will seldom be **less than £100,000** and may be measured in **hundreds of thousands of pounds or more**.

26. A plea of guilty should be recognised by the appropriate reduction.

E. Compensation   SG-451

27. The assessment of compensation in cases of death will usually be complex, will involve payment of sums well beyond the powers of a criminal court, and will ordinarily be covered by insurance.

28. In the great majority of cases the court should conclude that compensation should be dealt with in a civil court, and should say that no order is made for that reason.[438] There may be occasional cases, for example if the defendant is uninsured and payment may not otherwise be made, when consideration should be given to a compensation order in respect of bereavement and/or funeral expenses.[439]

F. Costs   SG-452

29. The defendant ought ordinarily (subject to means) to be ordered to pay the properly incurred costs of the prosecution.

G. Publicity Orders   SG-453

30. Publicity Orders are available in the case of corporate manslaughter only.[440] They may require publication in a specified manner of:
    (a)   the fact of conviction;
    (b)   specified particulars of the offence;
    (c)   the amount of any fine;
    (d)   the terms of any remedial order.

31. Such an order should ordinarily be imposed in a case of corporate manslaughter. The object is deterrence and punishment.
    (i)   The order should specify with particularity the matters to be published in accordance with section 10(1). Especial care should be taken with the terms of the particulars of the offence committed.
    (ii)   The order should normally specify the place where public announcement is to be made, and consideration should be given to indicating the size of any notice or advertisement required. It should ordinarily contain a provision designed to ensure that the conviction becomes known to shareholders in the case of companies and local people in the case of public bodies. Consideration should be given to requiring a statement on the defendant's website. A newspaper announcement may be unnecessary if the proceedings are certain to receive news coverage in any event, but if an order requires publication in a newspaper it should specify the paper, the form of announcement to be made and the number of insertions required.
    (iii) The prosecution should provide the court in advance of the sentencing hearing, and should serve on the defendant, a draft of the form of order suggested and the judge should personally endorse the final form of the order.
    (iv)   Consideration should be given to stipulating in the order that any comment placed by the defendant alongside the required announcement should be separated from it and clearly identified as such.

32. A publicity order is part of the penalty. Any exceptional cost of compliance should be considered in fixing the fine. It is not, however, necessary to fix the fine first and then deduct the cost of compliance.

H. Remedial Orders   SG-454

33. A remedial order is available both for corporate manslaughter[441] and HSWA offences.[442]

34. A defendant ought by the time of sentencing to have remedied any specific failings involved in the offence and if it has not will be deprived of significant mitigation.

---

[437] Observations in *Friskies Petcare (UK) Ltd* [2000] EWCA Crim 95; [2000] 2 Cr App Rep (S) 401 notwithstanding, it is no longer the case that fines of £500,000 are reserved for major public disasters

[438] Powers of Criminal Courts Act 2000, s.130(3)

[439] Under Powers of Criminal Courts Act 2000, s.130(9) and (10)

[440] Corporate Manslaughter and Corporate Homicide Act 2007, s. 10

[441] Corporate Manslaughter and Corporate Homicide Act 2007, s. 9

[442] Health and Safety at Work Act 1974, s. 42

35. If, however, it has not, a remedial order should be considered if it can be made sufficiently specific to be enforceable. The prosecution is required by section 9(2) CMCHA to give notice of the form of any such order sought, which can only be made on its application; although there is no equivalent stipulation in the HSWA it is good practice to require the same notice. The Judge should personally endorse the final form of such an order.

36. The cost of compliance with such an order should not ordinarily be taken into account in fixing the fine; the order requires only what should already have been done.

SG-455   I. Summary of approach to sentence

37. The normal approach to sentence should therefore be (in outline):
    (1) consider the questions at paragraph 6;
    (2) identify any particular aggravating or mitigating circumstances (paragraphs 7–11);
    (3) consider the nature, financial organisation and resources of the defendant (paragraphs 12–18);
    (4) consider the consequences of a fine (paragraphs 19–21);
    (5) consider compensation (but see paragraphs 27–28);
    (6) assess the fine in the light of the foregoing and all the circumstances of the case;
    (7) reduce as appropriate for any plea of guilty;
    (8) consider costs;
    (9) consider publicity order;
    (10) consider remedial order.

SG-456   Annex A: Financial information expected to be provided to the court

1. *For companies*: published audited accounts. Particular attention should be paid to (a) turnover, (b) profit before tax, (c) directors' remuneration, loan accounts and pension provision, (d) assets as disclosed by the balance sheet (note that they may be valued at cost of acquisition which may not be the same as current value). Most companies are required to lodge accounts at Companies House. Failure to produce relevant recent accounts on request may properly lead to the conclusion that the company can pay any appropriate fine.

2. *For partnerships*: annual audited accounts. Particular attention should be paid to (a) turnover, (b) profit before tax, (c) partner's drawings, loan accounts and pension provision, (d) assets as above. If accounts are not produced on request, see paragraph 1.

3. *For local authorities, police and fire authorities and similar public bodies*: the Annual Revenue Budget ('ARB') is the equivalent of turnover and the best indication of the size of the defendant organisation. It is published on www.local.communities.gov.uk/finance/bellwin.HTM. It is unlikely to be necessary to analyse specific expenditure or reserves unless inappropriate or grandiose expenditure is suggested. Such authorities also have attributed to them a 'Bellwin factor' which represents the level of exceptional and unforeseen expenditure that they are expected by central Government to meet themselves in any one year without any claim to recourse to central funds. But since that is arithmetically related to the ARB (currently 0.2%) it will ordinarily add little of significance beyond an indication of budgetary discipline.

4. *For health trusts*: the independent regulator of NHS Foundation Trusts is Monitor. It publishes quarterly reports and annual figures for the financial strength and stability of trusts from which the annual income can be seen, available via www.monitor-nhsft.gov.uk/home/our-publications. Detailed analysis of expenditure or reserves is unlikely to be called for.
   Note that Monitor has significant regulatory powers including over membership of the boards of directors or governors.

5. *For 'third sector' organisations*: it will be appropriate to inspect annual audited accounts. Detailed analysis of expenditure or reserves is unlikely to be called for unless there is a suggestion of unusual or unnecessary expenditure.

PART 20   BURGLARY OFFENCES

Definitive Guideline

Applicability of Guideline

In accordance with section 120 of the Coroners and Justice Act 2009, the Sentencing Council issues this definitive guideline. It applies to all offenders aged 18 and older, who are sentenced on or after 16 January 2012, regardless of the date of the offence.

Section 125(1) of the Coroners and Justice Act 2009 provides that when sentencing offences committed after 6 April 2010:

Every court —

(a)   must, in sentencing an offender, follow any sentencing guideline which is relevant to the offender's case, and

(b)   must, in exercising any other function relating to the sentencing of offenders, follow any sentencing guidelines which are relevant to the exercise of the function,

unless the court is satisfied that it would be contrary to the interests of justice to do so.

This guideline applies only to offenders aged 18 and older. General principles to be considered in the sentencing of youths are in the Sentencing Guidelines Council's definitive guideline, *Overarching Principles — Sentencing Youths* [see **SG-433**].

Structure, ranges and starting points

For the purposes of section 125(3)–(4) Coroners and Justice Act 2009, the guideline specifies offence ranges — the range of sentences appropriate for each type of offence. Within each offence, the Council has specified three categories which reflect varying degrees of seriousness. The offence range is split into category ranges — sentences appropriate for each level of seriousness. The Council has also identified a starting point within each category.

Starting points define the position within a category range from which to start calculating the provisional sentence. As in the Sentencing Council's Assault Definitive Guideline, this guideline adopts an offence based starting point. **Starting points apply to all offences within the corresponding category and are applicable to all offenders, in all cases.** Once the starting point is established, the court should consider further aggravating and mitigating factors and previous convictions so as to adjust the sentence within the range. Starting points and ranges apply to all offenders, whether they have pleaded guilty or been convicted after trial. Credit for a guilty plea is taken into consideration only at step four in the decision making process, after the appropriate sentence has been identified.

Information on community orders and fine bands is set out in the annex [not reproduced: see **SG-304** and **SG-330**].

Aggravated Burglary

Theft Act 1968 (section 10)

This is a serious specified offence for the purposes of section 224 of the Criminal Justice Act 2003

Triable only on indictment
Maximum: Life imprisonment

Offence range: 1–13 years' custody

STEP ONE   Determining the offence category

Category 1	Greater harm **and** higher culpability
Category 2	Greater harm **and** lower culpability **or** lesser harm **and** higher culpability
Category 3	Lesser harm **and** lower culpability

The court should determine the offence category using the table below.

The court should determine culpability and harm caused or intended, by reference only to the factors below, which comprise the principal factual elements of the offence. Where an offence does not fall squarely into a category, individual factors may require a degree of weighting before making an overall assessment and determining the appropriate offence category.

Factors indicating greater harm	Factors indicating higher culpability
Theft of/damage to property causing a significant degree of loss to the victim (whether economic, commercial, sentimental or personal value)	Victim or premises deliberately targeted (for example, due to vulnerability or hostility based on disability, race, sexual orientation)
Soiling, ransacking or vandalism of property	A significant degree of planning or organisation
Victim at home or on the premises (or returns) while offender present	Equipped for burglary (for example, implements carried and/or use of vehicle)
Significant physical or psychological injury or other significant trauma to the victim	Weapon present on entry
Violence used or threatened against victim, particularly involving a weapon	Member of a group or gang
Context of general public disorder	**Factors indicating lower culpability**
Factors indicating lesser harm	Offender exploited by others
No physical or psychological injury or other significant trauma to the victim	Mental disorder or learning disability, where linked to the commission of the offence
No violence used or threatened and a weapon is not produced	

STEP TWO Starting point and category range

Having determined the category, the court should use the corresponding starting points to reach a sentence within the category range below. The starting point applies to all offenders irrespective of plea or previous convictions. A case of particular gravity, reflected by multiple features of culpability or harm in step 1, could merit upward adjustment from the starting point before further adjustment for aggravating

Offence Category	Starting Point (*Applicable to all offenders*)	Category Range (*Applicable to all offenders*)
Category 1	10 years' custody	9–13 years' custody
Category 2	6 years' custody	4–9 years' custody
Category 3	2 years' custody	1–4 years' custody

or mitigating features, set out below.

The table below contains a **non-exhaustive** list of additional factual elements providing the context of the offence and factors relating to the offender. Identify whether any combination of these, or other relevant factors, should result in an upward or downward adjustment from the starting point. **In particular, relevant recent convictions are likely to result in an upward adjustment.** In some cases, having considered these factors, it may be appropriate to move outside the identified category range.

Factors increasing seriousness	Factors reducing seriousness or reflecting personal mitigation
Statutory aggravating factors:	Subordinate role in a group or gang
Previous convictions, having regard to a) the nature of the offence to which the conviction relates and its relevance to the current offence; and b) the time that has elapsed since the conviction	Injuries caused recklessly
	Nothing stolen or only property of very low value to the victim (whether economic, commercial, sentimental or personal)
Offence committed whilst on bail	Offender has made voluntary reparation to the victim
Other aggravating factors include:	No previous convictions or no relevant/recent convictions
Child at home (or returns home) when offence committed	Remorse
Offence committed at night	Good character and/or exemplary conduct
Abuse of power and/or position of trust	Determination, and/or demonstration of steps taken to address addiction or offending behaviour
Gratuitous degradation of victim	Serious medical conditions requiring urgent, intensive or long-term treatment
Any steps taken to prevent the victim reporting the incident or obtaining assistance and/or from assisting or supporting the prosecution	Age and/or lack of maturity where it affects the responsibility of the offender
Victim compelled to leave their home (in particular victims of domestic violence)	Lapse of time since the offence where this is not the fault of the offender
Established evidence of community impact	Mental disorder or learning disability, where not linked to the commission of the offence
Commission of offence whilst under the influence of alcohol or drugs	Sole or primary carer for dependent relatives
Failure to comply with current court orders	
Offence committed whilst on licence	
Offences Taken Into Consideration (TICs)	

STEP THREE   Consider any factors which indicate a reduction, such as assistance to the prosecution

The court should take into account sections 73 and 74 of the Serious Organised Crime and Police Act 2005 (assistance by defendants: reduction or review of sentence) and any other rule of law by virtue of which an offender may receive a discounted sentence in consequence of assistance given (or offered) to the prosecutor or investigator.

STEP FOUR   Reduction for guilty pleas

The court should take account of any potential reduction for a guilty plea in accordance with section 144 of the Criminal Justice Act 2003 and the Guilty Plea guideline.

STEP FIVE   Dangerousness

An aggravated burglary is a serious specified offence within the meaning of chapter 5 of the Criminal Justice Act 2003 and at this stage the court should consider whether having regard to the criteria contained in that chapter it would be appropriate to award a life sentence, imprisonment for public protection or an extended sentence. Where offenders meet the dangerousness criteria, the notional determinate sentence should be used as the basis for the setting of a minimum term.

STEP SIX   Totality principle

If sentencing an offender for more than one offence, or where the offender is already serving a sentence, consider whether the total sentence is just and proportionate to the offending behaviour.

STEP SEVEN   Compensation and ancillary orders

In all cases, courts should consider whether to make compensation and/or other ancillary orders.

STEP EIGHT   Reasons

Section 174 of the Criminal Justice Act 2003 imposes a duty to give reasons for, and explain the effect of, the sentence.

STEP NINE   Consideration for remand time

Sentencers should take into consideration any remand time served in relation to the final sentence at this final step. The court should consider whether to give credit for time spent on remand in custody or on bail in accordance with sections 240 and 240A of the Criminal Justice Act 2003.

DOMESTIC BURGLARY

SG-460

Theft Act 1968 (section 9)

This is a serious specified offence for the purposes of section 224 Criminal Justice Act 2003 if it was committed with intent to:

 (a)   inflict grievous bodily harm on a person, or
 (b)   do unlawful damage to a building or anything in it.

Triable either way

Maximum when tried summarily: Level 5 fine and/or 26 weeks' custody
Maximum when tried on indictment: 14 years' custody

Offence range: Community order — 6 years' custody

Where sentencing an offender for a qualifying third domestic burglary, the court must apply Section 111 of the Powers of the Criminal Courts (Sentencing) Act 2000 and impose a custodial term of at least three years, unless it is satisfied that there are particular circumstances which relate to any of the offences or to the offender which would make it unjust to do so.

STEP ONE   Determining the offence category

The court should determine the offence category using the table below.

Category 1	Greater harm **and** higher culpability
Category 2	Greater harm **and** lower culpability **or** lesser harm **and** higher culpability
Category 3	Lesser harm **and** lower culpability

(Sentencing Guidelines)

The court should determine culpability and harm caused or intended, by reference **only** to the factors below, which comprise the principal factual elements of the offence. Where an offence does not fall squarely into a category, individual factors may require a degree of weighting before making an overall assessment and determining the appropriate offence category.

Factors indicating greater harm	Factors indicating higher culpability
Theft of/damage to property causing a significant degree of loss to the victim (whether economic, sentimental or personal value)	Victim or premises deliberately targeted (for example, due to vulnerability or hostility based on disability, race, sexual orientation)
Soiling, ransacking or vandalism of property	A significant degree of planning or organisation
Occupier at home (or returns home) while offender present	Knife or other weapon carried (where not charged separately)
Trauma to the victim, beyond the normal inevitable consequence of intrusion and theft	Equipped for burglary (for example, implements carried and/or use of vehicle)
Violence used or threatened against victim	Member of a group or gang
Context of general public disorder	
Factors indicating lesser harm	**Factors indicating lower culpability**
Nothing stolen or only property of very low value to the victim (whether economic, sentimental or personal)	Offence committed on impulse, with limited intrusion into property
Limited damage or disturbance to property	Offender exploited by others
	Mental disorder or learning disability, where linked to the commission of the offence

STEP TWO Starting point and category range

Having determined the category, the court should use the corresponding starting points to reach a sentence within the category range below. The starting point applies to all offenders irrespective of plea or previous convictions.

Where the defendant is dependent on or has a propensity to misuse drugs and there is sufficient prospect of success, a community order with a drug rehabilitation requirement under section 209 of the Criminal Justice Act 2003 may be a proper alternative to a short or moderate custodial sentence.

Offence Category	Starting Point (*Applicable to all offenders*)	Category Range (*Applicable to all offenders*)
Category 1	3 years' custody	2–6 years' custody
Category 2	1 year's custody	High level community order — 2 years' custody
Category 3	High level Community Order	Low level community order — 26 weeks' custody

A case of particular gravity, reflected by multiple features of culpability or harm in step 1, could merit upward adjustment from the starting point before further adjustment for aggravating or mitigating features, set out below.

The table below contains a non-exhaustive list of additional factual elements providing the context of the offence and factors relating to the offender. Identify whether any combination of these, or other relevant factors, should result in an upward or downward adjustment from the starting point. **In particular, relevant recent convictions are likely to result in an upward adjustment**. In some cases, having considered these factors, it may be appropriate to move outside the identified category range.

When sentencing **category 2 or 3** offences, the court should also consider the custody threshold as follows:

- has the custody threshold been passed?
- if so, is it unavoidable that a custodial sentence be imposed?
- if so, can that sentence be suspended?

Factors increasing seriousness	Factors reducing seriousness or reflecting personal mitigation
Statutory aggravating factors: Previous convictions, having regard to a) the nature of the offence to which the conviction relates and its relevance to the current offence; and b) the time that has elapsed since the conviction* Offence committed whilst on bail *Other aggravating factors include*: Child at home (or returns home) when offence committed Offence committed at night Gratuitous degradation of the victim Any steps taken to prevent the victim reporting the incident or obtaining assistance and/or from assisting or supporting the prosecution Victim compelled to leave their home (in particular victims of domestic violence) Established evidence of community impact Commission of offence whilst under the influence of alcohol or drugs Failure to comply with current court orders Offence committed whilst on licence Offences Taken Into Consideration (TICs)	Offender has made voluntary reparation to the victim Subordinate role in a group or gang No previous convictions or no relevant/recent convictions Remorse Good character and/or exemplary conduct Determination, and/or demonstration of steps taken to address addiction or offending behaviour Serious medical conditions requiring urgent, intensive or long-term treatment Age and/or lack of maturity where it affects the responsibility of the offender Lapse of time since the offence where this is not the fault of the offender Mental disorder or learning disability, where not linked to the commission of the offence Sole or primary carer for dependent relatives

* Where sentencing an offender for a qualifying **third domestic burglary**, the court must apply section 111 of the Powers of the Criminal Courts (Sentencing) Act 2000 and impose a custodial term of at least three years, unless it is satisfied that there are particular circumstances which relate to any of the offences or to the offender which would make it unjust to do so.

STEP THREE   Consider any factors which indicate a reduction, such as assistance to the prosecution

The court should take into account sections 73 and 74 of the Serious Organised Crime and Police Act 2005 (assistance by defendants: reduction or review of sentence) and any other rule of law by virtue of which an offender may receive a discounted sentence in consequence of assistance given (or offered) to the prosecutor or investigator.

STEP FOUR   Reduction for guilty pleas

The court should take account of any potential reduction for a guilty plea in accordance with section 144 of the Criminal Justice Act 2003 and the Guilty Plea guideline.

Where a minimum mandatory sentence is imposed under section 111 Powers of Criminal Courts (Sentencing) Act, the discount for an early guilty plea must not exceed 20 per cent.

[Steps Five to Nine are identical to those for aggravated burglary: see **SG-459**.]

NON-DOMESTIC BURGLARY
 Theft Act 1968 (section 9)

SG-461

This is a serious specified offence for the purposes of section 224 Criminal Justice Act 2003 if it was committed with intent to:

    (a)   inflict grievous bodily harm on a person, or
    (b)   do unlawful damage to a building or anything in it.

Triable either way

Maximum when tried summarily: Level 5 fine and/or 26 weeks' custody
Maximum when tried on indictment: 10 years' custody

Offence range: Fine — 5 years' custody

STEP ONE Determining the offence category

The court should determine the offence category using the table below.

Category 1	Greater harm **and** higher culpability
Category 2	Greater harm **and** lower culpability **or** lesser harm **and** higher culpability
Category 3	Lesser harm **and** lower culpability

The court should determine culpability and harm caused or intended, by reference only to the factors below, which comprise the principal factual elements of the offence. Where an offence does not fall squarely into a category, individual factors may require a degree of weighting before making an overall assessment and determining the appropriate offence category.

Factors indicating greater harm	**Factors indicating higher culpability**
Theft of/damage to property causing a significant degree of loss to the victim (whether economic, commercial or personal value)	Premises or victim deliberately targeted (to include pharmacy or doctor's surgery and targeting due to vulnerability of victim or hostility based on disability, race, sexual orientation and so forth)
Soiling, ransacking or vandalism of property	A significant degree of planning or organisation
Victim on the premises (or returns) while offender present	Knife or other weapon carried (where not charged separately)
Trauma to the victim, beyond the normal inevitable consequence of intrusion and theft	Equipped for burglary (for example, implements carried and/or use of vehicle)
Violence used or threatened against victim	Member of a group or gang
Context of general public disorder	
Factors indicating lesser harm	**Factors indicating lower culpability**
Nothing stolen or only property of very low value to the victim (whether economic, commercial or personal)	Offence committed on impulse, with limited intrusion into property
Limited damage or disturbance to property	Offender exploited by others
	Mental disorder or learning disability, where linked to the commission of the offence

STEP TWO Starting point and category range

Having determined the category, the court should use the corresponding starting points to reach a sentence within the category range below. The starting point applies to all offenders irrespective of plea or previous convictions.

Where the defendant is dependent on or has a propensity to misuse drugs and there is sufficient prospect of success, a community order with a drug rehabilitation requirement under section 209 of the Criminal Justice Act 2003 may be a proper alternative to a short or moderate custodial sentence.

A case of particular gravity, reflected by multiple features of culpability or harm in step 1, could merit upward adjustment from the starting point before further adjustment for aggravating or mitigating features, set out [below].

Offence Category	**Starting Point** (*Applicable to all offenders*)	**Category Range** (*Applicable to all offenders*)
Category 1	2 years' custody	1–5 years' custody
Category 2	18 weeks' custody	Low level community order — 51 weeks' custody
Category 3	Medium level community order	Band B fine — 18 weeks' custody

The table below contains a non-exhaustive list of additional factual elements providing the context of the offence and factors relating to the offender. Identify whether any combination of these, or other relevant factors, should result in an upward or downward adjustment from the starting point. **In particular, relevant recent convictions are likely to result in an upward adjustment**. In some cases, having considered these factors, it may be appropriate to move outside the identified category range.

When sentencing **category 2 or 3** offences, the court should also consider the custody threshold as follows:

- has the custody threshold been passed?
- if so, is it unavoidable that a custodial sentence be imposed?
- if so, can that sentence be suspended?

When sentencing **category 3** offences, the court should also consider the community order threshold as follows:

- has the community order threshold been passed?

Factors increasing seriousness	Factors reducing seriousness or reflecting personal mitigation
Statutory aggravating factors: Previous convictions, having regard to a) the nature of the offence to which the conviction relates and its relevance to the current offence; and b) the time that has elapsed since the conviction Offence committed whilst on bail *Other aggravating factors include*: Offence committed at night, particularly where staff present or likely to be present Abuse of a position of trust Gratuitous degradation of the victim Any steps taken to prevent the victim reporting the incident or obtaining assistance and/or from assisting or supporting the prosecution Established evidence of community impact Commission of offence whilst under the influence of alcohol or drugs Failure to comply with current court orders Offence committed whilst on licence Offences Taken Into Consideration (TICs)	Offender has made voluntary reparation to the victim Subordinate role in a group or gang No previous convictions or no relevant/recent convictions Remorse Good character and/or exemplary conduct Determination, and/or demonstration of steps taken to address addiction or offending behaviour Serious medical conditions requiring urgent, intensive or long-term treatment Age and/or lack of maturity where it affects the responsibility of the offender Lapse of time since the offence where this is not the fault of the offender Mental disorder or learning disability, where not linked to the commission of the offence Sole or primary carer for dependent relatives

[Steps Three to Nine are identical to those for domestic burglary: see **SG-460**.]

ANNEX: FINE BANDS AND COMMUNITY ORDERS   **SG-462**

[The tables set out here are also set out in the Magistrates' Court Sentencing Guidelines, which includes further guidance on fines and community orders: see **SG-206** and **SG-330**.]

PART 21   DRUGS OFFENCES   **SG-463**
DEFINITIVE GUIDELINE

Applicability of Guideline

[Omitted: See **SG-457** for identical text save that this guideline has effect from 27 February 2012.]

Structure, ranges and starting points

[Omitted: See **SG-458** for identical text.]

FRAUDULENT EVASION OF A PROHIBITION BY BRINGING INTO OR TAKING OUT OF   **SG-464**
THE UK A CONTROLLED DRUG

Misuse of Drugs Act 1971 (section 3)

Customs and Excise Management Act 1979 (section 170(2))

Triable either way unless the defendant could receive the minimum sentence of seven years for a third drug trafficking offence under section 110 Powers of Criminal Courts (Sentencing) Act 2000 in which case the offence is triable only on indictment.

CLASS A

Maximum: Life imprisonment

Offence range: 3 years 6 months' – 16 years' custody

A Class A offence is a drug trafficking offence for the purpose of imposing a minimum sentence under section 110 Powers of Criminal Courts (Sentencing) Act 2000

Class B

Maximum: 14 years' custody and/or unlimited fine

Offence range: 12 weeks' – 10 years' custody

Class C

Maximum: 14 years' custody and/or unlimited fine

Offence range: Community order – 8 years' custody

SG-465   **STEP ONE**   **Determining the offence category**

The court should determine the offender's culpability (role) and the harm caused (quantity) with reference to the tables below.

In assessing culpability, the sentencer should weigh up all the factors of the case to determine role. Where there are characteristics present which fall under different role categories, the court should balance these characteristics to reach a fair assessment of the offender's culpability.

In assessing harm, quantity is determined by the weight of the product. Purity is not taken into account at step 1 but is dealt with at step 2.

Where the operation is on the most serious and commercial scale, involving a quantity of drugs significantly higher than category 1, sentences of 20 years and above may be appropriate, depending on the role of the offender.

Culpability demonstrated by offender's role One or more of these characteristics may demonstrate the offender's role. These lists are not exhaustive.	Category of harm Indicative quantity of drug concerned (upon which the starting point is based):
LEADING role: • Directing or organising buying and selling on a commercial scale; • Substantial links to, and influence on, others in a chain; • Close links to original source; • Expectation of substantial financial gain; • Uses business as cover; • Abuses a position of trust or responsibility.	**Category 1:** • Heroin, cocaine – 5kg; • Ecstasy – 10,000 tablets; • LSD – 250,000 squares; • Amphetamine – 20kg; • Cannabis – 200kg; • Ketamine – 5kg. **Category 2:** • Heroin, cocaine – 1kg; • Ecstasy – 2,000 tablets; • LSD – 25,000 squares; • Amphetamine – 4kg; • Cannabis – 40kg; • Ketamine – 1kg;
SIGNIFICANT role: • Operational or management function within a chain; • Involves others in the operation whether by pressure, influence, intimidation or reward; • Motivated by financial or other advantage, whether or not operating alone; • Some awareness and understanding of scale of operation. **LESSER role:** • Performs a limited function under direction; • Engaged by pressure, coercion, intimidation; • Involvement through naivety/exploitation; • No influence on those above in a chain; • Very little, if any, awareness or understanding of the scale of operation; • If own operation, solely for own use (considering reasonableness of account in all the circumstances).	**Category 3:** • Heroin, cocaine – 150g; • Ecstasy – 300 tablets; • LSD – 2,500 squares; • Amphetamine – 750g; • Cannabis – 6kg; • Ketamine – 150g. **Category 4:** • Heroin, cocaine – 5g; • Ecstasy – 20 tablets; • LSD – 170 squares; • Amphetamine – 20g; • Cannabis – 100g; • Ketamine – 5g.

STEP TWO Starting point and category range

Having determined the category, the court should use the corresponding starting point to reach a sentence within the category range below. The starting point applies to all offenders irrespective of plea or previous convictions. The court should then consider further adjustment within the category range for aggravating or mitigating features, set out [at **SG-467**]. In cases where the offender is regarded as being at the very top of the 'leading' role it may be justifiable for the court to depart from the guideline.

Where the defendant is dependent on or has a propensity to misuse drugs and there is sufficient prospect of success, a community order with a drug rehabilitation requirement under section 209 of the Criminal Justice Act 2003 can be a proper alternative to a short or moderate length custodial sentence.

*For **class A** cases, section 110 of the Powers of Criminal Courts (Sentencing) Act 2000 provides that a court should impose a minimum sentence of at least seven years' imprisonment for a third class A trafficking offence except where the court is of the opinion that there are particular circumstances which (a) relate to any of the offences or to the offender; and (b) would make it unjust to do so in all the circumstances.*

CLASS A	Leading role	Significant role	Lesser role
Category 1	**Starting point** 14 years' custody **Category range** 12 – 16 years' custody	**Starting point** 10 years' custody **Category range** 9 – 12 years' custody	**Starting point** 8 years' custody **Category range** 6 – 9 years' custody
Category 2	**Starting point** 11 years' custody **Category range** 9 – 13 years' custody	**Starting point** 8 years' custody **Category range** 6 years 6 months' – 10 years' custody	**Starting point** 6 years' custody **Category range** 5 – 7 years' custody
Category 3	**Starting point** 8 years 6 months' custody **Category range** 6 years 6 months' – 10 years' custody	**Starting point** 6 years' custody **Category range** 5 – 7 years' custody	**Starting point** 4 years 6 months' custody **Category range** 3 years 6 months' – 5 years' custody
Category 4	Where the quantity falls below the indicative amount set out for category 4 [at **SG-465**], first identify the role for the importation offence, then refer to the starting point and ranges for possession or supply offences, depending on intent. Where the quantity is significantly larger than the indicative amounts for category 4 but below category 3 amounts, refer to the category 3 ranges above.		

CLASS B	Leading role	Significant role	Lesser role
Category 1	**Starting point** 8 years' custody **Category range** 7 – 10 years' custody	**Starting point** 5 years 6 months' custody **Category range** 5 – 7 years' custody	**Starting point** 4 years' custody **Category range** 2 years 6 months' – 5 years' custody
Category 2	**Starting point** 6 years' custody **Category range** 4 years 6 months' – 8 years' custody	**Starting point** 4 years' custody **Category range** 2 years 6 months' – 5 years' custody	**Starting point** 2 years' custody **Category range** 18 months' – 3 years' custody
Category 3	**Starting point** 4 years' custody **Category range** 2 years 6 months' – 5 years' custody	**Starting point** 2 years' custody **Category range** 18 months' – 3 years' custody	**Starting point** 1 years' custody **Category range** 12 weeks' – 18 months' custody
Category 4	Where the quantity falls below the indicative amount set out for category 4 [at **SG-465**], first identify the role for the importation offence, then refer to the starting point and ranges for possession or supply offences, depending on intent. Where the quantity is significantly larger than the indicative amounts for category 4 but below category 3 amounts, refer to the category 3 ranges above.		

CLASS C	Leading role	Significant role	Lesser role
Category 1	**Starting point** 5 years' custody	**Starting point** 3 years' custody	**Starting point** 18 months' custody
	Category range 4 – 8 years' custody	**Category range** 2 – 5 years' custody	**Category range** 1 – 3 years' custody
Category 2	**Starting point** 3 years 6 months' custody	**Starting point** 18 months' custody	**Starting point** 26 weeks' custody
	Category range 2 years' – 5 years' custody	**Category range** 1 – 3 years' custody	**Category range** 12 weeks – 18 months' custody
Category 3	**Starting point** 18 months' custody	**Starting point** 26 weeks' custody	**Starting point** High level community order
	Category range 1 – 3 years' custody	**Category range** 12 weeks – 18 months' custody	**Category range** Medium level community order – 12 weeks' custody
Category 4	Where the quantity falls below the indicative amount set out for category 4 [at **SG-465**], first identify the role for the importation offence, then refer to the starting point and ranges for possession or supply offences, depending on intent. Where the quantity is significantly larger than the indicative amounts for category 4 but below category 3 amounts, refer to the category 3 ranges above.		

SG-467 The table below contains a **non-exhaustive** list of additional factual elements providing the context of the offence and factors relating to the offender. Identify whether any combination of these, or other relevant factors, should result in an upward or downward adjustment from the starting point. In some cases, having considered these factors, it may be appropriate to move outside the identified category range.

For appropriate **class C** ranges, consider the custody threshold as follows:

- has the custody threshold been passed?
- if so, is it unavoidable that a custodial sentence be imposed?
- if so, can that sentence be suspended?

Factors increasing seriousness	Factors reducing seriousness or reflecting personal mitigation
Statutory aggravating factors: Previous convictions, having regard to a) nature of the offence to which conviction relates and relevance to current offence; and b) time elapsed since conviction (see [italicised text at **SG-466**] if third drug trafficking conviction) Offender used or permitted a person under 18 to deliver a controlled drug to a third person Offence committed on bail *Other aggravating factors include:* Sophisticated nature of concealment and/or attempts to avoid detection Attempts to conceal or dispose of evidence, where not charged separately Exposure of others to more than usual danger, for example drugs cut with harmful substances Presence of weapon, where not charged separately High purity Failure to comply with current court orders Offence committed on licence	Lack of sophistication as to nature of concealment Involvement due to pressure, intimidation or coercion falling short of duress, except where already taken into account at step 1 Mistaken belief of the offender regarding the type of drug, taking into account the reasonableness of such belief in all the circumstances Isolated incident Low purity No previous convictions or no relevant or recent convictions Offender's vulnerability was exploited Remorse Good character and/or exemplary conduct Determination and/or demonstration of steps having been taken to address addiction or offending behaviour Serious medical conditions requiring urgent, intensive or long-term treatment Age and/or lack of maturity where it affects the responsibility of the offender Mental disorder or learning disability Sole or primary carer for dependent relatives

**STEP THREE Consider any factors which indicate a reduction, such as   SG-468
assistance to the prosecution**

The court should take into account sections 73 and 74 of the Serious Organised Crime and Police Act 2005 (assistance by defendants: reduction or review of sentence) and any other rule of law by virtue of which an offender may receive a discounted sentence in consequence of assistance given (or offered) to the prosecutor or investigator.

STEP FOUR Reduction for guilty pleas

The court should take account of any potential reduction for a guilty plea in accordance with section 144 of the Criminal Justice Act 2003 and the *Guilty Plea* guideline [see **SG-1**].

For class A offences, where a minimum mandatory sentence is imposed under section 110 Powers of Criminal Courts (Sentencing) Act, the discount for an early guilty plea must not exceed 20 per cent.

STEP FIVE Totality principle

If sentencing an offender for more than one offence, or where the offender is already serving a sentence, consider whether the total sentence is just and proportionate to the offending behaviour.

STEP SIX Confiscation and ancillary orders

In all cases, the court is required to consider confiscation where the Crown invokes the process or where the court considers it appropriate. It should also consider whether to make ancillary orders.

STEP SEVEN Reasons

Section 174 of the Criminal Justice Act 2003 imposes a duty to give reasons for, and explain the effect of, the sentence.

STEP EIGHT Consideration for remand time

Sentencers should take into consideration any remand time served in relation to the final sentence at this final step. The court should consider whether to give credit for time spent on remand in custody or on bail in accordance with sections 240 and 240A of the Criminal Justice Act 2003.

Supplying or Offering to Supply a Controlled Drug   SG-469
Misuse of Drugs Act 1971 (section 4(3))

Possession of a Controlled Drug with Intent to Supply it to Another
Misuse of Drugs Act 1971 (section 5(3))

Triable either way unless the defendant could receive the minimum sentence of seven years for a third drug trafficking offence under section 110 Powers of Criminal Courts (Sentencing) Act 2000 in which case the offence is triable only on indictment.

Class A

Maximum: Life imprisonment

Offence range: Community order – 16 years' custody
A class A offence is a drug trafficking offence for the purpose of imposing a minimum sentence under section 110 Powers of Criminal Courts (Sentencing) Act 2000

Class B

Maximum: 14 years' custody and/or unlimited fine

Offence range: Fine – 10 years' custody

Class C

Maximum: 14 years' custody and/or unlimited fine

Offence range: Fine – 8 years' custody

Sentencing Guidelines

SG-470   STEP ONE Determining the offence category

The court should determine the offender's culpability (role) and the harm caused (quantity/type of offender) with reference to the tables below.

In assessing culpability, the sentencer should weigh up all the factors of the case to determine role. Where there are characteristics present which fall under different role categories, the court should balance these characteristics to reach a fair assessment of the offender's culpability.

In assessing harm, quantity is determined by the weight of the product. Purity is not taken into account at step 1 but is dealt with at step 2. Where the offence is street dealing or supply of drugs in prison by a prison employee, the quantity of the product is less indicative of the harm caused and therefore the starting point is not based on quantity.

Where the operation is on the most serious and commercial scale, involving a quantity of drugs significantly higher than category 1, sentences of 20 years and above may be appropriate, depending on the role of the offender.

Culpability demonstrated by offender's role One or more of these characteristics may demonstrate the offender's role. These lists are not exhaustive.	Category of harm Indicative quantity of drug concerned (upon which the starting point is based):
LEADING role: • Directing or organising buying and selling on a commercial scale; • Substantial links to, and influence on, others in a chain; • Close links to original source; • Expectation of substantial financial gain; • Uses business as cover; • Abuses a position of trust or responsibility, for example prison employee, medical professional.	**Category 1** • Heroin, cocaine – 5kg; • Ecstasy – 10,000 tablets; • LSD – 250,000 squares; • Amphetamine – 20kg; • Cannabis – 200kg; • Ketamine – 5kg. **Category 2** • Heroin, cocaine – 1kg; • Ecstasy – 2,000 tablets; • LSD – 25,000 squares; • Amphetamine – 4kg; • Cannabis – 40kg; • Ketamine – 1kg.
SIGNIFICANT role: • Operational or management function within a chain; • Involves others in the operation whether by pressure, influence, intimidation or reward; • Motivated by financial or other advantage, whether or not operating alone; • Some awareness and understanding of scale of operation; • Supply, other than by a person in position of responsibility, to a prisoner for gain without coercion. **LESSER role:** • Performs a limited function under direction; • Engaged by pressure, coercion, intimidation; • Involvement through naivety/exploitation; • No influence on those above in a chain; • Very little, if any, awareness or understanding of the scale of operation; • If own operation, absence of financial gain, for example joint purchase for no profit, or sharing minimal quantity between peers on non-commercial basis.	**Category 3** Where the offence is selling direct to users [footnote indicates that this includes test purchase officers] ('street-dealing'), the starting point is not based on a quantity OR Where the offence is supply of drugs in prison by a prison employee, the starting point is not based on a quantity – see [italicised text above]. OR • Heroin, cocaine – 150g; • Ecstasy – 300 tablets; • LSD – 2,500 squares; • Amphetamine – 750g; • Cannabis – 6kg; • Ketamine – 150g. **Category 4** • Heroin, cocaine – 5g; • Ecstasy – 20 tablets; • LSD – 170 squares; • Amphetamine – 20g; • Cannabis – 100g; • Ketamine – 5g; OR Where the offence is selling directly to users [footnote indicates that this includes test purchase officers] ('street-dealing'), the starting point is not based on quantity – go to category 3.

STEP TWO   Starting point and category range

Having determined the category, the court should use the corresponding starting point to reach a sentence within the category range below. The starting point applies to all offenders irrespective of plea or previous convictions. The court should then consider further adjustment within the category range for aggravating or mitigating features, set out [at **SG-472**]. In cases where the offender is regarded as being at the very top of the 'leading' role it may be justifiable for the court to depart from the guideline.

Where the defendant is dependent on or has a propensity to misuse drugs and there is sufficient prospect of success, a community order with a drug rehabilitation requirement under section 209 of the Criminal Justice Act 2003 can be a proper alternative to a short or moderate length custodial sentence.

*For **class A** cases, section 110 of the Powers of Criminal Courts (Sentencing) Act 2000 provides that a court should impose a minimum sentence of at least seven years' imprisonment for a third class A trafficking offence except where the court is of the opinion that there are particular circumstances which (a) relate to any of the offences or to the offender; and (b) would make it unjust to do so in all the circumstances.*

CLASS A	Leading role	Significant role	Lesser role
Category 1	**Starting point** 14 years' custody **Category range** 12 – 16 years' custody	**Starting point** 10 years' custody **Category range** 9 – 12 years' custody	**Starting point** 7 years' custody **Category range** 6 – 9 years' custody
Category 2	**Starting point** 11 years' custody **Category range** 9 – 13 years' custody	**Starting point** 8 years' custody **Category range** 6 years 6 months' – 10 years' custody	**Starting point** 5 years' custody **Category range** 3 years 6 months' – 7 years' custody
Category 3	**Starting point** 8 years 6 months' custody **Category range** 6 years 6 months' – 10 years' custody	**Starting point** 4 years 6 months' custody **Category range** 3 years 6 months' – 7 years' custody	**Starting point** 3 years' custody **Category range** 2 – 4 years 6 months' custody
Category 4	**Starting point** 5 years 6 months' custody **Category range** 4 years 6 months' – 7 years 6 months' custody	**Starting point** 3 years 6 months' custody **Category range** 2 – 5 years' custody	**Starting point** 18 months' custody **Category range** High level community order – 3 years' custody

CLASS B	Leading role	Significant role	Lesser role
Category 1	**Starting point** 8 years' custody **Category range** 7 – 10 years' custody	**Starting point** 5 years 6 months' custody **Category range** 5 – 7 years' custody	**Starting point** 3 years' custody **Category range** 2 years 6 months' – 5 years' custody
Category 2	**Starting point** 6 years' custody **Category range** 4 years 6 months' – 8 years' custody	**Starting point** 4 years' custody **Category range** 2 years 6 months' – 5 years' custody	**Starting point** 1 years' custody **Category range** 26 weeks' – 3 years' custody
Category 3	**Starting point** 4 years' custody **Category range** 2 years 6 months' – 5 years' custody	**Starting point** 1 year's custody **Category range** 26 weeks' – 3 years' custody	**Starting point** High level community order **Category range** Low level community order – 26 weeks' custody

CLASS B	Leading role	Significant role	Lesser role
Category 4	**Starting point** 18 months' custody **Category range** 26 weeks' – 3 years' custody	**Starting point** High level community order **Category range** Medium level community order – 26 weeks' custody	**Starting point** Low level community order **Category range** Band B fine – medium level community order

CLASS C	Leading role	Significant role	Lesser role
Category 1	**Starting point** 5 years' custody **Category range** 4 – 8 years' custody	**Starting point** 3 years' custody **Category range** 2 – 5 years' custody	**Starting point** 18 months' custody **Category range** 1 – 3 years' custody
Category 2	**Starting point** 3 years 6 months' custody **Category range** 2 years' – 5 years' custody	**Starting point** 18 months' custody **Category range** 1 – 3 years' custody	**Starting point** 26 weeks' custody **Category range** 12 weeks – 18 months' custody
Category 3	**Starting point** 18 months' custody **Category range** 1 – 3 years' custody	**Starting point** 26 weeks' custody **Category range** 12 weeks – 18 months' custody	**Starting point** High level community order **Category range** Low level community order – 12 weeks' custody
Category 4	**Starting point** 26 weeks' custody **Category range** High level community order – 18 months' custody	**Starting point** High level community order **Category range** Low level community order – 12 weeks' custody	**Starting point** Low level community order **Category range** Band A fine – medium level community order

SG-472 The table below contains a **non-exhaustive** list of additional factual elements providing the context of the offence and factors relating to the offender. Identify whether any combination of these, or other relevant factors, should result in an upward or downward adjustment from the starting point. In some cases, having considered these factors, it may be appropriate to move outside the identified category range.

For appropriate **class B** and **C** ranges, consider the custody threshold as follows:

* has the custody threshold been passed?
* if so, is it unavoidable that a custodial sentence be imposed?
* if so, can that sentence be suspended?

For appropriate **class B** and **C** ranges, the court should also consider the community threshold as follows:

* has the community threshold been passed?

Factors increasing seriousness	Factors reducing seriousness or reflecting personal mitigation
Statutory aggravating factors: Previous convictions, having regard to a) nature of the offence to which conviction relates and relevance to current offence; and b) time elapsed since conviction (see [italicised text at **SG-471**] if third drug trafficking conviction) Offender used or permitted a person under 18 to deliver a controlled drug to a third person Offender 18 or over supplies or offers to supply a drug on, or in the vicinity of, school premises either when school in use as such or at a time between one hour before and one hour after they are to be used Offence committed on bail *Other aggravating factors include:* Targeting of any premises intended to locate vulnerable individuals or supply to such individuals and/or supply to those under 18 Exposure of others to more than usual danger, for example drugs cut with harmful substances Attempts to conceal or dispose of evidence, where not charged separately Presence of others, especially children and/or non-users Presence of weapon, where not charged separately Charged as importation of a very small amount High purity Failure to comply with current court orders Offence committed on licence Established evidence of community impact	Involvement due to pressure, intimidation or coercion falling short of duress, except where already taken into account at step 1 Supply only of drug to which offender addicted Mistaken belief of the offender regarding the type of drug, taking into account the reasonableness of such belief in all the circumstances Isolated incident Low purity No previous convictions **or** no relevant or recent convictions Offender's vulnerability was exploited Remorse Good character and/or exemplary conduct Determination and/or demonstration of steps having been taken to address addiction or offending behaviour Serious medical conditions requiring urgent, intensive or long-term treatment Age and/or lack of maturity where it affects the responsibility of the offender Mental disorder or learning disability Sole or primary carer for dependent relatives

[Steps Three to Eight are identical to those applicable to Fraudulent evasion of a prohibition by bringing into or taking out of the UK a controlled drug: see **SG-468**.] **SG-473**

Production of a Controlled Drug **SG-474**
Misuse of Drugs Act 1971 (section 4(2)(a) or (b))

Triable either way unless the defendant could receive the minimum sentence of seven years for a third drug trafficking offence under section 110 Powers of Criminal Courts (Sentencing) Act 2000 in which case the offence is triable only on indictment.

Class A

Maximum: Life imprisonment

Offence range: Community order – 16 years' custody

A class A offence is a drug trafficking offence for the purpose of imposing a minimum sentence under section 110 Powers of Criminal Courts (Sentencing) Act 2000

Class B

Maximum: 14 years' custody

Offence range: Discharge – 10 years' custody

Class C

Maximum: 14 years' custody

Offence range: Discharge – 8 years' custody

SG-475

CULTIVATION OF CANNABIS PLANT
Misuse of Drugs Act 1971 (section 6(2))

Maximum: 14 years' custody

Offence range: Discharge – 10 years' custody

STEP ONE Determining the offence category

The court should determine the offender's culpability (role) and the harm caused (output or potential output) with reference to the tables below.

In assessing culpability, the sentencer should weigh up all of the factors of the case to determine role. Where there are characteristics present which fall under different role categories, the court should balance these characteristics to reach a fair assessment of the offender's culpability.

In assessing harm, output or potential output is determined by the weight of the product or number of plants/scale of operation. For production offences, purity is not taken into account at step 1 but is dealt with at step 2.

Where the operation is on the most serious and commercial scale, involving a quantity of drugs significantly higher than category 1, sentences of 20 years and above may be appropriate, depending on the role of the offender.

Culpability demonstrated by offender's role One or more of these characteristics may demonstrate the offender's role. These lists are not exhaustive.	Category of harm Indicative quantity of drug concerned (upon which the starting point is based):
LEADING role: • Directing or organising buying and selling on a commercial scale; • Substantial links to, and influence on, others in a chain; • Expectation of substantial financial gain; • Uses business as cover; • Abuses a position of trust or responsibility	**Category 1** • Heroin, cocaine – 5kg; • Ecstasy – 10,000 tablets; • LSD – 250,000 squares; • Amphetamine – 20kg; • Cannabis – operation capable of producing industrial quantities for commercial use; • Ketamine – 5kg.
SIGNIFICANT role: • Operational or management function within a chain; • Involves others in the operation whether by pressure, influence, intimidation or reward; • Motivated by financial or other advantage, whether or not operating alone; • Some awareness and understanding of scale of operation; **LESSER role:** • Performs a limited function under direction; • Engaged by pressure, coercion, intimidation; • Involvement through naivety/exploitation; • No influence on those above in a chain; • Very little, if any, awareness or understanding of the scale of operation; • If own operation, solely for own use (considering reasonableness of account in all the circumstances).	**Category 2** • Heroin, cocaine – 1kg; • Ecstasy – 2,000 tablets; • LSD – 25,000 squares; • Amphetamine – 4kg; • Cannabis – operation capable of producing significant quantities for commercial use; • Ketamine – 1kg. **Category 3** • Heroin, cocaine – 150g; • Ecstasy – 300 tablets; • LSD – 2,500 squares; • Amphetamine – 750g; • Cannabis – 28 plants; [footnote indicates 'With assumed yield of 40g per plant'] • Ketamine – 150g. **Category 4** • Heroin, cocaine – 5g; • Ecstasy – 20 tablets; • LSD – 170 squares; • Amphetamine – 20g; • Cannabis – 9 plants (domestic operation); [footnote indicates 'With assumed yield of 40g per plant'] • Ketamine – 5g.

STEP TWO Starting point and category range

Having determined the category, the court should use the corresponding starting point to reach a sentence within the category range below. The starting point applies to all offenders irrespective of plea or previous convictions. The court should then consider further adjustment within the category range for aggravating or mitigating features, set out [at **SG-477**]. In cases where the offender is regarded as being at the very top of the 'leading' role it may be justifiable for the court to depart from the guideline.

Where the defendant is dependent on or has a propensity to misuse drugs and there is sufficient prospect of success, a community order with a drug rehabilitation requirement under section 209 of the Criminal Justice Act 2003 can be a proper alternative to a short or moderate length custodial sentence.

*For **class A** cases, section 110 of the Powers of Criminal Courts (Sentencing) Act 2000 provides that a court should impose a minimum sentence of at least seven years' imprisonment for a third class A trafficking offence except where the court is of the opinion that there are particular circumstances which (a) relate to any of the offences or to the offender; and (b) would make it unjust to do so in all the circumstances.*

CLASS A	Leading role	Significant role	Lesser role
Category 1	**Starting point** 14 years' custody	**Starting point** 10 years' custody	**Starting point** 7 years' custody
	Category range 12 – 16 years' custody	**Category range** 9 – 12 years' custody	**Category range** 6 – 9 years' custody
Category 2	**Starting point** 11 years' custody	**Starting point** 8 years' custody	**Starting point** 5 years' custody
	Category range 9 – 13 years' custody	**Category range** 6 years 6 months' – 10 years' custody	**Category range** 3 years 6 months' – 7 years' custody
Category 3	**Starting point** 8 years 6 months' custody	**Starting point** 5 years' custody	**Starting point** 3 years 6 months' custody
	Category range 6 years 6 months' – 10 years' custody	**Category range** 3 years 6 months' – 7 years' custody	**Category range** 2 – 5 years' custody
Category 4	**Starting point** 5 years 6 months' custody	**Starting point** 3 years 6 months' custody	**Starting point** 18 months' custody
	Category range 4 years 6 months' – 7 years 6 months' custody	**Category range** 2 – 5 years' custody	**Category range** High level community order – 3 years' custody

CLASS B	Leading role	Significant role	Lesser role
Category 1	**Starting point** 8 years' custody	**Starting point** 5 years 6 months' custody	**Starting point** 3 years' custody
	Category range 7 – 10 years' custody	**Category range** 5 – 7 years' custody	**Category range** 2 years 6 months' – 5 years' custody
Category 2	**Starting point** 6 years' custody	**Starting point** 4 years' custody	**Starting point** 1 years' custody
	Category range 4 years 6 months' – 8 years' custody	**Category range** 2 years 6 months' – 5 years' custody	**Category range** 26 weeks' – 3 years' custody
Category 3	**Starting point** 4 years' custody	**Starting point** 1 year's custody	**Starting point** High level community order
	Category range 2 years 6 months' – 5 years' custody	**Category range** 26 weeks' – 3 years' custody	**Category range** Low level community order – 26 weeks' custody

CLASS B	Leading role	Significant role	Lesser role
Category 4	**Starting point** 1 years' custody	**Starting point** High level community order	**Starting point** Band C fine
	Category range High level community order – 3 years' custody	**Category range** Medium level community order – 26 weeks' custody	**Category range** Discharge – medium level community order

CLASS C	Leading role	Significant role	Lesser role
Category 1	**Starting point** 5 years' custody	**Starting point** 3 years' custody	**Starting point** 18 months' custody
	Category range 4 – 8 years' custody	**Category range** 2 – 5 years' custody	**Category range** 1 – 3 years' custody
Category 2	**Starting point** 3 years 6 months' custody	**Starting point** 18 months' custody	**Starting point** 26 weeks' custody
	Category range 2 – 5 years' custody	**Category range** 1 – 3 years' custody	**Category range** High level community order – 18 months' custody
Category 3	**Starting point** 18 months' custody	**Starting point** 26 weeks' custody	**Starting point** High level community order
	Category range 1 – 3 years' custody	**Category range** High level community order – 18 months' custody	**Category range** Low level community order – 12 weeks' custody
Category 4	**Starting point** 26 weeks' custody	**Starting point** High level community order	**Starting point** Band C fine
	Category range High level community order – 18 months' custody	**Category range** Low level community order – 12 weeks' custody	**Category range** Discharge – medium level community order

SG-477 The table below contains a **non-exhaustive** list of additional factual elements providing the context of the offence and factors relating to the offender. Identify whether any combination of these, or other relevant factors, should result in an upward or downward adjustment from the starting point. In some cases, having considered these factors, it may be appropriate to move outside the identified category range.

Where appropriate, consider the custody threshold as follows:

- has the custody threshold been passed?
- if so, is it unavoidable that a custodial sentence be imposed?
- if so, can that sentence be suspended?

Where appropriate, the court should also consider the community threshold as follows:

- has the community threshold been passed?

Factors increasing seriousness	Factors reducing seriousness or reflecting personal mitigation
Statutory aggravating factors: Previous convictions, having regard to a) nature of the offence to which conviction relates and relevance to current offence; and b) time elapsed since conviction (see [italicised text at **SG-476**] if third drug trafficking conviction) Offence committed on bail *Other aggravating factors include:* Nature of any likely supply Level of any profit element Use of premises accompanied by unlawful access to electricity/other utility supply of others Ongoing/large scale operation as evidenced by presence and nature of specialist equipment Exposure of others to more than usual danger, for example drugs cut with harmful substances Attempts to conceal or dispose of evidence, where not charged separately Presence of others, especially children and/or non-users Presence of weapon, where not charged separately High purity or high potential yield Failure to comply with current court orders Offence committed on licence Established evidence of community impact	Involvement due to pressure, intimidation or coercion falling short of duress, except where already taken into account at step 1 Isolated incident Low purity No previous convictions **or** no relevant or recent convictions Offender's vulnerability was exploited Remorse Good character and/or exemplary conduct Determination and/or demonstration of steps having been taken to address addiction or offending behaviour Serious medical conditions requiring urgent, intensive or long-term treatment Age and/or lack of maturity where it affects the responsibility of the offender Mental disorder or learning disability Sole or primary carer for dependent relatives

[Steps Three to Eight are identical to those applicable to Fraudulent evasion of a prohibition by bringing into or taking out of the UK a controlled drug: see **SG-468**.]   **SG-478**

Sentencing Guidelines

Permitting Premises to be Used   **SG-479**
Misuse of Drugs Act 1971 (section 8)

Triable either way unless the defendant could receive the minimum sentence of seven years for a third drug trafficking offence under section 110 Powers of Criminal Courts (Sentencing) Act 2000 in which case the offence is triable only on indictment.

Class A

Maximum: 14 years' custody

Offence range: Community order – 4 years' custody

A class A offence is a drug trafficking offence for the purpose of imposing a minimum sentence under section 110 Powers of Criminal Courts (Sentencing) Act 2000

Class B

Maximum: 14 years' custody

Offence range: Fine – 18 months' custody

Class C

Maximum: 14 years' custody

Offence range: Discharge – 26 weeks' custody

STEP ONE   Determining the offence category   **SG-480**
The court should determine the offender's culpability and the harm caused (extent of the activity and/or the quantity of drugs) with reference to the table below.

In assessing harm, quantity is determined by the weight of the product. Purity is not taken into account at step 1 but is dealt with at step 2

Category 1	Higher culpability and greater harm
Category 2	Lower culpability and greater harm; or higher culpability and lesser harm
Category 3	Lower culpability and lesser harm

Factors indicating culpability (non-exhaustive)	Factors indicating harm (non-exhaustive)
Higher culpability: Permits premises to be used primarily for drug activity, for example crack house Permits use in expectation of substantial financial gain Uses legitimate business premises to aid and/or conceal illegal activity, for example public house or club *Lower culpability*: Permits use for limited or no financial gain No active role in any supply taking place Involvement through naivety	*Greater harm*: Regular drug-related activity Higher quantity of drugs, for example: Heroin, cocaine – more than 5g; Cannabis – more than 50g. *Lesser harm:* Infrequent drug-related activity Lower quantity of drugs, for example: Heroin, cocaine – up to 5g; Cannabis – up to 50g.

SG-481 **STEP TWO Starting point and category range**

Having determined the category, the court should use the table below to identify the corresponding starting point to reach a sentence within the category range. The starting point applies to all offenders irrespective of plea or previous convictions. The court should then consider further adjustment within the category range for aggravating or mitigating features, set out [at **SG-482**].

Where the defendant is dependent on or has a propensity to misuse drugs and there is sufficient prospect of success, a community order with a drug rehabilitation requirement under section 209 of the Criminal Justice Act 2003 can be a proper alternative to a short or moderate length custodial sentence.

*For **class A** cases, section 110 of the Powers of Criminal Courts (Sentencing) Act 2000 provides that a court should impose a minimum sentence of at least seven years' imprisonment for a third class A trafficking offence except where the court is of the opinion that there are particular circumstances which (a) relate to any of the offences or to the offender; and (b) would make it unjust to do so in all the circumstances.*

CLASS A

Offence category	Starting point (*applicable to all offenders*)	Category range (*applicable to all offenders*)
Category 1	2 years 6 months' custody	18 months' – 4 years' custody
Category 2	36 weeks' custody	High level community order – 18 months' custody
Category 3	Medium level community order	Low level community order – high level community order

CLASS B

Offence category	Starting point (*applicable to all offenders*)	Category range (*applicable to all offenders*)
Category 1	1 year's custody	26 weeks' – 18 months' custody
Category 2	High level community order	Low level community order – 26 weeks' custody
Category 3	Band C fine	Band A fine – low level community order

Class C

Offence category	Starting point (*applicable to all offenders*)	Category range (*applicable to all offenders*)
Category 1	12 weeks' custody	High level community order – 26 weeks' custody [footnote indicates that 'when tried summarily, the maximum penalty is 12 weeks' custody']
Category 2	Low level community order	Band C fine – high level community order
Category 3	Band A fine	Discharge – Band C fine

The table below contains a **non-exhaustive** list of additional factual elements providing the context of the offence and factors relating to the offender. Identify whether any combination of these, or other relevant factors, should result in an upward or downward adjustment from the starting point. In some cases, having considered these factors, it may be appropriate to move outside the identified category range.   **SG-482**

Where appropriate, consider the custody threshold as follows:

- has the custody threshold been passed?
- if so, is it unavoidable that a custodial sentence be imposed?
- if so, can that sentence be suspended?

Where appropriate, the court should also consider the community threshold as follows:

- has the community threshold been passed?

Factors increasing seriousness	Factors reducing seriousness or reflecting personal mitigation
Statutory aggravating factors: Previous convictions, having regard to a) nature of the offence to which conviction relates and relevance to current offence; and b) time elapsed since conviction (see [italicised text at **SG-481**] if third drug trafficking conviction) Offence committed on bail	Involvement due to pressure, intimidation or coercion falling short of duress Isolated incident Low purity No previous convictions **or** no relevant or recent convictions Offender's vulnerability was exploited Remorse
Other aggravating factors include: Length of time over which premises used for drug activity Volume of drug activity permitted Premises adapted to facilitate drug activity Location of premises, for example proximity to school Attempts to conceal or dispose of evidence, where not charged separately Presence of others, especially children and/or non-users High purity Presence of weapons, where not charged separately Failure to comply with current court orders Offence committed on licence Established evidence of community impact	Good character and/or exemplary conduct Determination and/or demonstration of steps having been taken to address addiction or offending behaviour Serious medical conditions requiring urgent, intensive or long-term treatment Age and/or lack of maturity where it affects the responsibility of the offender Mental disorder or learning disability Sole or primary carer for dependent relatives

[Steps Three to Eight are identical to those applicable to Fraudulent evasion of a prohibition by bringing into or taking out of the UK a controlled drug: see **SG-468**.]   **SG-483**

Possession of a Controlled Drug   SG-484
Misuse of Drugs Act 1971 (section 5(2))

Triable either way

CLASS A

Maximum: 7 years' custody

Offence range: Fine – 51 weeks' custody

CLASS B

Maximum: 5 years' custody

Offence range: Discharge – 26 weeks' custody

CLASS C

Maximum: 2 years' custody

Offence range: Discharge – Community order

SG-485   STEP ONE   **Determining the offence category**
The court should identify the offence category based on the class of drug involved.

Category 1	**Class A drug**
Category 2	Class B drug
Category 3	Class C drug

SG-486   STEP TWO   **Starting point and category range**
The court should use the table below to identify the corresponding starting point. The starting point applies to all offenders irrespective of plea or previous convictions. The court should then consider further adjustment within the category range for aggravating or mitigating features, set out [at **SG-487**].

Where the defendant is dependent on or has a propensity to misuse drugs and there is sufficient prospect of success, a community order with a drug rehabilitation requirement under section 209 of the Criminal Justice Act 2003 can be a proper alternative to a short or moderate length custodial sentence.

Offence category	Starting point (*applicable to all offenders*)	Category range (*applicable to all offenders*)
Category 1 (class A)	Band C fine	Band A fine – 51 weeks' custody
Category 2 (class B)	Band B fine	Discharge – 26 weeks' custody
Category 3 (class C)	Band A fine	Discharge – medium level community order

SG-487   The table below contains a **non-exhaustive** list of additional factual elements providing the context of the offence and factors relating to the offender. Identify whether any combination of these, or other relevant factors, should result in an upward or downward adjustment from the starting point. **In particular, possession of drugs in prison is likely to result in an upward adjustment**. In some cases, having considered these factors, it may be appropriate to move outside the identified category range.

Where appropriate, consider the custody threshold as follows:

* has the custody threshold been passed?
* if so, is it unavoidable that a custodial sentence be imposed?
* if so, can that sentence be suspended?

Where appropriate, the court should also consider the community threshold as follows:

* has the community threshold been passed?

Factors increasing seriousness	Factors reducing seriousness or reflecting personal mitigation
Statutory aggravating factors: Previous convictions, having regard to a) nature of the offence to which conviction relates and relevance to current offence; and b) time elapsed since conviction Offence committed on bail *Other aggravating factors include:* Possession of drug in prison Presence of others, especially children and/or non-users Possession of drug in a school or licensed premises Failure to comply with current court orders Offence committed on licence Attempts to conceal or dispose of evidence, where not charged separately Charged as importation of a very small amount Established evidence of community impact	No previous convictions **or** no relevant or recent convictions Remorse Good character and/or exemplary conduct Offender is using cannabis to help with a diagnosed medical condition Determination and/or demonstration of steps having been taken to address addiction or offending behaviour Serious medical conditions requiring urgent, intensive or long-term treatment Isolated incident Age and/or lack of maturity where it affects the responsibility of the offender Mental disorder or learning disability Sole or primary carer for dependent relatives

[Steps Three to Eight are similar to those applicable to Fraudulent evasion of a prohibition by bringing into or taking out of the UK a controlled drug (see **SG-468**) but the reference at Step Four to minimum mandatory sentences does not apply and Step Six merely states 'In all cases, the court should consider whether to make ancillary orders'.]   **SG-488**

Annex: Fine Bands and Community Orders   **SG-489**

[The tables set out here are also set out in the Magistrates' Court Sentencing Guidelines, which includes further guidance on fines and community orders: see **SG-306** and **SG-330**.]

PART 22   OFFENCES TAKEN INTO CONSIDERATION   **SG-490**

Definitive Guideline

Applicability of guideline

In accordance with section 120 of the Coroners and Justice Act 2009, the Sentencing Council issues this definitive guideline. It applies to all offenders whose cases are dealt with on or after 11 June 2012.

[Sets out the CAJA 2009, s. 125(1): see **SG-457**.]

This guideline applies where an offender admits the commission of other offences in the course of sentencing proceedings and requests those other offences to be taken into consideration.[443]

General principles   **SG-491**

When sentencing an offender who requests offences to be taken into consideration (TICs), courts should pass a total sentence which reflects *all* the offending behaviour. The sentence must be just and proportionate and must not exceed the statutory maximum for the conviction offence.

Offences to be Taken Into Consideration   **SG-492**

The court has discretion as to whether or not to take TICs into account. In exercising its discretion the court should take into account that TICs are capable of reflecting the offender's overall criminality. The court is likely to consider that the fact that the offender has assisted the police (particularly if the offences would not otherwise have been detected) and avoided the need for further proceedings demonstrates a genuine determination by the offender to 'wipe the slate clean'.[444]

---

[443]   s.305 Criminal Justice Act 2003 and s161(1) Powers of Criminal Courts (Sentencing) Act 2000
[444]   Per Lord Chief Justice, *R v Miles* [2006] EWCA Crim 256

It is generally **undesirable** for TICs to be accepted in the following circumstances:

- where the TIC is likely to attract a greater sentence than the conviction offence;
- where it is in the public interest that the TIC should be the subject of a separate charge;
- where the offender would avoid a prohibition, ancillary order or similar consequence which it would have been desirable to impose on conviction. For example:
  - where the TIC attracts mandatory disqualification or endorsement and the offence(s) for which the defendant is to be sentenced do not;
- where the TIC constitutes a breach of an earlier sentence;[445]
- where the TIC is a specified offence for the purposes of section 224 of the Criminal Justice Act 2003, but the conviction offence is non-specified; or
- where the TIC is not founded on the same facts or evidence or part of a series of offences of the same or similar character (unless the court is satisfied that it is in the interests of justice to do so).

SG-493 Jurisdiction

The magistrates' court cannot take into consideration an indictable only offence.

The Crown Court can take into account summary only offences provided the TICs are founded on the same facts or evidence as the indictable charge, or are part of a series of offences of the same or similar character as the indictable conviction offence.[446]

SG-494 Procedural safeguards

A court should generally only take offences into consideration if the following procedural provisions have been satisfied:

- the police or prosecuting authorities have prepared a schedule of offences (TIC schedule) that they consider suitable to be taken into consideration. The TIC schedule should set out the nature of each offence, the date of the offence(s), relevant detail about the offence(s) (including, for example, monetary values of items) and any other brief details that the court should be aware of;
- a copy of the TIC schedule must be provided to the defendant and his representative (if he has one) before the sentence hearing. The defendant should sign the TIC schedule to provisionally admit the offences;
- at the sentence hearing, the court should ask the defendant in open court whether he admits each of the offences on the TIC schedule and whether he wishes to have them taken into consideration;[447]
- if there is any doubt about the admission of a particular offence, it should not be accepted as a TIC. Special care should be taken with vulnerable and/or unrepresented defendants;
- if the defendant is committed to the Crown Court for sentence, this procedure must take place again at the Crown Court even if the defendant has agreed to the schedule in the magistrates' court.

SG-495 Application

The sentence imposed on an offender should, in most circumstances, be increased to reflect the fact that other offences have been taken into consideration. The court should:

1. Determine the sentencing starting point for the conviction offence, referring to the relevant definitive sentencing guidelines. No regard should be had to the presence of TICs at this stage.
2. Consider whether there are any aggravating or mitigating factors that justify an upward or downward adjustment from the starting point.

The presence of TICs should generally be treated as an aggravating feature that justifies an upward adjustment from the starting point. Where there is a large number of TICs, it may be appropriate to move outside the category range, although this must be considered in the context of the case and subject to the principle of totality. The court is limited to the statutory maximum for the conviction offence.

3. Continue through the sentencing process including:
   - consider whether the frank admission of a number of offences is an indication of a defendant's remorse or determination and/or demonstration of steps taken to address addiction or offending behaviour;
   - any reduction for a guilty plea should be applied to the overall sentence;
   - the principle of totality;

---

[445] *R v Webb* (1953) 37 Cr App 82
[446] s.40 Criminal Justice Act 1988
[447] *Anderson v DPP* [1978] AC 964

- when considering ancillary orders these can be considered in relation to any or all of the TICs, specifically:
  - compensation orders[448]- in the magistrate[s'] court the total compensation cannot exceed the limit for the conviction offence;
  - restitution orders.[449]

PART 23   TOTALITY

SG-496

Definitive Guideline

Applicability of guideline

In accordance with section 120 of the Coroners and Justice Act 2009, the Sentencing Council issues this definitive guideline. It applies to all offenders whose cases are dealt with on or after 11 June 2012.

[Sets out the CAJA 2009, s. 125(1): see **SG-457**.]

This guideline applies when sentencing an offender for multiple offences or when sentencing an offender who is already serving an existing sentence. In these situations, the courts should apply the principle of totality.

General principles

SG-497

The principle of totality comprises two elements:

1. all courts, when sentencing for more than a single offence, should pass a total sentence which reflects *all* the offending behaviour before it and is just and proportionate. This is so whether the sentences are structured as concurrent or consecutive. Therefore, concurrent sentences will ordinarily be longer than a single sentence for a single offence.
2. it is usually impossible to arrive at a just and proportionate sentence for multiple offending simply by adding together notional single sentences. It is necessary to address the offending behaviour, together with the factors personal to the offender as a whole.

Concurrent/consecutive sentences

SG-498

There is no inflexible rule governing whether sentences should be structured as concurrent or consecutive components. The overriding principle is that the overall sentence must be just and proportionate.

General approach (as applied to Determinate Custodial Sentences)

SG-499

1. **Consider the sentence for each individual offence, referring to the relevant sentencing guidelines.**
2. **Determine whether the case calls for concurrent or consecutive sentences.**

Concurrent Sentences will ordinarily be appropriate where:

a) offences arise out of the same incident or facts.

Examples include:

- a single incident of dangerous driving resulting in injuries to multiple victims;[450]
- robbery with a weapon where the weapon offence is ancillary to the robbery and is not distinct and independent of it;[451]
- fraud and associated forgery;
- separate counts of supplying different types of drugs of the same class as part of the same transaction.

b) there is a series of offences of the same or similar kind, especially when committed against the same person.

Examples include:

- repetitive small thefts from the *same* person, such as by an employee;
- repetitive benefit frauds of the same kind, committed in each payment period.

---

[448] s.131(2) Powers of Criminal Courts (Sentencing) Act 2000
[449] s.148 ibid.
[450] *R v Lawrence* (1989) 11 Cr App R (S) 580
[451] *R v Poulton and Celaire* [2002] EWCA Crim 2487; *Attorney General's Reference No 21 & 22 of 2003* [2003] EWCA Crim 3089

Where concurrent sentences are to be passed the sentence should reflect the overall criminality involved. The sentence should be appropriately aggravated by the presence of the associated offences.

Examples include:

- a single incident of dangerous driving resulting in injuries to multiple victims where there are separate charges relating to each victim. The sentences should generally be passed concurrently, but each sentence should be aggravated to take into account the harm caused;
- repetitive fraud or theft, where charged as a series of small frauds/thefts, would be properly considered in relation to the total amount of money obtained and the period of time over which the offending took place. The sentences should generally be passed concurrently, each one reflecting the overall seriousness;
- robbery with a weapon where the weapon offence is ancillary to the robbery and is not distinct and independent of it. The principal sentence for the robbery should properly reflect the presence of the weapon. The court must avoid double-counting and may deem it preferable for the possession of the weapon's offence to run concurrently to avoid the appearance of under-sentencing in respect of the robbery.[452]

Consecutive sentences will ordinarily be appropriate where:

a) offences arise out of unrelated facts or incidents.

Examples include:

- where the offender commits a theft on one occasion and a common assault against a different victim on a separate occasion;
- an attempt to pervert the course of justice in respect of another offence also charged;[453]
- a Bail Act offence;[454]
- any offence committed within the prison context;
- offences that are unrelated because whilst they were committed simultaneously they are distinct and there is an aggravating element that requires separate recognition, for example:
  - an assault on a constable committed to try to evade arrest for another offence also charged;[455]
  - where the defendant is convicted of drug dealing and possession of a firearm offence. The firearm offence is not the essence or the intrinsic part of the drugs offence and requires separate recognition;[456]
  - where the defendant is convicted of threats to kill in the context of an indecent assault on the same occasion, the threats to kill could be distinguished as a separate element.[457]

b) offences that are of the same or similar kind but where the overall criminality will not sufficiently be reflected by concurrent sentences.

Examples include:

- where offences committed against *different* people, such as repeated thefts involving attacks on several different shop assistants;[458]
- where offences of domestic violence or sexual offences are committed against the *same* individual.

c) one of more offence (s) qualifies for a statutory minimum sentence and concurrent sentences would improperly undermine that minimum[459]

However it is not permissible to impose consecutive sentences for offences committed at the same time in order to evade the statutory maximum penalty.[460]

Where consecutive sentences are to be passed add up the sentences for each offence and consider if the aggregate length is just and appropriate.

If the aggregate length is not just and proportionate the court should consider how to reach a just and proportionate sentence. There are a number of ways in which this could be achieved.

---

[452] *Attorney General's Reference Nos 21 & 22 of 2003*
[453] *Attorney General's Reference No 1 of 1990* (1990) 12 Cr App R (S) 245
[454] *R v Millen* (1980) 2 Cr App R (S) 357
[455] *R v Kastercum* (1972) 56 Cr App R 298
[456] *R v Poulton and Celaire* [2002] EWCA Crim 2487; *Attorney General's Reference Nos 21 & 22 of 2003* [2003] EWCA Crim 3089
[457] *R v Fletcher* [2002] 2 CAR (S) 127
[458] *R v Jamieson & Jamieson* [2008] EWCA Crim 2761
[459] *R v Raza* (2010) 1 Cr App R (S) 56
[460] *R v Ralphs* [2009] EWCA Crim 2555

Examples include:

- when sentencing for similar offence types or offences of a similar level of severity the court can consider:
    - whether all of the offences can be proportionately reduced (with particular reference to the category ranges within the sentencing guidelines) and passed consecutively;
    - whether, despite their similarity, a most serious principal offence can be identified and the other sentences can all be proportionately reduced (with particular reference to the category ranges within sentencing guidelines) and passed consecutively in order that the sentence for the lead offence can be clearly identified.
- when sentencing for two or more offences of differing levels of seriousness the court can consider:
    - whether some offences are of such low seriousness in the context of the most serious offence(s) that they can be recorded as 'no separate penalty' (for example technical breaches or minor driving offences not involving mandatory disqualification);
    - whether some of the offences are of lesser seriousness and are unrelated to the most serious offence(s), that they can be ordered to run concurrently so that the sentence for the most serious offence(s) can be clearly identified.
3. Test the overall sentence(s) against the requirement that they be just and proportionate.
4. Consider whether the sentence is structured in a way that will be best understood by all concerned with it.

Specific applications – Custodial sentences   **SG-500**

EXISTING DETERMINATE SENTENCE, WHERE DETERMINATE SENTENCE TO BE PASSED

Circumstance	Approach
Offender serving a determinate sentence (offence(s) committed before original sentence imposed)	Consider what the sentence length would have been if the court had dealt with the offences at the same time and ensure that the totality of the sentence is just and proportionate in all the circumstances. If it is not, an adjustment should be made to the sentence imposed for the latest offence.
Offender serving a determinate sentence (offence(s) committed after original sentence imposed)	Generally the sentence will be consecutive as it will have arisen out of an unrelated incident. The court must have regard to the totality of the offender's criminality when passing the second sentence, to ensure that the total sentence to be served is just and proportionate. Where a prisoner commits acts of violence in prison, any reduction for totality is likely to be minimal.[461]
Offender serving a determinate sentence but released from custody	The new sentence should start on the day it is imposed: s.265 Criminal Justice Act 2003 prohibits a sentence of imprisonment running consecutively to a sentence from which a prisoner has been released. The sentence for the new offence will take into account the aggravating feature that it was committed on licence. However, it must be commensurate with the new offence and cannot be artificially inflated with a view to ensuring that the offender serves a period in custody additional to the recall period (which will be an unknown quantity in most cases);[462] this is so even if the new sentence will, in consequence, add nothing to the period actually served.

---

[461] *R v Ali* (1998) 2 Cr App R 123
[462] *R v Costello* [2010] EWCA Crim 371

Circumstance	Approach
Offender subject to a s.116 return to custody The powers under s.116 Powers of Criminal Court (Sentencing) Act 2000 remain available where the offender: • has been released from a sentence of less than 12 months;[463] • committed his offence before 4 April 2005 and is released from a sentence of less than 4 years;[464] • committed his offence before 4 April 2005 and is released from a sentence of over 4 years following a Parole Board recommendation, or after serving two-thirds of his sentence under section 33(b) Criminal Justice Act 1991.[465]	The period of return under s.116 can either be ordered to be served before or concurrently with the sentence for the new offence. In either case the period of return shall be disregarded in determining the appropriate length of the new sentence.
Offender sentenced to a determinate term and subject to an existing suspended sentence order	Where an offender commits an additional offence during the operational period of a suspended sentence and the court orders the suspended sentence to be activated, the additional sentence will generally be consecutive to the activated suspended sentence, as it will arise out of unrelated facts.

SG-501　　　　EXTENDED SENTENCES FOR PUBLIC PROTECTION

Circumstance	Approach
Extended sentences – using multiple offences to calculate the requisite determinate term	In the case of extended sentences imposed under the Criminal Justice Act 2003, providing there is at least one specified offence, the threshold requirement under s.227(2B) Criminal Justice Act 2003 is reached if the total determinate sentence for all offences (specified or not) would be four years or more. The extended sentence should be passed either for one specified offence or concurrently on a number of them. Ordinarily either a concurrent determinate sentence or no separate penalty will be appropriate to the remaining offences.[466] The extension period is such as the court considers necessary for the purpose of protecting members of the public from serious harm caused by the offender committing further specified offences.[467] The extension period must not exceed five years (or eight for a sexual offence). The whole aggregate term must not exceed the statutory maximum. The custodial period must be adjusted for totality in the same way as determinate sentences would be. The extension period is measured by the need for protection and therefore does not require adjustment.

---

[463]　s.116 of the Powers of Criminal Courts (Sentencing) Act 2000 was repealed by s.332 of the Criminal Justice Act 2003 and Part 7 of Schedule 37. However, the effect of the saving in paragraph 29 of Schedule 2 to the Commencement No.8 and Transitional and Savings Provisions Order 2005 was that s.116 continued to apply where the earlier sentence was imposed for an offence committed before 4 April 2005, or was for a term of less than 12 months.

[464]　ibid.

[465]　ibid. The Criminal Justice & Immigration Act 2008 contains a further transitional provision. Paragraph 4 of Schedule 26 inserts an exclusion into s.116 which prevents prisoners released under s.33(1A) of the 1991 Act (i.e. eligible discretionary conditional release prisoners, who are released automatically at ½ point of their sentence, rather than on a recommendation from the Parole Board) from being returned to prison under s.116.

[466]　*R v Pinnell* [2010] EWCA Crim 2848

[467]　*R v Cornelius* [2002] EWCA Crim 138

INDETERMINATE SENTENCES   SG-502

Circumstance	Approach
Imposing multiple indeterminate sentences on the same occasion and using multiple offences to calculate the minimum term for an indeterminate sentence	Indeterminate sentences should start on the date of their imposition and so should generally be ordered to run concurrently. If any offence is a serious and specified one and it appears that the defendant is dangerous within the meaning of the dangerousness provisions of the Criminal Justice Act 2003 then: a) first assess the notional determinate term for all offences (serious, specified or otherwise), adjusting for totality in the usual way;[468] b) ascertain whether the total determinate term would be four years or more, or the offender has previously been convicted of a Schedule 15A offence; if so an indeterminate sentence may be passed; and c) the indeterminate sentence should generally be passed concurrently on all serious specific offences, but there may be some circumstances in which it suffices to pass it on a single such offence.
Indeterminate sentence (where the offender is already serving an existing determinate sentence)	It is generally undesirable to order an indeterminate sentence to be served consecutively to any other period of imprisonment on the basis that indeterminate sentences should start on their imposition.[469] The court should instead order the sentence to run concurrently but can adjust the minimum term for the new offence to reflect half of any period still remaining to be served under the existing sentence (to take account of the early release provisions for determinate sentences). The court should then review the minimum term to ensure that the total sentence is just and proportionate.
Indeterminate sentence (where the offender is already serving an existing indeterminate sentence)	It is generally undesirable to order an indeterminate sentence to be served consecutively to any other period of imprisonment on the basis that indeterminate sentences should start on their imposition. However, where necessary the court can order an indeterminate sentence to run consecutively to an indeterminate sentence passed on an earlier occasion.[470] The second sentence will commence on the expiration of the minimum term of the original sentence and the offender will become eligible for a parole review after serving both minimum terms.[471] The court should consider the length of the aggregate minimum terms that must be served before the offender will be eligible for consideration by the Parole Board. If this is not just and proportionate, the court can adjust the minimum term.
Ordering a determinate sentence to run consecutively to an indeterminate sentence	The court can order a determinate sentence to run consecutively to an indeterminate sentence. The determinate sentence will commence on the expiry of the minimum term of the indeterminate sentence and the offender will become eligible for a parole review after serving half of the determinate sentence.[472] The court should consider the total sentence that the offender will serve before becoming eligible for consideration for release. If this is not just and proportionate, the court can reduce the length of the determinate sentence, or alternatively, can order the second sentence to be served concurrently.

Sentencing Guidelines

---

[468] *R v Rahuel Delucca* [2010] EWCA Crim 710
[469] *R v O'Brien* [2006] EWCA Crim 1741
[470] *R v Hills* [2008] EWCA Crim 1871; *R v Ashes* [2007] EWCA Crim 1848
[471] s.28(1B) Crime (Sentences) Act 1997
[472] s.28 ibid.

SG-503   Specific applications – Non-custodial sentences

MULTIPLE FINES FOR NON-IMPRISONABLE OFFENCES

Circumstance	Approach
Offender convicted of more than one offence where a fine is appropriate	The total fine is inevitably cumulative. The court should determine the fine for each individual offence based on the seriousness of the offence[473] and taking into account the circumstances of the case including the financial circumstances of the offender so far as they are known, or appear, to the court.[474] The court should add up the fines for each offence and consider if they are just and proportionate. If the aggregate total is not just and proportionate the court should consider how to reach a just and proportionate fine. There are a number of ways in which this can be achieved. *For example:* • where an offender is to be fined for two or more offences that arose out of the same incident or where there are multiple offences of a repetitive kind, especially when committed against the same person, it will often be appropriate to impose for the most serious offence a fine which reflects the totality of the offending where this can be achieved within the maximum penalty for that offence. No separate penalty should be imposed for the other offences; • where an offender is to be fined for two or more offences that arose out of different incidents, it will often be appropriate to impose a separate fine for each of the offences. The court should add up the fines for each offence and consider if they are just and proportionate. If the aggregate amount is not just and proportionate the court should consider whether all of the fines can be proportionately reduced. Separate fines should then be passed. Where separate fines are passed, the court must be careful to ensure that there is no double-counting.[475] Where compensation is being ordered, that will need to be attributed to the relevant offence as will any necessary ancillary orders.
Multiple offences attracting fines – crossing the community threshold	If the offences being dealt with are all imprisonable, then the community threshold can be crossed by reason of multiple offending, when it would not be crossed for a single offence.[476] However, if the offences are non-imprisonable (e.g. driving without insurance) the threshold cannot be crossed.[477]

---

[473] s.164(2) Criminal Justice Act 2003
[474] s.164(3) ibid.
[475] *R v Pointon* [2008] EWCA Crim 513
[476] s.148(1) Criminal Justice Act 2003
[477] s.150A ibid. (in force since 14 July 2008) restricts the power to make a community order by limiting it to cases where the offence is punishable with imprisonment

FINES IN COMBINATION WITH OTHER SENTENCES

Circumstance	Approach
A fine may be imposed in addition to any other penalty for the same offence except:	• a hospital order;[478] • a discharge;[479] • a sentence fixed by law[480] (minimum sentences, EPP, IPP); • a minimum term imposed under s.110(2) or s.111(2) of the Powers of Criminal Courts (Sentencing) Act 2000;[481] • a life sentence imposed under s.225(2) Criminal Justice Act 2003 or a sentence of detention for life for an offender under 18 under s.226(2) Criminal Justice Act 2003.[482]
Fines and determinate custodial sentences	A fine should not generally be imposed in combination with a custodial sentence because of the effect of imprisonment on the means of the defendant. However, exceptionally, it may be appropriate to impose a fine in addition to a custodial sentence where: • the sentence is suspended; • a confiscation order is not contemplated; **and** • there is no obvious victim to whom compensation can be awarded; **and** • the offender has, or will have, resources from which a fine can be paid.[483]

COMMUNITY ORDERS

Circumstance	Approach
Multiple offences attracting community orders – crossing the custody threshold	If the offences are all imprisonable and none of the individual sentences merit a custodial sentence, the custody threshold can be crossed by reason of multiple offending.[484] If the custody threshold has been passed, the court should refer to the offence ranges in sentencing guidelines for the offences and to the general principles.
Multiple offences, where one offence would merit immediate custody and one offence would merit a community order	A community order should not be ordered to run consecutively to or concurrently with a custodial sentence. Instead the court should generally impose one custodial sentence that is aggravated appropriately by the presence of the associated offence(s). The alternative option is to impose no separate penalty for the offence of lesser seriousness.
Offender convicted of more than one offence where a community order is appropriate	A community order is a composite package rather than an accumulation of sentences attached to individual counts. The court should generally impose a single community order that reflects the overall criminality of the offending behaviour. Where it is necessary to impose more than one community order, these should be ordered to run concurrently and for ease of administration, each of the orders should be identical.

[478] s.37(8) Mental Health Act 1983
[479] *R v McClelland* [1951] 1 All ER 557
[480] s.163 Criminal Justice Act 2003
[481] ibid.
[482] ibid.
[483] This guidance is also provided at [SG-423] in the Fraud Guideline
[484] s.148(1) Criminal Justice Act 2003

Circumstance	Approach
Offender convicted of an offence while serving a community order	The power to deal with the offender depends on his being convicted whilst the order is still in force;[485] it does not arise where the order has expired, even if the additional offence was committed whilst it was still current.
	If an offender, in respect of whom a community order made by a magistrates' court is in force, is convicted by a magistrates' court of an additional offence, the magistrates' court should ordinarily revoke the previous community order and sentence afresh for both the original and the additional offence.
	Where an offender, in respect of whom a community order made by a Crown Court is in force, is convicted by a magistrates' court, the magistrates' court may, and ordinarily should, commit the offender to the Crown Court, in order to allow the Crown Court to re-sentence for the original offence and the additional offence.
	The sentencing court should consider the overall seriousness of the offending behaviour taking into account the additional offence and the original offence. The court should consider whether the combination of associated offences is sufficiently serious to justify a custodial sentence.
	If the court does not consider that custody is necessary, it should impose a single community order that reflects the overall totality of criminality. The court must take into account the extent to which the offender complied with the requirements of the previous order.

SG-506

DISQUALIFICATIONS FROM DRIVING

Circumstance	Approach
Offender convicted of two or more obligatory disqualification offences (s.34(1) Road Traffic Offender Act 1988)	The court must impose an order of disqualification for each offence unless for special reasons it does not disqualify the offender.[486]
	All orders of disqualification imposed by the court on the same date take effect immediately and cannot be ordered to run consecutively to one another.
	The court should take into account all offences when determining the disqualification periods and should generally impose like periods for each offence.
Offender convicted of two or more offences involving either: a) discretionary disqualification and obligatory endorsement from driving; or b) obligatory disqualification but the court for special reasons does not disqualify the offender and the penalty points to be taken into account number 12 or more (s.28 and 35 Road Traffic Offender Act 1988)	Where an offender is convicted on the same occasion of more than one offence to which s.35(1) Road Traffic Offender Act 1988 applies, only one disqualification shall be imposed on him.[487] However, the court must take into account all offences when determining the disqualification period. For the purposes of appeal, any disqualification imposed shall be treated as an order made on conviction of each of the offences.[488]
Other combinations involving two or more offences involving discretionary disqualification	As orders of disqualification take effect immediately, it is generally desirable for the court to impose a single disqualification order that reflects the overall criminality of the offending behaviour.

---

[485] Paragraphs 21–23 of Schedule 8 Criminal Justice Act 2003
[486] s.34(1) Road Traffic Offender Act 1988
[487] s.34(3) ibid.
[488] ibid.

COMPENSATION ORDERS

SG-507

Circumstance	Approach
Global compensation orders	The court should not fix a global compensation figure unless the offences were committed against the same victim.[489] Where there are competing claims for limited funds, the total compensation available should normally be apportioned on a pro rata basis.[490]

The court may combine a compensation order with any other form of order.

Compensation orders and fines	Priority is given to the imposition of a compensation order over a fine.[491] This does not affect sentences other than fines. This means that the fine should be reduced or, if necessary, dispensed with altogether, to enable the compensation to be paid.
Compensation orders and confiscation orders	A compensation order can be combined with a confiscation order where the amount that may be realised is sufficient. If such an order is made, priority should be given to compensation.[492]
Compensation orders and community orders	A compensation order can be combined with a community order.
Compensation orders and suspended sentence orders	A compensation order can be combined with a suspended sentence order.[493]
Compensation orders and custody	A compensation order can be combined with a sentence of immediate custody where the offender is clearly able to pay or has good prospects of employment on his release from custody.

PART 24   ALLOCATION

SG-508

Definitive Guideline

Applicability of guideline

In accordance with section 122(2) of the Coroners and Justice Act 2009, the Sentencing Council issues this definitive guideline. It applies to all defendants in the magistrates' court (including youths jointly charged with adults) whose cases are dealt with on or after 11 June 2012. It will not be applicable in the youth court where a separate statutory procedure applies.

[Sets out the CAJA 2009, s. 125(1): see **SG-457**.]

Statutory framework

SG-509

In accordance with section 19 of the Magistrates' Courts Act 1980, where a defendant pleads not guilty or has not indicated an intention to plead guilty to an offence triable either way, a magistrates' court must decide whether the offence should be sent to the Crown Court for trial.

When deciding whether an either way offence is more suitable for summary trial or trial on indictment, section 19 of the Magistrates' Courts Act 1980 provides that the court shall give the prosecutor and the accused the opportunity to make representations as to which court is more suitable for the conduct of the trial.[494]

---

[489] s.130(12) Powers of Criminal Courts (Sentencing) Act 2000
[490] *R v Mitchell* [2001] Crim LR 239
[491] s.118(5) Powers of Criminal Courts (Sentencing) Act 2000
[492] *R v Warton* [1976] Crim LR 520
[493] *R v Miller* [1976] Crim LR 694
[494] s.19(2) Magistrates' Courts Act 1980

The court must also have regard to:

a) the nature of the case;

b) whether the circumstances make the offence one of a serious character;

c) whether the punishment which a magistrates' court would have the power to inflict for the offence would be adequate; and

d) any other circumstances which appear to the court to make the offence more suitable for it to be tried in one way rather than the other.[495]

SG-510　Guidance

It is important to ensure that all cases are tried at the appropriate level. **In general, either way offences should be tried summarily unless it is likely that the court's sentencing powers will be insufficient.** Its powers will generally be insufficient if the outcome is likely to result in a sentence in excess of six months' imprisonment for a single offence.

The court should assess the likely sentence in the light of the facts alleged by the prosecution case, taking into account all aspects of the case including those advanced by the defence.

The court should refer to definitive guidelines to assess the likely sentence for the offence.

SG-511　Committal for sentence

There is ordinarily no statutory restriction on committing an either way case for sentence following conviction. The general power of the magistrates' court to commit to the Crown Court for sentence after a finding that a case is suitable for summary trial and/or conviction continues to be available where the court is of the opinion that the offence (and any associated offences) is so serious that greater punishment should be inflicted than the court has power to impose.[496] Where the court decides that the case is suitable to be dealt with in the magistrates' court, it should remind the defendant that all sentencing options remain open, including committal to the Crown Court for sentence at the time it informs the defendant of this decision.

However, where the court proceeds to the summary trial of certain offences relating to criminal damage, upon conviction there is no power to commit to Crown Court for sentence.[497]

SG-512　Linked cases

Where a youth and an adult are jointly charged, the youth must be tried summarily unless the court considers it to be in the interests of justice for both the youth and the adult to be committed to the Crown Court for trial. Examples of factors that should be considered when deciding whether to separate the youth and adult defendants include:

- whether separate trials can take place without causing undue inconvenience to witnesses or injustice to the case as a whole;
- the young age of the defendant, particularly where the age gap between the adult and youth offender is substantial;
- the immaturity of the youth;
- the relative culpability of the youth compared with the adult and whether or not the role played by the youth was minor; and
- the lack of previous convictions on the part of the youth.

SG-513　PART 25　DANGEROUS DOG OFFENCES

Definitive Guideline

Applicability of guideline

[Omitted: See **SG-457** for identical text save that this guideline has effect from 20 August 2012.]

SG-514　Structure, ranges and starting points

[Omitted: See **SG-458** for identical text.]

---

[495] s.19(1) and (3) ibid.

[496] s.3 Powers of Criminal Courts (Sentencing) Act 2000

[497] s.2 and s.33 Magistrates' Courts Act 1980

Sentencing Guidelines

OWNER OR PERSON IN CHARGE OF A DOG DANGEROUSLY OUT OF CONTROL IN A PUBLIC PLACE,   **SG-515**
INJURING ANY PERSON
Dangerous Dogs Act 1991 (section 3(1))

OWNER OR PERSON IN CHARGE ALLOWING A DOG TO BE IN A PRIVATE PLACE WHERE THE DOG IS NOT
PERMITTED TO BE, INJURING ANY PERSON
Dangerous Dogs Act 1991 (section 3(3)(a))

Triable either way

Maximum: 2 years' custody

Offence range: Discharge — 18 months' custody

STEP ONE Determining the offence category   **SG-516**

The court should determine the offence category using the table below.

Category 1	Greater harm and higher culpability
Category 2	Greater harm **and** lower culpability; **or** lesser harm **and** higher culpability
Category 3	Lesser harm **and** lower culpability

The court should determine culpability and harm caused or intended, by reference only to the factors below, which comprise the principal factual elements of the offence. Where an offence does not fall squarely into a category, individual factors may require a degree of weighting before making an overall assessment and determining the appropriate offence category.

Factors indicating greater harm	Factors indicating lower culpability
Serious injury (which includes disease transmission and/or psychological harm)	Attempts made to regain control of dog and/or intervene
Sustained or repeated attack	Provocation of dog without fault of the offender
Victim is a child or otherwise vulnerable because of personal circumstances	Evidence of safety or control measures having been taken
Factor indicating lesser harm	Mental disorder or learning disability, where linked to the commission of the offence
Minor injury	
Factors indicating higher culpability	
Statutory aggravating factors:	
Offence racially or religiously aggravated	
Offence motivated by, or demonstrating, hostility to the victim based on his or her sexual orientation (or presumed sexual orientation)	
Offence motivated by, or demonstrating, hostility to the victim based on the victim's disability (or presumed disability)	
Other aggravating factors:	
Failure to respond to warnings or concerns expressed by others about the dog's behaviour	
Goading, or allowing goading, of dog	
Dog used as weapon or to intimidate victim	
Offence motivated by, or demonstrating, hostility based on the victim's age, sex, gender identity (or presumed gender identity)	

STEP TWO Starting point and category range   **SG-517**

Having determined the category, the court should use the corresponding starting points to reach a sentence within the category range below. The starting point applies to all offenders irrespective of plea or previous convictions. A case of particular gravity, reflected by multiple features of culpability or harm in step 1, could merit upward adjustment from the starting point before further adjustment for aggravating or mitigating features, set out [below].

Offence Category	Starting Point (*Applicable to all offenders*)	Category Range (*Applicable to all offenders*)
Category 1	6 months' custody	Medium level community order – 18 months' custody
Category 2	Medium level community order	Band B fine – 6 months' custody
Category 3	Band B fine	Discharge – Band C fine

The table below contains a **non-exhaustive** list of additional factual elements providing the context of the offence and factors relating to the offender. Identify whether any combination of these, or other relevant factors, should result in an upward or downward adjustment from the starting point. In some cases, having considered these factors, it may be appropriate to move outside the identified category range.

When sentencing **category 1 or 2** offences, the court should also consider the custody threshold as follows:

- has the custody threshold been passed?
- if so, is it unavoidable that a custodial sentence be imposed?
- if so, can that sentence be suspended?

When sentencing **category 2** offences, the court should also consider the community order threshold as follows:

- has the community order threshold been passed?

Factors increasing seriousness	Factors reducing seriousness or reflecting personal mitigation
Statutory aggravating factors: Previous convictions, having regard to a) the nature of the offence to which the conviction relates and its relevance to the current offence; and b) the time that has elapsed since the conviction Offence committed whilst on bail *Other aggravating factors include:* Injury to another animal(s) Location of the offence Ongoing effect upon the victim and/or others Failure to take adequate precautions to prevent dog escaping Allowing person insufficiently experienced or trained, to be in charge of dog Ill treatment or failure to ensure welfare needs of dog, where not charged separately Dog known to be prohibited Lack or loss of control of dog due to influence of alcohol or drugs Offence committed against those working in the public sector or providing a service to the public Established evidence of community impact Failure to comply with current court orders Offence committed whilst on licence	No previous convictions or no relevant/recent convictions Isolated incident No previous complaints against, or incidents involving, the dog Remorse Good character and/or exemplary conduct Evidence of responsible ownership Determination and/or demonstration of steps taken to address addiction or offending behaviour Serious medical conditions requiring urgent, intensive or long-term treatment Age and/or lack of maturity where it affects the responsibility of the offender Mental disorder or learning disability, where not linked to the commission of the offence Sole or primary carer for dependent relatives

SG-518   **STEP THREE**   **Consider any factors which indicate a reduction, such as assistance to the prosecution**

The court should take into account sections 73 and 74 of the Serious Organised Crime and Police Act 2005 (assistance by defendants: reduction or review of sentence) and any other rule of law by virtue of which an offender may receive a discounted sentence in consequence of assistance given (or offered) to the prosecutor or investigator.

STEP FOUR   **Reduction for guilty pleas**

The court should take account of any potential reduction for a guilty plea in accordance with section 144 of the Criminal Justice Act 2003 and the *Guilty Plea* guideline.

STEP FIVE   **Compensation and ancillary orders**

In all cases, the court should consider whether to make a compensation order and/or other ancillary orders.

Compensation order

The court should consider compensation orders in all cases where personal injury, loss or damage has resulted from the offence.[498] The court must give reasons if it decides not to award compensation in such cases.

Other ancillary orders available include:

Disqualification from having custody of a dog

The court may disqualify the offender from having custody of a dog.[499] The test the court should consider is whether the offender is a fit and proper person to have custody of a dog.

Destruction order/contingent destruction order

In any case where the offender is not the owner of the dog, the owner must be given an opportunity to be present and make representations to the court.

The court **shall** make a destruction order unless the court is satisfied that the dog would not constitute a danger to public safety.[500]

In reaching a decision, the court should consider the relevant circumstances which include:

* the incident — what degree of harm was caused by the dog's behaviour?
* past behaviour of the dog — is this an isolated incident or have there been previous warnings or incidents? and
* owner's character — is the owner a fit and proper person to own this particular dog?

If the court is satisfied that the dog would not constitute a danger to public safety, it shall make a contingent destruction order imposing certain available conditions.[501] A contingent destruction order should specify the measures to be taken by the owner for keeping the dog under proper control, which include:

* muzzling;
* keeping on a lead;
* neutering in appropriate cases; and
* excluding it from a specified place.[502]

Where the court makes a destruction order, it may order the offender to pay what it determines to be the reasonable expenses of destroying the dog and of keeping it pending its destruction.[503]

STEP SIX   Totality principle

If sentencing an offender for more than one offence, or where the offender is already serving a sentence, consider whether the total sentence is just and proportionate to the offending behaviour.

STEP SEVEN   Reasons

Section 174 of the Criminal Justice Act 2003 imposes a duty to give reasons for, and explain the effect of, the sentence.

STEP EIGHT   Consideration for remand time

Sentencers should take into consideration any remand time served in relation to the final sentence at this final step. The court should consider whether to give credit for time spent on remand in custody or on bail in accordance with sections 240 and 240A of the Criminal Justice Act 2003.

Owner or Person in Charge of a Dog Dangerously Out of Control in a Public Place   **SG-519**

Dangerous Dogs Act 1991 (section 3(1))

---

[498]   s.130 Powers of Criminal Courts (Sentencing) Act 2000
[499]   s.4(1)(b) Dangerous Dogs Act 1991
[500]   s.4(1)(a) ibid
[501]   s.4A(4) Dangerous Dogs Act 1991
[502]   s.4A(5) ibid
[503]   s.4(4)(b) ibid

Sentencing Guidelines

OWNER OR PERSON IN CHARGE ALLOWING A DOG TO BE IN A PRIVATE PLACE WHERE THE DOG IS NOT PERMITTED TO BE, WHICH MAKES A PERSON FEAR INJURY

Dangerous Dogs Act 1991 (section 3(3)(b))

Triable summarily only

Maximum: 6 months' custody

Offence range: Discharge — 6 months' custody

SG-520 STEP ONE Determining the offence category

The court should determine the offence category using the table below.

Category 1	Greater harm and higher culpability
Category 2	Greater harm **and** lower culpability; **or** lesser harm **and** higher culpability
Category 3	Lesser harm **and** lower culpability

The court should determine culpability and harm caused or intended, by reference **only** to the factors below, which comprise the principal factual elements of the offence. Where an offence does not fall squarely into a category, individual factors may require a degree of weighting before making an overall assessment and determining the appropriate offence category.

Factors indicating greater harm	Factors indicating lesser harm
Presence of children or others who are vulnerable because of personal circumstances	Low risk to the public
Injury to another animal(s)	**Factors indicating lower culpability**
Factors indicating higher culpability	Attempts made to regain control of dog and/or intervene
Statutory aggravating factors:	Provocation of dog without fault of the offender
Offence racially or religiously aggravated	Evidence of safety or control measures having been taken
Offence motivated by, or demonstrating, hostility to the victim based on his or her sexual orientation (or presumed sexual orientation)	Mental disorder or learning disability, where linked to the commission of the offence
Offence motivated by, or demonstrating, hostility to the victim based on the victim's disability (or presumed disability)	
Other aggravating factors:	
Failure to respond to warnings or concerns expressed by others about the dog's behaviour	
Goading, or allowing goading, of dog	
Dog used as weapon or to intimidate victim	
Offence motivated by, or demonstrating, hostility based on the victim's age, sex, gender identity (or presumed gender identity)	

SG-521 STEP TWO Starting point and category range

Having determined the category, the court should use the corresponding starting points to reach a sentence within the category range below. The starting point applies to all offenders irrespective of plea or previous convictions. A case of particular gravity, reflected by multiple features of culpability or harm in step 1, could merit upward adjustment from the starting point before further adjustment for aggravating or mitigating features, set out [below].

Offence Category	Starting Point (*Applicable to all offenders*)	Category Range (*Applicable to all offenders*)
Category 1	Medium level community order	Band C fine – 6 months' custody
Category 2	Band B fine	Band A fine – Low level community order
Category 3	Band A fine	Discharge – Band B fine

The table below contains a **non-exhaustive** list of additional factual elements providing the context of the offence and factors relating to the offender. Identify whether any combination of these, or other relevant factors, should result in an upward or downward adjustment from the starting point. In some cases, having considered these factors, it may be appropriate to move outside the identified category range.

When sentencing **category 1** offences, the court should also consider the custody threshold as follows:

- has the custody threshold been passed?
- if so, is it unavoidable that a custodial sentence be imposed?
- if so, can that sentence be suspended?

When sentencing **category 1 or 2** offences, the court should also consider the community order threshold as follows:

- has the community order threshold been passed?

Factors increasing seriousness	Factors reducing seriousness or reflecting personal mitigation
Statutory aggravating factors:	
Previous convictions, having regard to a) the nature of the offence to which the conviction relates and its relevance to the current offence; and b) the time that has elapsed since the conviction	No previous convictions or no relevant/recent convictions
	Isolated incident
Offence committed whilst on bail	No previous complaints against, or incidents involving, the dog
Other aggravating factors include:	Remorse
Location of the offence	Good character and/or exemplary conduct
Ongoing effect upon the victim and/or others	Evidence of responsible ownership
Failure to take adequate precautions to prevent dog escaping	Determination and/or demonstration of steps taken to address addiction or offending behaviour
Allowing person insufficiently experienced or trained, to be in charge of dog	Serious medical conditions requiring urgent, intensive or long-term treatment
Ill treatment or failure to ensure welfare needs of dog, where not charged separately	Age and/or lack of maturity where it affects the responsibility of the offender
Dog known to be prohibited	Mental disorder or learning disability, where not linked to the commission of the offence
Lack or loss of control of dog due to the influence of alcohol or drugs	Sole or primary carer for dependent relatives
Offence committed against those working in the public sector or providing a service to the public	
Established evidence of community impact	
Failure to comply with current court orders	
Offence committed whilst on licence	

[Steps Three to Eight are almost identical to those applicable to Owner or person in charge of a dog dangerously out of control in a public place, injuring any person (see **SG-518**), but differ in relation to Destruction order/contingent destruction order. That aspect of Step 5 is set out below.]   **SG-522**

Destruction order/contingent destruction order

In any case where the offender is not the owner of the dog, the owner must be given an opportunity to be present and make representations to the court.

The court **may** make a destruction order.[504] Alternatively, it **may** make a contingent destruction order imposing certain available conditions.[505] A contingent destruction order should specify the measures to be taken by the owner for keeping the dog under proper control, which include:

- muzzling;
- keeping on a lead;
- neutering in appropriate cases; and
- excluding it from a specified place.[506]

In reaching a decision, the court should consider the relevant circumstances which include:

- the incident — what degree of harm was caused by the dog's behaviour?

---

[504] s.4(1)(a) ibid
[505] s.4A(4) ibid
[506] s.4A(5) ibid

- past behaviour of the dog — is this an isolated incident or have there been previous warnings or incidents? and
- owner's character — is the owner a fit and proper person to own this particular dog?

Where the court makes a destruction order, it **may** order the offender to pay what it determines to be the reasonable expenses of destroying the dog and of keeping it pending its destruction.[507]

SG-523   Possession of a Prohibited Dog
                              Dangerous Dogs Act 1991 (section 1(3))

                  Breeding, Selling, Exchanging or Advertising a Prohibited Dog
                              Dangerous Dogs Act 1991 (section 1(2))

Triable only summarily

Maximum: 6 months' custody

Offence range: Discharge — 6 months' custody

SG-524 **STEP ONE Determining the offence category**

The court should determine the offence category using the table below.

Category 1	**Greater harm and higher culpability**
Category 2	Greater harm **or** higher culpability
Category 3	**Neither** greater harm **nor** higher culpability

The court should determine culpability and harm caused or intended, by reference **only** to the factors below, which comprise the principal factual elements of the offence. Where an offence does not fall squarely into a category, individual factors may require a degree of weighting before making an overall assessment and determining the appropriate offence category.

Factors indicating greater harm	**Factors indicating higher culpability**
Injury to person	Possessing a dog known to be prohibited
Injury to another animal(s)	Breeding from a dog known to be prohibited
	Selling, exchanging or advertising a dog known to be prohibited
	Offence committed for gain
	Dog used to threaten or intimidate
	Permitting fighting
	Training and/or possession of paraphernalia for dog fighting

SG-525 **STEP TWO Starting point and category range**

Having determined the category, the court should use the corresponding starting points to reach a sentence within the category range below. The starting point applies to all offenders irrespective of plea or previous convictions. A case of particular gravity, reflected by multiple features of culpability or harm in step 1, could merit upward adjustment from the starting point before further adjustment for aggravating or mitigating features, set out [below].

Offence Category	Starting Point (*Applicable to all offenders*)	Category Range (*Applicable to all offenders*)
Category 1	Medium level community order	Band C fine – 6 months' custody*
Category 2	Band C fine	Band A fine – Medium level community order
Category 3	Band A fine	Discharge – Band B fine

* Imprisonment is not available if the provisions of s.1(7) Dangerous Dogs Act 1991 apply

---

[507] s.4(4)(b) ibid

The table below contains a **non-exhaustive** list of additional factual elements providing the context of the offence and factors relating to the offender. Identify whether any combination of these, or other relevant factors, should result in an upward or downward adjustment from the starting point. In some cases, having considered these factors, it may be appropriate to move outside the identified category range.

When sentencing **category 1** offences, the court should also consider the custody threshold as follows:

- has the custody threshold been passed?
- if so, is it unavoidable that a custodial sentence be imposed?
- if so, can that sentence be suspended?

When sentencing **category 1 or 2** offences, the court should also consider the community order threshold as follows:

- has the community order threshold been passed?

Factors increasing seriousness	Factors reducing seriousness or reflecting personal mitigation
Statutory aggravating factors:	No previous convictions **or** no relevant/recent convictions
Previous convictions, having regard to a) the nature of the offence to which the conviction relates and its relevance to the current offence; and b) the time that has elapsed since the conviction	Unaware that dog was prohibited type despite reasonable efforts to identify type
Offence committed whilst on bail	Evidence of safety or control measures having been taken by owner
Other aggravating factors include:	Prosecution results from owner notification
Presence of children or others who are vulnerable because of personal circumstances	Remorse
Ill treatment or failure to ensure welfare needs of dog, where not charged separately	Good character and/or exemplary conduct
Established evidence of community impact	Evidence of responsible ownership
Failure to comply with current court orders	Determination and/or demonstration of steps taken to address addiction or offending behaviour
Offence committed whilst on licence	Serious medical conditions requiring urgent, intensive or long-term treatment
	Age and/or lack of maturity where it affects the responsibility of the offender
	Lapse of time since the offence where this is not the fault of the offender
	Mental disorder or learning disability
	Sole or primary carer for dependent relatives

[Steps Three to Eight are almost identical to those applicable to Owner or person in charge of a dog dangerously out of control in a public place, injuring any person (see **SG-518**), but differ in relation to Destruction order/contingent destruction order. That aspect of Step 5 is set out below.]   **SG-526**

Destruction order/contingent destruction order

The court **shall** make a destruction order unless the court is satisfied that the dog would not constitute a danger to public safety.[508]

In reaching a decision, the court should consider the relevant circumstances which include:

- danger to the public — what is the potential risk of harm posed by the dog?
- behaviour of the dog — have there been any warnings or incidents involving the dog? and
- owner's character — is the owner a fit and proper person to own this particular dog?

If the court does not make a destruction order, the court **shall** make a contingent destruction order providing that unless the dog is exempted from the prohibition within two months it shall be destroyed.[509] Statutory procedures and conditions automatically apply to exempted dogs and no other conditions can be imposed.[510] Where the offender is the owner of the dog, it would not normally be appropriate to make a contingent destruction order in conjunction with a disqualification order.

---

[508] s.4(1)(a) ibid
[509] s.4A(1) ibid
[510] The Dangerous Dogs Compensation and Exemption Schemes Order 1991 SI No. 1744 (as amended by The Dangerous Dogs Compensation and Exemption Schemes (Amendment) Order 1991 SI No. 2297)

Furthermore, the court **must not** transfer ownership of the dog to another.[511]

Where the court makes a destruction order, it **may** order the offender to pay what it determines to be the reasonable expenses of destroying the dog and of keeping it pending its destruction.[512]

SG-527   ANNEX: FINE BANDS AND COMMUNITY ORDERS

[The tables set out here are also set out in the Magistrates' Court Sentencing Guidelines, which includes further guidance on fines and community orders: see **SG-306** and **SG-330**.]

PART 26   SEXUAL OFFENCES

[These Guidelines replace the Guidelines reproduced in Part 8 of the Sentencing Guidelines published in Supplement 1 with effect from 1 April 2014.]

SG-528   Applicability of guideline

In accordance with section 120 of the Coroners and Justice Act 2009, the Sentencing Council issues this definitive guideline. It applies to all offenders aged 18 and older, who are sentenced on or after 1 April 2014.

…This guideline applies only to offenders aged 18 and older. General principles to be considered in the sentencing of youths are in the Sentencing Guidelines Council's definitive guideline, *Overarching Principles – Sentencing Youths*.

SG-529   *Structure, ranges and starting points*

For the purposes of section 125(3)–(4) of the Coroners and Justice Act 2009, the guideline specifies *offence ranges* — the range of sentences appropriate for each type of offence. Within each offence, the Council has specified different *categories* which reflect varying degrees of seriousness. The offence range is split into *category ranges* — sentences appropriate for each level of seriousness. The Council has also identified a starting point within each category.

Starting points define the position within a category range from which to start calculating the provisional sentence. **Starting points apply to all offences within the corresponding category and are applicable to all offenders, in all cases.** Once the starting point is established, the court should consider further aggravating and mitigating factors and previous convictions so as to adjust the sentence within the range. Starting points and ranges apply to all offenders, whether they have pleaded guilty or been convicted after trial. Credit for a guilty plea is taken into consideration only at step four in the decision making process, after the appropriate sentence has been identified.

Information on ancillary orders is set out at Annex A [see **SG-657**]. Information on historic offences is set out at annexes B and C on [see **SG-658** and **SG-659**].

Information on community orders and fine bands is set out at Annex D [not reproduced here but see **SG-306** and **SG-330**].

SG-530   RAPE
                                Sexual Offences Act 2003 (section 1)

[For rape of a child under 13, see **SG-546**.]

Triable only on indictment
Maximum: Life imprisonment

Offence range: 4–19 years' custody

This is a serious specified offence for the purposes of sections 224 and 225(2) (life sentence for serious offences) of the Criminal Justice Act 2003.

---

[511] s.1(2)(b) Dangerous Dogs Act 1991
[512] s.4(4)(b) ibid

For offences committed on or after 3 December 2012, this is an offence listed in Part 1 of Schedule 15B for the purposes of sections 224A (life sentence for second listed offence) of the Criminal Justice Act 2003.

For convictions on or after 3 December 2012 (irrespective of the date of commission of the offence), this is a specified offence for the purposes of section 226A (extended sentence for certain violent or sexual offences) of the Criminal Justice Act 2003.

STEP ONE Determining the offence category   SG-531

The court should determine which categories of harm and culpability the offence falls into by reference **only** to the tables below.

Offences may be of such severity, for example involving a campaign of rape, that sentences of 20 years and above may be appropriate.

Harm	
Category 1	• The extreme nature of one or more category 2 factors or the extreme impact caused by a combination of category 2 factors **may** elevate to category 1
Category 2	• Severe psychological or physical harm • Pregnancy or STI as a consequence of offence • Additional degradation/humiliation • Abduction • Prolonged detention/sustained incident • Violence or threats of violence (beyond that which is inherent in the offence) • Forced/uninvited entry into victim's home • Victim is particularly vulnerable due to personal circumstances*
Category 3	Factor(s) in categories 1 and 2 not present

* for children under 13 please refer to the guideline [at **SG-546**]

Culpability	
A	**B**
• Significant degree of planning • Offender acts together with others to commit the offence • Use of alcohol/drugs on victim to facilitate the offence • Abuse of trust • Previous violence against victim • Offence committed in course of burglary • Recording of the offence • Commercial exploitation and/or motivation • Offence racially or religiously aggravated • Offence motivated by, or demonstrating, hostility to the victim based on his or her sexual orientation (or presumed sexual orientation) or transgender identity (or presumed transgender identity) • Offence motivated by, or demonstrating, hostility to the victim based on his or her disability (or presumed disability)	Factor(s) in category A not present

STEP TWO Starting point and category range   SG-532

Having determined the category, the court should use the corresponding starting points to reach a sentence within the category range below. The starting point applies to all offenders irrespective of plea or previous convictions. Having determined the starting point, step two allows further adjustment for aggravating or mitigating features set out below.

A case of particular gravity, reflected by multiple features of culpability or harm in step one, could merit upward adjustment from the starting point before further adjustment for aggravating or mitigating features, set out below.

Sentencing Guidelines

	A	B
Category 1	**Starting point** 15 years' custody **Category range** 13–19 years' custody	**Starting point** 12 years' custody **Category range** 10–15 years' custody
Category 2	**Starting point** 10 years' custody **Category range** 9–13 years' custody	**Starting point** 8 years' custody **Category range** 7–9 years' custody
Category 3	**Starting point** 7 years' custody **Category range** 6–9 years' custody	**Starting point** 5 years' custody **Category range** 4–7 years' custody

The table below contains a **non-exhaustive** list of additional factual elements providing the context of the offence and factors relating to the offender. Identify whether any combination of these, or other relevant factors, should result in an upward or downward adjustment from the starting point. **In particular, relevant recent convictions are likely to result in an upward adjustment.** In some cases, having considered these factors, it may be appropriate to move outside the identified category range.

Aggravating factors

Statutory aggravating factors

- Previous convictions, having regard to a) the nature of the offence to which the conviction relates and its relevance to the current offence; and b) the time that has elapsed since the conviction
- Offence committed whilst on bail

Other aggravating factors

- Specific targeting of a particularly vulnerable victim
- Ejaculation (where not taken into account at step one)
- Blackmail or other threats made (where not taken into account at step one)
- Location of offence
- Timing of offence
- Use of weapon or other item to frighten or injure
- Victim compelled to leave their home (including victims of domestic violence)
- Failure to comply with current court orders
- Offence committed whilst on licence
- Exploiting contact arrangements with a child to commit an offence
- Presence of others, especially children
- Any steps taken to prevent the victim reporting an incident, obtaining assistance and/or from assisting or supporting the prosecution
- Attempts to dispose of or conceal evidence
- Commission of offence whilst under the influence of alcohol or drugs

---

Mitigating factors

- No previous convictions **or** no relevant/recent convictions
- Remorse
- Previous good character and/or exemplary conduct*
- Age and/or lack of maturity where it affects the responsibility of the offender
- Mental disorder or learning disability, particularly where linked to the commission of the offence

* Previous good character/exemplary conduct is different from having no previous convictions. The more serious the offence, the less the weight which should normally be attributed to this factor. Where previous good character/exemplary conduct has been used to facilitate the offence, this mitigation should not normally be allowed and such conduct may constitute an aggravating factor.

In the context of this offence, previous good character/exemplary conduct should not normally be given any significant weight and will not normally justify a reduction in what would otherwise be the appropriate sentence.

STEP THREE Consider any factors which indicate a reduction, such as assistance to the prosecution   SG-533

The court should take into account sections 73 and 74 of the Serious Organised Crime and Police Act 2005 (assistance by defendants: reduction or review of sentence) and any other rule of law by virtue of which an offender may receive a discounted sentence in consequence of assistance given (or offered) to the prosecutor or investigator.

STEP FOUR Reduction for guilty pleas

The court should take account of any potential reduction for a guilty plea in accordance with section 144 of the Criminal Justice Act 2003 and the *Guilty Plea* guideline.

STEP FIVE Dangerousness

The court should consider whether having regard to the criteria contained in Chapter 5 of Part 12 of the Criminal Justice Act 2003 it would be appropriate to award a life sentence (section 224A or section 225(2)) or an extended sentence (section 226A). When sentencing offenders to a life sentence under these provisions, the notional determinate sentence should be used as the basis for the setting of a minimum term.

STEP SIX Totality principle

If sentencing an offender for more than one offence, or where the offender is already serving a sentence, consider whether the total sentence is just and proportionate to the offending behaviour.

STEP SEVEN Ancillary orders

The court must consider whether to make any ancillary orders. The court must also consider what other requirements or provisions may *automatically* apply. Further information is included at Annex A [see SG-657].

STEP EIGHT Reasons

Section 174 of the Criminal Justice Act 2003 imposes a duty to give reasons for, and explain the effect of, the sentence.

STEP NINE Consideration for time spent on bail

The court must consider whether to give credit for time spent on bail in accordance with section 240A of the Criminal Justice Act 2003.

ASSAULT BY PENETRATION   SG-534

Sexual Offences Act 2003 (section 2)

Triable only on indictment
Maximum: Life imprisonment

Offence range: Community order — 19 years' custody

[Repeats information as to the CJA 2003, ss. 224, 225(2), 224A and 226A which is set out at **SG-530**.]

STEP ONE Determining the offence category   SG-535

The court should determine which categories of harm and culpability the offence falls into by reference **only** to the tables below.

Harm	
Category 1	• The extreme nature of one or more category 2 factors or the extreme impact caused by a combination of category 2 factors **may** elevate to category 1
Category 2	• Severe psychological or physical harm • Penetration using large or dangerous object(s) • Additional degradation/humiliation • Abduction • Prolonged detention/sustained incident • Violence or threats of violence (beyond that which is inherent in the offence) • Forced/uninvited entry into victim's home • Victim is particularly vulnerable due to personal circumstances *
Category 3	Factor(s) in categories 1 and 2 not present

*for children under 13 please refer to the guideline [at **SG-550**]

Culpability	
A	**B**
• Significant degree of planning • Offender acts together with others to commit the offence • Use of alcohol/drugs on victim to facilitate the offence • Abuse of trust • Previous violence against victim • Offence committed in course of burglary • Recording of the offence • Commercial exploitation and/or motivation • Offence racially or religiously aggravated • Offence motivated by, or demonstrating, hostility to the victim based on his or her sexual orientation (or presumed sexual orientation) or transgender identity (or presumed transgender identity) • Offence motivated by, or demonstrating, hostility to the victim based on his or her disability (or presumed disability)	Factor(s) in category A not present

SG-536   **STEP TWO**   **Starting point and category range**

Having determined the category, the court should use the corresponding starting points to reach a sentence within the category range below. The starting point applies to all offenders irrespective of plea or previous convictions.

Having determined the starting point, step two allows further adjustment for aggravating or mitigating features, set out below.

A case of particular gravity, reflected by multiple features of culpability or harm in step one, could merit upward adjustment from the starting point before further adjustment for aggravating or mitigating features, set out below.

Where there is a sufficient prospect of rehabilitation, a community order with a sex offender treatment programme requirement under section 202 of the Criminal Justice Act 2003 can be a proper alternative to a short or moderate length custodial sentence.

	A	B
Category 1	**Starting point** 15 years' custody **Category range** 13–19 years' custody	**Starting point** 12 years' custody **Category range** 10–15 years' custody
Category 2	**Starting point** 8 years' custody **Category range** 5–13 years' custody	**Starting point** 6 years' custody **Category range** 4–9 years' custody
Category 3	**Starting point** 4 years' custody **Category range** 2–6 years' custody	**Starting point** 2 years' custody **Category range** High level community order—4 years' custody

The table below contains a **non-exhaustive** list of additional factual elements providing the context of the offence and factors relating to the offender. Identify whether any combination of these, or other relevant factors, should result in an upward or downward adjustment from the starting point. **In particular, relevant recent convictions are likely to result in an upward adjustment.** In some cases, having considered these factors, it may be appropriate to move outside the identified category range.

When sentencing appropriate **category 3** offences, the court should also consider the custody threshold as follows:

• has the custody threshold been passed?
• if so, is it unavoidable that a custodial sentence be imposed?
• if so, can that sentence be suspended?

Aggravating factors

Statutory aggravating factors
- Previous convictions, having regard to a) the nature of the offence to which the conviction relates and its relevance to the current offence; and b) the time that has elapsed since the conviction
- Offence committed whilst on bail

Other aggravating factors
- Specific targeting of a particularly vulnerable victim
- Blackmail or other threats made (where not taken into account at step one)
- Location of offence
- Timing of offence
- Use of weapon or other item to frighten or injure
- Victim compelled to leave their home (including victims of domestic violence)
- Failure to comply with current court orders
- Offence committed whilst on licence
- Exploiting contact arrangements with a child to commit an offence
- Presence of others, especially children
- Any steps taken to prevent the victim reporting an incident, obtaining assistance and/or from assisting or supporting the prosecution
- Attempts to dispose of or conceal evidence
- Commission of offence whilst under the influence of alcohol or drugs

Mitigating factors

- No previous convictions **or** no relevant/recent convictions
- Remorse
- Previous good character and/or exemplary conduct*
- Age and/or lack of maturity where it affects the responsibility of the offender
- Mental disorder or learning disability, particularly where linked to the commission of the offence

* [Repeats note as to distinction between previous good character/exemplary conduct and having no previous convictions and how to deal with them in respect of the offence: see **SG-532** for the full text.]

STEPS THREE to NINE

SG-537

[These are in the same terms as those applicable to rape: see **SG-533**.]

Sexual Assault

SG-538

Sexual Offences Act 2003 (section 3)

Triable either way
Maximum: 10 years' custody

Offence range: Community order—7 years' custody

For convictions on or after 3 December 2012 (irrespective of the date of commission of the offence), this is a specified offence for the purposes of section 226A (extended sentence for certain violent or sexual offences) of the Criminal Justice Act 2003.

STEP ONE Determining the offence category

SG-539

The court should determine which categories of harm and culpability the offence falls into by reference **only** to the tables below.

Harm	
Category 1	• Severe psychological or physical harm • Abduction • Violence or threats of violence • Forced/uninvited entry into victim's home
Category 2	• Touching of naked genitalia or naked breasts • Prolonged detention/sustained incident • Additional degradation/humiliation • Victim is particularly vulnerable due to personal circumstances *
Category 3	Factor(s) in categories 1 and 2 not present

*for children under 13 please refer to the guideline [at **SG-554**]

Culpability	
A	**B**
• Significant degree of planning • Offender acts together with others to commit the offence • Use of alcohol/drugs on victim to facilitate the offence • Abuse of trust • Previous violence against victim • Offence committed in course of burglary • Recording of offence • Commercial exploitation and/or motivation • Offence racially or religiously aggravated • Offence motivated by, or demonstrating, hostility to the victim based on his or her sexual orientation (or presumed sexual orientation) or transgender identity (or presumed transgender identity) • Offence motivated by, or demonstrating, hostility to the victim based on his or her disability (or presumed disability)	Factor(s) in category A not present

SG-540   STEP TWO   **Starting point and category range**

Having determined the category, the court should use the corresponding starting points to reach a sentence within the category range below. The starting point applies to all offenders irrespective of plea or previous convictions. Having determined the starting point, step two allows further adjustment for aggravating or mitigating features, set out below.

A case of particular gravity, reflected by multiple features of culpability or harm in step one, could merit upward adjustment from the starting point before further adjustment for aggravating or mitigating features, set out below.

Where there is a sufficient prospect of rehabilitation, a community order with a sex offender treatment programme requirement under section 202 of the Criminal Justice Act 2003 can be a proper alternative to a short or moderate length custodial sentence.

	A	**B**
Category 1	**Starting point** 4 years' custody **Category range** 3–7 years' custody	**Starting point** 2 years 6 months' custody **Category range** 2–4 years' custody
Category 2	**Starting point** 2 years' custody **Category range** 1–4 years' custody	**Starting point** 1 year's custody **Category range** High level community order–2 years' custody
Category 3	**Starting point** 26 weeks' custody **Category range** High level community order – 1 year's custody	**Starting point** High level community order **Category range** Medium level community order – 26 weeks' custody

The table below contains a **non-exhaustive** list of additional factual elements providing the context of the offence and factors relating to the offender. Identify whether any combination of these, or other relevant factors, should result in an upward or downward adjustment from the starting point. **In particular, relevant recent convictions are likely to result in an upward adjustment.** In some cases, having considered these factors, it may be appropriate to move outside the identified category range.

When sentencing appropriate **category 2 or 3 offences**, the court should also consider the custody threshold as follows:

- has the custody threshold been passed?
- if so, is it unavoidable that a custodial sentence be imposed?
- if so, can that sentence be suspended?

Aggravating factors
Statutory aggravating factors • Previous convictions, having regard to a) the nature of the offence to which the conviction relates and its relevance to the current offence; and b) the time that has elapsed since the conviction • Offence committed whilst on bail *Other aggravating factors* • Specific targeting of a particularly vulnerable victim • Blackmail or other threats made (where not taken into account at step one) • Location of offence • Timing of offence • Use of weapon or other item to frighten or injure • Victim compelled to leave their home (including victims of domestic violence) • Failure to comply with current court orders • Offence committed whilst on licence • Exploiting contact arrangements with a child to commit an offence • Presence of others, especially children • Any steps taken to prevent the victim reporting an incident, obtaining assistance and/or from assisting or supporting the prosecution • Attempts to dispose of or conceal evidence • Commission of offence whilst under the influence of alcohol or drugs

Mitigating factors
• No previous convictions **or** no relevant/recent convictions • Remorse • Previous good character and/or exemplary conduct* • Age and/or lack of maturity where it affects the responsibility of the offender • Mental disorder or learning disability, particularly where linked to the commission of the offence • Demonstration of steps taken to address offending behaviour

* Previous good character/exemplary conduct is different from having no previous convictions. The more serious the offence, the less the weight which should normally be attributed to this factor. Where previous good character/exemplary conduct has been used to facilitate the offence, this mitigation should not normally be allowed and such conduct may constitute an aggravating factor.

STEP THREE   SG-541
Consider any factors which indicate a reduction, such as assistance to the prosecution

The court should take into account sections 73 and 74 of the Serious Organised Crime and Police Act 2005 (assistance by defendants: reduction or review of sentence) and any other rule of law by virtue of which an offender may receive a discounted sentence in consequence of assistance given (or offered) to the prosecutor or investigator.

STEP FOUR Reduction for guilty pleas
The court should take account of any potential reduction for a guilty plea in accordance with section 144 of the Criminal Justice Act 2003 and the *Guilty Plea* guideline.

STEP FIVE Dangerousness
The court should consider whether having regard to the criteria contained in Chapter 5 of Part 12 of the Criminal Justice Act 2003 it would be appropriate to award an extended sentence (section 226A).

STEPS SIX to NINE

[These are in the same terms as those applicable to rape: see **SG-533**.]

SG-542   Causing a Person to Engage in Sexual Activity Without Consent

Sexual Offences Act 2003 (section 4)

Triable only on indictment (if penetration involved)
• otherwise, triable either way

Maximum: Life imprisonment (if penetration involved)
• otherwise, 10 years

Offence range: Community order — 7 years' custody (if no penetration involved) / 19 years' custody (if penetration involved)

[Repeats information as to the CJA 2003, ss. 224, 225(2), 224A and 226A which is set out at **SG-530**.]

SG-543   STEP ONE   **Determining the offence category**

The court should determine which categories of harm and culpability the offence falls into by reference **only** to the tables below.

Harm	
Category 1	• The extreme nature of one or more category 2 factors or the extreme impact caused by a combination of category 2 factors **may** elevate to category 1
Category 2	• Severe psychological or physical harm • Penetration using large or dangerous object(s) • Pregnancy or STI as a consequence of offence • Additional degradation/humiliation • Abduction • Prolonged detention/sustained incident • Violence or threats of violence • Forced/uninvited entry into victim's home • Victim is particularly vulnerable due to personal circumstances *
Category 3	Factor(s) in categories 1 and 2 not present

* for children under 13 please refer to the guideline [at **SG-546**]

Culpability	
A	B
• Significant degree of planning • Offender acts together with others to commit the offence • Use of alcohol/drugs on victim to facilitate the offence • Abuse of trust • Previous violence against victim • Offence committed in course of burglary • Recording of the offence • Commercial exploitation and/or motivation • Offence racially or religiously aggravated • Offence motivated by, or demonstrating, hostility to the victim based on his or her sexual orientation (or presumed sexual orientation) or transgender identity (or presumed transgender identity) • Offence motivated by, or demonstrating, hostility to the victim based on his or her disability (or presumed disability)	Factor(s) in category A not present

SG-544   STEP TWO   **Starting point and category range**

Having determined the category, the court should use the corresponding starting points to reach a sentence within the category range below. The starting point applies to all offenders irrespective of plea or previous convictions.

Having determined the starting point, step two allows further adjustment for aggravating or mitigating features, set out below.

A case of particular gravity, reflected by multiple features of culpability or harm in step one, could merit upward adjustment from the starting point before further adjustment for aggravating or mitigating features, set out below.

Where there is a sufficient prospect of rehabilitation, a community order with a sex offender treatment programme requirement under section 202 of the Criminal Justice Act 2003 can be a proper alternative to a short or moderate length custodial sentence.

Where offence involved penetration		
	A	**B**
Category 1	**Starting point** 15 years' custody **Category range** 13–19 years' custody	**Starting point** 12 years' custody **Category range** 10–15 years' custody
Category 2	**Starting point** 8 years' custody **Category range** 5–13 years' custody	**Starting point** 6 years' custody **Category range** 4–9 years' custody
Category 3	**Starting point** 4 years' custody **Category range** 2–6 years' custody	**Starting point** 2 years' custody **Category range** High level community order–4 years' custody

Where offence did not involve penetration		
	A	**B**
Category 1	**Starting point** 4 years' custody **Category range** 3–7 years' custody	**Starting point** 2 years 6 months' custody **Category range** 2–4 years' custody
Category 2	**Starting point** 2 years' custody **Category range** 1–4 years' custody	**Starting point** 1 year's custody **Category range** High level community order — 2 years' custody
Category 3	**Starting point** 26 weeks' custody **Category range** High level community order — 1 year's custody	**Starting point** High level community order **Category range** Medium level community order — 26 weeks' custody

The table below contains a **non-exhaustive** list of additional factual elements providing the context of the offence and factors relating to the offender. Identify whether any combination of these, or other relevant factors, should result in an upward or downward adjustment from the starting point. **In particular, relevant recent convictions are likely to result in an upward adjustment.** In some cases, having considered these factors, it may be appropriate to move outside the identified category range.

When sentencing appropriate **category 2 or 3** offences, the court should also consider the custody threshold as follows:

* has the custody threshold been passed?
* if so, is it unavoidable that a custodial sentence be imposed?
* if so, can that sentence be suspended?

Aggravating factors
Statutory aggravating factors
• Previous convictions, having regard to a) the nature of the offence to which the conviction relates and its relevance to the current offence; and b) the time that has elapsed since the conviction
• Offence committed whilst on bail

Other aggravating factors
- Specific targeting of a particularly vulnerable victim
- Ejaculation (where not taken into account at step one)
- Blackmail or other threats made (where not taken into account at step one)
- Location of offence
- Timing of offence
- Use of weapon or other item to frighten or injure
- Victim compelled to leave their home (including victims of domestic violence)
- Failure to comply with current court orders
- Offence committed whilst on licence
- Exploiting contact arrangements with a child to commit an offence
- Presence of others, especially children
- Any steps taken to prevent the victim reporting an incident, obtaining assistance and/or from assisting or supporting the prosecution
- Attempts to dispose of or conceal evidence
- Commission of offence whilst under the influence of alcohol or drugs

Mitigating factors

- No previous convictions **or** no relevant/recent convictions
- Remorse
- Previous good character and/or exemplary conduct*
- Age and/or lack of maturity where it affects the responsibility of the offender
- Mental disorder or learning disability, particularly where linked to the commission of the offence

* [Repeats note as to distinction between previous good character/exemplary conduct and having no previous convictions and how to deal with them in respect of the offence: see **SG-532** for the full text.]

SG-545 STEPS THREE TO NINE

[These are in the same terms as those applicable to rape: see **SG-533**.]

SG-546   Rape of a Child Under 13
                          Sexual Offences Act 2003 (section 5)

Triable only on indictment
Maximum: Life imprisonment

Offence range: 6–19 years' custody

[Repeats information as to the CJA 2003, ss. 224, 225(2), 224A and 226A, which is set out at **SG-530**.]

SG-547 STEP ONE Determining the offence category

The court should determine which categories of harm and culpability the offence falls into by reference **only** to the tables below.

> **Offences may be of such severity, for example involving a campaign of rape, that sentences of 20 years and above may be appropriate.**
> When dealing with the statutory offence of rape of a child under 13, the court may be faced with a wide range of offending behaviour.
>   Sentencers should have particular regard to the fact that these offences are not only committed through force or fear of force but may include exploitative behaviour towards a child which should be considered to indicate high culpability.
>   This guideline is designed to deal with the majority of offending behaviour which deserves a significant custodial sentence; the starting points and ranges reflect the fact that such offending merits such an approach. There may also be **exceptional** cases, where a lengthy community order with a requirement to participate in a sex offender treatment programme may be the best way of changing the offender's behaviour and of protecting the public by preventing any repetition of the offence. This guideline may not be appropriate where the sentencer is satisfied that on the available evidence, and in the absence of exploitation, a young or particularly immature defendant genuinely believed, on reasonable grounds, that the victim was aged 16 or over and that they were engaging in lawful sexual activity.
>   Sentencers are reminded that if sentencing outside the guideline they must be satisfied that it would be contrary to the interests of justice to follow the guideline.

Harm	
Category 1	• The extreme nature of one or more category 2 factors or the extreme impact caused by a combination of category 2 factors **may** elevate to category 1
Category 2	• Severe psychological or physical harm • Pregnancy or STI as a consequence of offence • Additional degradation/humiliation • Abduction • Prolonged detention /sustained incident • Violence or threats of violence • Forced/uninvited entry into victim's home • Child is particularly vulnerable due to extreme youth and/or personal circumstances
Category 3	Factor(s) in categories 1 and 2 not present

Culpability	
A	B
• Significant degree of planning • Offender acts together with others to commit the offence • Use of alcohol/drugs on victim to facilitate the offence • Grooming behaviour used against victim • Abuse of trust • Previous violence against victim • Offence committed in course of burglary • Sexual images of victim recorded, retained, solicited or shared • Deliberate isolation of victim • Commercial exploitation and/or motivation • Offence racially or religiously aggravated • Offence motivated by, or demonstrating, hostility to the victim based on his or her sexual orientation (or presumed sexual orientation) or transgender identity (or presumed transgender identity) • Offence motivated by, or demonstrating, hostility to the victim based on his or her disability (or presumed disability)	Factor(s) in category A not present

STEP TWO Starting point and category range

SG-548

Having determined the category, the court should use the corresponding starting points to reach a sentence within the category range below. The starting point applies to all offenders irrespective of plea or previous convictions. Having determined the starting point, step two allows further adjustment for aggravating or mitigating features, set out below.

A case of particular gravity, reflected by multiple features of culpability or harm in step one, could merit upward adjustment from the starting point before further adjustment for aggravating or mitigating features, set out below.

Sentencers should also note the wording set out at step one which may be applicable in exceptional cases.

	A	B
Category 1	**Starting point** 16 years' custody **Category range** 13–19 years' custody	**Starting point** 13 years' custody **Category range** 11–17 years' custody
Category 2	**Starting point** 13 years' custody **Category range** 11–17 years' custody	**Starting point** 10 years' custody **Category range** 8–13 years' custody
Category 3	**Starting point** 10 years' custody **Category range** 8–13 years' custody	**Starting point** 8 years' custody **Category range** 6–11 years' custody

The table below contains a **non-exhaustive** list of additional factual elements providing the context of the offence and factors relating to the offender. Identify whether any combination of these, or other relevant factors, should result in an upward or downward adjustment from the starting point. **In particular, relevant recent convictions are likely to result in an upward adjustment.** In some cases, having considered these factors, it may be appropriate to move outside the identified category range.

Aggravating factors

Statutory aggravating factors
- Previous convictions, having regard to a) the nature of the offence to which the conviction relates and its relevance to the current offence; and b) the time that has elapsed since the conviction
- Offence committed whilst on bail

Other aggravating factors
- Specific targeting of a particularly vulnerable child
- Ejaculation (where not taken into account at step one)
- Blackmail or other threats made (where not taken into account at step one)
- Location of offence
- Timing of offence
- Use of weapon or other item to frighten or injure
- Victim compelled to leave their home, school, etc
- Failure to comply with current court orders
- Offence committed whilst on licence
- Exploiting contact arrangements with a child to commit an offence
- Presence of others, especially other children
- Any steps taken to prevent the victim reporting an incident, obtaining assistance and/or from assisting or supporting the prosecution
- Attempts to dispose of or conceal evidence
- Commission of offence whilst offender under the influence of alcohol or drugs
- Victim encouraged to recruit others

Mitigating factors

- No previous convictions **or** no relevant/recent convictions
- Remorse
- Previous good character and/or exemplary conduct*
- Age and/or lack of maturity where it affects the responsibility of the offender
- Mental disorder or learning disability, particularly where linked to the commission of the offence

---

* [Repeats note as to distinction between previous good character/exemplary conduct and having no previous convictions and how to deal with them in respect of the offence: see **SG-532** for the full text.]

SG-549   **STEPS THREE TO NINE**

[These are in the same terms as those applicable to rape: see **SG-533**.]

SG-550   Assault of a Child Under 13 by Penetration
                               Sexual Offences Act 2003 (section 6)

Triable only on indictment
Maximum: Life imprisonment

Offence range: 2–19 years' custody
[Repeats information as to the CJA 2003, ss. 224, 225(2), 224A and 226A, which is set out at **SG-530**.]

SG-551   **STEP ONE Determining the offence category**

The court should determine which categories of harm and culpability the offence falls into by reference **only** to the tables below.

Harm	
Category 1	The extreme nature of one or more category 2 factors or the extreme impact caused by a combination of category 2 factors **may** elevate to category 1
Category 2	• Severe psychological or physical harm • Penetration using large or dangerous object(s) • Additional degradation/humiliation • Abduction • Prolonged detention /sustained incident • Violence or threats of violence • Forced/uninvited entry into victim's home • Child is particularly vulnerable due to extreme youth and/or personal circumstances
Category 3	Factor(s) in categories 1 and 2 not present

Culpability	
A	**B**
• Significant degree of planning • Offender acts together with others to commit the offence • Use of alcohol/drugs on victim to facilitate the offence • Grooming behaviour used against victim • Abuse of trust • Previous violence against victim • Offence committed in course of burglary • Sexual images of victim recorded, retained, solicited or shared • Deliberate isolation of victim • Commercial exploitation and/or motivation • Offence racially or religiously aggravated • Offence motivated by, or demonstrating, hostility to the victim based on his or her sexual orientation (or presumed sexual orientation) or transgender identity (or presumed transgender identity) • Offence motivated by, or demonstrating, hostility to the victim based on his or her disability (or presumed disability)	Factor(s) in category A not present

STEP TWO Starting point and category range   SG-552

Having determined the category, the court should use the corresponding starting points to reach a sentence within the category range below. The starting point applies to all offenders irrespective of plea or previous convictions. Having determined the starting point, step two allows further adjustment for aggravating or mitigating features, set out below.

A case of particular gravity, reflected by multiple features of culpability or harm in step one, could merit upward adjustment from the starting point before further adjustment for aggravating or mitigating features, set out below.

	A	**B**
Category 1	**Starting point** 16 years' custody **Category range** 13–19 years' custody	**Starting point** 13 years' custody **Category range** 11–17 years' custody
Category 2	**Starting point** 11 years' custody **Category range** 7–15 years' custody	**Starting point** 8 years' custody **Category range** 5–13 years' custody
Category 3	**Starting point** 6 years' custody **Category range** 4–9 years' custody	**Starting point** 4 years' custody **Category range** 2–6 years' custody

Sentencing Guidelines

The table below contains a **non-exhaustive** list of additional factual elements providing the context of the offence and factors relating to the offender. Identify whether any combination of these, or other relevant factors, should result in an upward or downward adjustment from the starting point. **In particular, relevant recent convictions are likely to result in an upward adjustment.** In some cases, having considered these factors, it may be appropriate to move outside the identified category range.

Aggravating factors

Statutory aggravating factors
- Previous convictions, having regard to a) the nature of the offence to which the conviction relates and its relevance to the current offence; and b) the time that has elapsed since the conviction
- Offence committed whilst on bail

Other aggravating factors
- Specific targeting of a particularly vulnerable child
- Blackmail or other threats made (where not taken into account at step one)
- Location of offence
- Timing of offence
- Use of weapon or other item to frighten or injure
- Victim compelled to leave their home, school etc
- Failure to comply with current court orders
- Offence committed whilst on licence
- Exploiting contact arrangements with a child to commit an offence
- Presence of others, especially other children
- Any steps taken to prevent the victim reporting an incident, obtaining assistance and/or from assisting or supporting the prosecution
- Attempts to dispose of or conceal evidence
- Commission of offence whilst under the influence of alcohol or drugs
- Victim encouraged to recruit others

Mitigating factors

- No previous convictions **or** no relevant/recent convictions
- Remorse
- Previous good character and/or exemplary conduct*
- Age and/or lack of maturity where it affects the responsibility of the offender
- Mental disorder or learning disability, particularly where linked to the commission of the offence

---

* [Repeats note as to distinction between previous good character/exemplary conduct and having no previous convictions and how to deal with them in respect of the offence: see **SG-532** for the full text.]

SG-553 STEPS THREE TO NINE

[These are in the same terms as those applicable to rape: see **SG-533**.]

SG-554   SEXUAL ASSAULT OF A CHILD UNDER 13
                              Sexual Offences Act 2003 (section 7)

Triable either way
Maximum: 14 years' custody

Offence range: Community order — 9 years' custody

For offences committed on or after 3 December 2012, this is an offence listed in Part 1 of Schedule 15B for the purposes of section 224A (life sentence for second listed offence) of the Criminal Justice Act 2003.

For convictions on or after 3 December 2012 (irrespective of the date of commission of the offence), this is a specified offence for the purposes of section 226A (extended sentence for certain violent or sexual offences) of the Criminal Justice Act 2003.

SG-555 STEP ONE Determining the offence category

The court should determine which categories of harm and culpability the offence falls into by reference **only** to the tables below.

Harm	
Category 1	• Severe psychological or physical harm • Abduction • Violence or threats of violence • Forced/uninvited entry into victim's home
Category 2	• Touching of naked genitalia or naked breast area • Prolonged detention/sustained incident • Additional degradation/humiliation • Child is particularly vulnerable due to extreme youth and/or personal circumstances
Category 3	Factor(s) in categories 1 and 2 not present

Culpability	
A	**B**
• Significant degree of planning • Offender acts together with others to commit the offence • Use of alcohol/drugs on victim to facilitate the offence • Grooming behaviour used against victim • Abuse of trust • Previous violence against victim • Offence committed in course of burglary • Sexual images of victim recorded, retained, solicited or shared • Deliberate isolation of victim • Commercial exploitation and/or motivation • Offence racially or religiously aggravated • Offence motivated by, or demonstrating, hostility to the victim based on his or her sexual orientation (or presumed sexual orientation) or transgender identity (or presumed transgender identity) • Offence motivated by, or demonstrating, hostility to the victim based on his or her disability (or presumed disability)	Factor(s) in category A not present

STEP TWO   Starting point and category range

SG-556

Having determined the category, the court should use the corresponding starting points to reach a sentence within the category range below. The starting point applies to all offenders irrespective of plea or previous convictions. Having determined the starting point, step two allows further adjustment for aggravating or mitigating features, set out below.

A case of particular gravity, reflected by multiple features of culpability or harm in step one, could merit upward adjustment from the starting point before further adjustment for aggravating or mitigating features, set out below.

Where there is a sufficient prospect of rehabilitation, a community order with a sex offender treatment programme requirement under section 202 of the Criminal Justice Act 2003 can be a proper alternative to a short or moderate length custodial sentence.

	A	**B**
Category 1	**Starting point** 6 years' custody **Category range** 4–9 years' custody	**Starting point** 4 years' custody **Category range** 3–7 years' custody
Category 2	**Starting point** 4 years' custody **Category range** 3–7 years' custody	**Starting point** 2 years' custody **Category range** 1–4 years' custody
Category 3	**Starting point** 1 year's custody **Category range** 26 weeks' — 2 years' custody	**Starting point** 26 weeks' custody **Category range** High level community order — 1 year's custody

Sentencing Guidelines

The table below contains a **non-exhaustive** list of additional factual elements providing the context of the offence and factors relating to the offender. Identify whether any combination of these, or other relevant factors, should result in an upward or downward adjustment from the starting point. **In particular, relevant recent convictions are likely to result in an upward adjustment.** In some cases, having considered these factors, it may be appropriate to move outside the identified category range.

Aggravating factors
Statutory aggravating factors • Previous convictions, having regard to a) the nature of the offence to which the conviction relates and its relevance to the current offence; and b) the time that has elapsed since the conviction • Offence committed whilst on bail *Other aggravating factors* • Specific targeting of a particularly vulnerable child • Blackmail or other threats made (where not taken into account at step one) • Location of offence • Timing of offence • Use of weapon or other item to frighten or injure • Victim compelled to leave their home, school, etc • Failure to comply with current court orders • Offence committed whilst on licence • Exploiting contact arrangements with a child to commit an offence • Presence of others, especially other children • Any steps taken to prevent the victim reporting an incident, obtaining assistance and/or from assisting or supporting the prosecution • Attempts to dispose of or conceal evidence • Commission of offence whilst under the influence of alcohol or drugs • Victim encouraged to recruit others

Mitigating factors
• No previous convictions **or** no relevant/recent convictions • Remorse • Previous good character and/or exemplary conduct* • Age and/or lack of maturity where it affects the responsibility of the offender • Mental disorder or learning disability, particularly where linked to the commission of the offence

* [Repeats note as to distinction between previous good character/exemplary conduct and having no previous convictions and how to deal with them in respect of the offence: see **SG-532** for the full text.]

SG-557 **STEP THREE Consider any factors which indicate a reduction, such as assistance to the prosecution**

The court should take into account sections 73 and 74 of the Serious Organised Crime and Police Act 2005 (assistance by defendants: reduction or review of sentence) and any other rule of law by virtue of which an offender may receive a discounted sentence in consequence of assistance given (or offered) to the prosecutor or investigator.

STEP FOUR Reduction for guilty pleas

The court should take account of any potential reduction for a guilty plea in accordance with section 144 of the Criminal Justice Act 2003 and the *Guilty Plea* guideline.

STEP FIVE Dangerousness

The court should consider whether having regard to the criteria contained in Chapter 5 of Part 12 of the Criminal Justice Act 2003 it would be appropriate to award a life sentence (section 224A) or an extended sentence (section 226A). When sentencing offenders to a life sentence under these provisions, the notional determinate sentence should be used as the basis for the setting of a minimum term.

STEPS SIX TO NINE

[These are in the same terms as those applicable to rape: see **SG-533**.]

SG-558

Causing or Inciting a Child Under 13 to Engage in Sexual Activity
Sexual Offences Act 2003 (section 8)

Triable only on indictment (if penetration involved)

- otherwise, triable either way

Maximum: Life imprisonment (if penetration involved)

- otherwise, 14 years' custody

Offence range: 1–17 years' custody

[Repeats information as to the CJA 2003, ss. 224, 225(2), 224A and 226A, which is set out at **SG-530**.]

STEP ONE Determining the offence category   SG-559

The court should determine which categories of harm and culpability the offence falls into by reference **only** to the tables below.

Harm	
Category 1	• The extreme nature of one or more category 2 factors or the extreme impact caused by a combination of category 2 factors **may** elevate to category 1
Category 2	• Severe psychological or physical harm • Penetration of vagina or anus (using body or object) by, or of, victim • Penile penetration of mouth by, or of, victim • Additional degradation/humiliation • Abduction • Prolonged detention/sustained incident • Violence or threats of violence • Forced/uninvited entry into victim's home • Child is particularly vulnerable due to extreme youth and/or personal circumstances
Category 3	Factor(s) in categories 1 and 2 not present

Culpability	
A	**B**
• Significant degree of planning • Offender acts together with others to commit the offence • Use of alcohol/drugs on victim to facilitate the offence • Grooming behaviour used against victim • Abuse of trust • Previous violence against victim • Offence committed in course of burglary • Sexual images of victim recorded, retained, solicited or shared • Deliberate isolation of victim • Commercial exploitation and/or motivation • Offence racially or religiously aggravated • Offence motivated by, or demonstrating hostility to the victim based on his or her sexual orientation (or presumed sexual orientation) or transgender identity (or presumed transgender identity) • Offence motivated by, or demonstrating, hostility to the victim based on his or her disability (or presumed disability)	Factor(s) in category A not present

STEP TWO Starting point and category range   SG-560

Having determined the category, the court should use the corresponding starting points to reach a sentence within the category range below. The starting point applies to all offenders irrespective of plea or previous convictions. Having determined the starting point, step two allows further adjustment for aggravating or mitigating features, set out below.

A case of particular gravity, reflected by multiple features of culpability or harm in step one, could merit upward adjustment from the starting point before further adjustment for aggravating or mitigating features, set out below.

Sentencing Guidelines

	A	B
Category 1	**Starting point** 13 years' custody **Category range** 11–17 years' custody	**Starting point** 11 years' custody **Category range** 10–15 years' custody
Category 2	**Starting point** 8 years' custody **Category range** 5–10 years' custody	**Starting point** 6 years' custody **Category range** 3–9 years' custody
Category 3	**Starting point** 5 years' custody **Category range** 3–8 years' custody	**Starting point** 2 years' custody **Category range** 1–4 years' custody

The table below contains a **non-exhaustive** list of additional factual elements providing the context of the offence and factors relating to the offender. Identify whether any combination of these, or other relevant factors, should result in an upward or downward adjustment from the starting point. **In particular, relevant recent convictions are likely to result in an upward adjustment.** In some cases, having considered these factors, it may be appropriate to move outside the identified category range.

Aggravating factors

Statutory aggravating factors
- Previous convictions, having regard to a) the nature of the offence to which the conviction relates and its relevance to the current offence; and b) the time that has elapsed since the conviction
- Offence committed whilst on bail

Other aggravating factors
- Specific targeting of a particularly vulnerable child
- Ejaculation (where not taken into account at step one)
- Blackmail or other threats made (where not taken into account at step one)
- Pregnancy or STI as a consequence of offence
- Location of offence
- Timing of offence
- Use of weapon or other item to frighten or injure
- Victim compelled to leave their home, school, etc
- Failure to comply with current court orders
- Offence committed whilst on licence
- Exploiting contact arrangements with a child to commit an offence
- Presence of others, especially other children
- Any steps taken to prevent the victim reporting an incident, obtaining assistance and/or from assisting or supporting the prosecution
- Attempts to dispose of or conceal evidence
- Commission of offence whilst offender under the influence of alcohol or drugs
- Victim encouraged to recruit others

Mitigating factors

- No previous convictions **or** no relevant/recent convictions
- Remorse
- Previous good character and/or exemplary conduct*
- Age and/or lack of maturity where it affects the responsibility of the offender
- Mental disorder or learning disability, particularly where linked to the commission of the offence
- Sexual activity was incited but no activity took place because the offender voluntarily desisted or intervened to prevent it

---

* [Repeats note as to distinction between previous good character/exemplary conduct and having no previous convictions and how to deal with them in respect of the offence: see **SG-532** for the full text.]

SG-561   **STEPS THREE TO NINE**

[These are in the same terms as those applicable to rape: see **SG-533**.]

SEXUAL ACTIVITY WITH A CHILD   SG-562
Sexual Offences Act 2003 (section 9)

CAUSING OR INCITING A CHILD TO ENGAGE IN SEXUAL ACTIVITY
Sexual Offences Act 2003 (section 10)

Triable only on indictment (if penetration involved)

• otherwise, triable either way

Maximum: 14 years' custody

Offence range: Community order — 10 years' custody

[Repeats information as to the CJA 2003, ss. 224A and 226A, which is set out at **SG-554**.]

Arranging or facilitating the commission of a child offence (section 14 of the Sexual Offences Act 2003 — [see SG-574])
The starting points and ranges in this guideline are also applicable to offences of arranging or facilitating the commission of a child offence. In such cases, the level of harm should be determined by reference to the type of activity arranged or facilitated. Sentences commensurate with the applicable starting point and range will ordinarily be appropriate. For offences involving significant commercial exploitation and/or an international element, it may, in the interests of justice, be appropriate to increase a sentence to a point above the category range. In exceptional cases, such as where a vulnerable offender performed a limited role, having been coerced or exploited by others, sentences below the starting point and range may be appropriate.

STEP ONE Determining the offence category   SG-563
The court should determine which categories of harm and culpability the offence falls into by reference **only** to the tables below.

This guideline also applies to offences committed remotely/online

Harm	
Category 1	• Penetration of vagina or anus (using body or object) • Penile penetration of mouth In either case by, or of, the victim
Category 2	Touching, or exposure, of naked genitalia or naked breasts by, or of, the victim
Category 3	Other sexual activity

Culpability	
A	**B**
• Significant degree of planning • Offender acts together with others to commit the offence • Use of alcohol/drugs on victim to facilitate the offence • Grooming behaviour used against victim • Abuse of trust • Use of threats (including blackmail) • Sexual images of victim recorded, retained, solicited or shared • Specific targeting of a particularly vulnerable child • Offender lied about age • Significant disparity in age • Commercial exploitation and/or motivation • Offence racially or religiously aggravated • Offence motivated by, or demonstrating, hostility to the victim based on his or her sexual orientation (or presumed sexual orientation) or transgender identity (or presumed transgender identity) • Offence motivated by, or demonstrating, hostility to the victim based on his or her disability (or presumed disability)	Factor(s) in category A not present

SG-564   STEP TWO Starting point and category range

Having determined the category, the court should use the corresponding starting points to reach a sentence within the category range below. The starting point applies to all offenders irrespective of plea or previous convictions. Having determined the starting point, step two allows further adjustment for aggravating or mitigating features, set out below.

A case of particular gravity, reflected by multiple features of culpability or harm in step one, could merit upward adjustment from the starting point before further adjustment for aggravating or mitigating features, set out below.

Where there is a sufficient prospect of rehabilitation, a community order with a sex offender treatment programme requirement under section 202 of the Criminal Justice Act 2003 can be a proper alternative to a short or moderate length custodial sentence.

	A	B
Category 1	**Starting point** 5 years' custody	**Starting point** 1 year's custody
	Category range 4–10 years' custody	**Category range** High level community order — 2 years' custody
Category 2	**Starting point** 3 years' custody	**Starting point** 26 weeks' custody
	Category range 2–6 years' custody	**Category range** High level community order — 1 year's custody
Category 3	**Starting point** 26 weeks' custody	**Starting point** Medium level community order
	Category range High level community order — 3 years' custody	**Category range** Low level community order — High level community order

The table below contains a **non-exhaustive** list of additional factual elements providing the context of the offence and factors relating to the offender. Identify whether any combination of these, or other relevant factors, should result in an upward or downward adjustment from the starting point. **In particular, relevant recent convictions are likely to result in an upward adjustment.** In some cases, having considered these factors, it may be appropriate to move outside the identified category range.

When sentencing appropriate **category 2 or 3 offences**, the court should also consider the custody threshold as follows:

* has the custody threshold been passed?
* if so, is it unavoidable that a custodial sentence be imposed?
* if so, can that sentence be suspended?

Aggravating factors

Statutory aggravating factors
* Previous convictions, having regard to a) the nature of the offence to which the conviction relates and its relevance to the current offence; and b) the time that has elapsed since the conviction
* Offence committed whilst on bail

Other aggravating factors
* Severe psychological or physical harm
* Ejaculation
* Pregnancy or STI as a consequence of offence
* Location of offence
* Timing of offence
* Victim compelled to leave their home, school, etc

- Failure to comply with current court orders
- Offence committed whilst on licence
- Exploiting contact arrangements with a child to commit an offence
- Presence of others, especially other children
- Any steps taken to prevent the victim reporting an incident, obtaining assistance and/or from assisting or supporting the prosecution
- Attempts to dispose of or conceal evidence
- Failure of offender to respond to previous warnings
- Commission of offence whilst under the influence of alcohol or drugs
- Victim encouraged to recruit others
- Period over which offence committed

Mitigating factors

- No previous convictions **or** no relevant/recent convictions
- Remorse
- Previous good character and/or exemplary conduct*
- Age and/or lack of maturity where it affects the responsibility of the offender
- Mental disorder or learning disability, particularly where linked to the commission of the offence
- Sexual activity was incited but no activity took place because the offender voluntarily desisted or intervened to prevent it

* [Repeats note as to distinction between previous good character/exemplary conduct and having no previous convictions and how to deal with them in respect of the offence: see **SG-532** for the full text.]

STEP THREE TO NINE   SG-565
[These are in the same terms as those applicable to sexual assault of a child under 13: see **SG-557**.]

SEXUAL ACTIVITY WITH A CHILD FAMILY MEMBER   SG-566
Sexual Offences Act 2003 (section 25)

INCITING A CHILD FAMILY MEMBER TO ENGAGE IN SEXUAL ACTIVITY
Sexual Offences Act 2003 (section 26)

Triable only on indictment (if penetration involved)

- otherwise, triable either way

Maximum: 14 years' custody

Offence range: Community order — 10 years' custody

[Repeats information as to the CJA 2003, ss. 224A and 226A, which is set out at **SG-554**.]

STEP ONE Determining the offence category   SG-567
The court should determine which categories of harm and culpability the offence falls into by reference **only** to the tables below. This offence involves those who have a family relationship with the victim and it should be assumed that the greater the abuse of trust within this relationship the more grave the offence.

Harm	
Category 1	• Penetration of vagina or anus (using body or object) • Penile penetration of mouth In either case by, or of, the victim
Category 2	Touching of naked genitalia or naked breasts by, or of, the victim
Category 3	Other sexual activity

Culpability	
A	**B**
• Significant degree of planning • Offender acts together with others to commit the offence • Use of alcohol/drugs on victim to facilitate the offence • Grooming behaviour used against victim • Use of threats (including blackmail) • Sexual images of victim recorded, retained, solicited or shared • Specific targeting of a particularly vulnerable child • Significant disparity in age • Commercial exploitation and/or motivation • Offence racially or religiously aggravated • Offence motivated by, or demonstrating, hostility to the victim based on his or her sexual orientation (or presumed sexual orientation) or transgender identity (or presumed transgender identity) • Offence motivated by, or demonstrating, hostility to the victim based on his or her disability (or presumed disability)	Factor(s) in category A not present

SG-568   **STEP TWO Starting point and category range**

Having determined the category, the court should use the corresponding starting points to reach a sentence within the category range below. The starting point applies to all offenders irrespective of plea or previous convictions. Having determined the starting point, step two allows further adjustment for aggravating or mitigating features, set out below.

A case of particular gravity, reflected by multiple features of culpability or harm in step one, could merit upward adjustment from the starting point before further adjustment for aggravating or mitigating features, set out below.

Where there is a sufficient prospect of rehabilitation, a community order with a sex offender treatment programme requirement under section 202 of the Criminal Justice Act 2003 can be a proper alternative to a short or moderate length custodial sentence.

	A	**B**
Category 1	**Starting point** 6 years' custody **Category range** 4–10 years' custody	**Starting point** 3 years 6 months' custody **Category range** 2 years 6 months' — 5 years' custody
Category 2	**Starting point** 4 years' custody **Category range** 2–6 years' custody	**Starting point** 18 months' custody **Category range** 26 weeks' — 2 years 6 months' custody
Category 3	**Starting point** 1 year's custody **Category range** High level community order — 3 years' custody	**Starting point** Medium level community order **Category range** Low level community order — High level community order

The table below contains a **non-exhaustive** list of additional factual elements providing the context of the offence and factors relating to the offender. Identify whether any combination of these, or other relevant factors, should result in an upward or downward adjustment from the starting point. **In particular, relevant recent convictions are likely to result in an upward adjustment.** In some cases, having considered these factors, it may be appropriate to move outside the identified category range.

When sentencing appropriate **category 3 offences**, the court should also consider the custody threshold as follows:

- has the custody threshold been passed?
- if so, is it unavoidable that a custodial sentence be imposed?
- if so, can that sentence be suspended?

Aggravating factors

Statutory aggravating factors
- Previous convictions, having regard to a) the nature of the offence to which the conviction relates and its relevance to the current offence; and b) the time that has elapsed since the conviction
- Offence committed whilst on bail

Other aggravating factors
- Severe psychological or physical harm
- Ejaculation
- Pregnancy or STI as a consequence of offence
- Location of offence
- Timing of offence
- Victim compelled to leave their home, school, etc
- Failure to comply with current court orders
- Offence committed whilst on licence
- Exploiting contact arrangements with a child to commit an offence
- Presence of others, especially other children
- Any steps taken to prevent the victim reporting an incident, obtaining assistance and/or from assisting or supporting the prosecution
- Attempts to dispose of or conceal evidence
- Failure of offender to respond to previous warnings
- Commission of offence whilst under the influence of alcohol or drugs
- Victim encouraged to recruit others
- Period over which offence committed

Mitigating factors

- No previous convictions **or** no relevant/recent convictions
- Remorse
- Previous good character and/or exemplary conduct*
- Age and/or lack of maturity where it affects the responsibility of the offender
- Mental disorder or learning disability, particularly where linked to the commission of the offence
- Sexual activity was incited but no activity took place because the offender voluntarily desisted or intervened to prevent it

---

* [Repeats note as to distinction between previous good character/exemplary conduct and having no previous convictions and how to deal with them in respect of the offence: see **SG-532** for the full text.]

STEPS THREE TO NINE   SG-569
[These are in the same terms as those applicable to sexual assault of a child under 13: see **SG-557**.]

ENGAGING IN SEXUAL ACTIVITY IN THE PRESENCE OF A CHILD   SG-570
Sexual Offences Act 2003 (section 11)

CAUSING A CHILD TO WATCH A SEXUAL ACT
Sexual Offences Act 2003 (section 12)

Triable either way
Maximum: 10 years' custody

Offence range: Community order — 6 years' custody

[Repeats information as to the CJA 2003, ss. 224A and 226A, which is set out at **SG-554**.]

> **Arranging or facilitating the commission of a child offence (section 14 of the Sexual Offences Act 2003 — guidance [at SG-574])**
>
> *The starting points and ranges in this guideline are also applicable to offences of arranging or facilitating the commission of a child offence. In such cases, the level of harm should be determined by reference to the type of activity arranged or facilitated. Sentences commensurate with the applicable starting point and range will ordinarily be appropriate. For offences involving significant commercial exploitation and/or an international element, it may, in the interests of justice, be appropriate to increase a sentence to a point above the category range. In exceptional cases, such as where a vulnerable offender performed a limited role, having been coerced or exploited by others, sentences below the starting point and range may be appropriate.*

SG-571   **STEP ONE Determining the offence category**

The court should determine which categories of harm and culpability the offence falls into by reference **only** to the tables below.

Harm	
Category 1	• Causing victim to view extreme pornography • Causing victim to view indecent/prohibited images of children • Engaging in, or causing a victim to view live, sexual activity involving sadism/violence/sexual activity with an animal/a child
Category 2	Engaging in, or causing a victim to view images of or view live, sexual activity involving: • penetration of vagina or anus (using body or object) • penile penetration of the mouth • masturbation
Category 3	Factor(s) in categories 1 and 2 not present

Culpability	
A	**B**
• Significant degree of planning • Offender acts together with others in order to commit the offence • Use of alcohol/drugs on victim to facilitate the offence • Grooming behaviour used against victim • Abuse of trust • Use of threats (including blackmail) • Specific targeting of a particularly vulnerable child • Significant disparity in age • Commercial exploitation and/or motivation • Offence racially or religiously aggravated • Offence motivated by, or demonstrating, hostility to the victim based on his or her sexual orientation (or presumed sexual orientation) or transgender identity (or presumed transgender identity) • Offence motivated by, or demonstrating, hostility to the victim based on his or her disability (or presumed disability)	Factor(s) in category A not present

SG-572   **STEP TWO Starting point and category range**

Having determined the category, the court should use the corresponding starting points to reach a sentence within the category range below. The starting point applies to all offenders irrespective of plea or previous convictions. Having determined the starting point, step two allows further adjustment for aggravating or mitigating features, set out below.

A case of particular gravity, reflected by multiple features of culpability or harm in step one, could merit upward adjustment from the starting point before further adjustment for aggravating or mitigating features, set out below.

Where there is a sufficient prospect of rehabilitation, a community order with a sex offender treatment programme requirement under section 202 of the Criminal Justice Act 2003 can be a proper alternative to a short or moderate length custodial sentence.

	A	B
Category 1	**Starting point** 4 years' custody **Category range** 3–6 years' custody	**Starting point** 2 years' custody **Category range** 1–3 years' custody
Category 2	**Starting point** 2 years' custody **Category range** 1–3 years' custody	**Starting point** 1 year's custody **Category range** High level community order — 18 months' custody
Category 3	**Starting point** 26 weeks' custody **Category range** High level community order — 1 year's custody	**Starting point** Medium level community order **Category range** Low level community order — Medium level community order

The table below contains a **non-exhaustive** list of additional factual elements providing the context of the offence and factors relating to the offender. Identify whether any combination of these, or other relevant factors, should result in an upward or downward adjustment from the starting point. **In particular, relevant recent convictions are likely to result in an upward adjustment.** In some cases, having considered these factors, it may be appropriate to move outside the identified category range.

When sentencing appropriate **category 2 or 3 offences**, the court should also consider the custody threshold as follows:

- has the custody threshold been passed?
- if so, is it unavoidable that a custodial sentence be imposed?
- if so, can that sentence be suspended?

Aggravating factors

Statutory aggravating factors
- Previous convictions, having regard to a) the nature of the offence to which the conviction relates and its relevance to the current offence; and b) the time that has elapsed since the conviction
- Offence committed whilst on bail

Other aggravating factors
- Location of offence
- Timing of offence
- Victim compelled to leave their home, school, etc
- Failure to comply with current court orders
- Offence committed whilst on licence
- Exploiting contact arrangements with a child to commit an offence
- Presence of others, especially other children
- Any steps taken to prevent the victim reporting an incident, obtaining assistance and/or from assisting or supporting the prosecution
- Attempts to dispose of or conceal evidence
- Failure of offender to respond to previous warnings
- Commission of offence whilst offender under the influence of alcohol or drugs
- Victim encouraged to recruit others

Mitigating factors

- No previous convictions **or** no relevant/recent convictions
- Remorse
- Previous good character and/or exemplary conduct*
- Age and/or lack of maturity where it affects the responsibility of the offender
- Mental disorder or learning disability, particularly where linked to the commission of the offence
- Demonstration of steps taken to address offending behaviour

---

* [Repeats note as to distinction between previous good character/exemplary conduct and having no previous convictions and how to deal with them in respect of the offence: see **SG-540** for the full text.]

Sentencing Guidelines

SG-573   STEPS THREE TO NINE

[These are in the same terms as those applicable to sexual assault of a child under 13: see **SG-557**.]

SG-574   ARRANGING OR FACILITATING THE COMMISSION OF A CHILD SEX OFFENCE

Sexual Offences Act 2003 (section 14)

Triable either way
Maximum: 14 years' custody

[Repeats information as to the CJA 2003, ss. 224A and 226A, which is set out at **SG-554**.]

*Sentencers should refer to the guideline for the applicable, substantive offence of arranging or facilitating under sections 9 to 12. See [**SG-570 et seq.**]. The level of harm should be determined by reference to the type of activity arranged or facilitated. Sentences commensurate with the applicable starting point and range will ordinarily be appropriate. For offences involving significant commercial exploitation and/or an international element, it may, in the interests of justice, be appropriate to increase a sentence to a point above the category range. In exceptional cases, such as where a vulnerable offender performed a limited role, having been coerced or exploited by others, sentences below the starting point and range may be appropriate.*

SG-575   MEETING A CHILD FOLLOWING SEXUAL GROOMING

Sexual Offences Act 2003 (section 15)

Triable either way
Maximum: 10 years' custody

Offence range: 1–7 years' custody

[Repeats information as to the CJA 2003, ss. 224A and 226A, which is set out at **SG-554**.]

SG-576   STEP ONE   Determining the offence category

The court should determine the offence category using the table below.

Category 1	Raised harm **and** raised culpability
Category 2	Raised harm **or** raised culpability
Category 3	Grooming **without** raised harm or culpability factors present

The court should determine culpability and harm caused or intended, by reference **only** to the factors below, which comprise the principal factual elements of the offence. Where an offence does not fall squarely into a category, individual factors may require a degree of weighting before making an overall assessment and determining the appropriate offence category.

Factors indicating raised harm

- Continued contact despite victim's attempts to terminate contact
- Sexual images exchanged
- Victim exposed to extreme sexual content for example, extreme pornography
- Child is particularly vulnerable due to personal circumstances

Factors indicating raised culpability

- Offender acts together with others to commit the offence
- Communication indicates penetrative sexual activity is intended
- Offender lied about age/persona
- Use of threats (including blackmail), gifts or bribes
- Abuse of trust
- Specific targeting of a particularly vulnerable child
- Abduction/detention
- Commercial exploitation and/or motivation
- Offence racially or religiously aggravated
- Offence motivated by, or demonstrating, hostility to the victim based on his or her sexual orientation (or presumed sexual orientation) or transgender identity (or presumed transgender identity)
- Offence motivated by, or demonstrating, hostility to the victim based on his or her disability (or presumed disability)

STEP TWO **Starting point and category range**   **SG-577**

Having determined the category, the court should use the corresponding starting points to reach a sentence within the category range below. The starting point applies to all offenders irrespective of plea or previous convictions. Having determined the starting point, step two allows further adjustment for aggravating or mitigating features, set out below.

A case of particular gravity, reflected by multiple features of culpability or harm in step one, could merit upward adjustment from the starting point before further adjustment for aggravating or mitigating features, set out below.

Category 1	**Starting point** 4 years' custody
	Category range 3–7 years' custody
Category 2	**Starting point** 2 years' custody
	Category range 1–4 years' custody
Category 3	**Starting point** 18 months' custody
	Category range 1 year — 2 years 6 months' custody

The table below contains a **non-exhaustive** list of additional factual elements providing the context of the offence and factors relating to the offender. Identify whether any combination of these, or other relevant factors, should result in an upward or downward adjustment from the starting point. **In particular, relevant recent convictions are likely to result in an upward adjustment.** In some cases, having considered these factors, it may be appropriate to move outside the identified category range.

Aggravating factors
Statutory aggravating factors • Previous convictions, having regard to a) the nature of the offence to which the conviction relates and its relevance to the current offence; and b) the time that has elapsed since the conviction • Offence committed whilst on bail
Other aggravating factors • Failure to comply with current court orders • Offence committed whilst on licence • Any steps taken to prevent the victim reporting an incident, obtaining assistance and/or from assisting or supporting the prosecution • Attempts to dispose of or conceal evidence • Victim encouraged to recruit others

Mitigating factors
• No previous convictions **or** no relevant/recent convictions • Remorse • Previous good character and/or exemplary conduct* • Age and/or lack of maturity where it affects the responsibility of the offender • Mental disorder or learning disability, particularly where linked to the commission of the offence • Demonstration of steps taken to address offending behaviour

* [Repeats note as to distinction between previous good character/exemplary conduct and having no previous convictions and how to deal with them in respect of the offence: see **SG-540** for the full text.]

STEPS THREE TO NINE   **SG-578**

[These are in the same terms as those applicable to sexual assault of a child under 13: see **SG-557**.]

SG-579

ABUSE OF POSITION OF TRUST: SEXUAL ACTIVITY WITH A CHILD

Sexual Offences Act 2003 (section 16)

ABUSE OF POSITION OF TRUST: CAUSING OR INCITING A CHILD TO ENGAGE IN SEXUAL ACTIVITY

Sexual Offences Act 2003 (section 17)

Triable either way
Maximum: 5 years' custody

Offence range: Community order — 2 years' custody

[Repeats information as to the CJA 2003, s. 226A which is set out at **SG-538**.]

SG-580 STEP ONE **Determining the offence category**

The court should determine which categories of harm and culpability the offence falls into by reference **only** to the tables below.

This guideline also applies to offences committed remotely/online

Harm	
Category 1	• Penetration of vagina or anus (using body or object) • Penile penetration of mouth In either case by, or of, the victim
Category 2	• Touching, or exposure, of naked genitalia or naked breasts by, or of, the victim
Category 3	Factor(s) in categories 1 and 2 not present

Culpability	
A	B
• Significant degree of planning • Offender acts together with others to commit the offence • Use of alcohol/drugs on victim to facilitate the offence • Grooming behaviour used against victim • Use of threats (including blackmail) • Sexual images of victim recorded, retained, solicited or shared • Specific targeting of a particularly vulnerable child • Commercial exploitation and/or motivation • Offence racially or religiously aggravated • Offence motivated by, or demonstrating, hostility to the victim based on his or her sexual orientation (or presumed sexual orientation) or transgender identity (or presumed transgender identity) • Offence motivated by, or demonstrating, hostility to the victim based on his or her disability (or presumed disability)	Factor(s) in category A not present

SG-581 STEP TWO **Starting point and category range**

Having determined the category, the court should use the corresponding starting points to reach a sentence within the category range below. The starting point applies to all offenders irrespective of plea or previous convictions. Having determined the starting point, step two allows further adjustment for aggravating or mitigating features, set out below.

A case of particular gravity, reflected by multiple features of culpability or harm in step one, could merit upward adjustment from the starting point before further adjustment for aggravating or mitigating features, set out below.

Where there is a sufficient prospect of rehabilitation, a community order with a sex offender treatment programme requirement under section 202 of the Criminal Justice Act 2003 can be a proper alternative to a short or moderate length custodial sentence.

	A	B
Category 1	**Starting point** 18 months' custody **Category range** 1–2 years' custody	**Starting point** 1 year's custody **Category range** 26 weeks' — 18 months' custody
Category 2	**Starting point** 1 year's custody **Category range** 26 weeks' — 18 months' custody	**Starting point** 26 weeks' custody **Category range** High level community order — 1 year's custody
Category 3	**Starting point** 26 weeks' custody **Category range** High level community order — 1 year's custody	**Starting point** Medium level community order **Category range** Low level community order — High level community order

The table below contains a **non-exhaustive** list of additional factual elements providing the context of the offence and factors relating to the offender. Identify whether any combination of these, or other relevant factors, should result in an upward or downward adjustment from the starting point. **In particular, relevant recent convictions are likely to result in an upward adjustment.** In some cases, having considered these factors, it may be appropriate to move outside the identified category range.

When sentencing appropriate **category 2 or 3 offences**, the court should also consider the custody threshold as follows:

- has the custody threshold been passed?
- if so, is it unavoidable that a custodial sentence be imposed?
- if so, can that sentence be suspended?

Aggravating factors

Statutory aggravating factors
- Previous convictions, having regard to a) the nature of the offence to which the conviction relates and its relevance to the current offence; and b) the time that has elapsed since the conviction
- Offence committed whilst on bail

Other aggravating factors
- Ejaculation
- Pregnancy or STI as a consequence of offence
- Location of offence
- Timing of offence
- Victim compelled to leave their home, school, etc
- Failure to comply with current court orders
- Offence committed whilst on licence
- Presence of others, especially other children
- Any steps taken to prevent the victim reporting an incident, obtaining assistance and/or from assisting or supporting the prosecution
- Attempts to dispose of or conceal evidence
- Failure of offender to respond to previous warnings
- Commission of offence whilst under the influence of alcohol or drugs
- Victim encouraged to recruit others

Mitigating factors

- No previous convictions **or** no relevant/recent convictions
- Remorse
- Previous good character and/or exemplary conduct*
- Age and/or lack of maturity where it affects the responsibility of the offender
- Mental disorder or learning disability, particularly where linked to the commission of the offence
- Sexual activity was incited but no activity took place because the offender voluntarily desisted or intervened to prevent it
- Demonstration of steps taken to address offending behaviour

* [Repeats note as to distinction between previous good character/exemplary conduct and having no previous convictions and how to deal with them in respect of the offence: see **SG-540** for the full text.]

SG-582   STEPS THREE TO NINE

[These are in the same terms as those applicable to sexual assault: see **SG-541**.]

SG-583   ABUSE OF POSITION OF TRUST: SEXUAL ACTIVITY IN THE PRESENCE OF A CHILD
Sexual Offences Act 2003 (section 18)

ABUSE OF POSITION OF TRUST: CAUSING A CHILD TO WATCH A SEXUAL ACT
Sexual Offences Act 2003 (section 19)

Triable either way
Maximum: 5 years' custody

Offence range: Community order — 2 years' custody

[Repeats information as to the CJA 2003, s. 226A, which is set out at **SG-538**.]

SG-584   STEP ONE **Determining the offence category**

The court should determine which categories of harm and culpability the offence falls into by reference **only** to the tables below.

Harm	
Category 1	• Causing victim to view extreme pornography • Causing victim to view indecent/prohibited images of children • Engaging in, or causing a victim to view live, sexual activity involving sadism/violence/ sexual activity with an animal/a child
Category 2	Engaging in, or causing a victim to view images of or view live, sexual activity involving: • penetration of vagina or anus (using body or object) • penile penetration of mouth • masturbation
Category 3	Factor(s) in categories 1 and 2 not present

Culpability	
A	**B**
• Significant degree of planning • Offender acts together with others to commit the offence • Use of alcohol/drugs on victim to facilitate the offence • Grooming behaviour used against victim • Use of threats (including blackmail) • Specific targeting of a particularly vulnerable child • Commercial exploitation and/or motivation • Offence racially or religiously aggravated • Offence motivated by, or demonstrating, hostility to the victim based on his or her sexual orientation (or presumed sexual orientation) or transgender identity (or presumed transgender identity) • Offence motivated by, or demonstrating, hostility to the victim based on his or her disability (or presumed disability)	Factor(s) in category A not present

SG-585   STEP TWO **Starting point and category range**

Having determined the category, the court should use the corresponding starting points to reach a sentence within the category range below. The starting point applies to all offenders irrespective of plea or previous convictions. Having determined the starting point, step two allows further adjustment for aggravating or mitigating features, set out below.

A case of particular gravity, reflected by multiple features of culpability or harm in step one, could merit upward adjustment from the starting point before further adjustment for aggravating or mitigating features, set out below.

Where there is a sufficient prospect of rehabilitation, a community order with a sex offender treatment programme requirement under section 202 of the Criminal Justice Act 2003 can be a proper alternative to a short or moderate length custodial sentence.

	A	B
Category 1	**Starting point** 18 months' custody **Category range** 1–2 years' custody	**Starting point** 1 year's custody **Category range** 26 weeks' — 18 months' custody
Category 2	**Starting point** 1 year's custody **Category range** 26 weeks' — 18 months' custody	**Starting point** 26 weeks' custody **Category range** High level community order — 1 year's custody
Category 3	**Starting point** 26 weeks' custody **Category range** High level community order — 1 year's custody	**Starting point** Medium level community order **Category range** Low level community order — High level community order

The table below contains a **non-exhaustive** list of additional factual elements providing the context of the offence and factors relating to the offender. Identify whether any combination of these, or other relevant factors, should result in an upward or downward adjustment from the starting point. **In particular, relevant recent convictions are likely to result in an upward adjustment.** In some cases, having considered these factors, it may be appropriate to move outside the identified category range.

When sentencing appropriate **category 2 or 3 offences**, the court should also consider the custody threshold as follows:

- has the custody threshold been passed?
- if so, is it unavoidable that a custodial sentence be imposed?
- if so, can that sentence be suspended?

Aggravating factors

Statutory aggravating factors
- Previous convictions, having regard to a) the nature of the offence to which the conviction relates and its relevance to the current offence; and b) the time that has elapsed since the conviction
- Offence committed whilst on bail

Other aggravating factors
- Location of offence
- Timing of offence
- Victim compelled to leave their home, school, etc
- Failure to comply with current court orders
- Offence committed whilst on licence
- Presence of others, especially other children
- Any steps taken to prevent the victim reporting an incident, obtaining assistance and/or from assisting or supporting the prosecution
- Attempts to dispose of or conceal evidence
- Failure of offender to respond to previous warnings
- Commission of offence whilst under the influence of alcohol or drugs
- Victim encouraged to recruit others

Mitigating factors

- No previous convictions **or** no relevant/recent convictions
- Remorse
- Previous good character and/or exemplary conduct*
- Age and/or lack of maturity where it affects the responsibility of the offender
- Mental disorder or learning disability, particularly where linked to the commission of the offence
- Demonstration of steps taken to address offending behaviour

---

* [Repeats note as to distinction between previous good character/exemplary conduct and having no previous convictions and how to deal with them in respect of the offence: see **SG-540** for the full text.]

STEPS THREE TO NINE   SG-586

[These are in the same terms as those applicable to sexual assault: see **SG-541**.]

Sentencing Guidelines

SG-587   POSSESSION OF INDECENT PHOTOGRAPH OF CHILD
Criminal Justice Act 1988 (section 160)

Triable either way

Maximum: 5 years' custody

Offence range: Community order — 3 years' custody

INDECENT PHOTOGRAPHS OF CHILDREN
Protection of Children Act 1978 (section 1)

Triable either way

Maximum: 10 years' custody

Offence range: Community order — 9 years' custody

[Repeats information as to the CJA 2003, ss. 224A and 226A, which is set out at **SG-554**.]

SG-588   STEP ONE **Determining the offence category**
The court should determine the offence category using the table below.

	Possession	Distribution*	Production**
Category A	Possession of images involving penetrative sexual activity Possession of images involving sexual activity with an animal or sadism	Sharing images involving penetrative sexual activity Sharing images involving sexual activity with an animal or sadism	Creating images involving penetrative sexual activity Creating images involving sexual activity with an animal or sadism
Category B	Possession of images involving non-penetrative sexual activity	Sharing of images involving non-penetrative sexual activity	Creating images involving non-penetrative sexual activity
Category C	Possession of other indecent images not falling within categories A or B	Sharing of other indecent images not falling within categories A or B	Creating other indecent images not falling within categories A or B

* Distribution includes possession with a view to distributing or sharing images.

** Production includes the taking or making of any image at source for instance the original image.

Making an image by simple downloading should be treated as possession for the purposes of sentencing.

In most cases the intrinsic character of the most serious of the offending images will initially determine the appropriate category. If, however, the most serious images are unrepresentative of the offender's conduct a lower category may be appropriate. A lower category will not, however, be appropriate if the offender has produced or taken (for example photographed) images of a higher category.

SG-589   STEP TWO **Starting point and category range**
Having determined the category, the court should use the corresponding starting points to reach a sentence within the category range below. The starting point applies to all offenders irrespective of plea or previous convictions. Having determined the starting point, step two allows further adjustment for aggravating or mitigating features, set out below.

Where there is a sufficient prospect of rehabilitation, a community order with a sex offender treatment programme requirement under section 202 of the Criminal Justice Act 2003 can be a proper alternative to a short or moderate length custodial sentence.

	Possession	Distribution	Production
Category A	**Starting point** 1 year's custody **Category range** 26 weeks — 3 years' custody	**Starting point** 3 years' custody **Category range** 2 — 5 years' custody	**Starting point** 6 years' custody **Category range** 4 — 9 years' custody
Category B	**Starting point** 26 weeks' custody **Category range** High level community order — 18 months' custody	**Starting point** 1 year's custody **Category range** 26 weeks — 2 years' custody	**Starting point** 2 years' custody **Category range** 1 — 4 years' custody
Category C	**Starting point** High level community order **Category range** Medium level community order — 26 weeks' custody	**Starting point** 13 weeks' custody **Category range** High level community order — 26 weeks' custody	**Starting point** 18 months' custody **Category range** 1 — 3 years' custody

The table below contains a **non-exhaustive** list of additional factual elements providing the context of the offence and factors relating to the offender. Identify whether any combination of these, or other relevant factors, should result in an upward or downward adjustment from the starting point. **In particular, relevant recent convictions are likely to result in an upward adjustment.** In some cases, having considered these factors, it may be appropriate to move outside the identified category range.

When sentencing appropriate **category 2 or 3 offences**, the court should also consider the custody threshold as follows:

- has the custody threshold been passed?
- if so, is it unavoidable that a custodial sentence be imposed?
- if so, can that sentence be suspended?

Aggravating factors
Statutory aggravating factors   • Previous convictions, having regard to a) the nature of the offence to which the conviction relates and its relevance to the current offence; and b) the time that has elapsed since the conviction   • Offence committed whilst on bail   *Other aggravating factors*   • Failure to comply with current court orders   • Offence committed whilst on licence   • Age and/or vulnerability of the child depicted^   • Discernable pain or distress suffered by child depicted   • Period over which images were possessed, distributed or produced   • High volume of images possessed, distributed or produced   • Placing images where there is the potential for a high volume of viewers   • Collection includes moving images   • Attempts to dispose of or conceal evidence   • Abuse of trust   • Child depicted known to the offender   • Active involvement in a network or process that facilitates or commissions the creation or sharing of indecent images of children   • Commercial exploitation and/or motivation   • Deliberate or systematic searching for images portraying young children, category A images or the portrayal of familial sexual abuse   • Large number of different victims   • Child depicted intoxicated or drugged

^ Age and/or vulnerability of the child should be given significant weight. In cases where the actual age of the victim is difficult to determine sentencers should consider the development of the child (infant, pre-pubescent, post-pubescent)

Mitigating factors
• No previous convictions **or** no relevant/recent convictions • Remorse • Previous good character and/or exemplary conduct* • Age and/or lack of maturity where it affects the responsibility of the offender • Mental disorder or learning disability, particularly where linked to the commission of the offence • Demonstration of steps taken to address offending behaviour

* [Repeats note as to distinction between previous good character/exemplary conduct and having no previous convictions and how to deal with them in respect of the offence: see **SG-540** for the full text.]

SG-590   **STEPS THREE TO NINE**

[These are in the same terms as those applicable to sexual assault of a child under 13: see **SG-557**.]

SG-591   CAUSING OR INCITING PROSTITUTION FOR GAIN
Sexual Offences Act 2003 (section 52)

CONTROLLING PROSTITUTION FOR GAIN
Sexual Offences Act 2003 (section 53)

Triable either way

Maximum: 7 years' custody

Offence range: Community order — 6 years' custody

[Repeats information as to the CJA 2003, s. 226A which is set out at **SG-538**.]

The terms 'prostitute' and 'prostitution' are used in this guideline in accordance with the statutory language contained in the Sexual Offences Act 2003.

SG-592   **STEP ONE   Determining the offence category**

The court should determine which categories of harm and culpability the offence falls into by reference **only** to the tables below.

Harm	
Category 1	• Abduction/detention • Violence or threats of violence • Sustained and systematic psychological abuse • Individual(s) forced or coerced to participate in unsafe/degrading sexual activity • Individual(s) forced or coerced into seeing many "customers" • Individual(s) forced/coerced/deceived into prostitution
Category 2	Factor(s) in category 1 not present

Culpability		
A	B	C
• Causing, inciting or controlling prostitution on significant commercial basis • Expectation of significant financial or other gain • Abuse of trust • Exploitation of those known to be trafficked • Significant involvement in limiting the freedom of prostitute(s) • Grooming of individual(s) to enter prostitution including through cultivation of a dependency on drugs or alcohol	• Close involvement with prostitute(s) for example control of finances, choice of clients, working conditions, etc (where offender's involvement is not as a result of coercion)	• Performs limited function under direction • Close involvement but engaged by coercion/intimidation/exploitation

STEP TWO Starting point and category range

Having determined the category, the court should use the corresponding starting points to reach a sentence within the category range below. The starting point applies to all offenders irrespective of plea or previous convictions. Having determined the starting point, step two allows further adjustment for aggravating or mitigating features, set out below.

A case of particular gravity, reflected by multiple features of culpability or harm in step one, could merit upward adjustment from the starting point before further adjustment for aggravating or mitigating features, set out below.

Where there is a sufficient prospect of rehabilitation, a community order with a sex offender treatment programme requirement under section 202 of the Criminal Justice Act 2003 can be a proper alternative to a short or moderate length custodial sentence.

	A	B	C
Category 1	**Starting point** 4 years' custody **Category range** 3–6 years' custody	**Starting point** 2 years 6 months' custody **Category range** 2–4 years' custody	**Starting point** 1 year's custody **Category range** 26 weeks' — 2 years' custody
Category 2	**Starting point** 2 years' 6 months' custody **Category range** 2–5 years' custody	**Starting point** 1 year's custody **Category range** High level community order — 2 years' custody	**Starting point** Medium level community Order **Category range** Low level community order — High level community order

The table below contains a **non-exhaustive** list of additional factual elements providing the context of the offence and factors relating to the offender. Identify whether any combination of these, or other relevant factors, should result in an upward or downward adjustment from the starting point. **In particular, relevant recent convictions are likely to result in an upward adjustment.** In some cases, having considered these factors, it may be appropriate to move outside the identified category range.

When sentencing appropriate **category 2 offences**, the court should also consider the custody threshold as follows:

- has the custody threshold been passed?
- if so, is it unavoidable that a custodial sentence be imposed?
- if so, can that sentence be suspended?

Aggravating factors
Statutory aggravating factors • Previous convictions, having regard to a) the nature of the offence to which the conviction relates and its relevance to the current offence; and b) the time that has elapsed since the conviction • Offence committed whilst on bail *Other aggravating factors* • Failure to comply with current court orders • Offence committed whilst on licence • Deliberate isolation of prostitute(s) • Threats made to expose prostitute(s) to the authorities (for example, immigration or police), family/friends or others • Harm threatened against the family/friends of prostitute(s) • Passport/identity documents removed • Prostitute(s) prevented from seeking medical treatment • Food withheld • Earnings withheld/kept by offender or evidence of excessive wage reduction or debt bondage, inflated travel or living expenses or unreasonable interest rates • Any steps taken to prevent the reporting of an incident, obtaining assistance and/or from assisting or supporting the prosecution • Attempts to dispose of or conceal evidence • Prostitute(s) forced or coerced into pornography • Timescale over which operation has been run

Mitigating factors
• No previous convictions **or** no relevant/recent convictions • Remorse • Previous good character and/or exemplary conduct* • Age and/or lack of maturity where it affects the responsibility of the offender • Mental disorder or learning disability, particularly where linked to the commission of the offence • Demonstration of steps taken to address offending behaviour

* [Repeats note as to distinction between previous good character/exemplary conduct and having no previous convictions and how to deal with them in respect of the offence: see **SG-540** for the full text.]

SG-594   STEPS THREE TO NINE

[These are in the same terms as those applicable to sexual assault: see **SG-541**.]

SG-595   KEEPING A BROTHEL USED FOR PROSTITUTION
Sexual Offences Act 1956 (section 33A)

Triable either way

Maximum: 7 years' custody

Offence range: Community order — 6 years' custody

The terms 'prostitute' and 'prostitution' are used in this guideline in accordance with the statutory language contained in the Sexual Offences Act 2003.

SG-596   STEP ONE   Determining the offence category

The court should determine which categories of harm and culpability the offence falls into by reference **only** to the tables below.

Harm	
Category 1	• Under 18 year olds working in brothel • Abduction/detention • Violence or threats of violence • Sustained and systematic psychological abuse • Those working in brothel forced or coerced to participate in unsafe/degrading sexual activity • Those working in brothel forced or coerced into seeing many "customers" • Those working in brothel forced/coerced/deceived into prostitution • Established evidence of community impact
Category 2	Factor(s) in category 1 not present.

Culpability		
A	B	C
• Keeping brothel on significant commercial basis • Involvement in keeping a number of brothels • Expectation of significant financial or other gain • Abuse of trust • Exploitation of those known to be trafficked • Significant involvement in limiting freedom of those working in brothel • Grooming of a person to work in the brothel including through cultivation of a dependency on drugs or alcohol	• Keeping/managing premises • Close involvement with those working in brothel e.g. control of finances, choice of clients, working conditions, etc. (where offender's involvement is not as a result of coercion)	• Performs limited function under direction • Close involvement but engaged by coercion/intimidation/exploitation

SG-597   STEP TWO   Starting point and category range

Having determined the category, the court should use the corresponding starting points to reach a sentence within the category range below. The starting point applies to all offenders irrespective of plea or previous convictions. Having determined the starting point, step two allows further adjustment for aggravating or mitigating features, set out below.

A case of particular gravity, reflected by multiple features of culpability or harm in step one, could merit upward adjustment from the starting point before further adjustment for aggravating or mitigating features, set out below.

Where there is a sufficient prospect of rehabilitation, a community order with a sex offender treatment programme requirement under section 202 of the Criminal Justice Act 2003 can be a proper alternative to a short or moderate length custodial sentence.

	A	B	C
Category 1	**Starting point** 5 years' custody **Category range** 3–6 years' custody	**Starting point** 3 years' custody **Category range** 2–5 years' custody	**Starting point** 1 year's custody **Category range** High level community order — 18 months' custody
Category 2	**Starting point** 3 years' custody **Category range** 2–5 years' custody	**Starting point** 12 months' custody **Category range** 26 weeks' — 2 years' custody	**Starting point** Medium level community order **Category range** Low level community order — High level community order

The table below contains a **non-exhaustive** list of additional factual elements providing the context of the offence and factors relating to the offender. Identify whether any combination of these, or other relevant factors, should result in an upward or downward adjustment from the starting point. **In particular, relevant recent convictions are likely to result in an upward adjustment.** In some cases, having considered these factors, it may be appropriate to move outside the identified category range.

When sentencing appropriate **category 1 offences**, the court should also consider the custody threshold as follows:

- has the custody threshold been passed?
- if so, is it unavoidable that a custodial sentence be imposed?
- if so, can that sentence be suspended?

Aggravating factors
Statutory aggravating factors • Previous convictions, having regard to a) the nature of the offence to which the conviction relates and its relevance to the current offence; and b) the time that has elapsed since the conviction • Offence committed whilst on bail *Other aggravating factors* • Failure to comply with current court orders • Offence committed whilst on licence • Deliberate isolation of those working in brothel • Threats made to expose those working in brothel to the authorities (for example, immigration or police), family/friends or others • Harm threatened against the family/friends of those working in brothel • Passport/identity documents removed • Those working in brothel prevented from seeking medical treatment • Food withheld • Those working in brothel passed around by offender and moved to other brothels • Earnings of those working in brothel withheld/kept by offender or evidence of excessive wage reduction or debt bondage, inflated travel or living expenses or unreasonable interest rates • Any steps taken to prevent those working in brothel reporting an incident, obtaining assistance and/or from assisting or supporting the prosecution • Attempts to dispose of or conceal evidence • Those working in brothel forced or coerced into pornography • Timescale over which operation has been run

Mitigating factors
• No previous convictions **or** no relevant/recent convictions • Remorse • Previous good character and/or exemplary conduct* • Age and/or lack of maturity where it affects the responsibility of the offender • Mental disorder or learning disability, particularly where linked to the commission of the offence • Demonstration of steps taken to address offending behaviour

* [Repeats note as to distinction between previous good character/exemplary conduct and having no previous convictions and how to deal with them in respect of the offence: see **SG-540** for the full text.]

SG-598   **STEPS THREE TO EIGHT**

[These are the same as those applicable to rape (see **SG-533**) but with the omission of the step relating to dangerousness.]

SG-599

CAUSING OR INCITING CHILD PROSTITUTION OR PORNOGRAPHY
Sexual Offences Act 2003 (section 48)

CONTROLLING A CHILD PROSTITUTE OR CHILD INVOLVED IN PORNOGRAPHY
Sexual Offences Act 2003 (section 49)

ARRANGING OR FACILITATING CHILD PROSTITUTION OR PORNOGRAPHY
Sexual Offences Act 2003 (section 50)

Triable either way

Maximum: 14 years' custody

Offence range: Victim aged under 13   1–13 years' custody
                       Victim aged 13–15   26 weeks' — 11 years' custody
                       Victim aged 16–17   Community order — 7 years' custody

[Repeats information as to the CJA 2003, ss. 224A and 226A which is set out at **SG-554**.]

The terms 'child prostitute', 'child prostitution' and 'child involved in pornography' are used in this guideline in accordance with the statutory language contained in the Sexual Offences Act 2003.

SG-600   **STEP ONE** **Determining the offence category**

The court should determine which categories of harm and culpability the offence falls into by reference **only** to the tables below.

For offences that involve wide scale commercial and/or international activity sentences above the category range may be appropriate.

Harm	
Category 1	• Victims involved in penetrative sexual activity • Abduction/detention • Violence or threats of violence • Sustained and systematic psychological abuse • Victim(s) participated in unsafe/degrading sexual activity beyond that which is inherent in the offence • Victim(s) passed around by the offender to other "customers" and/or moved to other brothels
Category 2	Factor(s) in category 1 not present

Culpability		
A	B	C
• Directing or organising child prostitution or pornography on significant commercial basis • Expectation of significant financial or other gain • Abuse of trust • Exploitation of victim(s) known to be trafficked • Significant involvement in limiting the freedom of the victim(s) • Grooming of a victim to enter prostitution or pornography including through cultivation of a dependency on drugs or alcohol	• Close involvement with inciting, controlling, arranging or facilitating child prostitution or pornography (where offender's involvement is not as a result of coercion)	• Performs limited function under direction • Close involvement but engaged by coercion/ intimidation / exploitation

STEP TWO Starting point and category range

Having determined the category, the court should use the corresponding starting points to reach a sentence within the category range below. The starting point applies to all offenders irrespective of plea or previous convictions. Having determined the starting point, step two allows further adjustment for aggravating or mitigating features, set out below.

A case of particular gravity, reflected by multiple features of culpability or harm in step one, could merit upward adjustment from the starting point before further adjustment for aggravating or mitigating features, set out below.

Where there is a sufficient prospect of rehabilitation, a community order with a sex offender treatment programme requirement under section 202 of the Criminal Justice Act 2003 can be a proper alternative to a short or moderate length custodial sentence.

SG-601

		A	B	C
Category 1	U13	**Starting point** 10 years' custody **Category range** 8–13 years' custody	**Starting point** 8 years' custody **Category range** 6–11 years' custody	**Starting point** 5 years' custody **Category range** 2–6 years' custody
	13–15	**Starting point** 8 years' custody **Category range** 6–11 years' custody	**Starting point** 5 years' custody **Category range** 4–8 years' custody	**Starting point** 2 years 6 months' custody **Category range** 1–4 years' custody
	16–17	**Starting point** 4 years' custody **Category range** 3–7 years' custody	**Starting point** 2 years' custody **Category range** 1–4 years' custody	**Starting point** 1 year's custody **Category range** 26 weeks' — 2 years' custody
Category 2	U13	**Starting point** 8 years' custody **Category range** 6–11 years' custody	**Starting point** 6 years' custody **Category range** 4–9 years' custody	**Starting point** 2 years' custody **Category range** 1–4 years' custody
	13–15	**Starting point** 6 years' custody **Category range** 4–9 years' custody	**Starting point** 3 years' custody **Category range** 2–5 years' custody	**Starting point** 1 year's custody **Category range** 26 weeks' — 2 years' custody
	16–17	**Starting point** 3 years' custody **Category range** 2–5 years' custody	**Starting point** 1 year's custody **Category range** 26 weeks' — 2 years' custody	**Starting point** 26 weeks' custody **Category range** High level community order — 1 year's custody

Sentencing Guidelines

The table below contains a **non-exhaustive** list of additional factual elements providing the context of the offence and factors relating to the offender. Identify whether any combination of these, or other relevant factors, should result in an upward or downward adjustment from the starting point. **In particular, relevant recent convictions are likely to result in an upward adjustment.** In some cases, having considered these factors, it may be appropriate to move outside the identified category range.

When sentencing appropriate **category 2 offences**, the court should also consider the custody threshold as follows:

- has the custody threshold been passed?
- if so, is it unavoidable that a custodial sentence be imposed?
- if so, can that sentence be suspended?

Aggravating factors

Statutory aggravating factors
- Previous convictions, having regard to a) the nature of the offence to which the conviction relates and its relevance to the current offence; and b) the time that has elapsed since the conviction
- Offence committed whilst on bail

Other aggravating factors
- Failure to comply with current court orders
- Offence committed whilst on licence
- Deliberate isolation of victim(s)
- Vulnerability of victim(s)
- Threats made to expose victim(s) to the authorities (for example immigration or police), family/friends or others
- Harm threatened against the family/friends of victim(s)
- Passport/identity documents removed
- Victim(s) prevented from seeking medical treatment
- Victim(s) prevented from attending school
- Food withheld
- Earnings withheld/kept by offender or evidence of excessive wage reduction or debt bondage, inflated travel or living expenses or unreasonable interest rates
- Any steps taken to prevent the victim reporting an incident, obtaining assistance and/or from assisting or supporting the prosecution
- Attempts to dispose of or conceal evidence
- Timescale over which the operation has been run

Mitigating factors

- No previous convictions **or** no relevant/recent convictions
- Remorse
- Previous good character and/or exemplary conduct*
- Age and/or lack of maturity where it affects the responsibility of the offender
- Mental disorder or learning disability, particularly where linked to the commission of the offence

---

* [Repeats note as to distinction between previous good character/exemplary conduct and having no previous convictions and how to deal with them in respect of the offence: see **SG-532** for the full text.]

SG-602　**STEPS THREE TO NINE**

[These are in the same terms as those applicable to sexual assault of a child under 13: see **SG-557**.]

SG-603　Paying for the Sexual Services of a Child

Sexual Offences Act 2003 (section 47)

Triable only on indictment (if involving penetration against victim under 16) – otherwise triable either way

Maximum:	Victim under 13 (penetrative)	Life imprisonment
	Victim under 13 (non-penetrative)	14 years' custody
	Victim aged 13–15	14 years' custody
	Victim aged 16–17	7 years' custody
Offence range:	Victim aged 16–17	Community order – 5 years' custody

This guideline should only be used where the victim is aged 16 or 17 years old. If the victim is under 13 please refer to the guidelines for rape of a child under 13, assault by penetration of a child under 13, sexual assault of a child under 13 or causing or inciting a child under 13 to engage in sexual activity, depending on the activity involved in the offence.

If the victim is aged 13–15 please refer to the sexual activity with a child guideline.

[Repeats information as to the CJA 2003, s. 226A, which is set out at **SG-538**.]

STEP ONE Determining the offence category   SG-604

The court should determine which categories of harm and culpability the offence falls into by reference **only** to the tables below.

This guideline should only be used where the victim was aged 16 or 17 years old.

Harm	
Category 1	• Penetration of vagina or anus (using body or object) by, or of, the victim • Penile penetration of mouth by, or of, the victim • Violence or threats of violence • Victim subjected to unsafe/degrading sexual activity (beyond that which is inherent in the offence)
Category 2	• Touching of naked genitalia or naked breasts by, or of, the victim
Category 3	• Other sexual activity

Culpability	
A	**B**
• Abduction/detention • Sexual images of victim recorded, retained, solicited or shared • Offender acts together with others to commit the offence • Use of alcohol/drugs on victim • Abuse of trust • Previous violence against victim • Sexual images of victim recorded, retained, solicited or shared • Blackmail or other threats made (including to expose victim to the authorities, family/friends or others) • Offender aware that he has a sexually transmitted disease • Offender aware victim has been trafficked	Factor(s) in category A not present

STEP TWO Starting point and category range   SG-605

Having determined the category, the court should use the corresponding starting points to reach a sentence within the category range below **for victims aged 16 or 17**. The starting point applies to all offenders irrespective of plea or previous convictions. Having determined the starting point, step two allows further adjustment for aggravating or mitigating features, set out below.

A case of particular gravity, reflected by multiple features of culpability in step one, could merit upward adjustment from the starting point before further adjustment for aggravating or mitigating features, set out below.

Where there is a sufficient prospect of rehabilitation, a community order with a sex offender treatment programme requirement under section 202 of the Criminal Justice Act 2003 can be a proper alternative to a short or moderate length custodial sentence.

	A	B
Category 1	**Starting point** 4 years' custody **Category range** 2–5 years' custody	**Starting point** 2 years' custody **Category range** 1–4 years' custody
Category 2	**Starting point** 3 years' custody **Category range** 1–4 years' custody	**Starting point** 1 year's custody **Category range** 26 weeks' — 2 years' custody
Category 3	**Starting point** 1 year's custody **Category range** 26 weeks' — 2 years' custody	**Starting point** 26 weeks' custody **Category range** High level community order — 1 year's custody

The table below contains a **non-exhaustive** list of additional factual elements providing the context of the offence and factors relating to the offender. Identify whether any combination of these, or other relevant factors, should result in an upward or downward adjustment from the starting point. **In particular, relevant recent convictions are likely to result in an upward adjustment.** In some cases, having considered these factors, it may be appropriate to move outside the identified category range.

When sentencing appropriate **category 3 offences**, the court should also consider the custody threshold as follows:

- has the custody threshold been passed?
- if so, is it unavoidable that a custodial sentence be imposed?
- if so, can that sentence be suspended?

Aggravating factors

Statutory aggravating factors
- Previous convictions, having regard to a) the nature of the offence to which the conviction relates and its relevance to the current offence; and b) the time that has elapsed since the conviction
- Offence committed whilst on bail

Other aggravating factors
- Ejaculation
- Failure to comply with current court orders
- Offence committed whilst on licence
- Any steps taken to prevent the victim reporting an incident, obtaining assistance and/or from assisting or supporting the prosecution
- Attempts to dispose of or conceal evidence

Mitigating factors

- No previous convictions **or** no relevant/recent convictions
- Remorse
- Previous good character and/or exemplary conduct*
- Age and/or lack of maturity where it affects the responsibility of the offender
- Mental disorder or learning disability, particularly where linked to the commission of the offence
- Demonstration of steps taken to address offending behaviour

---

* [Repeats note as to distinction between previous good character/exemplary conduct and having no previous convictions and how to deal with them in respect of the offence: see **SG-540** for the full text.]

SG-606   STEPS THREE TO NINE

[These are in the same terms as those applicable to sexual assault: see **SG-541**.]

SG-607

TRAFFICKING PEOPLE FOR SEXUAL EXPLOITATION
Sexual Offences Act 2003 (sections 59A)

(This guideline also applies to offences, committed before 6 April 2013, of trafficking into/within/out of the UK for sexual exploitation contrary to sections 57 to 59 of the Sexual Offences Act 2003)

Triable either way

Maximum: 14 years' custody

Offence range: Community order — 12 years' custody

[Repeats information as to the CJA 2003, s. 226A, which is set out at **SG-538**.]

The term 'prostitution' is used in this guideline in accordance with the statutory language contained in the Sexual Offences Act 2003.

SG-608

STEP ONE Determining the offence category
The court should determine which categories of harm and culpability the offence falls into by reference **only** to the tables below.

Harm	
Category 1	• Abduction/detention • Violence or threats of violence • Sustained and systematic psychological abuse • Victim(s) under 18 • Victim(s) forced or coerced to participate in unsafe/degrading sexual activity • Victim(s) forced/coerced into prostitution • Victim(s) tricked/deceived as to purpose of visit
Category 2	• Factor(s) in category 1 not present

Culpability		
A	B	C
• Directing or organising trafficking on significant commercial basis • Expectation of significant financial or other gain • Significant influence over others in trafficking organisation/ hierarchy • Abuse of trust	• Operational or management function within hierarchy • Involves others in operation whether by coercion/ intimidation/ exploitation or reward (and offender's involvement is not as a result of coercion)	• Performs limited function under direction • Close involvement but engaged by coercion/ intimidation/ exploitation

SG-609

STEP TWO Starting point and category range
Having determined the category of harm and culpability, the court should use the corresponding starting points to reach a sentence within the category range below. The starting point applies to all offenders irrespective of plea or previous convictions. Having determined the starting point, step two allows further adjustment for aggravating or mitigating features, set out below.

A case of particular gravity, reflected by multiple features of culpability or harm in step one, could merit upward adjustment from the starting point before further adjustment for aggravating or mitigating features, set out below.

Where there is a sufficient prospect of rehabilitation, a community order with a sex offender treatment programme requirement under section 202 of the Criminal Justice Act 2003 can be a proper alternative to a short or moderate length custodial sentence.

Sentencing Guidelines

	A	B	C
Category 1	**Starting point** 8 years' custody **Category range** 6–2 years' custody	**Starting point** 6 years' custody **Category range** 4–8 years' custody	**Starting point** 18 months' custody **Category range** 26 weeks' — 2 years' custody
Category 2	**Starting point** 6 years' custody **Category range** 4–8 years' custody	**Starting point** 4 years' custody **Category range** 2–6 years' custody	**Starting point** 26 weeks' custody **Category range** High level community order — 18 months' custody

The table below contains a **non-exhaustive** list of additional factual elements providing the context of the offence and factors relating to the offender. Identify whether any combination of these, or other relevant factors, should result in an upward or downward adjustment from the starting point. **In particular, relevant recent convictions are likely to result in an upward adjustment.** In some cases, having considered these factors, it may be appropriate to move outside the identified category range.

When sentencing appropriate **category 2 offences**, the court should also consider the custody threshold as follows:

- has the custody threshold been passed?
- if so, is it unavoidable that a custodial sentence be imposed?
- if so, can that sentence be suspended?

Aggravating factors

Statutory aggravating factors
- Previous convictions, having regard to a) the nature of the offence to which the conviction relates and its relevance to the current offence; and b) the time that has elapsed since the conviction
- Offence committed whilst on bail

Other aggravating factors
- Failure to comply with current court orders
- Offence committed whilst on licence
- Deliberate isolation of victim(s)
- Children of victim(s) left in home country due to trafficking
- Threats made to expose victim(s) to the authorities (for example immigration or police), family/friends or others
- Harm threatened against the family/friends of victim
- Exploitation of victim(s) from particularly vulnerable backgrounds
- Victim(s) previously trafficked/sold/passed around
- Passport/identity documents removed
- Victim(s) prevented from seeking medical treatment
- Food withheld
- Use of drugs/alcohol or other substance to secure victim's compliance
- Earnings of victim(s) withheld/kept by offender or evidence of excessive wage reduction, debt bondage, inflated travel or living expenses, unreasonable interest rates
- Any steps taken to prevent the victim reporting an incident, obtaining assistance and/or from assisting or supporting the prosecution
- Attempts to dispose of or conceal evidence
- Timescale over which operation has been run

Mitigating factors

- No previous convictions **or** no relevant/recent convictions
- Remorse
- Previous good character and/or exemplary conduct*
- Age and/or lack of maturity where it affects the responsibility of the offender
- Mental disorder or learning disability, particularly where linked to the commission of the offence

---

* [Repeats note as to distinction between previous good character/exemplary conduct and having no previous convictions and how to deal with them in respect of the offence: see **SG-532** for the full text.]

STEPS THREE TO NINE   **SG-610**

[These are in the same terms as those applicable to sexual assault: see **SG-541**.]

SEXUAL ACTIVITY WITH A PERSON WITH A MENTAL DISORDER IMPEDING CHOICE   **SG-611**

Sexual Offences Act 2003 (section 30)

CAUSING OR INCITING A PERSON, WITH A MENTAL DISORDER
IMPEDING CHOICE, TO ENGAGE IN SEXUAL ACTIVITY

Sexual Offences Act 2003 (section 31)

Triable only on indictment (if penetration involved)

• otherwise, triable either way

Maximum: Life imprisonment (if penetration involved)

• otherwise, 14 years' custody

Offence range: Community order — 19 years' custody

[Repeats information as to the CJA 2003, ss. 224, 225(2), 224A and 226A, which is set out at **SG-530**.]

STEP ONE **Determining the offence category**   **SG-612**

The court should determine which categories of harm and culpability the offence falls into by reference **only** to the tables below.

Harm	
Category 1	• The extreme nature of one or more category 2 factors or the extreme impact caused by a combination of category 2 factors **may** elevate to category 1
Category 2	• Severe psychological or physical harm • Pregnancy or STI as a consequence of offence • Additional degradation/humiliation • Abduction • Prolonged detention /sustained incident • Violence or threats of violence • Forced/uninvited entry into victim's home or residence
Category 3	Factor(s) in categories 1 and 2 not present

Culpability	
A	B
• Significant degree of planning • Offender acts together with others to commit the offence • Use of alcohol/drugs on victim to facilitate the offence • Grooming behaviour used against victim • Abuse of trust • Previous violence against victim • Offence committed in course of burglary • Sexual images of victim recorded, retained, solicited or shared • Deliberate isolation of victim • Commercial exploitation and/or motivation • Offence racially or religiously aggravated • Offence motivated by, or demonstrating, hostility to the victim based on his or her sexual orientation (or presumed sexual orientation) or transgender identity (or presumed transgender identity) • Offence motivated by, or demonstrating, hostility to the victim based on the victim's disability (or presumed disability)	Factor(s) in category A not present

SG-613 STEP TWO **Starting point and category range**

Having determined the category of harm and culpability, the court should use the corresponding starting points to reach a sentence within the category range below. The starting point applies to all offenders irrespective of plea or previous convictions. Having determined the starting point, step two allows further adjustment for aggravating or mitigating features, set out below.

A case of particular gravity, reflected by multiple features of culpability or harm in step one, could merit upward adjustment from the starting point before further adjustment for aggravating or mitigating features, set out below.

Where there is a sufficient prospect of rehabilitation, a community order with a sex offender treatment programme requirement under section 202 of the Criminal Justice Act 2003 can be a proper alternative to a short or moderate length custodial sentence.

Where offence involved penetration

	A	B
Category 1	**Starting point** 16 years' custody **Category range** 13–19 years' custody	**Starting point** 13 years' custody **Category range** 11–17 years' custody
Category 2	**Starting point** 13 years' custody **Category range** 11–17 years' custody	**Starting point** 10 years' custody **Category range** 8–13 years' custody
Category 3	**Starting point** 10 years' custody **Category range** 8–13 years' custody	**Starting point** 8 years' custody **Category range** 6–11 years' custody

Where offence did not involve penetration

	A	B
Category 1	**Starting point** 6 years' custody **Category range** 4–9 years' custody	**Starting point** 4 years' custody **Category range** 3–7 years' custody
Category 2	**Starting point** 4 years' custody **Category range** 3–7 years' custody	**Starting point** 2 years' custody **Category range** 1–4 years' custody
Category 3	**Starting point** 1 year's custody **Category range** 26 weeks' — 2 years' custody	**Starting point** 26 weeks' custody **Category range** High level community order — 1 year's custody

The table below contains a **non-exhaustive** list of additional factual elements providing the context of the offence and factors relating to the offender. Identify whether any combination of these, or other relevant factors, should result in an upward or downward adjustment from the starting point. **In particular, relevant recent convictions are likely to result in an upward adjustment.** In some cases, having considered these factors, it may be appropriate to move outside the identified category range.

When appropriate, the court should also consider the custody threshold as follows:

- has the custody threshold been passed?
- if so, is it unavoidable that a custodial sentence be imposed?
- if so, can that sentence be suspended?

Aggravating factors

Statutory aggravating factors
- Previous convictions, having regard to a) the nature of the offence to which the conviction relates and its relevance to the current offence; and b) the time that has elapsed since the conviction
- Offence committed whilst on bail

Other aggravating factors
- Ejaculation (where not taken into account at step one)
- Blackmail or other threats made (where not taken into account at step one)
- Location of offence
- Timing of offence
- Use of weapon or other item to frighten or injure
- Victim compelled to leave their home or institution (including victims of domestic violence)
- Failure to comply with current court orders
- Offence committed whilst on licence
- Presence of others, especially children
- Any steps taken to prevent the victim reporting an incident, obtaining assistance and/or from assisting or supporting the prosecution
- Attempts to dispose of or conceal evidence
- Commission of offence whilst under the influence of alcohol or drugs

---

Mitigating factors

- No previous convictions **or** no relevant/recent convictions
- Remorse
- Previous good character and/or exemplary conduct*
- Age and/or lack of maturity where it affects the responsibility of the offender
- Mental disorder or learning disability, particularly where linked to the commission of the offence
- Sexual activity was incited but no activity took place because the offender voluntarily desisted or intervened to prevent it

---

* [Repeats note as to distinction between previous good character/exemplary conduct and having no previous convictions and how to deal with them in respect of the offence: see **SG-532** for the full text.]

STEPS THREE TO NINE

[These are in the same terms as those applicable to rape: see **SG-533**.]

SG-614

ENGAGING IN SEXUAL ACTIVITY IN THE PRESENCE OF A PERSON WITH MENTAL DISORDER IMPEDING CHOICE

Sexual Offences Act 2003 (section 32)

SG-615

CAUSING A PERSON, WITH MENTAL DISORDER IMPEDING CHOICE, TO WATCH A SEXUAL ACT

Sexual Offences Act 2003 (section 33)

Triable either way
Maximum: 10 years' custody

Offence range: Community order — 6 years' custody

[Repeats information as to the CJA 2003, s. 226A which is set out at **SG-538**.]

STEP ONE Determining the offence category

SG-616

The court should determine which categories of harm and culpability the offence falls into by reference **only** to the tables below.

Harm	
Category 1	• Causing victim to view extreme pornography • Causing victim to view indecent/prohibited images of children • Engaging in, or causing a victim to view live, sexual activity involving sadism/violence/sexual activity with an animal/a child
Category 2	Engaging in, or causing a victim to view images of or view live, sexual activity involving: • penetration of vagina or anus (using body or object) • penile penetration of mouth • masturbation
Category 3	Factor(s) in categories 1 and 2 not present

Culpability	
A	B
• Significant degree of planning • Offender acts together with others in order to commit the offence • Use of alcohol/drugs on victim to facilitate the offence • Grooming behaviour used against victim • Abuse of trust • Use of threats (including blackmail) • Commercial exploitation and/or motivation • Offence racially or religiously aggravated • Offence motivated by, or demonstrating, hostility to the victim based on his or her sexual orientation (or presumed sexual orientation) or transgender identity (or presumed transgender identity) • Offence motivated by, or demonstrating, hostility to the victim based on his or her disability (or presumed disability)	Factor(s) in category A not present

SG-617   STEP TWO **Starting point and category range**

Having determined the category of harm and culpability, the court should use the corresponding starting points to reach a sentence within the category range below. The starting point applies to all offenders irrespective of plea or previous convictions.

Having determined the starting point, step two allows further adjustment for aggravating or mitigating features, set out below.

A case of particular gravity, reflected by multiple features of culpability or harm in step one, could merit upward adjustment from the starting point before further adjustment for aggravating or mitigating features, set out below.

Where there is a sufficient prospect of rehabilitation, a community order with a sex offender treatment programme requirement under section 202 of the Criminal Justice Act 2003 can be a proper alternative to a short or moderate length custodial sentence.

	A	B
Category 1	**Starting point** 4 years' custody **Category range** 3–6 years' custody	**Starting point** 2 years' custody **Category range** 1–3 years' custody
Category 2	**Starting point** 2 years' custody **Category range** 1–3 years' custody	**Starting point** 1 year's custody **Category range** High level community order — 18 months' custody
Category 3	**Starting point** 26 weeks' custody **Category range** High level community order — 1 year's custody	**Starting point** Medium level community order **Category range** Low level community order — Medium level community order

The table below contains a **non-exhaustive** list of additional factual elements providing the context of the offence and factors relating to the offender. Identify whether any combination of these, or other relevant factors, should result in an upward or downward adjustment from the starting point. **In particular, relevant recent convictions are likely to result in an upward adjustment.** In some cases, having considered these factors, it may be appropriate to move outside the identified category range.

When sentencing appropriate **category 2 or 3 offences**, the court should also consider the custody threshold as follows:

* has the custody threshold been passed?
* if so, is it unavoidable that a custodial sentence be imposed?
* if so, can that sentence be suspended?

Aggravating factors
Statutory aggravating factors   • Previous convictions, having regard to a) the nature of the offence to which the conviction relates and its relevance to the current offence; and b) the time that has elapsed since the conviction   • Offence committed whilst on bail   *Other aggravating factors*   • Location of offence   • Timing of offence   • Failure to comply with current court orders   • Offence committed whilst on licence   • Any steps taken to prevent the victim reporting an incident, obtaining assistance and/or from assisting or supporting the prosecution   • Attempts to dispose of or conceal evidence   • Commission of offence whilst under the influence of alcohol or drugs

Mitigating factors
• No previous convictions **or** no relevant/recent convictions   • Remorse   • Previous good character and/or exemplary conduct*   • Age and/or lack of maturity where it affects the responsibility of the offender   • Mental disorder or learning disability, particularly where linked to the commission of the offence   • Demonstration of steps taken to address offending behaviour

* [Repeats note as to distinction between previous good character/exemplary conduct and having no previous convictions and how to deal with them in respect of the offence: see **SG-540** for the full text.]

STEPS THREE TO NINE   SG-618

[These are in the same terms as those applicable to sexual assault: see **SG-541**.]

INDUCEMENT, THREAT OR DECEPTION TO PROCURE SEXUAL ACTIVITY WITH   SG-619
A PERSON WITH A MENTAL DISORDER

Sexual Offences Act 2003 (section 34)

CAUSING A PERSON WITH A MENTAL DISORDER TO ENGAGE IN OR AGREE TO ENGAGE
IN SEXUAL ACTIVITY BY INDUCEMENT, THREAT OR DECEPTION

Sexual Offences Act 2003 (section 35)

Triable only on indictment (if penetration involved); otherwise triable either way

Maximum: Life imprisonment (if penetration involved); otherwise 14 years' custody

Offence range: Community order — 10 years' custody

[Repeats information as to the CJA 2003, ss. 224, 225(2), 224A and 226A, which is set out at **SG-530**.]

SG-620 | **STEP ONE** **Determining the offence category**

The court should determine which categories of harm and culpability the offence falls into by reference **only** to the tables below.

This guideline also applies to offences committed remotely/online.

Harm	
Category 1	• Penetration of vagina or anus (using body or object) • Penile penetration of mouth In either case by, or of, the victim
Category 2	Touching, or exposure, of naked genitalia or naked breasts by, or of, the victim
Category 3	Other sexual activity

Culpability		
A		**B**
• Significant degree of planning • Offender acts together with others to commit the offence • Use of alcohol/drugs on victim to facilitate the offence • Abuse of trust • Sexual images of victim recorded, retained, solicited or shared • Commercial exploitation and/or motivation • Offence racially or religiously aggravated • Offence motivated by, or demonstrating, hostility to the victim based on his or her sexual orientation (or presumed sexual orientation) or transgender identity (or presumed transgender identity) • Offence motivated by, or demonstrating, hostility to the victim based on his or her disability (or presumed disability)		Factor(s) in category A not present

SG-621 | **STEP TWO** **Starting point and category range**

Having determined the category of harm and culpability, the court should use the corresponding starting points to reach a sentence within the category range below. The starting point applies to all offenders irrespective of plea or previous convictions. Having determined the starting point, step two allows further adjustment for aggravating or mitigating features, set out below.

A case of particular gravity, reflected by multiple features of culpability or harm in step one, could merit upward adjustment from the starting point before further adjustment for aggravating or mitigating features, set out below.

Where there is a sufficient prospect of rehabilitation, a community order with a sex offender treatment programme requirement under section 202 of the Criminal Justice Act 2003 can be a proper alternative to a short or moderate length custodial sentence.

	A	B
Category 1	**Starting point** 5 years' custody **Category range** 4–10 years' custody	**Starting point** 1 year's custody **Category range** High level community order — 2 years' custody
Category 2	**Starting point** 3 years' custody **Category range** 2–6 years' custody	**Starting point** 26 weeks' custody **Category range** High level community order — 1 year's custody
Category 3	**Starting point** 26 weeks' custody **Category range** High level community order — 3 years' custody	**Starting point** Medium level community order **Category range** Low level community order — High level community order

The table below contains a **non-exhaustive** list of additional factual elements providing the context of the offence and factors relating to the offender. Identify whether any combination of these, or other relevant factors, should result in an upward or downward adjustment from the starting point. **In particular, relevant recent convictions are likely to result in an upward adjustment.** In some cases, having considered these factors, it may be appropriate to move outside the identified category range.

When sentencing appropriate **category 2 or 3 offences**, the court should also consider the custody threshold as follows:

- has the custody threshold been passed?
- if so, is it unavoidable that a custodial sentence be imposed?
- if so, can that sentence be suspended?

Aggravating factors
Statutory aggravating factors • Previous convictions, having regard to a) the nature of the offence to which the conviction relates and its relevance to the current offence; and b) the time that has elapsed since the conviction • Offence committed whilst on bail *Other aggravating factors* • Severe psychological or physical harm • Ejaculation • Pregnancy or STI as a consequence of offence • Location of offence • Timing of offence • Victim compelled to leave their home or institution (including victims of domestic violence) • Failure to comply with current court orders • Offence committed whilst on licence • Any steps taken to prevent the victim reporting an incident, obtaining assistance and/or from assisting or supporting the prosecution • Attempts to dispose of or conceal evidence • Commission of offence whilst under the influence of alcohol or drugs

Mitigating factors
• No previous convictions **or** no relevant/recent convictions • Remorse • Previous good character and/or exemplary conduct* • Age and/or lack of maturity where it affects the responsibility of the offender • Mental disorder or learning disability, particularly where linked to the commission of the offence

* [Repeats note as to distinction between previous good character/exemplary conduct and having no previous convictions and how to deal with them in respect of the offence: see **SG-532** for the full text.]

STEPS THREE TO NINE   SG-622
[These are in the same terms as those applicable to rape: see **SG-533**.]

Engaging in Sexual Activity in the Presence, Procured by Inducement, Threat or Deception, of a Person with a Mental Disorder   SG-623
Sexual Offences Act 2003 (section 36)

Causing a Person with a Mental Disorder to Watch a Sexual Act by Inducement, Threat or Deception
Sexual Offences Act 2003 (section 37)

Triable either way

Maximum: 10 years' custody

Offence range: Community order — 6 years' custody

[Repeats information as to the CJA 2003, s. 226A, which is set out at **SG-538**.]

SG-624 **STEP ONE** **Determining the offence category**

The court should determine which categories of harm and culpability the offence falls into by reference **only** to the tables below.

Harm	
Category 1	• Causing victim to view extreme pornography • Causing victim to view indecent/prohibited images of children • Engaging in, or causing a victim to view live, sexual activity involving sadism/violence/sexual activity with an animal/a child
Category 2	Engaging in, or causing a victim to view images of or view live, sexual activity involving: • penetration of vagina or anus (using body or object) • penile penetration of mouth • masturbation
Category 3	Factor(s) in categories 1 and 2 not present

Culpability	
A	**B**
• Significant degree of planning • Offender acts together with others in order to commit the offence • Use of alcohol/drugs on victim to facilitate the offence • Abuse of trust • Commercial exploitation and/or motivation • Offence racially or religiously aggravated • Offence motivated by, or demonstrating, hostility to the victim based on his or her sexual orientation (or presumed sexual orientation) or transgender identity (or presumed transgender identity) • Offence motivated by, or demonstrating, hostility to the victim based on his or her disability (or presumed disability)	Factor(s) in category A not present

SG-625 **STEP TWO** **Starting point and category range**

Having determined the category of harm and culpability, the court should use the corresponding starting points to reach a sentence within the category range below. The starting point applies to all offenders irrespective of plea or previous convictions. Having determined the starting point, step two allows further adjustment for aggravating or mitigating features, set out below.

A case of particular gravity, reflected by multiple features of culpability or harm in step one, could merit upward adjustment from the starting point before further adjustment for aggravating or mitigating features, set out below.

Where there is a sufficient prospect of rehabilitation, a community order with a sex offender treatment programme requirement under section 202 of the Criminal Justice Act 2003 can be a proper alternative to a short or moderate length custodial sentence.

	A	B
Category 1	**Starting point** 4 years' custody **Category range** 3–6 years' custody	**Starting point** 2 years' custody **Category range** 1–3 years' custody
Category 2	**Starting point** 2 years' custody **Category range** 1–3 years' custody	**Starting point** 1 year's custody **Category range** High level community order — 18 months' custody
Category 3	**Starting point** 26 weeks' custody **Category range** High level community order — 1 year's custody	**Starting point** Medium level community order **Category range** Low level community order — Medium level community order

The table below contains a **non-exhaustive** list of additional factual elements providing the context of the offence and factors relating to the offender. Identify whether any combination of these, or other relevant factors, should result in an upward or downward adjustment from the starting point. **In particular, relevant recent convictions are likely to result in an upward adjustment.** In some cases, having considered these factors, it may be appropriate to move outside the identified category range.

When sentencing appropriate **category 2 or 3 offences**, the court should also consider the custody threshold as follows:

- has the custody threshold been passed?
- if so, is it unavoidable that a custodial sentence be imposed?
- if so, can that sentence be suspended?

Aggravating factors
Statutory aggravating factors • Previous convictions, having regard to a) the nature of the offence to which the conviction relates and its relevance to the current offence; and b) the time that has elapsed since the conviction • Offence committed whilst on bail *Other aggravating factors* • Location of offence • Timing of offence • Failure to comply with current court orders • Offence committed whilst on licence • Any steps taken to prevent the victim reporting an incident, obtaining assistance and/or from assisting or supporting the prosecution • Attempts to dispose of or conceal evidence • Commission of offence whilst under the influence of alcohol or drugs

Mitigating factors
• No previous convictions **or** no relevant/recent convictions • Remorse • Previous good character and/or exemplary conduct* • Age and/or lack of maturity where it affects the responsibility of the offender • Mental disorder or learning disability, particularly where linked to the commission of the offence • Demonstration of steps taken to address offending behaviour

* [Repeats note as to distinction between previous good character/exemplary conduct and having no previous convictions and how to deal with them in respect of the offence: see **SG-540** for the full text.]

STEPS THREE TO NINE   SG-626
[These are in the same terms as those applicable to sexual assault: see **SG-541**.]

CARE WORKERS: SEXUAL ACTIVITY WITH A PERSON WITH A MENTAL DISORDER   SG-627
Sexual Offences Act 2003 (section 38)

CARE WORKERS: CAUSING OR INCITING SEXUAL ACTIVITY
Sexual Offences Act 2003 (section 39)

Triable only on indictment (if penetration involved); otherwise triable either way

Maximum: 14 years' custody (if penetration involved); otherwise 10 years' custody

Offence range: Community order — 10 years' custody

[Repeats information as to the CJA 2003, s. 226A, which is set out at **SG-538**.]

STEP ONE   Determining the offence category   SG-628
The court should determine which categories of harm and culpability the offence falls into by reference **only** to the tables below.

This guideline also applies to offences committed remotely/online.

Harm	
Category 1	• Penetration of vagina or anus (using body or object) • Penile penetration of mouth In either case by, or of, the victim
Category 2	• Touching, or exposure, of naked genitalia or naked breasts by, or of, the victim
Category 3	Factor(s) in categories 1 and 2 not present

Culpability	
A	**B**
• Significant degree of planning • Offender acts together with others to commit the offence • Use of alcohol/drugs on victim to facilitate the offence • Grooming behaviour used against victim • Use of threats (including blackmail) • Sexual images of victim recorded, retained, solicited or shared • Commercial exploitation and/or motivation • Offence racially or religiously aggravated • Offence motivated by, or demonstrating, hostility to the victim based on his or her sexual orientation (or presumed sexual orientation) or transgender identity (or presumed transgender identity) • Offence motivated by, or demonstrating, hostility to the victim based on his or her disability (or presumed disability)	Factor(s) in category A not present

SG-629 STEP TWO Starting point and category range

Having determined the category of harm and culpability, the court should use the corresponding starting points to reach a sentence within the category range below. The starting point applies to all offenders irrespective of plea or previous convictions. Having determined the starting point, step two allows further adjustment for aggravating or mitigating features, set out below.

A case of particular gravity, reflected by multiple features of culpability or harm in step one, could merit upward adjustment from the starting point before further adjustment for aggravating or mitigating features, set out below.

Where there is a sufficient prospect of rehabilitation, a community order with a sex offender treatment programme requirement under section 202 of the Criminal Justice Act 2003 can be a proper alternative to a short or moderate length custodial sentence.

	A	B
Category 1	**Starting point** 5 years' custody **Category range** 4–10 years' custody	**Starting point** 18 months' custody **Category range** 1–2 years' custody
Category 2	**Starting point** 3 year's custody **Category range** 2–6 years' custody	**Starting point** 26 weeks' custody **Category range** Medium level community order — 1 year's custody
Category 3	**Starting point** 26 weeks' custody **Category range** High level community order — 3 years' custody	**Starting point** Medium level community order **Category range** Low level community order — High level community order

The table below contains a **non-exhaustive** list of additional factual elements providing the context of the offence and factors relating to the offender. Identify whether any combination of these, or other relevant factors, should result in an upward or downward adjustment from the starting point. **In particular, relevant recent convictions are likely to result in an upward adjustment.** In some cases, having considered these factors, it may be appropriate to move outside the identified category range.

When sentencing appropriate **category 2 or 3 offences**, the court should also consider the custody threshold as follows:

- has the custody threshold been passed?
- if so, is it unavoidable that a custodial sentence be imposed?
- if so, can that sentence be suspended?

Aggravating factors

Statutory aggravating factors
- Previous convictions, having regard to a) the nature of the offence to which the conviction relates and its relevance to the current offence; and b) the time that has elapsed since the conviction
- Offence committed whilst on bail

Other aggravating factors
- Ejaculation
- Pregnancy or STI as a consequence of offence
- Location of offence
- Timing of offence
- Victim compelled to leave their home or institution (including victims of domestic violence)
- Failure to comply with current court orders
- Offence committed whilst on licence
- Any steps taken to prevent the victim reporting an incident, obtaining assistance and/or from assisting or supporting the prosecution
- Attempts to dispose of or conceal evidence
- Failure of offender to respond to previous warnings
- Commission of offence whilst under the influence of alcohol or drugs

---

Mitigating factors

- No previous convictions **or** no relevant/recent convictions
- Remorse
- Previous good character and/or exemplary conduct*
- Age and/or lack of maturity where it affects the responsibility of the offender
- Mental disorder or learning disability, particularly where linked to the commission of the offence
- Sexual activity was incited but no activity took place because the offender voluntarily desisted or intervened to prevent it

---

* [Repeats note as to distinction between previous good character/exemplary conduct and having no previous convictions and how to deal with them in respect of the offence: see **SG-532** for the full text.]

STEPS THREE TO NINE   SG-630
[These are in the same terms as those applicable to sexual assault: see **SG-541**.]

CARE WORKERS: SEXUAL ACTIVITY IN THE PRESENCE OF   SG-631
A PERSON WITH A MENTAL DISORDER
Sexual Offences Act 2003 (section 40)

CARE WORKERS: CAUSING A PERSON WITH A MENTAL DISORDER TO WATCH
A SEXUAL ACT
Sexual Offences Act 2003 (section 41)

Triable either way

Maximum: 7 years' custody

Offence range: Community order — 2 years' custody

[Repeats information as to the CJA 2003, s. 226A, which is set out at **SG-538**.]

SG-632   STEP ONE **Determining the offence category**

The court should determine which categories of harm and culpability the offence falls into by reference **only** to the tables below.

Harm	
Category 1	• Causing victim to view extreme pornography • Causing victim to view indecent/prohibited images of children • Engaging in, or causing a victim to view live, sexual activity involving sadism/violence/sexual activity with an animal/a child
Category 2	Engaging in, or causing a victim to view images of or view live, sexual activity involving: • penetration of vagina or anus (using body or object) • penile penetration of mouth • masturbation
Category 3	Factor(s) in categories 1 and 2 not present

Culpability	
A	**B**
• Significant degree of planning • Offender acts together with others to commit the offence • Use of alcohol/drugs on victim to facilitate the offence • Grooming behaviour used against victim • Use of threats (including blackmail) • Commercial exploitation and/or motivation • Offence racially or religiously aggravated • Offence motivated by, or demonstrating, hostility to the victim based on his or her sexual orientation (or presumed sexual orientation) or transgender identity (or presumed transgender identity) • Offence motivated by, or demonstrating, hostility to the victim based on his or her disability (or presumed disability)	Factor(s) in category A not present

SG-633   STEP TWO **Starting point and category range**

Having determined the category of harm and culpability, the court should use the corresponding starting points to reach a sentence within the category range below. The starting point applies to all offenders irrespective of plea or previous convictions. Having determined the starting point, step two allows further adjustment for aggravating or mitigating features, set out below.

A case of particular gravity, reflected by multiple features of culpability or harm in step one, could merit upward adjustment from the starting point before further adjustment for aggravating or mitigating features, set out below.

Where there is a sufficient prospect of rehabilitation, a community order with a sex offender treatment programme requirement under section 202 of the Criminal Justice Act 2003 can be a proper alternative to a short or moderate length custodial sentence.

	A	B
Category 1	**Starting point** 18 months' custody **Category range** 1–2 years' custody	**Starting point** 1 year's custody **Category range** 26 weeks' — 18 months' custody
Category 2	**Starting point** 1 year's custody **Category range** 26 weeks' — 18 months' custody	**Starting point** 26 weeks' custody **Category range** High level community order — 1 year's custody
Category 3	**Starting point** 26 weeks' custody **Category range** High level community order — 1 year's custody	**Starting point** Medium level community order **Category range** Low level community order — High level community order

The table below contains a **non-exhaustive** list of additional factual elements providing the context of the offence and factors relating to the offender. Identify whether any combination of these, or other relevant factors, should result in an upward or downward adjustment from the starting point. **In particular, relevant recent convictions are likely to result in an upward adjustment.** In some cases, having considered these factors, it may be appropriate to move outside the identified category range.

When sentencing appropriate **category 2 or 3 offences**, the court should also consider the custody threshold as follows:

- has the custody threshold been passed?
- if so, is it unavoidable that a custodial sentence be imposed?
- if so, can that sentence be suspended?

Aggravating factors
Statutory aggravating factors
• Previous convictions, having regard to a) the nature of the offence to which the conviction relates and its relevance to the current offence; and b) the time that has elapsed since the conviction
• Offence committed whilst on bail
Other aggravating factors
• Location of offence
• Timing of offence
• Failure to comply with current court orders
• Offence committed whilst on licence
• Any steps taken to prevent the victim reporting an incident, obtaining assistance and/or from assisting or supporting the prosecution
• Attempts to dispose of or conceal evidence
• Failure of offender to respond to previous warnings
• Commission of offence whilst under the influence of alcohol or drugs

Mitigating factors
• No previous convictions **or** no relevant/recent convictions
• Remorse
• Previous good character and/or exemplary conduct*
• Age and/or lack of maturity where it affects the responsibility of the offender
• Mental disorder or learning disability, particularly where linked to the commission of the offence
• Demonstration of steps taken to address offending behaviour

* [Repeats note as to distinction between previous good character/exemplary conduct and having no previous convictions and how to deal with them in respect of the offence: see **SG-540** for the full text.]

STEPS THREE TO NINE   SG-634

[These are in the same terms as those applicable to sexual assault: see **SG-541**.]

Exposure   SG-635
Sexual Offences Act 2003 (section 66)

Triable either way

Maximum: 2 years' custody

Offence range: Fine — 1 year's custody

[Repeats information as to the CJA 2003, s. 226A, which is set out at **SG-538**.]

STEP ONE   Determining the offence category   SG-636
The court should determine the offence category using the table below.

Sentencing Guidelines

Category 1	Raised harm **and** raised culpability
Category 2	Raised harm **or** raised culpability
Category 3	Exposure **without** raised harm or culpability factors present

The court should determine culpability and harm caused or intended, by reference **only** to the factors below, which comprise the principal factual elements of the offence. Where an offence does not fall squarely into a category, individual factors may require a degree of weighting before making an overall assessment and determining the appropriate offence category.

| **Factors indicating raised harm** |
| • Victim followed/pursued
• Offender masturbated |

| **Factors indicating raised culpability** |
| • Specific or previous targeting of a particularly vulnerable victim
• Abuse of trust
• Use of threats (including blackmail)
• Offence racially or religiously aggravated
• Offence motivated by, or demonstrating, hostility to the victim based on his or her sexual orientation (or presumed sexual orientation) or transgender identity (or presumed transgender identity)
• Offence motivated by, or demonstrating, hostility to the victim based on his or her disability (or presumed disability) |

SG-637   STEP TWO **Starting point and category range**

Having determined the category, the court should use the corresponding starting points to reach a sentence within the category range below. The starting point applies to all offenders irrespective of plea or previous convictions. Having determined the starting point, step two allows further adjustment for aggravating or mitigating features, set out below.

A case of particular gravity, reflected by multiple features of culpability or harm in step one, could merit upward adjustment from the starting point before further adjustment for aggravating or mitigating features, set out below.

Where there is a sufficient prospect of rehabilitation, a community order with a sex offender treatment programme requirement under section 202 of the Criminal Justice Act 2003 can be a proper alternative to a short or moderate length custodial sentence.

Category 1	**Starting point** 26 weeks' custody **Category range** 12 weeks' — 1 year's custody
Category 2	**Starting point** High level community order **Category range** Medium level community order — 26 weeks' custody
Category 3	**Starting point** Medium level community order **Category range** Band A fine — High level community order

The table below contains a **non-exhaustive** list of additional factual elements providing the context of the offence and factors relating to the offender. Identify whether any combination of these, or other relevant factors, should result in an upward or downward adjustment from the starting point. **In particular, relevant recent convictions are likely to result in an upward adjustment.** In some cases, having considered these factors, it may be appropriate to move outside the identified category range.

When sentencing **category 2 offences**, the court should also consider the custody threshold as follows:

• has the custody threshold been passed?
• if so, is it unavoidable that a custodial sentence be imposed?
• if so, can that sentence be suspended?

When sentencing **category 3 offences**, the court should also consider the community order threshold as follows:

- has the community order threshold been passed?

Aggravating factors
Statutory aggravating factors • Previous convictions, having regard to a) the nature of the offence to which the conviction relates and its relevance to the current offence; and b) the time that has elapsed since the conviction • Offence committed whilst on bail   *Other aggravating factors* • Location of the offence • Timing of the offence • Any steps taken to prevent the victim reporting an incident, obtaining assistance and/or from assisting or supporting the prosecution • Failure to comply with current court orders • Offence committed whilst on licence • Commission of offence whilst under the influence of alcohol or drugs • Presence of others, especially children

Mitigating factors
• No previous convictions **or** no relevant/recent convictions • Remorse • Previous good character and/or exemplary conduct* • Age and/or lack of maturity where it affects the responsibility of the offender • Mental disorder or learning disability, particularly where linked to the commission of the offence • Demonstration of steps taken to address offending behaviour

* [Repeats note as to distinction between previous good character/exemplary conduct and having no previous convictions and how to deal with them in respect of the offence: see **SG-540** for the full text.]

STEPS THREE TO NINE   SG-638

[These are in the same terms as those applicable to sexual assault: see **SG-541**.]

VOYEURISM   SG-639
Sexual Offences Act 2003 (section 67)

Triable either way

Maximum: 2 years' custody

Offence range: Fine — 18 months' custody

[Repeats information as to the CJA 2003, s. 226A, which is set out at **SG-538**.]

STEP ONE Determining the offence category   SG-640
The court should determine the offence category using the table below.

Category 1	Raised harm **and** raised culpability
Category 2	Raised harm **or** raised culpability
Category 3	Voyeurism **without** raised harm or culpability factors present

The court should determine culpability and harm caused or intended, by reference **only** to the factors below, which comprise the principal factual elements of the offence. Where an offence does not fall squarely into a category, individual factors may require a degree of weighting before making an overall assessment and determining the appropriate offence category.

Sentencing Guidelines

Factors indicating raised harm
• Image(s) available to be viewed by others • Victim observed or recorded in their own home or residence

Factors indicating raised culpability
• Significant degree of planning • Image(s) recorded • Abuse of trust • Specific or previous targeting of a particularly vulnerable victim • Commercial exploitation and/or motivation • Offence racially or religiously aggravated • Offence motivated by, or demonstrating, hostility to the victim based on his or her sexual orientation (or presumed sexual orientation) or transgender identity (or presumed transgender identity) • Offence motivated by, or demonstrating, hostility to the victim based on his or her disability (or presumed disability)

SG-641   **STEP TWO Starting point and category range**

Having determined the category, the court should use the corresponding starting points to reach a sentence within the category range below. The starting point applies to all offenders irrespective of plea or previous convictions. Having determined the starting point, step two allows further adjustment for aggravating or mitigating features, set out below.

A case of particular gravity, reflected by multiple features of culpability or harm in step one, could merit upward adjustment from the starting point before further adjustment for aggravating or mitigating features, set out below.

Where there is a sufficient prospect of rehabilitation, a community order with a sex offender treatment programme requirement under section 202 of the Criminal Justice Act 2003 can be a proper alternative to a short or moderate length custodial sentence.

Category 1	**Starting point** 26 weeks' custody **Category range** 12 weeks' — 18 months' custody
Category 2	**Starting point** High level community order **Category range** Medium level community order — 26 weeks' custody
Category 3	**Starting point** Medium level community order **Category range** Band A fine — High level community order

The table below contains a **non-exhaustive** list of additional factual elements providing the context of the offence and factors relating to the offender. Identify whether any combination of these, or other relevant factors, should result in an upward or downward adjustment from the starting point. **In particular, relevant recent convictions are likely to result in an upward adjustment.** In some cases, having considered these factors, it may be appropriate to move outside the identified category range.

When sentencing **category 2 offences**, the court should also consider the custody threshold as follows:

• has the custody threshold been passed?
• if so, is it unavoidable that a custodial sentence be imposed?
• if so, can that sentence be suspended?

When sentencing **category 3 offences**, the court should also consider the community order threshold as follows:

• has the community order threshold been passed?

Aggravating factors

Statutory aggravating factors
- Previous convictions, having regard to a) the nature of the offence to which the conviction relates and its relevance to the current offence; and b) the time that has elapsed since the conviction
- Offence committed whilst on bail

Other aggravating factors
- Location of offence
- Timing of offence
- Failure to comply with current court orders
- Offence committed whilst on licence
- Distribution of images, whether or not for gain
- Placing images where there is the potential for a high volume of viewers
- Period over which victim observed
- Period over which images were made or distributed
- Any steps taken to prevent victim reporting an incident, obtaining assistance and/or from assisting or supporting the prosecution
- Attempts to dispose of or conceal evidence

Mitigating factors

- No previous convictions **or** no relevant/recent convictions
- Remorse
- Previous good character and/or exemplary conduct*
- Age and/or lack of maturity where it affects the responsibility of the offender
- Mental disorder or learning disability, particularly where linked to the commission of the offence
- Demonstration of steps taken to address offending behaviour

---

* [Repeats note as to distinction between previous good character/exemplary conduct and having no previous convictions and how to deal with them in respect of the offence: see **SG-540** for the full text.]

STEPS THREE TO NINE   SG-642

[These are in the same terms as those applicable to sexual assault: see **SG-541**.]

SEX WITH AN ADULT RELATIVE: PENETRATION   SG-643
Sexual Offences Act 2003 (section 64)

SEX WITH AN ADULT RELATIVE: CONSENTING TO PENETRATION
Sexual Offences Act 2003 (section 65)

Triable either way
Maximum: 2 years' custody

Offence range: Fine — 2 years' custody

[Repeats information as to the CJA 2003, s. 226A, which is set out at **SG-538**.]

STEP ONE Determining the offence category   SG-644
The court should determine the offence category using the table below.

Category 1	Raised harm **and** raised culpability
Category 2	Raised harm **or** raised culpability
Category 3	Sex with an adult relative **without** raised harm or culpability factors present

The court should determine culpability and harm caused or intended, by reference **only** to the factors below, which comprise the principal factual elements of the offence. Where an offence does not fall squarely into a category, individual factors may require a degree of weighting before making an overall assessment and determining the appropriate offence category.

Sentencing Guidelines

Factors indicating raised harm
• Victim is particularly vulnerable due to personal circumstances • Child conceived

Factors indicating raised culpability
• Grooming behaviour used against victim • Use of threats (including blackmail)

SG-645   **STEP TWO Starting point and category range**

Having determined the category, the court should use the corresponding starting points to reach a sentence within the category range below. The starting point applies to all offenders irrespective of plea or previous convictions. Having determined the starting point, step two allows further adjustment for aggravating or mitigating features, set out below.

A case of particular gravity, reflected by multiple features of culpability or harm in step one, could merit upward adjustment from the starting point before further adjustment for aggravating or mitigating features, set out below.

Where there is a sufficient prospect of rehabilitation, a community order with a sex offender treatment programme requirement under section 202 of the Criminal Justice Act 2003 can be a proper alternative to a short or moderate length custodial sentence.

Category 1	**Starting point** 1 year's custody **Category range** 26 weeks' — 2 years' custody
Category 2	**Starting point** High level community order **Category range** Medium level community order — 1 year's custody
Category 3	**Starting point** Medium level community order **Category range** Band A fine — High level community order

The table below contains a **non-exhaustive** list of additional factual elements providing the context of the offence and factors relating to the offender. Identify whether any combination of these, or other relevant factors, should result in an upward or downward adjustment from the starting point. **In particular, relevant recent convictions are likely to result in an upward adjustment.** In some cases, having considered these factors, it may be appropriate to move outside the identified category range.

When sentencing **category 2 offences**, the court should also consider the custody threshold as follows:

• has the custody threshold been passed?
• if so, is it unavoidable that a custodial sentence be imposed?
• if so, can that sentence be suspended?

When sentencing **category 3 offences**, the court should also consider the community order threshold as follows:

• has the community order threshold been passed?

Aggravating factors
Statutory aggravating factors • Previous convictions, having regard to a) the nature of the offence to which the conviction relates and its relevance to the current offence; and b) the time that has elapsed since the conviction • Offence committed whilst on bail

Other aggravating factors
- Failure to comply with current court orders
- Offence committed whilst on licence
- Failure of offender to respond to previous warnings
- Any steps taken to prevent reporting an incident, obtaining assistance and/or from assisting or supporting the prosecution
- Attempts to dispose of or conceal evidence

Mitigating factors

- No previous convictions **or** no relevant/recent convictions
- Remorse
- Previous good character and/or exemplary conduct*
- Age and/or lack of maturity where it affects the responsibility of the offender
- Mental disorder or learning disability, particularly where linked to the commission of the offence
- Demonstration of steps taken to address offending behaviour

* [Repeats note as to distinction between previous good character/exemplary conduct and having no previous convictions and how to deal with them in respect of the offence: see **SG-540** for the full text.]

STEPS THREE TO NINE   SG-646

[These are in the same terms as those applicable to sexual assault: see **SG-541**.]

ADMINISTERING A SUBSTANCE WITH INTENT   SG-647

Sexual Offences Act 2003 (section 61)

Triable either way

Maximum: 10 years' custody

Offence range: 1–9 years' custody

[Repeats information as to the CJA 2003, s. 226A, which is set out at **SG-538**.]

STEP ONE Determining the offence category   SG-648
The court should determine the offence category using the table below.

Category 1	Raised harm **and** raised culpability
Category 2	Raised harm **or** raised culpability
Category 3	Administering a substance with intent **without** raised harm or culpability factors present

The court should determine culpability and harm caused or intended, by reference **only** to the factors below, which comprise the principal factual elements of the offence. Where an offence does not fall squarely into a category, individual factors may require a degree of weighting before making an overall assessment and determining the appropriate offence category. Where no substantive sexual offence has been committed the main consideration for the court will be the offender's conduct as a whole including, but not exclusively, the offender's intention.

Factors indicating raised harm

- Severe psychological or physical harm
- Prolonged detention /sustained incident
- Additional degradation/humiliation

Factors indicating raised culpability
• Significant degree of planning • Specific targeting of a particularly vulnerable victim • Intended sexual offence carries a statutory maximum of life • Abuse of trust • Recording of offence • Offender acts together with others to commit the offence • Commercial exploitation and/or motivation • Offence racially or religiously aggravated • Offence motivated by, or demonstrating, hostility to the victim based on his or her sexual orientation (or presumed sexual orientation) or transgender identity (or presumed transgender identity) • Offence motivated by, or demonstrating, hostility to the victim based on his or her disability (or presumed disability)

SG-649   STEP TWO **Starting point and category range**

Having determined the category, the court should use the corresponding starting points to reach a sentence within the category range below. The starting point applies to all offenders irrespective of plea or previous convictions. Having determined the starting point, step two allows further adjustment for aggravating or mitigating features, set out below.

A case of particular gravity, reflected by multiple features of culpability or harm in step one, could merit upward adjustment from the starting point before further adjustment for aggravating or mitigating features, set out below.

Category 1	**Starting point** 6 years' custody **Category range** 4–9 years' custody
Category 2	**Starting point** 4 years' custody **Category range** 3–7 years' custody
Category 3	**Starting point** 2 years' custody **Category range** 1–5 years' custody

The table below contains a **non-exhaustive** list of additional factual elements providing the context of the offence and factors relating to the offender. Identify whether any combination of these, or other relevant factors, should result in an upward or downward adjustment from the starting point. **In particular, relevant recent convictions are likely to result in an upward adjustment.** In some cases, having considered these factors, it may be appropriate to move outside the identified category range.

Aggravating factors
Statutory aggravating factors • Previous convictions, having regard to a) the nature of the offence to which the conviction relates and its relevance to the current offence; and b) the time that has elapsed since the conviction • Offence committed whilst on bail *Other aggravating factors* • Location of offence • Timing of offence • Any steps taken to prevent reporting an incident, obtaining assistance and/or from assisting or supporting the prosecution • Attempts to dispose of or conceal evidence • Failure to comply with current court orders • Offence committed whilst on licence

Mitigating factors
• No previous convictions **or** no relevant/recent convictions • Remorse • Previous good character and/or exemplary conduct* • Age and/or lack of maturity where it affects the responsibility of the offender • Mental disorder or learning disability, particularly where linked to the commission of the offence • Demonstration of steps taken to address offending behaviour

* [Repeats note as to distinction between previous good character/exemplary conduct and having no previous convictions and how to deal with them in respect of the offence: see **SG-540** for the full text.]

STEPS THREE TO NINE

SG-650

[These are in the same terms as those applicable to sexual assault: see **SG-541**.]

Committing an Offence with Intent to Commit a Sexual Offence

SG-651

Sexual Offences Act 2003 (section 62)

Triable only on indictment (if kidnapping or false imprisonment committed)

• otherwise, triable either way

Maximum: Life imprisonment (if kidnapping or false imprisonment committed)

• otherwise, 10 years

[Repeats information as to the CJA 2003, ss. 224, 225(2), 224A and 226A which is set out at **SG-530**.]

The starting point and range should be commensurate with that for the preliminary offence actually committed, but with an enhancement to reflect the intention to commit a sexual offence.

The enhancement will vary depending on the nature and seriousness of the intended sexual offence, but 2 years is suggested as a suitable enhancement where the intent was to commit rape or assault by penetration.

Trespass with Intent to Commit a Sexual Offence

SG-652

Sexual Offences Act 2003 (section 63)

Triable either way

Maximum: 10 years' custody

Offence range: 1–9 years' custody

[Repeats information as to the CJA 2003, s. 226A, which is set out at **SG-538**.]

STEP ONE Determining the offence category

SG-653

The court should determine the offence category using the table below.

Category 1	Raised harm **and** raised culpability
Category 2	Raised harm **or** raised culpability
Category 3	Trespass with intent to commit a sexual offence **without** raised harm or culpability factors present

The court should determine culpability and harm caused or intended, by reference **only** to the factors below, which comprise the principal factual elements of the offence. Where an offence does not fall squarely into a category, individual factors may require a degree of weighting before making an overall assessment and determining the appropriate offence category. Where no substantive sexual offence has been committed the main consideration for the court will be the offender's conduct as a whole including, but not exclusively, the offender's intention.

Factors indicating raised harm
• Prolonged detention/sustained incident • Additional degradation/humiliation • Offence committed in victim's home

Factors indicating raised culpability
• Significant degree of planning
• Specific targeting of a particularly vulnerable victim
• Intended sexual offence attracts a statutory maximum of life imprisonment
• Possession of weapon or other item to frighten or injure
• Abuse of trust
• Offender acts together with others to commit the offence
• Commercial exploitation and/or motivation
• Offence racially or religiously aggravated
• Offence motivated by, or demonstrating, hostility to the victim based on his or her sexual orientation (or presumed sexual orientation) or transgender identity (or presumed transgender identity)
• Offence motivated by, or demonstrating, hostility to the victim based on his or her disability (or presumed disability)

SG-654   STEP TWO **Starting point and category range**

Having determined the category, the court should use the corresponding starting points to reach a sentence within the category range below. The starting point applies to all offenders irrespective of plea or previous convictions. Having determined the starting point, step two allows further adjustment for aggravating or mitigating features, set out below.

A case of particular gravity, reflected by multiple features of culpability or harm in step one, could merit upward adjustment from the starting point before further adjustment for aggravating or mitigating features, set out below.

Category 1	**Starting point** 6 years' custody **Category range** 4–9 years' custody
Category 2	**Starting point** 4 years' custody **Category range** 3–7 years' custody
Category 3	**Starting point** 2 years' custody **Category range** 1–5 years' custody

The table below contains a **non-exhaustive** list of additional factual elements providing the context of the offence and factors relating to the offender. Identify whether any combination of these, or other relevant factors, should result in an upward or downward adjustment from the starting point. **In particular, relevant recent convictions are likely to result in an upward adjustment.** In some cases, having considered these factors, it may be appropriate to move outside the identified category range.

Aggravating factors
Statutory aggravating factors
• Previous convictions, having regard to a) the nature of the offence to which the conviction relates and its relevance to the current offence; and b) the time that has elapsed since the conviction
• Offence committed whilst on bail
Other aggravating factors
• Location of offence
• Timing of offence
• Any steps taken to prevent reporting an incident, obtaining assistance and/or from assisting or supporting the prosecution
• Attempts to dispose of or conceal evidence
• Failure to comply with current court orders
• Offence committed whilst on licence

Mitigating factors
• No previous convictions **or** no relevant/recent convictions • Remorse • Previous good character and/or exemplary conduct* • Age and/or lack of maturity where it affects the responsibility of the offender • Mental disorder or learning disability, particularly where linked to the commission of the offence • Demonstration of steps taken to address offending behaviour

* [Repeats note as to distinction between previous good character/exemplary conduct and having no previous convictions and how to deal with them in respect of the offence: see **SG-540** for the full text.]

STEPS THREE TO NINE   SG-655

[These are in the same terms as those applicable to sexual assault: see **SG-541**.]

CHILD SEX OFFENCES COMMITTED BY CHILDREN OR YOUNG PERSONS   SG-656
(SECTIONS 9–12) (OFFENDER UNDER 18)
Sexual Offences Act 2003 (section 13)

SEXUAL ACTIVITY WITH A CHILD FAMILY MEMBER (OFFENDER UNDER 18)
Sexual Offences Act 2003 (section 25)

INCITING A CHILD FAMILY MEMBER TO ENGAGE IN SEXUAL
ACTIVITY (OFFENDER UNDER 18)
Sexual Offences Act 2003 (section 26)

Triable either way

Maximum: 5 years' custody

These are 'grave crimes' for the purposes of section 91 of the Powers of Criminal Courts (Sentencing) Act 2000.

[Repeats information as to the CJA 2003, s. 226A which is set out at **SG-538**.]

*Definitive guidelines for the sentencing of offenders under 18 years old are **not** included.*

When sentencing offenders under 18, a court must in particular:

- *follow the definitive guideline **Overarching Principles – Sentencing Youths**;and have regard to:*
- *the principal aim of the youth justice system (to prevent offending by children and young people); and*
- *the welfare of the young offender.*

ANNEX A   SG-657

ANCILLARY ORDERS

This summary of the key provisions is correct as at the date of publication but will be subject to subsequent changes in law. If necessary, seek legal advice.

Ancillary order	Statutory reference
Compensation The court must consider making a compensation order in any case in which personal injury, loss or damage has resulted from the offence. The court must give reasons if it decides not to make an order in such cases.	Section 130 of the Powers of Criminal Courts (Sentencing) Act 2000
Confiscation A confiscation order may be made by the Crown Court in circumstances in which the offender has obtained a financial benefit as a result of, or in connection with, his criminal conduct.	Section 6 and Schedule 2 of the Proceeds of Crime Act 2002

Sentencing Guidelines

Ancillary order	Statutory reference
Deprivation of property The court may order the offender is deprived of property used for the purpose of committing, or facilitating the commission of, any offence, or intended for that purpose.	Section 143 of the Powers of Criminal Courts (Sentencing) Act 2000
Disqualification from working with children From 17 June 2013 courts **no longer** have the power to disqualify offenders from working with children pursuant to the Criminal Justice and Court Services Act 2000.	Schedule 10 of the Safeguarding Vulnerable Groups Act 2006 Safeguarding Vulnerable Groups Act 2006 (Commencement No. 8 and Saving) Order 2012 (SI 2012/2231) Protection of Freedoms Act 2012 (Commencement No. 6) Order 2013 (SI 2013/1180)
Restraining order Following a conviction *or an acquittal*, a court may make a restraining order for the purpose of protecting the victim or another person from harassment or a fear of violence.	Sections 5 and 5A of the Protection from Harassment Act 1997
Serious crime prevention order (SCPO) An SCPO may be made by the Crown Court in respect of qualifying offenders, if the court is satisfied such an order would protect the public by preventing, restricting or disrupting the involvement of the offender in serious crime.	Section 19 and Schedule 1 of the Serious Crime Act 2007
Sexual offences prevention order (SOPO) A SOPO may be made against qualifying offenders if the court is satisfied such an order is necessary to protect the public or any particular member of the public from serious sexual harm from the offender. The terms of the SOPO must be proportionate to the objective of protecting the public and consistent with the sentence and other ancillary orders, conditions and requirements to which the offender is subject.	Section 104 and Schedules 3 and 5 of the Sexual Offences Act 2003

Automatic orders on conviction

The following requirements or provisions are **not** part of the sentence imposed by the court but apply automatically by operation of law. The role of the court is to inform the offender of the applicable requirements and/or prohibition.

Requirement or provision	Statutory reference
Notification requirements A relevant offender automatically becomes subject to notification requirements, obliging him to notify the police of specified information for a specified period. The court should inform the offender accordingly. *The operation of the notification requirement is not a relevant consideration in determining the sentence for the offence.*	Sections 80 to 88 and Schedule 3 of the Sexual Offences Act 2003
Protection for children and vulnerable adults A statutory scheme pursuant to which offenders *will* or *may* be barred from regulated activity relating to children or vulnerable adults, with or without the right to make representations, depending on the offence. The court should inform the offender accordingly.	Section 2 and Schedule 3 of the Safeguarding Vulnerable Groups Act 2006 Safeguarding Vulnerable Groups Act 2006 (Prescribed Criteria and Miscellaneous Provisions) Regulations 2009 (SI 2009/37) (as amended)

ANNEX B

Approach to Sentencing of Historic Sexual Offences

Details of the principal offences are set out in the table at Annex C [at SG-659].

When sentencing sexual offences under the Sexual Offences Act 1956, or other legislation pre-dating the 2003 Act, the court should apply the following principles[513]:

1. The offender must be sentenced in accordance with the sentencing regime applicable at the *date of sentence*. Under the Criminal Justice Act 2003[514] the court must have regard to the statutory purposes of sentencing and must base the sentencing exercise on its assessment of the seriousness of the offence.
2. The sentence is limited to the maximum sentence available at the *date of the commission of the offence*. If the maximum sentence has been reduced, the lower maximum will be applicable.
3. The court should have regard to any applicable sentencing guidelines for equivalent offences under the Sexual Offences Act 2003.
4. The seriousness of the offence, assessed by the culpability of the offender and the harm caused or intended, is the main consideration for the court. The court should not seek to establish the likely sentence had the offender been convicted shortly after the date of the offence.
5. When assessing the culpability of the offender, the court should have regard to relevant culpability factors set out in any applicable guideline.
6. The court must assess carefully the harm done to the victim based on the facts available to it, having regard to relevant harm factors set out in any applicable guideline. Consideration of the circumstances which brought the offence to light will be of importance.
7. The court must consider the relevance of the passage of time carefully as it has the potential to aggravate or mitigate the seriousness of the offence. It will be an aggravating factor where the offender has continued to commit sexual offences against the victim or others or has continued to prevent the victim reporting the offence.
8. Where there is an absence of further offending over a long period of time, especially if combined with evidence of good character, this may be treated by the court as a mitigating factor. However, as with offences dealt with under the Sexual Offences Act 2003, previous good character/exemplary conduct is different from having no previous convictions. The more serious the offence, the less the weight which should normally be attributed to this factor. Where previous good character/exemplary conduct has been used to facilitate the offence, this mitigation should not normally be allowed and such conduct may constitute an aggravating factor.
9. If the offender was very young and immature at the time of the offence, depending on the circumstances of the offence, this may be regarded as personal mitigation.
10. If the offender made admissions at the time of the offence that were not investigated this is likely to be regarded as personal mitigation. Even greater mitigation is available to the offender who reported himself to the police and/or made early admissions.
11. A reduction for an early guilty plea should be made in the usual manner.

ANNEX C

Historic Offences

Offence (Sexual Offences Act 1956 unless stated otherwise)	Effective dates	Maximum
Rape and assault offences		
Rape (section 1)	1 January 1957–30 April 2004	Life
Buggery with a person or animal (section 12)	1 January 1957–30 April 2004 (from 3 November 1994 non-consensual acts of buggery were defined as rape)	Life

---

[513] *R v H and others* [2011] EWCA Crim 2753
[514] Section 143

Sexual Offences Act 1956 (...ted otherwise)	Effective dates	Maximum
...nt assault on a woman (section 14)	1 January 1957–30 April 2004	1 January 1957–31 December 1960: 2 years 1 January 1961–15 September 1985: 2 years or 5 years if victim under 13 and age stated on indictment 16 September 1985 onwards: 10 years
Indecent assault upon a man (section 15)	1 January 1957–30 April 2004	10 years
Offences against children		
Sexual intercourse with a girl under 13 (section 5)	1 January 1957–30 April 2004	Life
Incest by a male person (section 10)	1 January 1957–30 April 2004	Life if victim under 13; otherwise 7 years
Incest by a female person (section 11)	1 January 1957–30 April 2004	7 years
Gross indecency (section 13)	1 January 1957–30 April 2004	Male offender over 21 with male under age of consent: 5 years Otherwise: 2 years
Indecency with a child (section 1 of the Indecency with Children Act 1960)	1 January 1961–30 April 2004	1 January 1961–30 September 1997: 2 years 1 October 1997 onwards: 10 years *Note: on 11 January 2001 the age definition of a child increased from 14 to 16.*
Incitement of a girl under 16 to commit incest (section 54 of the Criminal Law Act 1977)	8 September 1977–30 April 2004	2 years
Abuse of position of trust (section 3 of the Sexual Offences (Amendment) Act 2000)	8 January 2001–30 April 2004	5 years
Indecent images		
Taking indecent photographs of a child (section 1 of the Protection of Children Act 1978)	20 August 1978 — present	20 August 1978–10 January 2001: 3 years 11 January 2001 onwards: 10 years
Possession of indecent photographs of a child (section 160 of the Criminal Justice Act 1988)	11 January 1988 — present	11 January 1988–10 January 2001: 6 months 11 January 2001 onwards: 5 years
Exploitation offences		
Procurement of woman by threats (section 2) Procurement by false pretences (section 3) Causing prostitution of women (section 22) Procuration of girl under 21 for unlawful sexual intercourse in any part of the world (section 23) Detention in a brothel (section 24) Permitting a defective to use premises for intercourse (section 27) Causing or encouraging prostitution (etc) of a girl under 16 (section 28) Causing or encouraging prostitution of a defective (section 29)	1 January 1957–30 April 2004	2 years
Living on earnings of prostitution (section 30) Controlling a prostitute (section 31)	1 January 1957–30 April 2004	7 years

Offence (Sexual Offences Act 1956 unless stated otherwise)	Effective dates	Maximum
Trafficking into/within/out of the UK for sexual exploitation (sections 57–59 of the Sexual Offences Act 2003)	1 May 2005– 5 April 2013	14 years
Offences against those with a mental disorder		
Intercourse with a defective (section 7) Procurement of a defective (section 9)	1 January 1957–30 April 2004	2 years
Sexual intercourse with patients (section 128 of the Mental Health Act 1956)	1 November 1960–30 April 2004	2 years
Other offences		
Administering drugs to obtain or facilitate intercourse (section 4)	1 January 1957–30 April 2004	2 years
Burglary with intent to commit rape (section 9 of the Theft Act 1968)	1 January 1969–30 April 2004	14 years if dwelling; otherwise 10 years

With thanks to Sweet & Maxwell, HHJ Rook QC and Robert Ward CBE for their kind permission to reproduce parts of *Sexual Offences Law & Practice*.

ANNEX D   SG-660

Fine Bands and Community Orders

[The information set out here is also set out in the Magistrates' Court Sentencing Guidelines, which includes further guidance on fines and community orders: see **SG-306** and **SG-330**.]

[Intercourse with an animal and sexual penetration of a corpse   SG-661

The Sentencing Council did not consider it necessary to issue guidelines in respect of the offences under the SOA 2003, ss. 69 and 70 as these are relatively rare offences with relatively low maximum sentence offences. In those circumstances, it is arguable that the old guidelines still apply.]

PART 27   FRAUD, BRIBERY AND MONEY   SG-662
LAUNDERING: CORPORATE OFFENDERS

Definitive Guideline

Applicability of guideline
[Omitted: See **SG-457** for identical text save that this guideline has effect from 1 October 2014.]

Fraud, Bribery and Money Laundering: Corporate Offenders Fraud   SG-663
Conspiracy to defraud (common law)

Cheat the public revenue (common law)

Triable only on indictment

Fraud Act 2006 (sections 1, 6 and 7)

Theft Act 1968 (section 17)

Value Added Tax Act 1994 (section 72)

Customs and Excise Management Act 1979 (section 170)

Triable either way

Bribery

Bribery Act 2010 (sections 1, 2, 6 and 7)

Triable either way

Money laundering

Proceeds of Crime Act 2002 (sections 327, 328 and 329)

Triable either way

Maximum: Unlimited fine

Most cases of corporate offending in this area are likely to merit allocation for trial to the Crown Court.

Committal for sentence is mandatory if confiscation (see step two) is to be considered (Proceeds of Crime Act 2002 section 70).

SG-664   **STEP ONE   Compensation**

The court must consider making a compensation order requiring the offender to pay compensation for any personal injury, loss or damage resulting from the offence in such an amount as the court considers appropriate, having regard to the evidence and to the means of the offender.

Where the means of the offender are limited priority should be given to the payment of compensation over payment of any other financial penalty.

Reasons should be given if a compensation order is not made.

(See section 130 Power of Criminal Courts (Sentencing) Act 2000)

SG-665   **STEP TWO   Confiscation**

Confiscation must be considered if either the crown asks for it or the court thinks it may be appropriate.

Confiscation must be dealt with before, and taken into account when assessing, any other fine or financial order (except compensation).

(See Proceeds of Crime Act 2002 sections 6 and 13)

SG-666   **STEP THREE   Determining the offence category**

The court should determine the offence category with reference to **culpability** and **harm**.

Culpability	Harm	
The sentencer should weigh up all the factors of the case to determine **culpability. Where there are characteristics present which fall under different categories, the court should balance these characteristics to reach a fair assessment of the offender's culpability.**	Harm is represented by a financial sum calculated by reference to the table below	
	Amount obtained or intended to be obtained (or loss avoided or intended to be avoided)	
Culpability demonstrated by the offending corporation's role and motivation. May be demonstrated by one or more of the following **non-exhaustive** characteristics.		
A – High culpability		
Corporation plays a leading role in organised, planned unlawful activity (whether acting alone or with others)		
Wilful obstruction of detection (for example destruction of evidence, misleading investigators, suborning employees)	**Fraud**	For offences of fraud, conspiracy to defraud, cheating the Revenue and fraudulent evasion of duty or VAT, harm will normally be the actual or intended gross gain to the offender.
Involving others through pressure or coercion (for example employees or suppliers)		
Targeting of vulnerable victims or a large number of victims		
Corruption of officials performing a law enforcement role		
Abuse of dominant market position or position of trust or responsibility		

Culpability	Harm	
Offending committed over a sustained period of time Culture of wilful disregard of commission of offences by employees or agents with no effort to put effective systems in place (section 7 Bribery Act only) **B – Medium culpability** Corporation plays a significant role in unlawful activity organised by others	**Bribery**	For offences under the Bribery Act the appropriate figure will normally be the gross profit from the contract obtained, retained or sought as a result of the offending. An alternative measure for offences under section 7 may be the likely cost avoided by failing to put in place appropriate measures to prevent bribery.
Activity not unlawful from the outset Corporation reckless in making false statement (section 72 VAT Act 1994) All other cases where characteristics for categories A or C are not present **C – Lesser culpability**	**Money laundering**	For offences of money laundering the appropriate figure will normally be the amount laundered or, alternatively, the likely cost avoided by failing to put in place an effective anti-money laundering programme if this is higher.
Corporation plays a minor, peripheral role in unlawful activity organised by others Some effort made to put bribery prevention measures in place but insufficient to amount to a defence (section 7 Bribery Act only) Involvement through coercion, intimidation or exploitation	**General**	Where the actual or intended gain cannot be established, the appropriate measure will be the amount that the court considers was likely to be achieved in all the circumstances. In the absence of sufficient evidence of the amount that was likely to be obtained, 10–20 per cent of the relevant revenue (for instance between 10 and 20 per cent of the worldwide revenue derived from the product or business area to which the offence relates for the period of the offending) **may** be an appropriate measure. There may be large cases of fraud or bribery in which the true harm is to commerce or markets generally. That may justify adopting a harm figure beyond the normal measures here set out.

STEP FOUR Starting point and category range

SG-667

Having determined the culpability level at step three, the court should use the table below to determine the starting point within the category range below. The starting point applies to all offenders irrespective of plea or previous convictions.

The harm figure at step three is multiplied by the relevant percentage figure representing culpability.

Culpability Level

Harm figure multiplier	A	B	C
	Starting point 300%	**Starting point** 200%	**Starting point** 100%
	Category range 250% to 400%	**Category range** 100% to 300%	**Category range** 20% to 150%

Having determined the appropriate starting point, the court should then consider adjustment within the category range for aggravating or mitigating features. In some cases, having considered these factors, it may be appropriate to move outside the identified category range. (See below for a **non-exhaustive** list of aggravating and mitigating factors.)

Factors increasing seriousness	Factors reducing seriousness or reflecting mitigation
Previous relevant convictions or subject to previous relevant civil or regulatory enforcement action	No previous relevant convictions or previous relevant civil or regulatory enforcement action
Corporation or subsidiary set up to commit fraudulent activity	Victims voluntarily reimbursed/compensated
	No actual loss to victims
Fraudulent activity endemic within corporation	Corporation co-operated with investigation, made early admissions and/or voluntarily reported offending
Attempts made to conceal misconduct	
Substantial harm (whether financial or otherwise) suffered by victims of offending or by third parties affected by offending	Offending committed under previous director(s)/manager(s)
Risk of harm greater than actual or intended harm (for example in banking/credit fraud)	Little or no actual gain to corporation from offending
Substantial harm caused to integrity or confidence of markets	
Substantial harm caused to integrity of local or national governments	
Serious nature of underlying criminal activity (money laundering offences)	
Offence committed across borders or jurisdictions	

General principles to follow in setting a fine

The court should determine the appropriate level of fine in accordance with section 164 of the Criminal Justice Act 2003, which requires that the fine must reflect the seriousness of the offence and requires the court to take into account the financial circumstances of the offender.

Obtaining financial information

Companies and bodies delivering public or charitable services

Where the offender is a company or a body which delivers a public or charitable service, it is expected to provide comprehensive accounts for the last three years, to enable the court to make an accurate assessment of its financial status. In the absence of such disclosure, or where the court is not satisfied that it has been given sufficient reliable information, the court will be entitled to draw reasonable inferences as to the offender's means from evidence it has heard and from all the circumstances of the case.

1. *For companies*: annual accounts. Particular attention should be paid to turnover; profit before tax; directors' remuneration, loan accounts and pension provision; and assets as disclosed by the balance sheet. Most companies are required to file audited accounts at Companies House. Failure to produce relevant recent accounts on request may properly lead to the conclusion that the company can pay any appropriate fine.
2. *For partnerships*: annual accounts. Particular attention should be paid to turnover; profit before tax; partners' drawings, loan accounts and pension provision; assets as above. Limited liability partnerships (LLPs) may be required to file audited accounts with Companies House. If adequate accounts are not produced on request, see paragraph 1.
3. *For local authorities, fire authorities and similar public bodies*: the Annual Revenue Budget ("ARB") is the equivalent of turnover and the best indication of the size of the defendant organisation. It is unlikely to be necessary to analyse specific expenditure or reserves unless inappropriate expenditure is suggested.
4. *For health trusts*: the independent regulator of NHS Foundation Trusts is Monitor. It publishes quarterly reports and annual figures for the financial strength and stability of trusts from which the annual income can be seen, available via www.monitor-nhsft.gov.uk. Detailed analysis of expenditure or reserves is unlikely to be called for.
5. *For charities*: it will be appropriate to inspect annual audited accounts. Detailed analysis of expenditure or reserves is unlikely to be called for unless there is a suggestion of unusual or unnecessary expenditure.

STEP FIVE   Adjustment of fine   SG-668

Having arrived at a fine level, the court should consider whether there are any further factors which indicate an adjustment in the level of the fine. The court should 'step back' and consider the overall effect of its orders. The combination of orders made, compensation, confiscation and fine ought to achieve:

- the removal of all gain
- appropriate additional punishment, and
- deterrence

The fine may be adjusted to ensure that these objectives are met in a fair way. The court should consider any further factors relevant to the setting of the level of the fine to ensure that the fine is proportionate, having regard to the size and financial position of the offending organisation and the seriousness of the offence.

The fine must be substantial enough to have a real economic impact which will bring home to both management and shareholders the need to operate within the law. Whether the fine will have the effect of putting the offender out of business will be relevant; in some bad cases this may be an acceptable consequence.

In considering the ability of the offending organisation to pay any financial penalty the court can take into account the power to allow time for payment or to order that the amount be paid in instalments.

The court should consider whether the level of fine would otherwise cause unacceptable harm to third parties. In doing so the court should bear in mind that the payment of any compensation determined at step one should take priority over the payment of any fine.

The table below contains a **non-exhaustive** list of additional factual elements for the court to consider. The court should identify whether any combination of these, or other relevant factors, should result in a proportionate increase or reduction in the level of fine.

Factors to consider in adjusting the level of fine
Fine fulfils the objectives of punishment, deterrence and removal of gain
The value, worth or available means of the offender
Fine impairs offender's ability to make restitution to victims
Impact of fine on offender's ability to implement effective compliance programmes
Impact of fine on employment of staff, service users, customers and local economy (but not shareholders)
Impact of fine on performance of public or charitable function

STEP SIX   Consider any factors which would indicate a reduction, such as assistance to the prosecution   SG-669

The court should take into account sections 73 and 74 of the Serious Organised Crime and Police Act 2005 (assistance by defendants: reduction or review of sentence) and any other rule of law by virtue of which an offender may receive a discounted sentence in consequence of assistance given (or offered) to the prosecutor or investigator.

STEP SEVEN   Reduction for guilty pleas   SG-670

The court should take into account any potential reduction for a guilty plea in accordance with section 144 of the Criminal Justice Act 2003 and the Guilty Plea guideline.

STEP EIGHT   Ancillary Orders   SG-671

In all cases the court must consider whether to make any ancillary orders.

STEP NINE   Totality principle   SG-672

If sentencing an offender for more than one offence, consider whether the total sentence is just and proportionate to the offending behaviour.

STEP TEN   Reasons   SG-673

Section 174 of the Criminal Justice Act 2003 imposes a duty to give reasons for, and explain the effect of, the sentence.

PART 28   ENVIRONMENTAL OFFENCES

SG-674
DEFINITIVE GUIDELINE

Applicability of guideline

[Omitted: See **SG-457** for identical text save that this guideline has effect from 1 July 2014.]

This guideline applies only to individual offenders aged 18 and older or organisations. General principles to be considered in the sentencing of youths are in the Sentencing Guidelines Council's definitive guideline, *Overarching Principles – Sentencing Youths*.

Structure, ranges and starting points

[Omitted: See **SG-458**]

SG-675
ORGANISATIONS

Unauthorised or harmful deposit, treatment or disposal etc. of waste

Illegal discharges to air, land and water

Environmental Protection Act 1990 (section 33)

Environmental Permitting (England and Wales) Regulations 2010 (regulations 12 and 38(1), (2) and (3))

Also relevant, with adjustments, to certain related offences (see [**SG-685**])

Triable either way

Maximum: when tried on indictment: unlimited fine
　　　　　when tried summarily: £50,000 fine

Offence range: £100 fine – £3 million fine

Use this guideline when the offender is an organisation. If the offender is an individual, please refer to the guideline for individuals.

Confiscation

Committal to the Crown Court for sentence is mandatory if confiscation (see step two) is to be considered: Proceeds of Crime Act 2002 section 70. In such cases magistrates should state whether they would otherwise have committed for sentence.

Financial orders must be considered in this order: (1) compensation, (2) confiscation, and (3) fine (see Proceeds of Crime Act 2002 section 13).

SG-676　**STEP ONE Compensation**

The court must consider making a compensation order requiring the offender to pay compensation for any personal injury, loss or damage resulting from the offence in such an amount as the court considers appropriate, having regard to the evidence and to the means of the offender.

Where the means of the offender are limited, priority should be given to the payment of compensation over payment of any other financial penalty.

Reasons should be given if a compensation order is not made.

(See section 130 Powers of Criminal Courts (Sentencing) Act 2000)

SG-677　**STEP TWO   Confiscation (Crown Court only)**

Confiscation must be considered if either the Crown asks for it or the court thinks that it may be appropriate. Confiscation must be dealt with before any other fine or financial order (except compensation).

(See sections 6 and 13 Proceeds of Crime Act 2002)

STEP THREE   Determining the offence category   SG-678

The court should determine the offence category using only the culpability and harm factors in the tables below. The culpability and harm categories are on a sliding scale; there is inevitable overlap between the factors described in adjacent categories. Where an offence does not fall squarely into a category, individual factors may require a degree of weighting before making an overall assessment and determining the appropriate offence category.

Dealing with a **risk of harm** involves consideration of both the likelihood of harm occurring and the extent of it if it does. Risk of harm is less serious than the same actual harm. Where the offence has caused risk of harm but no (or less) actual harm the normal approach is to move down to the next category of harm. This may not be appropriate if either the likelihood or extent of potential harm is particularly high.   SG-679

Culpability	Harm	
Deliberate Intentional breach of or flagrant disregard for the law by person(s) whose position of responsibility in the organisation is such that their acts/omissions can properly be attributed to the organisation; **OR** deliberate failure by organisation to put in place and to enforce such systems as could reasonably be expected in all the circumstances to avoid commission of the offence.	Category 1	• Polluting material of a dangerous nature, for example, hazardous chemicals or sharp objects • Major adverse effect or damage to air or water quality, amenity value, or property • Polluting material was noxious, widespread or pervasive with long-lasting effects on human health or quality of life, animal health or flora • Major costs incurred through clean-up, site restoration or animal rehabilitation • Major interference with, prevention or undermining of other lawful activities or regulatory regime due to offence
Reckless Actual foresight of, or wilful blindness to, risk of offending but risk nevertheless taken by person(s) whose position of responsibility in the organisation is such that their acts/omissions can properly be attributed to the organisation; **OR** reckless failure by organisation to put in place and to enforce such systems as could reasonably be expected in all the circumstances to avoid commission of the offence.	Category 2	• Significant adverse effect or damage to air or water quality, amenity value, or property • Significant adverse effect on human health or quality of life, animal health or flora • Significant costs incurred through clean-up, site restoration or animal rehabilitation • Significant interference with or undermining of other lawful activities or regulatory regime due to offence • Risk of category 1 harm
Negligent Failure by the organisation as a whole to take reasonable care to put in place and enforce proper systems for avoiding commission of the offence.	Category 3	• Minor, localised adverse effect or damage to air or water quality, amenity value, or property • Minor adverse effect on human health or quality of life, animal health or flora • Low costs incurred through clean-up, site restoration or animal rehabilitation • Limited interference with or undermining of other lawful activities or regulatory regime due to offence • Risk of category 2 harm
Low or no culpability Offence committed with little or no fault on the part of the organisation as a whole, for example by accident or the act of a rogue employee and despite the presence and due enforcement of all reasonably required preventive measures, or where such proper preventive measures were unforeseeably overcome by exceptional events.	Category 4	• Risk of category 3 harm

Sentencing Guidelines

STEP FOUR   Starting point and category range

Having determined the category, the court should refer to the tables [below]. There are four tables of starting points and ranges: one for large organisations, one for medium organisations, one for small organisations and one for micro-organisations. The court should refer to the table that relates to the size of the offending organisation.

The court should use the corresponding starting point to reach a sentence within the category range. The court should then consider further adjustment within the category range for aggravating and mitigating features, set out [below].

General principles to follow in setting a fine

The court should determine the appropriate level of fine in accordance with section 164 of the Criminal Justice Act 2003, which requires that the fine must reflect the seriousness of the offence and the court to take into account the financial circumstances of the offender.

The level of fine should reflect the extent to which the offender fell below the required standard. The fine should meet, in a fair and proportionate way, the objectives of punishment, deterrence and the removal of gain derived through the commission of the offence; it should not be cheaper to offend than to take the appropriate precautions.

Obtaining financial information

Offenders which are companies, partnerships or bodies delivering a public or charitable service, are expected to provide comprehensive accounts for the last three years, to enable the court to make an accurate assessment of its financial status. In the absence of such disclosure, or where the court is not satisfied that it has been given sufficient reliable information, the court will be entitled to draw reasonable inferences as to the offender's means from evidence it has heard and from all the circumstances of the case.

Normally, only information relating to the organisation before the court will be relevant, unless it is demonstrated to the court that the resources of a linked organisation are available and can properly be taken into account.

1. *For companies*: annual accounts. Particular attention should be paid to turnover; profit before tax; directors' remuneration, loan accounts and pension provision; and assets as disclosed by the balance sheet. Most companies are required to file audited accounts at Companies House. **Failure to produce relevant recent accounts on request may properly lead to the conclusion that the company can pay any appropriate fine.**
2. *For partnerships*: annual accounts. Particular attention should be paid to turnover; profit before tax; partners' drawings, loan accounts and pension provision; assets as above. Limited Liability Partnerships (LLPs) may be required to file audited accounts with Companies House. **If adequate accounts are not produced on request, see paragraph 1.**
3. *For local authorities, fire authorities and similar public bodies*: the Annual Revenue Budget ("ARB") is the equivalent of turnover and the best indication of the size of the defendant organisation. It is unlikely to be necessary to analyse specific expenditure or reserves (where relevant) unless inappropriate expenditure is suggested.
4. *For health trusts*: the independent regulator of NHS Foundation Trusts is Monitor. It publishes quarterly reports and annual figures for the financial strength and stability of trusts from which the annual income can be seen, available via **www.monitor-nhsft.gov.uk**. Detailed analysis of expenditure or reserves is unlikely to be called for.
5. *For charities*: it will be appropriate to inspect annual audited accounts. Detailed analysis of expenditure or reserves is unlikely to be called for unless there is a suggestion of unusual or unnecessary expenditure.

At step four, the court will be required to focus on the organisation's annual turnover or equivalent to reach a starting point for a fine. At step six, the court may be required to refer to the other financial factors listed above to ensure that the proposed fine is proportionate.

Very large organisations

Where a defendant company's turnover or equivalent very greatly exceeds the threshold for large companies, it may be necessary to move outside the suggested range to achieve a proportionate sentence.

Large — Turnover or equivalent: £50 million and over.

Large	Starting Point	Range
Deliberate		
Category 1	£1,000,000	£450,000 – £3,000,000
Category 2	£500,000	£180,000 – £1,250,000
Category 3	£180,000	£100,000 – £450,000
Category 4	£100,000	£55,000 – £250,000
Reckless		
Category 1	£550,000	£250,000 – £1,500,000
Category 2	£250,000	£100,000 – £650,000
Category 3	£100,000	£60,000 – £250,000
Category 4	£60,000	£35,000 – £160,000
Negligent		
Category 1	£300,000	£140,000 – £750,000
Category 2	£140,000	£60,000 – £350,000
Category 3	£60,000	£35,000 – £150,000
Category 4	£35,000	£22,000 – £100,000
Low / No culpability		
Category 1	£50,000	£25,000 – £130,000
Category 2	£25,000	£14,000 – £70,000
Category 3	£14,000	£10,000 – £40,000
Category 4	£10,000	£7,000 – £25,000

Medium — Turnover or equivalent: between £10 million and £50 million.

Medium	Starting Point	Range
Deliberate		
Category 1	£400,000	£170,000 – £1,000,000
Category 2	£170,000	£70,000 – £450,000
Category 3	£70,000	£40,000 – £180,000
Category 4	£40,000	£22,000 – £100,000
Reckless		
Category 1	£220,000	£100,000 – £500,000
Category 2	£100,000	£40,000 – £250,000
Category 3	£40,000	£24,000 – £100,000
Category 4	£24,000	£14,000 – £60,000
Negligent		
Category 1	£120,000	£55,000 – £300,000
Category 2	£55,000	£25,000 – £140,000
Category 3	£25,000	£14,000 – £60,000
Category 4	£14,000	£8,000 – £35,000

Sentencing Guidelines

Medium	Starting Point	Range
Low / No culpability		
Category 1	£20,000	£10,000 – £50,000
Category 2	£10,000	£5,500 – £25,000
Category 3	£5,000	£3,500 – £14,000
Category 4	£3,000	£2,500 – £10,000

Small — Turnover or equivalent: between £2 million and £10 million.

Small	Starting Point	Range
Deliberate		
Category 1	£100,000	£45,000 – £400,000
Category 2	£45,000	£17,000 – £170,000
Category 3	£17,000	£10,000 – £70,000
Category 4	£10,000	£5,000 – £40,000
Reckless		
Category 1	£55,000	£24,000 – £220,000
Category 2	£24,000	£10,000 – £100,000
Category 3	£10,000	£5,000 – £40,000
Category 4	£5,000	£3,000 – £24,000
Negligent		
Category 1	£30,000	£13,000 – £120,000
Category 2	£13,000	£6,000 – £55,000
Category 3	£6,000	£3,000 – £23,000
Category 4	£3,000	£1,500 – £14,000
Low / No culpability		
Category 1	£5,000	£2,500 – £20,000
Category 2	£2,500	£1,000 – £10,000
Category 3	£1,000	£700 – £5,000
Category 4	£700	£400 – £3,500

Micro — Turnover or equivalent: not more than £2 million.

Micro	Starting Point	Range
Deliberate		
Category 1	£50,000	£9,000 – £95,000
Category 2	£22,000	£3,000 – £45,000
Category 3	£9,000	£2,000 – £17,000
Category 4	£5,000	£1,000 – £10,000
Reckless		
Category 1	£30,000	£3,000 – £55,000
Category 2	£12,000	£1,500 – £24,000
Category 3	£5,000	£1,000 – £10,000
Category 4	£3,000	£500 – £5,500

Micro	Starting Point	Range
Negligent		
Category 1	£15,000	£1,500 – £30,000
Category 2	£6,500	£1,000 – £13,000
Category 3	£2,500	£500 – £5,500
Category 4	£1,400	£350 – £3,000
Low / No culpability		
Category 1	£2,500	£500 – £5,000
Category 2	£1,000	£350 – £2,400
Category 3	£400	£175 – £1,000
Category 4	£200	£100 – £700

The table below contains a **non-exhaustive** list of factual elements providing the context of the offence and factors relating to the offender. Identify whether any combination of these, or other relevant factors, should result in an upward or downward adjustment from the starting point. **In particular, relevant recent convictions and/or a history of non-compliance are likely to result in a substantial upward adjustment.** In some cases, having considered these factors, it may be appropriate to move outside the identified category range.

Factors increasing seriousness	Factors reducing seriousness or reflecting mitigation
Statutory aggravating factors:	No previous convictions **or** no relevant/recent convictions
Previous convictions, having regard to a) the nature of the offence to which the conviction relates and its relevance to the current offence; and b) the time that has elapsed since the conviction	Evidence of steps taken to remedy problem
	Remorse
	Compensation paid voluntarily to remedy harm caused
	One-off event not commercially motivated
Other aggravating factors include:	Little or no financial gain
History of non-compliance with warnings by regulator	Effective compliance and ethics programme
Location of the offence, for example, near housing, schools, livestock or environmentally sensitive sites	Self-reporting, co-operation and acceptance of responsibility
	Good character and/or exemplary conduct
Repeated incidents of offending or offending over an extended period of time, where not charged separately	
Deliberate concealment of illegal nature of activity	
Ignoring risks identified by employees or others	
Established evidence of wider/community impact	
Breach of any order	
Offence committed for financial gain	
Obstruction of justice	

STEPS FIVE TO SEVEN   SG-680

The court should now 'step back' and, using the factors set out in steps five, six and seven, review whether the sentence as a whole meets, in a fair way, the objectives of punishment, deterrence and removal of gain derived through the commission of the offence. At steps five to seven, the court may increase or reduce the proposed fine reached at step four, if necessary moving outside the range.

SG-681   **STEP FIVE**   **Ensure that the combination of financial orders (compensation, confiscation if appropriate, and fine) removes any economic benefit derived from the offending**

The court should remove any economic benefit the offender has derived through the commission of the offence including:

- avoided costs;
- operating savings;
- any gain made as a direct result of the offence.

Where the offender is fined, the amount of economic benefit derived from the offence should normally be added to the fine arrived at in step four. If a confiscation order is made, in considering economic benefit, the court should avoid double recovery.

Economic benefit will not always be an identifiable feature of a case. For example, in some water pollution cases there may be strict liability but very little obvious gain. However, even in these cases there may be some avoidance of cost, for example alarms not installed and maintained, inadequate funding or security measures not installed. Any costs avoided will be considered as economic benefit.

Where it is not possible to calculate or estimate the economic benefit, the court may wish to draw on information from the enforcing authorities about the general costs of operating within the law.

SG-682   **STEP SIX**   **Check whether the proposed fine based on turnover is proportionate to the means of the offender**

The combination of financial orders must be sufficiently substantial to have a real economic impact which will bring home to both management and shareholders the need to improve regulatory compliance. Whether the fine will have the effect of putting the offender out of business will be relevant; in some bad cases this may be an acceptable consequence.

It will be necessary to examine the financial circumstances of the organisation in the round. If an organisation has a small profit margin relative to its turnover, downward adjustment may be needed. If it has a large profit margin, upward adjustment may be needed.

In considering the ability of the offending organisation to pay any financial penalty, the court can take into account **the power to allow time for payment or to order that the amount be paid in instalments.**

SG-683   **STEP SEVEN**   **Consider other factors that may warrant adjustment of the proposed fine**

The court should consider any further factors that are relevant to ensuring that the proposed fine is proportionate having regard to the means of the offender and the seriousness of the offence.

Where the fine will fall on public or charitable bodies, the fine should normally be substantially reduced if the offending organisation is able to demonstrate the proposed fine would have a significant impact on the provision of their services.

The non-exhaustive list below contains additional factual elements the court should consider in deciding whether an increase or reduction to the proposed fine is required:

- fine impairs offender's ability to make restitution to victims;
- impact of fine on offender's ability to improve conditions in the organisation to comply with the law;
- impact of fine on employment of staff, service users, customers and local economy.

SG-684   **STEP EIGHT**   **Consider any factors which indicate a reduction, such as assistance to the prosecution**

The court should take into account sections 73 and 74 of the Serious Organised Crime and Police Act 2005 (assistance by defendants: reduction or review of sentence) and any other rule of law by virtue of which an offender may receive a discounted sentence in consequence of assistance given (or offered) to the prosecutor or investigator.

STEP NINE   **Reduction for guilty pleas**

The court should take account of any potential reduction for a guilty plea in accordance with section 144 of the Criminal Justice Act 2003 and the Guilty Plea guideline.

STEP TEN   **Ancillary orders**

In all cases, the court must consider whether to make ancillary orders. These may include:

Forfeiture of vehicle
The court may order the forfeiture of a vehicle used in or for the purposes of the commission of the offence in accordance with section 33C of the Environmental Protection Act 1990.

Deprivation of property

Where section 33C of the Environmental Protection Act 1990 does not apply, the court may order the offender be deprived of property used to commit crime or intended for that purpose in accordance with section 143 of the Powers of Criminal Courts (Sentencing) Act 2000. In considering whether to make an order under section 143, the court must have regard to the value of the property and the likely effects on the offender of making the order taken together with any other order the court makes.

Remediation

Where an offender is convicted of an offence under regulation 38(1), (2) or (3) of the Environmental Permitting (England and Wales) Regulations 2010, a court may order the offender to take steps to remedy the cause of the offence within a specified period in accordance with regulation 44 of the Environmental Permitting (England and Wales) Regulations 2010.

STEP ELEVEN   Totality principle

If sentencing an offender for more than one offence, or where the offender is already serving a sentence, consider whether the total sentence is just and proportionate to the offending behaviour.

STEP TWELVE   Reasons

Section 174 of the Criminal Justice Act 2003 imposes a duty to give reasons for, and explain the effect of, the sentence.

Other environmental offences

In sentencing other relevant and analogous environmental offences, the court should refer to the sentencing approach in steps one to three and five to seven of the guideline, **adjusting the starting points and ranges bearing in mind the statutory maxima** for those offences. An indicative list of such offences is set out below.

SG-685

Offence	Mode of trial	Statutory maxima
Section 1 Control of Pollution (Amendment) Act 1989 – transporting controlled waste without registering	Triable summarily only	• level 5 fine
Section 34 Environmental Protection Act 1990 – breach of duty of care	Triable either way	• when tried on indictment: unlimited fine • when tried summarily: level 5 fine
Section 80 Environmental Protection Act 1990 – breach of an abatement notice	Triable summarily only	• where the offence is committed on industrial, trade or business premises: £20,000 fine • where the offence is committed on non-industrial etc. premises: level 5 fine with a further fine of an amount equal to one-tenth of that level for each day on which the offence continues after the conviction
Section 111 Water Industry Act 1991 – restrictions on use of public sewers	Triable either way	• when tried on indictment: imprisonment for a term not exceeding two years or a fine or both • when tried summarily: a fine not exceeding the statutory maximum and a further fine not exceeding £50 for each day on which the offence continues after conviction
Offences under the Transfrontier Shipment of Waste Regulations 2007	Triable either way	• when tried on indictment: a fine or two years' imprisonment or both • when tried summarily: a fine not exceeding the statutory maximum or three months' imprisonment or both

SG-686

Individuals

Unauthorised or harmful deposit, treatment or disposal etc. of waste

Illegal discharges to air, land and water

Environmental Protection Act 1990 (section 33)

Environmental Permitting (England and Wales) Regulations 2010 (regulations 12 and 38(1), (2) and (3))

Also relevant, with adjustments, to certain related offences (see [SG-685])

Triable either way

Maximum: when tried on indictment: unlimited fine and/or 5 years' custody
when tried summarily: £50,000 fine and/or 6 months' custody

Offence range: conditional discharge – 3 years' custody

Use this guideline when the offender is an individual. If the offender is an organisation, please refer to the guideline for organisations.

Confiscation

Committal to the Crown Court for sentence is mandatory if confiscation (see step two) is to be considered: Proceeds of Crime Act 2002 section 70. In such cases magistrates should state whether they would otherwise have committed for sentence.

If a fine is imposed, the financial orders must be considered in this order: (1) compensation, (2) confiscation, and (3) fine (see Proceeds of Crime Act 2002 section 13).

SG-687 **STEP ONE Compensation**

The court must consider making a compensation order requiring the offender to pay compensation for any personal injury, loss or damage resulting from the offence in such an amount as the court considers appropriate, having regard to the evidence and to the means of the offender.

Where the means of the offender are limited, priority should be given to the payment of compensation over payment of any other financial penalty.

Reasons should be given if a compensation order is not made.

(See section 130 Powers of Criminal Courts (Sentencing) Act 2000)

SG-688 **STEP TWO Confiscation (Crown Court only)**

Confiscation must be considered if either the Crown asks for it or the court thinks that it may be appropriate. Confiscation must be dealt with before any other fine or financial order (except compensation).

(See sections 6 and 13 Proceeds of Crime Act 2002)

SG-689 **STEP THREE Determining the offence category**

The court should determine the offence category using only the culpability and harm factors in the tables below. The culpability and harm categories are on a sliding scale; there is inevitable overlap between the factors described in adjacent categories. Where an offence does not fall squarely into a category, individual factors may require a degree of weighting before making an overall assessment and determining the appropriate offence category.

Dealing with a **risk of harm** involves consideration of both the likelihood of harm occurring and the extent of it if it does. Risk of harm is less serious than the same actual harm. Where the offence has caused risk of harm but no (or less) actual harm the normal approach is to move down to the next category of harm. This may not be appropriate if either the likelihood or extent of potential harm is particularly high.

Culpability	Harm	
Deliberate Where the offender intentionally breached, or flagrantly disregarded, the law **Reckless** Actual foresight of, or wilful blindness to, risk of offending but risk nevertheless taken **Negligent** Offence committed through act or omission which a person exercising reasonable care would not commit **Low or no culpability** Offence committed with little or no fault, for example by genuine accident despite the presence of proper preventive measures, or where such proper preventive measures were unforeseeably overcome by exceptional events	**Category 1**	• Polluting material of a dangerous nature, for example, hazardous chemicals or sharp objects • Major adverse effect or damage to air or water quality, amenity value, or property • Polluting material was noxious, widespread or pervasive with long-lasting effects on human health or quality of life, animal health, or flora • Major costs incurred through clean-up, site restoration or animal rehabilitation • Major interference with, prevention or undermining of other lawful activities or regulatory regime due to offence
	Category 2	• Significant adverse effect or damage to air or water quality, amenity value, or property • Significant adverse effect on human health or quality of life, animal health or flora • Significant costs incurred through clean-up, site restoration or animal rehabilitation • Significant interference with or undermining of other lawful activities or regulatory regime due to offence • Risk of category 1 harm
	Category 3	• Minor, localised adverse effect or damage to air or water quality, amenity value, or property • Minor adverse effect on human health or quality of life, animal health or flora • Low costs incurred through clean-up, site restoration or animal rehabilitation • Limited interference with or undermining of other lawful activities or regulatory regime due to offence • Risk of category 2 harm
	Category 4	• Risk of category 3 harm

STEP FOUR   Starting point and category range   SG-690

Having determined the category, the court should refer to the starting points [not reproduced here] to reach a sentence within the category range. The court should then consider further adjustment within the category range for aggravating and mitigating features, [not reproduced here].

General principles to follow in setting a fine

The court should determine the appropriate level of fine in accordance with section 164 of the Criminal Justice Act 2003, which requires that the fine must reflect the seriousness of the offence and the court to take into account the financial circumstances of the offender.

The level of fine should reflect the extent to which the offender fell below the required standard. The fine should meet, in a fair and proportionate way, the objectives of punishment, deterrence and the removal of gain derived through the commission of the offence; it should not be cheaper to offend than to take the appropriate precautions.

Obtaining financial information

In setting a fine, the court may conclude that the offender is able to pay any fine imposed unless the offender has supplied any financial information to the contrary. It is for the offender to disclose to the court such data relevant to their financial position as will enable it to assess what they can reasonably afford to pay. If necessary, the court may compel the disclosure of an individual offender's financial circumstances pursuant to section 162 of the Criminal Justice Act 2003. **In the absence of such disclosure, or where the court is not satisfied that it has been given sufficient reliable information, the court will be entitled to draw reasonable inferences as to the offender's means from evidence it has heard and from all the circumstances of the case.**

Sentencing Guidelines

Starting points and ranges

Where the range includes a potential sentence of custody, the court should consider the custody threshold as follows:

- has the custody threshold been passed?
- if so, is it unavoidable that a custodial sentence be imposed?
- if so, can that sentence be suspended?

Where the range includes a potential sentence of a community order, the court should consider the community order threshold as follows:

- has the community order threshold been passed?

However, even where the community order threshold has been passed, a fine will normally be the most appropriate disposal. Where confiscation is not applied for, consider, if wishing to remove any economic benefit derived through the commission of the offence, combining a fine with a community order.

Offence category	Starting Point	Range
Deliberate		
Category 1	18 months' custody	1 – 3 years' custody
Category 2	1 year's custody	26 weeks' – 18 months' custody
Category 3	Band F fine	Band E fine or medium level community order – 26 weeks' custody
Category 4	Band E fine	Band D fine or low level community order – Band E fine
Reckless		
Category 1	26 weeks' custody	Band F fine or high level community order – 12 months' custody
Category 2	Band F fine	Band E fine or medium level community order – 26 weeks' custody
Category 3	Band E fine	Band D fine or low level community order – Band E fine
Category 4	Band D fine	Band C fine – Band D fine
Negligent		
Category 1	Band F fine	Band E fine or medium level community order – 26 weeks' custody
Category 2	Band E fine	Band D fine or low level community order – Band E fine
Category 3	Band D fine	Band C fine – Band D fine
Category 4	Band C fine	Band B fine – Band C fine
Low / No culpability		
Category 1	Band D fine	Band C fine – Band D fine
Category 2	Band C fine	Band B fine – Band C fine
Category 3	Band B fine	Band A fine – Band B fine
Category 4	Band A fine	Conditional discharge – Band A fine

The table below contains a **non-exhaustive** list of factual elements providing the context of the offence and factors relating to the offender. Identify whether any combination of these, or other relevant factors, should result in an upward or downward adjustment from the starting point. **In particular, relevant recent convictions and/or a history of non-compliance are likely to result in a substantial upward adjustment.** In some cases, having considered these factors, it may be appropriate to move outside the identified category range.

Factors increasing seriousness	Factors reducing seriousness or reflecting mitigation
Statutory aggravating factors:	No previous convictions **or** no relevant/recent convictions
Previous convictions, having regard to a) the nature of the offence to which the conviction relates and its relevance to the current offence; and b) the time that has elapsed since the conviction	Remorse
	Compensation paid voluntarily to remedy harm caused
Offence committed whilst on bail	Evidence of steps taken to remedy problem
Other aggravating factors include:	One-off event not commercially motivated
History of non-compliance with warnings by regulator	Little or no financial gain
	Self-reporting, co-operation and acceptance of responsibility
Location of the offence, for example, near housing, schools, livestock or environmentally sensitive sites	Good character and/or exemplary conduct
Repeated incidents of offending or offending over an extended period of time, where not charged separately	Mental disorder or learning disability, where linked to the commission of the offence
Deliberate concealment of illegal nature of activity	Serious medical conditions requiring urgent, intensive or long-term treatment
Ignoring risks identified by employees or others	Age and/or lack of maturity where it affects the responsibility of the offender
Established evidence of wider/community impact	
Breach of any order	Sole or primary carer for dependent relatives
Offence committed for financial gain	
Obstruction of justice	
Offence committed whilst on licence	

STEPS FIVE AND SIX   SG-691

Where the sentence is or includes a fine, the court should 'step back' and, using the factors set out in steps five and six, **review whether the sentence as a whole meets, in a fair way, the objectives of punishment, deterrence and removal of gain derived through the commission of the offence.** At steps five and six, the court may increase or reduce the proposed fine reached at step four, if necessary moving outside the range.

STEP FIVE   Ensure that the combination of financial orders (compensation, confiscation if   SG-692
appropriate, and fine) removes any economic benefit derived from the offending

The court should remove any economic benefit the offender has derived through the commission of the offence including:

- avoided costs;
- operating savings;
- any gain made as a direct result of the offence.

Where the offender is fined, the amount of economic benefit derived from the offence should normally be added to the fine arrived at in step four. If a confiscation order is made, in considering economic benefit, the court should avoid double recovery.

Economic benefit will not always be an identifiable feature of a case. For example, in some water pollution cases there may be strict liability but very little obvious gain. However, even in these cases there may be some avoidance of cost, for example alarms not installed and maintained, inadequate funding or security measures not installed. Any costs avoided will be considered as economic benefit.

Where it is not possible to calculate or estimate the economic benefit derived from the offence, the court may wish to draw on information from the enforcing authorities about the general costs of operating within the law.

STEP SIX   Consider other factors that may warrant adjustment of the proposed fine   SG-693

The court should consider any further factors that are relevant to ensuring that the proposed fine is proportionate having regard to the means of the offender and the seriousness of the offence.

The **non-exhaustive** list below contains additional factual elements the court should consider in deciding whether an increase or reduction to the proposed fine is required:

- fine impairs offender's ability to make restitution to victims;
- impact of fine on offender's ability to improve conditions to comply with the law;
- impact of fine on employment of staff, service users, customers and local economy.

STEP SEVEN   Consider any factors which indicate a reduction, such as assistance to the prosecution

The court should take into account sections 73 and 74 of the Serious Organised Crime and Police Act 2005 (assistance by defendants: reduction or review of sentence) and any other rule of law by virtue of which an offender may receive a discounted sentence in consequence of assistance given (or offered) to the prosecutor or investigator.

STEP EIGHT   Reduction for guilty pleas

The court should take account of any potential reduction for a guilty plea in accordance with section 144 of the Criminal Justice Act 2003 and the Guilty Plea guideline.

STEP NINE   Ancillary orders

In all cases, the court must consider whether to make ancillary orders. These may include:

Disqualification of director

An offender may be disqualified from being a director of a company in accordance with section 2 of the Company Directors Disqualification Act 1986. The maximum period of disqualification is 15 years (Crown Court) or 5 years (magistrates' court).

Disqualification from driving

The court may order disqualification from driving where a vehicle has been used in connection with the commission of the offence (section 147 of the Powers of Criminal Courts (Sentencing) Act 2000).

The court may disqualify an offender from driving on conviction for any offence either in addition to any other sentence or instead of any other sentence (section 146 of the Powers of Criminal Courts (Sentencing) Act 2000).

The court should inform the offender of its intention to disqualify and hear representations.

Forfeiture of vehicle

The court may order the forfeiture of a vehicle used in or for the purposes of the commission of the offence in accordance with section 33C of the Environmental Protection Act 1990.

Deprivation of property

Where section 33C of the Environmental Protection Act 1990 does not apply, the court may order the offender to be deprived of property used to commit crime or intended for that purpose in accordance with section 143 of the Powers of Criminal Courts (Sentencing) Act 2000. In considering whether to make an order under section 143, the court must have regard to the value of the property and the likely effects on the offender of making the order taken together with any other order the court makes.

Remediation

Where an offender is convicted of an offence under regulation 38(1), (2) or (3) of the Environmental Permitting (England and Wales) Regulations 2010, a court may order the offender to take steps to remedy the cause of the offence within a specified period in accordance with regulation 44 of the Environmental Permitting (England and Wales) Regulations 2010.

STEP TEN   Totality principle

If sentencing an offender for more than one offence, or where the offender is already serving a sentence, consider whether the total sentence is just and proportionate to the offending behaviour.

STEP ELEVEN   Reasons

Section 174 of the Criminal Justice Act 2003 imposes a duty to give reasons for, and explain the effect of, the sentence.

STEP TWELVE   Consideration for time spent on bail

The court must consider whether to give credit for time spent on bail in accordance with section 240A of the Criminal Justice Act 2003.

Other environmental offences   SG-695

In sentencing other relevant and analogous environmental offences, the court should refer to the sentencing approach in steps one to three and five and six of the guideline, **adjusting the starting points and ranges bearing in mind the statutory maxima** for those offences. An indicative list of such offences is set out [at **SG-685 — the list is identical for organisations and individuals**].

ANNEX: FINE BANDS AND COMMUNITY ORDERS   SG-696

[The tables set out here are also set out in the Magistrates' Court Sentencing Guidelines, which includes further guidance on fines and community orders: see **SG-306** and **SG-330**.]

Index